# AMERICAN
# DECADES
## 1920-1929

# AMERICAN DECADES
## 1920-1929

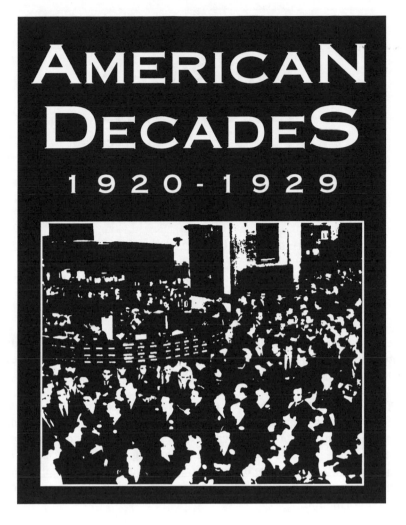

EDITED BY

## JUDITH S. BAUGHMAN

A MANLY, INC. BOOK

Gale Research Inc.

*An International Thomson Publishing Company*

I(T)P

**Changing the Way the World Learns**

NEW YORK • LONDON • BONN • BOSTON • DETROIT • MADRID
MELBOURNE • MEXICO CITY • PARIS • SINGAPORE • TOKYO
TORONTO • WASHINGTON • ALBANY NY • BELMONT CA • CINCINNATI OH

# AMERICAN
# DECADES
## 1920-1929

Matthew J. Bruccoli and Richard Layman, *Editorial Directors*

Karen L. Rood, *Senior Editor*

Printed in the United States of America

Published simultaneously in the United Kingdom
by Gale Research International Limited
(An affiliated company of Gale Research Inc.)

The paper used in this publication meets the minimum requirements of American National Standard for Information Sciences-Permanence Paper for Printed Library Materials, ANSI Z39.48-1984. ∞™

Library of Congress Catalog Card Number  95-080216
ISBN 0-8103-5724-0

I(T)P™

The trademark **ITP** is used under license.
10 9 8 7

# CONTENTS

# INTRODUCTION

**Prosperity.** The Jazz Age. The Roaring Twenties. The Lawless Decade. The Era of Wonderful Nonsense. The Boom. These labels pasted on the 1920s distort that decade: all such convenient labels are misleading just because they are convenient. For most all Americans the 1920s were not a ten-year debauch fueled by easy money and bootleg booze. Prosperity did not reach coal miners who earned between 75¢ and 85¢ an hour or public-school teachers who averaged between $970 and $1,200 per year.* Farmers never regained their wartime prosperity; farm acreage decreased as four million Americans left farms during the 1920s. Prosperity did not embrace American blacks, 85 percent of whom lived in the segregated South in 1920 — mostly in rural locations — and 23 percent of whom were illiterate. They were cut off from opportunity in the land of opportunity.

**Normalcy.** The serious side of the 1920s was as characteristic of the times as were the frivolities. The business-success ethic was widely accepted. Warren G. Harding declared that Americans wanted "not nostrums, but normalcy." He was right. *Normalcy* became the motto for a decade of abnormality. Calvin Coolidge stated that "The business of America is business." Herbert Hoover declared: "We in America are nearer to the final triumph over poverty, than ever before in the history of any land. . . . Given a chance to go forward with the policies of the last eight years, we shall soon with the help of God be in sight of the day when poverty will be banished from this nation." In 1922 Sinclair Lewis depicted the American businessman George F. Babbitt — whose name became synonymous with cultural and spiritual poverty; nonetheless, most Americans aspired to Babbitt's material comforts.

**Disillusionment.** It was a postwar decade, and, as is often the result of extended wars, the victors were disillusioned by the peace. Americans of the 1920s wanted no further involvements with Europe's problems. American participation in the League of Nations was defeated, and noble causes became suspect — especially foreign causes. The Russian Revolution was hailed as a great humanitarian event by some intellectuals, but most Americans regarded the Bolsheviks as menaces to The American Way or as ridiculous figures. Idealism — political, social or economic — was a luxury or a joke. The "noble experiment" of Prohibition was unenforceable and spawned the rackets.

**Change.** All was not business as usual. There were marked social changes, especially for women. Not only could women vote, they could smoke, drink, wear comfortable clothes, become educated, show their legs, and participate in a limited amount of sexual freedom. Birth control was openly discussed but not widely available to the working classes. As expressed in "Ain't We Got Fun" (1921) — "The rich get richer, and the poor get children." The term *Flaming Youth* implied not just an irresponsible, celebratory response to life: it expressed the revolt of the younger generation (that is, the generation after the war generation) against the standards and values of their elders. But youthful ebullience required money — parental money. Like so many of what have come to be regarded as defining qualities of the 1920s, the hedonistic conduct of the flappers and their sheiks† was an upper-middle-class phenomenon. Despite the hit song of 1927, the best things in life were not free.

**Heroes.** Yet there was a great deal of enduring worth or significance in the 1920s. There was a proliferation of genius, especially in the arts. The best books, music, and

---

*It is impossible to convert the purchasing power of 1920s dollars to 1990s dollars. The usual multipliers are from seven to ten. Thus, accepting the ten-times figure, the miners' 85¢ in 1920 might be worth $8.50 in 1995. But the value of the dollar involved other factors, such as income-tax rates: 1.5 percent on the first $7,500 of net income in 1929 compared to 15 percent of the first $17,850 in 1990.

---

† *Flapper* was originally a British term, describing women whose fiancés had been killed in World War I or younger women who had no one to marry. When the term was translated into American, it was thought to describe young women wearing unbuckled galoshes. *Sheik* as a term for a fashionable young man derived from the popularity of Rudolph Valentino's desert romance, *The Sheik*. Arabs were in vogue: *The Desert Song* was a Broadway hit, and Sheiks was a brand of condoms.

paintings of the decade retain their distinction; and their creators have become American cultural icons. The American capacity for hero worship found ready expression in sports, but the stars of the 1920s have proved to be enduring. The era and its heroes matched each other: Babe Ruth was a quintessential 1920s figure — not a celebrity, but a hero who personified the national mood. All the heroes were not artists or athletes. Every line of endeavor produced great figures: Harvey Williams Cushing, Rueben L. Kahn, George and Gladys Dick in medicine; Robert Goddard, Robert Millaken, and Edwin Hubble in science; Raymond Hood and Albert Kahn in architecture; Margaret Mead in anthropology; Margaret Sanger, Grace Abbott, and Maud Wood Park in social reform. These heroes — some of them immigrants who fulfilled the American Dream of success — embodied the key American quality of aspiration. If a label is required for the 1920s, *The Era of Aspiration* is appropriate. All that genius, talent, energy, confidence, and ambition drove the quest for new, more, bigger, better.

**Big Business.** "Never before, here or anywhere else, has a government been so completely fused with business," declared the *Wall Street Journal*. The 1920s fostered the growth of business and celebrated the men — many of them self-made — who made big business bigger: Walter P. Chrysler, Alfred P. Sloan, A. P. Giannini, Owen D. Young, Donald W. Douglas, David Sarnoff, Herbert Hoover ("The Great Engineer"), William C. Durant, Henry Ford. Although it was difficult for the unions to exercise power during a decade committed to business growth, labor generated its own great figures: John L. Lewis, David Dubinsky, Sidney Hillman, A. Philip Randolph, and Norman Thomas, leader of the United States Socialist Party, acquired respect but not power — especially on campuses — during a Republican decade.

American political activity was undistinguished during the 1920s. The most remarkable event was the Democrats' decision to run Al Smith, an anti-Prohibitionist Roman Catholic, for president in 1928 — possibly because Republican Hoover was unbeatable by any Democrat. Hoover broke the Solid South, and Smith did not carry his home state, New York.

**New Blood.** Sports remained segregated. But show business provided opportunities for blacks and Jews. Irving Berlin, George and Ira Gershwin, Richard Rogers and Lorenz Hart, and Jerome Kern wrote the Broadway songs of the 1920s; Al Jolson and Eddie Cantor performed the songs — often in blackface. The movie industry was organized by Jews who created the studio system: Jesse Lasky, Adolph Zukor, Marcus Loew, Louis B. Mayer, Carl Laemmle, Samuel Goldwyn, Irving Thalberg, the Warner brothers. American popular culture became increasingly dependent on infusions of new blood from abroad. Another pool of genius had been in place for a century. The jazz of the Jazz Age was black

Americans' most powerful influence on American — and ultimately — world culture. Louis Armstrong, Jelly Roll Morton, and Duke Ellington did it first; then whites made it pretty or respectable. Blocked from production or managerial control of music and theater, blacks were among the legendary performers of the era: singers Bessie Smith and Ethel Waters, singer-dancer Josephine Baker, comedian Bert Williams, and a regiment of instrumentalists.

Apart from the most notable figures of the Harlem Renaissance, American writers were white and mainly Protestant. But some of the most innovative and influential literary publishers of the 1920s were not members of the gentile club: Alfred A. Knopf, Bennett Cerf and Donald S. Klopfer (Random House), Horace Liveright, and Richard Simon and M. Lincoln Schuster.

**Mass Communication and Education.** At the same time that America became increasingly urbanized — and suburbanized — communication developments helped to close regional divisions. There were 18.5 million telephones in 1928. Paved roads and affordable cars connected towns with big cities — and ultimately killed the small towns. The most effective innovation in mass communication was radio. In 1921 no radios were manufactured in America; 4,428,000 were manufactured in 1929, and 10,250,000 households had radios.

More Americans stayed longer in school. Between 1919–1920 and 1927–1928 college enrollment almost tripled. Of the 919,000 college students in 1927–1928, 356,000 were women. Collegiate lifestyle influenced many aspects of the decade, including fashion, music, slang, and sexual mores. The big man on campus was a figure whose reputation extended off-campus — for a year or so.

**Hangovers.** During the 1930s there was an angry reaction against the 1920s and many of its representative figures. The Depression was blamed on the speculative irresponsibility of the boom years. The frivolity of the Jazz Age was condemned by the proletarian decade. Yet much of lasting worth was achieved during the 1920s — especially in the arts and media. Even the frivolity was serious frivolity, for the decade was characterized by satire, wit, and humor. There was a defining American quality of confidence that was never resuscitated after 1929 — except briefly at the end of World War II.

F. Scott Fitzgerald, who christened the Jazz Age, wrote its obituary:

> Now once more the belt is tight and we summon the proper expression of horror as we look back at our wasted youth. Sometimes, though, there is a ghostly rumble among the drums, an asthmatic whisper in the trombones that swings me back into the early twenties when we drank wood alcohol and every day in every way grew better and better, and there was a first abortive shortening of the skirts, and girls all looked alike in sweater

dresses, and people you didn't want to know said "Yes, we have no bananas," and it seemed only a question of a few years before the older people would step aside and let the world be run by those who saw things as they were — and it all seems rosy and romantic to us who were young then, because we will never feel quite so intensely about our surroundings any more.

— "Echoes of the Jazz Age," 1931

## PLAN OF THIS VOLUME

This is one of nine volumes in the *American Decades* series. Each volume will chronicle a single twentieth-century decade from thirteen separate perspectives, broadly covering American life. The volumes begin with a chronology of world events outside of America, which provides a context for American experience. Following are chapters, arranged in alphabetical order, on thirteen categories of American endeavor ranging from business to medicine, from the arts to sports. Each of these chapters contains the following elements: first, a table of contents for the chapter; second, a chronology of significant events in the field; third, Topics in the News, a series, beginning with an overview, of short essays describing current events; fourth, anecdotal sidebars of interesting and entertaining, though not necessarily important, information; fifth, Headline Makers, short biographical accounts of key people during the decade; sixth, People in the News, brief notices of significant accomplishments by people who mattered; seventh, Awards of note in the field (where applicable); eighth, Deaths during the decade of people in the field; and ninth, a list of Publications during or specifically about the decade in the field. In addition, there is a general bibliography at the end of this volume, followed by an index of photographs and an index of subjects.

# ACKNOWLEDGMENTS

This book was produced by Manly, Inc.

Production coordinator is James W. Hipp. Photography editor is Bruce Andrew Bowlin. Photographic copy work was performed by Joseph M. Bruccoli. Layout and graphics supervisor is Penney L. Haughton. Copyediting supervisor is Laurel M. Gladden. Typesetting supervisor is Kathleen M. Flanagan. Systems manager is George F. Dodge. Julie E. Frick is editorial associate. The production staff includes Phyllis A. Avant, Ann M. Cheschi, Patricia Coate, Denise W. Edwards, Joyce Fowler, Stephanie C. Hatchell, Margaret Meriwether, Kathy Lawler Merlette, Jeff Miller, Pamela D. Norton, Laura S. Pleicones, Emily R. Sharpe, William L. Thomas Jr., and Allison Trussell.

Walter W. Ross and Robert S. McConnell did library research. They were assisted by the following librarians at the Thomas Cooper Library of the University of South Carolina: Linda Holderfield and the interlibrary-loan staff; reference-department head Virginia Weathers; reference librarians Marilee Birchfield, Stefanie Buck, Cathy Eckman, Rebecca Feind, Jill Holman, Karen Joseph, Jean Rhyne, Kwamine Washington, and Connie Widney; circulation-department head Caroline Taylor; and acquisitions-searching supervisor David Haggard.

Michael L. Lazare contributed to the Sports and Media chapters. Robert W. Trogdon revised sections of the Education chapter and provided the Ernest Hemingway entry for the Arts chapter. Robert Moss provided supplementary material for the Lifestyles and Sports chapters. Devon Boan contributed to the World Events Chronology and provided the Langston Hughes and Harlem Renaissance material for the Arts chapter. Park Bucker, Cy League, and Anthony Perrello performed essential research labors.

# AMERICAN DECADES

## 1920-1929

# WORLD EVENTS: SELECTED OCCURENCES OUTSIDE THE UNITED STATES

## 1920

- Agatha Christie's *The Mysterious Affair at Styles*, introducing Hercule Poirot, is published.

- *Le Côté de Guermantes I* (*The Guermantes Way*, part 1), a section of Marcel Proust's *A la recherche du temps perdu* (*Remembrance of Things Past*), is published in France.

**10 Jan.** The Treaty of Versailles takes effect. Signed by the leaders of the victorious Allies — the United States, Great Britain, France, and Italy — the agreement redraws the map of Europe, imposes punitive reparations on Germany, and reassigns German colonies; Britain, for example, takes over German East Africa and renames it Tanganyika.

**13 Jan.** In a workers' attack on the Reichstag during rioting in Berlin, 44 people killed and 105 are wounded.

**17 Jan.** Premier Georges Clemenceau of France is defeated in general elections for the presidency by Paul Deschanel, who is succeeded on 23 September by Alexandre Millerand.

**7 Mar.** Russia invades Poland, which on 20 April invades Russia. The conflict between the two countries is temporarily ended by an armistice granting Polish terms on 6 October. Borders between Russia and Poland are established by the Treaty of Riga on 18 March 1921.

**10 Mar.** Three hundred thousand workers in India go on strike against British rule. In Jamshedpur British troops fire on protesting strikers.

**11 Mar.** The Syrian Congress declares Syria an independent nation and proclaims Prince Faisal king. On 24 March Faisal orders French troops out of his country. French forces under Gen. Pierre Gouraud, French high commander of Syria, occupy Damascus and dethrone King Faisal on 25 July. On 5 September Gouraud declares Lebanon a French mandate separate from Syria.

**13 Mar.** Berlin is seized in a coup d'état led by monarchist Dr. Wolfgang Kapp. The coup is put down within a week, and Kapp flees to Stockholm on 16 April.

**6 Apr.**    French troops occupy Darmstadt, Frankfurt, Hamburg, Hamau, and Dieburg in an attempt to force German troops to leave the Ruhr, Germany's industrial region. Germany agrees on 8 April to withdraw.

**7 Apr.**    Italy formally recognizes the state of Albania, which is occupied by Italian troops. Skirmishes between Italian and Albanian soldiers continue until a treaty insuring Albanian sovereignty is signed on 15 July by the two countries.

**23–25 Apr.**    The Allies grant Armenia independence under United States protection, pronounce Syria a French mandate, declare Mesopotamia a British mandate, and designate Palestine a Jewish state under British protection.

**16 May**    Joan of Arc is canonized by Pope Benedict XV.

Russia invades Persia, which is occupied by British troops. The British give ground but maintain uneasy control until early February 1921.

**17 May**    Mexican president Venustiano Carranza, defeated by the triumvirate of Plutarco Elías Calles, Álvaro Obregón, and Aldolfo de la Huerta, flees Mexico City but is captured in Puebla. On 21 May Carranza is assassinated in a Pueblan village by his escorts.

**14 June**    Max Weber, German economist and sociologist, dies at age fifty-six.

**10 July**    Peking is placed under martial law after conflict between President Hsu Shih-chang and the Chinese military.

**12 July**    Russia recognizes Lithuanian independence.

**23 July**    The British East Africa Protectorate is transformed into the colony of Kenya.

**24 July**    The Treaty of Saint-Germain, designating Austrian boundaries and conditions, takes effect.

**9 Aug.**    The Treaty of Trianon, defining Hungarian boundaries and conditions, is signed.

**10 Aug.**    The Treaty of Sèvres, stipulating Turkish boundaries and conditions, is signed.

**14 Aug.**    The Summer Olympics begin in Antwerp, Belgium.

**22 Aug.**    In Italy 500,000 workers take over more than five hundred factories in protests over economic and political difficulties.

**31 Aug.**    Wilhelm Wundt, German philosopher and one of the founders of modern psychology, dies at age eighty-eight.

**25 Sept.**    Twenty-five are killed in anti-Japanese protests in Gensan, Korea.

**26 Sept.**    After some five thousand attacks on individuals and property result in more than one hundred deaths, the British government orders a curfew in Belfast and other Irish cities.

**19 Oct.**    John Reed, an American writer who celebrated Russia's Bolshevik Revolution in *Ten Days That Shook the World* (1919), dies in Moscow at age thirty-three. He is the only American to be buried in the Kremlin wall.

**25 Oct.**    King Alexander I of Greece dies after being bitten by his pet monkey.

**18 Nov.**    The Jewish Quarter in Prague is plundered in three days of rioting by Czechs and nationalized Germans.

**26 Nov.**    Russia drives Turkish troops out of Armenia.

**29 Nov.**    Russian leader V. I. Lenin disavows all Soviet treaties and agreements.

**16 Dec.**    An earthquake in northern China kills more than 100,000 people.

**24 Dec.**    Russia conquers the country of Georgia.

**26 Dec.**    Karl Rudolph Legien, president of the German Federation of Labor Unions, dies at age sixty.

## 1921

- Luigi Pirandello's drama *Sei personaggi in cerca d'autore* (*Six Characters in Search of an Author*) premieres in Italy.

- Pablo Picasso paints *Three Musicians*.

- *Le Côté de Guermantes II* (*The Guermantes Way*, part 2) and *Sodome et Gomorrhe I* (*Cities of the Plain*, part 1), a section of Proust's *A la recherche du temps perdu* (*Remembrance of Things Past*), is published in France.

**9 Feb.**    The first Indian parliament under the Government of India Act of 1919 is convened in New Dehli.

**21 Feb.**    Gen. Reza Khan launches a coup d'état against British rule in Persia and establishes an independent government. On 26 February he concludes an agreement with Russian invaders who begin to withdraw from the country. On 1 May British troops leave Persia under Reza Khan's orders.

**8 Mar.**    Spanish premier Eduardo Dato Iradier is assassinated by rightists.

**24 Mar.**    Greece invades Turkey in an attempt to enforce the Treaty of Sèvres, establishing an Allies-supported government in Turkey.

**31 Mar.**    Coal miners strike in Great Britain. On 28 June the government agrees to provide miners a subsidy of £10 million.

**1 May**    Riots erupt in Jaffa, Palestine, between Arab and Jewish workers; twenty-seven, all Jews, are killed.

**May–July**    German war criminals are tried at Leipzig. France withdraws from the trial in protest over light sentences.

**29 June**    Lady Randolph Churchill, American-born mother of Winston Churchill, dies at age sixty-seven.

**21 July**    Moroccan rebels, led by Abd-el-Krim, defeat a Spanish force, killing twelve thousand, and establish the Republic of the Riff.

**27 July**    Canadian Frederick Grant Banting discovers insulin, for which he shares the 1923 Nobel Prize in medicine.

**29 July**    Adolf Hitler is elected chairman and absolute dictator of the Nazi Party centered in Munich, Germany.

**2 Aug.**    Enrico Caruso, internationally famous Italian tenor, dies at age forty-eight.

**16 Aug.**    Peter I, king of the Serbs, Croats, and Slovenes, dies and is succeeded by his son, Alexander I.

| | |
|---|---|
| **23 Aug.** | Emir Faisal becomes crowned head of the new kingdom of Iraq, formerly Mesopotamia. |
| **27 Aug.** | Dr. Alexander Wekerlé, five times premier of Hungary, dies at age seventy-one. |
| **28 Aug.** | Nicaragua is invaded by rebels based in Honduras; on 7 September these rebels are driven back into Honduras by the Nicaraguan army and captured by Honduran troops. |
| **12 Sept.** | Russia declares war on Bessarabia, a new Romanian province. |
| **22 Sept.** | Ivan Vazov, Bulgaria's national poet, dies. |
| **19 Oct.** | Premier António Granjó of Portugal and several other officials are assassinated after being arrested by the military. |
| **4 Nov.** | Hara Takashi, the first commoner to become premier of Japan, is assassinated by a fanatic; he is succeeded on 12 November by Korekiyo Takahashi, who is, in turn, succeeded by Baron Tomosaburo Kato on 11 June 1922. |
| **11 Nov.** | The Washington Armaments Conference, during which the United States, Japan, Great Britain, and France agree on Pacific boundaries and conditions, is convened. |
| **6 Dec.** | The British government signs a treaty with the Dail Eireann (Assembly of Ireland) to establish the Irish Free State. Nineteen members of the radical group Sinn Fein had already been executed during 1921 in the rebellion leading up to the signing of the treaty. |
| **8 Dec.** | The United States, Japan, England, and France sign the Four-Power Treaty for the arbitration and mediation of economic disputes. |
| **16 Dec.** | French composer Camille Saint-Saëns dies at age eighty-six. |

# 1922

- *Sodome et Gomorrhe II* (*Cites of the Plain*, part 2), a section of Proust's *A la recherche du temps perdu* (*Remembrance of Things Past*), is published in France.
- James Joyce's novel *Ulysses* is published in Paris.
- The silent movie classic of German expressionist horror, *Nosferatu*, directed by F. W. Murnau, is released.
- Centre Court at Wimbledon is built.
- *Siddhartha*, Hermann Hesse's novel of oriental mythology, is published in Germany.

| | |
|---|---|
| **22 Jan.** | Pope Benedict XV dies at age sixty-five. On 6 February Achille Cardinal Ratti, who takes the name Pius XI, is elected pope. |
| **15 Feb.** | The International Court of Justice is established at The Hague, in the Netherlands. |
| **18 Feb.** | Britain grants Egypt titular independence but maintains military bases throughout the country. |
| **25 Feb.** | Henri-Désiré Landru, the so-called modern Bluebeard, is guillotined in Versailles, France, for the murder of ten women and a young boy. |

| | |
|---|---|
| **3 Mar.** | Italian Fascists seize the disputed port city of Fiume, which briefly had operated as a state independent from either Italy or the new, loosely federated Yugoslavia. |
| **15 Mar.** | Four hundred followers of revolutionary Irish leader Eamon de Valera capture Limerick and evict more-conservative officials in the Free State government. |
| **18 Mar.** | The British government sentences Indian nationalist leader Mohandas Gandhi to six years in prison for sedition. |
| **1 Apr.** | Charles I, deposed emperor of Austria and king of Hungary, dies at age thirty-five. |
| **3 Apr.** | Joseph Stalin is elected general secretary of the Central Committee of the Russian Communist Party. |
| **16 Apr.** | The Treaty of Rapallo, insuring economic trade and military cooperation between Germany and Russia, is signed. |
| **24 June** | German foreign minister Walther Rathenau is assassinated by political opponents within his staff. |
| **12 Aug.** | Arthur Griffith, president of the Dáil Eireann, dies at age fifty. On 22 August Michael Collins, moderate leader of the Irish Free State, is assassinated by members of the Republican Society founded by de Valera. |
| **14 Sept.** | Great Britain sends a fleet of warships to the Dardanelles after Turkish troops rout the Greek army in Smyrna and destroy the city. On 28 November five Greek political leaders, including Premier Demetrios Gounaris and the head of the military, are executed in Athens after being blamed for the disaster at Smyrna. |
| **28 Oct.** | Italian Fascists march on Rome and demand the creation of a Fascist government. On 31 October Benito Mussolini, the military head (duce) of the Fascist Party, is named premier by King Victor Emmanuel III; on 25 November Mussolini is granted dictatorial powers. |
| **18 Nov.** | French novelist Marcel Proust dies at age fifty-one. |
| **20 Nov.** | The Lausanne Conference, called to rewrite the Treaty of Sèvres, convenes in Switzerland. |
| **26 Nov.** | Excavation begins on the tomb of ancient Egyptian king Tutankhamen near Luxor, Egypt. |
| **6 Dec.** | The provisional government in Ireland is superseded by the Free State government, formally establishing the Irish Free State. |
| **18 Dec.** | One week after his election, President Gabriel Narutowicz of Poland is assassinated by a madman. |
| **30 Dec.** | The Union of Soviet Socialist Republics is officially proclaimed. |

# 1923

- *La Prisonnière* (*The Captive*), a section of Proust's *A la recherche du temps perdu* (*Remembrance of Things Past*), is published posthumously in France.

- *The Prophet*, Kahlil Gibran's meditative prose poem, is published in London.

- *Ich und du* (*I and Thou*), Martin Buber's most famous work of philosophy, is published in Vienna.

- English-language production of Czech writer Karel Capek's drama *R.U.R.* (Czechoslovakia, 1921) introduces the term *robot*, which refers to a machine with human characteristics.

**10 Jan.**  France sends 100,000 troops into the Ruhr to seize German assets as war reparations. On 17 February German saboteurs sink a coal barge in the Rhine-Herne Canal, the first of many acts of sabotage in protest of French occupation.

**11 Jan.**  Constantine I, former king of Greece, dies at age fifty-four. He is succeeded by George II, a puppet of the military.

**1 Feb.**  Yaqui Indian soldiers put down a trolley car strike in Mexico City, killing fourteen and wounding thirty.

**10 Feb.**  Wilhelm Röntgen, the German scientist who discovered X rays in 1895 and was awarded the first Nobel Prize in physics in 1901, dies at age seventy-seven.

**26 Mar.**  Sarah Bernhardt, the celebrated French actress, dies at age seventy-eight.

**5 Apr.**  George Edward Stanhope Molyneux Herbert, Fifth Earl of Carnarvon, an Egyptologist who is financially backing explorations of the tomb of King Tutankhamen, dies in Cairo following an insect bite.

**5 Apr.**  Soviet troops massacre 340 Ukrainian peasants for protesting the execution of Roman Catholic vicar general Constantine Butchkavitch six days earlier.

**22 May**  Lady Constance Lytton, leader in the British woman's suffrage movement, dies at age fifty-four.

**9 June**  Aleksandur Stamboliyski, premier of Bulgaria and leader of the Peasant Party, is overthrown by right-wing military officers. On 14 June he is shot, allegedly in an escape attempt.

**20 July**  Mexican bandit Francisco "Pancho" Villa is shot and killed in ambush at Parral, Mexico.

**23 Aug.**  Baron Tomosaburo Kato, premier of Japan and hero of the Russo-Japanese War, dies at age sixty-two. On 28 August he is succeeded by Count Gombe Yamamoto, who is forced to resign on 29 December following an attempt on the life of Prince Regent Hirohito.

**27 Aug.**  The murders of an Italian delegation on the Greek-Albanian border leads to an international crisis.

**1 Sept.**  A major earthquake, with more than three hundred distinct shocks, destroys Tokyo and Yokohama, Japan, killing 143,000.

**10 Sept.**  The Irish Free State is unanimously elected to the League of Nations.

**13 Sept.**  Rightist general Miguel Primo de Rivera seizes power in Spain with the approval of King Alfonso XIII. Primo de Rivera exiles liberal opponents, such as writers Miguel de Unamuno y Jugo and Vicente Blasco Ibáñez.

**28 Sept.**  Ethiopia is admitted to the League of Nations despite British protests over Ethiopia's continued practice of slavery.

**22 Oct.**    A royalist revolt in Greece against the military government is quickly crushed but increases popular support for a republic. King George II is deposed and leaves Greece on 18 December.

**24 Oct.**    Clashes between police and Communist revolutionaries in Hamburg, Germany, kill 44 and wound 350.

**28 Oct.**    Reza Khan, minister of war in Persia, declares himself prime minister.

**29 Oct.**    Three weeks after Turkish nationalist troops occupy Constantinople, the Grand Assembly in Turkey proclaims the nation a republic and elects a new president, Mustafa Kemal, and a new premier, Ismet Pasha, ending six centuries of Ottoman rule.

**8 Nov.**    A putsch is launched in a Munich beer hall by Adolf Hitler and his Nazi followers but is crushed after one day. On 1 April 1924 Hitler is sentenced to nine months in prison, during which he writes *Mein Kampf*.

**5 Dec.**    Mexican rebels launch a revolt in Vera Cruz against the government of Álvaro Obregón. On 16 December, as rebel troops threaten Mexico City, the United States promises munitions to support the government.

**6 Dec.**    An international fleet of warships begins assembling at Canton after Sun Yat-sen, leader of southern China, threatens to close the free port.

**24 Dec.**    Martial law is declared in Honduras, and opponents of President Rafael López Gutiérrez are imprisoned. On 10 March 1924 Gutiérrez is killed by rebels supported by U.S. Marines.

**28 Dec.**    Alexandre-Gustave Eiffel, engineer on the Eiffel Tower and the Statue of Liberty, dies in Paris at age ninety-one.

# 1924

- E. M. Forster publishes his novel *A Passage to India* in London.

- *Der Zauberberg* (*The Magic Mountain*), Thomas Mann's symbolic novel set in a Swiss tuberculosis sanitarium, is published in Germany.

- I. A. Richards's *Principles of Literary Criticism*, which will influence literary criticism in the United States for more than thirty years, is published in England.

**18 Jan.**    A plot by the executive committee of the Communist International forces Russian Communist leader Leon Trotsky to retire to the Crimea. On 1 June he returns to Moscow to campaign against Leninist policies that prevail despite Lenin's death. Trotsky is expelled a second time on 10 December and dismissed as commissar of war on 18 January 1925.

**21 Jan.**    V. I. Lenin dies at age fifty-three.

**22 Jan.**    The British Labour Party wins its first election, making Ramsay MacDonald Britain's first Labour prime minister.

**25 Jan.**    The first Winter Olympics opens in Chamonix, France.

**27 Jan.**    The Treaty of Rome between Italy and Yugoslavia determines that Italy will take possession of the disputed port of Fiume but cede Porto Barros to Yugoslavia.

| | |
|---|---|
| **1 Feb.** | Britain becomes the first nation to formally recognize the Soviet Union. |
| **12 Feb.** | The sarcophagus of King Tutankhamen is opened after four thousand years. |
| **6 Apr.** | Rigged elections give Mussolini's Fascist Party a huge majority in the Italian parliament. |
| **13 Apr.** | Greek citizens vote to make their country a republic, and Greece is officially proclaimed a republic on 1 May. |
| **4 May** | The eighth Summer Olympics open in Paris. |
| **11 May** | Rioting between Communists and monarchists in Halle, Germany, kills thirty. |
| **3 June** | Franz Kafka, German-speaking Czech novelist, dies at age forty. |
| **10 June** | Socialist Giacomo Matteotti, an outspoken critic of Mussolini, is murdered by Fascists. In March 1926 the assassins are either acquitted or given light prison terms. |
| **5 July** | Gen. Isidor Lopes launches a bloody but unsuccessful rebellion in Brazil against the ineffectual government of Artur da Silva Bernardes, who then brings about minor economic reforms. |
| **3 Aug.** | Anglo-Polish novelist Joseph Conrad dies at age sixty-six. |
| **8 Sept.** | A military junta in Chile overthrows the liberal, reformist government of President Arturo Alessandri Palma. He is restored through a coup d'état on 23 January 1925 but resigns on 1 October 1925 because of continuing Chilean disorder. |
| **10 Sept.** | A revolt against the Soviet government breaks out in the Soviet republic of Georgia. |
| **12 Oct.** | Anatole France, France's leading literary figure and winner of the Nobel Prize in literature in 1921, dies at age eighty. |
| **13 Oct.** | Ibn Sa'ud, sultan of Nedj and leader of the Arabian Wahabis, captures Mecca in an attempt to expand his dominion in the Arabian Peninsula. By December 1925 he has also taken Medina, site of Muhammad's tomb. |
| **29 Oct.** | Frances Hodgson Burnett, British author of *Little Lord Fauntleroy* (1886) and *The Secret Garden* (1911), dies at age seventy-four. |
| **19 Nov.** | The assassination of Sir Lee Stack, commander of the Anglo-Egyptian army and British governor general of the Sudan, leads Britain to reassert its authority in Egypt; Stack's assassins are executed on 23 August 1925. |
| **29 Nov.** | Giacomo Puccini, Italian opera composer, dies at age sixty-five. |
| **30 Nov.** | Photographs are sent in a twenty-minute period by radio from London to New York. |
| **6 Dec.** | France begins wholesale arrests of Russian Communists in its country. |
| **27 Dec.** | Cesare Rossi, a former Mussolini lieutenant implicated in the murder of Matteotti, accuses Mussolini of serious crimes. |

# 1925

- The first volume of Adolf Hitler's *Mein Kampf* is published in Germany.

- Dmitry Shostakovich composes his first symphony.

- Sergey Eisenstein's movie *Potemkin* (*The Battleship Potemkin*) is produced.

- Franz Kafka's *Der Prozess* (*The Trial*) is published posthumously.

- *Albertine disparue* (*The Sweet Cheat Gone*), a section of Proust's *A la recherche du temps perdu* (*Remembrance of Things Past*), is published posthumously in France.

**7 Jan.** Germany elects a socialist, Paul Loebe, president of the Reichstag.

**24 Feb.** Kurdish rebels, under Sheik Said, launch a revolt against the Turkish government but are put down, and Said executed, within two months.

**28 Feb.** Friedrich Ebert, president of Germany, dies.

**12 Mar.** Sun Yat-sen, leader of China's Kuomintang party and president of the southern republic of China, dies at age fifty-nine.

**15 Apr.** Bolshevik agrarians in Bulgaria, backed by Soviet agents, attempt to assassinate the Bulgarian czar, Boris III. The following day they blow up the Cathedral of Sveti Krai in Sofia, killing 160 people.

**18–19 Apr.** Military leaders attempt a coup against the democratic government of Portugal's Manuel Teixeira Gomes. It fails, and in December Bernardino Machado, who had served as president from 1915 to 1917, is again elected to Portugal's highest office.

**26 Apr.** Field Marshal Paul von Hindenburg, at age seventy-eight, is elected president of Germany in a run-off election.

**14 May** H. Rider Haggard, English author of *King Solomon's Mines* (1885), dies at age sixty-nine.

**15 May** The Italian parliament grants women limited voting rights in certain elections.

**10 June** The Presbyterian, Methodist, and Congregational Churches in Canada merge to form the United Church of Canada.

**19 June** The French and Spanish armies, allied against the Riffs in Morocco, begin a blockade of all shipments entering Morocco in an attempt to prevent arms smuggling. On 26 July French forces reject an envoy from Riffian leader Abd-el-Krim attempting to negotiate Riffian autonomy. On 26 May 1926 the Franco-Spanish troops under the command of Marshal Henri Philippe Pétain conquer the Riffs and force Abd-el-Krim into exile. On 10 July 1926 France and Spain sign a treaty promising peace in Morocco between the two occupying forces.

**18 July** L'Exposition Internationale des Arts Décoratifs et Industriels Modernes (known as the Paris Exposition) opens and provides a venue and the name for art deco.

**7 Aug.** Druze rebels in Syria kill two hundred French soldiers and wound six hundred more in a revolt against the French mandate. The following day British troops in Transjordan mobilize on the Syrian border to prevent Druze rebels from fleeing Syria. On 20 September French troops attack Damascus and shell the native quarter.

**21 Aug.** A skirmish between Bulgarian and Greek troops near the tiny Turkish town of Demir Hissár launches a six-week border dispute between the two nations.

| | |
|---|---|
| **15 Sept.** | Russian Bolsheviks lead a revolt in Bessarabia, killing fifty Romanian troops, but the uprising is quickly put down. |
| **16 Oct.** | At Locarno, Switzerland, seven European nations negotiate a series of treaties that guarantee postwar borders and offer what Europeans consider the best hope for lasting peace. |
| **26 Nov.** | Rama VI, king of Siam, dies at age forty-four. |

## 1926

- *Metropolis*, director Fritz Lang's cinematic examination of power and technology, premieres in Germany.

- The production of Sean O'Casey's *The Plough and the Stars*, an unflattering portrayal of the Easter Rebellion, causes riots in Dublin.

- Britain's Academy of Choreographic Art, later the Royal Ballet, is founded by Ninette de Valois.

- English writer A. A. Milne publishes *Winnie-the-Pooh*, the first in this series of children's books.

| | |
|---|---|
| **3 Jan.** | Gen. Theodoros Pangalos leads a military coup in Greece and declares himself dictator. On 22 August Pangalos is overthrown by Gen. George Kondylas, who restores democracy. |
| **28 Jan.** | Viscount Takaakira Kato, premier of Japan since May 1924, dies at age sixty-six and is succeeded by commoner Reijiro Wakatsuki. |
| **8 Mar.** | The League of Nations calls a special session to admit Germany to membership but adjourns because of complications raised by Brazil and Spain over permanent seating on the council. On 11 June Brazil resigns from the League to protest nonrepresentation of Latin American states, and on 11 September Spain resigns when it is denied a permanent seat after Germany was unanimously admitted to the League of Nations on 7 September. |
| **7 Apr.** | Mussolini is shot and slightly wounded by a British woman, Violet Gibson. On 11 September he is unhurt when anarchist Gino Lucetti throws a bomb at his carriage, and on 31 October he is rescued by an angry mob that kills his fifteen-year-old would-be assassin, Anteo Zamboni. |
| **25 Apr.** | Reza Khan, prime minister of Persia, becomes shah, reigning as Reza Shah Pahlavi. He is first of the line that will remain in power in Iran until the Islamic revolution in 1979. |
| **1 May** | British coal miners go on strike, leading to a nationwide strike by millions of trade-union members. |
| **2 May** | Nicaraguan rebels, under Augusto César Sandino, launch a rebellion against the right-wing government of Emiliano Chamorro Vargas. In the early fall the uprising is quelled with the help of U.S. Marines, and on 11 November a conservative, Adolfo Díaz, is elected president. In December Juan Bautista Sacasa, the liberal vice president forced out by Sandino, sets up an opposition government, and civil war ensues. |
| **12 May** | A coup led by Marshal Józef Pilsudski overthrows the Polish government of Wincenty Witos. Pilsudski and his puppet president, Ignacy Moscicki, impose a highly repressive, rightist regime. |

**28 May**   Portuguese general Gomes da Costa leads a military coup that deposes President Bernardino Machado. On 9 July Gomes da Costa is, in turn, deposed in a second military coup led by Gen. António de Fragoso Carmona, who is elected president in March 1928.

**2 July**   Emile Coué, French psychotherapist who pioneered the use of auto-suggestion, dies at age sixty-nine.

**14 July**   President Mustafa Kemal Pasha of Turkey has fifteen members of the Young Turk Party executed for plotting against the government.

**23 Aug.**   Rudolph Valentino, Italian-born American movie actor, dies at age thirty-one following an appendectomy.

**5 Dec.**   French impressionist painter Claude Monet dies at age eighty-six.

**25 Dec.**   Yoshihito, emperor of Japan, dies at forty-seven and is succeeded by his son, Hirohito.

**29 Dec.**   Rainer Maria Rilke, German lyric poet, dies at age fifty-one.

## 1927

- *Napoléon,* director Abel Gance's ambitious silent film, premieres in France.

- *Le Temps retrouvé* (*Time Regained*), the final section of Proust's *A la recherche du temps perdu* (*Remembrance of Things Past*), is published in France, five years after Proust's death.

- Ivan Pavlov publishes *Conditioned Reflexes* in the Soviet Union.

- Martin Heidegger's classic of existentialist philosophy, *Sein und Zeit* (*Being and Time*), is published in Germany.

- *Der Steppenwolf* (*Steppenwolf*), Hermann Hesse's mystical novel of the outsider, is published in Germany.

**6 Jan.**   Wireless communication between London and New York City is established for public use.

**7 Mar.**   An earthquake in Osaka and Kobe, Japan, kills five thousand.

**7 Apr.**   The British government in India convicts eighteen men of antigovernment activity and sentences three to death.

**18 Apr.**   Nationalist Kuomintang leader Chiang Kai-shek splits with radical Chinese Communists and sets up a government at Nanjing. On 17 December he breaks diplomatic ties with the Soviet Union.

**4 May**   The United States negotiates an end to the civil war in Nicaragua. The two sides agree that President Adolfo Díaz will be allowed to remain in office until his successor is chosen through free elections supervised by Americans. On 4 November 1928 a liberal, José Moncado, is elected, and his party remains in power until it is overthrown by right-wing strongman Gen. Anastasio Somoza García in 1936.

**12 May**   British agents raid the headquarters of the Soviet propaganda office in London and seize documents intended to undermine the British government. Britain severs diplomatic ties with the Soviet Union on 26 May.

**15 May**   Excavation begins on the ancient Roman city of Herculaneum in southern Italy.

| | |
|---|---|
| **21 May** | Charles Lindbergh arrives in Paris and is greeted by ecstatic crowds after a thirty-three-and-one-half-hour nonstop flight from New York. |
| **22 May** | An earthquake in northern China kills more than 200,000 people. |
| **1 June** | Prohibition ends in Ontario, Canada, after eighteen years. |
| **15 July** | Irish Republican activist Constance Markievicz dies. |
| **15 July** | Rioting involving Socialists and monarchists in Vienna kills eighty-nine and injures more than six hundred. |
| **20 July** | King Ferdinand of Romania dies at age sixty-onc and is succeeded by his five-year-old grandson, Prince Mihai. |
| **29 Aug.** | Combat between Hindus and Moslems in India kills three hundred and injures almost three thousand. |
| **2 Oct.** | France expels the Soviet ambassador for encouraging revolution. |
| **3 Oct.** | Mexican rebels, led by Arnulfo Gómez and Francisco R. Serrano, revolt against the candidacy of former president Álvaro Obregón, who wishes to succeed Plutarco Elías Calles, president from 1924 to 1928. The rebels are defeated, and on 5 November Gómez is executed. |
| **12 Nov.** | Stalin expels Trotsky and his followers from the Communist Party and banishes them to the Soviet provinces. |
| **2 Dec.** | Olga Rudel-Zeunek is elected first female president of the Austrian senate. |
| **14 Dec.** | Britain grants Iraq a nominal independence but maintains military bases throughout the country. |

# 1928

- Eisenstein's film on the Russian Revolution, *October,* premieres in the Soviet Union.

- An early classic surrealist film, *Un Chien andalou* (*An Andalusian Dog*), by Luis Buñuel, Salvador Dali, and others, premieres in France.

- French composer Maurice Ravel produces *Boléro*.

- *Lady Chatterley's Lover,* D. H. Lawrence's controversial novel, is privately published in Florence, Italy. The full text is unavailable in Great Britain until 1960.

- Kurt Weill and Bertolt Brecht collaborate to produce *Die Dreigroschenoper* (*The Three-Penny Opera*) in Berlin.

- Evelyn Waugh's first novel, *Decline and Fall,* is published in London.

| | |
|---|---|
| **6 Jan.** | Pope Pius XI issues an encyclical condemning "Pan-Christian unity." |
| **11 Jan.** | Thomas Hardy, one of Britain's foremost men of letters, dies at age eighty-seven. |
| **28 Jan.** | Vicente Blasco Ibáñez, Spanish novelist best known for his popular 1916 work *Los cuatro jinetes del Apocalipsis* (*The Four Horsemen of the Apocalypse*), dies at age sixty-one. |

| | |
|---|---|
| **2 Feb.** | Transjordan signs a treaty with Britain creating an independent constitutional monarchy. |
| **11 Feb.** | The second Winter Olympics opens in Saint Moritz, Switzerland. |
| **2 Mar.** | Egypt rejects a treaty with Britain perceived to limit Egyptian sovereignty and is warned that British authority will not be compromised. |
| **22 Mar.** | Spain revokes its September 1926 decision to resign from the League of Nations. |
| **25 Mar.** | General Carmona is elected president of Portugal. In April he appoints rising statesman Antonio de Oliveira Salazar his minister of finance. |
| **12 Apr.** | German financier Gunther von Huenefeld completes the first successful east to west transatlantic flight. |
| **24 Apr.** | Chinese Nationalist forces led by Chiang Kai-shek capture Peking (Peiping). On 5 May Chiang Tso-Lin, warlord of Manchuria, is killed during a retreat from Peking after his defeat by nationalist forces. These forces clash on 14 May with Japanese troops at Tsinan-fu. On 8 June Chiang Kai-shek enters Peking after conquering much of northern China and dissipating the power of the feudal warlords. |
| **17 May** | The ninth Summer Olympics open in Amsterdam, Holland. |
| **7 June** | Hungary is cited by the League of Nations for importing five freight cars of machine-gun parts from Italy, thereby violating the Treaty of Trianon. |
| **14 June** | Emmeline Pankhurst, the original British suffragist organizer, dies at age sixty-nine. |
| **18 June** | Norwegian explorer Roald Amundsen disappears with his pilot and crew while attempting to rescue a stranded polar expedition. |
| **2 July** | Great Britain lowers the voting age for women from thirty to twenty-one, the voting age for British men. |
| **10 July** | Japan withdraws its troops from Shandong, China. |
| **17 July** | Álvaro Obregón, reelected president of Mexico on 1 July, is assassinated in Mexico City by forces convinced that he and former president Plutarco Elías Calles are using their reform movement to undermine the Roman Catholic Church. On 8 November José de Léon Toral is sentenced to death for the assassination, and a nun, Sister María Concepcíon Acevedo y de la Llata, is sentenced to twenty years as "intellectual author" of the crime. |
| **19 July** | King Faud of Egypt suspends the Egyptian parliament and assumes legislative control under British authority. |
| **21 July** | Ellen Terry, acclaimed British actress, dies at age eighty. |
| **27 Aug.** | The Pact of Paris, an ineffective agreement by twenty-three nations to outlaw war, is signed in Paris. |
| **27 Aug.** | Mustafa Kemal Pasha, president of Turkey, replaces the Arabic alphabet with the Roman alphabet for all future written communication in Turkey. |
| **12 Sept.** | Spain arrests more than two thousand protesters on the fifth anniversary of the dictatorship of Miguel Primo de Rivera. |

| | |
|---|---|
| **7 Oct.** | Ras Tafari becomes king of Ethiopia, and on 2 November 1930 he is named king of kings with the title Haile Selassie I. |
| **25 Nov.** | Mountain tribes in Afghanistan launch a major revolt against King Amanollah to protest his attempts at social reform. He abdicates on 14 January 1929 in favor of his brother, Inayatullah, who on 17 January is deposed by bandit leader Bacha-i-Saquao. On 3 November 1929 Gen. Mohammed Nadir Shah assumes the throne of Afghanistan and stabilizes the nation. |
| **24 Dec.** | Hungarian police arrest leaders of the Fascist Party and charge them with treason. |

## 1929

- Erich Maria Remarque's antiwar novel, *Im Westen nichts Neues* (*All Quiet on the Western Front*), is published in Germany.

- Virginia Woolf's groundbreaking examination of women and literature, *A Room of One's Own*, is published in England.

- Construction of the Maginot Line, a system of fortifications on the French-German border, begins in France.

| | |
|---|---|
| **5 Jan.** | Alexander I, king of the Serbs, Croats, and Slovenes since August 1921, proclaims himself dictator. On 3 October he officially renames the state Yugoslavia. |
| **16 Jan.** | Stalin expels Trotsky from European Russia and on 23 January arrests 150 of Trotsky's followers on charges of conspiracy. Trotsky takes refuge in Constantinople, then Norway, then Mexico, where in 1940 he is assassinated by Stalinists. |
| **11 Feb.** | The Lateran treaties between Italy and the Roman Catholic Church are signed, creating Vatican City — a 108.7-acre section of Rome encompassing Saint Peter's Church and the Vatican — as a sovereign state. |
| **12 Feb.** | English actress Lillie Langtry dies at age seventy-five. |
| **2 Mar.** | Gen. Jesús María Aguirre launches an unsuccessful two-month revolt in Vera Cruz against the government of Mexican president Emilio Portes Gil and the power behind Portes Gil, former president Plutarco Elías Calles. |
| **20 Mar.** | French general Ferdinand Foch, commander of the Allied expeditionary forces in World War I, dies at age seventy-eight. |
| **1 May** | Communist rioting in Berlin kills twenty and injures fifty. |
| **20 May** | Germany signs the Pact of Paris outlawing war. |
| **5 Aug.** | Millicent Garrett Fawcett, British suffragist organizer, dies at age eighty-two. |
| **19 Aug.** | Sergey Diaghilev, Russian ballet impresario in Paris, dies at age fifty-seven. |
| **22 Aug.** | A wave of Arab violence against Jews in the British mandate of Palestine kills hundreds. |
| **20 Oct.** | The new state of Tadzhikistan joins the U.S.S.R. |
| **6 Nov.** | Prince Maximilian, Germany's first republican chancellor, dies at age sixty-two. |

| | |
|---|---|
| **17 Nov.** | Moderate leader Nikolay Bukharin is expelled by the Politburo of the Central Committee of the Soviet Communist Party. Stalin is now clearly dictator of the U.S.S.R. |
| **24 Nov.** | Georges Clemenceau, former premier of France, dies. |
| **5 Dec.** | U.S. Marines put down a revolt against American control in Haiti. |
| **17 Dec.** | Gen. Gomes da Costa, former dictator of Portugal, dies in exile. |
| **21 Dec.** | Seventy are arrested in Mexico after the discovery of a plot to assassinate public officials. |

CHAPTER TWO

# THE ARTS

by MATTHEW J. BRUCCOLI and ARLYN BRUCCOLI

## CONTENTS

*Sidebars and tables are listed in italics.*

## 1920

**Movies**    *Dr. Jekyll and Mr. Hyde,* starring John Barrymore and Nita Naldi; *Way Down East,* starring Lillian Gish and Richard Barthelmess, directed by D. W. Griffith; *The Mark of Zorro,* starring Douglas Fairbanks; *Pollyanna,* starring Mary Pickford; *The Kid,* starring Charlie Chaplin.

**Fiction**    F. Scott Fitzgerald, *This Side of Paradise* and *Flappers and Philosophers;* Sinclair Lewis, *Main Street;* Sherwood Anderson, *Poor White;* Willa Cather, *Youth and the Bright Medusa;* Zane Grey, *The Man of the Forest;* Peter B. Kyne, *Kindred of the Dust;* Harold Bell Wright, *The Re-Creation of Brian Kent;* James Oliver Curwood, *The River's End;* Joseph C. Lincoln, *The Portygee.*

**Poetry**    T. S. Eliot, *Poems;* Ezra Pound, *Umbra* and *Hugh Selwyn Mauberley;* William Carlos Williams, *Kora in Hell;* Edna St. Vincent Millay, *A Few Figs from Thistles;* Carl Sandburg, *Smoke and Steel;* E. A. Robinson, *Lancelot.*

**Popular Songs**    Ted Lewis, "When My Baby Smiles at Me"; Paul Whiteman, "Whispering"; Al Jolson, "My Mammy" and "Avalon"; Bert Williams, "When the Moon Shines on the Moonshine"; Mamie Smith, "Crazy Blues"; Van & Schenck, "After You Get What You Want, You Don't Want It"; Ben Selvin, "Dardanella"; Nora Bayes, "Japanese Sandman"; Original Dixieland Jazz Band, "Margie"; Billy Murray, "I'll see You in C-U-B-A."

- Marcel Duchamp, Man Ray, and Katherine Dreier organize the New York Societé Anonyme for promoting modern art.

- The Pavley-Oukrainsky Ballet of the Chicago Civic Opera is the first American Ballet Company.

- The Julliard Foundation is established in New York to encourage music in the United States.

- Joseph Stella paints *Brooklyn Bridge.*

- Thomas Hart Benton paints *Portrait of Josie West.*

- Arturo Toscanini and the LaScala Orchestra give their first American performances.

- Jo Davidson sculpts *Gertrude Stein.*

- Lorado Taft sculpts *Fountain of Time.*

**2 Feb.**    Eugene O'Neill's *Beyond the Horizon* opens.

**7 June**    *George White Scandals* opens with songs by George Gershwin.

**1 Nov.**    Eugene O'Neill's *The Emperor Jones* opens.

**21 Dec.**    Zona Gale's *Miss Lulu Bett* opens.

## 1921

**Movies**    *The Four Horsemen of the Apocalypse,* starring Rudolph Valentino; *Tol'able David,* starring Richard Barthelmess; *The Three Musketeers,* starring Douglas Fairbanks; *Little Lord Fauntleroy,* starring Mary Pickford.

**Fiction**    John Dos Passos, *Three Soldiers;* Sherwood Anderson, *The Triumph of the Egg;* Ring W. Lardner, *The Big Town;* Donald Ogden Stewart, *A Parody Outline of History;* Booth Tarkington, *Alice Adams;* Dorothy Canfield, *The Brimming Cup;* Zane Grey, *The Mysterious Rider;* Edith Wharton, *The Age of Innocence.*

**Poetry**  Edna St. Vincent Millay, *Second April;* Marianne Moore, *Poems;* E. A. Robinson, *Collected Poems.*

**Popular Songs**  Fanny Brice, "Second Hand Rose"; Van & Schenck, "Ain't We Got Fun?"; Lottie Gee, "I'm Just Wild About Harry"; Eddie Cantor, "Ma! (He's Making Eyes at Me)"; Charles Davis, "Shuffle Along"; Eubie Blake, "Bandana Days"; Al Jolson, "April Showers"; Isham Jones, "Wabash Blues"; John Steel, "Say It With Music"; Zez Confrey, "Kitten on the Keys."

- Prokofiev's *The Love for Three Oranges* has its world premiere at the Chicago Civic Opera.

- Charles Ives composes *Thirty-Four Songs for Voices and Piano.*

- Howard Hansen composes Concerto for Organ, Strings, and Harp.

- The Eastman School of Music opens in Rochester, New York.

- Stuart Davis paints *Bull Durham.*

- Isadora Duncan opens a dance school in Moscow.

- Charles Demuth paints *Roofs and Steeples.*

- Arthur G. Dove paints *Thunderstorm.*

- John Marin paints *Off Stonington.*

- Phillips Gallery opens in Washington, D.C. — the first American museum of modern art.

**23 May**  *Shuffle Along,* with music by Eubie Blake and Noble Sissle, opens; it is the first black Broadway musical directed and written by blacks.

**1 June**  Eugene O'Neill's *Gold* opens.

**2 Nov.**  Eugene O'Neill's *Anna Christie* opens.

**10 Nov.**  Eugene O'Neill's *The Straw* opens.

# 1922

**Movies**  *The Prisoner of Zenda,* starring Ramon Novarro; *Orphans of the Storm,* starring Lillian and Dorothy Gish, directed by D. W. Griffith; *Blood and Sand,* starring Rudolph Valentino; *Foolish Wives,* directed by and starring Erich Von Stroheim; *Robin Hood,* starring Douglas Fairbanks; *Nanook of the North,* documentary directed by Robert Flaherty.

**Fiction**  Sinclair Lewis, *Babbitt;* James Joyce, *Ulysses;* E. E. Cummings, *The Enormous Room;* Willa Cather, *One of Ours;* Emerson Hough, *The Covered Wagon;* F. Scott Fitzgerald, *Tales of the Jazz Age.*

**Poetry**  T. S. Eliot, *The Waste Land.*

**Popular Songs**  Al Jolson, "Toot Toot Tootsie"; Paul Whiteman, "Chicago"; Harry Creamer & Turner Layton, "Way Down Yonder in New Orleans"; Irene Bordoni, "Do It Again"; Sophie Tucker, "Lovin' Sam the Sheik of Alabam' "; Gallagher & Sheean, "Mr. Gallagher and Mr. Sheean"; The Georgians, "I Wish I Could Shimmy Like My Sister Kate"; Van & Schenck, "Carolina in the Morning."

- George Antheil composes *Airplane Sonata* and *Death of the Machines.*

- Aaron Copland composes *Passacaglia for Piano.*

- George Bellows paints *The White House.*

- Maurice Prendergast paints *Acadia.*

- The Baltimore Museum of Art opens.

- Howard Hansen composes Symphony #1.

**9 Mar.**     Eugene O'Neill's *The Hairy Ape* opens.

**23 May**     *Abie's Irish Rose* by Anne Nichols opens; this much-ridiculed comedy about a Catholic/Jewish marriage sets a record of 2,327 Broadway performances.

**7 Nov.**     *Rain,* based on W. Somerset Maugham's "Miss Thompson," starring Jeanne Eagels, opens.

# 1923

**Movies**     *Safety Last,* starring Harold Lloyd; *The Ten Commandments,* starring Richard Dix and Rod LaRocque, directed by Cecil B. DeMille; *The Covered Wagon,* starring Lois Wilson; *The Hunchback of Notre Dame,* starring Lon Chaney; *The Pilgrim,* starring Charlie Chaplin.

**Fiction**     Sherwood Anderson, *Horses and Men* and *Many Marriages;* Willa Cather, *A Lost Lady;* Ernest Hemingway, *3 Stories & 10 Poems.*

**Poetry**     E. E. Cummings, *Tulips and Chimneys;* Robert Frost, *New Hampshire;* Edna St. Vincent Millay, *The Ballad of the Harp-Weaver;* Kahlil Gibran, *The Prophet;* Wallace Stevens, *Harmonium.*

**Popular Songs**     Billy Jones, "Yes, We Have No Bananas"; Jelly Roll Morton, "Mr. Jelly Lord"; Van & Schenck, "Who's Sorry Now?" and "That Old Gang of Mine"; Elisabeth Welch, "Charleston"; Wendell Hall, "It Ain't Gonna Rain No Mo' "; Jones & Hare, "Barney Google"; Sophie Tucker, "You've Got to See Mamma Ev'ry Night or You Can't See Mamma at All"; Bessie Smith, "Down Hearted Blues"; Paul Whiteman, "Linger Awhile" and "Three O'Clock in the Morning."

- Roger Sessions composes *The Black Maskers.*

- George Bellows paints *Between Rounds.*

- Charles Shuler paints *Bucks County Barn.*

- Rockwell Kent paints *Shadows of Evening.*

- Mikhail Mordkin ballet company, with Martha Graham, performs in the *Greenwich Village Follies.*

**10 Feb.**     *Icebound* by Owen Davis opens.

**16 Feb.**     Bessie Smith makes her first recordings ("Down Hearted Blues" and "Gulf Coast Blues").

**19 Mar.**     *The Adding Machine* by Elmer Rice opens; it is an early expressionistic drama.

**30–31 Mar.**     The first dance marathon in the United States is held in Audubon Ballroom, New York.

**1924**

| | |
|---|---|
| **6 Apr.** | Louis Armstrong records his first solo on "Chimes Blues" with King Oliver's Creole Jazz Band. |
| **29 Oct.** | *Runnin' Wild* opens; the all-black musical with songs by James P. Johnson and Cecil Mack introduces "Charleston." |

**Movies**  The Thief of Baghdad, starring Douglas Fairbanks; *Monsieur Beaucaire*, starring Rudolph Valentino; *Greed*, starring ZaSu Pitts, directed by Erich Von Stroheim; *He Who Gets Slapped*, starring Lon Chaney; *Sherlock Holmes, Jr.,* starring Buster Keaton; *The Iron Horse*, starring George O'Brien, directed by John Ford; *Beau Brummel*, starring John Barrymore.

**Fiction**  James Gould Cozzens, *Confusion;* Ring W. Lardner, *How to Write Short Stories;* Edith Wharton, *Old New York;* Louis Bromfield, *The Green Bay Tree;* Edna Ferber, *So Big;* Ernest Hemingway, *in our time;* Herman Melville, *Billy Budd;* Glenway Wescott, *The Apple of the Eye.*

**Poetry**  Robinson Jeffers, *Tamar;* Marianne Moore, *Observations;* Edgar Lee Masters, *The New Spoon River Anthology;* John Crowe Ransom, *Chills and Fever.*

**Popular Songs**  Blossom Seeley, "Alabamy Bound"; Marion Harris, "It Had to Be You"; Winnie Lightner, "Somebody Loves Me"; Mary Ellis & Dennis King, "Indian Love Call"; Isham Jones, "I'll See You in My Dreams"; Al Jolson, "California, Here I Come" and "The One I Love"; Fred & Adele Astaire & Cliff Edwards, "Fascinating Rhythm"; Walter Catlett, "Oh Lady, Be Good"; Grace Moore & John Steel, "What'll I Do?"; Cliff Edwards, "Just Give Me a June Night, the Moonlight, and You."

- Aaron Copland composes Symphony for Organ and Orchestra.

- John Alden Carpenter composes *Skyscrapers.*

- George Bellows paints *Dempsey and Firpo.*

- Georgia O'Keeffe paints *Dark Abstraction.*

- Michel Fokine forms the American Ballet.

- Arthur G. Dove paints *Portrait of Ralph Dusenberry.*

- Serge Koussevitsky is appointed head of the Boston Symphony.

- George Antheil composes *Ballet Mécanique.*

- Ferde Grofé composes *Mississippi Suite.*

- Charles Ives composes Three Pieces for Two Pianos.

- Metro-Goldwyn-Mayer is formed with Louis B. Mayer president and Irving Thalberg second vice president and head of production.

| | |
|---|---|
| **5 Feb.** | *Hell-Bent fer Heaven* by Hatcher Hughes opens. |
| **18 Feb.** | Bix Beiderbecke records "Fidgety Feet" and "Jazz Me Blues" with The Wolverines. |
| **24 Feb.** | George Gershwin's *Rhapsody in Blue* is performed by Paul Whiteman's orchestra in New York. |

**15 May**    Eugene O'Neill's *All God's Chillun Got Wings* opens — the play is controversial because its subject is miscegenation.

**2 Sept.**   *Rose Marie* opens with songs by Rudolph Friml and Otto Harbach.

**5 Sept.**   *What Price Glory?* by Maxwell Anderson and Lawrence Stallings opens, starring Louis Wolheim and William Boyd.

**Nov.**      Duke Ellington's Washingtonians make their first recordings ("Choo Choo" and "Rainy Nights").

**3 Nov.**    Eugene O'Neill's *S. S. Glencairn* opens.

**11 Nov.**   Eugene O'Neill's *Desire Under the Elms* opens.

**24 Nov.**   *They Knew What They Wanted* by Sidney Howard opens.

**1 Dec.**    *Lady, Be Good!* opens with songs by George and Ira Gershwin; it stars Fred and Adele Astaire.

**2 Dec.**    *The Student Prince* opens with music by Sigmund Romberg.

# 1925

**Movies**    *The Phantom of the Opera*, starring Lon Chaney; *Grass*, directed by Merian C. Cooper; *The Gold Rush*, starring Charlie Chaplin; *The Freshman*, starring Harold Lloyd; *The Merry Widow*, starring Mae Murray and John Gilbert, directed by Erich Von Stroheim; *The Big Parade*, starring John Gilbert; *Ben-Hur*, starring Ramon Novarro and Francis X. Bushman.

**Fiction**   F. Scott Fitzgerald, *The Great Gatsby;* Ernest Hemingway, *In Our Time;* Theodore Dreiser, *An American Tragedy;* Sinclair Lewis, *Arrowsmith;* John Dos Passos, *Manhattan Transfer;* Ellen Glasgow, *Barren Ground;* Anita Loos, *"Gentlemen Prefer Blondes";* John Erskine, *The Private Life of Helen of Troy.*

**Poetry**    E. E. Cummings, *&* and *XLI Poems;* T. S. Eliot, *The Hollow Men;* Robinson Jeffers, *Roan Stallion, Tamar and Other Poems;* Ezra Pound, *A Draft of XVI Cantos;* Amy Lowell, *What's O'Clock;* Countee Cullen, *Color.*

**Popular Songs**    Al Jolson, "Swanee" and "I'm Sitting on the Top of the World"; Louise Groody & Charles Winninger, "I Want to be Happy"; Louise Groody & John Barker, "Tea for Two"; Eddie Cantor, "If You Knew Susie Like I Know Susie"; Ben Bernie, "Sweet Georgia Brown"; Cliff Edwards, "Sleepy Time Gal"; Ethel Waters, "Dinah"; June Cochrane & Sterling Holloway, "Manhattan"; Fred Waring's Pennsylvanians, "Collegiate"; Vincent Lopez, "Always"; Gene Austin, "Yes Sir, That's My Baby" and "Five Foot Two, Eyes of Blue; — Has Anybody Seen My Girl?"

- John Alden Carpenter composes Jazz Orchestra Pieces.

- Paul Whiteman's orchestra performs George Gershwin's *135th Street* at Carnegie Hall in New York.

- Edward Hopper paints *House by the Railroad*.

- Man Ray paints *Sugar Loaves*.

- Paul Manship sculpts *Flight of Europa*.

- John D. Rockefeller funds the Cloisters in New York.

- The John Simon Guggenheim Memorial Foundation is founded.

**17 May**   *Garrick Gaieties* opens with songs by Richard Rodgers and Lorenz Hart.

**1 Sept.–**
**31 Oct.**   The Denishawn dancers are the first American dance company to tour the Orient.

**21 Sept.**   *The Vagabond King* opens with music by Rudolph Friml.

**22 Sept.**   *Sunny* opens with songs by Jerome Kern, Otto Harbach, and Oscar Hammerstein II; it stars Marilyn Miller, Clifton Webb, and Jack Donahue.

**12 Oct.**   *Craig's Wife* by George Kelly opens.

**12 Nov.**   Louis Armstrong makes his first recording with the Hot Five ("Gut Bucket Blues").

**3 Dec.**   George Gershwin's Concerto in F for Piano and Orchestra has its premiere at Carnegie Hall, New York.

**8 Dec.**   *The Coconuts* opens with songs by Irving Berlin; it stars the Marx Brothers.

# 1926

**Movies**   *Beau Geste,* starring Ronald Colman; *The Strong Man,* starring Harry Langdon; *The Sea Beast,* starring John Barrymore; *What Price Glory?,* starring Victor McLaglen and Edmund Lowe; *The Black Pirate,* starring Douglas Fairbanks (first Technicolor movie); *La Boheme,* starring Lillian Gish and John Gilbert; *The Son of the Sheik,* starring Rudolph Valentino; *The Torrent,* starring Greta Garbo.

**Fiction**   Ernest Hemingway, *The Sun Also Rises;* William Faulkner, *Soldiers' Pay;* Willa Cather, *My Mortal Enemy;* Edna Ferber, *Show Boat;* Ellen Glasgow, *The Romantic Comedians;* Ring W. Lardner, *The Love Nest;* Thornton Wilder, *The Cabala;* Thorne Smith, *Topper;* Earl Derr Biggers, *The Chinese Parrot;* F. Scott Fitzgerald, *All the Sad Young Men.*

**Poetry**   Hart Crane, *White Buildings;* Langston Hughes, *The Weary Blues;* Sara Teasdale, *Dark of the Moon.*

**Popular**
**Songs**   Ann Pennington, "Black Bottom"; Melody Sheiks, "The Blue Room" and "The Girl Friend"; McKinney's Cotton Pickers, "If I Could Be with You One Hour To-Night"; Georgie Price, "Bye Bye Blackbird"; Abe Lyman, "What Can I Say After I Say I'm Sorry?"; Al Jolson, "Breezin' Along With the Breeze"; Harry Richman, "The Birth of the Blues"; Eddie Cantor, "Baby Face"; Gertrude Lawrence, "Someone to Watch Over Me" and "Do-Do-Do"; Sophie Tucker, "When the Red, Red Robin Comes Bob, Bob, Bobbin' Along"; Louis Armstrong, "Heebie Jeebies"; Duke Ellington, "East St. Louis Toodle-oo."

- Walt Kuhn paints *Dressing Room.*

- Thomas Hart Benton paints *The Lord Is My Shepherd.*

- Paul Manship sculpts *Indian Hunter.*

- Bix Beiderbecke joins Frankie Trumbauer's band at the Arcadia Ballroom in Saint Louis.

- Margaret H'Doubler establishes the first dance department at the University of Wisconsin.

**23 Jan.**     Eugene O'Neill's *The Great God Brown* opens.

**17 Mar.**     *The Girl Friend* opens with songs by Richard Rodgers and Lorenz Hart.

**18 Apr.**     The first professional performance is given by Martha Graham & Trio at 48th Street Theater, New York.

**19 June**     George Antheil's *Ballet Mécanique* is performed in Paris.

**15 Sept.**     Jelly Roll Morton makes his first recordings with The Red Hot Peppers ("Black-bottom Stomp," "Smokehouse Blues," and "The Chant").

**8 Nov.**     *Oh, Kay!* opens with songs by George and Ira Gershwin; it stars Victor Moore and Gertrude Lawrence.

**30 Nov.**     *The Desert Song* opens with songs by Sigmund Romberg, Otto Harbach, and Oscar Hammerstein II.

**30 Dec.**     *In Abraham's Bosom* by Paul Green opens; it is an all-black drama.

# 1927

**Movies**     *The Jazz Singer,* starring Al Jolson; *The Scarlet Letter,* starring Lillian Gish; *It,* starring Clara Bow; *The General,* starring Buster Keaton; *Wings,* starring Buddy Rogers and Clara Bow; *Underworld,* starring George Bancroft, Evelyn Brent, and Clive Brook; *Flesh and the Devil,* starring John Gilbert and Greta Garbo; *Seventh Heaven,* starring Janet Gaynor and Charles Farrell; *Love,* starring John Gilbert and Greta Garbo; *The King of Kings,* directed by Cecil B. DeMille; *The Way of All Flesh,* starring Emil Jannings.

**Fiction**     Conrad Aiken, *Blue Voyage;* James Branch Cabell, *Something About Eve;* Willa Cather, *Death Comes to the Archbishop;* Julia Peterkin, *Black April;* Upton Sinclair, *Oil!;* Edith Wharton, *Twilight Sleep;* S. S. Van Dine, *The Canary Murder Case;* Thornton Wilder, *The Bridge of San Luis Rey;* Sinclair Lewis, *Elmer Gantry.*

**Poetry**     Countee Cullen, *The Ballad of the Brown Girl: An Old Ballad Retold, Caroling Dusk,* and *Copper Sun;* Langston Hughes, *Fine Clothes to the Jew;* Don Marquis, *Archy and Mehitabel;* E. A. Robinson, *Tristram.*

**Popular Songs**     Jules Bledsoe, "Ol' Man River"; Helen Morgan, "Bill"; and "Can't Help Lovin' Dat Man"; Norma Terris, Howard Marsh, Charles Winninger & Edna May Oliver, "Why Do I Love You?"; Fred Astaire, " 'S Wonderful"; Fain & Dunn, "Let a Smile Be Your Umbrella"; Belle Baker, "Blue Skies"; William Gaxton & Constance Carpenter, "My Heart Stood Still" and "Thou Swell"; John Price Jones & Mary Lawler, "The Best Things in Life are Free"; Frank Fay, "Me and My Shadow"; Gene Austin, "My Blue Heaven"; Ruth Etting, "It All Depends on You"; Vernon Dalhart, "Lindbergh, Eagle of the U.S.A."

- Roy Harris composes Concerto for Piano, Clarinet, and String Quartet.

- Roger Sessions composes Symphony in E Minor.

- Aaron Copland composes Concerto for Piano and Orchestra.

- Edward Hopper paints *Manhattan Bridge.*

- Georgia O'Keeffe paints *Radiator Building*.

- Charles Demuth paints *My Egypt*.

- Mahonri Young sculpts *Right to the Jaw*.

**26 Jan.** *Saturday's Children* by Maxwell Anderson opens.

**31 Jan.** *The Road to Rome* by Robert E. Sherwood opens; it stars Jane Cowl.

**25 Apr.** *Hit the Deck* opens with songs by Vincent Youmans and Lee Robin.

**6 Sept.** *Good News* opens with songs by Ray Henderson, B. G. DeSylva, and Lew Brown.

**8 Sept.** Bix Beiderbecke records "In a Mist."

**3 Nov.** *A Connecticut Yankee* opens with songs by Richard Rodgers and Lorenz Hart.

**22 Nov.** *Funny Face* opens with songs by George and Ira Gershwin; it stars Fred and Adele Astaire.

**4 Dec.** Duke Ellington's orchestra begins a long engagement at the Cotton Club in Harlem.

**27 Dec.** *Show Boat* opens with songs by Jerome Kern and Oscar Hammerstein II; it stars Helen Morgan, Charles Winninger, and Edna May Oliver.

**27 Dec.** *Paris Bound* by Philip Barry opens.

# 1928

**Movies** *The Wedding March,* starring Erich Von Stroheim and ZaSu Pitts, directed by Von Stroheim; *Lilac Time,* starring Colleen Moore and Gary Cooper; *The Circus,* starring Charlie Chaplin; *The Singing Fool,* starring Al Jolson; *Our Dancing Daughters,* starring Joan Crawford.

**Fiction** Djuna Barnes, *Ryder;* Upton Sinclair, *Boston;* Glenway Wescott, *Goodbye, Wisconsin;* Edith Wharton, *The Children;* Earl Derr Biggers, *Behind That Curtain;* Viña Delmar, *Bad Girl.*

**Poetry** Stephen Vincent Benét, *John Brown's Body;* Robert Frost, *West-Running Brook;* Robinson Jeffers, *Cawder;* Ezra Pound, *A Draft of Cantos XVII to XXVII;* Allen Tate, *Mr. Pope.*

**Popular Songs** Helen Kane, "I Wanna Be Loved By You"; Bix Beiderbecke with Paul Whiteman, "Thou Swell"; Gene Austin, "Ramona"; Evelyn Herbert, "Lover, Come Back to Me"; Ona Munson & Jack Whiting, "You're the Cream in My Coffee"; Ben Bernie, Peggy Chamberlin & June O'Dea, "Crazy Rhythm"; Ruth Etting, "Love Me or Leave Me"; Eddie Cantor, "Makin' Whoopee"; Rudy Vallee, "Sweet Lorraine"; Ruth Etting, "I'll Get By"; Jimmie Rodgers, "Blue Yodel."

- Virgil Thomson composes *Four Saints in Three Acts;* the libretto is by Gertrude Stein.

- John Alden Carpenter composes String Quartet.

- Arturo Toscanini becomes conductor of the New York Philharmonic.

- Walter Piston composes *Symphonic Piece*.
- Charles Demuth paints *I Saw the Figure 5 in Gold*.
- Charles Sheeler paints *River Rouge Industrial Plant*.
- John Steuart Curry paints *Baptism in Kansas*.
- John Sloan paints *Sixth Avenue Elevated at Third Street*.
- *Le Sacre du Printemps* is produced featuring Martha Graham.
- *The Oxford English Dictionary* is published.
- "Dance Derby of the Century" is closed after three weeks.
- The Doris Humphrey–Charles Weidman dance company is formed in New York.
- Louis Hart conducts the dance composition classes at the Neighborhood Playhouse, New York.

**9 Jan.** Eugene O'Neill's *Marco Millions* opens.

**10 Jan.** *Rosalie* opens with songs by George and Ira Gershwin, P. G. Wodehouse, and Sigmund Romberg; it stars Marilyn Miller, Frank Morgan, and Jack Donahue.

**30 Jan.** Eugene O'Neill's *Strange Interlude* opens.

**9 May** *Blackbirds of 1928* opens with songs by Jimmy McHugh and Dorothy Fields; the all-black cast stars Bill Robinson and Adelaide Hall.

**14 Aug.** *The Front Page* by Charles MacArthur and Ben Hecht opens; the newspaper melodrama stars Lee Tracy and Osgood Perkins.

**19 Sept.** *New Moon* opens with songs by Sigmund Romberg and Oscar Hammerstein II.

**23 Oct.** *Animal Crackers* opens with songs by Harry Ruby and Bert Kalamar; it stars the Marx Brothers.

**26 Nov.** *Holiday* by Philip Barry opens; it stars Hope Williams.

**4 Dec.** *Whoopee* with songs by Walter Donaldson and Gus Kahn opens; it stars Eddie Cantor and Ruth Etting.

**13 Dec.** George Gershwin's *An American in Paris* premieres at Carnegie Hall, New York.

# 1929

**Movies** *The Taming of the Shrew*, starring Mary Pickford and Douglas Fairbanks; *The Love Parade*, starring Jeanette MacDonald and Maurice Chevalier, directed by Ernst Lubitsch; *Hallelujah*, directed by King Vidor; *The Broadway Melody*, starring Charles King and Bessie Love; *Steamboat Willie*, produced by Walt Disney and starring Mickey Mouse; *In Old Arizona*, starring Warner Baxter; *Coquette*, starring Mary Pickford.

**Fiction**    Ernest Hemingway, *A Farewell to Arms;* Thomas Wolfe, *Look Homeward, Angel;* William Faulkner, *Sartoris* and *The Sound and the Fury;* Sinclair Lewis, *Dodsworth;* Frederic Dannay and Manfred Lee (Ellery Queen), *The Roman Hat Mystery;* Ellen Glasgow, *They Stooped to Folly;* Dashiell Hammett, *Red Harvest;* Theodore Dreiser, *A Galley of Women;* Ring W. Lardner, *Round Up;* Claude McKay, *Banjo;* John Steinbeck, *Cup of Gold;* Edith Wharton, *Hudson River Bracketed;* Chic Sale, *The Specialist;* Oliver LaFarge, *Laughing Boy;* Lloyd C. Douglas, *The Magnificent Obsession;* S. S. Van Dine, *The Bishop Murder Case.*

**Poetry**    Robinson Jeffers, *Dear Judas;* Conrad Aiken, *Selected Poems;* Louise Bogan, *Dark Summer;* Countee Cullen, *The Black Christ;* E. A. Robinson, *Cavender's House.*

**Popular Songs**    Nick Lucas, "Tiptoe Through the Tulips With Me"; Cliff Edwards, The Rounders & The Brox Sisters, "Singin' in the Rain"; Ethel Waters, "Am I Blue?"; Rudy Vallee, "I'm Just a Vagabond Lover"; Lillian Taiz & John Hundley, "With a Song in My Heart"; Louis Armstrong, "Ain't Misbehavin' "; William Gaxton & Genevieve Tobin, "You Do Something to Me"; Ruth Etting, "Button Up Your Overcoat"; Libby Holman, "Moanin' Low"; Helen Morgan, "Why Was I Born?"; Al Jolson, "Liza"; Charles King, "Broadway Melody."

- Samuel Barber composes Serenade for String Quartet.

- Walter Piston composes Viola Concerto.

- Roy Harris composes *American Portraits.*

- Edward Hopper paints *The Lighthouse at Two Lights.*

- Charles Shuler paints *Upper Deck.*

- Thomas Hart Benton paints *Georgia Cotton Pickers.*

- Arthur G. Dove paints *Foghorns.*

- Alexander Calder sculpts *Circus.*

- Saul Baizerman sculpts *Hod Carrier.*

- Isamu Noguchi sculpts *Martha Graham.*

- Fats Waller composes "Honeysuckle Rose," "Ain't Misbehavin'," and "Black and Blue."

**10 Jan.**    Elmer Rice's *Street Scene* opens.

**11 Feb.**    Eugene O'Neill's *Dynamo* opens.

**2 July**    *Showgirl* opens with songs by George and Ira Gershwin; it stars Ruby Keeler and Jimmy Durante.

**27 Nov.**    *Fifty Million Frenchmen* opens with songs by Cole Porter.

# OVERVIEW

**Post-War.** After World War I America replaced Britain and France as the strongest cultural force in the world. The shift resulted not only from America's financial power but from Europe's war casualties. Britain and France, as well as Germany, lost millions of their young men on the battlefields. Britain lost fifty thousand men on the first morning of the Somme battle in 1916. America's war losses were small in comparison to the slaughters of Ypres, the Marne, Passchendaele, Verdun, the Somme, and Gallipoli.

**Two Currents.** The development of American arts in the 1920s represented the confluence of two currents: 1) European influence; 2) indigenous materials and forms of expression. Before 1920 American high culture imitated European models, and there was the reiterated lament that it was impossible for an American artist to function in America. This complaint was more frequently applied to painting, sculpture, and music than to literature. Henry James (1843–1916) spent most of his literary life abroad writing Europeanized novels. Although Mark Twain (1835–1910) went to Europe as a visitor, his work remained rooted in America. When he wrote about his travels, Mark Twain wrote from the American perspective. Painter James Whistler (1834–1903) went abroad in 1855 and stayed there. Stephen Crane (1871–1900) moved to England to distance himself from rumors about his common-law wife — not for literary reasons.

**Foreign Study.** Most American writers, painters, and composers who participated in the American expatriate experience of the 1920s remained American in their choice of material and viewpoint. The material is the artist. Ernest Hemingway, who is regarded as a key expatriate figure in the 1920s, retained his American perspective in writing about American characters in another country. Ezra Pound and T. S. Eliot became totally Europeanized, and neither utilized American material. Painter-photographer Man Ray went to France in 1921 and produced a body of innovative work that had no nationality. During the 1920s aspiring painters, sculptors, and musicians went to France and Italy for study with influential teachers. The good apprentices learned the lessons of their foreign masters and applied them to American subjects. Brooklyn-born Aaron Copland studied in Paris with Nadia Boulanger and subsequently composed *Appalachian Spring*. It has been claimed that modern American art began when French Cubist paintings were exhibited at the 1913 Armory show in New York. Marsden Hartley, John Marin, and Charles Demuth studied in France and were influenced by Cubism, but they returned home to work with American material: the Maine coast, midwest grain elevators, skyscrapers.

**American Material.** The second current of 1920s art was what has been termed vernacular art: American material treated with American expression. The local-color movement in American literature had commenced in the mid nineteenth century, but in the twentieth century it endeavored to preserve or reassess America's recent past. Willa Cather extolled the strength and courage of Nebraska farm women in *My Ántonia* (1918). Sherwood Anderson's *Winesburg, Ohio* (1919), a key work in the revolt-from-the-village movement, depicts the American small town as a place of thwarted ambition, sexual frustration, and spiritual starvation. Sinclair Lewis satirized the provincialism and ignorance of the Midwest in *Main Street* (1920).

**Blacks and Jews.** Before World War I American artists and writers were almost all Anglo-Saxon. In the 1920s two rich infusions were injected into the mainstream of American culture: black music and the creative energy of Jewish immigrants. It is a truism that the most influential and most enduring forms of American music — blues, jazz, rhythm and blues — originated in Africa. During the 1920s these forms achieved national and international exposure through the work of the black American geniuses.

**White Jazz.** White composers and musicians popularized jazz — and in certain cases changed it into something else. Irving Berlin's "Alexander's Ragtime Band" (1911), which became the most widely played song of its time and was credited with triggering a ragtime craze, was not itself a ragtime composition. George Gershwin's *Rhapsody in Blue* (1924) was commissioned by Paul

Whiteman ("The Jazz King"). Whiteman's so-called symphonic jazz presentation was a long way from Louis Armstrong's New Orleans, but Gershwin became identified with jazz — in both white ("I Got Rhythm") and black (*Porgy and Bess*) idioms. Jewish composers and lyricists dominated popular American music during the 1920s.

**The Studio System.** The richest and most powerful medium of the decade, the movies, was controlled by brilliant and courageous Jews who developed the studio system. The great movie directors and the legendary stars were Gentiles, but the men who made their work possible and who expanded the scope of the industry were Jews: Marcus Loew (M-G-M), Louis B. Mayer (M-G-M), Irving Thalberg (M-G-M), Carl Laemmle (Universal), Adolph Zukor and Jesse Lasky (Paramount), Harry Cohn (Columbia), William Fox, the Warner Brothers, Samuel Goldwyn.

**Great Directors.** Thirty years before the French promulgated the concept of the director as auteur of the movie, the auteur system prevailed in Hollywood. Before sound and to a lesser extent after sound, the director was the dominant figure in moviemaking. The great directors of the 1920s became identified with certain movie genres, which they enlarged: D. W. Griffith (*Way Down East*, 1920), epic melodramas; Cecil B. DeMille (*The Ten Commandments*, 1923), biblical and outdoor epics; Erich Von Stroheim (*Greed*, 1923–1925), lavishly decadent drama; John Ford (*The Iron Horse*, 1924), westerns. But the industry did not accommodate directors, such as Rex Ingram and Marshall Nielan, who bucked the system.

**Catalogue of Genius.** No other decade in history — with the possible exception of 1590–1600 — produced a comparable burst of literary genius. These are some of the writers who published their first books during the 1920s: F. Scott Fitzgerald, Ernest Hemingway, E. E. Cummings, Thomas Wolfe, James Gould Cozzens, Edmund Wilson, Dashiell Hammett, William Faulkner, Hart Crane, Robert Penn Warren, Wallace Stevens, John Steinbeck, William Carlos Williams, Marianne Moore, Countee Cullen, John Dos Passos. These are some of the writers who continued to publish significant works in the 1920s: Willa Cather, Edith Wharton, Sinclair Lewis, Upton Sinclair, Ring W. Lardner, Sherwood Anderson, Theodore Dreiser, Booth Tarkington, E. A. Robinson, Robert Frost, Gertrude Stein, Ezra Pound, T. S. Eliot, Claude McKay, James Branch Cabell, Ellen Glasgow. These are some of the dramatists whose plays were first produced during the 1920s: George S. Kaufman, Elmer Rice, Langston Hughes, Robert E. Sherwood, Sidney Howard, Marc Connelly, Charles McArthur, Ben Hecht, Maxwell Anderson, Philip Barry. Eugene O'Neill's one-act plays were produced before the 1920s, but his major work commenced with *Beyond the Horizon* in 1920.

**Joyce and Proust.** Of the two cultural currents — the foreign and the indigenous — noted, in literature the American current surpassed European influences in the 1920s. The isms of Europe did not travel well; Dadaism, Expressionism, Vorticism, et al. did not take root in America. The strongest foreign influences were the work of Irishman James Joyce and Frenchman Marcel Proust. The stream-of-consciousness technique of Joyce's *Ulysses* (1922) permanently influenced the way other writers perceived actuality and conveyed thought processes. Proust's multivolume *Remembrance of Things Past* (published in English translation, 1922–1932) influenced the treatment of time in fiction and the structure of works with manifold themes. But serious American novelists did not try to write like Joyce or Proust. Except for Dos Passos and Faulkner, important younger American novelists did not experiment with form. They were more concerned with using American material and with developing styles that would accommodate the American language.

**Two Renaissances.** It is indicative of the decade's literary ambitions that the 1920s claimed two literary renaissances: the Southern Renaissance and the Harlem Renaissance. The South had not produced a strong body of literature between the Civil War and World War I. Black literature had been mostly oral or printed for restricted circulation. These renaissances provided national readerships for southern and black authors. (The Harlem Renaissance involved other arts as well.)

**Mass Media.** The expansion of media and the growth of the publishing industry in the 1920s secured national reputations for writers who might otherwise have been restricted to regional or racial reputations. It was also a time when successful writers began to make money. Newspaper syndicates and mass-circulation magazines paid writers fees commensurate with their reputations. A writer could support work on a novel by selling four short stories a year. After the advent of talkies Hollywood bought "literary properties" and paid what seemed huge salaries to writers who could write dialogue — conditions that led to exaggerated denunciations of Hollywood as the corruptor of talent and destroyer of genius. The movie industry also provided opportunities for composers, designers, and painters, as movie musicals became far more lavish than any productions the stage could provide.

**Culture Heroes.** "It was an age of miracles, it was an age of art, it was an age of excess, and it was an age of satire" — thus declared F. Scott Fitzgerald, the American writer most closely identified with the 1920s, in his essay "Echoes of the Jazz Age." But Fitzgerald omitted that it was also an age of heroes and hero worship; it was an age of genius. Every era requires its own heroes, and many heroes are manufactured to fill temporary needs. Consequently many twentieth-century heroes were only temporary celebrities. (A celebrity has been defined by historian Daniel Boorstin as someone who is well known for being well known.) Enduring heroes — those whose achievements and significance outlast their times — are rare figures in any decade. The 1920s generated heroes whose activities permanently changed their fields of endeavor or who provided gauges for the measurement of their successors. These observations are particularly justified in the arts. The 1920s produced culture heroes — geniuses who embody and express the aspirations of their time.

# TOPICS IN THE NEWS

## ARCHITECTURE

**Eclecticism.** Although he was already America's most interesting and innovative architect, Frank Lloyd Wright (1869–1959) produced no public architecture in the United States during the 1920s. His concept of organic integrity was significant in the California houses he designed, but his major work of the decade was the Imperial Hotel in Tokyo (having survived earthquake and fire in 1922, it was demolished in 1946); and he spent much of the decade in Japan. Important public architecture in the United States during the decade was relentlessly eclectic. (Built in 1922, Henry Bacon's Lincoln Memorial was a monument for neoclassic architecture, as its seated figure of Lincoln by Daniel Chester French was for academic sculpture.) The 1922 competition for the design of the Tribune Tower in Chicago was won by John Mead Howells and Raymond Hood; not until the end of the decade did they eschew eclectic embellishment. The second-place Tribune Tower design by Eliel Saarinen and Walter Gropius, though not built, attracted more attention than Howells and Hood's and proved of greater influence on urban architecture, the most important derivative being the Empire State Building.

Source:
Leland M. Roth, *A Concise History of American Architecture* (New York: Harper & Row, 1979).

## BROADWAY DRAMA

**The Stage.** Dramas of the "legitimate stage" (performed by live actors before successive audiences) flourished. Nineteen different work by Eugene O'Neill, the supreme American dramatist, were premiered — not all in New York City — in the 1920s (among them: *Anna Christie,* 1921; *Desire Under the Elms,* 1924; and *Strange Interlude,* 1928). George S. Kaufman was author or coauthor of eighteen productions and Marc Connelly of eleven — nine of them jointly (for example, *Beggar on Horseback,* 1924) during the decade. There were nine premiered works by Philip Barry (*Holiday* in 1928); sixteen by Sidney Howard (*They Knew What They Wanted* in

1924); and three by Robert E. Sherwood (*The Road to Rome* in 1927). The first, best, and most successful product of the long collaboration between Charles MacArthur and Ben Hecht was *The Front Page* in 1928. Three plays jointly by Maxwell Anderson and Lawrence Stallings were premiered (*What Price Glory?* in 1924), as well as other works by each. Though it would be eclipsed by the opera derived from it in 1935, *Porgy* by Dorothy and DuBose Heyward was a critical and popular success in 1927.

Source:
John MacNicholas, ed., *Dictionary of Literary Biography: Twentieth-Century American Dramatists* (Detroit: Bruccoli Clark/Gale, 1981).

## CENSORSHIP AND PURITANISM

**Prohibition.** The 1920s are now popularly perceived as an era of hedonistic rebellion against Victorian repression. Prohibition, the decade's defining institution, made dissipation a matter of principle and lawlessness chic. But the speakeasy would not have existed without the passage of the Eighteenth Amendment, a triumph for puritanism. Deriving from optimistic overconfidence in the power of law to promote human virtue, Prohibition — which became the law of the land in 1919 — was an experiment no less characteristic of the 1920s than other more rebellious experiments. Puritanism — contemporaneously defined as the fear that somebody somewhere is having a good time — remained a powerful force throughout the decade.

**Wartime Influences.** The battles between puritanism and the New Freedom were triggered by the marked changes in American society resulting from World War I. Young men who had never traveled went to France. A great war was fought, and boys died for idealistic slogans promulgated by old men. Women enjoyed previously unheard-of personal liberty, and many of them held what had been regarded as men's work during the war. The war brought new prosperity and new leisure. The issues were youth versus age, small town versus city, native-born versus immigrant, fundamentalism versus science. The

Rollin Kirby's *New York World* portrayal of Prohibition
in action

struggle was particularly evident in the arts. New ideas
were expressed in new ways, and new subjects were
treated in previously unprintable words. The huge movie
audiences saw things that had never appeared on the
stage. The moralists were under siege and fought back.

**Lewis and Fitzgerald.** Though neither was censored,
two novels published in 1920 fired opening shots in the
war against philistinism and repression. Sinclair Lewis's
*Main Street* proclaimed that the midwestern small town
was hell on earth populated by vulgarians and ig-
noramuses. F. Scott Fitzgerald's *This Side of Paradise* announced that there was "a new generation dedicated more
than the last to the fear of poverty and the worship of
success; grown up to find all Gods dead, all wars fought,
all faiths in man shaken. . . ."

*Jurgen.* Two organizations that vigilantly monitored
printed obscenity were the New York Society for the
Suppression of Vice and the New England Watch and
Ward Society. So many books and periodicals were prosecuted by the latter body that the words "banned in Boston" became a joke or a recommendation. The first unintended success achieved by the Society for the Suppression of Vice under its executive secretary, John S. Sumner, resulted from its action against James Branch
Cabell's *Jurgen* (1919). On 14 January 1920 the printing
plates and unsold copies were impounded, and Guy Holt,
Cabell's editor at McBride, was charged with violating
the New York antiobscenity laws. The alleged obscenity
had to do with double entendres and phallic symbolism: " 'There is a great deal in what I advance, I can
assure you. It is the most natural and most penetrating

kind of logic; and I wish merely to discharge a duty.' "
The two-year ban of *Jurgen* made a silly book important.
When the case came to trial in 1922, Judge Charles C.
Nott instructed the jury to acquit the publishers: "It is
doubtful if the book could be read or understood at all by
more than a very limited number of readers."

**Banned Books.** Books prosecuted in New York during
the 1920s included D. H. Lawrence's *Women in Love* and
a translation of Arthur Schnitzler's *Casanova's Homecoming.* Boni & Liveright editor T. R. Smith was tried and
cleared in connection with a translation of Petronius's
*Satyricon* and Maxwell Bodenheim's *Replenishing Jessica.*
In 1929 Radclyffe Hall's *The Well of Loneliness,* a novel
about lesbianism, was cleared by the New York court
after having been banned in England. The Bostonians
took action against Theodore Dreiser's *An American
Tragedy,* Lewis's *Elmer Gantry,* Sherwood Anderson's
*Dark Laughter,* John Dos Passos's *Manhattan Transfer,* an
issue of *Scribner's Magazine* in which Ernest Hemingway's *A Farewell to Arms* was serialized, and the issue of
*The American Mercury* with Herbert Asbury's "Hatrack," a
short story about a prostitute. Some sixty books were
suppressed in Boston during 1927.

*Ulysses.* The most egregious example of literary censorship in the 1920s was the ban against bringing copies
of James Joyce's *Ulysses* (1922) into the United States,
even as personal property. Customs agents were empowered to confiscate copies in the possession of ship passengers arriving in America. Again, the result was to call
attention to the novel, and *Ulysses* circulated in pirated
copies. Joyce was unable to secure an American copyright
for his work until 1933, when Bennett Cerf and Donald S.
Klopfer of Random House arranged a test case in which
Judge John M. Woolsey ruled that the book could be
published and sold in the United States.

**Clean Books.** In 1923 and 1925 unsuccessful attempts
were made to pass a "clean books bill" in the state of New
York. The puritans' relentlessness is testimony to their
belief in the power of literature — in contrast to the
flippant contempt expressed by Jimmy Walker, then a
member of the New York Assembly and later the flamboyant mayor of New York City, who commented that
"No girl was ever ruined by a book."

**Indecent Performances.** On 9 February 1927 the police served warrants against the actors and managers of
three New York plays — *The Captive, Sex,* and *The Virgin
Man* — for violation of section 1140A of the criminal
code forbidding indecent performances. The co-author
and star of *Sex,* Mae West, was fined $500 and sentenced
to ten days in jail, along with the producers. Similar
sentences were handed down for the authors and producers of the other plays.

**The Hays Office.** In the early 1920s the movie indus-
try was damaged by a series of scandals: the Fatty
Arbuckle rape trials, the drug-related death of Wallace
Reid, the unsolved murder of director William Desmond

## SOME BOOKS CENSORED OR BANNED IN AMERICA DURING THE TWENTIES

Anon, *A Young Girl's Diary*

Maxwell Bodenheim, *Replenishing Jessica*

James Branch Cabell, *Jurgen*

Floyd Dell, *Janet March*

Viña Delmar, *Bad Girl*

Mary Ware Dennett, *The Sex Side of Life*

Theodore Dreiser, *An American Tragedy*

René Fülop-Miller, *Rasputin, the Holy Devil*

Radclyffe Hall, *The Well of Loneliness*

Frank Harris, *My Life and Loves*

Ben Hecht, *Gargoyles*

Ben Hecht-Wallace Smith, *Fantazius Mallare, A Mysterious Oath*

J. K. Huysman, *La-Bas*

James Joyce, *Ulysses*

Robert Keable, *Simon Called Peter*

D. H. Lawrence, *Lady Chatterley's Lover*

Lawrence, *Women in Love*

Sinclair Lewis, *Elmer Gantry*

Frances Newman, *The Hard-Boiled Virgin*

Diana Patrick, *The Rebel Bird*

Erich Maria Remarque, *All Quiet on the Western Front*

*The Satyricon of Petronius Arbiter*

Arthur Schnitzler, *Casanova's Homecoming*

Upton Sinclair, *Oil!*

Marie C. Stopes, *Love in Marriage, or Married Love*

Jim Tully, *Circus Parade*

Arnold Zweig, *The Case of Sergeant Grischa*

---

lated a code to eliminate the production or distribution of movies that:

1. Dealt with sex in an improper manner
2. Were based on white slavery
3. Made vice attractive
4. Exhibited nakedness
5. Had prolonged passionate love scenes
6. Were predominantly concerned with the underworld
7. Made gambling and drunkenness attractive
8. Might instruct the weak in methods of committing crime
9. Ridiculed public officials
10. Offended religious beliefs
11. Emphasized violence
12. Portrayed vulgar postures and gestures, and
13. Used salacious subtitles or advertising[.]

By 1930 the thirteen points were elaborated into the Motion Picture Production Code, a document of some seven hundred words of more specific prohibition: actual childbirth, surgical operations, sex hygiene, cross-racial sexual relationships, "sexual perversion," and justified adultery were among the banned subjects; comic treatment of ministers of religion was not allowed; the presentation of "the use of liquor" was severely restricted; and the words "Gawd" and "damn" were examples of unpermitted profanity and obscenity. The code's prohibitions were wide-ranging but not exclusive: the omission of any reference to abortion, for example, demonstrates not that the subject was permissible but that it was unthinkable. The industry's reliance upon the code endured for more than twenty years, weakening — at first gradually — after World War II.

Sources:
Paul S. Boyer, *Purity in Print* (New York: Scribners, 1968);

Felice F. Lewis, *Literature, Obscenity, and Law* (Carbondale: Southern Illinois University Press, 1976);

Raymond Moley, *The Hays Office* (Indianapolis: Bobbs-Merrill, 1945).

---

Taylor implicating actresses Mary Miles Minter and Mabel Normand. Moreover, religious groups were calling for boycotts of movies featuring female nudity and sexual suggestion. Threatened with state and federal regulations, the movie industry acted to police itself by organizing the Motion Picture Producers and Distributors of America (MPPDA). Will Hays (1879–1954), postmaster general in the Harding cabinet, was hired to head the cleanup in 1922. His first act was to ban Arbuckle from the screen after the comedian had been acquitted. So firmly was Hays in control that the MPPDA became known as the Hays Office. In addition to imposing standards of behavior on performers, the Hays Office formu-

## DANCE

**Ballet.** Patrons of professional ballet in the early decades of the twentieth century tended toward a view of culture as a European import. At its best, American ballet was ardently derivative; resident companies hardly existed outside the major cities, and much of what little professional dancing was accessible to the public was both imported and of poor quality. Ballet schools were numerous — then, as now, ballet being considered an appropriate physical activity for young ladies. (The art of American modern dance would scarcely exist without the opportunity provided by regional ballet schools for early exposure to performance dance.)

Magazine cover by John Held Jr. featuring distorted
Charleston dancers

The Charleston dance step, permanently identified with the ebullience of the 1920s, was introduced in *Runnin' Wild*, an all-black 1923 show. The song "Charleston," by James P. Johnson and Cecil Mack, was supposedly inspired by the movements of black dancers in Charleston, South Carolina. The Charleston is a comic, sexy dance, adaptable to solo performance or chorus line. Danced by couples, it is synchronized rather than intimate. It is fast-paced and jerky of movement, performed with angled limbs and making frequent use of a buttocks-projecting semisquat. The feet rapidly alternate between heels-together/toes-together positions; the bent knees move in opposition; the splayed hands, moving in opposition or parallel, sometimes describe arcs in the air, palms forward and wrists extended, forearms pivoting from bent elbows, and sometimes shift back and forth from knee to opposite knee. It is a dance that displays the form of the body because it requires unconfining clothing, and if the woman performer is wearing the appropriate flapper attire, with rolled stockings and a short skirt constructed of beaded fringe, it displays a heretofore unprecedented expanse of bare thigh. But it is not a dance of erotic invitation; the effect is cheerfully — even innocently — impudent. The Charleston created a dance craze and an epidemic of Charleston contests. A 1924 Charleston marathon at the Roseland Ballroom in New York lasted for twenty-four hours.

The Charleston probably provoked another athletic dance of the decade, the Black Bottom, introduced by Ann Pennington ("The Girl With the Dimpled Knees") in the *George White Scandals of 1926*. The song was by B. G. DeSylva, Ray Henderson, and Lew Brown. The name of the dance referred to muddy river bottoms, but it was susceptible to other interpretations.

**Popular Dance.** The state of popular professional dancing at the time was no better. Modern-dance pioneer Ted Shawn, describing the situation that existed in his youth, said, "Dancers in musicals kicked 16 to the right, 16 to the left and kicked the backs of their heads. In vaudeville you had the soft shoe, the sand shuffle and the buck and wing."

**Denishawn.** The Denishawn School of Dance, founded in Los Angeles in 1915 by Ruth St. Denis (1878?–1968) and her newlywed husband, Shawn (1891–1972), reached the height of its considerable popularity in 1925. American modern dance emerged from the Denishawn company with the work of alumnae Martha Graham (1893–1991) and Doris Humphrey (1895–1958) in the late 1920s. Characteristics of modernism in dance include the discarding of shoes; unrealistic distortion of the body for purposes of emotional expressiveness rather than unrealistic elongation for elegance of line; homage to, rather than defiance of, gravity; suppression of personality (protagonists having designations like "One Who Seeks" rather than names like "Clara" or "Giselle"); and inspiration from primitive, exotic, or ancient cultures rather than European fairy tales.

**Graham and Humphrey.** Graham would become the most honored figure in American dance with her tension-filled, dynamic choreography created to "chart the graph of the heart." After seven years with Denishawn, she formed her own company and in 1929, three years after her first independent concert, presented her first distinctive and fully developed work, *Heretic*, in New York City with a group of fifteen other well-disciplined and identical-appearing dancers. Humphrey was with Denishawn eleven years, taking part in the company's 1925 tour of Asia. Less widely known than Graham, she is considered the greater choreographer by some critics and dancers.

Source:
Walter Terry, *The Dance in America* (New York: Harper, 1956).

Martha Graham in *Appalachian Spring*

Dust jacket for the great American novel of the 1920s
(Bruccoli Collection, Thomas Cooper Library,
University of South Carolina)

### EXPATRIATES

**Paree.** At certain times during the 1920s the centers of American literature, music, and art appeared to be located in the Montparnasse and Latin Quarter sections of Paris on the Left Bank of the Seine. There are ample explanations for this reverse migration. World War I had introduced Americans to France ("How Ya Gonna Keep 'em Down on the Farm After They've Seen Paree?"); transatlantic travel was cheap; the exchange rate (twenty francs to the dollar) enabled Americans to live better in France than at home; there was Prohibition and puritanism in America; there were opportunities for Americans to get published in Paris; everybody else was going there. Although there were pockets of Americans in Germany, England, and Italy, Paris was the preferred venue for creative figures, especially those serving their apprenticeships. There was also an American colony on the Riviera, about which F. Scott Fitzgerald wrote that "whatever happened seemed to have something to do with art."

**City Full of Geniuses.** The reputations of the now-famous expatriates have obscured the actuality that there were more fakers than workers. In one of his earliest dispatches from Paris in 1922 Ernest Hemingway declared: "The scum of Greenwich Village, New York, has been skimmed off and deposited in large ladlesful on that section of Paris adjacent to the Café Rotonde." Most of the Americans in Paris were tourists or pretenders, but an impressive number were serious workers. Major careers were launched, and masterpieces were achieved by expatriates: *The Great Gatsby* and *The Sun Also Rises* were written in France. Three early settlers who provided encouragement for creative Americans were Gertrude Stein, Ezra Pound, and Sylvia Beach. Stein had arrived in 1903. Although much of her own writing was negligible, she attracted a coterie of young expatriates. Pound's Paris tenure was limited to 1920–1924, but as editor, reviewer, and talent spotter he did more for the arts and artists than anyone else. Beach ran Shakespeare and Company, a bookshop and lending library, where she performed many services for expatriates. Her claim to literary immortality is that she published James Joyce's *Ulysses* in 1922. Hem-

Sylvia Beach at 8 rue Dupuytren, Paris, in 1920 before her move to 12 rue de l'Odéon

# THREE STORIES

Up in Michigan
Out of Season
My Old Man

# & TEN POEMS

Mitraigliatrice
Oklahoma
Oily Weather
Roosevelt
Captives
Champs d'Honneur
Riparto d'Assalto
Montparnasse
Along With Youth
Chapter Heading

# ERNEST HEMINGWAY

Front cover of Ernest Hemingway's first book, published in Paris by Contact Editions in 1923

ingway enjoyed the friendship and assistance of all three of these figures after he arrived in December 1921. The opportunities for publication were of prime importance for Hemingway and other young American writers in Paris. Robert McAlmon had the Contact Press; William Bird had the Three Mountains Press; Edward Titus had the Black Manikin Press; *The Little Review, Gargoyle, Transatlantic Review, This Quarter,* and *transition* were published in Paris. Fortunate composers studied with Nadia Boulanger, whose pupils included Virgil Thomson and Aaron Copland. Painters studied with Natalia Goncharova. Sergei Diaghilev brought the Ballets Russes to Paris. Cole Porter had studied composition at the Paris Schola Cantorum before the war, and his ballet *Within the Quota* was performed in Paris during 1923. The city seemed populated by geniuses: composers Darius Milhaud, François Poulenc, Erik Satie, Igor Stravinsky; artists Pablo Picasso, Joan Miró, Fernand Leger, Constantin Brancusi, Marc Chagall, Juan Gris. The Paris Art Deco exposition opened in 1925. The café talk was full of isms and new movements. Indeed, everything had something to do with art. In addition to those already noted, a partial roll call of the Americans who did serious work during extended stays in Paris includes artists Man

Ray, Alexander Calder, Jo Davidson; composer George Antheil; writers Djuna Barnes, Kay Boyle, E. E. Cummings, Hilda Doolittle, Janet Flanner, Glenway Wescott, and Archibald MacLeish.

**A Lost Generation.** Decades and generations acquire labels that stick, whether or not they are accurate. No label or slogan can accurately cover a generation. Moreover, there are several generations of artists working during any ten-year period. Nonetheless, the label "lost generation" stuck to the people who had been exposed to World War I, implying that they were permanent casualties. The term achieved currency through its appearance on the epigraph page of Ernest Hemingway's *The Sun Also Rises* (1926): " 'You are all a lost generation.' — Gertrude Stein *in conversation.*" Much later Hemingway explained that his use of "lost generation" was intended to be ironic, not literally defining. However, the war did cause a great and permanent change in the way people — especially artists — born after 1890 viewed the world. The old certainties and the old order were destroyed in the trenches: Antiwar novels published during the 1920s include Dos Passos's *Three Soldiers* (1921), Cummings's

**1920**

*Brownie's Book* — first issue of magazine for black children; edited by W. E. B. Du Bois and Jessie Redmon Fauset.

**1921**

*Shuffle Along* — first all-black Broadway show; score by Noble Sissle and Eubie Blake includes "Love Will Find a Way" and "I'm Just Wild About Harry."

*The Light* — weekly black newspaper — begins publication; subsequently renamed *Heebie Jeebies*.

**1922**

*The Book of American Negro Poetry*, edited by James Weldon Johnson.

**1923**

Cotton Club nightclub opens.

*Opportunity* — first issue of magazine sponsored by the Urban League.

*Runnin' Wild* — black musical produced on Broadway.

**1924**

Publication of Jean Toomer's *Cane*.

Publication of *There Is Confusion* by Jessie Redmon Fauset.

**1925**

*The Book of American Negro Spirituals*, edited by James Weldon Johnson and J. Rosamond Johnson.

Small's Paradise nightclub opens.

Publication of *The New Negro*, edited by Alain Locke.

**1926**

Savoy Ballroom opens.

*Fire!!* — only one issue published, edited by Wallace Thurman.

*Encore* — first issue.

Publication of Langston Hughes's *The Weary Blues*.

Arthur Schomburg's collection of African American books is acquired by The New York Public Library.

**1927**

*Plays of Negro Life*, edited by Alain Locke and Montgomery Gregory.

Publication of Langston Hughes's *Fine Clothes to the Jew*.

Publication of James Weldon Johnson's *God's Trombones: Seven Negro Sermons in Verse*.

Death of Florence Mills; 57,000 people pay their respect.

**1928**

*Harlem: A Forum of Negro Life* — only one issue published, edited by Wallace Thurman.

Publication of Claude McKay's novel *Home to Harlem*.

*Blackbirds of 1928* stars Florence Mills.

Fats Waller and Andy Razaf's *Keep Shufflin'* produced at Connie's Inn.

**1929**

Wallace Thurman's play *Harlem* produced on Broadway.

Publication of Wallace Thurman's novel *The Blacker the Berry*.

---

*The Enormous Room* (1922), Thomas Boyd's *Through the Wheat* (1923), and Hemingway's *A Farewell to Arms* (1929). Ezra Pound's poem *Hugh Selwyn Mauberley* (1920), an attack on the sterility of modern civilization, includes the lines:

> There died a myriad
> And of the best, among them,
> For an old bitch gone in the teeth,
> For a botched civilization. . . .

**Sources:**
Sylvia Beach, *Shakespeare & Company* (New York: Harcourt, Brace, 1959);

Malcolm Cowley, *A Second Flowering: Works and Days of the Lost Generation* (New York: Viking, 1973);

Hugh Ford, *Published in Paris: American and British Writers, Printers, and Publishers in Paris, 1920–1939* (New York: Macmillan, 1975).

## HARLEM RENAISSANCE

**Harlem.** In 1925 a *New York Herald Tribune* article announced, "we are on the edge, if not in the midst, of what might not improperly be called a Negro Renaissance." The causes of this renaissance — as with all such movements — were financial and educational. Blacks participated in the postwar prosperity — although to a

The only issue of the 1926 journal edited by Wallace Thurman

**Writers.** The brilliant achievements of black composers and musicians often deflected attention from the literary aspects of the movement. Nevertheless, literature became the focal point of the movement, and though, among the writers, only Langston Hughes became a familiar name, the fleet of young novelists and poets launched by the renaissance wrote a body of enduring works of American literature. The roll is stunning: biracial novelist and poet Jean Toomer; poet Hughes; poet Countee Cullen; novelist and poet McKay; writer and editor Jessie Fauset; novelist and folk anthropologist Hurston; novelist Nella Larson; poet and novelist Arna Bontemps; novelist and editor Wallace Thurman.

**Hughes.** Accomplished as a writer of fiction and drama, but known most extensively for his poetry, Hughes published his first great poem, and still perhaps his most anthologized, "The Negro Speaks of Rivers," in 1921 at age nineteen. His two poetry collections published in the 1920s were *The Weary Blues* (1926) and *Fine Clothes to the Jew* (1927).

**Cullen.** Cullen, sometimes called the poet laureate of the Harlem Renaissance, was the most popular black poet of his time. His poetry frequently addressed issues relating to social marginality, such as race, religious hypocrisy, and homosexuality. He published his first, and many think his best, collection, *Color*, in 1925. Other collections published during the 1920s are *Copper Sun* (1927), *The Ballad of the Brown Girl: An Old Ballad Retold* (1927), and *The Black Christ, and Other Poems* (1929).

**McKay.** McKay was second only to Langston Hughes in his influence on the Harlem Renaissance. He is principally remembered for his realistic novel *Home to Harlem* (1928), primarily because its portrayal of black life prompted sharp criticism from W. E. B. Du Bois and Alain Locke. Praise for the novel was widespread; it was awarded the medal of the Institute of Arts and Sciences. McKay, who had immigrated to the United States in 1914 from Jamaica, returned to Jamaica in 1922. His poetry volumes published in the 1920s are *Spring in New Hampshire and Other Poems* (1920) and *Harlem Shadows* (1922). He was posthumously proclaimed national poet of Jamaica.

**Toomer.** Toomer, though not as influential as other participants in the movement, was a creative force with his remarkable first novel, *Cane* (1923). The work, generally considered the first novel of the Harlem Renaissance, was a series of stories and poems held together by thematic similarities and a poetic style.

**Women Writers.** The contributions of women writers, important in the movement during their time, have lately been rediscovered. Fauset was editor of *The Crisis*, the journal of the NAACP. In that role she published much of the earliest and best work by Harlem Renaissance writers. Her own 1920s novels — *This is Confusion* (1924) and *Plum Bun* (1928) — were influenced by realism. By the time of her death in 1961, she had published

much lesser extent than did whites — and the young generation of literate and literary blacks made the best of it. Many of the most gifted gravitated to a center of black population north of 125th Street in Upper Manhattan that gave its name to the Harlem Renaissance. Harlem nightlife attracted white audiences, and black culture began to receive serious critical attention from white intellectuals.

**Locke and Van Vechten.** The movement was shaped significantly by the influence of Alain Locke, a Howard University philosopher, the first black Rhodes Scholar, and editor of *The New Negro*, in whose pages were published many of the best and most influential essays of the decade, and by Carl Van Vechten, a white editor and patron who became both literary patron and close friend to many of the best black writers of the period, including Langston Hughes, James Weldon Johnson, and Zora Neale Hurston.

**Desegregating the Arts.** The Harlem Renaissance is generally considered to have begun in 1917, when two events marked a turning point for black literary and artistic achievement: *Seven Arts* became the first desegregated white magazine in the twentieth century by publishing three poems by Claude McKay, and for the first time there were plays with black casts on Broadway, with three by white dramatist Ridgely Torrence.

Bix Beiderbecke (third from right in the back row) with Paul Whiteman's orchestra in 1927 or 1928

more novels than any other Harlem Renaissance writer. Hurston's best-known work and first novel, *Their Eyes Were Watching God,* was published in 1937, but her flamboyant personality and impressive early works made her a memorable figure in Harlem during the renaissance. Larson, like Toomer of mixed racial heritage, frequently dealt with issues of identity. Her best-known works, *Quicksand* (1928) and *Passing* (1929), led to her receiving the Harmon Medal in 1929 and a Guggenheim Fellowship in 1930, the first black woman so honored in creative writing.

**Bontemps and Thurman.** Bontemps, like Hurston, was an emerging voice throughout the 1920s but is best known for his novels written in the 1930s. Thurman was influential in his promotion of black artists and is perhaps best remembered as the driving spirit behind (and editor of ) *Fire!!* (1926), a remarkable literary journal, published only once.

**Termination.** The movement began to lose its energy with the Great Depression, when many of the black publications folded and as many as 25 percent of Harlem's residents were unemployed. Eventually artistic fervor gave way to social anger, and by the mid 1930s the level of artistic production among writers associated with the movement had dwindled significantly. Among the many talented writers of the period, only Langston Hughes and Zora Neale Hurston enjoyed general readership into the 1940s.

Sources:

*The Harlem Renaissance: An Historical Dictionary of the Era* (Westport, Conn.: Greenwood Press, 1984);

Nathan Irving Huggins, *Harlem Renaissance* (New York: Oxford University Press, 1977);

Huggins, ed., *Voices from the Harlem Renaissance* (New York: Oxford University Press, 1995).

## JAZZ

**Black Geniuses.** Another musician remarked that no trumpet player could do anything that Louis Armstrong had not already done. Armstrong's contemporaries included pianist-composer Jelly Roll Morton, blues singer Bessie Smith, and orchestra leader-composer Duke Ellington. The innovations and achievements of these and other black musicians in the 1920s proved to be the first widespread fulfillment of black American talent and genius. There were no doubt mute black geniuses in the arts before then who were deprived of the opportunity to utilize their genius. Art requires an audience, an interaction between the maker and the perceiver by means of the work; and artists, however compelling their creative urges, require incomes. Jazz provided black musicians with an art and a cross-racial public during the 1920s. The bootleggers functioned as patrons of American musical culture. The speakeasies were concert halls. The phonograph extended the popularity and the profitability of jazz.

**Definitions.** The term *jazz,* current before World War I (variably as *jass*), was applied to a way of dancing,

Label for Bessie Smith's first record, 1923

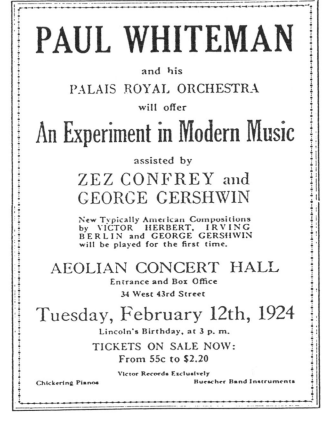

Advertisement for the concert at which George Gershwin's *Rhapsody in Blue* was first performed

to a type of music, and as a synonym for sexual intercourse — each meaning being disputably "the original." As music it is characterized by informality, syncopation, and a strong beat, and as dance by liberation from the more inhibited mating rituals that were — and are — traditional social dance. The erotic associations of jazz music were reinforced by its incubation in the brothels and saloons of New Orleans, especially in the Storyville district, closed by the government during World War I. There is disagreement about every aspect of jazz history except for the indisputable fact that it came out of New Orleans.

**Dixie.** Among the sources of jazz music were the brass marching bands of black New Orleans. Known generally as Dixieland but also called creole jazz because of the French-Spanish-African heritage of its early musicians, the style of jazz that flourished in New Orleans has four beats to the measure and features collective improvisations or, as it became more sophisticated and rehearsed, simulated collective improvisations.

**Black and Blue.** The blues — derived from "call and response" field-work songs and spirituals — became a major strain of jazz. The melancholy mood was achieved by what were called "blue notes" — flatted thirds and sevenths. W. C. Handy's 1914 "St. Louis Blues" became the most popular and influential blues composition, and a major portion of early or classic jazz was in the blues genre.

**Jelly Roll.** Nearly all of the great 1920s jazz figures were black. Jelly Roll Morton (Ferdinand La Menthe, 1885–1941), whose pride in the French portion of his ancestry offends some commentators and has diminished his current reputation, claimed that he "invented jazz"

around 1902 while playing ragtime piano in a New Orleans sporting house. A great bragger, he was also a genius and an innovator; critics who accept certain rhythmic intricacies and improvisational flourishes as definitive of jazz find merit in his claim. Other jazz pioneers were cornet players Buddy Bolden, King Oliver, and Bunk Johnson and clarinetist Johnny Dodds. A key event in the evolution of jazz occurred when Louis Armstrong was taught to play the cornet at the New Orleans Colored Waifs Home.

**Chicago.** From New Orleans, jazz worked its way up the Mississippi, without acquiring respectability. Chicago became the second major venue for jazz; the speakeasies employed jazz musicians, and white patrons became educated by exposure to jazz. Bix Beiderbecke (Leon Bismark Beiderbecke, 1903–1931) probably first heard Armstrong play on a riverboat in Davenport, Iowa, but as a schoolboy he developed his style by listening to the Chicago jazz greats. Beiderbecke was eventually labeled "The Greatest White Trumpet Player" — meaning that he did not threaten Armstrong's supremacy.

**Whiteman.** Paul Whiteman was the most influential figure in making jazz respectable by moving it from the speakeasies and black dance halls to theaters and cabarets patronized by whites. Promoted as the Jazz King, Whiteman provided smooth arrangements for relaxation and for dancing. The peak of Whiteman's successful efforts to enlarge the appeal of jazz was the 1924 concert for which he commissioned George Gershwin's *Rhapsody in Blue.* Whiteman's "symphonic jazz" was a long way from the spontaneity of Dixieland.

**Swing.** In the late 1920s and early 1930s jazz evolved into swing, which replaced improvisation with elaborate arrangements. As arranger and bandleader Fletcher Henderson was a key figure in the transition to swing and the big-band sound. Duke Ellington's 1931 composition "It Don't Mean a Thing If It Aint' Got That Swing" is sometimes credited with giving currency to the term *swing.*

**An American Art.** Jazz outlasted the Jazz Age, but during the 1920s it expressed the exuberance of the era. Jazz is regarded as the only art form generated in America, and it has reached a world audience. Change was inevitable as new talents appeared, but jazz has always been dominated by Americans.

**Popular Songs.** Many of the white songwriters and composers inspired by the innovations of black musicians were Jews. In the melting-pot tradition, American popular music in the 1920s represented a collaboration between Africa and Russia. Russian-born Irving Berlin and George Gershwin, the son of Russian immigrants, adapted black blues and jazz; and Russian-born Al Jolson sang their songs. Gershwin's hugely popular "Swanee" is representative of a cheerfully vulgarized amalgam of American emotions.

Sources:

James Collier, *The Making of Jazz: A Comprehensive History* (New York: Dell, 1979);

Gunther Schuller, *Early Jazz: Its Roots and Musical Development* (New York: Oxford University Press, 1968);

Barry Ulanov, *A History of Jazz in America* (New York: Da Capo, 1972).

## LITERARY MODERNISM

**Definition.** Certain writers, painters, and musicians found new ways of perceiving reality that came to be defined as modernism — not a period of time but a commitment to experimentation in techniques, freedom in ideas, originality in perceptions, and self-examination in emotions. In general it manifests a rejection of traditional techniques and unexamined values. It often — not invariably — expresses the plight of the individual in a world of machinery and commercialism. Perhaps the greatest influence on the ways writers endeavored to convey experience was the stream-of-consciousness or interior monologue of James Joyce's *Ulysses* (1922). Utilizing one day in Dublin, Joyce explored the interior lives of his characters by means of the association of ideas and sensory impressions. Novelist John Dos Passos adapted Joyce's techniques to American life. His *Manhattan Transfer* (1925) connects hundreds of episodes to convey a sense of New York City. The strongest influence on literary modernism was the new psychology with its analysis of the operations of the unconscious and myth. Sigmund Freud explicated

the id, ego, and superego; and Carl Jung identified "the collective unconscious."

**Difficulty.** Modern literature, like Cubism and abstraction in painting, required re-education for comprehension. In his 1929 novel *The Sound and the Fury* William Faulkner used the free-association steam-of-consciousness of a feeble-minded character for the development of the narrative. The poetry of Hart Crane (1899–1932), who published two volumes of verse — *White Buildings* (1926) and *The Bridge* (1930) — before his suicide, is dense and obscure. *The Bridge* is a long, uneven mystical brooding on American consciousness. The diversity and brilliance of many 1920s poets was concomitant with the diminishing readership for their difficult poetry. It is always true that writers write the best way they can, but in the 1920s poets wrote deliberately difficult verse as though challenging their readers. Serious poets were no longer expected to support themselves by poetry. William Carlos Williams was a doctor of medicine; Wallace Stevens was an insurance lawyer; T. S. Eliot was a publisher; Robert Frost was a writer-in-residence. The most financially successful and most popular poet of the 1920s was the relentlessly rhyming, reassuringly folksy nonmodernist Edgar A. Guest.

Source:

Frederic Hoffman, *The Twenties; American Writing in the Postwar Decade,* revised edition (New York: Collier, 1962).

## LITERARY MOVEMENTS

**Renaissances.** Stimulated by the aspiration and confidence that characterized the decade, the literary artists of the 1920s shared an ambition to make their work not just new but an expression of the possibilities of American creative force. The popularity of the term *renaissance* indicated a belief in the imminence of great developments in American culture. The Harlem Renaissance and the Southern Renaissance shared material but were segregated as to membership; no writer belonged to both.

**Southern Renaissance.** In 1920 the South was H. L. Mencken's "Sahara of the Bozart"; its literature was retrospective and trapped in the lost culture of Before-the-War. Two Richmond novelists who belonged to the Southern establishment, James Branch Cabell and Ellen Glasgow, led the attack on the old school of literature and urged the discovery of Southern writers who would treat Southern material in new ways. Cabell (1879–1958) utilized satire and fantasy in creating the kingdom of Poictesme. Glasgow (1873–1945) utilized satire and realism in portraying the postbellum South. The Richmond-based journal *The Reviewer* (1921–1925) published Julia Peterkin, DuBose Heyward, and Paul Green. Charleston, South Carolina; Nashville, Tennessee; and Chapel Hill, North Carolina, were also pockets of literary activity.

**Women.** Women writers were well represented in the Southern Renaissance. Julia Peterkin wrote about South

The 1956 Fugitives reunion at Vanderbilt: (front row) Allen Tate, John Crowe Ransom, and Donald Davidson; (middle row) Milton Starr, Alec Stevenson, and Robert Penn Warren; (back row) William Y. Elliott, Merrill Moore, Jesse Wills, and Sidney M. Hirsch

Carolina plantation blacks; her *Scarlet Sister Mary* (1928) won a Pulitzer Prize for fiction. Elizabeth Madox Roberts wrote about rural Kentucky with careful attention to details of speech and behavior; her best-known novel is *The Great Meadow* (1930). Other notable women writers were Frances Newman (*The Hard-Boiled Virgin*, 1926) and Evelyn Scott (*The Wave*, 1929).

**Faulkner.** William Faulkner (1897–1962) was the greatest figure of the Southern Renaissance. He influenced many writers, North and South, but he was not a joiner or leader. Although his technique and style were innovative, his material was the traditional concerns of Southern literature: the Civil War, slavery, the collapse of the old aristocracy, the effects of commercialism. Faulkner's Yoknapatawpha County — loosely based on Lafayette County, Mississippi — provides a historical microcosm of the Deep South. If there is an easily recognizable element in Southern writing, it is sense of place and the

history associated with place. Even when the writers denounce the pernicious influence of the past, they are nevertheless responding to it. In 1929 Faulkner published *Sartoris*, which formulated Yoknapatawpha, and *The Sound and the Fury*, his most technically influential novel. Three years younger than Faulkner, Thomas Wolfe (1900–1938) was the last major Southern writer to commence publication in the 1920s. His *Look Homeward, Angel* (1929) re-creates Asheville, North Carolina, as Altamont.

**Fugitives and Agrarians.** Nashville was the venue for the Fugitives and the Agrarians, as well as the incubator for the New Critics. The Fugitives — so designated because of their literary journal, *The Fugitive* (1922–1925) — were associated with Vanderbilt University; the leading figures in the group were John Crowe Ransom, Allen Tate, Robert Penn Warren, Donald Davidson, and Andrew Lytle. The Fugitives advocated Southern regionalism, opposing Northern industrialism and defending the South as a historical entity. The Agrarians and the Fugitives so thoroughly overlapped — same people, same place, same principles — that it is impossible to differentiate them. In 1930 the Agrarians published their manifesto, *I'll Take My Stand,* defending the traditional Southern land-based culture against the inroads of industrial capitalism.

**New Criticism.** Several of the Agrarians founded the New Criticism, a literary school that incubated in *The Southern Review,* edited by Warren and Cleanth Brooks at Louisiana State University. The New Critics applied close analysis to the language of a work — especially verse — scrutinizing metaphor and imagery. They endeavored to find the meanings of the work in the work itself, apart from biographical or historical considerations.

**New Humanism.** Of the academic critical movements of the period, only the New Critics enjoyed lasting influence, but the New Humanism was in force during the 1920s. It began as a reaction against the doctrine of scientific determinism, and it stressed the ethical value of experience and the freedom of will. More than the Fugitives and Agrarians, the New Humanists were connected with academic institutions. The principal figures were Irving Babbitt (Harvard), Paul Elmer More (Princeton), and Norman Foerster (University of North Carolina). Among the influential books generated by the New Humanism were Babbitt's *Rousseau and Romanticism* (1919), More's *Shelbourne Essays* (1904–1936), and Foerster's *American Criticism* (1928).

Sources:
Louise Cowen, *The Fugitive Group: A Literary History* (Baton Rouge: Louisiana State University Press, 1959);

*The Fugitive,* periodical;

Louis D. Rubin Jr., ed., *The History of Southern Literature* (Baton Rouge: Louisana State University Press, 1985);

John L. Stewart, *The Burden of Time: The Fugitives and Agrarians . . .* (Princeton: Princeton University Press, 1965).

## MOVIES

**Art and Money.** Periods of great artistic activity require wealth and leisure. The prosperity of the American 1920s and the rise of new classes provided a public and a market for artistic endeavors. It takes money to buy a theater ticket or concert ticket; it takes time to attend; it takes previous experience or education to understand the performance. During the 1920s the arts became important to classes of Americans who had heretofore been indifferent to them. This awareness of the arts was concomitant with the development of mass media. In previous decades American art was nurtured in certain big-city enclaves mainly in the Northeast, particularly New York, Boston, and Philadelphia. Newspapers did not have national distribution; there were no newsmagazines; there was no radio. But arts and letters became national news during the 1920s; artists and writers were newsworthy. Money makes headlines. The publicized record prices for

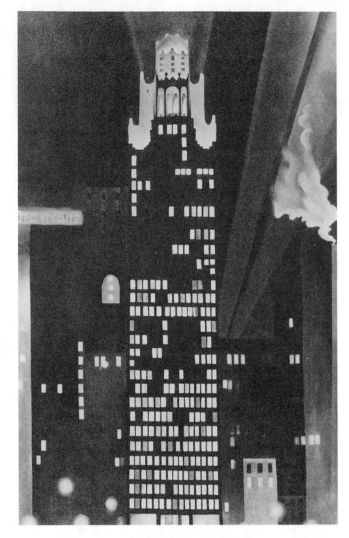

Georgia O'Keeffe, *The American Radiator Building*
(The Alfred Stieglitz Collection, Fisk University)

paintings, statues, and rare books impressed people and in some cases stimulated their interest. It was characteristic of the era that genius and materialism were linked. There was a general belief that if something was really important, then it ought to be worth a lot of money.

**Pioneers.** The most spectacular development occurred in the movies. Nickelodeons became picture palaces as the movies — before and after talkies — became the most popular and most flexible form of culture. The resources of the Hollywood studios far outstripped the capacities of staged drama. The movie epic was established as an American genre. The directors who invented and refined the American motion picture — D. W. Griffith, Erich Von Stroheim, Cecil B. DeMille, John Ford — were backed by extraordinary pioneer producers. The movie industry and studio system were nurtured by former garment manufacturers and salesmen, many of them foreign-born, who had the ability to think big and spend big. Often ridiculed by their intellectual hirelings for their mistakes of vocabulary and grammar, the important producers possessed the courage and ambition that made

Sheet music for the song associated with Fanny Brice, one of the *Follies* stars who became a legendary show-business figure

George Bellows's 1923 depiction of Jack Dempsey knocked out of the ring by Luis Angel Firpo (Metropolitan Museum of Art, New York)

a golden era for American movies. Metro-Goldwyn-Mayer, the top studio, was run by a former junkman, Louis B. Mayer, and his frail production genius, Irving Thalberg. The four Warner brothers gambled on sound. Former glove salesman Samuel Goldwyn — whose speech idiosyncrasies became known as Goldwynisms — concentrated on producing movies that satisfied his standards of quality.

**Stars.** Even before the advent of talkies in 1927, movies achieved a prodigious audience as productions became increasingly lavish. The Hollywood studio system consolidated the power of the big studios that controlled the stars and the movie theaters. Greta Garbo, Rudolph Valentino, Douglas Fairbanks, Mary Pickford, and Charlie Chaplin were among the most widely recognized figures on earth. Silent-movie comedians were particularly popular: Harold Lloyd and the team of Stan Laurel and Oliver Hardy.

Source:
Deems Taylor, *A Pictorial History of the Movies* (New York: Simon & Schuster, 1943).

## MUSICAL THEATER

**Broadway.** The movies and radio killed vaudeville, but Broadway provided a string of brilliant musical produc-

tions, many by younger composers and lyricists. The revue format consisting of a series of unconnected acts remained popular; in addition to the annual *Ziegfeld Follies* that had started before the war, there were the *George White Scandals*, Irving Berlin's *Music Box Revues*, Earl Carroll's *Vanities*, and others. The hit shows included *No, No, Nanette* (Vincent Youmans and Otto Harbach), *Show Boat* (Jerome Kern and Oscar Hammerstein II), *A Connecticut Yankee* (Richard Rodgers and Lorenz Hart), and *Lady, Be Good!* (George and Ira Gershwin).

Source:
Ethan Madden, *Better Foot Forward: The History of American Musical Theater* (New York: Grossman, 1976).

## PAINTING

**Schools.** "Ashcan," "Precisionist," "Regionalist"—several schools of American art flourished in the 1920s, as well as important painters unallied with any school.

**"Ashcan."** The "Ashcan School," developed from Impressionism, was realistic painting of informal subject and style. John Sloan (1871–1951) and George Bellows (1882–1925) were still producing important work in the 1920s (*Sixth Avenue Elevated at Third Street* by Sloan in 1928; *Lady Jean* by Bellows in 1924), though they are identified especially with the preceding decade.

**Stieglitz Group.** After the 1913 New York Armory Show launched modern art in America, the two principal clusters of American avant-garde artists were the Stieglitz Group and the Precisionists. All of these paint-

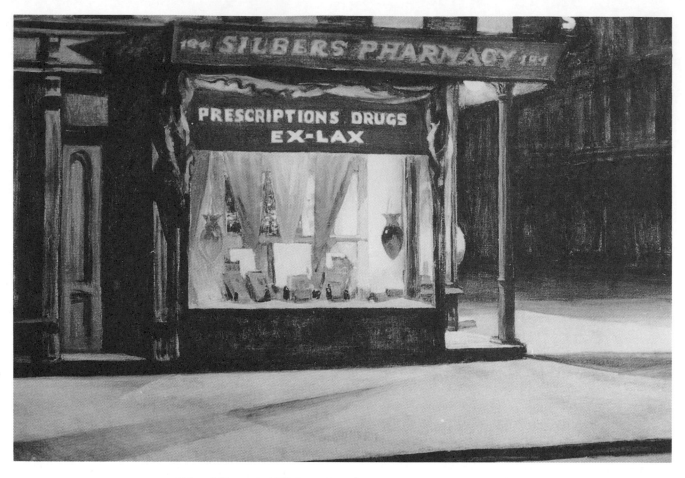

Edward Hopper's 1927 *Drug Store* (Museum of Fine Arts, Boston)

ers were born in the 1870s and 1880s, and they overlapped. The Stieglitz circle were painters who had been exhibited by photographer Alfred Stieglitz at his 291 Fifth Avenue gallery. Mostly European-trained and influenced by Cubism, they included Max Weber (1881–1961) and Arthur Dove (1880–1946), who had been in Henry Matisse's painting class in Paris in 1908; John Marin (1870–1953) and Marsden Hartley (1877–1943) had also studied in Europe. Weber, the first to develop a mature style, was a Cubist painter and sculptor. His *Tranquility* (1928) is a formal composition of three primitively massive female nudes in repose. Arthur Dove was an early innovator in nonobjective painting; his *Fog Horns* (1929) is a visual representation of three ominous, fog-muffled blasts of sound. Hartley (1877–1943) was influenced by German Expressionism; in the 1920s he worked in New Mexico, painting bold, abstract landscapes. Marin was a master of watercolor whose Cubist-influenced seascapes and cityscapes are full of movement; his *Sunset* was painted in 1922. Joseph Stella, an adjunct member of the Stieglitz group, was influenced by Italian Futurism with its geometric patterns and changing angles of vision. A repeated subject for Stella was the Brooklyn Bridge, as in one of his five panels collectively titled *New York Interpreted* (1922).

**Precisionism.** Precisionism (also known as Cubist-Realism or Cubo-Realism) presented an accurate realism with Cubist simplicity that achieved an abstract effect. Georgia O'Keeffe (1887–1986) was connected with the Stieglitz group (she and Stieglitz were married) and with the Precisionists for her closeups of flowers and plants, *Black Iris* being an example from 1926. Other principal Precisionists were Charles Sheeler (1883–1965) and Charles Demuth (1883–1935). Sheeler's austere, photo-realistic personal style is exemplified in *Upper Deck* (1929). Demuth's complexity and variety defy the narrowness of category, but in the 1920s he was a Precisionist painter, sometimes choosing industrial subjects (*Industry*, 1924?, and "My Egypt," 1927). His best-known work, *I Saw the Figure 5 In Gold* (1928), is an abstract representation of a clanging fire engine that was painted to illustrate a poem by William Carlos Williams.

**Davis.** The two-dimensional still lifes (notably *Lucky Strike*, 1921, and the *Egg Beater* series of 1927–1928) of Stuart Davis (1893–1967) prefigured the abstract art of post–World War II and provide a link between trompe-l'oeil (fool-the-eye) and pop art. Davis worked through and transcended almost every style and movement, and he is often identified as the most important American painter to emerge in the 1920s.

**Motley.** Archibald Motley Jr. (1891–1981), New Orleans born, Chicago educated, and influenced toward the abstract by a period of study in Paris, became in 1928 the first African American painter to have a solo exhibition in a commercial gallery.

**Regionalism.** Regionalism — a reaction against abstraction and formalism — is a movement in American painting associated with the 1930s. However, two of its important artists, Thomas Hart Benton (1889–1975) and John Steuart Curry (1897–1946), produced characteristic works — realistic in style (though Benton's use of distortion and unnatural color suggests a debt to Expressionism) and nonurban American in subject — in the 1920s. Benton's *Boom Town* (1928) is appropriately full of movement, an incident-filled painting unified by dynamic composition. Curry's *Tornado Over Kansas* (1929) is a survival drama of the pioneer-spirited western family.

**Hopper and Burchfield.** Edward Hopper (1882–1967) and Charles Burchfield (1893–1967) were essentially realistic painters who developed independently of art movements. Hopper's formal, spare compositions of urban or rural scenes are melancholy with the loneliness of motionless isolation. (*House by the Railroad* was painted in 1921.) Burchfield painted a natural world filled with hostile forces. His 1920s paintings of small-town malignancy (*House of Mystery*, 1924) were partly inspired by Sherwood Anderson's *Winesburg, Ohio.*

Sources:

John I. H. Baur, ed., *New Art in America: Fifty Painters of the 20th Century* (Greenwich, Conn.: New York Graphic Society, 1957);

Milton W. Brown, *American Painting from the Armory Show to the Depression* (Princeton: Princeton University Press, 1955).

## POETRY

**Pound.** Major poems were written during the 1920s by poets who were publishing before the war: Robert Frost (1874–1963), Ezra Pound (1885–1972), Edwin Arlington Robinson (1869–1935), Carl Sandburg (1878–1967), Vachel Lindsay (1879–1931). It is therefore misleading to identify the poets who began appearing in the 1920s without acknowledging their senior colleagues, especially Pound. Although Pound published his first book of verse in 1908, he was the most influential poet of the 1920s in terms of both his own work and his assistance to other writers. He encouraged gifted writers as different as Ernest Hemingway and T. S. Eliot; he edited journals, drafted manifestoes, and arranged for the publication of other poets' work. As a leader of the Imagists, Pound wrote a perfect Imagist poem, "In a Station of the Metro":

The apparition of these faces in the crowd,
Petals on a wet black bough.

# THE WASTE LAND

BY

T. S. ELIOT

"NAM Sibyllam quidem Cumis ego ipse oculis meis vidi in ampulla pendere, et cum illi pueri dicerent: Σίβυλλα τί θέλεις; respondebat illa: ἀποθανείν θέλω."

NEW YORK
BONI AND LIVERIGHT

Title page of the first edition of the most influential modernist poem

The first sixteen of Pound's most ambitious undertakings, the *Cantos* — poems drawing on a vast range of historical material — were published in 1925.

***The Waste Land.*** T. S. Eliot (1892–1965) dedicated *The Waste Land* (1922) to Pound with the words, "il migglior fabbro" (the better craftsman). *The Waste Land* was the most influential poem written in the English language during the twentieth century. Himself influenced by the seventeenth-century English metaphysical poets and the nineteenth-century French Symbolists, Eliot wrote exposing the spiritual and intellectual poverty of modern life.

**Older Generation.** The diversity of poetic styles and techniques during the 1920s is striking. The older generation — those born in the 1880s — who published key volumes during the 1920s were Wallace Stevens (1879–1955), Robinson Jeffers (1887–1962), William Carlos Williams (1883–1963), and Marianne Moore (1887–1972). Stevens's best work appeared in the 1930s, but his first book, *Harmonium,* was published in 1923, when he was forty-four. His elegant poems — described as epicurean — explored the nature of art. Williams and Moore were classified as Objectivists: poets for whom the object

T. S. Eliot

*The Black Mask* became the most influential magazine in the pulp mystery field.

was not just symbolic but a thing to be studied in its own right. Moore's cerebral poetry is praised for its precise observation; her 1924 volume was appropriately titled *Observations*. Robinson Jeffers published *Tamar and Other Poems* (1924), *Roan Stallion; Tamar and Other Poems* (1925), and *The Women at Point Sur* (1927) during the decade. His plotted long poems use violent material to express the theme that "civilization is a transient sickness."

**Millay and Cummings.** Among the younger poets were Edna St. Vincent Millay (1892–1950), E. E. Cummings (1894–1962), and Hart Crane (1899–1932). Millay's lyrical poetry expressed a hunger for beauty. Her best-known poem, "First Fig," from the 1920 volume *A Few Figs from Thistles*, caught the spirit of rebellion associated with the 1920s:

> My candle burns at both ends;
> It will not last the night;
> But ah, my foes, and oh, my friends —
> It gives a lovely light!

Cummings wrote typographically idiosyncratic verse with traditional themes: romantic love and self-reliance. He was a New England transcendentalist who wrote poems

of somewhat spurious modernism; they were not as difficult as they looked on the page:

> Buffalo Bill's
> defunct
>    Who used to
>     ride a watersmooth-silver
>         stallion
> and break onetwothreefourfive pigeonsjustlikethat[.]

His first volume of verse, *Tulips and Chimneys* (1923), was followed by volumes with Cummingsesque titles — *&* (1925) and *Is 5* (1926).

Sources:

Horace Gregory and Marza Zaturensha, *A History of American Poetry, 1900–1940* (New York: Harcourt, Brace, 1946);

David Perkins, *A History of Modern Poetry From the 1890s to the High Modern Mode* (Cambridge, Mass.: Harvard University Press, 1976).

## PULPS AND DETECTIVE FICTION

**Hard-Boiled.** The hard-boiled style, an enduring influence on American writing, began in what was regarded as the subliterary environment of pulp fiction — so named because the magazines were cheaply printed on

The Algonquin round table: (clockwise from upper left) Lynn Fontanne, Alfred Lunt, Robert Benchley, Frank Crowninshield, Alexander Woollcott, Heywood Broun, Marc Connelly, Frank Case, Franklin P. Adams, Edna Ferber, George S. Kaufman, Robert E. Sherwood, and Dorothy Parker

wood-pulp paper. This way of writing flourished in the pulps — also known as dime novels — that specialized in mystery-detective-crime fiction. The best and best known of these pulps was *Black Mask*. From the pulp racks grew what has been described as an authentic voice of American fiction. Raymond Chandler was a later *Black Mask* alumnus. The hard-boiled school outlived the demise of the pulps, achieved respectability, and flourishes in the 1990s.

**Definition.** Hard-boiled writing results from the use of violent or brutal action and the writer's response to that material. It is therefore realistic fiction with some or all of these elements: objective viewpoint, impersonal tone, colloquial speech, tough characters, and understated style.

**Hammett.** Dashiell Hammett (1894–1961) was the first major figure in the hard-boiled movement; if he did not invent it, he certainly perfected it. Hammett first appeared in *Black Mask* during 1922. In 1929 he was published by the respected imprint of Alfred A. Knopf with his first novel, *Red Harvest,* which had been serial-

ized in *Black Mask*. Hammett also formulated the believable working-detective character, The Continental Op.

**Sources:**
Ron Goulart, *The Hardboiled Dicks: An Anthology and Study of Pulp Detective Fiction* (Los Angeles: Sherbourne, 1965);

*The Hard-Boiled Omnibus; Early Stories from Black Mask* (New York: Simon & Schuster, 1949).

## SATIRE AND HUMOR

**Era of Satire.** Cynicism and ebullience coexisted during the 1920s and found joint expression as satire in words and in images. It was an era when ridicule was the weapon of choice. Politicians, financiers, intellectuals, puritans, reformers, feminists, and revolutionaries were popular targets. The main target was pomposity.

**Irreverence and Wit.** The defining characteristic of American humor is irreverence — the refusal to be impressed by or respectful of institutionalized power or conventional morality. Wit was prized during the 1920s, and reputations were built on the application of it. The reputations of literary humorists rarely outlive them because humor becomes identified with its time: a comic style often achieves its humor by originality of perception and expression; repeated and copied, it becomes corny. Satire and parody, however brilliant, depend on reader recognition of material that usually has a short literary life. Of the many 1920s humorists, the one who has achieved the greatest permanent stature and readership is Ring W. Lardner. His acutely observed misanthrope's sketches of personalities and human relationships, in particular, have retained an audience; and some of his topical material — baseball, for example — has acquired historical value.

**Parody and Verse.** The material ranged from literary humor to nonsense. Parody and satire were very popular. Donald Ogden Stewart, whose *Mr. and Mrs. Haddock Abroad* (1924) and *The Crazy Fool* (1925) were labeled "crazy humor," combined parody with nonsense. The most popular parodist of the decade was Robert Benchley, who moved from writing to performing his work. His "Treasurer's Report," a scatterbrained monologue, was widely reprinted and performed. The 1920s were also the last period when humorous verse was a form of mass entertainment. Samuel Hoffenstein (*Poems in Praise of Practically Nothing*, 1928) and Don Marquis (*Archy and Mehitabel*, 1927) were widely read. Franklin P. Adams's *New York World* column, "The Conning Tower," featured his own poems and welcomed the verse contributions of readers. His most widely known poem was based on the Chicago Cubs double-play combination and began —

These are the saddest of possible words:
"Tinker to Evers to Chance."

**Algonquin Group.** A group of the wits who wrote for New York publications formed the Vicious Circle, so named because they frequently lunched at a round table in the Algonquin Hotel. Since some of them had newspaper columns, they printed each other's witticisms and advanced their collective celebrity. This incestuous cadre, featuring Benchley, Adams, Dorothy Parker, Alexander Woollcott, Heywood Broun, and George S. Kaufman, raised the wisecrack into a literary genre. Parker achieved a permanent reputation on the basis of her wisecracking, self-triumphing contempt; reviewing *Winnie-the-Pooh* as *New Yorker* columnist "Constant Reader" she wrote "Tonstant weader fwew up."

**Magazine Satire.** *The New Yorker*, launched in 1925, initially had a strong component of parody or burlesque in its articles and drawings. The ridicule, as in the cartoons of Peter Arno, was intended as entertainment — not as social protest. But the radical journals cultivated angry satire intended to move readers to action, as did the drawings of Art Young for *The Masses*.

**College Humor.** College humor magazines had substantial readerships and served as incubators for verbal and cartoon humorists. The best known in the East were *The Yale Record*, *The Princeton Tiger*, *The Columbia Jester*, *The Dartmouth Jack-O'-Lantern*, and *The Harvard Lampoon*. Apprentice wits hoped to move from these publica-

Charlie Chaplin eating his shoes in *The Gold Rush* (1925)

tions to the commercial humor magazines such as *Judge*, *Life* (before the title was acquired for a photo-news magazine), and *The New Yorker*.

**Thurber.** James Thurber (ex *Ohio State Sundial*) and S. J. Perelman (ex *Brown Jug*) did their best work after the 1920s but published first books in the 1920s. Both became identified with *The New Yorker*. Thurber and E. B. White collaborated on *Is Sex Necessary? Or Why You Feel the Way You Do*, a travesty of psychology books. There were abundant targets for humor and receptive readers in the 1920s.

**Humor as Literature.** Several humorists ascended from journalism and commercial writing to the ranks of literature. Sportswriter Damon Runyon's low-life stories attained an enduring reputation. Screenwriter Anita Loos wrote a minor classic, "*Gentlemen Prefer Blondes.*" Both writers used the American language in innovative ways — as did Lardner — and one of the characteristics of 1920s humor was its linguistic resourcefulness.

**Lewis.** During the 1920s Sinclair Lewis's well-received novels — *Main Street*, *Babbitt*, *Arrowsmith*, *Elmer Gantry* — utilized exaggeration and caricature to ridicule the materialism and cultural poverty of American life. Foreign readers regarded Lewis's satires as documentary realism, and in 1930 he became the first American to receive the Nobel Prize for literature.

Sources:
Walter Blair and Hamlin Hill, *America's Humor* (New York: Oxford University Press, 1978);
Margaret Case Harriman, *The Vicious Circle: The Story of the Algonquin Round Table* (New York: Rinehart, 1951).

## SCULPTURE

**Naturalism to Modernism.** Naturalistic sculpture was ascendant at the start of the 1920s. The heroic in scale and theme was exemplified by Daniel Chester French's Lincoln Memorial statue begun in 1922 and Henry

The Keystone Kops: Ford Sterling on the phone, with Fatty Arbuckle at far right

Shrady's dynamic battle group for the Grant Memorial, seventeen years in progress and finished in 1922. Realistic portraiture (Malvina Hoffman's bronze *Paderewski the Artist: Head* in 1923, for example) began a shift to modernism with the simplified, expressionistic work of Jo Davidson (*Gertrude Stein* in 1920). Paul Manship's formal, decorative, elegantly simplified bronze figures (*Dancer and Gazelles*, 1916) defined the public concept of contemporary sculpture in the 1920s.

**Lachaise.** French-born and -educated, émigré Gaston Lachaise (1882–1935), who worked as an assistant to Manship, continued as an independent sculptor in the Beaux Arts tradition (*Dolphin Fountain*, 1924) but with greater originality in his bronze female nudes of monumental proportions (*Standing Woman*, 1912–1927, and especially *Floating Figure*, 1927).

**Zorach.** Lithuanian-born William Zorach (1887–1966) was a leader in the return to the direct carving of stone. Self-taught as a sculptor, he used abstraction and simplification of form to comform to the block being carved (*Floating Figure* of African mahogany in 1922).

The French-born prodigy Robert Laurent (1890–1970), educated in the United States with an apprenticeship in Paris, followed Zorach's lead in style and in respect for the material (*The Wave*, 1926).

**Calder.** Alexander Calder (1898–1976) was the great American sculptor in terms of creative originality. His concept of lightness and motion as attributes of sculpture was revolutionary. His wit and playfulness are apparent in his wire caricatures and portraits, in which he sometimes broke with three-dimensional tradition (*The Hostess*, 1928). Calder's activated sculptures became known as mobiles.

Source:
H. H. Arnason, *History of Modern Art: Painting • Sculpture • Architecture* (Englewood Cliffs, N.J.: Prentice-Hall / New York: Abrams, 1968).

## SILENT COMEDY

**Impact of Sound.** No matter how well photographed and directed, filmed drama is incomplete in the absence of audible spoken dialogue. The exaggerated mugging

Stan Laurel and Oliver Hardy in *Two Tars* (1928)

and pantomime required for communication between characters on screen impart a histrionic falsity to the most passionate declaration and turn tragedy into melodrama. With the advent of sound, movies fulfilled their potential and far outstripped the stage as a realistic dramatic medium. But sound killed the one movie genre that never needed to talk: the silent comedy.

**Shorts.** In the early years silent comedies were restricted to one-reelers and two-reelers — running for seven to fourteen minutes. These shorts did not permit the development of character or mixed emotions, but they were enormously popular throughout the silent era. One thousand reels of short comedies were released in 1925.

**The Little Tramp.** The golden period of silent comedy commenced in 1914 when Charlie Chaplin went to work at Mack Sennett's Keystone Studio, where he joined Fatty Arbuckle, Mabel Normand, Ben Turpin, and the Keystone Kops. Unhappy with the rush conditions at Keystone and wanting control over his work, Chaplin moved to other studios until he became his own producer in 1918. Unlike other comedians, who relied on slapstick or knockabout work, Chaplin developed the pathos of his Little Tramp figure.

**Keystone.** Sennett's comedy was physical, featuring custard-pie throwing and wild chases. Keystone's preeminence in the comedy field was diminished by the departure of Arbuckle and Normand. (Arbuckle's career was destroyed by his 1921–1922 rape trials even though he was acquitted.) Sennett's stable included Chester Conklin, Mack Swain, Charlie Chase, Charlie Murray, and Sydney Chaplin. Keystone's Harry Langdon was regarded as a potential Charlie Chaplin rival on the basis of *The Strong Man, Tramp Tramp Tramp,* and *Long Pants* (all 1927), in which he portrayed a character with child-like innocence, but his insistence on full control spoiled his movies. His career did not survive talkies.

**Hal Roach.** Audiences began to prefer comedies produced by Hal Roach, whose players included Stan Laurel and Oliver Hardy, and Harold Lloyd. Laurel and Hardy worked together for twenty years, successfully shifting to sound. Most of their best sound work was in the two-reel format, but their Academy Award winner, *The Music Box* (1932), was a three-reeler. They became the most enduring team in movie comedy. Lloyd's *Safety Last* (1923) and *The Freshman* (1925) were among the most popular silent comedy features. Because Chaplin spent so much time perfecting his movies, Lloyd became the biggest moneymaker during the 1920s. Like the other comedians of this genre, his humor was visual — frequently utilizing narrow escapes from perilous situations — but Lloyd also developed realistic characters. Lloyd's talkies during the 1930s did not match the success of his earlier work.

**Keaton.** By critical consensus Chaplin and Buster Keaton were the greatest silent clowns. Keaton's trademark was deadpan humor — his lack of expression in comic or dangerous situations. Like Chaplin, he di-

Al Jolson in *The Jazz Singer* (1927)

rected his movies. Keaton's movies were not popular; *The General* (1927), regarded as his masterpiece, lost money. Keaton did not enjoy Chaplin's control and ownership of his work after he became an M-G-M employee. His shift to talkies was disastrous, and by 1933 he was a has-been.

Some of the once-famous silent comedians continued to appear in small parts during the 1930s and 1940s, looking like ghosts.

Sources:
Walter Kerr, *The Silent Clowns* (New York: Knopf, 1975);

Richard Dyer MacCann, *The Silent Comedians* (Metuchen, N.J.: Scarecrow Press, 1993);

Mack Sennett, *King of Comedy* (Garden City, N.Y.: Doubleday, 1954).

## SOCIAL-PROTEST FICTION

**Radicals.** The full literary impact of Marxism came in the 1930s, but the Russian Revolution and the political suppressions during the 1920s influenced American writers who were socialists if not communists. These writers attempted to use literature as a class weapon. The most productive radical novelist of the decade was Upton Sinclair (1878–1968). A veteran of earlier protests, Sinclair published *Boston* (1929), a two-volume novel based on the Sacco-Vanzetti case. The younger literary radicals included Floyd Dell, Joseph Freeman, Max Eastman, and Michael Gold. John Dos Passos (1896–1970) was the most innovative — and the most talented — of the young radicals. Although he later moved to the Right, during the 1920s and 1930s he used news reports of oppression and injustice in his fiction-as-contemporary-history novels. Dos Passos experimented with techniques from cinema and modern painting to provide impressions of contemporary American social and political events.

Sources:
Daniel Aaron, *Writers on the Left* (New York: Harcourt, Brace & World, 1961);

Walter B. Rideout, *The Radical Novel in the United States 1900–1954* (Cambridge, Mass.: Harvard University Press, 1956).

## TALKIES

**Jolson Sings.** *The Jazz Singer* starring Al Jolson opened at the Warner Theatre in New York on 6 October 1927 and inaugurated the motion-picture talkie era. But the movie renowned as the first talkie was actually a silent with partial sound. It was not even the first feature movie with synchronized sound: *Don Juan* in 1926 had a synchronized music score and sound effects. Nonetheless, Jolson spoke the first line of dialogue in a full-length movie: "Wait a minute. Wait a minute. You ain't heard nothin' yet."

**Rush to Sound.** There was an apparent economic motive, apart from technological and personnel costs, to resist the change: the restoration of language to drama immediately limited the audience, which had been worldwide. With the transition to sound, the only universally accessible form of dramatic narrative ceased to exist. But, although some movie-industry people dismissed sound as a fad, audience demand was irresistible. The rush to sound was on, and all the studios eventually converted. Weekly movie attendance rose from 57 million in 1927 to 95 million in 1929.

**Vitaphone.** After more part-sound features, Warner premiered the first all-talking feature movie, *Lights of New York,* in July 1928. The Warner sound system, Vitaphone, used records synchronized with the film; and problems were frequent. The recording process necessitated that the actors talk into hidden microphones, limiting their mobility and constraining an acting style that depended upon exaggerated movement and gesture.

**Voices and Dialogue.** Writers who could write dialogue and actors who could speak it were imported from Broadway. Diction, accent, and vocal timbre were suddenly important. Careers of certain silent stars perished because they could not speak English or because their voices did not sound the way audiences expected. There is disagreement about whether John Gilbert's career as screen lover collapsed because his voice recorded as less manly than required or because audiences snickered at the bad dialogue he was provided. Gilbert's costar, Greta Garbo, retained her appeal by performing in roles that accommodated her foreign accent. Her first spoken line in *Anna Christie* (1930) was "Gimme a viskey. Ginger ale on the side. And don' be stingy, ba-bee."

**Movietone.** William Fox backed the Movietone sound-on-film system, which rapidly superseded Vitaphone. The first all-Movietone newsreel was shown on 28 October 1927. Thereafter newsreels became a staple of every movie theater program. General Electric developed the Photophone system in 1927, which was used by RKO; but Movietone became the preferred system for all studios.

**Musicals.** After *The Jazz Singer* the movie musical became an entertainment genre that eventually all but terminated the practice of taking Broadway musicals on tour. Movie musicals were more lavishly produced than stage shows, and the movies began to produce original musicals along with versions of hit shows. The first musical to win an Academy Award for best picture was *Broadway Melody* (1929) with an original score by Nacio Herb Brown and Arthur Freed. New singing stars were created by the movies; another hit 1929 musical, *The Love Parade* (Paramount-Famous Players-Lasky), paired Maurice Chevalier and Jeanette MacDonald.

Sources:
Richard Koszarski, *An Evening's Entertainment: The Age of the Silent Feature Picture 1915–1928* (New York: Scribners, 1990);

Frederic Thrasher, ed., *Okay for Sound . . . How the Screen Found Its Voice* (New York: Duell, Sloan & Pearce, 1946).

# HEADLINE MAKERS

## LOUIS ARMSTRONG

### 1901–1971

#### MUSICIAN

**An American Treasure.** Louis Armstrong was probably born on 4 August 1901, but he appropriated 4 July 1900 as his official birthday to reinforce his identification with American history. Born out of wedlock in New Orleans to Mary Albert and Will Armstrong, a laborer, he grew up surrounded by music. At twelve he was sent to the Colored Waifs Home for firing a gun on New Year's Eve. There Armstrong learned to play the cornet.

**Early Brilliance.** Supreme geniuses develop rapidly. In 1920 Armstrong was working with the Fate Marable Band on Mississippi steamboats. Then in 1922 he was invited to join King Oliver's Creole Jazz Band in Chicago. Oliver, then the leading cornet player, acted as Armstrong's mentor; but the apprentice excelled his master. His reputation among other musicians soared. His playing was distinguished by energy, clear tone, rich phrasing, lyricism, and complexity. Hoagy Carmichael described his first exposure to Armstrong playing "Bugle Call Rag": " 'Why,' I moaned, 'why isn't everybody in the world here to hear that?' I meant it. Something as unutterably stirring as that deserved to be heard by the world."

**Fame.** Although Armstrong was not ruthlessly ambitious, he knew when it was time for him to move ahead. In 1924 he joined the Fletcher Henderson Orchestra in New York, a musically sophisticated group led by an influential arranger. But Armstrong felt constricted in this orchestra and in 1925 formed his Hot Five with Kid Ory (trombone), Johnny Dodds (clarinet), Lil Armstrong (piano), and Johnny St. Cyr (banjo). The Hot Five was a studio group to serve the market for race records — rec-

ords sold to blacks, especially in the South. Armstrong's popularity cut across Jim Crow barriers, and he became the most popular black entertainer of his times. Armstrong recorded his first vocals with the Hot Five; "Heebie Jeebies" in 1926 was his first hit and his first scat-singing recording. The story that Armstrong improvised scat when he dropped his sheet music is almost certainly a fabrication.

**Entertainer.** Armstrong loved performing and clowning; his enjoyment of singing disturbed critics who wanted to hear him play, but audiences and record purchasers responded to his gravel voice and ebullience. By 1928 Armstrong had switched from cornet to trumpet. The 1928 recording of "West End Blues" — on which he plays and sings — has been praised as Armstrong's masterpiece. Music historian Gunther Scheller has noted the brilliant opening cadenza and the "Spectacular cascading phrases." So great was Armstrong's pleasure in work that in 1929 he was performing on Broadway in *Hot Chocolates,* leading his band at Connie's Inn in Harlem, and appearing in the late show at the Lafayette Theater. Two Fats Waller songs from *Hot Chocolates* became his biggest hits to date: "Ain't Misbehavin' "and "Black and Blue." He was twenty-eight.

**Satchmo.** At some point during the 1920s, Armstrong's nickname Satchmo (probably derived from satchel-mouth) gained currency, and as Satchmo he became a recognized world figure. In 1929 the Hot Five was succeeded by Louis Armstrong and his Orchestra, which went on the road. With this orchestra Armstrong's material evolved away from blues to include popular songs ("I Can't Give You Anything But Love, Baby") and novelty songs ("I'm a Ding Dong Daddy from Dumas"). Although purists complained that Armstrong was selling out, his public grew during the 1930s as he took his music to Europe. In 1937 Armstrong became the first black to host a network radio show, the *Fleischmann's Yeast Hour.* He appeared in Broadway shows and in the movies.

**The All Stars.** After World War II the jazz/swing scene changed as combos replaced big bands. In 1947 he formed the six-member All Stars which toured most of the time. The succession of one-night stands wore out other musicians, but Armstrong loved to perform. His last movie, *Hello, Dolly!* (1969), resulted in a hit record of the title song. He toured with the All Stars until shortly before his death from heart failure in 1971. He was mourned all over the world. If the term *lovable* means anything, Armstrong was lovable; his performances were love matches between the performer and his audience. It is possible to argue about the merits of any jazz musician, except Louis Armstrong. He was the greatest cornet and trumpet player. His recordings during the 1920s remain unsurpassed.

Sources:

Louis Armstrong, *Satchmo: My Life in New Orleans* (New York: Prentice-Hall, 1954);

James L. Collier, *Louis Armstrong: An American Genius* (New York: Oxford University Press, 1988);

Marc H. Miller, ed., *Louis Armstrong: A Cultural Legacy* (New York: Queens Museum of Art / Seattle: University of Washington Press, 1994);

*Louis Armstrong: Portrait of the Artist as a Young Man, 1923–1934* (Columbia/Legacy 57176).

## IRVING BERLIN

### 1888-1989

#### SONGWRITER

**America's Minstrel.** When asked to comment on Irving Berlin's place in American music, Jerome Kern famously declared: "Irving Berlin has no place in American music — he is American music." None of his contemporaries in an era of great songwriters that included Kern, George and Ira Gershwin, Richard Rodgers and Lorenz Hart, and Cole Porter wrote so many standard American songs. His fifteen hundred songs display an extraordinary range of material and moods: "White Christmas," "There's No Business Like Show Business," "Remember," "Always," "Blue Skies," "Cheek to Cheek," "Puttin' on the Ritz."

**Immigrant Orphan.** This intensely American troubadour was born in Russia and arrived in America when he was five. His father died when he was eight, and Israel Baline took to the streets of New York with less than two years of schooling. Working as a singing waiter in low saloons, he taught himself to pick out tunes on the black keys of the piano in the key of F-sharp. There is disagreement about whether he ever learned to read or write music. For the rest of his life he composed on the black keys and had the music taken down by an assistant.

**Tin-Pan Alley.** His first song lyric, "Marie from Sunny Italy," was published in 1907; a printer's error provided him with the surname Berlin. By 1909 he had his first hit, "My Wife's Gone to the Country, Hurrah! Hurrah!" (with George Whiting and Ted Snyder). Then came "Alexander's Ragtime Band" in 1911, one of the most popular of American songs. Berlin's stint on Tin-Pan Alley, the Manhattan locale for music publishers and song pluggers, was brief. In 1909 he began providing songs for Broadway shows, and in 1914 he wrote his first complete score for *Watch Your Step*, including "Play a Simple Melody." As a soldier during World War I, he wrote a show for the benefit of the troops, *Yip, Yip, Yaphank,* which featured "Oh, How I Hate to Get Up in the Morning."

**Broadway.** After the war Berlin wrote "A Pretty Girl Is Like a Melody" for the *Ziegfeld Follies*. At this point he was so successful that he was able to build his own theater, The Music Box, for which he wrote a series of annual shows, *The Music Box Revues*, from 1921 through 1924. His 1933 show, *As Thousands Cheer*, brilliantly demonstrated Berlin's ability to write in different styles: "Easter Parade," "Harlem on my Mind," "Heat Wave," and "Supper Time," the last a domestic lament for the victim of a lynching. His productivity and the variety of his songs fostered the slander that he had secret collaborators. Berlin became a newspaper celebrity during his 1925 courtship of Ellen Mackay, whose Roman Catholic millionaire father tried to prevent her marriage to a Jew.

**Hollywood.** With the advent of sound movies, Berlin began writing for the studios in 1928 and during the 1930s was primarily occupied with writing movie musicals. *Top Hat* (1935), with Ginger Rogers and Fred Astaire, became a classic of the genre. Always grateful to America for the opportunities it had provided him, in 1939 Berlin made a gift to the Girl Scouts of a song that had been cut from *Yip, Yip, Yaphank*: "God Bless America." During World War II he wrote and performed in *This Is the Army.* The show toured theaters and military bases; the proceeds were donated to military welfare.

**The Last Songsmith.** Irving Berlin was seventy-four when he wrote his last show, *Mr. President*, in 1962. When he died at 101, Berlin was the last of the group of great American songwriters whose work appealed to the entire nation during the first half of the twentieth century. His songs gave expression to the changing concerns of Americans decade by decade. Some of his colleagues were musically or poetically more sophisticated than Berlin. But no one else put the words and the music together as effectively and recognizably as Israel Baline. Among his most enduring songs are those about music: "A Pretty Girl Is Like a Melody," "Say It With Music," "Alexander's Ragtime Band," "I Love a Piano," "Let's Face the Music and Dance," "The Song Is Ended."

Sources:

Laurence Bergreen, *As Thousands Cheer: The Life of Irving Berlin* (New York: Viking, 1990);

Ian Whitcomb, *Irving Berlin and Ragtime America* (New York: Limelight, 1988);

*Irving Berlin: 100 Years* (Columbia 40035).

# CHARLIE CHAPLIN

## 1889-1977

### COMEDIAN

**Famous Face.** The American recognized more readily than any other throughout the world for more than seventy years was inhabited by an Englishman. Charles Spencer Chaplin, the child of English music-hall entertainers, grew up in English workhouses and orphanages, but his success story is a type of the American dream unrivaled by the imaginings of Hollywood: he became the supreme genius of movie comedy. His work has been analyzed by intellectuals and enjoyed everywhere by people wanting to be amused, and his Little Tramp is still such an identifiable Everyman that an impersonation of him has been used to sell electronic office equipment.

**Early Shorts.** At twelve Chaplin was on the stage, and at seventeen he was touring with the Fred Karno comedy troupe. In 1914 he was hired by Mack Sennett to appear in the silent shorts made by Mack Sennett's Keystone studio in Hollywood. The Sennett company included Fatty Arbuckle, Mabel Normand, and the Keystone Kops; the humor was physical, and the chase was mandatory. Sennett's mass-produced comedies provided Chaplin little opportunity to develop his comic ideas, as he appeared in thirty-five shorts in one year. One of these, *Kid Auto Races at Venice* (seven minutes), introduced Chaplin's tramp figure, who became the most popular movie character of all time. Told to put on a funny costume, Chaplin selected baggy trousers (borrowed from Fatty Arbuckle), oversize shoes (worn on the wrong feet), a cutaway coat that was too small, a derby, a bamboo cane, and a false mustache. The effect of seedy elegance — an insouciant absurd dignity — was a personification of unrealizable but resilient human aspiration.

**Writer and Director.** Although Chaplin began writing and directing at Keystone with *Caught in the Rain,* he was dissatisfied with the working conditions and remuneration. Possibly because of his impoverished childhood, Chaplin was a shrewd manager of his finances. Determined to acquire full control over his genius, Chaplin moved to the Essanay Studio (fourteen two-reelers, written and directed by Chaplin), thence to the Mutual Studio in 1916; at twenty-six he became the highest-paid performer in the world, receiving $670,000 for a dozen two-reelers — all of which he wrote and directed — including *The Floorwalker, The Fireman, One A.M., The Rink, The Cure, Easy Street,* and *The Immigrant.* During his year at Mutual, Chaplin refined his theories of comedy and movie construction. As he explained:

> I not only try to get myself into embarrassing situations, but I also incriminate the other characters in

the picture. When I do this, I always aim for economy of means. By that I mean that when one incident can get two big, separate laughs, it is much better than two individual incidents. In "The Adventurer" [ Mutual, 1917 ] I accomplished this by first placing myself on a balcony, eating ice cream with a girl. On the floor directly underneath the balcony I put a stout, dignified, well-dressed woman at a table. Then, while eating the ice cream, I let a piece drop off my spoon, slip through my baggy trousers and drop from the balcony onto this woman's neck. The first laugh came at my embarrassment over my own predicament. The second, and the much greater one, came when the ice cream landed on the woman's neck and she shrieked and started to dance around. Only one incident had been used, but it had got two people in trouble, and had also got two big laughs.

**Early Features.** In 1918 he moved to First National when he was paid $1 million for eight movies, including his first feature, *The Kid* (1921). A perfectionist who discarded much of his footage, Chaplin reduced his productions during the 1920s. While Fatty Arbuckle made nine features in a year, Chaplin spent one year on *The Kid.* Chaplin's Mutual and First National movies developed the character of the Little Tramp into a comic hero, weak and friendless but moved to quixotic exertion by acts of injustice or cruelty, confronting powerful figures. He may triumph through his wits or he may be defeated by brute force, but the Tramp's essential goodness and optimism are not impaired. Increasingly Chaplin built pathos into his hero's struggles.

**Independence.** He achieved total artistic and financial control over his movies in 1923 when Chaplin, Mary Pickford, Douglas Fairbanks, and D. W. Griffith formed United Artists. *The Gold Rush* (1925) — to which he devoted two years — was Chaplin's masterpiece in the 1920s. The episode of the tramp cooking and eating his shoes is the most famous movie comedy routine. Three years were spent on *The Circus* (1928).

**Sound.** Chaplin recognized that his comedy did not need sound and that spoken dialogue would limit his audience. Other silent clowns were destroyed by talkies, but Chaplin maintained his artistic independence and wealth. He spent another three years on *City Lights* (1931), which had sound effects and music but not dialogue. It is generally ranked as his greatest achievement. Chaplin's voice was not heard until *Modern Times* (1936), the last appearance of the Little Tramp.

**Messages.** Chaplin's career survived sexual and marital scandals that would have ruined any other star. He married two child brides and was involved in a messy paternity case. At age fifty-four he married eighteen-year-old Oona O'Neill, the daughter of dramatist Eugene O'Neill; the enduring marriage produced eight children. Chaplin generated further hostile attention by his political ideas. Beginning with *Modern Times,*

Chaplin used his movies to make political statements — with mixed results. *The Great Dictator* (1940) effectively ridiculed Hitler and Mussolini, but his postwar movies were didactic. Critics complained that his work had become pretentious.

**Exile.** During the war Chaplin advocated a second front in Europe to relieve the German pressure on the Soviet Union and became known as a friend of Russia. The fact that he had retained his British citizenship was cited as evidence of his un-American conduct. There were income-tax claims that Chaplin believed to be punitive. Boycotts were organized against *Monsieur Verdoux* (1947) and *A King in New York* (1957). *Limelight* (1952) was Chaplin's last major achievement. This evocation of the English music halls of his apprenticeship ends with a superb comedy routine by Chaplin and Buster Keaton. In 1952 while traveling abroad Chaplin was informed that the attorney general would not permit him to reenter the United States unless he could prove his "moral worth." Chaplin remained in Europe, settling in Switzerland, and returned to America only to accept a special Oscar in 1972. He was knighted by Queen Elizabeth II in 1975.

**Endurance.** During the 1920s there was never a minute when a Chaplin movie was not being shown somewhere. More people have watched his movies all over the world than those of any other performer. More than anyone else, he enlarged the range of comedy. Charlie Chaplin's audiences are still laughing.

Sources:

Charlie Chaplin, *Charlie Chaplin's Own Story* (Bloomington: Indiana University Press, 1985);

Chaplin, *My Autobiography* (New York: Simon & Schuster, 1964);

David Robinson, *Chaplin: His Life and Art* (New York: McGraw-Hill, 1985).

# F. SCOTT FITZGERALD

## 1896-1940

### WRITER

**Tales of the Jazz Age.** Francis Scott Key Fitzgerald is the American writer most closely identified with the 1920s, which he named the Jazz Age. Early success, alcoholism, and an appetite for glamorous society rendered him the subject for enduring literary gossip. Although Fitzgerald's popular reputation has been distorted into that of a playboy who squandered his genius, he was a productive author whose best fiction occupies a permanent place among the classics of American literature.

**Early Success.** The only son of a respectable merchant-class Roman Catholic family — on his father's side genteel and on his mother's prosperous — Fitzgerald left Saint Paul, Minnesota, for an academically precarious but socially and artistically profitable four years at Princeton University, leaving without a degree to serve stateside in World War I in 1917. In 1920 his first novel, *This Side of Paradise*, brought him celebrity and critical attention. Set at Princeton it was credited with defining the values of the postwar generation. *This Side of Paradise* introduced two character types whom Fitzgerald developed throughout his work: the aspiring young man seeking to fulfill his ideals ("the romantic egoist") and the magnetic, independent young woman whose radiant femininity masks a ruthless self-interest. From the start Fitzgerald's style was admired for its sensory appeal and charm. One reviewer exclaimed, "How that boy Fitzgerald can write!" *This Side of Paradise* established Fitzgerald's permanent connection with the publishing house of Charles Scribner's Sons and its legendary editor, Maxwell Perkins.

**Professional Author.** After his marriage to the fearless and unpredictable Alabama belle Zelda Sayre in 1920, Fitzgerald embarked on an extravagant life that required him to combine a career as a writer of remunerative short stories for the magazine market with his career as a serious novelist. Although Fitzgerald was a literary celebrity, his four novels were not best-sellers. During his working life he was more widely recognized as a story writer than as a novelist. His 160 short stories ranged from commercial romantic entertainment to the brilliant "May Day," "The Rich Boy," "The Diamond as Big as the Ritz," and "Babylon Revisited." His peak fee of $4,000 per story from *The Saturday Evening Post* was reached in 1929.

**The Great American Novel.** Fitzgerald's third novel, *The Great Gatsby* (1925), was written in France — where the Fitzgeralds' escape from the distractions of New York was nullified by the distractions of expatriate society. *The Great Gatsby* revealed a new control over structure and narrative point of view; Fitzgerald — not yet twenty-nine — had mastered his craft. Jay Gatsby, the idealistic racketeer who believes that he can repeat the past and re-create himself in his endeavor to recover Daisy, has become an archetypal American figure. The title for this novel that Fitzgerald regretted coming up with too late was "Under the Red, White, and Blue"— emphasizing that the main subject of the novel is the American Dream of success. The extraordinary achievement of *The Great Gatsby* was immediately recognized by some critics and fellow writers; its popular reputation has grown steadily. It is now read and studied throughout the world.

**Dissipation and Catastrophe.** Work on Fitzgerald's fourth novel was interrupted by his alcoholism and suspended in 1930 by Zelda Fitzgerald's schizophrenic breakdown; her expensive treatment made it necessary for Fitzgerald to concentrate on commercial work. Written in the hospital, her novel *Save Me the Waltz* has become a cult work, and her compelling personality and tragic collapse, from which she had only intermittent improvement thereafter, have become the subject of study.

**A Novel of Deterioration.** Published in 1934, *Tender Is the Night* examines Richard Diver, a brilliant American psychiatrist who is ruined by his marriage to a wealthy mental patient and the distractions of luxurious expatriate life in France. Fitzgerald's second masterpiece did not sell well and received mixed reviews. As the American Depression deepened during the 1930s, Fitzgerald experienced a series of personal and professional crises that he described in "The Crack-Up" essays.

**Hollywood.** In debt and increasingly unable to write commercial short stories, Fitzgerald went to work as a screenwriter in 1937. He earned a screen credit for *Three Comrades* in 1938 but was not a success in the movie industry. At the time of his death from a heart attack at forty-four, he was writing *The Love of the Last Tycoon*, a Hollywood novel with a hero based on M-G-M producer Irving Thalberg. The work in progress was posthumously published in 1941 and is regarded as the most brilliant fictional treatment of Hollywood.

**Restoration.** F. Scott Fitzgerald died believing himself a forgotten writer, but a series of reappraisals commencing in the late 1940s and early 1950s established him firmly among America's major writers. The admiration for his work is accompanied by interest in his life, and Fitzgerald has become an exemplary American figure. As he wrote to his daughter from Hollywood: "I am not a great man, but sometimes I think the impersonal and objective quality of my talent, and the sacrifices of it, in pieces, to preserve its essential value has some sort of epic grandeur."

Sources:
Matthew J. Bruccoli, *Some Sort of Epic Grandeur: The Life of F. Scott Fitzgerald*, revised edition (New York: Carroll & Graf, 1993);

Bruccoli, ed., *F. Scott Fitzgerald: A Life in Letters* (New York: Scribners, 1994);

Scottie Fitzgerald Smith, et al., eds., *The Romantic Egoists: A Pictorial Autobiography from the Scrapbooks and Albums of Scott and Zelda Fitzgerald* (New York: Scribners, 1974).

## GEORGE GERSHWIN

### 1898-1937

#### SONGWRITER/COMPOSER

**Brilliance.** Born Jacob Gershwine in Brooklyn, George Gershwin was the most brilliant figure among the cadre of brilliant songwriters of his time. Before his early death he had progressed from Broadway to classical forms and opera, treating the jazz idiom with increasing complexity.

**Song Plugger.** A gifted pianist, he was a song plugger on Tin Pan Alley at sixteen. In 1919 he wrote his first big hit, "Swanee," followed by scores for the *George White*

*Scandals* (1920–1924) that included "Stairway to Paradise," "Do it Again," and "Somebody Loves Me." Gershwin was handsome and attracted admiration. He behaved with the confidence of his genius.

**George and Ira.** George Gershwin wrote only the music for his songs. After 1924 his older brother, Ira, was his lyricist for a string of successful Broadway and Hollywood productions. George's fame overshadowed Ira's reputation, but the two artists worked together comfortably. Their first hit musical was *Lady, Be Good!* in 1924 (which introduced "Fascinating Rhythm").

**Symphonic Work.** That year George performed his *Rhapsody in Blue* with Paul Whiteman's orchestra. The next year the Gershwins wrote two shows, *Tell Me More* and *Tip-Toes;* and George performed his Concerto in F for Piano and Orchestra at Carnegie Hall with the New York Symphony Society. The brothers' scores during the 1920s included *Oh, Kay!* (1926) and *Funny Face* (1927). Some of their songs during this decade were "The Man I Love," "Do, Do, Do," "Someone to Watch Over Me," "Strike Up the Band," "Funny Face," " 'S Wonderful," and "Liza." In 1928 George's *An American in Paris* was performed at Carnegie Hall by the Philharmonic-Symphony Society of New York. He was thirty years old.

**Broadway and Opera.** The 1930 show *Girl Crazy* ("I Got Rhythm") was followed the next year by *Of Thee I Sing*. This political satire, the first musical comedy to win a Pulitzer Prize for drama, introduced "Love Is Sweeping the Country." George composed two symphonic works in 1932: *Second Rhapsody* and *Cuban Overture*. He then turned his energies to a project that had long interested him, an opera for black performers. As early as 1922 he had composed *Blue Monday* (*135th Street*), a short work in opera format for black performers. George and Ira selected the novel *Porgy*, set in Charleston, South Carolina, for the libretto and collaborated with its author, DuBose Heyward. *Porgy and Bess* included "Summertime," "I Got Plenty of Nothin'," and "It Ain't Necessarily So." The 1935 production ran for 124 performances, but it subsequently achieved a world reputation through frequent revivals.

**Hollywood.** The Gershwins' first movie score was for the 1937 Fred Astaire–Ginger Rogers vehicle *Shall We Dance*, which featured "Let's Call the Whole Thing Off" and "They Can't Take That Away from Me." Two more movies followed in 1937 and 1938 before George Gershwin died of a brain tumor at thirty-eight. The last song the brothers wrote was "Our Love Is Here to Stay." George Gershwin's name continues to evoke a sense of genius abruptly terminated and a nation deprived of the anticipated creations of that genius. Like so many of the celebrated figures of the 1920s, George Gershwin's career was intensely American. The son of Russian immigrants, he created another kind of art from the jazz and blues material of black American music.

Sources:

Edmund Jablonski, *The Gershwin Years* (Garden City, N.Y.: Doubleday, 1958);

Deena Rosenberg, *Fascinating Rhythm: The Collaboration of George and Ira Gershwin* (New York: Dutton, 1991);

Herman Wasserman, ed., *George Gershwin's Song-book,* revised edition (New York: Simon & Schuster, 1941);

*Gershwin Plays Gershwin* (Electra 79287).

# JOHN HELD JR.

## 1889-1958

### ILLUSTRATOR

**Illustrator of the Jazz Age.** The work of John Held Jr. so accurately delineated and parodied the new fashions of the 1920s that his illustrations became guides for the conduct and costume of flaming youth. He was the most popular and highest-paid artist of the decade, appearing in *Life, Judge, The New Yorker, College Humor,* and *Vanity Fair.* If a magazine had circulation problems, it commissioned a Held cover. He drew syndicated comic strips; he provided dust-jacket art; he made blockprints; he sculpted; he painted landscapes and cityscapes; he designed theater sets and costumes.

**Apprenticeship.** Held was born and raised in Salt Lake City, Utah, where his father was a musician and an illustrator. He had no formal art training, apart from working in his father's engraving shop. Held attended grade school and high school intermittently, but at fourteen he was a cartoonist for the *Salt Lake City Tribune.* As was the case with many gifted youths of his time, Held's higher education was provided by newspaper work. After moving to New York in 1910, Held became an increasingly successful freelance illustrator; however, his fame came in the 1920s, when his material perfectly matched the mood of the Jazz Age.

**Flappers and Sheiks.** Held's illustrations were immediately recognizable for their flappers and sheiks. The young women were slim, hipless, and flat-chested; skirts were short, and hair was bobbed. They were sexually appealing because of their youthful insouciance. The young men wore wide trousers and raccoon coats; their hair was slicked down. No one was more than twenty years old.

**From Satire to History.** Held's characters began as satire; their behavior and appearance were meant to be funny. But they became stereotypes. He caught the spirit of the time so wittily that his exaggerated figures provided models for American collegians. Among other labels, the 1920s were the collegiate decade. College fashions, college slang, college style, and college mores were emulated on and off campus. Held — who had not attended college — became the historiographer of a culture he invented.

**Gay Nineties.** Held also re-created another never-never land: the so-called Gay Nineties. When *New Yorker* editor Harold Ross asked him to make more of the blockprints that Held had made when they were boys in Utah, he provided a series of satires of the genteel society at the end of the century. Again, Held's parodies were received as reportage. The success of Held's work was due in part to his captions: "Horse Whipping The Masher and Good for Him A Moral Lesson Eng. By John Held Jr."

**Comeback.** Held's characters were unfashionable during the Depression. He continued to draw but put much of his work into writing books (*Grim Youth,* 1930) and sculpting. In the 1950s — a post-war period that had marked resemblances to the 1920s — his art was rediscovered, and he remains the Hogarth of the era of wonderful nonsense.

Sources:

Shelley Armitage, *John Held, Jr.: Illustrator of the Jazz Age* (Syracuse, N.Y.: Syracuse University Press, 1987);

*The Most of John Held Jr.,* introduction by Carl J. Weinhardt (Brattleboro, Vt.: Stephen Green Press, 1972).

# ERNEST HEMINGWAY

## 1899-1961

### WRITER

**The Writer as Celebrity.** Ernest Hemingway became America's most famous and recognizable writer, combining literary genius with a life of action. He may have been more widely celebrated as a sportsman, warrior, traveler, and drinker than as a literary figure. It has been frequently remarked that Hemingway's greatest fictional character was Hemingway.

**Early Fame.** The elder son in the large family of a devout doctor and a music teacher, Hemingway grew up in Oak Park, Illinois, summering at Walloon Lake in northern Michigan. Oak Park, a suburb of Chicago, was prosperous and puritanical. In Michigan Hemingway found the material for his early fiction: events of sudden tragedy and pathos endured by the local Indians; the life-and-death consciousness of the hunter and fisherman; and the adept participant and empathic witness that he discovered in himself. Hemingway did not attend college. After graduating from high school in 1917, he worked for a brief time as a cub reporter for the *Kansas City Star* before joining the Red Cross as an ambulance driver. During World War I Hemingway was wounded while serving on the Italian front. Married in 1921 to Hadley, the first of his four wives, assisted by the income of her trust fund, and encouraged by Sherwood Anderson, Hemingway returned to Europe as a correspondent for the *Toronto Star* with the intention of becoming a writer of fiction. In Paris he formed useful friendships with expatriate writers Ezra Pound, Gertrude Stein, F. Scott Fitzgerald, John Dos Passos, and Archibald MacLeish and with editors Ernest Walsh and Ford Madox Ford of, respectively, *This Quarter* and *Transatlantic Review*. Hemingway's resentment of the help he received found vent in insult — frequently in print; almost all of his literary friendships were eventually soured or destroyed. Hemingway's first book published in America, a short-story collection titled *In Our Time* (1925), like his two earlier collections of short pieces published in Paris, made use of heretofore nonliterary material: fishing and camping and bullfighting. After his Paris apprenticeship Hemingway published his first novel, *The Sun Also Rises*, in 1926. This well-received work about expatriates in Paris and the fiesta at Pamplona, Spain, formulated the Hemingway code of values and developed his recognizable style, utilizing detailed descriptions, clipped dialogue, inside dope, and simple sentences. The novel also provided a name for the aimless, post-war expatriates: the Lost Generation. *The Sun Also Rises* was followed in 1929 by *A Farewell to Arms,* an even more successful novel set in Italy during World War I. It recounts the love affair between an American ambulance driver, Frederic Henry, and an English nurse, Catherine Barclay, against the backdrop of the Italian retreat from Caporetto in 1917. The work was judged obscene by some readers. Hemingway also wrote some fifty stories, which included such widely anthologized and imitated classics as "The Killers," "The Snows of Kilimanjaro," and "Big Two-Hearted River."

**Sport and War as Literature.** In 1928 Hemingway settled in Key West, Florida, living there until 1940 when he moved to Cuba. During the 1930s Hemingway wrote nonfiction books about bullfighting (*Death in the Afternoon,* 1932) and big-game hunting (*Green Hills of Africa,* 1935). Hemingway seemed to spend more time fishing in Cuba or hunting in Wyoming or Montana than writing. Hemingway's exploits and tumultuous personal life made him good copy for newspapers and magazines. Accounts of his four marriages and fights with people like Morley Callaghan, Wallace Stevens, and Max Eastman placed his name and picture more often in gossip than in literary columns. Hemingway's critical standing and readership slipped during the 1930s. His activities as a correspondent during the Spanish Civil War produced *For Whom the Bell Tolls* (1940), which restored his reputation as a novelist. The novel describes a bridge-blowing operation behind Fascist lines by an American Spanish teacher, Robert Jordan, and a group of Loyalist partisans. It had the best reviews of any Hemingway work since *A Farewell to Arms* and sold over 500,000 copies. During

World War II Hemingway was again a correspondent but published no important fiction about this war. When it seemed that Hemingway was finished as a fiction writer, he achieved a comeback in 1952 with *The Old Man and the Sea,* an allegorical account of an old Cuban fisherman's fight with and eventual loss of a giant marlin. The novelette, which was first published in *Life,* helped secure for him the Nobel Prize in 1954.

**Endearing Reputation.** Suffering from hypertension and depression, Hemingway shot himself at his Ketchum, Idaho, home in 1961. At his death he left a large collection of unfinished writings, some of which have been edited and published by his estate. These include *A Moveable Feast* (1964), his reminiscences about Paris in the 1920s. Although his personal legend inevitably diminished after his death, Ernest Hemingway influenced more readers, nonreaders, and other writers than any other American writer.

Sources:

Carlos Baker, *Ernest Hemingway: A Life Story* (New York: Scribners, 1969);

John Raeburn, *Fame Became of Him: Hemingway as Public Writer* (Bloomington: Indiana University Press, 1984).

## LANGSTON HUGHES

### 1902-1967

#### Writer

**Early Writings.** The "poet laureate of the Negro race" was born into a troubled family, albeit one with a long history of abolitionist activism. Abandoned by his father's immigration to Mexico, young Langston and his mother moved in with his grandmother in Lawrence, Kansas, where he spent an unhappy, lonely childhood. In 1915 his mother moved the family to Cleveland, Ohio, where he began publishing stories and poems in the high-school magazine, reflecting his concerns with race and social justice.

**Travel and First Book.** After high school and a stay in Mexico with his father, Hughes returned to the United States for a year at Columbia University. Throughout a period that included odd jobs in New York, work as a messboy on ships traveling to Africa and Europe, and a job washing dishes in a Paris nightclub featuring black entertainers, Hughes was publishing poems in journals such as *The Crisis,* the journal for the NAACP, and *Opportunity,* the journal for the Urban League. As a result, even before he returned to Washington, D.C., in late 1924, he had developed a reputation among black poetry readers in America. He continued to work at menial jobs for a while, but in 1926 he published his first volume of poems, *The Weary Blues.* Soon after, he enrolled at Lincoln University, a predominantly black school in Pennsylvania.

**Major Black Poet.** By the time he graduated from Lincoln in 1929, Hughes had published a second volume of poetry, *Fine Clothes to the Jew* (1927), and had established himself as one of the major young poets of the Harlem Renaissance. His poetry was nontraditional in form and brutal in its honest look at black poverty and anger. Some black critics found his portrayal of black life demeaning, to which Hughes responded, "I have a right to portray any side of Negro life I wish to."

**Radicalism.** In the early 1930s he began to turn sharply toward the radical Left, writing for Communist journals and working for leftist causes. His defense of the Scottsboro Boys included a radical verse play titled *Scottsboro Limited* (1931). In 1932 he joined a team of black artists traveling to the Soviet Union to make a film on race relations. The project fell through, but Hughes was celebrated in the Soviet Union as a radical writer, and he reciprocated by producing the most radical poetry of his life (some of which he later disavowed). For the remainder of the decade he traveled in and out of the United States — to China, Japan, Mexico, Spain — and his literary interests turned toward fiction and drama.

**"Simple" and Later Work.** During this time he published an important volume of stories, *The Ways of White Folks* (1934), and saw his play on miscegenation, *Mulatto,* produced on Broadway (1935). He served briefly in 1938 as a war correspondent in Spain, then returned to the United States and founded the Harlem Suitcase Theatre. With the coming of World War II, Hughes abandoned the Left and became a columnist for *The Chicago Defender.* One of his most memorable creations was the character Jesse B. Semple, called "Simple," a black Everyman who would turn up regularly in his column. Hughes later compiled those "Simple" sketches into books and an Off-Broadway musical play. In the twenty years between the war and his death in 1967, he became prodigious in his production of literary works — highlighted by Broadway musicals, including *Street Scene* (1947) and *Black Nativity* (1961), a two-volume autobiography, a novel, two additional volumes of stories, a history of the NAACP, seven children's books on black culture, and five additional volumes of verse, including the highly acclaimed bebop collection, *Montage of a Dream Deferred* (1951). The most important literary figure of the Harlem Renaissance and one of America's representative poets, he died in New York in 1967.

Sources:

Langston Hughes, *I Wonder as I Wander: An Autobiographical Journey* (New York: Rinehart, 1956);

Arnold Rampersad, *The Life of Langston Hughes* (New York: Oxford University Press, 1986).

# AL JOLSON

## 1866-1950

### PERFORMER

**The World's Greatest Entertainer.** According to different sources Asa Yoelson was born in Russia or in Washington, D.C. As a boy he sang in the streets and in saloons, running away from his Orthodox Jewish home several times in attempts to break into show business. At fifteen he was performing in vaudeville. By 1906 Jolson was working in blackface.

**Mammy.** From the mid nineteenth century through the 1920s whites and blacks in burnt cork or grease paint performed exaggerated and distorted versions of black material. These acts — in and out of minstrel shows — were extremely popular with white audiences and frequently featured blacked-up whites yearning to return to the South. This nostalgia for a way of life that the audiences had never experienced may have resulted from the familial yearnings of immigrant groups. Jolson was by far the most successful of the mammy singers. In 1912 a runway from the stage was constructed in the Winter Garden on Broadway to enable Jolson to work closer to the audience. He probably introduced his mannerism of singing on one knee in 1913. The 1921 show *Bombo* included four songs that became Jolson standards: "My Mammy," "Toot, Toot, Tootsie," "California Here I Come," and "April Showers." Although he was a showman who put songs across with dancing and gesturing, his records were hits. Songwriters believed that he could do more than other singers to sell a song. It is unlikely that any other performer was so closely identified with so many songs — "Avalon," "Sonny Boy," "Swanee," "Waiting for the Robert E. Lee," "Rock-a-Bye Your Baby with a Dixie Melody," "The Red, Red Robin."

**"You Ain't Heard Nothin' Yet."** Jolson made *The Jazz Singer* for Warner Bros. in 1927. Although it is classified as the first talking movie, the sound was restricted to Jolson's singing and some dialogue. Jolson's line "You ain't heard nothin' yet" defined his performance style, for he loved to entertain audiences. He was successful in every medium and in the 1930s had radio programs.

**Comeback.** Jolson's material and style began to seem old-fashioned in the swing era, but he continued to perform with or without payment. During World War II he toured the war fronts, paying his own expenses. The 1946 movie *The Jolson Story,* in which his singing was dubbed for actor Larry Parks, restored Jolson's popularity, and he became a television star. The successful 1949 sequel, *Jolson Sings Again,* reinforced his reputation as the world's greatest entertainer. When he died in 1950 after returning from entertaining troops in Korea, he had been a star for forty years.

Sources:

Michael Freedland, *Jolson* (New York: Stein & Day, 1972);

Herbert G. Goldman, *Jolson* (New York: Oxford University Press, 1988);

*Al Jolson: Best of the Decca Years* (MCA 10505).

# RING W. LARDNER

## 1885-1933

### WRITER

**Sportswriter.** Ringgold Wilmer Lardner was the last master of American vernacular humor. Born in Niles, Michigan, he briefly studied engineering; but newspapers were his college at a time when most American writers came out of the newsrooms. Starting as a sports reporter for the *South Bend Times,* in 1919 he took over "In the Wake of the News," the widely read *Chicago Tribune* sports column. Lardner filled his daily columns with verse, parody, and short fiction.

*You Know Me Al.* In 1914 he published his first short story, "A Busher's Letters Home," which initiated the highly popular *You Know Me Al* series. These stories consist of quasi-literate letters written by an ignorant, boastful, dishonest, mean baseball pitcher. Known as the Busher stories, they established Lardner's reputation as a slang writer. H. L. Mencken observed in *The American Language* that "Lardner reports the common speech not only with humor, but also with the utmost accuracy." These stories solidified Lardner's fame as a writer of baseball fiction, although the range of his later stories extended to show business, the new leisure class, and marriage. His most widely reprinted story, "Champion" — about a corrupt fighter — appeared in 1916. The success of his magazine work enabled Lardner to give up the grind of a daily column. In 1919 he moved to Long Island to write a weekly "Letter" for the Bell Syndicate while writing short stories; he never wrote a novel.

**Best Stories.** Lardner wrote his best stories during the 1920s — including "Golden Honeymoon," "The Love Nest," "Hair Cut," "Some Like Them Cold," and "There Are Smiles" — which he published in volumes titled *How to Write Short Stories (with samples), The Love Nest,* and *Round Up.* His 1925 volume *What Of It?* included sketches that were credited with bringing Dada, a European avant-garde movement that proclaimed the absurdity of life and art, to American humor. Lardner's "I. Gaspiri (The Upholsterers)" had this stage direction:

"The curtain is lowered for seven days to denote the lapse of a week." He also worked in the theater, writing songs, sketches, and plays. *June Moon*, based on "Some Like Them Cold," on which he collaborated with George S. Kaufman in 1929, had a successful Broadway run.

**Lasting Achievement.** Lardner and F. Scott Fitzgerald became close friends when they were neighbors during 1923–1924. Fitzgerald brought him to Charles Scribner's Sons publishers and based Abe North in *Tender Is the Night* on Lardner. After Lardner died from tuberculosis, heart disease, and alcoholism, Fitzgerald wrote that "whatever Ring's achievement was, it fell short of the achievement he was capable of, and this because of a cynical attitude toward his work." It was Fitzgerald's analysis that Lardner was unable to develop high literary ambitions because he had been stifled by his sports-desk apprenticeship. Nonetheless, Ring Lardner's work holds up — not as curiosities or nostalgia, but as American literature.

Sources:

Donald Elder, *Ring Lardner: A Biography* (Garden City, N.Y.: Doubleday, 1956);

Ring Lardner, *Ring Around the Bases: The Complete Baseball Stories of Ring Lardner,* edited by Matthew J. Bruccoli (New York: Scribners, 1992).

# EUGENE O'NEILL

## 1888-1953

### PLAYWRIGHT

**The Greatest American Dramatist.** American drama is divisible into two periods: before and after Eugene O'Neill. The son of James O'Neill, a popular actor, Eugene O'Neill was born in a hotel at the corner of Broadway and 43rd Street and grew up in the theater. Rejecting the crowd-pleasing melodrama form, O'Neill enlarged the scope, material, and technique of American drama while setting high aspirations for himself and writing masterpieces that included *The Emperor Jones* (1920), *Anna Christie* (1921), *Desire Under the Elms* (1924), *Strange Interlude* (1928), *Mourning Becomes Electra* (1931), *The Iceman Cometh* (1946), *A Moon for the Misbegotten* (1947), and *Long Day's Journey Into Night* (1956).

**Apprenticeship.** O'Neill was dismissed from Princeton during his freshman year and spent his young manhood as a sailor, alcoholic, and beachcomber. The destructive love and guilt of his family inspired O'Neill's later family dramas: the father believed he had wasted his talent in moneymaking roles; the mother was addicted to morphine; the alcoholic son Jamie was an embittered failure. O'Neill began writing plays in 1913, developing themes of family guilt and strife, the destructive power of love, the constrictions of marriage, the necessity for sensitive and gifted characters to escape their environments, the need for "pipe dreams," and — perhaps his main recurring theme — the tragic effects on people who betray their temperaments or violate their natures. His most memorable characters are obsessed by fixed ideas or romantic ideals. It was necessary for O'Neill to develop new techniques for the revelation of the inner lives of his characters.

**Innovations.** While for the most part retaining realistic speech and detail, O'Neill moved from his early realism and naturalism to "supernaturalism" — the systematic use of symbolism in a realistic work. He introduced expressionistic techniques into American drama in his endeavor to objectify the inner experience of his characters; expressionism employed distortion, simplification, exaggeration, and symbolic settings. *The Emperor Jones* is regarded as the first American expressionist play, followed by *The Hairy Ape* (1922). In his endeavors to expand the scope of American drama, O'Neill recovered techniques from the classics and gave them expressionistic treatments. In *The Great God Brown* (1926) masks indicate the characters' efforts to hide their conflicts of mind and soul. *Lazarus Laughed* (1927) employs masks and chorus. The effective use of spoken thoughts — O'Neill's version of the aside — in *Strange Interlude* solidified his reputation as a technical genius. O'Neill also rejected the structural requirements of the conventional well-made plays; *Strange Interlude* ran from 5:15 to 11 P.M., with a dinner break. *Mourning Becomes Electra* was inspired by Aeschylus's *Oresteia;* O'Neill described this trilogy as the "modern psychological approximation of the Greek sense of fate."

**Later Work.** O'Neill married actresss Carlotta Monterey — his third wife — in 1929. She managed every aspect of his life in order to facilitate his work, and she made it possible for him to give up alcohol. He became a virtual recluse in France, Bermuda, Sea Island, and California. O'Neill won the Pulitzer Prize four times — once posthumously. In 1936 he received the Nobel Prize in literature. During the 1930s he worked on a nine-play cycle, "A Tale of Possessions Self-Dispossessed" — a study of the soul-destroying influence of business and property. But a tremor made it impossible for him to hold a pencil during his later years, and the work in progress on the cycle was destroyed, except for *A Touch of the Poet* and the unfinished *More Stately Mansions.* The last new play produced on Broadway during O'Neill's life was *The Iceman Cometh,* his most effective examination of the pipe-dream theme. The play concludes that humans require self-lies to sustain them; life without pipe dreams is too terrible for most people. This great play ran for only 136 performances in 1946, but subsequent productions have established its proper high position in the O'Neill canon.

**Late Plays.** During 1940–1943 O'Neill wrote two of his most personal plays about his family, renamed the Tyrones: *Long Day's Journey Into Night* and *A Moon for the Misbegotten.* He left instructions that *Long Day's Journey Into Night* was not to be performed until twenty-five years after his death; nevertheless, his widow allowed 1956 productions, and the success of this play solidified O'Neill's reputation with audiences who had not seen his plays in the 1920s or 1930s. *A Moon for the Misbegotten* closed on the road in 1947, but it was effectively revived in the 1950s. Both plays examine the open wounds that tormented the O'Neills and found expression in the most important body of drama since the death of William Shakespeare. Eugene O'Neill did not merely enrich American drama: he reinvented it and prepared the way for the playwrights who followed.

**Sources:**
Louis Sheaffer, *O'Neill: Son and Artist* (Boston: Little, Brown, 1973);
Sheaffer, *O'Neill: Son and Playwright* (Boston: Little, Brown, 1968).

# A. S. W. Rosenbach

## 1876-1952

### Bookman

"The Napoleon of the Auction Room." Dr. Abraham Simon Wolfe Rosenbach was the greatest rare-book dealer in the world during the 1920s; indeed, he is regarded as the greatest one who ever lived. Combining scholarship with salesmanship and showmanship, Rosenbach bought and sold more great books and manuscripts and built more major collections than anyone else. He boasted that the books and manuscripts in his vault were worth more than the total inventory of Macy's department store.

**An Era of Bibliophiles.** Great men match their times; their achievements are encouraged by the spirit of an era. The 1920s produced wealthy collectors who cherished their books and enjoyed the competition for rarities. By setting record prices in the auction rooms of New York and London, Rosenbach validated the cultural and investment values of books and manuscripts.

**Training.** A Philadelphian, Rosenbach was the nephew of antiquarian bookseller Moses Pollock and started pursuing books in his boyhood. Rosenbach planned an academic career, but after taking his Ph.D. at the University of Pennsylvania he began selling books in his brother Philip's antique store. A bon vivant who drank a bottle of whiskey a day, Rosenbach had the ability to develop friendships with his customers, thereby converting business dealings into collaborations. His Philadelphia and New York premises were clubs for favored buyers, and the hospitality was lavish. His early patrons included the Widener family, especially Harry Widener. After the young bibliophile perished in the

*Titanic* sinking, Rosenbach compiled the catalogue of the Widener collection at Harvard.

**Fulfillment.** The death of Rosenbach's rival George D. Smith in 1920 enabled "Dr. R" — as he became widely known — to acquire the business of Henry C. Folger, who was assembling what became the Folger Shakespeare Library, and Henry E. Huntington, who was responsible for the greatest library ever built by one man. Bidding for wealthy collectors as well as for stock, Rosenbach endeavored to dominate every major sale during the decade; he also developed the habit of retaining favorite items for his own collection. Thus, at the John Quinn sale during 1923–1924 he paid $1,950 for the manuscript of James Joyce's *Ulysses* and took it home. Rosenbach's strategy was to secure at least one headline-making item at any major auction he attended. In 1928 he paid £15,400 ($77,000) for the manuscript of *Alice In Wonderland*. He later sold it with two copies of the first edition for $150,000.

**The World of Literature.** Most antiquarian book dealers specialize in a field or a period, but Rosenbach embraced all literature from medieval manuscripts to twentieth-century fiction. He had a prodigious memory and knew the material. Rosenbach customarily bought books and manuscripts for stock because he believed in their literary value: at the Quinn sale he spent $72,000 on Joseph Conrad manuscripts, most of which he kept. His personal collection included Judaica and early American children's books. Although his customers were perforce wealthy individuals or institutions, his own activities and fame surpassed their prestige in proclaiming the importance of great books. The impressive printed catalogues of the Rosenbach Company were useful scholarly books on their own. The 1920 catalogue consisted of twenty-nine Shakespeare quartos — "the largest collection ever offered for sale of books by or relating to Shakespeare." In 1926 he marked the sesquicentennial of the Declaration of Independence with a catalogue that featured the original Declaration with the 1777 Articles of Confederation ($260,000). Rosenbach's activities were resented in England because he took many of the rarest British books to America. Not only did he dominate the London auction rooms, he plundered some of the richest private libraries in Britain. The most famous and most valuable book is the Gutenberg Bible (1454–1456), allegedly the first book printed from movable type. In 1926 Dr. R acquired a Gutenberg for Mrs. Edward Harkness at $106,000, the highest price for a printed book until 1947, when he paid $151,000 for the *Bay Psalm Book* (1640), allegedly the first book printed in North America. The last great book auction of the 1920s was the 1929 sale of the library of songwriter Jerome Kern: Rosenbach spent $410,000 of the $1,729,462 total.

**Change.** The book boom ended — not just because of the Depression but because many of the great collectors died. However, their deaths provided opportunities for Rosenbach to reacquire books he had previously sold.

Rosenbach maintained his position as the preeminent antiquarian bookman through the 1940s. After the deaths of the bachelor brothers, the Philip H. and A. S. W. Rosenbach Foundation has maintained a library in their Philadelphia home. The treasures of that institution are the books that Dr. R kept for himself.

Sources:

*The Collected Catalogues of Dr. A. S. W. Rosenbach, 1904–1951* (New York: Arno/McGraw-Hill, 1967);

Edwin Wolfe II and John F. Fleming, *Rosenbach* (Cleveland & New York: World, 1960).

## BESSIE SMITH

### 1894-1937

#### BLUES SINGER

**Empress of the Blues.** Born in poverty in Chattanooga, Tennessee, Bessie Smith became the greatest of blues singers. Supposedly discovered when she was eleven by blues singer Ma Rainey, Smith toured with the Rabbit Foot Minstrels and tent shows in the South. During her lifetime the blues was regarded as a form of black expression; she performed for mostly black audiences and recorded for what were classified as race records that were not stocked in record shops catering to whites. Unlike Louis Armstrong, who reached all audiences, Smith was unknown or unavailable to most white Americans during her career. She was a black artist working with traditional black material for a black public; nevertheless, Smith gave special performances for white audiences in some large cities.

**Recordings.** Smith reached her own audience through 160 records. She made her first identified recordings in 1923, "Gulf Coast Blues" and "Down-Hearted Blues." These two sides sold an extraordinary 780,000 copies, and Smith became the best-selling vocalist in the race-records field, where she competed with Ma Rainey, Mamie Smith, and Clara Smith. Her top recording fee was $200 per usable side; there were no royalties on sales. Smith's majestic voice was the vehicle for her versatility and technical mastery. Smith also differed from other blues singers in her range of material; her repertoire included vaudeville material and popular songs such as "Alexander's Ragtime Band." Her singing was lusty and profane, expressing misery, exuberance, and bitter humor. Her control of inflection and phrasing, lyricism, vocal wit, growling, moaning, and command of material set her above competing blues shouters. Smith's audiences required her to be more than a great blues singer: she was a commanding stage figure in lavish gowns. Carl Van Vechten, a white promoter of black artists, wrote lushly of her 1925 performance in a Newark, New Jersey, theater:

> Walking slowly to the footlights ... she began her strange, rhythmic rites in a voice full of shouting and moaning and praying and suffering, a wild, rough Ethiopan voice, harsh and volcanic, but seductive and sensuous, too, released between rouged lips and the whitest teeth, the singer swaying lightly to the beat, as is the negro custom.

> Now, inspired partly by the expressive words, partly by the stumbling strain of the accompaniment, partly by the powerfully magnetic personality of this elemental conjure woman with her pleasant African voice, quivering with passion and pain, sounding as if it had been developed at the sources of the Nile, the black and blue-back crowd, notable for the absence of mulattoes, burst into hysterical, semi-religious shrieks of sorrow and lamentations. Amens rent the air.

**Decline.** Smith's popularity declined markedly at the end of the 1920s as new forms of jazz made her singing seem old-fashioned. She never achieved a radio following. Smith's heavy drinking increased, and she became difficult to work with. She had squandered her substantial earnings. Smith had once commanded $2,000 a night, but in the 1930s she was working in a Philadelphia dive. Her last recording session came in 1933, for which she was paid $50 a side. Her death after an auto wreck near Coahoma, Mississippi, raised charges that she had been denied treatment at a white hospital in Clarksdale. The statement that "Bessie was the best" has never been seriously challenged.

Sources:
Chris Albertson, *Bessie* (New York: Stein & Day, 1972);

*The Complete Recordings,* 4 volumes (CBS 47091, 47471, 14744, 52838).

# Irving Thalberg

## 1899-1936

### Movie Producer

**Boy Wonder.** Irving Thalberg became an icon of American success mythology, but he did not rise from poverty; his German-Alsatian Jewish family was middle class. A Brooklyn boy who had not finished high school because of illness, Thalberg was employed at eighteen as a secretary in the New York office of Universal Pictures; he became general manager of the California studio when he was twenty. The story went around Hollywood that he was running a major studio before he was old enough to sign the payroll.

**M-G-M.** In 1923 Thalberg joined Louis B. Mayer as vice president of the Mayer Company. When Metro-Goldwyn-Mayer was formed by Loew's, Inc., in 1924, Thalberg became second vice president and supervisor of production. Mayer as president and Thalberg built the largest and most successful studio in Hollywood, based on its stable of stars and expensive productions. The M-G-M slogan was "More stars than in the heavens," and the studio roster included Greta Garbo, John Gilbert, Clark Gable, Lionel Barrymore, Wallace Beery, Spencer Tracy, and Thalberg's wife, Norma Shearer. His achievements resulted from his management skills, his decisiveness, and his movie sense. He had a strong understanding of movie structure and was able to supervise an entire production. Slim and handsome, Thalberg was mild-mannered; yet he imposed his will on associates and inspired their loyalty.

**Classic Movies.** The M-G-M reputation for movies with story value was credited to Thalberg, whose taste and expertise were especially well focused on screenplays. Working closely with writers whom he treated with the courtesy due to well-paid business employees, Thalberg routinely overruled them. He was responsible for the resented but effective system of double-teaming writers on the same project, often without informing them. His willingness to remake presumably completed movies salvaged the discarded *Sin of Madelon Claudet,* an Academy Award winner for Helen Hayes. The silent productions Thalberg took personal responsibility for included *The Merry Widow* (1925), *The Big Parade* (1925), *Ben-Hur* (1926), and *Flesh and the Devil* (1927). His first musical, *The Broadway Melody* (1929), won the Academy Award for best picture.

**Thalberg and Mayer.** Born with a heart defect and not expected to have a long life, Thalberg repeatedly worked until he collapsed. In 1933 while recuperating from overwork, he was removed by Mayer as head of production. Although Mayer claimed that the move was intended to prolong Thalberg's life, Hollywood insiders believed that Mayer had become resentful of Thalberg's eminence and irate at his insistence that his earnings be commensurate with his responsibilities. Thereafter Thalberg ran his own unit within M-G-M, producing *The Barretts of Wimpole Street* (1934), *Mutiny on the Bounty* (1935), *A Night at the Opera* (1935), *Romeo and Juliet* (1936), *The Good Earth* (1937), and *Camille* (1937). A paternalistic employer, Thalberg was credited with defeating a strike vote by the Screen Writers Guild.

**The Last Tycoon.** After Thalberg's death from pneumonia, Helen Hayes said, "He died of genius." Irving Thalberg has become a legendary American figure: the self-made business leader as culture hero. His legend has been perpetuated by F. Scott Fitzgerald's appropriating him as the model for Monroe Stahr, hero of the novel *The Love of the Last Tycoon.*

Sources:
F. Scott Fitzgerald, *The Love of the Last Tycoon: A Western* (Cambridge: Cambridge University Press, 1993);

Samuel Marx, *Mayer and Thalberg: The Make-Believe Saints* (New York: Random House, 1975);

Bob Thomas, *Thalberg* (Garden City, N.Y.: Doubleday, 1969).

# PEOPLE IN THE NEWS

Film comedian **Roscoe "Fatty" Arbuckle** was arrested for the rape and murder of a young actress found unconscious in his hotel room on 5 September 1921. Arbuckle was acquitted after three trials but his career was ruined.

In 1924 **George Pierce Baker** was named the director of Yale University's newly established department of drama, and he laid the groundwork for a program that would later be recognized as the best theater training center in the United States.

**Josephine Baker** became an immediate star in *La Revue Nègre*, Paris, in 1925.

Sculptor **Gutzon Borglum** abandoned work on the Lee-Jackson Confederate Memorial at Stone Mountain, Georgia, in March 1925. He shifted his attention to Mount Rushmore, South Dakota, where he commenced work on portraits of Washington, Jefferson, Lincoln, and Theodore Roosevelt in 1927.

In 1921 **Nadia Boulanger** became composition teacher at the American Conservatory in Fontainebleau, France.

In 1926 **Constantin Brancusi** had to pay an import fee for his *Bird in Flight* when it was classified as a taxable piece of metal — not a sculpture — by U.S. customs officials.

**A. P. Carter, Sara Dougherty Carter,** and **Maybelle Addington Carter** formed the Carter Family singing group in 1927.

The performances of Russian basso **Boris Chaliapin** in Mussorgsky's *Boris Godunov* at the Metropolitan Opera House in New York during 1921 and 1928 caused sensations.

Twenty-five-year-old English actor-playwright **Noel Coward** had five plays produced in New York during the 1925 season.

Mayor **James M. Curley** announced that the Chicago Opera Company would not be allowed to perform Richard Strauss's *Salome* in Boston during the 1923–1924 season.

**Isadora Duncan** was invited by the Soviet government to open a Moscow dance school in summer 1921. She met and married revolutionist poet **Sergei Yessenin** there.

**Mrs. H. O. Havemeyer** willed her collection to the Metropolitan Museum of Art, Manhattan, in 1929. In addition to Old Masters, the collection was strong in French impressionist paintings.

In 1929 **Albert Hirschfeld** began drawing caricatures of theater figures for *The New York Times*.

"Moanin' Low" sung by **Libby Holman** and danced by **Clifton Webb** stopped the show in the 1929 production of *The Little Show*.

Professor **Jay B. Hubbell** of Duke University edited the first issue of *American Literature* in 1929.

Composer **Jerome Kern** auctioned his rare-book collection in 1929. The 1,484 lots brought $1,729,462.50 — a record average of $1,165.41.

Harpsichord virtuoso **Wanda Landowska** made her triumphant American debut in Philadelphia, November 1923.

In 1927 **Stan Laurel** and **Oliver Hardy** made their first silent comedies as a team.

**Gertrude Lawrence** sang "Limehouse Blues" when *Charlot's Review* moved from London to New York in 1924.

Actress and director **Eva Le Gallienne** founded the Civic Repertory Company in New York City in 1926 to provide serious theater at inexpensive ticket prices.

**Sinclair Lewis** declined the Pulitzer Prize for his novel *Arrowsmith* in 1926, declaring that prizes corrupt writers. "And the Pulitzer Prize for novels is peculiarly objectionable because the terms of it have been constantly and grievously misrepresented."

Two years after their marriage, actors **Alfred Lunt** and **Lynn Fontanne** appeared together for the first time onstage in 1923 in Paul Kester's play *Sweet Nell of Old Drury*.

**Jelly Roll Morton** organized his band, The Red Hot Peppers, in 1926.

On 15 April 1925 **Vladimir Nabokov** married **Véra Slonom** in Berlin.

Cole Porter's score for *Within the Quota* was premiered by Les Ballets Suédois at the Théâtre des Champs-Elysees, Paris, on 25 October 1923. Darius Milhaud's ballet *La Création du Monde* premiered on the same bill.

Samuel (Roxy) Rothafel opened the world's largest theater, the Roxy, in New York on 21 March 1927. The cost was announced as $10 million.

Mamie Smith's 1922 recording of "Crazy Blues" launched a market for blues and "race" records.

Igor Stravinsky made his first American appearance conducting the Philharmonic Orchestra at Carnegie Hall, Manhattan, in January 1925. His ballet *Les Noces* had its American premiere at the Metropolitan Opera House in 1929.

Baritone **Lawrence Tibbett**, twenty-eight, brought down the house in Verdi's *Falstaff* at the Metropolitan Opera House in January 1925.

# AWARDS

## AMERICAN ACADEMY AND INSTITUTE OF ARTS AND LETTERS GOLD MEDAL

1922
Eugene O'Neill — drama

1923
Edwin H. Blashfield — painting

1924
Edith Wharton — fiction

1925
William C. Brownell — essays and belles lettres

1927
William M. Sloane — history and biography

1928
George W. Chadwick — music

1929
Edwin Arlington Robinson — poetry

## JOHN NEWBERY MEDAL (CHILDREN'S BOOKS)

1922
*The Story of Mankind,* by **Hendrik Van Loon**

1923
*The Voyages of Doctor Dolittle,* by **Hugh Lofting**

1924
*Dark Frigate,* by **Charles Hawes**

1925
*Tales from Silver Lands,* by **Charles Finger**

1926
*Shen of the Sea,* by **Arthur Chrisman**

1927
*Smoky, the Cowhorse,* by **Will James**

1928
*Gay Neck,* by **Dhan Mukerji**

1929

*The Trumpeter of Krakow,* by **Eric P. Kelly**

## PULITZER PRIZES

1920

Biography or Autobiography: *The Life of John Marshall,* by **Albert J. Beveridge**

Drama: *Beyond the Horizon,* by **Eugene O'Neill**

History: *The War with Mexico,* by **Justin H. Smith**

1921

Biography or Autobiography: *The Americanization of Edward Bok,* by **Edward Bok**

Drama: *Miss Lulu Bett,* by **Zona Gale**

Fiction: *The Age of Innocence,* by **Edith Wharton**

History: *The Victory at Sea,* by **William S. Sims** and **Burton J. Hendrick**

1922

Biography or Autobiography: *A Daughter of the Middle Border,* by **Hamlin Garland**

Drama: *Anna Christie,* by **Eugene O'Neill**

Fiction: *Alice Adams,* by **Booth Tarkington**

History: *The Founding of New England,* by **James Truslow Adams**

Poetry: *Collected Poems,* by **Edwin Arlington Robinson**

1923

Biography or Autobiography: *The Life and Letters of Walter Hines Page,* by **Burton J. Hendrick**

Drama: *Icebound,* by **Owen Davis**

Fiction: *One of Ours,* by **Willa Cather**

History: *The Supreme Court of the United States,* by **Charles Warren**

Poetry: *The Ballad of the Harp-Weaver* and *A Few Figs from Thistles,* by **Edna St. Vincent Millay**

1924

Biography or Autobiography: *From Immigrant to Inventor,* by **Michael Pupin**

Drama: *Hell-Bent fer Heaven,* by **Hatcher Hughes**

Fiction: *The Able McLaughlins,* by **Margaret Wilson**

History: *The American Revolution,* by **Charles H. McIlwain**

Poetry: *New Hampshire,* by **Robert Frost**

1925

Biography or Autobiography: *Barrett Wendell and His Letters,* by **M. A. DeWolfe Howe**

Drama: *They Knew What They Wanted,* by **Sidney Howard**

Fiction: *So Big,* by **Edna Ferber**

History: *A History of the American Frontier,* by **Frederic L. Paxson**

Poetry: *The Man Who Died Twice,* by **Edwin Arlington Robinson**

1926

Biography or Autobiography: *The Life of Sir William Osler,* by **Harvey Cushing**

Drama: *Craig's Wife,* by **George Kelly**

Fiction: *Arrowsmith,* by **Sinclair Lewis** (declined)

History: *The History of the United States,* by **Edward Channing**

Poetry: *What's O'Clock,* by **Amy Lowell**

1927

Biography or Autobiography: *Whitman,* by **Emery Holloway**

Drama: *In Abraham's Bosom,* by **Paul Green**

Fiction: *Early Autumn,* by **Louis Bromfield**

History: *Pinckney's Treaty,* by **Samuel Flagg Bemis**

Poetry: *Fiddler's Farewell,* by **Leonora Speyer**

1928

Biography or Autobiography: *The American Orchestra and Theodore Thomas,* by **Charles E. Russell**

Drama: *Strange Interlude,* by **Eugene O'Neill**

Fiction: *The Bridge of San Luis Rey,* by **Thornton Wilder**

History: *Main Currents in American Thought,* by **Vernon Louis Parrington**

Poetry: *Tristram,* by **Edwin Arlington Robinson**

1929

Biography or Autobiography: *The Training of an American: The Earlier Life and Letters of Walter Hines Page,* by **Burton J. Hendrick**

Drama: *Street Scene,* by **Elmer Rice**

Fiction: *Scarlet Sister Mary,* by **Julia Peterkin**

History: *The Organization and Administration of the Union Army,* by **Fred Albert Shannon**

Poetry: *John Brown's Body,* by **Stephen Vincent Benét**

## ACADEMY OF MOTION PICTURE ARTS AND SCIENCES AWARDS (THE OSCARS)

**1927–1928**

Actor: **Emil Jannings,** *The Way of All Flesh* and *The Last Command*

Actress: **Janet Gaynor,** *Seventh Heaven, Street Angel,* and *Sunrise*

Director: **Frank Borzage,** *Seventh Heaven;* **Lewis Milestone,** *Two Arabian Nights*

Picture: *Wings* (Paramount)

**1928–1929**

Actor: **Warner Baxter,** *In Old Arizona*

Actress: **Mary Pickford,** *Coquette*

Director: **Frank Lloyd,** *The Divine Lady*

Picture: *The Broadway Melody* (M-G-M)

**1929–1930**

Actor: **George Arliss,** *Disraeli*

Actress: **Norma Shearer,** *The Divorcee*

Director: **Lewis Milestone,** *All Quiet on the Western Front*

Picture: *All Quiet on the Western Front* (Universal)

# DEATHS

Brooks Adams, 78, historian (*The Degradation of the Democratic Dogma*), 13 February 1927.

James Lane Allen, 75, local-color novelist (*A Kentucky Cardinal*), 18 February 1925.

John Kendrick Bangs, magazine editor and humorist (*A Houseboat on the Styx*), 21 January 1922.

Nora Bayes, 47, singer ("Shine on Harvest Moon"), 19 March 1928.

Henry A. Beers, 79, literary critic, 7 September 1926.

George Bellows, 42, painter, 8 January 1925.

William Crary Brownell, 76, literary critic and editor, 22 July 1928.

Frances Hodgson Burnett, 74, author (*Little Lord Fauntleroy*), 29 October 1924.

John Burroughs, 83, naturalist writer, 29 March 1921.

Donn Byrne, 39, Irish American writer (*Messer Marco Polo*), 19 June 1928.

George Washington Cable, 80, local-color writer (*Old Creole Days*), 31 January 1925.

William Bliss Carman, 68, Canadian American poet (*Songs from Vagabondia*, with Richard Hovey), 8 June 1929.

Emma Carus, 48, singer, 18 November 1927.

Enrico Caruso, Italian tenor, 2 August 1921.

Mary Cassatt, 81, painter, 14 June 1926.

George Randolph Chester, 54, author (*Get Rich Quick Wallingford*), 26 February 1924.

George Cram Cook, 45, playwright and producer, January 1924.

Ina Coolbrith, 76, poet, 29 February 1928.

J. R. Coryell (Nick Carter and Bertha M. Clay), 76, pulp author, 15 July 1924.

Harry Crosby, 31, expatriate poet and publisher (Black Sun Press), 10 December 1929.

James Oliver Curwood, 49, adventure novelist, 13 August 1927.

Reginald de Koven, 60, composer (*Robin Hood*), 16 January 1920.

Frederick Van Renssalaer Dey (Nick Carter), 61, pulp writer, 26 April 1922.

John Drew, 73, member of illustrious acting family, 9 July 1927.

Isadora Duncan, 47, modern-dance pioneer, 14 September 1927.

Eleanora Duse, Italian actress, 21 April 1924.

Louise Imogen Guiney, 59, poet, 2 November 1920.

Silvio Hein, songwriter, 19 December 1928.

Victor Herbert, composer (*Babes in Toyland*) and founder of ASCAP, 26 May 1924.

Raymond Hitchcock, 64, comedian and actor, 25 November 1929.

Marietta Holley (Josiah Allen's Wife), 80, humorist, 1 March 1926.

Avery Hopwood, 46, playwright (*Getting Gertie's Garter*), 1 July 1928.

Harry Houdini (born Eric Weiss), 52, magician, 31 October 1926.

Emerson Hough, 65, writer (*The Covered Wagon*), 30 April 1923.

William Dean Howells, 83, novelist (*The Rise of Silas Lapham*), 11 May 1920.

James Gibbons Huneker, 61, literary and music critic, 9 February 1921.

George Innes, painter, 27 July 1926.

Barbara La Marr, 29, movie actress, 30 January 1926.

Charles B. Lewis (M. Quad), 82, journalist and humorist, 21 August 1924.

Harriet M. Lothrop (Margaret Sidney), 80, writer (*Five Little Peppers and How They Grew*), 2 August 1924.

Amy Lowell, 51, imagist poet, 12 May 1925.

June Mathis, 35, screenwriter, 25 July 1927.

Brander Matthews, 77, writer and professor, 31 March 1929.

George Barr McCutcheon, 62, romantic novelist (*Graustark*), 23 October 1928.

Henry Miller, 66, actor, 9 April 1926.

Florence Mills, 32, singer, 1 November 1927.

Mary Noailles Murfree (Charles Egbert Craddock), 72, local-color author (*In the Tennessee Mountains*), 31 July 1922.

Peter Newell, 62, painter and illustrator, 15 January 1924.

Frances Newman, 45, critic and novelist (*The Hard-Boiled Virgin*), 22 October 1928.

Thomas Nelson Page, 69, local-color writer (*In Ole Virginia*), 1 November 1922.

Vernon Louis Parrington, 57, literary historian (*Main Currents in American Thought*), 16 June 1929.

Joseph Pennell, 65, painter, 23 April 1926.

Eleanor Porter, 51, writer (*Pollyana*), 21 May 1920.

Maurice Prendergast, 61, painter, 1 February 1923.

John Quinn, 54, bibliophile and art collector, 28 July 1924.

John Reed, 32, radical journalist (*Ten Days That Shook the World*), 17 October 1920.

Wallace Reid, 30, movie actor, 18 January 1923.

Charles Rumsey, 42, sculptor, 21 September 1922.

Lillian Russell, 61, actress, 6 June 1922.

Edgar Saltus, 63, novelist, 31 July 1921.

John Singer Sargent, 69, painter, 15 April 1925.

Larry Semon, 39, movie comedian and cartoonist, 9 October 1928.

Harriet Spofford, 86, writer (*New-England Legends*), 15 August 1921.

George Sterling, 56, poet, 18 November 1926.

Grant Stewart, 63, a founder of Actors' Equity, 18 August 1929.

Gene Stratten-Porter, 56, novelist (*Freckles*), 6 December 1924.

Mary Virginia Hawes Terhune (Marion Harland), 81, romantic novelist, 3 June 1922.

Rudolph Valentino (born Rudolpho Alfonzo Raffaelo Pierre Filbert Guglielmi Di Valentina d'Antonguolla), 31, movie actor, 23 August 1926.

Elihu Vedder, 86, painter, 29 January 1923.

Kate Douglas Wiggin, 66, writer (*Mrs. Wiggs of the Cabbage Patch*), 23 August 1923.

Bert Williams, 45, comedian, 4 March 1922.

Jesse Lynch Williams, 58, writer, 14 September 1929.

Elinor Wylie, 42, poet and novelist, 16 December 1928.

# PUBLICATIONS

## General Reference

Frederick Lewis Allen, *Only Yesterday: An Informal History of the Nineteen-Twenties* (New York: Harper, 1931);

Charles and Mary Beard, *The Rise of American Civilization* (New York: Macmillan, 1927);

H. L. Mencken, *Prejudices: Second Series — Sixth Series* (New York: Knopf, 1920, 1922, 1924, 1926, 1927);

Samuel Eliot Morison, *The Oxford History of the United States* (New York: Oxford University Press, 1927);

Vernon Louis Parrington, *Main Currents in American Thought*, 3 volumes (New York: Harcourt, Brace, 1927–1930);

Gilbert Seldes, *The Seven Lively Arts* (New York: Harper, 1924);

Harold Stearns, *Civilization in the United States* (New York: Harcourt, Brace, 1922);

Mark Sullivan, *Our Times: The United States, 1900–1925* (New York: Scribners, 1926–1935).

## Movies

Eustace Hale Ball, *The Art of the Photoplay*, second edition (New York: Veritas, 1919);

Iris Barry, *Let's Go to the Movies* (New York: Payson & Clarke, 1926);

Daniel Blum, *A Pictorial History of the Silent Screen* (New York: Grosset & Dunlap, 1953);

Kevin Brownlow, *The Parade's Gone By . . .* (New York: Knopf, 1968);

John Emerson and Anita Loos, *Breaking Into the Movies* (New York: McCann, 1921);

Emerson and Loos, *How to Write Photoplays* (New York: McCann, 1990);

Samuel Goldwyn, *Behind the Screen* (New York: Doran, 1923);

Charles Harpole, ed., *History of the American Cinema*, 4 volumes to date (New York: Macmillan, 1990).

## Music

Samuel B. Charters, *Jazz, New Orleans, 1885–1963*, revised edition (New York: Oak, 1963);

Frank Driggs, *Black Beauty, White Heat: A Pictorial History of Classic Jazz, 1920–1950* (New York: Morrow, 1982);

Philip Furia, *The Poets of Tin Pan Alley: A History of America's Great Lyricists* (New York: Oxford University Press, 1990);

James Weldon Johnson, *The Book of American Negro Spirituals* (New York: Viking, 1925);

Neil Leonard, *Jazz and the White Americans: The Acceptance of a New Art Form* (Chicago: University of Chicago Press, 1962);

Alan Lomax, *Mister Jelly Roll: The Fortunes of Jelly Roll Morton, New Orleans Creole and Inventor of Jazz*, second edition (Berkeley: University of California Press, 1973);

H. W. Odom and G. B. Johnson, *The Negro and His Songs* (Chapel Hill: University of North Carolina Press, 1925);

Brian Priestley, *Jazz on Record: A History* (New York: Billboard Books, 1991);

Gunther Schuller, *Early Jazz: Its Roots and Musical Development* (New York: Oxford University Press, 1968);

Arnold Shaw, *The Jazz Age: Popular Music in the 1920's* (New York: Oxford University Press, 1987);

Frank Tirro, *Jazz: A History* (New York: Norton, 1977);

*Annual Review of Jazz Studies*, periodical;

*Journal of Jazz Studies*, periodical.

## Literature

Randolph Bourne, *The History of a Literary Radical* (New York: Huebsch, 1920);

Allen Churchill, *The Literary Decade: A Panorama of the Writers, Publishers, and Litterateurs of the 1920's* (Englewood Cliffs, N.J.: Prentice-Hall, 1971);

Irene and Allen Cleaton, *Books and Battles of the Twenties* (Boston: Houghton Mifflin, 1937);

Ann Douglas, *Terrible Honesty: Mongrel Manhattan in the 1920s* (New York: Farrar, Straus & Giroux, 1995);

Norman Foerster, *Humanism and America* (New York: Farrar & Rinehart, 1930);

Foerster, ed. *The Reinterpretation of American Literature: Some Contributions Toward the Understanding of its Historical Development* (New York: Harcourt, Brace, 1928);

Frederic Hoffman, *The Twenties,* revised edition (New York: Collier, 1962);

Jacob Zeitlin, *Life and Letters of Stuart P. Sherman* (New York: Farrar & Rinehart, 1929);

*The American Mercury,* periodical;

*Publishers' Weekly,* periodical;

*The Smart Set,* periodical;

*Vanity Fair,* periodical.

## Theater

Daniel C. Blum, *A Pictorial History of the American Theatre, 1860–1976,* fourth edition (New York: Crown, 1977);

Gerald M. Boardman, *American Musical Theatre: A Chronicle* (New York: Oxford University Press, 1992);

Walter Prichard Eaton, *The Theatre Guild: The First Ten Years* (Freeport, N.Y.: Books for Libraries, 1970);

Richard Lewine, *Encyclopedia of Theatre Music* (New York: Random House, 1961);

Oral S. Load and Edwin Mims Jr., *The American Stage* (New Haven: Yale University Press, 1929);

Kenneth Macgowan, *Footlights Across America* (New York: Harcourt, Brace, 1929);

George Jean Nathan, *The Critic and the Drama* (New York: Knopf, 1922);

Bernard Rosenberg, *The Broadway Musical: A Collaboration in Commerce and Art* (New York: New York University Press, 1993);

Joseph P. Swain, *The Broadway Musical: A Critical and Musical Survey* (New York: Oxford University Press, 1990);

Alexander Woollcott, *Enchanted Aisles* (New York: Putnam, 1924);

*Variety,* periodical.

## Art

Milton W. Brown, *American Painting from the Armory Show to the Depression* (Princeton: Princeton University Press, 1955);

S. B. Cheney, *Primer of Modern Art* (New York: Boni & Liveright, 1924);

Cedric Dover, *American Negro Art* (Greenwich, Conn.: New York Graphic Society, 1960);

Katherine Dreier, *Collection of the Societé Anonyme: Museum of Modern Art: 1920* (New Haven: Yale University Press, 1950);

Dreier, *Western Art and the New Era; An Introduction to Modern Art* (New York: Brentano's, 1923);

C. B. Ely, *The Modern Tendency in American Painting* (New York: Sherman, 1925);

Martin Friedman, *The Precisionist View in American Art* (Minneapolis: Walker Art Center, 1960);

W. Pach, *Modern Art in America* (New York: Kraushaar Galleries, 1928);

Paul Rosenfeld, *Port of New York: Essays on Fourteen American Moderns* (New York: Harcourt, Brace, 1924);

Lorado Taft, *The History of American Sculpture,* revised edition (New York: Macmillan, 1924);

Thomas E. Tallmadge, *The Story of American Architecture* (New York: Norton, 1927);

Dickran Tashjiaru, *Skyscraper Primitives: Dada and the American Avant-Garde, 1910–1925* (Middletown, Conn.: Wesleyan University Press, 1975);

Daniel Berkeley Updike, *Printing Types: Their History, Forms, and Use* (Cambridge, Mass.: Harvard University Press, 1922);

Forbes Watson, *American Printing Today* (Washington, D.C.: American Federation of Arts, 1929);

Mahonri Sharp Young, *Early American Moderns: Painters of the Stieglitz Group* (New York: Watson-Guptill, 1974);

*Art in America,* periodical;

*Art News,* periodical.

# BUSINESS AND THE ECONOMY

by HUGH NORTON

## CONTENTS

*Sidebars and tables are listed in italics.*

# 1920

- U.S. food prices are expected to fall 72 percent as farm prices plummet.

- The Census Bureau estimates that 1920 figures will show urban population outnumbering the rural; the total population is 105.7 million.

**2 Jan.** U.S. Attorney General A. Mitchell Palmer accuses the Industrial Workers of the World (IWW) of plotting to strike the railroads.

**5 Jan.** The Radio Corporation of America is founded with $20 million capital.

**16 Jan.** Prohibition begins; America goes dry.

**28 Feb.** The Esch-Cummins Act is passed; it restores railroads to private ownership and sets up the Railroad Labor Board.

**2 June** Congress passes the Merchant Marine Act to stimulate U.S. shipping.

**1 July** U.S. workers strike as railroads cut wages 10 to 20 percent and as the Railway Labor Board approves cuts of 12 percent.

**8 Sept.** U.S. transcontinental airmail service is begun with a flight from New York to San Francisco.

**26 Sept.** A bomb explodes in front of the J. P. Morgan offices on Wall Street, killing thirty and injuring twenty.

**2 Nov.** KDKA begins regular broadcasting from Pittsburgh, Pennsylvania.

**10 Dec.** Pitney-Bowes introduces the postage meter.

**19 Dec.** In *Traux* v. *Carrigan* the U.S. Supreme Court calls the Arizona picketing law unconstitutional.

**28 Dec.** Amalgamated Clothing Workers begins a six-month strike against clothing "sweat shops."

# 1921

- In recent years Dartmouth College, the University of Chicago, Harvard University, and other major colleges and universities have established business schools, following the example of the University of Pennsylvania.

- The Harding administration tries to relieve farm distress by an emergency tariff on imported farm products.

- The Ford Motor Company announces a schedule to produce one million vehicles each year.

- William Crapo Durant, formerly of General Motors, founds Durant Motors to produce the Durant 4, selling at $850.

- The Women's Bureau, a division of the Labor Department, says eight million females are in the labor force, 80 percent of them in clerical work.

- GM's market share rises to 12 percent under the leadership of Alfred P. Sloan.

- Cincinnati's WLW radio station, founded by auto parts manufacturer Powel Crosley, begins broadcasting.

- U.S. farmers overproduce, and prices fall to 85 percent of the levels of 1919; cotton falls to eleven cents per pound, down from forty-two cents.

**1922**

| | |
|---|---|
| **3 Jan.** | The U.S. Supreme Court rules that trade unions are answerable to the Sherman Anti-Trust Act, despite the Clayton Act, which seemed to have exempted unions. |
| **13 Jan.** | The Census Bureau says that 51 percent of Americans live in towns of more than twenty-five hundred. |
| **10 Mar.** | The first White Castle hamburger outlet, opens in Wichita, Kansas. |
| **10 May** | Ford Motor Company announces assets of more than $345 million. |
| **25 June** | Samuel Gompers is elected head of the American Federation of Labor for the fortieth time. |
| **26 Sept.** | Secretary of Commerce Herbert Hoover announces a plan to ease unemployment due to the 1920–1921 recession. |
| **31 Dec.** | According to the Census Bureau, the United States has 387,000 miles of surfaced roads, up from 190,476 in 1909. |

**1923**

- Standard Oil announces an eight-hour day for oil-field workers.
- Wills Sainte Claire announces the development of a new automobile to compete in the Stutz-Duesenberg market.
- Ford Motor Company acquires the Lincoln Company for $12 million.
- Durant Motors introduces its Stor, priced at $348 to compete with the Ford Model T, but Ford cuts its Model T prices to retaliate.
- The May Company acquires Hamburger and Sons in Los Angeles.

| | |
|---|---|
| **2 Feb.** | The Amoskeag Textile Mill in Manchester, New Hampshire, announces a wage cut of 20 percent and an increase in hours from forty-eight to fifty-two hours per week. |
| **9 Feb.** | Congress creates a War Foreign Debt Commission to negotiate settlements. |
| **1 July** | The U.S. Railroad Labor Board announces a 13 percent cut in wages affecting 400,000 workers. |
| **3 Aug.** | Station WGY in Schenectady, New York, uses the first sound effects on radio. |
| **18 Sept.** | Railway shopmen abandon their two-month strike. |
| **19 Sept.** | Congress passes the Fordney-McCumber Tariff Act, returning tariffs to the levels of the 1909 Payne-Aldrich Act. |
| **21 Sept.** | Congress passes the Commodity Exchange Act regulating trading. |

- GM puts its Chevrolet Division under the direction of William S. Knudsen, formerly of Ford, in an effort to make Chevrolet more competitive with Ford.
- Cotton prices drop to eleven cents per pound on U.S. markets.
- Zenith Radio is founded in Chicago.
- The Ethyl Corporation introduces a fuel additive to eliminate "knock" and reduce lead deposits in automobile engines.

- The U.S. Department of Commerce projects that over the next six years corporate profits will increase by 62 percent, dividends by 65 percent, and income to workers by 11 percent.

- PanAmerican Airways announces that it will buy nine navy flying boats to use in the New York City air-taxi service it is founding.

- Hudson Motors introduces a closed sedan selling for little more than its open model.

**4 Mar.**    Congress enacts the Agricultural Credits Act, which makes loans available to farmers.

**4 May**    The Supreme Court invalidates minimum-wage legislation in *Adkins* v. *Children's Hospital*.

**2 Aug.**    U.S. Steel reduces its standard twelve-hour workday to eight hours; the eight-hour day will allow the corporation to hire seven thousand additional workers.

**3 Aug.**    President Warren G. Harding dies, and Vice President Calvin Coolidge takes the helm.

**6 Aug.**    President Coolidge makes his first radio address.

# 1924

- A & P announces that it operates 11,913 stores.

- German dirigible ZR-3 flies from Friedrichshafen, Germany, to Lakehurst, New Jersey.

- Wall Street booms as 2.2 million shares are traded.

- The first U.S. diesel-electric locomotive is put into service by the Central Railroad of New Jersey.

- GM's Oakland becomes the first U.S. auto to be painted with Du Pont Duco paint, which cuts days off the time required to paint cars.

- Continental Baking Company is founded in Chicago; consolidating more than one hundred bakeries, it becomes the largest baking chain in the United States.

- Ford announces that it has ten thousand U.S. dealerships in operation.

- Southern Railway introduces the Crescent Limited that will run between New York and New Orleans; it has both a five-dollar premium fare and a regular fare.

- Luxury hotels opening during the spring and summer of this year include: the Mayflower (Washington, D.C.), the Parker House (Boston), the Palmer House (Chicago), the Peabody (Memphis), the Boca Raton (Palm Beach), The Breakers (Palm Beach), and the Miami Biltmore (Coral Gables).

- Union Carbide and Carbon Company introduces Prestone, an auto anti-freeze compound that costs five dollars per gallon.

- Ad man Bruce Barton says in his new book, *The Man Nobody Knows*, that Jesus was the world's best salesman in that he realized all good advertising is news.

**1 Jan.** Radios in American homes reach 2.5 million as compared to 2,000 in 1920.

**14 Feb.** Thomas J. Watson changes the name of his company to International Business Machines.

**1 Apr.** Dillon, Read and Company acquires Dodge Motor Company for $146 million, the largest automobile-industry transaction to date.

**16 Apr.** The Dawes Plan to stabilize the German economy in the war-debts issue is announced.

**June** Chrysler Corporation is founded; it announces that it will sell a new car for $1,500.

**4 Oct.** Nine days before his death at sixty-seven, tobacco millionaire James B. Duke gives $47 million to Trinity College, which becomes Duke University.

**4 Nov.** Calvin Coolidge is elected to his first full term; his vice president is Charles G. Dawes.

**30 Nov.** RCA sends photos by wireless transmitter from London to New York.

**17 Dec.** Gen. Billy Mitchell is found guilty of insubordination for advocating air power following a demonstration in which bombs dropped from planes sunk a battleship.

# 1925

**17 Jan.** In an address to the Society of American Newspaper Editors, President Coolidge says, "The business of America is business."

**2 Feb.** The Kelly Air Mail Act authorizes the U.S. Postal Department to contract for airmail carriage; rates are made high enough to attract air carriers.

- As cities and suburbs grow upward and outward, Americans spend more than $6 billion on building and construction.

- To fulfill a contract for transporting airmail from San Francisco to Chicago, William Boeing produces the 40A, the first plane that is capable of flying over the Sierra Nevada and Rocky Mountains with twelve hundred pounds of mail.

- After cautionary articles are published in influential northern newspapers, the boom of development in Florida begins to subside.

- Walter P. Chrysler produces the first Chrysler automobile.

**28 Feb.** Congress passes the Corrupt Practices Act to make it "unlawful for any national bank, or any corporation. . . to make a contribution or expenditure in connection with any election to any political office" but allows an individual donor to give up to $5,000 to a political campaign.

**2 Dec.** Gimbel Brothers acquires Philadelphia's Kaufmann & Bauer store.

**8 Dec.** President Coolidge tells Congress that he opposes cancellation of British and French war debts.

## 1926

- The Santa Fe *Super Chief* begins service from Chicago to Los Angeles in fifty-eight hours.

- Greyhound Corporation begins service with GM as its major stockholder.

- U.S. auto production reaches four million per year, up nearly eightfold from 1919.

- J. C. Penney Company opens its five hundredth store; it will soon reach 1,495 outlets.

- An automobile census shows that 72 percent of autos are closed models; in 1916 only 2 percent had been.

- Ford Motor Company takes over production of the Lincoln, adding a high-priced car to the Ford line.

- Scottish inventor John David introduces television.

- Sears, Roebuck distributes fifteen million catalogues and twenty-three million special announcements per year.

**26 Feb.** President Coolidge signs legislation reducing federal income and inheritance taxes.

**5 May** The United States and France sign an agreement on the war debt.

**9 May** Richard E. Byrd and pilot Floyd Bennett fly over the North Pole.

**20 May** Western Air Express begins service; it will later become Trans-World Airlines (TWA).

**6 July** A survey shows that one of six Americans owns an automobile.

## 1927

- President Coolidge signs a law to regulate radio broadcasting.

- The Franklin automobile, which has an air-cooled engine, is introduced.

- The New York Central Railroad refurbishes the *Twentieth Century Limited* with a new Hudson locomotive; archrival Pennsylvania Railroad upgrades its *Broadway Limited*.

- Calvin Coolidge announces he will not be a presidential candidate in 1928, leaving the Republican Party nomination open to Herbert Hoover.

- David Sarnoff's RCA splits into two networks (the Red and the Blue) to bring about more efficient management.

- Boston's Statler Hotel opens with 1,150 rooms.

- Washington's Hay-Adams Hotel opens on Lafayette Square.

- New Jersey's Newark Airport opens to relieve traffic to and from New York.

- Chrysler introduces the Plymouth and will soon introduce the DeSoto, a midpriced car.

- GM announces a $2.60-per-share dividend totaling $65 million, the largest dividend in American history.

**1928**

| | |
|---|---|
| **1 Feb.** | The Royal Hawaiian Hotel opens in Honolulu. |
| **7 Apr.** | Television is introduced in a U.S. demonstration, but potential investors are wary. |
| **27 May** | Charles A. Lindbergh arrives in Paris after a thirty-three-and-a-half-hour solo flight across the Atlantic to world acclaim. |
| **19 Oct.** | Juan Trippe of Pan American Airways announces airmail service to and from Cuba. |
| **5 Sept.** | Ford Motor Company announces that some of its workers will be put on a forty-hour week at the same pay they were receiving for working longer hours. |
| **Nov.** | The Model A Ford, announced on 25 May 1927, is introduced with worldwide publicity. |

- President Coolidge vetoes a farm subsidy plan, calling it a "price fixing scheme."
- Chrysler acquires Dodge Brothers and becomes one of the "big three."
- NBC broadcasts the Will Rogers program nationwide to an audience of millions.
- A. P. Giannini founds the TransAmerica Corporation.
- Wall Street is shaken as stock prices swing wildly.
- Presidential candidate Herbert Hoover declares that the end of poverty is in sight.
- New York Central Railroad earns $10 million as business travel soars.
- Movie producer Joseph Schenck calls "talkies" a passing fancy.
- Stearns-Knight introduces an automobile to compete at the high-price level.
- *Time* magazine inaugurates an aeronautics department.
- Marmon, a producer of expensive cars, introduces the Roosevelt to compete in the medium-price market.
- Stutz, which had produced the legendary Bear Cat, declares bankruptcy.
- Walter P. Chrysler announces plans for a seventy-seven-floor office building in Manhattan; the Chrysler Building, designed by architect William Van Alen, becomes a landmark of Art Deco style.
- Macy's department store announces that it has recently increased its sales staff to 12,500 and enlarged its floor space to 1.5 million square feet.
- David Gerber introduces improved baby foods to be sold through grocery stores.
- Ford brings out its popular wood-sided station wagon.
- Gruman Aircraft opens a plant on Long Island, New York.

| | |
|---|---|
| **7 Jan.** | "Coolidge optimism" spurs a Wall Street boom. |
| **27 May** | Congress passes the Jones-White Act providing subsidies to U.S. shipping. |
| **30 July** | George Eastman of Kodak introduces color motion pictures. |

**6 Nov.**     In the presidential election Herbert Hoover defeats New York's Alfred E. Smith by seven million votes.

## 1929

- Henry Ford is reported by the press to have a personal income in 1929 of $14 million.
- GM completes a Detroit office building that dominates the city and a New York office estimated to cost $60 million.
- Commercial airlines fly thirty million miles and carry 180,000 passengers.
- Seventy-one percent of U.S. families have incomes below $2,500; the average weekly wage is $28.
- Electric refrigerator sales reach eight hundred thousand, up from seventy-five thousand in 1925.

**12 Jan.**     James J. Hill, president of the Great Northern Railroad, dedicates the new eight-mile-long Cascade Tunnel.

**23 Feb.**     The Brotherhood of Sleeping Car Porters, headed by A. Philip Randolph, becomes the first Negro union to get an American Federation of Labor charter.

**17 Mar.**     GM announces plans to acquire the German auto firm Opel.

**7 June**     The Young Plan eases German war debts.

Curtiss-Wright is created by the merger of two pioneer aircraft builders.

**7 July**     Transcontinental Air Transport announces a plan to offer coast-to-coast service using air carriers over flatlands and rail carriers in the mountains.

**11 Sept.**     The Fokker F32, the world's longest passenger plane, is unveiled.

**29 Oct.**     Black Tuesday: the stock market collapses.

**29 Nov.**     Richard E. Byrd flies over the South Pole.

**31 Dec.**     President Hoover declares that the economy is sound.

# OVERVIEW

**America and the War.** World War I had ended in November 1918, and the impact of the war on the economic and business scene had been substantial. The war had passed through two phases: the first phase during which the United States functioned as a supplier of goods and services to the Allied European participants, and the second phase in which the United States provided economic assistance and combat troops. Before the war the United States had been relatively detached from the European economy, and London had played the role of international banker. Yet during the war the U.S. role as a supplier of goods was substantial. As a result, in America prices of most goods rose; labor was in short supply; and wages were high. Agricultural exports skyrocketed, and farmers prospered as never before.

**Economic Benefits.** Overall, the impact of the war on the economy was beneficial. Demand for manufactured goods rose in a spectacular fashion as American steel and all sorts of raw materials and other goods flowed toward Europe. These exports imposed no great strain on the economy — far less, for example, than during World War II, which resulted in considerable shortages of material and moderate rationing of consumer goods as well as the imposition of controls over labor. Little of that sort of activity took place during World War I, although railroad traffic was so high and resulting shortages of equipment were so severe that the federal government was forced to take over control of the railroads, which were not returned to their owners until 1921.

**Development of Technology.** One of the greatest long-range impacts of the war was the development of technology under the force of demand and through generous federal military spending. The automobile, airplane, and radio industries illustrate this case. All three existed by the turn of the century, but the latter two were generally experimental. The war changed this situation. By 1920 automobiles, airplanes, and radios were being produced in large quantities, and the workforce in these industries had accumulated vast experience in assembling these products. Plants were in place, and a sophisticated infrastructure of support existed: thousands of rural workers had moved to the industrial centers, and a corps of executives had emerged.

**Adjustments.** These changes were welcome, but as the extraordinary demand for goods began to decline, serious adjustments had to be made. Indeed, as many had predicted, layoffs began as soon as the end of the war was announced. Orders for ships, aircraft, and other military supplies were promptly canceled, as were orders for steel and other metals such as copper widely used in the production of military hardware. Yet the impact of these reductions was less than might have been expected since the output of many civilian products had not been sharply curtailed during the war, and consumers had cash on hand. Also, the return of servicemen to the economy was not terribly difficult since — again in contrast to World War II — only a relative handful of men had served. Much of the immediate reaction to the end of the war was relief and a wish to turn inward and forget about Europe, but the United States could never return to its prewar position. In the future the country would be locked into the world economy.

**Farmers.** With the exception of agriculture, the economy flourished in 1921–1923. Farmers suffered because European sources of supply had been restored. Many farmers had greatly overexpanded, buying high-priced land that was now unneeded. Bankers and merchants in the farm belt were plunged into severe difficulty (for example, a Kansas City haberdasher named Harry S Truman found himself with high-priced inventory he could not sell). But farmers apart, it was a booming decade.

**The Boom.** The election of Warren G. Harding in 1920 insured that the decade would be favorable to business, and after the death of Harding, Calvin Coolidge made it clear that he would continue his predecessor's probusiness policies. Demand for radios and automobiles seemed endless, and auto sales on credit became the order of the day. Hotels and office buildings rose in every city, housing starts increased, and the suburbs expanded. Prices were rising, but jobs were plentiful and wages were good. Chain stores appeared, beginning in the drug and grocery trades. Banks grew and consolidated. Movies and radio broadcasting became important; Herbert Hoover, the active secretary of commerce, championed the development of business, especially aviation and radio, as he put himself into position to win the presidency in 1928.

The stock-and-bond market began to be more active, and by middecade thousands of Americans who had never invested before were following the market avidly. In a 1929 study which asked respondents to name the most prestigious occupation, stockbrokers were the clear choice, far ahead of physicians or lawyers.

**Optimism.** Each year until the end of the decade all leading economic indexes rose. Politicians and clergymen spoke seriously of having eliminated poverty in the land. Young men who had formerly seemed destined for law or engineering began to enroll in business programs and major in marketing. Scientific management became fashionable. No day passed that the giant River Rouge plant of the Ford Motor Company did not entertain several delegations, many of them Europeans, studying Ford methods. Efficiency experts and management engineers roamed the shop floors with stopwatches and clipboards at the ready.

**Laissez-faire.** Both the Harding and Coolidge administrations adopted laissez-faire, or "hands off the economy," stances. Coolidge often said that the business of America was business, and he put that principle into practice. The antitrust laws were largely ignored; federal encouragement to business was more vigorous than ever before. Near the end of the decade some cautious observers were pointing out that the stock market was dangerously high, but no one took much note, certainly not the White House. Both Wall Street and Main Street were booming. Why should Pennsylvania Avenue interfere?

**Concerns.** Yet as the decade passed, some farseeing individuals began to have doubts. They speculated that perhaps demand for autos and other consumer goods was rising too rapidly and that too many people who had too little knowledge were in the stock market. Neither bankers nor consumers had experience in installment financing. Many worried about the plight of the farmers and of discontented workers who were not involved in the booming industries; railroad employees, the most organized members of the oldest labor group, had been forced to give up on a 1922 strike. It was also clear that prosperity was far from evenly distributed around the country. The Northeast, the Upper Midwest industrial belt, and the West Coast were booming, but the South and the agricultural Midwest were doing poorly. With the war over, blacks, coal miners, and other traditionally ill-paid workers had drifted back into their prewar status.

**Questions.** Was the frivolity of the Jazz Age — the orgy of dance crazes, speakeasies, flagpole sitting — masking the stock-market greed that seemed symbolic of problems in the rest of the economy? Were the truly positive aspects of the economy — the rise of the auto and aircraft industries, the refinements in air transportation and in communications, and the impressive buildings rising on every side — destined to be pushed into the background?

# TOPICS IN THE NEWS

## CARRIERS: TRANSPORTATION

**Railroads: Trends.** While the aviation and auto industries caught the public fancy, the railroads continued through the 1920s to provide the major share of intercity transportation, both passenger and freight. At the turn of the century the railroads transported the overwhelming share of intercity goods and passengers (about 70 percent of freight and an even larger percentage of passengers); by the end of the 1920s the railroad share of both passenger and freight movement had begun to decline slowly, but early in the decade this trend was not evident. Although revenue from passenger service fell from $1.2 million to $876,000, freight revenue rose slightly from $4.4 billion to $4.8 billion. Railroads were still regarded as the backbone of the national transportation system.

**Assumptions of the Railroads.** For the most part, railroad management in 1920 saw no reason to think that the industry might be headed for trouble. As the decade began, the railroads were still in federal hands, but management anticipated their quick return to private ownership. For a generation rail companies had enjoyed an almost total monopoly on intercity transportation, a monopoly that since 1887 had been reinforced by both federal and state regulation. Thus, spurred on by optimism, management investment in rail facilities and equipment rose by about $6 million in the 1920s. Obviously the auto industry was booming, and trucks were now engaged in freight transportation and the motor bus in passenger transportation. But from the railroad viewpoint, neither of these developments seemed worthy of serious concern. Most experts expressed the opinion that the truck and bus along with the private auto would be useful only for short hauls. Few thought that cars, trucks, and buses would be much of a factor in intercity movement. As for the aircraft, most transportation economists thought it might be useful for the carrying of mail but little else.

**Rail Improvements and Services.** The structure of the industry had changed little since 1900 (only one major railroad was constructed after that date), and the industry concentrated on internal technological improvements in the twentieth century. Locomotives and rolling stock had been consistently improved, and operating costs had declined. Many railroads operated hotels, restaurants, re-

The *Twentieth Century Limited* departing Grand Central Station, New York, for Chicago in 1925

sorts, and other subsidiary businesses. True, the number of cars that were loaded became smaller (this was a standard index of economic activity), but the industry employed about half a million people. The rail network by the turn of the century reached almost every major point in the United States. Class I roads (with revenues of a million dollars or more per year) served large geographic areas and jointly offered many transcontinental routes. Major railroads with nationwide sleeping-car service provided by the Pullman Company operated "name trains": *The Twentieth Century Limited, The Broadway Limited, The Overland Limited,* and *The Super Chief* became famous and provided settings for movies and novels.

**Railroad Predictions.** For most Americans in 1920, it would have been difficult to imagine a modern society in which railroads did not play a major role. In the years since the Civil War, railroads had significantly influenced the development of the national economy, especially in the West. But things were changing. Few knew it, but during the decade of the 1920s railroad passenger traffic would decline markedly. Much of the loss would be in commuter traffic that would be gradually taken over by the automobile.

**Motor Carriers and Roads.** The developing auto industry would have been useless, of course, without improvement in the primitive highways that had served horse-drawn vehicles. One of the attractions of the Model T Ford was that its design and rugged construction were suitable to the poor roads of the day. Though nothing like the interstate system existing in 1995 came into being, the 1920s were a decade of highway building. In 1916 the federal government had taken primary responsibility for constructing and financing intercounty and interstate roads, and national highway standards were created, giving rise to the system of north-south or east-west roads, such as US 1, US 50, US 66, and the like. To the modern generation these highways would seem totally inadequate, but to the motorists of the 1920s they were a major improvement over previous roads. These new highways stimulated not only the use of the private auto but the development of the commercial motor-carrier industry — trucks and buses that competed with the railroads. By the later part of the decade both the truck and the bus had gained a considerable foothold, and trucks would continue to gain in market share.

**Limitations of Truck and Bus Lines.** Like the air carriers, the truck and bus lines did not become fully effective on an intercity basis until the 1930s, and while by the late 1920s they had made considerable progress, they were still limited in their service. Long-distance trucking was hampered not only by the inadequate highway system but also by the lack of development in the vehicles themselves. Most trucks in the early part of the decade were merely somewhat larger versions of the automobile. The tractor trailer was still in its experimental stage and relatively little used, and both trucks and the bus were regarded as primarily useful for making short-distance runs and serving as feeders to the railroads. Many transportation economists regarded motor vehicles as suitable only to the inner city or the suburbs.

**Economics and the Motor Carriers.** The economic characteristics of the motor carriers and the railroads differed greatly. The railroad from the beginning was a capital-intensive industry. Even the smallest railroad required massive capital and therefore attracted corporate enterprise: land had to be acquired, tracks laid, tunnels drilled, bridges built, and equipment purchased. Consequently, by 1920 no one thought about building new railroads since the possibilities of profit would have been minuscule because of the huge costs. The motor carriers were in a completely different position. The typical truck or bus line in the mid 1920s was in effect a "mom and pop" operation. A used truck could be acquired for a few hundred dollars, overhead was low, and no right-of-way expenditures were required, since trucks used the public highways. The pioneer truck lines in the mid and late

1920s were very small scale, but as growth took place the firms expanded. The motor carriers became well established in the 1920s but made only a small dent in the railroads' share of ton miles carried by the end of the decade. For the motor carriers, the 1920s were a pioneering period. Their great growth would come in the following decade.

**Air Carriers.** By 1920 the term *carriers* did not accurately describe what would later become commercial airlines. The Wright brothers had flown their frail craft at

| PERCENTAGE SHARES OF TON MILES CARRIED, 1930 | |
| --- | --- |
| Railroad | 74.4 |
| Motor Carriers | 3.9 |
| Water Carriers | 16.5 |
| Pipelines | 17.7 |
| Airlines | *Too small to report |

Kitty Hawk, North Carolina, in 1903, and from the technological viewpoint progress had been rapid since then. The war had greatly increased public interest in flying with the performance of the Air Corps aces, such as Eddie Rickenbacker. And during the later 1920s the exploits of Charles Lindbergh and others had stimulated the imaginations of millions. Yet in 1920 few people thought that the airplane had much future as a serious partner in the transportation industry. Had someone suggested that fifty years later the airlines would far surpass the railroads as passenger carriers, he would not have been taken seriously. What the general public saw in the early years of the century were "barnstormers" flying rebuilt army planes from county fair to air circus, wing-walking and performing other stunts for a purse of $25. This was not a fledgling industry but a carnival.

**Air Carriers and the Army.** The army had some interest in the airplane as a weapon, but the army had no money. The war was over, and military appropriations were being slashed dramatically. Even at best the military was a poor market. Its custom was to buy a few experimental planes and test and modify them endlessly before placing orders (if indeed they were placed) with manufacturers. Few entrepreneurs were willing to invest money in such an uncertain venture. Moreover, it was clear that a stable commercial aviation system would never be developed without planes able to carry passengers safely and without sufficient numbers of passengers willing to fly.

**Airmail.** The army fliers made a breakthrough when in 1918 they were selected by the Wilson administration to fly selected airmail routes. The Air Corps was desperate to find some task that would keep them in the public eye, and they performed the airmail task well despite the fact that they had few planes and very little money. Although the business community came to depend on airmail, it was still a weak base on which to build air-passenger service comparable to that in some western European countries.

**Air Carriers and the Kelly Act.** In the mid 1920s the airmail service was put out into the private sector for bids, and in 1925 came the passage of the Kelly Act, which had been designed to subsidize the air carriers with the condition that they use the subsidy to provide facilities for transporting passengers as well as mail. The legislation

worked well. Almost immediately the carriers began a serious examination of the economics of air-passenger travel, and the aircraft producers on their part began to look seriously at designs for passenger-carrying planes.

**Air Carrier Developments.** During the middle to late 1920s relatively sophisticated planes came onto the market — the Dutch-built Fokker and Ford-built Tri-Motor, as well as Boeing, and, later, Douglas models. By later standards these aircraft were quite primitive, carrying only eight to twelve passengers; their noise levels were high, and their range limited. To aid in navigation the government built, along the airways, an emergency-field and beacon-light system that would be visible especially to the airmail carriers who did not fly at high altitudes (the mail planes of the early part of the decade had open cockpits). These additions helped, but the development of a full airline system was proceeding slowly, despite improvements in the Kelly Act in 1926. Yet the airlines would not play a major role in passenger carriage for many years (on the eve of World War II airlines accounted for only 2.3 percent of the total passenger carriage).

Sources:

Henry Ladd Smith, *Airways* (New York: Knopf, 1942);

Thurman W. Van Metre, *Transportation in the United States* (Chicago: Foundation Press, 1939);

Arch Whitehouse, *The Sky's the Limit: History of U.S. Airlines* (New York: Macmillan, 1971).

## CONSTRUCTION AND BUILDING

**Record Construction.** The 1920s set records for building and construction that would not be equaled until the 1950s. Total construction in 1925 reached more than $6 billion, having risen from slightly more than $919 million in 1916. Commercial buildings were a favorite vehicle for investment, combining a hoped-for profit with civic pride, commercial competitive spirit, and "boosterism." For example, dozens of large, up-to-date urban hotels opened their doors late in the era; they were the best in town, and many remained the best until the 1950s when they were replaced.

**Urban and Suburban Boom.** The great building boom of the decade was concentrated in the urban and suburban areas. By 1925 the downtown of most medium-sized and large cities was a thicket of scaffolding as office buildings, hotels, and apartment buildings vied with each other to reach the greatest heights, both financially and literally. In the suburbs construction spread in every direction as developers competed with each other to open the new "Castle Heights," "River View," or other fancifully named tract. Suburban residential construction was fueled by the increasing use of the automobile, which freed the commuter from the interurban railroads that had sprung up, and by the increasing availability of mortgage financing through the building or, later, savings-and-loan industry. These institutions, in turn, had been made possible by increasing incomes and by the expand-

Albert Kahn designed the Ford glass plant, built in 1922.

ing use of long-term payments for both homes and autos. The growing suburbs stimulated construction not only of shopping facilities, schools, and civic buildings but also of country clubs and golf courses.

**Educational and Civic Building.** Much construction was also taking place in private and public educational plants and in civic buildings. The 1920s were the golden era for industrialists and bankers to endow lavish academic buildings; Rockefeller, the Morgans, Duke, and other lesser lights poured money into their favorite institutions, and dozens of collegiate Gothic towers arose across the country. In addition, state and local governments took advantage of high tax revenues to make their marks in stone with courthouses, state office buildings, and university structures.

**Industrial Contruction.** Anxious for plant expansion to meet growing demands, industrialists were quick to build new factories and to incorporate the most recent technology and design into these plants. One of the leaders in this trend was Henry Ford, who completed the huge River Rouge plant in 1927, just in time to begin turning out the Model A. Freed from the city by the auto, plants could now be located in the outlying areas where they could be spread over a large site. Ford commissioned the well-known industrial architect Albert Kahn, who built many Ford plants in the 1920s. Few of these plants resembled those of the past, in that they were handsomely designed, well lighted and ventilated, and often looked more like schools than factories. The new plants made use of electricity to power machinery, and construction of power lines and generating facilities was a major part of the building activity of the era. Railroad construction was also important, with railroads upgrading lines, building new bridges and signal systems, and, in many cases, beginning the move to electrification. Highway building also assumed significance as the auto came into

wide use. A new type of building appeared on the scene in large cities, namely the parking garage, in many cases a multistory building in Art Deco style, a temple to the automobile.

**Workers and the Construction Boom.** Low-paid workers did not take much part in the housing construction boom. While a comfortable home could be had for $5,000 or often as little as $3,500, relatively few blue-collar workers earned more than $1,200 or $1,800 per year, and few even at that level had much income security. Even well-paid workers faced frequent layoffs during slack periods, which put long-term commitments out of reach. Nor was there much building by farmers; they had done all they needed (and more) in the previous decade.

**Glorious Failures.** Like much else in the decade, construction ended in a burst of glorious and dramatic failures. Symbolic was the completion of the Empire State Building, undertaken in late 1929 and opened in 1931. Alfred E. Smith, the colorful governor of New York and presidential candidate in 1928, had hoped that the building would make his fortune, but it remained largely untenanted until World War II began. Similarly, in cities throughout the country, hotels that opened in 1929–1930 would not experience a "full house" until World War II.

Sources:

Frederick Lewis Allen, *Only Yesterday* (New York: Harper, 1931);

Stewart Holbrook, *Age of the Moguls* (Garden City, N.Y.: Doubleday, 1954);

Charles P. Kindleberger, *The World in Depression, 1929–1939* (Berkeley: University of California Press, 1975).

## FARMS AND FARMERS

**Economic Characteristics.** Farmers, in general, did not share in the prosperity of the 1920s. As the decade began, the agricultural sector was faced with problems,

Technology down on the farm: the electric milker

many of them related to economic characteristics unique to the farm industry. This industry was made up of thousands of producers, each generating a minuscule portion of the total output and none having any control over the total market. Agriculture was dependent on good weather and was subject to pests and natural disorders of all types. National, regional, and often international markets for such products as grain and cotton were based on worldwide demand and supply. Furthermore, the farmer produced generally homogenous products. Wheat from farm X was the same as that from farm Y, and farmers had little opportunity, as economists said, to "differentiate" their products; therefore, advertising did not have the value in the farm industry that it had, for example, in the auto industry. In addition, farmers generally produced goods that were perishable. The steel mill might hold its output until better prices were available, but that strategy was impossible for most farmers. Moreover, although farming was an industrial enterprise, it was also a treasured way of life. Most farmers worked and lived on their farms, and they were extremely reluctant to leave them.

**Supply and Demand.** The farmer's immediate problem as the decade dawned was the dramatic change in supply and demand that had taken place during the past few years. European agriculture had been temporarily destroyed by the war, and the demand for food and other farm products there was met by suppliers in other parts of the world, especially the United States, Canada, and South America. To serve this demand farmers responded by expanding supply, an action that was not only rational but also encouraged by national policy. Farmers pur-

chased or leased land, borrowing money to do so, and from 1915 to 1919 they did very well indeed. Throughout the country, especially in the Midwest, prosperity became the norm. Prices were rising, credit was readily available, and farmers who had never been well-off as a class became relatively affluent. But by 1920 things had changed. Because Europe was recovering and beginning to rebuild its agricultural sector, it no longer needed to import huge amounts of farm products from abroad; the United States, Canada, and the Latin American nations thus were faced with enormous overproduction. Farmers found themselves with too much land, too much machinery, and too much debt. Land for which they had paid inflated prices was now far less valuable and, in many cases, unsalable. Rural banks were in trouble, and of course this crisis in the financial markets did not help. Mortgage foreclosures rose to new heights, and farmers were in real difficulty.

**Effects of Technology, Modernization.** Even though the farm sector was shrinking, the modern methods farmers had adopted were enabling them to maintain and, in fact, increase output more than enough to meet normal needs. Technology (both in machinery and chemical fertilizer) had made great strides; farmers operated with less hired help than formerly, and the number of workers devoted to agriculture was declining rapidly. The U.S. Department of Agriculture and the departments of agriculture at the land-grant colleges were encouraging efficiency in production, but in regard to the imbalance between supply and demand farmers were actually too efficient. Moreover, despite advances in technology and methods, much farmland had become overused, and little could be done to prevent the unusually high number of natural disasters — floods and the boll weevil, for example — that occurred during the decade.

**Lack of Attention.** Despite the enormous difficulties they confronted, farms and farming did not have a high profile. Both the Harding and the Coolidge administrations were much more interested in business than in the affairs of agriculture. The public tended to ignore farmers and direct its attention toward the glamorous auto and aviation industries, the fads and crazes of the Jazz Age, and certainly the stock market. Farming was not very exciting; indeed, the farmer's sons and daughters were themselves leaving the farm and going to the city, often in the industrial Northeast and Upper Midwest. Farm population was declining as was the farmer's political power.

**Advantages.** To be sure, not all farmers were in economic difficulty, nor were they isolated from the advancements in technology affecting the rest of society during the 1920s. Many Florida and California farmers were doing well as demand for their products, mainly citrus products, rose rapidly. And although cotton producers in the South and grain-crop producers in the Midwest were hard hit, livestock producers remained relatively prosperous as consumer incomes and demands for meat rose. And in a social sense, the farmer's quality of life was vastly improved: the auto, the truck, and the increasing availability of electricity, radio, and other amenities were giving the farmer a standard of living equal to that of city dwellers. Yet the farmer's economic problems remained.

Source:
Gerald Gunderson, *A New Economic History: America* (New York: McGraw-Hill, 1976).

## FINANCE AND BANKING

**Expansion of Commercial Banks.** Commercial banks greatly expanded during the 1920s. Led by such firms as the Bank of America and Chase Manhattan, commercial banks merged and consolidated and entered new fields, vastly increasing their construction and consumer loans. These banks also became deeply involved in the securities business and, to their future regret, put huge sums into brokers' loans and call money-market loans (short-term loans subject to recall at any time), many of which failed.

**Expansion of Investment Banks.** Perhaps the most startling expansion took place in the investment-banking field. The number of investment banks (that is, banks that did little or no commercial business, such as handling checking accounts, but instead lent funds to new entrepreneurs) rose from 277 in 1912 to 1,902 by 1929. These banks fueled the enormous increase, which took place during the great boom, in corporate offerings and in businesses.

**Consolidation.** Led by the Californian A. P. Giannini, who built his Bank of America (formerly the Bank of Italy) into a California chain that blanketed the state and who later founded the Trans-America Corporation, other banks began to merge rapidly throughout the nation. Banking, which had historically been a relatively local business, now increasingly operated in a chain system, depending much upon the laws of the states in which they were located. In many states throughout the South and West large numbers of banks became consolidated into a few hands, a factor that would be extremely troublesome in the next few years.

Sources:
John Brooks, *Once in Golconda* (New York: Norton, 1969);

F. Cyril James, *The Economics of Money Credit and Banking* (New York: Ronald Press, 1940).

## GOVERNMENT AND BUSINESS

**Laissez-faire.** In contrast to both the preceding and the succeeding decades, the 1920s were a period of little growth in federal or state regulation; instead, laissez-faire was the rule of the day. Except in regard to railroads, public utilities, radio broadcasting, and air carriers, regulation was at a low ebb. Warren G. Harding, in his desire to return to "normalcy," had little interest in regulation, and Coolidge felt much the same way. Although the antitrust laws were still in place, the so-called "rule of

reason" had rendered them of little use. There were no minimum-wage requirements on the federal level, no unemployment compensation, no National Labor Relations Act, no Environmental Protection Act, no Occupational Safety and Health Administration, no consumer protection laws, no Fair Employment Act, no Social Security Act, no Employment Act, and no federal programs for employment training. Taxes were generally low. Some historians have argued that the rapid shift to laissez-faire following the more interventionist mode of the Wilson era was not a reaction to the Wilson reforms but to the controls that had been put in place in wartime. In fact, much of the Wilson program was a casualty of the war. Whatever the reasons, the Harding-Coolidge years were certainly favorable to business and unfriendly, for the most part, toward regulation.

**Views of Government Leaders.** Harding, Coolidge, and the extremely conservative and influential Secretary of the Treasury Andrew W. Mellon (founder of ALCOA and Gulf Oil) strongly argued that low taxes and encouragement of business would promote prosperity and growth. Secretary of Commerce Herbert Hoover, who would become president after Coolidge stepped down in 1928, agreed, as did the business community and most of their fellow citizens. Certainly the nation seemed to be prosperous. Unemployment was low. Exports were at an all-time high, reaching $8.25 billion in 1920, three times the 1919 level. The federal budget was $8.23 billion (rather high for peacetime).

**Coolidge and the Stock Exchange.** When Coolidge took over after Harding's death, Wall Street had been a bit leery, feeling that he might be inclined to dampen things, but this fear proved groundless. The president greatly revered the business community, and he was certainly not one to intrude on its activities. When some of his advisers told him that perhaps the stock market was a bit freewheeling, he was somewhat concerned, but on finding that the New York Stock Exchange was under the jurisdiction of New York State, he happily abandoned the whole matter. There was of course no Securities and Exchange Commission, which no doubt pleased Coolidge. It can surprise no one that the business community for decades looked back on the 1920s as the golden age.

**Broadcasting and Air Carriers.** Two major exceptions to the government's generally "hands off" attitude toward regulation came in the radio-broadcasting and air-transport industries. The rapid entry of new commercial stations in the middle part of the decade had created intolerable conditions in regard to the frequencies at which they broadcast. Each station was free to choose (or change) its frequency, which resulted in a mishmash on the air. Without regulation, more powerful stations overwhelmed the less powerful. Radio owners enjoyed their nightly attempts to pick up distant signals and to brag of their accomplishments to their fellow workers the next day, but advertisers paying for air time were less amused. In 1927 President Coolidge signed legislation to create a regulatory body (later to become the Federal Communications Commission). This body did not attempt to oversee the economic structure of the industry or to involve itself in the morass of First Amendment issues of free speech or program content; it simply regulated the frequencies at which the various stations could operate. Similarly, the air-transport industry, which had grown haphazardly with a wide variety of aircraft and a cadre of informally trained pilots, presented a safety issue that could not be avoided. Both radio and aircraft operations were taken, at least on a temporary basis, under the umbrella of Hoover's Commerce Department.

**Transportation Act, Budget Act.** Two important matters did, in fact, emerge from the era. Though they were not dramatic and lacked wide public interest, they were of considerable value. First, Congress passed the Transportation Act of 1920, which returned the railroads to their owners and adjusted the program of railroad regulation that had been coming in bits and pieces for nearly half a century. Unfortunately, the legislation would soon be undermined by the onset of the Great Depression, and much of it would be moot. Secondly, the Congress passed the Budget Act of 1920 that would, for the first time in history, establish a budget for the federal government. To be sure, the act would not put the federal expenditures into a mode of rigid control, but it would enable lawmakers to have some understanding of what was being spent and for what. Hitherto the spending items were merely enacted at random, and no one had the slightest idea of how much was being spent overall.

Sources:

Jonathan Hughes, *The Governmental Habit* (New York: Basic Books, 1977);

H. H. Liebhafsky, *American Government and Business* (New York: Wiley, 1971);

Hugh S. Norton, *Economic Policy: Government and Business* (Columbus, Ohio: Merrill, 1966);

D. S. Watson, *Business and Government* (New York: McGraw-Hill, 1958).

## INDUSTRY: THE AIRCRAFT

**Beginnings.** Only seventeen years elapsed between the Wright brothers' experiments in 1903 and the arrival of the 1920s, yet the airline industry was second only to auto manufacturing in public interest. The industry consisted of a motley collection of poorly financed and, for the most part, poorly managed companies, each firm turning out a few aircraft per month. The entrepreneurs were an eclectic group: Air Corps veterans, barnstormers, a few speculators, a handful of businessmen who simply had some extra money to invest, and the relatively small number of businessmen who had somehow acquired an interest in the flying machine as well as investment funds. Many of the early figures were like the Wrights — small-town mechanics, men experienced in building bicycles — or they were pioneers in the auto industry and others who had no idea of the science of aeronautics.

## WALL STREET BIRDMAN

**M**ost pioneers in the airline industry were long-time fliers or aircraft builders who had little knowledge of finance. Juan T. Trippe (1899–1980) was an exception. A Yale graduate (1921) and a full decade younger than Eddie Rickenbacker, Trippe was not wealthy but from a well-connected family. While he did not become an influential figure until the 1930s, he was a 1920s type, both in his early business career and personal inclinations. Throughout his life he carefully listed his Yale club memberships and athletic prowess in his biographical material, and Yale served him well. He knew the wealthy, aviation-fancying Hambleton family, sportsman Jock Whitney, and Briton Hadden and Henry Luce of *Time*; he married into the Stettinius family (GM and U.S. Steel) and was a brother-in-law of the secretary of state. When Trippe decided to leave Wall Street to enter the aviation business in 1924, he could count on the support of his Ivy League friends, many of whom also had careers on Wall Street and interest in flying as a potential industry and as a sport.

Source: Marylin Bender and Selig Altschul, *The Chosen Instrument: Pan Am, Juan Trippe, the Rise and Fall of an American Entrepreneur* (New York: Simon & Schuster, 1982).

**The Military and the Aircraft Industry.** The end of the war had essentially closed down government demand for aircraft. The army and navy were anxious to proceed with development of their airplanes, but appropriations were minuscule, with contracts let for only about a half dozen planes, mainly for experimental purposes. When, during the so-called "air-mail scandals" in the early 1930s, the army briefly took over mail service from civilian contractors, it could muster only a handful of its own aircraft, most of them semiobsolete. The entire military Flying Service — then a division of the Signal Corps — had only eight hundred aircraft in inventory, and less than one hundred of these were suitable for the task.

**Civilian Demand.** Until the airmail contractors came on the scene, there was very slight civilian demand for aircraft. The barnstormers and the flying-circus trade made little money and, for the most part, depended on salvaged World War I military equipment. Used Air Corps planes, which were sold at sharply reduced prices to barnstormers and others, were readily available. These planes needed constant work to keep them flying, and even those in the best condition were so obsolete that the military was delighted to get rid of them. For each plane that flew, there were probably half a dozen that were cannibalized to get replacement parts.

William Boeing (right) and Eddie Hubbard with the Boeing Model C, which provided the first international airmail service

**Arrival of the Contractors: Boeing.** The salvation of the aircraft industry came with the arrival of the mail contractors following the Kelly Act in the mid 1920s. As the legislation had intended, the carriage of mail became sufficiently profitable to encourage manufacturers to produce planes suitable for the purpose. As in the auto industry, many of the early manufacturers were men who had made their money in totally unrelated fields but who had developed an interest in the new industry. Typical of these was William Boeing of Seattle, a lumberman who had learned to fly so that he could reach remote parts of the Northwest in order to fish. Gradually he moved into aircraft repair and manufacture (largely flying boats) and rather brashly bid on — and won — a contract to provide airmail from San Francisco to Chicago, a flight that required a plane not then available. Boeing thus produced, in 1925, the 40A, a durable plane of advanced design that sold for $25,000 and was capable of flying over the Sierra Nevada and Rocky Mountains with twelve hundred pounds of mail and, later, a few passengers. He wisely remained active in the timber and land business, which gave him a large and steady income not available to many of the other industry pioneers. He also had the good sense to concentrate on the business side of aircraft production and to leave the engineering to specialists.

Boeing was to become the largest aircraft manufacturer in the world.

**Industry Developments.** By the mid 1920s the aircraft industry had grown enormously. For one thing the military was beginning to show a greater interest and had more money to spend than earlier in the decade. Moreover, the major aircraft producers, while using the military market as a source of research and development, were beginning to perceive the importance of the commercial market. Indeed, some firms early on concentrated primarily on the civilian market, responding to the demands of the airmail contractors and, later on, passenger-plane contractors. By middecade the industry had become quite well organized, with adequate capital and qualified management; by late in the decade the industry had matured and assumed the configuration it would carry into World War II. Major aircraft producers included Boeing, Glenn L. Martin and his protégé Donald W. Douglas, Ryan, Lockheed, Curtiss-Wright, and, during the early period, Henry Ford, whose Tri-Motor (the famous tin goose) was the equal of anything then on the market. Douglas, whose company would become one of the largest aircraft manufacturers for the civilian market, had resigned the Naval Academy to attend MIT and was one of the few professional aeronautics engineers in the industry.

Henry Ford with his first car and his ten millionth, a Model T

**Conclusions.** From almost a backyard hobby operating on a shoestring, the production of aircraft had developed by 1930 into a major industry, and by 1940 it would be one of the nation's largest industries and the greatest producer of aircraft for the world market. The industry had essentially been created through the demand of fledgling airlines for suitable aircraft, which, in turn, had come into existence through the airmail subsidy, wisely used to stimulate the carriers to make provisions for passenger traffic. One might argue that these developments would ultimately have taken place anyway. No doubt they would have; but it was fortunate that by the beginning of the 1940s, with war on the horizon, the aircraft industry could capitalize on the foundations laid during the 1920s.

Sources:
Marilyn Bender and Seliq Altschul, *The Chosen Instrument: Pan Am, Juan Trippe, the Rise and Fall of an American Entrepreneur* (New York: Simon & Schuster, 1982);

John J. Nance, *Splash of Color: The Self-Destruction of Braniff International* (New York: Morrow, 1984);

Doris Rich, *Amelia Earhart: A Biography* (Washington: Smithsonian Institute Press, 1989).

## INDUSTRY: THE AUTOMOBILE

**Model T.** In 1908, when Henry Ford was forty-five years old and the president of the Ford Motor Company, he had an idea that must have made both his associates and competitors think he had taken leave of his senses. The Ford organization, following conventional wisdom, had been manufacturing the Ford Model N, a large, popular car. Auto producers generally believed that the car demanded by the public would be large and expensive, since by definition the auto attracted only those in the upper-income groups and would never be produced for the average man who could not afford it. But now Henry Ford wanted to manufacture a small car to sell to a mass

Interest in the automobile during the 1920s was immense, perhaps because there was no television or because in those days the various makes were quite distinctive. The introduction of new models in the local dealers' showrooms was a major event.

September and October were the magic months. In small communities new Fords, Chevrolets, Plymouths, and other makes would begin arriving at the local freight yard to be unloaded and driven to the nearest dealer, the process supervised by small boys and hangers-on. And when the cars reached the showroom, everyone came to see them. Brochures illustrating the new models were stacked on tables, and, in some cases, passed rather sparingly to those who gave some appearance of being likely customers (small boys not included).

Loud, sometimes heated discussions would get under way over the advantages of hydraulic brakes, "free wheeling," the "turret top," "knee action," "synchro-mesh" transmission, and so on.

Salesmen boosted the youngsters into front seats, opened hoods, pointed out improvements, and suggested trial spins. Serious negotiations began when a prospective customer and a salesman stepped outside to look over the trade-in.

The scene at the high-priced auto showrooms was a bit different from that at the Ford or GM dealerships. Packard, Cadillac, and Lincoln customers were older and clearly more affluent, the salesmen more restrained. The automobile brochures for up-scale cars were more attractive and often expensively produced. Later they would become collectors' items.

Henry Ford had many interests — farming, social issues, food fads, politics, and pacifism among them. During a legal proceeding he once said that history was "bunk," but around 1919 he began to re-create history on his property near Dearborn in the neighborhood of his River Rouge plant. Greenfield Village became over the next twenty years a potpourri of American history: a somewhat unstructured living museum filled with tradesmen's and workers' shops and historic buildings of various kinds (including Thomas Edison's laboratory moved from New Jersey and rebuilt on the Greenfield Village site). Ford and members of his family spent some $37 million on the project, far more than they put into their other philanthropic endeavors, such as the Ford Hospital and the Berry Schools.

**Source:** William S. Adams, *Henry Ford and Greenfield Village* (New York: Stokes, 1938).

Nash, Velie, Hudson, Franklin, Duesenberg, Chandler, Pierce-Arrow, and Rickenbacker enjoyed a reasonable share of the market, though many of them ultimately failed. Generally these smaller firms concentrated on the high-price/high-quality end of the market.

**The "Big Three."** Yet the smaller companies were of course overshadowed by the giant auto manufacturers. Founded in 1908 by William C. Durant, General Motors rose during the 1920s to the top of the industry, followed later in the decade by the Chrysler Corporation under the leadership of Walter P. Chrysler; both GM and Chrysler were amalgamations of other companies. The "big three" — GM, Chrysler, and Ford — accounted for well over 70 percent of the auto market, GM controlling about 40 percent of the market, and Ford and Chrysler dividing roughly 30 percent, though, as the decade passed, Ford began to lose its market share to the other two major firms. The greatest area of competition took place in the low end of the market occupied by Ford's Model T and, later, Model A; GM's Chevrolet; and Chrysler's Plymouth — the three most widely sold cars.

**Evolving Structure.** By middecade the industry had begun to change in structure and emphasis. The number of makes in autos had substantially declined, and while emphasis was still put on stylistic innovation and mechanical developments, increased attention was being given to management and the business side of the industry. The major figure of this era was Alfred P. Sloan Jr., who became the dominant personality in General Motors after the departure of Durant. Unlike many of the early giants of the industry, Sloan was a professional engineer, a graduate of MIT. Under Sloan, GM became a model of

market at a low price — less than $1,000 — an invitation to bankruptcy, the industry thought. Before the Model T went out of production, nearly twenty years later, the lowest-priced model was sold for $260. While his associates had predicted disaster, by 1920 Ford was the most famous figure in the industry, and his Model T the best-known car in the world, seventeen million having been sold.

**The Industry.** The industry was in great flux during the decade. Dozens of small firms merged with others or ultimately left the automobile field completely; from 1900 to 1930 some two thousand or more auto manufacturers were in business for at least some period of time. Such well-known smaller companies as Packard, Reo,

Henry M. Leland (1843–1932) was one of the great figures in the development of the automobile during the first two decades of this century. Beginning as a toolmaker, he rose to executive positions in several corporations, and in 1908 he won the Dewar trophy for automotive excellence. He had reassembled three knocked-down Cadillac automobiles that had interchangeable parts, and all ran successfully for five hundred miles or more.

After he sold Cadillac to General Motors in 1909, Leland and his son continued to operate the Cadillac division, where they introduced many technical improvements. In 1917 he left GM to manufacture Liberty airplane engines, and in 1920 he began to produce the Lincoln.

At first the Lincoln was well received, largely on the basis of Leland's reputation for high-quality work. But although the car was superbly engineered, it was poorly styled, and its production was slowed by Leland's insistence on quality and by the economic decline in the early 1920s. The car was soon in difficulty.

In 1922 the Lincoln passed to the control of the Ford Motor Company. Henry Ford and Leland were both strong-willed men. The Lelands, who had been slated to manage Lincoln production under Ford direction, soon left. Edsel Ford had the automobile restyled in the late 1920s and in the late 1930s produced the Lincoln Continental, a superb car. Henry M. Leland is remembered as the man who created the top cars of both the GM line (Cadillac) and the Ford line (Lincoln Continental).

Sources: Ottile M. Leland and Minnie M. Millbrook, *Master of Precision: Henry M. Leland* (Detroit: Wayne State University Press, 1966);

Allan Nevins and Frank E. Hill, *Ford: Expansion and Challenge, 1915–1933* (New York: McGraw-Hill, 1957).

the modern corporation, just as Ford earlier had become the symbol of mass production and low prices.

**Related Industries and Social Phenomena.** The auto industry produced a vast network of related industries and generated significant social phenomena. Among the related businesses were car dealerships; parts and supplies manufacturers and retailers; petroleum-products developers; service stations and garages. Highways were built linking almost every city, town, and village in the nation. As automobile ownership made distances easier to cover, schools were consolidated, and factories moved to the countryside. The suburbs mushroomed well beyond the limits of the electric interurban system, which had fueled the original exodus to the suburbs. Investments in motel-like tourist courts, gas stations, and other auto-support facilities rose to enormous levels by the end of the decade.

**Profits.** In the middle and later parts of the decade the auto industry was hugely profitable almost across the board but especially noticeably in the largest firms. When Henry Ford introduced his Model A (put on the market in November 1927 but generally unavailable to the public until 1928), the company took in more than fifty thousand orders (with cash deposits) before the model had entered production or many buyers had even seen the car. In the same year, GM declared a $65,250,000 dividend on its 17.4 million shares, the largest dividend in any firm to that date. Dealers throughout the nation prospered. And while most attention was fixed on the big three's low-priced entrants, demand was substantial and increasing, as the market boomed at the high-priced end of the market: Packard, Pierce-Arrow, Cadillac. In large cities some imported models, such as Rolls-Royce and Bentley, were seen. Other than these extremely expensive autos, the imported auto was unusual, and the idea that Japan would someday be a major supplier of U.S. cars would have been laughable.

**Automania.** Public interest in the automobile was intense. During the tooling-up period for the Model A, for example, rumors swept the country about what it would look like and how much it would cost. Newspapers ran pictures purporting to show the new car. On the day the Model A was introduced, Ford ran full-page ads in every paper in the country, and its introduction attracted worldwide attention. Crowds in showrooms were immense. In New York the major dealer had planned a show in the Waldorf Hotel lobby but had to shift to Madison Square Garden instead. In small towns the status symbol over the next few months was to own a new Model A. Although the old Model T was being phased out, it actually remained in production for months to fill orders, and Model T replacement parts were manufactured for years. Yet a new day had dawned. No longer would a standard model remain in production for twenty years, as the Model T had done, and, in fact, the Model A, of which about a million units were produced a year, was replaced by Ford in 1932.

**Strength of the Industry.** The auto industry would soon become the largest industry in the nation. In 1926, 4.2 million units were produced, and by 1930 the figure rose to 5.3 million. It has been estimated that by 1927 Americans owned 39 percent of all the autos in the world. Yet Ford and GM were also very strong in Europe where, during the 1920s, they established branch plants or bought interests in European firms. Even later, in the depth of the Depression, the demand for autos remained amazingly strong, partly because of the availability of used cars and partly because auto producers were among the first industries to adopt installment-buying plans.

## DISTRIBUTORSHIPS, DEALERSHIPS, AND AGENCIES

The structure of the automobile industry in the 1920s was built on the needs of the market at the time. High-priced cars sold poorly in small towns and rural areas, where incomes tended to be low. The Packard, with its $1,200 price tag, was beyond the reach of the lower-income groups, and in a small town or rural community there might be only three or four Packard owners. Ford, Chevrolet, and Plymouth, on the other hand, were popular in these markets, and it was a small town, indeed, that lacked dealers in these lines.

General Motors, Ford, and Chrysler produced makes of cars to fit most budgets, but the independents — Packard, Reo, and Pierce-Arrow, for example — found it impossible to maintain dealerships in small towns. These manufacturers relied instead on distributorships that were located in large cities and supplied cars to small-town "dealers," often local service stations or garages that sold on order only.

Dealers, in contrast, held franchises and maintained inventories of automobiles. The market was sliced up by the individual manufacturers into segments; a medium-sized town might have dealerships that sold two lines of cars only: Chevrolet/Oldsmobile or Buick/Cadillac or Buick/Pontiac, for instance. Chrysler might match up Dodge/Plymouth or Chrysler/Plymouth or Dodge trucks/Dodge cars or De Soto/Plymouth. Ford, since it had so many dealers and sold so many Ford cars and trucks compared to smaller companies, generally preferred dealers to offer the full line of Ford vehicles, although it was clear that few Lincolns would be sold in small communities. Only in the largest cities would one find dealers selling luxury cars and, only in the very largest, dealers in Rolls-Royce, Mercedes-Benz, and other costly European cars.

Source: Charles E. Edwards, *Dynamics of the United States Automobile Industry* (Columbia: University of South Carolina Press, 1965).

Source:
Alfred D. Chandler Jr., *Giant Enterprise: Ford, General Motors and the Automobile Industry* (New York: Harcourt, Brace & World, 1964).

## INDUSTRY: RADIO AND BROADCASTING

**Beginnings.** The development of radio and radio broadcasting caught the public fancy. During the *Titanic* disaster in 1912, the radios on the sinking ship and the various rescue boats played such a significant role in communicating events that David Sarnoff, a young New York telegraph operator handling the incoming signals, as well as other listeners, had visions of commercial radio being used for information and entertainment. In 1920 KDKA in Pittsburgh became the first radio station to enter commercial broadcasting; Sarnoff would, in the 1920s, give form to the Radio Corporation of America, which would become a star performer on the New York Stock Exchange.

**Costs.** Like the auto and the airplane, early radio was a crude affair, expensive and thought to be a toy of the rich; yet one of the attractions of the radio-broadcasting industry was that it could, in fact, be entered with a relatively small amount of money. A radio station complete with transmitter and a small building could be provided for a modest sum — perhaps $20,000 — an amount roughly equal to the cost of a small retail store. The greatest expense in broadcasting was for the technical expertise required to operate and maintain the equipment. It was clearly an advantage to operate as powerful a station as possible to increase the area covered by the signal.

**Mission.** The industry required some time to discover just what its mission was. Many of the early entrants were ham operators or former employees of the early wireless operators who envisioned the radio primarily as a means for conveying news and other general information. The idea that the radio might be used as a medium for entertainment or advertising had not yet taken hold. By the end of the decade, however, radio networks were vying with motion pictures as entertainment vehicles and had become major competitors with daily newspapers for the advertising dollar. From 1921 to 1929 the value of radios owned in the nation rose from $10.6 million to $411 million, a clear indication that the medium was fulfilling its mission of conveying news, entertainment, and advertisements throughout the United States.

**Issues.** Radio encountered all manner of issues not faced by other industries. Almost as soon as broadcasting became widespread, operators discovered that they needed to avoid trespassing on each other's frequencies lest the broadcasts become a mishmash of overlapping programs; with the encouragement of Herbert Hoover, who had established a bureau in his Department of Commerce to assist the pioneer industry, broadcasters embraced federal regulation as a means of eliminating congestion of the airways. Moreover, operators realized that if the radio were effectively to cover either general news or special national events such as presidential inaugurations, it needed to be coordinated through the development of networks. These networks would help in the dispersal not only of news stories but also of advertising. In addition, the radio industry understood that it must deal with such First Amendment issues as those raised by political or religious broadcasts.

KDKA Pittsburgh broadcasting the Harding-Cox election returns, 2 November 1920

**Electric Devices and Utilities.** Parallel to the manufacture of radios was the production of other electric devices — toasters, ranges, and refrigerators, for example. The industries that developed to manufacture these devices stimulated the demand for electricity, and the value of equipment to manufacture and distribute power rose from $809 million in 1921 to $2.3 billion in 1930. Investment in stocks and bonds related to electric utilities became one of the most important and popular elements in the bull market. The rapidly growing utilities were a fertile ground for consolidation and one of the most important segments of the emerging holding companies (companies that did not perform operations but simply owned and financially controlled working companies). Unfortunately, these holding companies were subject to abuse, although most of their flaws were not disclosed until the next decade.

Sources:

Neil Baldwin, *Edison: Inventing the Century* (New York: Hyperion, 1995);

Eugene Lyons, *David Sarnoff: A Biography* (New York: Harper & Row, 1966).

## LABOR: WORKERS AND UNIONS

**Skilled and Unskilled Workers.** The prosperity of the decade was generally shared by industrial workers in the form of relatively high wages and full employment; prosperity was not, however, universal, and certainly times were not good for unions. In part, unions did not thrive because they had for years concentrated their organizational efforts on workers who were members of skilled crafts — printers, carpenters, machinists, and the like; the group had, in fact, been the focus of the American Federation of Labor, which dated from the 1870s. As a consequence the unionized workers were concentrated in two major areas of the labor force, the railroads (through the railroad brotherhoods) and the skilled trades. The rising mass-production industries were not friendly to unions; their workers were largely unskilled (working on assembly lines was not a highly skilled trade), and many of these workers were recent arrivals from the rural South or immigrants from Europe.

**Unions.** Although the union movement would shake the mass-production industries during the 1930s, its growth would require a considerable shift in public opinion, which tended to be unsympathetic if not hostile toward unions in the 1920s. Many rural and small-town Americans considered unions a "foreign" influence; most envisioned union leaders as radical, bearded, bomb-throwing aliens, an image that was both a product and a cause of the Red Scare early in the decade. Moreover, farmers and small businessmen were resentful of the high wages that labor had commanded during the war.

**Industrial Workers.** The nation was experiencing the dislocations stemming from the shift from small- to large-scale industry. While employment in industry was growing, jobs in agriculture were shrinking rapidly, and population shifts from rural areas to the industrial sector were taking place. Instead of remaining on the land or learning a skilled trade, many men were entering factories to build autos, aircraft, or electrical equipment. Small towns were shrinking; small business was on the decline.

Young men who a decade before would have graduated from high school and learned a skilled trade were now joining the workforce of large industry. It was not easy for workers to fathom or to cope with the rapid changes in their world. Wages were fairly good, especially for people with little education or training; but while they paid quite well, these jobs were often unpleasant and almost always boring. They were also often unstable, with frequent layoffs and little possibility of advancement.

**How They Fared.** There were wide variations in how well segments of the workforce fared. Blacks did poorly. Many who had migrated to the North during the war to take industrial jobs now found themselves off the payroll; many of them had little or no education, and most fell victim to discriminatory labor policies. Farmworkers were in oversupply, and with the end of the war, workers in many of the basic industries, such as steel and mining, found few openings. During the war large numbers of women moved into industrial work, but for the most part they generally returned to their traditional "woman's work" when the war ended.

**Women.** Nor did women in any numbers take up professional work, other than teaching and nursing. Few women were found in law and medicine, fewer still in engineering, and not many in high-level administrative jobs in industry, except in the guise of administrative assistants, who were paid more than traditional secretaries. Few thought it wrong that men most often were paid more than women for the same work or that men were almost always put into higher positions than women of equal training. These attitudes also were reflected in higher education where, despite the move to coeducation, almost no women were found in the professional schools, outside education, and where even there most of them were destined to teach in secondary schools.

**Skilled Workers.** But workers skilled in industrial production — electricians, tool makers, and various other trades — were doing well. For the first time in the nation's history, workers were buying cars, houses, and a wide variety of consumer goods. Factory parking lots were filled with automobiles, and workers' homes boasted radio sets, electric stoves, and other products hitherto considered to be restricted to the higher income groups. Technical high schools were flourishing. Engineering schools were full. Completely new trades and professions were being established: automotive engineering, petroleum engineering, aeronautical engineering. On the trade level, capable auto mechanics were in demand and well paid; salesmen of all kinds, especially auto salesmen, enjoyed considerable success. Young women who had typing and office machine skills were doing relatively well; chain stores were hiring young women, albeit at low wages. Banks and brokerage houses were hiring in large numbers, and good securities salesmen were able to make large incomes.

## WAGES AND SALARIES

**W**ages and salaries varied widely during the decade. Manufacturing jobs generally paid well — $1,100 to $1,200 per year — though they were also affected by frequent layoffs. Farming paid poorly, with the average farmworker receiving $500 to $600 annually, though he might also save money by growing his own food. Most office workers earned around $1,200 — unless they were female and therefore brought home only $800 to $900 per year. Salaries for public-school teachers varied widely, but most earned $800 to $1,000 for nine months' service; college faculty collected between $1,200 and $1,800 for filling junior positions, $3,500 and $4,500 for attaining senior positions. Skilled tradesmen — carpenters, mechanics, and the like — pulled down about one dollar per hour, store clerks earned fifteen to twenty cents per hour, and bank clerks brought home about $25 weekly. Middle-level management positions averaged about $3,600 a year.

**Source:** U.S. Department of Labor, Bureau of Labor Statistics (1931).

Source:

David A. Shannon, *Twentieth Century America* (Chicago: Rand, McNally, 1963).

### THE MODERN CORPORATION

**History.** The years 1920–1930 were years of great growth and development for corporations. The corporation was, of course, not new; it had been used since the Middle Ages in Europe and since colonial days in America. But Americans had always distrusted the corporation, regarding it as a prelude to monopoly. The Sherman Anti-Trust Act of 1890 was an expression of their doubts, but aside from the Standard Oil case in 1911 and perhaps the Northern Securities case in 1904, the act had little impact after the end of the Theodore Roosevelt "trust busting" era, at least until the days of the New Deal. The formation of U.S. Steel by J. P. Morgan in 1901 had raised controversy, but by the time the case reached the courts in 1920 the judiciary had adopted the "rule of reason," holding that the matter of size or market share per se was not the sole factor in measuring monopoly power. Many large corporations were not by this reasoning "predatory." Although by the 1930s this doctrine had been abandoned, it in effect made the formation of large-scale business during the 1920s much easier from a standpoint of public policy.

**Purposes of the Corporation.** Clearly steel, auto manufacturing, and other large-scale industries could not be effective if they were organized on the principles of the corner grocery store. During the 1920s the modern corporation took on something of a new personality. Whereas in the early years of the century the goal of the large corporation was essentially the control of markets and the increase of power, its purposes now became maximization of efficiency and profit. J. P. Morgan had organized the United States Steel Corporation to monopolize the highly fragmented steel and wire business in order to control the market, and his methods had been brutal. The independents would join the corporation, or they would be frozen out. To be sure, the goal of W. C. Durant in organizing General Motors was to make money; however, the corporation was also organized to promote efficiency in production, and in a decade it became the model of corporate efficiency. Unfortunately Durant became entangled in speculation and was forced out, but he had laid the groundwork for GM. Alfred P. Sloan, who succeeded Durant, was typical of the new businessman, primarily manager and promotor rather than investor. U.S. Steel created a half dozen or so millionaires who sold out their original holdings; GM, on the other hand, made hundreds of thousands of stockholders comfortable amounts of money and set a pattern for management efficiency well into the future.

**Forms of Corporations.** The corporations of the nineteenth century were like the Ford Motor Company, closely held. During his lifetime Henry Ford owned 51 percent of the shares and ran the huge company like a family business insofar as decisions were concerned. In fact, the Ford Motor Company was a family business, although technically it was a corporation; but until long after Henry Ford died, no Ford shares were held by the public, only by the family. In contrast, GM, AT&T, General Foods, Standard Oil, RCA, and many other modern corporations had thousands of stockholders and were run by professional managers under boards of directors.

Source:
John Kenneth Galbraith, *The New Industrial State* (Boston: Houghton Mifflin, 1971).

## RETAIL TRADE AND MARKETING

**Changes.** The decade brought great changes in the product distribution system. Wholesaling generally declined in importance, and retailing increased. Chain stores came onto the scene, and department stores consolidated and assumed new importance. Many of these changes resulted from advancements in transportation and the growth of the suburbs. Increasing use of the automobile enabled consumers to shop beyond the confines of the immediate neighborhood, and this development had a negative impact on the corner store. Rising disposable incomes to many workers, increasing home ownership, and ascending levels of education created a wider and deeper consumer market.

**Growth of Chain Stores.** The chain-store movement grew rapidly as the 1920s passed. In 1912 only a handful

---

### J. C. PENNEY'S STORE

James Cash Penney (1875–1971) was probably the best-known retail merchant in the land. He got his start in Wyoming and at the height of his career operated the largest chain dry-goods business in the nation. His principles included cash-and-carry, profit sharing and stock ownership for managers, and high-quality but moderately priced goods. His stores were most often found in small communities.

Penney's store was always located downtown, usually on the main street; it was managed by a man and staffed by women. Its staples were men's work and dress clothing, women's and children's clothing and shoes, cloth sold by the yard, sewing supplies and patterns, stockings, and underwear. In small towns the store was a meeting place for housewives, and hours were designed to attract working folks.

Penney's was known as a good place for young men to begin a mercantile career; the company's policy was to hire promising youth just out of high school, train them, and place them in a store manager's job where they usually stayed for some time and became active in community affairs before being moved to larger stores. Penney lived to age ninety-five. By 1929 he had 1,495 stores and, by 1971, 1,660.

Sources: Beatrice Plumb, *J.C. Penney, Merchant Prince: A Biography of a Man Who Built a Business Enterprise on the Golden Rule* (Minneapolis: Denison, 1963);

Marvin Traub, *Like No Other Store: The Bloomingdale Legend* (New York: Times Books, 1993).

---

of firms had multiple outlets in more than one state, but by 1927 there were some 1,500 such firms operating nearly 70,000 outlets. The A & P, Kroger, and other food chains opened dozens of stores each week. Hotels (Statler), drugstores (Walgreen), candy stores (Fanny Farmer), and restaurants (Child's) became familiar landmarks in every part of the country. By 1927 W. T. Grant operated 109 outlets, Kresge 425, J. C. Penney (which served many small towns) more than 1,000 stores, and F. W. Woolworth more than 1,500. The growth in the number of chain stores was in part facilitated by the emergence of the truck, which was able to provide more flexible and less costly shipping for small lots than was the railroad.

**Chain-Store Employment Advantages.** Chain stores afforded their employees certain benefits not generally available elsewhere. Managers and other key personnel were allowed to purchase stock in the chain, and for many people this was an estate-building opportunity that was lacking in the traditional small business; J. C. Penney, in particular, was known for this fringe benefit. The chain store also provided the opportunity for a hardworking younger manager to move up in the chain, progressing from one store to another and increasing his responsibilities and earning potential.

**Chain Opponents.** The chains provided fierce competition for traditional merchants and mail-order houses. Many local merchants, especially in the South, tried to fight back with "fair-trade" legislation barring "loss leaders" and other chain tactics, but for the most part these antichain campaigns failed. The small-town drugstore and the "ma and pa" grocery were hardest hit by the emergence of the chain stores, though the chains also seriously impacted on the large mail-order houses that had flourished late in the nineteenth century. Sears, Roebuck and Montgomery Ward, which had served generations of farmers via the parcel post, began to languish, although Sears would, in the future, shift to the shopping-center pattern and become the nation's largest retailer.

**Department Stores.** In big cities major department stores became more luxurious and grew rapidly, especially through merger and consolidation. In New York, Saks Fifth Avenue opened with window displays of $1,000 raccoon coats, chauffeur livery, and a $3,000 pigskin trunk. Gimbel Brothers acquired Kaufman's in Pittsburgh, and in 1929 Lazarus Brothers founded Federated Department Stores by taking over Abraham & Straus, Filenes, Bullocks (on the West Coast), and other chains nationwide.

**Charge Accounts, Advertising.** By the middle of the decade both charge accounts and advertising had grown in importance. Most large department stores began to offer revolving credit on a contractual basis, although small neighborhood stores had offered credit informally for many years. Advertising, especially by radio, effectively boosted retail sales. Advertising became a specialty, and advertising firms, like law firms and accounting firms, began to move into the commercial world, where they offered their services in the creation of local and nationwide advertising campaigns. A newly developed field of psychology offered scientific advice in the psychology of advertising, especially for products sold to women.

**Marketing Science.** Just as scientific management had invaded the shop floor, marketing science invaded the sales floor and the advertising agency. The newly risen collegiate schools of business began to offer marketing as a field of study. The "drummer" of the 1890s was replaced by a young Harvard man or a University of Pennsylvania marketing consultant who spoke about such esoteric matters as "motivation" and "consumptionism."

**Responses.** The new marketing methods both appealed to and distressed customers. Many missed the personal atmosphere of the small store and disliked having to pick out their own merchandise to take to the checkout. But everyone had to admit that prices in the large outlets were lower and their products and services more varied than in the smaller stores. Perhaps the large-market concept reached its apogee in southern California where, by the latter part of the decade, the giant markets covering several full blocks arose. These huge stores combined farmers' markets, grocery outlets, and restaurants with such other amenities as movie theaters, bowling alleys, and child-care facilities.

Sources:

Leon A. Harris, *Merchant Princes: An Intimate History of Jewish Families Who Built Great Department Stores* (New York: Harper & Row, 1979);

William Leach, *Land of Desire* (New York: Pantheon, 1993);

Marvin Traub, *Like No Other Store: The Bloomingdale Legend* (New York: Times Books, 1993).

## SPECULATION IN LAND: THE FLORIDA BOOM AND CRASH

**Conditions.** Florida before the 1920s was a relatively undeveloped state. It was almost devoid of industry, except for agriculture and tourism, and it had an extremely shaky financial system. Economic development was largely in the hands of outsiders, speculators such as Standard Oil's Henry M. Flagler, who was a promoter of the Florida East Coast Railroad and builder of luxury hotels and resorts in the state.

**Promotion.** In the early 1920s Florida became increasingly attractive to Americans from other parts of the country. With its warm winters, exotic landscapes and seascapes, inexpensive real estate, and low cost of living, it seemed to be a paradise. Thus began a land rush southward from the cold, overpopulated northeastern states, propelled by newly adopted methods of promotion and publicity coming into use during the decade. Newspapers, radio commercials, elaborate brochures, and even William Jennings Bryan, who had been hired to promote Coral Gables, promised health, happiness, and prosperity with the purchase of a place in the Florida sun.

**Boom.** As middecade approached, development flourished, not only in luxury hotels but also in residential and commercial properties, many of them in the Miami area. Much of this development rested on a weak financial foundation with little supervision, a situation ripe for fraud and deception. Lots by the thousands were bought site unseen. Florida was a long way from the Northeast, where many prospective buyers lived, and thousands of customers signed contracts with nothing more than the word of a sales agent on the value and condition of the land they were buying. As the boom picked up steam, lots were sold for small amounts of money down and then were often immediately resold by their purchasers for higher prices; the profits they made would then be put into other Florida property, which would again be resold.

The cycle escalated; subdivisions were further subdivided as prices rose daily, if not hourly.

**Bust.** But by late 1925 the Florida boom was ending, impeded in part by cautionary articles in influential northern newspapers. The ardor of speculators and potential settlers began to cool. Then in September 1926 came the death blow. On the 18th of that month a hurricane of considerable force hit the eastern coast of the state, killing hundreds of people and causing enormous damage to the jerry-built houses strung out along the sea. In many ways the Florida land boom and crash predicted the financial boom and ultimate crash that would shake the financial structure of the nation three years later in October 1929.

Sources:
*The American Heritage History of the 20's and 30's* (New York: American Heritage, 1970);

Donald W. Curl, *Mizner's Florida: American Resort Architecture* (New York: Architectural History Foundation / Cambridge, Mass.: MIT Press, 1984).

## THE STOCK MARKET: BOOM

**Suspicion of Wall Street.** Before World War I only a small fraction of Americans had had anything to do with Wall Street and the securities markets. As the 1920s began, most Americans, especially those in the South and West, thought of Wall Street with fear and loathing. Populist politicians denounced the place as the center of financial shell games thought up by the likes of Vanderbilt, Gould, Drew, Morgan, and other millionaire operators. Middle-class citizens read in the newspapers about epic struggles among the superwealthy; but these common citizens were not part of the world of high finance, and most thought they never would be.

**New Interest in Wall Street.** With the conclusion of the war in 1918, however, many of them began to think again. Having been buyers of Liberty Bonds, they began to lose their fear of investing. Stockbrokers began to open offices not on Wall Street or LaSalle Street but on Main Street. Americans began to understand the advantages of investment and to become knowledgeable (or so they thought) about dividends, margin accounts, puts and calls, stock splits, and other esoteric stock-market concepts. Big corporations like U.S. Steel, General Electric, and General Motors offered common stock and bonds to a growing market; airlines, aircraft manufacturers, electric companies, radio corporations, steel- or copper-mining operations, and scores of other major industries were booming as never before and hungry for investment funds.

**Investment Opportunities.** There were certainly no good reasons for most investors to be alarmed at these growing opportunities or to shy away from them. General Motors, AT&T, Radio Corporation of America, Kennecott, U.S. Steel, and others were expanding rapidly to meet growing demand. They were stable firms honestly and capably run, producing good products, and offering thousands of jobs. To be sure, there was some evidence that investors were often uninformed or apt to go off on wild goose chases. For example, the Lindbergh flight generated a huge increase in sales of airline and aircraft stocks, and when stocks in Seaboard Air Line Railroad shot up on the market, Seaboard officials concluded that investors thought the company was an airline instead of a southeastern railroad.

**Investment Trusts.** Around middecade a new financial vehicle, the investment trust, offered a new approach to playing the market. Well known in Great Britain but not previously used in the United States, the investment trust was ideal for the unsophisticated investor who was sold mutual funds made up of the securities of various firms. Because all the stock-market research was done by professionals, the investor did not himself need to have knowledge of individual companies or the market. Moreover, if some of the companies whose stock was represented by the fund did poorly, others might do well; if all did well, so much the better. It was simply a matter of not putting all of one's eggs in one basket.

**Boom.** By 1929 the market was the center of conversation. It was talked about in the barbershop, the dining car, the locker room — everywhere, in every city. Many towns had brokerage offices located in lavish quarters in the best business building or on the ground floor of the most popular hotel, close at hand for traveling men. These offices were packed from 10:00 A.M. to 3:00 P.M., when the market closed. (On the West Coast brokers' offices were open from 7:00 A.M. until noon.) The rooms attracted a diverse crowd: retired schoolteachers, local tradesmen, professional men who dropped in on their lunch hours; all stood intently watching the board as clerks made continuous adjustments and the onlookers mentally calculated their gains for the day. Butlers, maids, hairdressers, waiters, and cabdrivers kept their ears open. Tales were told of nurses who were tipped off on good buys by grateful patients. No one was too far from a brokerage office to play the game. Cattle ranchers in Wyoming dealt with Denver brokers by telegraph; miners in Nevada left the saloons long enough to talk to their San Francisco brokerage offices; dowagers who had never made any pretense of being informed on business became avid devotees of the market.

**Market Madness.** By the summer of 1929 the financial community seemed to have taken leave of its collective sense. Men who developed a reputation for understanding the market became all-knowing. Academic economists began peddling their so-called expertise via the podium and the printed word. Hired by investment groups, some of them thereby lost what little credibility they might have had. Yale's Irving Fisher, a highly respected economist, predicted early in 1929 that "stock prices seem to have reached a permanent plateau," a statement he all too soon grew to regret. Any critical or cautionary statements were brushed off as spoilsport or worse — lack of faith in the U.S. economy, near treason. The banker Paul Warburg was regarded as beneath contempt for making mildly cautionary statements. Certainly it was hard to argue that trouble was on the way when during the summer months Westinghouse stock rose from 151 to 286, General Electric from 268 to 391, and U.S. Steel from 165 to 258. Even such a conservative stock as AT&T (recommended for widows and orphans) went from 209 to 303. And investment trusts also soared: Allegheny Corporation rose from 33 to 56. Summer was by custom a quiet time in the financial world; Wall Street nearly shut down. Brokers, bankers, and lawyers went to Newport, or traveled abroad, or spent most of their time up the Hudson in their summer places. But not in the summer of 1929. Brokers were too busy merely handling the paperwork that had become a serious problem. Back offices were snowed under with orders, most of them to buy. As the summer passed, offices worked through the weekends as well as into the night, as trading volume rose to new heights.

**Warning Signs.** Toward the end of summer, although the market continued to boom, certain warning signs began to appear. The number of shares traded rose to unheard-of heights — 4.4 million shares on 3 September (a small figure by today's standards but huge in 1929) — and still the market rose. AT&T shot to 304, U.S. Steel to 262, GE to 396, J. I. Case to 350, New York Central to 256, and RCA to 505. But brokers' loans, a critical sign, reached $137 million, and New York banks were in debt to the Federal Reserve $64 million. Throughout the nation were thousands of investors working on margin: buying stock on credit. This situation was tolerable if the market was rising but a disaster if the market started to fall, as many would soon learn.

Stock ticker invented by Thomas A. Edison

**Yellow Lights and Confusion.** The bull market seemed to be weakening, though signs were ambiguous. Most stocks continued to rise, and the volume of trading remained high. Cautious traders noted that the call-money rate — the rate banks charged for money subject to be paid "on call," or whenever lenders demanded it — went to 9 percent. This development was generally taken as a yellow light. On 5 September Roger Babson, a market analyst, warned that sooner or later a crash was on the way. Other figures such as Joseph P. Kennedy were quietly selling off stocks; Kennedy told associates that when he heard his hotel shoeshine boy dispensing market advice, he knew the time had come to get out. Information was becoming increasingly unreliable. The securities industry's paperwork, which was adequate for preboom conditions, was on the verge of collapse. The stock ticker, a machine that printed stock quotations on tape across the nation, was frequently behind the market in recording the quotations. In addition, while there was a vast flow of information spewing from the press on a daily basis, it was confusing and unreliable. Bankers, brokers, economics professors, clergymen, newspapermen, and others with no real credentials had little hesitation about giving advice, often completely in contradiction to the advice of other alleged experts. It was time to get out, some said. Nonsense, it was time to increase one's holdings, others countered.

| INDUSTRIAL AVERAGES FOR OCTOBER 1929 | | | |
|---|---|---|---|
| Date | Last | Net change | Day's sales |
| 1 | 431.13 | -4.06 | 4,524,810 |
| 2 | 434.66 | +3.53 | 3,367,610 |
| 3 | 415.14 | -19.52 | 4,747,330 |
| 4 | 408.64 | -6.50 | 5,634,900 |
| 5 | 424.96 | +16.32 | 2,451,870 |
| 6 | (Sunday) | | |
| 7 | 432.85 | +7.89 | 4,261,900 |
| 8 | 437.43 | +4.66 | 3,758,090 |
| 9 | 439.84 | +2.39 | 3,156,740 |
| 10 | 446.49 | +6.63 | 3,999,730 |
| 11 | 443.07 | -1.42 | 3,963,820 |
| 12 | (Holiday) | | |
| 13 | (Sunday) | | |
| 14 | 442.77 | -2.30 | 2,755,850 |
| 15 | 440.83 | -1.94 | 3,107,050 |
| 16 | 427.73 | -13.10 | 4,088,000 |
| 17 | 434.56 | +6.83 | 3,864,150 |
| 18 | 427.36 | -7.20 | 3,507,740 |
| 19 | 415.18 | -12.18 | 3,488,100 |
| 20 | (Sunday) | | |
| 21 | 409.23 | -5.95 | 6,091,870 |
| 22 | 415.07 | +5.84 | 4,129,820 |
| 23 | 384.10 | -30.97 | 6,374,960 |
| 24 | 371.91 | -12.19 | 12,894,650 |
| 25 | 372.66 | +0.75 | 5,923,220 |
| 26 | 367.42 | -5.25 | 2,087,660 |
| 27 | (Sunday) | | |
| 28 | 318.29 | -49.12 | 9,212,800 |
| 29 | 275.26 | -43.03 | 16,410,030 |
| 30 | 306.21 | +30.95 | 10,727,320 |
| 31 | 327.12 | +20.91 | 7,149,390 |

Source: *New York Times*, 1–31 October 1929.

Sources:

Bernard Baruch, *The Public Years* (New York: Holt, Rinehart & Winston, 1960);

S. H. Harris, *Twenty Years of Federal Reserve Policy* (Cambridge, Mass.: Harvard University Press, 1933);

John Maynard Keynes, *The General Theory of Employment, Interest and Money* (London: Macmillan, 1936);

Joseph Stagg Lawrence, *Wall Street and Washington* (Princeton: Princeton University Press, 1929);

George Soule, *Prosperity Decade: From War to Depression, 1917–1929* (New York: Rinehart, 1947).

## THE STOCK MARKET: CRASH

**Signs.** Although the signs had been clear for months, the crash clearly took many by surprise, perhaps because of the conflicting information to which they had been exposed or perhaps because of their own wishful thinking. The beginning of the end came quietly. In October freight-car loadings and housing starts, key economic indicators of the time, began to decline. As many later noted, the crash did not occur because investors suddenly decided it was time to leave but because they were pushed out. On the stock exchange, business seemed to be relatively normal; shares traded were in the four- to five-million range. But in September brokers' loans increased to $670 million — a good sign because it indicated there was still substantial interest in the market and a bad sign because it increased the outstanding balance of these volatile loans.

**Ominous Signs.** On 23 October two ominous events occurred: sales totaled six million shares, an enormous amount, and investors throughout the country began to discover how little they knew of what was afoot. The ticker fell more than an hour behind events, and by the end of the day investors had to wait an hour and forty minutes to know how much they had made or lost. Unfortunately, if they had lost, the delay often made it impossible to do anything about it, a plight especially alarming to those outside Manhattan who felt cut off from events. Many investors began to realize that they could be wiped out and not know it for several days. Thousands of orders to buy or sell had piled up in back offices. In 1929 office methods were still quite primitive: books were largely kept by hand, and there were no computers, no electronic transfers of funds. This situation was especially serious to people trading on margin.

**Margin Trading.** When the market was rising, margin trading had seemed like a magical way of making money. The margin trader bought stock by paying less than the full price (borrowing the margin — the difference — from the broker). If the customer paid 90 percent and a few days after the purchase the stock rose by a dozen points, the margin could be covered easily and a profit made. At this point the customer might pay off the margin, sell the stock, and get out, or he might pay off the margin, keep the stock, and increase his holdings by using the margin again. But this sort of account was extremely risky. If the stock fell, the customer had to put up more money to sustain the account. In the worst case, if the stock kept falling, the customer ultimately ran out of cash, and the broker, who in most cases had himself borrowed money from his banker, was forced to sell out

STAGE  BROADWAY  SCREEN

*VARIETY*

PRICE 25¢.

Published Weekly at 154 West 46th St., New York, N. Y., by Variety, Inc. Annual subscription, $10. Single copies, 25 cents.
Entered as second-class matter December 22, 1905, at the Post Office at New York, N. Y., under the act of March 3, 1879.

VOL. XCVII. No. 3          NEW YORK, WEDNESDAY, OCTOBER 30, 1929          88 PAGES

# WALL ST. LAYS AN EGG

The show-business newspaper printed this headline the day after the stock-market crash.

the account for what he could get. The greater the margin, the greater the difficulty when the market began to fall. If the customer could not pay the broker, the broker was unable to pay the banker, and all parties fell like a house of cards.

**Dangers of the Margin.** As the summer passed, there were increasing numbers of margin calls (delivered in uniquely distinguishable brown envelopes or, as matters deteriorated, by telephone). As stocks fell and the value of the buyers' holdings declined, they had to be "covered" by additional margins. Investors who had sufficient funds to pay the margin remained undisturbed, and brokers were relaxed and polite. There was really no problem, they said; it was just a matter of straightening out a few loose ends. If the customer continued to have the money to cover the margin, that statement was true. But as matters grew more serious for both investors and brokers, the calls became less polite. The brokers were desperate for cash to pay their banks. The banks were desperate to pay the federal lenders or the out-of-town banks whose spare cash they had poured into the call market.

**Collapse.** Thus, the slide turned into total collapse. The banks wanted their money from the brokers. The brokers wanted their money from the customers. The only way most customers could get the money was to sell the stock, and selling the stock depressed the market even more, increasing pressure all along the line. Again panic was fed by a shortage of information; the prices quoted on the ticker lagged well behind the actual prices on the exchange floor. On the evening of Thursday, 24 October, the ticker did not fall silent until eight and one-half minutes past 7:00 P.M., more than four hours after the market had closed. Nobody knew what current prices were or what they would be in the morning after some overnight revaluation had been made. The rancher in Wyoming might just as well have been in Tibet, but the

broker in Manhattan was little better off. On this one business day — 24 October 1929 — all the unthinkable crises and nightmares that had threatened during the preceding weeks came to pass.

**Prelude.** The day began quietly. Many brokers and bankers arrived in the Wall Street area early and found that the place was already crowded, not only with their colleagues, many of whom had spent the night in their offices or in nearby hotels, but also with a large number of customers and depositors, who were clearly in a hostile mood, although little was said. Obviously the crowd was frightened and confused by what was going on. One young broker from E. F. Hutton found the entrance to the stock exchange already crowded, and when the doorman recognized him and let him in, there was a rumble of displeasure from the throngs outside.

**Churchill.** On the exchange floor as the 10 A.M. opening hour neared, William Crawford, the longtime superintendent of the Exchange, received a call from Richard Whitney, acting president of the Exchange. Fearing that Whitney would close the Exchange, Crawford was relieved to find that the message concerned a visit from the British politician Winston Churchill, who was expected in midmorning. Crawford privately thought that Churchill might have picked a better day.

**Disaster.** For the first half hour after the opening bell had sounded, the situation looked somewhat better, but the resulting optimism was short-lived; by 10:45 A.M. the anemic recovery was over. Soon, communications broke down completely. Not only did the ticker begin to lag but switchboards were jammed, and bankers and brokers found that a call downstairs or across the street took a half hour to complete and that long-distance calls were nearly impossible. Immediately, huge blocks of stock were tendered for what they would bring, and after two and one-half hours had passed, sales had reached 12,894,650, more than twice the previous day's sales.

**Chaos.** By 11:00 A.M. the floor was a madhouse, as noisy as a steel mill. Crawford, a man who took his job seriously, noted that the rules of the Exchange were being violated on a wholesale basis. The rules in question prohibited traders on the floor from "shouting," "being coatless," "shoving," "running," or "cursing," and, so far as he could see, almost all the members were doing all of the above. But there were a few who appeared calm and collected, including John "Black Jack" Bouvier, future father-in-law of John F. Kennedy. Despite the few cool heads in the room, the air was filled with shouts to "sell at the market" — though no one knew what the market was at any given time.

**National Response.** In Detroit, Charles S. Mott, then chairman of GM, had laid careful plans for a stock-market emergency, but now his New York broker told him that almost nothing could be done from Detroit. In San Francisco, banker A. P. Giannini was holed up in his private hideaway in the Mark Hopkins Hotel. In New York, executive John J. Raskob, who weeks earlier had declared that everyone should be rich, was glued to the ticker, as were Joseph P. Kennedy and the "great bear" operator Jesse Livermore.

**Recovery Efforts.** At noon Acting President Whitney directed that the public gallery be closed (Churchill had already left), and at about the same time the leading bankers met to devise a plan, although they had some difficulty getting to the Morgan offices because of the crowd. En route they tried as best they could to radiate confidence, and rumors circulated that they and their banks would mount a rescue operation from the Morgan offices at 23 Wall Street. At 1:15 P.M. Richard Whitney, the bankers' representative, walked calmly onto the trading floor. Superintendent Crawford braced himself, thinking that Whitney would close the market, but instead he walked to the steel post and inquired politely, but in a loud voice to be heard over the bedlam, what the current price was. He was informed that it was 195. He ordered ten thousand shares at 205, and in the instantaneous hush he walked from post to post, ordering large blocks of choice issues.

**Whitney.** The bankers could hardly have chosen a better representative. A tall and handsome Harvard graduate with a patrician air, Whitney was Morgan's floor trader, and his elder brother, George, was a highly respected Morgan partner; the younger Whitney was clearly Morgan's man. Few men liked Richard Whitney — he was a consummate snob with a reputation for less than total honesty — but they had to respect him and his connections. (In 1938 he pleaded guilty to two indictments for grand larceny for looting his wife's estate and was sentenced to five-to-ten years in Sing Sing on each count. Always called "Mr. Whitney" by the prison staff and his fellow inmates, he was paroled three years later and lived comfortably until his death on 5 December 1974.) His performance on 24 October 1929 was, of course, great drama, but although the market briefly rallied, Whitney's gesture had no lasting effect. Later in the day, Thomas Lamont, head of the Morgan bank and an icon on Wall Street, received the press and talked bravely, but all to no avail.

**Terrible Reality.** The bankers were, in fact, in an impossible situation; to do what they knew should be done required them to act against their interests. Their instincts told them to sell, to get out from under as soon as possible. What the bankers had done on Thursday was to help restore some of the losses with the hope that further selling would stop; but that did not happen. Thursday's sales of close to thirteen million shares was followed by Friday sales of nearly six million shares, and the bankers (many of whom were not themselves as well-off as many thought) would have been superhuman if they had not joined the selling parade. The following Tuesday, 29 October — "Black Tuesday" — is regarded as one of the most devastating days in economic history, with 16,410,030 shares sold. By the evening of the 29th, no one had any illusions that the crisis was just a minor "adjustment" that would soon pass. The next day's edition of the show-business paper, *Variety*, summed it up, "WALL ST. LAYS AN EGG."

**Myths.** Not all stocks became worthless, and not everyone went flat broke. Over the next weeks some stocks rallied but remained far from their high points. Sound stocks like GM, U.S. Steel, and RCA still had value, and after a time they again became salable. But, sadly, many small investors were in fact wiped out, most of them caught in the margin trap. According to folklore, dozens of brokers jumped to their deaths from Manhattan skyscrapers. That story was largely mythical, though Edward Stone, a widely known broker, was forcibly restrained from jumping by his wife and his daughter. Rumors also flew of office boys making bids on good stock at fire-sale prices and having them accepted in the absence of other bids; but few of these accounts were really true.

**Bankers and Brokers.** One truth did emerge: bankers and brokers who had been lionized since the market boom began were now out of fashion. They were no longer invited to present commencement addresses, presented with honorary degrees, or featured in laudatory interviews. Instead they faced grillings from congressional committees and, in some cases, charges of mismanagement or even criminal prosecution. Never again in their lifetimes would the market or their positions be the same.

Sources:

John Brooks, *Once in Golconda* (New York: Norton, 1969);

John Kenneth Galbraith, *The Great Crash* (Boston: Houghton Mifflin, 1961);

Edwin Lefevre, *Reminiscences of a Stock Operator* (Garden City, N.Y.: Doubleday, 1930);

William E. Leuchtenburg, *The Perils of Prosperity, 1914–1932* (Chicago: University of Chicago Press, 1958);

Forrest McDonald, *Insull* (Chicago: University of Chicago Press, 1962);

Ferdinand Pecora, *Wall Street Under Oath* (New York: Simon & Schuster, 1939).

## THE STOCK MARKET: EFFECTS OF THE CRASH

**Improvements.** The weeks following the crash were surprisingly quiet. After the tumult died down, brokers directed their efforts to cleaning up the debris and bringing records up to date. To their surprise things looked better in many ways than they had expected. Although huge blocks of stock had been thrown onto the market willy-nilly, much of this stock was perfectly sound. It had been driven upward to artificially high levels by the bull market, and now it was artificially depressed by panic selling. When John D. Rockefeller Sr. announced that he and his sons were buying good common stocks, there were shouts of derision, and comedian Eddie Cantor responded, "Sure, who else has any money?"

**Bargains and Wariness.** But Rockefeller was right. Bargains were available, and although it might take weeks or months, the sound issues would rise. GM, RCA, U.S. Steel, and Pennsylvania Railroad, for example, were all still in business and their plants intact. Knowledgeable traders who had cash — Joseph P. Kennedy and Bernard Baruch, for example — were back in the market shopping carefully and picking up bargains. Yet they were in the minority. Many small speculators were not in any position to buy much at this point. Many were demoralized and for the rest of their lives refrained from any speculative activity or even credit transactions, such as borrowing money or taking out a mortgage on real estate.

**Other Americans.** Yet in the wake of the crash, the world west of the Hudson River was still there and still working. As strange as it may have seemed to the Wall Streeters, there were millions of Americans who cared not a whit for the stock market, who had never owned stocks and had no intention of ever doing so. Most of them had no market contacts and knew no one who had, and since most of them had incomes of less than $1,200 per year, they barely made ends meet, much less had funds to invest.

**Apparent Calm.** So far as they could see the crash of the market had no impact on them at all. They still had jobs. In most cases their bank accounts were sound, though there were exceptions. Some Michigan banks failed through overinvolvement in the auto industry, and some southern banks had suffered terrible losses in the call-money market, but relatively few banks closed their doors. Bank closings would not escalate until 1932. Moreover, stores and factories were still open and functioning. The big fuss seemed to involve only some rich folks in the East. In coffee shops and barbershops across

## IMMORTALITY FOR SALE

Joseph Duveen (1869–1939), who has been called the greatest salesman of his day, was an emblematic figure of the 1920s. Born in London to a large family of art dealers, Duveen (later Lord Duveen) was sent as a young man to New York to serve under his uncle, who headed the U.S. office of Duveen Brothers. For the next fifty years Joseph Duveen dominated the U.S. art market and had as his customers such tycoons as E. T. Stotesbury, William Randolph Hearst, S. H. Kress, Henry Goldman, Henry E. Huntington, and Andrew Mellon.

Duveen convinced the American millionaires that through the accumulation of fine art they could rise from the grubby world of trade and gain immortality by passing on their collections to posterity. He also convinced most of them that great art was available only from his firm and took it upon himself to tutor them in the more esoteric aspects of art collecting. He was a master salesman. Leaders of finance and industry lined up for the privilege of being his customers and, incidentally, for the right to pay the highest prices in the art world.

Duveen was instrumental in helping Huntington build his art collection for the world-famous Huntington Gallery and Library and was a principal influence on Mellon as he established the National Gallery of Art, to which Kress, under Duveen's counsel, added his own huge collection. As his biographer said, Duveen spent his career moving great art to the United States and American millionaires' fortunes to Europe.

**Source:** S. N. Behrman, *Duveen* (New York: Random House, 1952).

the land, conversations were more apt to center around the snappy new 1929 Chevrolet, GM's answer to the Ford Model A, and speculation about what Plymouth would think up in response.

**Hoover.** For the most part, ordinary Americans looked forward to the new decade with confidence in the economy. Herbert Hoover had been elected in 1928 by a margin of seven million votes, and so far things looked very good, indeed. Hoover was an engineer. He enjoyed a good reputation as an administrator and, since he had been food administrator under President Wilson, as a humanitarian. He was not a professional politician. He seemed to belong to the industrial scene of the decade: the spotless plants of the Ford Motor Company and the modern technology of the radio and aircraft industries. Hoover had lived in London for years and knew all about international finance; he was wealthy by his own efforts.

Born on the Iowa frontier in the 1870s, he was a Stanford graduate. The stock market aside, the decade had been good for the business community. Farmers were still not prosperous, but that was nothing new.

**Transition.** With the war a decade behind them, most Americans seemed to regard the 1920s as a transition period from war to full peace. Perhaps the 1930s would be a bit more organized and the new industries that had come on the scene fully integrated into the social and economic fabric.

**Building and Industrial Expansion.** Prosperity was still the order of the day. Hoover had taken office some eight months earlier, and so far the collapse of the market had almost no impact on building and on the future plans for industrial expansion. Hotels and office buildings were still under construction or on the drawing board. The Empire State Building, then the tallest structure in the world at 102 stories, was well underway. The aircraft, motor carrier, and radio industries were under development, and magazines were already speculating about something called television.

**Transportation.** Pullman traffic was at a high level, much of it business-related. In 1926 the New York Central had refurbished the *Twentieth-Century Limited* and assigned the famous Hudson-type locomotives to the train running on a sixteen-hour schedule between Chicago and New York. In 1926 the Central had transported more Pullman passengers than any other railroad, and the *Century* had grossed $10 million. Its archrival, the Pennsylvania Railroad, had achieved similar results with the *Broadway Limited.*

**Deluxe Cars.** High-priced automobiles were in great demand. Packard was doing well, as were Cadillac and Lincoln. Even more expensive makes — the Duesenberg, the Stutz, and the Pierce-Arrow — sold in respectable numbers. In fact, some new high-priced cars — the Willys Saint Claire and the Stearns-Knight — had recently been put on the market. The dealerships that sold these cars were palatial, the showrooms resembling lobbies in expensive hotels, with marble floors, mirrors, and potted palms. Except for Florida, where the bubble had burst in 1926, real estate was doing generally well. California — Los Angeles in particular — was booming.

**A Rosy Future.** Despite some isolated setbacks, the future of the economy seemed secure. The stock-market crash had been widely publicized — far too much, most people felt. Surely the new decade would be better. Certainly everyone said so.

Sources:

Karl Brunner, ed., *The Great Depression Revisited* (Boston: Martinus Nijhoff, 1981);

George Soule, *Prosperity Decade: From War to Depression, 1917–1929* (New York: Rinehart, 1947).

# HEADLINE MAKERS

## ROGER W. BABSON

### 1875-1967

#### PROGNOSTICATOR

**Speculator, Forecaster.** Roger W. Babson, a market speculator, gained fame as one of the few — including Joseph P. Kennedy — who forecast the market crash in 1929. He is often regarded as the "father" of the long line of market prognosticators, newsletter publishers, and other purveyors of financial information who have flourished over the years.

**Symbol.** In many ways Babson was symbolic of the extravagant era. He had been around Wall Street for years, but his background was never clear. He claimed to be an educator, philosopher, theologian, statistician, economist, and forecaster; he was clearly something of a con man. His forecasting methods, which involved charts, graphs, intersecting lines, and other hocus-pocus, were mysterious.

**Predictions.** Earlier in the decade Babson had predicted that if New York governor Alfred E. Smith were elected president in 1928, there would almost certainly be a serious depression, and on 5 September 1929 he noted that "sooner or later a crash is coming, and it may be terrific." When the crash did occur, Babson overnight became a prophet in his own land. Although earlier he had been largely ignored, he now gained a substantial following, and his Babson Institute and School of Management, his lectures, and his newsletters became staples of the financial world.

**Source:**
Irving Fisher, *The Stock Market Crash — and After* (New York: Macmillan, 1930).

# WALTER P. CHRYSLER

## 1881-1948

### AUTOMOTIVE TROUBLESHOOTER AND CONSOLIDATOR

**Early Years.** Even had Walter P. Chrysler not founded the corporation bearing his name, he would have been an important figure in heavy industry of the 1920s. Like Henry Ford, he rose rapidly from the ranks of labor; a machinist by trade, he worked in railroad shops for several years and eventually became general manager of the American Locomotive Company.

**Positions.** Drawn to the auto industry, he became something of a corporate "troubleshooter." In 1912 he took a position as works manager of Buick, a unit of General Motors, where he was named Buick president and General Motors vice president. After a brief retirement at the age of forty-five, he was asked to take over the troubled Willys-Overland Company but then moved on to the Maxwell Motor Company, which he renamed the Chrysler Corporation. By 1925 he had produced the first car bearing his own name.

**The Chrysler.** The Chrysler was an almost instant success; a mid- to upper-scale car, it sold for $1,595, the same as Buick. Its sales rose rapidly, but Chrysler desired to enlarge his line. In 1927 he developed and produced the lower-priced Plymouth, and in 1928 he acquired the Dodge Motor Company, which gave Chrysler a still-broader line of automobiles and made the corporation one of the so-called "big three."

**The Chrysler Building.** In 1929 Chrysler underwrote the construction of the magnificent seventy-seven-floor Chrysler Building in New York City, a skyscraper that immediately became an architectural landmark. Chrysler placed his toolbox with the handmade tools of his trade on display in the lobby.

**Sources:**
Walter P. Chrysler, *Life of an American Workman* (New York: Dodd, Mead, 1927);

Ralph Epstein, *The Automobile Industry: Its Economic and Commercial Development* (Chicago: University of Chicago Press, 1928).

# DONALD W. DOUGLAS

## 1892-1981

### PIONEER AIRCRAFT DEVELOPER

**Early Years.** A student at the U.S. Naval Academy in the early years of the century, Donald W. Douglas was inspired, by a demonstration of airplanes built by the Wright brothers, to transfer to MIT, where he studied aeronautical engineering and served as an instructor in the department. After graduation he joined the Glenn L. Martin Company in California, where he helped in the design and construction of a heavy bomber.

**Cloudster.** Douglas used his professional training and his skill at raising money to move rapidly into and upward in the aircraft industry. In 1920 he set up an office in a Los Angeles barbershop, and, with $40,000 in backing from sportsman David Davis, developed the *Cloudster*, a plane designed to fly across the country. The aircraft never actually achieved its goal, but it was the first plane in history able to carry a load that exceeded its own weight.

**Douglas Aircraft.** Bolstered by some navy contracts, Douglas incorporated his Douglas Aircraft Company in 1928. A few years later he made history with the DC-3, which was designed for the commercial airlines and represented a breakthrough in aircraft design. It was an airline workhorse for a decade or more and in its military version, the C-54, was a staple of the air force during World War II. Like the Model A Ford, Douglas's DC-3 seemed to go on forever and still flies in various parts of the world.

**Sources:**
Henry Ladd Smith, *Airways* (New York: Knopf, 1942);

Arch Whitehouse, *The Sky's the Limit: History of U.S. Airlines* (New York: Macmillan, 1971).

# PIERRE S. DU PONT

## 1870-1954

### AUTOMOTIVE INVESTOR

**Wide Interests.** Scion of the great chemical, gunpowder, and banking family, Pierre S. du Pont was one of the most successful businessmen and financiers of the 1920s. Active in the management of the Du Pont Company, he and the company had wide interests in other firms and finally took control of General Motors when William C. Durant was ousted in 1920.

**Venture Capital.** After World War I, the Du Pont Company, which had considerable cash on hand, began looking for what today would be called venture-capital possibilities, and GM looked attractive. The automobile industry was booming, and GM was the largest producer in the industry. Working through Pierre du Pont, the du Ponts became large holders in GM even before Durant's departure.

**Investment and Control.** Since GM had always been a major customer of the Du Pont Company, buying vast quantities of paint, finishes, man-made fabrics, and other such products, the automobile manufacturer seemed a wise investment possibility. Gradually, Pierre S. du Pont became a real force at GM and, when Durant's financial dealings appeared to become increasingly erratic, du Pont was a strong instrument in forcing out GM's founder and two-time president.

Sources:
Alfred D. Chandler Jr. and Stephen Salsbury, *Pierre S. duPont and the Making of the Modern Corporation* (New York: Harper & Row, 1971);

William S. Dutton, *DuPont: One Hundred and Thirty Years* (New York: Scribners, 1942).

## WILLIAM C. DURANT

### 1864-1947

#### AUTOMOTIVE PROMOTER

**Twenties Symbol.** The flamboyant William Crapo Durant became a symbol of the Roaring Twenties. Rising to great wealth and fame, he died in poverty and near obscurity as the result of his stock-market speculations. In 1908 he founded the General Motors Corporation, which became in the 1920s the largest corporation in the world. He was ousted as president of the company in 1910, regained control of it in 1916, and suffered a second ouster from GM in 1920.

**Promoter.** While Henry Ford and Walter P. Chrysler were production men, Durant was the epitome of the salesman and promoter, essentially a marketing specialist. But he also had a great eye for design and quality, putting together a line of cars that, under the GM banner, included Chevrolet, Pontiac, Oldsmobile, Buick, La Salle, and Cadillac.

**Flamboyance.** By the beginning of the decade GM was a company that attracted wide interest from investors and even more attention from a vast chain of suppliers. Durant was impatient and sometimes erratic in his methods. He disliked controls and rigidity, especially in financial matters, and he was apt to embrace innovative fi-

nancing methods if things moved too slowly. A great many officials, both inside and outside the firm, disliked this quality; they also felt that Durant was paying too much attention to his outside interests. Both factors contributed to his second ouster from GM. For a time Durant survived as an independent, manufacturing the Durant, a medium-priced car, and the Star, a lower-priced competitor to the Ford and to the GM Chevrolet, which Durant had originally developed.

**Aftermath.** Following Durant's departure, Pierre S. du Pont became GM's president with Alfred P. Sloan as manager. For several years the firm was essentially controlled by du Pont interests.

Sources:
Lawrence Gustin, *Billy Durant* (Grand Rapids, Mich.: Eerdmans, 1973);

Bernard M. Weisberger, *The Dream Maker* (Boston: Little, Brown, 1979).

## HENRY FORD

### 1863-1947

#### AUTOMOTIVE GENIUS

**Model T.** Henry Ford, a self-taught mechanical genius, was undoubtedly the most famous automaker and perhaps the most famous man of the era. Ford vastly improved the techniques of mass assembly and production and revolutionized the auto industry by producing the famous Model T, or "Tin Lizzie," an inexpensive, durable car that essentially democratized automobile ownership. The Model T, which was first produced in 1908 and remained in production until 1927, had sales of more than seventeen million during its nineteen years.

**Contradictions.** Ford was a man of many contradictions: an idealist who was a pacifist during World War I and health-food faddist all his life, he was also a pragmatist and sometime cynic; an obviously bright man, he also proved doggedly anti-intellectual, dismissing books and art as wastes of time. A would-be politician running for the Senate in 1918 and frequently mentioned as a presidential candidate, he did not have a politician's skills or instincts. His domain remained the auto industry.

**Ford Innovations.** In its early years the Ford Motor Company was considered a good place for labor. On 5 January 1914 Henry Ford introduced the five-dollar day and reduced the normal shift from nine to eight hours, innovations that generally horrified other industrialists but had obvious appeal for workers. He also became famous for his paternalistic Sociology Department, which attempted to offer humanitarian services to his workers but also closely monitored their private lives to be certain that they conformed to Ford's own standards.

He forbade his employees to smoke, for example, since he regarded tobacco as evil and disgusting.

**Twenties Accomplishments.** During the 1920s Ford and his company flourished. Journalists amused themselves by speculating on the size of his fortune, and, although he was often called the "last billionaire," he lived quite modestly compared to other tycoons. Between 1919 and 1927 his River Rouge production plant became a model of modern industrial design. In the early 1920s he bought Lincoln so that the Ford Motor Company could have and refine a luxury car and thus appeal to a different market from that of his Tin Lizzie. And his 1927 introduction of the replacement for Lizzie, the Model A, was one of the media events of the decade. During this period, too, Ford became a figure in aviation when he produced the fine Ford Tri-Motor aircraft. He personally hated to fly and did so only once, on a short flight piloted by Charles Lindbergh; he ultimately dropped the aviation operation after a crash in the early 1930s killed a pilot of whom he was fond.

**Final Years.** As Ford grew older he became more imperious. His one-man control of the giant corporation began to cause organizational difficulties, and the firm went into decline. During World War II Ford's son Edsel, who had been a stabilizing force in the company, died. Ford Motor Company was serving as a major military contractor, but its operations became so chaotic that officials felt it might be unable to meet its production goals. Consequently, the navy released young Henry Ford II, Henry Ford's grandson, from his military duties so that he could take leadership of the corporation. Under his direction Ford Motor Company was rebuilt and went public in 1961. It remains a major American auto producer in the mid 1990s.

Sources:

Harry Bennett, *We Never Called Him Henry* (New York: Fawcett, 1951);

Alan Nevins and Frank E. Hill, *Ford: Decline and Rebirth, 1933–1962* (New York: Scribners, 1962);

William C. Richards, *The Last Billionaire* (New York: Scribners, 1948);

Charles Sorenson, *My Forty Years With Ford* (New York: Norton, 1956).

# A. P. GIANNINI

## 1870-1949

### BANK OF AMERICA FOUNDER

**Early History.** A Californian of Italian descent, Amadeo Peter Giannini had in the early 1900s built his family produce business into a small bank. Looked down upon by the old-line San Francisco bankers as a newcomer, he was labeled the "Dago" banker. However, on the morning of 6 April 1906, when the great earthquake hit the city, he came into his own. His storefront Bank of Italy was destroyed almost immediately, but Giannini had secured $80,000 in his home, and with that money he opened a makeshift office tendering loans for rebuilding. The large downtown banks found their vaults covered with rubble or too hot from the fire to open, and weeks elapsed before they were back in business. Meanwhile, they were wiring New York banks for credit and cash while the Bank of Italy operated on its own resources. Giannini knew, of course, that he was on dangerous ground. His resources could not have begun to cover his demand deposits in case of a run; but that situation never developed, and the Bank of Italy (soon to be renamed the Bank of America) flourished.

**Accomplishments.** Over the next two decades Giannini rapidly expanded his network of banks, both in California and, later, in the East, until by 1927 the assets of his Bank of America were valued at more than $5 million. For the rest of his life he remained a great public figure and leader in the banking world. During his final years he became a major benefactor in his home state, giving millions to the foundation that bears his name and to the University of California, Berkeley.

Sources:

Julian Dana, *A. P. Giannini: Giant in the West* (New York: Prentice-Hall, 1947);

Thomas Gordon and Morgan Witts, *The Day the Bubble Burst* (New York: Doubleday, 1979).

# EDWARD V. RICKENBACKER

## 1890-1973

### AVIATION PIONEER

**Backgrounds.** One of the most famous of the Air Corps aces during World War I, Edward V. Rickenbacker also proved himself to be an effective and persistent businessman. President of Eastern Airlines for many years, he turned it into one of the most profitable and progressive airlines in the world.

**Early Efforts.** When the war ended and he returned home to the United States and a hero's welcome, Rickenbacker wanted to go into aviation. In 1918 he was sent by the War Department to tour the country on behalf of war bonds, and in the course of the tour he met many businessmen. But when he brought up the subject of commercial aviation, he was assured that, for the immediate future, there was little hope of being financially successful without abundant investment capital or congressional support, neither of which were apparently forthcoming.

**The Rickenbacker.** He consequently entered the auto industry, of which as a prewar race car driver he was knowledgeable. For about seven years he produced an automobile, the Rickenbacker, which was advertised as a "car worthy of the name." While it was never a big seller, the Rickenbacker was a well-regarded automobile in the upper price range. But competition from other car manufacturers was formidable, and by the mid 1920s conditions were not conducive to newcomers in the industry. The firm went bankrupt in 1927.

**Airline.** With the collapse of this venture, Rickenbacker bought a controlling interest in the Indianapolis Speedway, but all the while he remained hopeful that he would be able to move into aviation. Finally his chance came. After a long, complicated tour with General Motors, which had shown some interest in getting into aviation, and after having been caught in the tangle of the so-called "airmail scandals" early in the Roosevelt administration, he managed in 1934 to secure a major financial interest in the fledgling Eastern Airlines. Under his direction it grew over the next three decades into one of the nation's premier airlines. Rickenbacker also built a reputation as a tightfisted manager; he often said that he counted not only the pennies but also the mills (or one-tenth pennies) in the operation of the firm.

Sources:
Eddie Rickenbacker, *Rickenbacker* (Englewood Cliffs, N.J.: Prentice-Hall, 1967).

# ALFRED P. SLOAN JR.

## 1875-1966

### AUTOMOTIVE MANAGER

**Management Science.** Alfred P. Sloan Jr. was unlike most of the other early auto executives in that he had a university education. He had earned an engineering degree at MIT, but if he had attended the school in more recent years he would probably have majored in management science, an academic discipline that did not exist in his day. During his long career Sloan became the guru of industrial management, and he transformed GM into what was generally regarded as the best-managed corporation in the nation. Dozens of college professors and graduate students have written books, dissertations, and professional papers on the Sloan-imposed structure of the firm.

**Sloan's Accomplishments.** Backed strongly by the du Ponts who had come to control the organization in the early 1920s, Sloan took over the management of GM after William C. Durant's departure. His contribution was twofold. First, he installed effective cost controls over the sprawling enterprise, and, second, he structured the company so that its many parts worked together to produce maximum profits, while at the same time they retained individual identities and incentives. This was no

easy task since GM produced a wide range of products, including Cadillac limousines, off-the-road earthmoving equipment, intercity buses, refrigerators, spark plugs, and roller bearings. He also built a product line spanning the entire auto market — Chevrolet, Pontiac, Oldsmobile, Buick, La Salle (for a brief time), and Cadillac. The GM line thus provided something for everyone. For much of Sloan's long tenure, GM was the largest and most profitable manufacturing firm in the world.

Sources:
Alfred D. Chandler Jr., *Giant Enterprise: Ford, General Motors, and the Automobile Industry* (New York: Harcourt, Brace & World, 1964);

Ed Cray, *Chrome Colossus: General Motors and Its Times* (New York: McGraw-Hill, 1980);

Alfred P. Sloan Jr., *Adventures of a White Collar Man* (New York: Doubleday, Doran, 1941);

Sloan, *My Years With General Motors* (Garden City, N.Y.: Doubleday, 1964).

# BENJAMIN STRONG

## 1872-1928

### BANKER

**Reputation.** Benjamin Strong, governor of the New York Federal Reserve Bank from 1914 through 1928, was regarded by his contemporaries as the greatest central banker America had produced since Nicholas Biddle (president of the Bank of the United States from 1823 to 1836). He was considered more influential than his superior, the chairman of the Board of Governors of the Federal Reserve System in Washington. Strong died one year before the crash occurred, but controversy raged and continues to rage about what role his policies played in bringing on the crash.

**Policies.** In his first years as governor, Strong had advocated an extremely conservative and limited role for the Federal Reserve banks, but during World War I he condoned their expansion of services, particularly in regard to issuing Liberty Bonds. Following the war those in New York financial circles lobbied for the increased use of war-profits funds in the securities market and in foreign trade. Though Strong had reservations about "open-market powers" for the Federal Reserve System, he saw their potential and began to employ them. He hoped that the availability of so-called "easy money" would spur business activity and increase stock-market investments. His hopes were fulfilled; but by October 1929 speculation had reached such an extreme level that the stock market collapsed.

**Conclusions.** Whatever his actual culpability, Strong has gone down in history as one of those men in the banking community who mismanaged financial matters during the 1920s. Certainly the crash undermined the

American people's confidence in Wall Street and in the New York banking establishment, which would never again exercise such influence.

Sources:
Lester V. Chandler, *Benjamin Strong, Central Banker* (Washington: Brookings Institution, 1958);

John Kenneth Galbraith, *The Great Crash* (Boston: Houghton Mifflin, 1955);

Benjamin Strong, *Interpretations of Federal Reserve Policy* (New York: Harper, 1930).

# PEOPLE IN THE NEWS

**Bernard Baruch,** who made a fortune through stock-market speculation and who became famous during World War I as chairman of the War Industries Board, was an adviser to Presidents Harding, Coolidge, and Hoover during the 1920s.

Former newspaperman **Stuart Chase,** a widely quoted "economist," told the press in the fall of 1929, "We have probably three more years of prosperity ahead of us before we enter the tail-spin which has occurred in the eleventh year of the four great periods of commercial prosperity."

**Charles G. Dawes,** financier, banker, and vice president of the United States (1925–1929) under Calvin Coolidge, was noted for his quips about the uselessness of the office, but his most famous statement was that what the country needed was a good five-cent cigar.

In 1926 **Harvey S. Firestone** leased a one-million-acre rubber plantation in Liberia to provide his Firestone Tire and Rubber Company factories with raw rubber. He hoped to break the British monopoly on imported rubber.

Like many of his colleagues in academic economics, **Irving Fisher** of Yale made optimistic comments on the bull market only months before the October 1929 crash. However, his standing as a professional economist remained intact.

In 1922 **Edsel B. Ford,** president of Ford Motor Company and son of company founder Henry Ford, purchased the Lincoln Motor Car Company and took a keen interest in the development of the Lincoln luxury car.

Immediately after the October 1929 crash, hotel manager **Conrad Hilton** announced to the press that Hilton Hotels would initiate an economy plan to save on operating costs: stationery would be issued one sheet at a time.

During the 1920s **Samuel Insull** became active in electrical holding companies in the Midwest and, after their collapse in the 1929 crash, fled to Europe in 1932, was captured in 1934, and was tried for and acquitted of fraud later in the 1930s.

Throughout the 1920s **Joseph P. Kennedy** was widely quoted in the financial press regarding the several monetary coups he pulled off during the decade.

In 1921 **William S. Knudsen** resigned as production manager at Ford Motor Company to head the Chevrolet Division of General Motors Corporation (GM). (He rose to the presidency of GM in 1937.)

**Thomas W. Lamont** appeared almost daily in the news during the 1929 market crash. As senior partner in the Morgan bank, he served as the bankers' spokesman during the crisis.

**Jesse L. Livermore,** known to the press as the "Great Bear" operator or the "great plunger," survived the 1929 crash a wealthy man but continued to speculate until he finally went bankrupt.

In the days just before and after the October 1929 crash, **Charles E. Mitchell,** president of the National City Bank, was widely quoted; but when, following the crash, it became clear that his conduct had been less than completely honest, he faded from the scene.

**Charles S. Mott** became one of the General Motors millionaires after he merged his wheel-and-axle plant into GM in 1908. During the crash of 1929 he was serving as chairman of GM.

In 1927 **Charles W. Nash,** pioneer automaker and founder of the Nash Motor Company, introduced his Nash, an upper-medium-priced car.

**John J. Raskob,** for years an executive with the Du Pont Company and a leader at General Motors, was the author of the notorious "everyone should be rich" statement on the eve of the crash. He was one of the sponsors of the Empire State Building, begun in 1929.

On 8 November 1929 **James Riordan**, a widely admired self-made businessman and Wall Street speculator, committed suicide by shooting himself after he lost his fortune in the stock-market crash.

In 1921 **Charles E. Sorensen**, production guru of Ford Motor Company since the heyday of the Model T, became extremely influential after many of Henry Ford's lieutenants left the company.

In 1923 **Nathan Straus**, owner of Macy's department store, was voted the individual who had done the most for the welfare of New York City during the past twenty-five years.

In 1922 businessman **Gerard Swope**, who built International General Electric into a major General Electric (G.E.) subsidiary, was named president of G.E.

In early 1929 **Walter Teagle**, president of the Standard Oil Company, declared, "There has been no fundamental change in the petroleum industry."

**Samuel Vaculain**, chairman of the Baldwin Locomotive Company, used railroad terms to reassure the country after the 1929 crash: "The country is on the right track and steaming along."

In 1924 company president **Thomas John Watson** oversaw the renaming of the Computing-Tabulating-Recording Company to International Business Machines (IBM); he served as IBM president until 1949.

In 1928 **Robert Elkington Wood** — who had only joined the company in 1924 — became president of Sears, Roebuck and Company; under Wood's leadership Sears, Roebuck expanded to a $3-billion-a-year enterprise.

**Owen D. Young** became chairman of General Electric Corporation in 1922. In 1929 he worked with Charles G. Dawes on the German reparations problem, for which he developed the Young Plan.

# DEATHS

**Francis Wayland Ayer,** 75, "ad" pioneer, founder of advertising and public relations firm that later became N. W. Ayer and Son, 5 March 1923.

**William James Baldwin,** 79, pioneer skyscraper constructor, 7 May 1924.

**Ohio C. Barber,** 79, "Match King" of the Diamond Match Company, 4 February 1920.

**Clarence Walker Barron,** 70, pioneer in stock-market journalism, founder of Boston News Bureau (1887) and Philadelphia News Bureau (1897), publisher of the *Wall Street Journal* (1901–1928), founder of *Barron's Business and Financial Weekly* (1921), 20 October 1928.

**John Jacob Bausch,** 95, founder (1853), with Henry Lomb, and president of Bausch and Lomb Optical Company, 14 February 1926.

**William H. Beardsley,** 73, president of Florida East Coast Railway, 13 December 1925.

**Alexander Graham Bell,** 75, inventor of the telephone and founder, with Gardiner G. Hubbard and others, of Bell Telephone Company, 2 August 1922.

**Emil Berolzheimer,** 60, pencil manufacturer, 25 May 1922.

**Nicholas Biddle,** 44, financier and trustee of the Astor estate, member of the Biddle family of Philadelphia, influential in legal and financial affairs, 18 February 1923.

**Irving Ingersoll Bloomingdale,** 51, New York City department store owner, 15 October 1929.

**Peter Bosch,** 51, wallpaper manufacturer, 12 April 1922.

**John V. Bouvier,** stockbroker for fifty one years, 2 January 1926.

**David D. Buick,** 74, pioneer automobile inventor and manufacturer, founder of Buick Motor Company, 5 March 1929.

Burns D. Caldwell, 64, president of Wells Fargo Express, 24 September 1922.

A. G. Candler, 77, Coca-Cola founder, philanthropist, 12 March 1929.

Samuel Carr, Boston financier, 29 May 1922.

Henry J. Case, 84, pioneer inventor of harvesting machinery, partner in J. I. Case and Company, 31 August 1924.

William S. Champ, 55, Arctic explorer, baking powder manufacturer, 2 June 1924.

Frederick W. Chickering, 55, piano manufacturer, 14 October 1920.

J. W. Clark, 60, thread manufacturer, 15 July 1928.

William Andrews Clark, 86, copper magnate, financier, U.S. senator (D) from Montana (1899–1900, 1901–1907), 2 March 1925.

Louis W. Clarke, 79, pioneer telegrapher, 26 September 1921.

W. H. Coats, 62, chairman of J and P Coats thread-manufacturing company, 21 August 1928.

Herbert Seward Collins, 52, president of Union Tobacco Company, 22 September 1927.

James W. Corrigan, 47, steel manufacturer, 23 January 1928.

Eugene Victor Debs, 70, national secretary of Brotherhood of Locomotive Firemen (1880); founder (1893) and first president of American Railway Union; organizer of Social Democratic Party of America (1897); Socialist presidential candidate (1900, 1904, 1908, 1912, 1920); founder (1905), with others, of Industrial Workers of the World (IWW), 20 October 1926.

Charles Deering, 75, Chicago manufacturer of farm machinery, 5 February 1927.

Cleveland Hoadley Dodge, 66, founder of Phelps-Dodge Copper Corporation, 24 June 1926.

Horace E. Dodge, automobile manufacturer and cofounder, with John T. Dodge, of Dodge Motor Company, which merged with Chrysler Corporation, 10 December 1920.

John T. Dodge, 54, automobile manufacturer and cofounder, with Horace E. Dodge, of Dodge Motor Company, which merged with Chrysler Corporation, 14 January 1920.

Frank G. Drew, 55, president of Winchester Repeating Arms Company, 19 October 1928.

Alexis I. du Pont, 52, associate of E. I. Du Pont de Nemours and Company gunpowder manufacturer, 30 May 1921.

Biederman du Pont, 86, associate of E. I. Du Pont de Nemours and Company gunpowder manufacturer, 22 October 1923.

Philip F. du Pont, 49, associate of E. I. Du Pont de Nemours and Company gunpowder manufacturer, 17 May 1928.

William du Pont, 72, associate of E. I. Du Pont de Nemours and Company gunpowder manufacturer, 20 January 1928.

Benjamin N. Duke, 73, cigarette manufacturer; cofounder, with brother James B. Duke, of American Tobacco Company; major benefactor of Trinity College in Durham, North Carolina, renamed Duke University, 8 January 1929.

James B. Duke, 86, cigarette manufacturer; cofounder, with brother Benjamin N. Duke, and president of American Tobacco Company; major benefactor of Trinity College in Durham, North Carolina, renamed Duke University, 10 October 1925.

George Ehret, 91, brewer, 20 January 1927.

Edward H. Everett, 76, pioneer automobile manufacturer, 26 April 1929.

Leon Falk, 58, Pittsburgh Steel manufacturer, philanthropist, 20 October 1928.

Stuyvesant Fish, 71, railroad investor, banker, financier, associate of E. H. Harriman in development of rail systems, president of Illinois Central Railroad, 10 April 1923.

Julius Fleischman, 52, yeast manufacturer, 5 February 1925.

Jacob Gimbel, 71, coorganizer (1922), with brother Isaac Gimbel, of Gimbel Brothers, which by 1930 was the largest department store chain in the world, 7 November 1922.

Eugene Lewis Giroux, 66, mining engineer, associate of E. H. Harriman in development of rail systems, 31 March 1923.

Charles Jaspar Glidden, 70, pioneer in telephone industry, developer of far-reaching telephone system with his New England Telephone and Telegraph Company and Erie Telephone and Telegraph Company, promoter of long-distance automobile races such as the Glidden Tour, 11 September 1927.

Adolph Goble, 59, sausage manufacturer, Brooklyn, 25 March 1924.

Samuel Gompers, 74, organizer (1886), with others, and president (1886–1894, 1896–1924) of American Federation of Labor; member of Council of National Defense (1917) and Commission on International Labor Legislation at Treaty of Versailles (1919), 13 December 1924.

George Jay Gould, 59, president of Erie, Missouri Pacific, Texas and Pacific, Saint Louis Southwestern, and International and Great Northern Railroads, all inherited from his father, railroad tycoon Jay Gould, 16 May 1923.

Charles W. Gray, 52, president of Yellow Cab Company, 25 December 1927.

Isaac Guggenheim, 68, industrialist and mine owner, president of American Smelting and Refining Company, 10 October 1922.

Elwood Haynes, inventor of the automobile (1893–1894), who predated Ford's experiments by several years; organizer of Haynes-Apperson Company (1898) in Kokomo, Indiana, which continued as Haynes Automobile Company (1902–1925); discoverer of several alloys, including tungsten chrome steel and stainless steel, 13 April 1925.

William Dudley "Big Bill" Haywood, 58, labor leader and founder (1905), with others, of Industrial Workers of the World (IWW); member of Socialist Party (1901–1912); violence advocate; arrested and convicted of sedition (1917–1918) and fled to the Soviet Union while free on bail (1921), 18 May 1928.

Marcus Helm, 74, stockbroker and founder of Consolidated Exchange, 23 May 1929.

Percival S. Hill, 63, president of American Tobacco Company, 7 December 1925.

Clifford Milburn Holland, 40, chief engineer of the New York–New Jersey Interstate Bridge and Tunnel — subsequently named the Holland Tunnel — for vehicular traffic under the Hudson River, 27 October 1924.

Brian G. Hughes, 75, New York box manufacturer and practical joker, 8 December 1924.

Henry E. Huntington, 77, railroad executive and owner, organizer of urban and interurban transit systems in San Francisco and Los Angeles, founder of the public Huntington Library in San Marino, California, 23 May 1927.

James N. Jarvie, 75, American coffee importer, financier, philanthropist, 21 June 1929.

Jackson Johnson, 69, owner of the largest shoe-manufacturing company in the world, 23 January 1929.

George H. Jones, 81, chairman of Standard Oil Company of New Jersey, 22 November 1928.

William L. Jones, president of Jones and Laughlin Steel Company, one of the leaders of "little steel," 25 November 1926.

John Reese Kenly, 81, president of Atlantic Coast Line Railroad Company, 1 March 1928.

Henrietta M. King, 93, owner of King Ranch in Kingsville, Texas, the world's largest ranch, 31 March 1925.

Charles Morgan Kittle, 47, president of Sears, Roebuck and Company and former vice president of Illinois Central Railroad, 2 January 1928.

William Granville Lee, 69, twenty-year president of Brotherhood of Railroad Trainmen, 2 November 1929.

Marshall C. Lefferts, 79, celluloid manufacturer, book and art collector, 30 April 1928.

Edward Drummond Libbey, 71, glass manufacturer with Libbey-Owens-Ford Company, 13 November 1925.

Joseph S. Loose, 80, New York cracker manufacturer, 10 June 1922.

John M. Mack, motor-truck manufacturer, 14 March 1924.

Thomas Franklyn Manville Jr., 63, "Asbestos King" and president of Johns-Manville Company, 19 October 1925.

Jonathan Dixon Maxwell, 64, pioneer automobile maker whose company was taken over by Walter P. Chrysler and his Chrysler Corporation in 1925, 8 March 1928.

Ernest O. McCormick, vice president of Southern Pacific Railroad, 1 November 1923.

James Alexander McCrea, 48, vice president of Pennsylvania Railroad, 17 October 1923.

John McKesson Jr., 84, drug manufacturer with McKesson and Robbins Company, 5 September 1924.

Seth M. Milliken, 84, cotton manufacturer, 5 March 1920.

Charles H. Morse, 88, Chicago scales and machinery manufacturer, 5 May 1921.

William Herbert Murphy, 73, automobile manufacturer, art patron, 5 February 1929.

James Patrick Noonan, 51, president of International Brotherhood of Electrical Workers, vice president of American Federation of Labor, 4 December 1929.

James O'Sullivan, 83, rubber-heel maker who called himself "America's No. 1 Heel," 21 June 1929.

Henry T. Oxnard, 62, beet sugar manufacturer, 8 June 1922.

William Doud Packard, 62, engineer and inventor who, with brother James Ward Packard, founded Packard Electric Company (1890) and designed and built the Packard, a high-quality automobile (1899); associate in Packard Motor Company, 11 November 1923.

James A. Patten, 76, Chicago grain speculator known as the "Wheat King," philanthropist, 8 December 1928.

John Henry Patterson, 78, owner (1884–1922) of National Cash Register Company in Dayton, Ohio, developer of merchandising techniques such as exclusive sales territory, 7 May 1922.

W. A. Patterson, 82, automobile manufacturer, 9 September 1921.

F. S. Peabody, 66, coal operator with Peabody Coal Company, 27 August 1922.

Edward Butler Pillsbury, 73, macaroni manufacturer, 10 August 1929.

**Henry K. Porter,** 81, locomotive manufacturer, 10 April 1921.

**Terence V. Powderly,** 75, leader of Knights of Labor, a rival union of American Federation of Labor, 28 June 1924.

**J. T. Pratt,** 72, associate of John D. Rockefeller Sr., major stockholder in Standard Oil Company, developer of railroads and other industries, 23 August 1927.

**Harley T. Proctor,** 73, soap manufacturer with Proctor and Gamble Company, 15 May 1920.

**Eliphalet Remington,** 85, firearms manufacturer with Remington-Rand Company, 2 April 1924.

**William Rockefeller,** 81, brother of John D. Rockefeller who helped organize Standard Oil Company (1870) and managed company interests in New York; financier associated with copper interests, railways, and public-utility corporations, 24 June 1922.

**Washington Augustus Roebling,** 89, engineer and industrialist; associate of father John A. Roebling in designing and building the first suspension bridges in the United States, using steel cable; chief engineer of building the Brooklyn Bridge (1869–1883); director of Roebling cable-manufacturing plant (1888–1926) in Trenton, New Jersey, 21 July 1926.

**John Summer Runnels,** 84, former chairman of Pullman Company, 11 July 1929.

**Edward Larned Ryerson,** 73, steel producer, art patron, 19 January 1928.

**Horace A. Saks,** 43, department-store owner, 27 November 1925.

**Rudolph J. Schaefer,** 60, brewer, 9 November 1923.

**Henry F. O. Schwarz,** 59, toy dealer, 16 May 1925.

**Charles L. Seabury,** 61, yacht builder, 7 April 1922.

**Joseph Seep,** 89, pioneer petroleum producer and Rockefeller family associate, 1 April 1928.

**George Baldwin Selden,** 77, lawyer and inventor who patented the first gasoline-driven vehicle, or "road engine" (1895), and collected royalties on his patent until 1911 when Ford Motor Company refused to pay royalties and won its case in court, 17 January 1922.

**William George Sickel,** 60, former president of United American Lines, 1 May 1929.

**Sir Mortimer Singer,** 65, an heir to the I. M. Singer and Company sewing-machine fortune, 24 June 1929.

**Oberlin Smith,** 86, die inventor, former president of National Geographic Society, 18 July 1927.

**James M. Smyth,** 57, telephone pioneer, 9 March 1920.

**Edward Hamilton Squibb,** 77, physician and drug manufacturer, partner in E. R. Squibb and Sons chemical and pharmaceutical laboratory (1892) in Brooklyn, New York, 7 July 1929.

**B. M. Starks,** 60, general manager of Louisville and Nashville Railroad, 28 November 1923.

**Ellsworth Milton Statler,** 64, hotel owner who organized (1904) chain of Statler luxury hotels, 16 April 1928.

**Frederick T. Steinway,** 67, piano manufacturer with Steinway and Sons, 17 July 1927.

**Charles Chauncey Stillman,** 48, financier and banker for First National City Bank, 16 August 1926.

**James Jackson Storrow,** 61, Boston lawyer and banker, president of the executive council of Boy Scouts of America, 13 March 1927.

**Leo Sulzberger,** 40, merchant, philanthropist, 31 January 1927.

**J. W. Surbrug,** 66, tobacco and candy manufacturer, 29 May 1927.

**Edmund H. Taylor Jr.,** 93, distiller, 10 January 1923.

**C. P. Treat,** 78, railway builder, 27 January 1927.

**William Kissam Vanderbilt,** 71, grandson of railroad magnate Cornelius Vanderbilt; chairman of Lake Shore and Michigan Southern Railroad (1883–1903); president of New York, Chicago, and St. Louis Railway (1882–1887); yacht owner and competitor in 1895 America's Cup race, 23 July 1920.

**W. L. Velie,** 62, automobile, airplane, and agricultural machinery manufacturer, 24 October 1928.

**J. H. Wade,** 68, Cleveland, Ohio, financier and philanthropist, 6 March 1927.

**Samuel Wallach,** 67, clothing manufacturer, 23 June 1929.

**John Wanamaker,** 84, merchant who, with brother-in-law Nathan Brown, founded (1861) men's clothing store in Philadelphia — by 1871 the largest retail men's clothing store in the United States — and expanded it into a department store (1877); early exponent of advertising and promotion, 12 December 1922.

**Orville Taylor Waring,** 84, pioneer with Standard Oil Company, 19 May 1923.

**Hulbert Harrington Warner,** 81, Rochester, New York medicine manufacturer, 27 January 1923.

**John Isaac Waterbury,** 78, financier, art patron, 4 March 1929.

**W. S. Webb,** 75, official of New York Central Railroad, pioneer sleeping-car builder, 1926.

**Joseph H. Wesson,** 60, president of Smith and Wesson firearms-manufacturing company, 30 April 1920.

**Walter H. Wesson,** 71, firearms manufacturer with Smith and Wesson Company, 29 November 1921.

**Frank P. Wheeler,** carburetor manufacturer, Indianapolis, 27 May 1921.

Amos Nelson Whiteley, 86, reaper manufacturer, philanthropist, 3 August 1925.

Eli Whitney, 77, financier, 12 June 1924.

Payne Whitney, 51, financier, sportsman, 25 May 1927.

Everett Wilson, 67, meatpacker, 30 May 1921.

Arthur S. Winchester, 87, rifle manufacturer with Winchester Repeating Arms Company, 11 January 1925.

Howard E. Wurlitzer, 57, musical instrument manufacturer, 30 October 1928.

Benjamin Franklin Yoakum, 70, railroad builder and owner, financier, 28 November 1929.

# PUBLICATIONS

Arthur B. Adams, *Economics of Business Cycles* (New York: McGraw-Hill, 1925);

Roger W. Babson, *Making Good in Business* (New York: Revell, 1921);

William R. Basset, *How to Solve Typical Business Problems* (New York: Forbes, 1928);

Edward Bok, *Dollars Only* (New York: Scribners, 1926);

Glen Buck, *This American Ascendancy* (Chicago: Kroch, 1927);

Earnest Elmo Calkins, *Business the Civilizer* (Boston: Little, Brown, 1928);

John R. Commons, *Labor and Administration* (New York: Macmillan, 1923);

Earl Willis Crecraft, *Government and Business: A Study in the Economic Aspects of Government and the Public Aspects of Business* (Yonkers-on-Hudson, N.Y. & Chicago: World, 1928);

Charles Norton Fay, *Business in Politics: Suggestions for Leaders in American Business* (Cambridge, Mass.: Cosmos, 1926);

Abraham Filene with Burton Kline, *A Merchant's Horizon* (Boston: Houghton Mifflin, 1924);

Harvey S. Firestone with Samuel Crowther, *Men and Rubber: The Story of Business* (Garden City, N.Y.: Doubleday, Page, 1926);

William Byron Forbush, *Be Square* (New York: Scribners, 1924);

William Trufant Foster, *Business Without a Buyer* (Boston: Houghton Mifflin, 1927);

Foster and Waddill Catchings, *Profits* (Boston: Houghton Mifflin, 1925);

J. George Frederick, *The Great Game of Business: Its Rules, Its Fascination, Its Services and Rewards* (New York: Appleton, 1920);

Frederick, *Modern Industrial Consolidation* (New York: Frank-Maurice, 1926);

Charles W. Gerstenberg, *Personal Power in Business* (New York: Prentice-Hall, 1922);

George W. Grupp, *Economics of Motor Transportation* (New York: Appleton, 1923);

Lincoln Withington Hall, *Banking Cycles* (Philadelphia: University of Pennsylvania Press, 1927);

Edgar L. Heermance, *The Ethics of Business: A Study in Current Standards* (New York: Harper, 1926);

Charles L. Jamison, *Finance* (New York: Ronald, 1927);

Otto H. Kahn, *Our Economic and Other Problems: A Financier's Point of View* (New York: Doran, 1920);

Hazel Kyrk, *A Theory of Consumption* (Boston: Houghton Mifflin, 1923);

James Melvin Lee, *Business Ethics: A Manual of Modern Morals* (New York: Ronald, 1926);

Isaac Lippincott, *What the Farmer Needs* (New York: Appleton, 1928);

Paul Myer Mazur with Myron S. Silbert, *Principles of Organization Applied to Modern Retailing* (New York: Harper, 1927);

Wesley Clair Mitchell, *Business Cycles: The Problem and Its Setting* (New York: National Bureau of Economic Research, 1928);

Harold G. Moulton, *The Financial Organization of Society* (Chicago: University of Chicago Press, 1921);

Paul H. Nystrom, *Bibliography of Retailing: A Selected List of Books, Pamphlets, and Periodicals* (New York: Columbia University Press, 1928);

William Z. Ripley, *Main Street and Wall Street* (Boston: Little, Brown, 1927);

Edwin R. A. Seligman, *The Economics of Installment Selling: A Study in Consumers' Credit* (New York: Harper, 1927);

Fred W. Shibley, *The New Way to Net Profits* (New York: Harper, 1928);

James Gerald Smith, *The Development of Trust Companies in the United States* (New York: Holt, 1928);

Carl Snyder, *Business Cycles and Business Measurements: Studies in Quantitative Economics* (New York: Macmillan, 1927);

Rinehart John Swenson, *The National Government and Business* (New York: Century, 1924);

Harold Whitehead, *The Business of Selling* (New York: American Book, 1923);

*The Accounting Review*, periodical, founded in 1926;

*Administration: The Journal of Business Analysis and Control*, periodical, founded in 1921;

*Barron's: The National Financial Weekly*, periodical, founded in 1921;

*Bulletin of the Business Historical Society*, periodical, founded in 1926;

*Bureau Farmer*, periodical, founded in 1925;

*Business Bulletin*, periodical, founded in 1920;

*The Business Law Journal*, periodical, founded in 1923;

*Business Literature*, periodical, founded in 1928;

*Business Review*, periodical, founded in 1923;

*Cost and Management*, periodical, founded in 1926;

*Harvard Business Review*, periodical, founded in 1922;

*Independent Woman*, periodical, founded in 1920;

*Indiana Business Review*, periodical, founded in 1926;

*Journal of American Insurance*, periodical, founded in 1924;

*The Journal of Business of the University of Chicago*, periodical, founded in 1928;

*Journal of Economic and Business History*, periodical, founded in 1928;

*Journal of Retailing*, periodical, founded in 1925;

*Management Review*, periodical;

*The Marconi Review*, periodical, founded in 1928;

*Michigan Farmer*, periodical;

*Modern Machine Shop*, periodical, founded in 1928;

*Monthly Review*, periodical, founded in 1923;

*Popular Radio*, periodical, founded in 1922;

*Radio*, periodical;

*Research Monograph*, periodical, founded in 1928;

*Survey of Current Business*, periodical, founded in 1921;

*Texas Business Review*, periodical, founded in 1927;

*University Journal of Business*, periodical, founded in 1922;

*University of Denver Business Review*, periodical, founded in 1925.

# CHAPTER FOUR

# EDUCATION

by VINCENT A. LACEY, GEORGE S. REUTER JR., and JOHN E. KING

## CONTENTS

*Sidebars and tables are listed in italics.*

## 1920

- The U.S. Census shows that in a total U.S. population of more than 100,000,000 there are 21,578,000 students enrolled in public schools. College enrollment is 597,000 students.
- The Dalton Plan of instruction is first used by educators Ernest Jackman and Helen Parkhurst in Dalton, Massachusetts.
- The Lusk Laws requiring loyalty oaths for teachers in the state of New York are passed.
- Susan Miller Dorsey is appointed superintendent of the Los Angeles schools.
- Ellwood P. Cubberley of Stanford University publishes *The History of Education.*
- The first graduate school of geography is organized at Clark University.
- Junior colleges are established in Arizona and Iowa.

**4–10 Dec.** American Education Week is first celebrated.

## 1921

- About two hundred institutions of higher education are awarding master's degrees, and nearly fifty are offering doctorates.
- Junior colleges are established in Texas.

**18 Jan.** The New York State school commissioner makes public-school teachers subject to dismissal for active membership in the Communist Party.

**Fall** The fifth annual report of the federal Board of Vocational Education declares that between 1 July 1920 and 30 June 1921 the board cooperated with the states in the vocational training of 305,224 students in 3,859 schools. The most popular areas for training were home economics, trade and industry, and agriculture.

## 1922

- John Franklin Bobbitt's *Curriculum-making in Los Angeles* is published.
- George S. Counts's *The Selective Character of American Secondary Education* is published.
- John Dewey's *Human Nature and Conduct* draws national attention.

## 1923

- The Supreme Court rules in *Meyer* v. *Nebraska* that banning foreign-language instruction is unconstitutional.

**Winter** The Lusk Laws are repealed in New York State.

**16 Oct.** A law requiring mandatory educational and literacy tests for new voters is sustained by the New York State Court of Appeals.

## 1924

- William McAndrew is appointed superintendent of the Chicago School System.

**31 Mar.** The U.S. Supreme Court rules unconstitutional an Oregon law requiring all children to attend public schools.

**1925**

**21 May**    The teaching of the theory of evolution in schools is ruled untenable by the General Assembly of the Presbyterian Church at San Antonio, Texas.

**13 May**    The Florida House of Representatives passes a bill requiring daily Bible readings in all public schools.

**10 July**    John T. Scopes goes on trial in Dayton, Tennessee, for teaching evolution theory; on 21 July he is found guilty and fined $100.

**16 Oct.**    The Texas State Text Book Board bans the discussion of evolutionary theory in any of its school textbooks.

**29 Dec.**    Trustees of Trinity College in North Carolina agree to rename the institution Duke University, following a donation of $40 million by James B. Duke.

**1926**

- Carter Godwin Woodson wins the NAACP Spingarn Medal for his promotion of the study of African American history.

- A test case to require the White Plains, New York, school board to grant one hour of religious instruction for schoolchildren enters the court system.

**9 Feb.**    The Board of Education prohibits the teaching of the theory of evolution in Atlanta, Georgia, public schools.

**1927**

- William McAndrew is fired as superintendent of the Chicago School System.

- Samuel Morison's *The Oxford History of the United States* is published.

- New York University establishes seven summer schools in European universities; these summer schools will grant college credit for courses taught by American professors.

**1928**

- George S. Counts publishes *School and Society in Chicago*.

- Vernon Louis Parrington's *Main Currents in American Thought* wins the Pulitzer Prize for history.

**1929**

- The Carnegie Foundation for the Advancement of Teaching reports that intercollegiate athletics is a "Roman Circus."

- Susan Miller Dorsey retires as superintendent of the Los Angeles schools.

- The U.S. population is 121,770,000. Public-school enrollment is 25,678,000, and enrollment in colleges and universities is more than 1,000,000.

# OVERVIEW

**Changes.** The 1920s brought many changes in American education. The post–World War I baby boom led to dramatic increases in the numbers of students attending school and a marked rise in the demand for teachers. Social and economic factors produced such phenomena as the Red Scare, religious controversy, and political strife, which in turn influenced education in the United States. New classes in the sciences, physical education, home economics, geography, and industrial arts expanded the curriculum from the traditional focus on the Three Rs (readin', 'ritin', and 'rithmetic).

**Continuation of Segregation.** The doctrine of "separate but equal" schools for ethnic minorities had been established by *Plessy* v. *Ferguson,* a case argued before the United States Supreme Court in 1896. The "separate but equal" doctrine allowed states to maintain segregated schools as long as equal services were provided for blacks and whites. In arriving at this decision, the Supreme Court construed the Fourteenth Amendment as providing a sanction for segregation. The Court held that the object of the amendment, which declared that the rights of a U.S. citizen could not be abridged by the state in which he lived, was to "secure absolute equality of the two races before the law," but not in the same classrooms.

**Effects of Segregation.** The *Plessy* v. *Ferguson* precedent for "separate but equal" educational systems was maintained throughout the 1920s. Southern states and, in certain situations and localities, northern states used this principle primarily to keep blacks out of white schools, though it was also applied to other nonwhite ethnic groups through the Supreme Court decision in *Gong Lum* v. *Rice* in 1927. In fact, the "separate but equal" doctrine insured separation but not equality in education: the average expenditure of states and municipalities for the education of white students was far more than that for black students, and blacks were in essence prevented, through much of the country, from preparing themselves for certain occupations readily available to whites. It would be more than a quarter of a century after the 1920s ended before this doctrine would be legally reversed.

**Local School Districts.** As Howard A. Dawson and M. C. S. Noble Jr. report in *Handbook on Rural Educa-* *tion,* "A national high in numbers of school districts may have been reached in the 1920s with 189,227 one-room schools reported." The movement from the farm to the cities and suburbs and the development of the motorcar supported a national movement toward school-district reorganization. This movement was led by such figures as Ellwood P. Cubberley and Howard Dawson of the National Education Association's Department of Rural Education, along with Professors Julian Butterworth and E. N. Ferriss of Cornell University. Particularly noteworthy programs for school reorganization were begun in New York State in 1925 and in Arkansas in 1928. By the end of the 1920s the number of public-school districts had been reduced by consolidation to approximately 130,000. Simultaneously, the average number of school days in session per year increased from 161.9 to 172.7, and the average annual teacher's salary rose from $871 in 1920 to $1,420 in 1930.

**School Enrollments.** Public elementary and secondary school enrollments increased rapidly in the 1920s, as did the number of high-school graduates: 231,000 received diplomas in 1920 compared to 592,000 in 1930. The movement of the population from the rural areas to the cities brought about a new emphasis on providing students with the technical skills needed for jobs in business and industry. American colleges and universities, both public and private, also experienced huge increases in numbers of students, which, in turn, swelled the need for teachers, facilities, and funding, especially toward the end of the decade.

**Public versus Private.** During the early half of the 1920s, Americans debated the idea of forcing all students to attend public schools. The Ku Klux Klan and other groups wanted to close all parochial schools in Oregon, and the state legislature there passed a law requiring that all students attend public schools. In March 1924 the Supreme Court ruled that the Oregon law was unconstitutional; however, the debate over funding of private schools with public money continued throughout the decade.

**Religion in Schools.** The issue of separation of church and state loomed large but was not conclusively settled in the 1920s. Readings from the Bible and generally fundamentalist religious instruction remained a common part of public-school curricula. A huge conflict over the teaching of evolutionary theory arose, particularly in the South and Southwest, and culminated in the famous Scopes Trial of 1925.

**New Teaching Methods.** The Dalton Plan and the Contract Plan, two new approaches to teaching developed in the 1920s, enjoyed worldwide and enduring popularity (both plans are still used in the mid 1990s). The Dalton Plan required students to work on long-term individualized projects in a laboratory setting; the Contract Plan emphasized an individualized assignment agreed to by student and teacher in a written contract. This contract defined requirements to be fulfilled in order to earn a particular letter grade. Both plans emphasized individualized instruction and student responsibility.

# TOPICS IN THE NEWS

Voting lesson in a New York City Americanization class

## AMERICANIZATION AND EDUCATION

**Education for Immigrants.** The United States began as a "melting pot" of immigrants from all parts of the world. During the 1920s a major problem of American education involved the training of new immigrants. As the decade began, there were almost five million illiterate people, ten years of age or older, in the total population. Since most of the newly arriving immigrants settled in the larger cities, illiteracy in those cities rose as high as 15 percent. Among the foreign-born it was not unusual for the rate of illiteracy to be 25 to 35 percent. Therefore, many new educational programs were established to alleviate the illiteracy problem of these new Americans.

**Efforts toward Assimilation.** Following World War I, a national movement to assimilate immigrants into American society was organized. The Federal Bureau of Education and the naturalization division of the U.S. Immigration and Naturalization Service prepared a fed-

"When in the year 2000 the historian writes his account of the period through which we are now passing, how, I often wonder, will he appraise the various educational tendencies of our generation. He will no doubt have something to say about the extraordinary extension of educational opportunity, the structural reorganization of the educational system, the almost universal concern with curriculum making, the differentiation of the programs of higher education, the so-called progressive education movement, the development of teachers' colleges, the tremendous growth in educational expenditure, the widespread interest in the scientific study of education, and the numerous minor changes in the structure and procedure of our schools and colleges. . . .

"In at least one respect the historian of the future will, I think, find our attack upon the problem of education gravely deficient. . . . He will see, as we apparently do not, that we have been literally precipitated into a new world: a world which with a ruthless and relentless energy is destroying inherited values, creeds, and faiths; a world which is demanding new social arrangements, a new legal code, a new ethics, a new aesthetics, a new religion, and even a thorough-going revision of our ideas regarding the nature of man. He will see us in this strange fantastic industrial society repeating formulae handed down from an agrarian age when we should be searching with tireless effort for formulae suited to the world as it is; he will see us preoccupied with educational techniques and the minutia of school-keeping when we should be wrestling with the basic problem of life; he will see us greatly agitated over the construction of an algebra test or a marking scale, when we should be endeavoring to make the school function in the building of a new civilization. The social fabric, however, was no more simple than the lives which we led. . . .

"With the bodies bowed beneath the burdens of clearing forests, breaking virgin land, building homes, and bearing children, both men and women grew old in middle age. Life for us was a grim struggle with the elements. Material comforts were despised, physical prowess and courage were idealized, and the refinements of culture were unknown. Our recreations were crude, our religious beliefs primitive, our intellectual horizon narrow, and our educational needs limited. And yet an abundance of fertile land, the absence of hereditary social classes, and the participation of practically all members of society in manual labor made men socially and politically free—as they have seldom been free in human history. It was in a society of this type that the American system of public education took form."

Source: George S. Counts, *Secondary Education and Industrialism* (New York: Harcourt, Brace, 1929), pp. 5–6.

---

eral textbook on citizenship training. All accredited schools received the textbook free of charge. In 1921 the National Education Association (NEA) established a Department of Immigration Education to help introduce new immigrants to American culture. Americanization bureaus were established by statute in many states, and most of these bureaus are still in operation in the mid 1990s. During the 1920s churches, labor groups, and local civic organizations helped educate immigrants through classes organized to teach the English language, American history and civics, geography, and industrial arts.

**Immigration Acts.** In response to the rising number of immigrants, Congress passed immigration acts in 1921 and 1924. The more stringent of the two acts, the National Origins Act of 1924, restricted the admission of new immigrants to 2 percent of each foreign-born group resident in the United States in 1890. Because the major influx of immigrants from southern and eastern Europe occurred after 1890, the 1924 act in effect insured that most of the new immigrants would be from Great Brit-ain, Ireland, Germany, and Scandinavia. The act banned Oriental immigrants.

**Sources:**

Lawrence G. Brown, *Immigration: Cultural Conflicts and Social Adjustments* (New York: Longmans, Green, 1933);

Julius Drachsler, *Democracy and Assimilation* (New York: Macmillan, 1920);

Henry P. Fairchild, *The Melting-Pot Mistake* (Boston: Little, Brown, 1926).

## CITIZENSHIP AND EDUCATION

**Awakening the Spirit.** In order to meet the needs of an increasingly diverse society, educators developed new educational methods. Fundamental changes in the character, purpose, and direction of American education took place during the decade. Professor Ellwood P. Cubberley of Stanford University believed that education should be used to effect an "awakening of the spirit of fair play and good sportsmanship and to develop high ideals of honor and righteousness in social and civic life." In the 1920s educators throughout the country sought "to promote literacy and citizenship," primary focuses of the public schools.

**Education for Citizenship.** More and more citizens believed that knowledge was power and that education led to virtue. Voters thus supported the development of new courses and teaching methods that enlightened leaders of public schools recommended. "Education for citizenship" described the Cubberley principle that students who mastered the tools of learning and were trained for personal service and group cooperation would both develop their own ambitions and become better citizens. Cubberley argued that if public-school students "are given an understanding of industrial life and social institutions, the best of their personalities are developed, their ideals of life are awakened, and they are guided into lines of work where they are likely to make the greatest possible lasting results."

**Source:**
Ellwood P. Cubberley, *Public Education in the United States* (Boston: Houghton Mifflin, 1934).

## THE COURTS AND EDUCATION

**Lusk Laws of New York, 1920–1923.** Sen. Clayton R. Lusk, chairman of the legislative committee investigating sedition in the state of New York, led the New York legislature in passing a series of laws in 1920 and 1921 aimed at public-school teachers. These laws required teachers to obtain certificates of loyalty and character from the state commissioner of education. For nearly two years teachers called for the repeal of the so-called "Loyalty Laws," and in 1923, under the leadership of Gov. Alfred E. Smith, they were repealed.

**Ban on Teaching Foreign Languages.** During World War I, Nebraska, along with ten other states, passed laws that forbade the teaching of foreign languages, especially German, in public and private schools. These laws were instituted as safeguards against "dangerous" political and cultural influences from abroad. In 1923 the Supreme Court ruled, in *Meyer* v. *Nebraska,* that laws banning foreign-language teaching were unconstitutional.

**Private School Prohibition.** The Oregon legislature in 1922 passed a law to compel all schoolchildren to attend public schools. The Oregon law was aimed at closing parochial and other private schools, which were regarded as breeding grounds for unacceptable — that is, non-Protestant — religious beliefs. In *Pierce* v. *Society of Sisters of the Holy Names* (1924), the Supreme Court declared the Oregon statute unconstitutional because it unduly abridged the rights of parents to make a choice among schools.

**Sources:**
William C. Bagley and others, "Educators Demand Repeal of Lusk 'Loyalty' Law for New York Teachers," *School and Society,* 15 (3 June 1922): 605;

Newton Edwards, *The Courts and the Public Schools: The Legal Basis of School Organization and Administration* (Chicago: University of Chicago Press, 1933);

Edward A. Krug, *The Shaping of the American High School: Volume 2, 1920–1941* (New York: Harper & Row, 1972);

*Meyer* v. *Nebraska,* 262 U.S. 390, 43 S. Ct. 625 (1923);

*Pierce* v. *Society of Sisters of the Holy Names,* 268 U.S. 510 (1924).

## THE COURTS, POLITICS, AND THE CHICAGO SCHOOLS

**C.F.T.** The Chicago Federation of Teachers (C.F.T.) was founded in 1897 by a group of female elementary-school teachers. Led by Ella Flagg Young, Catherine Goggin, and Margaret Haley, the C.F.T. membership grew rapidly after the turn of the century, enrolling more members than did the National Education Association. One of the goals of the Chicago teachers was to win better working conditions and higher salaries. Discovering that, contrary to Illinois law, Chicago's public utility companies were not paying taxes upon the value of their franchises, the union brought lawsuits against these companies. C.F.T. lawyers won these suits, which forced the utilities to pay fair taxes. Similar lawsuits were filed and won against the Pullman and Swift Companies. Although the C.F.T. expected that the increased funding generated by these taxes would be spent on teachers' salaries, the board of education instead used these new revenues to build new schools and repair older ones.

**Thompson.** In *School and Society in Chicago* (1928), noted scholar George S. Counts argued that education and politics were intermingled in American society, especially in Chicago. "Machine politics" had been a part of American life since the Civil War, and Mayor William Hale "Big Bill" Thompson and his political machine meddled with the Chicago board of education and the teachers' pension funds. During his two terms as mayor (1915–1923), Thompson removed the superintendent, packed the board of education with his cronies, and raided the public funds for education.

**McAndrew.** In 1923 Mayor Thompson lost the mayoral election to a reform-minded candidate, who named William McAndrew superintendent of the Chicago schools. He proceeded to enact reforms, especially measures opposing political interference in the conduct of the public schools. Bitter opposition by vying political factions to McAndrew's reforms led to the re-election of Thompson in 1927. Fulfilling one of his campaign promises, Mayor Thompson fired McAndrew, ending a brief era of reform in the Chicago schools.

Sources:

H. Warren Button and Eugene F. Provenzo Jr., *History of Education and Culture in America* (Englewood Cliffs, N.J.: Prentice-Hall, 1983);

George S. Counts, *School and Society in Chicago* (New York: Harcourt, Brace, 1928).

## CURRICULUM CHANGES

**Fragmentation.** Between 1906 and 1908 the development of education as a field of study at universities commenced. In 1925 Cubberley strongly advocated requiring an introductory course in education for all students in universities, colleges, and normal schools. During the 1920s the growth of the number of professors in departments of education led to the division of this general introductory course into six or seven different courses, which would later be further subdivided. Certain educators questioned this fragmenting process because students who might have elected to take a more general education course often resisted taking several narrowly defined courses; they thus would miss pieces of the curriculum. Critics claimed that as a result many students studying to be teachers were lacking a comprehensive overview or philosophy of education and teaching methods.

Prof. Ellwood P. Cubberley of Stanford University

**In-Service Training of Teachers.** During the 1920s many small departments of education advanced into important schools and colleges of education throughout the United States. Typically the two-year normal school evolved into the four-year teachers' college, partly in response to increased demand for in-service training for already experienced teachers. There was a rapid growth in summer-school instruction for in-service teachers in all parts of America. Thousands of classroom teachers sat at the feet of scholars like Cubberley at Stanford or John Dewey and William Heard Kilpatrick at Columbia for a few weeks in the summer. Many of them traveled across the nation or from other countries to enroll in summer school.

**New Methods of Teaching.** Although there always was a tendency to try new approaches in education, educational theory was still in its formative years during the decade, and many teachers and members of the general public resisted any changes at all. Yet the relationship between child development and educational philosophy attracted increasing attention from scholars, and lessons in appreciation and expression replaced the "drill and exercise" approach in the classrooms of certain public-school teachers. This more "creative," less mechanical approach was intended to equip students for efficient participation in democratic life.

**Curriculum.** During the 1920s the actual curriculum was modified to stress citizenship as well as preparation for the workplace. The new curriculum emphasized algebra, geometry, civics, American government and history, industrial arts, home economics, and personal hygiene. These courses were intended to stimulate a student's personal ambition, ideals, and sense of service.

**Dalton Laboratory Plan.** The Dalton Laboratory Plan, which combined methods of Italian educator Maria Montessori and John Dewey, involved students' working on long-term individualized projects in a laboratory setting. Students were required to research a topic, write a lengthy report, and make an oral presentation of their materials. During the early 1920s Ernest Jackman and Helen Parkhurst implemented this method in the high school at Dalton, Massachusetts, and in the course of the decade the Dalton Plan became popular in schools throughout the United States and western Europe.

**The Contract Plan.** The Contract Plan, a modification of the Dalton Plan, was devised by Harry L. Miller who worked at Wisconsin High School, the campus school of the University of Wisconsin. Under the Dalton Plan the individualized assignment was agreed upon by student and teacher; under the Contract Plan the student and teacher created a contract that specified in advance

## PUPILS IN PUBLIC AND PRIVATE HIGH SCHOOLS 1869–1930

| Year | Number of Public High Schools | Students in Public and Private High Schools | Percentage of Students in Public High Schools | Percentage of Students in Private High Schools | Percentage of Total Population |
|---|---|---|---|---|---|
| 1869–1870 | c. 500 | 80,227 | | | 2.0 |
| 1879–1880 | c. 800 | 110,289 | | | 3.0 |
| 1889–1890 | 2,526 | 202,969 | 68.13 | 31.87 | 5.0 |
| 1894–1895 | 4,712 | 350,099 | 74.74 | 25.26 | 7.5 |
| 1899–1900 | 6,005 | 519,251 | 82.41 | 17.59 | 9.0 |
| 1904–1905 | 7,576 | 679,702 | 86.38 | 13.62 | 10.0 |
| 1909–1910 | 10,213 | 915,061 | 88.63 | 11.37 | 12.5 |
| 1914–1915 | 11,674 | 1,328,984 | 89.55 | 10.45 | 20.0 |
| 1919–1920 | 14,326 | 1,857,155 | 91.00 | 9.00 | 29.0 |
| 1924–1925 | c. 20,000 | 158,000 | 91.60 | 8.40 | 47.0 |
| 1929–1930 | c. 22,000 | | | | 52.0 |

Note: Accurate comparable figures for recent years are not available due to the rise of the junior high school and the inclusion of data for these as part of the secondary school figures.

**Source:** Ellwood P. Cubberley, *Public Education in the United States* (Boston: Houghton Mifflin, 1934), p. 627.

the grade the student wanted and the work required to achieve it. If all tasks for an assignment were satisfactorily completed, the student received the agreed-upon grade. The Contract Plan became popular in the 1920s, and it is still used in some schools today.

Sources:
Ellwood P. Cubberley, *Public Education in the United States* (Boston: Houghton Mifflin, 1934);

Ernest Jackman, "The Dalton Plan," *School Review,* 28 (November 1920): 688–696;

Harry L. Miller, *Creative Teaching and Learning* (New York: Scribners, 1927);

Helen Parkhurst, *Education on the Dalton Plan* (New York: Bell, 1922).

## DEMOGRAPHIC CHANGES

**Population Growth and Education.** Following World War I the population of the United States grew rapidly, with approximately thirteen million children not yet of school age, twenty-five million children between the ages of five and fifteen, and ten million students between the ages of sixteen and twenty. During the decade Americans became more and more interested in child education, health, and welfare. Total losses by death yearly in the population of the United States were approximately two and one-quarter million, a substantial reduction from previous decades. Since a greater number of children sur-

vived to adulthood than ever before, more of them were filling classrooms. Other facts concomitant with the increase in public-high-school enrollment during the decade included rural to urban population mobility, the increased influence of U.S. society, and a cultural awakening to the educational needs of children. The United States thus experienced great expansion in the public elementary and junior high schools.

**Junior High School Growth.** The junior high school system in the United States evolved rapidly during the 1920s. Even before 1910, reports of various professional education committees urged that schools be organized to include junior highs in a 6–3–3 plan. This plan consisted of six years of elementary school, three years of junior high school, and three years of high school. The two public school systems to gain nationwide attention for establishing a 6–3–3 plan were Columbus, Ohio, and Berkeley, California.

**Purpose of the Junior High.** In their early days, interest in junior highs — schools that housed grades 7 and 8 or grades 7, 8, and 9 — was largely administrative. Educators were trying to determine the relative effectiveness of the 6–3–3 school and the 8–4 school by focusing on such matters as achievement, pupil retention, and comparative costs. After the outbreak of World War I, how-

| PERCENT OF ALL SECONDARY PUPILS ENROLLED, 1920-1930 | | |
|---|---|---|
| Year | Reorganized 6-3-3 | In 8-4 Plan |
| 1920 | 14 | 86 |
| 1922 | 23 | 77 |
| 1924 | 30 | 70 |
| 1926 | 41 | 59 |
| 1928 | 46 | 54 |
| 1930 | 52 | 48 |

Source: Ellwood P. Cubberley, *Public Education in the United States* (Boston: Houghton Mifflin, 1934), p. 632.

| ANNUAL BILL FOR LUXURIES AND SCHOOL EXPENDITURES FOR 1920 | |
|---|---|
| For candy | $1,000,000,000 |
| For tobacco | 2,111,000,000 |
| For soft drinks | 350,000,000 |
| Perfumery and cosmetics | 750,000,000 |
| Theater admissions, dues, etc. | 800,000,000 |
| Ice cream | 250,000,000 |
| Cakes, confections, etc. | 350,000,000 |
| Luxurious food, delicacies, etc. | 5,000,000,000 |
| Joy-riding, races, boxing, and pleasure resorts | 3,000,000,000 |
| Furs | 300,000,000 |
| Carpets and luxurious clothing | 1,500,000,000 |
| Automobiles and parts | 2,000,000,000 |
| Toilet soaps | 400,000,000 |
| Pianos and phonographs | 250,000,000 |
| Total for the above luxuries | $21,811,000,000 |
| Total spent for education | 1,036,151,209 |

Source: Ellwood P. Cubberley, *An Introduction to the Study of Education and to Teaching* (Boston: Houghton Mifflin, 1925), p. 444.

ever, the primary emphasis in the junior high was on meeting the distinct needs of early adolescent youth, just as the central orientation of the high school was toward the socialization and vocational development of older teenagers. American society in the 1920s was becoming more complex, and it required a more specialized public-school system. In response the number of junior high and junior/senior high schools dramatically increased from one thousand to four thousand during the 1920s.

**High-School Enrollment.** Not only the number of high schools but also the number of students attending high schools spiraled during the 1920s, an increase that reflected the American people's change in attitude toward education during the decade. For the first time in the country's history, staying in school was regarded as an absolute measure of one's social class; moreover, as the workplace became technologically more sophisticated, a high-school education became almost mandatory. As a result the number of public high schools increased by nearly eight thousand, and the number of teachers increased by nearly sixty thousand during the 1920s.

Source:
Ellwood P. Cubberley, *Public Education in the United States* (Boston: Houghton Mifflin, 1934).

## FUNDING FOR EDUCATION

**Taxes and Education.** Although popular interest in education was widespread during the 1920s, troubling questions about its funding constantly arose. Before the institution of the federal income tax, which came with the ratification of the Sixteenth Amendment in February 1913, most schools were entirely dependent upon appeals to citizens for permission to tax and thereby fund their pedagogical or building programs. The federal income tax promised to provide a more reliable and equitable source of support for education throughout the nation.

But, in fact, federal funding was not substantial and therefore did not have much of an impact until after the 1920s; instead, public education remained largely dependent on state and local taxes for its financial support. In 1924, for example, school systems in the United States received approximately $4 million from the federal government, $262 million from the individual states, and $1⅓ billion from local sources. But the percentage of money allocated to education from these tax sources remained low, and many people, then as now, deplored taxation, however valuable the service it provided. In 1920 Americans invested more than twenty-one times as much in luxury items than they invested, through their tax dollars, in education.

**Equalization of Advantages.** The equalization of funding for education was a major argument for federal participation in this funding. The theory was that if the federal government allocated tax dollars to the states, each student who attended public school would receive equal financial support and enjoy equal facilities regardless of where he or she lived. But this expectation was never realized, since so much of money allocated to education instead was supplied by the states themselves (which might or might not be generous) or through local property taxes. In 1925 Delaware schools received 77.3 percent of their funding from the state and 22.7 percent from local taxation; Kansas schools, on the other hand, obtained only .4 percent of their funding from the state and 99.6 from local taxation. If a community were affluent and its property highly valued, its citizens paid substantial amounts of taxes to support schools; if a community were poor, containing little property of value or few property owners, little tax money for education would be generated. Thus, inequities between school districts, between states, and between regions of the United States existed. In Massachusetts, for example, financial support of children attending the public schools varied widely, ranging from $2,000 to $7,700 per child. In New York State, cities with populations of more than thirty thousand spent an average of 33 percent of their budgets on education, while the rural areas averaged 11 percent of their total spending.

**Administrative Changes.** During the 1920s proper professional school supervision became a joint local and state activity and a central concern of the National Education Association (NEA), which more than quadrupled its membership in the course of the decade. The local superintendent, often termed "city superintendent," became common. The first city superintendent had been appointed in Buffalo, New York, in 1837, with Louisville, Kentucky, installing one later that year; but the office was uncommon for many years until the 1920s. The American Association of School Administrators, a department of the NEA many years, pushed for the establishment of the superintendent's office for each school district having a high school and for a highly trained person to hold the post.

Sources:
Ellwood P. Cubberley, ed., *Readings in Public Education in the United States* (Boston: Houghton Mifflin, 1934);

*The Statistical History of the United States from Colonial Times to the Present* (Stamford, Conn.: Fairfield, 1965), p. 208.

## THE SCOPES TRIAL, 1925

**The Issue.** One of the most incendiary issues facing Americans in the 1920s was the teaching of the theory of evolution. The clash between religious fundamentalism and science resulted in the widely publicized trial of John T. Scopes. On 21 March 1925 the Tennessee legislature had enacted a law prohibiting the teaching of Darwin's theory of evolution in public schools. During the Scopes trial the right of teachers to convey to their students findings of biological science about the origins of human life rather than imparting the biblical account found in Genesis attracted worldwide attention.

In 1925 Joseph Wood Krutch, later an influential literary scholar, was a young reporter covering the Scopes Trial. The following excerpt presents his impressions of Darrow's courtroom presence and of Dayton, Tennessee:

"In Tennessee, as I said in a previous article, intellectual courage is almost dead. Whatever is done in the name of patriotism or religion may consider itself as exempt from any but the most respectful criticism, and anything like a vigorous liberal opinion seemed as unreal and remote in Dayton as the Daytonian psychology seems to a man who has spent his life in intellectual society. Even the State University had given the acquiescence of silence, but he, who came from afar, was a man who dared to do what no Tennessean had done — hold up a mirror that she might see herself as the world saw her — and the effect was electric. That Dayton was converted I should be far from maintaining, but she recognized courage and she respected it. For the first time the insolence of ignorance was shallow because for the first time it was questioned.

"What Darrow's speech would look like in cold print I do not know, but there was unquestionable greatness beheld in the passion with which it was uttered and in the calculation of the moment for utterance; and when he concluded with the solemn warning that 'with flying banners and beating drums we are marching backward to the glorious age of the sixteenth century when bigots lighted faggots to burn the men who dared to bring any intelligence and enlightenment and culture to the human mind' even Dayton stopped to think. However much or little it may have directly accomplished, it gave to Tennessee an invaluable example of the only possible way in which she can face the bigotry which is drawing her back into barbarism."

Source: Joseph Wood Krutch, "Darrow *vs.* Bryan," *Nation*, 121 (29 July 1925): 136.

**The Players.** In defiance of the new law prohibiting the teaching of Darwin's theory, John T. Scopes, a young, popular teacher in the small town of Dayton, Tennessee, presented evolutionary theory to his high-school class. Some of the leaders in the community decided to test the Tennessee law by putting Scopes on trial and enlisting the services of two of the best-known figures in the United States, William Jennings Bryan, who would direct the prosecution, and Clarence S. Darrow, who would lead Scopes's defense team.

The battle of the books in Dayton, Tennessee, on the eve of the Scopes trial

**The Decision.** Between 10 July and 21 July 1925, in the one-hundred-degree heat of the Dayton, Tennessee, courtroom, Bryan and Darrow waged a fierce battle over Scopes's right to teach Darwin's theory. Scopes was ultimately convicted and given a $100 fine, but a Tennessee appeals court overturned the verdict on a technicality. Scopes's conviction by the jury revealed that science and religion were still regarded as antithetical, especially in rural areas of America during the 1920s. In those areas fundamentalism impacted seriously upon the freedoms that teachers and educational administrators had.

Sources:

Mary Lee Settle, *The Scopes Trial: The State of Tennessee v. John Thomas Scopes* (New York: Watts, 1972);

Jerry R. Tompkins, ed., *D-days at Dayton: Reflections on the Scopes Trial* (Baton Rouge: Louisiana State University Press, 1965).

## SPORT AND EDUCATION

**Trends.** Throughout the twentieth century, college and university leaders have attempted to integrate athletics and physical education into student life. After World War I, intramural sports programs were developed; coaches of athletics became members of faculties; university administrators sought greater control over intercollegiate athletics; and critics called for reforms in intercollegiate sports.

**Intramural Athletics.** In the early 1920s Harvard and Yale developed intramural programs of competition in an attempt to provide "sports for all." These programs emphasized activities — tennis, swimming, canoeing, golf, horseback riding, and badminton, for example — that would be carried over to life beyond college. On many campuses physical-education teachers organized class, interfraternity, and interclub competitions in a wide variety of sports.

**Coaches as Teachers.** Although prior to World War I collegiate coaches were not usually members of faculties, during the 1920s many universities required these coaches to teach as well as coach and thus to become faculty members. The expectation that a coach would occupy not only the athletic field but also the formal classroom gave rise to more highly educated coaches in all sports. Moreover, these teacher-coaches became instrumental in establishing on their campuses departments of physical education, which began to appear during the decade.

## REGISTRATION ENROLLMENTS FOR VARIOUS UNIVERSITIES, 1885-1930

| University | 1885 | 1895 | 1905 | 1915 | 1925 | 1930 |
|---|---|---|---|---|---|---|
| California | 197 | 1,781 | 3,294 | 6,434 | 16,294 | 17,322 |
| Georgia | 184 | 299 | 483 | 651 | 1,390 | 1,840 |
| Illinois | 247 | 814 | 3,597 | 5,439 | 11,212 | 12,709 |
| Iowa | 234 | 1,133 | 1,560 | 2,680 | 5,082 | 4,860 |
| Michigan | 524 | 2,818 | 3,832 | 5,833 | 9,422 | 9,431 |
| Minnesota | 54 | 2,171 | 3,633 | 4,484 | 10,170 | 12,400 |
| Nebraska | 142 | 1,397 | 2,728 | 3,832 | 5,930 | 5,795 |
| North Carolina | 230 | 229 | 666 | 1,088 | 2,288 | 2,749 |
| Ohio State | 64 | 805 | 1,835 | 4,599 | 8,849 | 10,709 |
| Texas | 151 | 630 | 1,235 | 2,574 | 4,810 | 5,070 |
| Washington | 6 | 425 | 811 | 3,249 | 6,149 | 7,368 |
| Wisconsin | 313 | 1,520 | 3,010 | 5,128 | 7,760 | 9,401 |
| Chicago | | 1,265 | 2,373 | 3,803 | 5,484 | 5,679 |
| Columbia | 425 | 1,943 | 4,020 | 10,211 | 11,727 | 14,958 |
| Cornell | 461 | 1,638 | 3,230 | 5,598 | 5,397 | 5,725 |
| Harvard | 1,586 | 3,290 | 4,136 | 5,226 | 7,608 | 8,218 |
| Stanford | | 1,100 | 1,568 | 2,054 | 3,117 | 3,556 |
| Yale | 1,086 | 2,350 | 2,992 | 3,300 | 4,722 | 5,259 |

Data for the last two columns were taken from Walter's statistics for autumn registration, as printed annually in *School and Society*. Summer session, extension, and part-time students are not included.

Source: Ellwood P. Cubberley, *Public Education in the United States* (Boston: Houghton Mifflin, 1934), p. 653.

**Carnegie Report on Intercollegiate Athletics.** In 1929 the Carnegie Foundation for the Advancement of Teaching published a report claiming that the college sports establishment was "sodden" with "professionalism" and "commercialism." The most heavily criticized sport was collegiate football, which had become extremely popular and extremely profitable during the decade. Thirty million spectators had spent $50 million on football tickets in 1927. The obvious commercialism of athletics, which in turn led to its overemphasis on many campuses, produced what the Carnegie Report called a "Roman Circus" atmosphere. Although many agreed that the situation in college sports had gotten out of control, few reforms were enacted.

Sources:

John S. Brubacher and Willis Rudy, *Higher Education in Transition* (New York: Harper & Row, 1976);

Foster R. Dulles, *America Learns to Play* (Englewood Cliffs, N.J.: Prentice-Hall, 1940);

Howard J. Savage, *American College Athletics* (New York: Carnegie Foundation, 1929).

## UNIVERSITY ENROLLMENTS

**Spiraling Enrollments.** During the 1920s private and state universities enjoyed dramatic increases in enrollment. At the University of California, University of Georgia, and University of Minnesota enrollments nearly tripled between 1915 and 1930, while other universities doubled their numbers of students. Enrollments in the private colleges and universities also increased significantly during the 1920s.

**Growth in Higher Education.** The doubling of enrollments in colleges and universities during the decade was accompanied by increases in private donations from $7.5 million in 1915 to $25 million in 1930 and a rise in support from state and local governments from $62 million to $152 million. These increases were reversed by the devastating stock-market crash and resulting economic crisis that came in October 1929, but by the end of the decade nearly 150,000 college and university degrees were being granted annually, and the physical-plant value of these institutions totaled nearly $2 billion.

Source:
Ellwood Cubberley, *Public Education in the United States: A Study and Interpretation of American Educational History,* revised edition (Boston: Houghton Mifflin, 1948).

# HEADLINE MAKERS

## NICHOLAS MURRAY BUTLER

### 1862-1947

#### PRESIDENT OF COLUMBIA UNIVERSITY

**Accomplishments.** Nicholas Murray Butler was instrumental in remaking Columbia College into Columbia University during his tenure as a philosophy professor (1885–1901) and as the university's president (1902–1945). Under his leadership in the 1920s and 1930s, Columbia University experienced tremendous growth in staff, students, and facilities. Butler founded the Teachers College as a key part of the university in 1889, and during the 1920s he hired John Dewey, William Heard Kilpatrick, and George S. Counts to teach in the Teachers College. Butler also worked to standardize college-entrance and teacher-certification requirements. In addition, he was active in national and international politics, winning the Nobel Peace Prize in 1931 for his work on the Pact of Paris.

**Early Career.** Butler was born into a middle-class family in Elizabeth, New Jersey. After graduating from Paterson High School at the age of thirteen, he continued his studies privately until he enrolled in Columbia College in 1878. Upon graduating in 1882, he received a three-year fellowship in letters from the college and earned his M.A. in 1883 and his Ph.D. in 1884. After a year of study in Europe, Butler returned to Columbia. In addition to his teaching he served, from 1887 to 1895, on the New Jersey State Board of Education, through which he encouraged nonpartisan control of education, the abolishment of teacher certification by local authorities, and the creation of manual-training courses. After settling in New York City in 1894, Butler was instrumental in the centralization of the education system in the city. He also served as president (1894–1895) of the National Education Association, helping to establish nationwide standards for local school boards. In 1887, as president of the Industrial Education Association, he promoted the professional training of public-school teachers. In 1889 the association's school was chartered, with Butler as its president, as the New York College for the Training of Teachers (renamed the Teachers College in 1892). In 1893, due in large part to Butler's efforts, the Teachers College became affiliated with Columbia. Butler also assisted in the founding of the College Entrance Examination Board (1900), serving as its chairman from 1901 to 1914.

**Growth of Columbia University.** As a faculty member Butler was a leader among those who thought Columbia College should become Columbia University. In 1890 he presented to the trustees a plan to expand the school to provide advanced training for graduate students as well as Columbia College seniors. The plan was adopted with some modifications, and Butler was elected dean of the philosophy department by his fellow faculty members.

Following the resignation of Columbia president Seth Low in 1901, Butler became Columbia's acting president before becoming president in 1902. Under his administration Columbia University experienced unprecedented growth. More than any other university in the country, Columbia emphasized graduate education. Butler enlarged faculty ranks with some of the best individuals in their fields, creating at Columbia what has been called "the American Acropolis." He also increased administrative centralization at the university, justifying this move by claiming that it freed faculty from administrative chores so that they could devote more time to teaching. Critics complained that under Butler's tenure Columbia College's needs were slighted in deference to those of the university. They also pointed to the many resignations and dismissals of faculty members (among them critic Joel E. Spingarn, comparative-literature professor Henry W. L. Dana, and historian Charles A. Beard) who disagreed with Butler's policies as evidence of the president's dictatorial leadership. Butler produced no important book-length scholarship but did publish more than thirty-two hundred essays, speeches, reviews, press releases, and reports. His most famous writing is a two-volume autobiography entitled *Across the Busy Years* (1939–1940), which discusses his experiences during the years 1916 through 1939.

**Political Life.** Throughout his adult life Butler participated in national and international politics. Between 1901 and 1908 he was a close confidant of President Theodore Roosevelt. In 1913 he received Republican electoral votes for the vice presidency of the United States. In 1920 he briefly sought the nomination for president of the United States but soon shifted his support to Harding, believing that his election would be the best way to get the country into the League of Nations. But in the 1920s Butler became disenchanted with the Republican Party's support of Prohibition and high tariffs. In New York he led the campaign against the Eighteenth Amendment until its repeal. In 1927 the State Department asked his help in drafting what would become the Kellogg-Briand Pact. Butler delegated the task to Columbia professors Joseph P. Chamberlain and James T. Shotwell, then went on a public speaking campaign in support of its ratification. He was one of the founders of the Carnegie Endowment for International Peace and served as its president from 1925 to 1945. In 1931 he shared the Nobel Peace Prize with social reformer Jane Adams.

**Acclaim.** Butler was a proud man, and he took great pains to ensure that his biographical entry in *Who's Who* remained the longest entry, surpassing the biographies of Benito Mussolini, Joseph Stalin, and Franklin D. Roosevelt. H. G. Wells once referred to Butler as "the champion international visitor and retriever of foreign orders and degrees." In all, Butler received thirty-seven degrees from international universities and decorations from fifteen countries.

Sources:

Nicholas Butler, *Across the Busy Years: Recollections and Reflections*, 2 volumes (New York: Scribners, 1939–1940);

Albert Marrin, *Nicholas Murray Butler* (Boston: G. K. Hall, 1976).

# JOHN DEWEY

## 1859-1952

### EDUCATIONAL PHILOSOPHER AND PROFESSOR

**Pioneer.** John Dewey was an innovator in the fields of education, psychology, and philosophy. His theories of education were radically different from those previously employed in America and brought him to the forefront of the movement known as "progressive education." Dewey's influence was not limited to America, for at various times during his life he served as educational consultant to Japan, China, Turkey, and Mexico. He believed that research as well as teacher training should be part of the mission of any university's education department. In addition, Dewey was one of the most prominent moral philosophers of the twentieth century.

**The Laboratory School.** After graduating from the University of Vermont in 1879, Dewey taught high school for three years before entering Johns Hopkins University, where he received his doctorate in philosophy in 1884. After ten years at the University of Michigan, he became head of the department of philosophy, psychology, and pedagogy at the newly founded University of Chicago. In 1896 he organized the University Elementary School, better known as the Laboratory School. Here Dewey could test his pedagogical innovations as well as his more general philosophical principles. While in Chicago he formed personal and professional relationships with philosophers William H. Mead and James H. Tufts and reformer Jane Addams. In 1903 the Laboratory School was merged with the Francis W. Parker School. This merger precipitated to a series of disputes with University of Chicago president William Rainey Harper that ultimately led to Dewey's resignation in April 1904. In less than a month he had been hired by Columbia University president Nicholas Murray Butler. For the rest of his life Dewey was associated with Columbia, first holding a primary appointment in the department of philosophy and then a joint appointment at the Teachers College.

**Progressive Education.** Dewey was heavily influenced by the pragmatism of William James and developed it into a scientifically oriented theory of education known as "instrumentalism." Based on his research, Dewey saw education as the accumulation and assimilation of experience. He contended that a child learns through his or her experiences and activities, thereby developing into a balanced personality aware of many things. This theory changed the philosophy of children's education from an emphasis on lecture, memorization, and drill to a focus on students' becoming more actively involved in the learning process; this concept could be described as "learning by doing."

**Moral Philosopher.** Dewey's theories also stressed the moral aspects of education, and he bemoaned the separation of the moral and the intellectual in traditional educational systems. In many of his works Dewey outlined and defined his conception of the moral life. These works include *Ethics* (written with Tufts, 1908), *Democracy and Education* (1916), and *Human Nature and Conduct* (1922). He was a founder of the New School for Social Research (1919). In addition to his research and teaching duties, Dewey was the first president of the American Association of University Professors and was a charter member of the American Civil Liberties Union, the League for Industrial Democracy, and the League of Independent Political Action.

**Influence.** Dewey retired from Columbia and was named professor emeritus in 1930 but continued writing and consulting. His theories drew criticism from realists as being too vague and from theists for being too naturalistic. However, despite these charges Dewey had more influence on the direction of American education than any other theorist in the twentieth century.

Sources:

John Dewey, *Experience and Nature* (Chicago: Open Court, 1925);

Dewey, *Human Nature and Conduct: An Introduction to Social Psychology* (New York: Holt, 1922);

Dewey, *My Pedagogic Creed* (Washington, D.C.: Progressive Education Association, 1929);

Dewey, *The Philosophy of John Dewey* (New York: Holt, 1929);

Dewey, *The Quest for Certainty: A Study of the Relationship of Knowledge and Action* (New York: Minton, Balch, 1929);

Dewey, *Reconstruction in Philosophy* (New York: Holt, 1920);

Martin Dworkin, *Dewey on Education* (New York: Columbia University Teachers College Press, 1959);

George Dykhuizen, *The Life and Mind of John Dewey* (Carbondale: Southern Illinois University Press, 1973).

## SUSAN MILLER DORSEY

### 1857-1946

#### SUPERINTENDENT OF THE LOS ANGELES SCHOOL SYSTEM

**First Female Superintendent.** Susan Miller Dorsey made her mark as superintendent of the Los Angeles public-school system. During her tenure the system experienced huge growth in the number of students and employees. Dorsey managed this growth well, making the Los Angeles system a model for the country.

**Background as a Teacher.** Miller was born in Penn Yan, New York, the daughter of James and Hannah Benedict Miller. After attending the local public schools and Penn Yan Academy, she majored in the classics at Vassar and graduated with a B.A. in 1877. At Wilson College in Chamberburg, Pennsylvania, Miller taught Latin and Greek for a year before returning to Vassar to teach in the classics department. In 1881 Miller married a Baptist minister, Patrick William Dorsey, and they moved to Los Angeles where he accepted a position at the First Baptist Church. She was a social-welfare worker, and their only child, a son, was born in 1888.

**Joining the Los Angeles System.** Dorsey was teaching at Baptist College in Los Angeles when in 1894 her husband deserted her and took their son with him. Two years later she accepted a position at Los Angeles High School, again teaching Latin and Greek. Dorsey served as department chair from 1903 to 1907 and became vice principal of the school in 1907. Miller was chosen assistant superintendent of the Los Angeles city schools in 1913; she was the first woman to hold that position. In 1920 she was appointed superintendent of the Los Angeles school system.

**Growth of the System.** Dorsey served as superintendent of the Los Angeles high-school system from 1920 to 1929. During that time the public-school system experienced rapid growth. Miller saw the system swell from 47,000 students in 1920 to nearly 360,000 in 1929. To meet the demands of this increased enrollment, Dorsey hired more teachers, increasing their ranks from 750 in 1920 to 9,000 in 1929, and supervised a massive building program for the system. During her tenure Dorsey worked successfully with teacher committees in revising the curriculum in the Los Angeles city schools to accommodate the rapid growth in enrollment and the industrial-education needs of businesses in booming southern California. Dorsey looked out for her teachers through her support of higher salaries, sabbatical leaves, and job tenure. She advocated a strong vocational curriculum and special programs for both disabled and gifted students.

**Lasting Influence.** In addition to fulfilling her duties as superintendent, Dorsey was also in the California Teachers Association and the National Education Association (NEA), particularly as a member of the editorial council of the *NEA Journal*. After her retirement in 1929 she served as vice president of the Women's Law Observance Association. Many California colleges and universities, including the University of Southern California and Occidental College, gave Dorsey honorary degrees. She served as a member of the board of trustees of Scripps College (1927) and of the University of Redlands (1929–1933). She was made an honorary life member of the NEA in 1934. The system she did so much to shape honored her in 1937 by naming a school after her.

Sources:

John Franklin Bobbitt, *Curriculum-making in Los Angeles* (Chicago: University of Chicago Press, 1922);

W. E. Givens, "In Memoriam," *NEA Journal,* 35 (April 1946): 183;

James D. Hart, *A Companion to California* (New York: Oxford University Press, 1978);

Edward A. Krug, *The Shaping of the American High School,* volume 2 (New York: Harper & Row, 1972);

"Portrait," *NEA Journal,* 22 (October 1933): 173;

"A Tribute to a Great Leader," *NEA Journal,* 18 (April 1929): 136.

## WILLIAM HEARD KILPATRICK

### 1871-1965

#### PROFESSOR

**Progressive Educator.** William Heard Kilpatrick is commonly seen as a popularizer of John Dewey's theories of education. In a sense he was even more radical than Dewey, his former mentor. During his tenures as professor at Mercer College, Columbia University, and Bennington College, he expanded the scope of "progressive education," creating classes centered upon interaction with students rather than upon the authority of the teacher.

**No Report Cards.** Kilpatrick graduated from Mercer College in Macon, Georgia, with a B.A. in 1892 and an M.A. in 1893. Following a year of study in mathematics at Johns Hopkins, he served as teacher and principal in various Georgia public schools. While holding these positions, Kilpatrick did away with report cards and student punishments. After further training at Johns Hopkins, he returned to Mercer as a professor of mathematics in 1897. In 1904 he was made acting president of the college but left two years later because his liberal religious ideas were unacceptable to the school's trustees. After a year of teaching in Ohio, he studied under John Dewey at the Teachers College of Columbia University, receiving his Ph.D. in 1912.

**Popular Professor.** Kilpatrick began teaching at the Teachers College in 1909. He was an eloquent speaker, a handsome man, and a believer in Dewey's teachings. He became known as "Dewey's interpreter" by most in the educational world. Kilpatrick's classes were always held in the largest classrooms at Teachers College. He was sometimes referred to as the "Million Dollar Professor" because during one summer session students paid the university more than a million dollars in fees to enroll in his classes, a record intake for any professor during the 1920s and 1930s. Kilpatrick often held classes with as many as 650 students, and more than 35,000 students attended his classes during the course of his career.

**Emphasis on Students.** Building on Dewey's "learning by doing" approach, Kilpatrick introduced the project method of teaching to students at Columbia. Kilpatrick's project method called for learning activities in which students had the opportunity to choose, direct, or plan their own studies under conditions similar to those of real life. Kilpatrick went further than Dewey in rejecting a fixed curriculum and advocating pupil-centered instruction. He believed that the ideal class would be one in which students and teachers would work together as equals, learning what at the moment proved useful through "whole-hearted purposeful activity proceeding in a social environment." For Kilpatrick progressive education was essential since science had made the future so unpredictable that teaching had to be adaptable. He also felt that his program was the best method to instill a new system of morality based on internal authority because the older external authorities (like religion, family, and government) were breaking down. Kilpatrick's classes were not dominated by his lectures; rather, class discussion was his preferred manner of teaching.

**Lasting Impact.** In 1923 Kilpatrick became involved in the creation of Bennington College and later served on its board of trustees (1931–1939). He helped found *Social Frontier,* a journal of progressive education, in 1934. Kilpatrick retired from Columbia in 1938. From 1941 to 1951 he was the president of the New York Urban League. Through his teaching and writing (he published fourteen books and 375 articles) Kilpatrick profoundly shaped the direction of American education. Dean Melby of New York University once stated that "Kilpatrick influenced the lives of more teachers and children than any person who has lived in this generation. There isn't a child who hasn't been influenced by his living."

Sources:

Robert L. Church and Michael W. Sedlak, *Education in the United States: An Interpretive History* (New York: Free Press, 1976);

William H. Kilpatrick, *Foundations of Methods: Informal Talks on Teaching* (New York: Macmillan, 1925);

Samuel Tenenbaum, *William Heard Kilpatrick: Trail Blazer in Education* (New York: Harper, 1951).

## ABBOTT LAWRENCE LOWELL

### 1855-1943

#### PRESIDENT OF HARVARD UNIVERSITY

**Reform of Harvard.** A lawyer and a largely self-taught expert on government, Abbott Lawrence Lowell during his tenure as president of Harvard University (1909–1933) remade the university, both on the undergraduate and graduate levels. He stressed the importance of community at the school, revamping the residential system. Lowell was also instrumental in the installation of course concentrations. As president, Lowell attracted some of the best minds to Harvard's faculty, whose academic freedom he strongly defended. In politics Lowell played an important role in both the League of Nations debate and the case of Sacco and Vanzetti.

**Boston Brahmin.** Lowell was a member of one of the oldest and most prominent families in Boston and the brother of astronomer Percival Lowell and poet Amy Lowell. After attending private schools in Boston and Europe he enrolled at Harvard, where he excelled, especially in the field of mathematics. He graduated cum laude and entered Harvard Law School in 1877, from which he received his degree in 1880. With his cousin and brother-in-law, Francis Cabot Lowell, he formed a law firm in 1880; but although he had once aspired to a career on the bench, his energies and talents were soon attracted to education and the study of government. He succeeded his father as a member of the Corporation of the Massachusetts Institute of Technology in 1890, and, in 1900, as the only trustee of the Lowell Institute, a foundation for adult education. For three years, beginning in 1895, Lowell served on the Boston School Committee; his one reform of the system — making the superintendent responsible for teacher appointments — identified him with the rising professionalization of education.

**Scholar of Government.** While working as a lawyer, Lowell began publishing essays and books on various forms of government. In 1889 he published *Essays on Government,* which drew the attention of Woodrow Wilson. His two-volume *Governments and Parties in Continental Europe* (1896) was the first thorough study of its type published in America and led to an invitation to teach part-time at Harvard in 1897; Lowell immediately resigned from his law firm. In 1900 he accepted a professorship in government on the condition that he be allowed to teach half time for half pay so that he could pursue scholarship. His major study was *The Government of England* (1908), which successfully predicted the downfall of the British Empire.

**President Lowell.** Beginning in 1903 Lowell became involved with a movement to remake the educational system at Harvard. He believed that the free-elective system at the college produced mediocre albeit highly specialized students. As a professor and then as president beginning in 1909, Lowell helped replace the free-elective system with one requiring concentration and distribution in a student's choice of studies. He was also instrumental in establishing examinations in fields of concentration and a tutorial system, both based on English models. Believing that a strong sense of community was valuable to a college, Lowell in 1914 began requiring freshmen to live together in special halls and in 1930 opened the school's residential colleges, the Harvard House Plan, that distributed the student body into seven colleges. He established the business, architecture, and public-health schools at Harvard in the 1920s. Despite his belief in the educational value of community, Lowell did not allow African American students to live in the freshman dorms until he was forced to do so by protests in 1922 and 1923. Lowell also advocated limiting the number of Jewish students, a move blocked by Harvard's overseers.

**Controversies.** Lowell supported academic freedom, defending pro-German professor Hugo Münsterburg in 1917. Lowell disagreed with untenured lecturer Harold J. Laski over the Boston police strike of 1919, but when the overseers hinted that Laski should leave Harvard, Lowell responded, "If the Overseers ask for Laski's resignation they will get mine!" He helped found, with former president William Howard Taft, the League to Enforce Peace in 1915. He campaigned for the League of Nations Covenant. In 1927 he chaired an advisory committee for Massachusetts governor Alvan T. Fuller on executive clemency in the Sacco-Vanzetti case. After reviewing the trial record, the committee ruled that the trial had been fair and that the death sentences should be carried out. Lowell had to endure the vilification of opponents to the executions, claiming, "I have done my duty as a citizen with honesty and courage." In his last year at Harvard he created the Society of Fellows, a graduate program designed to encourage independent study. He retired in 1933 but remained active at Harvard and in politics, frequently criticizing New Deal policies and policies of appeasement in dealing with Japan and Germany. He died of a cerebral hemorrhage in January 1943.

Sources:

Abbott L. Lowell, *At War with Academic Traditions in America* (Cambridge, Mass.: Harvard University Press, 1934);

Lowell, *What a College President Has Learned* (New York: Macmillan, 1938);

Henry A. Yeomans, *Abbott Lawrence Lowell, 1856–1943* (Cambridge, Mass.: Harvard University Press, 1948).

# CARTER GODWIN WOODSON

## 1875-1950

### HISTORIAN AND PUBLISHER

**Foremost African American Historian.** Carter Godwin Woodson is widely known as the father of African American studies in the United States. As an educator he encouraged blacks and other Americans to learn more about African American contributions to the history of the United States. During his lifetime he did more to advance this field of study than any other person, producing seminal works in the field. In addition, through his efforts as a publisher he provided other scholars in the field with the means to disseminate their research.

**Difficult Background.** Woodson's parents were former slaves, and he was one of nine children who grew up on a farm near New Canton, Virginia. Work on the farm frequently required the children to miss school, which hampered Woodson's academic progress. In 1895, at the age of twenty, he finally entered high school, graduating two years later. While working as a teacher, Woodson studied at Berea College in Kentucky, graduating with a Litt. B. degree in 1903. He then enrolled at the University of Chicago, and, after teaching for four years in the Philippines, he received his B.A. in 1907 and his M.A. in 1908. In 1908 he became a student at Harvard, working on his doctorate (granted in 1912) while teaching high school in Washington, D.C. He was dean of the liberal arts college at Howard University in Washington, D.C., from 1919 to 1920 and served as dean at West Virginia State College between 1920 and 1922.

**Creation of African American Studies.** Woodson's impassioned desire to establish the study of African American history as a legitimate field was said to have been sparked by Harvard historian Edward Channing's statement that blacks had no history. In 1915 Woodson founded, in Chicago, the Association for the Study of Negro Life and History, the purpose of which was to disseminate information to students and the general public on African American history. This mission was furthered by the founding of the quarterly *Journal of Negro History* in 1916. During the early years of its existence, Woodson supported the journal almost solely from his income as a teacher. The journal published articles by some of the most respected African Americans of the day, including Woodson, Charles H. Wesley, W. E. B. Du Bois, and Marcus W. Jernegan. In 1921 Woodson created Associated Publishers Inc. in order to provide African American authors a means of publishing scholarly works on their history and culture. In order more easily to reach the general rather than academic public, Woodson helped establish Negro History Week in 1926. In 1936 he founded the monthly *Negro History Bulletin* as a means of providing information on African American history to the general public, schoolteachers, and schoolchildren.

**Respected Author.** As well as publishing works by other African American researchers, Woodson himself wrote numerous books on the history and culture of his people. In 1915 he published his first book, *The Education of the Negro Prior to 1861*. Perhaps his most influential work was the textbook *The Negro in Our History* (1922), which had gone into nine editions by 1950; sociologist Alain Locke claimed that more than any other book, it "bore the brunt of the movement for the popularization of Negro History." His published works in the 1920s included *The History of the Negro Church* (1921), *Free Negro Owners of Slaves in the United States* (1924), and *African Myths* (1928). In 1926 Woodson won the Spingarn Medal of the National Association for the Advancement of Colored People. Between 1944 and 1950 he edited the six-volume *Encyclopedia Africana*. At the time of his death, Associated Publishers had published more than fourteen books written or edited by Woodson and close to fifty by other authors.

Sources:

Frank J. Klingberg, "Carter G. Woodson, Historian, and His Contribution to American Historiography," *Journal of Negro History*, 41 ( January 1956): 66–68;

Charles H. Wesley, "Carter G. Woodson as a Scholar," *Journal of Negro History*, 36 ( January 1951): 12–24;

Carter Godwin Woodson, *Negro Makers of History* (Washington, D.C.: Associated Publishers, 1928).

# PEOPLE IN THE NEWS

**Katharine Lee Bates** retired in 1925 after a forty-year teaching career at Wellesley College. Among her collections of poetry, travel, and drama were *Yellow Clover* (1922) and *The Pilgrim Ship* (1926). Her poem "America the Beautiful" was put to music.

**Mary McLeod Bethune** was the founder of the Daytona Normal and Industrial Institute for Negro Girls, which was merged with the Cookman Institute for Men to form Bethune-Cookman College in Daytona Beach in 1923. Bethune served as president of Bethune-Cookman until 1942.

**Charles William Eliot,** who from 1909 to 1910 edited the fifty-volume Harvard Classics series known as "Dr. Eliot's Five-Foot Shelf of Books," published *A Late Harvest,* a collection of his writings, in 1924.

In 1922 **Bernhard Edward Fernow,** noted forester and educator, retired as editor of *Forestry Quarterly* and the *Journal of Forestry,* both of which he had founded.

Author and editor **Glenn Frank** in 1925 was chosen as president of the University of Wisconsin where he brought about educational reform and in 1927 recruited Alexander Meiklejohn to establish and run the Experimental College.

In memory of his son, **Simon Guggenheim** in 1925 founded the philanthropic John Simon Guggenheim Foundation to provide financial support for scholars and artists.

In 1923 **Granville Stanley Hall,** a Johns Hopkins University psychologist and educator who established one of the first psychological laboratories in the United States and wrote many books on child psychology, published his autobiography, *Life and Confessions of a Psychologist.*

**Luther Emmett Holt,** a physician and educator in New York City, retired from the College of Physicians and Surgeons in 1921, was elected president of the American Pediatric Society in 1923, and served as a visiting professor of pediatrics at the Union Medical College in Peking, China, in the fall of 1923.

**John Hope,** the first African American president of Morehouse College, became in 1929 president of the Atlanta University System, composed of Spelman College, Morehouse College, and Atlanta University. Under Hope's leadership, the Atlanta University System provided the first American graduate school for African Americans.

**Alvin Saunders Johnson,** a noted economist and educator who was one of the cofounders of the New School for Social Research in 1919, served as its director starting in 1923. Under his leadership it became one of the most successful institutions of adult education in the United States.

**Charles Hubbard Judd,** an educator and psychologist who was chairman of the department of education at the University of Chicago from 1909 until 1938, wrote *Psychology of Social Institutions* (1926), *Psychology of Secondary Education* (1927), and many other influential books in the field of education.

Art critic and educator **Alain LeRoy Locke,** who had been the first African American to be awarded a Rhodes scholarship, served as chairman of the philosophy department of Howard University during the 1920s. He gained national attention as a chronicler of the Harlem Renaissance that took place following World War I; among the works he published in the 1920s are *Four Negro Poets* (1927), *Plays of Negro Life* (1927), and *The Negro in America* (1936).

**Alexander Meiklejohn** served as president of Amherst College from 1912 until 1924 and taught at the University of Wisconsin in the philosophy department from 1926 until 1932. His influential books on educational issues include *The Liberal College* (1920), *The Experimental College* (1932), and *Free Speech and Its Relationship to Government* (1948). In 1963 he received the Presidential Medal of Freedom.

**Samuel Eliot Morison,** Harvard University and Oxford University history professor during the 1920s, published his *Maritime History of Massachusetts, 1783–1860* in 1921 and his two-volume *Oxford History of the United States* in 1927. Two of his twenty-five books won Pulitzer Prizes, and he was awarded the Presidential Medal of Freedom in 1964.

Arthur Amos Noyes, a chemist and teacher at the Massachusetts Institute of Technology, co-authored a monumental study, *A System of Qualitative Analysis for the Rare Elements,* and was elected president of the American Association for the Advancement of Science in 1927.

Vernon Louis Parrington, intellectual historian and educator, in 1927 published the first two volumes of *Main Currents in American Thought,* for which he won a Pulitzer Prize in 1928.

James Harvey Robinson, educator and historian who helped found the New School for Social Research, during the 1920s published two of his best-known books, *The Mind in the Making* (1921) and *The Ordeal of Civilization* (1926).

Harold Ordway Rugg, who taught at the University of Chicago from 1915 to 1919 and Columbia University from 1920 to 1951, produced the twelve-volume *Social Science Pamphlets* (1921–1928) and the fourteen-volume *Man and His Changing Society* series (1929–1945). His most important works in the field of education were *The Child-Centered School* (1928) and *Culture and Education in America* (1931). Rugg edited the *Journal of Educational Psychology* from 1920 to 1931.

University of Chicago anthropologist Edward Sapir, who was a pioneer in the field of descriptive linguistics, published his important *Language: An Introduction to the Study of Speech* in 1921.

In 1922 Martha Carey Thomas retired after thirty years as president of Bryn Mawr College. Thomas was the first woman academic in the United States to hold the title of dean. She helped establish the first graduate program at a women's college and helped organize the International Federation of University Women and the Association to Promote Scientific Research.

# DEATHS

Frank Frost Abbott, 64, Princeton University history professor and author of *Roman Political Institutions* (1901), 27 July 1924.

Henry A. Beers, 79, Yale English professor best known for his *History of English Romanticism* (1899), 7 September 1926.

T. G. Bergen, 81, president of the Brooklyn Board of Education, 13 March 1929.

Maximillan D. Berlitz, 67, teacher and founder of the Berlitz Schools of Languages, 6 April 1921.

Albert J. Beveridge, 64, former United States senator and historian whose best work was the two-volume, Pulitzer Prize–winning *Life of John Marshall* (1916, 1919), 27 April 1927.

Melville Madison Bigelow, 74, lawyer and professor at the University of Michigan and Harvard University; he wrote influential law textbooks and histories, including *History of Procedure in England from the Norman Conquest* (1896), 4 May 1921.

Ezra Brainerd, 80, former president of Middlebury College, 8 December 1924.

Oscar Browning, 86, historian, educator, and author of *An Introduction to the History of Educational Theories* (1888) and *History of the Modern World* (1912), 6 October 1923.

Ernest De Witt Burton, 69, University of Chicago religion professor who focused on New Testament interpretation and published many essays in the *American Journal of Theology,* 26 May 1925.

Albert Stanburrough Cook, 74, Yale University English professor, former president of the Modern Language Association of America, founder and president of the American Concordance Society, and author of *The Higher Study of English* (1906), 1 September 1927.

Archibald Cary Coolidge, 61, historian and director of Harvard University Library and author of *The United States as a World Power* (1908), 14 January 1928.

J. M. Coulter, 77, dean of American botanists, 23 December 1928.

David Duncan, 82, educator, private secretary to Herbert Spencer, and author of *The Life and Letters of Herbert Spencer* (1908), 18 May 1923.

G. M. Duncan, 70, professor, Yale University logician and metaphysician, 26 July 1928.

H. D. Foster, 64, Dartmouth historian for thirty-four years, 27 December 1927.

**Basil Lanneau Gildersleeve,** 92, Greek and Latin scholar at the University of Virginia and Johns Hopkins University, author of *Latin Grammar* (1867), and founder and editor of the *American Journal of Philology*, 9 January 1924.

**Frank Wakeley Gunsaulus,** 65, president of Armour Institute of Technology and lecturer in divinity at Yale; his best known works were *William Ewart Gladstone: A Biographical Study* (1898) and *Paths to the City of God* (1906), 17 March 1921.

**Emil G. Hirsch,** 71, rabbi, professor of rabbinics at the University of Chicago, and president of the Chicago Public Library, 7 January 1923.

**W. Harry Pratt Judson,** 77, president emeritus of the University of Chicago, professor of political science, author of *The Growth of the American Nation* (1895), and coeditor of the *American Historical Review* (1895–1902), 4 March 1927.

**W. C. B. Kemp,** 78, for sixty years a Columbia University student, 3 February 1929.

**W. V. Lawrence,** 85, founder of Sarah Lawrence College and Lawrence Hospital, 16 May 1927.

**Samuel Spahr Laws,** 97, former president of the University of Missouri from 1876 to 1889, who published many works on religion, 9 January 1921.

**J. H. Leete,** 60, educator and director from 1917 to 1928 of the Carnegie Library in Pittsburgh, 13 October 1929.

**Alice Longfellow,** 78, a daughter of poet Henry Wadsworth Longfellow and a founder of Radcliffe College, 7 December 1928.

**H. M. Reynolds,** 72, Greek professor at Yale University for thirty-nine years, 3 October 1929.

**William Scarborough,** 79, African American educator and president emeritus of Wilberforce University, 9 September 1926.

**William Thompson Sedgwick,** 56, professor of biology at the Massachusetts Institute of Technology and curator at the Lowell Institute, 25 January 1921.

**W. S. Simkins,** 86, professor at the University of Texas; he claimed to have fired the first shot at Fort Sumter, 27 February 1929.

**William Milligan Sloane,** 78, Seth Low Professor of History at Columbia University and former chancellor and president of the American Academy of Arts and Letters, 11 September 1928.

**M. S. Stratton,** 81, professor and dean at Wellesley College, 17 December 1925.

**William Jewett Tucker,** 87, president emeritus of Dartmouth College, 29 September 1926.

**J. M. Tyler,** 78, biologist on the Amherst College faculty for fifty years, 12 April 1929.

**H. H. Vail,** 86, schoolbook editor and publisher, 2 September 1925.

**Sarah F. Whiting,** 81, professor who was for forty years on the Wellesley College faculty, 13 September 1927.

**Woodrow Thomas Wilson,** 67, twenty-eighth president of the United States and former professor of political economy/jurisprudence at and president of Princeton University, 3 February 1924.

**Theodore Salisbury Woolsey,** 76, son of Yale University president Theodore Dwight Woolsey and a member of the Yale law faculty from 1879 to 1911, 24 April 1929.

**T. W. D. Worthen,** 82, mathematician who served forty-eight years on the Dartmouth faculty, 21 September 1927.

# PUBLICATIONS

John Franklin Bobbitt, *Curriculum-making in Los Angeles* (Chicago: University of Chicago Press, 1922);

Bobbitt, *How to Make a Curriculum* (Boston: Houghton Mifflin, 1924);

John Seiler Brubacher, *The Judicial Power of the New York State Commissioner of Education: Its Growth and Present Status with a Digest of Decisions* (New York: Teachers College, Columbia University, 1927);

Brubacher, *Scientific Method in Supervision: The Second Yearbook of the National Conference of Supervisors and Directors of Instruction* (New York: Teachers College, Columbia University, 1929);

Edmund de Schweinitz Brunner, *A Church and Community Survey of Pend Oreille County* (New York: Doran, 1922);

Julian Butterworth, *Principles of Rural School Administration* (New York: Macmillan, 1926);

M. M. Chambers, "Every Man a Brick," in *The Status of Military Training in American Universities* (Bloomington, Ill.: Public School Publishing, 1927);

George S. Counts, *School and Society in Chicago* (New York: Harcourt, Brace, 1928);

Counts, *Secondary Education and Industrialism* (New York: Harcourt, Brace, 1929);

Counts, *The Selective Character of American Secondary Education* (Chicago: University of Chicago, 1922);

Counts, *The Social Composition of Boards of Education: A Study in the Social Control of Public Education* (Chicago: University of Chicago, 1927);

Ellwood P. Cubberley, *The History of Education: Educational Practice and Progress Considered as a Phase of the Development and Spread of Western Civilization* (Boston: Houghton Mifflin, 1920);

Cubberley, *State School Administration: A Textbook of Principles* (Boston: Houghton Mifflin, 1927);

John Dewey, *Am I Getting an Education?* (Garden City, N.Y.: Doubleday, Doran, 1929);

Dewey, *Art and Education* (Merion, Pa.: Barnes Foundation Press, 1929);

Dewey, *Characters and Events: Popular Essays in Social and Political Philosophy* (New York: Holt, 1929);

Dewey, *Experience and Nature* (Chicago: Open Court, 1925);

Dewey, *Human Nature and Conduct: An Introduction to Social Psychology* (New York: Holt, 1922);

Dewey, *My Pedagogic Creed* (Washington, D.C.: Progressive Education Association, 1929);

Dewey, *The Philosophy of John Dewey* (New York: Holt, 1929);

Dewey, *The Quest for Certainty: A Study of the Relationship of Knowledge and Action* (New York: Minton, Balch, 1929);

Dewey, *Reconstruction in Philosophy* (New York: Holt, 1920);

Dewey, *The Sources of a Science of Education* (New York: Liveright, 1929);

Francis Wyche Dunn, *Interest Factors in Primary Reading Material* (New York: Teachers College, Columbia University, 1921);

Frank N. Freeman, *Mental Tests, Their History, Principles and Applications* (Boston: Houghton Mifflin, 1926);

Freeman, *Motion Pictures in the Classroom; An Experiment to Measure the Value of Motion Pictures as Supplementary Aids in Regular Classroom Instruction* (Boston: Houghton Mifflin, 1929);

Freeman, *Visual Education; A Comparative Study of Motion Pictures and Other Methods of Instruction; An Investigation Made with the Aid of a Grant From the Commonwealth Fund by Frank N. Freeman, A. P. Hollis, Lena A. Shaw, F. D. McClusky, Caroline Hoefer, D. E. Walker . . . and Others* (Chicago: University of Chicago Press, 1924);

Basil L. Gildersleeve, *Essays and Studies: Educational and Literary* (New York: Stechert, 1924);

Florence Goodenough, *The Kuhlman-Binet Tests for Children of Preschool Age; A Critical Study and Evaluation* (Minneapolis: University of Minnesota Press, 1928);

Goodenough, *Measurement of Intelligence by Drawings* (New York: Arno Press, 1926);

G. Stanley Hall, *Life and Confessions of a Psychologist* (New York: Appleton, 1923);

Hall, *Recreations of a Psychologist* (New York: Appleton, 1920);

John Louis Horn, *The American Elementary Schools; A Study in Fundamental Principles* (New York: Century, 1923);

Horn, *The Education of Exceptional Children: A Consideration of Public Schools Problems and Policies in the Fields of Differentiated Education* (New York: Century, 1924);

Horn, *Principles of Elementary Education* (New York: Century, 1929);

Herman Harrell Horne, *The Philosophy of Education: Being the Foundations of Education in the Related Natural and Mental Sciences* (New York: Macmillan, 1927);

Charles H. Judd, *New Materials of Instruction* (Bloomington, Ill.: Public School Publishing, 1920);

Judd, *Psychological Analysis of the Fundamentals of Arithmetic* (Chicago: University of Chicago, 1927);

Judd, *Psychology of Secondary Education* (Boston: Ginn, 1927);

Judd, *The Psychology of Social Institutions* (New York: Macmillan, 1926);

Judd, *Silent Reading: A Study of the Various Types* (Chicago: University of Chicago, 1922);

Judd, *Summary of Educational Investigations Relating to Arithmetic* (Chicago: University of Chicago, 1925);

Judd, *The Unique Character of American Secondary Education* (Cambridge: Harvard University Press, 1928);

William Heard Kilpatrick, *Education for a Changing Civilization: Three Lectures Delivered on the Luther Kellogg Foundation at Rutgers* (New York: Macmillan, 1926);

Kilpatrick, *Foundations of Method: Informal Talks on Teaching* (New York: Macmillan, 1925);

Robert S. Lynd and Helen M. Lynd, *Middletown: A Study in Contemporary American Culture* (New York: Harcourt, Brace, 1929);

Alexander Meiklejohn, *Freedom and the College* (New York: Century, 1923);

Meiklejohn, *The Liberal College* (Boston: Marshall Jones, 1920);

Meiklejohn, *Philosophy* (Chicago: American Library Association, 1926);

Walter S. Monroe, *Directing Learning in the High School* (Garden City, N.Y.: Doubleday, Page, 1927);

Monroe, *Educational Tests and Measurements* (Boston: Houghton Mifflin, 1924);

Monroe, *The High School* (Garden City, N.Y.: Doubleday, Doran, 1928);

Monroe, *An Introduction to the Theory of Educational Measurements* (Boston: Houghton Mifflin, 1923);

William Martin Proctor, *The Junior College: Its Organization and Administration* (Stanford: Stanford University Press, 1927);

Harold O. Rugg, *A Primer of Graphics and Statistics for Teachers* (Boston: Houghton Mifflin, 1925);

Rugg, *Resources, Industries and Cities of America* (New York: Columbia University Teachers College Press, 1926);

Rugg and Ann Shumaker, *The Child-Centered School: An Appraisal of the New Education* (Yonkers-on-Hudson, N.Y.: World Book, 1928);

Upton Sinclair, *The Goslings: A Study of the American Schools* (Pasadena: Upton Sinclair, 1924);

Edward Lee Thorndike, *Educational Psychology* (New York: Columbia University Teachers College Press, 1921);

Thorndike and Arthur I. Gates, *Elementary Principles of Education* (New York: Macmillan, 1929);

Thorndike and others, *Adult Learning* (New York: Macmillan, 1928);

Thorndike and others, *The Measurement of Intelligence* (New York: Columbia University Teachers College Press, 1927);

Thorndike and others, *The New Methodical Arithmetic* (New York: Rand, McNally, 1921);

Thorndike and others, *The Psychology of Algebra* (New York: Macmillan, 1923);

Thorndike and others, *The Psychology of Arithmetic* (New York: Macmillan, 1922);

Herbert Toops, *Trade Tests in Education* (New York: Columbia University Teachers College Press, 1921);

Mabel Barbara Trilling and others, *Home Economics in American Schools* (Chicago: University of Chicago, 1920);

Carter Godwin Woodson, *African Myths, Together with Proverbs: A Supplementary Reader Composed of Folk Tales from Various Parts of Africa, Adapted to the Use of Children in the Public Schools* (Washington, D.C.: Associated Publishers, 1928);

Woodson, *The Negro in Our History* (Washington, D.C.: Associated Publishers, 1922);

*American Educational Digest,* periodical; became *School Executives Magazine,* January 1929;

*Bulletin of the National Association of Secondary School Principals,* periodical; became *Bulletin of the Department of Secondary School Principals,* April 1928;

*California Journal of Secondary Education,* periodical;

*Curriculum Journal,* periodical; became *News Bulletin of the Society for Curriculum Study;*

*Frontiers of Democracy,* periodical; became *Social Frontiers;*

*General Science Quarterly,* periodical; became *Science Education,* May 1929;

*Harvard Teachers Record,* periodical; became *Harvard Educational Review,* January 1937;

*Historical Outlook,* periodical;

*Journal of Educational Method,* periodical; became *Educational Method,* October 1929;

*Junior High School Clearing House,* periodical; became *Junior High Clearing House,* April 1928, and *Junior-Senior High School Clearing House,* September 1929;

*Michigan Educational Journal,* periodical;

*Occupations,* periodical; became *Vocational Guidance Magazine.*

# FASHION

by JUDITH S. BAUGHMAN

## CONTENTS

*Sidebars and tables are listed in italics.*

# 1920

- Women's hems range from ankle length to calf length.

- A new three-button sports coat in cartridge cloth — the fabric used to hold powder charges during World War I — becomes a predecessor of the lightweight men's summer suit.

- Architect Addison Mizner constructs Palm Beach, Florida, Spanish-style mansions with exotic names (Villa de Sarmiento, El Mirasol) for such millionaires as A. J. Drexel Biddle, George and Isabel Dodge, and Harold S. Vanderbilt.

- John Manning Van Heusen introduces a semistiff three-ply detached collar.

- In New York City Raymond H. Dietrich and Thomas L. Hibbard found LeBaron Carrossiers, an "automotive architecture" firm.

- Men's suits with two pairs of pants become popular.

**16 Feb.** James H. Sherburne, chairman of a Massachusetts state commission, reports that working-class purchases of silk stockings and other "long-desired luxuries" have contributed to a 92 percent boost in the cost of living in the state since 1914.

**Sept.** Henry M. Leland introduces the Model L Lincoln, which he envisions as a "permanent car," so well made that it will never wear out or fail.

# 1921

- Jantzen presents a clinging knit one-piece bathing suit in men's and women's styles. Advertized as "the suit that changed bathing to swimming," it features a scoop-necked, sleeveless tunic attached to trunks and is decorated with stripes at the chest, hips, and thighs.

- High-buttoned shoes for men are replaced by oxfords, low-cut shoes that tie.

- Men's wristwatches become popular.

- Belted Norfolk jackets worn with either flannel slacks or knickers are popular sportswear for younger men.

- Among dress accessories for men are spats and canes.

- The Duesenberg Automobile and Motor Company introduces the Model A Duesenberg, the first U.S. straight-eight and first U.S. automobile with overhead camshaft and hydraulic brakes.

**4 Mar.** Warren G. Harding arrives at his inauguration in a Packard Twin-Six; he is the first president-elect to ride in an automobile to inaugural ceremonies.

**May** Construction begins on Chicago's Wrigley Building, which has a thirty-two-story tower and 442,000 square feet of office space; completed in 1924, its architects are Graham, Anderson, Probst, and White.

# 1922

- Architectural delineator Hugh Ferriss executes and publishes his influential drawings of the four stages of skyscraper construction.

- Industrial architect Albert Kahn begins construction on Henry Ford's new automobile production plant on the Rouge River in Michigan.

- The Ford Motor Company buys the Lincoln Motor Company from Henry M. Leland, who had also founded Cadillac in 1903; Edsel Ford, Henry Ford's son, plans to develop the Lincoln as Ford's luxury car.

- German architect Ludwig Mies van der Rohe introduces "ribbon windows" — glass evenly divided by concrete slabs — in plans for an office building; Mies van der Rohe later will use this style of window in many of his European and American buildings.

- Dr. Lulu Hunt Peters's *Diet and Health with Key to the Calories* (1918) appears on the best-seller lists, where it will remain through 1926; for two years — 1924 and 1925 — it heads the nonfiction list.

- Hat pins in onyx and crystal are popular in Paris, as are strapped, perforated, chunky-heeled pumps.

- The Prince of Wales wears a Fair Isles sweater with knickers while playing golf at St. Andrews, Scotland, and starts a rage in America and Europe for these brightly colored, patterned wool sweaters.

- The women's "slouch" suit, with jacket bloused over a hip-level belt, becomes popular.

| | |
|---|---|
| **5 May** | Coco Chanel introduces Chanel No. 5, which will become the world's best-known perfume. |
| **30 May** | The Lincoln Memorial is dedicated; the building has been designed by architect Henry Bacon, and the statue of the seated Lincoln has been sculpted by Daniel Chester French. |
| **July** | *Fruit, Garden and Home* is first published as a monthly magazine by Edwin Thomas Meredith in Des Moines, Iowa. In August 1924 it is renamed *Better Homes & Gardens*, and by 1928 it becomes the first magazine to achieve one million in circulation without featuring fiction or fashions. |
| **23 Dec.** | A Gothic-style plan by John Mead Howells and Raymond M. Hood is announced as the winner of the international competition for the design of Col. Robert R. McCormick's Chicago Tribune Tower; the second-place design is by Finland's Eliel Saarinen. |

## 1923

- Charles F. Kettering develops fast-drying Duco lacquer, which brings color to mass-produced cars.

- The "cake-eater's suit" is adopted by many noncollegiate young men.

- Ida Cohen Rosenthal founds the Maiden Form Brassiere Company, later renamed Maidenform.

- The "shingle" cut — an extremely short hairstyle with a single curl pulled forward from each ear onto each cheek — is increasingly seen in Europe and the United States.

- Felt cloche hats that are pulled down low on the forehead and feature small, slightly upturned brims in front and back are gaining popularity in Paris and America. The cloche is the perfect hat for the shingle cut.

- Artificial silk (rayon) stockings, often seamless and flesh-colored, are being worn with shorter skirts.

**1924**

- The excavation of King Tutankhamen's tomb, which began in late 1922, produces a rage for "Egyptian" accessories.

- The upscale Bergdorf Goodman women's fashion store opens a ready-to-wear department at its original Fifth Avenue location.

**22 Feb.**    The first successful U.S. chinchilla farm — which has seven males and four females — is established in Los Angeles.

**June**    Packard introduces its popular Single-Eight motor car.

- Architect Louis H. Sullivan publishes his influential book *The Autobiography of an Idea.*

- Lewis Mumford publishes his architectural study *Sticks and Stones: A Study of American Architecture and Civilization.*

- Henry Wright and Clarence S. Stein begin constructing the first of their planned communities, Sunnyside Gardens (completed in 1928) in Queens, New York; in 1928 they start work on a second "garden community," Radburn, New Jersey.

- Women adopt dramatic accessories, including long strings of pearls draped over the shoulders and bracelets circling the biceps.

- Heavy makeup and plucked, redrawn eyebrows are popular with women.

- Raymond Hood's black-and-gold American Radiator Building is completed in New York City.

- Loew's State Theater, one of Thomas W. Lamb's most famous "hard-top" movie palaces, opens in Saint Louis.

- Men adopt blue blazers and round-toed oxfords.

- Double-breasted suits worn with vests and bow ties remain popular with men.

- Macy's, one of the country's best-known retailers of men's and women's ready-to-wear fashions, completes an addition to its Thirty-fourth Street building. Further additions in 1928 and 1931 take up all but two small corners of the city block between Broadway and Seventh Avenue, making Macy's the world's largest department store under one roof. The store boasts two million square feet of floor space.

- Elsa Maxwell is hired as a press agent for couturier Jean Patou.

**29 Aug.**    Edward, Prince of Wales, arrives in New York; he charms the country and continues to exert a strong influence on men's fashion in Europe and America.

**Sept.**    Gimbel Brothers opens an upscale clothing store, Saks & Company, later to be called Saks Fifth Avenue.

- Addison Mizner begins construction of Boca Raton, but his plans for the city are abandoned when the Florida real-estate market collapses in spring 1926.

**Fall**    Jean Patou imports six American girls to help model fashions in his Paris couture house.

## 1925

- Chanel introduces her short, open, collarless cardigan jacket as part of her Chanel suit.
- Skirts rise to knee length.
- Oxford bags — voluminous pants — are adopted by American college men.
- Antoine de Paris opens a hair salon at Saks Fifth Avenue.
- Tans for women become popular, as do skin lotions and moisturizers.
- Inlaid and embossed linoleums are introduced.
- For the first time, more American men wear attached-collar shirts than wear detached-collar ones.
- Raymond H. Dietrich leaves LeBaron, Inc., and founds Dietrich, Inc., an automobile-custom-design firm in Detroit.
- Four-piece knickerbocker suits — knickers, jacket, vest, and traditional trousers — are widely sold.

**18 July** The Exposition Internationale des Arts Décoratifs et Industriels Modernes opens in Paris.

## 1926

- The cocktail dress becomes popular as speakeasy attire for women.
- French tennis player René Lacoste introduces the knit, short-sleeved Lacoste tennis or polo shirt with a crocodile emblem on the chest.
- New York's monumental Standard Oil Building, designed by Carrère and Hastings, is completed.
- Construction begins on William Van Alen's Chrysler Building (completed in 1930); this graceful New York City skyscraper becomes an embodiment of both Art Deco style and 1920s American exuberance.
- Chanel introduces the "little black dress," which *Vogue* labels "a Ford," a serviceable, enduring success.

**19 Feb.** The ballet *Skyscrapers*, scored by John Alden and commissioned by Sergei Diaghilev, premieres at the Metropolitan Opera House. The ballet uses jazz idiom to celebrate the most significant development in metropolitan architecture during the 1920s.

## 1927

- The Avalon, the greatest of John Eberson's "atmospheric" movie palaces, opens in Chicago.
- *Toward a New Architecture*, an English translation of Le Corbusier's *Vers une architecture* (1923), is published in New York.
- Elsa Schiaparelli makes her fashion debut with her trompe l'oeil (optical illusion) sweater.
- General Motors adds an Art and Colour Section, which is headed by the young automotive designer Harley J. Earl; it is the first styling department established by an American automobile company.

- Grauman's Chinese Theater (architects Meyer, designer Raymond Kennedy), one of the legendary American movie palaces, opens in Hollywood.

**11 Mar.** The Roxy Theater, the "Cathedral of the Motion Picture," opens at Seventh Avenue and Fiftieth Street in New York City with the premiere of Gloria Swanson's *The Love of Sunya*. The creation of Samuel L. Rothafel (Roxy), it is the most lavish of American movie palaces.

**25 May** Henry Ford announces that the Model A Ford will be produced and the Model T discontinued. Ford assembly lines begin manufacturing the new automobiles in October, and the first Model A display cars appear in November.

## 1928

- Architect R. Buckminster Fuller introduces his prefabricated Dymaxion House, a hexagonal module suspended from a central utility mast with outer walls of glass.

- The Packard, the most popular of the American luxury cars, achieves sales of fifty thousand.

- Fashion designer Hattie Carnegie opens a dress shop on East Forty-ninth Street in New York City.

- Hollywood costume designer Adrian introduces the slouch hat, which will supplant the cloche, in the Greta Garbo movie *A Woman of Affairs*.

- The trench coat and the similar French aviator coat replace the long yellow slicker as favorite rain wear on Ivy League campuses.

- The Model A Ford is offered in a wood-sided station-wagon version, the first large-scale production of this type of automobile body.

- The Model BB Splendid Stutz is introduced.

- The Designers' Gallery Show, which tours ten major American cities, displays modernistic designs.

**1 Jan.** The Milam Building, the first air-conditioned office building in the United States, opens in San Antonio, Texas.

**1 Dec.** The Model J Duesenberg, one of America's most spectacular automobiles, is introduced at the New York Automobile Salon.

## 1929

- Built-in furniture becomes popular.

- Mies van der Rohe premieres the Barcelona chair at the Barcelona Fair. This chair features curved steel legs and back supports topped by leather-covered foam-rubber cushions.

- *Middletown: A Study in American Culture*, by Robert S. Lynd and Helen Merrell Lynd, is published. Among the subjects it treats are the tastes in homes, clothing, and automobiles of the citizens of Middletown (actually Muncie, Indiana).

- Construction begins on Shreve, Lamb, and Harmon's Empire State Building in New York City; the tallest building in the world, it is completed in 1931.

- Ground is broken for Raymond Hood's modernist McGraw-Hill Building, which is finished in 1932.

- Howe and Lescaze's Philadelphia Savings Fund Society Building (completed in 1932) is under construction; it is an early expression of International Style in America.

- During this year American women purchase an average of one pound of powder and eight rouge compacts apiece.

- Hugh Ferriss's visionary *The Metropolis of Tomorrow* is published.

- The United States has 377 skyscrapers that are more than twenty stories high; 188 of them are in New York City.

**Feb.**    The Metropolitan Museum of Art opens its Contemporary American Decorative Arts Show, displaying modernist rooms by five major American designers.

**Spring**    Jean Patou's spring show restores the natural waistline and bustline to women's dresses.

**Fall**    In his fall show Patou drops skirt lengths. His 1929 shows are credited with killing the "garçonne" — or "little boy" — look and with ushering in the dominant style in women's fashion during the 1930s.

# OVERVIEW

**Force of Fashion.** In his 1928 study *Economics of Fashion* Columbia University marketing professor Paul H. Nystrom declared, "Fashion is one of the greatest forces in present-day life. It pervades every field and reaches every class. . . . It has always been a factor in human life but never more forceful, never more influential and never wider in scope than in the last decade, and it gives every indication of growing still more important." For Nystrom fashion included men's and women's clothing, of course, but also their cosmetic and hygiene products, their automobiles, and their household appliances and furnishings. Fashion, Nystrom said, was more than an expression of individual taste; it was instead a statement of group membership, of involvement in the currents of one's time. "To be out of fashion," he wrote, "is, indeed, to be out of the world."

**Communication.** At no time before the 1920s had fashion been so widely disseminated. During the decade technology vastly improved communication and thus began an actual uniting of the United States. By 1925 about 50 million Americans had access to radios, and smaller but still significant numbers regularly attended movies. Both radio and movies helped spread the word about what people were wearing and driving and how they were decorating their homes or designing their public buildings. Moreover, automobiles — more than 22 million of them were on U.S. roads by 1930 — allowed people not only to commute between home and job but also to travel beyond their city, state, or region. Increased ease of travel began to break down the cultural isolation of small towns and rural areas. Furthermore, magazines and newspapers of the 1920s increasingly addressed fashion issues through columns about and advertisements for the latest in clothing, autos, housing, and furnishings. Thus, improved communication meant that a large proportion of the general population was exposed to the latest fashion trends and responded, positively or negatively, to them.

**Foreign Influences in Attire.** During the 1920s the most distinctive clothing styles originated in Europe: in France for women's attire and in England for men's. The French designers Coco Chanel and Jean Patou were largely responsible for introducing the youthful, sporty, boyish look for women — and Patou for ending its popularity in 1929; the charming Prince of Wales and his youthful subjects at Oxford University variously popularized, among other items, knickers or plus fours, Fair Isles sweaters, dinner jackets as opposed to the more formal tails, and Oxford bags for young men. Their mothers no doubt felt most comfortable in clothing inspired by the more conservative French couture houses — Worth or Lanvin or Vionnet; their fathers always preferred suits influenced by the custom tailors of London's Savile Row.

**American Conditions and Young Women's Fashions.** Yet if young American women bobbed their hair, abandoned their corsets, and donned short skirts, their actions were prompted — or at least reinforced — as much by specific American conditions as by French fashion dictates. In 1920 the ratification of the Nineteenth Amendment won them the vote, or the promise of the vote when they turned twenty-one. They were enrolling in colleges or entering offices in record numbers, and they enjoyed driving automobiles and engaging in sports. Thus, their bobbed hair and their short, loosely fitted dresses made sense. Yet these fashions often shocked the young women's elders, who believed they signaled libertine behavior — licentious dancing, necking and petting, smoking, and drinking of the bootleg whiskey that resulted from Prohibition. Parents worried; clergymen preached; and several state legislatures tried unsuccessfully to pass laws fixing skirt lengths at six inches or nine inches or twelve inches from the ground. These responses from mature adults simply increased young women's fondness for their short skirts and cosmetics. What fun is it to rebel if nobody notices or cares?

**American Conditions and Young Men's Fashions.** Young men, too, often adopted their attire in response to specific American conditions. Their raccoon coats and baggy pants could be used to conceal illegal flasks (one mark of youthful rebellion against authority), and their blazers, flannel slacks, and camel-hair coats could communicate their status — affirming their memberships in Ivy League clubs or state-university fraternities. As young women became more apparently liberated from their traditional roles, young men seemed increasingly perplexed by the evolving nature of the male-female relationship (see, for example, F. Scott Fitzgerald's first novel, *This Side of Paradise,* 1920). College men's or even noncollege men's adoption of certain distinct styles could provide them with an "identity" that, in turn, functioned as a symbolic coat of armor as they confronted these "new women." So, too, could their tendency to idolize and imitate in dress the "heroes" of their day — the Prince of Wales, aviator Charles Lindbergh, and golfer Bobby Jones, for example. They wore their clothes as badges of their social memberships, which often supplanted their personal identities.

**The Automobile and Fashion.** As the decade progressed, the automobile increasingly became another definer of status and social class in America, both for young people and their parents. Henry Ford's Model T, which dominated the U.S. market until it went out of production in 1927, gave middle-class and even lower-middle-class citizens affordable, reliable transportation that was not bound to train or trolley-car schedules and routes. In so doing it afforded them the status of "owners" and often facilitated further ownership, as they were now able to travel to affordable suburban bungalow housing. The wealthy were always able to buy custom-built cars, but around middecade mass-produced automobiles (other than the Model T) began to develop style, and American consumers were drawn to them as expressions of their movement up the social ladder. Certain luxury cars also began to be partially mass-produced and then customized to individual specifications, and their consequent drop in price attracted the solidly middle-class buyer. Thus, with choice came further definition of status and taste. A family's automobile was an expression of the fashion it adopted, of its place in the world.

**Architecture and Fashion.** The quintessential expression of American energy and optimism in the 1920s was the skyscraper, the great tower that aspired toward heaven and dominated the earth (rather, the urban streets) below. As the decade progressed, the great towers tended to become both more massive and more utilitarian in structure, suggesting that their creators were in control of the vigorous, chaotic urban world. Yet in the suburban and country houses that many of these same architects designed, the emphasis was on traditional historical models — Dutch Colonial or French Provincial, for example — that harkened back to a seemingly more tranquil past. The same tendency was seen in the affordable planned communities and even in the small bungalows, all expressions of a desire for repose away from the invigorating but also exhausting city. Here fashion dictated, for the most part, a withdrawal from engagement with the modern world, though in a few cases toward the end of the decade the influence of modernist interior design began to be felt.

**Pervasiveness of Fashion.** Throughout the 1920s, then, a concern for fashion, for style as a social and cultural delineator, flourished. Fashion developments in attire, in architecture, and in automobiles helped to define the decade. And because the developments were disseminated by a new and constantly growing communication system that linked most areas of the country, these developments proved more pervasive and more influential than they had ever been in the past.

# TOPICS IN THE NEWS

## WOMEN'S FASHION

**Radical Changes.** Women's fashions in the 1920s reflected radical changes affecting many areas of post–World War I American society. In the first year of the decade the Nineteenth Amendment had given these women the vote, which, in turn, tended to color their expectations for their lives. Many of them rejected, at least temporarily, the traditional roles of wife and mother and instead entered the workforce of the thriving businesses of the period or enrolled in colleges and universities, which were also experiencing rapidly increasing enrollments. The working girl and the coed were typically young, simultaneously more liberated and more apparently frivolous than their mothers, and intoxicated by the attention lavished on them by the popular press. "Is the Younger Generation in Peril?" asked a long 1921 *Literary Digest* article. Typical of journalism investigating youth during the decade, it focused almost exclusively upon young women's fashions in dress and cosmetics.

**Licentious or Merely Sensible?** Articles of this kind inevitably linked short skirts, the rejection of the corset, and bobbed or shingled hair with "licentious" behavior — smoking, drinking bootleg whiskey, listening to jazz, dancing the Charleston or Black Bottom, necking, and petting. However, other assessments struck a calmer note. Writing at opposite ends of the decade, Frances Mathilda Abbott in a 1920 issue of *North American Review* and Fannie Hurst in a 1929 issue of the *New Republic* defended contemporary women's fashions for their utility and good sense. Short skirts, Abbott and Hurst argued, were more hygienic than skirts that dragged in the dirt. Knee-length dresses with loosely fitted bodices made it easier for women to drive automobiles, engage in sports, and function in their jobs, on their campuses, and in their homes. The replacement of torturous corsets by less constricting undergarments benefited women's health and increased their comfort. As Hurst claimed, these styles reflected the "new psychological, sociological, economic and political status" of the young woman of the 1920s. In so doing, the styles proved both shocking and appealing to her more conservative mother.

**French Couture, American Enterprise.** During the 1920s women's fashion largely originated in Paris,

## COUNTING CALORIES

**D**r. Lulu Hunt Peters's *Diet and Health with Key to the Calories* was a runaway best-seller during the figure-conscious 1920s. The book provided calorie-counting menus, advice on exercise and health in general, dialogues involving such characters as Mrs. Ima Gobbler and Mrs. Knott Little, line drawings purportedly by the author's young nephew, and Dr. Peters's personal confessions: "It is not in vain that all my life I have had to fight the too, too solid. Why, I can remember when I was a child I was always being consoled by being told that I would outgrow it, and that when I matured I would have some shape. Never can I tell pathetically 'when I was married I weighed only one hundred eighteen, and look at me now.' No, I was a delicate slip of one hundred sixty-five when I was taken."

Source: Lulu Hunt Peters, *Diet and Health with Key to the Calories* (Chicago: Reilly & Britton, 1918).

though couture styles were most often adapted for the American market. Only the most affluent Americans were fitted by the famous dress designers — Madeleine Vionnet, Coco Chanel, Paul Poiret, Jean Patou — in their Paris fashion houses (*Literary Digest* cites a "millionairess" who spent a mere $8,000 on her couturier-designed wardrobe in 1923, compared to her normal $20,000). More commonly, American designers and buyers from such firms as Bergdorf Goodman, Lord & Taylor, and John Wanamaker would attend the spring and fall Paris shows, where they would purchase couturier designs. (Less-scrupulous observers would simply sketch the dresses as they were being shown and thus steal the designs, a practice against which couturiers had little defense.) "Models," legitimately or illegitimately obtained, would then be brought to the United States, where they would be reproduced or redesigned for wealthy consumers or adapted for the substantially less pricey ready-to-wear trade. In December 1925 B. Altman

Patou and his six American models en route to Paris

advertised "Exact Copies of Vionnet Gowns" for $125 to $225 ($1,250 to $2,250 in 1995 figures); well-made ready-to-wear dresses of less-distinguished pedigree could be purchased for $8.98 to $13.95. The thriving American fashion magazines *Vogue* (which also published French and British editions) and *Harper's Bazaar* publicized the latest fashion trends, which in turn were picked up by fashion columns or advertisements in such general-interest magazines as *Collier's* and the *Saturday Evening Post* and in newspapers. The 1927 Sears, Roebuck catalogue offered a "Paul Poiret Model" fur-trimmed wool coat for $39.75 and an all-wool "Poiret Sheen" dress for $9.95. McCall's patterns provided simplified French styles to the American home seamstress who wanted to achieve the latest look in fashion at the lowest possible price.

**Garçonne.** Women's fashion in the 1920s was most fully embodied in the "garçonne" — or "little boy" — look. Adopted by the young, emancipated flappers in Europe and the United States, the style deemphasized the mature female form by flattening the breasts, dropping waists to the hipline, and, in 1925, shortening skirts to just below the knee. The look was basically "tubular," as it emphasized a straight line from shoulder to hem. Because in its most extreme form it exposed both the lower legs and the arms, the garçonne look required remarkable slenderness, and calorie counting became an obsession for women who adopted the style.

**Garçonne Variations.** Yet the look could be both more classic and "softer" than is suggested by the popular illustrations of John Held Jr. In the 1920s Gabrielle "Coco" Chanel, who is often credited with originating the boyish style, introduced her slightly bloused "little black dress" and her classic suit: a soft pleated or straight skirt topped by a short open jacket with edges bound in ribbon or braid. Chanel's preferred fabrics were jerseys and tweeds, which emphasized her taste for simplicity and understatement. Madeleine Vionnet, another great couturiere of the period, also softened the garçonne look by using the bias cut, often with delicate crepe fabrics, to produce a draped effect. Furthermore, the radical knee-length skirts were most popular between 1925 and 1927, with calf-length, frequently uneven hemlines dominating the earlier and later years of the decade.

**Evening Wear.** Women's evening fashion was typically elaborate — sewn, for example, in exquisite lamé and beaded chiffon fabrics and often accompanied by capes. Most formal wear was floor length, though the low-cut cocktail dress — introduced around 1926 and associated with nightclubs in Europe and speakeasies in the United States — might feature a shorter, irregular "handkerchief," or petal-shaped, hem. Backless evening dresses, which remained popular throughout the 1920s, sometimes accentuated their effect with long strings of beads cast over the shoulder and down the back. Hats were generally abandoned in the evening, though jeweled

Illustration of gentlemen in daytime formal wear and ladies in Chanel-inspired dresses or suits, complete with cloche hats

## THE NIGHT THE HEMS DROPPED

" . . . all the houses sent their hem lines plummeting, though it is pretty generally conceded, particularly by those associated with him, that it was Patou who fired the first gun. He fired it, so the story goes, after staring across a room at a group of women clad by Mademoiselle Chanel, and, because of the brevity of their skirts, seeing a good deal more of the ladies than is mandatory in the drawing room. His own dresses were equally scant, but his regurgitation of disgust was caused, fortuitously, by another. Suddenly desperate, he turned to his able lieutenant, Georges Bernard, and cried out, 'My God, my old, I can no more,' " and, rushing to his workroom, started feverishly designing frocks that swept the ground and waists that embraced the middle. He was in love with his inspiration until the evening his new collection was to be shown for the first time, when suddenly he was as terrified as any stage star on opening night who wonders why, in heaven's name, he ever went into the theater when fine, cozy jobs in Macy's basement are at hand. Patou didn't dare go out into the salons as the mannequins paraded. He sent Georges to face the music while he paced restlessly in his own office. About a quarter of the way through the ordeal Bernard returned. Patou grabbed him by the lapels. 'Well, what about it?' Bernard broke into a broad grin. 'It marches. All the women are squirming about in their chairs tugging at their skirts. Already they feel *démodée*!' "

Source: Edna Woolman Chase and Ilka Chase, *Always in Vogue* (Garden City, N.Y.: Doubleday, 1954).

combs or even ostrich-plume headdresses were occasionally worn.

**Accessories.** During the 1920s hats were a necessity for daytime wear, and the hat that prevailed through much of the decade was the cloche. Drawing its name from the French word for *bell*, which accurately described its shape, this small, deep-crowned hat fit snugly over its wearer's short hair and in the front reached almost to her eyebrows. Usually made of felt, the cloche might be decorated by a small jeweled pin at the side or front or by a wide ribbon band. For driving in open cars some women early in the decade adopted leather helmets with goggles, headgear worn with leather jackets or coats and with brightly colored long scarves thrown around the neck, a style inspired by World War I aviators. Shoes of the period tended to have pointed toes, some sort of strap — usually a T-strap — across the top of the foot, and thick, moderately high heels. Other accessories — jewelry, handbags, cigarette cases — often reflected the various fads, fancies, or cultural influences of the time. For exam-

ple, the excavation of King Tutankhamen's tomb in 1922 caused an explosion of "Egyptian"-motif scarves, compacts, earrings, and necklaces; the presence of avant-garde artists in Paris prompted Art Deco, Cubist, and Surrealist designs in fabrics and jewelry; Josephine Baker and the "Revue Nègre" sparked an interest in thick ivory African bracelets. And through it all, Chanel promoted fake jewelry, including long strings of cultured pearls.

**Hair, Cosmetics, Perfume.** As the decade began, bobbed hair, cut a bit shorter than shoulder length and often marcelled into deep, horizontal waves, was the standard in fashion. This style was later replaced, among the young or the daring, by the extremely short, slicked-down shingle or Eton cut, which featured a single curl pulled forward from each ear onto the cheek and which was totally hidden — except for the curl — by the cloche. In the 1920s cosmetics became respectable (for decades they had been associated with women of easy virtue), and by 1924 many women were wearing redrawn plucked eyebrows, heavy powder, dramatic rouge, scarlet lipstick that formed cupid-bow lips, and dark kohl eyeliner, the latter popularized by movie stars Pola Negri and Theda Bara. One source reports that in 1929 American women bought on average one pound of powder and eight rouge compacts each per year and that a skilled cosmetologist could earn sixty dollars a week plus tips. Around 1925 both heavily tanned skin and face creams were in vogue, and such designer perfumes as Chanel No. 5, Patou's Joy, and Jeanne Lanvin's Arpège were either available or about to be introduced.

**Lingerie.** Flappers allegedly "parked their corsets" in the ladies' room before joining their dates on the dance

## BRASSIERE HISTORY

Caresse Crosby, who with her poet husband Harry founded the Black Sun Press in Paris during the 1920s, claimed to have invented the brassiere when she was still New York debutante Mary Phelps "Polly" Jacob, a young rebel who hated the heavy corsetry of the time. She patented her creation — a simple garment made from two silk handkerchiefs and pink ribbon — in 1914 and a few years later sold the rights for $1,500 to Warner Brothers Corset Company. In the meanwhile Russian émigré Ida Cohen Rosenthal, who ran a women's dress shop in New York City, became convinced during the early 1920s that her full-figured customers would look better in their flapper dresses if they had a little "support." She therefore designed a brassiere with cups, substantial straps, and snap fasteners in the back. At first Rosenthal gave away the bras with dress sales, but the garments proved so popular that in 1923 she and her husband founded the Maiden Form Brassiere Company, later renamed Maidenform. During the 1920s and later, Warner and Maidenform turned this simple lingerie item into a multimillion-dollar industry.

Source: Ethlie Ann Vare and Greg Ptacek, *Mothers of Invention: From the Bra to the Bomb: Forgotten Women & Their Unforgettable Ideas* (New York: Morrow, 1988), pp. 54–60.

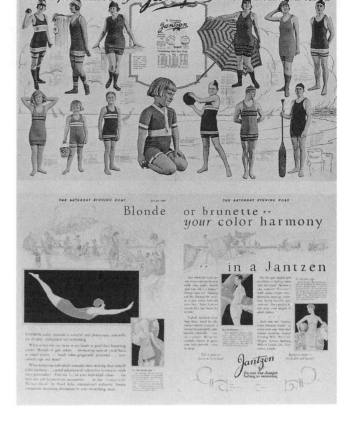

Bathing suit advertisements from 1922 and 1928

floor. Whatever the truth of this story, during the 1920s women's undergarments became progressively lighter in fabric and design. Torso-length corsets worn with linen or heavy cotton camisoles and long panties were replaced by lightweight rubber girdles and silk or rayon brassieres and cami-knickers, a combination of camisole and mid-thigh-length panties. During the 1920s the brassiere was used to flatten, not support, the breasts, though Ida Cohen Rosenthal invented the modern uplift bra during the same period. In 1923 rayon (then called "artificial silk") stockings became widely available, and women wore these flesh-colored hose supported by garter belts or rolled over garters above the knee.

**Sports Clothes.** Because during the 1920s women increasingly engaged in sports — golf, tennis, boating, swimming — designers were quick to provide them with fashionable outfits for these activities. Chanel created loose-fitting bell-bottom trousers to be worn while boating, and these pants quickly evolved into beach pajamas to be pulled over bathing suits on the Riviera or at Palm Beach. Women's swimsuits during the decade began as thigh-covering tight knit shorts topped either with sleeveless vests or with fitted knit tank tops, often striped at the breast or decorated with Cubist designs. In the

later 1920s, knit maillots — similar to present-day one-piece suits but extended several inches down the thigh — became extremely popular. Often worn with a belt and rolled stockings or beach booties, these daring suits tended to stir outrage from the guardians of American public morality. Typical tennis and golf wear for women was pleated, knee-length skirts with sleeveless cardigans for tennis and sleeved cardigans for golf. White was the only acceptable color for tennis clothes.

Sources:
Frances Mathilda Abbott, "As Seen by an Old Maid Grundy," *North American Review*, 212 (November 1920): 648–657;

Ernestine Carter, *The Changing World of Fashion* (New York: Putnam, 1977);

Diana de Marly, *The History of Haute Couture, 1850–1950* (New York: Holmes & Meier, 1980);

Jacqueline Herald, *Fashions of a Decade: The 1920s* (New York: Facts On File, 1991);

Fannie Hurst, "Let's Not Wear Them!" *New Republic*, 60 (30 October 1929): 293–294;

"Is the Younger Generation in Peril?" *Literary Digest*, 69 (14 May 1921): 9–12, 58, 61–64, 66–73;

Alan Jenkins, *The Twenties* (New York: Universe Books, 1974);

Lena Lençek and Gideon Bosker, *Making Waves: Swimsuits and the Undressing of America* (San Francisco: Chronicle, 1989);

Alan Mirken, ed., *The 1927 Edition of the Sears, Roebuck Catalogue* (New York: Bounty, 1970);

Jane Mulvagh, *Vogue History of 20th Century Fashion* (Harmondsworth, U.K.: Viking, 1988);

Maggie Pexton Murray, *Changing Styles in Fashion: Who, What, Why* (New York: Fairchild, 1989);

"What a Millionairess Spends on Her Clothes," *Literary Digest*, 81 (31 May 1924): 52–55.

The Prince of Wales, whose casually elegant style influenced men's fashion in Europe and America. Here he wears a Fair Isles sweater and tweed plus fours. Painting (1925) by John St. Helier Lander.

## MEN'S FASHION

**Youth Prevails.** During the 1920s men's fashion, like women's, was markedly more youthful, more casual than it had been during preceding decades. The boom in business and the general prosperity in the United States caused a huge increase in the numbers of young men attending colleges and universities throughout the country. And these institutions, whether Ivy League or Big Ten, developed codes of male fashion that only the most independent or misguided students ignored. Collegiate fashions were widely covered in the popular press and in such fashion journals as *Men's Wear* and *Gentlemen's Quarterly*, the latter founded as a haberdashery trade catalogue in December 1926.

**Heroes.** For collegians, as well as for their elders, the 1920s were an age of hero worship, and many of these heroes substantially influenced men's fashion of the day.

Such sports figures as golf's Bobby Jones and Walter Hagen, tennis's Bill Tilden, and swimming's Johnny Weissmuller not only set records in their fields but also provided sartorial models for their admirers, who were engaging in athletics — golf, tennis, and swimming, especially — in record numbers. The gridiron heroics of the University of Illinois's Red Grange or of Notre Dame's Four Horsemen provided a background for spectator fashion shows of raccoon coats, camel-hair polo coats, blue blazers, or Norfolk jackets. In 1927 aviation hero

An "Arrow Collar Man" by J. C. Leyendecker

Charles Lindbergh inspired a craze among young American men for leather driving jackets or coats. And, perhaps above all, Edward, Prince of Wales, strengthened England's claim as the men's fashion capital of the world. The dashing prince, with his easy charm and taste for casual but natty attire, became an icon of style. Covering his fall 1924 visit to the United States, *Vanity Fair* facetiously reported that the prince had endured 2,754,911 snapshots, had kissed 2,329 blondes, had drunk 19,218 quarts of champagne, and had appeared in 1,819 uniforms and 3,601 different hats. He was, in short, a model for young men of his time.

**Suits.** Throughout the decade most men's suits for business or the campus had a "tubular" look produced by the combination of narrow-shouldered jackets and quite wide, loose-fitting pants. The broad-shouldered, broad-chested suit coat characteristic of the prewar years was replaced by the more boyish-looking, unpadded, natural-shoulder jacket, which generally hung straight to the hips, though some versions were slightly tapered at the waist. Vented in the back, these suit jackets came in single- and double-breasted versions, with the single-breasted proving most popular among younger men. During the 1920s suit pants underwent two particularly notable style changes: sharp front and back creases replaced side creases, and cuffs replaced flat hems. Pants were fastened by buttons or hooks (zippers were not commonly used for this purpose until the mid 1930s) and were supported either by suspenders or belts, the latter just beginning to achieve popularity. Wool was the most common suit fabric; mature men favored wearing it in navy blue, medium gray, or brown, while younger men adopted paler colors, often in tweeds, during the late 1920s. Although Brooks Brothers was the retailer and label of choice in men's fashions at this time, less expensive men's stores offered serviceable three-piece suits for as little as $29.50.

**Vests, Shirts, Ties.** Men's single-breasted suits often included double-breasted vests or waistcoats, which, as the decade progressed, tended to be replaced by sleeveless V-neck pullover sweaters for comfort's sake. Until the mid 1920s shirts featured detached collars made of starched fabric, celluloid, or, most frequently, the softer three-ply cotton introduced by John Manning Van Heusen in 1920. Detached collars were often white, but when the attached-collar shirt became prevalent in 1925, shirts and collars normally matched in fabric and color. Common attached-collar styles included the button-down, the plain-pointed, and the pin-pointed (the points of the collar pinned under the tie). Though white shirts in broadcloth, oxford cloth, basket weave, and silk remained a staple of men's fashion, solid colors — particularly blue, tan, and yellow — and stripes became popular as the decade progressed. Ties, too, were becoming increasingly colorful; the traditional four-in-hand might appear in regimental or club stripes, plaids, or polka dots and be made of woven or crocheted silk or linen fabrics.

**Cake Eaters.** During the early 1920s many Ivy Leaguers attended tea dances in New York City hotels, where they socialized with young actresses, debutantes, and coeds. Since these dances usually served slivers of cake as refreshments and since the accepted male costume at these affairs was the narrow-shouldered, wide-trousered suit, this particular uniform became known as the "cake-eater's suit." By about 1923 the term was adopted — and the style adapted — by certain noncollege youth, "snappy" dressers of the sort that would have worn the jazz suit during the 1910s or the zoot suit during the 1940s. This version of the cake-eater's suit featured a slope-shouldered jacket that was rather snugly fitted at the waist and that had narrow, sharply notched lapels. It was worn with trousers that were quite narrow to the calves but then flared into wide bell bottoms. Accessories for this suit included soft high collars, narrow dark ties, and flat caps. Regarded as a flamboyant expression of lower-class, noncollegiate taste, this new version of the cake-eater's suit was emphatically rejected by college men, who may have turned to Oxford bags in part to escape the old "cake-eater" label.

**Collegiate Styles.** Whatever the stimulus, in 1925 many American college men adopted extraordinary pants originating at England's Oxford University, where students had developed them to cover knickers banned by university officials. Oxford bags, as they were called, were voluminous trousers measuring about twenty-five inches around the knees and twenty-two inches around the cuffs. Made usually of light-colored flannel and worn with short, natural-shouldered jackets or pullover turtleneck sweaters, Oxford bags retained some degree of popularity into the early 1930s. More generally accepted, especially on Ivy League campuses, were less voluminous but still loose flannel slacks worn with sports jackets and often with brightly colored cravats. Two styles of sports jackets were particularly popular: the blazer with a crest, or badgelike decoration, at the pocket and the modified Norfolk jacket with box pleats down each side and a belt at the back. College men also adopted the best-selling overcoats of the decade — the belted gabardine Burberry trench coat modeled on the waterproof garment worn by British officers during World War I; the camel-hair polo coat; the knee-length, velvet-collared chesterfield; and the raccoon coat.

**Fashion for the Links, Courts, and Shore.** No doubt the popularity of men's sportswear on campus during the 1920s reflected the growing interest of most Americans in both watching and participating in athletics. Properly dressed tennis players wore white flannel slacks with the white or cream-colored cable-knit sweater favored by American superstar Bill Tilden or with the short-sleeved knit tennis, or polo, shirt — complete with crocodile emblem on the chest — introduced in 1926 by French player René Lacoste, "the Crocodile." Golf, perhaps the most popular participant sport of the decade, was generally played in knickers — also known as plus fours — loose pants ending just below the knees and worn with brightly patterned long socks. Made in almost every fabric and color, knickers often had pleats at the waist and sharp creases in front and back. By 1925 they had evolved into four-piece knickerbocker suits — knickers, jacket, vest, and traditional trousers — for wear on the links, at resorts, or on the campus. In 1922 the Prince of Wales had worn a brightly colored pullover Fair Isles sweater with plus fours while playing golf at St. Andrews, Scotland, and this combination became another favorite in golfing attire. Men's bathing suits during the 1920s were one- or two-piece garments featuring sleeveless, scoop-necked tunics over — or attached to — trunks extending several inches down the thighs. Made of dark knits, these suits often featured horizontal stripes at the chest, hips, and thigh.

**Formal Wear.** Men's formal evening wear during the 1920s included black or deep blue single-breasted tailcoats (worn with white tie) or dinner jackets (known as tuxedos and worn with black tie) and narrow, sharply creased, uncuffed pants. Coat and pants were worn with a white starched shirt normally having a wing collar (a stiff, stand-up band that bent down at the top edges), a black bow tie, and a white or black double-breasted waistcoat. Formal day wear included the dark suit jacket or the tailed cutaway coat (also called a "morning coat"), which was closed by a single button and exposed the lower waist area. Either could be worn with gray, striped pants, a waistcoat, and a bow tie, four-in-hand, or ascot. Formal wear required black patent leather shoes or pumps, a top hat or collapsible opera hat, gloves, spats, and, often, a straight or crooked-neck cane of rosewood, bamboo, or malacca. Though an excellent cane could be purchased for five dollars in 1926, a full-bark malacca generally cost fifty dollars or more.

**Hair, Hats, Shoes, Underwear.** During the decade most men were clean-shaven and wore their hair slicked back and parted in the middle. For daytime wear the soft felt snap-brim fedora with a creased crown shared popularity with the stiffer, round-topped derby bowler, which had a narrow brim turned up at the sides; stiff, low-crowned straw hats were often adopted for casual summer wear, and short-billed caps for golfing. Shoes for every-day wear on campus or in town included broad-toed, low-cut oxfords, usually wing tip or saddle shoe in design. White or brown buckskin shoes, the latter popularized by the Prince of Wales during his fall 1924 visit to the United States, generally were reserved for resort or other casual wear. By 1921 wristwatches, introduced during the war, were beginning to replace pocket watches, especially among younger men. Underwear evolved from the long-sleeved, long-legged, one-piece union suit in the early 1920s to the sleeveless, short-legged, rayon one-piece with drop seat in the late 1920s. The latter coexisted with a quite modern-looking two-piece combination of sleeveless undershirt and loose-fitting shorts adjustable at the waist. During the 1920s men's nightshirts were replaced almost entirely by pajamas, and, according to one contemporary source, the best-selling models were white with blue or lavender stripes.

Sources:

John S. Capper, "Men Are Not Vain — They Want to Be Comfortable," *American Magazine,* 89 (May 1920): 32–33, 100, 102;

Diana de Marly, *Fashion for Men: An Illustrated History* (New York: Holmes & Meier, 1985);

Paul Gallico, *The Golden People* (Garden City, N.Y.: Doubleday, 1965);

"H. R. H., Edward Albert, Prince of Wales," *Vanity Fair,* 29 (October 1927): 81;

Jacqueline Herald, *Fashions of a Decade: The 1920s* (New York: Facts On File, 1991);

Alan Jenkins, *The Twenties* (New York: Universe, 1974);

Lena Lençek and Gideon Bosker, *Making Waves: Swimsuits and the Undressing of America* (San Francisco: Chronicle, 1989);

O. E. Schoeffler and William Gale, *Esquire's Encyclopedia of 20th Century Men's Fashion* (New York: McGraw-Hill, 1973);

Marion Sichel, *History of Men's Costume* (London: Batsford Academic and Educational, 1984).

## ARCHITECTURE: URBANIZATION, PHILOSOPHICAL DEBATE

**Urbanization.** The single most important influence on American architecture during the 1920s was the steady urbanization throughout the United States. The 1920 census revealed that for the first time in history more than 50 percent of Americans lived in towns or cities. By the end of the decade that figure had risen to 56 percent — or about 69 million — of which nearly 29 million lived in cities of more than 100,000. These commercial and industrial centers flourished not only on the East Coast but also in the upper Midwest, the Southwest, the far West, and Florida. Cities gave birth to skyscrapers, which required minimal horizontal space and which in their verticality suggested power, prosperity, and the latest technology. Cities also produced industrial plants, colossal movie houses, gas stations and tourist cabins (predecessors of motels) — and, by the mid 1920s, traffic jams and pollution. Thus, as these urban centers grew, so too did the desire to escape them. Miles of concrete roads led to suburbs that seemed to promise defense against the overcrowding, noise, and frantic pace increasingly identified with city life by the decade's end.

## WALTER GROPIUS ON THE BAUHAUS APPROACH TO ARCHITECTURE

"The most important condition for fruitful collaboration on architectural problems is a clear understanding of the new approach to architecture. Architecture during the last few generations has become weakly sentimental, esthetic and decorative. Its chief concern has been with ornamentation, with the formalistic use of motifs, ornaments and mouldings on the exterior of the building — as if upon a dead and superficial mass — not as part of a living organism. In this decadence architecture lost touch with new methods and materials; the architect was engulfed in academic estheticism, a slave to narrow conventions, and the planning of cities was no longer his job.

This kind of architecture we disown. We want to create a clear, organic architecture, whose inner logic will be radiant and naked, unencumbered by lying façades and trickeries; we want an architecture adapted to our world of machines, radios and fast motor cars, an architecture whose function is clearly recognizable in the relation of its forms.

With the increasing firmness and density of modern materials — steel, concrete, glass — and with the new boldness of engineering, the ponderousness of the old method of building is giving way to a new lightness and airiness. A new esthetic of the Horizontal is beginning to develop which endeavors to counteract the effect of gravity. At the same time the symmetrical relationship of parts of the building and their orientation toward a central axis is being replaced by a new conception of equilibrium which transmutes this dead symmetry of similar parts into an asymmetrical but rhythmical balance. The spirit of the new architecture wants to overcome inertia, to balance contrasts."

Source: Herbert Bayer, Walter Gropius, and Ise Gropius, eds., *Bauhaus 1919–1928* (New York: Museum of Modern Art, 1938).

---

**American Conservatism.** Like the U.S. political leaders of the decade — Harding, Coolidge, and Hoover — the major American architects of the 1920s were essentially conservative. Many had been trained in the prestigious Parisian Ecole des Beaux-Arts, which thereby exerted substantial influence on the courses taught in American architectural schools of the period. The Beaux-Arts ideal stressed form — mastery of design principles, materials, and historical prototypes — and deemphasized considerations of logic and function in buildings. During the 1920s the most vocal American critics of Beaux-Arts principles were either dead or in eclipse. Louis Henri Sullivan, the revolutionary Chicago architect who had

declared that "form ever follows function," died in April 1924, as did Bertram Grosvenor Goodhue, whose modernistic design for the Nebraska State Capitol (conceived in 1920) foreshadowed a public-building style that flourished in later decades. Frank Lloyd Wright was generally and erroneously regarded by his contemporaries as a has-been, and even he rejected what he regarded as the socialistic overtones of a radically new architecture developing in Europe.

**European Experimentation.** The leaders of this European movement included the Germans Walter Gropius and Ludwig Mies van der Rohe (both associated with the Bauhaus school of architecture and design in Weimar and Dessau and both later highly influential in America after fleeing Nazi Germany) and the Swiss Charles-Edouard Jeanneret (who called himself Le Corbusier and worked primarily in France). These practitioners of what eventually became known as the International Style advocated simple, unornamented, starkly geometric structures in which the demands of function prevailed over traditional aesthetic considerations. For these European architects function was related to the creation of a more egalitarian social order; they often focused on urban planning, characteristically on designing apartment buildings with landscaped commons for low-income laborers. If the results were sometimes boring, their inspiration was lofty. American architects adopted many of the technical features and some of the style of the European innovators as the decade progressed. In general, however, architects and engineers in the United States ignored the Europeans' social ideas, clinging instead to cherished American individualism, for better or worse.

Sources:
John Burchard and Albert Bush-Brown, *The Architecture of America: A Social and Cultural History* (Boston: Atlantic Monthly/Little, Brown, 1961);

Diane Maddex, ed., *Master Builders: A Guide to Famous American Architects* (Washington, D.C.: Preservation Press, 1985);

Leland M. Roth, *A Concise History of American Architecture* (New York: Icon Editions/Harper & Row, 1979).

## SKYSCRAPERS

**Quintessentially American.** Perhaps no structure more clearly expressed the optimism, energy, and ambition of the American 1920s than the skyscraper. As cities boomed, so too did the number of gigantic towers, proclaiming through their often startlingly individualistic forms the power and grandeur of American endeavors in general and American business in particular. The 1920s have been called the richest era in skyscraper design, primarily because of the theatrical romanticism of the buildings that appeared during the decade. The glistening white Wrigley Building in Chicago, begun in 1921 by Graham, Anderson, Probst, and White; the massive, curved-base Standard Oil Building, built by Carrère and Hastings on lower Broadway in 1926; and the ornately crowned tower — meant to suggest radio waves — of

The Chicago Tribune Tower (1925), designed by Raymond M. Hood and John Mead Howells

## SULLIVAN ON THE SECOND-PLACE FINISHER

"The Finnish master-edifice is not a lonely cry in the wilderness, it is a voice, resonant and rich, ringing amidst the wealth and joy of life. In utterance sublime and melodious, it prophesies a time to come, and not so far away, when the wretched and the yearning, the sordid, and the fierce, shall escape the bondage and the mania of fixed ideas.

..................

In its single solidarity of concentrated intention, there is revealed a logic of a new order, the logic of living things; and this incxorable logic of life is most graciously accepted and set forth in fluency of form. Rising from the earth in suspiration as of the earth and as of the universal genius of man, it ascends and ascends in beauty lofty and serene to the full height limit of the Chicago building ordinance, until its lovely crest seems at one with the sky."

Source: Louis Henri Sullivan, "The Chicago Tribune Competition," *Architectural Record,* 53 (February 1923): 151–157.

**The Chicago Tribune Competition.** Perhaps no event stirred more excitement in architectural circles of the decade than the competition sponsored by Col. Robert R. McCormick in 1922 for the design of a skyscraper home for his Chicago Tribune Company. McCormick offered a $50,000 first prize for a design that would be beautiful and distinctive as well as highly functional for the everyday operations of the Chicago newspaper. Some 281 drawings were submitted from around the world. A design by Gropius and another German, Adolf Meyer, combined the clean planes of Bauhaus architecture with the "solidity" of the Chicago Style of the 1880s, and a plan from Danish architect Knud Lönberg-Holm offset dark International Style rectangular towers with brightly colored, horizontally defined floors in the center of the building, an extremely avant-garde conception. Among the more eccentric submissions were a rectangular block topped by an enormous carved Indian holding a tomahawk raised assertively above his head (by German Heinrich Mossdorf) and a huge, capped Doric column, a shockingly obvious phallic symbol (by Frenchman Adolf Loos). The winning design came from Americans John Mead Howells and Raymond M. Hood, who envisioned a Gothic tower topped by a circle of buttresses and a simple spire. Second place was taken by a last-minute entry from Finland's Eliel Saarinen, who proposed a mountainlike structure that through setbacks at various levels receded to a square, narrow, undecorated top and achieved a soaring verticality. Led by Louis Henri Sullivan, architectural critics of the day almost unanimously denounced the decision of the Tribune Tower judges.

Cross and Cross's original RCA Building, erected in New York City in the late 1920s: all conveyed the imaginative spirit of the businesses that commissioned, and the architects that executed, them. By 1929 America could claim 377 skyscrapers that were greater than twenty stories high. Of the 188 that were in New York City, fifteen exceeded five hundred feet in height.

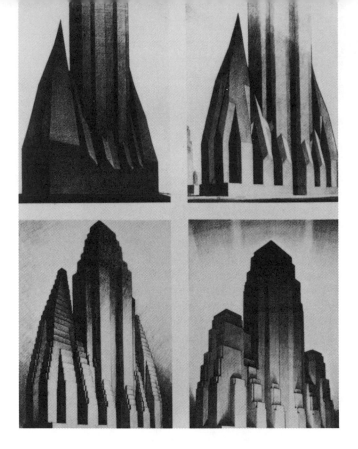

Hugh Ferriss's 1922 "Four Stages" drawings, which influenced skyscraper design throughout the 1920s

Even Hood, who seems to have been the primary formulator of the prize-winning drawing and whose reputation it launched, expressed regret that Saarinen's entry had not won. Saarinen, encouraged by his second-place finish in the competition, moved permanently to the United States, where he and his architect son Eero established substantial reputations. And the Howells-Hood Chicago Tribune Tower, completed in 1925 and so violently attacked in its own day, is now regarded as one of the handsomest Gothic landmarks in the United States.

**Evolution of the Skyscraper.** Although stylistic variety in American skyscrapers persisted throughout the 1920s, certain design tendencies also emerged. In the early years of the decade the rectangular corniced tower — often Gothic and sometimes incorporating several historical styles — prevailed. Lofty and romantic, it tended to invite extravagant decorative detail. Around 1924 this design began to give way to the ziggurat (a pyramidal structure created by a series of setback blocks as the building attained height). Emphasizing power and upward thrust, it normally minimized decorative detail. The ziggurat, in turn, began to surrender ground in the late 1920s and early 1930s to the slenderer, flat-roofed, horizontally defined slab that seemed more clearly to express the building's function.

**American Instincts.** These developments resulted in part from purely American conditions and instincts. A New York City zoning law of 1916 had limited the width of skyscrapers in an effort to ensure air circulation and light for streets below and buildings adjacent to these imposing structures. In the early 1920s, as construction of the tall buildings boomed, architect Harvey Wiley Corbett suggested that zoning requirements might be most practically met through the erection of clifflike pyramidal skyscrapers; progressively narrowing from base to crown, these towers would readily admit air and light and, to the delight of a business-driven society, would provide desirable windowed office space on the upper floors. Hugh Ferriss's extraordinary drawings of these mountainlike, soaring constructions explored the aesthetic possibilities of the ziggurat design, and among the skyscrapers that embodied it were the massive New York Telephone Company Building, also known as the Barclay-Vesey Building (Vorhees, Gmelin, and Walker, 1926) and the dramatically black — and in daylight apparently windowless — American Radiator Building (Raymond Hood, 1924).

**Foreign Influences.** If zoning laws and American inventiveness fueled developments in skyscraper design during the 1920s, so too did influences from abroad. Hood's American Radiator Building clearly had drawn some of its inspiration — especially its use of setbacks — from the Chicago Tribune entry of Finland's Eliel Saarinen, who had already created innovative public buildings in his native land. In some of its decorative touches, the American Radiator Building joined another New York City landmark, the Chrysler Building (William Van Alen, 1930), in revealing different foreign influences — notably, those showcased by the Exposition Internationale des Arts Décoratifs et Industriels Modernes, which began in Paris in July 1925 and which supplied the name for Art Deco style. Begun in 1926 and briefly the world's tallest skyscraper, the Chrysler Building was constructed of white brick and featured gray brick trim and eagle-headed gargoylelike projections modeled on the 1929 Chrysler hood ornament; the building was topped by a series of graceful stainless-steel arches containing triangular windows and peaking in a long spire. The skyscraper's flamboyant use of color, geometric decorative devices, and disparate materials made the Chrysler Building an embodiment of Art Deco style. It was also — perhaps more significantly — an expression of American exuberance in the 1920s.

**Encroaching Modernism.** In comparison to the Chrysler Building, the Empire State Building (begun in 1929 and completed in 1931 by Shreve, Lamb, and Harmon seemed sedate, even a little boring; yet its clean lines, the vertical indentations marking its tower, and, above all, its enormous height — 1,250 feet and 102 floors — gave it distinction and made it a symbol of American stability and power during the difficult Depression years of the 1930s. Two other buildings also begun in 1929 provided the first hints of a future trend in American skyscraper development, the flat-topped, rectangular slab. The McGraw-Hill Building (Raymond Hood, 1931) and the Philadelphia Savings Fund Society Building (George Howe and William Lescaze, 1932) punctuated their slab construction with horizontal strip windows and other clear structural expressions of the buildings' functions. They thus predicted the International Style modernism that would triumph in post-Depression, post–World War II America.

Sources:

John Burchard and Albert Bush-Brown, *The Architecture of America: A Social and Cultural History* (Boston: Atlantic Monthly/Little, Brown, 1961);

Paul Goldberger, *The Skyscraper* (New York: Knopf, 1981);

Leland M. Roth, *A Concise History of American Architecture* (New York: Icon Editions/Harper & Row, 1979);

Louis Henri Sullivan, "The Chicago Tribune Competition," *Architectural Record*, 53 (February 1923): 151–157.

## CITY HOMES

**Attractions of City Life.** During the 1920s, as in later decades of the twentieth century, huge numbers of Americans were drawn to the city by the perceived advantages it offered. The great urban centers — New York, Chicago, and Detroit, for example — seemed to promise the most exciting and most lucrative job opportunities, whether for stockbrokers, business entrepreneurs, factory workers, automobile salesmen, department-store clerks, or secretaries and receptionists. Cities offered a rich cultural life: theater, music and dance, and movies — particularly foreign movies like those of Sergei Eisenstein or Fritz Lang — that almost certainly would not be shown in small-town movie houses. Nightclub-speakeasies were primarily a phenomenon of the city, as were exotic ethnic restaurants, ethnic shops, or ethnic population centers. All these factors drew multitudes to America's great cities.

**Perils.** Yet with these advantages came pronounced urban problems. By the mid 1920s city streets were clogged with traffic — automobiles, trucks, taxicabs — and plans to relieve this vehicular congestion were either nonexistent or impractical, as was Harvey Wiley Corbett's vision of major city thoroughfares constructed many stories above existing streets. The internal-combustion engine also created increased levels of air pollution in cities: an 11 March 1924 *New York Times* story reported that on the preceding day scores of people had been poisoned by carbon monoxide in a Pittsburgh tunnel, and a 1928 issue of the *American Journal of Public Health* revealed that 133 Chicagoans had died from carbon monoxide poisoning between 1925 and 1927. Noise pollution, another threat to the quality of city life, could also be attributed chiefly to motor vehicles; the 31 March 1928 *Literary Digest* declared that the primary offenders to New York City ears were, in descending order of importance: trucks; elevated trains; street-cars; private automobiles and taxicabs; police cars, ambulances, fire engines; and the riveters busy with steel-frame building construction. If residents lived above the tenth floor of a high-rise, they would probably not be troubled by noise from the street below — unless that street were filled with high-rise buildings, in which case noise could echo upward as high as the twenty-fifth floor.

**Deluxe Apartment Living.** The decade saw the decline of the massive, one-family town house, the pride of the wealthy during earlier periods. The demise of the city mansion, with dining room capable of seating one hundred guests, resulted in part from the decreased availability of servants, who were now working for new masters in factories and department stores. It also resulted from the growing preference of tycoons and their wives for country estates or new homes in affluent suburbs, both quite easy commutes by rail or automobile to and from the commercial centers that provided or sustained tycoons' fortunes. Yet for those among the wealthy who desired elegant city living, facilities were available. The December 1925 *Vanity Fair* advertised a co-op apartment building at 1020 Fifth Avenue on the "Sunny Corner of Eighty-third Street." This Warren and Wetmore–designed high-rise offered one apartment per floor, ten to fourteen rooms and four to five baths per apartment, a price tag of $40,000 to $105,000, and, to serious inquirers, a list of the names of other tenant-owners.

**More-Affordable Apartment Living.** Desirable apartment housing in the heart of the city remained expensive during the decade, and people of moderate income tended to live in apartment buildings or duplexes on the city's periphery, from which they commuted to work by rail, streetcar, or automobile. Young professionals with promising futures might elect to buy into a cooperative apartment-building complex, such as Hudson View Gardens at 183rd Street and Pinehurst Avenue in New York City. According to the June 1925 *Vanity Fair*, this fifteen-building complex on seven acres overlooking the Hudson River offered a commissary, restaurant, beauty parlor and barber shop, steam laundry, post office, and infant nursery and playground. Its three- to six-room apartments came equipped with automatic refrigeration, garbage incinerators, built-in cabinets, radio receivers, and much more. The apartments were priced from $4,000 to $9,100, and buyers paid 25 percent down and the remainder in monthly installments, to which were added $37 to $85 monthly operating charges. Housing at Hudson View Gardens was no doubt too pricey for the majority of New York City office, department-store, or factory workers, but it served nicely those with higher incomes and the seemingly unlimited prospects that the 1920s promised.

Sources:

"Anti-Noise Campaign," *Literary Digest*, 96 (31 March 1928): 55–58;

"Auto Fumes Poison Scores in Tunnel," *New York Times*, 11 March 1924, I: 1;

Patio of Louwana, one of the Palm Beach "villas" designed by Addison Mizner

John Burchard and Albert Bush-Brown, *The Architecture of America: A Social and Cultural History* (Boston: Atlantic Monthly/Little, Brown, 1961);

Joel I. Connelly, Mathew J. Martinek, and John J. Aeberly, "The Carbon Monoxide Hazard in City Streets," *American Journal of Public Health*, 18 (November 1928): 1375–1383;

*Vanity Fair*, 24 ( June 1925): 29;

*Vanity Fair*, 25 (December 1925): 19.

## THE SUBURBS

**Suburbs and the Automobile.** The city offered economic opportunity and cultural excitement, but it also provoked in many Americans of the decade a nostalgia for the small-town or rural homes of their childhood — a desire for a private refuge from the traffic, noise, air pollution, and general commotion of the urban scene. The 1920s saw a boom in the housing industry, with 767,000 units built in 1922 and 1,048,000 units in 1925, most of these in the expanding suburbs. The middle class could elect to move to the suburbs because automobiles — the primary form of transportation between the job in the city and the home in the suburbs — were becoming more affordable. New and used Model Ts and other relatively inexpensive cars were widely available, and by 1930 more than 22 million of these vehicles were on American roads.

**Affordable Middle-Class Housing.** Although flight from the city had begun during the prewar period as an upper-class phenomenon, such exclusive suburban neighborhoods as Grosse Point, Michigan; Lake Forest, Illinois; or Tuxedo Park, New York, were gradually joined by humbler middle-class subdivisions. An annual family income of $2,500 and the newly popular installment plan made it possible for an upper-level bank clerk or a manager of a shoe store to purchase both an inexpensive automobile and a small suburban bungalow-style home. Standard contractor-designed bungalows, in a variety of styles, carried price tags of $3,000 to $10,000 in 1920. Although many of these less affluent bungalow-filled suburbs grew randomly, with little concern for consistency in architectural design or size of the homes in a given neighborhood, the 1920s also saw a movement toward regional styles, particularly in slightly more expensive middle-class housing. For example, the Southwest and Florida often produced Spanish-style homes —

Addison Mizner planned two-bedroom $7,000 Spanish-style villas for the working people of Boca Raton, and about twenty of these bungalows were completed before the collapse of the Florida real-estate market; California also embraced the Spanish style, as well as architect William W. Wurster's simple, modest houses in what would later be called the ranch style. On the lower end of the scale, inexpensive prefabricated homes were widely advertised but never popular in America. An Aladdin Company ad of 1923 offered plans, precut lumber, and hardware for a simple five-room frame house ($538) and for a twelve-room Dutch Colonial house ($1,932) in an effort to attract the less-well-off potential homeowner who had handyman skills.

**Planned Communities.** For the most part, suburbs in the 1920s haphazardly sprawled around cities, yet two American architects, Henry Wright (1878–1936) and Clarence S. Stein (1882–1975), countered this tendency as they campaigned for and designed several planned communities: Sunnyside Gardens in Queens, New York (1924–1928); Radburn, New Jersey (begun in 1928 and partially completed in the early 1930s); and Chatham Village, Pittsburgh, Pennsylvania (1931–1935). Each of these communities was different from the others, and both Radburn and Chatham Village contained buildings by other architects; but all three developments featured homes set back from major traffic thoroughfares and facing onto landscaped commons or parks. Sunnyside Gardens was filled with graceful two-story row houses on rectangular superblocks with garages grouped on the periphery of the "neighborhoods." Radburn placed single- and multifamily structures on amoeba-shaped superblocks. All three planned communities attempted to honor and preserve the topography of their sites with homes angling down the sides of hills and ancient trees and new hedges preserving the privacy of residents. Although these communities ultimately became middle- to upper-middle-class enclaves, Wright seized every opportunity to make them affordable to lower-income groups. Both he and Stein were firm believers in landscape architecture as an antidote to air pollution and noise, and Stein used his editorship of the *AIA Journal* (1918–1921) to support beautification and conservation causes. Although the planned communities that Wright and Stein designed did not have a strong influence on the direction of suburban development during the 1920s, they did provide models for city planners in later decades of the twentieth century.

**Estates and Wealthy Suburbs.** The country estates and great suburban houses of the 1920s combined the latest in modern technology — electricity, running hot and cold water, telephones, gas or electric stoves, electric refrigerators, steam heat — with a taste for the past in the designs of the homes themselves. Building on country estates might embody virtually any historical style from French Provincial to English Tudor to Spanish Colonial to rustic rural; the most popular of country-house archi-

tects during the period was Harrie T. Lindeberg, who designed estate homes in virtually every style. The finest suburban homes were also consciously "historicist," often blending styles to achieve what has been labeled "Tudorbethan" (from the words *Tudor* and *Elizabethan*) or "Stockbroker's Tudor." These luxurious homes might include stained glass, half-timbering, gables, exposed interior beams, paneling, and grand staircases. Even the innovative industrial architect Albert Kahn, whose factories embodied streamlined modern designs, produced romantic historicist homes for his auto-magnate clients in Grosse Point; the Cotswald style house — with paneling, slate, and even workmen imported from England — that Kahn designed for Edsel Ford in 1927 was among the best of these great suburban structures. The splendid, generically medieval homes that were built around a market square in Lake Forest, Illinois, some twenty miles from downtown Chicago, were largely the work of skilled society architect Howard Van Doren Shaw. During the 1920s a few modernistic luxury houses were being built in California by such architects as Frank Lloyd Wright and Richard Neutra. But the stockbrokers, automobile manufacturers, and captains of industry of every sort — men who daily immersed themselves in modern technology, business, and finance — chose to lead their private lives in homes that recalled a supposedly more leisurely, elegant, and romantic past.

Sources:

John Burchard and Albert Bush-Brown, *The Architecture of America: A Social and Cultural History* (Boston: Atlantic Monthly/Little, Brown, 1961);

Stephen Calloway and Elizabeth Cromley, eds., *The Elements of Style* (New York: Simon & Schuster, 1991);

Clifford Edward Clark Jr., *The American Family Home, 1800–1960* (Chapel Hill: University of North Carolina Press, 1986);

Donald W. Curl, *Mizner's Florida: American Resort Architecture* (New York: Architectural History Foundation / Cambridge, Mass.: MIT Press, 1984);

Grant Hildebrand, *The Architecture of Albert Kahn* (Cambridge, Mass.: MIT Press, 1974);

Edgar R. Jones, *Those Were the Good Old Days: A Happy Look at American Advertising, 1880–1930* (New York: Simon & Schuster, 1989): 286;

Leland M. Roth, *A Concise History of American Architecture* (New York: Harper & Row, 1979);

Vincent Scully, *American Architecture and Urbanism* (New York: Praeger, 1969).

## INTERIOR DESIGN

**Defining Lifestyles.** During the 1920s the interior design of homes, offices, and public buildings attracted greater general interest in America than it ever had in the past. Choice and arrangement of furnishings — whether chairs, lamps, floor coverings, or art objects — became subjects for professional training as well as measures of the homeowner's or apartment dweller's taste. The August 1924 *Vanity Fair* advertised eight schools of interior design, the majority centered in New York City; the others were in Boston and Cambridge, Massachusetts, and in San Francisco, and two of the eight claimed European branches in Paris and Florence. The decade saw the profusion of how-to books, such as Ethel Davis Seal's *Furnishing the Little House* (1924) and *The House Beautiful Furnishing Annual 1926* (1925) — the latter of which bore the subtitle *A Comprehensive and Practical Manual for the Guidance of All Who Seek Comfortable and Attractive Homes*. Interior design was treated regularly in such magazines as *House Beautiful, Arts & Decoration,* and *Fruit, Garden and Home* (founded in 1922 and renamed later in the decade *Better Homes & Gardens*). Home decoration also became a recurrent subject for fashion magazines, notably *Vogue* and *Harper's Bazaar*. In the 1920s fashion clearly extended beyond clothing and hairstyles to include the personal environment one created and inhabited. Thus, the Grosse Point matron might surround herself with reproductions, or even original pieces, of eighteenth-century French furnishings and the flapper with Art Moderne decor; each would be expressing her self-definition, her *lifestyle* (though that word did not come into common usage until the early 1960s).

**Historicism.** At the end of the decade both Art Deco and Bauhaus influences were being felt in American interior design, yet throughout the 1920s these modernistic elements were definitely a minority taste. Instead, home decor manuals and articles advised readers to choose "historical" styles in decoration but to modify them to accommodate modern conditions and modern conveniences. The author of the magazine article "Period Influences and Modernism in Home Decoration" declared in 1923: "more and more we prefer to adapt a 'period.' It is, as it were, Louis Seize [Sixteenth] up to date, or Charles II, with variations, or the aristocratic Jacobean and the gorgeous Italian, adjusted to our modern ways of living." Here, clearly, *modernism* meant the adaptation of the historical style to modern use — nothing more or less. Both Seal's book and *The House Beautiful Furnishing Annual 1926* provided descriptions and illustrations of furnishings (mostly reproductions) in a wide variety of traditional styles, and both reflected the taste of most professional interior decorators and molded the taste of amateurs. Seal, whose target was the presumably less affluent and experienced decorator of the "little" home, aggressively and unapologetically instructed her reader on how to blend period pieces into attractive, harmonious designs. Only the modern appliances in kitchen and bathroom were not generally forced into historical dress, though a "style" might be partially imposed through wall coverings, window treatments, and painted tables and chairs. Radiators were frequently concealed by decorative grillwork, and such contemporary technological innovations as the telephone, the radio, and the phonograph were normally hidden away in cabinets consistent with the rest of the period furniture in the room. Electric lighting — chandeliers, wall lamps, and floor lamps — often was styled to resemble old-fashioned candles or a candelabra.

## THE ART DECO EXHIBITION

L'Exposition Internationale des Arts Décoratifs et Industriels Modernes (the International Exhibition of Decorative and Industrial Arts) officially opened in Paris on 18 July 1925. Built in the center of the city, the exhibition included some 130 different pavilions and galleries from more than twenty nations and a multitude of French cities. Exhibits were supposed to display the most advanced technological and artistic innovations in architecture, furnishings (wood, leather, metal, textiles, books, playthings, musical instruments, means of transport), theater and gardening and street art, decoration (clothes and their accessories, flowers and feathers, perfumery, jewelry), and teaching. Filled with huge glass fountains, Cubistic man-made trees, floodlights, gardens, rides, and music, the exposition created an almost surrealistic, carnival-like setting. Pavilions ranged from Emile-Jacques Ruhlmann's ornately decorated private house for a wealthy collector, to the publisher Crès's building shaped like books, to the couturier Paul Poiret's exotically fitted-out barges moored on the Left Bank of the Seine River, to Le Corbusier's starkly rectangular concrete, steel, and glass house filled with mass-produced furniture and Cubist paintings. Though one critic called it "the most serious and sustained exhibition of bad taste the world has ever seen," the majority of commentators saw in the Art Deco Exposition the birth of a new decorative style.

**Sources:** Patricia Bayer, *Art Deco Interiors: Decoration and Design Classics of the 1920s and 1930s* (Boston: Bullfinch Press/Little, Brown, 1990);

Carolyn Hall, "The Art Deco Exhibition," *The Twenties in Vogue* (New York: Harmony, 1983), pp. 92–97;

Allan Ross MacDougall, "The Beginning of Summer in Paris," *Arts & Decoration,* 23 (July 1925): 47, 66.

**Birth of Modernism.** When the French government invited the United States to participate in the 1925 Exposition Internationale des Arts Décoratifs et Industriels Modernes in Paris, Interior Secretary Herbert Hoover declined, saying that there was "no modern decorative art movement in America." Hoover may have overstated the case — the United States was, after all, erecting increasingly modernistic skyscrapers and industrial plants — but these structures could hardly be exported to the Paris Exposition site. Yet, in truth, modernistic interior design did not have much impact in America until 1928. In that year the Designers' Gallery Show, which featured streamlined, functional, well-crafted interiors in such materials as glass, aluminum, formica, and chrome, began a tour of ten major cities. The exhibition displayed works by such rising modernist designers as Joseph Urban, Donald Deskey, Paul T. Frankl, and Ruth Reeves. In February

1929 the Metropolitan Museum of Art in New York City opened its Contemporary American Decorative Arts Show of modernist rooms designed by Urban, Eugene Schoen, Eliel Saarinen, Ely Jacques Kahn, and Raymond Hood. The show attracted enormous crowds and generally favorable reviews.

**Art Moderne.** This new, late-1920s interior-design style, often labeled Art Moderne in America, married French Art Deco opulence with German Bauhaus functionalism. Though Art Deco and the Bauhaus style in many ways seemed diametrically opposed, the two movements were united by their common rejection of conventional historicist tastes and standards in interior decoration. Art Moderne was most frequently embraced in homes by young, affluent urban sophisticates and in public buildings by businesses eager to project forward-looking images.

**Art Deco.** Art Deco combined such diverse elements as oriental lacquered screens; veneered ivory- or ebony-inlaid dressing tables and desks; geometrically patterned carpets and linoleums; stained-glass windows in sunburst, fountain, or scarab patterns; sleek tubular chairs or floor lamps; vivid, often metallic wall coverings; and stylized ceramic figurines. Austrian-American Paul T. Frankl created opulent Art Deco interiors, one of which included a half-moon-shaped desk and triangular chair finished in bright red lacquer with black trim and placed under a large, round, tasselled mirror. Almost anything could be labeled Art Deco — if it seemed "modern," finely crafted, and expensive and if it contributed to a "total" look in a room, apartment, or house.

**Bauhaus.** Bauhaus interior style stressed geometric, streamlined designs, the use of new, often synthetic materials, and mass production of the objects created. For the architects and other designers of the Bauhaus the beauty of a building and its interiors lay in the simplest possible expression of function. Ludwig Mies van der Rohe, who immigrated to the United States in 1936, created a classic piece of Bauhaus-inspired furniture in his 1929 Barcelona chair; still produced in the 1990s, it has curved steel legs and back supports, which are covered by leather-covered foam-rubber cushions. Frankl complemented his Art Deco taste for Oriental effects with his Bauhaus-inspired skyscraper bookcases and cabinets with their set-back silhouettes. The influence of the Bauhaus was also largely responsible for the popularity of built-in furniture toward the end of the decade.

**Commercial Moderne.** Chief among the public structures that adopted Art Moderne interiors during the late 1920s were nightclubs, rail terminals (many air terminals followed suit in the 1930s), movie theaters, and businesses that were unafraid to project exuberance instead of staid respectability. In 1926 the French Line, often used by Americans traveling to and from Europe, launched its luxury liner the *Ile-de-France,* an Art Deco masterpiece that included among its wonders a dining room with gray marble walls punctuated by squares of lighted Lalique glass; a piano, tables, and chairs in white ash; and wall and ceiling panels depicting wealthy people at play. The Carlton Hotel in Washington, D.C., had a lounge decorated with small round tables, boldly striped clean-lined chairs, and a huge, round, glass-paneled bar with etchings of grapes and Roman figures topped by a moving sculpture of a goddess and hunting dog. The Cincinnati Union Terminal, begun in 1929, displayed rings of color ranging from yellow to orange circling its dome, a glass-mosaic mural on its wall, and linoleum wall panels decorated with jungle animals in its ladies' room. The lobby of Manhattan's Chrysler Building featured red marble walls; geometrically patterned floors; ornamental metalwork; a ceiling fresco; recessed lighting in support columns, ceiling, and walls; and elevator doors veneered with plant-like shapes. It is perhaps the most famous and impressive of commercial Art Deco buildings. During the 1930s Art Moderne interiors would move closer to the streamlined Bauhaus ideal.

**Sources:**

Herbert Bayer, Walter Gropius, and Ise Gropius, eds., *Bauhaus 1919– 1928* (New York: Museum of Modern Art, 1938);

Patricia Bayer, *Art Deco Interiors: Decoration and Design Classics of the 1920s and 1930s* (Boston: Bullfinch Press/Little, Brown, 1990);

Stephen Calloway, *Twentieth-Century Decoration: The Domestic Interior From 1900 to the Present Day* (London: Weidenfeld & Nicolson, 1988);

*The House Beautiful Furnishing Annual 1926* (Boston: Atlantic Monthly, 1925);

John Loring, "Architectural Deco," *Connoisseur,* 200 ( January–April 1979): 48–54;

"Period Influences and Modernism in Home Decoration," *Arts & Decoration,* 20 (December 1923): 50, 52, 69;

Mary Jane Pool, ed., *20th-Century Decorating, Architecture & Gardens: 80 Years of Ideas & Pleasure From House & Garden* (New York: Holt, Rinehart & Winston, 1980);

Franz Schulze, *Mies van der Rohe: A Critical Biography* (Chicago: University of Chicago Press, 1985);

Ethel Davis Seal, *Furnishing the Little House* (New York: Century, 1924).

## MOVIE PALACES

**Pleasure Domes.** Among the most extravagant public buildings of the 1920s were the great movie theaters that sprung up in major cities throughout America. Shrines to prosperity, technology, and entertainment, these huge pleasure domes often combined vaudeville-style acts (dance troops, orchestras, vocal ensembles) with a movie — usually last on the bill — accompanied by a "mighty Wurlitzer" organ that was raised on a platform from the orchestra pit. For the price of a twenty-five-cent ticket (before 6 P.M.), a housewife could drop of her young children at the theater nursery, which included baby sitters and a resident nursing staff. She would then pass through an opulently decorated lobby and, if so inclined, an equally opulent ladies' lounge before being escorted to her first-balcony seat by a grand personage: a scrupulously polite, impeccably white-gloved usher in a tuxedo or military-cadet-style uniform with rows of brass buttons and shoulder braid on its jacket. In her seat she would be delighted by carved and inlaid and gilded and magnificently lighted walls and ceilings, statuary and paintings, elaborately decorated and draped stage curtains, wondrous air conditioning, and plush velvet seats. All this for two bits, with the show yet to come.

**Impresarios.** Providing the vision and raising the funding for most of these movie palaces were great impresarios of the decade. Chief among them were two men: Samuel Lionel Rothafel (born Rothapfel), who was known as Roxy and whose theaters dotted Manhattan, and Sidney Patrick Grauman, whose movie palaces seemed to define the glittering character of Hollywood. Both of these men lived the rags-to-riches, American Dream stories that so often filled their theaters. Roxy, the son of a shoemaker, joined the U.S. Marines at age sixteen, traveled with a minor-league baseball team, worked as a book salesman, and tended bar in Forest City, Pennsylvania, where he married his boss's daughter and ultimately convinced his father-in-law to show moving pictures to paying customers in the tavern. By the late 1920s, bolstered by the promotional value of his weekly radio program, Roxy had become the most successful and famous movie-theater impresario in America. During the early 1930s he directed interior decoration for the Radio City Music Hall, but his greatest triumph came with the March 1927 opening of the $10 million, sixty-two-hundred-seat "Cathedral of the Motion Picture: The Roxy" (architect W. W. Ahlschlager, decorator Harold Rambusch). Located a few blocks from Times Square, the Roxy inspired the kind of awe-stricken response recorded in Helen E. Hokinson's 1929 *New Yorker* cartoon of a little girl asking her mother, "Mama — does God live here?" Sid Grauman, who spent his youth traveling through America with his father's not-very-successful minstrel show, in 1906 convinced the older Grauman to settle in San Francisco and try to make a living showing movies in a converted store. The venture was successful enough that Sid Grauman decided to move on to the film capital of America, Hollywood, where he opened his first bona fide movie palace, the Million Dollar (architects Woollett) in 1918. It was followed in 1922 by the first of his "exotic" theaters, the Egyptian (architects Meyer and Holler), an eighteen-hundred-seat temple with cast heads of pharaohs at the doorway and pseudo-Egyptian artifacts throughout. His masterpiece was Grauman's Chinese Theater (architects Meyer and Holler, designer Raymond Kennedy). Built in 1927, it immediately became a Hollywood landmark, with its glitzy, movie-set-Chinese architecture and interior decor and its handprints, footprints, and signatures of the stars in the concrete walkways outside.

**Architects.** Theater-chain owner Marcus Loew declared, "We sell tickets to theaters, not movies," and one of his primary theatrical architects was Thomas W. Lamb, who built more than three hundred movie houses

Proscenium and lobby of Loew's Paradise (1929), the Bronx

during his career. Born in Scotland, Lamb used his classical architectural training to create some of the most elegant of the so-called hard-top theaters, which had elaborately decorated ceilings and resembled true opera houses. Loew's State Theater, built by Lamb in Saint Louis in 1924, featured Corinthian columns with Wedgwood bases, marble balustrades and staircases, and ornate fountains. In 1927 Lamb designed his most lavish theater (said to be Marcus Loew's favorite), the Midland in Kansas City, Missouri. This four-thousand-seat baroque/rococo temple contained 6.5 million square inches of silver and gold leaf, mahogany walls topped by plasterwork cherubs, and a dome hung with two elaborate crystal chandeliers. The interior work required fifteen sculptors, and their labors were complemented by antiques purchased from one of the Vanderbilt homes. While Lamb was the master of the "hard-top" theater, Austrian-born John Eberson was the inventor and presiding genius of the "atmospheric" theater, which had a plain concrete ceiling onto which images — clouds, moon, stars, and even the occasional airplane — were projected by a machine called the Brenograph Junior. Eberson's greatest theater, the Avalon (Chicago, 1927), was a Persian "mosque" filled with domes, minarets, and handmade tiles; the combination of authentic-looking Eastern decor and projected ceiling atmospherics created a breathtaking fantasy world for audiences. Yet another of Eberson's splendid theaters was Loew's Paradise, built in the Bronx

| | | | |
|---|---|---|---|
| Ford Motor Company | $590 | Kissel Motor Car Company | 2,385 |
| Durant Motors, Inc. | 785 | Stutz Motor Car Company | 2,550 |
| Chevrolet Motor Company | 795 | DuPont Motors, Inc. | 3,050 |
| Willys-Overland Company | 850-1,550 | McFarlan Motor Corporation | 3,100–6,600 |
| Essex (Hudson-Essex Company) | 945 | Packard Motor Car Company | 3,275–4,900 |
| Maxwell Motor Corporation | 1,095 | Peerless Motor Car Company | 3,295–3,690 |
| Dodge Brothers Company | 1,250 | Apperson Automobile Company | 3,485 |
| Nash Motors Company | 1,295 | Cadillac Motor Car Company | 3,885–4,550 |
| Reo Motor Car Company | 1,595 | Pierce-Arrow Motor Car Company | 3,895–6,900 |
| Studebaker Corporation | 1,595-2,785 | Dorris Motor Car Company | 4,310 |
| Buick Motor Company | 1,665-2,350 | Lincoln Motor Company | 4,800 |
| Auburn Automobile Company | 1,795 | Daniels Motor Company | 7,600 |
| Chrysler Motor Car Company | 1,825 | Duesenberg Automobile & Motor Company | 7,800 |
| Hudson Motor Car Company | 2,150 | Locomobile Company of America, Inc. | 9,990 |
| Rickenbacker Motor Company | 2,195-2,795 | Rolls-Royce of America, Inc. | 10,895 chassis only |
| Franklin Manufacturing Company, 2,250 | | | |

Source: "The Scientific American Annual Automobile Guide," *Scientific American*, 132 (January 1925): 68–71.

---

for Loew in 1929. This extravagant Venetian palace featured a Carrara marble fountain in its grand lobby and statues, stuffed birds, and imitation poplar trees in its elaborately decorated auditorium. Though Lamb and Eberson were the acknowledged geniuses of movie palace design, Chicagoans C. W. and George Rapp and Californians Marcus Priteca and S. Charles Lee also created splendid theaters during the 1920s.

Sources:

Ben M. Hall, *The Best Remaining Seats: The Story of the Golden Age of the Movie Palace* (New York: Clarkson N. Potter, 1961);

David Naylor, *Great American Movie Theaters* (Washington, D.C.: Preservation Press, 1987);

Ave Pildas and Lucinda Smith, *Movie Palaces* (New York: Clarkson N. Potter, 1980).

## AUTOMOBILES: IN SEARCH OF STYLE

**The Amazing Tin Lizzie.** Henry Ford's Model T — popularly labeled the "Tin Lizzie" or "flivver" — revolutionized American society. This simple, tough, affordable car, which was produced between October 1908 and May 1927, put America on wheels. Nearly 15.5 million Model Ts were manufactured, and an astonishing 75 percent of them were still being driven when the car went out of production in 1927. Priced as low as $260 (for a new roadster in 1925; a good used Model T could be bought for about $50), the Tin Lizzie was the answer to the workingman's prayers. She was also frequently the object of his curses as he backed her up steep grades (reverse was her most powerful gear), pushed her through mud holes, and tried to start her on cold mornings. Yet no other car so captured the imagination of the American public: the Model T spawned songs, doggerel verse, jokes, camaraderie among owners, and a multitude of appreciative letters to Henry Ford, who was widely regarded as the common man's friend and benefactor because of his automobile.

**Model T Style.** Throughout its years the Model T featured a four-cylinder engine, rear-wheel brakes, and a pedal-controlled planetary transmission with two forward speeds; on a good, flat road (too often a rarity in the 1920s) it might reach forty-five miles per hour. The first Model T's were available in four body styles — the most

Prestige · · The Packard owner, however high his station, mentions his car with a certain satisfaction—knowing that his choice proclaims discriminating taste as well as a sound judgment of fine things.

For the Packard is one of the world's few fine cars universally approved by the enthusiastic owners of other famous makes.

Recognized everywhere, as supremely typifying America's genius for perfection

in things mechanical, Packard cars go further in possessing to a marked degree that subtle attribute—prestige.

Packard prestige, sensed if not defined by every Packard owner, is reflected in the car's aristocratic beauty, its distinction, its luxury and comfort, its superb performance—unexcelled in traffic or on the open road.

## PACKARD

ASK THE MAN WHO OWNS ONE

An advertisement for the Packard, America's most popular luxury car, which offered restrained elegance and engineering excellence

popular being the five-passenger touring car and the two-passenger roadster — and in a variety of colors, though between 1913 and 1926, when mass production really picked up, Tin Lizzies were invariably black. Until Charles F. Kettering developed fast-drying Duco lacquer in 1923, colored paints required several applications and two weeks to dry — absurd wastes of labor and time on Ford's assembly lines. Henry Ford allegedly quipped that the Model T customer could "have a car painted any color he wants so long as it is black." And although colors did reappear on the Model T in its final year of production, the only other major style changes that occurred during its lifetime were those imposed by customer-handymen served by Ford accessory stores that sprung up all over the country. Thus, the car might sport fancy spare-wheel covers or bumpers with a nickel finish. In general, however, the Tin Lizzie was not a dressy lady; she was simply a plain, hardworking, honest one.

**Chevy.** The Model T's chief competitor during the 1920s was the Chevrolet, developed in 1911 by the flamboyant William Crapo Durant, who in the previous year had been ousted as head of General Motors; in 1916 he

again seized control of GM, where he remained until November 1920, when he was ousted for a second time. Durant brought to GM his four-cylinder Chevy and his philosophy that a single auto company should offer vehicles "for every purse and purpose." Alfred P. Sloan Jr., who would become president of GM in 1923, convinced Durant's immediate successor, Pierre du Pont, to retain the money-losing Chevy and to boost it as an attractive alternative to Ford's Model T. GM could not match Ford's low price; but, Sloan reasoned, many potential buyers of the Tin Lizzie would be willing to pay $150 to $250 more for a better-looking, slightly more powerful, and better-riding car. According to the January 1925 *Scientific American*, the lowest-priced Chevy of that year cost $490 to the Model T's $260, had a wheelbase of 103 inches to the Model T's 100 inches, and boasted a forty-two-horsepower engine to the Model T's forty. The Chevy also might have, though *Scientific American* did not mention it, Kettering's Duco lacquer finish, available in a variety of colors. Sloan's hunch was correct. GM's Chevy sold extremely well, finishing a respectable second in sales to the Model T through much of the decade. Clearly, by the mid 1920s style and the status-consciousness it implied were beginning to influence substantial numbers of even the least well-to-do auto buyers.

**The Major Companies and Style.** The major automobile companies responded to consumer demand for stylistic choice by expanding their model lines and by placing a new emphasis on the aesthetic appeal of their products. Expansion was often achieved through buying up smaller companies. For example, Ford acquired the upscale Lincoln marque from Henry M. Leland in 1922, and Walter P. Chrysler, who had developed his luxury Imperial in 1926, purchased the Dodge company for its line of mid-priced "Dependability Cars" in 1928. But interest in stylistic diversity and development was most clearly reflected through the establishment of aesthetic design components or departments in the major companies. In 1925 Henry Ford finally agreed with his son Edsel that the new Lincoln should be professionally styled and that custom designer Raymond H. Dietrich should be brought to Detroit for that purpose. Moreover, Henry Ford's belated recognition that "beauty of line and color has come to be considered a necessity in a motor car today," as one of Ford's ads proclaimed, was the primary impetus for his introduction of the Model A in 1927. Responding even more strongly to the demands for style, General Motors (which by 1927 offered seventy-two car models) had created the automotive industry's first separate design department, the Art and Colour Section, headed by Harley J. Earl. One of Earl's most memorable creations was the sleek, sporty La Salle, which Sloan called "the first stylist's car to achieve success in mass production." Thus, the offerings of each major automobile company were expanded through the acquisition of smaller companies' stock and through a new industry-wide emphasis on design as an attractor of customers.

Automobile manufacturers were both responding to a need and creating it.

Sources:

C. Edson Armi, *The Art of American Car Design: The Profession and Personalities* (University Park: Pennsylvania State University Press, 1988);

*Handbook of Automobiles 1924* (New York: National Automobile Chamber of Congress, 1924);

"The Scientific American Annual Automobile Guide," *Scientific American,* 132 ( January 1925): 68–71;

Stephen W. Sears, *The American Heritage History of the Automobile in America* (New York: American Heritage, 1977);

Alfred P. Sloan Jr., *My Years with General Motors* (Garden City, N.Y.: Doubleday, 1964), p. 269.

## AUTOMOBILES: THE OLYMPIAN CARS

**Magnificence.** The period of the "Olympian Cars," a phrase coined by Richard Burns Carson, began around 1925 and extended into the early 1930s. These magnificent automobiles were brilliantly engineered and meticulously styled, and many of them were personalized by the custom coachwork of the great coach-making companies of the period — Brunn, LeBaron, Fleetwood, Dietrich, and Brewster. The January 1929 issue of *Arts & Decoration* illustrated several of the fine vehicles of the year, including a convertible Lincoln detailed by Dietrich; a Pierce-Arrow with "luxurious cushions" and gold ornamental hardware designed for Mrs. Calvin Coolidge; and a Cadillac convertible coupé with bodywork by Fisher and interior colors — "suggested by Vermeer's 'Head of a Young Girl' " — of pale blue, gold, and gray. These upscale cars made up no more than 5 percent of the American automobile market, but they spurred the imagination of the first generation in which a person's motorcar became an important indicator of his or her social class. Automobile historian Stephen W. Sears has declared that old wealth tended to choose the "dignified" marques — Cunningham, Pierce-Arrow, American Rolls-Royce, or (rather surprisingly, considering its quite recent origins) Lincoln; new wealth gravitated toward Cadillac, Stutz, Franklin, and Chrysler; the adventurous few chose America's most splendid automobile, the Duesenberg Model J, introduced in 1928. Some of the grand marques spawned the sporty roadsters (cousins of the earlier Stutz Bearcat and Mercer Raceabout) that were so closely associated in the mind of the public with the so-called flaming youth of the 1920s.

**Packard.** By far the most popular of the Olympian cars was the Packard, which became a symbol of wealth and status in movies, short stories, and popular songs, and which, astonishingly, achieved sales of fifty thousand in 1928. The Packard's most successful models during the 1920s were the Twin-Six (a twelve-cylinder car produced between 1915 and 1922) and the Single-Eight (an eight-cylinder vehicle introduced in June 1923). Packard consistently featured a yoke-shaped radiator, a long hood with carefully defined accents, low sleek lines, and a wide variety of cosmetic options, such as spare-tire covers,

## THE AUTOMOBILE AS SOCIAL DEFINER

"In the city of Zenith, in the barbarous twentieth century, a family's motor indicated its social rank as precisely as the grades of the peerage determined the rank of an English family. . . . The details of precedence were never officially determined. There was no court to determine whether the second son of a Pierce Arrow limousine should go into dinner before the first son of a Buick roadster, but of their respective social importance there was no doubt; and where Babbitt as a boy had aspired to the presidency, his son Ted aspired to a Packard twin-six and an established position in the motored gentry."

Source: Sinclair Lewis, *Babbitt* (New York: Harcourt, Brace, 1922), pp. 74–75.

hood ornaments, spotlights, and deluxe wheels. The Twin-Six was priced from $2,600 to $4,600 in 1922, and the Single-Eight from $3,650 to $4,950 in 1924. The 1924 model was offered in Packard blue, Brewster green, Packard maroon, and Westminster gray — with black accents. A great favorite of tycoons and royalty, the Packard was the first automobile to deliver an American president to his inauguration; Warren G. Harding arrived for the ceremony on 4 March 1921 in a Twin-Six.

**Lincoln.** The Lincoln, which became Edsel Ford's chief responsibility in the mid 1920s, was known for its quietly refined styling and its sturdy construction (its body, for example, was framed by hardwood cut from a single piece of lumber). Preferred by doctors, lawyers, and bankers for its understated elegance, the Lincoln was also the favorite car of gangsters and police because of its power and acceleration. Indeed, from 1924 on, the car was produced in special police models with bulletproof glass, shotgun racks, spotlights, and other features. The 1924 *Handbook of Automobiles* lists nine models ranging in price from $3,800 to $5,100; available colors included Cobalt blue, Brewster green, and Orriford Lake maroon. Beginning in 1925 the Lincoln enjoyed sales of more than eight thousand cars a year, and in 1926 it began to feature coordinated interior and exterior designs, some of which — the Egyptian, for example — must have ruffled the most staid of Lincoln devotees.

**Stutz.** The Stutz was known for its speed and road ability. All the models of this marque were readily identifiable by their extremely low, racy appearance and their vivid colors, including yellow and royal red. During the mid 1920s the Stutz company came under the control of Charles M. Schwab, president of Bethlehem Steel, who oversaw production of two classic Stutz cars: the Model AA (also called the Vertical Eight) in 1926 and the appropriately named Model BB Splendid Stutz in 1928.

The Model J Duesenberg (1928), which provided brute power and customized styling

Prices were not generally advertised for these sporty cars, which were the first to include safety glass as a standard feature. Stutz fell victim to the Great Depression.

**Pierce-Arrow.** Pierce-Arrow, one of the oldest auto companies in America, produced its first car in 1901. During the 1920s advertising for this marque usually featured paintings of "The Pierce-Arrow Sort of People": well-dressed ladies and gentlemen in elegant settings, with a view through a window of their Pierce-Arrow closed sedans or limousines priced in 1925 between $5,250 and $7,000. Never extravagantly styled, these huge, well-made Olympians projected a solid, "corporate" image. Large, cone-shaped headlights that swept upward from the front fenders were their most recognizable trademarks. The Pierce-Arrow rarely invented new names for its models, preferring instead to use Series numbers — the Pierce-Arrow Series 80, for example. This labeling system was probably meant to suggest that the automobile had achieved near perfection and therefore should not change but instead slowly evolve. The Pierce-Arrow line was bought by Studebaker in 1929 and disappeared forever in 1938.

**The Duesenberg.** One of the greatest American cars of the 1920s and 1930s was the Duesenberg, whose name provided the slang word *doozy* — meaning "the best," "the tops," "the most splendid." The line of cars bearing this name developed through the work of a pair of German-born, Iowa-raised brothers, Frederick and Au-gust Duesenberg, who through their engineering and mechanical genius moved from the production of bicycles, motorcycles, and early two-cylinder automobiles to racing cars and, in the 1920s, passenger cars. The Duesenberg brothers' entry into the passenger-car market came in 1921 with a vehicle (later called the Model A) that was the first automobile to have a straight-eight motor, four-wheel hydraulic braking, and substantial amounts of aluminum in its engine construction. It was an extremely powerful car, but with a $5,000 to $10,000 price tag and rather ungainly styling, it had poor sales; of the roughly six hundred models produced in the Duesenbergs' Indianapolis plant, only ninety sold in 1921. In 1926, however, Erret Lobban Cord, president of Auburn Automobile Company, purchased Duesenberg and, retaining the Duesenberg brothers in the engineering department, determined to invest the next Duesenberg with style. The result appeared on 1 December 1928 — the Model J Duesenberg, a nearly twenty-foot-long beauty with an elevated hood, curved back end, and exquisite detailing. Fred Duesenberg's engineering gave it a straight-eight engine, twin overhead camshafts, aluminum hydraulic brakes on all four wheels, and the capacity to reach a speed of 116 miles per hour. The Model J cost $8,500 for the chassis alone, and with body work by one of the major custom coach makers (most of whom designed bodies for the car), its price reached nearly $20,000. One commentator has suggested that the Duesenberg Model J was the perfect embodiment of the extravagant, extraordinary 1920s. The automobile was, in fact, succeeded in 1932 by the Model SJ Duesenberg, an even more powerful and elaborately styled vehicle, in which Fred Duesenberg suffered fatal injuries that same year. The marque that he and August Duesenberg founded also soon died, a victim in 1937 of the Great Depression.

Sources:

Kevin Brazendale and Enrica Enceti, eds., *Classic Cars: Fifty Years of the World's Finest Automobile Design* (New York: Exeter, 1981);

Richard Burns Carson, *The Olympian Cars: The Great American Luxury Automobiles of the Twenties & Thirties* (New York: Knopf, 1976);

*Handbook of Automobiles 1924* (New York: National Automobile Chamber of Commerce, 1924);

"Modern Cars Notable for Beauty of Line and Luxurious Fittings," *Arts & Decoration*, 30 ( January 1929): 64–65;

"The Scientific American Annual Automobile Guide," *Scientific American*, 132 ( January 1925): 68–71;

Stephen W. Sears, *The American Heritage History of the Automobile in America* (New York: American Heritage, 1977);

Louis William Steinwedel and J. Herbert Newport, *The Duesenberg: The Story of America's Premier Car* (Philadelphia: Chilton, 1970);

Brock Yates, "Duesenberg," *American Heritage*, 45 ( July/August 1994): 88–99.

# HEADLINE MAKERS

## HATTIE CARNEGIE

## 1886-1956

### FASHION ENTREPRENEUR

**Fashion and Business Sense.** Hattie Carnegie, who first achieved prominence in American fashion during the 1920s, was known for both her sophisticated taste in women's clothing and her genius in business. Having little talent for drawing, cutting, or sewing, Carnegie was not a designer in the usual sense; she instead altered original fashions imported from France and directed and polished the work of her own design assistants to ensure understated elegance and excellent workmanship in the clothing she sold. Carnegie was reportedly the first American to produce both custom-made and ready-to-wear garments under a single label, and she was among the first to complement her clothing stores with separate millinery, jewelry, cosmetics, and perfume establishments, thereby creating a multimillion-dollar empire.

**Early Life.** Born Henrietta Kanengeiser in a Vienna ghetto, Carnegie came with her family to Manhattan's Lower East Side when she was six years old. As a teenager she worked as a messenger at Macy's, made hats for acquaintances, and adopted the surname of steel tycoon Andrew Carnegie, whose rags-to-riches story she hoped to duplicate. Hattie Carnegie's energy, her tiny, trim figure (she was less than five feet tall), and her personal flair drew the attention of Rose Roth, a seamstress, who hired Carnegie to model Roth-designed dresses in restaurants, theaters, opera houses, and other public places. The two women joined forces to found a dress and millinery shop on East Tenth Street, moving it later to more fashionable West Eighty-sixth Street. Primarily through Carnegie's energy and sophisticated appearance, they began to attract a clientele that included Mrs. William Randolph Hearst and opera singer Alma Gluck.

**Success.** In 1919 Carnegie bought out Roth's interest in the shop and made the first of her more than one hundred trips to Paris, where she bought couturier dress designs that she resold in — or restyled for — the American market. Her colorful Paris forays, during which she often held court at the Ritz Hotel, earned her the attention of *Vogue* and *Harper's Bazaar*, which publicized both her label and her fashion opinions. In 1928 Carnegie established her most famous dress shop on East Forty-ninth Street. Among her notable clients during the decades that followed were actresses Joan Crawford, Tallulah Bankhead, and Gertrude Lawrence; heiress Barbara Hutton; and the Duchess of Windsor.

**Enduring Elegance, Rising Talent.** Throughout her career Carnegie insisted that the designs bearing her name be elegant, sophisticated, and enduring rather than faddish. She was particularly noted for her beaded and embroidered evening suits and for her tailored daytime suits, often gray, with finely detailed collars and jeweled buttons. Perhaps her best-remembered suit, which she introduced in the early 1950s, featured a straight skirt topped by a jacket fitted at the waist and flared over the hips. Throughout her career Carnegie discovered and employed as her assistants talented young designers, among them James Galanos, Pauline Trigère, Norman Norell, and Claire McCardell. In 1939 Hattie Carnegie received the Neiman-Marcus Award and in 1948 the Coty American Fashion Critics' Award, the latter recognizing her lifetime contribution to "American elegance."

Sources:

*New York Times,* 23 February 1956, p. 27;

Anne Stegemeyer, *Who's Who in Fashion,* second edition (New York: Fairchild, 1988);

*Time,* 67 (5 March 1956): 20–21.

## GABRIELLE "COCO" CHANEL

### 1883-1971

#### COUTURIERE, LIBERATOR, LEGEND

**Legend.** Coco Chanel once declared, "Legend is the consecration of celebrity," and no other fashion designer in history has exceeded either Chanel's celebrity or her legend. She was a fiercely independent lover of dukes, industrialists, and artists; a confidante of many of the creative geniuses of her day — among them, writer Jean Cocteau, painter Pablo Picasso, ballet impresario Sergei Diaghilev, and composer Igor Stravinsky; and a self-created image of the free-spirited "new woman" of the 1920s. Through her personal example and the fashion empire she established, Chanel launched and sustained the movement toward simplicity, practicality, and unfussy elegance in women's clothing. "A fashion that does not reach the streets is not a fashion," she said, and by the early years of the 1920s, Chanel fashion had reached streets throughout Europe and the United States.

**Early Life.** Chanel both obscured and embroidered upon the facts of her early life; as one of her biographers declared, "She was herself a Chanel creation." Though she claimed to have been born in Auvergne in 1893, records show that she was actually born in the poorhouse of the town of Saumur ten years earlier. Her mother, a poorhouse employee, and her father, an itinerant tradesman, were not married until fifteen months after her birth. Her mother died when Chanel was six, and her father disappeared after placing his five children under the care of relatives. Chanel and her two sisters seem to have spent most of their adolescence as nonpaying residents of a religious, orphanage-like boarding school in Moulins, but by 1903, when she was twenty, Chanel had become the mistress of a well-to-do young military officer, Etienne Balsan. In 1907 she fell in love with Balsan's friend, Arthur "Boy" Capel, a wealthy English industrialist, and around 1910 Balsan and Capel helped Chanel set up a millinery shop at 21 rue Cambon in Paris. Her simple, elegant hats charmed the society women to whom Balsan and Capel introduced her, and by 1915 she was able to open additional shops in the resort towns of Deauville and Biarritz. In that year she also moved into couture, designing dresses, skirts, and sweaters in jersey, a fabric not previously used in the French fashion houses. Legend has it that during the war years Chanel put on a polo player's or sailor's sweater, belted it around her waist, pushed up the sleeves, and liked the effect so much that she produced smaller-sized versions for women. Whatever the facts of the sweater's origin, it became a staple of Chanel's house and remained popular through the 1920s and beyond.

**The Chanel Look.** In December 1919 Boy Capel was killed in an automobile accident, and a grieving Chanel threw herself even more fervently into her work. By the early 1920s she was directing a huge staff in four buildings on the rue Cambon, had introduced the simple chemise dress that became the embodiment of her "garçonne," or "little boy," look, and had started a vogue for bell-bottom pants and lounging pajamas. In 1922 she began to market Chanel No. 5 in its simple, square bottle; the perfume became the most popular and one of the most prestigious scents in the world. Chanel favored sweater sets — a cardigan worn over a matching or contrasting round-necked sweater — with short, loosely fitted straight or pleated skirts. Her simple, youthful daytime attire usually came in neutral colors — beige was a favorite — and her more elaborate evening wear normally appeared in pastels. In 1925 she produced her short, open, collarless cardigan jacket, which became a signature of the classic Chanel suit, and in 1926 she brought out her little black dress, which *Vogue* labeled a "Ford" for its serviceable and enduring quality. Chanel's personal tastes set the style of the decade, both in Europe and America: she adored mixing costume jewelry — lots of it — with authentic gems; she bobbed her hair and was among the first women to sunbathe; she wore strapped sandals and low beige pumps; and she smoked cigarettes in public. Chanel both embodied, and in many ways dictated, the revolution in women's fashion that occurred in the 1920s.

**Connections.** Chanel's influence was in part the result of the personal and social contacts she made in postwar Europe. In 1917 she became a protégée of the wealthy, beautiful Misia Edwards — later Misia Sert — who introduced her to the circle of avant-garde writers and artists with whom Edwards associated. During the 1920s Chanel herself hosted parties for these intellectuals as well as for the wealthiest and best-known members of European and American society. In 1924 she designed the costumes for Diaghilev's ballet *Train Bleu,* for which

Cocteau had written the story and Picasso had designed sets. During the 1920s and early 1930s Chanel also formed intense but generally brief liaisons with fascinating men: Russian Grand Duke Dmitri Pavlovich, who had participated in the assassination of the mad Russian monk Rasputin; Hugh Richard Arthur Grosvenor, Duke of Westminster, among the wealthiest men in England; brooding French poet Pierre Revedy; and French artist Paul Iribe. Each of these men seems to have proposed marriage, but Chanel — always protective of her independence — declined. Most biographers agree, however, that her often-repeated retort to the duke of Westminster's proposal — "There are already three Duchesses of Westminster, but there is only one Coco Chanel" — is almost certainly apocryphal.

**Retirement and Comeback.** In 1938 Chanel retired from the couture scene and lived comfortably in Europe — during World War II under the protection of a German officer, a situation which earned her the contempt of many of her countrymen and led her to self-exile in Switzerland. In 1954, angered by the constrictions on women of Christian Dior's "New Look" — tightly pinched waists, padded busts, long bouffant skirts — she decided, at the age of seventy, to try a comeback. "Fashion has become a joke," she said. "The designers have forgotten that there are women inside the dresses. Most women dress for men and want to be admired. But they must also be able to move, to get into a car without bursting their seams! Clothes must have a natural shape." Her 1954 collection was greeted by lukewarm reviews from the critics but by enthusiastic responses from women around the world. Once again her casually elegant attire, epitomized by updated versions of the Chanel suit, had succeeded in liberating women from repressive fashion norms. In 1957 Chanel was presented with the Neiman-Marcus Award. She continued to produce distinguished collections until her death at age eighty-seven.

Sources:
Pierre Galante, *Mademoiselle Chanel,* translated by Eileen Geist and Jessie Wood (Chicago: Regnery, 1973);

Marcel Haedrich, *Coco Chanel: Her Life, Her Secrets,* translated by Charles Lam Markmann (Boston: Little, Brown, 1972).

# RAYMOND M. DIETRICH

## 1894-1980

### AUTOMOBILE ARCHITECT

**Artists.** In the 1920s, for the first time, styling became a focus for mass-produced cars. During the preceding two decades body design had been a significant concern for only the most expensive of automobiles. Often a grand-marque auto company would manufacture a chassis — the frame and working parts — and then turn it over to a custom coach builder, who would construct the body with the particular styling features specified by the wealthy customer (he would have to be extremely well-to-do, since in 1920 a custom-built automobile cost between $12,000 and $15,000 — the equivalent of $120,000 to $150,000 in 1995 figures). Among the great coach-building companies were Brewster, Healy, Judkins, and Derham, all of which enjoyed reputations for splendid work and all of which had moved into automobile-body construction and design when their original roles as producers of horse-drawn carriages had become obsolete. During the mid and late 1920s custom coach builders again felt the burdens of progress, as manufacturers of expensive cars moved toward mass production and toward setting up their own design departments or coachbuilding subsidiaries. One of the key figures in this transition was Raymond H. Dietrich, a genuine artist in the evolving automobile industry.

**Early Life.** Dietrich, who was born and raised in Brooklyn, New York, found his first work as an engraver for the American Bank Note Company. In 1913 he signed on as a designing and drafting apprentice with Brewster, where he was joined in 1919 by another young designer, Thomas L. Hibbard, just back from the war in Europe. Although both draftsmen were pleased with their Brewster connection, they also felt that their creative ideas were being stifled by the company's rigid traditions, particularly those elevating metal craftsmen over draftsmen and designers. They complained to the company president and were fired as a result.

**LeBaron Carrossiers.** In 1920 Dietrich and Hibbard scraped together enough money to rent an office at 2 Columbus Circle in New York City. There they founded LeBaron Carrossiers, a suitably fancy name that the Francophile Hibbard had chosen. The idea behind the company was even more inventive — and more revolutionary — than its name, for LeBaron Carrossiers offered wealthy customers "automotive architecture," individual custom designs with complete plans and drawings that any good coach maker could then execute. Thus, Dietrich and Hibbard did not sell automobiles but instead their services as designers. Their plan proved enormously successful; they were soon providing auto designs to such celebrities as Gloria Swanson, Rudolph Valentino, and Florenz Ziegfeld. Unfortunately, however, on a 1923 trip to promote the company's services in Europe, Hibbard succumbed to his love for France, resigned his partnership in LeBaron Carrossiers, and joined another expatriate American, Howard "Dutch" Darrin, to form Hibbard & Darrin, which was to become one of the premier coach-designing firms on the Continent.

**LeBaron, Inc.** Hibbard's departure and the growing tendency among the major coach builders to incorporate Dietrich and Hibbard–like design departments within their own companies increased pressures for Dietrich. Although at present he had more work orders than he could easily handle, he clearly saw that the large coach builders with resident designers would soon cut into his business. He therefore worked out a merger between LeBaron Carrossiers and the Bridgeport Body Company to form LeBaron, Inc., a combination coach-building and design operation. At LeBaron, Dietrich honed the design principles he had been developing for years. For both safety and aesthetic reasons he lowered the roof and window levels of automobiles. He emphasized the horizontal flow between engine and passenger areas by using continuous molding that ran from the radiator, under the windows, and around the rear of the body. He added other detailing features — swept back front fenders, for example — that increased the appearance of length and the overall harmony of his designs. Dietrich was, in short, imposing a coherent style to automobile bodywork.

**Edsel Ford and Catalogue Customizing.** In 1923 Edsel Ford, who was attempting to develop the Ford Motor Company's newly acquired luxury car, the Lincoln, came up with a brilliant idea — catalogue customizing. He decided to choose a variety of attractive body styles, mass-produce perhaps twenty-five unfinished cars in each style, and then allow the customer for each car to specify the trim and finish he wanted. This procedure would substantially lower the price of the automobile — to around $5,000 — but would ensure that the product remained a superb one. Since Edsel Ford had been pleased with work Dietrich had done for him in the past, he offered to bring LeBaron to Detroit under the sponsorship of a larger body-building company, the Murray Corporation. Dietrich was intrigued by the design possibilities of catalogue customizing, and in 1925, when his partners refused to move from New York City to Detroit, he resigned from LeBaron and, with Edsel Ford's help, founded Dietrich, Inc., a custom-design firm, near the Ford and Lincoln plants. During the next six years Dietrich continued producing individual designs for a few clients, but most of his work was done in catalogue customizing — for Lincoln, of course, but also for Packard, for the new Chrysler Imperial, for Franklin, and, in 1929, for Pierce-Arrow. Both his custom designs and his catalogue-customizing designs generated elegant automobiles.

**Later Years.** In the early 1930s the Great Depression devastated Dietrich's company, since the prosperous customers for whom catalogue customizing proved attractive were then disappearing. In 1932 his old friend Walter P. Chrysler offered him a design job in Chrysler Corporation's mass-production plant. Dietrich enjoyed some degree of success there, but when Walter P. Chrysler died in 1940, the designer was again without a job. He returned to custom work in a small way until 1949, when he established Ray Dietrich, Inc., in Grand Rapids, Michigan. Until his retirement in 1969 he supplied design advice for Checker, Lincoln, and Mercury and created the plans for an $87,000 parade car used by Presidents Harry S Truman and Dwight D. Eisenhower. Though

Dietrich's major accomplishments occurred within a short eleven-year period, the automobile bodies he designed are regarded as among the finest in automobile history.

Sources:
Richard Burns Carson, *The Olympian Cars: The Great American Luxury Cars of the Twenties & Thirties* (New York: Knopf, 1976);

Hugo Pfau, "The Master Craftsmen: The Golden Age of the Coachbuilder in America," in *The American Car Since 1775* (New York: Bailey, 1971), pp. 144–147.

## HUGH FERRISS

### 1889-1962

#### ARCHITECTURAL DELINEATOR

**Recorder and Inspirer.** Hugh Ferriss was a trained architect whose preferred tools were paper and charcoal pencils. For more than three decades beginning in the 1920s, he was America's most-respected "delineator" — artistic renderer — of urban architecture. As delineator he provided both early design sketches and fully developed presentation drawings for more than one hundred architectural firms during the 1920s. Many of these commissioned drawings were published in trade journals, popular magazines, and newspapers, as were Ferriss's noncommercial visions of the urban scene. Recording the evolution of city architecture, particularly of the skyscraper, Ferriss's drawings also helped inspire and direct the changes that occurred during the decade.

**Early Life and Career.** Ferriss was born in Saint Louis, where he earned an architectural degree from Washington University in 1911. After a year as an apprentice draftsman with the architectural firm of Mariner and La Beaume, he left Saint Louis to take a draftsman position in the New York office of Cass Gilbert, architect of the Woolworth Building, then nearing completion. Following two years with Gilbert and with his encouragement, Ferris decided in 1915 to try to establish a career for himself as an independent architectural delineator. He lived with his wife, Dorothy Lapham, a *Vanity Fair* illustrator, in Greenwich Village and found freelance work as an artist for magazines, newspapers, and building-industry manufacturers and trade associations. By 1921 Ferriss had become quite well known, and his drawings were regularly exhibited in architectural shows and in the print media.

**The Four Stages.** In 1916 New York had passed a zoning law that regulated the upper-level mass of tall buildings by prescribing setbacks to ensure light and air circulation to the streets below. During the war years and the recession that followed, the zoning law was virtually ignored, but as construction boomed in 1921, architects began to question how they could fulfill the requirements of the law while providing interesting and functional buildings. In 1922 Ferriss produced, at the invitation of skyscraper designer and city planner Harvey Wiley Corbett, a set of drawings illustrating what the two envisioned as the "Four Stages" of skyscraper construction. These drawings began with a carved out pyramidal mass and concluded with a structure cut away into aesthetically pleasing setbacks that provided maximum office space and fulfilled the requirements of both steel-cage construction and the zoning law. Ferriss's designs — which were exhibited in architectural and art shows throughout the country and widely reprinted in newspapers and magazines — caused a sensation in the architectural community. They clearly provided skyscraper builders with exciting alternatives to the simple piling up of ever smaller rectangles from base to summit. Ferriss declared in a *New York Times Magazine* article: "We are not contemplating the new architecture of a city. We are contemplating the new architecture of a civilization." With the profusion of pyramidal, setback skyscrapers in American cities during the mid to late 1920s, Ferriss's statement proved less hyperbolic than it might at first have seemed.

**Influences: Corbett and Hood.** Although he provided delineations for architectural firms ranging from the most conservative to the most experimental, Ferriss was primarily influenced by the two visionary skyscraper designers, Corbett and Raymond M. Hood. Corbett engaged Ferriss to illustrate multilevel traffic systems to alleviate the automobile congestion that was one of Corbett's chief concerns; he also invited the delineator to participate in a futuristic exhibition, the Titan City, at the New York John Wanamaker department store, a show that included drawings of skyscrapers with businesses in their lower levels and penthouse apartments and terraced roofs above, aircraft landing areas, and a skyscraper church. With Hood, Ferriss developed drawings of slender, tall, widely spaced towers, one group covered in masonry and a later group in glass. Hood also was the inspiration for Ferriss's illustration of luxury apartments built into an enormous expansion bridge. Both Corbett and Hood tended to streamline form and do away with extraneous decoration in their skyscrapers, and these characteristics were also favored by their delineator.

**The Metropolis of Tomorrow.** In 1929 Ferris published *The Metropolis of Tomorrow,* a magnificent collection of his drawings with an evocative accompanying text. In its three sections the book examines what Ferriss regarded as the best of contemporary urban buildings; his prophecies for architectural developments in the future; and his formulations for an urban utopia. The buildings that he praises in the first part of *The Metropolis of Tomorrow* — including Chicago's Tribune Tower, Detroit's Penobscot Building, and New York's Chanin Building

and Chrysler Building — are all massive, monumental, and, in Ferriss's drawings at least, stripped of excessive decoration. "Projected Trends," part 2 of the book, focuses particularly upon setback buildings with terraces, penthouses, and roof gardens, and includes visual warnings of the dire situations that would develop — building and traffic congestion, for example — if urban planning were not embraced. In section three of *The Metropolis of Tomorrow* Ferriss presents his ideal city divided into three major zones, Business, Science, and Art, in which giant pyramidal structures on bases covering four to eight city blocks were surrounded by low-rise buildings laid out on geometric grids. At the center of this "Imaginary City" sat a large park. The diagram of the city as a whole, with its three major zones and assorted subzones, resembled a six-pointed star. Impractical due to its failure to illustrate or discuss institutional buildings such as schools and hospitals, the placement and design of factories, and the various forms of residential structures, *The Metropolis of Tomorrow* nonetheless stirred considerable discussion about the nature — and the future — of the city in America.

**Final Years.** The years during which building construction almost entirely ceased hit Ferriss hard. There was little work available for delineators, and he was forced to return to illustrating advertisements to support himself and his family. In 1936, however, he was appointed delineator and design consultant for the 1939 New York World's Fair, the theme of which was "Building the World of Tomorrow." Yet the fair, with its emphasis on air travel and superhighways, proved to be more the vision of industrial designers Norman Bel Geddes and Henry Dreyfuss than of Ferriss. In the early 1940s the Architectural League of New York awarded him a Brunner travel grant to visit and draw outstanding structures built in American since 1929. Among the structures on which he focused were hydroelectric dams, airports, bridges, grain elevators, factories, highways, and housing projects, with only a few representations of skyscrapers. These drawings from the early 1940s later appeared as part of his 1953 collection *Power in Buildings.* Between 1946 and 1949 he served as design consultant and delineator for the United Nations Building in New York City, his last major project. Though he produced distinguished work during the 1930s and 1940s, Hugh Ferriss secured his enduring reputation in the 1920s. During that decade he both recorded and significantly influenced the development of urban architecture in America.

Sources:
Hugh Ferriss, "The New Architecture," *New York Times Magazine,* 19 March 1922, p. 8;

Ferriss, *Power in Buildings: An Artist's View of Contemporary Architecture* (New York: Columbia University Press, 1953);

"Hugh Ferriss, 72, Architect Here," *New York Times,* 30 January 1962, p. 29;

Carol Willis, "Drawing Towards Metropolis," in *The Metropolis of Tomorrow* (Princeton: Princeton Architectural Press, 1986 — facsimile reprint of Ferriss's 1929 book), pp. 148–199.

# RAYMOND M. HOOD

## 1881-1934

### SKYSCRAPER ARCHITECT

**Currents and Contradictions.** During the 1920s America was noted for its distinguished skyscraper architects — Harvey Wiley Corbett, Ralph Walker, Ely Jacques Kahn, William Van Alen — but no single figure so fully embodied the currents and contradictions of the decade as Raymond Mathewson Hood. Classically trained in the United States and Paris and apprenticed in one of America's major architectural firms, Hood proved amazingly independent. In the course of his brief twelve-year career he evolved from an adherent of the Gothic style to a practitioner of modernism. Born into a prosperous, conservative family, he preferred the commotion of the urban scene to the respectability of the stately architectural firm. As one commentator remarked, during a decade in which most well-known architects were in the *Social Register,* Raymond Hood was in the phone book. Yet he designed and built several of the notable commercial buildings of the 1920s and early 1930s.

**Beginnings.** Hood, the son of a well-to-do Providence, Rhode Island, box manufacturer, attended Brown University for two years and then enrolled in the Massachusetts Institute of Technology, where he earned an architectural degree in 1903. Following his graduation he worked as a draftsman in Boston for the Gothic architectural firm of Cram, Goodhue and Ferguson and then in the New York office of Palmer and Hornbostel. Unsuccessful on his first attempt to be admitted to Paris's Ecole des Beaux-Arts, Hood finally was accepted and took a degree there in 1911. On his return to the United States he spent three years in Hornbostel's Pittsburgh office, where he not only assisted in executing building commissions but also created several prize-winning designs for the architectural competitions that the firm regularly entered. In 1914 he and another young architect set up their own office in New York City. Hood was sustained during World War I and the recession of 1920–1921 mostly by renovation jobs, notably for Placido Mori's restaurant-speakeasy, and by a small but steady salary from the American Radiator Company, for which he designed radiator covers. His increasing success in architectural competitions bolstered his optimism about his potential success as an architect, and in 1920 he married Elsie Schmidt, his secretary, with whom he would have three children.

**Success.** In 1922 John Mead Howells, one of the well-known American architects who had been specially invited to submit designs for the heavily publicized Chicago Tribune competition, asked Hood to join him in the project. The exact nature of each man's contribution to the competition design is unclear; apparently, however, Howells provided a sketch that Hood then radically modified in his drawing. Amid a storm of controversy the anonymously submitted Howells-Hood entry narrowly won the competition over the entry of Finland's Eliel Saarinen. At the time, Saarinen's design was felt by certain critics to be more modern, more experimental than that of Howells and Hood. Yet retrospective examinations of their graceful Gothic tower have generally praised the sophistication of its setbacks and its elevator plans as well as the flexibility of its office space, thereby confirming the original judges' decision. Despite the controversy — or perhaps because of it — Hood's reputation was made, and his $10,000 share of the $50,000 first-place prize money helped remedy his rather precarious financial situation.

**American Radiator Building.** Before the Chicago Tribune Tower was completed in 1925, Hood in 1924 had finished his second distinctive skyscraper, an office building for his old friends at the American Radiator Company. With the assistance of architect Frederick Godley and engineer J. André Fouilhoux he designed a structure that, despite its midblock location and its mere twenty-story height, would project an impression of massiveness. Hood achieved this end by erecting a building that shot straight up from its base and culminated in a series of sharp setbacks near its top. Constructed of black brick so that during daylight hours its dark-appearing windows would not "punch holes" in and thereby destroy its solid appearance, the American Radiator Building had a startling gold-gilded top, which was lighted at night, and abstract gold-gilded decorations at setback points. This stylized ornamentation was regarded by some critics as an early example of Art Deco style in America. Others saw the black-and-gold structure as the perfect example of the marriage of skyscrapers and commercialism — a torchlike building advertising a company that sold furnaces and heaters.

**Daily News and McGraw-Hill Buildings.** In 1929 Hood again teamed with his Chicago Tribune Tower collaborator, Howells, to design an office-building production plant for Capt. Joseph Medill Patterson's tabloid, the *New York Daily News.* The building, a nine-story production-plant base topped by a thirty-six-story office tower, was a white, massive, vertically defined structure with dramatic setbacks and a flat crown. Its only significant exterior decoration was hung over the entryway: an enormous marble panel containing a skyscraper skyline, drawings of tradesmen, and a quotation from Abraham Lincoln ("He made so many of them" — referring, of course, to God and the common man). Inside this modernistic structure Hood placed a black glass lobby with a sunken center that contained a huge revolving globe, an extremely dramatic touch. The Daily News Building was completed in 1931, the same year as another modernistic structure, the McGraw-Hill Building, designed by Hood in collaboration with Fouilhoux. A setback, green terracotta structure, it had on each floor almost uninterrupted windows, giving it a horizontal appearance similar to that found in many of the European International Style buildings. Hood's structure was crowned by a mesalike penthouse, which bore in huge letters the company's name.

**Rockefeller Center.** Throughout his career Hood accepted commissions for buildings other than skyscrapers — private homes, apartment complexes, public buildings — though none of these projects was particularly notable for its architecture. He was a major designer for the Century of Progress Exposition, which opened in Chicago in 1933. He also toyed with such speculative but unfulfilled ventures as apartments in bridges and a tower city surrounded by broad highways and open countryside. His final major work, before his death of heart and circulatory problems at the age of fifty-three, was on Rockefeller Center, begun in 1930 and completed ten years later. Designed by a consortium of architects, this skyscraper complex cannot in any real sense be credited to Hood. However, he has been described as the "key man" in its development, and the massing of the buildings, their monochromatic exteriors, and their rooftop landscape gardens almost certainly reflect his influence. Whatever the case, Raymond M. Hood was the greatest skyscraper architect of the 1920s, embodying and inspiring the evolution of skyscraper design in America during the decade.

### Sources:

Walter H. Kilham Jr., *Raymond Hood, Architect: Form Through Function in the American Skyscraper* (New York: Architectural Book Publishing, 1973);

Robert A. M. Stern, with Thomas P. Catalano, *Raymond Hood* (New York: Institute for Architecture and Urban Studies/Rizzoli, 1982);

Allene Talmey, "Man Against the Sky," *New Yorker*, 6 (11 April 1931): 24–27.

# ALBERT KAHN

## 1869-1942

### INDUSTRIAL ARCHITECT

**"Beautiful Factories."** Detroit-based architect Albert Kahn has been called the father of the modern American factory. By the 1920s Detroit had become the center of the flourishing U.S. automobile industry, and Kahn provided what he described as "beautiful factories" — streamlined and functional — for many of the great Detroit manufacturers. Packard, Chrysler, General Motors, and Ford were among his clients, as were giants in such worldwide industries as food, textiles, chemicals, and business machines. During the early 1930s Kahn helped establish factories and engineering education in the Soviet Union; later in the 1930s and in the first years of World War II he developed plants for the construction of tanks and military aircraft. Throughout his career he also designed notable nonindustrial structures: the Detroit Athletic club, office buildings for General Motors and Fisher, the Hill Auditorium and Clements Library at the University of Michigan, and handsome private homes for such Grosse Point auto magnates as H. E. Dodge and Edsel Ford. But it is for his more than two thousand factories that Albert Kahn is remembered.

**Life.** Kahn, the oldest son of an itinerant rabbi, was born in Germany but spent his early childhood in Luxembourg. In 1880 the family immigrated to Detroit, where young Kahn did not attend school but instead worked at odd jobs and took free Sunday-morning art lessons from sculptor Julius Melchers. Discovering that his pupil was color-blind, Melchers recommended that he take up architecture instead of art and in 1885 helped him earn an apprentice position with the Detroit firm of Mason and Rice. Kahn proved an apt student of design and in 1890 won a scholarship that allowed him to travel for a year in Europe, where he met and became friends with another young architect, Henry Bacon. Returning to Detroit, Kahn rose to the position of chief designer with Mason and Rice. He refused an offer to replace Frank Lloyd Wright in Louis Sullivan's firm during the early 1890s, instead remaining with Mason and Rice until 1896. In that year he married Ernestine Krolik and set up an architectural partnership with two colleagues from Mason and Rice. By 1902 Kahn had established his own practice, which grew during the next forty years to a company of nearly four hundred people.

**Early Industrial Accomplishments.** Kahn's first significant industrial commission came from Henry B. Joy, manager of the Packard Motor Car Company, who asked him to design a ten-building production plant in Detroit. Completed between 1903 and 1905, the project included nine conventional buildings and a tenth constructed of reinforced concrete, a material that had rarely been used before in factory construction. In 1908 Henry Ford had introduced the Model T, and late that year Ford contracted with Kahn to design a factory that would place all aspects of the auto's production under a single roof. This Highland Park construction (1909–1914) combined reinforced concrete with large, steel-framed windows, thus providing improved lighting and ventilation for assembly-line workers. Through this project Kahn and Ford established a long and mutually beneficial relationship: both were energetic, inventive, self-educated men who sought innovative but practical solutions to problems in the workplace.

**River Rouge.** In early 1918 Ford asked Kahn to design and construct a single-building production plant for the Eagle Submarine Chaser, which Ford wanted to produce as part of the U.S. war effort. In fourteen weeks Kahn erected a huge, one-story, steel-framed, lavishly windowed structure on a new two-thousand-acre Ford site on the Rouge River near Detroit. After the war the building was converted to a Model T body shop, and its site became the nucleus of Ford's expanding empire. Between 1922 and 1926 Kahn constructed at River Rouge a complex of innovative factory buildings, including the Glass Plant (1922), the Motor Assembly Building (1924–1925), and the Open Hearth Building (1925). In most cases these one-story structures incorporated steel frames, windowed walls, roofs with monitors (raised sections containing additional windows or louvers), and interior planning built around assembly-line organizational systems. Clean and attractive, River Rouge was America's first truly modern industrial complex because its design and construction fully expressed the architecture of utility.

**Later Career.** Following the stock-market crash in October 1929, automobile production radically declined, but Kahn and his company remained busy renovating plants so that they could produce vehicles in the most economical way possible. Between 1929 and 1932 he also directed the construction of 521 factories and the training of more than four thousand engineers in the Soviet Union as part of the Soviets' First Five-Year Plan of industrialization. By 1937 Kahn's firm was performing nearly one-fifth of all architect-designed factory construction in the United States. And as World War II approached he developed Ford's giant Willow Run bomber plant (1941–1943), the Glenn Martin Assembly Building and its additions (1937–1941) for the manufacture of other military aircraft, and the Chrysler Tank Arsenal (1941), all models of modern design. In the course of his career Albert Kahn seized the opportunity — and the responsibility — to transform the architecture of American industry. Toward the end of his life he recalled, with obvious satisfaction and with tongue firmly in cheek: "When I began, the real architects would design only museums, cathedrals, capitols, monuments. The office boy was considered good enough to do factory buildings. I'm still that office boy designing factories. I have no dignity to be impaired."

Sources:
*Architectural Forum,* 69 (August 1938): 87–142;

Grant Hildebrand, *The Architecture of Albert Kahn* (Cambridge, Mass.: MIT Press, 1974).

# ADDISON MIZNER

## 1872-1933

### PALM BEACH ARCHITECT

**Genius or Fraud?** Because of the extravagance of his vision and his connection with the Florida boom during the 1920s, Addison Mizner has been described both as a genius of American architecture and as one of architecture's great frauds. An early biographer quipped that his flamboyant Palm Beach "villas" embodied a "Bastard-Spanish-Moorish-Romanesque-Gothic-Renaissance-Bull-Market-Damn-the-Expense style." Yet his work was praised by such notable figures as Frank Lloyd Wright, skyscraper designer Harvey Wiley Corbett, and sculptor Jo Davidson. Whatever the final assessment of his work, Mizner undeniably embodied the ebullient, gaudy, expansive spirit of the decade.

**Early Life.** Mizner was born into a prominent California family who encouraged his youthful interest in drawing. A year in Guatemala, where his father served as an American diplomat, inspired Mizner's love for Spanish architecture and artifacts, a passion that was sharpened by a few months' residence at the University of Salamanca in Spain. Never much of a student, he avoided the usual avenue to architectural success in his time — the Ecole des Beaux-Arts in Paris — and instead became an apprentice in 1893 with San Francisco architect Willis Polk. Soon running up substantial debts, Mizner fled San Francisco for Alaska, where he joined the Klondike gold rush with his younger brother, Wilson, who was just beginning his long career as con man and wit. Addison Mizner returned to San Francisco in 1899 and then embarked on a two-year voyage through the South Pacific, where he claimed to have worked as an artist in ivory and charcoal, an exporter of antiques, a coffin-handle salesman, a prize fighter, and a restorer of family portraits for Hawaiian Queen Liliuokalani, who knighted him. In 1903 he co-authored, with Ethel Watts Mumford, *The Cynic's Calendar,* a collection of twisted aphorisms such as "Where there's a will, there's a lawsuit" and "A word to the wise is resented." The volume sold relatively well, and Mizner returned to San Francisco with the notion of becoming an importer of Guatemalan coffee so that he could marry a lumber heiress whose father had just died. The heiress committed suicide, and the coffee plan did not work out, but while in Guatemala Mizner bought vestments, tapestries, candlesticks, and even altars from impoverished churches — loot that he was able to sell to collectors for substantial sums.

**New York.** With his newfound fortune and the help of a childhood friend, Mrs. Hermann Oelrichs, a star in the New York social scene, Mizner set himself up in 1904 as a society architect. Mrs. Oelrichs introduced him to Stanford White, the premier society architect, who sent small jobs his way. Mrs. Oelrichs also introduced him to other of her wealthy friends, who were charmed by Mizner's wit and his exotic history, which he amusingly and racily embroidered. The brief marriage of his brother Wilson to the much older widow of tycoon Charles T. Yerkes — a match lavishly covered by the newspapers — brought even further attention to the Mizner name. Between 1904 and 1917 Addison Mizner built a successful career as an architect who designed luxury homes in a variety of styles. His New York period ended when World War I slowed the construction of these homes and when a debilitating injury required that he find a warmer climate.

**Arrival in Palm Beach.** In January 1918 Mizner became the houseguest of Paris Singer, a wealthy heir to the sewing machine fortune and kingpin of Palm Beach society. Singer commissioned Mizner to design and construct a hospital–convalescent home for affluent American combat veterans, and Mizner responded with a brick-and-stucco tile-roofed Spanish-style building surrounded by small, identically styled villas. The war ended in November 1918, and when the complex opened in January 1919 it was not as a hospital but instead as the exclusive Everglades Club. The Everglades Club quickly became the center of Palm Beach social life and the inspiration for dozens of Mizner-built mansions along the city's beachfront.

**Palm Beach Style.** Commissioned by the elite of Palm Beach — Stotesburys, Vanderbilts, Biddles, Dukes, Wanamakers — the huge "villas" featured red-tiled roofs and spectacular loggias (roofed, often glassed-in or screened-in galleries) that opened onto patios and gardens and views of the sea. These homes were furnished by Mizner with tapestries, woodwork, grillwork, and flooring from ancient homes and churches in Europe and Latin America or with replicas — tile, wrought iron, carved wood, stained glass, pottery, furniture — manufactured by Mizner Industries, which Mizner established for the purpose. It is said that he hired men in hobnail boots to trod on drying concrete steps or workers with hatchets and files to scar newly installed woodwork — thus investing new homes with an antique appearance. His intention was not to deceive his wealthy customers but instead to provide them with his own picturesque, romantic version of history. As he told a contemporary interviewer, "My houses are full of history. I can afford to have a great deal because I make it up." No doubt many of the most outrageous tales about his architectural practices — that he once forgot to include a door in the design of a boathouse and a staircase in the design of a multistory villa — were self-created. He loved to repeat the story that when a client had asked to see the blueprints for the house he had commissioned, Mizner had replied that they were not available because the house had not been *built* yet. First the completed house, then the plans, he suggested.

**Boca Raton.** In addition to the Everglades Club and private villas, Mizner also provided Palm Beach with commercial and public buildings — Spanish-style shops and offices with stone walkways, sheltering loggias, and attractive landscaping. During the fall of 1924 he seized the opportunity to design an entire Spanish-style city — Boca Raton — which would include mansions, moderately priced housing, a commercial district, polo fields and golf courses, extraordinarily wide main streets, and an extensive canal system featuring electric gondolas. Caught up in the frenzy of the Florida boom, Mizner hoped to attract investors of all sorts to his model city

and, in turn, make his own fortune. Instead, despite frenzied building and promotion on his part, his project was doomed when the Florida real-estate market collapsed entirely in the spring of 1926.

**The Comedy Goes On.** After the Boca Raton disaster Mizner continued to erect a few buildings in Palm Beach and elsewhere — The Cloister at Sea Island, Georgia, for example. However, his reputation and the popularity of his architectural style rapidly declined, although both have enjoyed something of a revival since the early 1980s. Mizner spent much time during his final years writing *The Many Mizners* (1932), an account of his life until 1915. He was able to maintain his lifestyle only with the help of affluent former clients who often paid his household bills. Yet Mizner seems not to have lost his shrewd, if eccentric, perspective on life. A telegram from Wilson Mizner exhorted him, only hours before his death: "Stop dying. Am trying to write comedy." Addison Mizner replied: "Am going to get well. The comedy goes on."

Sources:

Donald W. Curl, *Mizner's Florida: American Resort Architecture* (New York: Architectural History Foundation / Cambridge, Mass: MIT Press, 1984);

Alva Johnston, *The Legendary Mizners* (New York: Farrar, Straus & Young, 1953);

Mary Fanton Roberts, "Exotic Beauty of Palm Beach Homes," *Arts & Decoration*, 20 (December 1923): 22–25.

## JEAN PATOU

### 1880?-1936

#### FRENCH FASHION INNOVATOR

**Spirit of the 1920s.** Jean Patou may have been the couturier who most fully embodied the spirit of the 1920s. A handsome, high-stakes gambler in both the casinos and the fashion world, Patou aligned himself with the restless international café society of Paris and the newly popular Riviera. He helped define the youthful, athletic look of the mid 1920s by producing exquisitely cut short dresses, often pleated or fitted with geometric inserts to ensure freedom of movement, and by introducing "Cubist" sweaters and bathing suits. He identified this style as particularly "American" and stunned the fashion world by importing six young women from the United States to model in his Paris shows. Yet with his 1929 collections Patou almost single-handedly killed the "boyish" look by, during his spring show, reintroducing the natural bustline and waistline to women's fashion and, during his fall show, dropping skirt lengths to at least midcalf, a style that took hold as the Great Depression began.

**Life.** Born in Normandy, Patou was the son of an affluent tanner known for the fine leathers he produced for specialty bookbinders. Supported by family money, the young Patou tried his hand as a furrier, a tailor, and, finally, a Paris dressmaker, opening "Maison Parry" in 1912 and moving to the rue St. Florentin and a shop under his own name in early 1914. His first major collection was scheduled to appear that fall but was delayed for five years by the Great War; Patou enlisted in the crack Zouave infantry unit, rising to captain before the Armistice in November 1918. Like many other combat survivors of that war, Patou seemed marked by determination to cast off old values and to embrace — almost recklessly — new ones.

**Cultural and Social Influences.** Upon his return to Paris, Patou commissioned interior designer André Mare and architect Louis Sue, Art Deco leaders, to redecorate his couture house and to design elegant bottles for his various fragrances, including Joy — advertised as "The most expensive scent in the world." He drew upon the influence of Georges Braque and Pablo Picasso as he employed geometric figures and dramatic colors in his "Cubist" sweaters and swimsuits during the mid 1920s. In 1924 he established sportswear shops, among the first of their kind, in the resorts of Deauville and Biarritz, where the international expatriate society gathered. It has also been claimed that he predated both Coco Chanel and Hermès in employing visible initials identifying the designer of a garment, thus assuring his frequently nouveau riche clientele that their good taste would be recognized. Thus, like his contemporary and rival Chanel, he brought into his designs and his promotional strategies major cultural and social currents of his time.

**Patou and the Americans.** Although Patou's first major triumph was his designing of the revolutionary tennis ensembles — short pleated skirts, sleeveless sweaters, and brightly colored headbands — for French star Suzanne Lenglen, he was soon providing similarly elegant but wearable tennis garb for the American player Helen Wills, who substituted an eyeshade for Lenglen's headband. He also outfitted the portly American society hostess Elsa Maxwell, a close friend and vigorous promoter of his endeavors, and such American movie stars as Gloria Swanson and Mary Pickford. But his most sensational "American" gesture came in late 1924, when, with a jury including *Vogue* editor Edna Woolman Chase, Broadway showman Florenz Ziegfeld, *Vogue* and *Vanity Fair* publisher Condé Nast, and fashion photographer Edward Steichen, he chose six American girls to join the French models already working in his Paris fashion house. He thus secured athletic, slender "American Dianas" to complement his more voluptuous "French Venuses" and to show his "Cubist" look to best advantage. He also created enormous goodwill with American consumers and New York fashion merchants.

**Triumph and Decline.** When Patou, in the months before the stock-market crash, restored the natural feminine waistline and bustline and dropped hemlines, he announced the prevailing style of the next decade but ironically killed the look that had sustained him during the 1920s. His perfumes, notions, and a backless white satin evening gown were all that sustained him and his fashion house until his death of a heart attack in March 1936. The Jean Patou line did rebound, however, under the management of his brother-in-law Raymond Barbas and a series of notable young designers, including Marc Bohan, Karl Lagerfeld, and Christian Lacroix.

Sources:
Edna Woolman Chase and Ilka Chase, *Always in Vogue* (Garden City, N.Y.: Doubleday, 1954);

Meredith Etherington-Smith, *Patou* (New York: St. Martin's Press/Marek, 1983);

Elsa Maxwell, *R.S.V.P.: Elsa Maxwell's Own Story* (Boston: Little, Brown, 1954);

*New York Times,* 9 March 1936, p. 17.

# PEOPLE IN THE NEWS

M-G-M costume designer **Adrian** (born Adrian Adolph Greenburg), who had worked with Irving Berlin on Broadway and Rudolph Valentino in Hollywood, began a revolution in millinery by costuming Greta Garbo in a slouch hat in the 1928 movie *A Woman of Affairs,* a tepid version of Michael Arlen's 1924 novel *The Green Hat.* The slouch hat, a soft-crowned felt with a flexible brim pulled down over one eye, replaced the cloche in the late 1920s and early 1930s as the most popular women's hat style.

Famous hairdresser **Antoine de Paris** (born Antek Cierplikowski in Sieradz, Poland) opened the first of his American salons at Saks Fifth Avenue in 1925. Monsieur Antoine claimed to have invented the shingle bob in 1917.

In 1925 **Walter W. Birge** established the Industrial Rayon Corporation, a holding company for his Industrial Fibre Corporation, the fourth largest rayon producer in the United States; Birge had been a member of the five-man committee that adopted the word *rayon* when U.S. government officials requested that manufacturers stop calling their product "artificial silk."

Chicago-born **Main Rousseau Bocher** left Paris *Vogue* — where he had served successively as illustrator, fashion editor, and editor in chief — to found his own Paris fashion house in 1929 under the name **Mainbocher.** He was the first American to run a successful salon in Paris, and his establishments there and, later, in New York flourished until his retirement in 1971.

In 1928 Duesenberg's young factory stylist **Gordon Buehrig,** who would become one of America's great automotive designers, created several body types for the legendary Duesenberg Model J.

In 1928 **John Cavanagh** established on Park Avenue a men's hat shop that became one of the most prestigious in the United States. In the 1930s he would create the Hat Corporation of America and the Cavanagh Research Corporation, both of which promoted hat development and trade.

*Toward a New Architecture,* the English translation of *Vers une architecture* (1923), was published in New York in 1927. This collection of essays by Swiss architect **Le Corbusier** defines his design principles and prints several statements — including "A house is a machine for living in" — that influenced the development of modernist architecture in America.

**Paul Philippe Cret,** a French-born Philadelphia architect best remembered for public buildings in modern classical style, began construction of his masterpiece, the Folger Shakespeare Library, in 1928; the Washington, D.C., building, near the Library of Congress, was completed in 1932.

The twenty-year-old **Lilly Daché** immigrated to the United States from France in 1924. After one week's work as a millinery salesgirl at Macy's, she set up her own New York City shop, which she operated for forty-five years; she became the best-known women's hat designer in America.

In 1927 **Donald Deskey** founded Deskey-Vollmer, an interior-design firm that executed modernistic apartment renovations for such well-known New Yorkers as cosmetics queen Helena Rubinstein, literary critic Gilbert Seldes, and Saks Fifth Avenue president Adam Gimbel. In 1932 Deskey designed the interiors for Radio City Music Hall.

Decorator **Elsie de Wolfe,** who had earlier made her fortune by introducing "New American money to Old French furniture," was one of the popularizers of modernist white-on-white rooms in 1929.

A design for a Dymaxion House — a hexagonal, glass-covered, steel and aluminum structure hung from a central column and powered by sunlight — was introduced in 1928 by **R. Buckminster Fuller,** later celebrated for his geodesic domes.

In 1928 architect **Cass Gilbert** began work on the U.S. Supreme Court Building; the most important of the three structures Gilbert designed for the national capital, the Supreme Court Building was completed in 1935.

**Ruzzie Green,** art director at the Stehli Silk Corporation, in 1928 introduced a dress fabric printed with the word *It;* the design capitalized on the sex appeal of movie star Clara Bow, the "It Girl."

In 1928 German-born **Walter Gropius** resigned as director of the revolutionary Bauhaus school of design, which he had founded in his native country in 1919. Gropius fled Nazi Germany in 1934 and four years later became chairman of the Harvard University Architecture Department, where he was a vigorous campaigner for modern, socially relevant design.

French designer **Madame Jeanne Lanvin** in 1926 opened the world's first boutique for men. Located across the street from her couturiere house on the rue du Faubourg St. Honoré in Paris, this men's shop was managed by Madame Lanvin's nephew, Maurice Lanvin.

In the fall of 1925 **Lois Long,** under the pseudonym "Lipstick," began writing a shopping column for *The New Yorker.* Eventually titled "On and Off the Avenue," the column often treated fashion designers or retail-clothing establishments.

In 25 April 1925 **Man Ray** (born Emmanuel Radnitsky in Philadelphia) photographed couturier fashions on display in the Pavillon de l'Elégance, a section of the Art Deco Exposition in Paris, which would officially open in July. His pictures of designer-dressed wood-and-wax mannequins were regarded both as effective advertisements for fashion and as expressions of Surrealist art.

By 1927 **Marion Morehouse,** whom photographer **Edward Steichen** called "the best fashion model I ever worked with," had become the most recognizable photographic model in America. In 1933 she left modeling to marry poet E. E. Cummings; their union survived until his death in 1962.

**Julia Morgan,** the first woman to attend the Ecole des Beaux-Arts in Paris, was architect for William Randolph Hearst's castle complex at San Simeon in central California. She worked on the project from 1919 to 1939, and Hearst first occupied the main castle, "La Casa Grande," in December 1925.

American cultural historian **Lewis Mumford** published the first of his several important architectural studies, *Sticks and Stones: A Study of American Architecture and Civilization,* in 1924. From 1931 to 1963 Mumford wrote the "Sky Line" column as architectural critic for *The New Yorker.*

In 1928 **Charles Nessler,** inventor of the permanent wave in 1905 and purported inventor of false eyelashes some time later, published *The Story of Hair: Its Purposes and Its Preservation.* In his book Nessler attempts to define "the relationship between the fundamental nature of the individual and the covering of his scalp" and predicts the eradication of male baldness before the end of the twentieth century. Known to his customers as Father Nestle, he operated a hair salon on East Forty-sixth Street in New York City.

Vienna-born architect **Richard Neutra,** who later would become a master of the International Style, in 1929 completed the first private house to be framed entirely in steel; the Los Angeles home of Dr. Phillip Lovell featured dramatic balconies poised over a ravine.

In 1928 **Norman Norell,** later one of America's best-known fashion designers, began a twelve-year apprenticeship with Hattie Carnegie, who honed his taste for precision tailoring and conservative elegance.

**Frank Alvah Parsons,** who in 1905 had become president of the New York School of Fine and Applied Art and who taught interior design as a system of principles, established his Paris Ateliers, or workshops, for American and European students in 1921. The New York School was renamed the Parsons School in 1941.

In 1927 French couturier **Paul Poiret** prophesied in *Forum* that within thirty years women would routinely wear pants in public; his remarks sparked considerable disagreement from readers.

**Gilbert Rohde,** who had spent two years in Europe, where he admired German and French applied arts, in 1929 began creating chromium-plated metal and Bakelite tables in his New York City studio. During the 1930s he became well known for designing wooden, tubular-metal, and wicker furniture.

In 1926 architect **Eliel Saarinen** became director of the art academy at Cranbrook, the Bloomfield Hills, Michigan, estate of publisher and art patron George Gough Booth; Saarinen assembled at Cranbrook a stable of artists and craftsmen that included furniture designers **Harry Bertoia, Charles Eames,** and **Eero Saarinen,** Eliel Saarinen's son.

In 1927 **Elsa Schiaparelli** introduced her trompe l'oeil (optical illusion) sweater, featuring a white collar and bow pattern knitted into a black background; an enormous success in Paris and the United States, the sweater was the first of Schiaparelli's experiments with Surrealist effects.

The 1924 publication of *Spanish Farm Houses and Minor Public Buildings* by **Winsor Soule** provided plans for simple one-story homes with patios or porches; the book stimulated interest in ranch-style homes and villas, especially in California.

In 1923 artist and designer **Ethel Traphagen** founded the Traphagen School of Fashion at 1680 Broadway in New York City. Both the Traphagen School and the Fashion Academy, founded at 4 East Fifty-third Street by **Emil Alvin Hartman** in 1917, were major American schools of fashion design during the 1920s.

**Joseph Urban,** a Vienna-born architect who during his career created sets for sixteen Ziegfeld Follies, fifty-four Metropolitan Opera productions, and thirty movies, designed the spectacular Ziegfeld Theatre on Sixth Avenue and Forty-fourth Street in New York City. Completed in 1927 and razed in 1966, the structure featured a revolutionary egg-shaped auditorium;

it was the first modern theater created exclusively for musicals.

**Valentina** (Nicholaevna Sanina Schlee), a ballerina refugee from the Russian Revolution, opened a New York City dressmaking shop in 1928. Her dramatic style, which included long, draped gowns, turbans, and veils, made her a major fashion voice until her retirement in 1957.

In 1921 **Carmel White** was hired as an assistant fashion editor by American *Vogue*. Under her married name, **Carmel Snow**, she became one of the most influential voices in fashion until her death in 1961. In line to succeed **Edna Woolman Chase** as editor in chief of *Vogue*, Snow defected to archrival *Harper's Bazaar* in 1932.

**Bertram G. Work,** president of B. F. Goodrich Company, allegedly gave the zipper its name (to capture its "zip") when Goodrich introduced the zippered rubber boot in 1923; the company registered the name as a trademark in 1925, but gradually *zipper* became the generic name for all hookless or slide fasteners.

Out of architectural fashion during the 1920s, **Frank Lloyd Wright** supported himself primarily through commissions for private homes in the Midwest and southern California. Several of these homes, including the Millard House built in Pasadena in 1923, employed Mayan Cubistic designs in patterned concrete blocks and threads of steel.

# AWARDS

## AMERICAN INSTITUTE OF ARCHITECTS GOLD MEDAL

(American Institute of Architects)

1920 — No award

1921 — No award

1922 — Victor Laloux

1923 — Henry Bacon

1924 — No award

1925 — Bertram Grosvenor Goodhue

— Sir Edwin Landseer Lutyens

1926 — No award

1927 — Howard Van Doren Shaw

1928 — No award

1929 — Milton Bennett Medary

## THOMAS B. CLARKE PRIZE

(National Academy of Design for Interior Design)

1920 — James Hopkins

1921 — Leon Kroll

1922 — Gertrude Fiske

1923 — Eugene F. Savage

1924 — Clifford Addams

1925 — Gertrude Fiske

1926 — Will Foster

1927 — John E. Costigan

1928 — Alice K. Stoddard

1929 — Ettore Caser

## ROYAL GOLD MEDAL FOR ARCHITECTURE

(Royal Institute of British Architects)

1922 — Thomas Hastings

## AMERICAN ACADEMY AND INSTITUTE OF ARTS AND LETTERS GOLD MEDAL

(American Academy and Institute of Arts and Letters)

1921 — Cass Gilbert, architecture

# DEATHS

Benjamin L. Armstrong, 85, known as the "dean of silk producers"; for sixty-eight years Armstrong was associated with the silk industry, founding several production companies in New London, Connecticut, 20 October 1929.

Henry Bacon, 57, architect best remembered for designing public monuments, particularly the Lincoln Memorial, with seated figure of Lincoln by sculptor Daniel Chester French, 16 February 1924.

Alvah Norton Belding, 86, last of four brothers who founded Belding Brothers, a pioneer manufacturer and distributor of silk thread, 19 December 1925.

Carl Benz, 84, German engineer who in 1886 developed what was probably the world's first motorcar, 3 April 1929.

Charles I. Berg, 70, designer of one of New York City's first skyscrapers, the twenty-story Gillenger Building erected in 1897 at Wall Street and Nassau Street, 13 October 1926.

Alfred Cartier, 84, son of the founder of the legendary French jewelry firm. During the twentieth century the Cartier empire flourished under the direction of Alfred Cartier's three sons: Louis, who managed the Paris branch; Jacques, who ran the London branch; and Pierre, who headed the New York branch, 15 October 1925.

Theophilus Parsons Chandler, 82, specialist in ecclesiastical architecture; he was the organizer and first director of the University of Pennsylvania School of Architecture, 16 August 1928.

Count Hilaire de Bernigaud de Chardonnet, 84, French chemist known as "father of the Rayon Industry"; in 1891 his plant at Besançon began regular commercial production of "artificial silk," 12 March 1924.

Col. Austen Colgate, 64, for more than thirty years a director of Colgate soap and perfume manufacturers, 5 September 1927.

Michael Dreicer, 53, a leading New York jeweler and investor in Fifth Avenue real estate; in 1924 Cartier's of New York acquired the remaining stock of Dreicer & Company for $2.5 million, 26 July 1921.

John H. Duncan, 76, architect chiefly remembered as the designer of Grant's Tomb, 18 October 1929.

Cyrus Lazelle Warner Eidlitz, 68, architect who supplied the plans for the *New York Times* building on Forty-third Street, 5 October 1921.

Bertram Grosvenor Goodhue, 55, architect primarily known for his Gothic churches, including the chapel of the United States Military Academy at West Point; the most notable of his several New York City buildings is St. Thomas's Church Fifth Avenue, which includes a dollar sign among other engravings on its door, 23 April 1924.

John H. Hanan, 71, a director of the United Shoe Machinery Company of Boston and the Hanan Shoe Company of New York, 25 August 1920.

Harry Hart, 79, a founder and for fifty years president of the Chicago-based Hart, Schaffner & Marx, pioneer manufacturer of men's clothing, 20 November 1929.

Thomas Hastings, 69, cofounder with John Merven Carrère of Carrère & Hastings architectural firm, which numbered among its achievements the United States Senate and House Office Buildings, the New York Public Library, and the Memorial Amphitheatre at the Tomb of the Unknown Soldier in Arlington National Cemetery, 22 October 1929.

William D. Hewitt, 76, Philadelphia architect best known as a designer of churches and the Hull School Memorial Building in Pottstown, Pennsylvania, 23 April 1924.

William Holabird, 68, Chicago architect who developed the idea introduced by William Le Baron Jenney of using load-bearing metal as structural support for tall buildings, a crucial principle in the construction of skyscrapers, 19 July 1923.

Richard Hudnut, 72, millionaire New York perfume manufacturer, 30 October 1928.

Robert I. Ingersoll, 68, founder of a New York watchmaking company best remembered for the Ingersoll one-dollar watch, of which more than 70 million were sold through the Ingersoll mail-order business, 4 September 1928.

Col. Jacob J. Janeway, 86, president of Janeway & Carpenter Wall Paper Manufacturing Company, one of the largest wall-covering producers in the United States, 31 July 1926.

Jackson Johnson, 69, a founder of the International Shoe Company, the largest shoe manufacturer in the world; Johnson was credited with moving the shoemaking industry from New England to the Midwest, thereby improving distribution of his product, 23 January 1929.

Jonas Kuppenheimer, 66, founder with his father, Bernard, and two brothers, Louis B. and Albert B., of the Chicago-based House of Kuppenheimer, men's clothing manufacturers, 4 May 1921.

Edward Drummond Libbey, 71, Toledo, Ohio, glass manufacturer who introduced an automatic glass-blowing machine and a revolutionary method for making window glass in flat, continuous sheets, 13 November 1925.

Austin Willard Lord, 62, member of the architectural firm Lord & Hewlett and from 1912 to 1915 director of Columbia University's School of Architecture, 19 January 1921.

Henry Rutgers Marshall, 74, New York architect who published books on philosophy, psychology, and aesthetics; he served terms as president of the American Psychological Association and president of the New York chapter of the American Institute of Architects, 3 May 1927.

William Rutherford Mead, 81, founding partner and business manager of the prestigious New York architectural firm McKim, Mead & White, 20 June 1928.

Milton Bennett Medary, 55, architect who designed the Washington Memorial Chapel at Valley Forge, Pennsylvania, the Carillon Tower for the Edward Bok Bird Sanctuary at Mountain Lake, Florida, and the Department of Justice office building, on which he was working at the time of his death, 7 August 1929.

Theodore Frelinghuysen Merseles, 65, director of two pioneer mail-order houses, National Cloak and Suit Company (1903–1921) and Montgomery Ward and Company (1921–1927), 7 March 1929.

John Charles Olmsted, 67, nephew, adopted son, and partner of Frederick Law Olmsted, landscape architect of Central Park; John Charles Olmstead, who served as first president of the American Society of Landscape Architects, was principally known as landscape designer for the Chicago World's Fair in 1893, for Smith and Mount Holyoke Colleges, and for urban parks and playgrounds throughout the United States, 24 February 1920.

William Doud Packard, 62, founder with his brother, James Ward Packard, of the Packard Motor Car Company, producer of luxury automobiles, 11 November 1923.

Frederick Forrest Peabody, 65, former president of Cluett, Peabody collar company, which produced the Arrow shirt, 23 February 1927.

Charles Poynter Redfern, 76, son of English designer John Redfern, dressmaker to Queen Victoria and the British aristocracy. In 1891 Charles Poynter Redfern established a fashion house in Paris, where he became known for his elegant blue ladies' suits and for the elaborate costumes he created for actress Sarah Bernhardt; in 1911 he declared that "the cultured American lady is the best-dressed lady in the world," 16 June 1929.

Horace Saks, 43, a founder of Saks Thirty-fourth Street and first president of the upscale Saks Fifth Avenue, 27 November 1925.

Howard Van Doren Shaw, 56, architect best known for designing fashionable, vaguely medieval houses in the Chicago area, particularly in Lake Forest; he also planned the model town built in Indiana Harbor, Indiana, 6 May 1926.

Louis Henri Sullivan, 67, revolutionary Chicago architect whose modernist declaration that "form ever follows function" proved highly influential to later generations of architects, including his disciple Frank Lloyd Wright; among Sullivan's most famous buildings are Chicago's acoustically perfect Auditorium Theater, built with Dankmar Adler, and Saint Louis's Wainwright Building, perhaps the first true skyscraper, 14 April 1924.

Samuel Breck Parkman Trowbridge, 62, head of the Fifth Avenue architectural firm Trowbridge & Livingston, known for designing banks — among them New York City's Bankers Trust, Chemical National Bank, J. P. Morgan, and Bank of America, 29 January 1925.

William Burnet Tuthill, 74, architect who was chief designer, with assistance from Louis Henri Sullivan and Dankmar Adler, of New York City's Carnegie Hall, 25 August 1929.

Julien Stevens Ulman, 54, leather exporter who was president of F. Blumenthal in New York, the Amalgamated Leather Company, the Transocean Products Corporation, and the Fashion Publicity Company, 7 May 1920.

Zealie Van Raalte, 54, a founder and vice president of the Van Raalte silk-producing and importing firm headquartered on Fifth Avenue, 16 May 1921.

John Wanamaker, 84, founder of the John Wanamaker department stores in Philadelphia and New York; an innovative businessman who began his career as a men's clothier, he emphasized quality goods, customer satisfaction, and effective newspaper advertising, 12 December 1922.

Lewis Rodman Wanamaker, 65, son of John Wanamaker; as buyer for and later director of both the Philadelphia and New York stores, Rodman Wanamaker imported gowns, antiques, and other expensive goods from Paris, thereby providing the John Wanamaker establishments with a more upscale image, 9 March 1928.

**Dr. Lucien C. Warner,** 84, director of Warner Chemical Company who, with his brother, Dr. Ira De Ver Warner, also created the Warner Company, manufacturer of women's foundation garments, 30 July 1925.

**Lloyd Warren,** 55, architect who was a founder and the first director of the New York Beaux Arts Institute of Design, an organization through which established architects provided mentoring and competitions for students enrolled in architectural schools throughout the United States, 25 October 1922.

# PUBLICATIONS

---

Le Corbusier, *Vers une architecture* (Paris: Crès, 1923); *Toward a New Architecture* (New York: Payson & Clarke, 1927);

Nathaniel Cortlandt Curtis, *Architectural Composition* (Cleveland: Jansen, 1923);

Hugh Ferriss, *The Metropolis of Tomorrow* (New York: Ives Washburn, 1929);

B. C. Forbes and O. D. Foster, *Automotive Giants of America: Men Who Are Making Our Motor Industry* (New York: Forbes, 1926);

John F. Harbeson, *The Study of Architectural Design With Special Reference to the Program of the Beaux-Arts Institute of Design* (New York: Pencil Points Press, 1927);

Werner Hegemann and Elbert Peets, *The American Vitruvius: An Architects' Handbook of Civic Art* (New York: Architectural Books, 1922);

Henry-Russell Hitchcock, *Modern Architecture, Romanticism and Reintegration* (New York: Harcourt, Brace, 1929);

Hitchcock and Philip Johnson, *The International Style: Architecture Since 1922* (New York: Norton, 1932);

*The House Beautiful Furnishing Annual 1926* (Boston: Atlantic Monthly, 1925);

Fiske Kimball, *American Architecture* (Indianapolis: Bobbs, Merrill, 1928);

Erich Mendelsohn, *Amerika* (Berlin: Mosse, 1928);

Lewis Mumford, *Sticks and Stones: A Study of American Architecture and Civilization* (New York: Boni & Liveright, 1924);

Richard Neutra, *Amerika* (Vienna: Schroll, 1930);

Rexford Newcomb, *The Spanish House for America* (Philadelphia: Lippincott, 1927);

Paul H. Nystrom, *Economics of Fashion* (New York: Ronald Press, 1928);

Augusta Owen Patterson, *American Homes of To-Day: Their Architectural Style, Their Environment, Their Characteristics* (New York: Macmillan, 1924);

Geoffrey Scott, *The Architecture of Humanism,* second edition (New York: Scribners, 1924);

Winsor Soule, *Spanish Farm Houses and Minor Public Buildings* (New York: Architectural Books, 1924);

Louis Henri Sullivan, *The Autobiography of an Idea* (New York: A.I.A., 1924);

Thomas Eddy Tallmadge, *The Story of Architecture in America* (New York: Norton, 1927);

Bruno Taut, *Modern Architecture* (London: Studio, 1929);

*American Architect,* periodical;

*American Automobile,* periodical;

*Architectural Forum,* periodical;

*Architectural Record,* periodical;

*Architectural Review,* periodical;

*Architecture,* periodical;

*Arts & Decoration,* periodical;

*Better Homes & Gardens,* periodical, begun in 1922;

*Gentlemen's Quarterly,* periodical, begun in 1926;

*House and Garden,* periodical;

*House Beautiful,* periodical;

*Ladies' Home Journal,* periodical;

*McCall's,* periodical;

*Men's Wear,* periodical, begun in 1924;

*Pencil Points,* periodical, begun in 1920.

# GOVERNMENT AND POLITICS

by JANET HUDSON

## CONTENTS

*Sidebars and tables are listed in italics.*

## 1920

- The 1920 census reports that 105,710,620 people live in the United States and that for the first time rural residents number fewer than urban residents.

**16 Jan.** Secured by ratification of the Eighteenth Amendment to the Constitution in January 1919, national prohibition of the manufacture, sale, and transportation of alcoholic beverages goes into effect.

**19 Mar.** In a victory for opponents of the Treaty of Versailles, the Senate rejects U.S. membership in the League of Nations.

**8–14 May** At its national convention in New York City, the Socialist Party nominates its presidential candidate Eugene V. Debs — who since 1918 has been serving a ten-year prison sentence for violating the Espionage Act.

**8–12 June** At its national convention in Chicago, the Republican Party nominates Sen. Warren G. Harding from Ohio for president of the United States.

**28 June–
5 July** At the Democratic National Convention in San Francisco, Gov. James M. Cox of Ohio is nominated for president of the United States. Democrats select former secretary of the navy Franklin Delano Roosevelt as vice presidential candidate.

**2 Nov.** With his campaign slogan "back to normalcy," Warren G. Harding receives 404 electoral votes and 60 percent of the popular vote to win the presidency of the United States.

## 1921

- Polio strikes rising political star Franklin D. Roosevelt. Doctors suspect that he will never walk again.

**4 Mar.** Warren G. Harding is inaugurated as twenty-ninth president of the United States.

**19 May** Harding signs the Emergency Immigration Act, restricting immigration to the United States from any European country to 3 percent of the individuals of that nationality in the United States at the time of the 1910 census. The act also creates an annual ceiling of 355,000 immigrants.

**20 June** Alice Robertson of Oklahoma becomes the first woman to preside over the U.S. House of Representatives, remaining at the podium for thirty minutes.

**30 June** President Harding names former president William Howard Taft chief justice of the U.S. Supreme Court.

**25 Aug.** Because the United States never ratified the Versailles Treaty, U.S. and German representatives sign a peace treaty in Berlin to officially recognize the end of World War I.

**11 Oct.** The U.S. House Committee on Rules launches an investigation of the Ku Klux Klan.

**2 Nov.** Congress votes to designate 11 November — Armistice Day — a national holiday.

## 1922

**6 Feb.** The Washington Conference on arms reduction ends with agreements on three important treaties — the Four-Power Treaty, the Five-Power Treaty, and the Nine-Power Treaty.

**1923**

| | |
|---|---|
| **15 Apr.** | The Senate launches an investigation that Secretary of the Interior Albert B. Fall was involved in illegal activities surrounding the lease of the Teapot Dome oil fields and other federal oil reserves to private oil companies. |
| **15 May** | The U.S. Supreme Court declares the Federal Child Labor Law unconstitutional. |
| **14 June** | In a silent march in Washington, D.C., African Americans from every state demonstrate their support for the Anti-Lynching Bill. |
| **19 Sept.** | President Harding vetoes the Veteran's Bonus Bill. |
| **3 Oct.** | Rebecca Felton, age eighty-seven, of Georgia becomes the first female U.S. senator. Her term, to which the governor of Georgia appointed her following the death of Sen. Thomas Watson, lasts only one day. |

| | |
|---|---|
| **4 Mar.** | Congress passes the Agricultural Credits Act, making low-interest loans available to farmers. |
| | Secretary of the Interior Albert B. Fall resigns as the Senate investigation into the Teapot Dome scandal escalates. |
| **9 Apr.** | The U.S. Supreme Court rules the minimum-wage law for women and children in Washington, D.C., to be unconstitutional in *Adkins* v. *Children's Hospital*. |
| **2 Aug.** | President Harding dies of apoplexy at a San Francisco hotel. |
| **3 Aug.** | Calvin Coolidge is sworn in as the thirtieth president of the United States. |
| **15 Sept.** | Although the Ku Klux Klan has become a powerful political force in midwestern politics, Oklahoma governor J. C. Walton places his state under martial law to counteract the escalation of racial violence caused by the Ku Klux Klan and its white supremacy philosophy. |

**1924**

| | |
|---|---|
| • | The Senate continues its high-profile investigation into allegations that former Secretary of the Interior Albert B. Falls leased government oil reserves to private oil companies for his personal financial gain. |
| **3 Feb.** | Former president Woodrow Wilson dies. |
| **10 Mar.** | J. Edgar Hoover is appointed acting director of the Federal Bureau of Investigation. |
| **15 Apr.** | The U.S. Senate votes unanimously to bar all Japanese immigrants except for ministers, educators, and their families. |
| **17 May** | Congress overrides President Coolidge's veto of the Veterans' Bonus Bill, which allocates $2 billion for veterans of the Great War. |
| **26 May** | Congress passes the National Origins Act, lowering the European immigration quota to 150,000 per year and making the 1890 census the basis for determining each nation's share of that quota. |
| **2 June** | President Coolidge signs the Income Tax Reduction Bill, which becomes known as the Revenue Act of 1924. |

**1925**

**10–12 June**    At its national convention, held in Cleveland, the Republican Party nominates Calvin Coolidge as its presidential candidate and Charles Gates Dawes of Illinois as its vice presidential candidate. For the first time proceedings of the convention are broadcast live by radio throughout the country.

**19 June**    At its national convention, held in Saint Paul, Minnesota, the Farm Labor Party nominates Duncan MacDonald of Illinois as its presidential candidate and William Bouck, a farmer from Washington, as its vice presidential candidate.

**24 June–
10 July**    At its national convention, held in New York City, the Democratic Party nominates John W. Davis of West Virginia for the presidency of the United States and William Jennings Bryan's brother Charles W. Bryan for vice president.

**4 July**    The Progressive Party chooses Sen. Robert M. La Follette of Wisconsin as its presidential candidate and Sen. Burton K. Wheeler of Montana as its vice presidential candidate.

**1 Sept.**    The Dawes Plan — negotiated loans to assist Germany in paying its war reparations — goes into effect.

**18 Oct.**    The Texas Supreme Court rules that Miriam A. "Ma" Ferguson is a legally qualified candidate for governor.

**4 Nov.**    Calvin Coolidge wins the presidency of the United States with 382 electoral votes and 54 percent of the popular vote. Republicans regain control of both the House and the Senate.

- Vice President Charles Gates Dawes wins the Nobel Peace Prize for his plan to scale down and reorganize Germany's payment of war reparations.

**5 Jan.**    Nellie Taylor Ross of Wyoming becomes the first woman in the United States to complete her late husband's term as governor.

**4 Mar.**    Calvin Coolidge is inaugurated and begins his first full term as president.

**8 Aug.**    Forty thousand Ku Klux Klan members from all over the nation march on Washington, D.C., hoping to broaden support for their organization.

**14 Nov.**    The governor of North Dakota appoints Non-Partisan League leader Gerald P. Nye to the U.S. Senate to fill the unexpired term of the late Sen. Edwin Ladd.

**1926**

**26 Feb.**    President Coolidge signs the Revenue Act, reducing income taxes and other taxes.

**3 Mar.**    The Senate ratifies a treaty with Mexico to prevent smuggling of narcotics, liquor, and aliens across the border.

**7 Apr.**    The U.S. attorney general informs the Senate Prohibition Committee that the national bootleg trade is estimated at $3.6 billion since the passing of the Volstead Act.

**23 June**    The Senate Campaign Fund Investigating Committee learns that the Anti-Saloon League of America received $3,444,624 in contributions between 1920 and 1925 and spent $3,430,285.

**25 Oct.**    The U.S. Supreme Court upholds the president's exclusive power to remove executive officers from their positions.

## 1927

- Secretary of State Frank Billings Kellogg and Foreign Minister Aristide Briand of France draft the Kellogg-Briand Pact, which renounces war as an option for resolving international conflict. Sixty-two nations eventually sign the pact.

**7 Mar.**    The U.S. Supreme Court rules unconstitutional a Texas law excluding African Americans from voting in the Democratic primary. Justice Oliver Wendell Holmes Jr. maintains that the law is a direct infringement of the Fourteenth Amendment.

**6 Apr.**    President Coolidge vetoes a resolution of the Philippine legislature declaring its independence from the United States.

**2 Aug.**    President Coolidge announces that he will not seek reelection to the presidency in 1928.

**10 Oct.**    The U.S. Supreme Court invalidates the leases of the Teapot Dome government oil reserves in Wyoming made by former Secretary of the Interior Albert B. Fall in 1922.

## 1928

**12–15 June**    At its national convention, held in Kansas City, Missouri, the Republican Party nominates Herbert Hoover of California for the presidency of the United States. Sen. Charles Curtis of Kansas receives the vice presidential nomination.

**26–29 June**    At its national convention, held in Houston, Texas, the Democratic Party nominates Alfred E. Smith of New York for the presidency of the United States. Joseph T. Robinson of Arkansas balances the ticket as the vice presidential nominee.

**6 Nov.**    Republican candidates Herbert Hoover and Charles Curtis capture the White House in a landslide, carrying 40 states, 444 electoral votes, and 58 percent of the popular vote.

**27 Nov.**    "To keep the crooks out" of government work, the U.S. Civil Service Commission announces plans to install fingerprinting systems in 250 cities.

## 1929

- Frank Billings Kellogg wins the Nobel Peace Prize for his contribution to the Kellogg-Briand Pact.

**1 Jan.**    Franklin D. Roosevelt is sworn in as New York's new governor, succeeding Alfred Smith, defeated Democratic candidate for the presidency of the United States.

**15 Jan.**    The Senate ratifies the Kellogg-Briand multilateral treaty, which renounces war as a national policy.

**4 Mar.**    Herbert Hoover is inaugurated as the thirty-first president of the United States.

**18 June**    President Hoover signs the reapportionment bill, which gives the president the authority to reapportion Congress after each decennial census if Congress fails to act. Hoover finds this legislation necessary because Congress has so far refused to reapportion congressional districts on the basis of the 1920 census.

**29 Oct.**    On what comes to be known as "Black Tuesday," the Dow Jones Industrial Average on Wall Street plummets 30.57 points and $30 billion disappears.

# OVERVIEW

**Postwar Reaction.** When the decade of the 1920s began, Americans were anxious to forget the world war they had recently fought and eager to roll back the clock to an era of innocence, a time that doubtless never existed. The reluctance of the Senate to ratify the Treaty of Versailles — which officially ended the war with Germany and established the terms of the peace that followed — loomed large in the early months of the new decade. Reflecting popular opinion the Senate resisted President Woodrow Wilson's proposed League of Nations. Isolationist sentiment also prevailed in the Senate debate over the ratification of the treaty, revealing Americans' unwillingness to accept the responsibilities of world leadership. Americans sought to keep the world at bay, clamoring for immigration restrictions to protect their culture against the perceived threat of foreign radicals, to reduce economic competition from immigrant workers, and to prevent a general bombardment of the United States with heterogeneous religious beliefs and cultural values.

**Republican Hegemony.** Frustrated with an expanding federal government, the growing centralization of power in the executive branch, and President Wilson's domestic and international activism, voters eagerly expelled the Democrats and ushered in twelve years of Republican hegemony with Warren G. Harding's landslide victory in 1920. Harding died in office in 1923. His vice president, Calvin Coolidge, completed Harding's term and was elected to a full term of office in 1924. Choosing not to run for reelection in 1928, Coolidge paved the way for Herbert Hoover, secretary of commerce for both Harding and Coolidge, who won the largest electoral-college victory of the decade. In addition to controlling the White House for three terms, the probusiness Republicans also held majorities in both houses of Congress throughout the 1920s, enabling them to control the legislative agenda.

**A Probusiness Political Environment.** The prevailing political sentiment of the 1920s sanctioned a retreat from the increased government activism that had characterized the Progressive Era of 1910–1917 and had accelerated with American participation in World War I. In later decades — with the challenges presented by the Great Depression, World War II, the Cold War, and the civil rights movement — the nation once again turned to the federal government for solutions, but in the 1920s, the interlude decade between World War I and the Great Depression, the majority of Americans endorsed the Republicans' commitment to minimal government and probusiness economics. Republicans preached and practiced economy in government, making significant spending and tax cuts. Agriculture, arguably the largest sector of the American economy, however, suffered during this era of general business prosperity, and Republicans ignored farmers' calls for federal government assistance.

**Corruption and Scandal.** Emanating from the secure relationship between business and government were a seemingly endless array of scandals and allegations of corruption, which have earned the 1920s a reputation as an era of excess. Charges of public corruption in President Harding's administration set the tone for the decade. Attorney General Harry Daugherty and the director of the Veterans' Bureau, Charles Forbes, both resigned over separate instances of fraud. By far the most sensational scandal of the decade was Teapot Dome. Secretary of the Interior Albert B. Fall accepted a bribe from wealthy oil magnates to lease government oil reserves in California and Wyoming to major oil companies. In 1923 Fall and Secretary of the Navy Edwin Denby resigned because of their roles in this scandal.

**"Politics of Provincialism."** Conflicts over cultural issues such as prohibition of alcoholic beverages, immigration restriction, teaching the theory of evolution in the schools, race relations, and the Ku Klux Klan illustrated how many Americans resisted the march of modernity. On many of these issues the primary cultural cleavage lay between rural and urban Americans. The 1920 census revealed that Americans were moving to the cities. For the first time in the nation's history urban dwellers outnumbered their rural counterparts. Rural Americans — overwhelmingly native-born, Protestant, and "dry" — responded defensively to this changing character of American life. They perceived that urban Americans — heavily immigrant, Catholic, and "wet" — threatened their culture. Politics became an arena for defending traditional rural values. The revival of the Ku Klux Klan in the 1920s illustrated the worst aspects of this political struggle to preserve the eroding hegemony of white, Protestant, Anglo-Saxon culture. With a campaign of intimidation and terror, hooded Americans refused to accept the consequences of social heterogeneity.

**Politics of Prohibition.** In January 1920 the long-anticipated American experiment with Prohibition officially began. Ratified the previous year, the Eighteenth Amendment to the Constitution forbade the manufacture, sale, and transportation of intoxicating liquors. Dubbed the "Noble Experiment" by its supporters, Prohibition was a catalyst for political controversy throughout the decade and intensified the growing cultural divide between town and country in American life. Rural Protestants, especially Baptists and Methodists, hailed the measure as progressive reform, while immigrant, Catholic urban dwellers viewed Prohibition as a repression of personal freedoms. Besides the cultural conflict, Prohibition fueled the growth of organized crime, whose ruthless bosses readily supplied the American demand for illegal alcohol. Opponents of this Draconian experiment continually cried for its repeal, but repeal of Prohibition did not come until the darker economic times of the 1930s, when the prospects of legal profits and taxes from liquor were too important to ignore.

# TOPICS IN THE NEWS

## AFTER THE GREAT WAR: ISOLATIONISM AND THE TREATY OF VERSAILLES

**The Stage Is Set.** As the 1920s began, the United States still struggled to bring World War I to an official end. Although the actual fighting had ceased in November 1918 and peace negotiations had been concluded during the spring of 1919, the U.S. Senate had not ratified the Treaty of Versailles — the peace agreement the Allies forced on a defeated Germany. The Senate's failure to ratify the treaty was testimony to bitter divisions over the controversial peace agreement. President Woodrow Wilson, who had negotiated the treaty, was paralyzed, having suffered two debilitating strokes in late 1919, and was unable to spearhead a campaign for its passage. The fate of the treaty rested with a divided Senate, which had failed to produce the two-thirds majority needed for ratification on its first vote, taken on 19 November 1919.

**Wilson's Plan.** Wilson had supported the entry of the United States into the European war primarily in the hope of influencing the peace that followed. Yet in January 1919, when he faced his allies — Prime Minister David Lloyd George of Great Britain, Premier Georges Clemenceau of France, and Prime Minister Vittorio Orlando of Italy — at the peace conference in Paris, he learned that they had a vision of a peace radically different from his own. The European leaders planned to reap the traditional spoils of war and punish the perceived aggressor, Germany. Wilson wanted to implement national self-determination, a principle asserted in the president's well-known Fourteen Points, his list of post-war goals. Confronted with overwhelming opposition to his peace plans, Wilson was compelled by necessity to compromise many of his Fourteen Points. "Open diplomacy" gave way to closed-door negotiations. Instead of Wilson's "peace without victory," the treaty made Germany the villain with a "guilt clause," and oppressive reparations accompanied this judgment. Wilson yielded on these and other points to retain his most cherished goal — the League of Nations. With the formation of this international organization committed to settling future disputes among nations, Wilson believed he could accept a less-than-perfect peace. He was depending on the League of Nations to compensate for the shortcomings of the treaty.

**Republican Victory of 1918.** In the 1918 midterm elections that preceded his negotiations in Paris, President Wilson campaigned for fellow Democrats, hoping to win a mandate for the League of Nations before traveling to Europe, but his party lost. Instead of an endorsement of Wilson's foreign policy, the American electorate handed the Democratic president two Republican-controlled houses of Congress. The Republican triumph signaled serious trouble for Wilson and the League of Nations. Resentful of Wilson's wartime powers and his growing international activism, Republicans were determined to curb his power by preventing American participation in the League of Nations that Wilson worked so hard to create.

**Degrees of Dissent.** Yet Republicans were not united in their opposition to the treaty or American participa-

## THE DAWES PLAN

**A**s Woodrow Wilson had feared, a punitive peace against Germany that required heavy reparations payments proved counterproductive for general European postwar economic recovery. Crippled by runaway inflation and frustrated by its debt burden, Germany stopped paying reparations in 1923. Without German reparations, France, Great Britain, Italy, and other nations were unable to repay their war debts to the United States. The United States compounded the international economic crisis with the highest protective tariff ever: the Fordney-McCumber Tariff of 1922, named for its sponsors — Republican representative Joseph Fordney of Michigan and Republican senator Porter McCumber of North Dakota. With limited access to American markets, European nations experienced difficulty raising the capital needed to repay wartime loans.

Secretary of State Charles E. Hughes, preferring an economic to a political solution, invited Charles G. Dawes, a Chicago banker, to represent the United States as head of an international "Committee of Experts" to analyze European economic instability and to propose a solution to the current crisis. The Dawes Committee, as it became known, devised an economic plan that addressed the escalating international debt crisis. Completed in April 1924, the Dawes Plan scaled down German reparations payments and called on American bankers to make substantial loans to Germany in order to stabilize its currency and help it meet its reparations obligations to the Allied nations, who in turn would use the money to repay their war debts to the United States. The plan worked as designed for five years. The European press hailed Dawes's committee as "the saviors of civilization." Later that year the Republicans selected Dawes to run as their vice presidential candidate with President Calvin Coolidge. In 1925 Dawes won the Nobel Peace Prize for his contribution to the plan.

**Source:** Bascom N. Timmons, *Portrait of an American: Charles G. Dawes* (New York: Holt, 1953).

committed the United States to collective security. Between these two groups was the majority faction, the strong reservationists. These senators, led by Henry Cabot Lodge of Massachusetts, exhibited determination to have the League of Nations on their terms or not have it at all.

**Lodge's Opposition.** Republican victories in 1918 positioned Lodge, Wilson's most bitter critic, to become chairman of the Senate Foreign Relations Committee, a committee he quickly packed with his supporters. Zealous partisanship motivated Lodge to oppose ratification of the treaty in order to prevent Wilson and Democrats from taking credit for it in the November election. Combining his partisan opposition to Wilson with a lifelong passion to defend American freedom of action in foreign affairs, Lodge waged a fierce campaign against Wilson's version of the peace. He led the Foreign Relations Committee to adopt forty-five amendments to the treaty, which he later condensed to fourteen — mimicking Wilson's Fourteen Points. During this struggle over the treaty Wilson suffered his paralyzing strokes. In November 1919, when the Senate voted on the treaty as amended by Lodge's committee, Democrats dutifully opposed the treaty as Wilson had instructed. The combined opposition of Democrats and Republican "irreconcilables" defeated this version of the treaty.

**Wilson's Dream Dies.** Supporters of the treaty earnestly looked for ways to bridge the differences among the factions and ratify an acceptable treaty. Public opinion grew weary of Senate intransigence. Lodge became the object of much criticism even from fellow Republicans. Yet Wilson and Lodge both remained immovable. The final vote on the treaty with Lodge's amendments came 19 March 1920. This time twenty-one Democrats abandoned Wilson's extreme position and voted for this version of the treaty. Forty-nine senators, a bare majority, voted for passage, but ratification required a two-thirds vote, and the Senate was seven votes short of that goal. Wilson's dreams of postwar peace died with the Senate's rejection of the treaty. The United States never signed the Treaty of Versailles or joined the League of Nations.

**Source:**
Ralph Stone, *The Irreconcilables: The Fight Against the League of Nations* (Lexington: University Press of Kentucky, 1970).

tion in the League of Nations. Republican dissenters were roughly divided into three groups: "irreconcilables," "mild reservationists," or "strong reservationists." Irreconcilables were extreme isolationists philosophically opposed to any international involvement. By contrast, mild reservationists stood much closer to Wilson's position, agreeing with the underlying principle of the organization but expressing reservations about Article X of the League of Nations Covenant, a controversial section that

### AFTER THE GREAT WAR: ANTIRADICALISM AND THE RED SCARE

**The Palmer Raids.** The xenophobia that underlay immigration restrictions and the revitalization of the Ku Klux Klan was also apparent in the Red Scare of 1920. On 2 January 1920 federal agents under the direction of Attorney General A. Mitchell Palmer raided pool halls, restaurants, and private homes in thirty-three American cities, arresting more than four thousand alleged radicals or communists, often without proper warrants. Arrested radicals who lacked citizenship papers were held for de-

Relatives of the 6,000 people arrested during Attorney General A. Mitchell Palmer's "Red Scare" demonstrating in front of the White House

portation hearings. Known as the Palmer Raids, this on-slaught against civil liberties marked the height of a government campaign begun in 1919 to fight a perceived "red menace" that many believed to be a threat to American democracy.

**Fear of Communism.** After the Bolshevik Revolution in Russia in 1917, an unprecedented fear of radicalism gripped the United States. In March 1919 news that the Third Communist International was encouraging its members to foment global revolution compounded Americans' fears. By 1920 there were three rival American Communist parties — the Proletarian Party and two opposing factions both calling themselves the Communist Labor Party. These parties remained small but vocal. Together, the widespread fear of communism and the mere existence of Communist parties in the United States provided ammunition for Americans who interpreted the nation's postwar problems as the product of Communist infiltration rather than as predictable consequences of adjustment to a peacetime economy.

**Postwar Problems.** After the war rapid and haphazard demobilization brought inflation and unemployment. A startling wave of strikes — steelworkers, coal miners, Boston policemen, and a general strike in Seattle — began. Organized labor used the cessation of hostilities to push for wage increases it had forgone during the war. Ambitious politicians, antiunion employers, and enthusiastic journalists magnified the gravity of labor unrest through exaggerated claims about the radical origins of labor protest. In late April 1919 thirty-six government officials, including Supreme Court Justice Oliver Wendell Holmes Jr. and Attorney General Palmer, received

"May Day" bombs through the mail, heightening the growing fear of radical subversion.

**Antiradical Campaign.** In autumn 1919 the federal government launched a crusade to halt what was believed to be a concerted Communist plot to destroy the United States. Ironically, Palmer, who led this crusade against domestic radicalism, had been a staunch defender of individual rights in his early months as attorney general, but his receipt of a mail bomb and his presidential aspirations had prompted a political metamorphosis. He became an enthusiastic leader for the "100 percent Americanism" philosophy. On 7 November 1919 Palmer began coordinated nationwide raids to round up and detain alleged radicals. Soon Americans clamored for their deportation, and Palmer readily obliged. Just before Christmas the *Buford,* an Army transport with 249 aliens on board, set sail for Finland, where they were sent by rail to the Soviet Union. Palmer followed up with the even more sweeping raids of January 1920. He also used Americans' fear of radicals to destroy the Industrial Workers of the World (IWW, also known as the "Wobblies"), a militant industrial union whose mission was to end capitalist exploitation of workers.

**The Red Scare Subsides.** By late 1920 the Red Scare waned as Americans turned away from the trauma of war to the calm of peace. As the bombings, Palmer Raids, and immigrant deportations subsided, many Americans realized that warnings of a radical Bolshevik threat had been greatly exaggerated. Ironically, Americans' most basic and cherished civil liberties, such as freedom of speech, freedom of the press, and representative government, had been threatened more by the aggressive tactics of the federal government than by alleged radicals and foreign subversives.

**Source:**
Robert K. Murray, *Red Scare: A Study in National Hysteria, 1919–1920* (Minneapolis: University of Minnesota Press, 1955).

## AFTER THE GREAT WAR: NATIVISM

**Fear and Resentment.** In the shaky peacetime economy that followed the Great War in Europe, Americans, especially organized labor, feared economic competition from immigrants, who willingly worked for low wages. White Protestants resented the flood of Catholics and Jews from southern and eastern Europe into the United States. Prohibitionists condemned the drinking habits of most immigrants. Many Americans distrusted foreigners in general, perceiving them as stereotypical anarchists bent on importing communism and destroying Americans' freedom. Although the United States already restricted Asian immigration, it had always had an open-door policy in regard to the European immigrants. In the 1920s, Americans' anxieties about foreigners resulted in the first European-immigration laws, designed to keep potential troublemakers out of the country.

**Immigration Restrictions.** Congress readily accommodated constituents who clamored for immigration restrictions. In 1921 Republican senators Hiram Johnson of California and Henry Cabot Lodge of Massachusetts led congressional passage of an emergency immigration restriction act that established a limit of 355,000 European immigrants per year. Each nation was given a quota equal to 3 percent of the foreign-born persons from that country in the United States at the time of the 1910 census. This first restriction on European immigration represented a dramatic departure from the nineteenth-century ideal of the United States as an asylum for downtrodden Europeans.

**The Quest for Racial Homogeneity.** The 1921 restriction legislation was only a temporary measure, and its passage did not quell the fervor for immigration restriction. After the economy rebounded from the postwar slump, business, seeking a ready supply of cheap labor, returned to its customary posture of supporting unrestricted immigration, but anti-immigrant sentiment continued to prevail. No longer fueled by economic concerns, the political debate became driven by ethnic theories about racial homogeneity. Racial theorists posited that the greatness of the United States flowed from its racially and culturally homogeneous Anglo-Saxon founders. Thus, they argued, the influx of allegedly inferior alien races and cultures since the 1890s threatened national unity and even the future existence of the nation. As restrictionists linked racial homogeneity with the preservation of American democracy, congressional debate soon reflected the broad popularity of these ideas, which rejected the traditional "melting pot" theory — the belief that the many ethnic groups who came to America soon shed their old traditions and became part of a homogenous national culture.

**National Origins Act.** The debate culminated in 1924 when Congress passed the National Origins Act, lowering the European-immigration quota. The act permanently capped annual European immigration at 150,000 and based each nation's quota at 2 percent of the foreign-born persons from that country in the United States at the time of the 1890 census, a change directed at southern and eastern Europeans, who had begun arriving in large numbers after that date. Congress also banned Asian immigration outright. In endorsing the concept of racial homogeneity, Congress rejected the established principle of judging individual initiative and ability rather than accepting national stereotypes.

**Source:**
Robert A. Divine, *American Immigration Policy, 1924–1952* (New Haven: Yale University Press, 1957).

## AFTER THE GREAT WAR: NATIVISM AND THE KU KLUX KLAN

**A Revitalized Klan.** Immigration restriction was not the only visible symptom of nativism during the 1920s. The decade also witnessed the revival of the long-dormant Ku Klux Klan, founded during Reconstruction to intimidate African Americans newly freed from slavery. In 1915 William J. Simmons reorganized the fraternal order in Atlanta, Georgia, and hailed its mission as the defense of "comprehensive Americanism." Following World War I the newly organized Klan spread across the United States. Membership increased rapidly, mushrooming to 4.5 million in 1924, when the organization reached it zenith. Unlike the nineteenth-century Ku Klux Klan, which targeted its violence primarily against African Americans and their scarce white allies in the South, the resurgent Klan of the 1920s broadened its geographical scope and expanded its list of enemies. The Anglo-Saxon-glorifying, white supremacist organization lashed out at immigrants, especially Catholics and Jews, and any group that conflicted with the Klan's cherished beliefs in nativism, white supremacy, and Protestantism.

**Congressional Hearings.** A *New York World* exposé on the Klan's violence, corruption, and religious intolerance was the catalyst for a House investigation that began in October 1921 and lasted just over a week. The House Rules Committee hearings evolved into a forum not only for those speaking against the Klan but also for members of the "Invisible Empire" pleading its case. Simmons, the Klan's organizer, stressed the organization's fraternal and benevolent nature while publicly distancing himself from its violence. The result was little more than frustration for Klan opponents. The only casualty from the hearings appeared to be the Rules Committee chair — Philip Campbell, a Republican from Kansas, who suffered defeat in the next election. Campbell's loss testified to the

In 1925 the Ku Klux Klan made a show of strength with a 40,000-man parade on Pennsylvania Avenue, Washington, D.C.

Klan's extensive political influence and alerted other politicians to their potential fate if they crossed the Klan.

**Political Influence.** As Campbell's 1922 defeat illustrates, violent persuasion and intimidation were not the Klan's only avenue of influence. Politicians at all levels of government actively sought the Klan's endorsement and support. Americans resentful of new immigrants and their influence on national culture supported and sympathized with the Klan and its mission. Prohibition particularly interested the Klan, which contended that violators were largely foreign-born, Catholic, and un-American. In 1922 the Klan participated in local elections throughout the country and helped to elect governors in Georgia, Alabama, California, and Oregon. The election that year of Klansman Earl Mayfield as a U.S. senator from Texas stood as the crowning political achievement of the Invisible Empire.

**The Height of Klan Power.** By 1924 the Klan's political power had grown so formidable that it sought to parlay its local and state victories into success at the national level. Despite tremendous pressure from some party regulars, the Democratic Party refused to condemn the Ku Klux Klan specifically in its 1924 party platform, fearing the political consequences. Klan support crossed partisan lines, as Republicans — especially in the Midwest — also counted on support from hooded Americans. John Davis, the Democratic presidential nominee, and Robert La Follette, the Progressive candidate, campaigned against the Klan, but Republican President Cal-

vin Coolidge remained silent on the issue, hoping to retain support from both pro-Klan and anti-Klan Republicans.

**The Decline of the Klan.** After 1925, support for the Klan declined rapidly. A partial explanation for dwindling pro-Klan sentiment was the diminished threat to nativism and white supremacy. Congress closed the doors to massive immigration in 1924, and African Americans remained disenfranchised across the South. The race riots of the postwar years had ended, and Prohibition was in place. The immorality and ineptness of Klan leaders, such as Grand Dragon David Stephenson of Indiana, who was found guilty of second-degree murder in 1925, also contributed to the decline of the Invisible Empire. Over time community leaders across the country had observed the Klan's violence and rejected the legitimacy of this extremist organization that relied fundamentally on intimidation and terror.

Sources:

David M. Chalmers, *Hooded Americanism: The History of the Ku Klux Klan* (Durham, N.C.: Duke University Press, 1981);

U.S. Congress, House Committee on Rules, *Ku Klux Klan Hearings, October 11–17, 1921, 67th Congress,* First Session (Washington, D.C., 1921).

## AFTER THE GREAT WAR: THE "NOBLE EXPERIMENT" OF PROHIBITION

**Prohibition Begins.** The cultural diversity of Americans in the rapidly changing society of the 1920s power-

**B**y the 1920s nearly all African Americans in the South had been barred from participation in the political process. Beginning in the 1890s and continuing through the first decade of the twentieth century, southern states erected barriers and passed statutes that disfranchised blacks. The array of legal obstructions preventing blacks from registering and voting included property, literacy, and employment requirements; poll taxes; "understanding" clauses that required blacks to explain selected clauses from the Constitution; and even laws demanding that a would-be black voter must have a "good reputation." Even most blacks who met these strict standards were kept from exercising the franchise by fraud and intimidation. In 1920 in Mississippi 290,782 of the 453,663 African American adults over twenty-one could read and write. Yet fewer than a thousand of them were registered to vote. "Grandfather clauses," which extended voting rights to those who had voted before 1865 and their descendants, prevented the disfranchisement of most whites who could not meet voter-registration requirements. County registration officers employed liberal interpretations of voting restrictions to exempt even illiterate whites from literacy requirements and "understanding" clauses.

Another feature of southern political culture disfranchised African Americans: the white primary. The region was characterized as the "Solid South" because of the dominance of the Democratic Party. Without a viable Republican Party to compete against the Democrats, the Democratic primary election effectively served as the real election. By custom, and by law in some states, the Democratic primary was for whites only. The National Association for the Advancement of Colored People (NAACP) and W. E. B. Du Bois, one of its founders, mounted a legal challenge to the white primary in Texas. In 1927 the Supreme Court sided with the NAACP, ruling unconstitutional the exclusion of blacks from the Democratic primary.

Source: "Democracy in Mississippi: A Study of Negro Suffrage," *Crisis*, 34 (November 1927): 296.

fully manifested itself in the political conflicts associated with Prohibition, which divided Americans according to their religious beliefs, cultural practices, and residential patterns. For almost a century reformers had longed for implementation of this "Noble Experiment," which officially began on 16 January 1920, according to the provis-

ions of the Eighteenth Amendment to the Constitution. Protestant moralists viewed this ban on the production, transportation, and sale of intoxicating liquor in the United States as a progressive reform that would root out the sins associated with alcohol consumption. The Volstead Act, passed by Congress in September 1919 to codify the newly ratified constitutional amendment, defined "intoxicating liquor" as any beverage that contained as much as 0.5 percent alcohol (thus including beer as well as hard liquor in the forbidden category). The law permitted consumption of existing supplies of liquor for religious and medicinal purposes.

**The Cultural Divide.** Political debate surrounding Prohibition did not cease with ratification of the Eighteenth Amendment, however, as the ban on alcohol consumption remained a divisive issue in every election until the nation abandoned the failed experiment in 1933. The political cleavage over Prohibition — which displayed a strong class and cultural bias — resembled divisions on other controversial issues of the decade. Urban areas with large immigrant populations resisted the liquor ban openly, although defiance of the law occurred nationwide. It altered the lifestyles of ethnic and other working-class Americans more than that of the largely Anglo-Protestant middle class. Immigrants and workers lost more than the privilege to drink. Prohibition closed the neighborhood saloon, a working-class meeting place and haven. Illegal speakeasies, which replaced saloons, appealed more to middle- and upper-class clientele than workers. Moreover, the rich managed to continue drinking good liquor while less-affluent Americans often consumed homemade alcoholic beverages, which were sometimes made with poisonous wood alcohol.

**Organized Crime.** Alcohol consumption declined during Prohibition, but it was by no means eliminated. Creating and supplying bootleg liquor for Americans who would not relinquish lifelong drinking habits was a multimillion-dollar business. Because the business was illegal, the entrepreneurs who ran it were criminals. Thus, Prohibition had the unintended consequences of lining the pockets of organized crime and giving rise to notorious gangsters such as Al Capone, who made a fortune by providing illegal liquor to the hard-drinking city of Chicago and nearby areas. Crime associated with the underground liquor trade ballooned as federal, state, and local governments committed woefully inadequate resources to the enforcement of Prohibition.

**The Push for Repeal.** Gov. Alfred E. Smith of New York, the 1928 Democratic presidential nominee and an outspoken critic of Prohibition, blamed the restriction of alcohol for increased crime in his state and elsewhere. Total prohibition of alcoholic beverages, he argued, was an unreasonable restriction of personal freedom that encouraged public corruption and disrespect for the law. By campaigning for modification of Prohibition the New York governor defied his party's stated intention to enforce the Eighteenth Amendment. Urban wets like

Smith, who had always opposed Prohibition, lobbied diligently for its repeal on the grounds that it granted organized crime an opportunity it could exploit at the expense of law and order in the nation's urban areas. Yet Smith spoke only for one wing of the Democratic Party, which was deeply divided over the issue. As the decade wore on, the failings of Prohibition became apparent to more Americans, and organized efforts for repeal were mounted, but not until the Great Depression convinced the nation that liquor production might boost the languishing economy was Prohibition finally repealed.

Source:
Andrew Sinclair, *Era of Excess: A Social History of the Prohibition Movement* (New York: Harper & Row, 1962).

## GOVERNMENT AND BUSINESS

**Unprecedented Prosperity.** Immediately following World War I the United States experienced a postwar boom, but in 1920–1921 this brief economic surge was followed by the sharpest short-term recession in American history. Inflation remained under control despite an unemployment rate of 3–4 percent. Between 1922 and 1927 the economy grew at a rate of 7 percent per year. As the national industrial and manufacturing base produced more consumer goods, prosperity increasingly depended on consumption.

**The Revival of Conservative Economics.** Politicians and business leaders of the 1920s resurrected the conservative economic philosophy that dominated the late nineteenth century. Government took a backseat while business drove the nation. Successful businessmen commanded enormous respect and deference, and their reputations as leaders outpaced those of politicians. President Calvin Coolidge sounded the theme for the decade in 1925, when he declared: "The business of America is business. The man who builds a factory builds a temple. The man who works there worships there." Businessmen often espoused the belief that their material success confirmed their innate ability to lead the rest of society. Conversely, they maintained that poverty was the consequence of squandered opportunities. Therefore, business leaders reasoned, the government should not burden the virtuous rich to help the undeserving poor.

**Drastic Tax Cuts.** This philosophy found an able and willing spokesman in Secretary of the Treasury Andrew W. Mellon, who held his cabinet post under all three Republican presidents of the decade. He worked diligently to insure minimal government intrusion on business. Dear to Mellon's heart was tax reform. In 1921 he initiated the first of many tax cuts he proposed during the decade. Reductions in government spending and taxing, Mellon believed, were essential to a healthy economy. Moreover, he argued, removing the tax burden from wealthy Americans would stimulate the economy. Instead of paying taxes, they would invest in job-creating industries from

Alcohol was ferried by fast motorboats from offshore freighters; this rum-runner was caught by the Coast Guard with 2,000 bottles of booze.

which all Americans would eventually profit as the benefits trickled down.

**Government as the Facilitator of Business Growth.** The role of government in the 1920s was essentially to provide a favorable legal climate, then step back and let business operate unfettered by restrictions and regulations. The Commerce Department, under the direction of Herbert Hoover, facilitated cooperation between government and the private sector. Hoover promoted the use of the principles of efficiency in business and emphasized "cooperative capitalism," which attempted to strike a balance between unregulated capitalism and aggressive government intervention.

**Labor.** The heyday for labor radicalism had passed by 1920. Union membership declined from 5.1 million in 1920 to 3.6 million in 1929. "Welfare capitalism," a paternalistic system of services and benefits that businesses provided their employees, characterized the relationship between management and labor in this decade. Since the federal government did not yet provide unemployment compensation or Social Security pensions, business promoted welfare capitalism as a self-interested strategy for promoting worker loyalty and keeping unions and government regulations out of the workplace. Yet the system was wholly inadequate. Because businesses were expected to act voluntarily, most companies did not participate, leaving workers without adequate benefits or protection.

Those corporations that had welfare programs often reduced them when hard times hit, precisely at the moment they were most needed.

Source:
William J. Barber, *From New Era to New Deal: Herbert Hoover, the Economists, and American Economic Policy, 1921–1933* (New York: Cambridge University Press, 1985).

## GOVERNMENT AND THE FARMERS

**The Farmers' Economic Travail.** The 1920s afforded unprecedented economic opportunities for many Americans, but not for the nation's farmers. They had enjoyed unusual prosperity during World War I, owing to the increased demand for American agricultural products in war-torn Europe, but in the 1920s they were plagued by low prices for agricultural products, high costs for producing these goods, and heavy debt. Increases in the American farmers' productivity created surpluses that drove commodity prices down and lowered their income. While prices for agricultural products remained low, costs for land, machinery, equipment, labor, transportation, and taxes were rising, creating greater disparity between a farmer's costs and income.

**An Inaccurate Diagnosis.** The pervasive "farm problem" of the 1920s was complex. The market compensated a farmer's increased productivity and efficiency with a lower standard of living. Collectively, Americans devoted too many resources — land, labor, and capital — to agriculture. Consequently, the supply of agricultural products far outstripped the demand for them. The problem, however, is much easier to diagnose in retrospect than it was during the 1920s. Arguing that the problem with American agriculture was overproduction seemed paradoxical to contemporaries who closely associated the independent farmer with the essence of American virtue and character, someone to be emulated, not discouraged, from increasing his crop yields. Instead of realizing the link between low prices and overproduction, farmers blamed their adversity on insufficient credit, high interest rates, inadequate tariffs, and declining world trade. Overwhelmed by the seriousness of their problems, farmers looked to the federal government for assistance.

**An Unreceptive Republican Ear.** Farmers' demands for federal help ran against the popular political mood of the 1920s, which demanded a reduction in government involvement in business. Moreover, the growing urban character of the nation weakened farmers' political influence. Yet agriculture had powerful allies in Congress. In 1921 two Republican legislators from Iowa, Sen. William Kenyon and Congressman L. J. Dickinson, organized the "farm bloc," a bipartisan group of congressmen that exerted political pressure for legislation to alleviate the farmers' economic misery. During President Harding's administration this legislative caucus advocated generous credit, higher tariffs, and cooperative marketing, all proposals that treated symptoms rather than the core problems — production surpluses and price disparities.

## ORGANIZED LABOR SQUEEZED OUT

In the period between the prosperity of the World War I years and the reforms of the New Deal, the American labor movement experienced a diminution in its status. Full employment during the war and the domination of the Democratic Party in Washington generally strengthened the bargaining power of labor during the presidency of Woodrow Wilson, but the antiradical and anti-immigrant sentiments that emerged during the war and continued through the Red Scare of 1920 silenced many radical spokesmen for labor. Samuel Gompers, president of the American Federation of Labor (AFL), had always been outspokenly antiradical, but Gompers's profession of "pure and simple unionism" was not enough to shield his union and others from the socialist label. The fear of labor radicalism weakened union bargaining power during the period of increased unemployment that accompanied the recession of 1920–1921. Moreover, the return of Republican political hegemony fostered close ties between government and business during the 1920s. Business leaders organized "open shop" committees designed to promote union busting. AFL membership declined by more than 30 percent between 1920 and 1923, and strike activity waned, reaching an all-time low during the decade. Labor had to bide its time until a more favorable political environment emerged. The 1920s ended with unrest among textile workers in the South, and efforts to organize workers in that region quickly escalated into violence. The 1929 Loray strike in Gastonia, North Carolina, foreshadowed the labor turmoil of the 1930s.

Source: Irving L. Bernstein, *The Lean Years: A History of the American Worker 1920–1933* (Boston: Houghton Mifflin, 1960).

**The McNary-Haugen Debates.** George N. Peek, of the Moline Plow Company, understood the problem and developed a plan to achieve economic equality for agriculture. Formalizing and promoting an idea known as parity prices for farmers, Peek advocated raising agricultural commodities prices to a level at which farmers would have the same purchasing power they held in the prosperous period of 1909–1914. Congressional supporters of Peek's parity plan incorporated it into the McNary-Haugen Bill, named for its sponsors, Sen. Charles McNary of Oregon and Congressman Gilbert Haugen of Iowa — both Republicans. Introduced in 1924, the bill, which called for federal price supports for agricultural products, shaped agricultural debate the remainder of the decade. Congress debated and defeated modified versions of McNary-Haugen in 1924, 1925, and 1926. Each defeat prompted new compromises to accommodate criticism of the surplus-control legislation. McNary-Haugen proponents eked out their first victory in 1927 with congressional approval of the bill. But the long-awaited legislative accomplishment was quickly vetoed by President Coolidge. A second veto in 1928 — followed by the election of Herbert Hoover, an emphatic opponent of the bill — effectively killed the reform effort. Rather than direct federal intervention, Hoover favored strengthening farmers' private cooperative marketing organizations. In 1929 Congress passed the Agricultural Marketing Act to implement Hoover's self-help objectives.

**Limited Successes.** The McNary-Haugen campaign succeeded in bringing attention to the farmers' plight even if reformers could not translate their proposals into law. While the McNary-Haugen Bill did not advocate acreage reduction as part of the solution to the nation's agricultural problems, its emphasis on pernicious agricultural surpluses helped legitimize acreage-reduction schemes as possible methods for combating overproduction. Also, during congressional debates over the bill the parity price concept gained wide acceptance in the agricultural community. Thus, even though the McNary-Haugen Bill never passed, it contributed ideas important to later agriculture reform efforts. Yet the nation would have to experience its worst depression, and all sectors of the economy would turn to the federal government for help, before a major reorganization of the agricultural sector pushed acreage reduction and parity pricing measures into law.

Source:
Gilbert C. Fite, "The Farmer's Dilemma, 1919–1929," in *Change and Continuity in Twentieth-Century America: the 1920s,* edited by John Braeman (Columbus: Ohio State University Press, 1968).

## NATIONAL POLITICS: THE 1920 REPUBLICAN NOMINATION RACE

**Potential Candidates.** As the party controlling the executive branch in 1920, the Democrats suffered the fallout from postwar restlessness. Moreover, Democratic presidential hopefuls hesitated to launch their candidacies, awaiting President Woodrow Wilson's decision about seeking a third term. Not only were Democrats on the defensive but Republicans enjoyed momentum because they had gained congressional seats in the midterm elections of 1918. Given these advantages Republicans seemed poised for victory in 1920, but which Republican would occupy the Oval Office? The choice was not obvious, especially after former president Theodore Roosevelt's death in January 1919. The list of prominent Republicans vying for the nomination included Gen. Leonard Wood of New Hampshire, Sen. Hiram Johnson of California (Roosevelt's Progressive Party running mate in 1912), Gov. Frank O. Lowden of Illinois, Sen. Warren G. Harding of Ohio, and Gov. Calvin Coolidge of Massachusetts. These candidates and others competed for delegates during the preconvention selection process.

**Republican Primaries.** In 1920 only twenty states held presidential preference primaries, and many of them did not bind delegates to the winner, but Republican Party primary voting still surpassed participation in the two previous presidential elections. The primary process yielded confusion rather than a consensus candidate. Candidates did not enter all of the primaries, limiting the public's opportunity to choose. For example, Harding competed in only two primaries — Ohio, his home state, which he won, and Indiana, which he lost.

**Republican Hopefuls.** Leonard Wood became the early front-runner, having received the endorsement of Theodore Roosevelt. With a promise of tough action against striking labor unions and an emphasis on nationalism and anti-Bolshevism, Wood appealed to party conservatives. His policies earned Wood huge campaign contributions, but he attracted criticism from his opponents for his lavish campaign spending. Hiram Johnson garnered much of the progressive Republican vote with his record of fighting against monopolies, defending civil liberties, and adamantly opposing the League of Nations. Although out of step with party regulars, Johnson made his appeal to the people and regularly criticized Wood and Frank O. Lowden for their large campaign funds. Lowden ran on his effectiveness as governor of Illinois. Unlike Johnson, Lowden favored ratification of the Treaty of Versailles, with reservations. Independently wealthy, he could finance his own campaign, but some Republicans believed that his lack of indebtedness to campaign contributors made him too independent. Lowden appealed to those favoring efficiency and economy in government. Warren G. Harding, a newspaper publisher, had little ambition for the presidency himself, but his campaign manager, Harry M. Daugherty, had more than enough for them both. Harding's reputation for moderation on all issues and his staunch party loyalty stood as his greatest assets.

**Republican Platform.** On Tuesday, 8 June 1920, Republicans convened in Chicago for their five-day national convention. Debate on the party's platform position on the League of Nations presented the greatest challenge to party unity, but Elihu Root resolved the controversy with a compromise that satisfied those adamantly opposed to the organization and internationalists who were willing to endorse the Treaty of Versailles if Wilson would accept revisions. After resolving the delicate issue of the League of Nations, Republican delegates endorsed a platform that reflected the growing strength of conservatives in the party and the waning influence of its progressive wing, whose minority report met with resounding rejection. Along with the standard condemnation of Democratic policies, the platform advocated governmental economy, tax revision, and deflation of credit and currency to control inflation. It included a plank condemning strikes and lockouts as well as one promising immigration limits, especially for non-Europeans.

**Presidential Balloting.** Wood arrived at the convention with 124 delegates, more than any of his competitors. Johnson was not far behind with 112 delegates, while Lowden had 72, and Harding came to the convention with 39. No candidate was close to having the 493 delegates necessary for the nomination. On the first ballot, taken Friday evening, Wood maintained his front-runner's position with 287.5 votes; he was followed by Lowden with 211.5, Johnson with 133.5, and twelve other candidates who shared 351.5 votes. Three more ballots produced similar results. The convention then adjourned for the day despite objections from Wood and Lowden delegates.

**"Smoke-Filled Room" Politics.** After the adjournment, backroom strategy began in earnest, as old-guard Republicans maneuvered to find a consensus candidate. Johnson's refusal to accept second place on a ticket headed by Wood thwarted the most likely combination, one that would have held Roosevelt supporters together. Increasingly, it became apparent that delegates pledged to the top three candidates were unwilling to commit to rivals. They needed a compromise candidate that all could accept. In the now-famous "smoke-filled room" convention chairman Henry Cabot Lodge allegedly moved to make Harding, one of the minor candidates, the party's nominee. Harding had an unblemished record as a party regular, making it easy for many Republicans to accept him. While he had done nothing to demonstrate presidential capability, he also had done nothing to demonstrate his inability to master the job. Moreover, Harding was from Ohio, an important swing state for the Republicans, especially if the Democrats nominated James Cox, governor of the Buckeye State. While the logic of choosing Harding was compelling for some Republicans, his supporters could not garner enough support to win him the nomination when balloting resumed Saturday morning. Instead the informal deal makers gave Wood, Johnson, and Lowden another chance to break their deadlock. On the fifth, sixth, and seventh ballots the deadlock remained, and support for Harding was slowly mounting. After the eighth ballot (Lowden 307, Wood 299, Harding 133.5, and Johnson 87), Chairman Lodge called a recess. Following a three-hour recess, Harding led on the ninth ballot with 374.5 delegates. He secured the nomination on the tenth and final ballot with a comfortable majority.

**Selecting a Running Mate.** While maneuvering among inside power brokers characterized Harding's nomination, spontaneity distinguished the vice presidential nomination. The architects of Harding's nomination selected Irvine L. Lenroot of Wisconsin, an unusual choice since Lenroot, who was also a senator and from the same geographic region as Harding, did not offer the traditional balance a vice presidential candidate is expected to bring the ticket. In defiance of these leaders an Oregon delegate unexpectedly nominated Calvin Coolidge of Massachusetts, a highly respected candidate who

had distanced himself from those running the convention. Delegates demonstrated wildly following Coolidge's nomination, thwarting convention managers' control of the process. With 674.5 votes Coolidge captured the nomination on the first ballot.

**Sources:**

Richard C. Bain and Judith H. Parris, *Convention Decisions and Voting Records*, second edition (Washington, D.C.: Brookings Institution, 1973);

"Chicago 1920," *New Republic*, 23 (23 June 1920): 108–110;

Donald R. McCoy, "Election of 1920," in *History of American Presidential Elections 1789–1968*, edited by Arthur M. Schlesinger Jr., volume 3 (New York: Chelsea House/McGraw-Hill, 1971), pp. 2349–2455.

## NATIONAL POLITICS: THE 1920 DEMOCRATIC NOMINATION RACE

**Incumbency Blues.** The Democrats' greatest liability in 1920 was their two-term sitting president, Woodrow Wilson. Wilson's public support had dwindled with the conclusion of World War I and the ensuing chaos that enveloped Europe. The ongoing bitter struggle between Wilson and the Senate over the League of Nations heightened public dissatisfaction with the president and minimized the Democrats' opportunity for victory in November 1920. Furthermore, Wilson's ambivalence about seeking an unprecedented third term for himself complicated other candidates' decisions to pursue the office. Despite candid advice from close political friends who urged him not to seek reelection, Wilson refused to renounce the possibility. Thus, potential candidates, reluctant to challenge a sitting president from their own party, muddled through the nomination process, which produced little more than weak candidates with a small core of committed delegates.

**Likely Democratic Contenders.** William Gibbs McAdoo, Wilson's son-in-law and secretary of the treasury, exemplified the hesitancy Wilson's indecision introduced to the campaign. While McAdoo neither entered primaries nor campaigned on the stump, he privately declared his intentions to run. As a "dry" southern liberal, McAdoo developed considerable support. Yet less than two weeks before the convention, McAdoo announced that he would not seek the nomination. Supporters wondered if his declaration was strategic or sincere. Gov. James M. Cox of Ohio declared his candidacy in February 1920, but he also did little public campaigning, hoping his strong home-state support would spread. Cox — who had been a three-time governor, unprecedented in Ohio, and had served a brief term in Congress (1909– 1913) — had the advantage of not being associated with Wilson and his faltering image. Moreover, since the Republicans had nominated Harding, a senator from Ohio, the state became strategically important. One candidate who was not deterred by the idea of an aggressive campaign for the Democratic nomination was Attorney General A. Mitchell Palmer, known for his aggressive tactics in the Red Scare of 1920. He openly sought the nomination with a vigor reminiscent of his Bolshevik-hunting methods. As a member of Wilson's cabinet, Palmer enjoyed much administration support, but he had to share that with McAdoo, who also amassed a following among administration insiders.

**The Democratic Convention.** Democrats gathered in San Francisco on Monday, 28 June 1920, almost three weeks after the Republican Convention. This delay bolstered the growing impression that the Democrats were trailing in the campaign. Leading the list of issues on the Democrats' lengthy platform was a predictable endorsement of the League of Nations, declaring that it was for the idea of the league that "America broke away from traditional isolation and spent her blood and treasure to crush a colossal scheme of conquest." Democrats also highlighted their continued support for a revenue-producing tariff, agricultural interests, and "adequate compensation" for labor. The platform endorsed the Nineteenth Amendment, which would grant women equal suffrage, and encouraged Democrats from states that had not yet ratified it to support ratification. Reacting to criticism of Palmer's anti-Bolshevik raids, the party reiterated its support for free speech and freedom of the press but promised "no toleration of enemy propaganda or the advocacy of the overthrow of the government." The platform concluded with a dig at Republicans for their "lavish use of money" in seeking the presidential nomination.

**Choosing from the Multitude.** Most delegates came to San Francisco uncommitted, encouraging a crowded field of presidential hopefuls and a tedious nomination process. On the first ballot delegates divided their votes among twenty-four nominees. Although ambivalent about his intentions, McAdoo led the vote with 266 votes. Palmer was close behind with 256, and Governor Cox received 134 votes. The remaining delegates divided their votes between twenty-one other nominees, who included Gov. Alfred E. Smith of New York, Sen. Carter Glass of Virginia, Agriculture Secretary Edwin T. Meredith of Iowa, Sen. Robert L. Owen of Oklahoma, and Ambassador to the Court of St. James John W. Davis of West Virginia. Little changed on the second ballot, so the convention adjourned Friday night.

**Keeping Wilson Out.** That weekend the specter of a Wilson candidacy frightened convention leaders. Bainbridge Colby, Wilson's secretary of state, notified the president that he anticipated a convention deadlock and was prepared to place Wilson's name into nomination. Others close to the president argued forcefully against this gambit, and they prevailed. Having suffered two strokes the previous year, Wilson was in failing health and an unlikely candidate, but Wilson yielded to this reality only reluctantly. Keeping Wilson out required convincing him that the convention would not deadlock, a task that relied largely on fiction since there seemed little evidence to support this assertion. The balloting on Saturday demonstrated the difficulty of avoiding a deadlock. Delegates cast twenty ballots; yet the day concluded without a nominee. While the same three candidates led, the order had changed, and the field had narrowed considerably. On the twelfth ballot Cox pulled ahead for the first time, but he gained little momentum with the ten subsequent ballots.

**Cox Emerges Victorious.** When voting resumed on Monday the slow pace continued. Finally, after the thirty-eighth ballot, Palmer realized he had reached his maximum level of support and released his delegates, who divided themselves between Cox and McAdoo. Following Palmer's exit, Cox, with the aid of his campaign manager, Edmond H. Moore, gradually garnered enough votes that on the forty-fourth ballot a McAdoo delegate could successfully move, just before 2:00 A.M., that the convention unanimously nominate Cox.

**The Vice-Presidential Nomination.** Selecting Cox's running mate was simple. Nominated by acclamation, Assistant Secretary of the Navy Franklin D. Roosevelt became the Democratic vice presidential nominee. Roosevelt, a New Yorker and administration insider, provided the balance Cox needed as a midwestern governor whose political career had been mostly outside Washington.

Sources:

Richard C. Bain and Judith H. Parris, *Convention Decisions and Voting Records*, second edition (Washington, D.C.: Brookings Institution, 1973);

Robert Hale, "Another Convention — The Democratic," *Nation*, 111 (17 July 1920): 69–70;

Donald R. McCoy, "Election of 1920," in *History of American Presidential Elections 1789–1968*, edited by Arthur M. Schlesinger Jr., volume 3 (New York: Chelsea House/McGraw-Hill, 1971), pp. 2349–2455.

## NATIONAL POLITICS: THE 1920 ELECTIONS

**Harding Campaigns on Image.** The Republicans' strategy reflected their growing confidence and the prevailing attitude that the 1920 election was theirs to lose. Warren G. Harding and Calvin Coolidge conducted a low-risk campaign. Rather than center the campaign on debates over issues and jeopardize his front-runner status, Harding opted to campaign on his image, which was consistent with Americans' desires for peace and tranquillity. The major obstacle for Harding was his lack of a national reputation. Instead of taking to the time-honored stump to overcome this handicap, Harding campaigned from another favorite American icon — the front porch. He invited all interested Americans to his home in Marion, Ohio, and delegations of voters appeared there regularly. Drawing on his experience as a newspaper publisher, Harding successfully wooed the press. Nearly 90 percent of newspaper editors around the country supported him, and reporters regularly gave him favorable press.

**Low-Key Coolidge.** Coolidge readily imitated Harding's campaign style, spending most of the campaign season conducting business as usual as governor of Massachusetts. In the fall he ventured briefly outside his home state. In late October, at the insistence of the Republican National Committee, Coolidge reluctantly made an eight-day tour through the South, where he sounded the popular themes of patriotism, common sense in government, and general "thrift and industry."

**The Democrats' Aggressive Style.** James Cox and Franklin D. Roosevelt conducted a more aggressive campaign than their Republican opponents, making the League of Nations their central issue. Democrats also recognized the strategic importance of criticizing the Republicans' extravagant campaign spending. Unlike Harding, James Cox, a millionaire and divorcé, could not wage an image-oriented campaign for the presidency. He was also hampered by Wilson's growing unpopularity. To overcome these negative images Cox packaged himself as a dynamic problem solver both at home and abroad. Roosevelt complemented Cox's campaign style with energy and vigor. Roosevelt campaigned across the country, logging more than eighteen hundred miles and averaging ten speeches a day, quite a contrast to his Republican counterpart.

**A Harding Landslide.** Cox was unable to distance himself from the discredited Wilson, and Harding's "image campaign" succeeded. Frustrated with postwar inflation and recession, Americans embraced the Republicans' promise of lower taxes and less government. Voters could not resist Harding's promise of "normalcy" and

| Senate | 66th Congress | 67th Congress | Net Gain/Loss |
|---|---|---|---|
| Democrats | 47 | 37 | -10 |
| Republicans | 49 | 59 | +10 |

| House | 66th Congress | 67th Congress | Net Gain/Loss |
|---|---|---|---|
| Democrats | 190 | 131 | -59 |
| Republicans | 240 | 301 | +61 |
| Other | 3 | 1 | -2 |

| Governors | 1918 | 1920 | Net Gain/Loss |
|---|---|---|---|
| Democrats | 25 | 20 | -5 |
| Republicans | 22 | 27 | +5 |
| Other | 1 | 1 | 0 |

gave the Republican ticket a landslide victory. They carried thirty-seven states, captured 404 electoral votes to 127 for Cox and Roosevelt, and received almost twice the popular vote of Cox and Roosevelt: 16,152,200 (60 percent) to 9,147,353 (37 percent). Only the South (with the exception of Tennessee) remained loyal to the Democratic Party in the 1920 election. The Republicans' courting of black votes, rather than Cox's appeal, accounted for much of the southern loyalty to the Democrats.

**Sources:**
"Eclipse of Progressivism," *New Republic,* 24 (27 October 1920): 210–216;

Donald R. McCoy, "Election of 1920," in *History of American Presidential Elections 1789–1968*, edited by Arthur M. Schlesinger Jr., volume 3 (New York: Chelsea House/McGraw-Hill, 1971), pp. 2349–2455.

## NATIONAL POLITICS: THE 1922 ELECTIONS

**Democratic Gains in Congress.** Following Harding's landslide victory in 1920, the Democrats' political future seemed bleak. But the Democrats rebounded in the next election. The postwar recession worsened in 1921 and 1922. Economic malaise, along with Harding's ineffectiveness and rifts between progressives and conservatives, weakened the Republicans' stronghold. Traditionally in midterm elections voters have favored the party out of power, and the 1922 election verified this generalization with a vengeance. Democrats retained all of their congressional seats and gained more than seventy seats formerly held by Republicans. No other midterm election had produced such a sizable victory for the party out of power. Republicans narrowly retained control of the House of Representatives.

**Potential for the Future.** The 1922 gains foreshadowed future successes for Democrats, whose greatest sup-

| Senate | 67th Congress | 68th Congress | Net Gain/Loss |
|---|---|---|---|
| Democrats | 37 | 43 | +6 |
| Republicans | 59 | 51 | -8 |
| Other | 0 | 2 | +2 |

| House | 67th Congress | 68th Congress | Net Gain/Loss |
|---|---|---|---|
| Democrats | 131 | 205 | +74 |
| Republicans | 301 | 225 | -76 |
| Other | 1 | 5 | +4 |

| Governors | 1920 | 1922 | Net Gain/Loss |
|---|---|---|---|
| Democrats | 20 | 15 | -5 |
| Republicans | 27 | 33 | +6 |
| Other | 1 | 0 | -1 |

port in this election came from urban areas. Democrats were particularly strong among new citizens who resided in larger northern cities. The urban upsurge, while important to Democratic gains, was less than it might have been because congressional district lines had not been redrawn to reflect the population shift reported in the 1920 census. Democrats would have benefited from prompt district remapping, which the Constitution required, but they did not push the issue since Republican-controlled state legislatures would have done the redrawing. The sizable gains of 1922 encouraged Democrats about their presidential chances in 1924, a dismal prospect just two years earlier.

Sources:
David Burner, "Election of 1924," in *History of American Presidential Elections 1789–1968*, edited by Arthur M. Schlesinger Jr., volume 3 (New York: Chelsea House/McGraw-Hill, 1971), pp. 2459–2581;

"The Electoral Turnover in America," *New Statesman*, 20 (18 November 1922): 195–196.

## NATIONAL POLITICS: THE 1924 REPUBLICAN NOMINATION RACE

**Coolidge Meets the Progressive Challenge.** Calvin Coolidge had been president only a few months when the 1924 presidential campaign season began. Harding's unexpected death in August 1923 put Coolidge in the White House, but it did not earn him the confidence of the Republican old guard or the party's progressive senators. Coolidge used the presidential primaries as an opportunity to unite his party and solidify support for his nomination. Yet two Republican mavericks, Sen. Hiram Johnson of California and Sen. Robert La Follette of Wisconsin, complicated Coolidge's task. Both progressive senators challenged their party's incumbent president for the Republican nomination. Senator Johnson criti-

cized the administration's tax-reduction plan, advised against involvement in the World Court, and advocated the termination of all immigration from Asia. Johnson's determined efforts, however, delivered him only one primary victory, in South Dakota. Coolidge even prevailed comfortably in Johnson's home state of California. While Johnson entered nearly every primary, La Follette selected his fights more judiciously. Running in only two states, La Follette defeated Coolidge in Wisconsin, La Follette's home state, and the progressive senator placed second among the three contenders in North Dakota. Besides the progressive challenge Coolidge also had to contend with repercussions from the Teapot Dome scandal, with its allegations of corruption in Harding's administration.

**The Republican Convention.** When the Republicans convened on 10 June 1924 in Cleveland, Ohio, most of their business seemed pro forma. Their nominee was apparent. One new rule reflected the broadened electorate. Because women had entered national politics after the ratification of the Nineteenth Amendment, the Republican National Committee provided for equal representation, one woman and one man from each state and territory, on the committee. The convention received unprecedented attention, with gavel-to-gavel radio coverage for the first time in American history. As the party in power, Republicans opted for a concise and noncontroversial platform, which trumpeted the party's accomplishments since 1921: lowering taxes and keeping the country out of the League of Nations. La Follette's supporters put forth an alternative platform that blasted the government and private monopoly, but it was defeated without a vote.

**Coolidge Is Nominated.** Having met the progressive challenge during the primaries and demonstrated his ability to quell negative fallout from Teapot Dome, Coolidge assured himself a first-ballot victory. Since Coolidge's nomination was certain, nomination speeches, rather than balloting, occupied conventioneers' attention. Dr. Marion L. Burton's speech, one of the longest nominating speeches in convention history, praised Coolidge, "The Man, The American, and the Human Being." After nine seconding speeches, delegates bestowed a near-unanimous vote on Coolidge. Only thirty-four die-hard delegates maintained their commitments to La Follette and Johnson.

**Selecting a Vice President.** Harding's death and Wilson's near death in office persuaded delegates of the importance of the vice presidential candidate selection. Coolidge had not designated a running mate, so several names emerged. On the first ballot six candidates divided the vote. Frank Lowden led the field with 222, despite his repeated assertions that he was not interested in and would not accept the position. After three ballots Lowden won, and he still refused to accept the nomination. Herbert Hoover and Charles G. Dawes then stood as the two most likely contenders. Despite broad popu-

Calvin Coolidge was vacationing in rural Vermont when President Warren G. Harding died; the new president took the oath of office from his father, a justice of the peace.

larity, each man was unpopular with at least one bloc of voters. Hoover's role in fixing agriculture prices during the war had alienated farmers, and Dawes was unpopular with organized labor because of his opposition to strikes. By a vote of 682–234 Dawes secured the nomination, reflecting the Republicans' greater interest in agrarian support than the labor vote. Moreover, Dawes's criticism of the closed shop endeared him to many conservatives. Dawes was the author of the Dawes Plan, which renegotiated German reparations payments.

Sources:

Richard C. Bain and Judith H. Parris, *Convention Decisions and Voting Records,* second edition (Washington, D.C.: Brookings Institution, 1973);

David Burner, "Election of 1924," in *History of American Presidential Elections 1789–1968,* edited by Arthur M. Schlesinger Jr., volume 3 (New York: Chelsea House/McGraw-Hill, 1971), pp. 2459–2581;

"National Affairs," *Time,* 3 (21 June 1924): 1–7.

## NATIONAL POLITICS: THE 1924 DEMOCRATIC NOMINATION RACE

**Trouble for the Democrats.** In the early months of the campaign season Democrats eagerly anticipated recapturing the presidency, especially since President Harding, a well-loved Republican, had died and the Teapot Dome scandal promised to taint the Republican Party. The Democrats' hopes waned as Coolidge successfully distanced himself from the scandal, and their leading candidate, William McAdoo — President Wilson's treasury secretary and son-in-law — became more closely associated with the scandal, as well as with the Ku Klux Klan. Democratic success in 1924 depended on party unity, but Democrats could not find a single issue that could bring together the party's disparate constituents. Prohibition loomed as one divisive issue. "Wets" and "dries" each had a candidate who shared their views. The increasingly prominent Ku Klux Klan attracted many Democrats but repelled many others. As was evident in the 1922 election, Democrats were gaining voters in large urban areas. These new urbanites, however, clashed with the party's established rural base.

**The Leading Contender.** McAdoo received strong support from labor, primarily because of his administration of the railroad crisis during World War I. As an unequivocal dry, McAdoo had great support in the rural South. His silence on the Klan, when most politicians were openly denouncing the reactionary organization, curried favor among Klan members and sympathizers. Yet McAdoo's willingness to accept Klan support diminished his support among reformers and urban Democrats, especially Catholic voters. The Klan issue merely compounded McAdoo's earlier image problems, which began when his connections with Edward L. Doheny, who was deeply involved in the Teapot Dome scandal, were exposed.

**The Urban Candidate.** McAdoo's opponents lined up behind a host of favorite sons, but his most serious opposition came from New York governor Alfred E. Smith. Smith, wet, Catholic, and part of the eastern urban political machine, was anathema to the party's dry, Protestant, rural constituents. The stark contrast between McAdoo and Smith further solidified rural/urban divisions within the Democratic Party, and the nomination of either man promised to alienate a substantial core of Democratic supporters. During the primaries McAdoo made a strong showing in the South and West while Smith carried heavily populated states such as Massachusetts, New York, and Illinois, states whose electoral votes could swing the November presidential race.

**The Democratic Convention.** On 24 June 1924 delegates assembled at Madison Square Garden in New York, a controversial host city given the heightened cultural division displayed during the primaries. Dry delegates never passed up an opportunity to express outrage at New Yorkers' flagrant violation of Prohibition, and the city supplied endless opportunities for criticism.

**The Platform and the Ku Klux Klan.** The Democrats' platform opened with the lofty statement that the party stood for "equal rights to all, and special privilege to none." Moreover, they pronounced their commitment to "human rights" to be above the Republicans' shallow commitment to "material things." Yet the Democratic platform lacked specific recommendations that would give substance to their rhetoric. William Jennings Bryan managed to slip a bit of radicalism into the otherwise bland political document by adding calls for federal aid to education, "vigorous enforcement of existing laws governing monopoly," government control of natural resources, and a public referendum on any declaration of war. The bulk of excitement surrounding the platform, however, came from debate over an excluded plank. Smith's supporters, wanting to embarrass McAdoo for accepting Klan support, proposed a plank denouncing the Klan by name rather than accepting a milder condemnation of efforts "to arouse religious or racial dissension." McAdoo forces argued that Smith's plank would destroy the harmony of the convention, and delegates defeated it by a margin of one vote, the closest in convention history.

**A Nine-Day Stalemate.** The vote on the anti-Klan plank foreshadowed the difficulty the divided convention had in selecting a candidate, but still no one seemed prepared for the lengthy stalemate that ensued. The Democrats' procedural rule requiring that a nominee receive two-thirds of the delegates' votes to win the nomination further complicated an already complex situation. McAdoo and Smith had similar strategies. Each planned to understate their support initially and then increase his vote total slowly. The field was not limited to McAdoo

and Smith. Delegates nominated and supported fourteen favorite sons and dark-horse candidates. Instead of dropping out as usual, many of the other candidates — each hoping to become a compromise choice in the face of a deadlocked convention — remained in the balloting, which began on Monday, 30 June. By the end of the week there had been seventy-seven rounds of balloting and neither McAdoo nor Smith was close to the 733 votes he needed to win the nomination. Several attempts to break the deadlock with rule changes were all defeated. The candidates' strategies reflected their escalating frustration. Each side began to hold out for his opponent's delegates to leave town. Balloting resumed the next Monday, 7 July. Increasingly, it became clear that delegates would not accept McAdoo or Smith, and they would have to choose a nominee from among the alternate candidates. Finally, on the 103rd ballot, after nine days of voting, the convention nominated John W. Davis, who had been the third-place candidate through most of the balloting. Davis, a cultivated gentleman and corporate lawyer, had served as ambassador to Great Britain in Wilson's administration. While the eleventh-hour decision was hardly a victory for anyone, Davis's nomination represented a strategic win for Smith's forces because Davis had the support of urban politicians.

**The Vice-Presidential Candidate.** Choosing Davis's running mate from among thirteen candidates, the delegates nominated Gov. Charles W. Bryan of Nebraska, brother of William Jennings Bryan, for the vice presidency with the minimum two-thirds vote. Bryan's nomination seemed to be an attempt to mollify the radical fringe of the party, and many dissatisfied delegates booed and hissed when Bryan's victory was announced.

Sources:

Richard C. Bain and Judith H. Parris, *Convention Decisions and Voting Records,* second edition (Washington, D.C.: Brookings Institution, 1973);

David Burner, "Election of 1924," in *History of American Presidential Elections 1789–1968,* edited by Arthur M. Schlesinger Jr., volume 3 (New York: Chelsea House/McGraw-Hill, 1971), pp. 2459–2581;

"The Garden Party," *Nation,* 119 (9 July 1924): 29–31.

## NATIONAL POLITICS: THE PROGRESSIVE PARTY, 1924

**A Third-Party Challenge.** While Sen. Robert La Follette of Wisconsin lacked the political support to keep the Republican Party from nominating Coolidge, he had the support to challenge Coolidge and Davis in the general election as a third-party candidate. La Follette bolted the Republican Party and ran as the Progressive Party candidate with Sen. Burton K. Wheeler, a Democrat from Montana, as his running mate. Different from Theodore Roosevelt's Progressive Party of 1912, La Follette's Progressive Party, founded in 1924, was the outgrowth of the progressive activism of the Committee of Forty-Eight, a political action group formed in 1919, and the Conference for Progressive Political Action. The new Progressive Party was a coalition of organized labor, farm groups, Socialists, and independent radicals, all of whom were dissatisfied with the two mainstream parties, which had both nominated conservative candidates. La Follette and the Progressives strove to unite workers from the factory and the farm.

**Party Issues.** The party platform reflected the Progressives' strident opposition to monopolies and embraced popular progressive causes such as public ownership of water power, nationalization of the railroads, direct election of the president, increased taxes on wealth, termination of child labor, and popular election of judges (because the courts had become such an enemy of labor legislation). Progressives also called for a national referendum on any declaration of war, an outgrowth of their isolationist stance. La Follette and the Progressives distanced themselves from the Communists and would not accept their support. La Follette also denounced the Klan, a tactic that alienated a core of otherwise sympathetic voters.

Sources:

Richard C. Bain and Judith H. Parris, *Convention Decisions and Voting Records,* second edition (Washington, D.C.: Brookings Institution, 1973);

David Burner, "Election of 1924," in *History of American Presidential Elections 1789–1968,* edited by Arthur M. Schlesinger Jr., volume 3 (New York: Chelsea House/McGraw-Hill, 1971), pp. 2459–2581.

## WOMEN CHOSEN TO LEAD

**T**hree women, all Democrats, won political contests against male competition in 1924. Each of these victories was unprecedented. Voters from the Twelfth Congressional District of New Jersey elected Mary T. Norton to the House of Representatives, making her the first Democratic woman ever elected to that body and the first woman to represent any state in the East. Two other women became the first women elected to governorships. In a special election held in November Wyoming elected Nellie T. Ross to complete the unexpired term of her husband, William B. Ross, who had been elected governor in 1922 and died on 2 October 1924. Texas voters elected Miriam A. "Ma" Ferguson as their governor in 1924. Ferguson's husband, James E. Ferguson, had served as governor of Texas from 1915 until August 1917, when he was impeached and removed from office. Miriam Ferguson campaigned on the commitment to follow her husband's advice if elected, promising "two governors for the price of one." Norton's 1924 triumph marked the beginning of a career in the House that spanned more than a quarter of a century. Ross and Ferguson both lost reelection bids in 1926.

Source: "National Affairs," *Time,* 4 (17 November 1924): 5–6.

## NATIONAL POLITICS: THE 1924 ELECTIONS

**Coolidge's Quiet Campaign.** As in 1920 Coolidge stayed close to home and ran a low-key campaign. Rather than engage Davis and La Follette in debates on particular issues, Coolidge preferred to campaign on general principles such as economy in government. When Coolidge did not speak in generalities, he did not speak. Silence became a major part of his strategy, as he essentially ignored both the issues and his opponents. He left the hard-core campaigning to his running mate, Charles Dawes, whose direct and competitive style often led to conflict, especially with La Follette, who became Dawes's favorite target after early polls indicated La Follette was ahead of Davis in California and a *Literary Digest* postcard canvass, hardly an accurate poll, showed strong support for La Follette throughout the nation. Dawes willingly engaged in demagoguery, falsely associating La Follette with communism.

**Davis's Conservatism.** The Democrats' problems persisted into the fall campaign. Not only was the party divided, but its conservative compromise candidate, John Davis, had difficulty distinguishing himself from Coolidge. Davis endorsed "The American's Creed," which included Thomas Jefferson's maxim "that government is best which governs least," a sentiment popular with busi-

| Senate | 68th Congress | 69th Congress | Net Gain/Loss |
|---|---|---|---|
| Democrats | 43 | 39 | -4 |
| Republicans | 51 | 56 | +5 |
| Other | 2 | 1 | -1 |

| House | 68th Congress | 69th Congress | Net Gain/Loss |
|---|---|---|---|
| Democrats | 205 | 183 | -22 |
| Republicans | 225 | 247 | +22 |
| Other | 5 | 4 | -1 |

| Governors | 1922 | 1924 | Net Gain/Loss |
|---|---|---|---|
| Democrats | 15 | 26 | +11 |
| Republicans | 33 | 22 | -11 |

nessmen in 1924. As a corporate lawyer, Davis was closely associated with Wall Street, and in several cases he had sided with management over labor — both liabilities for a Democrat.

**The Candidate of a Divided Party.** Davis was also reluctant to attack. Except on the corruption issue, he did not challenge Republicans. In many respects the Democrats themselves had tied Davis's hands. Except on the Klan issue, where Davis boldly joined La Follette in condemning the Klan by name (a stand only Coolidge refused to take), Davis avoided controversial issues, attempting to prevent further divisions within the party. In frustration Davis lamented that McAdoo supporters ran away when he reached out to the eastern group, and that Smith's group did the same when he appealed to McAdoo's forces.

**Coolidge Wins.** The election results revealed the strength of the Republican Party. Coolidge won with 382 electoral votes. Davis captured the solid Democratic South, twelve southern states with 136 electoral votes. La Follette carried only Wisconsin but received 17 percent of the popular vote nationwide. Coolidge's victory with 54 percent of the popular vote was a significant win for Republicans in a three-way race. Since La Follette had been a Republican, many assumed he drew most of his support from his former party. Yet historian David Burner argues that the Progressive candidate hurt both parties, but that he took away more votes from the Democrats than the Republicans. A comparison of party strength in the presidential race and the congressional contests — where the Progressives fielded no candidates — reveals that Coolidge's vote was 4 percent below the vote the Republicans won in the House, but Davis's vote dropped 13 percent below the overall Democratic House vote. While the results varied by region, Democrats were

best served by the rapid demise of the Progressive Party. Davis's support came from the extremes — large metropolitan wards and wholly rural districts. Coolidge prevailed in the middle of the political spectrum. Ultimately the Democrats' internal weaknesses and the Progressives' radical identity facilitated the Republicans' victory in 1924.

**Sources:**

David Burner, "Election of 1924," in *History of American Presidential Elections 1789–1968*, edited by Arthur M. Schlesinger Jr., volume 3 (New York: Chelsea House/McGraw-Hill, 1971), pp. 2459–2581;

"Business Wins," *Nation*, 119 (12 November 1924): 510;

*Congressional Quarterly's Guide to U.S. Elections*, second edition (Washington, D.C.: Congressional Quarterly, 1985).

## NATIONAL POLITICS: THE 1926 ELECTIONS

**Minimal House Losses for the Republicans.** Even though Republicans emerged from the midterm elections with a smaller majority in the House of Representatives, President Calvin Coolidge insisted that he and his administration had not experienced a political setback. After all, midterm reverses for the party in power were common and expected, and the probusiness Republicans had suffered their fewest losses of the decade.

**Significant Senate Losses.** The most significant change resulting from the midterm elections came in the Senate, where Democrats gained seven seats. The most embarrassing for Coolidge was the defeat in Massachusetts of Sen. William Butler by Democrat David Walsh. Butler, from Coolidge's home state, was the only candidate for whom the president campaigned personally. Yet Coolidge argued that personal and local concerns, rather than national issues, determined the outcome of this and the other Senate races in which Republicans fared poorly. Despite their gains the Democrats were still short of the majority they needed to take control of the Senate, but the increased Democratic presence effectively neutralized the Republicans' ability to push their legislative agenda. An opposition coalition of Democrats, Farmer-Laborite Henrik Shipstead of Minnesota, and a half-dozen Republican insurgents presented potential trouble for Coolidge because this group could block Republican legislation until the next presidential election, when the Democrats hoped to capture control of the presidency and Congress.

**Sources:**

"Mr. Coolidge, the Election, and the Future," *Nation*, 123 (17 November 1926): 498;

"National Affairs," *Time*, 8 (15 November 1926): 8–11.

## NATIONAL POLITICS: THE 1928 REPUBLICAN NOMINATION RACE

**Coolidge Rules Out Renomination.** "I do not choose to run for President in 1928," President Coolidge announced in a statement issued in August 1927. His decision was hard to understand given the popularity of the

| Senate | 69th Congress | 70th Congress | Net Gain/Loss |
|---|---|---|---|
| Democrats | 39 | 46 | +7 |
| Republicans | 56 | 49 | -7 |
| Other | 1 | 1 | 0 |

| House | 69th Congress | 70th Congress | Net Gain/Loss |
|---|---|---|---|
| Democrats | 183 | 195 | +12 |
| Republicans | 247 | 237 | -10 |
| Other | 4 | 3 | -1 |

| Governors | 1924 | 1926 | Net Gain/Loss |
|---|---|---|---|
| Democrats | 26 | 24 | -2 |
| Republicans | 22 | 24 | +2 |

Republicans and the booming economy. Friends speculated that Coolidge's pronouncement left the door open for a draft at the convention if a favorable candidate did not emerge, but one did — Herbert Hoover of California. Hoover had sought the nomination in 1920, and as secretary of commerce in the Harding and Coolidge administrations he had continued to develop his presidential potential. During the 1928 primaries he aggressively sought nationwide support for the Republican nomination. Frank O. Lowden, the only other candidate who competed nationwide, entered primaries only where his chances of success seemed promising, leaving Hoover unopposed in many contests and enabling him to acquire many committed delegates before the convention.

**The Republican Convention and Platform Debate.** Republicans convened in Kansas City, Missouri, for their four-day convention on 12 June 1928. Their platform, not surprisingly, endorsed the policies of the Coolidge administration, especially the lowering of taxes and federal debt. Isolationism continued to receive Republican support. The only controversies in the platform debate were over Prohibition and agricultural policy. A minority plank proposed by a New York delegate advocated the repeal of the Eighteenth Amendment. Equally at odds with the majority was a substitute platform proposed by a delegation from eight states, led by Sen. Robert La Follette Jr. of Wisconsin, following in the tradition of his late father. Among other things, this group called for liberalization of the Volstead Act, the legislation passed to implement the Eighteenth Amendment, by allowing each state to hold a referendum on Prohibition. Neither anti-Prohibition plank prevailed. Contentious debate surrounded the disagreement over the party's commitment to agriculture. La Follette's group, favoring stronger support for farmers than the majority platform included, wanted either the same commitment to agricul-

ture that was given to industry or passage of the McNary-Haugen Bill, which proposed a federal subsidy for agricultural products. Coolidge and Hoover both adamantly opposed this bill. Since their forces dominated the convention, the majority platform passed 807 to 277 without alteration.

**Hoover Is Nominated on the First Ballot.** The convention, as expected, received Hoover enthusiastically. Lowden surprised delegates by dropping out of the nomination race at the eleventh hour. Instead of hearing a nomination speech for Lowden, the convention listened to a letter announcing his withdrawal because the platform failed to address the serious needs of farmers. Although the probability of stopping Hoover was minimal, many of Lowden's delegates felt he had betrayed and abandoned them. Hoover won the nomination on the first ballot, but 25 percent of the delegates voted for other candidates, including Lowden, Coolidge, and a host of favorite sons.

**Curtis Joins the Ticket.** Four candidates were nominated for the vice presidential slot, and three withdrew in favor of Charles Curtis of Kansas, the Senate majority leader, who was selected because of his popularity with midwestern farmers. Curtis received all but thirty-seven of the delegates' votes, and these delegates — hard-core Progressives — did not vote against him but merely abstained, making Curtis's nomination unanimous.

Sources:

Richard C. Bain and Judith H. Parris, *Convention Decisions and Voting Records,* second edition (Washington, D.C.: Brookings Institution, 1973);

Lawrence H. Fuchs, "Election of 1928," in *History of American Presidential Elections 1789–1968,* edited by Arthur M. Schlesinger Jr., volume 3 (New York: Chelsea House/McGraw-Hill, 1971), pp. 2585–2704;

"National Affairs," *Time,* 11 (25 June 1928): 9–15.

## NATIONAL POLITICS: THE 1928 DEMOCRATIC NOMINATION RACE

**The Obvious Candidate.** As Democrats prepared for the 1928 presidential campaign, divisions within their party were as deep as they had been in the previous presidential election. Once again the party was divided into rural versus urban, wet versus dry, and Catholic versus Protestant. Increasingly Democrats depended on the recent ethnic voters who resided primarily in large urban areas. The necessity of maintaining the loyalty of these voters made New York a must-win state for the Democrats, and this reality boosted the candidacy of Alfred E. "Al" Smith, the governor of that state. A leading contender in 1924, Smith used the recognition he had gained in that loss to launch a four-year campaign for the 1928 nomination. Smith organized his urban, wet, liberal forces early, working to avoid another 103-ballot, deadlocked convention. Smith was not unchallenged, but the opposing rural, dry, conservative forces lacked leadership. Many drys hoped William McAdoo would run, but the

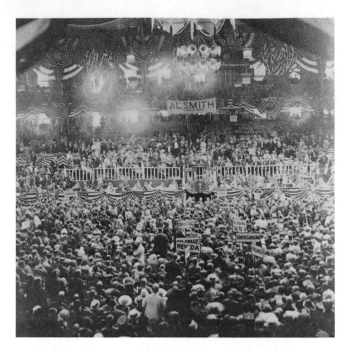

Demonstration for Alfred E. Smith during the 1928 Democratic National Convention

bitter McAdoo announced in December 1927 that he would not seek the nomination. Democrats who disapproved of Smith's wet connections turned to weaker favorite sons, whose organizations lacked the strength to compete with Smith's forces.

**The Wet/Dry Conflict.** Democrats gathered on 26 June in Houston, Texas, a city carefully selected to placate southerners who did not want Smith. Business moved more quickly than at the 1924 convention. The absence of William Jennings Bryan, who had died in 1925, probably contributed to a lower level of tension. Claiming to represent a million voters from the southern states, Smith's opposition expressed its antagonism toward the New Yorker with a protest petition against any candidate who favored the repeal of Prohibition. While the convention took no action on the petition, it exposed a growing cleavage in the party over the alcohol issue. The platform acquiesced to the dry delegates with a plank that pledged "an honest effort to enforce the eighteenth amendment," but Smith openly defied the party's declaration by campaigning for modification of Prohibition, which he considered a sham that encouraged public corruption and disrespect for the law.

**A First-Ballot Victory.** For the third consecutive convention Franklin D. Roosevelt nominated Smith to be the Democratic presidential nominee. On the first roll call Smith fell ten votes short of the two-thirds he needed for the nomination, but many delegates quickly changed their votes, putting Smith over the requisite number on the first ballot.

**A Southern Running Mate.** In selecting a running mate Smith had to reach out to the rural, dry forces for balance. The convention chairman, Sen. Joseph T. Robinson of Arkansas, seemed the obvious choice, and he secured the nomination by a comfortable margin on the first ballot, becoming the first resident southerner to run on a national presidential ticket since the Civil War. As a dry, Protestant, rural southerner, Robinson's presence on the ticket was essential.

Sources:

Richard C. Bain and Judith H. Parris, *Convention Decisions and Voting Records,* second edition (Washington, D.C.: Brookings Institution, 1973);

Lawrence H. Fuchs, "Election of 1928," in *History of American Presidential Elections 1789–1968,* edited by Arthur M. Schlesinger Jr., volume 3 (New York: Chelsea House/McGraw-Hill, 1971), pp. 2585–2704;

"National Affairs," *Time,* 12 (2 July 1928): 9–10.

## NATIONAL POLITICS: THE 1928 ELECTIONS

**Smith's Challenge.** Besides needing to unite his own fractured party, Smith had the unenviable task of convincing Americans that in an era of unprecedented prosperity they should put a different party in control of the White House. Both of these challenges were complicated by Smith's background, religion, and opposition to Prohibition. Smith's wife, Katie, attracted considerable criticism for her lack of social grace and excessive talking, which tended to cause political trouble for her husband. For many voters, especially rural Democrats, Smith embodied the essence of what they perceived as a threat to America and its future: he was an Irish Catholic New Yorker with connections to the corrupt Tammany Hall political machine that ran New York City, and he favored the termination of Prohibition. For Americans who feared radicalism, sympathized with the anti-Catholicism of the Ku Klux Klan, supported immigration restrictions, and agreed with the "100 percent American" philosophy, Smith's credentials as a loyal, lifelong Democrat did little to win their support.

**Campaigning on the Issues.** Smith conducted an issues-oriented campaign, and his stands worked against him. He endorsed open immigration at a time when the majority of Americans wanted the nation's doors closed, especially to non-Anglo-Saxon ethnic groups. The most promising tactic for Democrats was to attack Republican policies that inflicted suffering on American farmers, but rural, Protestant voters had little fondness for the New York politician. The campaign became increasingly focused on Smith himself. Unwilling to renounce either his anti-Prohibition stance or his Tammany Hall connection, Smith weathered criticism on these issues, as he tried to combat voters' fears about his Catholicism.

**A Catholic President?** Opponents raised questions about Smith's allegiance to the United States, insinuating that his first loyalty would be to the Pope. Voters ignored the New York governor's long-standing support for the separation of church and state, confirming the adage that

| Senate | 70th Congress | 71st Congress | Net Gain/Loss |
|---|---|---|---|
| Democrats | 46 | 39 | -7 |
| Republicans | 49 | 56 | +7 |
| Other | 1 | 1 | 0 |

| House | 70th Congress | 71st Congress | Net Gain/Loss |
|---|---|---|---|
| Democrats | 195 | 167 | -28 |
| Republicans | 237 | 267 | +30 |
| Other | 3 | 1 | -2 |

| Governors | 1926 | 1928 | Net Gain/Loss |
|---|---|---|---|
| Democrats | 24 | 21 | -3 |
| Republicans | 24 | 27 | +3 |

perception rather than reality usually prevails in politics. Prominent Protestant leaders inflamed church members' anxieties about Smith's religion. Methodist bishop James Cannon Jr. led strong attacks against Smith in the South. As the organizer of the Southern Dry Democratic Conference, Cannon broke ranks with traditional Solid South Democrats and campaigned for the "moral necessity" of electing Hoover rather than the wet Catholic.

**A Referendum on Prosperity.** Despite cultural and religious conflicts the 1928 presidential campaign ultimately became a referendum on the national economy, and Hoover had the benefit of being identified with continued prosperity. Realizing that he had the advantageous position, Hoover refused to debate Smith on the issues, preferring instead an aloof approach that linked the self-made millionaire with general Republican popularity. An unprecedented economic calamity was only one year away, but from the vantage point of 1928 the economy seemed strong, and the majority of Americans willingly endorsed the party it perceived as responsible for their prosperity.

**Hoover's Victory.** Hoover received 444 electoral votes to 87 for Smith, who won only eight states, less than either Cox in 1920 or Davis in 1924. Hoover cracked the Solid South, winning in Tennessee, Virginia, North Carolina, Texas, Oklahoma, and Florida. This defection by southern Democrats was more a rejection of Smith's Catholicism and anti–Prohibitionism than an affirmation of Hoover. In the next decade the Depression sent southerners scrambling back into the Democratic fold.

**Smith's Coalition.** For a candidate with so many liabilities, Smith showed surprising strength despite Hoover's overwhelming victory. Although Smith carried only eight states, he won 41 percent of the popular vote and made significant advances for Democrats in the nation's

large metropolitan counties. Voter turnout was a remarkable 67.5 percent, up almost 11 percent from 1924, and Smith successfully lured many northeastern and midwestern urban ethnic voters away from the Republicans. Many of these eastern, second-generation Americans would never have defected from the GOP if the populist, dry, rural crusaders had remained in control of the Democratic Party. Smith's success at attracting these urban ethnic voters in 1928 began the major political realignment of the twentieth century, which Franklin D. Roosevelt completed in the 1930s when he forged his New Deal coalition by joining these voters to the Democrats' traditional Solid South base.

Sources:

*Congressional Quarterly's Guide to U.S. Elections,* second edition (Washington, D.C.: Congressional Quarterly, 1985);

Lawrence H. Fuchs, "Election of 1928," in *History of American Presidential Elections 1789–1968,* edited by Arthur M. Schlesinger Jr., volume 3 (New York: Chelsea House/McGraw-Hill, 1971), pp. 2585–2704;

"The Meaning of Hoover's Victory," *New Republic,* 56 (14 November 1928): 336–339.

## RURAL AND URBAN CONFLICT: CONGRESSIONAL REAPPORTIONMENT

**Population Shift to the Cities.** The 1920 national census revealed that the population of the United States had increased by 14 million and that — for the first time in American history — the majority of Americans resided in urban rather than rural areas. The population of New York City had passed 7 million, and the population of Los Angeles had doubled since 1910, reaching more than 1.2 million. By 1929 ninety-three cities in the United States had populations exceeding 100,000. Approximately 6 million Americans moved from farms to urban areas during the 1920s. In that number were many African Americans, who left the segregated South in search of greater economic, personal, and political freedom in northern cities.

**Rural-Urban Tensions.** This population shift represented more than a demographic change. Economic, social, and political changes accompanied Americans' migration to cities. As urban areas grew and promoted their interests in the political arena, rural Americans, who had long considered themselves the custodians of traditional values, arose to defend their way of life against the perceived urban onslaught. Many of the political conflicts of the 1920s — over Prohibition, immigration restriction, the Ku Klux Klan, and agricultural subsidies — were framed by a rural/urban tension. For rural Americans the city symbolized all that threatened rural cultural hegemony.

**Congress Stalls Reapportionment.** The Constitution mandates that every ten years, after each national census, Congress must adjust the apportionment of seats in the House of Representatives to reflect shifts in the population. Following the census of 1920 Congress failed to

## OUTLAWING WAR: THE KELLOGG-BRIAND PACT

**A**mericans hoped that World War I had indeed been "the war to end all wars," but once the peace treaty was negotiated they rejected the League of Nations and the Permanent Court of International Justice (World Court) — two institutions created to insure long-term international peace. Near the end of the 1920s, American idealists supported the notion of outlawing war. In April 1927 Aristide Briand, foreign minister of France, suggested that his country and the United States formally renounce war with a bilateral agreement. Believing such an agreement constituted an "entangled alliance," President Calvin Coolidge resisted Briand's overture, but the American public's enthusiasm for Briand's proposal became so great that Coolidge could not continue to ignore it. Therefore, in June Secretary of State Frank B. Kellogg countered with a proposed multilateral treaty that invited "all the principal Powers of the world to a declaration renouncing war as an instrument of national policy." After some negotiations and revision, Kellogg's proposal was accepted by the international community. Responding to the extraordinary popularity of the pact with American voters, the Senate approved it by a vote of eighty-five to one. An editor for *The Nation* wrote, "A vote for it is like a vote for the Ten Commandments, perfectly proper and in no wise affecting the existing status of the world." In August 1928 fifteen nations met in Paris to sign the Kellogg-Briand Pact, which was eventually endorsed by more than sixty countries. The pact that outlawed war had only the moral force of world opinion to uphold it and was thus completely powerless to achieve world peace.

**Source:** Stephen J. Kneeshaw, *In Pursuit of Peace: The American Reaction to the Kellogg-Briand Pact, 1928–1929* (New York: Garland, 1991).

Source:
Charles W. Eagles, *Democracy Delayed: Congressional Reapportionment and Urban-Rural Conflict in the 1920s* (Athens: University of Georgia Press, 1990).

## THE TEAPOT DOME SCANDAL

**Scandals in the Harding Administration.** Late in his presidency Warren G. Harding commented to journalist William Allen White that his enemies were not a problem, "but my damned friends . . . they're the ones that keep me walking the floor nights!" During the early 1920s Harding's cronies were involved in one scandal after another. Attorney General Harry Daugherty was caught accepting bribes from former clients to protect them from federal prosecution, and the Veterans' Bureau director, Charles Forbes, was jailed for fraud. The most sensational case of public corruption during the Harding administration was the Teapot Dome scandal. Contemporaries believed that this scandal, which involved public officials making secret deals for personal profit at public expense, epitomized politics of the 1920s. Many historians have blamed the flurry of public corruption in the 1920s on the excessive privileges granted to business by its friends in government.

**Conservation Struggle.** What eventually mushroomed into a scandal of national proportion began as a conservation policy struggle within the Republican Party. During the prewar Progressive Era, reformers and conservationists, fearing the reduction of domestic oil supplies, tightened federal oil-leasing policies. Republican president William Howard Taft created two naval petroleum reserves in California exclusively for government use, and in 1915 President Woodrow Wilson created a third reserve — Teapot Dome in Wyoming. As soon as these reserves were created, debate began over the possibility of leasing these reserves to private oil companies. Business interests advocated public access to the reserves, while conservationists opposed any private leases.

**Albert Fall's Machinations.** While businessmen and conservationists both had political allies, Harding tipped the balance with the appointment of Sen. Albert B. Fall of New Mexico, an outspoken anticonservationist, as secretary of the interior. In 1921, with the tacit approval of Secretary of the Navy Edwin Denby, Fall maneuvered to have Harding issue an executive order transferring control of the naval oil reserves from the Navy Department to the Interior Department. Fall granted drilling rights in the California reserves to Edward L. Doheny, owner of Pan-American Petroleum and Transport Company, and that same year Fall leased the Teapot Dome reserve to Harry Sinclair of Mammoth Oil Company. Within weeks Sinclair also had access to Elk Hills, one of the California reserves.

**Conservation Retaliation.** Although he had no hard evidence, Harry A. Slattery, a staunch conservationist, heard rumors of Fall's covert manipulations and began working to expose him, soliciting the assistance of Sen.

fulfill this task. Because the American population had shifted to the cities, rural voters were slated to lose representation to their underrepresented urban counterparts. Nearly all opponents of reapportionment were rural congressmen, who feared that a new urban majority would repeal Prohibition and end immigration restriction.

**Reapportionment Endorsed.** In 1929, after nearly a decade of ignoring its responsibility, Congress passed a bill that granted the president authority to reapportion House seats after each decennial census if Congress failed to fulfill its constitutional responsibility to do so. Congress stalled until the 1930 census before carrying out reapportionment. Never before had Congress so consistently refused to reapportion representation in the House.

Secretary of the Interior Albert B. Fall, who went to prison for taking bribes from oil tycoons Harry Sinclair and Edward Doheny to lease federal oil reserves to their companies.

Edward Doheny with his wife, being congratulated by his chief defense attorney, Frank J. Hogan, after being acquitted of bribing Albert B. Fall.

Robert La Follette of Wisconsin, a longtime conservationist who launched a Senate investigation. Chaired by Democrat Thomas J. Walsh of Montana, the Senate Committee on Public Lands and Surveys reluctantly "studied" the situation privately for sixteen months before public hearings opened in October 1923. By then Fall had resigned as interior secretary and Harding had died, diminishing the urgency of the investigation.

**The Scandal Breaks.** For two months the fairly routine Senate investigation attracted little attention. But Fall's conspicuous personal spending led to inquiries that forced him to admit that he had borrowed $100,000 dollars from an unnamed source. This admission attracted national attention to the Teapot Dome investigation. Next Doheny admitted that he was the "source" of the "loan," which he defended as assistance to a longtime friend.

**A Media Frenzy.** From January to March 1924 the Teapot Dome hearings were a national sensation. At the Senate hearings politicians hurled charges and countercharges. Since it was an election year, Democrats seldom missed an opportunity to exploit the Republican scandal. Journalists enjoyed the fallout, covering every possible angle and extrapolating broadly. Eventually Attorney General Daugherty and Secretary of the Navy Denby resigned under intense criticism. As the investigation continued into the spring, Democrats cast wider and wider nets to snag more Republicans, attempting with little success to link President Coolidge with the scandal simply on the grounds of guilt by association.

**Ironic Consequences.** Remarkably, the Teapot Dome scandal had little effect on the Republicans, who managed to taint their fiercest Democratic rival, William McAdoo, one of Doheny's legal advisers, with fallout from the scandal. Revelations of Doheny's role in the scandal tarnished McAdoo by association. Coolidge's image as an honest, frugal New Englander committed to small government helped the Republicans to avoid the worst of the backlash from the scandal, as did the president's willingness to press the investigation. In the 1924 election voters refused to punish Coolidge for corruption in Harding's administration.

**Final Fallout.** State trials in California and Wyoming between 1924 and 1929 divulged the passing of more money from oil barons to Fall and the Republican National Committee. Fall, who reportedly received at least $409,000 from Sinclair and Doheny, was convicted of accepting bribes in 1929 and became the first cabinet officer in the nation's history to serve a prison sentence. Sinclair and Doheny were acquitted of paying bribes. The Supreme Court eventually overturned Fall's oil-leasing policy and nullified the Sinclair and Doheny leases. In December 1924 Coolidge established a Federal Oil Conservation Board to promote the preservation of the government oil supply, and the next Republican president, Herbert Hoover, announced "complete conservation of government oil in this administration."

Source:
Burl Noggle, *Teapot Dome: Oil and Politics in the 1920s* (Baton Rouge: Louisiana State University Press, 1962).

# HEADLINE MAKERS

## CALVIN COOLIDGE

### 1872-1933

PRESIDENT OF THE UNITED STATES, 1923-1929

**Massachusetts Governor.** Over the course of a quarter-century Calvin Coolidge successfully climbed the political ladder. Beginning in 1898 as city councilman of Northampton, Massachusetts, he proceeded through local and state offices, finally reaching the White House in 1923. As governor of Massachusetts, Coolidge attracted national attention in 1919, when he called in the National Guard to end the Boston police strike, which had turned violent. Although it made him unpopular with Samuel Gompers and organized labor, Coolidge's strikebreaking endeared him to Americans who considered labor protests a radical threat to public safety.

**Balancing the Ticket in 1920.** Coolidge's dramatic termination of the Boston police strike earned him national attention and sparked rumors about a presidential bid. He did not campaign vigorously in 1920, but his name was placed in nomination at the 1920 Republican National Convention that year, and he received thirty-four votes on the first ballot. The old-guard Republicans who helped to secure the presidential nomination for Warren G. Harding wanted Sen. Irvine L. Lenroot of Wisconsin for vice president, but in defiance of the party establishment the delegates chose the cautious, aloof New England governor to balance a ticket headed by the gregarious midwestern senator.

**Coolidge Inherits Harding's Mess.** Following Harding's sudden death in 1923, "Silent Cal" assumed the presidency and effectively calmed a nation mourning a beloved president. He masterfully distanced himself from Harding administration corruption scandals. Coolidge's reputation for honesty and frugality was exactly what the Republican Party needed to preclude a public backlash. With decisiveness and speed Coolidge created an in-vestigative commission and prosecuted all alleged violators of the public trust.

**Lackluster President.** Coolidge was easily nominated and elected to a full term as president in 1924. That he lacked imagination, leadership skills, idealism, and compassion for suffering farmers mattered little to Americans who admired his support for big business and willingness to maintain the status quo. He kept tariffs high, taxes low, and immigrants out. Twice he vetoed the McNary-Haugen Bill to provide government price supports for agriculture. "The business of America is business," Coolidge often asserted, and he committed his presidency to that maxim.

Source:
Donald R. McCoy, *Calvin Coolidge: The Quiet President* (New York: Macmillan, 1967).

## WARREN GAMALIEL HARDING

### 1865-1923

PRESIDENT OF THE UNITED STATES, 1921-1923

**A Lovable President.** A former journalist and senator from Ohio, Warren G. Harding ushered in a decade of Republican ascendancy with his landslide election to the presidency in 1920. Republican hegemony lasted until 1932, when Americans finally rejected the laissez-faire Republican policies that had thrust them into the Great Depression. Unlike his Democratic predecessor, Woodrow Wilson, Harding was popular, personable, approachable, and loved by the American people. His down-home image was familiar to millions. Harding's popularity persisted despite attempts to arouse racist sentiment against him with accusations that his great-grandmother Elizabeth Madison was black and that his great-grandfather had African American ancestors. While these claims were never definitively verified, they were widely accepted in the South.

**Politics of Normalcy.** Harding's 1920 presidential campaign popularized the term *normalcy*. In defining this concept Harding explained, "I don't mean the old order, but a regular steady order of things. I mean normal procedure, the natural way, without excess." Harding wanted to create a partnership between government and business, to make government "business friendly." His administration supported higher tariffs and reduced government spending while overhauling the federal tax structure to reduce the burden on wealthy Americans. Moreover, the Republican president promoted industrial standardization, efficiency, expansion of business, and elimination of waste. Harding appealed to all Americans frustrated with Wilson and the Democrats. The slogan "Let's be done with wiggle and wobble" highlighted Harding's determination to abandon Wilson's policies and tactics.

**A Cabinet of Contrasts.** To fulfill his campaign promise to make government more like business, Harding brought some of the "best minds" of American business to Washington. Among the new president's most able recruits were Charles Evans Hughes as secretary of state, Henry C. Wallace as secretary of agriculture, Herbert Hoover as secretary of commerce, and Andrew W. Mellon as secretary of the treasury. Yet Harding did not confine his selection of policy advisers strictly to accomplished men with respected reputations. The former Ohio senator also appointed several political cronies who later betrayed his trust and tarnished his administration. Harding rewarded his longtime friend and campaign manager Harry M. Daugherty with the post of attorney general. He later resigned in the midst of scandal and was tried but acquitted of charges that he conspired to defraud the federal government. The most notorious corruption scandal involving the Harding administration involved another of the president's friends, Albert B. Fall, who was appointed secretary of the interior. Implicated in the notorious Teapot Dome scandal, Fall resigned, was tried for accepting bribes from private oil companies, and became the first cabinet officer in American history to be sent to prison for committing a felony.

**Harding's Death.** Elected to the presidency on his fifty-fifth birthday, 2 November 1920, Harding died unexpectedly on 2 August 1923, while in San Francisco during a transcontinental speaking tour. Just before and soon after his death, the scandals involving members of his administration began to erupt, revealing the degree to which Harding had been victimized by his friends. While the preponderance of evidence indicates that Harding was not an accomplice to their illegal activities, he bore the responsibility for appointing the culprits. His reputation was also damaged when Nan Britton published *The President's Daughter* (1927), in which she told of her affair with the president and the birth of her daughter, Elizabeth Ann, who, Britton insisted, was Harding's child.

**Source:**
Robert K. Murray, *The Harding Era: Warren G. Harding and His Administration* (Minneapolis: University of Minnesota Press, 1969).

## HERBERT HOOVER

### 1874-1964

SECRETARY OF COMMERCE, 1921-1929

PRESIDENT OF THE UNITED STATES, 1929-1933

**From Rags to Riches.** Herbert Hoover was one of the most admired public figures in the United States before his reputation was tarnished by the onset of the Great Depression during his presidency. Hoover's life seemed like that of a Horatio Alger hero. Son of an Iowa farmer and orphaned at age ten, Herbert Clark Hoover earned a degree from Stanford University, became a mining engineer, and was a self-made millionaire before he reached forty. During World War I he directed the Belgian Relief Commission and headed the U.S. Food Administration, an arm of Woodrow Wilson's war mobilization effort. Hoover spent most of the 1920s as secretary of commerce under Presidents Warren G. Harding and Calvin Coolidge.

**Secretary of Commerce.** Known to insiders as "Secretary of Commerce and Under Secretary of Everything Else," Hoover made Commerce one of the most active cabinet departments. Not a doctrinaire conservative like many other Republican cabinet officers of the decade, Hoover championed progressive capitalism, attempting to balance laissez-faire dogma with humanitarian values. Hoover strove to implement his principles of "cooperative capitalism" by forging an alliance between government and business that relied on experts and volunteers to promote efficiency and self-regulation. To accomplish these goals he organized hundreds of national conferences to study business and economic trends, bringing together experts, amassing information, and disseminating new ideas for making business more efficient and profitable. One of Hoover's crowning achievements was his encouragement of western states to cooperate in building a major dam, later named in his honor, on the Colorado River. He also coordinated relief efforts after the Mississippi River flood of 1927, one of the worst natural disasters of the decade.

**President Hoover.** Hoover's success as secretary of commerce helped in his campaign for the presidency in 1928, when he handily defeated Gov. Alfred E. Smith of New York. During the first eight months of his presidency Hoover exhibited his progressive tendencies through conservation policy, prison reform, a conference on child welfare, and the promotion of humanitarian treatment of African Americans. After the stock-market crash of October 1929 ushered in the Great Depression of the 1930s, however, Hoover's philosophy of self-help and voluntary cooperation proved inadequate to resolve the nation's economic problems and left the once-revered

Hoover one of the nation's most criticized political figures for decades to come.

Source:
David Burner, *Herbert Hoover: The Public Life* (New York: Knopf, 1978).

## ROBERT M. LA FOLLETTE

### 1855-1925

UNITED STATES SENATOR FROM WISCONSIN, 1906-1925

PROGRESSIVE PARTY PRESIDENTIAL CANDIDATE, 1924

**Progressive Reformer.** In 1906 Robert La Follette moved from the governor's office in Wisconsin, where he had served three two-year terms, to the United States Senate, where he served as an active member of the progressive wing of the Republican Party until his death in 1925. Resented by fellow Republican senators, La Follette constantly fought against privilege, corruption, and political bossism to produce a more viable and equitable democracy. Invariably defending unpopular positions, La Follette was often resented, even by those whose cause the senator believed he championed.

**"Irreconcilable."** La Follette opposed entry into World War I, and after Wilson negotiated the peace, he led the hard-core resisters — known as "irreconcilables" — in opposition to ratification of the Treaty of Versailles. Sounding isolationist themes, La Follette argued that the treaty betrayed the powerless and served only as preparation for a future bloodbath. The document omitted Wilson's Fourteen Points, which had been the basis for American entry into the war. The treaty failed to liberate the victors' colonies, La Follette insisted, making a mockery of "self-determination." Moreover, La Follette completely distrusted the League of Nations, which, he argued, would be dominated by governments who revered the status quo. La Follette's opposition to the League had a higher motivation than the partisan animosity expressed by Henry Cabot Lodge and the "strong reservationists," but together all opponents of the League, whom Wilson called a "little group of willful men," prevailed with the Senate's rejection of the Treaty of Versailles.

**Presidential Bid in 1924.** Although La Follette constantly contested conservative business interests, his major domestic battle came in 1924. Disappointed with the two conservative, mainstream presidential candidates — Calvin Coolidge and John Davis — progressive reformers mobilized for a third-party challenge in 1924. Leaders of the Conference for Progressive Political Action — an or-

ganization of farm leaders, social workers, organized labor, former Bull Moosers, and Socialists — formed the new Progressive Party and selected La Follette as their presidential candidate. La Follette attempted to unite discontented farmers and organized labor. In the campaign La Follette and the Progressives called for public ownership of utilities, nationalization of the railroads, increased taxes on the wealthy, curbing the power of the Supreme Court, popular election of the president, elimination of child labor, and a national referendum on declarations of war. During the campaign Republicans constantly attacked La Follette's "radicalism," and the *Wall Street Journal* referred to the party's agenda as "Wisconsin Bolshevism." Yet the Communist Party labeled the Progressive Party's platform "the most reactionary document." Although La Follette had been a fiery progressive leader and radical by some standards, the Wisconsin senator had always staunchly opposed communism.

**Ultimate Victory.** While La Follette's third-party candidacy was not as successful as Theodore Roosevelt's had been in 1912, the Progressive candidate carried his home state, Wisconsin, and attracted almost 5 million votes. La Follette's bid for the presidency was his final political contest: he died less than a year later at age seventy. Although La Follette lost many of his political battles in life, most of his "radical" ideas were enshrined into law after his death, apparently vindicating the soundness of his principles.

Source:
Bernard A. Weisberger, *The La Follettes of Wisconsin: Love and Politics in Progressive America* (Madison: University of Wisconsin Press, 1994).

## WILLIAM GIBBS MCADOO

### 1863-1941

CANDIDATE FOR THE DEMOCRATIC PRESIDENTIAL NOMINATION, 1920, 1924

**Secretary of the Treasury.** Born in Georgia during the Civil War, William G. McAdoo received his college education at the University of Tennessee, became a lawyer, and left his native South, at age twenty-nine, for opportunities in New York, where he developed considerable experience as an attorney of high finance. Although never elected to public office, McAdoo's political activism began when he worked in Woodrow Wilson's 1910 campaign for governor of New Jersey and continued through Wilson's successful presidential bid in 1912. After winning the presidency Wilson appointed McAdoo as secretary of the treasury because the New York lawyer had financial expertise but was not tainted by Wall Street connections. McAdoo's most important responsibility was financing the war, a duty that ultimately made the treasury secretary unpopular with progressives when he endorsed a tax plan that drew heavily upon middle- and lower-class incomes. Overburdened by the stresses associated with his wartime responsibilities, McAdoo resigned his cabinet office when the European conflict ended.

**Presidential Aspirations, 1920.** Since McAdoo was Woodrow Wilson's son-in-law and secretary of the treasury, many anticipated that he would become Wilson's political successor. But McAdoo, along with other Democratic hopefuls, fell victim to Wilson's indecisiveness regarding his own third-term candidacy. Without Wilson's endorsement, McAdoo hesitated to declare his intentions to seek the nomination. While privately McAdoo solicited support for himself, publicly he remained quiet about the idea. McAdoo's name, however, was placed in nomination at the Democratic convention in 1920, and he remained in the balloting until a fellow progressive, Ohio governor James Cox, won the presidential nomination on the forty-fourth ballot.

**Advocate of Rural, Dry Forces.** The 1920 loss did not end McAdoo's aspirations for the presidency. As part of his strategy for 1924, McAdoo, realizing he could never win the support of the New York delegation, made California his home. Instead of seeking the eastern urban vote, the former secretary of the treasury opted to pursue a West-South coalition. With his new ties in California and his native roots in the South, the strategy seemed plausible. As an outspoken advocate of Prohibition, McAdoo quickly endeared himself to rural Americans. But once he decided to pursue this course, he inevitably needed to solicit Ku Klux Klan support. McAdoo's acceptance of the Klan's endorsement diminished his appeal to immigrants and progressives, and it helped polarize the Democratic party into rival rural and urban camps. McAdoo's association with Edward L. Doheny, an oil millionaire who bribed Secretary of the Interior Albert B. Fall to lease government oil reserves, further diminished his appeal to progressives.

**McAdoo's Defeat.** Despite advice to the contrary, McAdoo waged a bitter fight throughout 1924 with New York governor Al Smith. Yet neither man could garner the two-thirds vote needed for the nomination. So following an intense convention struggle, McAdoo, along with Smith, had to capitulate to compromise candidate John Davis. Unwilling or unable to mount another fight against Al Smith, McAdoo ended his quest for the presidency long before the 1928 campaign season began, paving the way for Smith's triumph at the Democratic Convention. McAdoo returned to his private law practice in Los Angeles and served as chairman of the board of the government-owned American President Lines until his death in 1941.

**Progressive Career.** The 1924 campaign was, in many respects, an aberration from McAdoo's otherwise progressive career. Reactionary forces such as the Klan supported McAdoo generally because he was the only strong rural candidate. He had advocated lower tariffs, federal regulation of American shipping, federal financing of elections, and federal insurance of bank deposits. McAdoo served as a transitional figure between the Progressive reform movement of the early twentieth century and the more government-sponsored reform of the 1930s — the New Deal that Franklin Roosevelt fashioned to address the problems of the Great Depression.

Source:
David Burner, *The Politics of Provincialism: The Democratic Party in Transition, 1918–1932* (New York: Norton, 1968).

# ANDREW W. MELLON

## 1855-1937

### SECRETARY OF THE TREASURY, 1921-1932

**Millionaire Cabinet Secretary.** As President Warren Harding's secretary of the treasury, Andrew Mellon, a Pittsburgh multimillionaire, molded the relationship between government and business during the 1920s, a relationship that influenced politics throughout the decade. Before entering government service, Mellon had an exceptionally successful career as a financier in various businesses, including oil and aluminum. Harding appointed Mellon as treasury secretary on the advice of Philander Knox, a prominent Republican senator from Pennsylvania and a longtime friend of Mellon. Mellon's age, wealth, career banking experience, and conservative Republican connections suggested he would probably endorse traditional, old-line conservative policies, and he did.

**Mellon's Economic Philosophy.** Committed to retrenchment and economy in government, Secretary of the Treasury Mellon reduced federal spending vigorously. He consistently opposed the veterans' bonus bill and the McNary-Haugen farm bills. But even more central to Mellon's financial vision than spending reduction was tax reduction, especially for the rich. Mellon rejected the progressive philosophy of taxation that insisted those Americans most able to pay should pay more taxes. Instead the he articulated a philosophy later known as "trickle-down economics." Taxing the rich, Mellon argued, inhibited their investment ability, thus impeding job growth and the entire economy. Without a heavy tax burden, the wealthy would invest, create jobs, and ultimately all participants in the economy would become beneficiaries of investors' tax-free profits as prosperity filtered down to workers and farmers, Mellon argued.

**Mellon's Tax Program.** Republicans eagerly returned America to a peacetime budget, dramatically reducing government spending that had grown substantially during World War I. Mellon complemented these spending reductions with major tax revision. Mellon proposed that Congress repeal the excess-profits tax, which taxed corporate profits above 8 percent, and that it reduce the surtax on income from 65 percent to 40 percent and steadily lower it to 25 percent. (The surtax was an additional tax on existing taxes for wealthy Americans.) These reductions applied only to wealthy Americans, and Congress balked. While blunting Mellon's extreme cuts, Congress did, however, approve substantial tax cuts in 1921. This was the first of many tax reductions enacted during the decade at Mellon's instigation, as he was reappointed secretary of the treasury during both Coolidge's and Hoover's administrations. During Coolidge's administration a Nebraska progressive commented that "Mr. Mellon himself gets a larger personal reduction than the aggregate of practically all the taxpayers in the state of Nebraska." Mellon eventually convinced Congress to eliminate gift taxes, to cut estate taxes by 50 percent, and to reduce the maximum income-tax rate from 40 percent to 20 percent.

**Source:**
George Soule, *Prosperity Decade: From War to Depression 1917–1929* (New York: Rinehart, 1947).

## ALFRED E. SMITH

### 1873-1944

NEW YORK GOVERNOR, 1919-1921, 1923-1929

DEMOCRATIC NOMINEE FOR PRESIDENT, 1928

**Smith's Early Career.** With only an eighth-grade education, Alfred E. Smith, an Irish Catholic New Yorker raised in the Fourth Ward of the city's Lower East Side, entered the rough-and-tumble world of New York City politics as a Tammany Hall loyalist. He began his political career in 1903 as a representative in New York's state assembly. During his legislative career Smith earned a reputation as a hardworking, progressive legislator. In 1918 New York elected the aggressive politician as its governor. In 1920 Smith lost his reelection bid when the rising conservative, xenophobic tide swept Republicans into office in New York, as well as across the nation. But Smith easily recaptured the governorship in 1922 and served three consecutive terms following that victory.

**Progressive Governor.** While governor, Smith developed a reputation as a progressive reformer. Consistent with national progressive reform efforts to increase governmental efficiency, Smith reorganized New York's state government, eliminating overlapping agencies and reducing costs. He worked for a forty-eight-hour workweek for labor and strengthened the State Labor Department's hand in enforcing safety requirements and administering workmen's compensation. Smith also developed low-cost housing projects and an extensive parks and recreation system in New York. Determined to defend civil liberties in an era of repression, the governor vetoed several antisedition bills, thwarting the legislature's attempts to curtail the civil liberties of Socialists. Throughout his governorship Smith opposed Prohibition and called for its repeal. His accomplishments made him a viable candidate for national office, but his sometimes controversial views on major issues made him a target of substantial criticism.

**Presidential Hopeful.** Always the ambitious politician, the successful New York governor soon set his sights on the presidency. At the 1920 Democratic convention Smith was included in the crowded field of favorite sons and dark-horse candidates, but he was hardly a serious contender that year. Four years later Smith made a serious bid for the Democratic presidential nomination, but his urban, wet forces clashed with the Democratic Party's rural, dry, Protestant wing. Thus, a bitterly divided convention in 1924 could not nominate either Al Smith or his chief opponent, William McAdoo. Smith's open opposition to the Ku Klux Klan, which included virulent anti-Catholicism among its prejudices, thwarted his opportunity to secure the necessary two-thirds majority. After an unprecedented 103 ballots, delegates settled for John Davis, a compromise candidate.

**Campaign of 1928.** Determined not to repeat the mistakes that divided the 1924 Democratic convention, Smith campaigned early and long, assuring himself the party's nomination in 1928. Although the rural opposition in the Democratic Party was without a national leader, it was determined to be a menacing force. Smith could not unite his party, and he continually reaped dissenters' criticism for his anti-Prohibition stance, his Tammany connections, and his Catholic beliefs. Smith's controversial candidacy diverted attention from the reality of a formidable opponent, Herbert Hoover, and a strong economy. Historian Richard Hofstadter observed, "There was not a Democrat alive, Protestant or Catholic, who could have beaten Hoover in 1928."

**Source:**
David Burner, *The Politics of Provincialism: The Democratic Party in Transition, 1918–1932* (New York: Norton, 1968).

# PEOPLE IN THE NEWS

On 15 January 1929 Sen. **John J. Blaine** of Wisconsin, a progressive Republican, cast the only dissenting vote against the Kellogg-Briand Pact, which renounced war as a national policy. Blaine argued, "This pact commits our Nation to an impossible peace, unworthy of the traditions of America, and forgetful of that which made this Republic possible."

On 19 July 1928 Bishop **James Cannon Jr.** of the Methodist Episcopal Church, South, pledged at the Southern Dry Democratic Conference in Asheville, North Carolina, to vote against and work against his party's presidential nominee, Alfred E. Smith, who took a "wet" stance on Prohibition.

On 28 March 1924 Attorney General **Harry M. Daugherty,** who had been indicted on charges of conspiracy to defraud the government, resigned at President Coolidge's request.

On 14 June 1929 former vice president **Charles G. Dawes** arrived in London to begin his new position as American ambassador to Great Britain.

On 18 February 1924 **Edwin Denby** resigned as secretary of the navy under pressure from the Senate's investigation into the Teapot Dome scandal.

On 30 January 1925 Col. **Charles R. Forbes,** director of the Veterans' Bureau, was convicted of conspiracy to loot the funds of that agency. A Federal District Court judge fined him $10,000 and sentenced him to two years in prison.

On 1 October 1923 at the forty-third annual convention of the American Federation of Labor (AFL) in Portland, Oregon, **Samuel Gompers,** the president of AFL, declared, "I believe the Republic of the United States of America is the best form of government on the earth today." Gompers added, however, "It is still not good enough for us nor good enough for those who are to come after. . . ."

On 3 December 1929, a month after the Great Stock Market Crash, President **Herbert Hoover,** in his annual message to Congress, declared business sound, promised an income-tax cut, requested urgent passage of tariff legislation, and requested stronger Prohibition laws.

On 8 September 1928 the Council and the Assembly of the League of Nations elected former secretary of state **Charles E. Hughes** to be a member of the Permanent Court of International Justice.

On 16 February 1925 the Senate confirmed **Frank B. Kellogg** of Minnesota, the U.S. ambassador to England, as President Calvin Coolidge's new secretary of state.

In December 1928 President Coolidge restored the citizenship rights of **John W. Langley,** congressman from Kentucky from 1907 until 1925, when he was convicted of conspiracy to remove twelve hundred cases of liquor from a distillery in Lawrenceburg, Kentucky. Langley served eleven months of his two-year sentence.

In December 1929 **Gail Laughlin,** a Maine state legislator, declared, "There may be too much lobbying going on in Washington, but there is not nearly enough of the right kind." She urged that there be more lobbying for the proposed Equal Rights Amendment.

In May 1929 the Louisiana State Senate voted to acquit Gov. **Huey P. Long** of all allegations against him regardless of the evidence, charging the Louisiana House of Representatives impeachment proceedings against Governor Long were illegal because they took place in a special session that extended without authorization. The impeachment charges included attempted bribery of the legislature, failure to account for state funds, intimidation of the press, and "friskiness with a woman" at a New Orleans studio party.

On 28 November 1924 Sen. **James Reed** and the caucus of Republican Senators adopted a resolution excluding Senators Robert La Follette, Edwin Ladd, Smith Brookhart, and Lynn Frazier from Republican conferences and appointments to Republican vacancies in Senate committees because they had supported the Progressive Party in the recent election.

On 1 January 1929 **Franklin D. Roosevelt,** in his first inaugural address as governor of New York, said, "Our civilization cannot endure unless we, as individuals, realize our personal responsibility to and dependence on the rest of the world. For it is literally true that the 'self-supporting' man or woman has become as extinct as the man of the Stone Age."

On 12 October 1921 Imperial Wizard **William J. Simmons,** founder of the revived Ku Klux Klan, testified before the House inquiry of the Klan and denied hostility to "negroes, Jews or Catholics." This vicious allegation, Simmons maintained, came from an attempt by the *New York World* to boost its circulation.

On 17 April 1927 Gov. **Alfred Smith** of New York responded in the *Atlantic Monthly* to an open letter from Charles Marshall demanding to know if Smith's allegiance were to the U.S. Constitution or the Roman Catholic Church. Smith replied, "I believe in absolute freedom of conscience for all men and in equality of all churches, all sects, and all beliefs . . . I believe in the absolute separation of Church and State."

In May 1929 Chief Justice **William Howard Taft** spoke to his Yale fraternity, Psi Upsilon, in Washington, D.C., lamenting, "When a man grows old as I have, he then feels like resorting to profanity, as he ought not to do, at the misconception of life and the use of the universities by feather-headed young men that don't look ahead to know the opportunities they have."

On 4 February 1924, following the death of former president Woodrow Wilson, **Edith Wilson** wrote to Henry Cabot Lodge, longtime political adversary of her husband, "I note in the papers that you have been designated by the Senate of the U.S. as one of those to attend Mr. Wilson's funeral. As the funeral is private and not official and realizing that your presence would be embarrassing to you and unwelcome to me I write to request that you do *not* attend."

On 10 November 1923, the eve of Armistice Day, former president **Woodrow Wilson** proclaimed in a radio address: "Happily the present situation in the world of affairs affords us the opportunity to retrieve the past and to render mankind the inestimable service of proving that there is at least one great and powerful nation which can turn away from programs of self-interest and devote itself to practicing and establishing the highest ideals of disinterested service and the consistent maintenance of exalted standards of conscience and of right."

# DEATHS

---

**Elias Milton Ammons,** 64, governor (D) of Colorado (1913–1915), 20 May 1925.

**Simeon Eben Baldwin,** 86, governor (D) of Connecticut (1911–1915), associate justice (1893–1907) and chief justice (1907–1910) of Connecticut's Supreme Court, 30 January 1927.

**Richard Achilles Ballinger,** 63, secretary of the interior (1909–1911) under President William Howard Taft, 6 June 1922.

**Thomas Walter Bickett,** 42, governor (D) of North Carolina (1917–1921), 29 December 1921.

**Horace Boies,** 95, governor (D) of Iowa (1890–1894), 4 April 1923.

**William Jennings Bryan,** 65, representative (D) from Nebraska (1891–1895), Democratic presidential candidate (1896, 1900, 1908), 26 July 1925.

**Joseph Gurney "Uncle Joe" Cannon,** 90, representative (R) from Illinois (1873–1891, 1893–1913, 1915–1923), Speaker of the House (1903–1911), ousted as speaker for using autocratic methods to control House procedure, 12 November 1926.

**Joseph Maull Carey,** 79, senator (R) from Wyoming (1890–1895), governor (D) of Wyoming (1911–1915), 5 February 1924.

**George Earle Chamberlain,** 74, governor (D) of Oregon (1903–1909), senator (1909–1921), 9 July 1928.

**James Beauchamp "Champ" Clark,** 70, representative (D) from Missouri (1893–1895, 1897–1921), Speaker of the House (1911–1919), candidate for 1912 Democratic presidential nomination, 2 March 1921.

**William Andrews Clark,** 86, senator (D) from Montana (1899–1900, 1901–1907), mining tycoon, 2 March 1925.

LeBaron Bradford Colt, 78, senator (R) from Rhode Island (1913–1924), 18 August 1924.

William Rufus Day, 64, secretary of state under President William McKinley (1898), judge of U.S. circuit court of appeals (1899–1903), U.S. Supreme Court associate justice (1903–1922), 9 July 1923.

Eugene Victor Debs, 70, Socialist activist, organizer of Social Democratic party of America (1897), Socialist presidential candidate (1900, 1904, 1908, 1912, 1920), imprisoned (1918–1921) for violating Espionage Act, 20 October 1926.

Edwin Denby, 58, representative (R) from Michigan (1905–1911), secretary of the navy (1921–1924) during President Warren G. Harding's administration, tainted by the Teapot Dome scandal, resigned in February 1924, 8 February 1929.

Chauncey Mitchell Depew, 93, president (1885–1899) and chairman of the board (1899–1928) of New York Central Railroad, senator (R) from New York (1899–1911), delegate to every Republican National Convention from 1888 to 1924, 5 April 1928.

Sanford Ballard Dole, 82, president of the Republic of Hawaii (1894–1900), first governor of the Territory of Hawaii (1900–1903), 9 June 1926.

Henry Algernon du Pont, 88, U.S. army officer (1861–1875) serving through Civil War, senator (R) from Delaware (1906–1917), associate of E. I. Du Pont de Nemours & Company gunpowder manufacturer, 31 December 1926.

Woodbridge Nathan Ferris, 75, governor (D) of Michigan (1913–1917), senator (1923–1928), 23 March 1928.

Murphy James Foster, 72, governor (D) of Louisiana (1892–1900), senator (1901–1913), 12 June 1921.

David Rowland Francis, 76, governor (D) of Missouri (1889–1893), secretary of the interior (1885–1889) under President Grover Cleveland, promoter and official of the Louisana Purchase Exposition (1903–1904), ambassador to Russia (1916–1917) during President Woodrow Wilson's administration, 15 January 1927.

Lyman Judson Gage, 90, secretary of the treasury (1897–1902) during the McKinley and Theodore Roosevelt administrations, staunch defender of the gold standard, 26 January 1927.

Helen Hamilton Gardener, 72, woman's suffrage activist, first female member of the U.S. Civil Service Commission, 26 July 1925.

Martin Henry Glynn, 53, representative (D) from New York (1899–1901), governor (1913–1915), 14 December 1924.

Samuel Gompers, 74, labor leader, organizer (1886), with others, and president (1886–1894, 1896–1924) of American Federation of Labor, member of Council of National Defense (1917) and Commission on International Labor Legislation at Treaty of Versailles (1919), 13 December 1924.

Frank R. Gooding, 68, governor (R) of Idaho, (1905–1909), senator (1921–1928), 24 June 1928.

Warren Gamaliel Harding, 57, senator from Ohio (1915–1921), twenty-ninth U.S. president (1921–1923), 2 August 1923.

Dudley Mays Hughes, 78, representative (D) from Georgia (1909–1917), leader of agricultural interests, 20 January 1927.

Claude Kitchin, 54, representative (D) from North Carolina (1901–1923), 31 May 1923.

William Walton Kitchin, 48, representative (D) from North Carolina (1897–1909), governor (1909–1913), 9 November 1924.

Philander Chase Knox, 68, attorney general (R, 1901–1904) during President Theodore Roosevelt's administration who drew up legislation creating U.S. Department of Commerce and Labor (1903), senator from Pennsylvania (1904–1909, 1917–1921), secretary of state (1909–1913), under President Taft, 12 October 1921.

Edwin Fremont Ladd, 65, senator (R) from North Dakota (1921–1925), 22 June 1925.

Robert Marion La Follette, 70, representative (R) from Wisconsin (1885–1891), governor (1901–1906), senator (1906–1925), conservationist who helped launch senatorial investigation into Teapot Dome oil-reserve leasing, Progressive Party presidential candidate in 1924, 18 June 1925.

Robert Lansing, 64, secretary of state (D) during President Wilson's administration (1915–1920), arranged purchase (1917) of Danish West Indies (later named Virgin Islands), 30 October 1928.

Robert Todd Lincoln, 82, son of Abraham Lincoln, secretary of war (1881–1885) during President James Garfield's administration, minister to Great Britain (1889–1893), 26 July 1926.

Charles Augustus Lindbergh Sr., 65, representative (R) from Minnesota (1907–1917), 24 May 1924.

Henry Cabot Lodge, 74, representative (R) from Massachusetts (1887–1893), senator (1893–1924), 9 November 1924.

Meyer London, 54, labor leader, founder (1899–1901), with others, of Socialist party of America, representative (Socialist) from New York (1915–1919, 1921–1923), 6 June 1926.

Martin Barnaby Madden, 73, representative (R) from Illinois (1905–1928), 27 April 1928.

James Robert Mann, 66, representative (R) from Illinois (1897–1922), 30 November 1922.

Thomas Riley Marshall, 71, governor (D) of Indiana (1909–1913), vice president of the United States under Woodrow Wilson (1913–1921), 1 June 1925.

Samuel Walker McCall, 72, representative (R) from Massachusetts (1893–1913), governor (1916–1919), 4 November 1923.

Medill McCormick, 47, representative (R) from Illinois (1917–1919), senator (1919–1925), 25 February 1925.

Frank Joseph McNulty, 53, representative (D) from New Jersey (1923–1925), labor leader, 26 May 1926.

Thomas Chipman McRae, 77, representative (D) from Arkansas (1887–1903), governor (1921–1925), 2 June 1929.

Edwin Thomas Meredith, 51, secretary of agriculture (D, 1920–1921) during President Wilson's administration, 17 June 1928.

William W. Morrow, 86, representative (R) from California (1885–1891), federal judge (1891–1923), 24 July 1929.

Levi Parsons Morton, 96, representative (R) from New York (1879–1881), U.S. minister to France (1881–1885), vice president of the United States under Benjamin Harrison (1889–1893), governor of New York (1895–1897), 16 May 1920.

Knute Nelson, 80, representative (R) from Minnesota (1883–1889), governor (1893–1895), senator (1895–1923), 28 April 1923.

Alton Brooks Parker, 73, Democratic presidential candidate in 1904, 10 May 1926.

Austin Peay, 51, governor (D) of Tennessee (1923–1927), 2 October 1927.

Boies Penrose, 61, senator (R) from Pennsylvania (1897–1921), 31 December 1921.

Richard Franklin Pettigrew, 78, first senator (R) from South Dakota (1889–1901), 5 October 1926.

Pinckney Benton Stewart Pinchback, 84, son of a white planter and Negro slave who organized volunteer Negro company for service with Union army in the Civil War (1862–1863), Louisiana Reconstruction politician, lieutenant governor (1871), acting governor (1872–1873), elected as U.S. representative (1872) and senator (1873) but was not seated, 21 December 1921.

Terence Vincent Powderly, 75, labor leader, general master workman for Knights of Labor (1883–1893), U.S. commissioner general of immigration (1897–1902) under President McKinley, chief of Division of Information in Bureau of Immigration (1907–1921), 24 June 1924.

Samuel Moffett Ralston, 67, governor (D) of Indiana (1913–1917), senator (1923–1925), 14 October 1925.

Willard Saulsbury Jr., 55, senator (D) from Delaware (1913–1919), 20 February 1927.

John Franklin Shafroth, 67, representative (D) from Colorado (1895–1905), governor (1909–1913), senator (1913–1919), 20 February 1922.

William Graves Sharp, 63, representative (D) from Ohio (1909–1915), ambassador to France during World War I, 17 November 1922.

Isaac Ruth Sherwood, 90, representative (D) from Ohio (1907–1921, 1923–1925), 15 October 1925.

Harry Skinner, 73, representative (Populist) from North Carolina (1895–1899), 19 May 1929.

Walter Inglewood Smith, 59, representative (R) from Iowa (1901–1911), served on Eighth Circuit Court of Appeals (1911–1922), 27 January 1922.

William Cameron Sproul, 57, governor (R) of Pennsylvania (1919–1923), 21 March 1928.

Watson Carvosso Squire, 88, governor of the Territory of Washington (1884–1887), senator (R) from Washington (1889–1897), 7 June 1926.

Edward Reilly Stettinius, 60, partner (1916–1925) in J. P. Morgan & Co., chief purchasing agent in United States for the allied governments during World War I, 3 September 1925.

Joseph Kemp Toole, 77, first governor (D) of Montana (1889–1893, 1901–1908), 11 March 1929.

Lawrence Davis Tyson, 68, senator (D) from Tennessee (1925–1929), 24 August 1929.

Oscar Wilder Underwood, 66, representative (D) from Alabama (1895–1896, 1897–1915), senator (1915–1927), chairman of the Committee on Ways and Means (1911–1915), 25 January 1929.

Henry Cantwell Wallace, 58, secretary of agriculture (R, 1921–1924) in Harding and Coolidge administrations, 25 October 1924.

Francis E. Warren, 85, senator (R) from Wyoming (1890–1893, 1895–1929), 24 November 1929.

Thomas Edward Watson, representative (Populist) from Georgia (1891–1893), Populist nominee for vice president in 1896 and president in 1904, senator (1921–1922), publisher of violent segregationist and anti-Semitic newspaper *Weekly Jeffersonian*, 26 September 1922.

John Wingate Weeks, 66, representative (R) from Massachusetts (1905–1913), senator (1913–1919), secretary of war (1921–1925) in Harding and Coolidge administrations, 12 July 1926.

Thomas Woodrow Wilson, 67, twenty-eighth U.S. president (1913–1921), 3 February 1924.

Maj. Gen. Leonard Wood, 66, military governor of Cuba (1899–1902), U.S. army chief of staff (1910–1914), governor general of the Philippines (1921–1927), candidate for the Republican nomination for the presidency in 1916 and 1920, 7 August 1927.

Luke Edward Wright, 76, secretary of war during President Theodore Roosevelt's administration, 17 November 1922.

# PUBLICATIONS

---

Hayes Baker-Crothers, *Problems of Citizenship* (New York: Holt, 1924);

Nan Britton, *The President's Daughter* (New York: Elizabeth Ann Guild, 1927);

Nicholas Murray Butler, *Faith of a Liberal: Essays and Addresses on Political Principles and Public Policies* (New York: Scribners, 1924);

William Seal Carpenter, *Democracy and Representation* (Princeton: Princeton University Press, 1925);

Carrie Chapman Catt, *Woman Suffrage and Politics: the Inner Story of the Suffrage Movement* (New York: Scribners, 1923);

Calvin Coolidge, *Autobiography of Calvin Coolidge* (New York: Cosmopolitan Book Corporation, 1929);

Albert Russell Ellingwood, *Government and Labor* (Chicago: A. W. Shaw, 1926);

Charles Norman Fay, *Business in Politics: Suggestions for Leaders in American Business* (Cambridge, Mass.: Cosmos Press, 1926);

Charles Grove Haines, *Principles and Problems of Government* (New York: Harper, 1926);

Florence Jaffray Harriman, *From Pinafores to Politics* (New York: Holt, 1923);

Frederic J. Haskin, *American Government* (Washington, D.C.: F. J. Haskin, 1924);

Frederick Emory Haynes, *Social Politics in the United States* (Boston: Houghton Mifflin, 1924);

Arthur Norman Holcome, *Political Parties of Today: A Study in Republican and Democratic Politics* (New York: Harper, 1924);

Herbert Hoover, *American Individualism* (Garden City, N.Y.: Doubleday, Page, 1922);

Hoover, *New Day: Campaign Speeches of Herbert Hoover* (Stanford: Stanford University Press, 1928);

David Franklin Houston, *Eight Years with Wilson's Cabinet, 1913 to 1920: With a Personal Estimate of the President* (Garden City: N.Y.: Doubleday, Page, 1926);

Will Irwin, *Herbert Hoover: A Reminiscent Biography* (New York: Century, 1928);

Sinclair Lewis, *The Man Who Knew Coolidge, Being the Soul of Lowell Schmaltz, Constructive and Nordic Citizen* (New York: Harcourt, Brace, 1928);

Philip H. Love, *Andrew W. Mellon, the Man and His Work* (Baltimore: F. H. Coggins, 1929);

Jay Lovestone, *Government — Strikebreaker: A Study of the Role of the Government in the Recent Industrial Crisis* (New York: Workers Party of America, 1923);

Chester Collins Maxey, *Problem of Government, with Special Reference to American Institutions and Conditions* (New York: Knopf, 1925);

William Gibbs McAdoo, *The Challenge: Liquor and Lawlessness Versus Constitutional Government* (New York: Century, 1928);

Gaston Bullock Means, *The Strange Death of President Harding, from the Diaries of Gaston B. Means, as Told to May Dixon Thacker* (New York: Guild Publishing, 1930);

Andrew William Mellon, *Taxation: The People's Business* (New York: Macmillan, 1924);

Conference Committee on the Merit System, *Merit System in Government* (New York: National Municipal League, 1926);

Charles Merriam, *American Party System: An Introduction to the Study of Political Parties in the United States* (New York: Macmillan, 1924);

William Bennett Munro, *Government of the United States: National, State, and Local* (New York: Macmillan, 1925);

Louise Overacker, *The Presidential Primary* (New York: Macmillan, 1926);

Edith May Phelps, *Restriction of Immigration* (New York: Wilson, 1924);

William Gunn Shepherd, *The Boys' Own Book of Politics for Uncle Sam's Young Voters* (New York: Macmillan, 1923);

Alpheus Henry Snow, *American Philosophy of Government* (New York: Putman, 1921);

Mary Synon, *McAdoo, the Man and His Times: A Panorama in Democracy* (Indianapolis: Bobbs-Merrill, 1924);

Robert Morris Washburn, *Calvin Coolidge; His First Biography: From Cornerstone to Capstone to the Accession* (Boston: Small, Maynard, 1923);

William Allen White, *Calvin Coolidge, the Man Who is President* (New York: Macmillan, 1925);

Leonard Wood, *Leonard Wood on National Issues, the Many-Sided Mind of a Great Executive Shown by his Public Utterances* (Garden City, N.Y.: Doubleday, Page, 1920);

James Albert Woodburn, *American Politics: Political Parties and Party Problems in the United States* (New York: Putnam, 1924);

*Atlantic Monthly*, periodical;

*Congressional Digest*, periodical, founded in 1921;

*The Independent*, periodical;

*The Nation*, periodical;

*The New Republic*, periodical;

*Time*, periodical, founded in 1923.

# LAW AND JUSTICE

by MILES RICHARDS

## CONTENTS

*Sidebars and tables are listed in italics.*

## 1920

**2 Jan.**     Federal agents begin nationwide raids on suspected political radicals. More than four thousand people are detained in thirty-three cities.

**5 Jan.**     The U.S. Supreme Court upholds the constitutionality of the Volstead Act, the legislative measure passed to implement the Eighteenth Amendment, which Congress had declared ratified on 29 January 1919. The amendment prohibits the manufacture, sale, or transport of alcoholic beverages in the United States.

**16 Jan.**    Prohibition officially begins.

**19 Apr.**    The U.S. Supreme Court rules that to implement an international treaty, Congress may enact legislation that otherwise might be construed as a violation of an individual state's sovereignty.

**5 May**      Nicola Sacco and Bartolomeo Vanzetti, known anarchists, are arrested for the murder of two men during a payroll robbery in South Braintree, Massachusetts, some weeks earlier.

**15 May**     Chicago gangster "Big Jim" Colosimo, who has been shot to death, is given the first "gangland funeral." It is attended by movie and opera stars, judges, and, Johnny Torrio, who was suspected of having arranged the hit.

**7 June**     The U.S. Supreme Court rules that the Eighteenth Amendment is constitutional. This ruling abrogates all existing state laws that permit the sale of light wines and beer. The justices also declare that Congress has the authority to define what constitutes an intoxicating liquor.

**26 Aug.**    By proclamation President Woodrow Wilson declares the ratification of the Nineteenth Amendment, which prohibits the denial of suffrage based solely on gender.

## 1921

**3 Jan.**     The U.S. Supreme Court rules that a secondary labor boycott initiated during a strike constitutes an illegal restraint of trade, as defined by the Clayton Anti-Trust Act. Such boycotts can therefore be prohibited by federal-court injunctions.

**30 June**    The Senate confirms the appointment of William Howard Taft as chief justice of the U.S. Supreme Court. He is the only former president to serve on that court.

**10 Sept.**   Sacco and Vanzetti are convicted on all charges, including murder. After they are sentenced to death their supporters start a concerted public-defense campaign.

**19 Dec.**    The U.S. Supreme Court voids an Arizona state law forbidding employers to seek court injunctions to bar picketing by striking workers.

**23 Dec.**    President Warren G. Harding pardons Eugene V. Debs, Congressman Victor Berger of Wisconsin, and all others convicted under the Sedition Act of 1918 and other measures designed to curb dissent during World War I.

## 1922

**27 Mar.**    The U.S. Supreme Court declares it lawful for a state judge to issue an order that directs federal authorities to remand a federal prisoner to state custody for prosecution. Such transfers must have the prior assent of the U.S. Department of Justice.

**22 Apr.** A New York State court judge rules that Dr. William J. Johnston, a physician, has violated a state obscenity law by printing and distributing a booklet titled *Love In Marriage.* Johnston is fined $250.

**15 May** The U.S. Supreme Court voids a federal law that places a flat tax on the net profits of a business that employs child labor to produce goods sold through interstate commerce. The majority of the justices view the tax as a retributive measure and as a violation of the sovereign powers reserved to the various states in the Tenth Amendment.

**26 May** President Harding signs a measure creating the Federal Narcotics Control Board.

**22 Sept.** Congress enacts a statute allowing an American woman to retain her citizenship when she marries an alien but denying a foreign woman automatic citizenship upon marrying an American national.

**1 Dec.** The U.S. Supreme Court rules that federal and state authorities both may prosecute a person caught in a specific instance of bootlegging, stating that such joint prosecutions do not violate the double-jeopardy clause of the Fifth Amendment.

# 1923

**9 Apr.** The U.S. Supreme Court rules that a law setting a minimum wage for female workers in the District of Columbia is unconstitutional.

**4 May** The New York General Assembly passes an act that repeals a state prohibition enforcement law. Despite the protest of President Harding, Gov. Alfred E. Smith signs the measure.

**4 June** The U.S. Supreme Court strikes down a Nebraska law that bars the teaching of all foreign languages to grammar-school pupils.

**8 June** The U.S. Supreme Court affirms that an existing New York state law on sedition is constitutional because a "clear and present danger" need not exist to warrant official punitive action.

**15 Sept.** Gov. J. C. Walton of Oklahoma declares martial law because of widespread violence perpetrated by the Ku Klux Klan. Over the next three weeks several thousand Klansmen are detained by state military forces.

**13 Oct.** The administration of President Calvin Coolidge declares its intention to enforce Prohibition stringently through the policing procedures included in the Volstead Act.

# 1924

**28 Mar.** President Coolidge dismisses Attorney General Harry Daugherty for his involvement in various scandals during the Harding administration. Daugherty is succeeded by Harlan Fiske Stone, the dean of Columbia University Law School.

**26 May** President Coolidge signs the National Origins Act, which places strict quotas on the number of European immigrants allowed to enter the United States each year. This legislation also forbids all immigration to the United States from East Asia.

**2 June** Nathan Leopold and Richard Loeb are arrested in Chicago for the kidnap-murder of young Robert Franks. The wealthy Leopold and Loeb families retain famous trial lawyer Clarence Darrow, who mounts an "insanity defense."

**1925**

**15 June** President Coolidge signs legislation making all Native Americans citizens of the United States.

**10 Sept.** Leopold and Loeb are found guilty of murder but are sentenced by "reason of insanity" to life imprisonment rather than death.

**9 Dec.** President Coolidge nominates Attorney General Stone to fill a vacancy on the U.S. Supreme Court.

**19 Dec.** Stone persuades Coolidge to appoint Acting Director J. Edgar Hoover as the permanent head of the Federal Bureau of Investigation (FBI).

**28 Jan.** Stone is questioned by the full Senate Judiciary Committee, becoming the first Supreme Court nominee to undergo scrutiny by the committee.

**2 Feb.** The Senate confirms Stone's appointment to the U.S. Supreme Court by an overwhelming margin of 71–6.

**4 Feb.** Charles R. Forbes, head of the Veterans' Bureau under President Harding, is sentenced to two years in prison for fraud, conspiracy, and bribery.

**Mar.** After escaping an attempt on his life, Chicago gang boss Johnny Torrio hands over his crime empire to Al Capone and retires to Italy with between $10 million and $30 million.

**3 Mar.** The U.S. Supreme Court upholds the right of federal prohibition agents to confiscate all alcoholic beverages that are found during routine searches of automobiles. The court rules that such searches are not violations of the Fourth Amendment.

**5 May** John T. Scopes, a high-school science teacher, is arrested in Dayton, Tennessee, for violating a state law that bars the teaching of evolution in public schools.

**6 May** The U.S. Treasury Department uses U.S. Coast Guard vessels to wage an all-out campaign against rumrunners who have been increasing the scope of their activities along the Atlantic Seaboard.

**1 June** The U.S. Supreme Court abrogates an Oregon law that makes it compulsory for all children between the ages of eight and sixteen to attend public school.

**28 June** At a conference in Chicago a coalition of radical political groups creates the International Labor Defense Fund (ILDF) to help various "political prisoners" procure legal assistance against criminal prosecution.

**10 July** In Dayton, Tennessee, the Scopes "Monkey" Trial begins. Clarence Darrow leads the defense; William Jennings Bryan assists the prosecution.

**21 July** Scopes is found guilty and pays a minimal fine.

**9 Sept.** A white mob in Detroit, Michigan, attacks the home of Dr. Ossian Sweet, an African American physician who has recently moved into an all-white neighborhood. After firing on the crowd in self-defense and killing one attacker, Sweet and eleven associates are arrested for murder.

**21 Nov.** David C. Stephenson, grand dragon of the Ku Klux Klan in Indiana, is found guilty of second-degree murder. His conviction damages the prestige of the Klan in the Midwest.

## 1926

**27 Jan.** The Senate approves a treaty that permits U.S. membership in the Permanent Court of International Justice at The Hague, Netherlands.

**12 Feb.** After two inconclusive trials prosecutors drop murder charges against all defendants in the Sweet case except one, Ossian Sweet's brother Henry.

**19 Feb.** The U.S. Supreme Court rules that a defendant's right to a fair trial, as guaranteed by the Sixth Amendment, would be denied if a "mob atmosphere" dominates trial proceedings.

**14 May** With Clarence Darrow as his defense attorney, Henry Sweet is declared innocent by an all-white jury.

**24 May** The U.S. Supreme Court declares the constitutionality of restrictive property covenants, discriminatory pacts designed to prevent members of various minorities from residing within a community. The court rules that such covenants violate neither the Fourteenth nor the Fifteenth Amendment.

## 1927

**5 Jan.** The Massachusetts General Court (legislature) enacts the first compulsory auto-insurance law in the United States, requiring all Massachusetts drivers to have $5,000 to $10,000 of liability coverage.

**28 Feb.** The U.S. Supreme Court declares that all oil contracts and leases granted to oil magnate Edward L. Doheny by former secretary of the interior Albert B. Fall are illegal, fraudulent, and corrupt.

**3 Mar.** President Coolidge signs legislation that amplifies the Prohibition Bureau within the U.S. Treasury Department.

**7 Mar.** The U.S. Supreme Court orders the state of Texas to pay an indemnity of $5,000 to L. A. Nixon, an African American who had been denied the right to vote in the Texas Democratic primary election of 1924.

**10 June** After reviewing all surviving evidence, the three-member Lowell Commission, appointed by Gov. Alvan T. Fuller of Massachusetts, declares Sacco and Vanzetti guilty as charged.

**23 Aug.** After the U.S. Supreme Court refuses to grant a final reprieve, Sacco and Vanzetti are executed at the Charlestown (Mass.) State Penitentiary.

**21 Nov.** The U.S. Supreme Court upholds the right of the state of Mississippi to place all nonwhite pupils in segregated public schools.

## 1928

**9 Feb.** The U.S. Supreme Court strikes down a New Jersey law that has created a commission to regulate the business practices of employment agencies operating in that state.

**4 June** The U.S. Supreme Court sustains the right of federal agents to wiretap private telephones during investigations of persons suspected of violating Prohibition laws.

## 1929

**14 Feb.**     Gunmen working for Al Capone, the leading racketeer in Chicago, execute seven members of a rival gang. This crime becomes known as the Saint Valentine's Day Massacre.

**9 Apr.**      The Canadian government protests the sinking of *I'm Alone,* a vessel of Canadian registry, some two hundred miles off the Florida coast by a U.S. Coast Guard cutter whose crew had suspected that the ship was being used by rumrunners.

**20 May**      President Herbert Hoover creates the National Commission on Law Observance and Enforcement to investigate the enforcement of Prohibition and other related problems.

**7 May**       The U.S. Supreme Court sustains the right of the federal government to deny citizenship to any immigrant who directly declares an unwillingness to fulfill military service, whatever the circumstance.

# OVERVIEW

The Advent of Normalcy. For the two decades that preceded the 1920s, the American people had witnessed progressive domestic reform legislation. Millions of them, in varying capacities, had participated in a foreign war to "make the world safe for democracy." By late 1919 public sentiment in the United States favored a return to more tranquil times. The massive Republican electoral triumph in 1920 resulted in Warren G. Harding's ascent to the presidency and comfortable majorities for his party in both houses of Congress. In essence "normalcy" meant a conservative status quo in which few bold initiatives of any sort were attempted. President Harding and his Congressional supporters began filling the federal judiciary with appointees who held an equally conservative perspective in the area of jurisprudence.

The "Great Red Scare." During World War I many resident aliens, citizens of German descent, and antiwar activists were subjected to various forms of official persecution. In fact, the basic civil liberties of all Americans were restricted during the war years. After the conclusion of the fighting in November 1918 this trend was not reversed because there was widespread concern about the activities of radical political leftists. Many observers came to believe that a violent upheaval resembling the Russian Revolution of November 1917 could occur in the United States. Such thinking included a note of xenophobia because so many radicals, especially Marxists, were foreign born. In early January 1920 systematic nationwide round-ups of more than four thousand political dissidents by agents of the U.S. Department of Justice met with great public approval. Some 3,550 detainees of alien extraction were slated for deportation, but President Woodrow Wilson personally abrogated many expulsion orders, and only 556, including the noted radical Emma Goldman, were actually expelled.

A Conservative Supreme Court. The appointment of Chief Justice William Howard Taft in June 1921 accelerated a trend that had existed on the Supreme Court for some years. Taft joined a bloc of sitting justices, including James McReynolds and Edward Sanford, who were confirmed advocates of judicial restraint, the view that it was not the jurists' role to initiate bold change through court rulings. Taft and his allies saw themselves as "legal stewards" who promoted stability by upholding long-standing precedents and doctrines. In the 1920s the conservative majority on the Taft Court remained predominant. Republican presidents filled the court vacancies with nominees loyal to this philosophy. Two progressive associate justices, Oliver Wendell Holmes Jr. and Louis Brandeis, challenged this prevailing assumption in a series of judicial dissents, especially in the area of individual rights. This tandem became popularly known as the "great dissenters." Also in this decade plans were first formulated, at Taft's urging, to remove the Supreme Court from its longtime headquarters in the Capitol Building to a permanent new building.

Modest Challenges to Jim Crow. By the 1920s the virulent white racism of the two preceding decades was subsiding somewhat. Yet segregation remained prevalent in most states, especially in the Deep South. African Americans were still being lynched by white mobs throughout the United States. Powerful southern lawmakers in Congress continued to thwart all efforts to enact national antilynching legislation. The conservative bloc on the Supreme Court consistently declined to challenge the "separate but equal" doctrine first elucidated in 1896 in the case of *Plessy* v. *Ferguson.* The Taft Court, however, was willing in various decisions to make modest modifications in the racial status quo. Also during these years black law schools, such as Howard University in Washington, D.C., were training young lawyers who would later successfully confront Jim Crowism in the legal arena.

The Rise of the G-Man. Although the Bureau of Investigation, an arm of the U.S. Department of Justice, had existed since 1906, it had not been a notable force in American criminal justice prior to the 1920s. Too many agents and supervisors had gained their positions through official patronage, regardless of merit. In December 1924 J. Edgar Hoover began his long tenure as the director of the newly reorganized bureau, which was renamed the Federal Bureau of Investigation (FBI) at Hoover's insistence. He successfully weeded out many of the political hacks and incompetents who had given the organization a reputation for corruption. Beginning in the 1920s, his agents became noted for their strong sense of professionalism.

**A Noble Experiment.** In January 1920 the Eighteenth Amendment to the U.S. Constitution went into legal effect, banning the manufacture, sale, and consumption of alcoholic beverages. For decades organizations such as the Women's Christian Temperance Union and the Anti-Saloon League had lobbied Congress to legislate this amendment. Various states in the predominantly rural South and Midwest had already passed prohibition laws in the 1910s. Prohibition was generally popular among "old stock" Americans who were middle-class, resided in small towns, and were affiliated with the major Protestant denominations. Many of their countrymen living in the major urban areas were opposed to this "noble experiment." Ethnic Americans, many of whom had recently emigrated from eastern and southern Europe, were never able to appreciate the basic thinking behind such legislated morality.

**Law Enforcement and Prohibition.** The enforcement of Prohibition proved difficult from the outset. The respective state and local law enforcement agencies were singularly incapable of coordinating such efforts. The Eighteenth Amendment became law before a federal police entity was organized to enforce its provisions. J. Edgar Hoover repeatedly spurned all requests that the FBI assume such a role, and the Department of Justice never wanted any such an agency to operate under its control. It was not until March 1927 that Congress passed legislation that strengthened the enforcement powers of the Prohibition Bureau, which was under the jurisdiction of the Department of the Treasury.

**The Rise of the Bootlegger.** Those individuals who manufactured liquor in defiance of the Eighteenth Amendment were popularly called bootleggers. Prior to Prohibition, urban juvenile street gangs, usually based in ethnic working-class neighborhoods, had engaged in a wide range of petty lawbreaking activities. After January 1920 these gangs turned their primary attention to bootlegging. Any criminal with good local political connections could pursue a career that offered the potential for wealth.

**The Bootleggers and Chicago.** Many American cities witnessed lethal battles between rival gangs who sought to dominate the illicit liquor business within their designated "territories." In the public mind, though, such bloody "turf wars" were invariably associated with Chicago. That city was the headquarters of such notorious major bootleggers as Al Capone, Dion O'Banion, and Johnny Torrio.

**A Result of Prohibition.** Prior to the end of Prohibition in 1933, bootlegging outfits began to diversify their criminal endeavors. Besides controlling such long-standing illicit activities as prostitution and gambling, gangsters invested their "booze" profits in legitimate businesses. To avoid the bloody gang warfare of the Prohibition Era, major underworld figures such as Meyer Lansky and Frank Costello of New York City sought to create a national criminal syndicate. A lasting, unintended legacy of the "noble experiment" was modern organized crime.

his family to join him. In northern cities blacks quickly re-created their own communities, establishing churches, southern-style restaurants, and businesses run by former neighbors down south. But not only did African Americans face job discrimination once they came north, they also confronted severe housing discrimination. Blacks were forced to live in severely crowded segregated neighborhoods where rents were exorbitant. Their migration to northern cities resulted not in an end to Jim Crow segregation but rather in the establishment of new forms of de facto urban segregation in schools, swimming pools, restaurants, and theaters.

**First Black Mass Movement.** The New Negro contributed to urban culture in the 1920s through the flourishing in jazz, art, and literature known as the Harlem Renaissance; this increasingly militant figure also became part of the first black mass movement of the twentieth century, the Back to Africa Movement led by Marcus Garvey. Garvey, who had established the Universal Negro Improvement Association in Jamaica in 1914 to "draw the peoples of the race together," delivered a message of pride that attracted urban blacks in the United States. He hoped to establish in Africa a strong black nation that would offer protection and opportunity to blacks everywhere. Garvey's movement lost steam after his conviction for mail fraud in 1925, but it continued to stimulate positive racial identity and militancy in many African Americans of the 1920s and later.

Sources:
James R. Grossman, *Land of Hope: Chicago, Black Southerners, and the Great Migration* (Chicago: University of Chicago Press, 1989);

Nathan Huggins, *Harlem Renaissance* (New York: Oxford University Press, 1971);

Judith Stein, *The World of Marcus Garvey: Race and Class in Modern Society* (Baton Rouge: Louisiana State University Press, 1986).

## BACKLASH

**History.** Ku Klux Klan (KKK) activism and violence in the 1920s represented a reaction by some native-born, Protestant whites to the growing diversification of American society and an effort to impose their version of law and order on it. Based on the vigilante group that sprung up in the post–Civil War South, a new KKK emerged in 1915 at Stone Mountain, Georgia, when sixteen men lit a cross symbolizing the Klan's resurrection. Between 1920 and 1925 the group quickly grew until it had five million members. Klansmen, who viewed themselves as embodying "100 percent Americanism," shared an antipathy to blacks, Jews, Catholics, and immigrants.

**KKK Methods.** The Klan primarily used violent viligantism to terrorize so-called moral offenders, but it also worked through political channels. In the early 1920s the Klan dominated politics in Indiana, Texas, Oklahoma, and Colorado. It deadlocked the 1924 Democratic National Convention by successfully opposing the condemnation of the Klan by name. The group lobbied on the national level for laws restricting immigration. Be-

cause of its excesses, the organization lost most of its strength by the end of the decade.

Source:
David Mark Chalmers, *Hooded Americanism: The History of the Ku Klux Klan*, third edition (Durham, N.C.: Duke University Press, 1987).

## THE BIRTH CONTROL MOVEMENT

**The Campaigner.** Women from all economic classes gained greater ability to limit pregnancy in the 1920s as a result of the effort of nurse and birth control advocate Margaret Sanger, who vowed to "do something to change the destiny of mothers whose miseries were as vast as the sky." By 1914 Sanger was determined to remove the stigma of obscenity from contraception and to set up a nationwide network of advice centers on birth control for women. She first had to find a safe, reliable method of birth control and, in 1915, traveled to Europe, where she learned about the diaphragm. By the 1920s Sanger broke her ties with radical colleagues, a shift in approach that won her the support of powerful, conservative groups such as physicians, philanthropists, and wealthy women.

**The Triumph.** In 1921 Sanger organized the American Birth Control League, which changed its name to the Planned Parenthood Federation of America in 1942. In 1923 she opened the Birth Control Clinical Research Bureau in New York City, the first doctor-staffed birth-control clinic in the United States. The bureau, which refuted claims that diaphragms cause cancer and madness, became a model for the network of more than three hundred clinics established by Sanger across the country by 1938. Throughout the 1920s and 1930s Sanger worked tirelessly to raise money for these clinics and fought for the reversal of laws that had labeled birth control information obscene. In 1937 the mailing of contraceptive material became legal, and birth control was affirmed as a legitimate medical service to be taught in medical schools.

Sources:
Ellen Chesler, *Women of Valor: Margaret Sanger and the Birth Control Movement in America* (New York: Simon & Schuster, 1992);

David M. Kennedy, *Birth Control in America: The Career of Margaret Sanger* (New Haven: Yale University Press, 1991).

## BOOSTERISM

**Civic Philosophy.** Although the concept of "boosting" a town or region began in the late nineteenth century, the phenomenon of boosterism reached its peak of popularity during the 1920s. Boosterism was a civic philosophy that aimed to advertise towns and cities, promote economic development, foster tourism, and increase civic pride. Business, boosters claimed, was an indispensable part of society: commercial development led directly to improvements in all aspects of life in a town or city. This philosophy manifested itself loudly and brashly during the decade. Citizens, boosters insisted, should have "pep" and aim continuously to "push" their communities' advantages. Anyone criticizing elements of local life were likely to be labeled "knockers" and opponents to progress. The phenomenon of boosterism was a product of the changing nature of American economic life. The sharp increase in commercial occupations such as sales, management, and advertising left more and more men in an ambiguous social position. They fit neither the traditional category of professionals, such as doctors and lawyers, nor that of skilled craftsmen. The philosophy of boosterism gave these Americans a sense of purpose and value in their communities. The emphasis placed on community service by civic clubs and chambers of commerce allowed businessmen to consider themselves motivated by more than personal financial gain; it allowed them to claim an important contributing role in their towns and cities.

**Service Clubs.** During the 1920s the number of civic and service clubs for businessmen grew rapidly. The Kiwanis Club expanded from 205 chapters in 1920 to 1,800 in 1929. The first Lions Club was founded in 1917; by 1930 there were more than 1,200 worldwide. The Rotary Club — the oldest service organization in the country — had been founded in 1905 and saw its ranks swell to 150,000 members by the end of the 1920s. Although these clubs were established to foster fraternity among local businessmen, as they grew they increasingly emphasized community service as part of their purpose. The Lions Club, for example, became well known for campaigns to raise money for the blind. The Shriner's Club united behind an effort to aid crippled children. Other activities of the clubs included monthly luncheons featuring motivational speakers and group songs and programs designed to promote belief in business and commerce. For businessmen, the service clubs offered a means of establishing friendship with their peers, furthering their own commercial interests, and contributing to the improvement of their communities.

**Chambers of Commerce.** More formal than the service clubs were the hundreds of local chambers of commerce that flourished during the 1920s. At the turn of the century most chambers of commerce had existed solely to improve the business climate in their respective towns. Over the course of the decade the organizations increasingly took on the role of advancing social cohesion and enriching municipal life. Chamber activities were varied: erecting street signs; organizing local celebrations such as festivals, field days, and parades; conducting campaigns for fire prevention and civic beautification; and erecting billboards to promote their cities' attractions and historical sites. Sociologists Robert and Helen Lynd reported that during a single month in 1924, 151 different meetings sponsored by 41 organizations were conducted in the chamber of commerce building in Muncie, Indiana. By the end of the decade chambers of commerce had become a permanent part of American civil life.

**Intellectual Backlash.** As boosterism became popular among the nation's businessmen, it drew attacks from

Shipwreck Kelley, the best known of the 1920s flagpole sitters

writers and other critics. Service clubs and town promotion campaigns, they claimed, typified the conformity, tastelessness, and greed which underlay American society. Sinclair Lewis, who satirized boosters in novels such as *Main Street* (1920) and *Babbitt* (1922), became the leading voice in the antiboosterism vanguard. Lewis and other satirists focused on the trappings and excesses of boosterism — particularly on the slogans and rhetoric of service-club members — and rarely discussed its more serious characteristics. As a result, boosterism is remembered today as a pejorative term for the offensive aspects of business culture in the 1920s. The noise and silliness of booster rhetoric would be tempered by the Depression, but the essential philosophy behind boosterism remains widely accepted.

Sources:

Frederick Lewis Allen, *Only Yesterday* (New York: Harper & Row, 1931);

Robert S. Lynd and Helen Merrell Lynd, *Middletown: A Study in Contemporary American Culture* (New York: Harcourt, Brace, 1929);

Elmer T. Peterson, "A Defense of Boosters," *Saturday Evening Post*, 198 (30 January 1926): 16, 88, 93.

## FADS AND CRAZES

**Crossword Puzzles.** In 1924 Richard Leo Simon and Max Lincoln Schuster published their first volume, *The Cross Word Puzzle Book*, which was also the world's first collection of crossword puzzles. Simon and Schuster were

"By 1920 there were at least five types of places for dancing open to the public. There were dances sponsored by social-work agencies, particularly those concerned with juvenile behavior. Some municipalities, in fact, established their own dancehalls where, under close supervision, young people could dance free or for a small charge. These, of course, tended to draw almost wholly adolescents. Second, there were club dances, lodge dances, 'charity balls,' and the like, sponsored by ethnic groups, police or firemen, athletic clubs, fraternal societies, and similar organizations, open to the public for a token 'membership fee.' These dances had been traditionally part of city life since the earlier nineteenth century, chiefly at the lower and lower-middle class economic and social level. The 'fireman's ball,' since the days of volunteer firefighters, had always meant rowdyism, deservedly or not. Third, there was public dancing at hotels, restricted to guests or a socially desirable clientele; at restaurants; and at cabarets or night clubs, which often provided vaudeville-type entertainment in addition to food and drink. (Beyond city limits these were usually termed 'roadhouses.') Since high costs naturally restricted attendance to the urban minority who could afford it, the hotel ballroom and cabaret were almost exclusively big-city places.

The fourth kind of public dancehall, the 'taxi-dance' ballroom, drew more customers and much more criticism. A few so-called 'open' taxi-dance halls allowed women to enter; most were 'closed,' that is, for men only, offering 'hostesses' or "instructresses" for partners. Taxi-dance halls charged an admission fee and sold tickets to be exchanged for each dance, which lasted about 60 seconds, followed by an intermission of 30–60 seconds. The standard price was 10 cents a dance, sometimes two for 25 cents or 40 cents for three in better establishments, the girls retaining half of the ticket charge plus tips. Large city dancehalls offered 200 to 300 hostesses; a survey in New York in 1925 showed about 8,000 girls so employed in the city. A hostess, by collecting 70–100 tickets per night plus tips, could make about $30 a week, as compared to $18–$20 a week for office work.

Although licensed and regulated, these taxi-dance halls were under constant attack throughout the twenties and thirties. The Commissioner of Licenses for New York City, after a four-month survey in 1924, found 'immoral behavior' in twenty per cent of them, that is, drinking, drug peddling, 'sensual and promiscuous dancing' and prostitution 'A fringe of immorality is constant with every dancehall' of this type, an investigator for the Women's City Club reported that year. All were closed in the early thirties and allowed to reopen only after close inspection; they were banned completely from the grounds of the Chicago World's Fair of 1933. Nonetheless the hardy ones survived, and a few still do, although in depleted numbers since the mid-forties.

The fifth type of public dancehall, and by far the most widely attended in the twenties, was the 'dance palace' (which might also be at an amusement park or outdoor pavilion) a direct descendant of the original Grand Central of the pre-World War I years. Huge, brilliantly lighted, elaborately decorated with gilt, drapes, columns, mirrors, and ornate chandeliers, often with two bands, these became synonymous with glamor and romance. Capable of holding crowds of 5,000, these Gardens, Palaces, Parks, and Ballrooms attracted millions of patrons yearly — six million in New York City alone in 1924, nearly that many in Chicago. Every city or country town had one or more, for singles of both sexes and young and older marrieds. The range of age was about 16–50, most patrons in their twenties, men usually outnumbering women by about 20%. An admission fee — $1 to $1.50 for singles and $2.00 for a couple — ordinarily entitled one to 3–5 dances, after which tickets at 5–10 cents admitted a couple to the floor which was guarded by velvet ropes and uniformed ticket-takers. New York's Roseland and Savoy, Chicago's Trianon and Aragon, Boston's Raymor, the Hollywood Palladium and the Palomar in Los Angeles, Detroit's Greystone, Cleveland's Crystal Slipper, Cincinnati's Castle Farms, Denver's Elitch's Garden, and many more had nation reputations, but every small town had its Avalon, Dreamland, or Paradise."

so concerned the book might fail that they published it under a separate imprint, Plaza Publishing Company, to conceal their identities. They attached a pencil to each copy, vigorously advertised it, and turned crosswords into a nationwide rage. The Baltimore and Ohio Railroad put dictionaries on their trains to help puzzle players. A headline in the Ohio State University student newspaper in February 1925 read: "Cross Word Puzzle Craze Gripping American Campuses." College newspapers published puzzles, college teams competed in puzzle contests, and the University of Kentucky offered a course in crosswords, approved by a dean who commented that

The Mah-Jongg craze intensified during the 1920s; but this photo is a posed publicity gimmick.

crosswords were "educational, scientific, instructive and mentally stimulative as well as entertaining."

**Emile Coué's Twelve-Word Mind Cure.** "Day by day in every way I am getting better and better." This sentence, repeated over and over, was French pharmacist Emile Coué's simple formula for health and happiness. When Coué, a supersalesman, brought his system of "Self-Mastery by Auto-Suggestion" to the United States, masses of suggestible Americans swallowed his prescription whole. Coué's notion was that a person's imagination was his strongest faculty, capable of winning any contest with internal or external negative forces. Coué made his first tour of the United States in 1923 and had to fight off crowds of followers.

**Cures — and Denunciations — of Coué.** The American Medical Association attacked Coué as "a purveyor of cloudy stuff" whose system of healing would bring "tears of laughter and pity" from real doctors. In spite of this denunciation, the Frenchman conducted a second popular cross-country lecture tour in 1924. Although his followers insisted that his cure healed varicose veins and

grew hair on bald heads, Coué himself claimed more modest results. He announced that a man seized by yawning cut his yawns from seven per minute to one every ninety minutes under his "treatment"; he also demonstrated that two stuttering boys could say "good morning" and "I won't stutter anymore" without a slip. Coué Institutes opened in cities across the country, but by the middle of the decade patients abandoned them. In truth sick people did not get "better and better" with Coué's mind cure.

**Mah-Jongg.** The ancient Chinese game of Mah-Jongg, introduced in the United States in 1922, had millions of enthusiasts playing within a year. Members of women's Mah-Jongg clubs shouted Mah-Jongg words — "Pung" and "Chow" — at one another and donned silk kimonos to play in proper attire. The game also caught on in colleges, rivaling bridge as a staple of fraternity and dormitory entertainment. Mah-Jongg, a combination of dominoes and dice, required a set of 144 carved bone tiles. In 1923 Mah-Jongg sets outsold radios, and Chinese manufacturers ran out of calf bones used to make the

John B. Watson's theories of Behaviorism became widely influential during the 1920s.

tiles. American manufacturers soon entered production, and beef packers in Chicago sent bones to China for carving by Chinese artisans. A fine Mah-Jongg set from China sold for $500 in the United States, though American-made celluloid copies soon sold for just a few dollars. The difficult and constantly changing rules of the game inspired more than twenty rule books during the decade, and Chinese Americans often were recruited to teach novice American enthusiasts.

**Flagpole Sitting.** Alvin "Shipwreck" Kelly, the most famous flagpole sitter of the 1920s, called himself "The Luckiest Fool Alive." Kelly, a former boxer, started sitting on flagpoles in Hollywood in 1924 when a theater hired him to draw crowds. He balanced himself on a small disk with stirrups to prevent him from falling, took five minute naps every hour, and consumed only liquids hoisted to him on ropes. Kelly was quickly in demand as a publicity gimmick for hotels and theaters, and in 1929 he sat for a total of 145 days on various flagpoles. Kelly popularized flagpole sitting across the country; in Baltimore twenty flagpole sitters — three of them women — were in action during a single week in 1929.

**Dance Marathons.** "Of all the crazy competitions ever invented, the dancing marathon wins by a considerable margin of lunacy." So exclaimed the *New York World* in 1923. At contests across the country, couples danced for days on end and competed for thousands of dollars in prize money. Since winning the contest depended on being the last couple to drop out or collapse, dancers used

every method to keep their partners awake: some offered smelling salts and ice packs, others kicked and punched their partners. In 1928 ninety-one couples lasted nearly three weeks in the $5,000 "Dance Derby of the Century," which was closed down after 482 hours.

**First American Dance Marathoner.** The first American to set a record was Alma Cummings. A thirty-two-year old dance teacher at the Audubon Ballroom in New York City, Cummings had six male partners, all younger than she, and remained in motion on the dance floor for twenty-seven hours. She conserved enough energy to end with a flourish, spinning to the middle of the floor in a whirlwind waltz to the cheers of her audience. Her achievement, on 1 April 1923, surpassed the existing record set in England. It also, according to one observer, challenged the primacy of youth and the preeminence of male fortitude. Within weeks dance-endurance contests spread to cities across the country.

**Dance Marathon Records.** Less than a month after Alma Cummings's triumph, eight young people, who had already danced a record twenty-eight hours and fifty minutes at the Audubon Ballroom, were warned that the police were about to raid the place. Law enforcement officers were invoking an old statute that pertained to six-day bicycle races and made it illegal for any contestant to participate in a race or contest for more than twelve hours in a twenty-four hour period. The contestants eluded the police with the help of parents and friends, who at midnight provided them with a van that transported the still-moving dancers to the Edgewater Dock in New York. They danced off the van and onto a ferry that took them across the Hudson River to New Jersey. Urged by Fort Lee, New Jersey, police to move on, they reached a hospitable destination in Connecticut, where Vera Shepard finally set a new record: sixty-nine hours of continuous dancing in three states, two dance halls, one private parlor, four moving vans, and a ferry. But her record had already been topped in Cleveland — by June Curry, who danced for ninety hours and ten minutes.

Sources:

Frank M. Calabria, "The Dance Marathon Craze," *Journal of Popular Culture*, 10, no. 1 (1976): 54–67;

Paul Sann, *Fads, Follies and Delusions of the American People* (New York: Bonanza Books, 1968);

*This Fabulous Century* (New York: Time-Life Books, 1988).

## FREUDIANISM

**Freud's Idea.** Sigmund Freud's theories enjoyed great popularity in the 1920s. Aspects of his work made their way into everyday conversation, journalism, and literature. Before his time, psychology had been overwhelmingly concerned with the intellect, regarding conscious perceptions and ideas as the fundamental factors of mental health. In opposition to this focus on the surface of the mind, Freud claimed that "subconscious" urges, desires, and inhibitions dominated human behavior. According to his theories, traumas suffered in childhood were often forgotten or "repressed" by the conscious mind only to dominate the subconscious, manifesting themselves in neurotic behavior or even serious mental illness. The practical goal of Freud's psychoanalytic method was to cure mental illness by discovering its hidden causes, which, when brought to the surface, could be addressed and resolved.

**Freudianism's Vogue in the 1920s.** Many people from nonscientific backgrounds were fascinated by the idea of searching for the subconscious causes of their thoughts and actions. Few laypeople, however, actually read Freud. Most often they took their information from one of the many accessible summaries of Freud's work that were available by 1920. Such summaries tended to reduce and distort the original for the mass audience. One successful popularizer was André Tridon, who in 1921 presented a series of lectures in the United States on Freudian psychoanalysis. The simplicity of his talks prompted H. L. Mencken to comment sarcastically that "even a college professor or politician can understand Tridon on 'Psychoanalysis.' "

**Freudianism by the Masses.** By the 1920s such Freudian terms as *repression, sublimation,* and *complex* were in general usage, wielded by citizens who were otherwise ignorant of the intricacies of Freud's theories. Engaging in small talk at parties, people often sought to psychoanalyze one another, to discover the subconscious motivations of themselves and their friends. In this receptive atmosphere, such a concept as personality typing (developed by Carl G. Jung, an early disciple of Freud) was turned into a popular game in which people calculated their own type on the basis of forty simple questions. The game included for comparison the personality types of various celebrities who had taken the test.

**Critics on Popularity.** Such popularity based on accessible catchphrases and ill-understood bits of sophisticated ideas raised objections. Freud himself believed that the immense popularity of his theories was a liability rather than an asset. He felt that laypeople grabbed at the exciting aspects of his ideas, made simple by summaries that omitted complexities, and applied them recklessly and indiscriminately. This viewpoint was shared by many social critics of the period. Critics of Freudianism predominantly chose to attack the popularity of his ideas rather than the scientific validity of the concepts themselves. Within the field of professional psychology, rigorous debate raged over Freud's work, but social commentators tended to reserve their ridicule for amateurs who appropriated ideas and methods that they did not fully understand. Karl Menninger, for instance, claimed that regardless of its scientific accuracy psychoanalysis had "suffered . . . at the hands of those amateurs who think or pretend that they understand it well enough to apply its principles."

**Critics on Vulgarity.** Freudianism's critics were disturbed by more than what they perceived as it vulgar accessibility. Freud's emphasis on sexual repression as a cause of neurosis also offended many sensibilities. Many commentators claimed that by citing the harmful effects of sexual repression, Freudians were encouraging immoral, licentious behavior. Such critics believed that the alleged excesses of the 1920s could be accounted for this way. There was also a mistrust of the hidden, esoteric nature of psychoanalysis's conception of the subconscious. Anti-Freudians were suspicious of attempts to look for obscure motivations for abnormal behavior that might have a simple, obvious cause.

Sources:

Sigmund Freud, *Delusion and Dream,* translated by Helen M. Downey (New York: Moffatt, 1917);

Freud, *Dream Psychology; Psychoanalysis for Beginners* (New York: J. A. McCann, 1921);

Freud, *A General Introduction to Psychoanalysis* (New York: Boni & Liveright, 1920);

Freud, *Group Psychology and the Analysis of the Ego* (New York: Boni & Liveright, 1922);

J. C. Furnas, *Great Times: An Informal Social History of the United States* (New York: Putnam, 1974);

Frederick Hoffman, *The Twenties: American Writing in the Postwar Decade* (New York: Viking, 1955).

## THE IMPACT OF TECHNOLOGY ON DAILY LIFE

**Electricity and Water.** During the 1920s the spread of technology transformed the way average Americans lived their daily lives. In 1920 only 34.7 percent of American dwellings had electricity; by 1930 67.9 percent had electric power. In the cities the growth was even more dramatic: 84.8 percent of all urban homes were wired for electricity by 1930, compared to only 47.4 percent a decade earlier. Hot and cold running water, which had been available only to the upper classes at the turn of the century, also became common, particularly in urban areas. In 1929 the President's Conference on Home Building and Home Ownership reported that 71 percent of urban homes had indoor bathrooms. A 1926 survey of the residents of Zanesville, Ohio, revealed that 91 percent of the city's houses were equipped with running water and that 61 percent had complete plumbing systems. This increased availability of electricity and water made possible the proliferation of appliances and conveniences that changed daily life in American society.

**The Middle Classes.** At the turn of the century, families with a comfortable income depended on servants, hired labor, and delivery men to support their day-to-day lives. The new technology available in the 1920s — combined with a diminishing supply of people willing to work as servants — caused more and more middle-class families to do their own housework. By 1926 80 percent of American homes with incomes more than $3,000 had vacuum cleaners and washing machines. These devices reduced the heavy labor involved in housework and made the tasks more acceptable to middle- and upper-class women. Electric washing machines in the 1920s had no automatic cycles and did not spin clothes semidry, but they eliminated the hauling of water and manual wringing that once made clothes-washing such a difficult chore. Early vacuum cleaners, though heavy and clumsy, cleaned more thoroughly than brooms and ended the grueling semiannual removal of carpets and rugs for cleaning. Electric refrigerators allowed families to store perishable food for longer periods and, with the help of the automobile, eliminated the need for regular delivery service by retailers. However, the number of hours housewives devoted to maintaining their homes did not change: the average mother in the 1920s spent fifty to sixty hours a week on domestic tasks, roughly the same as she had at the turn of the century. Rather than supervising maids and ordering food deliveries, housewives were operating appliances and going to stores.

**The Lower Classes.** The fabled economic prosperity of the decade was not enjoyed by the majority of Americans. Though industrial production boomed and wages for skilled and unskilled workers rose, unpredictable layoffs and the absence of sick leave and worker's compensation made employment and a steady income uncertain. A 1929 Brookings Institution study reported that 59 percent of the nation's families still lived below a minimal level of "health and decency." Labor-saving electric appliances such as vacuum cleaners and washing machines remained too expensive for most lower-class families. A new washing machine in the 1920s cost between $60 and $200, and the average factory worker earned about $100 a month. The technology that did change working-class families' lives was the expansion of basic utility services such as electricity, water, and natural gas. Electricity brought better lighting and reduced the danger of fires caused by kerosene lamps and gas lights. Indoor plumbing ended the discomfort of using outhouses in cold months and reduced the danger of typhoid fever in the summers. Gas ranges were cooler in the summer than continuously burning stoves and did not fill houses with coal dust and kerosene fumes. The benefits of technology were compounded by new public-health measures such as pure food regulations, water and sewage treatment, and garbage-collection services. The primary influence of technology on the lower classes was that it raised their standard of living in general: infant morality rates fell, epidemic diseases were drastically reduced, and diets improved. Although the income and daily workload of poor people saw little improvement, they lived healthier lives.

**Cleanliness and Social Divisions.** One of the side effects of expanding access to technology was the narrowing of the social gap between rich and poor. Before World War I, the circumstance that most lower-class homes had no hot and cold running water made bathing and washing clothes extremely difficult. As a result, most working-class people bathed no more than once a week, wore a shirt for weeks without washing it, and seldom changed their underclothes. Cleanliness was a condition strictly for the upper classes. As a natural result of their low hygiene standards, the poor looked and smelled repulsive to the rich. Cleanliness was important for getting a good job because members of the comfortable classes often interacted with the poor only when seeking to hire employees. When running water became available to most lower-income families, bathing and washing clothes became easier, and cleanliness increased. Immigrants and poor people looking for jobs as clerks, waiters, shop-girls, or servants were encouraged to learn habits of good hygiene. Although the economic prosperity of the decade was enjoyed primarily by the rich, access to technology helped lessen the most basic physical distinctions between the classes — cleanliness, dress, and health.

**Rural Areas.** The spread of technology in the 1920s remained primarily an urban phenomenon. Only 10 percent of the nation's farm families had electric power in 1930 (compared to the 85 percent of the families in cities and towns). Indoor plumbing was also slow to reach rural areas. By 1930, 33 percent of rural homes (compared to 71 percent of urban homes) had running water. Not until the 1930s and 1940s would utility service reach rural areas on a large scale.

Sources:

Ruth Schwartz Cowan, *More Work for Mother* (New York: Basic Books, 1983);

Earl Lifshey, *The Housewares Story: A History of the American Housewares Industry* (Chicago: National Housewares Manufacturers Association, 1973);

*Statistical History of the United States from Colonial Times to the Present* (Stamford, Conn.: Fairfield, 1965);

Susan Strasser, *Never Done* (New York: Pantheon, 1982).

## MASCULINITY AND THE EXPERIENCE OF MEN

**New Heroes: Athletes.** In his 1921 novel *Three Soldiers*, John Dos Passos described soldiers wounded in World War I as "discarded automatons, broken toys laid away in rows." World War I was a war without heroes, and veterans returned to America disillusioned and cynical. They searched at home for new male heroes and affirmations of manhood. Some men gave hero status to athletes, and popular excitement over spectator sports became intense. The 1920s have been called the "Golden Age of Sport," when athletics were "seated on the American throne." Baseball was the national pastime, but football nearly "became a national religion." One found "real men" on the gridiron and the diamond: the Sultan of Swat (Babe Ruth), the Four Horsemen of Notre Dame (Harry Stuhldreher, Don Miller, Jim Crowley, and Elmer Layden), the Galloping Ghost (Red Grange). A journalist for *Collier's* wrote in 1929, "I've seen moral courage in football as often as physical. I've seen football make men out of condemned material."

**Aviator Hero.** Another male hero of the 1920s was Charles Lindbergh. Within days of his pioneering solo flight across the Atlantic in 1927, he became a symbol of American dreams. Lindbergh "stands out in a grubby world as an inspiration," declared one newspaper. But the elation over Lindbergh was fleeting, ending with the ticker-tape parade. Journalist Joseph Hart lamented, "We . . . go back to the contracted routines of our institutional ways because ninety-nine percent of us must be content to be shaped and moulded by the routine ways and forms of the world to the routine tasks of life."

**On the Job.** For most American men those routine tasks meant their jobs, and in the 1920s men worked at least eight hours a day, six days a week, fifty weeks a year. They typically labored in factories or offices along with hundreds of other employees, not on their own farms or in their own businesses. For middle-class men, proportionately fewer were professionals than in the past, and proportionately more were middlemen — salesmen or agents. At their jobs men now needed an accommodating personality, not the go-getting individualism of prior decades, because few men worked autonomously in the 1920s. Factory workers encountered increasingly routine tasks on the shop floor, and as their jobs became specialized and repetitive, workers became bored, tired, and unhappy. They responded by joining together to manipulate employer efficiency strategies for their own benefit. For example, workers at a meatpacking plant undermined a time-motion observer by deliberately using extra motions to wrap bacon when a rate setter was present and then speeding it up after the observer left.

**At Home.** Men turned to home and family for affirmation of their worldly achievements and reassurance about the moral order; but things at home were different, too. Husbands who looked toward home at the end of their day for "an asylum and a refuge, a feather-bed for aching limbs and an opiate for bruised self-esteem" had to adjust to marriage as a partnership in which his wife handed him his crying baby instead of his pipe and slippers. As more wives expected to share domestic responsibilities with their mates and sought reciprocity in marriage, male authority eroded at home as well as work, and if a man insisted on "playing a patriarchal role," he might discover, according to a 1926 claim in the *Ladies' Home Journal,* "that modern families won't put up with it anymore." But while shifts in sex roles were felt in the 1920s, they were subtle, and most men and women still held to more deeply imprinted gender patterns. As it would for many decades, "female equality threatened men, and sexual equality confused them."

Source:
Peter Feline, *Him/Her Self: Sex Roles in Modern America* (New York: New American Library, 1974).

## "THE NOBLE EXPERIMENT"

**Cultural Conflict.** The Eighteenth Amendment, outlawing the sale of liquor, was the culmination of the campaigns of the Anti-Saloon League and the Women's Christian Temperance Union to dry up the United States. Forty-six states ratified the amendment, which went into effect in January 1920. The fight for Prohibition was a cultural conflict between white, native, Protestant Americans and new immigrants, as well as a conflict between women and men. Mainstream Protestants associated the saloon with the working-class and immigrant cultures they wished to bring in line with their own values. Women fought for Prohibition to protect their homes and families, recognizing that drunken husbands used up a family's income on liquor and often physically or sexually abused their wives and children.

**A Fool's Errand.** Resistance to Prohibition had been fierce: 1919 New Jersey Democratic gubernatorial candidate Edward I. Edwards pledged to "make New Jersey as wet as the Atlantic Ocean." While Prohibition curbed alcohol consumption in the 1920s, strict enforcement was clearly, as one historian has said, "a fool's errand." If people wished to drink, they could easily find liquor, especially in the cities. Enforcement was estimated as 95 percent effective in rural, conservative Kansas but only 5 percent effective in urban, liberal New York. In January 1920 portable stills went on sale at hardware stores for six dollars. Speakeasies opened almost as soon as saloons closed, and these new settings ironically made drinking more genteel and sophisticated. Speakeasies provided opportunities for "new women" to smoke, order cocktails, enjoy conversation, and mix with men. Flappers were conspicuously present at the fancier speakeasies, although there was no overall increase in women's drinking in the 1920s. Since liquor became more expensive with Prohibition, an appearance at a speakeasy identified middle- and upper-class young women with fashionable and chic society, rather than with the lower-class drunks rightly or wrongly associated with the neighborhood saloon.

Source:
Mark Edward Lender and James Kirby Martin, *Drinking in America* (New York: Free Press, 1987).

## SCIENTIFIC CHILD REARING

**Fewer Children, More Attention.** In the 1920s families were smaller than in the past and continued to get smaller: the average number of children born to a woman who lived the usual number of childbearing years was 3.56 in 1900, 3.17 in 1920, 2.5 in 1925, and 1.8 in 1935. There were fewer children in the population and more adults per child. These changes meant that adult attention could be focused on the individual child. For most families by the 1920s, children lived at home until they were fully grown and attended school longer than any generation in the past. The experience of children of the same age group was increasingly uniform. Childhood now tended to be quite leisured, sheltered from adult concerns, and focused on preparation for adulthood.

**"Sacralized" Children.** New attitudes toward children and new economic conditions affecting them freed children from work and other adult responsibilities by the 1920s. After the turn of the century, children were "sacralized" — that is, invested with new religious and sentimental meaning — and they were held above financial considerations. Child labor laws signaled this change: the laws removed children from the labor force, in part because it became more efficient to educate children than to employ them. Child labor laws also reflected the idea that the only acceptable work for the sacralized child was instructional and educational in nature. Even less well-to-do parents were expected to subsidize their children's expenses by providing them with an allowance. Children were economically "useless" but emotionally "priceless," their value measured in the parents' joy in a child's smile or goodnight kiss.

**Democratic Families.** Smaller families also became more democratic. The formerly rigid roles that defined interaction between children and parents were relaxed in the 1920s, giving way to more spontaneous expressions of ideas and emotions throughout the family. The decline in the number of children per family and the focus on emotional satisfaction and nurturance made hierarchically defined relationships between parents and children — and, indeed, between the parents themselves — both unnecessary and undesirable.

**Watson's Influence.** Despite the movement toward more open, affectionate parent/child relationships, the advice of child psychologist John B. Watson influenced many parents. Watson, a behavioral psychologist, promoted a strict model of child rearing. His model appealed to parents in the mid 1920s since it offered a "scientific approach" to parents anxious about raising children equipped to deal with modern life. Watson believed that

the child's personality was shaped through systematic habit training early in life. He was a most severe behaviorist, asserting that families overindulged their children and that affection was responsible for social maladaption. He advised parents to curb their displays of affection. Mothers were instructed to enforce a strict regimen of habit training and to resist their emotional responses to the child. Watson's harshness limited his popularity, but his behavioral emphasis on rigid adherence to "scientific" rules and schedules of feeding, toilet training, and discipline influenced the behavior of many middle-class parents in the 1920s.

Sources:
Paula Fass, *The Damned and the Beautiful: American Youth in the 1920s* (New York: Oxford University Press, 1977);

Margo Horn, *Before It's Too Late: The Child Guidance Movement in the United States, 1922–1945* (Philadelphia: Temple University Press, 1989);

Viviana Zelizer, *Pricing the Priceless* (New York: Basic Books, 1985).

## WOMEN GET THE VOTE

**"Hurrah! And Vote for Suffrage."** So shouted Harry Burn, at twenty-four the youngest member of the U.S. House of Representatives, on 18 August 1920, when he heeded his mother's admonition and cast the final vote for the passage of the Nineteenth Amendment, giving women the right to vote. Twenty-six million women were enfranchised, and a battle for women's suffrage that began at the Seneca Falls Woman's Rights Convention in 1848 finally was won.

**No Panacea.** Initially elated, activist women quickly discovered that the vote was not the panacea for women they hoped. First, women did not vote in blocs or uniformly support women's issues; they voted according to race, social class, religious background, and geographic location. Furthermore, women's groups did not agree on the best strategy for further reform, and some women did not believe additional reform was necessary at all. As suffrage leader Anna Howard Shaw lamented in 1920, "I am sorry for you young women who have to carry on the work for the next ten years, for suffrage was a symbol, and now you have lost your symbol."

**Factionalism.** After 1920 the suffrage movement fragmented into factions: social feminists who sought reform of society in general; feminists who focused on expanded roles for women; women who were dedicated to pacifism; and women who campaigned for labor and professional reform. The moderate League of Women Voters attracted many women who sought social reform, education for women, and the elimination of laws discriminating against women. The more radical National Women's Party, led by Alice Paul, believed in the necessity of an Equal Rights Amendment (ERA) and single-mindedly struggled for it during the 1920s. The issue served to divide women, since many thought protective legislation preferable to a constitutional amendment and viewed the ERA as too extreme.

Suffragettes celebrating ratification of the Nineteenth Amendment in August 1920

**Black Women Activists.** Black suffragists felt abandoned by white activists after suffrage passed. They thus turned from feminist politics to issues of racial justice, to the Back to Africa Movement led by Marcus Garvey, and to the antilynching movement. In 1922 black leader Mary B. Talbert founded the Anti-Lynching Crusade, and by 1923 seven hundred black and white women had joined the effort to stop these murders. Black and white southern feminists, who addressed specific issues facing southern black women, formed the Committee on Negro Problems in 1924 and the Southern Council on Women and Children in Industry in 1931. In a 1927 issue of *Current History* devoted to the "new woman," suffragists and other activist women noted with satisfaction feminist accomplishments since the passage of the Nineteenth Amendment.

Sources:

Dorothy M. Brown, *Setting a Course: American Women in the Twenties* (Boston: Twayne, 1987);

Nancy M. Cott, *The Grounding of Modern Feminism* (New Haven: Yale University Press, 1987).

## WOMEN GO TO WORK

**"There is a tacit understanding that women should not make over twenty-five cents an hour."** In 1920 women composed 23.6 percent of the labor force, and 8.3 million women older than the age of fifteen worked outside the home. By 1930 the percentage of women in the work force rose to 27, and their numbers increased to 11 million. World War I had expanded women's employment in new sectors of the economy, and by 1920, 25.6 percent of employed women worked in white-collar office-staff jobs, 23.8 percent in manufacturing, 18.2 percent in domestic service, and 12.9 percent in agriculture. While the first generation of college-educated women entered professions in the 1920s, they found opportunities only in nurturing "women's professions," such as nursing, teaching, social work, and, within medicine, pediatrics. And in factories, while male factory workers on federal contracts in 1920 started at forty cents an hour, women started at twenty-five cents.

**The Women's Bureau and WTUL.** The Women's Bureau, a new federal agency approved by Congress in June 1920, was charged with reporting the conditions of women in industry and promoting the welfare of working women. The Women's Trade Union League (WTUL) also fought to improve women's labor conditions in the 1920s. The WTUL argued that protective legislation based on women's special position as childbearers not be used to jeopardize women workers by restricting their access to certain jobs.

**Working Hours.** Women laborers worked long hours, and both the Women's Bureau and WTUL fought for shorter workdays. By the early 1920s all but five states upheld the ten-hour-per-day/fifty-hour-per-week schedule, while those five embraced the fifty-four-hour workweek. Women's Bureau director Mary Anderson reported a typical workday in an early 1920s tobacco factory of a Virginia woman deserted by her husband: "Rising at 5:30 A.M, she cooked breakfast, dressed the children, took them to a day nursery, and was at the factory by 7:30 A.M. When the factory closed at 6:00 P.M., she picked up the children and arrived home at 7:00 P.M. to cook dinner, do the housework, and sew the children's clothes, usually going to bed at midnight." Anderson commented: "Ten hours at the factory and the double duty at home was bad not only for the woman's health but bad for family life." This quote captured the central problem of women's work: meshing the necessity to work with family responsibilities. Efforts to improve working conditions for women were consistently undermined by society's ambivalence about combining the roles of wife and mother with those of worker and professional. But ever-increasing numbers of married women worked as the decade progressed: the percentage of married women among all women workers rose from 23.6 percent in 1920 to 29 percent in 1930.

**Education and Training.** The 1920s saw pioneering efforts to educate and train women workers. Most notable was Bryn Mawr College's Summer Schools for Women Workers in Industry. Launched by Byrn Mawr's president, M. Carey Thomas, in 1921 and operating for ten years, the school provided academic training, union-organizing skills, and lessons in participatory democracy to women recruited by unions and the YMCA. The 1920s continued the historical trend of increasing labor-force participation for women, but women continued to work long hours for poor pay, and they performed undervalued "women's work," in whatever sphere of the economy they worked.

Sources:

Rita R. Heller, "The Bryn Mawr Workers' Summer School, 1921–1930: A Surprising Alliance," in *History of Higher Education Annual* (1981): 110–131;

Alice Kessler-Harris, *Out to Work: A History of Wage-Earning Women in the United States* (New York: Oxford University Press, 1982).

## YOUTH CULTURE

**Peer Socialization.** A flamboyant youth subculture with its own ways of speaking, dressing, and acting flourished in the 1920s. Youth peer culture grew in the context of the family's retreat into a private emotional world and of the extended length of time teenagers and young adults spent in school. In the 1920s the high school, college, and peer group replaced the family's role in so-

John Held Jr. titled this drawing "The Dance-Mad Younger Set" to make the point that more than dancing occurred at dances.

cializing adolescents; now these institutions defined the world of youth.

**Mass Phenomenon.** The new importance of schooling in creating peer culture was indicated by the marked acceleration in rates of attendance: between 1900 and 1930 high-school enrollments increased 650 percent, and attendance in colleges and universities went up threefold. Of the three decades, the 1920s witnessed the greatest rate of increase. By 1930 school attendance was a mass phenomenon for the first time: close to 60 percent of the high-school age population and almost 20 percent of those of college age enrolled in school. Thus school peer culture now reached youth from a wide range of economic classes and racial and ethnic groups, blending and homogenizing patterns of behavior and attitudes among these diverse groups.

**Boy/Girl Relationships.** According to *Middletown*, sociologists Robert S. and Helen Merrell Lynd's classic study of life in Muncie, Indiana, in the 1920s high school became "a place from which [youth] go home to eat and sleep." Young men and women met in classes, at evening socials, and in after-school activities. They found privacy in cars and went out with friends four or more evenings each week. Teenagers saw movies together, drove to the next town on the weekend for dances, and parked in lovers' lanes on the way home. According to the Lynds, nearly one-half of Muncie's male high-school students and one-third of its female students took part in the new practice of petting, which came into vogue because of the youths' economic independence and freedom from adult supervision. Petting parties attracted these youths, and girls who did not attend became less popular. The youth culture of the 1920s, in Muncie and beyond, provided a setting for sexual experimentation and changing moral attitudes toward sexual behavior. The new practice of dating permitted paired relationships without implying a commitment to marriage; it tested compatibility and encouraged experimental relationships with different partners. The privacy afforded by dating encouraged sexual exploration, and the practice of petting permitted a range of erotic physical contacts, while respecting the taboo against sexual intercourse.

**Collegiate Style.** Nowhere did the youth culture of the 1920s flourish more than on college and university campuses. Campus fads and behaviors (the emblems of group membership) symbolized youth culture and spread widely off campus. Magazines, movies, and advertising spread the word across the country about "collegiate fashions" and lifestyles, creating a mass culture and a big business.

In clothing a special "flapper line" of styles and sizes was brought out, and according to a UCLA newspaper in 1923, "'College style' has a definite meaning. To the layman it spells — debonair smartness — an individual trimness that is particularly the insignia of the young man of today. Fall '23 can almost be called the young man's season with the style pace set by the collegian." Everyone wanted to look and act "collegian," and the nation became obsessed with what glamorous college youth were doing, wearing, smoking, singing, and dancing.

Sources:

Paula Fass, *The Damned and the Beautiful: American Youth in the 1920s* (New York: Oxford University Press, 1977);

Robert S. Lynd and Helen Merrell Lynd, *Middletown: A Study in Contemporary American Culture* (New York: Harcourt, Brace, 1929);

John Modell, *Into One's Own: From Youth to Adulthood in the United States, 1920–1975* (Berkeley: University of California Press, 1989);

Barbara Miller Solomon, *In the Company of Educated Women* (New Haven: Yale University Press, 1985).

# HEADLINE MAKERS

## GRACE ABBOTT

### 1878-1939

#### SOCIAL WORKER AND DIRECTOR, FEDERAL CHILDREN'S BUREAU

**Passion to Reform.** Grace Abbott inherited her inclination toward public affairs from her father, who was active in Nebraska politics and the state's first lieutenant governor. From her mother, an abolitionist and suffragist, she derived her passion to reform the world. Abbott grew up on the expansive Nebraska prairies and in 1898 graduated from Grand Island College in her hometown. She taught high school in Grand Island for eight years and in 1907 followed her sister, social worker Edith Abbott, to Chicago to attend graduate school in political science at the University of Chicago. Grace Abbott earned a master's degree in 1909.

**Hull House.** During the first decade of the twentieth century, Chicago was home to a vital circle of women intellectuals and social reformers. Grace Abbott was immediately attracted to Hull House, Jane Addams's pioneer social settlement, where she became a resident in 1908 and lived for nine years. Hull House placed her in the midst of social activism: she participated in the Chicago garment workers' strike of 1910–1911, she worked for the election of Theodore Roosevelt in 1912, she was involved in the successful Illinois woman-suffrage campaign of 1913, and she went with Jane Addams to the International Congress of Women at The Hague in 1915.

**Immigrants' Protective League.** Abbott first gained public attention as head of the Immigrants' Protective League (IPL), an organization founded to shelter new immigrants from abuse by unscrupulous lawyers, travel agents, and operators of fraudulent savings banks and employment agencies. Particularly sympathetic to the situations of people removed from a foreign rural setting into a bustling American city, Abbott worked to remedy the exploitation of immigrants, and her first book, *The Immigrant and the Community* (1917), was based on her experience at the IPL. She also taught a course on immigration at the newly established Chicago School of Civics and Philanthropy. Abbott secured state legislation regulating employment agencies and persuaded officials at Ellis Island to take responsibility for the immediate situation of the immigrants they admitted.

**Child Labor.** In 1917 Abbott accepted the longstanding invitation of her Hull House friend and director of the Children's Bureau, Julia Lathrop, to join the bureau's staff in Washington. Turning her focus to child welfare since the flood of immigration to the United States had slowed, she became director of the bureau's child-labor division. Abbott was responsible for the detailed investigation of the dates of birth of working children, information necessary for the enforcement of the first federal child-labor law, passed in 1916. When that law was declared unconstitutional in 1918, Abbott saw the need for a constitutional amendment abolishing child labor, an issue for which she campaigned the rest of her life. She turned to the preparation of Children's Year conferences at the bureau in 1919 and returned to Illinois that autumn to become director of the new Illinois State Immigrants' Commission.

**Children's Bureau.** In the summer of 1921 Abbott was appointed director of the federal Children's Bureau, a position she held for thirteen years. Her first task was to administer the 1921 Sheppard-Towner Act, the first federal law providing direct federal aid to states to provide programs combating infant and maternal disease and mortality. The act was controversial; many who carried on the Red Scare mentality claimed it was "under direct orders from Moscow." Abbott eloquently and vigorously fought back, administering the Children's Bureau and the Sheppard-Towner Act with painstaking care throughout the 1920s. She established three thousand child-health and prenatal-care centers throughout the country and instituted an enduring model of state-federal cooperation in social-welfare programs. But in 1929, Abbott's vehement opposition, Sheppard-Towner was killed in Congress. In the face of this defeat, she asserted the continued authority of the Children's Bureau over all aspects of child welfare.

**Other Accomplishments.** In addition to her leadership of the Children's Bureau, Abbott served as an unofficial U.S. delegate to the League of Nations Advisory Committee on Traffic in Women and Children and as president of the National Conference of Social Work. In the early 1930s she greeted the New Deal with enthusiasm, though she commented ironically, "I am beginning to feel quite unnecessary. During the past few years one felt that the few liberals in the federal government who were ready to speak up when necessary could not be spared. Now I have the com-

fortable feeling that my job will be taken care of if I leave." Abbott remained at the Children's Bureau until 1933 in order to assist her friend, Frances Perkins, President Franklin D. Roosevelt's new secretary of labor. In late 1933 Abbott organized the Child Health Recovery Conference. As a member of Roosevelt's Council on Economic Security in 1934–1935, she helped draft the Social Security Act, which greatly expanded the philosophy of Sheppard-Towner.

**Final Years.** In 1934, her health failing, Abbott returned to Chicago to become professor of public welfare at the University of Chicago's School of Social Service Administration (successor to the School of Civics and Philanthropy), where her sister, Edith, was dean. Abbott's final book, *The Child and the State*, appeared in 1938. Although she never saw the ratification of an amendment banning child labor, Abbott was gratified to see the passage of the Fair Labor Standards Act in 1938, which restricted child labor.

Source:
Lela B. Costin, *Two Sisters for Social Justice: A Biography of Grace and Edith Abbott* (Urbana & Champaign: University of Illinois Press, 1983).

## ABRAHAM EPSTEIN

### 1892-1945

#### PIONEER OF SOCIAL SECURITY

**Beginnings.** A pioneer of the American social-insurance movement, Abraham Epstein was born in Luban, near Pinsk, Russia, and came to the United States at the age of eighteen. He lived in New York City and worked at factory jobs for one and one-half years, until a friend got him a job teaching Hebrew in Pittsburgh, Pennsylvania. Soon after his arrival, he walked into an exclusive private boys' school, asked about enrollment, passed the entrance examination, and won a tuition scholarship to attend East Liberty Academy. Another scholarship enabled him to enter the University of Pittsburgh, where he received a B.S. in 1917. That same year he became an American citizen.

**Commission on Old Age Pensions.** Epstein continued to do graduate work in economics at the university and conducted a detailed survey of employment and housing conditions of Pittsburgh's black population. This study, *The Negro Migrant in Pittsburgh* (1918), won him offers of several university fellowships, but he instead took a position at the Pennsylvania Commission on Old Age Pensions. He remained there until 1927, securing the passage of a state-financed old-age-pension program in 1923, despite vigorous business opposition. The pension act was declared unconstitutional in 1924, and before the decision could be appealed, the commission had been disbanded.

**Social Insurance.** After leaving the commission, Epstein founded the American Association for Old Age Security in 1927, which changed its name to the American Association for Social Security in 1933. By 1927 he had published several books on aging and lectured widely for social welfare and unions. Epstein led one of the two dominant groups favoring social insurance in the 1930s: he advocated government-financed programs aimed at redistributing wealth and caring for the underprivileged. The other, more conservative group, led by John D. Andrews, favored private social-insurance programs as a means of preventing suffering and poverty. The two approaches came into conflict during the Depression: Andrews's "American plan" was adopted in Wisconsin in 1932, and Epstein's "European plan" won in the New York State legislature in 1935.

**Social Security Act.** A rift between Andrews and Epstein resulted in the Roosevelt administration's failure to consult Epstein on the drafting of the Social Security Act of 1935, a blow from which he never recovered. He criticized the Social Security Act for failing to provide for government contributions, for leaving unemployment compensation to the states, and for the large reserve fund it set up that reduced spending power. Many of his criticisms still plague the program today.

Source:
*New York Times,* 3 May 1942, p. 43.

# LAWRENCE K. FRANK

## 1890-1968

### FOUNDATION EXECUTIVE AND BEHAVIORAL SCIENTIST

**Foundations.** Anthropologist Margaret Mead said in her obituary of Lawrence K. Frank that he "used [philanthropic] foundations the way the Lord meant them to be used." Frank grew up in Cincinnati, Ohio, and received his B.A. degree in economics from Columbia University in 1912. As a graduate student he met Columbia economist Wesley C. Mitchell, who with his wife, the educator Lucy Sprague Mitchell, became friends and influential mentors of Frank.

**Laura Spelman Rockefeller Memorial.** In 1923 Frank was selected as director of the Laura Spelman Rockefeller Memorial, a new foundation that was part of the Rockefeller family philanthropies and devoted exclusively to the well-being of children. Instead of using the foundation's considerable resources to aid existing child-welfare agencies, Frank decided to create new preventive facilities studying the psychological development of normal children. He designed a university-based child-study program including research on child growth and development along with parent education on child rearing.

**Child Welfare Research Institutes.** Frank's new program included conducting practical research that would lead to the establishment of norms for the behavior of the "average American child" at each age, as well as publicizing and applying the results of this research in nursery and elementary schools, parent-training programs, and medical settings. Under Frank's leadership, by 1930 the Laura Spelman Rockefeller Memorial had funded nine Child Welfare Research Institutes in major universities in the United States and Canada. Research at these institutes amassed enormous amounts of data that shaped the fields of developmental child psychology, early childhood education, and pediatrics for decades.

**Achievements.** When the Laura Spelman Rockefeller Memorial was terminated in 1929, Frank continued to direct the child-development program, first as part of the larger Rockefeller Foundation, then, beginning in 1933, as part of its General Education Board. He maintained his philanthropic work on behalf of children and in education at the Josiah Macy Foundation from 1936 to 1942 and at the Caroline B. Zachry Institute of Human Development from 1945 to 1950. Frank wrote prolifically for both scientific and popular audiences. His books include *Nature and Human Nature* (1951); *Babies are Puppies, Puppies Are Babies* (1953); and *Feelings and Emotions* (1954). In 1950 he shared the *Parents Magazine* Award with his wife, Mary, for their article "How to Help Your Child in School." In 1947 he had shared, with Catherine MacKenzie of *The New York Times,* a Lasker Award for his contributions to popular adult education in mental health, especially regarding parent/child relationships. Frank, an intellectual collaborator and mentor to many in the behavioral sciences, expanded the work of foundations in child-study research and its practical application.

Source:
*New York Times,* 24 September 1968, p. 44.

# BEN LINDSEY

## 1869-1943

### JUDGE

**Early Life.** In 1901 Ben Lindsey became judge of the Juvenile and Family Court of Denver, which in the 1920s was the best-known court of its kind in the world. Lindsey grew up in Jackson, Tennessee, until he was eleven, when his family moved to Denver. He returned to Tennessee and went to high school at Southwestern Baptist

University. In these years he became close to his aunt's husband, who had unorthodox views about politics and economics and who influenced Lindsey's thinking.

**Lawyer and Judge.** Lindsey returned to Denver at the age of sixteen, and his father, plagued by debt, committed suicide. Ben and his younger brother became family breadwinners. He was unable to finish high school but worked in a law office and began to read law. When he was nineteen, he attempted suicide out of fatigue and despair. After this crisis, as Lindsey later described it, he resolved to continue in the law and was admitted to the bar in 1894 at the age of twenty-four. Lindsey entered Democratic politics and in 1901 was appointed to an unexpired term in a county judgeship, an office he held through many heated elections for the next twenty-six years. During his term and through his efforts, the court evolved into the Juvenile and Family Court of Denver, an innovative center of the new juvenile-court movement.

**Compassionate Justice.** Lindsey led in the practice of compassionate juvenile justice and progressive thinking about family life. One of his most original legislative achievements was the Colorado Adult Delinquency Act of 1903, establishing the principle that adults contributing to the delinquency of a minor were legally responsible. By 1920 forty states adopted laws based on the Colorado statute. As juvenile-court judge Lindsey emphasized probation and rehabilitation rather than punishment. He often became involved with offending youth and their families: when he sentenced one youth to reform school for stealing coal and his mother became hysterical in court, Lindsey visited the boy's home that night. The judge discovered that the boy stole the coal to heat his parents' shanty, where his father was dying of lead poisoning contracted as a miner. Lindsey placed the youth on informal probation and used the case to fight for social legislation.

**Companionate Marriage.** In the 1920s Lindsey became interested in the so-called sexual revolution then underway. He coined the term *companionate marriage* in his 1927 book by that title. In it he advocated compulsory education in sex, including contraception, and liberalization of divorce laws to allow childless couples whose marriages did not work to divorce without fees and lawsuits. Though not especially radical, Lindsey's proposals won him the media title of spokesman for flaming youth.

**Final Years.** Lindsey's liberal views made him the target of the Ku Klux Klan, which was active in Colorado in the 1920s. His narrow electoral victory in 1924 was reversed when the state supreme court invalidated his votes in a predominantly Jewish district. He was disbarred in 1929 for receiving money for legal services while he was a judge, a decision widely called excessive and personally motivated since the services were rendered in New York, outside his jurisdiction. Although the Colorado bar readmitted him in 1935, he spent the rest of his life in California where he was overwhelmingly elected county judge

of Los Angeles in 1934. He remained judge and continued to work on behalf of children until his death in 1943.

Source:
*New York Times,* 16 April 1924, p. 40.

# ROBERT S. LYND
# AND
# HELEN MERRELL LYND

## 1892-1970, 1896-1982

### SOCIOLOGISTS

**Pioneer Sociologists.** With their two groundbreaking studies of American life, *Middletown* (1929) and *Middletown in Transition* (1937), Robert S. and Helen Merrell Lynd helped found the field of modern sociology. Their research made available for the first time an in-depth account of how average Americans lived their daily lives during the 1920s.

**Background.** Robert Staughton Lynd was born in New Albany, Indiana, and raised in Louisville, Kentucky. He graduated from Princeton in 1914 and for four years served as the managing editor of *Publishers' Weekly.* Following a year of service in World War I, Lynd worked briefly for Charles Scribner's Sons and *The Freeman Magazine* before entering Union Theological Seminary. Helen Merrell was born in La Grange, Illinois, and attended Wellesley College, from which she graduated Phi Beta Kappa in 1919. For two years she taught in girls' schools in New York, where she met Robert Lynd. They were married in 1922. After Robert Lynd received his divinity degree in 1923, the Lynds became missionaries in the oil fields of Montana. Their experiences in the oil fields convinced them of the inequities in American society, and their interests shifted from religion to sociology. In the mid 1920s Robert Lynd directed a series of "Small City" studies for the Institute of Social and Religious Research. As a result of these studies, he and his wife were selected to conduct a study of religious life in Muncie, Indiana. They found it impossible to focus solely on the single aspect of religion in community life and instead wrote a sweeping study of the community as a whole.

**Middletown.** The Lynds' first book was intended to be a factual, objective description of all aspects of life in Muncie, Indiana. They selected the city because they found it to be as representative as possible of average American life in the 1920s. The Lynds and a small team of researchers spent eighteen months — from January 1924 to June 1925 — conducting interviews, compiling statistics, and distributing surveys to the city's residents. The published book examined such aspects of everyday life as earning a living, making a home, training children, and engaging in leisure and recreational activities. The study reflects the 1920s' concern with analyzing and describing American society. Though the Lynds did not moralize or attempt to evaluate the propriety of what they found, the book devotes much attention to the values and beliefs of Middletown's residents and depicts a materialistic elite, conspicuous consumption, and sharp class differences within the city.

**Reception.** Though the city is referred to throughout not as Muncie but as Middletown, Muncie residents identified themselves easily and denounced the study as slanted and disparaging. *Middletown,* however, gained instant popularity, with six printings in 1929. Its success created a demand for more social surveys and led other researchers to begin compiling facts about life in the United States. The book, moreover, was seized upon by writers and social critics as evidence of the vacuity and sterility of American culture.

**Academic Sociology.** Although Robert Lynd had no formal training as sociologist, *Middletown* created for him a reputation as a leading figure in the modern social sciences. In 1930 he became the secretary of the Social Science Research Council, a body organized to promote research and foster cooperations between anthropologists, economists, historians, statisticians, and sociologists. In 1931 Lynd joined the faculty of Columbia University as professor of sociology. His emphasis on research and "down-to-earth" methodology brought him into conflict with colleagues who advocated abstract theory, but Lynd's career at Columbia was instrumental in establishing sociology as an accepted academic discipline.

**Return to Middletown.** In the mid 1930s Robert and Helen Lynd returned to Muncie, Indiana, to investigate how the city had changed as a result of the Depression. Unlike its predecessor, *Middletown in Transition* was less descriptive and did not aim for detached objectivity. The Lynds instead focused on social change in the city, particularly the effects of industrialization and class stratification. The book analyzed the economic and social power structure of the city and was critical of the dominance of a small number of powerful families over the lives of Muncie's residents.

**Contributions.** Though they published no more major studies, both of the Lynds enjoyed long teaching careers, Robert Lynd at Columbia University and Helen Lynd at Sarah Lawrence College, and contributed to sociological journals and nonacademic periodicals such as *The Nation.* Helen Lynd became active in academic reform, arguing for interdisciplinary curricula, flexible scheduling, and the replacement of grades with written evaluations.

Sources:

John Madge, *The Origins of Scientific Sociology* (New York: Free Press of Glencoe, 1962);

Charles H. Page, *Fifty Years in the Sociological Enterprise: A Lucky Journey* (Amherst: University of Massachusetts Press, 1982);

"Robert S. Lynd, Co-Author of 'Middletown,' Dies," *New York Times,* 3 November 1970, p. 38.

## MAUD WOOD PARK

### 1871-1955

#### SUFFRAGIST, CIVIC LEADER

**Beginnings.** Maud Wood Park became first president of the League of Women Voters, a nonpartisan organization to educate new voters following the passage of woman's suffrage in 1920. Maud Wood grew up in Boston and earned money by teaching in Chelsea High School in order to attend Radcliffe College. In 1898 she graduated summa cum laude from Radcliffe, where she was one of only two students in a class of seventy-two to favor the vote for women. While still a student, she married Charles Edward Park, a Boston architect, in 1897. The couple lived near the Boston settlement Denison House, introducing Maud Wood Park to social-reform work. Charles Park died in 1904.

**Suffrage.** For fifteen years Maud Wood Park was active in suffrage and civic work in Boston. She became chair of the Massachusetts Woman Suffrage Association in 1900 and executive secretary of the Boston Equal Suffrage Association for Good Government, which was devoted to combining work for suffrage with activities for civic betterment. A charismatic speaker, Park traveled widely to enlist college women in the cause of suffrage. In 1916 her friend Carrie Chapman Catt, president of the National American Woman's Suffrage Association (NAWSA), persuaded Park to join the NAWSA's Congressional Committee and to go to Washington to lobby directly for the federal suffrage amendment. Thus Park led the "front-door lobby" to win suffrage.

**League of Women Voters.** Park agreed to serve as first president of the League of Women Voters (LWV), the organization that succeeded the NAWSA. She said that the league's purpose should be to "promote reforms in which women will naturally take an interest in a greater degree than men — protection for working women, children, public health questions, and the care of dependent and delinquent classes." Under Park's leadership the LWV adopted a thirty-eight-point program of legislative measures. Though women's organizations divided in the 1920s, Park helped form the Women's Joint Congressional Committee (WJCC) in 1920, with representatives from nine other women's organizations, and then became its head. The WJCC succeeded in winning two important pieces of legislation: the Sheppard-Towner Maternity and Infancy Protection Act of 1921 and the 1922 Cable Act, which granted independent citizenship to married women. The league also served to pressure the Women's Bureau to end child labor and promote social legislation on behalf of women. Because of serious illness, Park resigned from the presidency of the league in 1924, but she continued for the rest of her life to lecture and work on behalf of women.

Source:
Eleanor Flexner, *Century of Struggle: The Woman's Rights Movement in the United States* (Cambridge: Harvard University Press, 1959).

## EMILY PRICE POST

### 1872-1960

WRITER, AUTHORITY OF ETIQUETTE, INTERIOR DECORATOR

**Genteel Beginnings.** Raised in a genteel, upper-class Manhattan home, young Emily Price personally embodied the ideals of etiquette that later made her famous. She was born in Baltimore but moved with her family to New York City in 1877, when her father, Bruce Price, gained national prominence as an architect. Price was reared by a governess and educated at Miss Graham's finishing school. Her extraordinary beauty and manners attracted wide attention.

**Young Matron.** Soon after her New York society debut, Emily Price married Edwin M. Post, a businessman. The couple lived on Staten Island and then in Manhattan, and Emily Post made frequent trips to Europe. She wrote long, lively letters home while abroad, which she turned into her 1904 novel, *The Flight of a Moth*. The Posts had two sons, Edwin Jr. and Bruce Price, the latter of whom died in 1927, but her husband's extramarital affairs led to the couple's divorce in 1905.

**Novels and Sentimentalism.** Forced to supplement her income to raise her sons, Mrs. Price Post, the name she preferred after her divorce, turned to freelance writing. During the next twenty years, she wrote six novels and many essays and short stories on life, adventure, and romance among the wealthy. Her writing met with instant success. She continued to travel and in 1915 motored from New York to California with her son Edwin to attend the Panama-Pacific Exposition in San Francisco. She published her travel journal, first in magazines and then as a book, *By Motor to the Golden Gate* (1916).

**Etiquette.** In 1921 Richard Duffy, an editor at Funk and Wagnalls, asked Post to write a guide to American etiquette. After discovering that no such work existed, Post enthusiastically took on the project. She worked zealously for ten months and produced *Etiquette in Society, in Business, in Politics, and at Home*, published in 1922. An immediate best-seller, the book made Post a celebrity and the nation's arbiter of proper social behavior. Post wrote with humor, good judgment, detail, and authority, thereby answering postwar Americans' need for order in their changing relationships. Her book, the title of which changed to *Etiquette: and The Blue Book of Social Usage*, codified and modified traditions and informal practices, defining proper behavior in the unconventional 1920s.

**Final Years.** In the 1930s and 1940s, while she was in her sixties and seventies, Post wrote a *McCall's* magazine etiquette column that was later syndicated, and she had a weekly radio show. She organized a cooperative-apartment building in New York City and built a summer home on Martha's Vineyard, Massachusetts. In her later years Post turned to gardening and home decorating and published several editions of her own favorite book, *The Personality of a House*, on interior decorating. She established the Emily Post Institute in 1946 and, with her son Edwin as adviser, managed her business empire. Never condescending, Post was embraced by the anxious middle class, who turned to her witty fictional families named Wellborn and Highbrow for standards of politeness and decor in America's mobile, democratic society.

Source:
Edwin Post, *Truly Emily Post* (New York: Funk & Wagnalls, 1961).

# PEOPLE IN THE NEWS

In 1922 **Charles Atlas** (born Angelos Sicilano) was named "America's Most Perfectly Developed Man" in a Madison Square Garden physical culture exhibition, launching his popular mail-order body-building course.

In 1920 **Mary Ritter Beard,** a suffrage activist and pioneering historian of women, published *A Short History of the Labor Movement.* Her later works included *On Understanding Women* (1931), and *Women As a Force in History* (1946).

**Gertrude Bonnin,** a Native American who preferred the Indian name **Zitkala-Sa —**, worked tirelessly for Indian rights. In 1921, after she moved to Washington, D.C., she conducted a survey of conditions of Native Americans for the Indian Welfare Commission and thereafter worked for years for improvements in health and education and for the conservation of Indian lands.

In 1922 seventeen-year-old **Clara Bow,** who, during the 1920s, became a major star of films and was dubbed the "It Girl," won a fan-magazine contest for "The Most Beautiful Girl in the World."

In February 1926 *Vanities* producer **Earl Carroll** offered seventeen-year-old **Joyce Hawley** $1,000 to sit nude in a bathtub of champagne at his party. Hawley started to cry when guests arrived.

In January 1925, **Floyd Collins,** a young Kentuckian exploring a cave, became trapped 125 feet underground. The effort to free Collins was chronicled on the front pages of newspapers across the nation. The news sensation ended eighteen days later when rescuers discovered Collins's dead body on 16 February.

Physician and social reformer **Alice Hamilton** was the first woman professor at Harvard Medical School. She worked throughout the 1920s on treating industrial diseases and promoting industrial safety, on promoting protective labor legislation for women, and for instituting child-labor laws.

In 1925 **Mary Belle Harris** was appointed superintendent of the first federal women's prison, which was located in West Virginia. Selected because of her service as superintendent of the New Jersey Home for Girls,

Harris was known as an innovator in prison reform. At the West Virginia prison she instituted educational programs, including a beauty school and a classification system to determine the women's best skills and thus prepare them to reenter society.

In 1924 social worker **Elizabeth Ross Haynes** was the first black woman elected to the national board of the YMCA.

By 1929 **Howard Johnson** had developed the twenty-eight brands of ice cream that became his trademark; the same year **Reginald Sprague,** hoping to capitalize on the superior reputation of Johnson's food products, opened the first Howard Johnson restaurant.

**Will Keith Kellogg,** who had almost single-handedly converted Americans to a nation of cold-cereal breakfast eaters, retired as president of W. K. Kellogg Company in 1929.

**Freida Loehmann** decided brand-name women's clothes that stores had been unable to sell could be sold at a discount. In 1920 she became the pioneer of off-price retailing. She offered wholesalers cash for their unsold preseason merchandise and then retailed the garments in her Brooklyn store. Within ten years Loehmann built a business worth $3 million.

On 24 January 1922 an ice cream bar called the Eskimo Pie was patented by Iowan **C. K. Nelson.**

In 1924 **Leonard (Kip) Rhinelander,** heir to a $100 million fortune, married **Alice Beatrice Jones,** the daughter of a New York City cab driver. The couple became a newspaper sensation when Rhinelander sued for an annulment, charging that his bride had hidden the fact that her father was black. The annulment was denied, but Rhinelander negotiated a divorce settlement that paid his wife $31,500 in cash and $300 a month for the rest of her life.

An organizer of the Knights of the Ku Klux Klan, **William Simmons,** hired the Southern Publicity Association, an Atlanta public-relations firm, to develop the strategy that resulted in the recruitment of two million initiated members by the early 1920s.

In 1925 the credibility of the Ku Klux Klan was hurt when its Grand Dragon, **David C. Stephenson,** was convicted of murdering his secretary and made statements damaging to leading pro-Klan Indiana politicians.

On 5 August 1926 **Ehrich Weiss (The Great Houdini)** stayed underwater ninety-one minutes with only five to six minutes of air supply.

# DEATHS

**Antionette Louisa Brown Blackwell,** 96, abolitionist, woman's rights advocate, and first woman ordained as a minister in the United States (by the Congregational Church in 1853), 5 November 1921.

**Richard Henry Boyd,** 79, who was born a slave, became a Baptist minister in 1870, and built Baptist churches all over Texas, 27 August 1922.

**Charles Horton Cooley,** 65, University of Michigan professor who, through his reading and writings, laid the groundwork for the study of sociology; he was a founder and the first president of the American Sociological Society, 8 May 1929.

**John Cotton Dana,** 72, librarian who introduced open shelves, children's departments, and branch libraries during his forty years of public-library service in Denver, Colorado; Springfield, Massachusetts; and Newark, New Jersey, 21 July 1929.

**Lucy Flower,** 84, social reformer who worked for the establishment of the first juvenile court, in Cook County, Illinois, 27 April 1921.

**Frederick Taylor Gates,** 78, educational fundraiser and philanthropist who organized the planning of the University of Chicago, advised John D. Rockefeller on the establishment of Rockefeller's General Education Board, the Rockefeller Institute for Medical Research, and the Rockefeller Foundation, 6 February 1929.

**Granville Stanley Hall,** 80, psychologist, educator, and pioneer in the field of child psychology who established the psychological basis of the adolescent stage of life in his 1904 study, *Adolescence,* 24 April 1924.

**Sophie Loeb,** 53, social reformer and journalist who worked on behalf of poor families and orphans and secured major social-welfare legislation, including passage of the Sheppard-Towner Act of 1921, which provided federal funds for infant- and maternal-health care, 18 January 1929.

**Juliette Gordon Low,** 80, founder of the Girl Scouts in 1915 and president of the organization from 1915 to 1920, 18 January 1927.

**Phoebe Anne Oakley Mozee (Annie Oakley),** 66, markswoman who starred in vaudeville and circuses, shot cigarettes from her husband's lips, and could split a playing card into thirty pieces, 2 November 1926.

**Allen Bartlett Pond,** 71, architect and humanitarian who built in Chicago the Hull House settlement house devoted to social and civic work, 17 March 1929.

**Mary Richmond,** 67, social worker and social-work educator who endeavored to make social work a profession and reform marriage laws; she published *Social Diagnosis* (1917), in which she described social evidence and a systematic method to study social problems, 12 September 1928.

**Louisa Schuyler,** 98, welfare worker who helped establish the Bellevue Hospital School of Nursing in 1873; she lobbied for the 1875 New York legislation removing children younger than age three from poorhouses and for 1890 laws turning over the care of the mentally ill to the state. In 1915 she helped establish the National Committee for the Prevention of Blindness, 10 October 1926.

**Victoria Claflin Woodhull,** 88, women's rights and free-love advocate who was also the first woman to be nominated for the U.S. presidency (by her own National Radical Reform Party), 10 June 1927.

# PUBLICATIONS

Richard O. Beard, ed., *Parent Education* (Minneapolis: University of Minnesota Press, 1927);

Phyllis Blanchard, *The Care of the Adolescent Girl* (London: Paul, Trench, Trubner, 1921);

George A. Coe, *What Ails Our Youth?* (New York: Scribners, 1925);

John Dewey, *Human Nature and Conduct* (New York: Holt, 1922);

Dewey, *Individualism, Old and New* (New York: Minton, Balch, 1930);

V. F. Claverton, *The Bankruptcy of Marriage* (New York: Macaulay, 1928);

Katherine Bement Davis, *Factors in the Sex Life of Twenty-Two Hundred Women* (New York: Harper, 1929);

Arnold L. Gesell, *Infancy and Human Growth* (New York: Macmillan, 1928);

G. V. Hamilton, *A Research in Marriage* (New York: Boni, 1929);

Jesse F. Hayden, *The Art of Marriage* (High Point, N.C.: Book Sales Agency, 1926);

Ben Lindsey, *Companionate Marriage* (New York: Boni & Liveright, 1927);

Lindsey and Wainwright Evans, *The Revolt of Modern Youth* (New York: Boni & Liveright, 1925);

Robert S. Lynd and Helen Merrell Lynd, *Middletown: A Study in Contemporary American Culture* (New York: Harcourt, Brace, 1929);

Alfred E. Smith, *Up to Now* (New York: Bobbs-Merrill, 1929);

Douglas Thom, *Everyday Problems of the Everyday Child* (New York: Appleton, 1927);

William I. and Dorothy S. Thomas, *The Child in America* (New York: Knopf, 1928);

Mabel Walker Willebrandt, *The Inside of Prohibition* (Indianapolis: Bobbs-Merrill, 1929);

John B. Watson, *Psychological Care of Infant and Child* (New York: Norton, 1928);

Thomas Woody, *A History of Women's Education in the United States* (New York: Science Press, 1929);

*American Magazine*, periodical;

*Atlantic Monthly*, periodical;

*Better Homes & Gardens*, periodical founded as *Fruit, Garden and Home* in 1922;

*Century*, periodical;

*Current Opinion*, periodical;

*Harper's*, periodical;

*Ladies' Home Journal*, periodical;

*The New Yorker*, periodical founded in 1925;

*Scribner's Magazine*, periodical;

*Survey*, periodical;

*Time*, periodical founded in 1923;

*Woman's Home Companion*, periodical.

# MEDIA

by MATTHEW J. BRUCCOLI and ARLYN BRUCCOLI

## CONTENTS

*Sidebars and tables are listed in italics.*

## 1920

- AT&T, GE, and RCA enter into a cross-licensing agreement for radio broadcasting.

- *The Freeman* is founded in New York by Francis Neilson and Albert Jay Nock as a mildly radical journal.

- *Screenland* magazine is founded.

- *The Dial* is founded by Scofield Thayer as a journal receptive to avant-garde literature.

**20 Aug.**   The first radio news bulletins are broadcast by station 8MK Detroit.

**16 Sept.**   Enrico Caruso makes his final recording session for Victor.

**2 Nov.**   KDKA Pittsburgh broadcasts the Harding-Cox presidential election returns.

## 1921

- *Love Story* magazine (Street & Smith) commences publication; it begins as a quarterly but soon becomes a weekly.

- George T. Delacorte Jr. launches the Dell Publishing Company, which becomes a prolific publisher of pulp, comic, and fan magazines.

- The first regularly scheduled children's radio program, *The Man on the Moon,* commences twice-weekly broadcasting on WJZ Newark.

**11 Apr.**   The first radio sports broadcast is the Johnny Ray–Johnny Dundee bout over KDKA Pittsburgh.

**5–14 Oct.**   In the first World Series radio broadcast (Yankees-Giants) by WJZ Newark, Sandy Hunt telephones play-by-play from the Polo Grounds in Manhattan to announcer Tommy Cowan.

**11 Nov.**   President Warren G. Harding broadcasts the Armistice Day address from the Tomb of the Unknown Soldier, Arlington National Cemetery.

## 1922

- *Fruit, Garden and Home* begins publication in Des Moines, Iowa; its name is changed to *Better Homes and Gardens* in 1924.

- Haldeman-Julius Publishing Company is founded in Girard, Kansas — publishers of Little Blue Books.

- *True Confessions* is launched by Fawcett Publications.

- *The Reader's Digest* is founded by DeWitt and Lila Wallace.

- *The Fugitive* is founded in Nashville as a magazine of verse.

- Will H. Hays is appointed head of the Motion Picture Producers and Directors of America (the Hays Office) after the Fatty Arbuckle rape case, the unsolved murder of William Desmond Taylor, and the drug-related death of Wallace Reid.

- President Harding's address to Congress and the first presidential news conference are broadcast.

- *The New York Times Book Review* begins publication as a separate section.

- NANA (North American Newspaper Alliance) is formed by American and Canadian newspapers as a features syndicate.

**8 Feb.** President Harding has a radio installed in the White House.

**3 Aug.** The first radio broadcast of a full-length play, Eugene Walter's *The Wolf*, over WGY Schenectady, is two and one-half hours long.

**28 Aug.** The first radio commercial is broadcast by WEAF New York; the station "rents" air time at $100 for ten minutes.

**2 Oct.** The first broadcast of a football game is Princeton vs. the University of Chicago, over WEAF New York; the broadcast from Chicago uses long-distance telephone lines.

## 1923

- *Time* magazine begins publication.

- *The Happiness Boys* (Billy Jones and Ernie Hare) radio program begins.

- The *A&P Gypsies*, the *Ipana Troubadours*, and the *Cliquot Club Eskimos* radio programs begin.

- In *Hoover* v. *Intercity Radio Co., Inc.* (286 F. 1003) the U.S. Court of Appeals rules that the secretary of commerce could assign radio wavelengths but not otherwise regulate broadcasting.

- H. V. Kaltenborn becomes the first radio news commentator.

## 1924

- Presidential political conventions are broadcast for the first time.

- Richard L. Simon and M. Lincoln Schuster publish *Cross Word Puzzle Book* (Plaza Publishing Co.).

- The *Herald* and the *Tribune* merge into the *New York Herald Tribune*.

- *The Saturday Review of Literature* begins publication under the editorship of Henry Seidel Canby.

- Two lurid picture tabloids are launched in New York City: William Randolph Hearst's *Daily Mirror* and Bernarr Macfadden's *New York Evening Graphic*.

- The *New York Daily Worker* is launched as the Communist Party newspaper.

**Jan.** *The American Mercury* begins publication under the editorship of H. L. Mencken and George Jean Nathan.

**20 Sept.** Walter Winchell's "Your Broadway and Mine" begins in the *Graphic*.

## 1925

- *EWSM Barn Dance* begins broadcasting from Nashville; it is later renamed *Grand Ole Opry*.

- *The New Yorker* begins publication.

- *Cosmopolitan* begins publication.

- *Children* begins publication; its title is changed to *Parents' Magazine* in 1929.

- Electrical recordings utilizing microphones and amplifiers replace acoustical recordings. The first electronic phonograph with a loudspeaker was the Brunswick Panatrope.

- *Screen Play* magazine begins publication.

## 1926

- The Book-of-the-Month Club is launched. The first selection, *Lolly Willowes* by Sylvia Townsend Warner, is sent to 4,750 members.

- GE, Westinghouse, and RCA form the National Broadcasting Company.

- The movie *Don Juan* (Warner Bros.) has music and sound effects.

- *The New Masses* begins publication as a radical magazine emulating *The Masses,* which had been suppressed by the government in 1917 because of its militant pacifism.

**12 Jan.** *Sam 'n' Henry* (Freeman Gosden and Charles Correll) begins broadcasting on WGN Chicago.

**15 Nov.** Regular network broadcasting is initiated with a variety show originated by WEAF New York and carried by twenty-one NBC-affiliated stations, with remote pick-ups from Chicago and Kansas City.

## 1927

- The Literary Guild of America is founded.

- The Jack Dempsey–Gene Tunney heavyweight championship fight is broadcast.

- Arthur Judson organizes the Columbia Phonograph Broadcasting System, which becomes CBS.

- Paramount News begins.

- Car radios are introduced by the Philadelphia Storage Battery Co. (Philco).

- *transition* is founded in Paris by Eugene Jolas and Elliot Paul as a journal for the publication of experimental writing.

- The Fox Movietone sound newsreels begin.

**1 Jan.** The Rose Bowl football game is the first coast-to-coast broadcast.

**23 Feb.** President Calvin Coolidge signs a bill creating the Federal Radio Commission, the predecessor of the Federal Communications Commission. Sponsored by Secretary of Commerce Herbert Hoover, the FRC is empowered to grant licenses for assigned radio channels.

## 1928

Clarence Mackay merges his Commercial Cable and Postal Telegraph companies with the International Telephone and Telegraph Corporation, thereby forming the first organization to combine radio, cable, and telegraph services.

- The first commercial television receiver is offered for sale by the Daven Corporation of Newark, New Jersey; the price is seventy-five dollars.
- NBC forms two networks: Red and Blue.
- The *Dictionary of American Biography* commences publication.
- The RKO movie studio is formed by GE, Westinghouse, and RCA.
- *The Lights of New York* (Warner Bros.) is the first all-talking movie.
- Walt Disney releases his first animated movie, *Plane Crazy,* and his first animated movie with synchronized sound, *Steamboat Willie* — both with Mickey Mouse.
- The first license for a television station (W2XBS) is issued to RCA.

**11 May**      WGY Schenectady offers the first scheduled television service, on Tuesdays, Thursdays, and Fridays between 1:30 and 2:00 P.M..

**22 Aug.**      WGY airs the first televised news broadcast, the nomination of Al Smith for president.

**11 Sept.**      WGY broadcasts the first televised play, J. Hartley Manners's *The Queen's Messenger.*

## 1929

- *The Fleischmann Hour* starring Rudy Vallee begins.
- *Amos 'n' Andy* is broadcast on the NBC network.
- Hearst Metrotone News begins distribution through M-G-M.
- *Screen Romances* and *Screen Stories* begin publication.
- A broadcasting rating service is introduced by Crossley's Cooperative Analysis of Broadcasting.
- RCA acquires the Victor Talking Machine Company.

**June**      The issue of *Scribner's Magazine* with the second installment of Ernest Hemingway's *A Farewell to Arms* is banned in Boston.

**19 Aug.**      *Amos 'n' Andy* moves to the NBC Blue Network.

# OVERVIEW

**Radio vs. Print.** The shift from a print-based culture to an electronic culture commenced during the 1920s. Nonetheless, the decade witnessed major publishing developments. The print and the sound media did not engage in open combat because radio was not yet a strong threat to the financial well-being of newspapers and magazines. Moreover, radio was not yet an effective news medium. People listened to radio bulletins, but they relied on newspapers to "read all about it."

**Ad Revenue.** No matter how large their circulation figures are, twentieth-century newspapers and magazines do not survive on income from selling copies, unless the sample-copy price is prohibitively high. (Even *The Reader's Digest* was eventually compelled to withdraw its ban on advertising.) Advertising revenue supports all newspapers and unsubsidized magazines. Ad rates are based on circulation; the larger the circulation, the higher the rates. When a periodical loses its advertising, it dies.

**Commercials.** The first radio commercial — an ad for a New York apartment building — was heard in August 1922. The advertiser reportedly paid $100. By the end of the decade almost $20 million was spent by advertisers for network time. Nonetheless, print culture continued to thrive in the early years of radio. Hugely successful new magazines and major book publishing houses were born in the 1920s.

**Phonograph Records.** Other electronic media competed for the time and attention of Americans. Although phonograph recordings had been popular since the turn of the century, the quality of the recordings and the players was so poor that record sales flagged during the early 1920s before the development of electrical recordings and the electrical phonograph. Even so, the phonograph was largely responsible for the demise of the player piano, formerly the pride of American parlors. Although the sound fidelity of the improved equipment was very poor by later standards, phonograph records were influential in enlarging the audience for classical music, making serious music available to people who otherwise could not have heard it. Thus, the 1923 Columbia Records catalogue featured cellist Pablo Casals, soprano Emmy Destinn, soprano Mary Garden, pianist Percy Grainger, pianist Josef Hofmann, soprano Rosa Ponselle, the Chi-

cago Symphony Orchestra, the Metropolitan Opera House Orchestra, and the Philharmonic Orchestra of New York.

**Radio Programs.** Radio exerted a stronger appeal than records, and the increase in the number of receivers coincided with a drop in record sales. After the receiver was paid for, radio was free, and listening to radio was more convenient than cranking the phonograph and changing records every four minutes. Initially the radio broadcasters didn't know what to do with their medium. Programming — that is, the quality and appeal of the programs — was not a particular concern. People would listen to anything. There was an abundance of music, but comparatively little air time was given to programs developed for the capabilities of the medium. Radio drama was slow to develop, possibly because the station owners thought that radio drama could not compete with movies, especially after sound was introduced in 1927. The long-enduring American ritual of going to the movies every week was established during the 1920s.

**Tabloid Papers.** All classes of Americans read newspapers, and each paper was edited for its constituency. (One reason for spending two cents on a newspaper was to find out what was on radio that day.) The most striking development in 1920s journalism was the introduction of tabloid-size papers, mainly intended for an uneducated or immigrant readership. The tabs printed material that was not heard over the airwaves. Moreover, radio could not attempt the service features that the working-class papers provided. The advice columns, instructional articles, and pro-bono crusades built reader trust and loyalty. At that time newspapers published short stories and serialized novels, usually in the weekend editions. There were more than a thousand foreign-language periodicals published in America during the 1920s.

**Newspaper Chains.** Newspapers closed or were merged during the 1920s — just as in previous decades — but radio was not to blame. Apart from the rise of the tabloids, the most significant development was the growth of the chains. Frank Munsey, known as the "Grand Executioner" because of his policy of consolidating weak papers, died in 1925. In 1929 the Scripps-Howard chain had twenty-five dailies. The most famous

American newspaper tycoon, William Randolph Hearst, had twenty dailies and eleven Sunday papers in 1922; he also owned wire services, King Features syndicate, magazines, the Hearst Metrotone newsreel, and the *American Weekly* Sunday supplement with the largest periodical circulation in the world. Hearst had been a crusading publisher, even a populist, in the 1890s, but by the 1920s he was widely distrusted or feared as an abuser of power. Whatever was the actual extent of Hearst's political power, he was unable to get himself elected to any major office. His papers were not admired for their journalistic standards; many of them were frankly sensationalist, featuring scare headlines. Smaller chains that operated during the 1920s were those of Frank E. Gannett, James M. Cox, and the Ridder brothers. Starting in 1923 Cornelius Vanderbilt Jr. tried to build a chain of respectable tabloids in Los Angeles, San Francisco, and Miami — all of which perished.

**Newsmagazines.** New magazines with successful new editorial rationales developed during the 1920s; the most influential innovation was of the newsmagazine with packaged news. *Time,* the pioneer of the type, was not a newspaper in magazine format; it organized the events of the week into topics and summarized the most important events within each topic. The announced intention was to enable busy people to keep up with world news, as well as cultural events. The prodigious success of *Time* and *The Reader's Digest,* also a selector and packager for busy people, signaled a shift in American magazine-reading habits away from long articles that required time and concentration. Perhaps busy people really were too busy to read much, but it is likely that there were more diverting claims on their leisure time in the new era of mass media.

**Books.** The book publishers were responsible for the most enduring cultural events of the decade. During the 1920s Americans became the most influential young writers in the English language. Great writers require great editors and publishers, and publishers achieve greatness through their authors. The movement inaccurately named Modernism coincided with the formation of new publishing houses, most of which still exist in some corporate form. But much of the best writing of the 1920s had nothing to do with the experiments of Modernism: it was good writing without isms.

**Circulation of Print.** Novels sold well at $1.75 to $2 in cloth binding. There were no mass-market paperbacks until 1939, but Grosset & Dunlap and A. L. Burt sold hardbound reprints for fifty cents. Many fiction readers obtained current books from the circulating or rental libraries, which lent books for a nickel a day. Many of these libraries were located in drug stores or other retail businesses. There were many venues for printed matter in the 1920s. Boys sold newspapers and *The Saturday Evening Post* in the streets. Newsstands abounded. Railroad stations had extensive selections of reading material. Despite the rapid expansion of radio networks and the radio audience, printed words continued to dominate American culture and information communication.

# TOPICS IN THE NEWS

## ADVERTISING AND PUBLIC RELATIONS

**Buy! Buy!** The 1920s brought a boom in advertising as postwar consumerism and the cult of salesmanship coincided. Existing ad agencies expanded, and new agencies (Young & Rubicam, Dancer-Fitzgerald-Sample, and Benton & Bowles) were founded. J. Walter Thompson's agency's billings went from $10.7 million in 1922 to $37.5 million in 1929. Albert Lasker, the head of Lord & Thomas, worked with George Washington Hill of the American Tobacco Company (Lucky Strike) to increase that company's earnings from $12 million in 1926 to $40 million in 1930.

**Slogans.** Most advertising still appeared in print during the 1920s, and ad revenue promoted the growth of the mass-circulation magazines, called slicks because they were printed on paper that would reproduce quality ad art. Cigarette advertising produced a war among Lucky Strike, Camel, and Chesterfield. The untapped market was women; before the 1920s no respectable woman smoked in public. Lucky Strike urged women to "Reach for a Lucky instead of a sweet," and the young woman in the famous 1926 Chesterfield ad asked her male companion to "Blow some my way." It was an era of slogans and heretofore-unsuspected maladies: Woodbury Facial Soap "For the skin you love to touch"; Palmolive to "Keep that schoolgirl complexion"; Lifebuoy to prevent "B.O."; Listerine to cure halitosis because "Even Your Best Friend Won't Tell You"; and Absorbine Jr. "Kills Athlete's Foot Fungi on contact."

**"Somewhere West of Laramie."** Edward S. Jordan's prose-poem for the Jordan Playboy first appeared in the 23 June 1923 *Saturday Evening Post*. The Jordan was an assembled car — put together from chassis and engine supplied by other manufacturers — but Jordan's effusion did not mention his car's mechanical qualities. He sold youth, sex appeal, and the spirit of adventure: "Somewhere West of Laramie there's a broncho-busting, steer-roping girl. . . ."

**Bernays.** The prodigious propaganda efforts during World War I elevated the shady press agent, or publicity agent, into the respectable opinion maker and the public-relations counsel. The leader of this new field was Ed-

This 1922 ad stated the populist editorial policy of the *Daily News*.

ward L. Bernays (1891–1995), who coined the term "public relations counsel" and dignified it in his books and pronouncements.

> The public relations counsel supervises and directs the contacts of business and other organizations with the public. He ascertains the state of public opinion toward a given company, product, or idea, and directs his efforts to strengthen favorable impressions or dispel ungrounded prejudices. His function is to crystallize public opinion and to make articulate ideas and events that are already in existence and that are favorable to company policy. It is also an essential part of his services to create the circumstances or the news which will themselves eventuate in the desired expression from the public.
>
> — "The Business of Propaganda," 1928

Two of the most successful cigarette ads of the 1920s, top and left, were aimed at the new market of women smokers.

Below, Edward Bernays and his wife at the Paris Exposition des Arts Decoratifs, 1927.

## Somewhere West of Laramie

SOMEWHERE west of Laramie there's a broncho-busting, steer-roping girl who knows what I'm talking about. She can tell what a sassy pony, that's a cross between greased lightning and the place where it hits, can do with eleven hundred pounds of steel and action when he's going high, wide and handsome.

The truth is—the Playboy was built for her.

Built for the lass whose face is brown with the sun when the day is done of revel and romp and race.

She loves the cross of the wild and the tame.

There's a savor of links about that car—of laughter and lilt and light—a hint of old loves—and saddle and quirt. It's a brawny thing—yet a graceful thing for the sweep o' the Avenue.

Step into the Playboy when the hour grows dull with things gone dead and stale.

Then start for the land of real living with the spirit of the lass who rides, lean and rangy, into the red horizon of a Wyoming twilight.

# JORDAN
JORDAN MOTOR CAR COMPANY, Inc., Cleveland, Ohio

The best-known automobile advertisement of the 1920s sold an unexceptional car.

## The best new book each month selected for you by this committee—

AND SENT TO YOU REGULARLY ON AP-
PROVAL—A UNIQUE SERVICE FOR THOSE
WHO WISH TO KEEP ABREAST OF
THE BEST NEW BOOKS AS THEY APPEAR

CERTAINLY there is nothing more satisfying, to a person who loves books, than to keep abreast of the best new works of our present-day writers, *as they appear*. And, inversely, there are few things more annoying than to miss the outstanding books, when everybody else of intelligence is reading, discussing and enjoying them. Yet how frequently most of us disappoint ourselves in this way!

Think over the last few years. How often have interesting books appeared, widely discussed and widely recommended, books you were really anxious to read and fully intended to read when you "got around to it," but which nevertheless you missed! Why does this happen to you so often?

The true reason lies in your habits of book-buying. Through carelessness, or through the driving circumstances of a busy life, you simply *overlook* obtaining books that you really want to read. Or you live in a district remote from bookstores, where it is impossible to get the best new books without difficulty.

This need be true no longer. A unique service has been organized, *which will deliver to you every month, without effort or trouble on your part*, the best book of that month, whether fiction or non-fiction. And if the book you receive is not one you would have chosen yourself, *you may exchange it for a book you prefer*, from a list of other new books that are recommended. In this way, automatically, you keep abreast of the best literature of the day.

These "best books" are chosen for you, *from the books of all publishers*, by a group of unbiased critics and writers, whose judgment as to books and whose catholicity of taste have been demonstrated for many years before the public. The members of

this Selecting Committee, who have agreed to perform this service, are listed above. With each book sent there is always included some interesting comment by a member of the committee upon the book and the author.

The price at which the books are billed to you is in every case the publisher's retail price. There are no extra charges for the service.

A very interesting prospectus has been prepared, explaining the many conveniences of this plan. This prospectus will convince you of several things: that the plan will really enable you always to "keep up" with the best of the new books; that you will never again, through carelessness, miss books you are anxious to read; that the recommendations of this unbiased committee will guide you in obtaining books that are really worth-while; that there is no chance of your purchasing books that you would not choose to purchase anyway; and that, in spite of the many conveniences of the plan, the cost of the books you get is no greater than if you purchased them yourself.

Send for this prospectus, using the coupon below or a letter. Your request will involve you in no obligation to subscribe.

BOOK-OF-THE-MONTH CLUB, INC.
218 West 40th St.    Dept. 25    New York, N.Y.

BOOK-OF-THE-MONTH CLUB, INC.
218 West 40th St., Dept. 25, New York, N.Y.
Please send me, without cost, your Prospectus confirming the details of the Book-of-the-Month Plan of Reading. This request involves me in no obligation to subscribe to your service.

Name_____
Address_____
City_____  State_____

Advertisement for the Book-of-the-Month Club (*Time*, 1926)

Bernays was his own best client. Ivy Lee, another celebrated PR figure, represented the Rockefeller family and endeavored to make old John D. likable — or less detestable — by having the robber baron give dimes to children. These manipulators relied primarily on the print media to convey their messages. When a public event was staged, it had to be covered in the newspapers in order to make it effective. They were still press agents.

**Sources:**
Edward L. Bernays, *Crystallizing Public Opinion* (New York: Boni & Liveright, 1923);

Bernays, *Propaganda* (New York: Liveright, 1928);

Roy S. Durstine, *This Advertising Business* (New York: Scribners, 1928);

Ivy Lee, *Publicity: Some of the Things It Is and Is Not* (New York: Industries Publishing Co., 1925).

## BOOK CLUBS

**A Book a Month.** Mass-media and mass-marketing stimulated each other during the 1920s. The most successful publishing development was distribution through book clubs. At the start of the decade most Americans did not have access to bookstores. Many potential members of the emerging reading public did not know what to

read or how to obtain books. The founding of the Book-of-the-Month Club (BOMC) by Robert K. Haas and Harry Scherman filled a well-defined need.

**Judges.** The monthly selections were chosen by a panel of judges — critic Henry Seidel Canby, columnist Heywood Broun, author Dorothy Canfield Fisher, man-of-letters Christopher Morley, and newspaper publisher William Allen White — who exercised complete freedom to pick any current book that was not priced more than three dollars. The first selection, distributed in April 1926, established the integrity of the judges: Sylvia Townsend Warner's *Lolly Willowes: or, the Loving Huntsman*, an English feminist fantasy that was hardly a crowd pleaser, went to 4,750 members. Subsequent 1926 selections positioned the BOMC as upper middlebrow. In certain social groups membership in the BOMC was regarded as a badge of intelligence; in others, of pretentiousness; in still others, of intellectual conformity.

**Literary Guild.** The BOMC prospered, rapidly. By the end of its first season there were 46,539 members. Inevitably the BOMC spawned imitators and competitors, of which the most successful was the Literary Guild of America, launched in 1927. The first Guild selection was *Anthony Comstock: Roundsman of the Lord,* by Hey-

The 1920s were a boom period for movie-fan magazines. This cover depicts Rudolph Valentino.

wood Broun and Margaret Leech. At first booksellers and some publishers opposed the BOMC. Although the club took away bookstore customers, it also brought in new buyers who wanted a book because it was the BOMC selection. Publishers initially resisted making the price discounts required by the club. Nonetheless, it was clear that the BOMC — and its progeny — put books in the hands of readers who otherwise would not have known about them or purchased them. Both the BOMC and the Literary Guild began on a subscription basis. Members paid an annual fee for twelve books. The negative-option system that allowed members to decline selections was a later improvement. Guild members received special inexpensive editions (twelve books for eighteen dollars), whereas the BOMC distributed copies of the trade edition. The Guild also began with a panel of judges, which was dropped.

**Specialization.** The next movement in the book-club industry was from general to specialized selections. The hundred-odd American book clubs that eventually emerged were aimed at professions (lawyers), hobbyists (gardeners), and particular fields (history). Their impact on American readers has been prodigious and salutary.

Sources:

*The Book of the Month: Sixty Years of Books in American Life* (Boston: Little, Brown, 1986);

Charles Lee, *The Hidden Public: The Story of the Book-of-the-Month Club* (Garden City, N.Y.: Doubleday, 1958).

## GENRE MAGAZINES

**Fan Mags.** Movie-fan and movie-romance magazines flourished during the 1920s. These were overlapping categories; both covered the Hollywood scene, but the content of the movie-romance publications stressed the mar-

ital adventures and romantic attachments of Hollywood, much of it invented. Among the many magazines in this field were *Screenland* (1920), *Screen Play* (1925), *Screenbook* (1928), *Screen Stories* (1929), and *Screen Romances* (1929).

**Macfadden.** Health faddist Bernarr Macfadden (1868–1955), who had become wealthy from his magazine *Physical Culture,* introduced what became known as the confession magazine with *True Story* in 1919. It reached a weekly circulation of more than 2 million. The success of this magazine was attributed in large part to its sexual frankness. However, *True Story* was not salacious or intended to arouse erotic feelings; Macfadden treated sexual problems in a quasi-clinical way. *True Story* inspired imitations, including Macfadden's *True Romances* (1923) and *True Experiences* (1925). Fawcett Publications had a success in 1922 with *True Confessions,* which began as a crime magazine but converted to women's romantic experiences. Having discovered that the word *true* sold copies, Macfadden introduced the first quasi-factual detective magazine, *True Detective Mysteries,* in 1924. Other publishers reached the same conclusion, and both *True Marriage Stories* and *True Love Stories* commenced in 1924. (Writers of subliterary popular fiction often used multiple pseudonyms; "true"-magazine writers used a different one for each appearance, author recognition being

A display of Macfadden magazines

## American Literature
*A Journal of Literary History, Criticism, and Bibliography*

Volume One      MARCH, 1929      Number One

### CONTENTS

Contents page for the first journal devoted to American
literary scholarship, founded by Jay B. Hubbell

a distinct disadvantage.) Bernarr Macfadden's magazines were innovative and very profitable; but his newspaper ventures, including the *New York Evening Graphic*, were failures.

**Better Homes and Gardens.** In the home-magazine field one of the great publishing successes of the decade was *Better Homes and Gardens* — which began in 1922 as *Fruit, Garden, and Home*. E. T. Meredith, its publisher and editorial director, built his magazine on the policy of providing practical information and advice for middle-class families; much of each issue was given over to how-to-do-it instructions that were practicable for non-professionals.

**Whiz Bang.** *Captain Billy's Whiz Bang* was a surprising success in the 1920s magazine field, and its popularity provides a reminder that the literary decade — like any decade — had its vulgar component. Captain Billy was Wilford H. Fawcett of Minneapolis, and a Whiz Bang was a type of World War I shell. In 1919 Fawcett began

preparing joke sheets that were sold in hotels for twenty-five cents. The jokes were suggestive, lewd, and coarse, leaning heavily on what was then called barnyard and outhouse humor. Whatever else it was, the *Whiz Bang* was a cultural phenomenon; although it attracted imitators, none of them constituted real competion. By the mid 1920s *Captain Billy's Whiz Bang* was selling almost half a million copies of each issue and financed the Fawcett publishing empire, which grew to include *True Confessions* (1922), *Mechanix Illustrated* (1928), and paperback books.

**Sources:**

William R. Hunt, *Body Love: The Amazing Career of Bernarr Macfadden* (Bowling Green, Ohio: Bowling Green University Popular Press, 1989);

Theodore Peterson, *Magazines in the Twentieth Century* (Urbana: University of Illinois Press, 1956);

John Tebbel and Mary Ellen Zuckerman, *The Magazine in America, 1741–1990* (New York: Oxford University Press, 1991).

**1920**

*Contact* (terminated 1923), ed. William Carlos Williams and Robert McAlmon. New York.

**1921**

*The Double Dealer* (1926). New Orleans.

*The Reviewer* (1925). Richmond, Va.

*Broom* (1924). Rome; Berlin; New York.

*Gargoyle* (1922). Paris.

**1922**

*The Fugitive* (1925). Nashville, Tenn.

*Secession* (1924), ed. Gorham Munson with Matthew Josephson and Kenneth Burke. Vienna; Berlin; Reutte; Florence; New York.

*The Wave* (1924), ed. Vincent Starrett. Chicago; Copenhagen.

**1923**

*The Chicago Literary Times* (1924), ed. Ben Hecht.

*The Modern Quarterly* (1940), ed. V. F. Calverton. Baltimore.

**1924**

*The Transatlantic Review* (1925), ed. Ford Madox Ford. Paris.

**1925**

*This Quarter* (1932), ed. Ernest Walsh and Ethel Moorhead. Paris; Milan; Monte Carlo.

*Two Worlds* (1927), ed. Samuel Roth. New York.

**1926**

*Fire!!*, ed. Wallace Thurman. New York.

**1927**

*Hound and Horn* (1934). Portland, Maine.

*transition* (1938), ed. Eugene Jolas and Elliot Paul. Paris; The Hague.

*Exile* (1928), ed. Ezra Pound. Dijon.

**1929**

*Blues* (1930), ed. Charles Henri Ford. Columbus, Miss.

*Tambour* (1930). Paris.

## LITTLE MAGAZINES

**Art vs. Money.** Because printing costs were still relatively low in America — and very cheap in Europe — many so-called "little magazines" sprang up during the 1920s. The term "little" did not refer to format but to circulation. The standard work, *The Little Magazine: A History and a Bibliography*, states that "A little magazine is a magazine designed to print artistic work which for reasons of commercial expediency is not acceptable to the money-minded periodicals or presses." Virtually all little magazines existed for the purpose of publishing avant-garde or experimental writing, often by their editors. A writer is not a writer unless he or she is published somewhere, somehow. The little magazines provided a place for writers — typically younger writers — to break in. Ezra Pound was the most important figure involved with the little magazines as editor or adviser during the 1920s. Nearly all of these magazines had a short life span as the editors ran out of money or lost interest.

**University Sponsorship.** The regional literary magazines resembled the little magazines in publishing material that could not find a commercial market, but the regionals were less experimental. Some of these were *Frontier* (University of Montana, 1920), *The Southwest Review* (Southern Methodist University, 1924; previously *The Texas Review*), and *The Prairie Schooner* (University of Nebraska, 1927). Since the regional literary magazines nearly always had university sponsorship, their life expectancies were better than those of the privately funded little magazines. However, the university-sponsored magazines were not necessarily parochial; some, such as *The Virginia Quarterly Review* (The University of Virginia, 1925), were national in scope. The universities also supported scholarly or critical journals that were not actually little magazines; Duke's *American Literature* became the most important journal in its field.

Sources:

Hugh Ford, *Published in Paris: American and British Writers, Printers, and Publishers in Paris, 1920–1939* (New York: Macmillan, 1975);

Frederick J. Hoffman, Charles Allen, and Carolyn F. Ulrich, *The Little Magazine: A History and a Bibliography* (Princeton: Princeton University Press, 1946).

## NEWSPAPERS

**Stop the Presses!** During the 1920s, now-legendary writers worked on papers that aggressively competed for news and readers. *The Front Page,* the 1928 hit play by ex-reporters Charles MacArthur and Ben Hecht, established the public's idea of how newspapers operated. In 1920 there were 2,042 English-language dailies in 1,295 American cities; their total circulation was 27.8 million. Americans habitually read newspapers, which cost two cents; many households took morning and evening papers. Most cities had papers with different ownerships and editorial policies — usually, Republican and Democrat.

**Tabloids.** The most influential innovation in Jazz Age journalism was the successful introduction of tabloid or sensationalized journalism by Joseph Medill Patterson's *The New York Daily News* in 1919. It was followed by William Randolph Hearst's *The New York Daily Mirror*

Composograph from the *New York Evening Graphic* depicting Daddy Browning with child-bride Peaches

and Bernarr Macfadden's *New York Evening Graphic* in 1924. There were also nonsensational tabloids that used the tab size for the sake of convenience. The *Graphic,* the most blatantly vulgar of the tabloids, was inevitably known as the "Porno-Graphic." It ignored most national or world events to concentrate on the coverage of sex and crime — preferably sex crime. Two of the crimes that sold tabloid papers were the 1922 Hall-Mills case (an unsolved lover's-lane murder of a minister and a choir singer) and the 1927 Snyder-Gray case (the murder of a husband by an adulterous wife and her corset-salesman lover). Tabloid journalism also fed on the Kip Rhinelander divorce/miscegenation trial and the antics of Daddy Browning and his child bride, Peaches. The most egregious feature of the *Graphic* was the "composograph" — a faked photograph, such as the depiction of actor Rudolph Valentino's arrival in heaven. Jazz journalism was not restricted to New York. *The Denver Post* was not a tabloid, but it was sensational and successful in the 1920s.

**Comics.** Comic strips (also known as the funnies) were effective circulation builders, especially for the tabloids. The Chicago Tribune–New York News syndicate and Hearst's King Features syndicate developed some of the most widely printed strips during the 1920s. Three long-running popular strips began in 1919: Frank King's *Gasoline Alley,* Billy DeBeck's *Barney Google,* and E. C. Segar's *Thimble Theatre* — which introduced Popeye in 1929. Harold Gray's *Little Orphan Annie* began in 1924, as did Roy Crane's *Wash Tubbs,* the first adventure strip. Other popular strips that began during the decade were Martin Branner's *Winnie Winkle* (1920), Russ Westover's *Tillie the Toiler* (1921), and Frank Willard's *Moon Mullins* (1923). Older comic artists whose work remained popular included Rube Goldberg, George McManus, and Tad (Thomas Aloysius Dorgan).

**The** *World.* By general consent *The New York World* was the best paper in America during the decade, and it had a national influence. Under Herbert Bayard Swope, executive editor from 1920 to 1929, the *World* was regarded as "the newspaperman's newspaper." The *World* did not try to provide broad coverage of the news; instead, it relied on good reporting and writing: "THE WORLD does not believe that all the news that is fit to print is worth reading." The independently liberal editorial page was edited by Walter Lippmann, who became

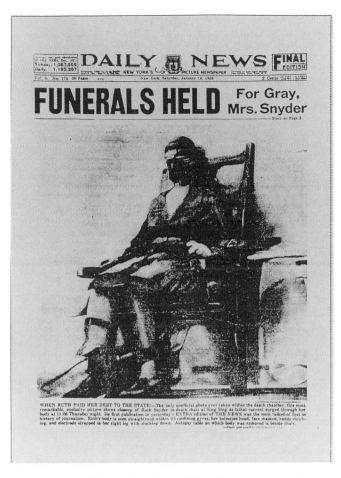

A reporter violated the rules of Sing Sing prison by taking this photo with a camera strapped to his leg.

Grantland Rice broadcasting the 1923 World Series

one of the most influential political writers in America. The editorial page featured the drawings of Rollin Kirby and H. T. Webster, two of the most widely admired cartoonists of their time. But the glory of the *World* was its op-ed page (the right-hand page opposite the editorial page), featuring Heywood Broun ("It Seems to Me"), Frankin P. Adams ("The Conning Tower"), the theatre reviews of Alexander Woollcott, and other columns. The sale of the *World* to the Scripps-Howard chain by the Pulitzer family and the paper's merger into the *World-Telegram* in 1931 was a black day in newspaper history.

**The *Trib*.** The glory years of the *World* coincided with the great years of the *New York Herald Tribune* — formed when the *Tribune* purchased the *Herald* in 1924 — an acquisition that included *The Paris Herald,* the best of the three American dailies published in Paris. Although the *Trib* was regarded as the best-written and best-edited paper in New York, it could not match the circulation or advertising revenue of *The New York Times.*

**Grantland Rice.** The sports department of the *Trib* featured columns by W. O. McGeehan and Grantland Rice. McGeehan was an exponent of what city editor Stanley Walker called the "Aw-Nuts" school of sportswriting; Rice wrote "Hurrah" columns, and it was remarked that he covered games as though he were re-porting on the Trojan War. Rice's account of the 1924 Notre Dame–Army football game had the most famous lead in American sports writing:

> Outlined against a blue-gray October sky, the Four Horsemen rode again. In dramatic lore they are known as Famine, Pestilence, Destruction and Death. These are only aliases. Their real names are Stuhldreher, Miller, Crowley and Layden.

He also wrote the most widely recognized couplet of sports verse:

> For when the One Great Scorer comes to write against your name,
>
> He marks — not that you won or lost — but how you played the game.

**By-Lines.** Columnists and feature writers were celebrities during the 1920s. The line-up included Damon Runyon, Walter Winchell, O. O. McIntyre, Floyd Gibbons, Paul Gallico, Will Rogers, Arthur Brisbane, Westbrook Pegler, Ring W. Lardner, Franklin P. Adams (F.P.A.), Heywood Broun, Walter Lippmann — all of whom had national reputations.

Sources:

Simon Michael Bessie, *Jazz Journalism: The Story of Tabloid Newspapers* (New York: Dutton, 1938);

Sidney Kobre, *Development of American Journalism* (Dubuque, Iowa: Braun, 1969);

Frank Luther Mott, *American Journalism: A History, 1690–1960*, third edition (New York: Macmillan, 1962);

Jerry Robinson, *The Comics: An Illustrated History of Comic Strip Art* (New York: Putnam, 1974).

## NEWSREELS

**Silent newsreels.** The first newsreel produced in America was the Pathé Weekly, commencing in 1911. Audiences at first-run movie theaters soon came to expect silent newsreels, especially during World War I.

**Movietone.** There were experimental sound newsreels with synchronized recordings, but the talkie newsreel was not practical until Theodore Case developed his sound-on-film system. The Fox Film Corporation purchased Case's system in 1926 and established the Fox Movietone Corporation. The first Fox Movietone News release showed Charles Lindbergh's takeoff on 20 May 1927. Combined with footage of the Washington ceremonies welcoming Lindbergh, it was exhibited as a special feature five months before the premiere of *The Jazz Singer*. The first all-sound Movietone newsreel was shown at the New York Roxy Theatre on 28 October 1927; it included segments on Niagara Falls, "The Romance of the Iron Horse," the Army-Yale football game, and a rodeo. On 3 December Movietone News was released as a regular weekly feature; this newsreel covered the Vatican Choir at the Tomb of the Unknown Soldier, the blowing of the Conowingo Bridge in Maryland, and the Army-Navy football game.

**Competition.** The great success of Movietone News compelled the other movie studios to produce competing newsreels. Paramount News began in 1927 as "The Eyes of the World" and soon became "The Eyes and Ears of the World." Hearst Metrotone News (later the News of the Day) began releasing through Metro-Goldwyn-Mayer in 1929. Pathé News added sound, and Universal Studios established its own sound-newsreel service. There were other short-lived newsreel production companies. At the peak of their popularity the newsreels ran for ten minutes and were changed twice a week. But the newsreels were not restricted to straight news coverage; human-interest and humorous features were included.

**Newsreel Theaters.** The newsreels were so popular that theaters showing only newsreels opened in large cities. The first newsreel theater was the Embassy at Broadway and 46th Street in Manhattan, which opened on 2 November 1929 and operated until 1949. Some of these newsreel theaters claimed to add new material every day. The movie theater newsreel died in the 1950s, one of the many things killed by television.

**Source:**
Raymond Fielding, *The American Newsreel, 1911–1967* (Norman: University of Oklahoma Press, 1972).

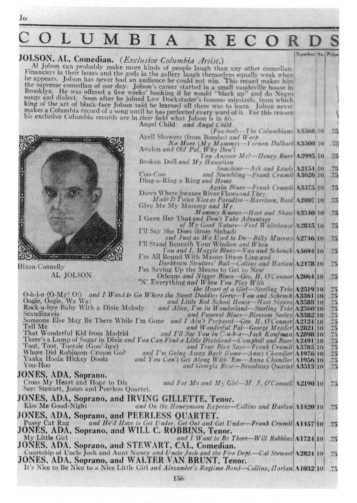

A page from the 1923 Columbia record catalogue

## PHONOGRAPH RECORDS

**Low Fidelity.** Sales of phonographs and records decreased during the early years of the 1920s after reaching a peak in 1920. The chief cause of the decline was the radio craze, but the poor sound quality of the recordings and the phonographs impeded the growth of the industry. The recordings were made by the acoustical or mechanical system, which did not use amplifiers or microphones. These records did not reproduce the overtones of the sound, and the players used a large horn to magnify the sound. The result was scratchy and failed to provide a realistic sound reproduction. Most phonographs had to be hand-cranked every three or four records. In 1925 the wind-up cabinet-model Victrolas were priced from $110 to $250.

**Victor.** The industry was stimulated by the development in 1925 of an electrical recording process by Western Electric Company, which also developed the all-electric Orthophonic phonograph with a loudspeaker. Victor, the largest record-phonograph manufacturer, was the first to bring out electrical recordings for the Orthophonic Victrola. Sales increased steadily until 65 million records were sold in 1929, almost half of which were from Victor.

**Inconvenience.** Even at their best, records in the 1920s were fragile, short-lived, inconvenient, and relatively expensive. The lacquer or wax records were easily cracked; they melted in hot weather; they became scratchy after a few playings; the ten-inch records played for four minutes. Popular music and comedy routines were recorded on the ten-inch disks that sold at an average price of seventy-five cents. Classic or serious music was on twelve-inch disks that cost $1.25 or $1.50. There were no record changers.

**Recording Stars.** The leading producers were Victor, Columbia, Okeh, Gennett, and Brunswick. The best-selling orchestra leader of the 1920s was Paul Whiteman, whose "Whispering"/"Japanese Sandman" sold more than a million copies for Victor in 1920. Dance-music records were very popular throughout the decade, and Victor had another best-seller in 1920 with bandleader Ben Selvin's "Dardanella." Victor also introduced the yodels of Jimmie Rodgers. Columbia lured Whiteman away from Victor in 1928 and gave him his own label. Singer-bandleader Ted Lewis ("When My Baby Smiles at Me") also had his own Columbia label; one of his hits was "Goodnight" in 1928. The Columbia roster boasted Bessie Smith. Brunswick hits included Isham Jones's "Wabash Blues" in 1921 and Al Jolson's "Sonny Boy" in 1924.

**Race Records.** The major companies developed "Race" series aimed at black buyers. Okeh was particularly attentive to black performers. Mamie Smith's "Crazy Blues"/"It's Right Here for You" sold an exceptional seventy-five thousand copies in 1920. Okeh sought out what was described as "Americana" (music by obscure or local performers) and had country and western and Yiddish record series. Black Swan, launched in 1921, was the first black-owned label. Its biggest success was Ethel Waters's "Oh Daddy"/"Down Home Blues." Records enlarged the audience for black jazz and blues — exposing whites to music they had never before heard and could hear only on records. Gennett recorded some of the most famous jazz figures of the 1920s, including King Oliver, Louis Armstrong, and Jelly Roll Morton. Bix Beiderbecke made his early records for Gennett.

**Radio Stars.** Most of the recording stars of the early 1920s — for example, Al Jolson, Bessie Smith, and Eddie Cantor — had previously made their reputations on the stage. However, at the end of the decade the reputations of the most popular recording entertainers had been achieved through radio exposure. Billy Jones and Ernie Hare (The Happiness Boys), Moran and Mack (The Two Black Crows), and Charles Correll and Freeman Gosden (Amos 'n' Andy) were obscure vaudeville performers before radio made them national figures.

Source:
Roland Gelatt, *The Fabulous Phonograph: From Edison to Stereo* (New York: Appleton-Century, 1966).

## PUBLISHING HOUSES LAUNCHED DURING THE 1920S

| | |
|---|---|
| 1920 | Thomas Seltzer |
| 1921 | Harcourt, Brace (reorganized from Harcourt, Brace & Howe, 1919) |
| 1922 | Haldeman-Julius |
| 1923 | Albert & Charles Boni |
| 1923 | Dial |
| 1924 | International Publishers |
| 1924 | Simon & Schuster |
| 1924 | Payson & Clarke |
| 1924 | Greenberg: Publisher |
| 1924 | Minton, Balch |
| 1925 | Viking |
| 1925 | Norton |
| 1926 | William Morrow |
| 1926 | John Day |
| 1926 | Vanguard |
| 1927 | Random House (reorganized from Modern Library, 1925) |
| 1928 | Horace Liveright (reorganized from Boni & Liveright, 1917) |
| 1928 | Covici-Friede |
| 1928 | Coward-McCann |
| 1929 | Cape & Smith |
| 1929 | Farrar & Rinehart |
| 1929 | University of New Mexico Press |

## PUBLISHING

**New Houses.** Writers require publication, and publishers need books. The 1920s were a golden era for American writing and publishing. During the decade twenty influential trade publishing houses and seven university presses were launched. (An influential publisher is one that publishes significant authors and widely read books, good or bad; the longevity of the imprint is also a factor in its influence.) More enduring major American houses were founded during the 1920s than in any other decade.

**Opportunity.** Apart from the availability of ambitious young men who wanted their own companies, the cause for this proliferation was economic. A publishing com-

Conrad Aiken, *Blue Voyage* (1927)

————, *Costumes by Eros* (1928)

Edward W. Bok, *The Americanization of Edward Bok* (1920)

James Boyd, *Drums* (1925)

————, *Marching On* (1927)

Thomas Boyd, *Through the Wheat* (1923)

Morley Callaghan, *Strange Fugitive* (1928)

————, *A Native Argosy* (1929)

Calvin Coolidge, *The Price of Freedom* (1924)

F. Scott Fitzgerald, *This Side of Paradise* (1920)

————, *Flappers and Philosophers* (1920)

————, *The Beautiful and Damned* (1922)

————, *Tales of the Jazz Age* (1922)

————, *The Vegetable* (1923)

————, *The Great Gatsby* (1925)

————, *All the Sad Young Men* (1926)

Ernest Hemingway, *The Torrents of Spring* (1926)

————, *The Sun Also Rises* (1926)

————, *Men Without Women* (1927)

————, *A Farewell to Arms* (1929)

Will James, *Cowboys North and South* (1924)

————, *The Drifting Cowboy* (1925)

————, *Smoky: The Story of A Cow Pony* (1926)

————, *Cow Country* (1927)

————, *Sand* (1929)

Ring W. Lardner, *How to Write Short Stories* (1924)

————, *What of It?* (1925)

————, *The Love Nest and Other Stories* (1926)

————, *Round Up* (1929)

John P. Marquand, *The Unspeakable Gentleman* (1922) [first novel]

————, *The Black Cargo* (1925)

Thomas Nelson Page, *The Red Riders* (1924)

Theodore Roosevelt, *An Autobiography* (1920)

————, *Diaries of Boyhood and Youth* (1928)

Theodore and Kermit Roosevelt, *East of the Sun and West of the Moon* (1926)

George Santayana, *Character and Opinions in the United States* (1920)

————, *Soliloquies in England, and Later Soliloquies* (1922)

————, *Dialogues in Limbo* (1925)

————, *Platonism and the Spiritual Life* (1927)

————, *The Realm of Essence* (1927)

Robert E. Sherwood, *The Road to Rome* (1927)

John W. Thomason Jr., *Fix Bayonets!* (1926)

Arthur Train, *Tut! Tut! Mr. Tutt* (1924)

————, *Page Mr. Tutt* (1926)

————, *When Tutt Meets Tutt* (1927)

S. S. Van Dine, *The Benson Murder Case* (1926)

————, *The Canary Murder Case* (1927)

————, *The Greene Murder Case* (1928)

————, *The Bishop Murder Case* (1929)

Edith Wharton, *In Morocco* (1920)

————, *A Son at the Front* (1924)

————, *The Writing of Fiction* (1925)

Edmund Wilson, *I Thought of Daisy* (1928)

Thomas Wolfe, *Look Homeward, Angel* (1929)

pany could be started with comparatively little financing: Richard L. Simon and Max L. Schuster launched their house with a $4,000 bankroll and hit pay dirt with their first book, the first crossword-puzzle book. The culture of America was print-based. Despite the increasing competition from radio, reading was still the chief source of pleasure and instruction.

**Personal Publishing.** As impressive as the number of new imprints was the range of their editorial rationales. Most of the lists represented the taste and judgment of one or two men — the owner or the partners. Publishing was personal; some of the young owners regarded themselves as crusaders. Thus, Emanuel Haldeman-Julius of Girard, Kansas, published some two thousand titles of the Little Blue Books at ten cents each. These paper-cov-

ered books were 3 ½" x 5" in format and had from 32 to 128 pages. Some of the titles expressed Haldeman-Julius's socialist convictions, and some had titillating titles (*Confidential Chats with Husbands* by Dr. Lay); but most of the Little Blue Books provided worthwhile literature (Greek and Roman classics) and self-education (*Botany for Beginners*) for millions of readers who would otherwise not have had access to it. Vanguard Press was started by Charles Garland to disburden himself of his inheritance; its purpose was to publish inexpensive books to promote social justice. W. W. Norton organized his firm for the main purpose of educating readers, and it developed into an important trade and textbook publisher.

**Autodidactism.** The 1920s' concern with education was evidenced by the success of books that made accessi-

Advertisement for one of the correspondence schools that were popular during the 1920s

ble the things that educated people are supposed to know. The most successful one-volume works were H. G. Wells's *The Outline of History* (1920) and Hendrik Van Loon's *The Story of Mankind* (1921). Will Durant's *The Story of Philosophy: The Lives and Opinions of the Greater Philosophers* (1926) started in the Little Blue Books series and grew into the multivolume *The Story of Civilization*. All of these volumes actually became best-sellers; Van Loon's book — which was originally published for juveniles — earned him $200,000 in two years. The popularity of these volumes was probably more an indication of the social insecurity of the new leisure class than an expression of a hunger for knowledge for its own sake. The organization of education in convenient, time-saving packages was characteristic of the 1920s. The self-made man and the woman he had married before they had time or money for culture were buyers of books that would allow them to become self-educated. The market for autodidactism cut across class boundaries. Newspaper and magazine ads offered correspondence courses that would teach salesmanship, piano playing, and grammar. A long-running ad asked, "Do you make these mistakes in English?"

**The Five-Foot Shelf.** Autodidactism achieved respectability with *The Harvard Classics*. Having stated

## BONI & LIVERIGHT HIGHSPOTS (1920-1929)

Sherwood Anderson, *Dark Laughter* (1925)
Anderson, *Tar: A Midwest Childhood* (1926)
Gertrude Atherton, *Black Oxen* (1923)
Djuna Barnes, *A Book* (1923)
Barnes, *Ryder* (1928)
Hart Crane, *White Buildings* (1926)
E. E. Cummings, *The Enormous Room* (1922)
Cummings, *Is 5* (1926)
Cummings, *Him* (1927)
Hilda Doolittle, *Collected Poems of H. D.* (1925)
Theodore Dreiser, *Hey Rub-a-Dub-Dub* (1920)
Dreiser, *A Book About Myself* (1922)
Dreiser, *An American Tragedy* (1925)
Dreiser, *Chains* (1927)
Dreiser, *A Gallery of Women* (1929)
Isadora Duncan, *My Life* (1927)
T. S. Eliot, *The Waste Land* (1922)
William Faulkner, *Soldiers' Pay* (1926)
Faulkner, *Mosquitoes* (1927)
Ben Hecht, *Gargoyles* (1922)
Hecht, *The Florentine Dagger* (1923)
Ernest Hemingway, *In Our Time* (1925)
James G. Huneker, *Painted Veils* (1920)
Robinson Jeffers, *Roan Stallion; Tamar and Other Poems* (1925)
Jeffers, *The Women at Point Sur* (1927)
Jeffers, *Cawder* (1929)
Jeffers, *Dear Judas* (1929)
Anita Loos, *"Gentlemen Prefer Blondes"* (1925)
Loos, *"But Gentlemen Marry Brunettes"* (1928)
Edgar Lee Masters, *The New Spoon River* (1924)
Eugene O'Neill, *Beyond the Horizo*n (1920)
O'Neill, *The Emperor Jones, Diff'rent, The Straw* (1921)
O'Neill, *Gold* (1921)
O'Neill, *The Hairy Ape, Anna Christie, The First Man* (1922)
O'Neill, *All God's Chillun Got Wings and Welded* (1924)
O'Neill, *Desire Under the Elms* (1925)
O'Neill, *The Great God Brown, The Fountain, The Moon of the Caribbees and Other Plays* (1926)
O'Neill, *Marco Millions* (1927)
O'Neill, *Lazarus Laughed* (1927)
O'Neill, *Strange Interlude* (1928)
O'Neill, *Dynamo* (1929)
Dorothy Parker, *Enough Rope* (1926)
Parker, *Sunset Gun* (1928)
Ezra Pound, *Poems, 1918–21* (1921)
Pound, *Personae* (1926)
Upton Sinclair, *Oil!* (1927)
Sinclair, *Boston* (1928)
Jean Toomer, *Cane* (1923)

Covers for two of Hugo Gernsback's pulp magazines

that a man could acquire an education in the liberal arts by reading for fifteen minutes a day from books that would occupy five feet of shelf space, Harvard president Charles W. Eliot backed his assertion by editing a set of fifty volumes with selections from hundreds of great books. Sold mainly by mail during the 1920s, the "five-foot shelf" became a fixture in many American homes.

**Sources:**

Peter Dzwonkoski, ed., *American Literary Publishing Houses, 1900–1980: Trade and Paperback; Dictionary of Literary Biography*, volume 46 (Detroit: Bruccoli Clark/Gale, 1986);

Emanuel Haldeman-Julius, *The First Hundred Million* (New York: Simon & Schuster, 1928);

John Tebbel, *A History of Book Publishing in the United States*, volume 3 (New York: Bowker, 1978).

## PULP MAGAZINES

*Black Mask.* The terms "pulp magazine" and "dime novel" have become interchangeable, but the two types of magazines had separate histories. The dime novels were paper-covered thin books that resembled magazines and usually had one long story. They became popular during the Civil War, and the contents were mostly adventure or western stories. Ned Buntline's Buffalo Bill stories were widely read in this format. Publisher Frank Munsey created the first pulp magazine, *Argosy,* in 1896: a 7" x 10" collection of fiction, printed on wood-pulp paper. Later, pulps featured lurid or exciting covers. Each issue included stories and novelettes; some pulps serialized novels. Most sold for ten cents or fifteen cents. Not all magazines printed on pulp paper were regarded as pulp magazines; the term also indicated content or editorial rationale. The authentic pulps were almost always restricted to a particular subject or setting (the West, sports, crime, aviation) and intended for an unsophisticated readership. Thus, *The Smart Set*, which H. L. Mencken and George Jean Nathan took over writing in 1914, was printed on pulp paper but was not classified as a pulp because it was a journal of opinion and literature with high editorial standards. However, Mencken and Nathan launched three pulps — *Parisienne* (1915), *Saucy Stories* (1916), and *Black Mask* (1920) — for the purpose of making quick profits. *Black Mask* became the most celebrated mystery-detective-crime pulp under the editorship of Joseph Shaw, who took over in 1926. Shaw and his star contributor, Dashiell Hammett, formulated what became known as the hard-boiled school of writing — stories in which tough characters engage in violent action and use what is supposed to be the vernacular speech. Although

## CRIME/MYSTERY/DETECTIVE PULPS, 1920-1929

*Black Mask* (1920)

*Love Story Magazine* (1921)

*Detective Tales* (1922)

*Midnight* (1922)

*Midnight Mysteries* (1922)

*Weird Tales* (1923)

*Flynn's* (1924)

*Real Detective Tales* (1924)

*Real Detective Tales and Mystery Stories* (1925)

*Clues* (1926)

*Flynn's Weekly* (1926)

*Mystery Stories* (1927)

*Flynn's Weekly Detective Fiction* (1927)

*Thrilling Tales* (1927)

*Underworld* (1927)

*Secret Service Stories* (1927)

*Sensational Startling Stories* (1927)

*Crime Mysteries* (1927)

*Cabaret Stories* (1928)

*Dragnet Magazine* (1928)

*Tropical Adventures* (1928)

*Detective Fiction Weekly* (1928)

*Gangster Stories* (1929)

*Fire Fighters* (1929)

*Best Detective* (1929)

*Detective Classics* (1929)

*Murder Mysteries* (1929)

*Price Detective Magazine* (1929)

*Spy Stories* (1929)

*Thrills of the Jungle* (1929)

*Underworld Magazine* (1929)

*Zeppelin Stories* (1929)

the pulps were regarded as subliterary, the best pulp writers — particularly in the mystery and science-fiction genres — influenced the material and style of modern fiction. Hammett serialized *Red Harvest*, *The Dain Curse*, and *The Maltese Falcon* in *Black Mask* during 1928–1929.

**Sci Fi.** The pioneer of pulp science fiction was editor-publisher Hugo Gernsback, who launched *Amazing Stories, The Magazine of Scientifiction* in 1926. It reached 150,000 circulation at twenty-five cents an issue. Gernsback also initiated *Science Wonder Stories* and *Air Wonder Stories* in 1929.

**Categories.** There is no complete record of pulp magazines because many of them published only one or two issues, but hundreds of new pulps appeared during the 1920s. Each aimed at a particular market. Sports and westerns spawned the most magazines. In the sports field there were pulps devoted to baseball, football, boxing, and other games. Frederick Faust, who wrote as Max Brand among other pseudonyms, was almost certainly the most prolific western writer. There were successful romance pulps aimed at the female market, but the pulp readership was predominantly male. The "spicy" pulps, whose covers promised titillation and eroticism that the contents did not deliver, were obviously aimed at men. The pulps survived through the 1940s.

Source:

Ron Goulart, *Cheap Thrills: An Informal History of the Pulp Magazines* (New Rochelle, N.Y.: Arlington House, 1972).

## RADIO PROGRAMMING

**Battery Power.** Radios were first marketed for home use in 1920; 5 million were sold annually by 1929. The leading brands were RCA, Atwater Kent, and Crosley — all of which were battery-powered. The batteries were expensive, heavy, and inconvenient. RCA's Radiola was the most widely advertised make; the basic model with earphones, but not loudspeaker, sold for thirty-five dollars (batteries and antenna extra) in 1924. The price range for better models was $150 to $350.

**Mostly Music.** Broadcasting began for the purpose of selling radio receivers. Before the later years of the 1920s, radio programming was unimaginative, offering mainly speeches, lectures, and music. The fact of radio was still so remarkable that people would listen to anything just for the sake of hearing sound coming out of the box — just as in 1947 people would watch anything on television, and still do. There were such radio-broadcast anomalies as bridge and basket-weaving lessons. In 1925 more than 70 percent of air time was given over to music, .1 percent to drama, .7 percent to news, and .2 percent to sports. Every week the stations broadcast speeches from meetings of civic and professional organizations, such as The Commercial Law League of America, The Foreign Policy Association, The Pennsylvania Society, The Woodrow Wilson Foundation, The Government Club, and The Advertising Club. Radio tried to be respectable, and the entertainment it provided was presumably high-class. Most of the air time was allotted to music, with a considerable portion of classics and opera. Many orchestras were named for a sponsor: the Ipana (toothpaste) Troubadours, the A&P (grocery chain) Gypsies, the Cliquot Club (soda water) Eskimos, the Champion (spark plugs) Sparkers, the Hoover (vacuum cleaner) Sentinels, the Cities Service (gasoline) Orchestra, the Wrigley (chewing gum) Orchestra, and the Seiberling (tires) Singers. The Goodrich (tires) Silvertown Orchestra featured the anonymous Silver Masked Tenor who wore a mask when he sang. The most popular variety

The Atwater-Kent five-tube receiver was a popular model in 1924.

program was *Roxy and his Gang,* hosted by movie-palace builder Samuel Rothafel (Roxy). Commencing in 1927 on NBC, the opening show included a chorus of 100 singers, a complete symphony orchestra of 110 musicians, and a studio orchestra with 60 musicians. Roxy later broadcast the first complete symphony and the first complete opera. Rudy Vallee's *Fleischmann* (yeast) *Hour,* a variety show that began in 1929, included drama written especially for radio; previously radio programs relied on recycled stage plays. Yet at the end of the decade there were only a few radio stars — that is, performers around whom the program was organized — Rudy Vallee, who had his own orchestra, being one.

**Comedy and Sports.** There were surprisingly few radio comedy stars. The earliest comedians to have their own network program were Billy Jones and Ernie Hare, a song-and-patter team sponsored by the Happiness Candy Company and accordingly billed as the Happiness Boys, on the NBC network in 1923. They were renamed the Interwoven Pair on CBS when Interwoven Socks became their sponsor in 1929. They invariably opened their program with this song:

How do you do, every-body, how do you do?

Gee it's great to say hell-o to all of you;
I'm Billy Jones
I'm Ernie Hare,
And we're a silly-looking pair;
How do you doodle-doodle-doodle-doodle-do?

But *Amos 'n' Andy,* which was broadcast six times a week on NBC, outdrew any other program. There were no regularly scheduled sports broadcasts, but major events were covered. The Jack Dempsey–Georges Carpentier heavyweight championship bout was broadcast on 2 July 1921. The first baseball-game broadcast (Pirates and Phillies) was presented by KDKA Pittsburgh on 5 August 1921. The first World Series broadcast came in 1921, facilitated by the circumstance that the Yankees and Giants both played at the Polo Grounds. On 1 January 1927 the Rose Bowl football game provided the first coast-to-coast broadcast. Graham McNamee became the best-known sports announcer of the 1920s. Radio news programs were slow to develop, and news commentators — as differentiated from news announcers — were regarded as a breakthrough. H. V. Kaltenborn began his weekly news commentary or analysis over WEAF New York in

| Sponsor | Program | Sponsor | Program |
| --- | --- | --- | --- |
| **General Variety** | | Iodent | *Iodent Program* |
| Eveready | *Eveready Hour* | Ipana | *Ipana Troubadours* |
| | | Royal Typewriters | *Royal Music Makers WEAF Musical Comedy Hour* |
| **Concert Music** | | | |
| Atwater Kent | *Atwater Kent Hour* | **Light Music** | |
| | *Boston Symphony Orchestra* | Wonder Bread | *Jolly Wonder Bakers* |
| | *Capitol Theater Concert* | Happiness Candy | *Jones & Hare* |
| Brunswick | *Chicago Civic Opera* | | *The Vikings:* male quartette |
| La France | *La France Orchestra* | Smith Brothers | Trade & Mark: songs, patter |
| Maxwell House | *Maxwell House Hour* | **News, Commentary** | |
| | *Midweek Hymn Sing* | | *Frederick William Wile:* Political Situation |
| Baulkite | *National Symphony Orchestra:* Walter Damrosch | **Religious Talk Programs** | |
| RCA | *RCA Radiotrons:* John Charles Thomas | | *Men's Conference:* Rev S. Parkes Cadman |
| **Musical Variety** | | | *St. George Vesper Service* |
| A&P | *A&P Gypsies:* string ensemble | | *Synagogue Service* |
| Champion | *Champion Spark Plug Hour* | | *Young People's Conference:* Rev Dan Poling |
| Cliquot Club | *Cliquot Club Eskimos* | **Miscellaneous Talk Programs** | |
| Coward Shoes | *Coward Comfort Hour:* familiar music | Work-Whitehead | *Auction Bridge Game:* panel on bridge |
| Davis | *Davis Saxophone Octette* | Cook & Sons | *Cook's Travelogue:* travel talk |
| Amazo Cook Oil | *Don Amazie, Wizard:* musical travelogue | **Daytime Homemakers' Talks** | |
| Goodrich Tires | *Goodrich Zippers:* banjo ensemble | General Mills | *Betty Crocker:* food talk |
| Hires | *Hires Harvesters* | | |

Source: Harrison B. Summers, ed., *History of Broadcasting* (New York: Arno & New York Times, 1971).

Ernie Hare and Billy Jones, the Happiness Boys, were the first successful radio comedy team.

Newspaper advertisement announcing the formation of NBC in 1926

October 1923, and his readily recognizable clipped speech was still heard on radio in 1950.

**Molly and Others.** Serial drama — programs with a continuing story line involving the same characters — was a late development. The longest-running serial, *The Rise of the Goldbergs,* began in 1929 on NBC; it was written by Gertrude Berg, who also performed the role of Molly Goldberg. It was the first major Jewish comedy on radio and was on television a quarter of a century later. Other enduring programs that dated from the 1920s were *The National Barn Dance* (WLS Chicago, 1924), the *Grand Ole Opry* (WSM Nashville, 1925), and *The National Farm and Home Hour,* a public-service program (NBC Blue Network, 1928).

**NBC and CBS.** The quality of programming improved markedly with the competition between the National Broadcasting Company and Columbia Broadcasting System networks for listeners, affiliated stations, and advertising revenue. In 1926 NBC linked twenty-four stations into the first network, which was inaugurated on 15 November with a four-and-a-half hour show from

New York and other cities. In 1927 NBC formed two networks: the Red Network (anchor station WEAF New York) and the Blue Network (anchor station WJZ New York).

**Who Was Listening.** CBS was launched at the end of 1928 and had forty-nine affiliated stations in January 1929. Radio advertising revenue rose from $4 million in 1927 to $40 million in 1929. At the end of 1929 more than 12 million American families — 40 percent of the population — had radios. New York led with 58 percent; only 5 percent of Mississippi families owned radios. Yet while the networks were competing for listeners during the 1920s, they had no clear sense of how many listeners they had or what the listeners were listening to. A radio ratings system, the Cooperative Analysis of Broadcasting, was developed in 1929 by Archibald M. Crossley to determine how many people listened to NBC and CBS.

**Early TV.** Through the second half of the decade there were confident predictions of the advent of television, which was successfully demonstrated by 1927. Although there were television broadcasts for the public in 1928 and 1929, the Depression postponed the development of television.

Lila and DeWitt Wallace, founders of *The Reader's Digest*

condensed articles published in other magazines to provide a monthly selection of "enduring value" cut for people who did not have time to read many magazines or long articles; there was no fiction. Because there were no ads, the price of twenty-five cents (three dollars per year) was high at a time when most magazines cost ten cents or fifteen cents. The no-ad policy held until 1955. The first issue, dated February 1922, went to 1,500 subscribers. By 1929 there were 216,000 subscribers, and *The Reader's Digest*, which ultimately reached a world circulation of more than 30 million, was on its way to becoming the most successful magazine in history. From the start *The Reader's Digest* had critics who charged that it was cheerfully lowbrow and oversimplified complex ideas. Nonetheless, the editorial formula worked: readership extended to 163 countries with editions in sixteen languages. The digest concept was widely imitated, but none of the imitations succeeded.

**Editorial Policy.** The extraordinary popularity of *The Reader's Digest* resulted from the nature of the material and the character of the magazine as much as from its readability. Until the operation became too big for one editor to control, DeWitt Wallace was responsible for selecting all the articles: "I simply hunt for things that interest me, and if they do, I print them." In the early years he worked in the New York Public Library, making condensations himself in longhand, and until the 1930s he was not charged reprint fees. The *Digest* began including book condensations in 1934. The overall tone of each issue was optimistic and wholesome, with a certain spiritual quality; the *Digest* was politically conservative, but it had a progressive attitude toward sex education. The *Digest* had a missionary aspect, engaging in medical crusades and campaigning for safer driving. It was among the earliest magazines to publish the connection between cigarettes and lung cancer.

**Sources:**
Gleason L. Archer, *History of Radio to 1926* (New York: Arno/New York Times, 1971);

Erik Barnouw, *A Tower in Babel*, volume 1 (New York: Oxford University Press, 1966);

Samuel L. Rothafel and Raymond F. Yates, *Broadcasting, Its New Day* (New York: Century, 1925);

Robert Sobel, *RCA* (New York: Stein & Day, 1986);

Christopher H. Sterling and John M. Kittross, *Stay Tuned: A Concise History of American Broadcasting,* second edition (Belmont, Cal.: Wadsworth, 1990).

## THE READER'S DIGEST

**Small Wonder.** The digest magazine was introduced in the 1920s; the term *digest* applied to both the format (5" x 7½") and the editorial policy. The first and only enduring digest magazine — which gave its name to the category — was *The Reader's Digest,* founded by newlyweds DeWitt and Lila Wallace in 1922. DeWitt Wallace

**Sources:**
John Bambridge, *Little Wonder, or, The Reader's Digest and How it Grew* (New York: Reynal & Hitchcock, 1946);

John Heidenry, *Theirs Was the Kingdom: Lila and DeWitt Wallace and the Story of the Reader's Digest* (New York: Norton, 1993).

# HEADLINE MAKERS

## HEYWOOD BROUN

### 1888-1939

#### COLUMNIST

**Apprenticeship.** In an era of brilliant newspapermen, some of whom acquired national reputations and legendary status, Heywood Broun was probably the columnist most respected by his readers and colleagues. Broun was born into a well-off Brooklyn family and attended Harvard as a member of the class of 1910. The extracurricular pleasures of the poker table and the Red Sox and an inability to pass French prevented him from graduating. He went to work as a reporter — at that time the normal move for someone with literary ambition. In 1912 he began covering sports for the *New York Tribune*, and his articles were admired for their detail and vivid description. After going to France as a correspondent during World War I — where he criticized the American leadership — he returned to the *Tribune* as drama critic and literary editor.

**"It Seems to Me."** Broun's national fame and influence commenced in 1921 with his daily column, "It Seems to Me," on the op-ed page of *The New York World*. As its title indicated, Broun's column had no controlling subject; he often wrote what were identified as "whimsy" pieces, such as "The Fifty-First Dragon," which has been widely reprinted. A large man who was described as looking "like an unmade bed," Broun was a member of the Algonquin Hotel Round Table group of wits and a greatly admired figure in the New York literary-journalistic world. Although Broun cultivated a reputation for carelessness and even laziness, he published twelve books.

**Sacco and Vanzetti.** Broun became increasingly interested in social matters and questions of injustice. He was committed to the defense of Nicola Sacco and Bartolomeo Vanzetti, anarchists who were sentenced to death for murder. His 1927 column on the committee — which included the presidents of Harvard and MIT — appointed to review the trial ended with a denunciation: "I've said these men have slept, but from now on it is our business to make them toss and turn a little, for a cry should go up from many million voices before the day set for Sacco and Vanzetti to die. We have the right to beat against tight minds with our fists and shout into the ears of the old men. We want to know, we will know — 'why?' " A subsequent column asked: "From now on, I want to know, will the institution of learning in Cambridge which once we called Harvard be known as Hangman's House?" Although the *World* was regarded as a liberal paper, two of Broun's columns were withheld. Broun maintained his position that a signed column — particularly one headed "It Seems to Me" — was the writer's responsibility and could not be required to conform to the newspaper's policies. After he criticized the *World* and its publisher in print, Broun was fired. In 1928 he moved his column to *The New York Telegram* — later *The New York World-Telegram* — where he enjoyed more editorial freedom. His column was syndicated by the Scripps-Howard chain and had an estimated readership of one million. He has been credited with establishing the syndicated opinion column as a feature independent of the policies of the newspapers that printed it.

**Politics.** Broun became increasingly involved in politics and causes during the Depression. He joined the Socialist Party and ran unsuccessfully for Congress. In 1933 he was one of the founders of the American Newspaper Guild, which fought for improved working conditions for journalists. He was the first Guild president and was reelected to that position for the rest of his life.

Heywood Broun died of pneumonia at fifty-one after writing his first column for *The New York Post*.

Sources:
Dale Kramer, *Heywood Broun* (New York: Current Books, 1949);
Richard O'Connor, *Heywood Broun* (New York: Putnam, 1975).

# BENNETT A. CERF
## AND
# DONALD S. KLOPFER

## 1898-1971, 1902-1986

### PUBLISHERS

**Partners.** Extrovert Bennett Cerf and quiet Donald Klopfer built Random House into the best of the publishing houses founded during the 1920s. It became a commercially successful firm with a commitment to literature and a list of distinguished authors.

**The Modern Library.** In 1925 twenty-seven-year-old Cerf, a Columbia University graduate, had the title of vice president at the publishing house of Boni & Liveright, having acquired that position by lending money to Horace Liveright. Always in need of money, Liveright offered to sell the Modern Library series to Cerf for $215,000. It was a splendid opportunity because the Modern Library, a list of more than one hundred clothbound ninety-five-cent reprints of classics, sold widely with little attention from Liveright. Cerf's family was prosperous, but he could not raise the purchase price alone. He asked his twenty-three-year-old friend Klopfer to put up half. Klopfer, who had attended Williams College, was working for his family's diamond-cutting business and had no publishing experience. They refurbished the drab Modern Library volumes, added new titles, and aggressively promoted the series. In 1931 they launched the Modern Library Giants series — six-hundred-page volumes that sold for one dollar. The first Giants title was Leo Tolstoy's *War and Peace*, followed by James Boswell's *Life of Johnson*, Victor Hugo's *Les Miserables*, *The Complete Poems of Keats and Shelley*, *Plutarch's Lives*, and a three-volume set of Edward Gibbons's *Decline and Fall of the Roman Empire*. By 1928 they had sold a million copies and established the Modern Library as the standard American inexpensive line before the paperback revolution. The Modern Library became a cultural force, establishing a canon for self-educating readers.

**Random House.** In 1927 the partners changed the name of the imprint from the Modern Library to Random House, indicating a commitment to variety — in subject, format, and price. They began copublishing deluxe editions with the English Nonesuch Press. The first independent Random House volume was a 1928 limited illustrated edition of Voltaire's *Candide*. Publication of trade books (books intended for bookstore sale to general readers) commenced in 1929. During the early 1930s Random House became a literary house with the addition of Eugene O'Neill, William Faulkner, Marcel Proust, and Gertrude Stein to its list. In 1932 Cerf and Klopfer challenged the ban on the importation of James Joyce's *Ulysses* into America. After the case was decided in their favor, Random House published the first legal American edition in 1934.

**Outside/Inside.** Cerf functioned effectively as outside-man/inside-man. Although Klopfer was primarily responsible for management, he earned the trust of the Random House authors and was respected in the publishing world. Through his visibility as a columnist, lecturer, anthologist, and ultimately television panelist, Cerf, Eudora Welty, and John O'Hara.

**Growth.** Random House achieved extraordinary growth and influence when it acquired the house of Alfred A. Knopf in 1960. The company, begun with a $215,000 investment in 1925, was worth $40 million when Bennett Cerf and Donald Klopfer sold Random House to RCA in 1966.

Source:
Bennett Cerf, *At Random* (New York: Random House, 1977).

# CHARLES CORRELL
## AND
# FREEMAN GOSDEN

## 1890-1972, 1899-1982

### RADIO COMEDIANS

**Blackface and Blackvoice.** Two white men, Charles Correll and Freeman Gosden, wrote and performed *Amos 'n' Andy*, a radio program about black characters that was the first radio serial and the most popular program of its time. Correll (born in Peoria, Illinois) and Gosden (born in Richmond, Virginia) had both been vaudeville song-and-chatter performers when they became friends in 1920, as the result of working for the Joe Bren Producing Company of Chicago, which produced minstrel shows. In 1925 they began singing and telling jokes in radio stations. Their breakthrough came in January 1926, when they began nightly ten-minute WGN broadcasts about *Sam 'n' Henry*, two Southern black men who had moved to Chicago. Described as a "radio comic strip," *Sam 'n'*

*Henry* was the first radio program with a continuing story line; previously, every broadcast was expected to complete the narrative.

**Amos 'n' Andy.** The program was a success from the start, and in 1928 WMAQ Chicago hired them away, but WGN retained rights to the *Sam 'n' Henry* characters. Correll and Gosden created Amos Jones and Andrew H. Brown, two residents of Harlem. Amos, performed by Gosden, was hard-working; Andy, performed by Correll, was lazy but likable. They were partners in the Fresh Air Taxi Company, so named because their only car was roofless. More characters were developed, including the larcenous Kingfish and his wife, Saphire, all of whose voices were provided by Correll and Gosden. *Amos 'n' Andy* was broadcast six nights a week in fifteen-minute installments and was even more successful than *Sam 'n' Henry*. In the era of blackface entertainment, there were no protests against the material of *Amos 'n' Andy*.

**A Radio Institution.** In August 1929 Correll and Gosden moved to the NBC Red Network for $100,000 a year. *Amos 'n' Andy* immediately became the most popular show on network radio. Movie theaters stopped their projectors and turned on the radio during the 7:00 P.M. broadcast; restaurants played the programs during dinner. The characters' mispronunciations became popular usages — "I'se regusted." The program went to five broadcasts a week in 1931 and then to once a week in 1943. The partners wrote and performed more than five thousand radio broadcasts.

**TV and New Standards.** *Amos 'n' Andy* retained its popularity through the 1940s. CBS bought rights to the program for $2.5 million in 1948, but the change to television with black actors was not successful, the reality of the image being in conflict with the cartoonishness of the characters. There had been a growing criticism of the program, especially from the NAACP. Correll and Gosden were hurt by the charges of bigotry, insisting that their portrayals were unprejudiced and affectionate; but public sensitivity to racism had become strong, and no new *Amos 'n' Andy* television episodes were produced after 1954.

Source:
Melvin Patrick Ely, *The Adventures of Amos 'n' Andy: A Social History of an American Phenomenon* (New York: Free Press, 1991).

## HORACE LIVERIGHT

### 1886-1933

#### PUBLISHER

**Jazz Age Publisher.** Horace Liveright was another of the flamboyant figures whose careers are inseparable from the 1920s. His style of success and his spectacular failure are emblematic of the decade. As head of Boni & Liveright he published an exciting list of books while hosting a perpetual party and spending himself into insolvency.

**Boni & Liveright.** Liveright did not bother to complete high school. At sixteen he was working for a stock-brokerage office, and at eighteen he wrote the libretto and lyrics for an unproduced operetta. In 1917, after a series of unsuccessful business ventures, he was staked to a publishing partnership with Albert Boni by his wealthy father-in-law. Liveright had no publishing experience, but he had read widely and admired writers. The first Boni & Liveright project, the Modern Library, became the best-known American series of inexpensive classic reprints. Bound in so-called limp leather and priced at sixty cents, the first twelve volumes were Oscar Wilde's *The Picture of Dorian Gray*, August Strindberg's *Married*, Rudyard Kipling's *Soldiers Three*, Robert Louis Stevenson's *Treasure Island*, H. G. Wells's *The War in the Air*, Henrik Ibsen's *A Doll's House*, Anatole France's *The Red Lily*, Guy de Maupassant's *Mlle. Fifi*, Friedrich Nietzsche's *Thus Spake Zarathustra*, Fyodor Dostoyevsky's *Poor People*, Maurice Maeterlinck's *St. Antony*, and Arthur Schopenhauer's *Pessimism*. Always in need of ready cash, Liveright sold the Modern Library to Bennett Cerf and Donald Klopfer in 1925, thereby terminating a dependable source of income.

**Gambler.** Disagreement about other publishing projects led to Boni's departure in 1918, supposedly after a coin toss. The firm name remained Boni & Liveright until 1928, when the imprint became Horace Liveright. It was Liveright's company during the 1920s; he operated it as a private fiefdom and treated it as a personal bank. He was largely responsible for its brilliant list, and he was solely responsible for its frenzied finances. Liveright was a gambler: he gambled on authors; he gambled on the stock market; he gambled on Broadway shows. He was an alcoholic and a womanizer. He published T. S. Eliot, Ezra Pound, Eugene O'Neill, Theodore Dreiser, Sherwood Anderson, William Faulkner, and Ernest Hemingway. An avowed Socialist, he published Leon Trotsky's *The Bolsheviki and World Peace* (1918) and John Reed's *The Ten Days that Shook the World* (1919). In 1920 he published Sigmund Freud's *A General Introduction to Psychoanalysis*, the book that Freudianized America.

**Patron of Writers.** Liveright was a generous backer of writers, and it was asserted that he would make a $300 advance to anyone with an idea for a book. He provided Anderson and Dreiser with steady incomes to support them while they were writing — a publishing practice Liveright may have introduced. He flouted accepted practice in the way books were publicized and marketed. Before Liveright, books were expected to sell through dignified announcements and word of mouth. He aggressively promoted books and treated them as newsworthy events, employing pioneer public-relations consultant Edward L. Bernays. Liveright also fought censorship — not only of his own books. With little support from other publishers, he victoriously opposed the "Clean Books Bill" in the New York legislature.

**Fall.** As long as next year's best-seller could be expected to pay last year's bills, Horace Liveright — the company and the individual — defied insolvency. After the 1929 Wall Street crash, arithmetic destroyed him. In 1930 Liveright left publishing and went to Hollywood as a producer, but he did not succeed there. He returned to New York and failed to make a comeback as a theater producer. Horace Liveright died broke of alcoholism and pneumonia at forty-seven.

Source:
Tom Dardis, *Firebrand: The Life of Horace Liveright* (New York: Random House, 1995).

## GEORGE HORACE LORIMER

### 1867-1937

#### MAGAZINE EDITOR

**The Great American Magazine.** During the 1920s *The Saturday Evening Post* was the most successful magazine in America, perhaps in the world. It reached a peak circulation of 3 million; for a nickel its readers bought two hundred pages with fiction and articles by the most popular and best-paid writers. The man responsible was George Horace Lorimer, a devout proponent of the gospel of business and a good judge of writing.

**Success Story.** Lorimer lived the American success story. The son of a Baptist minister, he dropped out of Yale after one year at the urging of Philip D. Armour, head of the meatpacking firm, and rose to head of the Armour canning department. After his own grocery business failed, Lorimer became a reporter. In 1898 he was hired as literary editor of *The Saturday Evening Post*, published by Cyrus H. K. Curtis, owner of *The Ladies' Home Journal.* The *Post* was moribund, its chief asset a shaky claim to having been founded by Benjamin Franklin. Lorimer was assigned to edit the magazine while Curtis was recruiting an editor in chief. Lorimer did it so well that he was made editor in chief, a position he held for thirty-nine years. For more than twenty years Lorimer's *Post* had a significant influence in shaping American values and American taste through its fiction, nonfiction, and advertising. Lorimer read everything that was printed in his magazine and was personally responsible for the editorial pages, which were probusiness and isolationist. He was the author of three books — one of which, *Letters from a Self-Made Merchant to his Son* (1902), a highly successful work of business fiction, was serialized in the *Post.*

**Contributors.** Lorimer treated writers generously and recruited a corps of contributors who became associated with the *Post* and thereby built reader loyalty. Although intellectuals dismissed the *Post* stories as escapism and commercial entertainment, the *Post* published Ring W. Lardner, F. Scott Fitzgerald, William Faulkner, John P. Marquand, Sinclair Lewis, John Galsworthy, Rudyard Kipling, Booth Tarkington, and Kenneth Roberts during the 1920s. Prominent illustrators worked for the *Post*, and Norman Rockwell's many covers became identified with the magazine. The 6 March 1926 issue had 238 pages with ten articles, ranging in subject from the export trade to the making of dictionaries, and ten stories, including Fitzgerald's "Adolescent Marriage." There were 117 full-page ads, many of them for automobiles or automotive products.

**Loss of Influence.** During the 1930s Lorimer opposed President Franklin D. Roosevelt's New Deal, and *The Saturday Evening Post*, out of touch with prevailing public opinion, gradually lost much of its political and cultural influence. George Horace Lorimer retired in 1936, the year before his death.

Sources:
Jan Cohn, *Creating America: George Horace Lorimer and The Saturday Evening Post* (Pittsburgh: University of Pittsburgh Press, 1989);

John Tebbel, *George Horace Lorimer and The Saturday Evening Post* (Garden City, N.Y.: Doubleday, 1948).

## HENRY R. LUCE
## AND
## BRITON HADDEN

### 1898-1967, 1898-1929

#### MAGAZINE PUBLISHERS

**New Departures.** Henry Luce and Briton Hadden invented the newsmagazine when they launched *Time* in 1923. Their magazine developed innovative approaches to news coverage, such as packaging the news in topical units; utilizing group journalism, by which an article resulted from the work of teams of researchers, reporters, writers, and editors; and replacing standard newspaper prose with a catchy narrative style.

**School Days.** Luce was born in China to Presbyterian missionaries and retained a missionary zeal in his approach to publishing. At fifteen he came to America and attended the Hotchkiss School in Connecticut. At Hotchkiss he encountered Briton Hadden, the Brooklyn-born offspring of a well-connected family. Luce edited the school literary magazine and was assistant managing editor of the newspaper; Hadden was managing editor of the paper. They went to Yale, where Hadden became chairman of *The Yale Daily News* and Luce the managing editor.

**Prospectus.** College was interrupted when both served as army lieutenants during World War I. At Camp Jackson, South Carolina, they planned a newsmagazine. After graduating from Yale in 1920 — Hadden was voted most likely to succeed and Luce most brilliant — both became newspaper reporters. While working on *The Baltimore News* in 1922 they drafted a prospectus for their newsmagazine and quit their jobs to raise $100,000.

Their prospectus announced:

> People are uninformed BECAUSE NO PUBLICATION HAS ADAPTED ITSELF TO THE TIME WHICH BUSY MEN ARE ABLE TO SPEND ON SIMPLY KEEPING INFORMED.
>
> *Time* is a weekly news-magazine, aimed to serve the modern necessity of keeping people informed, created on a new principle of COMPLETE ORGANIZATION.

**Editorial Bias.** On the subject of editorial bias, the prospectus declared that "the editors recognize that complete neutrality on public questions and important news is probably as undesirable as it is impossible, and are therefore ready to acknowledge certain prejudices which may in varying measure predetermine their opinions on the news." From the start *Time* was attacked for slanting its coverage, especially in the fields of politics, government, and economics, for Luce and Hadden were conservatives who opposed government interference with business.

**Timestyle.** The partners decided to go ahead with $86,000 from seventy-two investors. The first issue, dated 3 March 1923, had former House Speaker Joseph Cannon on the cover; it sold for fifteen cents, and there were twenty-two departments in twenty-eight pages. That Hadden was the editor and Luce the business manager was supposedly decided by a coin flip. Hadden was responsible for inventing what became known as Timestyle, influenced by Homeric texts he had studied as a schoolboy: compound epithets ( jut-jawed) and inverted sentences ("Backward ran sentences until reeled the mind" in a *New Yorker* parody). There were also combined words (cinemaddict), puns (sexsational), and the use of phrases with special connotations ("great and good friend"). In the beginning there was little reportorial work; most of the *Time* articles were written or rewritten from newspaper clippings. The first issue reached 9,000 subscribers and a few thousand newsstand purchasers. Circulation grew to 136,000 in 1927 and 200,000 in 1929.

**Luce without Hadden.** In 1927 Hadden and Luce exchanged responsibilities and titles. Hadden died of a streptococcus infection in 1929. Luce went on to build an international media empire including magazines (*For-*

*tune*, 1930; *Architectural Forum*, 1932; *Life*, 1936; *Sports Illustrated*, 1954), radio (1931) and newsreel (1935) versions of *The March of Time*, and Time-Life books. *Life* developed photojournalism. Luce and his publications remained staunchly Republican, although most of his writers were liberals. "For some goddamn reason Republicans can't write," he remarked.

**"The American Century."** The missionary boy used his publications to deliver sermons, particularly on the theme of the postwar world as "the American Century," the era in which the well-being of the world would be America's responsibility. Henry Luce did not exert as much influence over national and international policy as he wanted to — or as much as his detractors thought he did. His major and enduring influence was on the effective presentation of information.

Sources:

Noel Busch, *Briton Hadden: A Biography of the Co-founder of Time* (New York: Farrar, Straus, 1949);

John Kobler, *Luce: His Time, Life, and Fortune,* (Garden City, N.Y.: Doubleday, 1968);

W. A. Swanberg, *Luce and his Empire* (New York: Scribners, 1972).

# H. L. MENCKEN

## 1880-1956

### CRITIC & EDITOR

**Great Debunker.** During the 1920s few Americans matched Henry L. Mencken's influence as a writer and as an independent thinker. He was the decade's great debunker, aiming ridicule at the cowardice and ignorance of what he called the "booboisee."

**"The Baltimore Anti-Christ."** Mencken graduated from the Baltimore Polytechnic School and became a reporter on the *Baltimore Herald* in 1899. He moved to the *Baltimore Sun* in 1906, and was associated with the Sunpapers as editor, correspondent, and columnist ("The Free Lance") for the rest of his working life. The force of Mencken's mind and the breadth of his learning enabled him to combine journalism with simultaneous careers as magazine editor, philologist, and literary-social critic. As editor of *The Smart Set* and *The American Mercury*, as well as a prolific contributor to other journals, Mencken had a strong influence on American iconoclasm during the 1920s. He denounced puritanism, censorship, fundamentalism, political corruption, and human folly, among other targets of opportunity. His powerful jeremiads earned him the titles of "The Sage of Baltimore" and "The Baltimore Anti-Christ." Even when most actively involved in New York publishing activities he commuted from his permanent residence in Baltimore.

**And Nathan.** With George Jean Nathan, Mencken edited *The Smart Set* from 1914 to 1923 and founded *The American Mercury* in 1924. Nathan's primary interest was the theater, and he was much less concerned with political and philosophical ideas than Mencken; but their combined attacks on the inadequacies and absurdities of American culture, along with Mencken's Germanophilia, led their admirers to coin the slogan "Mencken, Nathan, und Gott." As a literary critic, Mencken ridiculed both popular and academic taste while promoting the work of writers he regarded as truthful and courageous: particularly Theodore Dreiser, Sinclair Lewis, Joseph Conrad, Arnold Bennett, Henrik Ibsen, and George Bernard Shaw. His support was crucial to the recognition of Dreiser as a major American novelist.

**Prejudices and Philology.** Mencken wrote more than thirty books on literature, philosophy, politics, and women, as well as autobiographies. His articles and essays were collected in six volumes correctly titled *Prejudices*. Mencken's major literary achievement was *The American Language: A Preliminary Inquiry into the Development of English in the United States*, first published as one volume in 1919 but revised and enlarged into three volumes during the next twenty-five years. This extraordinary philological work was accomplished by a self-educated independent scholar without academic or financial support.

**Courage and Independence.** Never pompous or self-righteous, Mencken was at his best when declaring the emperor's nudity. His courageous positions were often expressed by means of irony and hyperbole. He destroyed many of his targets by exposing them to ridicule. A man who acted on his own convictions, Mencken was unimpressed and unintimidated by power or numbers. He opposed America's involvement in both world wars; he attacked powerful religious and political leaders; he ridiculed the cultural poverty of the hinterlands — especially the South, which he labeled "the Sahara of the Bozart" (the desert of the beaux arts); he challenged censorship and risked jail by selling a copy of a banned issue of *The American Mercury* on the Boston Common in 1926; he took on all comers, including Woodrow Wilson and Franklin Delano Roosevelt. Mencken consistently fought for American freedom, declaring that "no man can be dignified as long as he is afraid."

**Hero.** H. L. Mencken's reputation diminished during the 1930s and 1940s because his insistence on individualism and self-reliance was perceived as irresponsible or outdated by new generations committed to mass causes. Nonetheless, he was a culture hero in his own time; his work liberated American thought.

Sources:
Allison Bulsterbaum, *H. L. Mencken: A Research Guide* (New York: Garland, 1988);

William Manchester, *Disturber of the Peace: The Life of H. L. Mencken* (New York: Harper, 1951);

H. L. Mencken, *My Life as Author and Editor* (New York: Knopf, 1992).

## WILLIAM S. PALEY

### 1901-1990

#### RADIO TYCOON

**Conflicting Assessments.** William S. Paley, the head of the Columbia Broadcasting System, has been classified as a genius with an unerring instinct for entertainment and as a megalomaniac motivated by greed. When he died, *Video Age International* published conflicting assessments: "No one can deny that Paley was a programming genius, and that he was one of the architects of modern society"; and "He had a fine feel for creating a mix of popular and special interest programming, but he took credit for a great many achievements that distinctly belong to others." Undeniably, under his autocratic leadership the Columbia Broadcasting System rewrote the nation's definition of entertainment and news.

**Family Fortune.** William Paley was born in Chicago on 28 September 1901, the son of Samuel and Goldie Drew Paley, Ukrainian Jewish immigrants. Making money was in Paley's blood: his father had been apprenticed to a cigar maker while in his teens; within a decade he owned a cigar factory and had made a fortune. His most popular brand was La Palina.

**Starting at the Top.** William Paley attended the University of Chicago, but when the elder Paley moved the Congress Cigar Company to Philadelphia, William transferred to the University of Pennsylvania. He received a B.S. from the Wharton School and was named vice president and secretary of the cigar company at the then-enormous salary of $50,000 a year. In 1928 the younger Paley bought $50 worth of advertising weekly on Philadelphia station WCAU. The sale of La Palina Cigars increased. Some sources claim that William immediately grasped radio's potential and urged his father to invest $300,000 to buy WCAU and a controlling interest in the struggling United Independent Broadcasters Network. Others say the purchase was Samuel's idea and that William resisted it. In any case, the family bought the network. Paley became president of the network on 26 September 1928, one day before his twenty-seventh birthday, and renamed it the Columbia Broadcasting System.

**Building and Dealing.** In December 1928 CBS bought WABC New York as its flagship station for $390,000, bringing the Paleys' investment to $1.5 million. Paley aggressively recruited affiliate stations for the network, and on 8 January 1929 he announced that CBS had forty-nine stations in forty-two cities. Unlike his rival David Sarnoff of NBC, Paley had little interest in the technical aspects of broadcasting. He was a promoter and a deal maker. While still in his twenties he sold half of CBS to Paramount Pictures for $3.8 million and reacquired it after the 1929 stock-market crash. Consequently the Paleys and his family retained all of their CBS stock, but Paramount owed them $5 million.

**CBS News.** In 1933, when newspapers kept wire services from giving radio full access to their news, Paley set up his own CBS news organization. Two years later he hired Edward R. Murrow to recruit on-air news reporters. In 1937 he sent Murrow to London to supervise public affairs programming as the war in Europe neared. Part of Murrow's job was to hire and assemble able newsmen to report and broadcast the news. The names of these men read like an honor roll of broadcast journalism: Walter Cronkite, William Shirer, Eric K. Sevareid, Elmer Davis, Charles Collingwood, Howard K. Smith, and Winston Burdett. In effect they set the course for CBS News, the nation's premier broadcast-news organization until Cronkite retired in 1981. Murrow himself proved a superb newsman.

**Tastemaker.** Because of the quality of its stars and its programs, CBS became known as the "Tiffany Network," and Paley became renowned as a tastemaker. For twenty-six years CBS led both NBC and ABC in audience ratings. Many credited other CBS executives with the success, notably Dr. Frank Stanton, a longtime CBS executive who labored behind his flamboyant, publicity-conscious, high-living boss. Paley's second wife was the former Barbara (Babe) Cushing, a prominent social figure. At the time of his death Paley's fortune was estimated at $500 million, including his 8 percent share of CBS, valued at $356 million.

Sources:

William S. Paley, *As It Happened: A Memoir* (Garden City, N.Y.: Doubleday, 1979);

Sally Bedel Smith, *In All His Glory: The Life of William S. Paley* (New York: Simon & Schuster, 1990).

# JOSEPH MEDILL PATTERSON

## 1879-1946

### NEWSPAPER PUBLISHER

**Newspaper Family.** Joseph Patterson published the first and most successful tabloid newspaper in America. A man of eccentricities and contradictions who acted on impulse, he might have been classified as unbalanced — except that he was a journalist with a sure sense of what interested his readers. Patterson was born into a wealthy and powerful newspaper family. His maternal grandfather was Joseph Medill, publisher and editor of the *Chicago Tribune*, and his father became editor of that paper. Patterson's sister, Eleanor (Cissy), later became publisher of the *Washington Times-Herald*. Although he dressed carelessly and rejected the requirements of his social position, he was educated at the upper-class Groton School in Massachusetts and graduated from Yale in 1901. All of his life he felt comfortable with the proletariat, living with bums in Chicago's First Ward and New York's Bowery. Patterson was certain that he understood working-class people, and he endeavored to improve their living conditions. Failing that, he wanted to provide them with a newspaper.

**Friend of the Proletariat.** After Yale, Patterson joined the *Tribune* as a reporter, but his proletarian concerns directed him to reform politics — often in opposition to the policies of the *Tribune*. Patterson left the *Tribune* when he learned that his election to the Illinois House of Representatives had been rigged by the paper. In 1906 he joined the Socialist Party and wrote plays (*Dope* and *The Fourth Estate*) and a novel (*A Little Brother of the Rich*, 1908) denouncing capitalism and the corrupt rich. But his experiences as an author convinced him of the validity of the profit motive, and he withdrew from socialism.

**The Captain and the Colonel.** Patterson returned to the *Tribune* in 1910 as coeditor with his cousin Robert McCormick, a conservative and aristocrat. They disagreed about editorial policy. Patterson joined the army during World War I, participated in battle, and earned the rank of captain. McCormick rose to colonel. Both retained the use of their military titles in civilian life.

*The Daily News.* During the war the cousins agreed that they should not continue to coedit the *Tribune*. In 1919 Captain Patterson met with Lord Harmsworth, publisher of the London tabloid *Daily Mirror*, who convinced him that an American tabloid would succeed. Patterson started rush work on a New York tabloid at the same time that William Randolph Hearst was developing one. Patterson published first; *The Illustrated Daily News* appeared on 26 June 1919. The term "tabloid" indicated more than format (11½" x 13¾"): it also indicated content and style. *The Daily News* (*Illustrated* was soon dropped from is name) featured sensational photographs, scandal, crime, sex, comics, and contests. The paper's most famous scoop was the 1928 front-page photo of Ruth Snyder dying in the electric chair for the murder of her husband — a photo taken with a concealed camera. The tabloid size supposedly made it convenient for the subway strap-hangers, but *The Daily News* succeeded because it appealed to people who did not find the traditional newspapers interesting. The critics of tabloid journalism referred to *The Daily News* as "the servant-girl's bible," and advertisers were initially wary of becoming associated with a vulgar publication. Nonetheless, Patterson did know what his readers wanted. In the 1930s *The Daily News* reached the largest circulation in America, and *The Sunday News* had the largest circulation in the world at over 3 million.

**Competition.** In 1924 both Hearst's morning *Daily Mirror* and Bernarr Macfadden's *Evening Graphic* entered the New York tabloid field. Neither matched the success of *The Daily News*. The *Graphic* tried to out-sensationalize the *News* but lacked Patterson's sure sense of his readers' taste.

**Editorial Policy.** Until 1925 Patterson ran his paper by telephone from Chicago. His principal interests were the circulation-building features and the editorials. He developed comic strips and provided ideas for "The Gumps," "Dick Tracy," and "Little Orphan Annie." He controlled the editorial page and collaborated in writing the editorials. Initially a strong supporter of Franklin Roosevelt, Patterson became a bitter opponent of the president's foreign policy, which he saw as designed to force America into World War II. Patterson's attacks on communism earned the proletariat's friend the enmity of the Left.

**Self-Reliance.** Ralph Waldo Emerson's observation that "An institution is the lengthened shadow of one man" was strikingly exemplified by Joseph Medill Patterson. His unlikely collection of qualities and emotions were responsible for the prodigious success of *The Daily News*.

Sources:
Jack Alexander, "Vox Populi," *New Yorker* (6, 13, 20 August 1938);
John W. Tebbel, *American Dynasty: The Story of the McCormicks, Medills, and Pattersons* (Garden City, N.Y.: Doubleday, 1947).

# MAXWELL E. PERKINS

## 1884-1947

### EDITOR AND PUBLISHER

**Editor of Geniuses.** Maxwell Perkins was the most renowned editor to practice his craft at an American publishing house. It has been remarked that his career was based on a quest for an American Tolstoy, whose *War and Peace* he regarded as the supreme work of fiction. Perkins's reputation is permanently linked with those of three geniuses he published at Scribners: F. Scott Fitzgerald, Ernest Hemingway, and Thomas Wolfe. The 1920s were a golden decade for American literature; brilliant writers and great publishers reinforced each other. Boni & Liveright had a stimulating list of titles; but no house matched the distinction of Charles Scribner's Sons, which entered the 1920s as a conservative firm and became the imprint of exciting young fiction writers.

**Allegiance to Talent.** Though raised in New Jersey, Maxwell Perkins came from New England stock and was Harvard-educated. His Yankee reserve and integrity characterized his relationships with his authors, who depended on him for more than editorial guidance. After working as a reporter on *The New York Times*, Perkins became advertising manager at Charles Scribner's Sons in 1910 and moved to the editorial department in 1914. Because he had the right background and family connections, he was able to persuade his older colleagues to undertake departures from their traditional publishing policies. Although he was unable to convince the firm to take a chance on the novel Fitzgerald wrote in the army during 1918, Perkins compelled acceptance of the rewritten novel, *This Side of Paradise,* by telling Charles Scribner: "My feeling is that a publisher's first allegiance is to talent. . . . If we're going to turn down the likes of Fitzgerald, I will lose all interest in publishing books." Published in 1920, Fitzgerald's novel was a surprise success and initiated Perkins's reputation as a discoverer of literary talent.

**Fitzgerald and Hemingway.** The relationship between Fitzgerald and Perkins grew increasingly close, and Fitzgerald brought two of his friends, Ring W. Lardner and Ernest Hemingway, into the Perkins stable. Hemingway had published a volume of short stories in America in 1925, and Perkins contracted for his novel without reading it in 1926. When the typescript of *The Sun Also Rises* arrived, Perkins again had trouble convincing his colleagues that a book that featured promiscuity and drunkenness should bear the Scribners imprint. And it was in this case necessary for Perkins to persuade an extremely touchy author to make certain revisions and deletions for the sake of propriety.

**Editorial Technique.** As with Fitzgerald, Perkins's working relationship with Hemingway became a warm and lasting friendship, an extraordinary circumstance in view of Hemingway's suspicious nature and history of broken friendships. There were frequent eruptions by Hemingway, but Perkins always placated him, reassuring the writer of the editor's loyalty. Perkins's rule was that "The book belongs to the author." It was the editor's responsibility to help the writer but not to take control of the work. His commitment to his authors' talent was as crucial to Perkins's achievements as his editorial skills. The writers trusted him; therefore, they trusted his advice. He did not rewrite the books; he offered suggestions for improvement. Perkins's particular strength was in suggesting structural revisions, as he did for *The Great Gatsby.*

**Wolfe.** The editorial task for which Perkins became celebrated was his work with Thomas Wolfe on *Look Homeward, Angel,* published in 1929. In a process unusual for Perkins, he was required to become virtually a collaborator as he worked closely with Wolfe night after night to cut and restructure the long, unpublishable drafts. Fitzgerald and Hemingway could have succeeded without Perkins, but *Look Homeward, Angel* would not have been published without Perkins's editorial interposition. The friendship between Wolfe and Perkins was intense, but in the year after the publication of *Of Time and the River* (1935), the pathologically suspicious writer broke with Perkins and Scribners in reaction to the charges that he could not write publishable books without Perkins. When Wolfe died in 1938, he had not published another novel.

**Role Model.** In addition to the famed geniuses, Perkins's roster of writers included Morley Callaghan, Erskine Caldwell, Taylor Caldwell, Marjorie Kinnan Rawlings, S. S. Van Dine, Arthur Train, Will James, and James Boyd. He was working with James Jones on *From Here to Eternity* when he died. Because of his connection with some of the greatest figures in American literature and the distorted accounts of his editorial miracles, Maxwell Perkins has inspired aspiring editors and dignified a profession in which the bookkeepers outvote the bookmakers.

Sources:

A. Scott Berg, *Maxwell Perkins: Editor of Genius* (New York: Dutton, 1978);

*Editor to Author: The Letters of Maxwell E. Perkins* (New York: Scribners, 1950).

# HAROLD W. ROSS

## 1892-1951

### EDITOR

**Ross of *The New Yorker*.** Harold Ross was a tramp reporter from Aspen, Colorado, who conceived and ran a cosmopolitan magazine that developed some of the best American writers for twenty-five years. Ross of *The New Yorker* became the subject of many anecdotes about his eccentricities and alleged lack of sophistication ("Is Moby Dick the Man or the whale?"), yet he was an editorial genius who permanently influenced the rationale of American magazine publishing and developed new literary forms.

**Shaky Start.** Ross left high school to work as a reporter at a string of newspapers. In 1918 he became de facto editor in chief of *The Stars and Stripes*, the American expeditionary force newspaper published in Paris, with the permanent rank of private. He had discovered his genius: the ability to run a periodical in accordance with his high editorial standards. After the war he worked for magazines in New York while planning his own magazine. His wife, Jane Grant, whom he married in 1920, encourged the plan, and they pooled their earnings toward starting his magazine. Their $25,000 was matched by the same amount from Raoul Fleischmann, a member of a wealthy family who had no literary or journalistic background. Ross wrote the prospectus that included the famous statement: "*The New Yorker* will be the magazine which is not edited for the old lady in Du-

buque." He planned a magazine of "gaiety, wit and satire." His prospectus explained that "It will be what is commonly called sophisticated, in that it will assume a reasonable degree of enlightenment on the part of its readers. It will hate bunk." The first issue, dated 21 February 1925, had thirty-six pages and sold for fifteen cents; it was not well received. Early contributors included Ross's friends from the Algonquin Round Table group: Alexander Woollcott, Robert Benchley, and Dorothy Parker. *The New Yorker* lost money steadily during 1925 and was kept alive by infusions of Fleischmann's personal wealth. At one point Ross lost $30,000 in a poker game while trying to save the magazine. Fleischmann (publisher and treasurer) and Ross (editor) became permanent enemies. In 1926 the magazine turned the corner as Ross refined the deparments and tone.

**Editors and Writers.** Ross's rationale for running a magazine was: "An editor prints what pleases him. If enough people like what he does he is a success." With the help of a brilliant staff of editors and writers — including Katharine Angell White, E. B. White, James Thurber, Wolcott Gibbs, St. Clair McKelway — Ross published the best-edited magazine in America. The high-school dropout was committed to excellence in grammar, syntax, and punctuation. The former tramp reporter enforced factual correctness. During the 1920s Ross encouraged the introduction and improvement of the departments with which *The New Yorker* became identified: "Reporter at Large," "The Wayward Press," the profile, and "Shouts and Murmurs." Gradually the magazine's humorous or satiric content was replaced by factual articles that grew in length. Ross catagorized anything that was not a factual piece or a contribution to one of the departments as a "casual." Although *The New Yorker* nurtured some of the best short-story writers of the century, Ross was not personally committed to "casuals"; nonetheless, he was partly responsible for the development of what became known as "the *New Yorker* story" — an elliptical, underplotted work of short fiction that was often introspective. The fiction writers during Ross's tenure included John O'Hara, Sally Benson, Vladimir Nabokov, Clarence Day, J. D. Salinger, John Cheever, and Robert Coates.

**Ross's Masterpiece.** Ross's commitment to editorial integrity was so strong that he eventually sold most of his *New Yorker* stock to reinforce the separation between editorial and business departments. If a magazine can really be the product of one person's work over the course of twenty-seven years, *The New Yorker* was Harold Ross's masterpiece. He retained final editorial control and attempted to read everything that he published; his detailed editorial queries became legendary: "Who he?" "What means?" "When happen?" "Don't get." "Fix." The man who became the subject of anecdotes that emphasized his innocence or imperfect education or bias was the genius who made possible the work of many important talents and thereby had a permanent effect on American literature.

**Sources:**

Thomas Kunkel, *Genius in Disguise: Harold Ross of the New Yorker* (New York: Random House, 1995);

James Thurber, *The Years with Ross* (Boston: Little, Brown, 1959).

# DAVID SARNOFF

## 1891-1971

### COMMUNICATIONS TYCOON

**Radio and Television Leader.** David Sarnoff, an immigrant boy with a grammar-school education, became the most powerful figure in the communications and media industries. As president of the Radio Corporation of America he created the National Broadcasting Company radio network and developed television.

**Pluck and Luck.** Sarnoff was born in Russia and arrived in America at ten. When he was fifteen he left school to support his family after the death of his father. His first job was as messenger boy for the Commercial Cable Company, and in 1906 he moved to the Marconi Wireless Telegraph Company of America as a $5.50-per-week office boy. Sarnoff taught himself telegraphy and was encouraged by Guglielmo Marconi. On the night of 14 April 1912 he was managing the experimental radio station on the roof of the Wanamaker Department store in New York when the *Titanic* hit an iceberg. He remained at his equipment for seventy-two hours.

**Radio Music Box.** Sarnoff became manager of the Marconi Wireless Telegraph Company of America, which in 1919 was merged into the new Radio Corporation of America — owned by General Electric, Westinghouse, American Telephone and Telegraph, and the United Fruit Company. As an RCA executive, Sarnoff resubmitted a memo to the Marconi Company in 1915: "I have in mind a plan of development that would make radio a household utility in the same sense as a piano or a phonograph. The idea is to bring music into the home by wireless. The receiver can be designed in the form of a simple 'Radio Music Box' and arranged for several different wave-lengths, which should be changeable with the throwing of a single switch or pressing of a single button." He was allowed $2,000 to develop the "radio music box," which sold $83 million worth of units between 1922 and 1924. In 1926 he organized for RCA the first radio network, the National Broadcasting Company, and acquired station WEAF New York from AT&T, which withdrew from broadcasting. Sarnoff steadily enlarged the scope of RCA activities. He purchased the Victor Talking Machine Company in 1929 and was credited with putting the phonograph and radio in the same unit;

he acquired a major share of the RKO movie studio in 1928; and in 1929 he formed a new company with General Motors to manufacture car radios.

**Advent of Television.** Sarnoff had a knowledge of the technical aspects of broadcasting, but his genius was prognostic. He was able to anticipate developments in communications media, and he possessed the drive and business ability to bring his predictions to successful reality. He became president of RCA in 1930 and was credited with saving the firm when the government ordered GE and Westinghouse to sell their RCA interests in 1932. As president he consistently invested substantial amounts in research, often against the opposition of his associates. A 1923 Sarnoff prediction took twenty-five years to fulfill: "I believe that television, which is the technical name for seeing as well as hearing by radio, will come to pass in the future." As president of RCA he was in a position to provide Vladimir Zworykin with $100,000 for work on television. The research investment reached $50 million before black-and-white television was perfected. During World War II, RCA manufactured radar, shoran, loran, and other electronic devices; Sarnoff went on active duty and became a brigadier general. After the war Sarnoff, who retained his rank, devoted his full attention to television, sensing that the consumer market was ready for it. He accomplished the task of persuading radio stations to invest in television facilities. Then he undertook the responsibility to make color television feasible, successfully competing against the Columbia Broadcasting System to develop a system that would receive FCC approval.

**Research and Manufacture.** Although he had financed the NBC Symphony for Arturo Toscanini, Sarnoff was more interested in developing network radio and television than in program content: "Of course we have a certain responsibility for creating programs, but basically we're delivery boys." He often stated that "The heart of RCA is its scientific laboratories." Sarnoff's unrivaled achievements resulted from the circumstance that he was the only network head who was head of a manufacturing operation; RCA made the equipment to send and receive radio and television broadcasts. In many instances RCA scientists and engineers developed that equipment.

**Fulfillment.** David Sarnoff represented one of the great American success stories from the last waves of nineteenth-century immigration. He became rich, but wealth was not his primary interest. His chief ambition was to enlarge the applications of the electronic media through research, development, and production. Consequently he permanently changed not just the means of mass communication but American life and culture.

**Sources:**

Eugene Lyon, *David Sarnoff* (New York: Harper & Row, 1966);

Robert Sobel, *RCA* (New York: Stein & Day, 1986).

# WALTER WINCHELL

## 1897-1972

### COLUMNIST

**Gossip.** The claim that Walter Winchell created the modern gossip column has been disputed, but he was indisputably the most widely known and widely read columnist in American journalism. By various estimates the readers of his column and the listeners to his radio broadcasts totaled between 25 million and 50 million at the peak of his fame.

**Show Biz.** Raised in poverty in Manhattan, Winchell left school in the sixth grade to become a vaudeville singer. He was a song-and-dance man in second-rate vaudeville circuits in 1919 when he began posting pages of gossip and news backstage. In 1922 he began writing the "Stage Whispers" news column for *The Vaudeville News*. This trade paper had a limited circulation, but it provided him connections with people who assisted his rise. His two early mentors were speakeasy hostess Texas Guinan and Mark Hellinger. A columnist and reporter on *The Daily News*, Hellinger is regarded as the first Broadway columnist; but sentimental vignettes — not gossip — were his stock in trade.

**"On Broadway."** In 1924 Winchell moved to the *Evening Graphic*, a sensational tabloid owned by health faddist Bernarr Macfadden. The *Graphic* featured crime and scandal articles. Winchell's column, "Your Broadway and Mine," began as show-business news. In 1925 he inaugurated what became the recognizable Winchell format — short items of personal information about celebrities connected by dots: "It's a girl at the Carter de Havens. . . . Lenore Ulric paid $7 income tax. . . . Fanny Brice is betting on the horses at Belmont. . . . S. Jay Kaufman sails on the 16th via the Berengaria to be hitched to a Hungarian. . . . " The column proved so popular that Winchell was hired away by William Randolph Hearst's *Daily Mirror*, which was engaged in a struggle with the *The Daily News* for New York morning tabloid circulation. Many readers bought the *Mirror* just for Winchell's "On Broadway," and the column reached a peak syndication to 800 newspapers.

**Winchellese.** The content of "On Broadway" evolved away from bits of show-biz gossip. Winchell included items about politics and business, recommendations or dismissals of movies and books, and predictions; and he conducted his many bitter feuds in print. The material was expressed by means of a punning language that became known as Winchellese: "That Way" (in love), "Closerthanthis" (in love), "Infanticipate" (pregnant),

"Chicagorilla" (gangster from Chicago), "Renovated" (divorced), "Phfft" (broken, ended, or spoiled) and "the Mister and Miseries" (marital difficulties). Some were coined by Winchell and some were provided by a growing cadre of contributors, but he accepted credit for all of the neologisms and thereby acquired a reputation as a language innovator and wit.

**Influence.** The influence of the column became prodigious. A favorable mention in Winchell could make a novel a best-seller; any mention in Winchell could make a person an instant celebrity. Moreover, Winchell's readership cut across several boundaries; he was read by subway straphangers and by intellectuals. Lyricist Lorenz Hart wrote: "I follow Winchell and read every line. That's why the lady is a tramp." Ernest Hemingway allegedly stated that "Winchell is the greatest newspaperman that ever lived." Inevitably, Winchell inspired a journalistic genre. His column was widely imitated as it became necessary for most papers — in and out of New York — to run a column of metropolitan gossip. Winchell's clones included Ed Sullivan (his bitter enemy), Sidney Skolsky, Earl Wilson, and Leonard Lyons, but none came close to matching his influence.

**Radio.** Compulsively driven to seek more influence and more recognition, Winchell appeared in vaudeville and movies, but his greatest media exposure resulted from his weekly radio broadcasts that began in 1930. Opening with "Good evening, Mr. and Mrs. America and all the ships at sea," Winchell delivered items of the sort that appeared in his column at the rate of 227 words per minute punctuated by a clicking telegraph key to provide a sense of urgency.

**Runyon Fund.** Winchell developed a devoted friendship with Damon Runyon, another legendary newspaperman. When Runyon had lost the ability to speak and was dying of cancer, he and Winchell sat together in the Stork Club night after night. Winchell raised $32 million for the cancer research fund named for Runyon.

**Times Change.** During the 1930s Winchell embraced Franklin Delano Roosevelt's New Deal and denounced Hitler, thereby eliciting attacks as a radical from the right wing. When he became a strong foe of communism after the war, he was denounced as a fascist by the Left. By the end of the 1950s Winchell seemed old-fashioned. The world he had written about no longer existed; the things that had seemed scandalous were out in the open; his powerful friends were dead. His style and personality did not translate well into television broadcasting. Walter Winchell died in California without a column and without an audience.

**Source:**

Neal Gabler, *Winchell: Gossip, Power, and the Culture of Celebrity* (New York: Knopf, 1994).

# PEOPLE IN THE NEWS

**Moses Annenberg** acquired the *Daily Racing Form* in 1922; it was the start of his racing wire service providing results to bookies and gamblers, which bankrolled his other publishing ventures.

**Clarke Fisher Ansley** joined Columbia University Press on 1 January 1928 to commence work on the *Columbia Encyclopedia*, which was published in 1935.

**Harold W. Arlin** of KDKA Pittsburgh became the first full-time radio announcer in 1922.

**Edwin Howard Armstrong** sold his regeneration and superheterodyne radio patents to Westinghouse for $335,000 in 1920. He later develops FM.

**William Bird**'s Paris-based Three Mountains Press published its first book — Ezra Pound's *Indiscretions* — in 1923.

**Dr. S. Parkes Cadman,** prominent minister and syndicated columnist, began a weekly religious program for NBC in 1928.

The **Cohn** brothers — **Jack** and **Harry** — founded Columbia Pictures in 1924.

Poet-publisher **Harry Crosby** murdered his mistress and commited suicide on 10 December 1929.

**Harry** and **Caresse Crosby**'s Paris-based Black Sun Press published its first book, her *Crosses of Gold*, in 1925.

**Mrs. Mary Ware Dennett,** author of *The Sex Side of Life*, a pamphlet for children, was fined $300 by a Brooklyn federal court in 1929. She refused to pay the fine, and her conviction was reversed by the U.S. Circuit Court of Appeals.

**Philo T. Farnsworth** transmited the first television pictures in 1927.

**Milton Feasley** and **Gordon Seagrove** wrote the first "Even your best friend won't tell you" ads for Listerine in 1922.

**Robert Flaherty** produced *Nanook of the North*, the first documentary, in 1922.

**Dr. Edgar J. Goodspeed**'s *The New Testament: An American Translation*, published in 1923, became the best-selling modern-speech Bible.

**Ben Gross** became radio editor of *The New York Daily News* in 1925.

**Warren Harding** was the first American president to broadcast a formal address, for the 1922 dedication of the Francis Scott Key monument at Fort McHenry, Baltimore, Maryland.

Director **Rex Ingram** (*The Four Horsemen of the Apocalypse*) transferred movie production to France in 1925 in order to evade Louis B. Mayer's control.

**Herbert T. Kalmus** developed the Technicolor process in 1923.

**H. V. Kaltenborn**'s news commentary is canceled by WEAF New York in 1924, after a complaint from the State Department.

**Marcus Loew** founded the Loew's, Inc., theater chain in 1920. He organized Metro-Goldwyn-Mayer in 1924, thereby providing quality movies for his theatres.

**Robert McAlmon**'s Paris-based Contact Editions published its first book — his *A Hasty Bunch* — in 1922.

**Eugene F. McDonald Jr.,** 33, established Zenith Radio in 1923.

**H. L. Mencken** is arrested on the Boston Common on 5 April 1926 for selling a copy of *The American Mercury* with Herbert Asbury's "Hatrack"; he was tried and acquitted of publishing obscenity.

**A. C. Nielsen** founded his market-research service in 1923; the Nielsen ratings subsequently became a standard gauge for broadcasters.

**Harry Pace** and **W. C. Handy** established Black Swan — the first record company owned by blacks — in May 1921.

**Emily Post** published *Etiquette, In Society, In Business, In Politics, and At Home*, followed by *Etiquette: The Blue Book of Social Usage* in 1927.

**Julius Rosenwald,** chairman of Sears, Roebuck, acquired the *Encyclopaedia Britannica* in 1929.

Actor **Chic Sale** published *The Specialist,* a booklet about building outhouses. It sold more than 200,000 copies in 1929, and "Chic Sale" became another term for outhouse.

**Upton Sinclair** addressed two thousand people on the Boston Common on 12 June 1927 to protest the banning of his *Oil!* He subsequently published an edition of the novel with fig leaves over the pages cited by the authorities.

Presidential candidate **Al Smith** became identified with his pronunciation of the word *raddio* during his 1928 campaign.

**Dr. Jules Styne,** twenty-eight, established the Music Corporation of America in 1924; MCA became a powerful agency representing orchestras and radio and movie performances.

**Horace A. Wade,** age eleven, published a thirty-thousand-word novelette, *In the Shadow of the Great Peril,* in February 1920.

The four **Warner** brothers — **Albert, Harry, Jack,** and **Sam** — incorporated Warner Bros. Pictures in 1923.

**Ed Wynn's** *The Perfect Fool,* the first stage show to be broadcast, was heard over WJZ Newark on 19 February 1922.

**Vladimir Zworykin** and Westinghouse patented the iconoscope, the first electronic camera tube for a television system, in 1923.

# AWARDS

## PULITZER PRIZES FOR JOURNALISM

1920

Editorial Writing: Harvey E. Newbranch, *Omaha Evening World Herald*

Reporting: John J. Leary Jr., *New York World*

1921

Public Service: *Boston Post*

Reporting: Louis Seibold, *New York World*

1922

Cartoon: Rollin Kirby, *New York World*

Editorial Writing: Frank M. O'Brien, *New York Herald*

Public Service: *New York World*

Reporting: Kirke L. Simpson, Associated Press

1923

Editorial Writing: William Allen White, *Emporia Gazette*

Public Service: *Memphis Commercial Appeal*

Reporting: Alva Johnson, *The New York Times*

1924

Cartoon: Jay Norwood Darling, *Des Moines Register and Tribune*

Editorial Writing: *Boston Herald* and Frank I. Cobb, *New York World*

Public Service: *New York World*

Reporting: Magner White, *San Diego Sun*

1925

Cartoon: Rollin Kirby, *New York World*

Editorial Writing: *Charleston* (S.C.) *News and Courier*

Reporting: James W. Mulroy and Alvin H. Goldstein, *Chicago Daily News*

1926

Cartoon: D. R. Fitzpatrick, *St. Louis Post-Dispatch*

Editorial Writing: Edward M. Kingsbury, *The New York Times*

Public Service: *Columbus* (Ga.) *Enquirer Sun*

Reporting: William Burke Miller, *Louisville Courier-Journal*

1927

Cartoon: Nelson Harding, *Brooklyn Daily Eagle*

Editorial Writing: F. Lauriston Bullard, *Boston Herald*

Public Sevice: *Canton* (Ohio) *Daily News*

Reporting: John T. Rogers, *St. Louis Post-Dispatch*

1928

Cartoon: Nelson Harding, *Brooklyn Daily Eagle*

Editorial Writing: Grover Cleveland Hall, *Montgomery Advertiser*

Public Service: *Indianapolis Times*

1929

Cartoon: Rollin Kirby, *New York World*

Editorial Writing: Louis Isaac Jaffe, *Norfolk Virginian-Pilot*

Reporting: Paul Y. Anderson, *St. Louis Post-Dispatch*

# DEATHS

**Charles Alexander,** 55, editor and publisher of black magazines, 5 September 1923.

**Daniel Appleton,** 77, book publisher, 16 March 1929.

**W. W. Appleton,** 78, book publisher, 27 January 1924.

**Francis W. Ayer,** 75, pioneer advertising executive (N. W. Ayer & Son) and publisher of Ayers's *American Newspaper Annual and Directory,* 5 March 1923.

**Clarence W. Barron,** 73, publisher of *The Wall Street Journal* and *Barron's Financial Weekly,* 2 October 1928.

**W. L. Bobbs,** 65, book publisher, 11 February 1926.

**Edward L. Burlingame,** 74, book editor, 15 November 1922.

**Frank I. Cobb,** 54, newspaper editor, 21 December 1923.

**Elizabeth Cochrane** (Nellie ), 55, reporter, 22 January 1922.

**M. H. de Young,** publisher of *The San Francisco Chronicle,* 15 February 1925.

**T. A. Dorgan** (Tad), 52, cartoonist, 2 May 1929.

**E. P. Dutton,** 92, book publisher, 6 September 1923.

**Otto Floto,** 66, circus owner, 4 August 1929.

**Charles Forepaugh,** 91, circus owner, 17 July 1929.

**Richard K. Fox,** 76, publisher of *The National Police Gazette,* 14 November 1922.

**Eddie Foy,** 72, musical comedy star and hero of the Iroquois Theatre fire, 16 February 1928.

**Charles H. Grasty,** 61, newspaper editor and publisher (Baltimore Sunpapers), 19 January 1924.

**Briton Hadden,** 31, cofounder of *Time,* 27 February 1929.

**Henry Holt,** 86, book publisher, 13 February 1926.

**Thomas H. Ince,** 42, movie producer, 19 November 1924.

**Victor F. Lawson,** editor and publisher of *The Chicago Daily News,* 19 August 1925.

**Marcus Loew,** 57, movie theatre and M-G-M proprietor, 5 September 1927.

**Col. William D'Alton Mann,** 81, publisher of *Town Topics,* 17 May 1920.

**Orison Swett Marden,** 74, founder and editor of *Success,* 10 March 1924.

**W. B. (Bat) Masterson,** 67, gunfighter and journalist, 25 October 1921.

**Frank A. Munsey,** 71, newspaper and magazine publisher, 22 December 1925.

**James O'Neill,** 73, actor (*The Count of Monte Cristo*), 10 August 1920.

**R. F. Outcault,** 65, cartoonist (*The Yellow Kid* ), 25 September 1928.

**William Marion Reedy,** 58, editor and publisher of *Reedy's Mirror,* 28 July 1920.

**Charles Ringling,** 62, circus owner, 3 December 1926.

**E. W. Scripps,** 72, newspaper chain owner (Scripps-Howard), 12 March 1926.

**Frank L. Stanton,** 70, *Atlanta Constitution* columnist, 7 January 1927.

**Melville E. Stone,** 81, founder of the *Chicago Daily News* and general manager of the Associated Press, 15 February 1929.

**Bert Leston Taylor,** 55, *Chicago Tribune* columnist ("A Line o' Type or Two"), 19 March 1921.

**Buck Taylor,** Wild West showman, 28 April 1924.

**Charles H. Taylor,** editor and publisher of the *Boston Globe,* 22 June 1921.

**William Desmond Taylor,** 45, movie director, 1 or 2 February 1922.

**J. Walter Thompson,** 81, advertising executive who convinced businessmen and media of the value of advertising and built America's largest advertising agency, 16 October 1928.

**A. W. Wagnalls,** 80, book publisher, 3 September 1924.

**S. L. Warner,** 40, movie producer, 5 October 1927.

**Henry Watterson,** 81, editor of the *Louisville Courier-Journal,* 22 December 1921.

**Florenz Ziegfeld Sr.,** 82, impresario, 20 May 1923.

# PUBLICATIONS

Hugh E. Agnew, *Advertising Media* (New York: Van Nostrand, 1932);

Frank A. Arnold, *Broadcast Advertising* (New York: Wiley, 1933);

William Peck Banning, *Commercial Broadcast Pioneer: The WEAF Experiment 1922–1926* (Cambridge, Mass.: Harvard University Press, 1946);

Erik Barnouw, *A Tower in Babel: A History of Broadcasting in the United States to 1933* (New York: Oxford University Press, 1966);

James Boylan, ed., *The World and the 20's: The Golden Years of New York's Legendary Newspaper* (New York: Dial, 1973);

Frank Buxton and Bill Owen, *The Big Broadcast 1920–1950* (New York: Viking, 1972);

Nelson A. Crawford, *The Ethics of Journalism* (New York: Knopf, 1924);

Frederick G. Detweiler, *The Negro Press in the United States* (Chicago: University of Chicago Press, 1922);

Orrin E. Dunlap Jr., *Radio in Advertising* (New York: Harper, 1931);

Gene Fowler, *Skyline: A Reporter's Reminiscences of the 1920s* (New York: Viking, 1961);

George French, *20th Century Advertising* (New York: Van Nostrand, 1926);

Herman S. Hettinger, *A Decade of Radio Advertising* (Chicago: University of Chicago Press, 1933);

Frank J. Kahn, ed., *Documents of American Broadcasting* (New York: Appleton-Century-Crofts, 1968);

Al Laney, *Paris Herald* (New York: Appleton, 1947);

Tom Lewis, *Empire of the Air: The Men Who Made Radio* (New York: Burlingame/HarperCollins, 1991);

Walter Lippmann, *Public Opinion* (New York: Harcourt, Brace, 1922);

J. Fred MacDonald, *Don't Touch That Dial! Radio Programming in American Life, 1920–1960* (Chicago: Nelson-Hall, 1979);

Robert E. Park, *The Immigrant Press and its Control* (New York: Harper, 1922);

Joan Shelley Rubin, *The Making of Middlebrow Culture* (Chapel Hill: University of North Carolina Press, 1992);

Paul Schubert, *History of Broadcasting: Radio to Television: The Electric Word: The Rise of Radio* (New York: Arno Press & New York Times, 1971);

George Seldes, *You Can't Print That! The Truth Behind the News, 1918–1928* (New York: Payson & Clarke, 1929);

Melville E. Stone, *Fifty Years a Journalist* (Garden City, N.Y.: Doubleday, Page, 1921);

Oswald Garrison Villard, *Some Newspapers and Newspaper Men* (New York: Knopf, 1923);

Caulton Waugh, *The Comics* (New York: Macmillan, 1947);

David Manning White and Robert H. Abel, *The Funnies: An American Idiom* (New York: Free Press of Glencoe/Macmillan, 1963);

*Billboard,* periodical;

*Editor and Publisher,* periodical;

*Publishers' Weekly,* periodical;

*Radio Broadcast,* periodical;

*Variety,* periodical.

CHAPTER TEN

# MEDICINE AND HEALTH

by SUZANNE CAMERON LINDER and EMILY LINDER JOHNSON

## CONTENTS

*Sidebars and tables are listed in italics.*

## 1920

- George Whipple cures anemia in dogs by feeding them large amounts of raw liver.

- Phenobarbital (discovered in 1911) is introduced in the treatment of epilepsy.

- Harvey Cushing pioneers new techniques in brain surgery.

## 1921

- Frederick Banting and Charles Best extract insulin from the pancreas and begin experiments using the substance on dogs.

- James Collip isolates pure insulin.

- Alexander Fleming discovers an antibacterial substance, lysozyme, in saliva, mucus, and tears.

- The inkblot test for the study of personality is introduced by Hermann Rorschach.

- Albert Calmette and Camille Guerin develop tuberculosis vaccine.

- The first American birth control conference convenes in New York City.

## 1922

- Frederick Banting and Charles Best successfully use insulin to treat a diabetic.

- Elmer McCollum uses vitamin D, found in cod liver oil, to treat rickets.

- Herbert Evans discovers vitamin E, which he believes to be vital to fertility.

- Joseph Erlanger and Herbert Gasser use an oscilloscope to study electrical impulses in a single nerve fiber.

- Frederick Hopkins discovers glutathione, a sequence of three amino acids essential for the utilization of oxygen by a cell.

## 1923

- George and Gladys Dick, who discover that streptococcus causes scarlet fever, develop an antitoxin.

- Reuben Kahn makes available a faster and more sensitive test for syphilis.

- The first birth control clinic opens in New York City under the leadership of Margaret Sanger.

## 1924

- Harry Steenbock finds that the ultraviolet component of sunlight increases vitamin D in food.

- Theodor Svedberg invents the ultracentrifuge, which makes it possible to isolate viruses.

- Acetylene is used as an anesthetic.

- Willem Einthoven invents the electrocardiograph.

- Rudolph Matas introduces the use of intravenous saline solution to prevent dehydration.

## 1925

- George Whipple demonstrates that iron is a major factor in the formation of red blood cells.
- James Collip discovers parathormone, a hormone secreted by the parathyroid gland.

## 1926

- George Whipple, George Minot, and William Murphy show that a diet rich in liver can control pernicious anemia, usually a fatal disease.
- Urease is the first enzyme to be crystallized by James Sumner, Massachusetts biochemist.
- A chemical (later identified as acetylcholine) is shown to be involved in the transmission of nerve impulses.
- Spiroptera carcinoma, a cancer caused by a parasite, is discovered.

## 1927

- Frank A. Hartman isolates cortin from the adrenal glands.

## 1928

- Alexander Fleming discovers penicillin in molds.
- Albert Szent-Györgyi isolates hexuronic acid, later proved to be vitamin C.
- George Papanicolaou develops the Pap test for diagnosing uterine cancers.
- Philip Drinker and Louis Shaw develop the iron-lung respirator.
- Research by Oscar Riddle shows that prolactin, a pituitary hormone, causes the production of milk in the breasts.

## 1929

- Hans Berger develops the electroencephalograph (EEG).
- Edward Doisy discovers theelin, a female sex hormone, in urine of pregnant women.
- Adolph Butenandt, German biochemist, determines the chemical structure of estrone, a female sex hormone.
- Adenosine triphosphate (ATP) is isolated from muscle.
- Manfred J. Sakel uses insulin shock as a treatment for schizophrenia.
- The Nobel Prize goes to Christiaan Eijkman for discovering vitamin B and to Frederick Hopkins for discovering vitamin A.
- The first human heart catheterization is performed.

# OVERVIEW

**Increase in the Rate of Progress.** As America entered the twentieth century, the rate of progress seemed to increase exponentially, especially in the medical field. On 15 May 1930 Rufus Cole, physician and director of the Hospital of the Rockefeller Institute for Medical Research, addressed the Academy of Medicine in New York City on the progress of medicine during the past twenty-five years. He said that the concept of progress was relatively new. It dated from the eighteenth-century Enlightenment when new discoveries in natural science amplified knowledge of the environment and man became more hopeful of the future. "Today we have to ask ourselves," he said, "not whether medicine has progressed but at what rate progress has occurred."

**Change from the Art of the Physician to the Science of Medicine.** The medical progress that was so apparent to Cole as the decade of the 1920s came to an end was largely a result of the change in emphasis from the art of the physician to the science of medicine. In 1900 the average doctor had few effective drugs and little laboratory equipment beyond the microscope. His role was that of sage and comforter, and with his relatively superior education and genuine concern for the patient, he often could offer commonsense solutions to practical problems. The physician ministered at the patient's bedside much as did the clergy, but unfortunately, comfort was frequently the best the doctor had to provide. However, many people tended to live and die in the same vicinity, and the family doctor had an intimate knowledge of the patient's medical and social history as well as his or her family history and genetic predispositions.

**The Secret of Patient Care.** In 1926 Francis W. Peabody, a physician at Boston City Hospital, spoke to the students of Harvard Medical School on care of the patient. He said that the most common criticism made by older practitioners was that young graduates had been taught a great deal about the mechanism of disease but very little about the practice of medicine: ". . . they are too 'scientific' and do not know how to take care of patients." Peabody also discussed the depersonalization that accompanied hospital care and asserted that the good physician must know his patients thoroughly. He concluded that "the secret of the care of the patient is in caring for the patient." When Peabody had attended medical school a generation earlier, patient care was the primary tool of the physician.

**Conditions at the Turn of the Century.** At the turn of the century smallpox was the only disease for which there was an effective immunization. Diphtheria, typhoid, or scarlet fever might constitute a death sentence for the patient. Moreover, maternal and infant mortality rates were high, for the psychological and nutritional aspects of well-baby care were yet undefined. Physicians did not have the knowledge or the diagnostic tools to deal with a large number of the problems they encountered.

**Scientific Medicine.** Lawrence J. Henderson, a professor of medical history at Harvard, estimated that before the 1920s, the patient had less than a fifty-fifty chance of benefiting from seeing a doctor. During the decade other aspects of medicine began to eclipse the art of the physician. In 1920, for the first time, the nation's urban dwellers outnumbered the rural population. Better transportation made office visits more common, while specialization and the growth of hospitals contributed to the depersonalization of services. As the doctor's semi-clerical role declined, scientific developments and highly improved educational opportunities contributed to his effectiveness.

**The Flexner Report on Medical Education.** One of the main influences on the improvement in medical education was the Flexner Report. In November 1908 the trustees of the Carnegie Foundation authorized a study of medical education in the United States. They chose Abraham Flexner, a specialist in the field of education, to undertake the study. Flexner pointed out the great discrepancy that had occurred between medical science and medical education. While science had progressed, education had failed to keep pace. Flexner found that many teaching hospitals were antiquated and unsanitary and that many proprietary institutions — privately owned schools not associated with universities — existed solely for the profit of their owners. His recommendation was that 120 medical schools be closed, and within the next few years most of them were.

**Better Education Meant Increase in Income and Prestige.** Due to the influence of the Flexner Report and to more-stringent licensing requirements, an undergraduate degree was generally a prerequisite to medical school in 1920, and almost all of these schools provided hospital facilities and clinical instruction as well as a requirement that the student complete an internship. The average medical graduate in the 1920s was far better trained than his predecessors had been, and as a result, both the income and prestige of physicians increased.

**Influence of Feminist Reformers.** After women gained the right to vote in 1920, female reformers were largely responsible for persuading Congress to pass the Sheppard-Towner Act in 1921. It provided matching funds to states for prenatal and children's health centers. Operated mainly by public-health nurses and women physicians, these centers sought to reduce rates of maternal and infant mortality by giving pregnant women advice on personal hygiene and infant care.

**The American Medical Association Opposed Free Medical Care.** The growing authority of the medical profession was apparent in the fate of the Sheppard-Towner Act. Government support for maternal and child health programs that became available under the act in 1921 was discontinued when the American Medical Association, fearful of competition from free health centers, persuaded Congress to discontinue the program in 1927. However, the decade of the 1920s was characterized by increased interest in and support for the health of women and children.

**The "Age of the Child."** In 1923 the *American Journal of Public Health* declared, "This is indeed the age of the child. The rapid growth of the maternal and child hygiene movement is one of the most striking developments in the public-health field." With impetus from the Sheppard-Towner Act, many state health departments obtained funds for bureaus of child hygiene, and these children's bureaus helped organize examinations, immunizations, and school health programs.

**The Role of Nurses.** The number of professionally trained nurses increased dramatically during World War I. After the war the additional nurses proved useful in the programs for maternal and child health when the idea that the nurse's role should include helping families prepare for new members gained acceptance. Some nurses, specially trained as midwives, took responsibility for prenatal, delivery, postpartum, and infant care. In 1930 a study that compared outcomes of care provided by physicians and trained nurse-midwives demonstrated that care provided by the midwives was as good as, or superior to, that provided by doctors.

**Nursing Education.** Accompanying the increase in the prestige and numbers of nurses, there was growing interest in nursing education, which in the early twentieth century had been administered by hospitals. In 1923 the first major study of nursing and nursing education recommended that professionals be prepared in universities.

**Birth Control and Women's Health.** Another type of education under scrutiny in the 1920s involved the controversial issue of birth control. Some states had passed legislation prohibiting dissemination not only of contraceptives but also of information about birth control. Due to the leadership of Margaret Sanger and other feminists, information about procreation became more readily available. In addition, medical researchers developed the first effective tests for pregnancy and for detection of uterine cancer and discovered prolactin, the hormone that causes the production of breast milk.

**Nutrition.** Nutrition and vitamin deficiencies were other areas of emphasis in the 1920s. Casimir Funk, a Polish scientist who became an American citizen in 1920, coined the term *vitamin*. During the decade researchers discovered vitamins A, B, D, and E, and isolated hexuronic acid, which later proved to be vitamin C. Physicians also made progress in treating pellagra, a vitamin-deficiency disease, and pernicious anemia, which later proved to be caused by a lack of assimilation of vitamin $B_{12}$.

**Diabetes.** One outstanding accomplishment of the 1920s was the use of insulin in treating diabetes, a disease that had previously been treated by controlling the diet. This method was not always effective, and in many cases diabetes was fatal. Juvenile diabetes was a frequent killer of young people. Work by Frederick Banting, Charles Best, John J. R. MacLeod, and James Collip was instrumental in the development of insulin.

**Scarlet Fever.** Another childhood disease that was brought under control was scarlet fever. Dr. George F. Dick and his wife, Dr. Gladys H. Dick, developed a skin test for susceptibility, an immunization, and an antitoxin that if given early could help the patient fight the disease more effectively.

**Penicillin.** Alexander Fleming, a British physician, discovered the antibiotic properties of a mold, *penicillium notatum*. He was not able to make the drug available for practical use, and it was not until the 1940s that other doctors would bring it into general application. Fleming's discovery opened the way for the development of antibiotic drugs, which revolutionized the field of medicine.

**Neurosurgery.** Harvey Cushing, professor of surgery at Harvard, pioneered in the field of neurosurgery in the first decades of the twentieth century and published studies in the 1920s. He was also interested in the history of medicine, and in 1925 he won the Pulitzer Prize for a biography of Sir William Osler, physician, teacher, and author of a widely used medical textbook of the period.

**Osler's Textbook.** Osler died in 1919, but he continued to exert an influence through the widespread use of his textbook *The Principles and Practice of Medicine*. The text, first printed in 1895, continued to be adapted to incorporate advances until 1947 when the sixteenth edition was published. Osler wrote, "Everywhere the old order changes and happy they who can change with it."

**The End of the Decade.** The changes brought about by laboratory experimentation made a profound impact in the 1920s. Undoubtedly the impact was much greater in cities or areas in close proximity to medical schools. It took much longer for progress in science to filter down to the rural physician. Because few physicians lived and worked in rural areas, a wide discrepancy existed in the quality of medical care available to rural and urban citizens. Nevertheless, while the medical profession in 1900 was characterized by art rather than by science, by the end of the decade of the 1920s the emphasis was on the science of medicine.

# TOPICS IN THE NEWS

## COMMUNICABLE DISEASES

**Measles.** Measles, a childhood disease characterized by high fever, sore throat, and skin rash, was widespread in the 1920s, but was not usually fatal when patients received good care. However, in foundling hospitals half the patients might die from terminal bronchopneumonia. There was also the danger of developing blindness. Although the microorganism, or "germ," that caused measles had not been indentified, a serum made from the blood of convalescent patients was used after 1920 to provide some resistance to the disease for children who were exposed to measles. It was not completely effective in immunizing the exposed children, but those who became infected usually had a lighter case.

**Scarlet Fever.** Before 1923 scarlet fever was a danger faced by children and adults on a daily basis. Through the work of a husband-and-wife scientific team, the germ responsible for the disease was recognized, and an inoculation was created to prevent its deadly complications. By 1924 there was still no cure for scarlet fever, but new preventive measures introduced by George and Gladys Dick removed the danger of a disease that might cause deafness, blindness, heart and kidney disease, permanent crippling, or death.

**Research Accelerates.** Although research into the diseases of typhoid and diphtheria had proved fruitful, little was known about scarlet fever despite the great amount of work that was being done in that area. In order to remedy this situation, the John McCormick Institute for Contagious Diseases was founded by Mr. and Mrs. Harold McCormick of Chicago in honor of the son they lost

### SCARLET FEVER

Emily Breeden, who had scarlet fever when she was a little girl in Marlboro County, South Carolina, recalled how the quarantine program worked in the early 1920s before George and Gladys Dick developed the antitoxin in 1923. The county board of health posted a yellow flag in Emily's front yard and a printed notice on the door to ward off any visitors. The patient and her mother stayed in one room while another member of the family left food on a tray outside the door. The mother carefully washed the dishes with disinfectant before placing them outside the door again. Confinement lasted one month, and then the room had to be fumigated. Emily carefully hung the homework papers she had prepared for school on a clothesline tied across the room so that they could be fumigated, too. After she and her mother left the room at the end of the quarantine period, rags were stuffed around the windows and doors to make the room as airtight as possible, and a quart of formaldehyde was poured into a fourteen-quart container with thirteen and one-half ounces of permanganate potash. The resulting fumes were supposed to kill any scarlet fever germs that remained in the room, including those on the homework papers, which Emily then took to school.

Source: Suzanne C. Linder, *Medicine in Marlboro County, 1736–1980* (Baltimore: Gateway Press, 1980), pp. 75-76.

to scarlet fever. The Dicks went to work trying to identify the scarlet fever microbe.

**Identifying the Germ.** In 1923 the germ hemolytic streptococcus was definitely identified as the cause of scarlet fever. The germ was isolated from the sore on the finger of a nurse with the disease and then swabbed on the tonsils of several volunteers. When a typical case of scarlet fever resulted, the Dicks deemed the experiment conclusive.

**Developing the Antitoxin.** Experimentation with the newly discovered germ showed that when subjects were injected with a diluted version, a reaction would appear if that subject had never had the disease. This meant that the subject was susceptible to contracting scarlet fever. Subjects who had had the disease showed no reaction at all. Thus, the Dick test became a conclusive method of determining susceptibility or immunity to the disease. Finally, when larger amounts of the scarlet fever toxin were injected into subjects previously showing a positive reaction to the Dick test, the skin test became negative and the subject was now immune to the disease. The scarlet fever inoculation was born.

**Prevention, Not Cure.** These experiments in the 1920s virtually eliminated the threat of scarlet fever in epidemic proportions. The Dick skin test and the immunization that followed were not cures for scarlet fever, but preventive measures. Nevertheless, as long as people were willing to be tested and immunized if that test was positive, they were protected from the ravages of the disease.

**Tuberculosis.** In 1922 Census Bureau compilations showed that 90,452 people in the United States died of tuberculosis, a deadly and contagious disease caused by the bacterium *Mycobacterium tuberculosis,* which was first identified in 1882 by Robert Koch. Although the disease can involve almost any organ or tissue of the body, between 92 percent and 94 percent of infection is pulmonary. The most common mode of transmission is by inhalation of bacilli from the sputum of persons with ulcerative pulmonary tuberculosis. Minute droplets discharged by cough or sneeze from the infected person may float in the air for hours.

**Skin Test.** Since tuberculosis is easily spread and can be deadly, scientists realized early the necessity of identifying unknowing carriers of the disease. Thus, the first step in limiting the spread of tuberculosis was taken in 1890 when Koch developed the tuberculin skin test. The test, if positive, resulted in a reddened, inflamed patch when small amounts of tuberculin were injected beneath the skin. Tuberculin was a chemical released from the tuberculosis bacterium that caused an allergic reaction (the inflamed patch of skin) in tuberculosis-infected individuals.

**Mortality Rates.** The tuberculin skin test was a valuable tool in diagnosing victims of tuberculosis, but the mortality rate from the disease remained high in the 1920s. The death rate in 1922 was 97 per 100,000 population. Colorado showed the highest rate at 172.6 per 100,000, probably because infected persons migrated there to take advantage of the cool, dry climate. Nebraska had the lowest rate at 36.1.

**Vaccine.** Although the death rate from tuberculosis was 2.4 percent lower in 1922 than in 1921, merely identifying carriers of the disease was not enough to stop its progression. The most significant development in reducing the tuberculosis death count came in 1921 when two French microbiologists, Albert Calmette and Camille Guerin, produced the first vaccine. Calmette was a student of Louis Pasteur in Paris, and Guerin was a veterinarian who joined Calmette to study the microbiology of infectious diseases, particularly tuberculosis. The research of the two scientists showed that exposure to tuberculosis or suffering a mild infection of the disease led to eventual resistance. This resistance was caused by the immune system's response to the bacteria in the body.

**Calmette and Guerin.** From 1906 to 1921 Calmette and Guerin cultured the tuberculosis bacteria from cattle and found that the bacteria lost ability to cause the disease over many generations. Despite their weakened form, these harmless bacteria were able to stimulate the cow's immune system to produce antibodies and protect against the disease.

**BCG.** Although there was some concern regarding the vaccine's transference to humans, Calmette and Guerin produced a harmless vaccine in 1921, a strain called Bacillus Calmette-Guerin (BCG). The immunization was harmless because the avirulent strain could not damage lung tissue. The vaccine was used in Paris in 1922 and throughout Europe and Asia by 1930. The United States and England were less receptive to the vaccine and insisted on extensive testing before beginning BCG immunizations in the 1950s. With worldwide acceptance, the incidence of tuberculosis declined.

**U.S. Response.** The vaccine was controversial in the United States because it used specially bred live bacteria, and it conflicted with the widely used skin test as developed by Koch. The skin test was designed to identify carriers of the disease for treatment, but anyone vaccinated showed a positive skin test even when not infected. Nevertheless, the vaccine was eventually accepted worldwide by the 1950s, and tuberculosis was finally reduced to a disease that could be prevented, or identified and treated.

Sources:

Barbara Bates, *Bargaining for Life: A Social History of Tuberculosis, 1876–1938* (Philadelphia: University of Pennsylvania Press, 1992);

George F. Dick and Gladys H. Dick, "The Etiology of Scarlet Fever," *Journal of the American Medical Association* (*JAMA*), 82 (26 January 1924): 301–302;

Dick and Dick, "Scarlet Fever," *American Journal of Public Health,* 14 (December 1924): 1022–1028;

Ernest Gruening, "Another Germ Bites the Dust," *Collier's*, 74 (4 October 1924): 26;

"The Mortality From Tuberculosis and Cancer," *Science*, 58 (13 July 1923): 510;

Herbert T. Wade, ed., *The New International Year Book for 1926* (New York: Dodd, Mead, 1927), p. 459;

Gene H. Stollerman, "The Historical Role of the Dick Test," *JAMA*, 250 (9 December 1983): 3097–3099.

## DIAGNOSIS TECHNOLOGY

**Electrocardiograph.** The electrocardiograph, an instrument designed to measure the electrical currents of the heart, was invented in 1924. Willem Einthoven was responsible for this new invention, which grew out of his work regarding the nature of heart action in disease as well as in health.

**Unsatisfactory Instrumentation.** Einthoven at first attempted to measure these currents by using the Lippmann capillary electrometer and various other instruments Einthoven built to aid his research. He found the capillary electrometer to be severely restrictive, but he was able to develop a way to correct its limitations. Still not satisfied with the available instrumentation and frustrated by the time and labor required for the current mechanisms to be effective, he searched for another means of recording the electrical currents attending the heartbeat.

**A New Invention.** The string galvanometer was Einthoven's answer to the limitations of other instruments. He described his new instrument and its relation to his experiments in electrocardiography in a series of papers. These papers dealt so completely with the field that little of major importance has been added that Einthoven did not at least touch on in his original research. For example, his first paper on electrocardiography noted a case of auricular fibrillation, although he was not yet aware of its significance. More than half a century after its invention, the electrocardiograph is still a major diagnostic tool in heart disease.

**Psychophysiology Faces Change.** As neurologists and psychiatrists in the later nineteenth century searched for a better understanding of brain function and its relation to mental processes, a renegade German scientist and psychiatrist developed a new approach. Always considered an outsider, Hans Berger dismissed the popular theories regarding the mind-brain relationship and sought a method grounded in the natural sciences. Berger's research led him on a search for a method to measure human brain-wave patterns and culminated in the development of the electroencephalograph.

**Early Attempts.** After disillusioning attempts at measuring changes in brain circulation and changes in the temperature of the brain during mental activity, Berger realized that studying the electrical activity of the brain would provide more insight into mental functioning and disturbances. Although Berger's knowledge of electro-

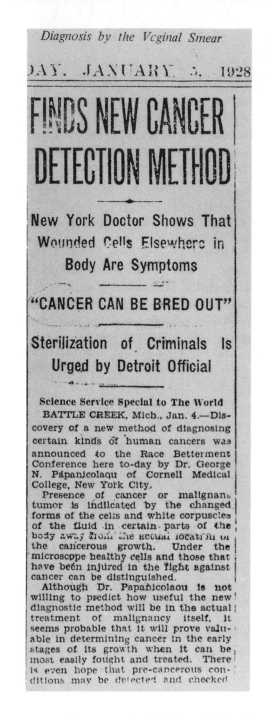

*Diagnosis by the Vaginal Smear*

**DAY, JANUARY 5, 1928**

# FINDS NEW CANCER DETECTION METHOD

**New York Doctor Shows That Wounded Cells Elsewhere in Body Are Symptoms**

**"CANCER CAN BE BRED OUT"**

**Sterilization of Criminals Is Urged by Detroit Official**

Science Service Special to The World
BATTLE CREEK, Mich., Jan. 4.—Discovery of a new method of diagnosing certain kinds of human cancers was announced to the Race Betterment Conference here to-day by Dr. George N. Papanicolaou of Cornell Medical College, New York City.

Presence of cancer or malignant tumor is indicated by the changed forms of the cells and white corpuscles of the fluid in certain parts of the body away from the actual location of the cancerous growth. Under the microscope healthy cells and those that have been injured in the fight against cancer can be distinguished.

Although Dr. Papanicolaou is not willing to predict how useful the new diagnostic method will be in the actual treatment of malignancy itself, it seems probable that it will prove valuable in determining cancer in the early stages of its growth when it can be most easily fought and treated. There is even hope that pre-cancerous conditions may be detected and checked

Newspaper article announcing Dr. Papanicolaou's smear test for cervical and uterine cancer

physiology and physics was limited, he made his first attempt at recording the electrical impulses of the brain in 1920. This first experiment consisted of stimulating the cortex of patients with skull defects by applying electrical current to the skin covering the defect. The attempt was unsuccessful, but Berger continued his research and successfully recorded the first electroencephalogram (EEG), or brain-wave pattern, in 1929.

**An Exciting Discovery.** Berger's success was primarily due to his creating the appropriate instrument, the electroencephalograph. The instrument used pairs of electrodes placed on the scalp to transmit a signal to one of

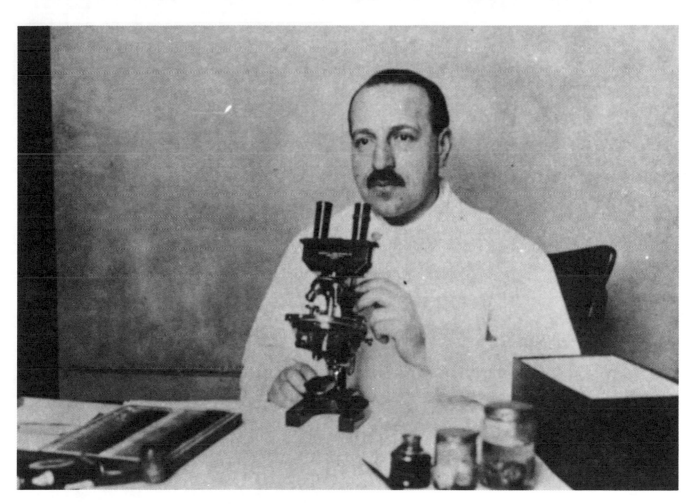

Dr. George N. Papanicolaou, developer of the Pap test

several recording channels of the electroencephalograph. The signal conveyed the difference in voltage between the pair, and the rhythmic fluctuation of the difference was shown as waves on a line graph.

**Doubts.** Berger's research was monumental, and the potential impact of such a discovery was great, but the scientific world regarded this new diagnostic tool with open disbelief. Even Berger himself was not completely confident in the reliability of the EEG. However, as he continued to study the working of the brain and the connections between parts of the central nervous system, he became convinced of the significance of the EEG. He published a series of fourteen papers in an effort to explain his research and win over the scientific community, and interest in the EEG eventually spread throughout the Western world.

**Significance.** By the time Berger published his last paper in 1938, the EEG was firmly entrenched as a medical diagnostic method. The EEG was somewhat limited as a research tool because it recorded only a small sample of electrical activity from the brain surface. Nevertheless, electroencephalography has proved to be vital in cases of serious head injury, brain tumors, cerebral infections, and various degenerative diseases of the nervous system. The electroencephalograph may be viewed as initiating a new era in neurophysiology, and Hans Berger may be called a true pioneer of medicine.

**Cancer Test.** In medical research the study of one subject often leads to a momentous discovery in another area. Such was the case with the research of George N. Papanicolaou, a Greek physician who immigrated to the United States in 1913. Papanicolaou worked at New York's Cornell Medical College in the area of cytology, specifically studying sex determination in guinea pigs. His research eventually led to a modern method for early detection of cancer in humans.

**A Better Understanding.** Papanicolaou's research required that he design a way to examine vaginal discharges of female guinea pigs. By microscopically studying the discharged cells, the doctor noted changes in their size and shape that correlated with the changes in the uterus and ovaries during the guinea pig menstrual cycle. Extending his theories to humans, Papanicolaou identified similar changes in the vaginal cells of women. More important, research showed clearly abnormal cells in the vaginal fluid from a woman diagnosed with cervical cancer. It was a short step from this discovery to Papanicolaou's development of the "Pap smear" as a method of early cancer detection.

**Irrefutable Findings.** A paper on the new cancer detection method was published in 1928 with Papanicolaou predicting that "a better understanding and more accurate analysis of the cancer problem is bound to result from use of this method. It is possible that analogous methods will be developed for the recognition of cancer in other organs." Although gynecologists initially preferred older methods of uterine cancer diagnosis to the new Pap smear, Papanicolaou's findings became irrefutable and were widely accepted by 1948.

**Significance.** Clearly, the Pap smear was a critical discovery. The method was able to detect cancer of the uterus five to ten years before symptoms appeared, and, as Papanicolaou predicted, the use of the Pap smear was extended to diagnosing cancer in other tissues of the body, such as the colon, kidney, bladder, prostate, lungs, breast, and sinuses.

Sources:

Daniel E. Carmichael, *The Pap Smear: Life of George Papanicolaou* (Springfield, Ill.: Thomas, 1973);

Mary Erlichman, *Electroencephalographic (EEG) Video Monitoring* (Rockville, Md.: United States Department of Health and Human Services, 1990);

L. J. Rather, *The Genesis of Cancer: A Study in the History of Ideas* (Baltimore: Johns Hopkins University Press, 1978);

Donald F. Scott, *Understanding EEG: An Introduction to Electroencephalography* (Philadelphia: Lippincott, 1976);

Wrynn Smith, *A Profile of Health and Disease in America: Cancer* (New York: Facts On File, 1987), pp. 52, 100;

H. B. Williams, "Willem Einthoven," *Science,* 67 (4 May 1928): 456–457.

## HEALTH OF WOMEN AND CHILDREN

**Mortality Rates.** The improvement of maternal and child hygiene, a trend throughout the 1920s, was set in motion by disturbing mortality rates. In 1921 there were 18,000 maternal deaths, or 68 maternal deaths for every 10,000 live births. The statistics for children were not any better, with 248,432 deaths recorded for children under five in 1920.

**Significant Reforms.** The astonishing data in the early 1920s was enough to rouse public interest and evoke changes in the state of public health and welfare. The changes were many and varied, including the establishment of divisions of child hygiene, infant welfare stations, and additional public-health nursing services. In addition, the American Child Health Organization was formed by the merging of six national organizations. The leadership of Herbert Hoover, later president of the United States, assured that the children's health movement would receive increased financial and social support.

**The Sheppard-Towner Act.** One of the most significant milestones on the road to health reform for women and children was the passage of the Sheppard-Towner Act in 1921. The purpose of the act was to assist the states in setting up programs to protect the health of women and children. The act planned to meet the goals

---

## CHILD CARE

**D**r. L. Emmett Holt, author of a textbook on pediatrics and a manual for child care, was to the 1920s what Dr. Benjamin Spock became for later generations, an expert on child-rearing practices. Holt's advice was archaic and repressive as compared to Spock's, and a mother who followed Holt's recommendations in the modern day might be accused of child abuse.

Dr. Holt warned of serious objections to kissing infants. He declared, "Babies under six months old should never be played with; and the less of it at any time the better for the infant." According to Holt, the most common bad habits of children were sucking, nail biting, dirt eating, bed-wetting, and masturbation. He recommended wearing mittens or fastening the hands to the sides during sleep. "In more obstinate cases, it may be necessary to confine the elbow by small pasteboard splints. . . ." Children should be carefully watched at the time of going to sleep and first waking to prevent masturbation because in that case, Holt said, "Punishments and mechanical restraint are of little avail except with infants."

**Sources:** L. Emmett Holt, *The Care and Feeding of Children,* twelfth edition (New York: Appleton, 1923), pp. 38, 192–195;

Holt, *The Diseases of Infancy and Childhood, for the Use of Students and Practitioners of Medicine* (New York: Appleton, 1926).

---

of better infant care through the teaching of mothers, better care for mothers through education as to the need of supervision during pregnancy and childbirth, and a wider distribution of medical and nursing facilities.

**Standards Developed.** The act's program was largely under the guidance of the Children's Bureau, a division of the Department of Labor set up to administer the first Child Labor Act. Under the bureau's leadership a conference of the state directors of maternity and child hygiene was held in October of 1924. One result of the conference was the promise of the bureau to formulate a code of standards for child care and prenatal care. For example, the code regarding prenatal care covered obstetrical examinations and the care and advice which should be given to pregnant women. In drafting the codes, the bureau enlisted the help of the American Pediatric Society, the American Medical Association, and the American Child Health Association.

**Mortality Rate Decreases.** By 1927 the infant mortality rate had decreased markedly and seemed to be generally on the decline. According to the report by the Children's Bureau, of 1,849,902 babies born, 119,093 died. In other words, there were 65 deaths per 1,000 births, as compared with 73.3 deaths per 1,000 births in

**A**lthough Lydia Pinkham began selling her patent medicine in 1875, it was still popular in the 1920s. In 1925 it sold almost three times as much as it had sold in any previous year. Mrs. Pinkham was one of the first women to establish a flourishing business. Her advertising catered to "women's complaints" and took advantage of lack of satisfaction at home and antagonism to males in general. The increased interest in feminism that accompanied the right to vote for women in 1920 provided encouragements for such hostility.

Robert C. Washburn, writing for the *American Mercury*, explained, "If part of Lydia Pinkham's success was thus due to the fact that she filled her sails with wind from the fringes of the feminist hurricane that was sweeping the country, another source of strength was that she put her finger on the crying need of her sex (no pun intended), the need for some sympathetic soul to talk to." Advertisements encouraged women to write to Mrs. Pinkham and air their grievances.

Pinkham's dour countenance continued to appear in ads long after her death. The sincere sourness of the Pinkham approach led to a plague of wit which swept the country and contributed to the success of the nostrum. One popular jingle taunted:

Mrs. X had bosom trouble
She was flat across the bow
Then she took three bottles of Compound
Now they milk her like a cow!
Oh we sing, we sing, we sing
Of Lydia Pinkham, Pinkham, Pinkham
And her love for the human race.

Pinkham's appeal to feminism and the jokes which helped to make her product easily recognizable probably contributed to sales, but the fact that the compound was 15 percent alcohol during Prohibition also added to its popularity.

Sources: J. C. Furnas, *The Americans* (New York: Putnam, 1969), p. 907;

Robert Collyer Washburn, "Lydia Pinkham," *American Mercury*, 22 (February 1931): 172–176.

1926. Similarly, the maternal death rate was also moving downward. The report stated that a key factor in the statistics was the effect of the Sheppard-Towner Act. A comparison of mortality rates showed a reduction in every state that had accepted the act and cooperated with its program for four years or more.

**Health Education.** Although important steps were taken in the public health field to protect women and children, educational leaders were also interested in the issues. This interest led to the establishment of health education courses in teacher-training institutions and the addition of health instruction to the public school curriculum.

**The Age of the Child.** These beneficial government programs were discontinued in 1927 because of pressure from the American Medical Association, whose members feared the competition presented by free health centers. Nevertheless, much good work had already been accomplished, and the benefits of the program were long lasting. The 1920s were characterized by increased support for women and children, and as stated in the *American Journal of Public Health* in 1923, it was indeed "the age of the child."

Sources:
Walter H. Brown, M.D., "The Trend of Maternal and Child Hygiene," *The American Journal of Public Health*, 13 (August 1923): 636–638;

Herbert T. Wade, ed., *The New International Year Book, A Compendium of the World's Progress for the Year 1925* (New York: Dodd, Mead, 1926), p. 415;

Wade, ed., *The New International Year Book, A Compendium of the World's Progress for the Year 1927* (New York: Dodd, Mead, 1928), p. 438.

## INSULIN

**Insulin.** Diabetes mellitus, also known as "sugar disease," is a disease that killed thousands every year until the discovery of insulin in 1921. Diabetes is often seen in children, and before the treatment existed, the disease was essentially a death sentence. It is caused by a defect in the pancreas, which is then unable to produce the hormone insulin needed by muscle cells to utilize glucose. Without glucose the tissues are deprived of their main energy and are forced to produce energy from fat. High blood levels of toxic ketone bodies (acetone) result.

**Symptoms.** The diabetic shows a high level of glucose in blood and urine. Symptoms of the disease include increased thirst and hunger, increased urination, weakness, and a loss of weight. If left untreated, the acetone accumulates in the blood, brain function ceases, and the patient may slip into a coma and die.

**Pancreas Defect Responsible for Disease.** Although a disease thought to be diabetes was recognized by the Egyptians as early as 1500 B.C., it was not until 1899 that the causative factor in the disease was discovered to be a defect in the pancreas. This was a major step forward because scientists were then able to produce the disease in laboratory animals. However, even with these advances, no scientist was able to isolate the exact substance that was causing the pancreatic malfunction.

**Banting Resolves to Find Cure.** Many experiments were conducted in the early 1900s in the search for the elusive pancreatic substance, but no real progress was made until the 1920s when Frederick Grant Banting was

Charles Best and Frederick Grant Banting, codevelopers of insulin, in 1921

physiologists in the world had been trying without success for thirty years. The door of opportunity remained closed.

**A Determination to Succeed.** However, Banting learned that MacLeod was going to Scotland for twelve weeks in the summer of 1921. Banting asked if he could use one of MacLeod's laboratories while he was away. He would need ten dogs and a helper who could run blood-sugar determinations. MacLeod agreed to his request if he would work without compensation and without standing at the university. Charles Best, age twenty-one, who was just graduating with a degree in biochemistry, agreed to help. Best was concerned with a recent diabetic death in his family. Between them, Banting and Best had less than $500. They cooked on a Bunsen burner in the lab and frequently slept there. By the end of July they were able to induce diabetic coma by removing the pancreas of a dog and restore the animal to health using a substance they had isolated from the pancreas of another dog, a substance they called the "X Factor."

**"X Factor" Isolated and Purified.** The animal's recovery was short-lived, and it became evident that an additional injection of the X Factor would be necessary every day. Banting and Best would have to find another method of producing the substance in quantity. When MacLeod returned from Europe, he insisted that the researchers repeat the experiments with dogs before trying to work with humans. After the second experiment worked, MacLeod offered Banting and Best sixty dollars a month each and dedicated the entire efforts of his department to the project. James Collip, who had a doctorate in chemistry, worked on purifying the X Factor, which MacLeod named "insulin."

**First Successful Treatment of Diabetes.** In January 1922 Banting and Best first tested insulin on themselves to show that it was not harmful, then administered an injection to Leonard Thompson, a twelve-year-old boy dying of diabetes. His recovery seemed nothing less than

allowed access to a proper laboratory. Banting was a young Canadian physician whose life had been altered by diabetes at the age of fifteen when his sweetheart and his best friend died of the disease. Banting served as a pall-bearer for both, and this experience influenced his resolve in later life to find a cure for diabetes.

**Banting Proposes Research.** After studying medicine at the University of Toronto and serving as a battlefield surgeon in World War I, Banting set up practice as an orthopedic surgeon in London, Ontario. He also took a part-time teaching assignment in the School of Medicine at the University of Western Ontario. While preparing a lecture on physiology, he became interested in the pancreas and began to wonder how it might have influenced the death of his friends years earlier. He proposed to research the subject at Western Ontario, but the faculty refused him with the recommendation that he discuss his ideas with professor John J. R. MacLeod at the University of Toronto, an authority on diabetes research. Banting met with MacLeod in 1920, but the elder physician contemptuously questioned how a young nonscientist could hope to find a cure for diabetes when the best miraculous, and other diabetics quickly came forward for treatment. There was soon difficulty in producing the substance in the quantities needed.

**Banting and MacLeod Honored.** While Banting and Best worked on problems of mass production, MacLeod traveled around reading papers on "his" discovery. The 1923 Nobel Prize for medical research was awarded to MacLeod and Banting as "codiscoverers" of insulin. Banting gave half of his money and half of the credit to Best, after which MacLeod decided to give half of his money to Collip.

**Insulin Promises New Life.** The discovery of insulin has been called one of the most revolutionary events in the history of medicine. Although not a cure, insulin changed the devastating effects of a previously deadly disease. Insulin promised sufferers of diabetes a full and healthy life. Today, there are an estimated fifteen million diabetics alive due to insulin.

Sources:

Michael Bliss, *Banting: A Biography* (Toronto: McClelland & Stewart, 1984);

Bliss, *The Discovery of Insulin* (Toronto: McClelland & Stewart, 1982);

Wayne Martin, *Medical Heroes and Heretics* (Old Greenwich, Conn.: Devon–Adair, 1977), pp. 2–19;

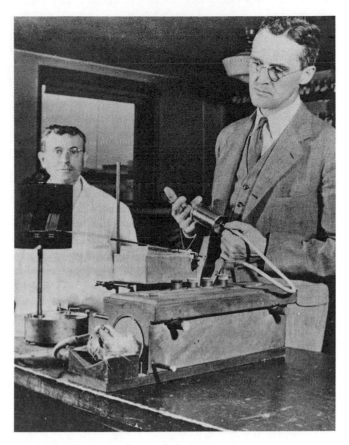

Philip Drinker with his respirator in 1928

## NEW MEDICAL MACHINERY

**Poliomyelitis.** Poliomyelitis was still a deadly disease in the 1920s, but victims of polio were given new hope by the invention of the iron lung in 1928. Polio, also called infantile paralysis, is a disease causing destruction of nerve cells, crippled limbs, and the wasting away of muscles. In "anterior" polio the respiratory muscles are paralyzed, often causing death within a few hours of the first respiratory distress. Due to its infectious nature, polio was a widespread and dangerous disease until the Salk vaccine was introduced in the 1950s.

**Early Experiments Lead to the Iron Lung.** The invention of the iron-lung mechanical respirator allowed paralyzed polio patients to remain alive indefinitely, thus saving many lives. The iron lung was created by Philip Drinker after he observed several physiological experiments to design artificial respiration methods for use after surgery. The experiments, which were conducted by his brother Cecil and Louis Shaw, involved placing a cat inside an airtight box with his head protruding from an airtight collar. Volume changes were then measured to identify normal breathing patterns.

**The Prototype.** Philip Drinker continued to experiment similarly with paralyzed cats. He was able to keep them alive by inducing breathing artificially with the use of a hypodermic syringe connected to the box. Next, a larger box, or plethysmograph, was built with a $500 grant from the New York Consolidated Gas Company and the help of a tinsmith and the Harvard Medical School machine shop.

**Operation.** The workable iron lung breathed for the patient using an electric bellows to interchange the air. The patient would lie on a stretcher secured with a rubber collar. The stretcher would then be slipped into a metal cylinder, and the iron lung was secured until it was airtight. During inspiration, the bellows expanded and sucked air out of the tank. When the pressure surrounding the lungs became less than that of the air outside in the atmosphere, the lungs expanded and drew in air from the outside. During expiration, the bellows contracted and the pressure in the tank returned to that of the atmosphere, causing the lungs to contract.

**A Lifesaving Invention.** The first use of the iron lung was with an eight-year-old girl who had respiratory paralysis caused by poliomyelitis. The respirator kept her alive five days until she died of other complications. The next patient was a Harvard University student who used the iron lung for several weeks and then recovered.

**Dependency an Issue.** The iron lung was considered indispensable by many, but it was criticized by some physicians because the doctors feared that patients would become chronically dependent on the breathing apparatus. This fear led to unnecessary delays in treatment using the respirator, and it was eventually shown that only a small percentage of patients fell into the dependent category.

**Impact of the First Mechanical Respirator.** John Meyer, a thoracic surgeon and author of "A Practical

"Among the hundred or more types of healing offered to the sophisticated is aerotherapy. Obviously aerotherapy means treatment by air, but in this instance hot air is particularly concerned. The patient is baked in a hot oven. Heat relieves pain and produces an increased flow of blood to the part heated. The blood aids in removing waste products and brings to the part the substances that overcome infection. There is nothing essentially wrong about hot air therapy.

"Since the time of Hippocrates and indeed even in Biblical legend men have availed themselves of the healing powers existing in nature. The light and heat of the sun, the burning steam from natural hot springs, the dry air of the desert, and even the buffeting of the waves of the sea have been used for physical stimulation in overcoming disease. It has remained for the astute commercial minds of our progressive land to incorporate these qualities for their personal gain.

"Aerotherapy as one department of physical therapy becomes a cult when it is used to the exclusion of all other forms of healing. In New York a progressive quack established an institute equipped with special devices for pouring hot air over various portions of the body. He issued a beautiful brochure, illustrated with the likenesses of beautiful damsels in various states of negligee, smiling the smile of the satisfied, under his salubrious ministrations. In this document appeared incidentally the claim that hot air will cure anything from ague to zoster. . . . "

Source: Morris Fishbein, *The New Medical Follies: An Encyclopedia of Cultism and Quackery in These United States, with Essays on The Cult of Beauty, The Craze for Reduction, Rejuvenation, Eclecticism, Bread and Dietary Fads, Physical Therapy, and a Forecast as to the Physician of the Future* (New York: Boni & Liveright, 1927), pp. 16–17.

"One Dr. Fitzgerald of Hartford, Connecticut, has divided the body into zones, lengthwise and crosswise, and heals disease in one zone by pressing of others. To keep the pressure going he developed little wire springs. For instance, a toothache on the right side may be 'cured' by fastening a little spring around the second toe of the left foot. Naturally, Fitzgerald has never convinced any one with ordinary reasoning powers that there is anything in his system — except what he gets out of it."

Source: Morris Fishbein, *The New Medical Follies: An Encyclopedia of Cultism and Quackery in These United States, with Essays on The Cult of Beauty, The Craze for Reduction, Rejuvenation, Eclecticism, Bread and Dietary Fads, Physical Therapy, and a Forecast as to the Physician of the Future* (New York: Boni & Liveright, 1927), pp. 16–17, 64.

**Svedberg Determines Need for New Instrument.** Svedberg's interest in the chemistry of colloids, mixtures of tiny particles suspended in another substance, made him realize the need for the ultracentrifuge. In his experiments, Svedberg was unable to measure the exact size of colloid particles and believed that his problem might be solved by subjecting them to the increased gravitational field of a high-speed centrifuge. Svedberg originally tried to develop an "optical centrifuge" which would photograph the sedimentation of the particles. When this effort proved elusive due to convection problems, Svedberg joined with Herman Rinde and created a working convection-free centrifuge in 1924.

**A Significant Research Tool.** The Svedberg creation, called the ultracentrifuge, became an important research tool. The ultracentrifuge allowed scientists to measure the sizes and shapes of proteins, allowed scientists to shift their focus from the whole organism to smaller and smaller parts, and led to the isolation of viruses and identification of the basis for their method of attacking cells. Other research aided by the ultracentrifuge included the separation of subcellular organelles, the development of understanding DNA, and the discovery of the methodology for carrying out genetic engineering.

Sources:
John Meyer, "A Practical Mechanical Respirator, 1929: The 'Iron Lung,'" *Annals of Thoracic Surgery*, 50 (1990): 490–493;

Peter Sebel and others, *Respiration: The Breath of Life* (New York: Torstar, 1985), pp. 114–115;

Tyler Wasson, ed., *Nobel Prize Winners* (New York: Wilson, 1987), pp. 1030–1033.

### PENICILLIN

**Penicillin: A Fortunate Accident.** In September 1928 Alexander Fleming, a young physician at Saint Mary's Hospital in London, noticed an unusual finding on the culture plate he was about to discard. Several weeks ear-

Mechanical Respirator, 1929: The 'Iron Lung,'" notes that the Drinker respirator was the first successful mechanical respirator and that it provided a "lifeline for thousands of patients afflicted with respiratory failure caused by poliomyelitis." In addition, Drinker's invention was a key factor in the development of modern respiratory treatment.

**The Ultracentrifuge.** The Nobel Prize in chemistry was awarded to Theodor Svedberg, a Swedish physical chemist, in 1926 for the invention of the ultracentrifuge. The ultracentrifuge was a fast centrifuge, a machine used to separate colloid particles and materials of different densities through the use of a rotor spinning around a central axis to create centrifugal force.

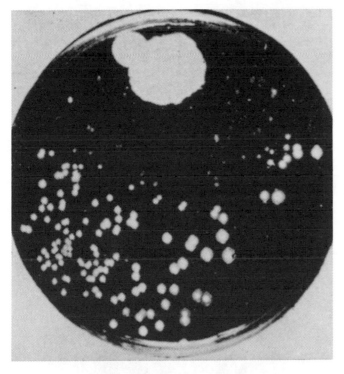

The original mold growth of *penicillium notatum*

## A COUNTRY DOCTOR

"William James Crosland (1873–1921) practiced medicine in Bennettsville, South Carolina, a small town of about 5,000. Like most country doctors of his era, he cared deeply about his patients and took whatever action he could to insure their return to health. When he faced his own last battle with cancer, his patients had an opportunity to return some of that kindness. His daughter, Kirby, recalled that the heat was unbearable one September day during the last long illness of her father. The family had done everything they could to make him more comfortable, but his wife kept murmuring, 'If only it would rain!' There was not a cloud in the sky, but suddenly rain fell in sheets — pouring across the roof and splattering the windows, fresh and cool. Kirby continued, 'We rushed to a window. There in front of the house stood the town's fire truck, with the volunteer firemen playing hoses on the roof. They were making it rain for 'Doc,' and they didn't stop until the air in the room was cool."

Source: Lulu Crosland Ricaud, *The Family of Edward and Ann Snead Crosland, 1740–1957* (Columbia, S.C.: State Commercial Printing, 1958), p. 389.

lier he had streaked the culture plate with staphylococci. A contaminant mold was growing near one edge of the plate. The unusual thing was that something was coming from the mold that was actually destroying the disease-causing bacteria in the vicinity. Fleming's colleague, Dr. C. J. La Touche, identified the mold as *penicillium notatum*. A derivative of the mold, which Fleming named penicillin, would become the first effective antibiotic.

**Effectiveness.** Later experiments demonstrated that the mold must have been on the plate before the staphylococci rather than following it, because penicillin was effective against the organism only in the stage of active division. It had little effect on mature bacteria. Given that fact and the fact that *penicillium notatum* proved to be one of the most effective strains of the penicillium molds, Fleming's discovery appears to be fortunate indeed.

**Fleming's Previous Work.** Fleming had worked for many years searching for an antimicrobial agent that would be effective against bacteria yet not harmful to delicate tissues. In 1921 he discovered lysozyme, a naturally occurring substance in tears, saliva, and blood that inhibited bacterial growth. His work with lysozyme helped him to recognize the potential value of penicillin.

**Disappointing Data.** Fleming was disappointed that further experiments showed that penicillin took several hours to act as an antibacterial agent but that it was removed from the bloodstream very quickly. In his landmark paper which appeared in the *British Journal of Experimental Pathology* in 1929, the shortcomings of the drug were emphasized more than its possible use as a clinical agent.

**Eventual Success.** It was not until the 1940s that Howard Walker Florey and Ernst Boris Chain and their "Oxford group" conducted animal experiments and showed the effectiveness of penicillin. Fleming, Florey, and Chain shared the Nobel Prize for physiology or medicine in 1945 for the discovery of penicillin and its curative effect in various infectious diseases.

**Uses in World War II.** Using the mold that Fleming discovered in 1928, pharmaceutical companies in America were able to produce large quantities of penicillin before the close of World War II. It proved effective against syphilis, gonorrhea, and infections caused by pneumococci, staphylococci, and streptococci. It was especially useful to military physicians who were called upon to treat battle injuries as well as rampant venereal disease.

Sources:
Lois A. Magner, *A History of Medicine* (New York: Marcel Dekker, 1992), pp. 350–356;

John C. Sheehan, *The Enchanted Ring: The Untold Story of Penicillin* Cambridge: MIT Press, 1982);

Allen B. Weisse, *Medical Odysseys* (New Brunswick, N.J.: Rutgers University Press, 1991), pp. 69–86.

## RORSCHACH TEST

**Rorschach.** The ink-blot test devised to study personality and diagnose psychopathologic conditions was introduced in 1921 by Hermann Rorschach. Rorschach, a

Swiss psychiatrist, created the test as a series of ten symmetrical ink spots that a patient would be asked to interpret. Although previous psychiatrists used the ink-blot test in free-association exercises, they used the test to study thematic content. Rorschach believed that the test could be used for more complete evaluation of a patient's condition. Through systematic analysis of factors cited by the patient, such as attention to wholes or details, color, shading, and apparent movement in human form, Rorschach could detect psychological processes or structure of the patient's personality. He also believed patterns as reported by the patient would lead to the diagnosis of certain clinical disorders. The accuracy of the Rorschach ink-blot test has been challenged by some scientists. Nevertheless, it is widely used in many countries.

Source:
Ruth Bochner, *Clinical Application of the Rorschach Test* (New York: Grune & Stratton, 1942).

## RURAL DISEASES

**Hookworm.** Hookworm, or ancylostomiasis, is a condition caused by a parasite found in tropical and subtropical climates, especially where the inhabitants do not wear shoes and where the soil is contaminated by human excrement. In the early twentieth century Dr. Charles Wardell Stiles of the United States Public Health Service found that hookworm was epidemic in the southern United States. The parasite entered the sole of the foot and made its way to the intestine, resulting in pain, diarrhea, anemia, and listlessness. Victims sometimes experienced a craving to eat a certain type of white clay.

**Sanitary Commission.** The Rockefeller Foundation established a sanitary commission that educated people about the problem and encouraged practical measures for permanent sanitation. In sixteen southern counties surveyed by Rockefeller workers between 1910 and 1915, the rate of hookworm infection was 59.2 percent. By 1923 the rate had fallen to 23.9 percent. Hookworm remained a problem in the South throughout the 1920s. Adequate control was made possible only by the vast social and economic changes and improvement in sanitation practices of the late 1930s and early 1940s.

**Pellagra.** Pellagra in its early stages was sometimes confused with sunburn or poison oak. A skin rash symmetrically marked the victim's hands and feet and sketched an ugly red butterfly across the patient's face. The effect of this very apparent symptom of the disease was to set pellagrins apart. Because the cause of the disease was unknown, some hospitals refused to admit sufferers because of the fear of contagion.

**Symptoms, Treatment.** Other symptoms included diarrhea, delusions of persecution, and depression. The disease was often fatal, not only because of the debilitating effects of the symptoms, but also because patients were prone to commit suicide, especially by drowning. Victims were frequently confined to mental hospitals. In 1914 the

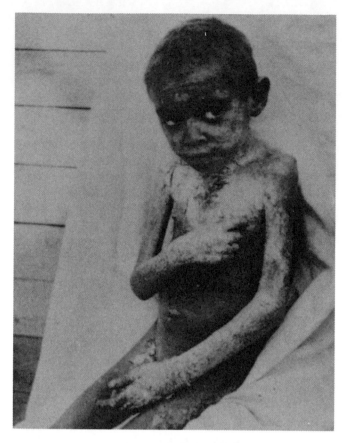

A severe case of pellagra

United States Public Health Service assigned Dr. Joseph Goldberger, a dedicated and determined investigator, to study the disease, which was most prevalent in the southern states, a region that was still suffering from poverty resulting from the Civil War and its aftermath. Goldberger postulated that a faulty diet was the cause of pellagra. Despite the fact that he never identified the specific deficiency, Goldberger found that brewer's yeast was an effective treatment for pellagra. The mortality rate for pellagra between 1924 and 1928 was 58 percent, and the United States Public Health Service estimated 170,000 cases in 1927. Between 1927 and 1932 the Red Cross distributed three quarters of a million packages of garden seeds and more than 200,000 pounds of brewer's yeast. In 1937 Dr. Conrad A. Elvehjem and his colleagues at the University of Wisconsin identified nicotinic acid as the specific ingredient which cured pellagra.

**Tularemia.** A man working in a Washington, D.C., meat market went to his physician, Dr. J. Lawn Thompson, in 1921 for treatment of what he told the physician was well known among butchers who handled rabbits as "rabbit fever." Other cases with similar symptoms were known in Utah as "deer-fly fever" and in Idaho as "glandular type of tick fever."

**Francis.** In a landmark article in the *Journal of the American Medical Association* in 1925, Edward Francis, a surgeon with the United States Public Health Service, synthesized various reports and presented evidence that all were caused by one organism, *Bacterium tularense*, which grew in the blood of infected rodents. Infection could occur through a skin lesion when hunters or butchers handled contaminated meat or when a tick or deer fly which had bitten an infected animal bit a human. Although Edward Francis was not the first to describe symptoms, he was the first to synthesize reports and present data to show how the disease was transmitted. He also named it tularemia.

**Symptoms, Treatment.** Symptoms of the disease included chills, fever, headache, body pains, vomiting, tender and enlarged lymph glands, prostration, and a punched-out circular sore about one-fourth inch in diameter at the site of the infection. Diagnosis was by agglutination of the bacteria in the blood serum of the patient. Treatment in the 1920s was primarily bed rest, and convalescence might take from two months to a year. Death was rare but did occur in more serious cases.

**Sources:**

John Duffy, *The Healers: The Rise of the Medical Establishment* (New York: McGraw-Hill, 1976); republished as *The Healers: A History of American Medicine* (Urbana: University of Illinois Press, 1979), pp. 240–241, 424–423;

Elizabeth Etheridge, *The Butterfly Caste: A Social History of Pellagra in the South* (Westport, Conn.: Greenwood Press, 1972), pp. 160–163, 192–193;

Edward Francis, "Tularemia," *JAMA*, 84 (15 April 1925): 1243–1250;

Alan I. Marcus, "The South's Native Foreigners: Hookworm as a Factor in Southern Distinctiveness," *Disease and Distinctiveness in the American South*, edited by Todd L. Savitt and James Harvey Young (Knoxville: University of Tennessee Press, 1988), pp. 79–99;

*The Rockefeller Foundation Annual Report*, 1913–1914, p. 11–12; 1923, p. 111;

Jay P. Sanford, "Tularemia Revisited," *JAMA*, 250 (16 December 1983), 3225–3226.

## SYPHILIS

**Modern Syphilis.** Although a particularly devastating disease since the sixteenth century, syphilis in the 1920s was commonly found in a milder form. It was usually transmitted via sexual contact, but occasionally was caused by contact with objects used by someone infected with the disease. Regardless of how syphilis was trans-

mitted, it was known that the disease was caused by a spirochete, or spiral-shaped germ, that entered the body through breaks in the skin or through the mucous membranes.

**Phases of the Disease.** The primary phase of syphilis, also the most contagious phase, is during the first two to six weeks after infection when the primary lesion, or chancre, appears at the site of infection. The chancre is a single, small, painless ulcer that heals during the primary phase. Secondary syphilis appears after a latent period of six to eight weeks and is identified by flulike symptoms, including a feeling of malaise and a skin rash. After a few weeks, secondary lesions and accompanying symptoms disappear. Late or tertiary syphilis occurs after another latent period of one to twenty years and is without symptoms. The phase begins when the spirochetes have spread through the body and localized in the brain and heart. Paralysis, mental derangement, and death may result. Late syphilis develops in only about one-third of untreated cases and, in the mid 1990s, has almost disappeared entirely as a result of antibiotic therapy.

**Detection and Early Treatment.** Syphilis can be fatal if left untreated, and there is no vaccine to prevent the disease. The first treatment of syphilis was in the sixteenth century and included the use of various metal preparations such as mercury. By 1910 the common treatment was Salvarsan, the trade name for the drug arsphenamine, discovered by Paul Ehrlich in 1909. Salvarsan was an organic arsenic compound that rendered the patient noninfectious but did not always result in a cure. The drug also caused toxic effects in the nervous system, kidneys, and skin of some patients. In the 1940s the revolutionary cure provided by antibiotics replaced the use of Salvarsan and placed primary importance on early detection of the disease.

**Early Tests.** August von Wassermann created the first test for syphilis in 1906. The Wassermann test consisted of examining blood samples from the infected person. The test was based on the idea that the blood sample would show antibodies formed in order to fight the disease. Although the Wassermann test was a useful tool in a majority of cases, it was complex and time-consuming. In the February 1923 issue of the *American Journal of Public Health*, the Director of Laboratories at the Michigan State Department of Health reported that "[g]ranting the importance of correct serum diagnosis of syphilis, it must be admitted that the Wassermann test does not entirely supply such a diagnosis. The many variable elements of this test give it numerous sources of error, so many indeed, that it is not uncommon for even dependable workers to vary in their findings on the same specimen of blood."

**The Kahn Test.** It was widely recognized in the 1920s that the Wassermann test needed standardizing in order to enhance its diagnostic value. Several other tests were developed during this time, but none proved to be more effective than the Wassermann test until Reuben Leon Kahn introduced his method in 1923. The Kahn test evolved in the laboratories of the Michigan Department of Health and was simpler, faster, and more sensitive than any other available method of detecting syphilis. By 1925 this test was routinely used by the United States Navy and soon after was utilized around the world.

Sources:

Kenneth F. Kiple, ed., *The Cambridge World History of Human Disease* (New York: Cambridge University Press, 1993), pp. 1025–1033;

Claude Puetel, *History of Syphilis* (Baltimore: Johns Hopkins University Press, 1992);

C. C. Young, "The Kahn Test For Syphilis In The Public Health Laboratory," *American Journal of Public Health*, 13 (February 1923): 6–99.

## VITAMINS AND MINERALS

**Vitamin C.** Although Albert Szent-Györgyi was awarded the Nobel Prize in 1937 for the discovery of vitamin C, it is clear that the work of scientists such as Axel Holst, Theodor Frolich, Sylvester Zilva, Charles Glen King, and Joseph L. Svirbely, led to his success. The search for vitamin C gained momentum after it was determined that scurvy was a disease caused by defective nutrition, as opposed to a germ, and that the ingestion of certain fruits and vegetables offered prevention or cure. Scurvy, which caused bleeding gums and general debility, was common among sailors who had access only to non-perishable foods. The British navy began providing lime juice for long voyages after 1795, hence the name *limeys* for British sailors.

**Early Experiments Provide Basis for Discovery of Vitamin C.** In 1907 bacteriologist Holst and pediatrician Frolich announced that they could produce scurvy in guinea pigs through changes in diet. They found that hay and oats, foods deficient in vitamin C, led to scurvy, while a diet of fresh fruits and vegetables did not. After World War I, Zilva obtained samples of the ingredient that seemed to prevent scurvy and determined some of its properties.

**An Accidental Discovery.** Meanwhile, Szent-Györgyi spent the 1920s studying biological oxidation. He was interested in why some plants turn brown after being cut and some do not and hoped to link a similar occurrence in humans, the bronzelike color change in skin that accompanied a disorder of the adrenal gland, to a new hormone in the adrenal cortex. His research was unproductive until a collaborative effort was attempted. In 1926 he joined with Frederick Gowland Hopkins in order to continue his studies and try to isolate this potential new hormone. It was during this research that Szent-Györgyi found a new substance that would eventually be termed vitamin C. At this point the scientist knew only that the substance was not a new hormone but a carbohydrate related to the sugars and consisting of six carbon atoms, eight hydrogen atoms, and six oxygen atoms. After Szent-Györgyi's original name *Ignose* (from the Latin *ignosco*,

Albert Szent-Györgyi, discoverer of vitamin C

meaning "I don't know," and *ose*, the suffix for sugars) was rejected, the new substance was named *hexuronic acid* because it contained six carbon atoms and was acidic.

**Is Hexuronic Acid Vitamin C?** The publication of the discovery of hexuronic acid in 1928 is generally believed to be the discovery of vitamin C, although the article never identified the two as the same. In 1929 Charles Glen King of the University of Pennsylvania became aware that hexuronic acid might be vitamin C and began experiments to prove that the speculations were indeed true. King published results of his experimentation that same year and explained the preparation and properties of vitamin C, although he also was not ready to link it to hexuronic acid.

**Svirbely Gives Proof.** The work of Svirbely at a research center in Szeged, Hungary, provided the crucial proof. Svirbely had previously studied vitamin C with King at the University of Pittsburgh. Since Svirbely was able to tell if something contained vitamin C, Szent-Györgyi gave him hexuronic acid to test. Svirbely's experiments with guinea pigs showed that animals without hexuronic acid in their diets contracted scurvy, and those receiving it were healthy. Svirbely's results proved that Szent-Györgyi's hexuronic acid was vitamin C.

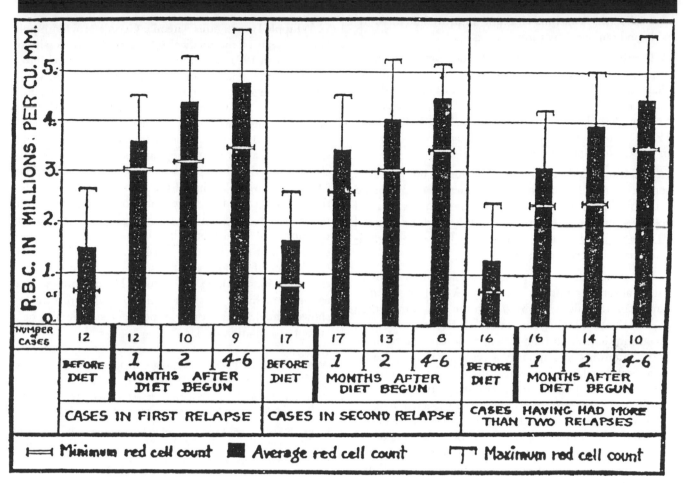

Source: George R. Minot and William Murphy, "Treatment of Pernicious Anemia by a Special Diet," *JAMA*, 87 (14 August 1926): 470–476.

**A Bitter Controversy.** At Szent-Györgyi's request, Svirbely kept King apprised of the experimentation. In 1932, after learning of Svirbely's research, King announced in *Science* that hexuronic acid was vitamin C. This publication beat Svirbely and Szent-Györgyi, who published their results in *Nature* two weeks later. A bitter controversy arose over which scientist could actually claim the discovery of vitamin C.

**Szent-Györgyi Recognized.** Although the controversy between Szent-Györgyi and King continued throughout their lifetimes, the Nobel Prize committee chose to recognize Szent-Györgyi. Most scientists now agree that Szent-Györgyi was primarily responsible for the discovery of the important vitamin.

**Vitamin D and Rickets.** First described in the second century A.D., rickets was a widespread and damaging disease until the identification of vitamin D in 1922. Usually seen in children, rickets is caused by a deficiency of vitamin D, which leads to insufficient calcification of a child's growing bones. The disease was so common in the

early 1900s that many studies showed at least one quarter of infants in low-income families showed indications of the disease. The bones became so soft that they twisted and curved into abnormal shapes, and growth was stunted. If treatment was not begun early, the bones later hardened but the abnormalities, such as spine curvature, bowlegs, and knock-knees, remained. The ribs might also take on a beady appearance at their juncture to the breast-bone, and a narrowed chest and pelvis might lead to an increased susceptibility to lung diseases and difficulties in childbearing later in life.

**Symptoms.** Early symptoms of rickets include restlessness, profuse sweating, lack of muscle tone, softening of bones in the skull, delay in learning to sit, crawl, and walk, and delay in the eruption of teeth. Spasms of the hands and feet, cramps, and muscle twitching are also indications of the disease.

**Discovery Leads to Prevention.** The discovery of vitamin D by Elmer McCollum in 1922 all but eradicated incidence of rickets in developed countries. He recommended that children drink more milk and take cod liver oil to supply vitamin D. The identification of vitamin D, also called the "sunshine vitamin," improved diets worldwide and removed the threat of rickets.

**Pernicious Anemia.** In the 1920s doctors made significant progress in treating pernicious anemia, a disease characterized by an insufficient number of red blood cells (erythrocytes). Dr. Thomas Addison of Guy's Hospital in London described the condition as early as 1849, and by 1926 approximately six thousand patients died annually in the United States from the disease.

**Red Blood Cell Production.** The human body requires certain dietary factors for the production of red blood cells. In addition to protein and minerals such as iron and copper, numerous vitamins such as folic acid, $B_6$, $B_2$, and $B_{12}$ are required. Cyanocobalamin, or $B_{12}$, is the significant factor in pernicious anemia.

**Symptoms.** Several steps are necessary for an individual to absorb vitamin $B_{12}$ properly. A protein found in normal gastric juice must bind with the $B_{12}$. It must then pass to the terminal ileum, a part of the small intestine, for absorption. A chronic inflammation of the stomach lining resulting from an immune response to the patient's own tissues makes it impossible for a patient with pernicious anemia to produce the necessary gastric protein for $B_{12}$ binding and absorption. The result is anemia or insufficient production of red blood cells to carry the necessary oxygen to all parts of the body. Because parts of the spinal cord require $B_{12}$ for normal functioning, pernicious anemia patients develop tingling in the hands and feet, suffer lack of coordination, and have problems with motor and sensory functions.

**Early Treatment.** In the early 1920s physicians did not comprehend the cause of the disease. They some-times treated patients with arsenic, blood transfusions, or even removal of the spleen.

**Whipple Investigates Anemia.** George Hoyt Whipple became dean of the medical school at the University of Rochester in 1921 and brought with him a research project on anemia in laboratory dogs. He found that he could improve the overall condition of the dogs by feeding them pig liver. At Rochester, George Minot and William Parry Murphy, two younger physicians, worked with Whipple on the anemia experiments. Minot and Murphy showed that a diet containing large amounts of liver was clearly beneficial to patients with anemia. Whipple, Minot, and Murphy shared the Nobel Prize in 1934 for their work on the dietary treatment of anemia. Although the pioneering research was accomplished in the 1920s, it was not until 1936 that Whipple discovered the importance of iron deficiency in causing anemia. William B. Castle, one of Minot's assistants, experimented with gastric acids in searching for a cure. He demonstrated a connection, but it was not until 1954 that researchers showed the definitive cause of pernicious anemia to be a lack of assimilation of $B_{12}$.

Sources:

William H. Crosby, "Pernicious Anemia-Study and Therapy," *JAMA,* 250 (23/30 December 1983): 3336–3338;

Kenneth F. Kiple, ed., *The Cambridge World History of Human Disease* (New York: Cambridge University Press, 1993), pp. 978–980;

George R. Minot and William P. Murphy, "Treatment of Pernicious Anemia by a Special Diet," *JAMA,* 87 (14 August 1926): 470–476;

Ralph W. Moss, *Free Radical: Albert Szent-Györgyi and the Battle over Vitamin C* (New York: Paragon House, 1988);

Tyler Wasson, ed., *Nobel Prize Winners* (New York: Wilson, 1987), pp. 1034–1036;

Allen B. Weisse, *Medical Odysseys* (New Brunswick, N.J.: Rutgers University Press, 1991), pp. 112–124.

# HEADLINE MAKERS

## HARVEY WILLIAMS CUSHING

### 1869-1939

#### NEUROSURGEON

**Early Life.** A native of Cleveland, Ohio, Harvey Williams Cushing was born 9 April 1869, the sixth son and youngest in a family of ten children. His father, grandfather, great-grandfather, and an older brother were all physicians. Harvey Cushing received his B.A. degree from Yale in 1891 and his M.D. from Harvard in 1895. He was drawn to surgery by his talent for dissecting and handling delicate tissue. He interned in surgery at Massachusetts General Hospital and took residency training at the Johns Hopkins Hospital in Baltimore. He was surgical assistant to William Stewart Halsted, one of the foremost figures in the history of American surgery. Halsted taught Cushing his slow, meticulous technique.

**Early Career.** Cushing spent one year in Europe (1900–1901) meeting and studying with some of the best surgeons in the world. He began general surgical practice in Baltimore in the summer of 1901 and received a minor appointment at the Johns Hopkins Hospital. He gradually turned his interest toward surgery of the pituitary gland and other branches of neurological surgery. In 1910 he successfully removed a tumor from the right parietal hemisphere of the brain of Gen. Leonard Wood, and this operation enhanced Cushing's reputation as a neurosurgeon. His original and increasingly skillful operative procedures resulted in dramatic reductions in mortality equaled by no other neurosurgeon of his time.

**Boston.** In September 1912 Cushing moved to Boston to become surgeon in chief of the Peter Bent Brigham Hospital, the teaching institution of the Harvard Medical School. He contributed to drawing up specifications for the hospital, which was new at the time. At Brigham other doctors carried the burden of general surgery, thus freeing Cushing to concentrate on neurological surgery.

**Neuilly.** When World War I broke out, Cushing took a volunteer group from Harvard to work in the military hospital at Neuilly, France, in 1915 before the United States had entered the war. Later he organized a large army medical unit which served first with the British and then with American forces. In the winter of 1917 Cushing operated constantly, generally in hospitals near the front. He subsequently published a classic paper on wartime injuries of the brain.

**Brain Surgery.** Throughout his career Cushing published books and articles on various aspects of brain surgery. Some of his most important works appeared between 1925 and his formal retirement in 1932. Topics included tumors of the glioma group, intracranial physiology and surgery, acromegaly, and tumors arising from the blood vessels of the brain. His monograph on intracranial tumors included his original description of pituitary basophilism, now known as Cushing's disease, one of his greatest contributions to clinical medicine.

**Pulitzer Prize.** Cushing wrote a two-volume biography of Sir William Osler, a professor at Johns Hopkins who had influenced his career. Osler was influential not only as a teacher and physician, but also as the author of a textbook on medicine which was widely used for nearly half a century. Harvey Cushing won the Pulitzer Prize in 1925 for his work.

**Book Collector.** One influence Osler had on Cushing was to stimulate the latter's interest in book collecting. Throughout his career Cushing accumulated an extensive personal library of historical medicine. He bequeathed his library to Yale and persuaded some of his friends to do likewise, thus providing for the establishment of the Historical Library at the new Yale Medical Library in June 1941.

**Source:**
John Farquhar Fulton, *Harvey Cushing: A Biography* (Springfield, Ill.: Thomas, 1946).

## GEORGE AND GLADYS DICK

### 1881-1967, 1881-1963

### SCIENTISTS

**Achievements.** George and Gladys Dick, a husband-and-wife team of scientists, were able to control scarlet fever, a disease that had taken its toll on thousands. The Dicks did not find a cure for scarlet fever, but they were responsible for creating a test to determine an individual's susceptibility and for creating a way to prevent the disease.

**Early Lives.** Dr. George Francis Dick was born in Fort Wayne, Indiana, attended Indiana University, and was a graduate of the Rush Medical School in Chicago. Dick found his calling in the area of researching contagious diseases. It was during his studies in this area that George Dick met Gladys Henry. Henry earned a bachelor of science degree at the University of Nebraska and went on to receive the M.D. at Johns Hopkins in 1907. She did postgraduate work at Hopkins and at the University of Berlin. In 1911 Henry moved to Chicago, where her career and personal paths intersected with those of George Dick when both served as research pathologists at the University of Chicago. They were married in 1914.

**Searching for the Germ.** George Dick soon went to work at the McCormick Institute for Contagious Diseases, while Henry was in charge of the laboratory of the Childs Memorial Hospital. Both of the doctors devoted their research to the identification of the germ that causes scarlet fever, for as they stated in the *American Journal of Public Health,* "the intelligent prevention treatment of a disease must depend on a definite knowledge of its cause. Attempts to learn the etiology of scarlet fever have long been hampered by failure to obtain the disease experimentally."

**Early Investigation.** The initial research was conducted using animals such as guinea pigs, mice, rabbits, dogs, pigeons, and small white pigs as subjects. Although some of the animals became sick, none exhibited all of the symptoms of scarlet fever. The Dicks were forced to conclude that human subjects were necessary if their research was to continue. Luckily, several of the Dicks' friends believed in their research and volunteered to be infected with the disease in the name of science. The

Dicks also never hesitated to try upon themselves the treatments meant for the volunteers.

**First Human Experiments.** The first series of volunteers in 1921 were inoculated with fresh whole blood, blood serum, or throat mucus from acute cases of scarlet fever, but results were negative. The next group was inoculated with the organism most usually associated with the disease, hemolytic streptococcus, but the disease did not fully manifest itself.

**Success.** Producing experimental scarlet fever was not an easy task since the causative agent was unknown and less than half of those exposed to scarlet fever ever contracted the disease. After many tests with no success, the Dicks decided that their failure was perhaps due to an insusceptibility on the part of the volunteers. The Dicks started new experimentation with a group of volunteers who could give a complete family history and who had never been exposed to the disease. This group of volunteers was inoculated with a pure culture of hemolytic streptococcus which had been isolated from a lesion on the finger of an infected nurse. In 1923 the Dicks had their first case of experimentally produced scarlet fever. After additional research, the Dicks concluded that hemolytic streptococcus was the germ that caused scarlet fever.

**Preventive Measures Introduced.** With their medical knowledge of the immune system, the Dicks knew that the germ would produce a toxin in the body which would stimulate the creation of an antitoxin to fight the disease. Using a laboratory-created toxin from the scarlet fever germ, the Dicks found that injecting subjects with a diluted form of the toxin would produce a skin reaction if the subject was susceptible to the disease. Subjects who had had the disease showed no reaction. Therefore, this new skin test conclusively showed susceptibility or immunity and identified those in need of inoculation.

**Immunization Developed.** The immunization developed after the Dicks discovered that larger amounts of this toxin injected into subjects with a positive skin test made the skin test negative. Experience showed that three doses of toxin given at five-day intervals gave the best protection. However, the immunization had to be carried to the point of a negative skin test.

**Use of the Process.** Practical use of the Dick skin test and immunization began immediately. The New York City Board of Health sent for the toxin as soon as the experimentation was complete. Health officials seemed to agree with what the Dicks wrote in the *American Journal of Public Health* in 1924: "Because complications may occur so early in scarlet fever, and the damage done by the disease is to be estimated not so much in the number of deaths as in the after effects, the importance of preventive immunization is apparent."

Sources:
George F. Dick and Gladys H. Dick, "Scarlet Fever," *American Journal of Public Health,* 14 (December 1924): 1022–1028;

Ernest Gruening, "Another Germ Bites the Dust," *Colliers*, 74 (4 October 1924): 26.

## ABRAHAM FLEXNER

### 1866-1959

#### MEDICAL EDUCATOR

**Report.** Abraham Flexner, brother of Simon Flexner, was born in Louisville, Kentucky, and became well known as an educational reformer and an expert on medical education. In the early 1900s many medical schools existed solely for the profit of their owners, and even students without a high-school education were accepted and graduated as long as their tuition was paid. In his critical report Flexner referred to such schools as "proprietary institutions." Many of the teaching hospitals were unsanitary and lacked the necessary clinical facilities. An in-depth study by Abraham Flexner was partially responsible for bringing these practices to an end and reforming medical education in order to produce a better-educated medical community.

**Flexner's Education.** The education of Abraham Flexner consisted of a B.A. from Johns Hopkins University in 1886, a master's degree in psychology from Harvard University in 1906, and the study of comparative education at the University of Berlin. Throughout his schooling Flexner came to believe in the superiority of German universities and believed that the United States should restructure its educational system in like fashion. This opinion was expressed in 1908 in a book published by Flexner called *The American College*. The book was a wealth of information gained by Flexner throughout his years as a preparatory-school teacher and administrator, and its publication was a definitive point in his career.

**A Study of Medical Schools.** *The American College* identified Flexner as an educational reformer and led to his employment by the Carnegie Foundation for the Advancement of Teaching. The head of the foundation, Henry Pritchett, read the book and thought that Flexner should undertake a study for his organization "to ascertain the facts concerning medical education and the medical schools themselves."

**The Need for Reform.** After two years of extensive research and after visiting all of the medical schools in the United States and Canada, Flexner published his report in 1910. The report, *Medical Education in the United States and Canada*, not only exposed the appalling conditions prevalent in medical education but also offered creative suggestions as methods of reform.

**Recommendations.** Flexner recommended that 120 of the 155 medical schools in existence be closed. His main objective was to "reduce the number and increase the output of medical schools." Flexner was critical of the way medical schools had been developed "regardless of need, regardless of the proximity of competent universities, regardless of favoring local conditions," and offered that a medical school is ideally "a university department; it is most favorably located in a large city, where the problem of procuring clinical material, at once abundant and various, solves itself." Flexner's report was influential and far-reaching. His book and the one following it, *Medical Education in Europe*, changed professional and public opinion, as well as the practices of universities.

**Raising Educational Standards.** In 1913 Flexner joined the staff of the General Education Board, created by the Rockefeller Foundation to improve the educational standards of the United States. He served on the board for fifteen years as assistant secretary, secretary, and head of the Division of Studies and Medical Education. He published several reports during this time, including *Medical Education: A Comparative Study* in 1925. Flexner's work at the General Education Board was varied and included awarding research grants in the area of humanities, establishing research facilities at medical schools, and disbursing the $50 million given by the Rockefellers to improve medical education.

**Realizing His Ideas.** Flexner's primary interest remained medical education, and many of his ideas were realized when he was given $5 million by Louis Bamburger and his sister, Mrs. Felix Fuld. Flexner used the money to establish the Institute for Advanced Study at Princeton in 1930. The institute brought scholars, including Albert Einstein, together and gave them freedom to pursue conceptual research. The institute remains a leading educational center and is a testament to Flexner's belief in scholastic excellence.

Sources:

Abraham Flexner, *Abraham Flexner: An Autobiography* (New York: Simon & Schuster, 1960);

Geoffrey Marks and William K. Beatty, *The Story of Medicine in America* (New York: Scribners, 1973), pp. 203–209.

## SIMON FLEXNER

### 1863-1946

#### PATHOLOGIST

**Accomplishments.** The accomplishments of Simon Flexner, pathologist and director of the Rockefeller Institute for Medical Research, were extraordinary in their diversity and impact. Flexner was the fourth of nine children born to Morris and Esther Flexner in Louisville, Kentucky. Abraham

Flexner, the education specialist, was his brother. As a young man Simon Flexner was apprenticed to a druggist who sent him to the Louisville College of Pharmacy. After graduating in 1882, Flexner's interest in medicine led him to study at the University of Louisville where he earned an M.D. in 1889. This early education and Flexner's investigative nature set the stage for his remarkable career.

**Early Work.** After medical school Flexner turned his talents to research in the fields of pathology and bacteriology. He began his work at the Johns Hopkins Hospital where he became an associate in pathology in 1892. Flexner conducted his research under the tutelage of William H. Welch, whom he considered a major influence in his life. Flexner also studied in Europe at Strasbourg and at Prague.

**Meningitis.** An outbreak of cerebrospinal meningitis in Maryland in 1893 gave Flexner experience in the area of infectious diseases. This experience proved valuable while Flexner was in Manila studying the diseases of the Philippine Islands. There he was able to isolate a widespread strain of dysentery, since known as the Flexner type.

**Academic Career.** By 1898 Flexner was promoted to full professor of pathological anatomy at Johns Hopkins. He moved to the University of Pennsylvania as a professor of pathology from 1899 to 1903. While in Pennsylvania Flexner researched problems in the areas of pathology, bacteriology, and immunology, and managed a governmental commission investigating bubonic plague in San Francisco. He also influenced the career of a brilliant Japanese physician, Hideyo Noguchi.

**The Rockefeller Institute.** Flexner is widely known for his work as the director of the Rockefeller Institute for Medical Research, which was created in 1901. Excited by the possibilities presented by this new corps of investigators devoting all their time to medical research, Flexner accepted a position as one of the seven members of the institute's board of scientific directors. The board was headed by Flexner's mentor, William Welch. With Welch's advice Flexner organized the institute into several laboratory departments, instead of limiting its work to one particular subdivision of medical research. In 1924 Flexner was formally recognized for his outstanding contributions and named as director of the institution.

**Research Breakthroughs.** The Rockefeller Institute was gradually becoming internationally famous, partly due to the scientific achievements of Simon Flexner. Throughout his tenure at the institute Flexner still continued his research. In 1905, when New York was faced with an epidemic of cerebrospinal meningitis, Flexner conceived the idea of injecting serum into the spinal canal. This method reduced the death rate from the disease by half. In 1907, during a poliomyelitis epidemic, Flexner found that the infectious agent was a filterable virus rather than a bacterial organism. His work in this area laid the groundwork for the development of the polio vaccine.

**Honors and Achievements.** Flexner was the editor of the *Journal of Experimental Medicine* for nineteen years and published reports on his research in pathology and bacteriology. He was chairman of the Public Health Council of New York State and a trustee of the Johns Hopkins University and of the Carnegie Foundation of New York. His most notable achievement may be that of melding a group of individualistic senior colleagues into the renowned Rockefeller Institute.

**Source:**
Abraham Flexner, *Abraham Flexner: An Autobiography* (New York: Simon & Schuster, 1960).

## REUBEN LEON KAHN

### 1887-1974

#### SEROLOGIST

**Achievements.** Reuben L. Kahn was a Russian-born American serologist and immunologist whose primary impact was the development of a more sensitive test for syphilis. Syphilis is one of the chief venereal diseases, a group of diseases generally transferred through sexual contact. If not treated promptly, syphilis can cause paralysis, mental derangement, and death. Syphilis can also be passed to the unborn children of pregnant mothers resulting in insanity, heart disease, and paralysis in the affected child. There is no vaccine for the disease, but treatment is relatively inexpensive and simple.

**The Kahn Test.** The first effective test for syphilis was developed in 1906 by August von Wassermann. The Wassermann test was welcomed as the best way to detect the disease, but the test also required a two-day incubation period, and its complexity provided many sources for error. While many physicians and scientists tried to improve the Wassermann test, none succeeded until Reuben Kahn did so in 1923. Kahn's modified syphilis test was simpler, took only a few minutes to complete, and was more accurate than any other available method for detecting syphilis. Kahn's test became the standard test for syphilis detection in the United States Navy in 1925 and was soon recognized worldwide.

**Kahn's Study of Immunology.** While applying his test to other diseases, Kahn realized that it produced some false positive and false negative reactions. This discovery led him to a broader study of the role of different tissues in immunity, as differentiated from the role of white blood cells and blood antibodies. His research led to Kahn's "universal serological reaction" in 1951. This new discovery was, as Kahn remarked, "a potential serologic indicator of various situations in health and in different diseases."

**Kahn's Career.** The career of Reuben Kahn spanned the fields of serology and immunology and produced over

170 scientific publications. He conducted his research at the Michigan Department of Health, the University of Michigan, and Howard University. Although most widely known for his improvements to the test for early syphilis detection, Kahn's universal serological reaction is considered a landmark in the science of immunology. His research was carried out at the Michigan Department of Health, the University of Michigan, and Howard University, but he also received honorary degrees and awards from other institutions.

Sources:

W. Montague Cobb, "Reuben Leon Kahn, D.Sc., LL.D., M.D., Ph.D. — 1887," *Journal of the National Medical Association,* 63 (September 1971): 388–394;

Reuben L. Kahn, *The Kahn Test: A Practical Guide* (Baltimore: Williams & Wilkins, 1928);

Kahn, "Rapid Precipitation Phase of the Kahn Test for Syphilis, with New Method for Indicating Results," *JAMA,* 81 (14 July 1923): 88–92;

C. C. Young, "The Kahn Test for Syphilis in the Public Health Laboratory," *American Journal of Public Health,* 13 (February 1923): pp. 96–99.

## KARL LANDSTEINER

## 1868-1943

### SEROLOGIST

**Achievement.** Karl Landsteiner transformed serology from a mere collection of unrelated phenomena to a branch of chemical science. Although this achievement was one of his greatest legacies, Landsteiner's interests led him to study many different areas of medicine, and his discoveries have lasting impact.

**Life.** Born in Vienna, Austria, Landsteiner studied medicine at the University of Vienna and received the M.D. degree in 1891. He spent an extensive period studying with eminent scientists in Zurich, Munich, and Vienna. This preparation contributed to his work at the Rockefeller Institute in New York beginning in 1922, which provided a significant contribution to immunological knowledge in the United States.

**Blood Types Discovered.** Landsteiner's primary interests lay in the fields of immunology and serology. He found that when certain blood samples were mixed, agglutination (clumping) occurred. This area of research led to one of Landsteiner's most important discoveries, the existence of different types of blood. For a transfusion to be successful, it is necessary that the blood of the donor and that of the recipient be compatible. Neither must have present antagonistic substances or agglutinins that could dissolve or clump the cells in the blood of the other.

**Bloodtyping.** The recognition that human blood was of type A, B, AB, or O was monumental because it increased the safety of blood transfusions and eliminated much of the danger of operations. Previously, transfusions were considered too risky for general use because of the problems inherent in mingling different blood types. In 1930 Landsteiner received the Nobel Prize in physiology or medicine for his important contribution to medical science.

**The Study of Infectious Disease.** Landsteiner used his talents to combat the infectious diseases syphilis and poliomyelitis. In 1906 he was able to transmit syphilis to apes, and his research led to important observations regarding immunity to the disease. Landsteiner produced poliomyelitis in monkeys for the first time and disclosed many facts that led to the later discovery of the virus causing the disease.

**New Blood Factors Discovered.** In 1940 Landsteiner announced the finding of a new series of factors in human blood, designated M, N, and P, in addition to the initial four discovered in 1901. These factors found practical application in cases of disputed paternity.

**The Rh Factor.** More important, Landsteiner and his associates found the Rh factor, which is present in 85 percent or more of human subjects. Those who lack the Rh factor are Rh negative. Under ordinary circumstances, the presence or absence of the Rh factor has no bearing on life or health. It becomes important in cases of blood transfusion or pregnancy. Because the factor may cause serious disturbances in an individual carrying antibodies against it, infants in utero may be in danger if the mother and father carry different Rh types. Likewise, the Rh factor must be compatible for safe blood transfusion.

Source:

Stanhope Bayne-Jones, "Dr. Karl Landsteiner," *Science,* 73 (5 June 1931): 599–604.

## ELMER VERNER MCCOLLUM

## 1879-1967

### BIOCHEMIST

**Rickets.** Once a widespread condition commonly found in young children, rickets has essentially been eradicated due to the pioneering efforts of Elmer McCollum, an American biochemist who dedicated his life to the study of the relationship between diet and health. He began his work in the field of biochemistry at the Connecticut Agricultural Experiment Station during his doctoral training in organic chemistry at Yale University. He earned his Ph.D. in 1907 and proceeded to develop the first white rat colony in the United States created to study the effects of nutrition. At the time he was working with the Wisconsin College of Agriculture, and although assigned to study the food and excrement of cattle, McCollum found that the use of rats circumvented the complicated methodology required when studying larger animals.

**Existence of Vitamins.** McCollum's study of rats led to the realization that a fat-deficient diet resulted in growth retardation which could be reversed by feeding "an extract of egg or butter." By 1915 McCollum had identified the substances that were found necessary for normal growth and named them vitamins A and B. It was during these initial experiments that McCollum also developed the letter system of naming *vitamins.* The term originated in 1906 when Casimir Funk, a colleague of Sir Frederick Gowland Hopkins, professor of biochemistry at Cambridge University, proposed that substances necessary for health be called vitamins.

**Vitamin D Found to Prevent Rickets.** In 1922 McCollum began the research for which he is best known. Through his study of vitamins and nutrition, McCollum was able to isolate and identify vitamin D. This was a major breakthrough in the treatment of rickets, a bone disease caused by a lack of vitamin D that results in the improper and incomplete absorption of calcium into a child's bones. McCollum also created the "line test" for measuring vitamin D in foods.

**A Balanced Diet.** McCollum's study of nutrition is a basis for many of today's nutritional standards. In 1923 *American Magazine* sought McCollum's advice about the basics of good nutrition. In the resulting article McCollum stated that a satisfactory diet required several essentials. First, he recommended the generous use of dairy products. Second, McCollum suggested that fruits and the leafy parts of vegetables contained dietary properties that could not be found in other foods or in root vegetables. Finally, he stressed that a safe rule of thumb was never to eat meat more than once a day and always avoid overeating. These principles have repeatedly been proven to be keys of healthy living.

**A Noteworthy Career.** McCollum's valuable contributions in the field of nutrition were recognized throughout his career. He was a professor of agricultural chemistry at the University of Wisconsin and an emeritus professor of biochemistry at Johns Hopkins University, where the McCollum-Pratt Institute was created in his honor. McCollum also published *The Newer Knowledge of Nutrition* in 1918 which greatly influenced dietitians of the time. The identification of vitamins A, B, and D, the essential eradication of rickets, the vitamin nomenclature as used today, and general knowledge of how diet affects human health can all be attributed to the work of Elmer McCollum.

Sources:

Elmer V. McCollum, *From Kansas Farm Boy to Scientist* (Lawrence: University of Kansas Press, 1964);

McCollum, *A History of Nutrition* (Boston: Houghton Mifflin, 1957);

McCollum, *The Newer Knowledge of Nutrition* (New York: Macmillan, 1922);

M. K. Wisehart, "What to Eat," *American Magazine*, 95 (January 1923): 14–15, 112.

## GEORGE RICHARDS MINOT

### 1885-1950

**Preparation.** George Minot's father, grandfather, and several other members of the family were all outstanding physicians in Boston, Massachusetts. After a private-school education in Boston, Minot graduated from Harvard where he received the B.A. degree in 1908 and the M.D. in 1912. In an era when postgraduate study was still unusual for physicians, he went on to intern at Massachusetts General Hospital and to take a residency at Johns Hopkins. He was especially interested in the relation of diet to disease, but he also studied problems of blood coagulation.

**Study of Pernicious Anemia.** In 1915 Minot returned to Massachusetts General where his interest in blood coagulation led to a more specific study of pernicious anemia. Minot and his colleagues found that splenectomy resulted in only temporary improvement in patients with the disease.

**Influence of Diabetes.** Minot began working at the Collis P. Huntington Memorial Hospital in Boston in 1917, where he became chief of the medical service in 1923. In the same year he developed severe diabetes. He pursued a course of rigorous dietary regulation, the only method of controlling the disease known at the time, and insulin became available soon enough to save his life. His personal experience with the importance of diet possibly influenced his pursuit of a dietary treatment of pernicious anemia.

**A Cure for Pernicious Anemia.** George Hoyt Whipple, pathologist and dean at the University of Rochester School of Medicine, showed that a diet rich in liver was beneficial to dogs rendered anemic by repeated bleeding. Minot invited his associate William Parry Murphy to join him in an effort to test the benefits to sufferers of pernicious anemia of a diet containing as much as half a pound of liver a day. In 1926 they were able to report that such a diet led to rapid improvement. The following year, along with Edwin J. Cohn, professor of physical chemistry at Harvard, they developed an effective liver extract for oral use. Whipple, Minot, and Murphy received the 1934 Nobel Prize in physiology or medicine for their discovery of liver therapy in anemias.

**Later Career.** In 1928 Minot became director of the Thorndike Memorial Laboratory and chief of the Fourth (Harvard) Medical Service at the Boston City Hospital. In addition to doing research, he also taught at the Harvard Medical School. One of his junior colleagues at Thorndike, William D. Castle, built upon Minot's research to show that the cause of pernicious anemia was the inability to absorb the vitamin B12. Other associates made significant contributions in several fields, including the treatment of hemophilia.

**Lasting Influence.** In addition to publishing some 150 papers, principally about blood disorders and the effects of nutritional deficiencies, Minot also found time to stimulate and encourage his students. By 1956 sixteen graduates of the Thorndike or its affiliated medical services held distinguished positions abroad, and nearly fifty more held professorships in American medical schools.

Sources:

William H. Crosby, "Pernicious Anemia — Study and Therapy," *JAMA,* 250 (23 December 1983): 3336–3338;

George R. Minot and William P. Murphy, "Treatment of Pernicious Anemia by a Special Diet," *JAMA,* 87 (4 August 1926): 470–476;

Allen B. Weisse, *Medical Odysseys* (New Brunswick, N.J.: Rutgers University Press, 1991), pp. 112–124.

## THOMAS MILTON RIVERS

### 1888-1962

#### VIROLOGIST

**Life and Work.** Known for his research in the area of viral disease, Thomas Milton Rivers was also a compassionate physician and gifted administrator. Born in Jonesboro, Georgia, he graduated from Emory College in 1909 with a Bachelor of Arts degree. Immediately following graduation, Rivers was admitted to the Johns Hopkins Medical School. Although a talented student, Rivers's dream of becoming a physician was not to be soon realized. He was diagnosed with an often fatal neuromuscular degeneration and left medical school to become a laboratory assistant at a hospital in the Panama Canal Zone. By 1912 the illness had not progressed, and Rivers returned to Johns Hopkins and graduated in 1915.

**An Interest in Virology Develops.** After an internship and residency in pediatrics at Johns Hopkins, Rivers spent time investigating an outbreak of pneumonia as a member of the army medical corps. This may have been the beginning of his productive career researching viral diseases. Three years of research in bacteriology at Johns Hopkins led to an appointment to the hospital staff of the Rockefeller Institute for Medical Research in New York City as head of the infectious disease ward. The Rockefeller Institute also offered Rivers the opportunity to pioneer a new field of research, virology.

**Valuable Contributions.** The work of Thomas Rivers helped to establish virology as a separate division of microbiology. In 1926 Rivers announced findings that were contrary to the beliefs of many of his colleagues, including Hideyo Noguchi and his superior, Simon Flexner.

Rivers's controversial announcement was that unlike most bacteria, the reproduction of viruses depends upon living cells of the host. Rivers adamantly insisted upon the validity of his theory, which was later found to be correct. Rivers made other valuable observations in the field of virology, such as the latency of certain pathogenic viruses, the passive immunity induced by viral infection, and the pathological effects of virus infection, including cell necrosis and cell proliferation. In 1928 Rivers summarized current thinking on viral infections as editor of *Filterable Viruses.*

**A Brave Experimenter.** Rivers was an experienced clinician and scientist and was willing to conduct research into diseases considered to be too dangerous by other experimenters. For example, an outbreak of "parrot fever" in New York and California proved to be so dangerous and contagious that research was abandoned almost everywhere except the laboratory of Thomas Rivers. The doctor also made thorough clinical studies of other rare viruses, including those causing Rift Valley fever, lymphocytic choriomeningitis, and "louping ill" of sheep. Under his guidance the Rockefeller Institute became a leading center of research in viral diseases.

**Positions of Leadership.** After the 1920s Rivers assumed other positions of leadership at the Rockefeller Institute. In 1937 he succeeded Rufus Cole as director of the hospital, and was vice president of the Rockefeller Institute by 1953. Meanwhile, Rivers was a member of the New York City Board of Health, and he directed the formation of Naval Medical Research Unit Number 2. Rivers retired from the Rockefeller Institute in 1955, only to become vice president for medical affairs of the National Foundation — March of Dimes, an organization having headquarters in Washington, D.C., that raised funds for poliomyelitis and other medical research.

Source:

Gerald Astor, *The Disease Detectives: Deadly Medical Mysteries and the People Who Solved Them* (New York: New American Library, 1984).

## HARRY STEENBOCK

### 1886-1967

#### VITAMIN RESEARCHER

**Background.** In the 1920s research into the effects of vitamins was extensive and carried out in laboratories throughout the world. Harry Steenbock played an important role in this field of research. Steenbock studied at the University of Wisconsin in 1907 when noted biochemist Elmer McCollum was pursuing dietary and nutritional research as a member of the faculty.

**Sunlight Increases Vitamin D.** McCollum's belief that substances called vitamins were essential to life, and his discovery of vitamin D as a cure for rickets, provided a starting point for Steenbock. McCollum's research had shown that both vitamin D and sunlight were effective in the treatment of rickets, but it was not known whether these treatments were independently effective or part of a single therapeutic process. Steenbock's research would provide an answer to this question. In 1924 he was able to prove that sunlight converted chemicals in food into vitamin D. Although the conversion was not fully understood, Steenbock found that foods exposed to sunlight were effective treatments for patients suffering from rickets.

**Other Nutritional Studies.** Steenbock continued research into nutrition and was able to isolate carotene, found in yellow vegetables and containing vitamin A. He also used livestock in his study of nutrition, and his experimentation led to the beginning of the use of live animals in nutritional studies.

**Steenbock's Contribution Overlooked.** There were many noteworthy scientists conducting research into nutrition and vitamins, namely Christiaan Eijkman, Frederick Gowland Hopkins, McCollum, Alfred Hess, and Adolf Windaus. In 1928 Windaus was awarded the Nobel Prize in chemistry, but *The Scientific Monthly* (April 1929) devoted an article to the reasons that other deserving scientists were ignored. The article stated that Hess and Steenbock were specifically deserving of recognition for the discovery that vitamin D could be activated through exposure to ultraviolet light.

Source:
Herbert Bailey, *The Vitamin Pioneers*, (Emmaus, Pa.: Rodale Books, 1968).

## GEORGE HOYT WHIPPLE

### 1878-1976

#### CONQUEROR OF PERNICIOUS ANEMIA

**Early Career.** The work of George Hoyt Whipple was often ridiculed, but it saved thousands of lives and led to the understanding of organisms as intricately interconnected systems. Whipple attended the Johns Hopkins Medical School in Baltimore, Maryland, and earned his medical degree in 1905. His primary interest was in the research of blood and liver disorders, which he studied with a colleague, John H. King. Whipple and King concentrated on the study of obstructive jaundice (icterus), a disease in which liver damage results in the release of yellowish bile pigments that appear in the skin of the patient. Whipple continued his study of the disease with Charles Hooper at the University of California in San Francisco. In 1914 their research led them to consider the possibility that the liver might be involved in pernicious anemia.

**Pernicious Anemia.** Pernicious anemia is a type of anemia in which the number of red blood cells in a patient's bloodstream is severely reduced. This leads to a reduction in the level of blood hemoglobin, which transports oxygen to the cells of the body. These cells then cannot produce enough energy to create the chemical reactions needed to survive. The result is the death of the cell and often the death of the patient.

**A Treatment for Anemia Is Found.** Whipple and Hooper began their research in pernicious anemia using dogs from a local pound. They were tying to determine how the animals reacted to artificially induced anemia. Next, they tried to increase rapidly the production of hemoglobin through a variation in the dogs' diet. They were able to produce dramatic results by feeding the dogs a diet of liver, lean scrap meat, and beef heart. On this diet complete hemoglobin regeneration occurred within two to four weeks. Although ridiculed by the medical community for thinking that a specific diet could cure a disease, Whipple and Hooper created liver and meat extracts that produced favorable results. Hooper was the first doctor to use these extracts as a treatment for a human patient suffering from pernicious anemia, but due to the ridicule, Hooper discontinued the research. Whipple continued the experiments with the help of Frieda S. Robscheit-Robbins at the New School of Medicine and Dentistry at Rochester University in New York. This research led to a definition of the necessary dietary requirements for treatment of pernicious anemia and, with the help of George Minot at Harvard University and the Eli Lilly Pharmaceutical Company, to the development of extracts that would save thousands of lives.

**The Importance of Iron.** In 1925 Whipple and his associate discovered that the mineral iron was the most essential element for the production of hemoglobin. This important finding was announced in the *American Journal of Physiology* in an article titled "Blood Regeneration in Severe Anemia: III. Iron Reaction Favorable — Arsenic and Germanium Dioxide Almost Inert." Whipple and Robscheit-Robbins continued their research into the 1940s.

**Nobel.** In addition to the discovery of a treatment for pernicious anemia, Whipple also described several basic recycling enzymatic pathways within the body and improved the understanding of human liver and blood physiology. In 1934 Whipple's lifesaving research was recognized when he was awarded the Nobel Prize in physiology or medicine with George Minot and William Murphy.

Sources:
Tyler Wasson, ed., *Nobel Prize Winners* (New York: Wilson, 1987), pp. 1112–1114;

George Whipple, "Blood Regeneration in Severe Anemia, II, Favorable Influence of Liver, Heart and Skeletal Muscle in Diet," *American Journal of Physiology*, 72 (1925): 408–418.

# PEOPLE IN THE NEWS

In 1927 the Children's Bureau of the Labor Department under the leadership of **Grace Abbott** announced the lowest infant mortality rate in the history of birth registration.

In 1925 **Dr. John J. Abel** purified and concentrated insulin, making it several times more effective than the common product then available.

New Jersey police confiscated twelve thousand fliers advertising magic powders for sale by voodoo doctor **D. Alexander** in August 1925.

In 1923 surgical assistant **Dr. Duff S. Allen** perfected the cardioscope, an instrument that made it possible to see inside a beating heart.

**Edgar Allen** and **Edward A. Doisy** in the 1920s pioneered in female sex hormone research. Their article, "An Ovarian Hormone," (*JAMA*, 81:819), was a milestone in the field.

**Dr. William L. Bettison** of the University of Michigan published an account of trichinosis infestation among Michigan football fans in *Journal of the American Medical Association* in 1926. The infestation occurred when the fans ate undercooked pork in Champaign, Illinois, before a Michigan-Illinois game in the fall of 1924.

**Edwin G. Boring** became director of the psychological laboratory at Harvard in 1924.

**Drs. Henry I. Bowditch** and **Ralph D. Leonard** in March 1923 advanced the theory that the use of X rays cured whooping cough.

In 1929 **Detlev Wulf Bronk** became professor of medical physics at the University of Pennsylvania.

**James B. Collip** discovered parathormone, a hormone secreted by the parathyroid gland, in 1925.

In 1923 **Drs. George W. Crile** and **Dennis R. W. Crile** revived patients who had been pronouced dead by injecting adrenalin directly into their hearts.

Leper **John R. Early** broke quarantine for the fourth time when he left the federal leprosarium at Carville, Louisiana, in July 1923. He surrendered to District of Columbia health officials three weeks later.

**Dr. Byron E. Eldred** demonstrated his electronic ear trumpet to the New York Otological Society in 1925. The society remained skeptical about its usefulness.

**Morris Fishbein** increased the power of the American Medical Association after he became editor of its journal in 1924.

Stating "I am loath to subscribe to the proposition that knowledge of birth preventive methods would materially lessen morality," **Circuit Judge Fisher** of Chicago granted a mandamus petition in November 1923 to compel the city to issue a license for a proposed birth control clinic in that city.

**Drs. E. A. Graham, G. H. Copher,** and **W. H. Cole** in 1923 perfected a technique of using a combination with iodine and bromine salts to aid in X-raying the gallbladder in 1923.

In July 1925 **Dr. W. E. Gye** reported in *The Lancet* that cancer was caused by a virus or a group of viruses.

In 1925 **Dr. George T. Harding,** father of President Warren G. Harding, scorned treatment of his diabetes by insulin, advocating to reporters change in diet as the only logical treatment.

**Frank A. Hartman** isolated cortin from the adrenal glands in 1927. The absence of cortin was thought to cause Addison's disease.

Scopolamine, a derivative of deadly nightshade, was promoted as a truth serum by **Dr. R. E. House** at the meeting of the American Association of Anaesthetists in July 1923.

In 1923 **Theodor Koppanyi** arrived in America from Vienna to continue his experiments with eye transplants in animals.

**Paul de Kruif**'s *The Microbe Hunters* in 1926 became a popular book about bacteriology.

In 1923 a doctor grafted a portion of a pig's eye onto the eyeball of **Alfred Lemonowicz,** which allowed the blind boy to see slightly. Lemonowicz received many contracts to appear in vaudeville with the pig.

The **London Fields Distemper Council** revealed an elaborate plan of experiments to find a cure for distemper in dogs in September 1924.

In February 1924 **Alfred W. McConn** charged that the American Medical Association was keeping "10,000,000 people from recovery" by banning "lime starvation" McConn had advocated as a treatment for tuberculosis.

**Thomas Hunt Morgan,** professor of experimental zoology at Columbia University, moved to the California Institute of Technology in 1928. There he pioneered in genetics, experimenting with the fruit fly.

In the *Journal of the American Medical Association* in 1921, **Reuben Ottenberg** reported on the medicolegal application of blood grouping in determining paternity.

Plans for the "greatest medical center in the world," to be built jointly by Presbyterian Hospital and Columbia College of Physicians and Surgeons, were announced by the hospital's president, **Dean Sage,** in October 1923. Cost of the center was estimated to be $20 million.

In 1923 **Margaret Sanger** organized the National Committee on Federal Legislation for Birth Control.

**George Bernard Shaw** in October 1925 blasted the General Medical Council of England for blacklisting osteopaths and physicans who assisted osteopaths as anesthetists.

Creditors threatened to seize the property of Swiss tubculosis researcher **Dr. Henry Spahlinger** in December of 1925.

Radium was used for the first time to eradicate birthmarks in 1923; **Dr. Lawrence R. Taussig** of the University of California perfected the technique.

**Edward Lee Thorndike** in *The Measurement of Intelligence* described in 1926 how to use tests to develop numerical measures of intelligence.

In 1924 **Dr. I. Toyama** helped prove that the lacquer on Mah Jongg boxes was the cause of dermatitis, an inflammation of the skin.

# DEATHS

**John Henry Abegg,** 64, Red Cross official, 4 December 1920.

**Albert Abrams,** 60, president of American Society for Psycho-Physical Research, 13 January 1924.

**Jasper W. Babcock,** 66, pellagra expert, 3 March 1922.

**Robert Bell,** 80, cancer expert, 20 January 1926.

**Edward Hickling Bradford,** 75, former dean of the Harvard Medical School, 7 May 1926.

**Nathaniel E. Brill,** 65, president of Medical Board of Mount Sinai Hospital and discoverer of Brill's Disease, 13 December 1926.

**Willem Einthoven,** 67, heart expert and Nobel Prize winner (1924), 29 September 1928.

**Joseph Goldberger,** 54, who postulated dietary etiology of pellagra, 17 January 1929.

**William Crawford Gorgas,** 65, who helped eradicate yellow fever in Cuba and Panama Canal Zone, 3 July 1920.

**Frederick Robin Green,** 59, former editor of *Health Magazine* and secretary and executive officer of the American Medical Association, 26 April 1929.

**Hugh Reed Griffin,** 72, Red Cross official, 5 May 1922.

**Granville Stanley Hall,** 90, first president of the American Psychological Association and educator, 24 April 1924.

**J. F. Hall-Edwards,** 68, pioneer X-ray operator, 15 August 1926.

**William Stewart Halsted,** 69, developer of surgical techniques, 7 September 1922.

**Luther Emmett Holt,** 68, pioneer in the field of pediatrics, 14 January 1924.

**S. Andral Kilmer,** 83, cancer expert, 14 January 1924.

**H. E. Lewis,** 52, editor of *American Medicine,* 6 August 1927.

**Jacques Loeb,** 64, researcher of tropisms and sexual attraction in animals, 11 February 1924.

Joseph McDowell Mathews, 80, America's first proctologist and former president of American Medical Association, 2 December 1928.

Hideyo Noguchi, 51, developer of skin test for syphilis, 21 May 1928.

Henry Irving Ostrom, 73, senior member of the American Institution of Homeopathy, 5 April 1925.

J. Y. Porter, 79, yellow fever expert, 16 March 1927.

Charles Andrews Powers, 64, president of the American Society for the Control of Cancer, 23 December 1922.

Charles Alfred Lee Reed, 72, former president of the American Medical Association, 28 August 1928.

Rear Adm. Presley Marion Rixey, 75, former surgeon general, 18 June 1928.

Charles F. Roberts, 87 or 88, pioneer in the New York Health Department, 26 September 1920.

Lucius Elmer Sayre, 78, former president of the American Pharmaceutical Association, 20 July 1925.

Stephen Smith, 99, founder of the American Public Health Association, 26 August 1922.

Edward Bradford Titchener, 60, leader of the "structuralists" school of psychology, 3 August 1927.

August von Wassermann, 59, originator of the blood test for syphilis, 16 March 1925.

Robert Fulton Weir, 89, former president of the American Surgical Association, 6 April 1927.

H. M. Whelpley, 65, former president of the American Pharmaceutical Association, 26 June 1926.

J. A. Witherspoon, 65, former president of American Medical Association, 25 April 1929.

# PUBLICATIONS

---

The Atlas of Life and Its Opposing Forces (N.p.: World Naturalists League, 1927);

Claude Bernard, An Introduction to the Study of Experimental Medicine (New York: Macmillan, 1927);

Theodor Billroth, The Medical Sciences in the German Universities (New York: Macmillan, 1924);

Gilbert Edward Brooke, Aids to Tropical Medicine, third edition, revised (New York: Wood, 1927);

Bernard Brouwer, Anatomical, Phylogenetical and Clinical Studies on the Central Nervous System (Baltimore: Johns Hopkins University Press, 1927);

Alan Mason Chesney, Immunity in Syphilis (Baltimore: Williams & Wilkins, 1927);

David Marvel Reynolds Culbreth, A Manual of Materia Medica and Pharmacology (Philadalphia: Lea & Febiger, 1927);

Harvey Cushing, The Life of Sir William Osler (Oxford: Clarendon Press, 1925);

Cushing, The Personality of a Hospital. Ether Day Address, the Massachusetts General Hospital, October 18, 1920 (Boston: Jamaica Printing, 1921);

Charles Loomis Dana, Text-book of Nervous Diseases (New York: Wood, 1925);

Frederick Myers Dearborn, American Homeopathy in the World War (Chicago: American Institute of Homeopathy, 1923);

Lavinia Dock and Isabel M. Stewart, A Short History of Nursing (New York: Putnam, 1920);

Emilius Clark Dudley, The Medicine Man; Being the Memoirs of Fifty Years of Medical Progress (New York: Sears, 1927);

Walton Forest Dutton, Intravenous Therapy; Its Application in the Modern Practice of Medicine (Philadelphia: Davis, 1925);

Morris Fishbein, The New Medical Follies: An Encyclopedia of Cultism and Quackery in These United States with Essays on the Cult of Beauty, The Craze for Reduction, Rejuvenation, Eclecticism, Bread and Dietary Fads, Physical Therapy, and a Forecast as to the Physician of the Future (New York: Boni & Liveright, 1927);

Abraham Flexner, Medical Education: A Comparative Study (New York: Macmillan, 1925);

Alfred Friedlander, Hypotension (London: Bailliere, Tindall & Cox, 1927);

Casimir Funk, *The Vitamins* (Baltimore: Williams & Wilkins, 1922);

Joseph Goldberger, *A Study of Endemic Pellagra in Some Cotton-mill Villages of South Carolina* (Washington: U. S. Government Printing Office, 1929);

Henry Simms Hartzog, *Triumphs of Medicine* (New York: Doubleday, Page, 1927);

Philip Bovier Hawk, *Practical Physiological Chemistry*, eighth edition (Philadalphia: Blakiston, 1923);

L. Emmett Holt, *The Diseases of Infancy and Childhood, for the Use of Students and Practitioners of Medicine* (New York: Appleton, 1926);

Reuben L. Kahn, *The Kahn Test: A Practical Guide* (Baltimore: Williams & Wilkins, 1928);

Robert J. S. McDowall, *Clinical Physiology (a Symptom Analysis) in Relation to Modern Diagnosis and Treatment; A Text for Practitioners and Senior Students of Medicine* (New York: Appleton, 1927);

John James Rickard Macleod, *Insulin; Its Use in the Treatment of Diabetes* (Baltimore: Williams & Wilkins, 1925);

Macleod, *Physiology and Biochemistry in Modern Medicine*, fifth edition (Saint Louis: Mosby, 1927);

Elmer Verner McCollum, *The American Home Diet; an Answer to the Ever Present Question, What Shall We Have for Dinner* (Detroit: Mathews, 1920);

McCollum, *Food, Nutrition and Health* (Baltimore: Published by the author, 1925);

McCollum, *The Newer Knowledge of Nutrition* (New York: Macmillan, 1922);

McCollum, *A Textbook of Organic Chemistry for Students of Medicine and Biology*, second edition, revised (New York: Macmillan, 1920);

Nathan Clark Morse, *Emergencies of a General Practice*, second edition (Saint Louis: Mosby, 1927);

Sir William Osler, *The Principles and Practice of Medicine*, tenth edition (New York: Appleton, 1925);

Francis W. Palfrey, *The Specialties in General Practice* (Philadelphia: W. B. Saunders, 1927);

John Ritter, *Handbook of Tuberculosis for Medical Students and Practitioners of Medicine* (Chicago: Craftsmen, 1923);

George Louis Rohdenburg, *Clinical Laboratory Procedures* (New York: Macmillan, 1927);

Milgon J. Rosenau, *Preventive Medicine and Hygiene*, fifth edition (New York: Appleton-Century, 1927);

Lee Herbert Smith, *Nursing in the Home*, sixth edition revised (Buffalo, N.Y.: World's Dispensary Medical Association, 1920);

Ernest Henry Starling, *The Action of Alcohol on Man* (New York: Longmans, Green, 1923);

James Campbell Todd, *Clinical Diagnosis by Laboratory Methods: A Working Manual of Clinical Pathology* (Philadelphia: Saunders, 1927);

John Broadus Watson, *Behaviorism* (New York: Norton, 1925);

Hans Zinsser, *A Textbook of Bacteriology*, fifth edition (New York: Appleton, 1922);

*American Journal of Roentgenology*, periodical (1913–1922); retitled *American Journal of Roentgenology and Radium Therapy* (1923–1951);

*American Journal of Tropical Medicine*, periodical, begun 1921;

*Annals of Internal Medicine*, periodical, begun 1927;

*Annals of Medicine, with Abstracts of the World's Literature*, periodical, begun 1920;

*Archives of Pathology and Laboratory Medicine*, periodical, begun 1926;

*Archives of Physical Therapy*, periodical, begun 1926;

*Bulletin* [Academy of Medicine], periodical, begun 1920;

*Clinical Excerpts*, periodical, begun 1927;

*Clinical Medicine*, periodical, begun 1924;

*Clinical Medicine and Surgery*, periodical, begun 1927;

*Journal of Clinical Investigation*, periodical, begun 1924;

*Journal of Medicine* [Cincinnati, Ohio], periodical, begun 1927;

*Journal of Preventive Medicine*, periodical, begun 1926;

*Medicine*, periodical, begun 1922;

*Medical Insurance*, periodical, begun 1923;

*Medical Life*, periodical, begun 1920;

*Nation's Health*, periodical, begun 1921;

*The New England Journal of Medicine*, periodical, begun 1928;

*Pediatrics*, periodical, begun 1924;

*Quarterly Cumulative Index Medicus*, periodical, begun 1927.

CHAPTER ELEVEN

# RELIGION

by JOHN SCOTT WILSON

## CONTENTS

*Sidebars and tables are listed in italics.*

## 1920

- The Hartford Theological Seminary in Hartford, Connecticut, announces that it will no longer require female applicants for admission to declare they do not intend to seek ordination.

## 1921

- The American Association of Women Preachers begins publication of *Woman's Pulpit*.

- Junior Hadassah is founded as an auxiliary of Hadassha, the Women's Zionist Organization of America.

- The Greek Orthodox Archdiocese of North and South America is created by the Ecumenical Patriarch.

**25 May**    The General Assembly of the Presbyterian Church U.S.A. (Northern) urges federal marriage and divorce laws.

**2 Nov.**    Margaret Sanger founds the American Birth Control League in New York City. It is a combination of the Birth Control League, which she founded in 1914, and the Voluntary Parenthood League, founded by Mary Ware Dennett in 1919. The issue of contraception becomes a major topic in religious circles, with liberals such as Harry Emerson Fosdick and the Universalist Church approving and conservatives such as the Protestant Episcopal House of Bishops and the Roman Catholic Church opposing.

## 1922

**21 May**    Harry Emerson Fosdick, Baptist but associate pastor of First Presbyterian Church in New York City, preaches his widely circulated sermon "Shall the Fundamentalists Win?" This intensifies the debate between modernist and Fundamentalist Protestants.

**12 Sept.**    The House of Bishops of the Protestant Episcopal Church vote to remove the word *obey* from the marriage service.

**Nov.**    Bishop Platon is elected Metropolitan of the Orthodox Church of All the Americas and Canada, the former Diocese of the Aleutians and North America of the Russian Orthodox Church.

## 1923

- The Vatican reaffirms its recognition of the National Catholic Welfare Conference as an official body. This organization, which coordinates welfare activities for all the nation's dioceses, is the outgrowth of the National Catholic Warfare Committee, the first attempt to create a national agency to represent and coordinate actions by all the nation's dioceses.

- Rabbi Ben Frankel founds Hillel Foundation at the University of Illinois. This campus religious group is patterned after the Methodist Wesley Foundation. In 1925 B'nai B'rith assumes responsibility for this largest Jewish campus organization.

**18 May**    The all-male General Assembly of the Presbyterian Church U.S.A. (Northern) votes to merge the Women's Board of Home Missions with the Presbyterian Board of Home Missions, ending the female control of this aspect of church work.

## 1924

- The Methodist Episcopal Church begins to allow ordination of women for local congregations. They are not allowed to belong to the General Conference, however, thus limiting their activities and careers.

- The Presbyterian Church U.S. (Southern) elects women to national service boards for the first time.

- The Woman's Branch of the Union of Orthodox Jewish Congregations of America is founded.

- Aimee Semple McPherson begins broadcasting from her new radio station KFSG (Kall Full Square Gospel) from her Angelus Temple in Los Angeles. This is the first full-time religious radio station in America.

- The editors and critics of *Film Daily* choose Cecil B. DeMille's *The Ten Commandments* as one of the best movies of 1923.

- Metropolitan Platon declares the Diocese of All America and Canada autonomous from the Russian Patriarch.

**31 Mar.**    The Supreme Court strikes down a law of the state of Oregon that requires all children to attend public schools. The law was intended to end parochial education, particularly Catholic schools.

**27 May**    The General Conference of the Methodist Episcopal Church ends its ban on dancing and theater attendance.

**2 June**    A proposed amendment to the Constitution ending child labor is sent to the states. While twenty-six states ratify the amendment, it fails of passage. A major force in opposition is the Roman Catholic Church, which fears giving the state excessive control over children.

## 1925

- The Presbyterian Church U.S.A. (Northern) publishes The Auburn Affirmation, a revision of the points established in the Westminster Confession of Faith. The affirmation permits Presbyterians to have differing interpretations of the principles of their faith.

- Bruce Barton's *The Man Nobody Knows*, a life of Jesus, enters the best-seller list, where it stays for two years. More than 750,000 copies are sold.

- The largest Buddhist temple in the United States is opened in Los Angeles.

- The Jewish Institute of Religion graduates its first class.

- The Protestant Episcopal Church expels Bishop William M. Brown for heresy because he supported communism as a modern form of Christianity.

**13 May**    The state of Florida passes a law requiring daily Bible reading in public schools.

**6 July**    Francis E. Clark, the founder and head of the United Society of Christian Endeavor, retires. He founded this largest of Protestant youth groups in 1881.

**10-21 July**   The trial of John T. Scopes in Dayton, Tennessee, for teaching evolution in a science class attracts the nation's attention. This is one of the first media events in the nation's history. The radio station WGN of Chicago arranges for remote broadcast of the event. The high point of the trial comes on 20 July, when William Jennings Bryan, serving as a lawyer for the prosecution, agrees to take the witness stand. His testimony fails to satisfy his Fundamentalist allies. Sophisticates, however, enjoy the humiliating questioning Bryan endures from defense lawyer Clarence Darrow, who focuses on the inconsistencies in the Bible with questions frequently used by village atheists in the previous century. Scopes is found guilty of teaching evolution, and fined $100.

**16 Oct.**   The Texas State Text Book Board prohibits the discussion of the theory of evolution in its school textbooks.

**9 Nov.**   The cornerstone of the nave of St. John the Devine, the largest Episcopal church in the United States, is laid.

## 1926

- Henry Sloane Coffin becomes professor of homiletics and president of Union Theological Seminary in New York City, positions he will hold until 1945.

- Bob Jones founds the college with his name in Clearwater, Florida. After a period in Tennessee the school moves to Greenville, South Carolina, in 1946.

**18 May**   Aimee Semple McPherson, founder of the Full Square Gospel Church and pastor of the Angelus Temple in Los Angeles, disappears while swimming in the ocean. She reappears six weeks later in the Arizona desert claiming to have been kidnapped. The sensational charge that she spent part of that time with a man in Carmel, California, makes her a national figure.

**20 June**   The first Eucharistic Congress in the United States opens in Chicago.

**26 July**   The Sanctuary of Our Lady of Victory in Lackawanna, New York, becomes the first Roman Catholic church in the United States to be consecrated as a basilica.

## 1927

- Mary Katherine Jones Bennett, former president of the Women's Board of Home Missions of the northern Presbyterian Church publishes "Causes of Unrest Among Women of the Church" reflecting a growing feminist current in that denomination. In 1929 she publishes "Status of Women in the Presbyterian Church, U.S.A. with References to Other Denominations."

- Sinclair Lewis's biting satire on a get-ahead Protestant minister, *Elmer Gantry*, immediately goes on the best-seller list.

**17 Apr.**   Gov. Alfred E. Smith of New York, leading contender for the Democratic presidential nomination, responds to a question whether his religion might involve a conflict between his church and the Constitution by stating, "I recognize no power in the institution of my Church to interfere with the operations of the Constitution of the United States or the enforcement of the law of the land."

**1928**

**26 Apr.** Archimandrite Mardariye is consecrated bishop of the Serbian Orthodox Church in North America. He arrives to take up his reign for new dioceses.

**8 May** The Serbian Orthodox Church holds its first American National Church Assembly in Chicago.

**10 May** The Evangelical Church rules that only celibate women may be ordained.

- Governor Smith of New York becomes the first Roman Catholic to be nominated for the presidency by a major party. Although both candidates try to keep religious prejudice out of the campaign, the issue of Smith's religion becomes both a positive factor, bringing Catholic votes to the Democratic column, and a negative issue, pushing dry Protestants into the Republican column. Hoover wins in this Republican year and carries five states in the Democratic Solid South.

**1929**

- The General Assembly of the Presbyterian Church U.S.A. (Northern) reorganizes Princeton Theological Seminary, weakening the conservative dominance both on the board of trustees and in the curriculum. J. Gresham Machen resigns in protest and begins the Westminster Seminary in Philadelphia.

- The Daughters of the American Revolution demand a Senate investigation into communist influences in the Federal Council of Churches of Christ.

**16 Oct.** The Federal Council of Churches of Christ pledges its support for the textile strikes in Elizabethton, Tennessee, and Gastonia, North Carolina.

# OVERVIEW

**Normalcy.** *Normalcy* is one word that could be used to describe American life and culture, including religion, in the 1920s. In his 1920 race for the presidency Warren G. Harding used this word, which captures both the reality of the dramatic changes that were taking place in the United States and the efforts of many of its citizens to ignore the challenges these changes presented. Americans wanted both the future, which seemed to be limitless, and an idealized past, which moderated the terrors of rapid change. This same apprehension of threat and promise also affected the major American religious communities. While each religious group continually congratulated itself on its seeming successes, each also operated from strongly defensive positions.

**Religion and Culture.** In understanding religion in American history it is essential to remember that the various faiths of the country were deeply fused with various cultures, and while one thinks and talks of churches and denominations, those official organizations were in large part manifestations of cultural communities that operated on both the local and national level. Religion was more than congregations, denominations, or even large bodies such as those composed of Protestants, Catholics, Jews, or Orthodox believers, and the actions of those groups reflected and affected the divisions that had always existed in the nation.

**Stasis and the Roots of Change.** Some things in American religious life seemed not to have changed in the 1920s. Protestants still dominated in their denominations and in their combined membership. Members of the mainline denominations made up the business elite, controlled major cultural institutions from colleges and universities down to local country clubs, and ran most elected bodies. No matter what their actual social class was, white Protestants considered themselves the "real" Americans. From their perspective other groups — Roman Catholics, Orthodox Catholics, Jews, and black Protestants — were more "American" the closer they were to the white Protestant "standard." But this white Anglo-Saxon Protestant dominance was already beginning to erode, and the nation was well on its way to becoming a multicultural society.

**Signs of Decline.** However, serious signs of decline in the mainline Protestant groups could be seen. There seemed to be a sharp decline in religious commitment. Denominational giving dropped, and although membership in the major denominations continued to grow, those who looked more closely could see that they failed to grow as quickly as the whole population. Smaller sectarian groups saw the most expansion during the decade. But this growth went unnoticed, since they started from small bases. Further evidence of the weakening attraction of religion, often cited by conservatives, was the decline in the number of applicants for the foreign-mission field. In 1920 2,700 people offered themselves for missionary training. In 1928 that number had dropped to 252.

**Protestants and Prohibition.** Although the collapse of the Interchurch World Movement disappointed many people, the Protestant community took action to assert its dominant position in the nation's culture. The most obvious of these efforts was national Prohibition, secured by the ratification of the Eighteenth Amendment in 1919 and defined by the Volstead Act, which went into effect on 16 January 1920. The Anti-Saloon League, which continued to monitor the support of Prohibition, called itself the Protestant Church in action. The amendment prohibited the manufacture, sale, or transportation of alcoholic beverages in the United States and its territories. The Volstead Act defined alcoholic beverages as those with more than 0.5 percent alcohol by volume. A dry America was a longtime Protestant dream and had been the basis for contention with Roman Catholics for decades. Now it was achieved, and the whole nation once more was under the sway of Protestant moral values.

**Catholics and Prohibition.** The many Roman Catholic communities in the large industrial cities and states of the country were offended by Prohibition, which not only was imposed upon them, but interfered with the cultural use of alcohol that they brought with them from their native lands. Instead of actually solving tensions between Catholics and Protestants, Prohibition and its enforcement intensified the social and political struggles of the decade.

**Protestants and Immigration.** Protestants were also partly responsible for the new immigration laws that went into effect during the decade, although Catholic union members had also long opposed unrestricted immigration. Both the immigration acts of 1921 and 1924 placed a cap on the number of immigrants who could be admitted to the United States each year. In addition to limiting the absolute number of immigrants who could be admitted, these laws placed a quota on the number of people who could immigrate to the United States from particular countries. These quotas were based on the national origin of the American population at various times. Initially this quota reflected the percentage in the census of 1910, but the permanent immigration act of 1924 moved the quota base back to the level of the census of 1890 in order to exclude more of the "undesirable" types, which meant Jews, Roman Catholics, and Orthodox Catholics, who had come to the United States at the turn of the century. Even as the process of acculturation was taking place, large numbers of old-stock Protestants concluded these new immigrants could never be assimilated, at least not in large numbers.

**The Decline of Protestant Power.** But the Protestant hegemony was collapsing in spite of its apparent successes in this decade. To the concern of militant Protestants, Roman Catholics grew in number and continued to be the largest distinct Christian group. Roman Catholics were also earning more money than in previous decades and rising in social status. Some families, such as the Kennedys, had moved to the trappings of great wealth and the manners of the Protestant elite. Catholic colleges such as Notre Dame University, Fordham University, Georgetown University, and Boston College were preparing their students to take important places in American political, economic, and intellectual life.

**The Ku Klux Klan.** While Prohibition and immigration restrictions relied on the federal government to carry out the desires of white Protestants, a few from that community took direct action to try to ensure their social and political dominance. In the early years of its existence the nation paid little attention to the Ku Klux Klan, which experienced a revival in 1915. This second Klan was loosely based on the political terrorist organization that had run rampant in the post–Civil War South and in its early years had limited growth. But in the social turmoil that followed the Great War, this new Klan with new, ambitious organizers suddenly expanded in numbers and influence. The urban press began to report on the organization's nativist beliefs. The Klan was convinced that only white Protestants could be true Americans and was militantly prejudiced against not only blacks but also Jews and Roman Catholics. In spite of the violent racial outrages that erupted in various places and were attributed to the Klan, many middle-class and lower-middle-class Protestants saw the hooded order as a fraternal organization that sought to validate small-town Protestant values in a rapidly changing society.

**The Klan and Politics.** Some astute Klansmen saw a political role for the organization for advancing either traditional ends or their careers. The Invisible Empire, as it called itself, became a major force in Democratic states such as Oklahoma and Alabama as well as in Indiana. The organization was nonpartisan in its climb to power. By middecade the nature of the Klan and its proper place in the nation were a subject for bitter debate between its supporters and people who insisted that its violence and extralegal actions raised questions as to whether it was not actually un-American. In 1924 the Democratic Party split over a resolution condemning the Klan, and in a year with three major parties campaigning for the presidency the party experienced galling defeat. But the repeated acts of violence, the various political and criminal scandals, the virulence of the Klan's racism, and the revelations that Klan leaders were profiting from the organization led to the crumbling of the organization and the decline of its importance.

**Religion and Class.** The Protestant community, as always, was as greatly splintered as the Democrats, both on the basis of race and class. In spite of a general American belief in a classless society, Protestants were divided, with the tall-steeple churches of the business class aloof from working-class churches within their own denominations, and even more sharply, divided from the emerging Pentecostal and Holiness Churches of the poor. Sociologists Robert and Helen Lynd reached this conclusion in *Middletown* (1929), their study of Muncie, Indiana, where business-class congregations had few members from the working class and denominations tended to attract people of the same social background. Liston Pope, later dean of the Yale Divinity School, analyzed the class function of Protestant churches in his study of Gastonia, North Carolina, in the great textile strike there in 1929.

**Churches and Class.** The class nature of American Protestant churches was studied by H. Richard Niebuhr. The distinguished theologian noted in his first notable book, *The Social Sources of Denominationalism* (1929), that the various denominations that proliferated in the United States tended to follow a particular path: from the creation of a sect, with members from lower social status, gradually moving to church and denominational positions as the members rose in economic and social status. While outsiders seemed to encounter a united Protestant community, people inside sensed how deeply they were divided.

**Churches and Race.** White Protestants generally ignored the way class divided denominations and congregations, and even fewer noticed the split between white and black Protestants. While most large, white Protestant groups had some minority members, the vast majority of African Americans belonged to Methodist and Baptist groups and were deeply alienated from their white counterparts. The northern and southern Methodist churches failed to unite during the decade in part over the issue of how to organize the black members of these two largely white denominations, which had virtually no contact with the various African American Methodist denominations. Nor was there any familial contact between white Baptists and the various black Baptist denominations. Each race had its own churches, which seemed natural and right at the time. Even the Pentecostal movement, whose early leaders were both black and white, spilt along racial lines during the decade and organized themselves on a racial basis.

**Theological Differences.** While the class and race divisions of the Protestant community were widely ignored, differences over theological issues were not. In the 1920s the struggle between the *fundamentalists,* a new word coined to describe conservative Protestants who had adopted a premillennialist view, and Protestant liberals and moderates who were willing to accept changes in both religious doctrines and social behavior, became one of the most bitter religious struggles in the nation's history.

**Religion and Evolution.** Newspapers and magazines paid primary attention to this struggle in the public debate over teaching evolution in public schools. Fundamentalist groups organized to press state legislatures to ban the teaching of evolution to schoolchildren, convinced that such teachings would undermine students' faith and contribute to what was perceived as the generally weakening moral tone of the nation. The effort to ban the teaching of evolution reached its climax in Tennessee, which became to first state to adopt this Fundamentalist program. The Tennessee law led to the great Scopes "Monkey" Trial in the small town of Dayton, whose city fathers hoped the publicity from a challenge to the law would put Dayton on the map and lead to economic growth. The trial linked Fundamentalism to rural, Protestant values in the minds of most Americans, even though antievolution efforts came from big cities such as New York, Minneapolis, and Fort Worth. Sophisticates believed that the Dayton trial proved the silliness of the antievolution effort, although other states, mostly in the Protestant South, continued to pass laws prohibiting teaching children that the world was ancient and that the human race did not begin with Adam and Eve.

**Fundamentalism.** The questions surrounding Fundamentalism constituted a Protestant quarrel, but the battle was limited to a few important denominations. The struggle had little impact on liturgical communities such as the Protestant Episcopal Church and the various Lutheran groups, being largely confined to the Evangelical community. Even there, however, not every denomination was affected. Conservative Protestant churches such as the Southern Baptist Convention, the southern Presbyterians, and the Church of Christ had no major battles because they had so few modernists. The Congregationalists; the Christian Church (Disciples of Christ), which had congregational autonomy; and the Northern Methodists, because of the their willingness to accept a broad range of views and opinions, were relatively peaceful about the matter. The real battles took place in the northern Presbyterian Church and the Northern Baptist Convention. The modernists seemed to win the denominational battles and even the struggle for public opinion, at least for a time.

**The Place of Roman Catholicism.** While the Roman Catholic Church in America was one of the largest, richest, and most powerful groups in the Roman Catholic world, it still acted as if it were an immigrant church, a newcomer to American society. This self-perception was reinforced in part by the Vatican, which still had not made its peace with the modern world and still feared the effects of liberal democracy. The Vatican even hesitated to allow Americans to create a national organization to coordinate the church's American charities and only begrudgingly permitted the reorganization of the National Catholic Warfare Committee as the National Catholic Welfare Conference (NCWC) in 1923. But permission to create the NCWC was given, and finally a basis for a national Catholic Church was found. Now the bishops had at least a limited forum for discussion of some of their common problems.

**Entering Mainstream America.** Another event with symbolic significance came with the raising of George Mundeline to the College of Cardinals. He was the first non–Irish American cardinal in the history of the American church. While the Irish would continue to dominate the American Catholic Church for the coming decades, its hierarchy was beginning to reflect the various national origins of the church's population in the United States. In spite of the Ku Klux Klan, the humiliating defeat of Alfred E. Smith in 1928, and the continuing fears of Protestants, the Roman Catholic Church was becoming a fully American institution.

**A Divided Role.** Two events in the 1920s gave symbolic evidence of the divided place of the Roman Catholic Church in American culture. In 1926 a Eucharistic Congress held in Chicago culminated in a celebratory Mass for tens of thousands of worshipers in Soldier Field. Protestant America watched as the holy sacrament of the Mass was taken from the dark, mysterious altars of hundreds of sanctuaries and celebrated in public, in the open air of the American heartland. Two years later Smith, the first Roman Catholic nominated for the U.S. presidency, was resoundingly trounced by his Protestant, Republican opponent, Herbert Hoover; mainstream America was not ready for a wet, urban Catholic who spoke with a New York accent to serve as president. Only John F. Kennedy, a Harvard-educated Catholic with the style, manners, and accent of the northeastern elite, would achieve that goal — thirty-two years later.

**Jews in America.** More than the Protestant and Catholic communities, Jews were both an ethnic group as well as a religious one, and most American Christians saw them that way in the 1920s. In spite of the concerns of American nativists and others who wondered if the cultures of the "New Immigrants" would allow assimilation, the Jews who poured into the United States from central and eastern Europe at the turn of the century moved quickly in the process of adapting to America. This process took time, of course, and during this time the culture of the past was retained.

**Jewish Diversity.** A part of the religious and cultural vibrancy of these Yiddish-speaking Jews was reflected in new Orthodox congregations, schools, and other institutions that sprang up in the industrial cities, particularly on New York City's Lower East Side. American Reform congregations, composed of nineteenth-century immigrants from Germany, found themselves facing fellow Jews they loved, feared, and sometimes understood. These fully assimilated German Jews, many of whom had found an established place in the community, were often as much offended by the actions, manners, and religious practices of these immigrants from eastern Europe as were old-stock Americans.

**Questioning Assimilation.** Yet the efforts to establish their fellow Jews, to provide health and education for people eager to seize opportunities for freedom, caused many assimilated Jews to examine whether they had gone too far in their efforts to adapt to the larger American culture. In 1926 the Reform congregations adopted the Columbus Platform, a restatement of their values and practices. This platform provided for a return to traditional rituals and practices that had been abandoned decades earlier in an attempt to assimilate. In addition, all Jews, long established or newly arrived, joined to protest when their sons and daughters encountered the rising tide of anti-Semitism in the decade. They were particularly offended by quotas on Jewish admissions adopted by private colleges and graduate programs. In spite of those quotas, particularly those at Ivy League schools, the number of Jewish lawyers, physicians, and dentists rapidly increased, and the Jewish middle class rapidly expanded. Not all Jews chose the traditional professions as an exit from the working class. Meyer Lansky was the most prominent of those Jews who went into organized crime, one of the fastest ways to wealth in the 1920s, when criminal groups consolidated their activities into a loose national organization. If it was American, even if it was illegal, Jews could do it too.

**Jews and Politics.** Morris Hillquit was only the best known of those who remained politically committed to working-class Jews. He earned a handsome living through labor law but devoted most of his energies to trying to advance the Socialist Party and bring about a Marxist state. His efforts were of little use in the conser-

vative political mood of the 1920s. The Socialist Party saw a sharp drop in votes, many from Jewish and German communities, from those given to Indiana-born Eugene V. Debs in 1920 to the tiny vote the Presbyterian minister Norman Thomas received in his Socialist campaign in 1928. As nativist antiradicals pointed out, Jews were an important component of radical politics, but the presidential nominees were old-stock white Protestants.

**Anti-Semitism.** The rapid ascent of Jewish immigrants and their high visibility in certain industries, particularly movies and radio, helped trigger new waves of anti-Semitism that partially reflected growing anti-Semitism in Europe. The Ku Klux Klan listed Jews among the many groups they considered dangerous to "traditional" values.

**Henry Ford and Anti-Semitism.** While it was easy to dismiss these "drivers of second-hand Fords," as some urban critics did during the early stages of the Klan, it was more difficult to dismiss the maker of the Ford Model-T himself. In 1920 Henry Ford, one of the most admired men in America and one of the richest, began publishing in his *Dearborn Independent* a series of scurrilous attacks on Jews that culminated by reprinting the Russian anti-Semitic forgery *The Protocols of the Elders of Zion*. Protests from the Jewish community and some Christian leaders such as former presidents Woodrow Wilson and William Taft were swift but took time to have an effect. Ford refused for a long time to admit that he had published material that not only was untrue but damaging to a significant part of the population, and he only reluctantly issued an apology for his actions in 1927. But by that time the poison he endorsed was not only circulating in the United States but had added to the rising tide of anti-Semitism in Germany and other parts of the world.

**Changes.** The end of the 1920s came not on 31 December 1929 but on 29 October, when the stock market crashed, which preceded the Depression that characterized the coming decade. Just as the stock market was based on unfounded speculation, so was much of the religious fervor of the 1920s. And, just as wise investors knew that a speculation market must inevitably decline, so many religious people during the decade sensed that underlying forces were changing American religious life more than they could comprehend. On the surface the decade seemed to end much as it had begun. Crises had occurred, but they had been surmounted, and "normalcy" continued. But deep structural changes were taking place, and the American religious landscape was in the slow process of stunning change.

# TOPICS IN THE NEWS

## THE PRESBYTERIANS AND THE AUBURN AFFIRMATION

**The Conflict between Modernism and Traditionalism.** The Presbyterian Church U.S.A. (Northern) was deeply split at the turn of the century between conservative traditionalists and those more responsive to changes in biblical scholarship and the surrounding world. The modernists, as they would soon be called, believed it was time for a reexamination of the Westminster Confession of Faith (1647), which was still the foundation of Presbyterian doctrines. Conservatives not only opposed such a reexamination but saw no reason for it. In 1910, at the close of the annual General Assembly, the conservatives succeeded in adopting a set of five "essential and necessary" doctrines for its ministers. They quickly became known as the Five Points. The Five Points included a belief in the inerrancy of the Bible, the virgin birth of Christ, his substitutionary atonement, his bodily resurrection, and the authenticity of miracles. These were similar to the Five Points of Fundamentalism, although the Fundamentalists substituted the imminent return of Christ for the belief in miracles. Even though the last points were sharply different, the conservatives and the Fundamentalists worked together effectively against their more liberal common enemies during the 1920s.

**The Auburn Affirmation.** As the struggle between Fundamentalists and modernists heated up in the 1920s, self-described moderates attempted to find a middle way between the more extreme factions. In 1925 a group of more than a thousand clergymen signed an "Affirmation of Faith," usually called The Auburn Affirmation, that reiterated the Five Points of 1910 but allowed members of the denomination to have various, valid means of explaining these truths. In short, the signers believed that the denomination should tolerate those who might affirm alternate versions of Christian doctrines and extend confidence and fellowship to all believers as they defined themselves.

**Quelling Unrest.** The Auburn Affirmation became the basis for peace in the denomination. Nonetheless, conservatives, led by J. Gresham Machen of the Princeton Theological Seminary, insisted that the modernists were not Christians and should leave the denomi-

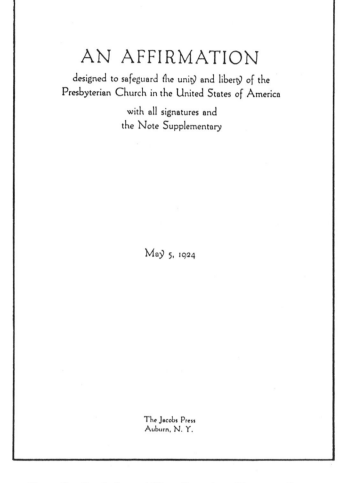

AN AFFIRMATION
designed to safeguard the unity and liberty of the
Presbyterian Church in the United States of America

with all signatures and
the Note Supplementary

May 5, 1924

The Jacobs Press
Auburn, N. Y.

Cover for the Auburn Affirmation, signed by more than one thousand clergymen, which held that the Presbyterian denomination permitted a diversity of belief

nation. The threat of a split caused the moderator, Prof. Charles R. Erdman of the Princeton Theological Seminary, a conservative himself, to appoint a Committee of Fifteen to study the "causes of unrest" in the Presbyterian Church and report back to the General Assembly in 1927.

**Supporting the Affirmation.** The committee's report repudiated Machen's position that conservatives and lib-

Charles R. Erdman, moderator of the General Assembly of the Presbyterian Church U.S.A.

erals belonged to different religions, and the report urged toleration within the denomination, saying, "The Presbyterian system admits diversity of view where the core of truth is identical." Further, the committee limited the power of the General Assembly to define doctrine, as conservatives had done with the Five Points. Doctrine was too important to rest in the hands of a temporary majority, it said. Essentially, this was a recapitulation of The Auburn Affirmation, and it served to end the bitter struggles in the denomination after some of the more militant Fundamentalists eventually followed Machen out of the denomination.

**Setting a Pattern.** The struggle between the Fundamentalists and modernists set the path of the Presbyterian Church for the rest of the century. In the coming decade questions over the role of missionaries and who could go into the mission field racked the church once again, and the conservatives left what they perceived as a hollow shell of the Reform tradition.

Sources:
Randall Balmer and John R. Fitsmeier, *The Presbyterians* (Westport, Conn.: Greenwood Press, 1993);

Ned B. Stonehouse, *J. Gresham Machen: A Biographical Memoir* (Grand Rapids, Mich.: Eerdmans, 1954).

## HENRY FORD AND THE DEARBORN INDEPENDENT

**Henry Ford, Publisher.** In 1919 Henry Ford, the man who put America on wheels with his Model T, purchased *The Dearborn Independent*, a weekly publication, to present his views to his many admirers. While Ford himself did not exercise direct editorial control over the publication, it reflected his opinions and beliefs.

**Perpetuating Old Lies.** In 1920 *The Dearborn Independent* began a series of articles attacking the alleged power of Jews in the international banking community and their relation to the recent World War, which Ford had bitterly opposed. The articles, later published as *The International Jew: The World's Foremost Problem* (1922), reflected many of the anti-Semitic assumptions of nineteenth-century American rural culture. *The Dearborn Independent* charged that Jewish financiers had gained control of the money supply and manipulated it to advance their interests. (Ford himself regretted that he had borrowed from eastern banks to finance the expansion of his automobile company and acted as quickly as possible to regain total control over the Ford Motor Company.) The articles went further, charging that these Jewish bankers had pulled the world into the recent World War. The articles culminated by repeating the old lie that Jews were plotting to overthrow Christian civilization.

**The Protocols of the Elders of Zion.** In 1920 *The Dearborn Independent* began publishing a translation of *The Protocols of the Elders of Zion*. The *Protocols* were alleged to be a recounting of the centennial meeting of "learned elders" of the Jewish nation during which they detailed how they had tormented Christian society in the past hundred years and discussed plans to destroy Christian civilization in the next century. This virulently anti-Semitic document had been forged by the secret police of czarist Russia in 1905 as the government attempted to divert Russians from their growing disgust with its corruption and incompetence by turning them to a standard target of hatred — the Jews. While it is difficult to determine how many people read Ford's publication, the poison of *The International Jew* and *The Protocols of the Elders of Zion* spread into American culture backed by Ford's name.

**Response.** The Jewish community was divided as to how to respond to this torrent of anti-Semitism. The American Jewish Committee, the largest and most influential Jewish voice, continued its cautious practice of avoiding contention with anti-Semites in an effort to minimize and contain the old Christian hatreds of Jews. They believed that it was best not to call attention to topics that might trigger even more serious acts against them. But periodicals such as *The American Hebrew* called on Jews to band together to protest and boycott Ford products. Christians also sought to end the inflammatory lies coming out of Dearborn. More than a hundred people, including former presidents William Howard Taft

**The Ford International Weekly**

# THE DEARBORN INDEPENDENT

$1.50     Dearborn, Michigan, April 12, 1924     Ten Cents

## Exploiting Farm Organizations

Jewish Monopoly Traps Operate Under Guise
of Co-operative Marketing Associations

## Europe and the Next War

## Antics of the Antique Hunter

## "The Eighteenth of April '75"

## Pulitzer Races Promote Flying

CHRONICLER OF THE NEGLECTED TRUTH

Henry Ford sponsored this weekly that published
anti-Semitic articles.

and Woodrow Wilson, and prominent political and religious leaders, such as William Jennings Bryan and Cardinal William O'Connell, signed a letter asking Ford to stop the continued publication of "vicious propaganda" — to no avail.

**Continued Attacks.** Between May 1920 and December 1921 *The Dearborn Independent* ran its charges and falsehoods, and then they stopped without explanation. However, various parts of the original attacks were collected and published as *The International Jew*. The book circulated widely in the United States, Europe, and South America. Adolf Hitler was one of its readers, and Ford's detractors and many other people believed, without proof, that Ford offered financial support to the growth of the Nazi movement. In 1924 *The Dearborn Independent* returned to its anti-Semitic campaign, this time attacking a Jewish lawyer active in organizing farm cooperatives. The series, "The Jewish Exploitation of Farmers' Organizations," once more linked Jewish bankers and others to a purported effort to undermine American institutions. The outraged target of the attack sued *The Dearborn Independent* and Ford himself.

**Trial.** In spite of Ford's efforts, the issue went to trial in 1927. Ford avoided having to testify under oath as to his actual role in the publication when he was injured in an automobile accident the day before he was scheduled to appear in court. Before Ford recovered and had to go to court, a juror gave a newspaper interview about the trial, which forced the judge to declare a mistrial.

**Ford's Problems.** By this time the Ford Motor Company was in financial difficulty. Ford had refused to follow the lead of the revitalized General Motors Corporation into annual model changes and had dropped in market share. In 1927 Ford closed his factory and began retooling to introduce the Model A. He was eager to walk away from his money-losing publication and end the constant criticism of his social views. He arranged an interview with Louis Marshall, spokesman for the American Jewish Committee, and agreed to retract the anti-Semitic statements in *The Dearborn Independent* and apologize for any damage the articles had done. Marshall drafted a statement to that effect and Ford signed it without change. He then closed *The Dearborn Independent*, ending his publishing career.

**Lingering Rumors of Anti-Semitism.** Charges that Ford was anti-Semitic declined in intensity but continued to circulate, as did copies of *The International Jew*. Rumors continued to link Ford to Hitler into the 1930s. In 1937 he once again apologized for publishing anti-Semitic material. He lost his credibility, however, when he accepted a medal from Hitler in 1938, the year of Kristallnacht, one of the worst pogroms of the century to that time. Many Jews could not forgive Ford for his part, direct or indirect, in contributing to the flood that swept away so many of their fellow Jews in Hitler's Holocaust.

Sources:

Carol W. Gelderman, *Henry Ford: The Wayward Capitalist* (New York: Dial, 1981);

David L. Lewis, *The Public Image of Henry Ford* (Detroit: Wayne State University Press, 1976).

## PROTESTANT EVANGELISM

**Cooperative Evangelism.** The self-assurance of American Protestants reached a high in 1919 as the various leading denominations agreed to cooperate with each other in evangelizing the world. The euphoric optimism that followed the end of World War I convinced many Protestants leaders that now the world was ready for mass conversion. Under the terms of the Interchurch World Movement, the denominations agreed to coordinate their benevolent activities. Among other things, the world's mission fields would be divided among the various denominations to eliminate competition and improve efficiency. In addition, the Interchurch Movement promised to raise $200 million, as a start to fund this effort. The total budget for the next decade was estimated at $1 billion.

**Failed Effort.** The Interchurch World Movement began its fund-raising drive in 1920 using advertising as a basis:

Christ was big, was He not? None bigger.
Christ was busy, was He not? None busier.
He was always about His Father's business.
Christ needs big men for big business.

However, the campaign was a failure. Some denominations declined to cooperate from the beginning. The Southern Baptist Convention refused to permit any agency to stop its missionaries from preaching to anyone anywhere in the world. When the Interchurch Movement published its critical report on the suppression of the great steel strike of 1919, businessmen charged that the organization was simply another form of un-American radicalism. Contributions dropped from their already-low level, and more denominations severed their ties with the movement. It collapsed into ignominy.

**A Mask of Prosperity.** The failure of the Interchurch Movement was only one symptom of the decline of Protestant vigor. This decline was hidden in part, as the prosperity of the decade permitted many urban congregations to build splendid new sanctuaries. In New York City work continued on the great Cathedral of St. John the Divine, and the members of the Park Avenue Baptist Church moved into a new sanctuary, only to agree to move by the end of the decade to the enormous Riverside Church. Many congregations, such as the Calvary Baptist Church in New York City, followed the assurances of political and business leaders that the problems of poverty had essentially been solved and went deeply into debt to construct new buildings. These mortgages would haunt their accounts in the coming decade of depression.

Source:
Marshall Olds, *Analysis of the Interchurch World Movement Report on the Steel Strike* (New York & London: Putnam, 1923).

## THE RISE AND RETREAT OF FUNDAMENTALISM

**The Fundamentalist Challenge.** In the 1920s, to the surprise of many observers, American Protestants returned to issues that had seemingly been resolved decades earlier, and the nation was presented with a series of spectacular clashes between people calling themselves Fundamentalists and their opponents, whom they called modernists. In the early years of the decade the Fundamentalists seemed to be riding high, challenging their opponents for control of denominational machinery and of American culture itself. But they failed to drive their enemies from their denominations, and the farcical aspects of the so-called Scopes "Monkey" Trial in Dayton, Tennessee, along with the weaknesses of Prohibition, signaled their loss in the conflict. The Fundamentalists were forced to the sidelines and obscurity, into

Professor J. Gresham Machen of the Princeton Theological Seminary was a conservative Calvinist who rejected Fundamentalism.

a quiescence in which they licked their wounds and prepared for the renewal of the struggle that would come at the end of the century.

**Modern Scholarship.** In the last decades of the nineteenth century a series of scholarly breakthroughs led to a revolution in the way many people regarded the earth and humanity and how they looked at the Bible. Charles Darwin's theory of evolution provided a way to explain changes in animals and plants over the millions of years of life on the earth. Although some American scientists, most notably Louis Agassiz, refused to accept the Darwinian approach, other scientists found the new theory a persuasive way to explain the complicated history of life on earth. In the coming decades the theory would be greatly modified, but the revolution in thought that began with Darwin became a foundation of modern science.

**Science and Religion.** In the nineteenth century science was already becoming the touchstone of knowledge, replacing old standards, including religious faith, for the

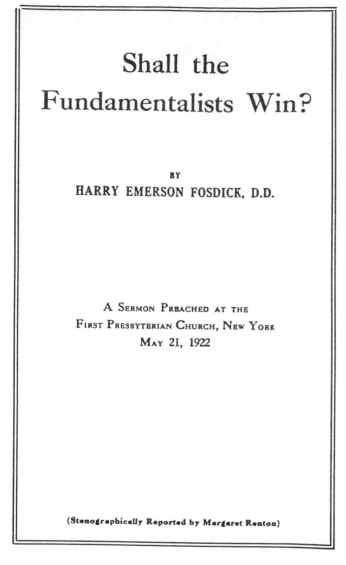

# Shall the Fundamentalists Win?

### BY
### HARRY EMERSON FOSDICK, D.D.

A Sermon Preached at the
First Presbyterian Church, New York
May 21, 1922

(Stenographically Reported by Margaret Renton)

Harry Emerson Fosdick, a Baptist who became minister at the
First Presbyterian Church in New York, delivered this
widely publicized sermon.

better-educated parts of the Western population. Christians leaders then were forced to chose between older reconciliations between science and biblical faith or develop a new means to harmonize the two. For Roman Catholics such as Father John A. Zahm of Notre Dame the answer was simple: religious truth was beyond the mere truth of science, and the two could not conflict in their separate spheres. More-progressive Protestants — including liberals such as Henry Ward Beecher, the best-known preacher of his day — simply jettisoned Bible stories about the origins of humanity as scientific truth and accepted evolution. The Bible contained the word of God, such people believed, but many of those words were poetry and myths that held deeper truths than their surface meanings.

**Against Evolution.** Even though the scientific community, and many in the religious community who concerned themselves with such issues, had fully accepted Darwinism, in the 1920s the World's Fundamentals Association, an organization of Fundamentalist Protestants, attempted to drive evolution from the public schools. They believed the theory of evolution not only was unbiblical but also undermined Christian faith and led to what they considered to be the evident depravity of the times. Led by William Jennings Bryan, an active Presbyterian and former presidential candidate, legislatures in state after state, school board after school board, and state and local textbook committees were forced to wrestle with questions of how to deal with this scientific theory that said, according to popular distortion, that humanity's ancestors were monkeys. The theory of evolution challenged the idea of the special creation of the human race as found in the story of Adam and Eve. Scholars who found stories in other ancient texts of great floods and other myths similar to stories in the Bible seemed to erode the unique qualities of Christianity, thus apparently undermining its claim to the true faith.

**Against Modern Biblical Interpretation.** While the question of teaching evolution in schools was the most visible public topic in the 1920s, Fundamentalists were convinced that a more insidious enemy had infiltrated the churches' seminaries and there were undermining the foundations of the Christian faith. This enemy, they believed, consisted of new scholarly approaches to studying the Bible. The essence of the Protestant separation from the Roman Catholic Church in the sixteenth century was that the Catholic Church, Protestants charged, had drifted away from Christianity's biblical roots. The Protestant reformers sought to return the church to its biblical sources, what they believed to be the actual words of God.

**The Higher Criticism.** But in the nineteenth century German scholars, followed by scholars and theologians in other Western nations, insisted that the Bible was a human product and could and should be studied like any other human document. This textual analysis proved stimulating, provocative, and dangerous. Not only was it clear to such scholars that the Bible was a collection of writings completed over time, but there was evidence that there had been a variety of writers in the various books for this foundation of Protestant faith. Further, the Bible itself could be placed in its own historical times and in the cultural settings in which it was composed. Most of these scholars believed that the Bible contained the word of God, but few believed that every word was essentially dictated by God, including the King James Version, the most popular English translation.

**The Social Gospel.** Another challenge to conservatives came as Protestants found themselves in richer, more urban settings by the turn of the century. As wealth grew, questions were raised about how fortunes were made and how money was spent. A movement appeared called the Social Gospel, which insisted that Christian ethics should be applied to the larger world rather than restricted to private life. According to advocates of the Social Gospel, the longtime preoccupation of American evangelicals with personal salvation should be shifted to the saving of society. Baptist theologian Walter Rauschenbush devised a theology of the Social Gospel, insisting that when Jesus told his followers that the Kingdom of God was within them, he meant just what he said. The Kingdom of God is within people in the twentieth century, he said, and Christians have a responsibility to work to advance that kingdom. Rauschenbush moved beyond the pale for social conservatives when he declared his support for a type of Christian socialism.

**Churches and Change.** Evolution, German scholarship, and the Social Gospel were not of great concern to most Americans at the turn of the century. Instead, people worried about living their lives, and for the white middle class those lives were being lived with a multitude of new choices. The restraints and restrictions of rural and small-town America earlier in the century no longer seemed to apply. The most socially distinguished congregations began to build larger and more lavish sanctuaries. People could easily distinguish between the socially powerful tall-steeple churches and the more humble buildings

of the lower and middle classes, even of the great middle-class Methodist and Baptist denominations.

**Changes in the Churches.** As buildings grew larger and architecturally more interesting, these congregations introduced more-sophisticated music, replacing the old gospel songs of worshipers' childhoods with organs, trained choirs, and the centuries-old music of the Western Christian church. Evangelical churches, which before had focused on the sermon, now borrowed the liturgical trappings of the Protestant Episcopal Church. In the eyes of conservatives these churches were adapting to the world, not rejecting it.

**Conservative Concerns.** Conservatives worried about such developments as feminism, the actions of young people, and birth control (which many Christians supported), although they tended to focus on theological issues. In 1910, at the end of the annual General Assembly, conservatives in the Presbyterian Church U.S.A. (Northern) adopted five "essential and necessary" doctrines to check what they perceived as a slide into doctrinal softness.

**Premillennialism.** In the late nineteenth century many of the conservatives who would later be called Fundamentalists added a new component to the doctrines that served as the foundation of their beliefs. In response to new ways of reading the Bible, they became convinced that Jesus would fulfill his promise to return before the thousand years of his promised rule would begin. This premillennialist tenet reflected a growing dismay among conservative Protestants about the direction of modern life. Instead of improving, as liberals insisted, the world was actually in a state of decline according to traditionalists, and the increasing drift from what they saw as sound doctrine indicated to them that the future could only be worse. The signs of the times, as they read them, indicated that the imminent return of Jesus must be near. He was coming soon, but was America ready? Certainly those churches drifting into modernism, as they called it, were not, they believed.

**Fundamentalism.** Between 1910 and 1915 Lyman and Milton Stewart, two California oil millionaires, funded a mass mailing of twelve booklets on the main points of conservative Protestant doctrine. *The Fundamentals: A Testimony to the Truth,* as the collection was called, went to many Protestant ministers in an effort to check what the Stewarts saw as a drift from religious truth. World War I only convinced Fundamentalists that they had read Bible prophecies correctly. Jesus was coming soon, they believed, and the battle with those who were betraying the faith had to be joined now.

**Perceptions of Fundamentalism.** In the aftermath of the Scopes "Monkey" Trial in Dayton, Tennessee, in 1925, Fundamentalism came to be seen by many as a doctrine that appealed to the ignorant and the unsophisticated. Journalists and even historians suggested that this movement, like the Ku Klux Klan, was restricted to the

## THE CHALLENGE TO FUNDAMENTALISM

In 1922 the controversy between newly organized Fundamentalists and moderate and liberal Protestants boiled over when Harry Emerson Fosdick of the First Presbyterian Church in New York City gave a sermon, "Shall the Fundamentalists win?," that attracted extensive attention and forced a confrontation between the opposing forces for control of the northern Baptist and Presbyterian Churches.

Fosdick said that the Fundamentalist controversy "threatens to divide the American churches as though already they were not sufficiently split and riven," noting that the Fundamentalists' "apparent intention is to drive out of the evangelical churches men and women of liberal opinions." Distinguishing Fundamentalism as an "essentially illiberal and intolerant" type of conservatism, Fosdick criticized its refusal to take into account "new knowledge about the physical universe, its origin, its forces, its laws; new knowledge about human history and in particular about the ways in which the ancient peoples used to think in matters of religion and the methods by which they phrased and explained their spiritual experiences; and new knowledge, also, about other religions and the strangely similar ways in which men's faiths and religious practices have developed everywhere."

"The Fundamentalists," Fosdick continued, "insist that we must all believe in the . . . virgin birth of our Lord; that . . . the original documents of the Scripture, which of course we no longer possess, were inerrantly dictated to men a good deal as a man might dictate to a stenographer; that we must believe . . . that the blood of our Lord, shed in a substitutionary death, placates an alienated Deity and makes possible welcome for the returning sinner; and that we must believe in the second coming of our Lord upon the clouds of heaven to set up a millennium here as the only way in which God can bring history to a worthy denouement." Fosdick had no quarrel with anyone's right to these beliefs; rather, he was troubled by Fundamentalist claims that all Christians must possess these beliefs. He concluded, "There are many opinions in the field of modern controversy concerning which I am not sure whether they are right or wrong, but there is one thing I am sure of: courtesy and kindliness and tolerance and humility and fairness are right. Opinions may be mistaken: love never is."

Source: Harry Emerson Fosdick, "Shall the Fundamentalists Win?," *Christian Work*, 102 (10 June 1922): 716–722.

more benighted sections of the nation, particularly the rural South and the more backward parts of the Midwest and West. In actuality, Fundamentalism laid claim to men with learning and in many cases highly trained minds. The best example was J. Gresham Machen, New Testament professor at Princeton Theological Seminary, though Machen refused to be called a Fundamentalist and rejected their premillenialist ideas. He spoke for a long tradition of conservative Calvinism that had been developed at Princeton early in the nineteenth century and continued into the 1920s. This theology, based on Scottish common-sense philosophy, rested on a complex set of approaches to both scientific and theological issues. In 1923 Machen published a spirited defense of traditional Protestantism, *Christianity and Liberalism*, which rejected the modernists' arguments out of hand. Liberalism, he concluded, was not Christianity but some other religion, and those who accepted it should withdraw from Christian churches. Ironically, Machen was put on the defensive, and in 1929 he left Princeton and established Westminster Seminary to teach his conservative views. In time he would be expelled from the Presbyterian Church for his refusal to work with those whose theology he abhorred.

**Prominent Fundamentalists.** If Machen was a scholar, some self-proclaimed Fundamentalists were at least college and seminary trained, and several were pastors of large congregations in major cities. Three of most prominent in the movement were William Bell Riley of the First Baptist Church of Minneapolis, J. Frank Norris of the First Baptist Church of Fort Worth, and John Roach Straton of Calvary Baptist Church in New York City. These men were strident voices for Fundamentalism within their denominations and militant warriors for their faith against those who spoke for modernism or even compromise. While they worked individually for the most part, they also worked together in organizations such as the World's Fundamentals Association and the Baptist Bible Union.

**Speaking Out against Fundamentalism.** In 1922 Harry Emerson Fosdick, a minister at the First Presbyterian Church in New York City even though he was a Baptist, delivered a widely noticed sermon called "Shall the Fundamentalists Win?" Fosdick was more moderate than his enemies thought, but the title of the sermon and its wide distribution by public-relations agent Ivy Lee brought the issue fully into the public eye. Fosdick spoke in an effort to keep the Fundamentalists from purging the modernists in the Northern Baptist and Presbyterian denominations. He believed that Christians could share a common set of beliefs even though they might disagree about the meanings of those beliefs and that, because they shared common beliefs, they could work together within the denominations. Conservatives such as Machen and Fundamentalists were outraged by this inclusionist approach, since they doubted that the modernists were even Christian. The battle was joined.

The ideas and doctrines of Fundamentalism were codified and preached by urban Protestants, yet the public during the 1920s and later tended to attribute the movement to the more "backward" and rural parts of the nation. H. L. Mencken, the acerbic newspaperman and editor of the *American Mercury*, was one of the many reporters who covered the trial of John T. Scopes in Dayton, Tennessee, for violating state law by teaching evolution. Mencken's report, "The Hills of Zion," was widely read and helped to establish this viewpoint.

"In the big cities of the Republic, despite the endless efforts of consecrated men, [evangelical Christianity] is laid up with a wasting disease," Mencken wrote. "Even in Dayton . . . [the] nine churches of the village were all half empty on Sunday, and weeds choked their yards." He went on to elaborate upon the squalor and ignorance of the people he encountered in the Tennessee hills, including a visit to a rural church. Then he and other journalists returned to Dayton. "It was nearly eleven o'clock — an immensely late hour for those latitudes — but the whole town was still gathered in the courthouse yard, listening to the disputes of theologians. The Scopes trial had brought them in from all directions. There was a friar wearing a sandwich sign announcing that he was the Bible champion of the world. There was a Seventh Day Adventist arguing that Clarence Darrow was the beast with seven heads and ten horns described in Revelation XIII, and that the end of the world was at hand. There was an ancient who maintained that no Catholic could be a Christian. There was the eloquent Dr. T. T. Martin, of Blue Mountain, Miss. come to town with a truck-load of torches and hymn-books to put Darwin in his place. There was a singing brother bellowing apocalyptic hymns. There was William Jennings Bryan, followed everywhere by a gaping crowd. It was better than the circus."

Source: H. L. Mencken, "The Hills of Zion," in *The Vintage Mencken* (New York: Knopf, 1955), pp. 153–161.

**Fundamentalists versus Modernists.** The struggle took various forms. Fosdick declined to become a Presbyterian and left First Presbyterian Church in 1925 to lead the Park Avenue Baptist Church and then, with Rockefeller money, to lead the Riverside Church on Morningside Heights. The northern Presbyterian Church finally adopted the Auburn Affirmation, which essentially said that interpretation of doctrine was an individual matter. The Fundamentalists won some battles, as colleges such as Baylor University were purged of their evolutionist faculty. But the Fundamentalists were unable to gain control of any of the denominations they contested with the modernists and were forced to leave or to learn to live with people whose ideas they despised. Conservatives continued to control some denominations, such as the Lutheran churches, the Presbyterian Church U.S. (Southern), and the Southern Baptist Convention. But the more tenacious Fundamentalists, including Bell Riley, J. Frank Norris, and Bob Jones, were convinced that even these denominations were too soft and organized their own schools and colleges to prevent the world's corrupting influences from weakening the faith of their students. Struggles over denominational machinery and colleges and seminaries were primarily important for those directly affected. While these battles attracted press attention from time to time, essentially most Americans took little interest in these internecine quarrels. The Scopes "Monkey" Trial was another matter.

**Stopping Evolution in the Schools.** The World's Fundamentals Association was organized in 1919 to fight what was perceived as a decline in the nation's moral values, which many Fundamentalists believed was caused by the unchecked entry of evolution into the public schools. Children who were told that they had descended from animals, they believed, would behave like animals. They thought that Christians should check this corrupting force on the young by banning evolution from the schools. William Jennings Bryan, former Democratic presidential candidate, secretary of state, and moderator of the northern Presbyterian Church, became the figurehead of this effort.

**Banning Evolution from the Classroom.** In 1925 Tennessee became the first state to pass a law prohibiting the teaching of evolution in the state's schools. Essentially this was an expression of principle, since punishment would be a modest $100 fine. The recently organized American Civil Liberties Union (ACLU) quickly offered to defend any of Tennessee's teachers who might be charged with the crime. The ACLU was convinced that excluding an accepted scientific theory from the classroom violated a teacher's freedom of speech in teaching science as scientists understood it.

**Challenging the Law.** Soon after the ACLU offer was made, a group of businessmen in the small river town of Dayton decided to beat neighboring Chattanooga to the courts and put Dayton on the map by testing the antievolution law first. They asked a young teacher, John T. Scopes, if he had taught evolution when he took over the high-school biology class earlier that year. Scopes was not certain but assured the men gathered in the town drugstore that if it were in the textbook, he had taught it. In April Scopes made a point of teaching evolution to a biology class and was subsequently arrested.

**A Well-Publicized Trial.** The trial that summer was one of the first media circuses of the twentieth century, as newspaper and magazine journalists were joined by radio reporters. WGN, the radio station of the *Chicago Tribune,* made arrangements for remote broadcasts. H. L. Mencken, the best known and most acerbic social observer of his day, was in town for the *Baltimore Sun.* The journalists had a field day with the crowd of publicity seekers who poured into town to warn that the punishment of Sodom soon awaited those who abandoned the faith for the sins of modernism.

**Conviction.** Scopes's legal defense intended to call scientists to testify as to the place of evolution in biological theory, but the presiding judge insisted that the issue was not the validity of science but whether Scopes had broken the law by teaching evolution. Since he agreed that he had, there seemed to be no defense. It was in this context that Clarence Darrow, perhaps the best known defense lawyer in the country, persuaded Bryan, who was with the prosecution, to take the stand. Bryan was subjected to a scathing examination. Darrow asked all the old questions made familiar by village atheists in the previous century — Where did Cain find his wife? Could a fish actually swallow a man? — and so on. Bryan answered with a combination of naive faith and a view that the words in the Bible might not mean exactly what they seemed to mean to contemporary readers. Sophisticates such as Mencken believed that even though Scopes was convicted, the Fundamentalists had actually lost, as the nation laughed at the absurdity of Bryan's testimony. Scopes's conviction was later overturned by the Tennessee Supreme Court, but the damage to Fundamentalism had already been done. The movement, even with its complex set of underlying ideas, seemed suitable only for hicks and yokels.

**The Decline of Fundamentalism.** This same attitude quickly linked Fundamentalism with what many considered to be other remnants of the nation's small-town and rural past. Prohibition was the most obvious example. As enforcement seemed only to breed crime and disrespect for the law, as the new popular music influenced by jazz attracted more and more young people, as drinking became not only a way to strike a blow for liberty but also to show that one was sophisticated, the Eighteenth Amendment was linked to the most reactionary of its Protestant supporters. Fundamentalism was widely seen as connected with the most "backward" parts of the nation. It became linked not only with intolerance for Protestant moderates but with also all religious intolerance. This feeling was intensified in the presidential election of 1928, in which religious prejudice stirred up by Fundamentalists such as J. Frank Norris and John Roach Straton played a role in Alfred E. Smith's defeat. By the end of the decade Fundamentalism seemed beyond the concerns of sophisticated people, whatever their religious views. Its seeming crudity and vulgarity, its antiintellectualism, and its nativism eroded what little appeal it might have possessed at the beginning of the decade.

| MEMBERSHIP IN THE LARGEST RELIGIOUS BODIES IN 1926 | |
| --- | --- |
| Roman Catholic Church | 18,005,003 |
| Jewish Congregations | 4,081,242 |
| Methodist Episcopal Church | 4,080,777 |
| Southern Baptist Convention | 3,524,378 |
| Negro Baptist Churches | 3,196,623 |
| Methodist Episcopal Church, South | 2,487,694 |
| Presbyterian Church U.S.A. (Northern) | 1,894,030 |
| Protestant Episcopal Church | 1,859,085 |
| Christian Church (Disciples of Christ) | 1,377,595 |
| Northern Baptist Convention | 1,289,966 |
| United Lutheran Church | 1,214,340 |
| Lutheran, Missouri Synod | 1,040,275 |
| Congregational Church | 881,696 |
| African Methodist Episcopal Church | 545,814 |
| Church of Jesus Christ of Latter-Day Saints | 542,194 |
| Norwegian Lutheran Church | 496,707 |
| African Methodist Episcopal Church, Zion | 456,813 |
| Presbyterian Church U.S. (Southern) | 451,043 |
| Church of Christ | 433,714 |

Source: *Census of Religious Bodies, 1926,* volume 1 (Washington, D.C.: Government Printing Office, 1930).

The modernists in all fields seemed to have won, at least for the present.

Sources:
Randall Balmer and John R. Fitzmier, *The Presbyterians* (Westport, Conn.: Greenwood Press, 1993);

George Marsden, *Reforming Fundamentalism: Fuller Seminary and the New Evangelicalism* (Grand Rapids, Mich.: Eerdmans, 1987).

## RELIGION AND POPULAR CULTURE

**The Place of Religion in American Culture.** When sociologists Robert and Helen Lynd studied the people of

Biblical epics were highly successful in the 1920s; in this still from Cecil B. DeMille's *The Ten Commandments*, Estelle Taylor worships the Golden Calf.

Muncie, Indiana, for *Middletown* (1929), they found a decline in church attendance and a widespread belief that the old-time religious values of the late nineteenth century were eroding. One resident of this Middle American city had a word for it: "A-U-T-O." But in spite of this erosion of traditional American Christianity, deep currents of belief and the search for solace intensified the struggle between Fundamentalist and modernist Protestants. But other issues were also raised by popular culture. What was its role in changing the standards of modern America? What could and should be done about it?

**Hollywood.** The most troubling issue for many religious leaders and many of their parishioners was Hollywood, as the movie industry was now known. Frequently movies raised questions about relationships between parents and children, with young people's clearly modern, hedonistic values shown as preferable; between husbands and wives, with the wife's right to happiness more important than the sanctity of marriage; or the glamour of crime, sin, and corruption. While movies rarely attacked the church directly, its simple presentation of new behavior was enough to arouse demands for censorship and reform.

**Scandals.** These demands were intensified when in the early 1920s a series of scandals erupted in Hollywood, ranging from rape charges against the popular comedian Roscoe "Fatty" Arbuckle, who was found not guilty, and the mysterious death of director William Desmond Taylor. That death was linked to drugs and the careers of two prominent actresses, Mabel Normand and Mary Miles Minter, when their love letters to him were found in Taylor's bungalow. The movie industry was then stunned by an anonymous account of life on the industry's edge, *The Sins of Hollywood* (1922).

**The Hays Office.** In panic, movie leaders bowed to critics and established a committee to ensure the morality of their products, preferring self-censorship to a proliferation of local censorship boards or the federal censorship many politicians demanded. Will Hays, whose background as a Presbyterian elder and term as postmaster general in the scandal-ridden administration of President Warren G. Harding suggested he would know sin when he met it, was named president of the board, popularly called the Hays Office. The Hays Office, its critics charged, was more cosmetic than effective in cleaning up Hollywood.

A controversial best-seller in the 1920s was *The Man Nobody Knows* (1925), a life of Jesus written by advertising executive Bruce Barton. The book was widely criticized by intellectuals and conservatives at the time for its crude efforts to link Jesus to the commercial culture of twentieth-century America.

Barton dismissed the idea that Jesus was a weakling, noting that he was a carpenter who slept outdoors. "His muscles were so strong that when he drove the money-changers out, nobody dare to oppose him!" He also claimed that Jesus was "the most popular dinner guest in Jerusalem!" He also praised Jesus' ability to pick up "twelve men from the bottom ranks of business and [forge] them into an organization that conquered the world."

"Surely no one will consider us lacking in reverence," Barton wrote, "if we say that every one of the 'principles of modern salesmanship' on which business men so much pride themselves, are brilliantly exemplified in Jesus' talk and work." Barton then explicitly linked Jesus' ministry and modern business, suggesting that "if [Jesus] were to live again, in these modern days, he would find a way to make . . . [his works] known — to be advertised by his service, not merely by his sermons. One thing is certain: he would not neglect the market-place . . . [and] the present day market-place is the newspaper and the magazine. He would be a national advertiser today . . . as he was the great advertiser of his own day."

Source: Bruce Barton, *The Man Nobody Knows* (Indianapolis: Bobbs-Merrill, 1925).

**Religious Movies.** Religious films persuaded some critics and many viewers that movies could present religious stories clearly, provided there was enough spectacle along with the religious theme. Director and producer Cecil B. DeMille showed the way to the new subject matter. After a series of provocative, sophisticated melodramas such as *Male and Female* (1919), with its sensational flashback showing Gloria Swanson taking a bath in milk, DeMille turned to religion in the 1920s. In 1923 he released his spectacular first version of *The Ten Commandments*. His critics charged that this biblical epic, one of the greatest in Hollywood's history, was only an excuse to present scantily clad dancing girls while seeming to present the source of Jewish and Christian laws and morality. Audiences, however, were stunned by its extravagance and loved the production. In 1926 he released a silent version of the 1880 best-seller *Ben-Hur*, which traced the effects of Jesus' life on fictional contemporaries. The spectacular film starred Ramon Novarro as Ben-Hur and Francis X. Bushman as his nemesis. The chariot-race scene was one of the great spectacles of the decade. In 1927 DeMille produced what is still considered among the best lives of Jesus in another spectacular film, *The King of Kings*, starring Herbert Baxter Warner. Even the most conservative Christians who had serious reservations about everything connected with Hollywood had difficulty in denouncing the apparent intent of these films, if not their trappings.

**Hear No Evil.** But religious films and movies presenting solid family life were not enough to silence Hollywood's critics. They became more insistent when sound was added to movies at the end of the decade. Now parents had to worry not only about the images their children saw but the language they heard. While obscenities were shunned, vulgarity and sexual innuendo became issues as Hollywood moved into a decade of Depression.

**Radio.** Sound was also important in another new medium in popular culture, radio, which became a fad at the beginning of the decade. Many observers believed that it would vanish quickly, like fads in the past, but like crossword puzzles and bridge, radio proved to be lasting. The new wireless sound system quickly developed ties with religion. Early in the decade KDKA, often considered the first commercial radio station, broadcast evening vesper services from Calvary Protestant Episcopal Church in Pittsburgh. The program was such a success that it became a regular Sunday feature.

**Religious Radio.** In the early days of radio, religious broadcasting established a new medium for spreading the gospel to untold thousands, many of whom would never appear in a church. Paul Rader of the Chicago Gospel Tabernacle found the prospect of such a new audience so enticing that he arranged for his own station to use another Chicago station's frequency when it was silent on Sundays. In 1922 Rader began his long radio career on WJST (Where Jesus Saves Thousands). The following year R. R. Brown began a radio career that would last more than fifty years when he began to broadcast his Radio Chapel Services over WOW in Omaha, Nebraska. He estimated that he had more than half a million listeners before the decade was over. In 1924 Aimee Semple McPherson arranged for a license for a weak-frequency station in Los Angeles, KFSG (Kall Full Square Gospel), usually considered the first fully religious radio station.

**Regulation.** Religious broadcasters were only part of the many people who poured into the new industry. Competing stations were set up; equipment was primitive, as were the skills of radio engineers; and the result was a babble of voices in the ether. In 1927 the federal government established the Federal Radio Commission (FRC), later the Federal Communications Commission (FCC), to regulate and monitor the airwaves. One of the FRC's first actions was to straighten out frequency allocations to limit overlap. A variety of smaller stations, including several operated by religious groups, were forced to give up their broadcasting rights. Full-time religious stations reached their peak in 1927, when about sixty stations were committed to or owned by religious groups. That number was cut in half within seven years.

**Radio Preachers.** The FRC was in agreement with the leaders of mainstream religious groups, who believed that radio was too important to allow just any message to be sent out into the world. Nor would the FRC permit the complete commercialization of radio, at least in the beginning. The agency insisted that stations provide time for public service, including religious service for the public. This fell quickly into the hands of mainstream groups such as the Federal Council of Churches, which had established the National Radio Pulpit in 1926. Here some of the leading Protestant preachers of the time, among them Ralph W. Sockman, S. Parkes Cadman, and Harry Emerson Fosdick, spoke to the nation. These men were so successful and filled such a need that many, such as Fosdick, became even more widely known. For the time it seemed that the mainline churches had won the airwaves away from their Fundamentalist and Pentecostal brethren.

**Publishing.** The struggle between religious conservatives and liberals was less visible in the area of books. While a vigorous Fundamentalist and conservative religious press was developing, commercial publishing was dominated by liberals, who tended to buy more books. This can be seen in the popularity of Hendrik Van Loon's *The Story of Mankind*, which stayed on the best-seller list for two years after its publication in 1921. This first of several of Van Loon's popularizations of history paid no attention to Fundamentalist beliefs about the origins of life. He started human history in the primordial soup of an emerging world and traced it down to the present. The people who bought Van Loon's work were the people who also read James Harvey Robinson's *The Mind in the Making* (1921) or Will Durant's *The Story of Philosophy* (1926), both best-sellers in the decade. Humanism had answers to questions of existence as well as religion. For those who wanted more-religious material there was Bruce Barton's life of Jesus, *The Man Nobody Knows* (1925), which tried to link Jesus to modern life and modern businessmen. A more serious biography of the founder of Christianity but hardly a choice of conservatives was a translation of Giovanni Papini's *Life of Christ* (1923), which gave a pragmatist view of Jesus.

**Attacks on Religious Leaders.** Even though there were no successful debunkings of Jesus or the leaders of Christianity, H. L. Mencken and his followers subjected contemporary religious figures to scathing review. Mencken's *American Mercury*, which he edited with George Jean Nathan, continually targeted the credulity of the American "booboisie," as he called the American middle class, and the excesses of religious figures. In 1929 Wilbur J. Cash denounced the Protestant establishment of his native North Carolina in the pages of the *American Mercury* in a bitter article called "The Mind of the South." Cash was willing to join Mencken and other urban sophisticates to charge that ignorance and religious Fundamentalism were linked to the backwardness and depravity of the rural regions of the nation.

**Satire.** This same urge to debunk and denounce characterized Sinclair Lewis's novel *Elmer Gantry*, which stayed on the best-seller list for two years after it was published in 1927. He had attended the services and read the newspaper accounts of New York's John Roach Straton to find material to build his satire of a preacher who almost persuades himself that he believes what he says. Aimee Semple McPherson was the prototype of one of the minor figures in the novel. Hollywood was unwilling to adapt this exposé of revival religion until 1960.

**Religious Best-Seller.** A longer-lasting best-seller appeared in 1929, when a minister turned professional writer, Lloyd C. Douglas, published *The Magnificent Obsession*. The novel's central plot device is based on a newspaper story of a man who dies while the life-saving equipment that could prevent his death is being used to revive another victim. The religious part of Douglas's novel, and probably the center of its attraction for many readers, was his assurance that the Golden Rule would make life richer and deeper if it were practiced completely. Douglas followed this novel with others with religious themes, and the novel would be filmed with great success twice.

# HEADLINE MAKERS

## BRUCE BARTON

### 1886-1967

### WRITER

**Religious Writer.** Bruce Barton attempted to apply to the business and political world of twentieth-century America the religious values he had learned from his father, a Congregationalist minister. Instead of following his father's footsteps into the ministry, when Barton finished his bachelor's degree at Amherst College he moved into journalism and from there into the growing advertising industry. He had immediate success, and in 1918 he was one of the founders of the advertising firm Barton, Durstine, and Osborn, later Barton, Batten, Durstine, and Osborn (BBD&O), which became the third-largest advertising firm in the nation. Even though he was in the secular world, he used his talents for his religious responsibilities. For instance, he coined the slogan later used by the Salvation Army, "A man may be down, but he's never out."

**Becoming a Writer.** In 1914 Barton published his first book, *A Young Man's Jesus*, which in its efforts to make the historical Jesus accessible to young men like himself anticipated his better-known work in the following decade. In 1925 he published *The Man Nobody Knows*, which spent two years on the best-seller list. This was followed by *The Book Nobody Knows* (1926) and *What Can a Man Believe?* (1927). Barton took from the Gospels the familiar stories that had lost their meaning to many through their constant repetition and tried to revitalize the experiences, words, and actions of Jesus. He sought to make Jesus real to a world far different from Palestine of two thousand years earlier. *The Man Nobody Knows* has become one of the artifacts from the 1920s used to condemn the superficiality of American life and culture. How else can one read Barton's assertion that Jesus was "the Founder of Modern Business"? Or that the great parables of the Gospels were the first examples of modern advertising and that the Parable of the Good Samaritan was the greatest advertisement ever written? How else to understand Barton's statement that if Jesus were alive, "He would be a national advertiser today"?

**Reaching Out to Men.** *The Man Nobody Knows* was part of an attempt in the early decades of the twentieth century to bring men back into the churches and reinvigorate their religious commitment. While men filled the pulpits, made up vestries and boards of deacons, and were the delegates to denominational bodies, they were a distinct minority of the membership and an even smaller part of congregations that filled the pews on Sundays. Barton believed that the reason for the lack of commitment of ordinary men to the church was that they had difficulty identifying with the effeminate Jesus as portrayed by religious leaders and women in the nineteenth century. Barton believed that the meek and mild Jesus failed to attract men eager for action who, in the increasingly complicated machine civilization of the twentieth century, needed an example of masculinity as well as religion.

**Barton's Jesus.** Barton's best-seller did not engage in the contemporary debate between the Fundamentalists and modernists, although his casual treatment of some doctrines that were being debated placed him in the modernist camp. Instead, he told the old story of Jesus but stressed his human masculinity. Barton's Jesus was an outdoorsman. He worked with his hands as a carpenter, one of the many things he learned from his father, Joseph. He was physically strong, as seen in his cleansing of the temple. Jesus liked women, and they in turn liked him. He was a sociable man who laughed, ate, drank, and visited with the interesting people of his time and community. Most important, Jesus worked; he was not a man of mere words. He expressed his message in what he did and how he did it, and he acted in the marketplaces of Palestine, where his actions would be reported to others. He was also a man who understood organization. He took twelve ordinary men from ordinary walks of life and created the church, the largest organization in history. Modern men, including middle-class businessmen, should be about their Father's business too, Barton suggested.

**Success.** If the sale of books is a measure of success, then Barton's work achieved success. *The Man Nobody*

*Knows* sold more than 750,000 copies in two years. How successful Barton and his work were in revitalizing faith, bringing people into Christianity, or changing behavior is unknown, although his critics might point to the apparent decline in religious sentiment during the decade. Nonetheless, Barton believed that Jesus was too important to be kept in the churches. While he was not able to follow his father's path into the ministry, he understood how to sell and tried to do that with Jesus.

Sources:

James A. Neuchaterlein, "Bruce Barton and the Business Ethos of the 1920's," *South Atlantic Quarterly*, 76 (Summer 1977);

Leo P. Ribuffo, "Jesus Christ as Business Statesman: Bruce Barton and the Selling of Corporate Capitalism," *American Quarterly*, 33 (Fall 1981).

## JAMES CANNON JR.

## 1864-1944

### BISHOP

**Religious Leader.** After graduating from Randolph-Macon College and the Princeton Theological Seminary, James Cannon Jr. committed himself to advancing the cause of Jesus; the Methodist Episcopal Church, South; and himself. His enemies — and he had many inside and outside his denomination — believed that he actually followed these priorities in reverse order. Shortly after Cannon's ordination he became president of the Blackstone School for Girls, a Methodist school in Virginia, and quickly managed to place it and himself on solid financial footing. The money he saved he invested in the Richmond Virginian, which became a leading weekly Methodist newspaper and his voice to his fellow Methodists. He also served as the head of the Virginia Anti-Saloon League, the most prominent Prohibition organization in the country.

**Bishop Cannon.** Cannon rose quickly in Southern Methodist ranks, in time serving as chair of the Southern Methodist Board of Temperance and Social Service. In 1918 he was elected a bishop of his denomination. From these various positions Cannon was one of the most noted and effective voices for Prohibition. Even though most southern states were already dry, Cannon worked vigorously to secure their ratifications of the Eighteenth Amendment, which went into effect in 1920.

**Prominence.** The 1920s were Bishop Cannon's decade. He seemed to be everywhere, as he became the effective head of the National Anti-Saloon League before and after the death of Philip Scanlon in 1927. From this position Cannon operated in the presidential election of 1928, in which he turned the political skills he had mastered in the politics of Virginia and his denomination to the national level.

**Politics.** Cannon attracted much attention when he organized southern opposition to the presidential race of Alfred E. Smith, the Democratic nominee in 1928. Cannon insisted that he fought against Smith because the New York governor openly advocated modification of Prohibition. Cannon charged that the governor had failed to enforce Prohibition laws in New York and that he would not only allow them to be ignored in the entire nation but would even work for repeal. Evangelical Christians could not tolerate such a betrayal of a reform they had spent so many decades and so much money to achieve. Although Cannon always denied the charge, there was a darker side to his actions, coming from his concern that Smith was a Roman Catholic. Whether Cannon was motivated by anti-Catholic prejudice or not, he certainly was willing to use Southern Protestant fears of Roman Catholicism to bring them to the Republican voting column. In 1928, with funds from the Republican National Committee and the Anti-Saloon League, Cannon called a meeting of anti-Smith southerners in Asheville, North Carolina, to rally the vote against Smith. There are questions about Cannon's actual contributions in the election, but he was highly visible, giving interviews and speeches and campaigning extensively, and many observers accepted his claim to have organized the Upper South for the Republican Party.

**Victory?** But more important than anti-Catholic prejudice in Herbert Hoover's victory that year was national prosperity, Hoover's pledge that with God's help he would end poverty in the country. It is doubtful that any Democrat could have won in 1928, and probably none could have done as well as Smith. But when the results were in, Hoover carried five southern states. Bishop Cannon demanded the credit for the split vote in the South, but he would welcome attention less in the next decade, when he would be the target of blame when questions would be raised about his gambling on the stock market before the crash, his use of campaign funds, and his initial relations with the woman who became his second wife.

Source:

Virginius Dabney, *Dry Messiah: The Life of Bishop Cannon* (New York: Knopf, 1949).

## RUSSELL H. CONWELL

## 1843-1925

### PREACHER

Outstanding Minister. In the year before his death, the Christian Century named Russell H. Conwell one of the twenty-five outstanding preachers in the United States. His death ended a long and colorful life. After serving in the military in the Civil

War and a successful career in law and as a public lecturer, Conwell turned to the ministry. In 1882 he became pastor of Grace Baptist Church in Philadelphia, a floundering congregation with about ninety members. Within a decade the church had more than three thousand members and soon broke ground for a sanctuary with four thousand seats, making it one of the largest churches in America.

**Promoting Growth.** The Baptist Temple of Philadelphia not only had an extensive Sunday program, but Conwell expanded its activities to provide for the secular needs of his parishioners and the surrounding community. In 1884 he began an informal "college" for the young men in the area, a night school that quickly grew into Temple College and then Temple University, with a variety of schools and divisions; he served as the first president. (In 1969 the Conwell School of Theology moved from Temple to Massachusetts and became part of the Gordon-Conwell Theological Seminary.) Conwell also established hospitals in the area. In many ways Conwell's church led the way in the creation of the modern institutional church.

**Speaker.** While Conwell was widely admired for his church work, he was better known for his skills as a public speaker. One of the conditions he made before moving to Philadelphia was to have the freedom to continue his career on the lecture circuit. He averaged 175 lectures a year, earning an estimated $11 million over the course of his career. He gave most of the money to charity, particularly education. Conwell's best-known lecture was "Acres of Diamonds," which alone earned him more than $2 million in his lifetime. This was only one of the many well-known self-help sermons of the late nineteenth century. The point of the lecture-sermon came from a story Conwell said had been given to him by an Arab guide on one of his trips. A farmer dreamed that he discovered great wealth, acres of diamonds. Convinced that the dream was a true vision, he sold his land and wandered the earth. Finally, in despair, the man killed himself. Meanwhile, the land he left was discovered to contain one of the largest diamond concentrations in the world, making the people who bought it rich. The point, Conwell said, was that we should begin our lives, even the search for wealth, right where we are.

**The Pursuit of Wealth.** And Conwell believed that people should seek wealth. As he pointed out, "I have come to tell you . . . you ought to be rich and it is your duty to get rich." He concluded the lecture by saying that "to make money is to preach the gospel." Conwell was careful to distinguish between seeking money for its own sake and seeking wealth to do good. Like other self-help spokesmen at the end of the nineteenth century, he believed in the stewardship of wealth. "The man that worships the dollar instead of the purposes for which it ought to be used, the man who idolizes simply money, the miser that hoards his money in the cellar, or hides it in his stocking, or refuses to invest it where it will do the world

good, that man who hugs the dollar until the eagle squeals has in him the root of all evil." In his life Conwell seemed to personify his own precepts. He earned wealth, gave it away, found the limelight, and he tried to use it to encourage his listeners to turn their lives to good purpose. He was greatly loved and admired.

**Sources:**

Daniel W. Bjork, *The Victorian Flight: Russell H. Conwell and the Crisis of American Individualism* (Washington, D.C.: University Press of America, 1979);

Irvin G. Wylie, *The Self-Made Man in America: The Myth of Rags to Riches* (New Brunswick, N.J.: Rutgers University Press, 1954).

## HARRY EMERSON FOSDICK

### 1878-1969

#### MINISTER

**Modernist Preacher.** Through his collected sermons, his public stands on issues, and his radio services, Harry Emerson Fosdick became not only the best-known preacher of his day but also a representative of the modernist forces that struggled with Fundamentalists during the 1920s.

**Early Career.** In 1919 the dwindling congregations of the First Presbyterian Church in New York City, the University Place Presbyterian Church, and the Madison Square Presbyterian Church agreed to merge to concentrate their combined resources and efforts. Fosdick, a graduate of Colgate College and Union Theological Seminary in New York and already widely known for his sermons, was asked to become the congregation's preaching minster. The fact that he was and would remain a Baptist in this Presbyterian church was considered irrelevant.

**Success and Publicity.** Fosdick's services attracted large crowds, and the experiment seemed a splendid success. In 1922 Fosdick entered the growing war between the increasingly militant Fundamentalists and the modernists. In his sermon "Shall the Fundamentalists Win?" he condemned the exclusionary practices of the Fundamentalists and pleaded for a church where individual beliefs on issues such as the virgin birth of Jesus, the inerrancy of the Scriptures, and the question of the Second Coming of Christ were left to individual interpretation while all Christians worked together for the common good. The sermon attracted extensive publicity, particularly after public-relations man Ivy Lee republished it as "New Knowledge and Christian Faith" and distributed it to the nation's Protestant clergy.

**Contention.** The line between Fundamentalists and modernists was now drawn in the northern Presbyterian Church. Fundamentalists and their conservatives allies, particularly the faculty of the denomination's Princeton

Theological Seminary at Princeton University, responded with outrage. Not only was Fosdick unsound in doctrine, he was an interloper in one of the denomination's leading congregations. For the next two years the issue of Fosdick and his place in the denomination was fought at meetings of the various governing bodies of the Presbyterian Church, including the annual meetings of the General Assembly, the church's governing body. Here Fosdick's rejection of the Five Points of Fundamentalist belief was condemned by a large minority of the delegates, but church governance would not allow the annual body to remove him from his congregation.

**Resignation.** The New York Presbytery tried to protect Fosdick, as did First Presbyterian Church, which adamantly refused his offer to resign. In 1925 a seeming compromise was reached: the New York Presbytery proposed that Fosdick join the denomination and regularize his relationship with the church and his congregation. On the surface this would resolve the issue of Fosdick's denominational loyalties; but as a Presbyterian, he would also be subject to denominational control, and some sort of heresy trial was likely if he accepted that route. Fosdick concluded that the Fundamentalists would eventually expel him, and he resigned from First Presbyterian in March 1925.

**Moving On.** Fosdick was more than a symbol — he was a brilliant preacher. As the controversy whirled, a new pulpit was found for him. He was offered the ministry of the Park Avenue Baptist Church, also in New York City, a congregation that included some of the nation's leading businessmen, including John D. Rockefeller Jr. The congregation had completed an expensive new sanctuary in 1922. In negotiations with the directors of the church, Fosdick insisted that the church modify its requirement that only those who had been baptized by immersion be accepted for membership, a tenet that had long been a key principle of Baptists. Park Avenue Baptist agreed to open admission, and the offer was sweetened when Rockefeller offered to provide much of the funding for a sanctuary in Morningside Heights, outside the silk-stocking district of the city, to create a church inclusive in class as well as in doctrine.

**Becoming Established.** Fosdick later recalled that in his talks with Rockefeller in regard to the move, he speculated about the effects of his relationship with one of the world's richest men. Rockefeller responded, "Do you think more people will criticize you on account of my wealth, than will criticize me on account of your theology?" The agreement to create an interdenominational Protestant church was made. The building on Park Avenue was sold, and the money from the sale, combined with a generous gift from Rockefeller, led to the construction of the great Riverside Church in Morningside Heights in New York. The new sanctuary was officially opened in 1930 and remained Fosdick's home and the location of the studio for his popular radio services until his retirement.

Sources:

Harry Emerson Fosdick, *The Living of These Days* (New York: Harper & Row, 1956);

Robert Moats Miller, *Harry Emerson Fosdick: Preacher, Pastor, Prophet* (New York: Oxford University Press, 1985).

## AIMEE SEMPLE McPHERSON

### 1890-1944

#### PREACHER

**Early Life.** Sister Aimee, as the followers of Aimee Semple McPherson called her, was one of the few women in the United States to form her own denomination — although that was in the process of what she considered her true calling, saving souls. Born Beth Kennedy in Canada into a family dominated by her mother's commitment to the Salvation Army, in 1907 Aimee, as she by then called herself, attended a Pentecostal tent meeting and was converted. She soon married revivalist Robert Semple and went on the revival trail with him. While she was never ordained, she took naturally to preaching, which was sufficient for her and those she brought to the altar. In 1910 the couple went into the missionary field in China, where her daughter was born and her husband died.

**Finding a Place.** Distraught, the young widow returned to the United States and two years later married Harold S. McPherson. Family life was not enough to keep Sister Aimee from the revival circuit, and she left her husband to return to saving souls. (He divorced her in the 1920s on grounds of desertion.) For several years, with her mother serving as manager of the ministry, Sister Aimee wandered the country until she arrived in Los Angeles in 1918 and found the permanent site of her ministry and church.

**Local Fame.** McPherson's message was salvation, but she recognized the need to attract attention in order to present her message. By the time she reached Los Angeles she had developed the flamboyant style that attracted not only attention but notoriety. In her new setting the crowds grew, as did the converts, and McPherson put down roots, building a stunning pie-shaped sanctuary for her Full Square Gospel Church, as she called it. The Angelus Temple opened in 1923, and the crowds poured in, to be entertained as much by McPherson's show-business antics as by her sermons of hope. In 1924 she opened her own radio station, KFSG (the letters stood for Kall Full Square Gospel), the first full-time religious radio station. Sister Aimee became locally famous.

**Gossip.** While McPherson could dress and look like an angel in her pulpit, and while her resonant voice caressed her followers with her words of eternal hope, she was stubborn, hardheaded, and impulsive in private life.

In the middle of the decade she paid little attention to the gossip that linked her to her station's former radio engineer.

**A Colorful Story.** McPherson liked to swim for relaxation. One May evening in 1926 she went to Ocean Park with her secretary, and while the secretary stayed on shore McPherson took her customary swim out beyond the breakers. She failed to swim back and had apparently disappeared. The distraught secretary called McPherson's mother, and a full-scale search was organized. Hundreds of the members of the Angelus Temple scoured the beaches looking for her body. One overwrought follower committed suicide in despair. The body was not found. McPherson's mother assumed her daughter dead or perhaps raised directly up to heaven in advance of her death. The national press had a splendid time with the mysterious disappearance of such a colorful character, and, as stories about the disappearance continued to sell papers, rumors about sightings of McPherson circulated. There was even speculation that she was with the radio engineer, whose wife had returned to Australia, claiming McPherson had taken up with her husband. Nearly six weeks after the disappearance, a letter arrived at the Angelus Temple demanding $500,000 in ransom for McPherson's return. If the money were not handed over, the letter said, she would be sold into white slavery in Mexico. Her mother, who had given her up for dead, was stunned. She was even more stunned when a few days later McPherson called from Douglas, Arizona, saying that she had finally managed to escape from her kidnappers.

**McPherson's Story.** By the time McPherson's mother arrived in Douglas, Sister Aimee was talking to the press, detailing the story that she would always repeat. According to McPherson, while she was at the beach a couple had come up to her asking her to come to their car to see and possibly heal their sick child. At the automobile, she said, she was chloroformed, restrained, and held hostage by two men and a woman. She was tortured to make her cooperate with her kidnappers and eventually taken to an adobe shack in Mexico. One day, when all of her captors were out of the house, McPherson cut her ropes, escaped through a window, and crawled and staggered through the desert until she was found and taken to Douglas.

**Triumphal Entry.** Sister Aimee returned to Los Angeles to a triumphal welcome from her followers. The press and the police were less credulous. Stories were published that a woman who looked like McPherson had spent ten days in the resort town of Carmel, California, with McPherson's former radio engineer. The press also wondered over McPherson's failure to show any evidence of her alleged mistreatment or of the ordeal of staggering through the desert for hours. In a matter of weeks a grand jury was convened, and McPherson and her mother were forced to testify. Both were bound over, and after six weeks of considerable publicity they were charged with a variety of crimes, including a conspiracy to manufacture evidence.

**Fame.** The case came to nothing, and McPherson was now famous. Leaving the Angelus Temple to her mother, she went on an extended revival tour of the East. She was now a national celebrity, and crowds poured out to see her. She began to dress fashionably and even bobbed the luxuriant hair that had captivated the grand jury when she let it down for them during the hearings. In New York City she made a highly publicized visit to Texas Guinin, a speakeasy, and even addressed the revelers there. Reporters always noted her doings; Sister Aimee was good copy and was always willing to talk. When asked about the disappearance and kidnapping, her response was a smiling "That's my story and I'm sticking to it."

**Later Ministry.** McPherson returned to Los Angeles and continued her ministry. Although she had no original intention to begin a new denomination, her central church developed new congregations in the spreading Pentecostal movement. She remained a celebrity, and crowds continued to pack her temple into the next decade. Some came to watch and were converted — which was what she intended.

Sources:

Edith Blumhofer, *Aimee Semple McPherson: Everybody's Sister* (Grand Rapids, Mich.: Eerdmans, 1993);

Daniel M. Epstein, *Sister Aimee: The Life of Aimee Semple McPherson* (New York: Harcourt Brace Jovanovich, 1993);

Amiee Semple McPherson, *The Story of My Life*, edited by Raymond W. Becker (Hollywood, Cal.: International Correspondence Publishers, 1951).

# J. FRANK NORRIS

## 1877-1952

### MINISTER

**Flamboyant Fundamentalist.** Pastor of the First Baptist Church in Fort Worth, Texas, J. Frank Norris was one of the most flamboyant figures in the Southern Baptist Convention until he was forced from the denomination. Sensation naturally followed Norris. Once he was charged with burning his own church; on another occasion he was declared not guilty on grounds of self-defense for killing one of the many men he offended. A strident voice in Fundamentalist circles, he was widely loved and admired by those who shared his views and were swayed by his sermons.

**Early Life and Career.** Norris was born in rural Alabama and moved with his family to Texas as a child. He experienced an early conversion, and after graduating from Baylor University and the Southern Baptist Seminary in Louisville, Kentucky, he took a church in Dallas, Texas, which he quickly developed into one of the largest congregations in the state. In 1909 he became pastor of the First Baptist Church in Fort Worth, where he spent the rest of his career, although he also assumed the pastorate of Temple Baptist Church in Detroit in the 1930s, somehow managing to run both churches at the same time.

**Provocative Preacher.** Norris was acknowledged as one of the greatest preachers of his time. He devoted his preaching to winning souls and to blasting his enemies, he accumulated a multitude of both. By 1926 his Sunday school boasted more than five thousand members, and some Sundays more than ten thousand people would attend his Fort Worth church. It was definitely Norris's church: he ran it as he saw fit and associated with other Southern Baptists as he saw fit, which was from an attack position.

**Controversy in the Convention.** In 1919 Norris became convinced that some of the faculty at Baylor were teaching evolution, and he made such charges in his newspaper, the *Fence Rail* (after 1927 the *Fundamentalist*). This attack offended many alumni and supporters of the university. They were further offended by his refusal to contribute money from his congregation to the Southern Baptist Convention and its agencies. The convention was based on the agreement of individual congregations to contribute to a central set of agencies, most of them involved with domestic and foreign missions run by the annual convention. In 1923 the Texas Baptist Convention refused to accept a delegate from First Baptist Church of Fort Worth and the following year officially expelled Norris and his congregation, effectively severing his and the church's ties with the Southern Baptist Convention. Nevertheless, the faculty of Baylor was purged, and Norris was pleased with his actions.

**Efforts at Organization.** Although Norris was instinctively an independent, in 1923 he helped organize the Fundamentalists' Baptist Bible Union, and after the collapse of that organization in 1932 he cooperated with the World's Christian Fundamentals Association, but neither of these organizations was large or had real influence.

**Scandal.** Norris had a penchant for scandal. When his church burned in 1912, he was charged with, but not convicted for, arson. In 1926 he became involved in another scandal when he shot and killed an enemy in his church office. Norris had been conducting a running battle with the Roman Catholic mayor of Fort Worth over Norris's charges that the mayor had illegally favored a Catholic organization. An ally of the mayor, a wealthy lumberman, called to say that he was coming to Norris's study one Saturday afternoon. Norris insisted that he had been threatened on the telephone and, fearing for his life, defended himself by killing his visitor. He was charged with murder. His devoted congregation quickly raised funds for his defense, at one time collecting $16,000 in cash in a washtub. Norris was acquitted on the first ballot by the jury, who agreed that it really was a case of self-defense.

**Fiery Personality.** By the end of the 1920s Norris was one of the best known and most outspoken of the nation's Fundamentalists. He believed the mission of the church was simple and clearly defined: to preach Christ and Him crucified. The social issues that preoccupied others were irrelevant to Norris, whose goal was to save as many souls as possible. While his commitment was clear, his personality was fiery. It seemed that when no enemies were available Norris would make some. For his followers he represented the old-time religion; for his many enemies he besmirched his church, religion, and region.

Sources:

Norman Anderson, "The Shooting Parson of Texas," *New Republic*, 48 (1 September 1926): 35–37;

George W. Dollar, *A History of Fundamentalism in America* (Greenville, S.C.: Bob Jones University Press, 1973).

## WILLIAM BELL RILEY

### 1861-1947

#### MINISTER

**Early Ministry.** William Bell Riley was educated at Hanover College in Indiana and then studied at the Southern Baptist Seminary in Louisville, Kentucky. After serving a series of small churches, he became pastor of the First Baptist Church of Minneapolis in 1897, which he quickly developed into one of the largest congregations in the country and a major force in the struggle for Fundamentalism. In 1902 he founded the Northwestern Bible and Missionary Training School, which was later expanded with the addition of a seminary and then a college and now is called the Northwestern Schools.

**Fundamentalism.** Riley was one of most successful proponents to a general audience of the imminent return of Christ, the premillennialist doctrine that became one of the principles of Fundamentalism in the late nineteenth century. But Riley led the struggle with modernism in his own Northern Baptist Convention and in Protestant circles less over the doctrine of premillennialism than over the inerrancy of the Bible. He was convinced that the perceived drift from the true foundations of Christianity came from the scholarly examination of the Bible in theological schools — examinations that regarded the Bible as a human document that could be studied like any other human document, with a belief that its value lies in its ability to inspire. His response was straightforward: "(1) the Bible was finished in heaven and handed down, (2) the King James Version was absolutely inerrant, and (3) its literal acceptance was alone correct."

**Fighting Modernism.** In 1919 Riley organized and led the World's Christian Fundamentals Association. The organization was committed to battling modernists wherever they might be but soon fixed on the issue of evolution for battle. It sought to prohibit the teaching of the theory in public schools. In 1925 Tennessee passed such a law, leading to the Scopes "Monkey" Trial in Dayton, which subjected Fundamentalists to the ridicule of their many enemies in religious and secular circles.

**Other Efforts.** Riley directed much of his energy to the struggle with modernists in the Northern Baptist Convention, although his congregation never severed its ties with the denomination. In 1923 he joined J. Frank Norris to form the Baptist Bible Union, which attempted to purge the Baptist conventions of their perceived weaknesses and to coordinate members' contributions into activities at home and abroad that met their theological standards. The Baptist Bible Union collapsed not long after taking over Des Moines University in Iowa and discovering that it could not meet the financial commitments that had been made. The decade ended on a sour note for Riley, who turned his attention back to his church and schools in Minneapolis.

Sources:

George W. Dollar, *A History of Fundamentalism in America* (Greenville, S.C.: Bob Jones University Press, 1973);

"Faith of the Fundamentalists," *Current History*, 26 (19 June 1927): 26;

"Portrait of William Bell Riley," *Literary Digest*, 76 (13 January 1923): 31.

# JOHN A. RYAN

## 1865-1945

### PRIEST

**American Priest.** Father John A. Ryan was America's best-known liberal Catholic cleric in the 1920s. The son of Irish immigrants, he grew up in Minnesota and was deeply affected by the attempts of Archbishop John Ireland of Saint Paul to acculturate the Roman Catholic Church to America without compromising its essential beliefs and structures. Father Ryan was also touched by the message to the laboring classes expressed in Pope Leo XIII's *Rerum Novarum 1891; Of New Things*, which warned of the dangers of socialism but also condemned the excesses of capitalism.

**Academic Career.** Ryan earned a Ph.D. at the Catholic University. His dissertation, published in 1906 as *The Living Wage*, presented his belief that American capitalism could and should be reformed according to Christian principles. Christianity offered more hope to the workingman, he said, than any form of socialism. It also offered a better life for Christian capitalists. In 1915 Father Ryan returned to the Catholic University, where he developed a distinguished teaching career.

**Social Action.** When the United States entered World War I in 1917, Father Ryan worked closely with the National Catholic Warfare Conference, a national agency that coordinated the charitable activities of the independent bishoprics. When the Vatican finally agreed to allow the conference to reorganize as the permanent National Catholic Welfare Conference, the first national structure for the American Roman Catholic Church, Ryan was named head of the social action department. From this position he called the attention of the church, its parishioners, and the American public to problems in a society dominated by unrestrained capitalism. The clearest expression of his developing views came with the publication of *Social Reconstruction* in 1920.

**On Catholicism in America.** While Father Ryan's economic and social views placed him at the left of the political and social spectrum, he also aroused Protestants, many of whom had long feared and opposed the Roman Catholic Church, believing that it stifled religious liberty in nations where it was dominant. In 1922 Ryan published with Moorhouse F. X. Millar *The State and the Church*, which spelled out the Roman Catholic Church's traditional position that where it had the ability and consequent responsibility, it should restrict the teaching and preaching of heresy and misguided (i.e., non-Catholic) forms of Christianity. Ryan always insisted that such a situation did not obtain in the United States. Too many religious groups already existed for anyone to hope for a totally Catholic nation, he said, adding that he believed religious liberty was best for America.

**Politics.** Nevertheless, his outspoken views haunted the presidential campaign of Roman Catholic candidate Alfred E. Smith in 1928. Smith's opponents used Father Ryan's high visibility in the campaign and his well-publicized views on church-state relations outside the United States to confirm old fears of American Protestants. Few Protestants who knew Father Ryan believed the widespread rumors that if Smith were elected, one of the first actions of the new Catholic president would be to move the Vatican to the United States. Nor could a president repeal Prohibition by himself or close the public schools, but even relatively open-minded Protestants were troubled by Ryan's position and its implications if Smith should be elected. Even a liberal such as Ryan seemed to support the sort of religious intolerance that Protestants saw in nations dominated by the Roman Catholic Church, such as Spain. In some ways his advanced reputation reinforced Protestant fears of Catholic actions.

**Disappointment.** Ryan was deeply disappointed with the failure of the Smith campaign and believed that anti-Catholic prejudice was a major cause, ignoring the Republican majority among the general public and the widespread prosperity of the decade. Probably no Democrat could have been elected in 1928, but the openly anti-Catholic sentiment, not only among the ignorant but also among intellectuals, was damaging to the Catholic community.

Source:

Robert D. Cross, *The Emerging of Liberal Catholicism in America* (Cambridge, Mass.: Harvard University Press, 1958).

# JOHN ROACH STRATON

## 1874-1929

### MINISTER

**Major Fundamentalists.** John Roach Straton was born into a Baptist preacher's home and early in his life dedicated himself to the ministry. He attended Mercer University and the Southern Baptist Theological Seminary but did not earn any degrees. After serving a series of churches in the South, in 1918 he was called to Calvary Baptist Church in New York City, where he became a leading public figure in city life and a major force in the Fundamentalist struggles of the 1920s.

**Public Figure.** Straton quickly became a public figure in New York with his attacks on vice and corruption, which he charged made the city a modern Babylon suitable for God's wrath. In 1920 he singled out the Broadway play *Aphrodite* as a target, charging that it marked a new low in morality and a "degrading bondage to Mammon." He was disgusted, he said, by this "nightmare of nude men and women slobbering over each other, lolling on couches, and dancing together in feigned drunken revelry."

**The Man Who Fought Broadway.** Straton continued his attacks on the theater through out the decade, engaging in a series of public debates with defenders of Broadway. He assumed he was always the winner. By 1924 his church bulletin was listing him as the "Man Who Fights Broadway," calling him "a crusader, a two-fisted fighting man of God, always the defendant at the bulwarks of Christianity" who "fights with both hands with unmitigated fervor." In the mid 1920s he conducted tours of cabarets where the "licentious" dancing sometimes led to arrests. He was one of the prototypes for Sinclair Lewis's publicity-seeking preacher Elmer Gantry.

**Fundamentalist Battles.** Straton was a major force among Fundamentalists during the decade, challenging the popular assumption then and later that the movement was essentially rural and specifically southern. He was particularly offended by Harry Emerson Fosdick's 1922 sermon "Shall the Fundamentalists Win?" He answered the sermon with his own "Shall the Funny Monkeyists Win?" When Fosdick, a Baptist serving in the First Presbyterian Church of New York City, left that congregation to assume the pastorate of the new sanctuary of the Park Avenue Baptist Church, Straton was incensed. He became even more furious when that congregation accepted Fosdick's demand that the congregation accept all confessed Christians without requiring total immersion for membership. For Straton, Fosdick and his congregation had abandoned Baptist as well as Christian principles.

**Attacking Liberalism.** Straton was an outspoken proponent of Fundamentalism in the Northern Baptist Convention, protesting from the floor at the convention's 1923 meeting a speaker he thought too weak in essential beliefs. He attacked the most liberal seminaries and theological schools, charging that they were teaching their students the false tenets of German philosophy and theology that he claimed had led to the outrages of World War I, adding that their graduates were weakening the faith of their parishioners.

**Politics.** In 1928 Straton was an outspoken opponent of Alfred E. Smith's presidential candidacy. He focused his opposition on Smith's ties with the Democratic machine of Tammany Hall and his anti-Prohibition stance, but an underlying issue was Smith's Roman Catholic faith. Like most Protestants in the decade, Straton was part of a long Protestant mistrust of the Roman Catholic Church.

**Depression.** At the end of the decade Straton attracted widespread attention when he announced that his congregation had agreed to raze their structure and build a hotel to share the site with the church. He was convinced that the income from the hotel on its valuable piece of property on West Fifty-seventh Street would later support the congregation and its activities. However, the Salisbury Hotel opened just as the great stock-market crash ended the hectic prosperity of the 1920s, leaving the church with a staggering debt of more than $2 million. Straton himself was not around to pay off the sum. He died unexpectedly on 29 October 1929, the day of the worst plunge of the stock market, and did not see the effects of the Depression that followed.

Sources:

George W. Dollar, *A History of Fundamentalism in America* (Greenville, S.C.: Bob Jones University Press, 1973);

Samuel Walker, "The Fundamentalist Pope," *American Mercury*, 8 ( July 1926): 257–265.

# WILLIAM "BILLY" SUNDAY

## 1862-1935

### EVANGELIST

**The Best-Known Evangelist in America.** Billy Sunday entered the 1920s as the best-known revivalist in America. His great campaign in New York City in 1917 coincided with America's entry into the Great War, and in his sermons Sunday managed to fuse Christianity and American patriotism to the delight of millions. His success was even greater when he was able to celebrate the death of his longtime enemy, "John Barleycorn," with the adoption of Prohibition. He even attained some wealth. In 1920 Dun and Bradstreet estimated his worth at $1.4 million.

**Decline.** However, the 1920s were not pleasant for Sunday and his wife. While he continued to attract large audiences and led thousands to hit the "sawdust trail" that led to the altars of the tabernacles he had put up for his revivals, these special buildings no longer went up in the largest cities of the North, and he found himself working medium-sized cities in the South and Midwest.

**Scandals.** He also faced a series of scandals that raised questions about his ethics and abilities. He was sued by men who claimed they had ghostwritten some of his books and had not been properly paid. Questions were raised about his ministry's finances, which were skillfully handled by his wife. Sunday's expensive organization depended on love offerings, but questions were raised as to whether he played fair with the local groups that raised the initial funds for his revivals and bore much of the cost. These financial questions became more pointed as Sunday and his wife began to live more lavishly and as Mrs. Sunday's clothes began to look like those of the society matrons who had long been targets of her husband's scorn. In addition, his son abandoned his wife for another woman and began to frequent speakeasies.

**Problems with Prohibition.** Finally there was the issue of Prohibition itself. Fighting "demon rum" had long been one of Sunday's main preoccupations, but alcohol seemed to be everywhere as the Eighteenth Amendment failed to be enforced and supported. By the end of the 1920s many Christians had begun to question the methods used to advance Prohibition, the effectiveness of its enforcement, and its relationship to the growing disdain for the law that seemed to have swept the nation. For many what had seemed a great victory had began to look like a mistake. Perhaps Sunday himself, some believed, was responsible for some of these problems through his excessive demands for a totally dry America.

**Left on the Sidelines.** Sunday's sermons had long been criticized by the refined, who accused him of vulgarity and crudeness. A former baseball player, Sunday did not hide that he was poorly educated. His dramatic, flamboyant sermons were given in the language of his audience. He believed that too many ministers spoke in language their listeners could not understand and so the Word failed to be heard. If volume and slang were enough, Sunday was the answer. But he was no longer the answer for many. His strident, simplistic approach, his focus on alcohol and fast living, his alliance with the Fundamentalists, and his opposition to Alfred E. Smith all made him seem out of date at best, if not reactionary. For urban sophisticates in and out of the church, Billy Sunday was the link between all they disliked about the past and much of what they wanted to forget. That he was still popular in what they considered the more benighted regions of the nation only confirmed, all evidence to the contrary, that conservative, even Fundamentalist, Protestantism had no connection with them and no place in modern American life. His time was past.

Sources:
Lyle W. Dorset, *Billy Sunday and the Redemption of Urban America* (Grand Rapids, Mich.: Eerdmans, 1990);

William G. McLoughlin, *Billy Sunday Was His Real Name* (Chicago: University of Chicago Press, 1955);

*Modern Revivalism: Charles Grandison Finney to Billy Graham* (New York: Ronald Press, 1959).

# PEOPLE IN THE NEWS

In November 1920 Secretary of War **Newton D. Baker** signed prison-release authorizations for thirty-three conscientious objectors who had refused to comply with conscription or to give alternative service during World War I. They based their stand on their Christian conviction that cooperation with any war effort and its destruction of life was wrong. Their release triggered loud protests from the American Legion and other patriotic groups.

In June 1929 **Reverend William St. John Blackshear,** the Texas-born rector of St. Matthew's Protestant Episcopal Church in Brooklyn, read a statement in which he noted that there were Episcopal churches for African Americans nearby and that therefore he discouraged "members of that race" from attending his church. The five African American members of St. Matthews were deeply upset, and several stopped attending the church. When the incident attracted protests from the

National Association for the Advancement of Colored People (NAACP), Reverend Blackshear said he was surprised at the response.

In June 1921 **Charles Carver,** rector of Christ Episcopal Church in New Haven, Connecticut, played the leading role in nine performances of *The Divorce Question* at the Hyperion Theater. The former actor said he hoped "to bring to the attention of the people of New Haven the great divorce evil."

In February 1924, when **W. S. Crawford,** pastor of the Boulevard Methodist Episcopal Church in Binghamton, New York, preached a sermon condemning divorce, most of the church choir went on strike. Nearly half of its thirty members were divorced. Most of the singers returned after Reverend Crawford expressed his regrets, but the choirmaster, who was divorced and married to a divorcée, never came back.

In March 1929 theatrical producer **Abraham Lincoln Erlanger** purchased Rabbi Jacob ben Asher's *Arba'ah Turim* (circa 1490; *Code of the Jews*) for an undisclosed price. He donated this first printed account of Orthodox life, published some thirty years after the Gutenberg Bible, to the Jewish Theological Seminary in New York City.

In 1922 **Father Edward Joseph Flanagan** incorporated his Home for Homeless Boys outside Omaha, Nebraska, as a municipality, calling it Boys Town. Father Flanagan's successful work seemed to justify his often-quoted remark, "There's no such thing as a bad boy."

In 1923 **Edgar Johnson Goodspeed** published *The New Testament: An American Translation,* his translation from the original Greek into American English. With the aid of J. M. P. Smith he finished *The Complete Bible: An American Translation* in 1939.

In December 1929 **Rev. Adelbert J. Helm** resigned as pastor of Bethel Evangelical Church in Detroit after the church council refused membership to an African American candidate.

In June 1929 the **Very Reverend Dr. Herbert Lansdowne Johnson,** dean of St. Paul's Protestant Episcopal Cathedral in Detroit, resigned after he upset his parish by complaining that he could not freely voice his views on Prohibition because six of the nine members of the cathedral vestry kept liquor cellars.

In 1924 **William Gibbs McAdoo,** former secretary of the treasury, responded to Ku Klux Klan charges that the 1917 printing of the dollar bill included Roman Catholic propaganda — such as images of the Pope and a rosary — by affirming that the 1917 printing came from plates adopted during the Lincoln administration in the 1860s.

In June 1923 **William McLeod,** governor of South Carolina, issued a call for a day of prayer to deliver the state's cotton crop from the boll weevil. He also made arrangements for the aerial spraying of pesticides.

In 1923 **J. Gresham Machen,** a professor at the Princeton Theological Seminary, entered the struggle between the Fundamentalists and modernists when he published *Christianity and Liberalism,* one of the most intellectual defenses of the Fundamentalist position. While he disliked the personalities of those who led the Fundamentalist crusade, Machen believed their views were close to biblical truth. He charged that liberals were not true Christians because they had departed from this ideal and therefore should leave the true Christian churches. Bitterly defending his position, he was forced out of Princeton Theological Seminary in 1929, when it was reorganized. He then established the Westminster Seminary outside Philadelphia to continue preaching his conservative views.

In 1925 the **Right Reverend John Gardner Murray,** Protestant Episcopal bishop of Maryland, became the first elected presiding bishop of his church when the House of Clerical and Lay Deputies of the triennial convention approved his election by the House of Bishops.

In 1924 **Arthur "Golden Rule" Nash** distributed the stock of his A. Nash Tailoring Company to his employees, arranging for the eventual transfer of ownership to them. Strongly affected in his early years by membership in the Seventh Day Adventist Church, Nash said he feared becoming a millionaire and would feel like a criminal if he took the profits of a business based on the labor of others.

In October 1922 **Graham Patterson,** publisher of *The Christian Herald,* announced the creation of the Christian Herald Motion Picture Bureau. The new syndicate would distribute its movies to churches and schools in an effort to present "clean pictures for clean people."

In February 1926 **Dr. A. S. W. Rosenbach** purchased the Melk edition of the Gutenberg Bible — one of the forty-five known copies of the work — for an auction price of $106,000 (the equivalent of more than a million in 1995 dollars). Dr. Rosenbach had bought his first Gutenberg Bible in 1923 for $43,350.

In the summer of 1925 **Mrs. John Seebach** disturbed the the small congregation of the Lutheran Memorial Church in western Philadelphia, Pennsylvania, when she took her husband's pulpit while he was vacationing in Europe. Church members had long speculated that she wrote her husband's sermons. Some women in the church protested to the presiding bishop of the United Lutheran Church, who noted that a person did not have to be ordained to preach and agreed with Mrs. Seebach's argument that she was only preaching, not performing full pastoral duties.

On 12 October 1928 **Augusta E. Stetson,** who had established the first Christian Science Church in New York City, surprised many — including herself — when she died. Rumored to be the successor to Mary Baker

Eddy, the founder of Christian Science, Mrs. Stetson claimed until her last months that she was immortal.

In 1922 **Rev. Boyd Vincent**, Protestant Episcopal bishop of Michigan, released the results of a three-year study on the role of religion in matters of health. The commission affirmed that "God has infinite blessings of power in store for those who seek them by prayer, communion, and active trust."

# DEATHS

---

**Lyman Abbott**, 87?, former pastor of the Plymouth Church in Brooklyn and editor of *The Independent*, 22 October 1922.

**Robert Case Beebe**, 72, founder and director of a medical mission and hospital in Nanking who later served as executive secretary of the China Medical Missionary Association, 13 March 1928.

**Antoinette Brown Blackwell**, 96?, suffragette and one of the first women to pastor a church in America, though never ordained, 2 November 1921.

**Olympia Brown**, 91, the first woman ordained by a major denomination when the Universalist Church gave her a pastorate in 1863, 23 October 1926.

**Francis E. Symmes Clark**, 75, Congregationalist minister who founded the youth group Christian Endeavor, which became the largest interdenominational youth group in the world and generated a variety of denominational imitations, 26 May 1927.

**H. N. Couden**, 79, chaplain of the U.S. House of Representatives, 1895–1921, 22 August 1922.

**Frank Crane**, 67, Methodist Episcopal clergyman for twenty-five before becoming a journalist who wrote brief essays focusing upon the brighter aspects of life, 6 November 1928.

**Churchill Hunter Cutting**, 83, president emeritus of the American Bible Society, 23 April 1924.

**E. M. Deems**, 77, chaplain of Sailors' Sung Harbor, a mission to sailors on Staten Island, 7 August 1929.

**M. K. "Mother" Edwards**, 98, missionary to the Zulu since 1869, 24 September 1927.

**Mary Hannah Fulton**, 73, one of the early graduates of the Women's Medical College of Pennsylvania, in 1884 sent by the Presbyterian Board of Foreign Missions to southern China, 7 January 1927.

**Cardinal James Gibbons**, 87?, second American cardinal, founder and first chancellor of the Catholic University in Washington, D.C., 24 March 1921.

**John F. Goucher**, 79, Methodist Episcopal minister who founded the Woman's College of Baltimore, later Goucher College, in 1889 and served as its president until 1908, 19 July 1922.

**John G. Hallimond**, 67, head of the Bowery Mission for twenty-five years, 21 November 1924.

**G. C. Houghton**, 71, rector of the "Little Church Around the Corner," the Protestant Episcopal Church of the Transfiguration, celebrated for its connection with Broadway, 17 April 1923.

**Alvah Hovey**, 92, founder of the Women's American Baptist Missionary Society, one of the largest of the women's missionary organizations, 7 November 1923.

**Solomon E. Jaffe**, 66, chief rabbi of the Orthodox synagogues of greater New York, 15 November 1923.

**Ellen Toy Knowles**, 94, one of the founders of the Women's Christian Temperance Union (WCTU), 10 November 1929.

**Joseph Krauskopf**, 65, immigrant from Germany who became one of the leading Reform rabbis in the nation; founded the National Farm School at Doylestown, Pennsylvania; and was a leading promoter of the Jewish Publication Society of America, 12 June 1923.

**Robert Stuart MacArthur**, 82, founder and pastor of Calvary Baptist Church in New York City, president of the Baptist World Alliance, 23 February 1923.

**Newton Mann**, 91, Unitarian minister said to have been the first clergyman in the United States to expound the doctrine of evolution from the pulpit, 25 July 1926.

D. N. McKee, former head of the Mother Church, First Church of Christ, Scientist, in Boston, 11 August 1929.

Richard Carey Morse, 86, active in the expansion of the Young Men's Christian Association (YMCA), 26 December 1926.

Edgar Page, 85, prolific writer of gospel hymns, including "Beulah Land" and "Trusting Jesus," 8 January 1923.

Sigmund Rosenbaum, 76, founder of the International Order of B'nai B'rith, 16 February 1920.

Philip Scanlon, 57, head of the Board of Temperance and Moral Welfare of the Presbyterian Church for twenty years and president of the National Temperance Society and the Anti-Saloon League, 21 March 1927.

Augusta E. Stetson, 86?, founder of the first Christian Science Church in New York City, 12 October 1928.

John Roach Straton, 55?, Fundamentalist minister, 29 October 1929;

John Heyl Vincent, 92, editor of the *Sunday School Journal*, which helped to standardize Sunday school curricula, and founder of the Chautauqua self-education movement, 9 May 1920.

John Wanamaker, 84, the first full-time secretary of the YMCA in the United States, 1857–1861, Philadelphia department store magnate, supporter of evangelism, 12 December 1922.

# PUBLICATIONS

---

Harry E. Banner, *Twilight of Christianity* (New York: Smith, 1929);

Bruce Barton, *The Book Nobody Knows* (Indianapolis: Bobbs-Merrill, 1926);

Barton, *The Man Nobody Knows* (Indianapolis: Bobbs-Merrill, 1925);

Barton, *What Can a Man Believe?* (Indianapolis: Bobbs-Merrill, 1927);

William Jennings Bryan, *The Bible and Its Enemies In His Image* (New York: Revell, 1922);

Shirley Jackson Case, *Jesus: A New Biography* (Chicago: University of Chicago Press, 1928);

Henry Sloane Coffin, *A More Christian Industrial Order* (New York: Macmillan, 1920);

Lloyd C. Douglas, *The Magnificent Obession* (New York: Grosset & Dunlap, 1929);

Will Durant, *The Story of Philosophy* (New York: Simon & Schuster, 1926);

Harry Emerson Fosdick, *Adventurous Religion and Other Essays* (New York: Harper, 1926);

Fosdick, *Christianity and Progress* (New York: Revell, 1922);

Fosdick, *The Modern Use of the Bible* (New York: Macmillan, 1924);

Fosdick, *Religion's Debt to Science* (Chicago: American Institute of Sacred Literature, 1928);

James George Frazer, *Folk-lore in the Old Testament: Studies in Comparative Religion, Legend and Law* (New York: Macmillan, 1923);

Frazer, *The Golden Bough: A Study in Magic and Religion* (New York: Macmillan, 1922);

Edgar Johnson Goodspeed, trans., *The New Testament: An American Translation* (Chicago: University of Chicago Press, 1923);

Sinclair Lewis, *Elmer Gantry* (New York: Harcourt, Brace, 1927);

Robert S. Lynd and Helen Merrell Lynd, *Middletown: A Study in American Culture* (New York: Harcourt, Brace, 1929);

J. Gresham Machen, *Christianity and Liberalism* (New York: Macmillan, 1923);

Shailer Mathews, *The Contributions of Science to Religion* (New York: Appleton, 1924);

Mathews, *The Faith of Modernism* (New York: Macmillan, 1924);

Alfred McCann, *God — Or Gorilla?* (New York: Devin Adair, 1922);

H. Richard Niebuhr, *The Social Sources of Denominationalism* (New York: Holt, 1929);

Marshall Olds, *Analysis of the Interchurch World Movement Report on the Steel Strike* (New York & London: Putnam, 1923);

Henry Fairfield Osborn, *Purposive Evolution: The Link Between Science and Religion* (New York: Holt, 1926);

Giovanni Papini, *Life of Christ,* translated by Dorothy Canfield Fisher (New York: Harcourt, Brace, 1923);

James Harvey Robinson, *The Mind in the Making: The Relation of Intelligence to Social Reform* (New York & London: Harper, 1921);

John A. Ryan and Moorhouse F. X. Millar, *The State and the Church* (New York: Macmillan, 1922);

John T. Scopes, *The World's Most Famous Court Trial* (Cincinnati: National, 1925);

Robert E. Speer, *Race and Race Relations, A Christian View of Human Contacts* (New York: Revell, 1924);

Charles Stelzle, *A Son of the Bowery: The Life Story of an East Side American* (New York: Doran, 1926);

John Roach Straton, *Fighting the Devil in Modern Babylon* (Boston: Stratford, 1929);

Straton, *The Menace of Immorality in Church and State* (New York: Doran, 1920);

Richard Henry Tawney, *Religion and the Rise of Capitalism: A Historical Study* (New York: Harcourt, Brace, 1926);

Hendrik Van Loon, *The Story of Mankind* (New York: Boni & Liveright, 1921);

Alfred North Whitehead, *Religion in the Making: Lowell Lectures, 1926* (New York: Macmillan, 1926);

Whitehead, *Science and the Modern World: The Lowell Lectures, 1925* (New York: Macmillan, 1925);

*America,* periodical;

*Christian Century,* periodical;

*Christian Herald,* periodical;

*Commonweal,* periodical;

*World Tomorrow,* periodical.

# SCIENCE AND TECHNOLOGY

by ALLAN CHARLES

## CONTENTS

*Sidebars and tables are listed in italics.*

## 1920

- The first hearing aid using vacuum tubes is invented by Earl Charles Hanson. It is marketed in 1921 as the Vactuphone.

- Physicist Otto Stern begins developing the theory of particle spin, whereby subatomic particles such as electrons have a spin expressible in either whole numbers (bosons) or half numbers (fermions).

- John Thompson, a retired U.S. Army officer, receives a patent for his machine gun, later nicknamed the "tommy gun."

- The existence of the neutron, a subatomic particle, is inferred by William D. Harkins. The uncharged particle is not actually discovered until 1932.

**2 Nov.** Station KDKA in Pittsburgh transmits the first regular licensed radio broadcast.

**13 Dec.** At the Mount Wilson Observatory in California, physicist Albert Michelson uses a stellar interferometer to calculate the diameter of the large star Betelgeuse, the first star — other than the sun — ever measured.

## 1921

- Thomas Midgley Jr. invents an improved gasoline by adding tetraethyl, which increases octane and prevents engine knock. It is marketed as Ethyl gasoline.

- The lie detector, or polygraph, is invented by John Augustus Larson and Leonarde Keeler, policemen in Berkeley, California. It can detect untruths by measuring changes in pulse rate, blood pressure, respiration, and perspiration.

- German-born physiologist Otto Loewi propounds his theory of the chemical basis for the transmission of nerve impulses.

- Intercontinental communication by shortwave radio is demonstrated by the American Radio League and Paul Godley in Scotland.

## 1922

- A team of scientists at Johns Hopkins University, headed by Elmer V. McCollum, discovers vitamin D, an antirickettic substance they found in cod liver oil.

- Herbert Evans and K. J. Scott suggest the existence of another vitamin in foods such as wheat germ, alfalfa, and lettuce. Barnett Sure names it vitamin E in 1923, and Evans's team finally isolates it in 1936.

- Mathematician John R. Carson describes a possible new form of radio broadcasting, frequency modulation (FM), as distinct from the original type of broadcasting, amplitude modulation (AM), in which the size of the wave is modulated.

- William Howell discovers heparin, a new phospholipid useful as an anticoagulant in blood transfusions.

- Herbert T. Kalmus produces the first full-length technicolor motion picture, *The Toll of the Sea.*

**27 Feb.** Secretary of Commerce Herbert Hoover convenes a national conference of radio, telephone, and telegraph experts.

## 1923

- The Compton effect is discovered by physicist Arthur Holly Compton, who notes that the wavelengths of X rays and gamma rays increase when they collide with electrons, illustrating that X rays and gamma rays are particles.

- Russian-born Vladimir Zworykin invents the first television camera, a light-ray-tube scanning device that he calls the iconoscope. In 1924 he patents the kinescope, a television picture tube using a cathode-ray tube.

- Edwin H. Armstrong constructs the first FM radio, using the mathematics developed in 1922 by John R. Carson.

- Two U.S. Army pilots perform the first in-flight refueling operation.

- At the Mount Wilson Observatory astronomer Edwin Hubble discovers that nebulae (fuzzy points of light seen in the sky) are clusters of stars.

- George Eastman produces 16-mm film for use by the general public, beginning the era of home movies. In 1923 Bell and Howell Company market a 16-mm camera, and Victor Animatograph offers a projector.

## 1924

- Harvard Observatory publishes the Henry Draper Catalogue, compiled by Annie J. Cannon, giving the spectra of 225,300 stars.

- Transatlantic radio transmission of still photographs begins.

- FM radio is introduced.

- Hubble proves that the clusters of stars he discovered in 1923 are independent galaxies, not parts of the Milky Way, the galaxy in which the Earth is located.

- American Telephone and Telegraph and General Electric join forces to found Bell Telephone Laboratories.

## 1925

- Zworykin applies for a patent for color television; it is not granted until 1928.

- George Whipple, a pathologist at the University of Rochester School of Medicine and Dentistry, demonstrates that iron is an essential element in red blood cells.

- Using large nickel crystals to diffract X rays, physicist Clinton J. Davisson confirms Louis de Broglie's 1924 theory that particles have wavelike properties.

- American physicist Robert A. Millikan names cosmic rays, first suggested in 1911 by Austrian Victor Hess.

- G. L. McCarthy patents a microfilm camera for use by banks to make reduced copies of checks.

**July**   High-school teacher John Scopes is found guilty in Dayton, Tennessee, of violating a state law that forbids the teaching of Charles Darwin's theory of evolution in the public schools.

**3 Sept.**   The U.S. Navy dirigible *Shenandoah* is destroyed in a storm over Ava, Ohio.

**12 Sept.**  President Calvin Coolidge appoints a National Aircraft Board with Dwight Morrow as chairman.

## 1926

- The National Broadcasting Company (NBC) links twenty-four radio stations into a "network."

- Harold Sinclair develops one of the earliest fluid-drive automatic transmissions for automobiles.

- The mule-drawn cotton stripper is introduced, marking the beginning of the end for picking cotton by hand.

- Physicist Enrico Fermi and British scientist Paul Dirac compile the Fermi-Dirac statistics regarding the spin of subatomic particles.

- Bell Labs produces a voiceprint machine, the voice coder, to analyze the frequency (pitch) and energy content of speech.

- James B. Sumner proves that enzymes are proteins and that they aid in bringing about biochemical reactions in the body.

- Vitamin B1 is discovered. Its existence has been presumed since 1896.

**18 Feb.**  Harcourt, Brace publishes Paul de Kruif's *Microbe Hunters*, probably the most popular book on bacteriology ever to appear.

**16 Mar.**  In Auburn, Massachusetts, Robert H. Goddard launches first rocket propelled by liquid fuel.

**6 Aug.**  The first commercial motion picture with sound, *Don Juan*, is released by Warner Bros.

## 1927

- J. A. O'Neill invents the first magnetic recording tape. It is first made of paper, which is replaced by plastic in 1932.

- Hermann J. Muller at the University of Texas uses irradiation techniques to induce mutations artificially in the fruit fly.

**7 Jan.**  The first radiotelephone connection is made between New York and London.

**23 Feb.**  Congress creates the Federal Radio Commission.

**7 Apr.**  Walter Gifford, president of AT&T, makes first successful demonstration of television, in the Washington, D.C., office of Secretary of Commerce Herbert Hoover.

**20–21 May**  Charles A. Lindbergh makes the first nonstop, solo flight across the Atlantic Ocean, flying from New York to Paris in thirty-three and a half hours.

**Oct.**  The first feature-length talking picture, *The Jazz Singer*, is released by Warner Bros.

## 1928

- Philip Drinker and Louis Shaw at Harvard University invent the "iron lung" as an aid to breathing, especially for polio sufferers.

- Vannevar Bush and associates at the Massachusetts Institute of Technology invent an analog computer to solve differential equations.

- Minnesota Mining and Manufacturing (3M) markets cellophane tape as Scotch Tape.

- Richard E. Byrd establishes a base in Antarctica from which he flies over the South Pole.

- Margaret Mead publishes *Coming of Age in Samoa*, a popular, classic anthropological study whose conclusions remain unchallenged until the 1980s.

- Vitamin C is discovered by Charles G. King at the University of Pittsburgh. Hungarian scientist Albert Szent-Gyorgyi, working independently, makes the same discovery two weeks later.

- General Electric and New York radio station WRNY make the first primitive efforts at television broadcasting.

- Austrian-born physician George Goldberger, working on a cure for pellagra, finds that a heated yeast extract, later shown to contain the B vitamin niacin, will cure blacktongue, a dog disease analogous to pellagra in humans.

**12 Dec.** Delegates from forty countries assemble in Washington, D.C., for a conference on civil aeronautics.

## 1929

- Further efforts at television broadcasting are made. NBC puts on the air a station with a scanning rate of sixty lines per second.

- Bell Labs produces a color television prototype using a scanning rate of fifty lines per second.

- The Dunlop Rubber Company develops the first foam rubber.

- Hubble recalculates the distance to the Andromeda galaxy as 930,000 light years.

**17 July** Goddard launches the first instrumented rocket, complete with camera, barometer, and thermometer.

# OVERVIEW

**A Climactic Decade.** The 1920s were a decade of culmination in technology and science. Ideas and inventions on which scientists and engineers had been working for years came out of the developmental stage and into people's lives for the first time.

**Cars.** Henry Ford opened his assembly line in 1913, but World War I slowed the growth of automobile ownership. During the 1920s the private car become a fixture of everyday American life. As late as 1919 there were 6.8 million passenger cars on the road in a country of about 105 million people. By 1929 there were 23 million cars for about 122 million people.

**Airplanes.** Orville and Wilbur Wright made the first successful manned flight in 1903, but little progress was made until World War I (1914–1918) provided the impetus for improved aeronautic technology. In 1920 the airplane was still mainly a county-fair curiosity. By the late 1920s the major U.S. cities were linked by regularly scheduled airline service. Another fixture of modern life had appeared.

**Movies.** Though it has roots in the first two decades of the twentieth century, the modern motion picture is for the most part a product of the 1920s. In the first decade of the century movies were little more than video-parlor curiosities viewed by one person at a time. In the 1910s movie houses were set up to show flickering, jerky, silent, black-and-white motion pictures. During the 1920s large, Art Deco motion-picture houses were constructed. By the mid 1920s movies had started coming out in color, and sound was added in the late 1920s.

**Radio and Television.** Wireless telephony was still so experimental in 1912 that when the *Titanic* struck an iceberg and began to sink, the only ship close enough to come to the aid of the passengers was unaware of the disaster. The accident occurred at night, and that ship kept its radio on only in the daytime. Radio, as it is known by the public, was born in the 1920s. The first commercial radio station went on the air in 1920, and by 1929 there was a well-regulated industry of hundreds of stations. Although a commercially viable television prototype was not developed until the 1930s, a primitive form of black-and-white television was publicly demonstrated in the late 1920s, and active experimentation with color television was under way.

**Discovering New Galaxies.** Astronomy went through a period of rapid change in the 1920s. Before the 1920s everybody, including scientists, thought that the Milky Way — the galaxy that includes our solar system — was the entire universe. By the end of the decade astronomers had found that the Milky Way is just one ordinary galaxy among a multitude of others. (In a bit of whimsy astronomers named one of the new galaxies "Snickers" to make fun of a popular candy bar named after our own galaxy.)

**The Big Bang Theory.** Scientists also considered the universe to be fairly static, until the Big Bang theory of the origin of the universe was set forth in the late 1920s. Suddenly the universe was described as rapidly expanding and ever-changing.

# TOPICS IN THE NEWS

## AUTOMOBILES

**A Decade of Transformations.** When the 1920s began, the Stanley Company of Newton, Massachusetts, was still manufacturing its Stanley steamers. During the decade the internal-combustion, gasoline-powered car completed its triumph over the efficient but slow-starting steam-powered car. A steam engine, which operates by external combustion, is basically simpler than an internal-combustion engine. In the steam engine a liquid-fueled fire is used to boil water, and the resulting steam drives a turbine that powers the car. Its simplicity was partially negated by the fact that pumps had to be serviced, but what really killed the steam car was the fact that it took at least twenty minutes to build up a head of steam and get going. Although the time required to start it was reduced, the steam car was injured by gossip — such as false reports of boiler explosions. No Stanley or White steamer blew up. The steam car was faster, quieter, and easier to maintain than the gasoline-powered, internal-combustion car. The Stanley brothers' company, which had produced some eighteen thousand steam cars in twenty-seven years, went out of business in 1925.

**Henry Ford.** The story of the motorcar in the 1920s was still the story of Henry Ford, who continued to dominate the fields of automotive engineering and production. In December 1927 the first Model A rolled off the gigantic River Rouge assembly line. It was not a retooled Model T; it was a completely new automobile with a safety-glass windshield, hydraulic shock absorbers, an all-wheel braking system, and a higher-geared transmission replacing the planetary transmission.

**The Chevies Keep Rolling.** Chevrolet kept pressure on Ford by means of style and engineering improvements. In 1927, the year Ford shifted models, Chevrolet outsold Ford for the first time, manufacturing 1,001,880 units to become the world's largest automaker. In 1928, with the Model A in full production, Ford regained the lead, only to lose it again in 1929. The resurgence of Chevrolet in 1929 was partly because of a bold innovation — the "valve-in-head" engine design, in which the valve compartments are parts of a single precast engine block. That design has since become standard in the automotive industry.

---

## "BOSS KETT"

**S**ome of the most important innovations in the automobile industry were the work of Charles Franklin Kettering (1876–1958), known to his employees as "Boss Kettering" or "Boss Kett." By 1920 he was already well known as the inventor of the first electric self-starter, an electric motor that turned over the engine of the car, eliminating the necessity of laborious and dangerous hand cranking. That invention, which made it easier for women to become drivers, was introduced in the 1912 Cadillac.

During the 1920s, as vice president for research at General Motors, Kettering worked with Thomas Midgley to develop leaded gasoline, which increased octane and prevented engine knock. *Ethyl* gasoline, a name coined by Kettering, went on sale in Dayton, Ohio, on 1 February 1923. Kettering also helped to develop Duco, a quick-drying durable lacquer finish for auto bodies, a considerable improvement over older slow-drying auto paints. When Duco was introduced in 1925, it came in only one color, light blue, but GM chemists gradually came up with other colors. Perhaps Kettering's greatest breakthrough of the 1920s, however, was the development of a high-speed, two-cycle diesel engine. Beginning in the 1930s this GM diesel revolutionized the way the world powered its ships, locomotives, and trucks.

Sources: Thomas A. Boyd, *Professional Amateur: The Biography of Charles Franklin Kettering* (New York: Dutton, 1957);

Stuart W. Leslie, *Boss Kettering: Wizard of General Motors* (New York: Columbia University Press, 1983).

Sources:

Frederick Lewis Allen, *Only Yesterday: An Informal History of the Nineteen-Twenties* (New York: Harper, 1931);

*Automotive Industry,* 175 ( July 1995);

Roger Burlingame, *Henry Ford: A Great Life in Brief* (New York: Knopf, 1954);

General Motors Company, Chevrolet Motor Division, *The Chevrolet Story, 1911–1970* (Detroit: The Division, 1969);

Lt. James H. "Jimmy" Doolittle poses with his Curtiss R3C after winning the Schneider Cup race, 25 October 1925. Doolittle went on to set the world's speed record for land planes in 1932 and to earn the Medal of Honor for leading the 1942 "Tokyo Raid" during World War II.

Lyman Nash, "The Steam-Driven Automobile in America," *American Legion Magazine,* 87 (August 1969):26–31, 44–45.

## AVIATION

**Peacetime.** During World War I, which ended in November 1918, military aircraft technology went through prodigious and rapid development, especially by the Europeans. By contrast the 1920s were devoted to civilian aviation pursuits.

**Barnstormers.** Unemployed former fighter pilots roamed the country, each having spent a few hundred dollars for a war-surplus plane, usually a two-seater Curtiss JN-4 "Jenny" trainer. They buzzed from county fair to county fair, giving one person at a time a ride for the then significant fare of five or ten dollars. The daredevil barnstormers became the subjects of many movies depicting their exploits of flying under bridges and through barns. Flying upside down and doing barrel rolls and loop-the-loops were standard practices, and even wing walking was performed to attract attention. Charles A. Lindbergh, too young to have been in the war, always wore a parachute when wing walking and ended his act by floating to the ground to the astonishment of the crowd.

**Regulation.** There was no official inspection of aircraft, no mandatory training of pilots, no rules of flight. Anyone old enough to buy a horse could buy a plane and treat either means of transportation with equal abandon. In 1926 Congress passed an Air Commerce Act, creating an Aeronautics Branch connected with the Department of Commerce. Planes and their pilots became subject to qualification standards and licensing, and the recklessness of the old-time barnstormers came to an end.

**Airmail.** In the 1920s the best way to make steady money in aviation was to land a government contract to deliver mail. Passenger service was slower to develop. The first regular airmail route had been established in 1918 between New York and Washington, D.C. In 1920 the Post Office Department expanded its airmail service to transcontinental proportions, initiating a route from New York to San Francisco with stops at major interior cities. At first mail was airborne only by day and was transported by train during the night. Day-and-night air transportation was attempted in 1921 but discontinued because with only rudimentary instrumentation night flying was dangerous. In fact it was the main reason thirty-one of the first forty airmail pilots crashed and died. Not until mid 1924 was day-and-night service permanently established. By 1925 private airlines had emerged, and Congress authorized the post office to put mail on regularly scheduled flights. Those mail contracts were a boon to the infant airline industry and helped attract investment.

**Sikorsky.** One of the greatest American aircraft designers of the 1920s and after was Igor Sikorsky, who arrived in the United States in 1919 as a refugee from Communism in the Soviet Union. In February 1920 he formed a partnership with Ivan Prokofieff and Joseph Michael to manufacture large airplanes capable of carrying freight or passengers. Emerging as leader of the enterprise, Sikorsky reorganized it in March 1923 as Sikorsky Aero Engineering Company.

**Long Island.** Sikorsky rented space at a Long Island airfield, where in 1924 he successfully tested a transport plane, the fourteen-passenger S-29-A. The two-engine

Mail plane, 1926

S-29-A was quite an innovation because it was entirely made of metal at a time when wood was still much used in aircraft construction. Charles A. Lindbergh's history-making solo, nonstop transatlantic flight in 1927 over-shadowed Sikorsky's aeronautic accomplishments. At that time Sikorsky was building a transatlantic plane, the twin-engine S-37. He sold his prototype S-37 to American Airways International, and in 1929 it flew seven thousand miles from San Francisco to Santiago, Chile. From there it flew over the Andes to Buenos Aires, Argentina, attaining an altitude of nineteen thousand feet. Meanwhile Sikorsky had attracted the attention of Pan American Airways, whose technical adviser, Charles Lindbergh, became interested in Sikorsky's S-38, a twin-engine amphibian plane. Starting in 1929 a total of 111 S-38s were sold, mainly to Pan Am but also to other companies, private individuals, and the military. Those planes were the beginning of the famous Pan American Clippers of the 1930s. Though Sikorsky is best known for his work on helicopters in the 1930s, during the 1920s he restricted himself to developing fixed-wing aircraft.

**Army Planes.** Although the 1920s were not an active decade for research and development of military aircraft, the services were not completely out of the picture. The champion of military aviation was U.S. Army Air Corps Brig. Gen. William "Billy" Mitchell. In a 1921 experiment off the Virginia Capes, he demonstrated that airplanes could sink large naval vessels (in this case battleships captured from Germany). Yet skeptics pointed out that the ships were motionless in the water and were not firing back at the planes. General Mitchell continued to harass his superiors in Washington until they demoted him to colonel and banished him to Fort Sam Houston, Texas. When the giant U.S. Navy dirigible *Shenandoah* crashed in Ohio in 1925, Mitchell blamed it on "incompetency and criminal neglect" that was "almost treasonable." The army was stung and moved to court-martial Mitchell, who was suspended from duty for five years. At the urging of Secretary of Commerce Herbert Hoover, President Calvin Coolidge convened a nine-man investigatory panel, headed by financier Dwight Morrow, the future father-in-law of aviator Charles Lindbergh. The Morrow report led to some strengthening of the Air Corps within the U.S. Army, but no new funds were appropriated for the corps, and it was not until after World War II that Mitchell's dream of an independent U.S. Air Force was realized.

**The Verville Scout.** In foreign flying meets during the early 1920s Americans, though the inventors of the airplane, commanded little respect. There were four American entries in the 1920 Gordon Bennett Aviation Cup race, held near Paris. The most sophisticated American plane in the contest was a Verville Scout, partially designed by Orville Wright and built by the Dayton-Wright Airplane Company of Ohio. It was a monoplane at a time when most manufacturers felt that the mutually reinforcing wings of the double-winged biplane were the only safe way to achieve the strength required for racing competition. Fears about the Verville Scout were allayed with a photograph showing twelve men standing on its wings, which boasted variable camber, arching or curvature to adjust the wind flow over the wings (achieved today by wing flaps). The plane also had retractable landing gear to reduce drag and was powered by a 250-horsepower Hall-Scott engine, which unfortunately malfunctioned, taking the plane out of the race. With the other American entries so amateurish as to occasion mirth among the European spectators, the French retained the cup.

**Naval Aviation.** Along with Mitchell, navy fliers were able to obtain some funds during the first half of the 1920s to have the Curtiss Company produce racing airplanes for the services. From 1920 to 1925 navy Curtiss planes competed with army Curtiss versions and civilian sport planes in the National Air Races from 1920 to 1925. In a 1923 seaplane competition, the Schneider Trophy Race, held in the English Channel off the Isle of Wight, the Americans made up for earlier embarrassments. The U.S. Navy sent four single-seat biplanes: two Curtiss CR-3's with Curtiss D-12 engines, a Navy-Wright NW-2 racer, and a Naval Aircraft Factory TR3-A. The 650-horsepower high-compression engine in the NW-2 blew up in a preliminary race, and the engine in the TR3-A malfunctioned on takeoff, but the two streamlined CR-3's swept lap after lap at the amazingly high speeds of 177 and 173 MPH, astounding European aviators. Before the end of the year a Curtiss R-2C1 navy racer — with an improved Curtiss D-12 engine and two wing-mounted radiators — won the American Pulitzer Trophy race, averaging 244 MPH. The D-12 was a water-cooled engine with twelve in-line cylinders. It had one-eighth inch greater bore than earlier Curtiss engines and therefore 50 additional horsepower.

**The Curtiss R3C.** In 1925 the army ordered the Curtiss R3C-1 (the wheeled version), and the navy bought the R3C-2 (the seaplane version) of a single-seat biplane constructed mostly of wood (spruce, birch, ash, and hickory) and powered by a 610-horsepower Curtiss engine. That year the army plane took the Pulitzer Trophy with a speed of 249 MPH. Unsatisfied, the army took the wheels off, attached streamlined pontoons, and entered it in the Schneider Trophy Race, hosted by the navy as the defending champions from 1923 and held off Baltimore. With Lt. James H. "Jimmy" Doolittle as pilot, the army plane won the race averaging just under 233 MPH. The next day he set a world speed record of 245.7 MPH.

Igor Sikorsky with a mock-up for the S-38

**Fighters.** There were a few prototype fighter planes produced in the decade, including the navy O2U Corsair, but because it was peacetime they were not put into mass production. To test its planes at sea in the early 1920s, the navy converted a collier (coal-carrying ship) as its first aircraft carrier — the *Langley*. Both services went to monoplane designs and preferred lower-powered radial engines; that is, the cylinders were arranged in a circle so they could be air cooled. In-line engines had to be water cooled, and the water lines were subject to rupture by enemy gunfire. Nevertheless, Europeans largely ignored this problem and produced fighter planes with water-

Announcement of the first solo transatlantic flight: "Take your hats off to Lucky, Lucky Lindy, the Eagle of the U.S.A."

cooled engines that were more powerful than those of the Americans. During the 1920s American fighter planes still had the same armaments as World War I planes — two machine guns. The fall of Gen. Billy Mitchell in 1925 hurt efforts to win congressional appropriations for military aviation in the late 1920s. In 1928 the Boeing Company of Seattle sold the army and navy planes from its F4B/P-12 series. Powered by a single, air-cooled, rotary 550-horsepower Pratt and Whitney engine, the plane was the last of the old wooden biplanes. It went into limited mass production in the 1930s and was still in use during the first years of World War II.

**The Guggenheim Fund.** In the late 1920s private aeronautics was greatly assisted financially by the Guggenheim Fund for the Promotion of Aeronautics, a philanthropic fund set up by Daniel Guggenheim, a wealthy American mining entrepreneur. Guggenheim's son Harry F. Guggenheim, who had been a U.S. Navy pilot in France during World War I, inspired his father's creation of a fund to ensure further research and development in aeronautics. From 1926 to 1930 seven major grants were made to universities, including New York University, Massachusetts Institute of Technology, Stanford University, and California Institute of Technology. The fund also sponsored international contests to demonstrate improvements that came out of their research — such as increases in takeoff angle, decreases in stalling, and other safety improvements. The fund enlisted Doolittle to perform experiments that led to the development of instrument flying, thus minimizing crashes caused by fog or night blindness. The fund also assisted Comdr. Richard Byrd in his polar explorations, and after Charles Lindbergh's groundbreaking nonstop transatlantic flight, the fund sponsored a nationwide tour for Lindbergh and his plane, *The Spirit of St. Louis*. Lindbergh's flight helped to convince the public that long-distance flying could be a safe means of transportation, and the tour contributed greatly to the popularization of air travel.

**A Ford Airplane.** Patterned rather closely on a German Fokker aircraft, Henry Ford's 4AT trimotor, first flown in 1926 and featuring three Pratt and Whitney 420-horsepower radial engines, was one of the safest airplanes of its time. With its inherent stability it could climb with two engines and maintain level flight with one. It had an enclosed cockpit with side-by-side dual controls and carried eleven to fourteen passengers. With a cruising speed of 107 MPH and a range of 570 miles, it could attain a ceiling of 16,500 feet, higher than any mountain in the forty-eight states. Some 199 of the 4AT and its 1928 successor, the 5AT, had been produced by 1933.

Sources:

Enzo Angelucci, *Airplanes from the Dawn of Flight to the Present Day* (New York: McGraw-Hill, 1973);

Terry Gwynn-Jones, *Farther and Faster: Aviation's Adventuring Years, 1909–1939* (Washington, D.C.: Smithsonian Institution Press, 1991);

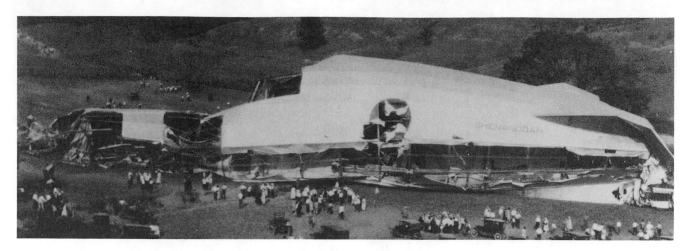

Wreckage of the stern section of the dirigible *Shenandoah* at Ava, Ohio, on 3 September 1925

James J. Halley, *The Role of the Fighter in Air Warfare* (London: Barrie & Jenkins, 1979);

Richard P. Hallion, *Legacy of Flight: The Guggenheim Contribution to American Aviation* (Seattle: University of Washington Press, 1977);

H. F. King, comp., *Kitty Hawk to Concorde: Jane's 100 Significant Aircraft* (London: Jane's Yearbooks, 1970);

Claudia M. Oakes and Kathleen L. Brooks-Pazmany, comps., *Aircraft of the National Air and Space Museum,* fourth edition (Washington, D.C.: Smithsonian Institution Press, 1991);

Lowell Thomas and Lowell Thomas Jr., *Famous First Flights That Changed History* (Garden City, N.Y.: Doubleday, 1969).

## DIRIGIBLES

**Dirigibles and Blimps.** Lighter-than-air craft include both dirigibles, with rigid hull structures, and blimps, with limp hull structures that fall flat when deflated. Blimps were used during both world wars, but they were too small to carry many bombs in wartime or many passengers in peacetime. The large dirigibles could perform either mission.

**The Zeppelin.** The French invented the airship in the late eighteenth century, but the craft remained strictly experimental for a century until Graf Ferdinand von Zeppelin caused the Germans to move permanently into the forefront of the field. Indeed the word *zeppelin* became a generic term for the dirigible. Americans did little in the early period of experimenting with lighter-than-air craft, but when they saw the power of German zeppelins on bombing raids over England in World War I and watched while the huge craft soaked up anti-aircraft fire and then floated away, they vowed to get into the program. Separate gas bags within the hulls of the zeppelins meant that a few holes would not disable a ship, although some, of course, were shot down.

**The R38.** In 1920 the U.S. Navy contracted with the British government to purchase their R38 dirigible and sent an aviation crew to be trained in operating the ship and to fly it back to America. Before the turnover was complete, however, the airship broke in half during a strenuous test run over Hull, England, on 23 August 1921. Like the German airships, the R38 was filled with hydrogen, which is highly flammable, and the breakage started fires, which increased the number of casualties. Forty-four men were killed, sixteen of them Americans. It was the worst aviation disaster in history up to that time. Since the transfer to the U.S. Navy was not complete, the British refunded half a million dollars to the United States.

**Billy Mitchell.** In 1919 Brig. Gen. William "Billy" Mitchell, the fiery and controversial advocate of military air power, tried to get the Germans to build a dirigible for the U.S. Army. Unauthorized by higher authorities and opposed by the Navy Department, the negotiations fell through. The army settled for a small, Italian, semirigid airship, the *Roma*. Bought in June 1920 and brought to America disassembled, the *Roma* crashed and burned in November 1921 on her maiden U.S. flight, causing the deaths of thirty-four men.

**The *Shenandoah*.** In summer 1923 the first American-made dirigible went airborne. Christened the *Shenandoah*, she was also the world's first rigid airship to be filled with helium. Unlike hydrogen, helium is not flammable, but it is the second lightest element, whereas hydrogen is the lightest. Thus helium has less lifting ability than hydrogen. Another disadvantage with helium was its cost: some two hundred times as much as hydrogen. During the years between the two world wars the United States was the sole significant producer of helium, and it had only one plant, in Fort Worth, Texas. In late 1924, when the *Shenandoah* was joined at her home hanger in Lakehurst, New Jersey, by her German-made sister ship *Los Angeles*, there was not enough helium for both dirigibles, and the *Shenandoah* was out of commission until June 1925.

**Disaster.** The *Shenandoah* was used on reconnaissance missions for the naval fleet, but the navy considered the airship most useful in public relations. Most of the time it was on exhibit to large crowds in various cities. On 2 September 1925 the *Shenandoah* left Lakehurst for its

The first successful helicopter; Berliner's prototype rose vertically and flew horizontally.

fifty-seventh flight, a public-relations tour of big cities and state fairs in the Midwest. The *Shenandoah* had successfully been flown from coast to coast, but conditions on this flight were more severe. The weather in the American Midwest is the worst of any populated area on earth, with numerous tornadoes and violent thunderstorms. In 1925 there was no radar, and weather forecasting was still rudimentary. On 3 September the *Shenandoah* encountered a fierce line of thunderstorms near Ava, Ohio, as a cold front overriding a warm front set a tremendous vertical windshear.

**Final Moments.** The giant airship rose uncontrollably with violent rolling and pitching. Structural failures began to occur. The ship then dived out of control, dropping more than three thousand feet in less than three minutes. The crew discharged ballast, and the ship leveled out, only to be caught two minutes later in another updraft. This time the stricken vessel broke in half, spilling out some of the crew. The control gondola broke free and fell to earth, killing the captain, Lt. Comdr. Zachary Lansdowne, along with five of his men. Of a crew of forty-three there were twenty-nine survivors. They free-ballooned the forward part of the ship to a relatively soft landing. In an era not yet accustomed to aerial disasters, law enforcement officials were unable to cordon off the crash site, and looters made off with many pieces of wreckage.

*Los Angeles.* At about the same time they were building the *Shenandoah* the U.S. Navy was attempting to buy a German-made dirigible. Faced with opposition from Britain and France, the Americans persisted in difficult negotiations with their recent enemy. Finally the *Los Angeles* — built by the world's leading airship company, Luftschiffbau Zeppelin, and filled with helium at the insistence of the Americans — flew from Friedrichshafen, Germany, to Lakehurst, New Jersey, in October 1924.

**Eight Years of Service.** The *Los Angeles* was in active service for eight years, a long time for a dirigible, making 331 flights. After it was retired from active duty in 1932, it was used in various experiments for another seven years until finally being broken up for scrap in 1939. The United States built two more dirigibles in the 1930s, the *Akron* and the *Macon*. Each was lost after only two years of service, the *Akron* in 1933 off New England and the *Macon* in 1935 off California. There was no long-range reconnaissance by dirigibles during World War II, only coastal scouting by a few blimps. Many U.S. Navy men, all volunteers, had given their lives to test a different kind of airship — one that ultimately was abandoned.

Sources:

Guy Hartcup, *The Achievement of the Airship: A History of the Development of Rigid, Semi-Rigid and Non-Rigid Airships* (Newton Abbot, U.K. & North Pomfret, Vt.: David & Charles, 1974);

Douglas H. Robinson and Charles L. Keller, *"Up Ship!" A History of the U.S. Navy's Rigid Airships, 1919–1935* (Annapolis, Md.: Naval Institute Press, 1982).

## HELICOPTERS

**The Prototype.** In summer 1922 the well-known inventor of the microphone, Emile Berliner, and his son Henry A. Berliner made the first successful flight in a helicopter. It attained an altitude of only fifteen to twenty feet and flew at just 20 MPH. The significance of the flight was that the machine rose vertically from the ground and proceeded to fly horizontally. Other experimental craft at the time were able to rise vertically and set down vertically, but they were incapable of horizontal movement.

**Sikorsky.** Russian American Igor Sikorsky, who directed his efforts solely to fixed-wing aircraft during the 1920s, had built two prototype helicopters before he emigrated from the Soviet Union in 1919, but neither the helicopter he built in Kiev in 1909 nor his 1910 model would fly. Having decided that the helicopter needed to wait for "better engines, lighter materials, and experi-

During the early years of electric power, one of the most challenging problems for engineers was how to minimize the destructive force of lightning on electrical-transmission systems. Some advances had been made by 1920, but further developments were hampered by the fact that no one was exactly sure what happened when lightning struck. One morning in August 1920, Charles P. Steinmetz, chief consulting engineer for the General Electric Research Laboratory in Schenectady, New York, was inspired by a chance occurrence to find a way to learn more about lightning. Arriving at his camp on the Mohawk River, he found that it had been struck by lightning, leaving dangling electrical wires, a broken window, damaged beams, and a shattered mirror on the cabin floor. Instead of being dismayed at the mess, Steinmetz was excited at the opportunity to examine the undisturbed evidence. He and an assistant spent the day taking photographs, collecting every splinter of wood from damaged beams, and picking up every last particle of the mirror. After examining and measuring the splinters, Steinmetz was able to calculate the power of the lightning stroke as it took various paths through the cabin. Once he and his assistant pieced the mirror back together, they could see the path of the electric discharge in the fused silvering on the back of the mirror.

From this chance opportunity Steinmetz developed a methodology for studying lightning. Next he wanted to be on hand at the moment a lightning bolt struck. He became determined to build a lightning generator in the laboratory despite the difficulty of duplicating the ultrahigh voltage and extremely heavy current of a natural lightning bolt. Within two years he and his assistants had developed an apparatus that could discharge 10,000 amperes at 120,000 volts in a few millionths of a second, creating the phenomenal force of more than one million horsepower. To make the device they assembled a high-voltage power source, a "kenotron" (a recently developed two-element rectifier tube), and a huge condenser with glass plates covered with lead foil and arranged to discharge the current across a gap in which a test object could be placed. The first time they tested the device, the artificial lightning shattered a tree limb into tiny fragments.

The invention gave engineers a means of testing insulation, lightning arresters, and other electrical equipment, but no one knew how to measure real lightning, which Steinmetz estimated to be as much as five hundred times more powerful than the lightning he created in the laboratory. Steinmetz, who died suddenly in 1923, did not live to see the solution of this problem, which came in 1928. GE engineers developed the surge-voltage recorder, installed some of them on the tall metal towers carrying a new high-voltage transmission line across the Pocono Mountains, settled into a nearby corrugated iron shack filled with instruments, and waited for lightning to strike one of the recorders. Late that summer they were finally able to measure the wave shape of a lightning bolt within a few feet of the point where it struck.

Source: John Anderson Miller, *Workshop of Engineers: The Story of the General Engineering Laboratory of the General Electric Company, 1895–1952* (Schenectady, N.Y.: General Electric, 1953).

enced mechanics," Sikorsky returned to work on rotary-bladed aircraft in the 1930s and became famous for developing the first truly workable helicopters.

**Sources:**
"At Last the Helicopter," *Scientific American,* 127 (September 1922): 158;

Dorothy Cochrane, Von Hardesty, and Russell Lee, *The Aviation Careers of Igor Sikorsky* (Los Angeles: Washington University Press for the National Air and Space Museum, 1989);

"A Helicopter that Flies — The Berliner Machine," *Scientific American,* 127 (September 1922): 160.

## THE LIE DETECTOR

**Policemen Inventors.** In the early 1920s John Augustus Larson, a Berkeley, California, police officer, developed the first practical polygraph. With three pens swinging back and forth on a slowly moving strip of paper, it worked like a seismograph to record changes in the subject's blood pressure, heart rate, and breathing rate. Larson's fellow police officer Leonarde Keeler added a fourth measurement. Increases in perspiration were detected by measuring the "galvanic skin response." An electric current passing over the skin gains strength when salty water (a good conductor) appears on the skin surface. Because these indicators were supposed to increase when a subject lied, the moving pens were supposed to swing more widely when untruths were uttered.

**Doubters.** The inventors never claimed that their machine was infallible, and many skeptics have maintained that a person being examined would be so nervous that many false readings would be obtained. The trained operator always asks a series of innocuous "control" questions at first in order to establish a base pattern of readings against which to compare deviations. Early examiners

Vitaphone, the first successful sound system for movie theater projectors, invented by Hugh M. Stoller and Harry Pfannenstiel of AT&T Bell Laboratories, utilized synchronized phonograph records. This system was used for *The Jazz Singer* in 1927.

often employed the technique of mixing relevant and irrelevant questions. That method was faulted even by Larson himself and was largely abandoned by the 1950s. Although polygraphs and polygraph operators have become more sophisticated over the years, reservations about the reliability of lie-detector readings remain, and they continue to be inadmissible as evidence in a court of law.

**Sources:**
Eugene B. Block, *Lie Detectors: Their History and Use* (New York: McKay, 1977);

David T. Lykken, *A Tremor in the Blood: Uses and Abuses of Lie Detectors* (New York: McGraw-Hill, 1981).

## MOTION PICTURES WITH SOUND

**Flickers.** The 1920s were the golden age of silent films, which flickered on the screen as a pianist played to enhance the mood set by the action. Large metropolitan theaters even had full orchestras to play live music for their patrons. There were rumors that a marriage might be arranged between the flickers and the phonograph, but

the greatest American inventor of all time, Thomas A. Edison, had been working on the problem since 1888 and had succeeded in producing only the 1895 and 1913 Kinetophones — ignominious failures. The problem of synchronizing sound and picture seemed insurmountable, and other early-twentieth-century attempts — the Synchroscope, the Cinematophone, and the Cameraphone — had also failed.

**Silence Is Golden.** The sound fidelity of available audio systems was not good. Screen actors had been selected for their ability to act out roles physically, not for their speaking voices, while stage actors tended to over-project their voices, an acting style that would spoil the intimate effect created by the close-in cameras. Furthermore, producers had another reason to oppose sound: it would cost them most of their lucrative foreign market. The printed titles (dialogue cards) could easily be translated into any language, while a talking picture would have to be "dubbed," and nobody was sure how that inevitably expensive process could be accomplished.

**Development of "Talkies."** In the mid 1920s radio engineers at Western Electric and telephone engineers at Bell Labs worked on a system for making sound pictures. Sam Warner, one of the four brothers who founded Warner Bros. studio, heard about the effort and thought talkies that actually worked might get their young, struggling movie company into the big time. When he broached the subject to his brother Harry, Harry replied, "Who the hell wants to hear actors talk?" Nevertheless, Harry came around, and he and Sam worked out a deal with Western Electric in 1925. The new system needed a name by which to market it, and Warner Bros. settled on Vitaphone (life sound).

**New Problems.** The culmination of years of effort at synchronizing an electronically driven sound system with a mechanically driven motion-picture projector, Vitaphone was a sound-on-disk system. (The innovation of putting the sound track on the same strip of film as the pictures came later.) With the advent of Vitaphone the old, hand-cranked movie camera had to be abandoned because the human arm could not be precise enough to synchronize audio and video accurately. Early power-driven cameras, however, had noisy motors whose sound was recorded along with the actors' voices. The Warners' first solution to the problem was to place cameras and cameramen in portable, stifling-hot soundproof booths. (Cameras with silent motors were eventually developed.) Traffic noises from outside the studio would also be picked up. Thus it was not just the climate and scenery of southern California that led Warner Bros. to join the exodus of movie studios from New York City to Hollywood. There they set up a thirteen-acre studio lot that was easier to soundproof than their studio in New York.

**The First Sound Motion Picture.** Warner Bros. made the first sound movie, *Don Juan* (1926), in New York City before their move to Hollywood. It was not a feature-length motion picture, and the actors did not talk. The only sound was a synchronized musical score and sound effects.

*The Jazz Singer. Don Juan* did not totally capture the public's imagination, but the following year Warner Bros. produced a real blockbuster, *The Jazz Singer,* filmed in Hollywood. The movie starred Al Jolson, a nationally known stage actor and singer who was eager to explore the new medium of sound pictures. The first full-length feature film with synchronized dialogue and singing, the movie took four months to shoot and cost Warner Bros. a half million dollars, a colossal sum of money in 1927. Sam Warner died the evening before the New York premiere of the movie in October 1927. He never lived to see the great success of *The Jazz Singer,* a pioneering effort in the history of technology that put Warner Bros. into the big time at last.

**All Aboard.** Walt Disney, the pioneer in movie cartoons, made his first sound cartoon in 1928. Fox Studios released the first talking western, *In Old Arizona,* in late

## HERBERT HOOVER'S DECADE

**A**s secretary of commerce from 1921 to 1928 and as president of the United States from 1929 to 1933, Herbert Hoover left his mark on business, industry, and technology during the 1920s. Always vitally interested in the development and regulation of aeronautics and radio, he called or caused to be called various conferences to deal with problems arising in those growth industries. Standards of licensing and performance had to be established, and confusion and overlapping claims had to be eliminated. In his memoirs Hoover recalled one of the problems he faced in trying to regulate the radio industry. During the early 1920s evangelist Aimee Semple McPherson was broadcasting randomly and widely all over the AM band and ignored frequent warnings to restrict her broadcasting to her own wavelength. Finally Hoover's local inspector "sealed up her station," and an enraged McPherson wrote Hoover:

> Please order your minions of Satan to leave my station alone. You cannot expect the Almighty to abide by your wavelength nonsense. When I offer my prayers to Him I must fit into His wave reception. Open this station at once.

"Finally," said Hoover, "our tactful inspector persuaded her to employ a radio manager of his own selection, who kept her upon her wave length."

Source: Herbert Hoover, *The Memoirs of Herbert Hoover,* volume 2: *The Cabinet and The Presidency, 1920–1933* (New York: Macmillan, 1952).

1928. Silent westerns had died a natural death earlier in the decade, but *In Old Arizona* revived the popularity of the genre. In 1929 Fox announced it was abandoning silent films. Paramount, M-G-M, and Universal soon did so as well.

**Things in the Offing.** Technological advances of the late 1920s quite literally "set the stage" for the golden age of movies in the 1930s and 1940s. By the mid 1930s Vitaphone had been replaced. This separate-disk sound system got out of sync if the film broke during a showing and a few frames had to be clipped away in making a splice. Every time the film broke the picture got farther ahead of the audio. As early as 1928 Walt Disney was using an optical-sound-on-film system, a variation on the method invented by Lee De Forest in 1920. De Forest's method eliminated all need for synchronization gear, as the soundtrack was on the edge of the picture film itself.

Sources:
Daniel Blum, *A New Pictorial History of the Talkies,* revised and enlarged by John Kobal (New York: Putnam, 1982);

During the 1920s Vannevar Bush and a team of scientists at Massachusetts Institute of Technology worked on a "differential analyzer" — the first modern analog computer. As their name suggests, analog computers work by physical analogy. For example, the spaces on a slide rule, which is a simple analog computer, correspond to numerical values. In contrast a digital computer, of which the abacus is the earliest and simplest example, works by counting discrete units. The modern electronic computers that started coming into use after World War II are digital.

Bush needed an analog computer to help him in his research on electric power transmission, which required measurement of continuously varying electrical currents flowing in a power grid — a time-consuming task because it involved solving high-order differential equations by hand. Electrically operated, not electronic, the machine Bush and his colleagues completed in 1928 was a complicated mechanical apparatus containing an electrical meter, mechanical integrators, servo motors, torque amplifiers, and printers. With advent of the electrical analog computer it became possible to create simulations of proposed automobiles, aircraft, missiles, nuclear-power plants, and other technological designs. To build and test all envisaged systems would be prohibitively expensive. Analog computers gave manufacturers a relatively inexpensive way to determine what probably would work and what probably would not.

Source: James M. Nyce and Paul Kahn, eds., *From Memex to Hypertext: Vannevar Bush and The Mind's Machine* (Boston: Academic Press, 1991).

Alexander Walker, *The Shattered Silents: How the Talkies Came to Stay* (London: Elm Tree Books, 1978);

Curt Wohleber, "How the Movies Learned to Talk," *Invention and Technology*, 10 (Winter 1995).

## MOTION PICTURES IN COLOR

**Technicolor.** The use of color film in motion pictures was pioneered by Herbert T. Kalmus, a graduate of the Massachusetts Institute of Technology who began work on color photography in 1913. Kalmus made a short, one-reel color movie, *The Gulf Between*, in 1917, but it attracted little notice. In 1920 Kalmus tried to obtain backing for his infant Technicolor Company from George Eastman, founder of the Eastman Kodak Company in Rochester, New York. The film-manufacturing giant turned Kalmus down, saying his manufacturing technique was faulty.

**A Two-Component Process.** During the 1920s Kalmus, who used a two-primary-color technique to make his pioneer movie, developed two significant improvements to the process, which he called Process Number Two and Process Number Three. Process Number Two, though experimental, met with some success. Kalmus used it in 1922 for the first full-length technicolor movie, *The Toll of the Sea*. The following year Cecil B. DeMille used it for the prologue to his *The Ten Commandments*. Parts of *Cytherea* and *The Uninvited Guest* were filmed in Process Number Two technicolor in 1924, the year in which Jesse Lasky used it for the second all-technicolor movie, *Wanderer of the Wasteland*. The same film was used in 1926 for the third all-color movie, *The Black Pirate*, starring Douglas Fairbanks. The panels of Process Number Two film had a tendency to become somewhat cup shaped, creating a blurred focus of the picture on the screen. Process Number Three film, first used for *The Viking* in 1928, solved that problem.

**Exploding Color.** Impressed with *The Viking*, Warner Bros. signed a fat contract with Kalmus and became the first studio to move wholeheartedly into color. Investor Joseph P. Kennedy, father of the future president, brought RKO into color pictures, and M-G-M soon followed. By the end of the 1920s color was no longer experimental, but it would not be until the end of the 1940s that technicolor would almost completely displace black and white in Hollywood filmmaking.

Source:
Herbert T. Kalmus and Eleanore King Kalmus, *Mr. Technicolor* (Absecon, N.J.: MagicImage Filmbooks, 1990).

## RADIO

**An Experimental Apparatus.** In 1920 radio was still in the experimental stage. Guglielmo Marconi invented wireless telegraphy in 1899. The wireless telegraph sent a series of dot and dash signals through space, using the same code invented in the 1840s by Samuel Morse. In 1906 an actual voice communication was transmitted, and wireless telephony was invented. Both forms of communication were commonly called "wireless," but in 1912 the U.S. Navy ordered that the terms *radiotelegraphy* and *radiotelephony* be employed instead. The American public rapidly accepted the change, but by 1920 the simple term *radio* had become the American name for the still experimental invention. The British, however, continued using the term *wireless* for most of the twentieth century.

**Vacuum Tubes.** The earliest radios were crystal sets, difficult to tune and operate. During World War I, however, developments in vacuum tubes, devices similar to light bulbs and the ancestors of the modern transistors, allowed the sending and receiving of radio signals to become much more precise and powerful.

**The First Radio Station.** The first commercial radio station was started by Dr. Frank Conrad, an engineer with Westinghouse in East Pittsburgh, Pennsylvania,

Dr. Frank Conrad, a Westinghouse engineer, started the first commercial radio, KDKA Pittsburgh.

who was working on voice-transmitting equipment for the U.S. Navy. He set up what amounted to a ham radio operation in his garage and tested the navy's equipment by talking to the Westinghouse plant some four or five miles away. In April 1920, as his transmissions became of more than research interest, he received a license to use the call letters 8XK and began communicating with a circle of radio-buff friends in the Pittsburgh area. To save his voice and his time he began playing phonograph records over the air. A local department store heard about the broadcast music and placed an advertisement in the *Pittsburgh Sun* hoping to sell radio receivers to those who could not make their own.

**Marketing Radio.** At that point Harry P. Davis, a Westinghouse vice president with a mind for marketing, foresaw that voices and music coming over the airways would appeal to the public at large, not just technically minded hobbyists. At Davis's urging Westinghouse set up Conrad in the plant with a more powerful transmitter,

and on 27 October 1920 the Department of Commerce licensed the station to operate on the wavelength of 360 meters and assigned it a four-letter, nautical call sign, KDKA, as if Conrad were broadcasting from a ship. The first commercial radio station was born, and a new era had dawned.

**The Radio Boom.** With litigation over some twelve hundred vacuum-tube patents still unresolved, additional new stations did not pop up overnight. The navy joined the chorus of those wanting an end to the patent squabbling, which was literally stopping progress, and the situation was substantially improved by agreements made in July 1921. Some legal wrangling, however, persisted for years. Nevertheless, commercial radio stations — mostly small, shoestring operations — began springing up nationwide. The second station, WEAF in New York, started to broadcast in September 1921; by the end of 1922 there were 508 stations. In April 1923 the editors of *Scientific American* proclaimed, "1922 will stand out in the history of radio. For it was during the past year that radio broadcasting became a regular feature of every-day life, and radio entered the average home life of the average man." In 1921, before the boom began, only $9 million worth of radio equipment was sold. In 1923 that figure had increased to some $46 million, and in 1926 the total national expenditure on radio equipment was $400 million. With this tremendous growth came the need for regulation, and in February 1927 the Federal Radio Commission was established.

**The Superhet.** In 1922 Edwin Armstrong made a significant scientific breakthrough for broadcasting when he invented the superheterodyne receiver. In the "superhet" the incoming signal is mixed (heterodyned) with another nearby frequency. When one frequency is subtracted from the other the resultant signal is more easily and cleanly amplified — leading to increased fidelity. The invention eventually came to be included in virtually all radio receivers. In 1922 there were already some sixty thousand households with radios. By 1933 there would be close to twenty million.

**FM Radio.** By 1929 Armstrong had successfully tested frequency modulation (FM), a new form of broadcasting in which the radio-wave frequency itself is varied to transmit the signal. All original radio broadcasting used amplitude modulation (AM), in which the size (amplitude) of the wave is varied to transmit the signal. FM signals are less susceptible to noise interference than AM and are less likely to overlap each other in cases of poor reception. They do, however, have to be spaced farther apart on the radio band. Because of the onset of the Depression and difficulty in convincing broadcast companies that FM radio would work, it would be another ten years before Armstrong would be able to put an FM station on the air.

Sources:

Hugh G. J. Aitken, *The Continuous Wave: Technology and the American Radio, 1900–1922* (Princeton: Princeton University Press, 1985);

Gleason Archer, *History of the Radio to 1926* (New York: American Historical Society, 1938);

Susan J. Douglas, *Inventing American Broadcasting, 1899–1922* (Baltimore: Johns Hopkins University Press, 1987);

Thomas S. W. Lewis, "Radio Revolutionary: Edwin Armstrong's Innovations," *Invention and Technology*, 1 (Fall 1985);

John Liston, "Twelve Months of Radio," *Scientific American*, 128 (April 1923): 242, 286–287;

Paul Schubert, *The Electric Word: The Rise of Radio* (New York: Macmillan, 1928).

## THE RED SHIFT: DISCOVERING AN EXPANDING UNIVERSE

**Clouds in the Heavens.** In the early 1920s Vesto M. Slipher, an astronomer working at the Lowell Observatory near Flagstaff, Arizona, was examining spiral-shaped nebulae in the night sky. According to contemporary scientific opinion these nebulae were cloudy patches of light caused by gases, but Slipher came to the conclusion

---

## BIRD PSYCHOLOGIST

**A**mong the most significant ornithological studies of the 1920s was the work of a child psychologist, Margaret Morse Nice (1883–1974), who had a master's degree in psychology and wrote articles on that subject at the same time she was studying birds. Nice's consuming interest was the observation of behavior, whether in her five daughters (the "research subjects" of her writings on psychology) or birds.

By 1920 Nice had decided she preferred bird-watching to people-watching and published the first of thirty-five articles that led to *The Birds of Oklahoma* (1924), the first complete study of that subject, which she wrote with her husband, Leonard Blaine Nice, head of the physiology department at the University of Oklahoma.

Margaret Nice's early bird studies are largely descriptive, but by the mid 1920s she had begun careful observations of their behavior, inspired by watching captive wild birds that she kept as pets. (Guests often found themselves sharing the dinner table with sparrows.) After the Nices moved to Ohio in 1927, she began her most important work, her studies of the behavior of song sparrows. She kept track of individual birds in the wild by placing colored bands on their legs and giving each one a name and a number. Never before had anyone followed a species of birds so closely, and when the final compilation of her research was published in two volumes as *Studies in the Life History of the Song Sparrow* in 1937 and 1943, it established her reputation as one of the foremost ornithologists in the world.

Source: Christopher Cornog, Entry on Margaret Nice, in *Notable American Women: The Modern Period, A Biographical Dictionary*, edited by Barbara Sicherman and Carol Hurd Green, with Ilene Kantrov and Harriette Walker (Cambridge, Mass.: Harvard University Press, 1980).

---

that they were entire, separate galaxies like the Milky Way.

**The Doppler Effect.** By 1923 he had measured the Doppler shifts of some forty-one of these star clusters. Discovered by Austrian scientist Christian Doppler, the Doppler effect describes the changes in sound or light waves transmitted from one body to another as they get closer together or farther apart. As objects move closer, waves get shorter and their frequency gets higher, and as light-wave frequencies get higher their color shifts toward the blue range. An object moving away emits longer waves with a lower frequency, and thus light waves in this category exhibit a red shift. Slipher detected red shifts in thirty-six of the galaxies he examined, meaning that they were moving away from Earth. The remaining five nebulae exhibited a blue shift, which seemed to mean that they were getting closer to Earth, but in 1925 it was discovered that the Milky Way is itself rotating rapidly. Failure to account for this spin had led to false blue-shift readings. After correcting for this factor, it was found that only two galaxies, both comparatively near to our own, showed a net blue shift. Slipher's work supported the research Edwin Hubble was doing at the same time on the expanding universe.

Source:
Isaac Asimov, *Asimov's New Guide to Science* (New York: Basic Books, 1984).

## TELEPHONES

**Many Advances.** The 1920s were a period of continuous advancement in telephone technology, beginning with the first completely automatic switching office, established in Omaha, Nebraska, in 1921. During that same year the first deep-sea telephone cable was laid, between Key West, Florida, and Havana, Cuba. (It is not to be confused with submarine cables for telegraph signals which had been laid since the 1850s on the ocean floor.) In 1926 American telephone transmitters and receivers were first placed in the same unit, the handset, while in 1929 telephone linemen began using the power-driven auger to bore holes for telephone poles — a great advance over hand digging.

Source:
C. D. Hanscom, ed., *Dates in American Telephone Technology* (New York: Bell Telephone Laboratories, 1961).

## TELEVISION

**Zworykin.** In 1923 Russian immigrant Vladimir Zworykin applied for a patent for his iconoscope, a television camera or transmission tube. Many scientists and inventors had been working on the possibility of transmitting pictures ever since the first primitive telegraphs of the 1830s. By 1884 a German inventor, Paul Gottlieb Nipkow, had patented a sort of picture transmitter that used a mechanical scanner projecting onto a photosensitive rotating disk. The problem with Nipkow's invention and other primitive mechanical television prototypes was that they employed hand- or electric-motor-driven devices that projected either light or a stream of electrons sequentially onto a photosensitive surface to "draw" a quick series of pictures that the eye would interpret as a moving picture. Through a phenomenon called "persistence of vision" the eye perceives a series of still pictures as actual motion.

**Trial Runs.** In 1927 Bell Labs publicly demonstrated the transmission of mechanically scanned television over the telephone lines from New York to Washington, D.C. By 1928 General Electric was attempting the actual open-air broadcasting of such images, and in 1929 NBC

Vladimir Zworykin with early kinescope picture tube, Pittsburgh, 1929

put a station on the air with a scanning rate of sixty lines per second. These early efforts were not commercially successful, partly because of the scarcity of receivers, which still resembled Nipkow disks, but also because mechanical scanners could not reach a rapid enough scanning rate to present a high-resolution picture.

**Zworykin's Kinescope.** In 1924 Zworykin, who had been working toward an all-electronic system, applied for a patent for his kinescope, an electronic scanning device that uses a glass cathode-ray tube (CRT or picture tube). In this wedge-shaped tube a current of electricity at the small end sends a stream of electrons to the wide end. Starting at the upper left and working to the lower right, this stream of electrons "paints" a series of pictures on the photosensitive coating on the inside surface of the glass at the big end of the picture tube. The scanning is controlled by an electrostatic or electromagnetic grid in which a current, varying with the transmission signal, guides and deflects the stream of electrons so as to leave either a black dot or no dot for a split second on each part of the screen. These tiny dots form the overall picture.

**Color.** In 1925 Zworykin applied for a patent for color television, but he received little support from his employer, Westinghouse. Color television uses compound photosensitive spots, each one with specific portions of red, green, and blue. The stream of electrons must hit a precise portion of a spot to show a particular color, and the mixture of the three colors then creates others, displaying an overall multicolored picture. Bell Labs demonstrated a color-television prototype in 1929, a year after the British developed theirs.

Source:

C. D. Hanscom, ed., *Dates in American Telephone Technology* (New York: Bell Telephone Laboratories, 1961).

# HEADLINE MAKERS

## ARTHUR HOLLY COMPTON

### 1892-1962

#### PARTICLE PHYSICIST

**Nobel Prize Winner.** Arthur Holly Compton shared the 1927 Nobel Prize in physics for his discovery of the Compton effect, which lent strong support to Albert Einstein's important law of the photoelectric effect (1905).

**Background.** Born in Wooster, Ohio, Compton received a B.S. from the College of Wooster (1913) and an M.A. (1914) and a Ph.D. (1916) from Princeton University. After teaching at the University of Minnesota (1916–1917) and working on airplane-instrument design with the U.S. Army Signal Corps during World War I, Compton spent a year at Cambridge University, where he did research with Ernest Rutherford, the discoverer of the nucleus of the atom. He then accepted a post at Washington University in Saint Louis, where he taught physics from 1920 to 1923. He was at the University of Chicago from 1923 to 1945, after which he returned to Washington University, where he was chancellor (1945–1953) and Distinguished Service Professor of Natural Philosophy (1954–1961). During World War II he worked on the project to develop the atomic bomb.

**The Compton Effect.** In his research during the early 1920s Compton noticed that when an X ray or gamma ray strikes an electron, it bounces off at an angle to its original trajectory and loses energy in the process. This loss of energy is demonstrated by the fact that the X or gamma ray exhibits a longer wavelength, a characteristic of its drop in speed. As the gamma ray data was less conclusive than the data on X rays, when Compton published the results of his research in 1923, he limited his claims about this effect to X rays, but further research demonstrated that the Compton effect applied to gamma rays as well. Compton's discovery was a major breakthrough in determining that X rays and gamma rays were really particles, although people continue to call them rays. Physicists now speak of them as "wavy particles" because the subatomic particles do have wavelike characteristics, such as frequency and wavelength.

**Backing Up Einstein.** Compton's work supported Einstein's employment of Max Planck's quantum theory (1900) to explain the photoelectric effect, whereby a light ray striking a metal plate "kicks out" electrons. Experiments showed that the frequency of the incoming light determined the number of electrons ejected. More electrons were dislodged from their atoms by blue light than by red light, which has a lower frequency than blue. Further, the speed of the ejected electrons varies according to the frequency of the light used. Thus, high-frequency ultraviolet light is the most efficient at producing the effect. By assuming that light rays are actually quanta (packets of energy) Einstein was able to devise equations to account mathematically for the photoelectric effect. Today light quanta are generally referred to as *photons*, a term coined by Compton in 1928.

Sources:

Niels H. de V. Heathcote, *Nobel Prize Winners in Physics, 1901–1950* (New York: Schuman, 1953);

Marjorie Johnston, ed., *The Cosmos of Arthur Holly Compton* (New York: Knopf, 1967).

# ROBERT H. GODDARD

## 1882-1945

### ROCKET SCIENTIST

**Overview.** The best rocket research anywhere in the world took place in the United States in the 1920s, and one man, Robert Goddard, was responsible for it. His work on rocketry in the 1920s lay the groundwork for the exploration of outer space that began in the 1960s.

**Roots.** Robert Hutchings Goddard was born and raised in Worcester, Massachusetts, receiving a B.S. from Worcester Polytechnic Institute in 1908 and earning a Ph.D. in physics at Clark University three years later. After a year of postdoctoral research at Princeton University, the young scientist returned to Clark to teach physics in 1914 and became a full professor in 1919.

**Rocket Man.** While still in public school Goddard had developed an interest in rockets when he read H. G. Wells's *The War of the Worlds* (1898). He came to realize that rockets would be essential for travel in the vacuum of space because they carry not only their own fuel but also the oxidants necessary for the combustion of the fuel. At first Goddard experimented with traditional solid-fuel propulsion, but he soon turned to liquid fuel, taking out a patent for a liquid-fuel system in 1914. During World War I Goddard worked on shoulder-held rocket launchers. Not perfected in time for that war, the weapon became the bazooka used in World War II. He also helped develop larger surface-to-surface and surface-to-air rockets for tactical use on the battlefront.

**Space Travel.** By 1919 Goddard had realized that liquid fuel was better than solid fuel for achieving the slow, smooth takeoff thrust and the subsequent high-nozzle velocities required for lifting a large vehicle into space. He worked on that project during the first half of the 1920s, largely alone and with a shoestring budget. Finally in 1926, in an event now shrouded in myth, Goddard made his breakthrough.

**Liftoff.** On the clear, cold day of 16 March 1926 Goddard and two assistants stood on a frozen farm field in Auburn, Massachusetts, and detonated the world's first liquid-fuel rocket. History was made. Goddard had shown that it could be done. Continuing his research, Goddard went on to launch the first instrumented rocket — which carried a barometer, a thermometer, and a camera — on 17 July 1929.

**German Advances.** Goddard was a loner — almost a hobbyist — and his experiments were underfunded. In the 1930s a heavily funded team of German scientists, led by Werner von Braun, surged ahead of American scientists in rocketry. Yet the Germans built on Goddard's discoveries for their V-2 rocket. Developed in time for use in World War II, it was the first IRBM (intermediate-range ballistic missile), a rocket that actually enters space on the way to its target.

Sources:

Esther C. Goddard and G. Edward Pendray, eds., *The Papers of Robert H. Goddard*, 3 volumes (New York: McGraw-Hill, 1970);

Robert H. Goddard, *Rockets* (New York: American Rocket Society, 1946).

# EDWIN P. HUBBLE

## 1889-1953

### ASTRONOMER

**Hubble's Law.** Edwin Hubble's discovery that galaxies are constantly moving away from each other changed forever the conception of a stable universe shared by many of his contemporaries and paved the way for the Big Bang theory, the most widely accepted explanation for the origin of the universe.

**Background.** Born in Marshfield, Missouri, Edwin Powell Hubble studied under astronomers Robert Millikan and G. E. Hale at the University of Chicago. An amateur heavyweight boxer, Hubble was a Rhodes Scholar at Oxford University, where he studied law and ran track, and earned a B.A. in 1913. He soon decided to return to the study of astronomy and earned a Ph.D. in astrophysics from the University of Chicago in 1917, just in time to join the army and fight in France in World War I. He rose to the rank of major before being demobilized and taking up his life's work as an astronomer in 1919.

**Studying Andromeda.** In 1923 Hubble aimed the powerful 100-inch telescope at Mount Wilson Observatory in Pasadena, California, at the Andromeda nebula. He believed that a nebula was not merely a gas cloud or a fuzzy single star but a collection of stars, perhaps even an entire galaxy like the Milky Way. Andromeda seemed closer than many other nebulae, and Hubble zeroed in on its spiral arms, employing Cepheid variables — tables of the varying magnitude (brightness) of certain stars — to enable him to gauge distance. He calculated that Andromeda was almost a million light-years away from Earth — far, far beyond the edges of the Earth's own galaxy, the Milky Way, and thus a separate galaxy. (A light-year is about six trillion miles, the distance light travels in a year.) Hubble published his findings in 1924, and as late as 1929 had only slightly revised his estimate of the distance to

Andromeda. In the 1930s, however, other astronomers, using larger telescopes and revised Cepheid variable tables, recalculated the distance to Andromeda as approximately 2.5 million light-years. Even at that far remove, Andromeda is one of the nearest galaxies to the Earth, as the average distance between galaxies is about twenty million light-years.

**Hubble's Law and the Expanding Universe.** Building on Vesto M. Slipher's discovery that most galaxies had strong red shifts in their spectra, Hubble next began next to examine various galaxies and calculate their Doppler shifts. The faster a star is moving away from Earth, the greater the shift in the red portion of the light spectrum received from that star. Hubble found that almost all galaxies were moving away from Earth, and those farthest from Earth were moving away at an even faster rate. In 1929 he expressed this proportionality as Hubble's law. The only conclusion possible, given Hubble's law, is that the universe is rapidly expanding — even exploding. Thus Hubble's law supports the beginning of the Big Bang theory of the origin of the universe, expounded in 1927 and in the early 1930s by the mathematician-philosopher-cleric Georges Lemaitre.

Source:
Alexander S. Sharov and Igor D. Novikov, *Edwin Hubble, The Discoverer of the Big Bang Universe*, translated by Vitaly Kisin (Cambridge: Cambridge University Press, 1993).

## CHARLES A. LINDBERGH

### 1902-1974

#### PIONEER AVIATOR

"Lucky Lindy." The greatest aeronautic feat of the 1920s, and indeed one of the greatest and most-publicized events of the decade in any sense, was Charles Augustus Lindbergh's solo, nonstop crossing of the Atlantic in 1927. More important than the personal fame the flight brought Lindbergh was its impact on the history of aviation. It proved that it was possible to build planes capable of flying long distances safely, paving the way for the development of commercial airlines and specialized military aircraft.

**The Orteig Prize.** Lindbergh's flight was not the first Atlantic crossing by air. Eight years earlier five navy men in a seaplane, the NC-4, had flown from Newfoundland to the Azores to Portugal and then to England. Still, nobody had ever flown solo directly from an American city to a European capital, and the Orteig prize of $25,000 was offered for the first individual to accomplish such a feat.

**Richard Byrd.** Navy Comdr. Richard E. Byrd had flown over the North Pole in 1926 and was keen to win the honor of being the first to cross the Atlantic solo. He had had the runway at Roosevelt Field on Long Island lengthened to enable a plane laden with extra gasoline tanks to take off. Unfortunately for Byrd, a minor crash delayed his departure, and he approved the request of a long and lean midwestern mail pilot, Charles Lindbergh, to use the field.

**Backing.** Lindbergh, who was backed by Saint Louis civic boosters and aviation buffs, named his plane *The Spirit of St. Louis.* (It is now hanging in the National Air and Space Museum in Washington, D.C.) He wanted a specially constructed plane for the flight and finally signed a contract with Ryan Airlines of San Diego, California, to build the aircraft for $10,580. It had a nine-cylinder, air-cooled Curtiss-Wright engine with redundancies — back-up parts. It had two ignition systems, a double carburetor, and no radiator to spring a leak. Lindbergh not only supervised but assisted in the construction, which was accomplished in only sixty days.

**In the Air.** Lindbergh left San Diego for New York on 10 May 1927, stopping only for a brief layover in Saint Louis. On 12 May the bleary-eyed, twenty-five-year-old aviator taxied to a stop on at Roosevelt Field. After a week of last-minute preparations, interviews, and weather watching — during which Lindbergh is said to have gotten little sleep — the U.S. Weather Bureau finally issued a guardedly optimistic forecast for the North Atlantic on 20 May 1927. It was pouring rain on Long Island, but Lindbergh ordered his plane pushed out of the hanger and into takeoff position. With agonizing slowness the plane bumped across the muddy airstrip, barely getting up enough speed to clear a parked tractor and some overhead wires at the end of the runway. Finally at 7:52 A.M. *The Spirit of St. Louis* went airborne carrying 425 gallons of gasoline — its biggest load ever. The stripped-down cockpit contained no radio and no parachute. To save even more weight the cockpit seat was made out of wicker, and the only food Lindbergh carried was five sandwiches. The airplane had no windshield, only side windows, and to see ahead Lindbergh had to use a movable periscope.

**Over the Waves.** Lindbergh's plane, a monoplane in an era of biplanes, was the finest available, and the chances of its failing him were not great. The primary difficulty was in the takeoff, in which a crackup would almost certainly have created a blazing inferno. In a time before automatic pilots — and with thirty-seven course changes to make in thirty-three hours — Lindbergh was aware that his greatest enemy was sleep. He had prepared for the flight by deliberately depriving himself of sleep for long periods, but it is doubtful that such "training" was of any real benefit. His youth and stamina were his real strengths. Lindbergh had not even reached Nova Scotia when he first fell asleep, waking up with a jolt. When he opened a window to blow cold air on his face, his Mercator chart, on which he had plotted his great-circle course, almost got sucked out of the plane. He buzzed Saint John's, Newfoundland, to let people know he had made it to the extreme tip of North America, and then he headed out over the vastness of the open Atlantic.

**No Deicers.** Flying blind in dense clouds, Lindbergh rose to more than ten thousand feet, trying to get above them. He could not, and the wings began to ice up. By descending and maneuvering, he finally escaped the clouds and the ice, but sleepiness continued to dog him. He hallucinated, saw mirages, and sometimes snapped awake just as the plane was on the verge of setting down in the sea. Finally he saw the coast of Ireland, got a fix on his position, and steadied his course for Paris. At Le Bourget Airport on 21 May a tumultuous crowd of 100,000 excited Frenchmen surged onto the runway as he taxied to a stop. Lindbergh's epic flight of 3,610 miles had taken thirty-three and a half hours. The American was borne off the field in triumph on their shoulders, as souvenir seekers ripped off parts of the plane. President Calvin Coolidge had the national hero brought home on the navy cruiser *Memphis.* In his younger days Lindbergh had been a reserve second lieutenant in the U. S. Army Air Service. Now he was made a colonel. His safe landing on 21 May 1927 in France put American aviation on the high level it had been seeking for some time. A new era in aviation had dawned.

Sources:
Charles A. Lindbergh, *Of Flight and Life* (New York: Scribners, 1948);

Lindbergh, *"We"* (New York & London: Putnam, 1927).

# MARGARET MEAD

## 1901-1978

### ANTHROPOLOGIST

**A Classic Study.** Margaret Mead's *Coming of Age in Samoa,* a classic study of the influence of culture on individual personality, was a best-seller when it was published in 1928 and made her one of the best-known anthropologists in American history.

**Background.** Born in Philadelphia, Mead earned a B.A. at Barnard College (1923) and a Ph.D. at Columbia University (1929), where she studied anthropology under Franz Boas, who became her mentor. Boas removed the weight of racism from anthropology by denying the existence of "higher" or "lower" forms of humanity. He also denied that genetic inheritance was the primary determining factor in creating human capabilities, falling back on the view of John Locke that the environment in which the individual matures has a far greater influence on human development.

According to Boas — and Mead — it was not "nature" but "nurture" that was significant.

**Samoa.** Encouraged by Boas, Mead spent the period from November 1925 to June 1926 in the Samoan Islands, where she lived with an American family, studied the Samoan language, and interviewed about fifty adolescent females. This fieldwork convinced her that adolescence was a calm and peaceful period for the Samoans, in contrast to that of Americans, who as a culture underwent great emotional upheavals during that stage of life. To Mead the fact that adolescent Samoans were different from adolescent Americans proved that culture, not biology, was responsible for American teenagers' difficulties. When her *Coming of Age in Samoa* was published in 1928, it was hailed as a triumph for nurture over heredity.

**Rebuttal.** Shortly before she died, Mead was shown the manuscript for a reply to *Coming of Age in Samoa.* Derek Freeman had started his anthropological career as a great admirer of Mead, but after spending six years in Samoa, living with native families, and developing a complete mastery of the language, he came to the conclusion that Mead's research had been shallow, imprecise, and basically incorrect. In fact, Freeman maintained that the Samoans themselves felt the book was not factually correct. In his *Margaret Mead and Samoa: The Making and Unmaking of an Anthropological Myth* (1983), Freeman attempted to set the record straight. Some have called Freeman's book a polemic, but it is scholarly in substance and moderate in tone.

Sources:
Derek Freeman, *Margaret Mead and Samoa: The Making and Unmaking of an Anthropological Myth* (Cambridge, Mass.: Harvard University Press, 1983);

Jane Howard, *Margaret Mead: A Life* (New York: Simon & Schuster, 1984).

# ALBERT A. MICHELSON

## 1852-1931

### PHYSICIST

**Nobel Prize Winner.** The first American to win the Nobel Prize for physics, awarded in 1907, Albert Abraham Michelson is still renowned for his measurements of the speed of light and his calculation of the size of Betelgeuse, the first star other than the sun to be measured.

**Background.** Born to Jewish parents in a small Polish town that was at the time part of Prussia, Michelson immigrated to the United States with his family when he was four years old. He graduated from Annapolis in 1873 and served in the fleet until returning to the Naval Academy as an instructor in 1875. After study in Germany and France (1880–1882), he taught at Case School of Applied Science (1882–1889), Clark University (1889–1892), and the University of Chicago (1892–1931).

**Early Work.** In 1878–1879 Michelson measured the speed of light with impressive accuracy and found it to be a constant. He refined his measurements in 1882, coming up with 299,853 kilometers per second (a little over 186,000 miles per second), the accepted figure until 1927, when he was able to find an even more precise measurement. After moving on to Case in Cleveland, Michelson worked with Edward Morley on an experiment to prove the existence of the ether, the substance that was believed to fill outer space. Their failure to find ether eventually led scientists to abandon the ether theory and prepared the way for the conception of light rays as particles.

**Star Size.** While Michelson was at the University of Chicago he spent his summers at the California Institute of Technology and the nearby Mount Wilson Observatory. Using the 100-inch telescope, then the largest in the world, he built an interferometer onto it so that he could measure the diameter of a star. He selected Betelgeuse, the largest star in the constellation Orion, and with only the light from the opposite edges of Betelgeuse shining through the slits in the interferometer, he was able to gauge the star's angular diameter. Already knowing the distance of the star from Earth, Michelson then used trigonometry to calculate the actual diameter of Betelgeuse as 386 million kilometers, or 240 million miles. The final calculations and the dramatic announcement that Michelson was the first man ever to measure the size of a star (other than the sun) were made in December 1920.

Sources:

Bernard Jaffe, *Michelson and the Speed of Light* (Garden City, N.Y.: Doubleday, 1960);

Dorothy Michelson Livingston, *The Master of Light* (New York: Scribners, 1973).

## ROBERT A. MILLIKAN

### 1868-1953

#### PHYSICIST

**Nobel Prize Winner.** Robert Millikan won the Nobel Prize for physics in 1923 for his work on the charge of the electron and the photoelectric effect, work essentially completed by 1917. During the 1920s he devoted his attention to radioactivity from outer space, naming and investigating the phenomenon of cosmic rays.

**Early Life.** Robert Millikan was born in Morrison, Illinois, and graduated from Oberlin College in 1921. He received his doctorate in physics from Columbia University in New York City in 1895. After further study at

Göttingen and Berlin, Germany, he taught and did research at the University of Chicago until 1921, when he accepted a post at the California Institute of Technology in Pasadena, where he remained until his retirement in 1945.

**The Electronic Charge.** In 1906 Millikan began the work that led to his determination of the precise value of $e$ — the charge of the electron. By 1909 he had invented an oil-drop apparatus for use in his experiments. He sprayed droplets of oil about .001 mm in diameter into a chamber. Some of the drops fell by gravity through a pinhole into a lower chamber, where their speed — varied by an electric current — could be measured by a telescope aimed at a set of crosshairs. By causing the drop to fall at the same speed whether or not the current was applied, Millikan could determine that the drop (containing a single ion) was neutral. When an ion captured one or more electrons, its speed would increase, but always as a multiple of a certain quantity, which was analogous to the basic charge of a single electron. Millikan filled his chambers with various gases and used thousands of drops of various sizes and substances, but he obtained the same result. He reported his results in 1912 but continued to refine his determinations for the value of $e$ until 1917.

**Photoelectric Effect.** Millikan's next project was testing Albert Einstein's mathematical explanation for the photoelectric effect (1905), whereby light knocks negatively charged particles (electrons) out of a metal plate. Einstein used Max Planck's quantum theory to develop an equation stating that a particle, or quantum, of light, especially ultraviolet light, produces the photoelectric effect. Beginning in 1912 Millikan and his research team at Cal Tech conducted lengthy laboratory experiments, bombarding cylinders of the alkali metals sodium, potassium, and lithium with light rays of various frequencies (not just ultraviolet). The results, published in 1916, confirmed Einstein's equation, for which Millikan won a Nobel Prize in 1923.

**Cosmic Rays.** Millikan's next major project was his research on the charged particle of particularly high energy discovered by Swiss physicist Albert Gockel in 1910. At first this "air ionization" was thought to have been caused by radioactive elements on Earth, but the following year Austrian Victor Hess suggested that they came from outer space — a theory Millikan proved in 1925. He called this mysterious energy *cosmic rays,* but physicist Arthur Holly Compton maintained (correctly, as it turned out) that the cosmic rays were really particles with wave characteristics. Hoping to disprove Compton, Millikan assigned one of his best assistants, Carl Anderson, the task of researching cosmic radiation. In the process of carrying out the research, Anderson accidentally discovered a new particle, the antielectron or positron, which had been predicted to exist but which had never been found. Anderson was awarded a Nobel Prize for this discovery in 1936.

**Sources:**
Niels H. de V. Heathcote, *Nobel Prize Winners in Physics, 1901–1950* (New York: Schuman, 1953);

Robert H. Kargon, *The Rise of Robert Millikan: Portrait of a Life in American Science* (Ithaca, N.Y. & London: Cornell University Press, 1982).

# PEOPLE IN THE NEWS

In 1921–1922 naturalist **Carl Ethan Akeley** used the motion-picture camera he had patented in 1916 to make the first movies of gorillas in their natural habitat in Africa.

In May 1922 **George Frost,** eighteen-year-old president of the Lane High School Radio Club in Chicago, fitted the first automobile radio to the passenger door of a Ford Model T.

In 1928 pioneer astronomer **George Ellery Hale** secured a grant from the Rockefeller Foundation to construct an observatory on Mount Palomar for the California Institute of Technology. The telescope at this observatory was larger than the one at Cal Tech's Mount Wilson Observatory, for which Hale had also secured funding and which he directed from 1908 until 1923.

In the 10 July 1920 issue of *Scientific American* **Ralph Howard** expounded on the importance of the heat- and wear-resistant fiber asbestos, detailing its use as a fireproof insulation material for pipes, boilers, automobile spark plugs and brakes, stove lining, and domestic roofs, walls, and ceilings. He wrote that the material "contributes to the world's progress and makes life safer and more complete in an almost infinite number of ways."

In October 1923 **Reuben Leon Kahn** brought attention to his newly developed test for syphilis by testing forty serum samples in fifteen minutes. The standard Kahn test proved to be simpler, faster, and more sensitive than the widely used Wassermann test for syphilis.

In 1927 **Irving Langmuir,** a chemist with the General Electric research laboratory, invented atomic-hydrogen welding, making it possible to weld stainless steel, which could not be joined by older welding methods.

In November 1922 **A. C. Mace,** associate curator of the Egyptian Division of the Metropolitan Museum of Art in New York City, participated in the excavation of King Tutankhamen's tomb at the Thebes Necropolis in Egypt. Mace was part of a team led by the British archaeologist **Howard Carter.**

On 3 August 1921 **Lt. John B. Macready** performed the first aerial crop dusting. Working for the Ohio Agricultural Experimental Station, he used a light airplane to dust a six-acre catalpa grove infested with leaf caterpillars in Troy, Ohio.

In the 20 March 1920 issue of *Scientific American* **H. W. Nieman** and **C. Wells Nieman** proposed a method of communicating with intelligent Martians by using wireless telegraphy or flashes of light to send a series of Morse code signals that could be graphed as increasingly complex patterns and pictures.

In 1923 paleontologist **George Olsen** found the first fossilized dinosaur eggs. A member of the Central Asiatic Expedition to the Gobi Desert led by **Roy Chapman Andrews** and sponsored by the American Museum of Natural History in New York City, Olsen found the 95-million-year-old eggs in a cluster near the bones of the newly discovered dinosaur *Protoceratops andrewsi.*

On 27 February 1920 airplane pilot **Major Schroeder** set a new altitude record of 32,020 feet. After his oxygen supply ran out, he became unconscious and lost control of the plane. Never fully regaining consciousness, he leveled the plane at 2,000 feet and landed safely. When witnesses found him, they discovered that the frigid temperature at the extreme altitude he had reached had frozen the fluids in his eyes.

In 1920 pioneer biochemist **Harry Steenbock** isolated carotene, which is found in orange and yellow vegetables and contains vitamin A. By 1924 he and German chemist Adolf Windaus, working independently, had discovered that the ultraviolet rays in sunlight increase the amount of vitamin D in some foods.

In May 1922 **H. E. Winlock,** director of the archaeological excavations sponsored by the Metropolitan Museum of Art at the Thebes Necropolis in Egypt, described one of the greatest finds of the dig season (December 1921–May 1922): the Hekanakht Papers. Dating from 2004 B.C. and detailing agricultural practices of that time, these letters and scrolls are among the oldest documents in the world.

# AWARDS

## THE GUGGENHEIM AWARD

The Guggenheim Fund for the Promotion of Aeronautics established an award for significant progress in aviation research in 1929. The award for that year was given in April 1930.

1929: **Orville Wright,** for his role in inventing the first workable airplane.

## NOBEL PRIZE WINNERS

During the 1920s there were two Nobel Prizes awarded to Americans in the sciences. Both were in physics. (Albert Einstein, who became a resident of the United States in 1930 and a citizen in 1944, won the Nobel Prize for physics in 1921, while still a citizen of his native Germany.) The Nobel Prize represents worldwide recognition of a scientist's work and is widely considered the highest honor a scientist can receive.

1923: **Robert Millikan** won the Nobel Prize for physics for his work on measuring the charge of the electron and the photoelectric effect.

1927: **Arthur Holly Compton** shared the Nobel Prize for physics with British scientist C. T. R. Wilson for their research on X rays and cosmic rays.

# DEATHS

**Frank Stephen Baldwin,** 86, inventor of Baldwin calculator and other calculating machines, 8 April 1925.

**Edward E. Barnard,** 66, first astronomer to combine the camera and the telescope, taking photographs of plants, comets, nebulae, and the Milky Way, 6 February 1923.

**Alexander Graham Bell,** 75, inventor of the telephone, 2 August 1922.

**Emile Berliner,** 78, inventor of the microphone, the disk phonograph record, and the first workable helicopter, 3 August 1929.

**Hezekiah Bissel,** 93, the only engineer with the Union Pacific Railroad to see the construction of the transcontinental railway from start to finish (1862–1869), 23 June 1928.

**Bertram B. Boltwood,** 57, chemist and physicist who researched the properties of the radioactive elements uranium and thorium, discovering ionium, an isotope of thorium, and pioneering radioactive dating of geological strata, 15 August 1927.

**Charles Francis Brush,** 80, pioneer in methods of electric lighting, inventor of Brush electric arc light system used on the streets of Cleveland, Ohio, and New York City, 15 June 1929.

**Luther Burbank,** 77, botanist, the father of modern plant breeding, 11 April 1926.

**John Hoffman Dunlap,** 41, inventor of the diagonal-jet drinking fountain, which replaced the less-sanitary vertical-jet fountain, 29 July 1924.

**George Washington Goethals,** 69, chief engineer in charge of the construction of the Panama Canal (1907–1914), 21 January 1928.

**Granville Stanley Hall,** 80, widely regarded as the founder of educational and child psychology, 24 April 1924.

**John Fillmore Hayford,** 56, engineer who developed the theory of isostasy, which states that the surface materials of the Earth are so distributed as to exert an overall even pressure on the interior of the planet, 10 March 1925.

**John Wesley Hyatt,** 82, inventor of composition billiard ball, water filter and purifier, roller bearing, lock-stitch sewing machine, and celluloid, 10 May 1920.

**Henrietta Swan Leavitt,** 53, astronomer who found that Cepheid-variable stars — those with regular periods (cycles of fluctuation in brightness) — have periods proportional to their absolute magnitude (that is, the brighter the star the longer its period), a factor important in measuring the distance of such stars from Earth, 12 December 1921.

**Jacques Loeb,** 64, physiologist who conducted groundbreaking experiments on tropisms, parthogenic reproduction, and regeneration in lower animals, 11 February 1924.

**Hudson Maxim,** 74, explosives inventor, 6 May 1927.

**James Mooney,** 60, ethnologist with the Smithsonian Institution Bureau of American Ethnology, best known for his study of the Cherokee, Kiowa, and Sioux tribes, 22 December 1921.

**Edward W. Morley,** 85, chemist who worked with Albert Michelson on ether experiments, 24 February 1923.

**Raphael Pumpelly,** 85, geologist, first professor of mining at Harvard University and author of the survey of

U.S. mineral resources for the 1880 census, 10 August 1923.

**Ira Remsen,** 81, chemist, codiscoverer of saccharin, 4 March 1927.

**Theodore William Richards,** 60, winner of the 1914 Nobel Prize for chemistry for his determination of the atomic weights of sixty elements, 2 April 1928.

**John Martin Schaeberle,** 71, astronomer and engineer who invented instruments to improve astronomical observations, 17 September 1924.

**Charles Proteus Steinmetz,** 58, electrical engineer whose studies of alternating current (AC) helped to make its use commercially feasible, 26 October 1923.

**Edward Bradford Titchener,** 60, a leader of the structuralist school of psychologists, who helped to establish the scientific basis of his field, author of the two-volume *Experimental Psychology* (1901, 1905), editor of psychological journals, and founder of the Society of Experimental Psychology, 3 August 1927.

**Charles Doolittle Walcott,** 76, assistant geologist for the U.S. Geological Survey under Clarence King and J. Wesley Powell (1879–1893) and chief geologist for the survey (1894–1907); secretary of the Smithsonian Institution (1907–1927); a founder of the National Research Council, the National Advisory Committee on Aeronautics (which he directed during World War I), and the national airmail service (1918); president of the National Academy of Sciences (1917–1923); author of the Air Commerce Act of 1926 and various works on geology; 9 February 1927.

**John Findlay Wallace,** 68, engineer, a pioneer in the construction of elevated railroad tracks, 3 July 1921.

**Burt Green Wilder,** 83, professor of neurology and invertebrate zoology at Cornell University (1867–1910), known for his studies of the animal and human brain and his collection of brains willed to him by prominent intellectuals such as psychologist Edward Titchener, economist Jeremiah Whipple Jenks, pathologist Theobald White, and pacifist Rosika Schwimmer; willed his own brain to the collection; 22 January 1925.

# PUBLICATIONS

Wilhelm Bolsche, *Love-Life in Nature: The Story of the Evolution of Love* (New York: A. & C. Boni, 1926);

Gamaliel Bradford, *Darwin* (Boston & New York: Houghton Mifflin, 1926);

William H. Bragg, *Creative Knowledge: Old Trades and New Science* (New York & London: Harper, 1927);

C. D. Broad, *Scientific Thought* (New York: Harcourt, Brace, 1923);

Otis W. Caldwell and Edwin E. Slosson, eds., *Science Remaking the World* (Garden City, N.Y.: Doubleday, Page, 1923);

Herdman F. Cleland, *Our Prehistoric Ancestors* (New York: Coward-McCann, 1928);

A. P. Coleman, *Ice Ages, Recent and Ancient* (New York: Macmillan, 1926);

Henry Crew, *The Rise of Modern Physics: A Popular Sketch* (Baltimore: Williams & Wilkins, 1928);

J. T. Cunningham, *Hormones and Heredity* (New York: Macmillan, 1921);

Paul de Kruif, *Hunger Fighters* (New York: Harcourt, Brace, 1928);

de Kruif, *Microbe Hunters* (New York: Harcourt, Brace, 1926);

George A. Dorsey, *Hows and Whys of Human Behavior* (New York & London: Harper, 1929);

Dorsey, *Why We Behave Like Human Beings* (New York & London: Harper, 1925);

Charles R. Gibson, *Machines & How They Work: All Explained in an Easy Fashion* (Philadelphia: Lippincott, 1926);

George Ellery Hale, *Beyond the Milky Way* (New York & London: Scribners, 1926);

Hale, *The Depths of the Universe* (New York & London: Scribners, 1926);

Hale, *The New Heavens* (New York: Scribners, 1922);

Benjamin Harrow, *From Newton to Einstein: Changing Conceptions of the Universe*, second edition, revised and enlarged (New York: Van Nostrand, 1920);

Charles Homer Haskins, *Studies in the History of Mediæval Science* (Cambridge, Mass.: Harvard University Press, 1924);

William T. Hornaday, *The Minds and Manners of Wild Animals: A Book of Personal Observations* (New York: Scribners, 1922);

William J. Humphreys, *Physics of the Air* (Philadelphia: Lippincott, 1920; revised and enlarged edition, New York: McGraw-Hill, 1929);

Julian Huxley, *Essays in Popular Science* (New York: Knopf, 1927);

Thornwell Jacobs, *The New Science and the Old Religion* (Atlanta: Oglethorpe University Press, 1927);

Waldemar Kaempffert, ed., *A Popular History of American Invention*, 2 volumes (New York: Scribners, 1924);

Vernon L. Kellogg, *Human Life as the Biologist Sees It* (New York: Holt, 1922);

Kellogg, *Mind and Heredity* (Princeton: Princeton University Press, 1923);

Marion F. Lansing, *Great Moments in Science* (Garden City, N.Y.: Doubleday, Page, 1926);

Gilbert N. Lewis, *The Anatomy of Science* (New Haven: Yale University Press, 1926);

William A. Locy, *The Growth of Biology* (New York: Holt, 1925);

Oliver Lodge, *Evolution and Creation* (New York: Doran, 1926);

H. A. Lorentz, *Problems of Modern Physics* (Boston: Ginn, 1927);

Matthew Luckiesh, *Foundations of the Universe* (New York: Van Nostrand, 1925);

Margaret Mead, *Coming of Age in Samoa* (New York: Morrow, 1928);

George P. Merrill, *The First Hundred Years of American Geology* (New Haven: Yale University Press, 1924);

Robert A. Millikan, *Evolution in Science and Religion* (New Haven: Yale University Press, 1927);

S. A. Mitchell, *Eclipses of the Sun* (New York: Columbia University Press, 1923);

Louis T. More, *The Dogmas of Evolution* (Princeton: Princeton University Press, 1925);

Thomas Hunt Morgan, *Evolution and Genetics* (Princeton: Princeton University Press, 1925);

Joseph Needham, ed., *Science, Religion, and Reality* (New York: Macmillan, 1925);

Henry F. Osborn, *Evolution and Religion in Education: Polemics of the Fundamentalist Controversy of 1922 to 1926* (New York: Scribners, 1926);

Osborn, *From the Greeks to Darwin: The Development of the Evolution Idea through Twenty-four Centuries,* second edition, revised and enlarged (New York: Scribners, 1929);

Osborn, *Impressions of the Great Naturalists: Reminiscences of Darwin, Huxley, Balfour, Cope and Others* (New York: Scribners, 1928);

Osborn, *Man Rises to Parnassus: Critical Epochs in the Prehistory of Man* (Princeton: Princeton University Press, 1927);

James Edward Peabody and Arthur Ellsworth Hunt, *Biology and Human Welfare* (New York: Macmillan, 1924);

Raymond Pearl, *The Biology of Population Growth* (New York: Knopf, 1925);

Michael Pupin, *From Immigrant to Inventor* (New York: Scribners, 1923);

Pupin, *The New Reformation, From Physical to Spiritual* (New York: Scribners, 1927);

William S. Sadler, *Race Decadence: An Examination of the Causes of Racial Degeneracy in the United States* (Chicago: McClurg, 1922);

George Sarton, *Introduction to the History of Science,* volume 1 (Baltimore: Carnegie Institute, 1927);

Samuel Schmucker, *Man's Life on Earth* (Chatauqua, N.Y.: Chatauqua Press, 1925);

Paul Schubert, *The Electric Word: The Rise of Radio* (New York: Macmillan, 1928);

Robert Shafer, *Progress and Science: Essays in Criticism* (New Haven: Yale University Press, 1922);

Maynard Shipley, *The War on Modern Science: A Short History of the Fundamentalist Attacks on Evolution and Modernism* (New York: Knopf, 1927);

Charles Joseph Singer, *From Magic to Science, Essays on the Scientific Twilight* (New York: Boni & Liveright, 1928);

Edwin E. Slosson, *Chats on Science* (New York: Century, 1924);

Charles Proteus Steinmetz, *Four Lectures on Relativity and Space* (New York: McGraw-Hill, 1923);

John M. Stillman, *Theophrastus Bombasticus von Hohenheim Called Paracelsus* (Chicago & London: Open Court, 1920);

J. W. N. Sullivan, *Aspect of Science* (New York: Knopf, 1925);

J. Arthur Thomson, *The Outline of Science: A Plain Story Simply Told* (New York: Putnam, 1922);

William Morton Wheeler, *Foibles of Insects and Men* (New York: Knopf, 1928);

Wheeler, *Social Life Among the Insects* (New York: Harcourt, Brace, 1923);

Milton Whitney, *Soil and Civilization: A Modern Concept of the Soil and the Historical Development of Agriculture* (New York: Van Nostrand, 1925);

Harris Hawthorne Wilder, *The History of the Human Body,* second edition, revised (New York: Holt, 1923);

Wilder, *The Pedigree of the Human Race* (New York: Holt, 1926);

Clark Wissler, *Man and Culture* (New York: Crowell, 1923);

*National Geographic,* periodical;

*Scientific American,* periodical.

# SPORTS

by RONALD BAUGHMAN

## CONTENTS

*Sidebars and tables are listed in italics.*

# 1920

| | |
|---|---|
| **1 Jan.** | In the Rose Bowl Harvard beats the University of Oregon 7–6. |
| **3 Jan.** | Babe Ruth is sold by the Boston Red Sox to the New York Yankees. |
| **12 Feb.** | The National Negro Baseball League (NNBL) is founded. |
| **1 May** | The Brooklyn Dodgers play the Boston Braves to a 1–1 tie in twenty-six innings. Boston's Joe Oeschger and Brooklyn's Leon Cadore pitch the entire game. |
| **6 May** | Johnny Wilson wins the middleweight championship by a decision over Mike O'Dowd. |
| **12 June** | Man o' War runs the mile and 3/8 in 2 minutes 14⅕ seconds at Belmont. |
| **1 July** | Walter Johnson of the Washington Senators pitches a no-hitter against the Boston Red Sox. |
| **3 July** | William Tatem Tilden II becomes the first American to win the men's singles title at Wimbledon by defeating Australian Gerald Patterson 2–6, 6–3, 6–2, 6–4. |
| **10 July** | Man o' War beats John P. Grier in a match race at Aqueduct. He sets a new world record of 1 minute 49⅕ seconds for the mile and 1¹⁄₁₆ distance. |
| **15–27 July** | The U.S. yacht *Resolute* defeats Great Britain's *Shamrock IV* in the America's Cup race. |
| **16 July** | Jock Hutchison, a Scot living in the United States, wins the Professional Golfers' Association (PGA) title. |
| **16 Aug.** | The Cleveland Indians' Ray Chapman is killed when he is hit in the head by a ball pitched by the Yankees' Carl Mays. |
| **22 Aug.** | Fidel LaBarba wins the flyweight boxing championship by outpointing Frankie Genaro. |
| **4 Sept.** | Man o' War runs the mile and 5/8 in 2 minutes 40⅘ at Belmont. |
| **7 Sept.** | "Big Bill" Tilden beats fellow American "Little Bill" Johnston to claim the men's title at the U.S. Championships 6–1, 1–6, 7–5, 5–7, 6–3. |
| **15 Sept.** | Exterminator runs two miles in 3 minutes 21⅘ seconds at Belmont. |
| **17 Sept.** | The American Professional Football Association (APFA) is formed with Jim Thorpe as president; franchises are sold for $100. |
| **19 Sept.** | Norwegian-born Molla Bjurdstedt Mallory defeats American Marion Zinderstein 6–3, 6–1 for the women's title at the U.S. Championships. |
| **28 Sept.** | Eight Chicago White Sox players are indicted by a Chicago grand jury on charges that they conspired to throw the 1919 World Series. |
| **30 Sept.** | Babe Ruth finishes the season with fifty-four home runs, breaking his previous record of twenty-nine for the Boston Red Sox in 1919. |
| **2 Oct.** | Cincinnati and Pittsburgh schedule a triple-header but are forced to call the third game because of darkness. |
| **10 Oct.** | William "Wamby" Wambsganss, the Cleveland Indians second baseman, makes an unassisted triple play in the World Series. |
| **12 Oct.** | In his last race, the Kenilworth Gold Cup, Man o' War beats Sir Barton, the 1919 Triple Crown winner. |

The Cleveland Indians defeat the Brooklyn Dodgers in the World Series, 5 games to 2.

**25 Nov.**    WTAW, College Station, Texas, broadcasts the University of Texas–Texas A&M game, which the University of Texas wins 7–3.

The first international airplane race in the United States is held at Mitchel Field on Long Island and draws a crowd of twenty-five thousand to forty thousand. Known as the Pulitzer Race, it becomes an annual event; when other races are added to the program in 1924, the meet becomes known as the National Air Races.

**14 Dec.**    Notre Dame's All-American halfback George Gipp dies of pneumonia.

**22 Dec.**    Joe Lynch wins the bantamweight championship from Pete Herman on a decision.

**30 Dec.–**
**1 Jan. 1921**    The U.S. Davis Cup tennis team defeats Australasia 5–0 in Auckland, New Zealand.

# 1921

•    The U.S. Figure Skating Association is founded.

**1 Jan.**    In the Rose Bowl the University of California, Berkeley, beats Ohio State University 28–0.

**12 Jan.**    Judge Kenesaw Mountain Landis is appointed commissioner of baseball.

**23 Apr.**    Charles Paddock runs the 100 meters in 10.4 seconds and the 300 meters in 33.2 seconds.

**19 June**    During the first National Collegiate Athletics Association (NCAA) track-and-field championships, Paddock runs 220 yards twice in 20.8 seconds.

**25 June**    Pete Herman regains the bantamweight championship from Joe Lynch on a decision.

**26 June**    Jock Hutchison wins the British Open championship with a score of 296.

**3 July**    Bill Tilden defeats South Africa's Brian Ivan Cobb "Babe" Norton 4–6, 2–6, 6–1, 6–0, 7–5 in the Wimbledon men's final.

**21 July**    Jack Dempsey defends his heavyweight crown against Georges Carpentier in the first boxing match to have a "million-dollar gate."

**2 Aug.**    When testimony disappears, the eight members of the Chicago White Sox accused of fixing the 1919 World Series are found not guilty. Commissioner Landis subsequently bans them for life.

**14 Aug.**    English-born American golfer Jim Barnes wins the U.S. Open with a score of 289.

**21 Aug.**    Molla Bjurdstedt Mallory defeats American Mary K. Browne to take the women's crown at the U.S. Championships 4–6, 6–4, 6–2.

**2, 3, 5 Sept.**    In New York the United States beats Japan in Davis Cup play.

**20 Sept.**    Bill Tilden beats American Wallace Johnson 4–6, 6–4, 6–2 for the men's title at the U.S. Championships.

**1922**

**23 Sept.**  Johnny Buff wins the bantamweight championship from Pete Herman on a decision.

**29 Sept.**  Walter Hagen wins his first PGA Championship.

**13 Oct.**  The New York Giants defeat the New York Yankees in the World Series, 5 games to 3.

**25 Nov.**  The American Olympic Association, an organizing board for U.S. teams, is established.

- The American Professional Football Association (APFA) changes its name to the National Football League (NFL).

- George Halas renames his Chicago Staleys professional football team; they will now be known as the Chicago Bears.

- Jim Furey assembles the first true professional basketball team, which he calls the "Original Celtics."

**1 Jan.**  In the Rose Bowl the University of California, Berkeley, ties with Washington & Jefferson, 0–0.

**17 Mar.**  Edward "Mickey" Walker wins the welterweight championship from Jack Britton in a decision.

**30 Apr.**  Charles Robertson of the Chicago White Sox pitches a no-hitter against the Detroit Tigers.

**7 May**  Jesse Barnes of the New York Giants pitches a no-hitter against the Philadelphia Phillies.

**24 June**  Walter Hagen becomes the first American-born winner of the British Open golf tournament with a score of 300.

**9 July**  Molla Bjurdstedt Mallory reaches the women's final at Wimbledon but loses to France's Suzanne Lenglen 2–6, 0–6.

**10 July**  Joe Lynch regains the bantamweight championship by knocking out Johnny Buff.

**16 July**  Gene Sarazen wins the U.S. Open golfing championship with a score of 288.

**19 Aug.**  Gene Sarazen wins the PGA title.

**20 Aug.**  Molla Bjurdstedt Mallory beats Helen Wills 6–3, 6–1 to take the U.S. Championships women's title.

**20 Aug.**  Bill Tilden defeats Bill Johnston for the U.S. Championships men's title 4–6, 3–6, 6–2, 6–3, 6–4.

**26 Aug.**  The first Walker Cup golf matches are played at the National Links of America, Southampton, Long Island. The United States defeats Great Britain and Ireland 8–4.

**1, 2, 5 Sept.**  In New York the United States defeats Australasia 4–1 in Davis Cup play.

**1 Oct.**  Glenna Collett wins her first Women's National Championships golfing crown.

**8 Oct.**  The New York Giants defeat the New York Yankees in the World Series, 4 games to 0, plus one tie.

**28 Oct.** WEAF, New York, is the first radio station to broadcast a football game coast to coast: Princeton beats Chicago 21–18.

**29 Oct.** In the first game they play together, Stuhldreher, Miller, Crowley, and Layden — the Four Horseman of Notre Dame — lead their team to victory over Georgia Tech 13–3.

# 1923

- The National Negro Baseball League (NNBL) draws more than four hundred thousand spectators and earns $200,000 in gate receipts.

**1 Jan.** The University of Southern California beats Pennsylvania State University 14–3 in the Rose Bowl.

**17 Mar.** Mike McTigue wins the light heavyweight championship, outpointing Battling Siki in 20 rounds.

**2 June** Eugene Criqui wins the featherweight championship from Johnny Kilbane on a knockout.

**18 June** Pancho Villa wins the flyweight championship by knocking out Jimmy Wilde.

**8 July** Bill Johnston wins the men's title at Wimbledon by defeating fellow American Francis T. Hunter 6–0, 6–3, 6–1.

**16 July** Bobby Jones wins his first U.S. Open title with a score of 296.

**26 July** Johnny Dundee wins the featherweight championship from Eugene Criqui on a decision.

**Aug.** A new tennis stadium opens at Forest Hills, New York; a permanent concrete structure, it is the first of its kind for the sport. The Wightman Cup matches are the inaugural event for the facility.

**11, 13 Aug.** In the first Wightman Cup tennis competition the U.S. women defeat the British women 7–0.

**19 Aug.** Helen Wills wins her first singles title at the U.S. Championships by defeating Molla Bjurdstedt Mallory 6–2, 6–1.

**31 Aug.** Harry Greb wins the middleweight championship by a decision over Johnny Wilson.

**31 Aug.–
3 Sept.** The U.S. Davis Cup team defeats Australia 4–1 in New York.

**2 Sept.** Howard Ehmke of the Boston Red Sox pitches a no-hitter against the Philadelphia Athletics.

**14 Sept.** Jack Dempsey defends his heavyweight crown against Luis Angel Firpo.

**16 Sept.** Bill Tilden takes the men's U.S. Championships title by overpowering Bill Johnston 6–4, 6–1, 6–4.

**23 Sept.** Christopher "Battling" Battalino wins the featherweight championship from André Routis on a decision.

**30 Sept.** Gene Sarazen takes the PGA Championship for the second time in a row.

**15 Oct.** The New York Yankees defeat the New York Giants in the World Series, 4 games to 2.

**25 Oct.** The American Power Boat Association (APBA), adopting the rules of the Mississippi Valley Power Boat Association, begins to sanction power-boat races.

## 1924

- The Boston Bruins become the first U.S. team to join the National Hockey League (NHL).

**1 Jan.** In the Rose Bowl the University of Washington ties Navy 14–14.

**21 Mar.** Abe Goldstein wins the bantamweight championship from Joe Lynch by a decision.

**7 June** American golfer Cyril Walker wins the U.S. Open Championship with a score of 297.

**18–19 June** Great Britain defeats the United States in the Wightman Cup 6–1.

**28 June** Walter Hagen wins his second British Open with a score of 301.

**6 July** American tennis star Helen Wills plays for the women's singles title at Wimbledon but loses to Great Britain's Kathleen "Kitty" McKane 6–4, 4–6, 4–6.

**17 July** Jesse Haines of the Saint Louis Cardinals pitches a no-hitter against the Boston Braves.

**16 Aug.** Helen Wills defeats Molla Bjurdstedt Mallory 6–1, 6–2 to retain her women's title at the U.S. Championships.

**3 Sept.** Bill Tilden wins the U.S. Championships men's singles title with a 6–1, 9–7, 6–2 victory over Bill Johnston.

**11–13 Sept.** The United States wins 5–0 over Australia in Davis Cup play.

**21 Sept.** Walter Hagen wins the PGA title.

**28 Sept.** Paddy Driscoll of the Chicago Cardinals drop-kicks a fifty-yard field goal; he repeats this feat on 11 October 1924.

Bobby Jones wins his first U.S. Amateur Championship.

**5 Oct.** Rogers Hornsby of the Saint Louis Cardinals finishes the season with a .424 average — the highest in the history of major-league baseball.

**10 Oct.** The Washington Senators defeat the New York Giants in the World Series, 4 games to 3.

**18 Oct.** Halfback Harold "Red" Grange of the University of Illinois scores 4 touchdowns in 12 minutes against the University of Michigan on runs of 95 yards, 67 yards, 56 yards, and 44 yards.

**19 Dec.** Eddie Martin wins the bantamweight championship from Abe Goldstein on a decision.

## 1925

**1 Jan.** In the Rose Bowl Notre Dame defeats Stanford 27–10.

**20 Mar.** Phil Rosenberg wins the bantamweight championship from Eddie Martin in a decision.

| | |
|---|---|
| **3 May** | Paul Berlenbach wins the light heavyweight championship by outpointing Mike McTigue. |
| **1 June** | Lou Gehrig begins his record of playing 2,130 consecutive games when he pinch-hits for Yankees shortstop Pee Wee Wanninger. |
| **6 June** | American Willie MacFarlane defeats Bobby Jones in a play-off to take the U.S. Open with a score of 291. |
| **27 June** | Jim Barnes wins the British Open with a score of 300. |
| **14–15 Aug.** | Great Britain beats the United States in the Wightman Cup. |
| **25 Aug.** | Helen Wills defeats England's Kathleen "Kitty" McKane 3–6, 6–0, 6–2 to win her third straight title at the U.S. Championships. |
| **10–12 Sept.** | The United States defeats France 5–0 in Davis Cup play. |
| **13 Sept.** | Dazzy Vance pitches a no-hitter against the Philadelphia Phillies. |
| **20 Sept.** | Bill Tilden defeats Bill Johnston 4–6, 11–9, 6–3, 4–6, 6–3 in the men's U.S. Championships finals. |
| **27 Sept.** | Walter Hagen takes his second consecutive PGA Championship. |
| **5 Oct.** | Glenna Collett wins her second Women's National Championships golfing crown. |
| **15 Oct.** | The Pittsburgh Pirates defeat the Washington Senators in the World Series, 4 games to 3. |
| **26 Nov.** | Red Grange plays his first professional football game with the Chicago Bears against the Chicago Cardinals. It is the first professional football game to be broadcast on a nationwide hookup. |
| **28 Nov.** | A new Madison Square Garden designed by architect Thomas W. Lamb opens on Eighth Avenue between Forty-ninth and Fiftieth Streets. It remains in operation until February 1968. |
| **7 Dec.** | Rocky Kansas wins the lightweight boxing championship from Jimmy Goodrich on a decision. |

# 1926

| | |
|---|---|
| **1 Jan.** | In the Rose Bowl Alabama beats the University of Washington 20–19. |
| **16 Feb.** | At Cannes, Suzanne Lenglen defeats Helen Wills in the tennis "Match of the Century." |
| **28 Feb., 7 Mar.** | In two thirty-six-hole rounds on consecutive Sundays, Walter Hagen beats Bobby Jones. |
| **Apr.** | The New York Rangers, the Chicago Blackhawks, and the Detroit Cougars join the National Hockey League. |
| **May** | Branch Rickey is replaced by Rogers Hornsby as manager of the Saint Louis Cardinals. |
| **20 May** | Pete Latzo wins the welterweight championship from Mickey Walker on a decision. |

**17, 18 June**    The United States defeats Great Britain in Wightman Cup competition 4–3.

**26 June**    Bobby Jones wins the British Open with a score of 291.

**3 July**    Sammy Mandell wins the lightweight championship from Rocky Kansas on a decision.

**3 July**    American Howard Kinsey plays in the Wimbledon men's finals but loses to France's Jacques Boratra 6–8, 1–6, 3–6.

**11 July**    Bobby Jones wins the U.S. Open with a score of 293; he becomes the first American to win the British and U.S. titles in a single year.

**6 Aug.**    Gertrude Ederle becomes the first woman to swim the English Channel; her time is 14 hours 31 minutes.

**19 Aug.**    Tiger Flowers retains the middleweight championship, winning by a decision over Harry Greb.

**21 Aug.**    Ted Lyons of the Chicago White Sox pitches a no-hitter against the Boston Red Sox.

**24 Aug.**    Molla Bjurdstedt Mallory wins her eighth and final U.S. Championships singles title with a 4–6, 6–4, 9–7 victory over Great Britain's Elizabeth Ryan.

**9–11 Sept.**    The United States defeats France 4–1 in Davis Cup competition.

**23 Sept.**    In Philadelphia, Gene Tunney wins the heavyweight championship from Jack Dempsey in a ten-round unanimous decision.

**26 Sept.**    Walter Hagen takes his third consecutive PGA Championship.

**6 Oct.**    Babe Ruth hits 3 home runs in a World Series game.

**10 Oct.**    The Saint Louis Cardinals defeat the New York Yankees in the World Series, 4 games to 3.

**3 Dec.**    Mickey Walker wins the middleweight championship by a controversial decision over Tiger Flowers.

# 1927

**1 Jan.**    In the Rose Bowl Alabama ties Stanford 7–7.

**5 Apr.**    Johnny Weissmuller sets a record of 51 seconds in 100-yard freestyle swimming.

**4 May**    Weissmuller sets swimming records for 200 yards (1 minute 56⅘ seconds), 200 meters (2 minutes 2 seconds), and 220 yards (2 minutes 9 seconds).

**3 June**    Joe Dundee wins the welterweight championship from Pete Latzo by a decision.

**5 June**    The first Ryder Cup golf competition is played at the Worcester, Massachusetts, Country Club. The United States defeats Great Britain 9 1/2 to 2 1/2.

**3 July**    American Helen Wills wins the first of her eight Wimbledon singles titles by defeating Lili de Alvarez of Spain 6–2, 6–4.

**16 July**    Bobby Jones wins his second British Open title with a score of 285.

**12, 13 Aug.**    The United States beats Great Britain 5–2 in the Wightman Cup.

**31 Aug.**     Helen Wills defeats England's Betty Nuthall 6–1, 6–4 to take the women's title at the U.S. Championships.

**8–10 Sept.**     France defeats the United States 3–2 in Davis Cup competition; Bill Tilden loses to René Lacoste, and Bill Johnston loses to Lacoste and Henri Cochet.

**12 Sept.**     Benny Bass wins the featherweight championship by outpointing Red Chapman.

**17 Sept.**     Walter Hagen wins his fourth consecutive PGA title, which is his fifth PGA Championship of the decade.

**18 Sept.**     Bill Tilden loses to René Lacoste 9–11, 3–6, 9–11 in the men's final of the U.S. Championships.

**22 Sept.**     The Gene Tunney–Jack Dempsey heavyweight championship fight at Soldier Field, Chicago, draws $2.65 million — the first sports gate to top $2 million; Tunney keeps his title because of the legendary "long count" in the seventh round.

**30 Sept.**     Babe Ruth hits his sixtieth home run of the season.

**7 Oct.**     Tommy Loughran wins the light heavyweight championship by a decision over Mike McTigue.

**8 Oct.**     The New York Yankees defeat the Pittsburgh Pirates in the World Series, 4 games to 0.

# 1928

**1 Jan.**     In the Rose Bowl Stanford beats Pittsburgh 7–6.

**10 Feb.**     Tony Canzoneri wins the featherweight championship from Benny Bass on a decision.

**15 Apr.**     The New York Rangers are the first American team to win the National Hockey League Stanley Cup.

**12 May**     Walter Hagen wins his third British Open title with a score of 292.

**15–16 June**     Great Britain defeats the United States in the Wightman Cup 4–3.

**25 June**     American Johnny Farrell beats Bobby Jones in a play-off to win the U.S. Open with a score of 294.

**8 July**     Helen Wills defends her Wimbledon title by defeating Lili de Alvarez 6–2, 6–3.

**27–29 July**     The United States loses 4–1 in Davis Cup play against France; Bill Tilden gets the only U.S. victory by beating René Lacoste.

**18 Sept.**     Francis Hunter loses to France's Henri Cochet 6–4, 4–6, 6–3, 5–7, 3–6 in the men's final of the U.S. Championships.

**25 Sept.**     Helen Wills defeats American Helen Jacobs 6–2, 6–1 to take the women's singles final of the U.S. Championships.

**28 Sept.**     André Routis wins the featherweight championship from Tony Canzoneri on a decision.

**30 Sept.**     Glenna Collett wins her third Women's National Championships golfing crown.

**9 Oct.** The New York Yankees defeat the Saint Louis Cardinals in the World Series, 4 games to 0; this is the Yankees's second Series sweep in a row, and for the second time in his career Babe Ruth hits three home runs in a single game.

**6 Nov.** American Leo Diegel wins the PGA Championship.

**26 Dec.** Johnny Weissmuller retires from competition after having set sixty-seven world swimming records.

## 1929

**1 Jan.** Roy Riegels runs sixty-three yards to the wrong goalpost and sets up a score for Georgia Tech, who beat Riegels's team, the University of California, Berkeley, 8–7, in the Rose Bowl game.

**8 May** Carl Hubbell of the New York Giants pitches a no-hitter against the Pittsburgh Pirates.

**11 May** Walter Hagen wins his fourth British Open title with a score of 292.

**1 July** Bobby Jones beats Al Espinosa to win the U.S. Open with a score of 294.

**6 July** In the Wimbledon women's singles title match, which features America's two Helens — Wills and Jacobs — Wills defeats Jocabs 6–1, 6–2; Wills will win the title again in 1930, 1932, 1933, 1935, and 1938.

**9–10 Aug.** The United States beats Great Britain in Wightman Cup play 4–3.

**25 Aug.** Helen Wills wins the women's title at the U.S. Championships with a victory over Mrs. P. H. Watson 6–4, 6–2; Wills will win again in 1931 for a total of seven U.S. Championships singles titles.

**13 Sept.** Bill Tilden defeats Francis Hunter 3–6, 6–3, 4–6, 6–2, 6–4 in the men's finals of the U.S. championships; this is Tilden's seventh and last U.S. Championships singles title.

**6 Oct.** Glenna Collett wins her fourth Women's National Championships golfing crown; she will take her fifth in 1930 and her sixth in 1935.

**14 Oct.** The Philadelphia Athletics defeat the Chicago Cubs in the World Series, 4 games to 1.

**24 Oct.** The Carnegie Foundation for the Advancement of Teaching releases *American Collegiate Athletics,* a report documenting abuses in college-athletics programs, especially football, and calls for reforms.

**7 Dec.** Leo Diegel wins his second consecutive PGA Championship.

# OVERVIEW

---

**Legends.** The 1920s have been called the Golden Age of Sports. From the very beginning of the decade extraordinary athlete-heroes emerged in virtually every sport — baseball, football, tennis, golf, polo, and the Olympic sports. Babe Ruth, Ty Cobb, Lou Gehrig, Red Grange, Knute Rockne, Helen Wills, Bill Tilden, Bobby Jones, Walter Hagen, Jack Dempsey, Benny Leonard, and Tommy Hitchcock established records and, in the process, became legends.

**Prosperity and Play.** After the war America was eager both to work and to play. Prosperity, or at least the expectation of prosperity, characterized the nation. Citizens in increasing numbers were leaving farms to take jobs in the burgeoning industrial cities, and Americans' personal incomes improved significantly. By 1925, 40 percent of workers in the United States earned at least $2,000 annually — which would adequately if not extravagantly support a family of four — and many enjoyed shortened workweeks, which gave them increased leisure time. The nation went on a spending spree, buying, among other items, automobiles, radios, and tickets to movies and athletic events. In 1928 Stuart Chase wrote in "Play," collected in C. A. Beard's *Whither Mankind*: "Not far from one quarter of the entire national income of America is expended for play and recreation broadly interpreted. Perhaps half that sum is expended in forms of play new since the coming of the industrial revolution, and requiring more or less complicated machinery for their enjoyment."

**The New Machinery of Play.** Part of the expenditure for play was invested in giant stadiums — particularly for college football and professional baseball games — that were being built across the nation. As college football began to rival professional baseball in popularity, more than twenty universities with major football programs erected new stadiums during the 1920s. The most notable of these stadiums were at the University of Washington (built in 1920, capacity of 46,000); Stanford (1921, 86,011); Ohio State (1922, 85,339); Nebraska (1923, 73,650); Illinois (1923, 70,538); Purdue (1924, 67,861); Texas A&M (1925, 72,387); Missouri (1926, 62,000); Michigan (1927, 101,701); and Alabama (1929, 70,123). The New York Yankees' Bronx baseball stadium held

62,000 fans; called "The House that Ruth Built" in recognition of the home-run king's drawing power, it opened in 1923. A new $6-million, 18,000-seat Madison Square Garden opened on 28 November 1925. In 1923 the West Side Tennis Club built the country's first permanent tennis facility at Forest Hills, New York; the concrete stadium had a seating capacity of 14,000. These huge venues for sporting events also encouraged a building boom in public and private golf courses, tennis courts, swimming facilities, and multisport athletic clubs across the nation. Americans were not just watching sports; they were also participating in them.

**The Amateur Model.** Athletes were exalted as models for American youth, and sports were often regarded as builders not only of physical skills but also of moral character. Notre Dame coach Knute Rockne preached, and no doubt fervently believed, that football taught the individual to triumph over adversity and attain glory. For many, the amateur, who played for honor rather than money, could be the only true athlete-hero. The "Father of American Football" wrote in his 1893 volume *Walter Camp's Book of College Sports*, "A gentleman never competes for money, directly or indirectly. Make no mistake about this. No matter how winding the road may be that eventually brings the sovereign into the pocket, it is the price of what should be dearer to you than anything else — your honor." The great amateur athletes — Helen Wills, Bobby Jones, Tommy Hitchcock, and a legion of college football players — were regarded as ultimate exemplars of this athletic ideal.

**The Strain between Amateurism and Professionalism.** Athlete-heroes attracted large followings, which in turn generated huge gate receipts. For many amateur athletes during the 1920s, sport-for-sport's-sake began to be less attractive than sport-for-a-substantial-financial-reward. Although Bobby Jones remained an amateur and retired from golf never having earned a cent from his sport, others responded positively to the promise of big money and turned pro. In 1925 Red Grange left the University of Illinois immediately following his final college football game and joined the Chicago Bears, with whom he could earn more than $100,000 a year. He had become a client of the sports promoter C. C. Pyle, who in the following year, 1926, financed a professional tennis tour that lured both French star Suzanne Lenglen and the rising young American player Vincent Richards out of the amateur ranks. These defections to the professional arena were generally regarded as shocking, as affronts to the purity of sport. Through most of his career Bill Tilden denounced professionalism, asserting that those who played for pay were "turning whore," yet he too became a professional in 1931. Curiously, in the minds of the American public, paying athletes was allowable in certain sports but not in others. Professional football was, in its early years, regarded as somewhat disreputable while professional baseball was elevated to the national pastime. Baseball players usually received salaries of between $4,000 and $10,000 a year, and giants such as Babe Ruth and Ty Cobb were paid much more. Yet throughout much of the sports world in the 1920s, the conflict between amateurism and professionalism would remain a troublesome issue.

**Racism in Sports.** During the decade Jim Crow laws prevented most gifted black athletes from participating in the American Dream of success that was so much a part of the sports culture. Notable black athletes had appeared in the nineteenth century, particularly as jockeys, but after the turn of the century African Americans, generally speaking, were not allowed to compete with whites. There were black boxers, but only one, Tiger Flowers, held a title during the 1920s. Convinced that a mixed boxing match would have little gate appeal, many white boxers refused to face black fighters or, if they did, virtually required the African American fighters to lose. Yet, in at least one sport, blacks found a remedy. Since professional baseball excluded black athletes, African Americans founded, owned, and operated the Negro National Baseball League and the Eastern Colored League, which were established before the 1920s but achieved their highest level of stability during the decade.

**Sports and Media.** For Americans in general, participating in and watching sporting events became part of the good life. Radio broadcasts of college football and professional baseball began early in the 1920s and helped transform local athlete-heroes into national icons. Movie houses showed clips of sports contests and helped create stars. Newspapers and magazines gave the sports reporter a new authority as the media brought information about athletes and athletics to large, receptive audiences. Moreover, radio, movies, and the print media contributed to the "ballyhoo," or inflated dramatic interest, surrounding certain sporting events. They reported every rumor of secret "killer punches" or "evil eyes" being developed by Jack Dempsey and his various heavyweight opponents. They covered every unfolding development during the weeks preceding the 1926 Suzanne Lenglen–Helen Wills match in Cannes. The media supplied news but also manufactured it and, in the process, created and satisfied an eager audience. The 1920s roared with play. The decade was truly, for fans and athletes alike, the Golden Age of Sports.

# TOPICS IN THE NEWS

## BASEBALL: ADVANCEMENTS AND LEGENDS

**Baseball in Evolution.** Baseball in the 1920s was filled with superlative players, managers, and teams and with game-altering changes in strategy, equipment, and ballparks. For decades baseball had been played as a game of hit-and-run, choked-bat singles and bunts, and base-stealing; it had focused on the play among pitchers, short-ball hitters, and infielders. Such great singles hitters and base runners as the Detroit Tigers' Ty Cobb and the Pittsburgh Pirates' Honus Wagner epitomized this approach to the game. But change came as the decade began and Babe Ruth made his debut as a New York Yankee after being sold by the Boston Red Sox. The preceding year he had hit an astonishing twenty-nine home runs for Boston, and in 1920, his first season with the Yanks, he smashed an almost unbelievable fifty-four homers. League owners and managers — and the fans — fell in love with the drama of the long ball.

**Changes.** To increase the number of homers, which made games seem more exciting and caused gate receipts to rise dramatically, the ball was altered from the cork-and-rubber-centered "dead ball" to a more responsive so-called "rabbit ball." New baseball parks, too, were designed to help batters by means of outfields bounded by bleachers and fences. Rules were imposed forbidding pitchers to improve their odds with batters by scuffing or adding foreign substances to balls. All these changes in the game were intended to help batters hit long balls. The fans voiced their approval by coming to games in ever-increasing numbers through the decade. In turn, players' salaries, especially the salaries of those who hit often and long, improved as well. Yet some features of the game did not change much — for example, the well-publicized, colorful rowdiness that endeared such players as Ruth to an adoring nation.

**The Great Players.** The 1920s provided an extraordinary gathering of legendary players. In the outfield were the Yankees' Ruth (lifetime batting average of .342), the Tigers' Cobb (.367), and the Cleveland Indians' Tris Speaker (.344). The infield also had its fabled figures. At third base the Pittsburgh Pirates' Harold "Pie" Traynor, who was perhaps the decade's most skillful infielder, had

Rogers Hornsby hit over .400 three times; his .424 in 1924 has never been equaled.

a lifetime batting average of .320. At second base were the Saint Louis Cardinals' seven-time National League batting champion Rogers Hornsby (.358), the Chicago White Sox's Eddie Collins (.333), and the New York Giants' Frankie Frisch (.316). At first base were the Yankees' Lou Gehrig (.339) and the Saint Louis Browns' George Sisler (.340), and, at shortstop, Travis Jackson (.291), who was a standout infielder with the Giants.

## TY COBB'S UNBROKEN RECORD OF HOME PLATE STEALS

| GAME DATE | TEAMS AND SCORE | OPPOSING PITCHER/CATCHER | INNING |
|---|---|---|---|
| 22–7–09 | Boston 0, Detroit 6 | Wolter/Donohue | 7 |
| 16–8–10 | Detroit 8, Washington 3 | Groom/Ainsmith | 4 |
| 12–5–11 | New York 5, Detroit 6 | Caldwell/Sweeney | 7 |
| 12–7–11 | Philadelphia 0, Detroit 9 | Krause/Thomas | 1 |
| 18–8–11 | Detroit 9, New York 4 | Killalay/Carrigan | 1 |
| 20–4–12 | Detroit 6, Cleveland 5 | Gregg/Easterly | 1 |
| 1–5–12 | Detroit 2, Chicago 5 | Benz/Block | 1 |
| 13–5–12 | New York 15, Detroit 4 | Vaughn/Street | 1 |
| 21–6–12 | Detroit 2, Cleveland 6 | Blanding/O'Neill | 6 |
| 4–7–12(1) | St. Louis 3, Detroit 9 | Baumgardner/Krichell | 5 |
| 18–5–13 | Detroit 1, Washington 2 | Johnson/Ainsmith | 7 |
| 20–5–13 | Detroit 8, Philadelphia 7 | Houck/Lapp | 3 |
| 25–8–13 | Detroit 6, Washington 5 | Bedient/Nunamaker | 5 |
| 15–9–13 | New York 5, Detroit 7 | Warhop/Sweeney | 5 |
| 9–6–14 | Philadelphia 7, Detroit 1 | Shawkey/Lapp | 4 |
| 28–4–15 | St. Louis 3, Detroit 12 | James/Agnew | 3 |
| 4–6–15 | Detroit 3, New York 0 | Caldwell/Nunamaker | 9 |
| 9–6–15 | Detroit 15, Boston 0 | Collins/Carrigan | 3 |
| 18–6–15 | Detroit 5, Washington 3 | Boehling/Henry | 1 |
| 18–6–15 | Detroit 5, Washington 3 | Boehling/Williams | 5 |
| 23–6–15 | St. Louis 2, Detroit 4 | Lowdermilk/Agnew | 8 |
| 23–8–16 | Detroit 10, Philadelphia 3 | Sheehan/Picinich | 8 |
| 9–7–18(2) | Detroit 5, Philadelphia 4 | Perry/Perkins | 5 |
| 23–8–19 | Boston 4, Detroit 8 | Hoyt/Walters | 3 |
| 18–5–20 | Philadelphia 2, Detroit 8 | Martin/Myatt | 8 |
| 19–9–20(1) | Washington 7, Detroit 9 | Bono/Gharrity | 4 |
| 2–10–23 | Detroit 7, Chicago 5 | Castner/Crouse | 7 |
| 22–4–24 | Chicago 3, Detroit 4 | Bayne/Collins | 3 |
| 27–4–24 | Chicago 3, Detroit 4 | Lyons/Crouse | 5 |
| 10–8–24 | Detroit 13, Boston 7 | Ross/Picinich | 7 |
| 3–7–27 | Detroit 5, Cleveland 7 | Uhle/Sewell | 1 |
| 19–4–27 | Philadelphia 3, Washington 1 | Crowder/Ruel | 6 |
| 26–4–27 | Philadelphia 9, Boston 8 | Welzer/Hartley | 7 |
| 6–7–27 | Boston 1, Philadelphia 5 | Lundgren/Hartley | 1 |
| 15–6–28 | Philadelphia 12, Cleveland 5 | Grant/Sewell | 8 |
| World Series | | | |
| 9–10–09 | Detroit 7, Pittsburgh 2 | Willis/Gibson | 3 |

Source: Al Stump, *Cobb: A Biography* (Chapel Hill, N.C.: Algonquin, 1994).

# BABE RUTH'S 1927 RECORD OF SIXTY HOME RUNS

In 1927 New York Yankee Babe Ruth hit 60 home runs, one of which bounced from the field into the stands. Today this home run would be scored a double. His 60-home-run record stood until another Yankee, Roger Maris, broke it with 61 homers on 1 October 1961, but the 1961 season had eight more games (162) than did the 1927 season (154).

| HR/ Game | Date | Opposing Pitcher / Club | Where Made | HR/ Game | Date | Opposing Pitcher / Club | Where Made |
|---|---|---|---|---|---|---|---|
| 1 / 4 | 15 Apr. | Ehmke (R) / Phil. | N.Y. | 31 / 94 | 24 July | Thomas (R), Chi. | Chi. |
| 2 / 11 | 23 Apr. | Walberg (L), Phil. | Phil. | 32 / 95 | 26 July | Gaston (R), St. Louis | N.Y. |
| 3 / 12 | 24 Apr. | Thurston (R), Wash. | Wash. | 33 / 95 | 26 July | Gaston (R), St. Louis | N.Y. |
| 4 / 14 | 29 Apr. | Harriss (R), Bost. | Bost. | 34 / 98 | 28 July | Stewart (L), St. L. | N.Y. |
| 5 / 16 | 1 May | Quinn (R), Phil. | N.Y. | 35 / 106 | 5 Aug. | G. Smith (R), Det. | N.Y. |
| 6 / 16 | 1 May | Walberg (L), Phil. | N.Y. | 36 / 110 | 10 Aug. | Zachary (L), Wash. | Wash. |
| 7 / 24 | 10 May | Gaston (R), St. L. | St. L. | 37 / 114 | 11 Aug. | Thomas (R), Chic. | Chi. |
| 8 / 25 | 11 May | Nevers (R), St. L. | St. L. | 38 / 115 | 17 Aug. | Connally (R), Chi. | Chi. |
| 9 / 29 | 17 May | Collins (R), Det. | Det. | 39 / 118 | 20 Aug. | Miller (L), Clev. | Clev. |
| 10 / 33 | 22 May | Karr (R), Clev. | Clev. | 40 / 120 | 22 Aug. | Shaute (L), Clev. | Clev. |
| 11 / 34 | 23 May | Thurston (R) Wash. | Wash. | 41 / 124 | 22 Aug. | Nevers (R), St. L. | St. L. |
| 12 / 37 | 28 May | Thurston (R), Wash. | N.Y | 42 / 125 | 28 Aug. | Wingard (L), St. L. | St. L. |
| 13 / 39 | 29 May | MacFayden (R), Bost. | N.Y. | 43 / 127 | 31 Aug. | Welzer (R), Bost. | N.Y. |
| 14 / 41 | 30 May | Walberg (L), Phil. | Phil. | 44 / 128 | 2 Sept. | Walberg (L), Phil. | Phil. |
| 15 / 42 | 31 May | Ehmke (R), Phil. | Phil. | 45 / 132 | 6 Sept. | Welzer (R), Bost. | Bost. |
| 16 / 43 | 31 May | Quinn (R), Phil. | Phil. | 46 / 132 | 6 Sept. | Welzer (R), Bost. | Bost. |
| 17 / 47 | 5 June | Whitehill (L), Det. | N.Y. | 47 / 133 | 6 Sept. | Russell (R), Bost. | Bost. |
| 18 / 48 | 7 June | Thomas (R), Chi. | N.Y. | 48 / 134 | 7 Sept. | MacFayden (R), Bost. | Bost. |
| 19 / 52 | 11 June | Buckeye (L), Clev. | N.Y. | 49 / 134 | 7 Sept. | Harriss (R), Bost. | Bost. |
| 20 / 52 | 11 June | Buckeye (L), Clev. | N.Y. | 50 / 138 | 11 Sept. | Gaston (R), St. L. | N.Y. |
| 21 / 53 | 12 June | Uhle (R), Clev. | N.Y. | 51 / 139 | 13 Sept. | Hudlin (R), Clev. | N.Y. |
| 22 / 55 | 16 June | Zachary (L), St. L. | N.Y. | 52 / 140 | 13 Sept. | Shaute (L), Clev. | N.Y. |
| 23 / 60 | 22 June | Wiltse (L), Bost. | Bost. | 53 / 143 | 16 Sept. | Blankenship (R), Chi. | N.Y. |
| 24 / 60 | 22 June | Wiltse (L), Bost. | Bost. | 54 / 147 | 18 Sept. | Lyons (R), Chi. | N.Y. |
| 25 / 70 | 30 June | Harriss (R), Bost. | N.Y. | 55 / 148 | 21 Sept. | Gibson (R), Det. | N.Y. |
| 26 / 73 | 3 July | Lisenbee (R), Wash. | Wash. | 56 / 149 | 22 Sept. | Holloway (R), Det. | N.Y. |
| 27 / 78 | 8 July | Whitehill (L), Det. | Det. | 57 / 152 | 27 Sept. | Grove (L), Phil. | N.Y. |
| 28 / 79 | 9 July | Holloway (R), Det. | Det. | 58 / 153 | 29 Sept. | Lisenbee (R), Wash. | N.Y. |
| 29 / 79 | 9 July | Holloway (R), Det. | Det. | 59 / 153 | 29 Sept. | Hopkins (R), Wash. | N.Y. |
| 30 / 83 | 12 July | Shaute (L), Clev. | Clev. | 60 / 154 | 30 Sept. | Zachary (L), Wash. | N.Y. |

**Source:** *The Official Encyclopedia of Baseball*, sixth edition, edited by Hy Turkin and S. C. Thompson (New York: Barnes, 1972).

Two remarkable catchers were the Philadelphia Athletics' Mickey Cochrane (.320) and the Chicago Cubs' Gabby Hartnett (.297). Brilliant pitchers included the Washington Senators' Walter Johnson (416–279), the Philadelphia Athletics' Lefty Grove (300–141), the Cardinals' Grover Cleveland Alexander (373–208), the Brooklyn Dodgers' and then Pirates' Burleigh Grimes (270–212), and the Red Sox's and later Yankees' Herb Pennock (240–161).

**The Yankees and Huggins, the Cardinals and Rickey.** The greatest team of the era and probably of all baseball history was the 1927 Yankees, managed by the diminutive but iron-willed Miller Huggins. Under Huggins's direction was one of the finest home-run duos, Ruth and Gehrig, who between them hit 107 homers in 1927. Along with these two legendary players, the Yankees had Bob Muesel, Earl Combs, and Tony Lazzeri, who were also .300-plus hitters. With Huggins directing the team

(and often banging heads with the rambunctious Ruth), the Yankees won the 1923, 1927, and 1928 World Series. The 1926 Cardinals were also an outstanding team. It had been built by the remarkable Branch Rickey, who had been replaced as manager in May 1926 by second baseman Rogers Hornsby. Hornsby acquired thirty-nine-year-old pitcher Grover Cleveland Alexander from the Cubs, and in the 1926 Series, Alexander beat the Yankees twice and then, reportedly suffering from a hangover, came out of the bullpen to strike out Lazzeri with the bases loaded in the seventh inning of the seventh game. The Cards took the game and the world championship when Ruth was thrown out while trying to steal second.

**The Giants and McGraw, the Athletics and Mack.** The Giants' longtime manager John J. McGraw led his team to National League pennants from 1921 through 1924. His 1921 and 1922 teams defeated the Yankees in the World Series but his team lost to them in 1923. McGraw's 1924 team, his tenth and final pennant winner, faced the Senators and Walter Johnson in the Series. Johnson came in as a relief pitcher to win the final game four-to-three in the twelfth inning and thus gave the Senators their only championship during Johnson's twenty-year career with the team. As the 1920s came to an end, Connie Mack, baseball's grand old man and manager of the team since 1901, led his Philadelphia Athletics to a four-games-to-one 1929 Series victory over the Chicago Cubs, with splendid play by Mickey Cochrane and Lefty Grove. Mack's team also took the 1930 Series against the Saint Louis Cardinals in what would prove to be the last of his five world championships. In 1931 his team lost to the Cards, dashing Mack's hopes to be the first manager to win three consecutive World Series. Mack retired as the Athletics' manager on 18 August 1950 at the age of eighty-six. He had been with the team for nearly fifty years, and with his retirement the golden age of baseball in the 1920s seemed also to have come finally to a close.

Sources:

J. C. Furnas, *Great Times: An Informal Social History of the United States* (New York: Putnam, 1974);

*The History of Baseball,* edited by Allison Danzig and Joe Reichler (Englewood Cliffs, N.J.: Prentice-Hall, 1959);

*The Official Encyclopedia of Baseball,* sixth edition, edited by Hy Turkin and S. C. Thompson (New York: Barnes, 1972).

## BASEBALL: THE BLACK SOX SCANDAL

**The Conspiracy.** On 28 September 1920 a Chicago grand jury indicted eight Chicago White Sox baseball players for conspiring to throw the 1919 World Series, which they had played against the Cincinnati Reds. The players accused were pitchers Eddie Cicotte and Claude "Lefty" Williams, first baseman Arnold "Chick" Gandil, shortstop Charles "Swede" Risberg, third baseman George "Buck" Weaver, left fielder "Shoeless Joe" Jackson, center fielder Oscar "Happy" Felsch, and substitute

The 1919 Chicago "Black Sox," eight of whom were banned from baseball for conspiring to throw the World Series against the Cincinnati Reds

infielder Fred McMullen. The gamblers accused of fixing the Series were Arnold Rothstein, who had New York gangland connections; Abe Attell, a former feather-weight boxing champion; John "Sport" Sullivan from Chicago; and Billy Maharg from Philadelphia. Roth-stein's files revealed that he had paid the players bribes totaling $80,000.

**The Teams.** The 1919 Chicago White Sox were a strong team. During the regular season they had won eighty-eight games and lost fifty-two. Their opponents, the Cincinnati Reds, had gone ninety-six and forty-four that season and had won their first National League pennant since the team had become a charter member of the league in 1876. On the strength of their play during the 1919 season, the White Sox were five-to-one favor-ites to win the Series. National interest in this Series was so great that baseball officials changed the number of games played from the usual best four out of seven to the best five out of nine.

**The Games.** The Series opened in Cincinnati on 1 October, and suspicious events immediately occurred. Ty Cobb, who attended the games, later told a friend he had heard rumors that the Series had been fixed and that the White Sox pitcher would hit the Reds' first hitter with a pitched ball in the first inning to signal that the fix was on. Pitcher Cicotte hit Maury Rath, the Reds' lead-off batter. In the fourth inning of the game the Reds got five runs against Cicotte, a twenty-nine-game regular-season winner, to break a 1–1 tie and force Cicotte out of the game, which Cincinnati won 9–1. Although outhit 10 to 4, the Reds won the second game 4–2, with another fourth-inning explosion that knocked out White Sox pitcher Lefty Williams, a regular-season twenty-three-game winner. In the third game White Sox left-hander Dutch Ruether pitched a 3–0 shutout against Adolfo Luque. Cincinnati took the fourth game in a 2–0 pitcher's battle, with the Reds' Jimmy Ring allowing only three hits to loser Cicotte's five. In the fifth inning of this game Cicotte badly played an infield grounder and then

Judge Kenesaw Mountain Landis was appointed first baseball commissioner to clean up after the "Black Sox" scandal.

threw the ball into the outfield, allowing the runner to reach second; later he bobbled a throw from the outfield and a Reds player scored. Cincinnati, which now led the Series three games to one, took the next game 5–0, a shutout earned in part through White Sox fielding errors. The White Sox's Dickie Kerr won both the sixth game, 5–4, and the seventh game, 4–1. The Series ended with a 10–5 game when the Reds routed Lefty Williams in a four-run first-inning barrage, although Shoeless Joe Jackson hit a three-run homer to bring the Sox back from a 10–1 deficit.

**Immediate Doubts.** White Sox manager William "Kid" Gleason suspected something was amiss early in the first game and reported his concerns to White Sox owner Charles A. Comiskey. Comiskey allegedly related Gleason's apprehensions to National League president John Heylander, who dismissed them and did nothing. Throughout the winter and next summer, American League president Ban Johnson, who hoped to disprove the conspiracy rumors, gathered evidence to present to Judge Charles A. McDonald.

**Investigation and Trial.** In the course of his investigation Johnson discovered that Chick Gandil had, in fact, arranged a fix, for which he received $15,000 from Abe Attell, the go-between for the players and gamblers. Cicotte admitted that he had received $10,000 "for being a crook," and Shoeless Joe Jackson confessed that he had been present at the planning sessions and had been paid $5,000. Yet he hit .375 during the Series, knocking in six runs. Weaver claimed — and evidence supported him — that he had neither gone along with the fix nor received money; his requests for a dismissal were denied. The trial took place in Chicago in July 1921, but since player confessions and other documentary evidence had mysteriously disappeared, the eight were found not guilty of intent to defraud. It was rumored that after the verdict some jury members held a drunken party in the courtroom and carried the acquitted ball players around on their shoulders.

**The New Commissioner's Judgment.** Even before the 1919 scandal, owners had become increasingly dissatisfied with the three-man baseball commission, which had proved ineffective against gamblers' influence on the game and player rebelliousness. The owners therefore decided to appoint a single commissioner who would be granted virtually unlimited power to clean up baseball. In January 1921 Judge Kenesaw Mountain Landis was named first commissioner. A devoted baseball fan, Landis disregarded the Chicago jury's verdict and banned the eight players from baseball for life. "Regardless of the verdict of juries, no player that throws a ball game, no player that entertains proposals or promises to throw a game, no player that sits in conference with a bunch of crooked players and gamblers where the ways and means of throwing games are discussed and does not promptly tell his club about it, will ever play professional baseball," Landis stated. The two players most hurt by this lifetime disbarment were Jackson and Cicotte. Jackson, a hitter with Hall-of-Fame credentials, had a lifetime batting average of .356 when he stopped playing, while Cicotte had a 211–147 record and had reached his peak as a pitcher, winning in his last three seasons 28, 29, and 21 games, respectively. Because of the fix the 1919 White Sox would forever be remembered as the Black Sox, the team that tarnished their own name and that of baseball in general.

Sources:

Eliot Asinof, *Eight Men Out: The Black Sox and the 1919 Series* (New York: Holt, Rinehart & Winston, 1977);

Leo Katcher, *The Big Bankroll: The Life and Times of Arnold Rothstein* (New York: Harper, 1959);

Richard Scheinin, *Field of Screams: The Dark Underside of America's National Pastime* (New York: Norton, 1994).

## BASEBALL: THE NEGRO LEAGUES

**Jim Crow.** Throughout the early decades of the twentieth century, all sports — boxing, tennis, golf, basketball, football, racing, the Olympics — strongly discour-

The "Black Babe Ruth," catcher Josh Gibson was the most prolific home-run hitter in the Negro Leagues. He is credited with an unverified 962 homers.

but the most systematic structuring for the black game came with the founding of the National Negro Baseball League (NNBL) in 1920 and the Eastern Colored League (ECL) in 1923. In 1929 the ECL became the American Negro League (ANL) but collapsed after the season, and the NNBL disbanded after its 1931 season. Team membership in the various leagues was fluid, but, in all, sixty-three teams played baseball within or outside leagues from 1920 until 1949.

**Organizing Giant.** Andrew "Rube" Foster, the NNBL's black founder and president, had considerable executive skill; he enforced a 5 percent charge on all NNBL games as a means of shoring up the league's financial structure. The black clubs often had to pay stiff rents to play in white-owned ballparks, but despite such economic strains, the NNBL drew more than 400,000 spectators and earned $200,000 in gate receipts in 1923, and Foster's team, the American Giants, averaged $85,000 a game. Salaries and expenses, however, stretched profits thin. Black baseball players' salaries varied enormously, but the truly great pitchers and hitters might earn $1,000 a month, and they often played as many as two hundred games a season. Teams frequently folded or moved from city to city; they came and went with little notice.

**The Negro World Series in the 1920s.** Unlike records for white baseball, statistics for the Negro leagues tend to be unreliable. Press coverage of black games tended to be nonexistent or inaccurate, although accounts of the Negro World Series between the NNBL and the ECL are fuller and more reliable. In 1924 the Kansas City Monarchs of the NNBL defeated the Philadelphia Hilldales of the ECL five games to four. These two teams were owned by white men, J. L. Wilkinson (Kansas City) and Ed Bolden (Philadelphia). In 1925 the Hilldales got revenge on the Monarchs by beating them five games to one, and in 1926 the American Giants (NNBL) won five games to four over the Bacharach Giants (ECL). In 1927 the American Giants repeated as champions, taking the Bacharach Giants five games to three. Financial difficulties in the Eastern Colored League brought an end to these games at the end of the decade.

**Hall of Fame Players.** In an attempt to rectify at least partially the inequities of the past, Major League Baseball officials in the 1970s searched records for great black players of the Jim Crow years. As a result certain players have been inducted into the Cooperstown Hall of Fame. The first inductee was the flamboyant pitcher Leroy "Satchel" Paige (inducted in 1971), who played for twenty-one years in the NNBL with such teams as the Birmingham Black Barons and then spent six years in the majors, pitching from 1948 to 1953 for the Cleveland Indians and the Saint Louis Browns and, in 1965, for the Kansas City Athletics. Other players from the black leagues to receive Hall of Fame honors include power-hitting catcher Josh Gibson (1972), who starred for the

aged or, more often, prohibited African Americans from engaging in athletic activities with whites, though there were notable exceptions. Boxing's Joe Gans was lightweight champion between 1901 and 1908; Jack Johnson defeated Tommy Burns in 1908 for the heavyweight crown (and defended against Jim Jeffries in 1910, causing race riots in many cities); and Tiger Flowers held the middleweight title in 1926. But throughout the 1920s Jack Dempsey was reluctant to face such black boxers as John Lester Johnson or Harry Wills, the "New Orleans Brown Panther." In the nineteenth century nearly all jockeys had been black (Isaac Murphy won the Kentucky Derby three times), but at the turn of the twentieth century white jockeys formed an "anticolored union" that prohibited blacks from participating in the sport. As John Rickards Betts states, "No minority group has suffered so deeply or reaped such benefits from sport as has the American black."

**Leagues of Their Own.** Banned from white professional baseball, African Americans were playing in loosely organized teams and leagues during the 1890s,

**O**n 10 October 1920 William "Wamby" Wambsganss, Cleveland Indian second baseman, made the only unassisted triple play in World Series history and one of seven such plays in baseball history. With the Series between Cleveland and the Brooklyn Dodgers tied at two games each, the play occurred in the fifth inning of the fifth game. With Dodgers on first and second, Dodger relief pitcher Clarence Mitchell hit a hard line drive to Wamby for the first out. Wamby stepped on second for an automatic out against Brooklyn second baseman, Pete Kilduff, who had not returned to second after the catch but instead was heading toward third. Wamby then tagged catcher Otto Miller, who was approaching second from first. The same game produced other Series firsts: Cleveland outfielder Elmer Smith hit a grand-slam home run, Cleveland pitcher Jim Bagby became the first pitcher to hit a home run, and Clarence Mitchell, in two at bats, produced five outs against his own team. Cleveland won the game 7–0, and the Series 5–2.

**Source:** George K. Leonard, "Wambsganss' Wonder," *Yesterday in Sports*, edited by John Durant (New York: Barnes, 1956), p. 132.

Crawford Colored Giants and later the Homestead Grays; outfielder John Thomas "Cool Papa" Bell (1974), who played for the Saint Louis Stars; and outfielder Oscar Charleston (1976), who was a member of the Indianapolis ABCs, the Saint Louis Giants, the Harrisburg Giants, and the Philadelphia Hilldales. Shortstop and second baseman John Henry "Pop" Lloyd (1977), "the black Honus Wagner," hit and fielded for the Brooklyn Royal Giants, the Bacharach Giants, the Hilldale Giants, and the Lincoln Giants. William Julius "Judy" Johnson (1977) was a great third baseman for the Philadelphia Hilldales. Martin Dighigo (or DiHigo) (1977) played every position except catcher for the Cuban Stars (West), the Homestead Grays, and the Philadelphia Hilldales. Ray Dandridge (1987) was a standout third baseman for the Houston Eagles. NNBL president Rube Foster, who had been an outstanding turn-of-the-century pitcher, was inducted into the Hall of Fame in 1981.

**What Might Have Been.** As sports historian Mark Ribowsky notes, "Latter-day revisionists have combed over the eye-popping but poorly verified statistics of the Negro league greats and over-romanticized, even sanctified, men who lived not to engender a legend but only for the next game they could get. . . . But while the veracity of these records is surely open to question, we learn from them how surprisingly stable a good many black teams were. Despite tremendous hardships, the Negro leagues played set schedules. They kept their buses rolling through the East, the South, and the Midwest, lodged their players in hotels and rooming houses, rented stadiums, printed and sold tickets, even traveled with portable lights a decade before the first big league night game. Above all, the men of the Negro leagues played serious ball."

Sources:
John Rickards Betts, *America's Sporting Heritage: 1850–1950* (Reading, Mass.: Addison-Wesley, 1974);

Mark Ribowsky, *Don't Look Back: Satchel Paige in the Shadows of Baseball* (New York: Simon & Schuster, 1994).

## BASKETBALL

**A Lackluster Game: College Basketball.** Having been invented by James Naismith in the winter of 1891, basketball was not quite thirty years old as the decade of the 1920s began. In its adolescence the game had difficulties that tended to discourage both athletic participation and spectator interest. The interpretation of rules varied from game to game and court to court, thereby resulting in inconsistent officiating and confused players and observers. One set of referees often repeatedly officiated games for a single team and thus became virtually part of that team. As a consequence the phrase "home court advantage" carried real meaning, and few teams were eager to gamble their win-loss record at another school's gymnasium where they would be under the control of another team's officials. With two twenty-minute halves, games were short and extremely low-scoring, and until 1923 only one player from each team was allowed to shoot foul shots.

**Few Intersectional Games.** Only a few college conferences, such as the Big Ten or the Eastern Intercollegiate Basketball League, had any degree of regular play with actual schedules. Games between colleges from different sections of the country were even rarer. During the 1920s no single team dominated, though Penn was regarded as a power in the Eastern League. College basketball was not a major sport during the Golden Age, except perhaps once a year during the national championships, which had only recently been established. At the conclusion of the 1919–1920 season New York University traveled to Atlanta, Georgia, to win the National Amateur Athletic Union (AAU) basketball tournament and become the first national collegiate basketball champion of the decade.

**Professional Basketball.** Professional basketball, which in the 1920s attracted far more spectators than did college basketball, was extremely disorganized. A player might be part of one team one night and another the next, according to whoever offered him more money. A good professional player could earn anywhere from $40 to $125 a game, and he would possibly play one hundred or more games per season with a dozen or more teams. Sophisticated, well-planned-out team play, as a consequence, did not exist as the decade began.

**Birth of Team Identity: The "Original Celtics."**
Around 1922 Jim Furey assembled the first true professional basketball team and called it the "Original Celtics." As manager he contracted with players — Johnny Beckman, Pete Barry, Ernie Reich, Dutch Dehnert, Horse Haggerty, and Joe Trippe — to play only for him during the season. Furey hired a coach, Johnny Witte, and guaranteed his players a straight salary so that they could concentrate on developing their basketball skills rather than on finding teams to play with and against. There had been other teams called the Celtics before Furey's, but the Original Celtics were the first truly organized team. They dominated professional basketball in the 1920s because for the first time the same athletes played together game after game from the beginning to the end of the season. They developed plays and tactics that revolutionized the sport. During the decade shooting skill was regarded as a good player's major attribute, with the ability to take a physical beating a close second. The Original Celtics instead stressed individual and team speed and strategy; these qualities allowed them to get more shots than their opponents and to avoid a certain amount of the rough play.

**Influences.** Because of their skill and team cohesiveness, the Celtics defeated opponents by great margins. After building up substantial leads, they experimented with new plays and maneuvers during the game. Their successes soon prompted others to follow their lead and to develop similarly cohesive teams: for example, the New York Whirlwinds, the Cleveland Rosenblums, and the Washington Palace Five (named after the Washington, D.C., laundry of owner George Preston Marshall). Marshall, who also owned the National Football League's Washington Redskins, became professional basketball's greatest advocate during the 1920s.

**Game Boosters.** The Celtics themselves served as important boosters of professional basketball by playing 125 to 150 games per season and maintaining a win average of over .900. They tried to play every night and twice on Sunday, if possible. The Celtics eventually became part of professional basketball's American League, which adopted the same rules as intercollegiate basketball and eliminated the two-handed dribble. These changes eased the transition of such college stars as Vic Hanson of Syracuse University into the professional ranks. The Original Celtics' Beckman, who had previously been a top scorer for Nanticote in the Pennsylvania State League, was considered the best professional basketball player of the decade.

Source:
Tom Meany, "Basketball," in *Sport's Golden Age*, edited by Allison Danzig and Peter Brandwein (New York: Harper, 1948).

## BOXING

**The Rise in Popularity.** Throughout all weight divisions, from flyweight to heavyweight, the 1920s pro-

Tex Rickard, promoter of five million-dollar boxing gates

duced splendid boxers, including two of the greatest fighters of all time: heavyweight Jack Dempsey and lightweight Benny Leonard. Before World War I, boxing in the United States had been largely regarded as disreputable, practiced by rough characters in saloons and attracting spectators of uncertain character. After the war many of the laws that had banned boxing were rescinded, and the sport was brought under the control of commissions intended to reduce the undesirable criminal and gambling elements so often associated with it. With legal impediments lifted, boxing spread rapidly throughout the country and became one of the popular athletic spectacles for both the privileged classes and the common man.

**Dempsey's and Rickard's Long Shadows.** Jack Dempsey was one of the most compelling boxers in the ring and thus contributed to the rising interest in the sport during the decade. Promoter Tex Rickard helped elevate the financial rewards for boxers and bring a new glamour to their matches. The undisputed champion of boxing promoters, he produced the first million-dollar gate in the Dempsey–Georges Carpentier fight and then set up later matches that generated even more revenue.

Benny Leonard, the undefeated lightweight champion between 1917 and 1924, widely regarded as the greatest small boxer

**The Lighter Weights.** In the flyweight class (not over 112 pounds), Frankie Genaro, Pancho Villa, and Fidel LaBarba, a gold medalist in the 1924 Paris Olympics, were three standout fighters. Among the bantamweights (not over 118 pounds) Panama Al Brown, Pete Herman, and Joe Lynch were three of the best. The featherweight class (not over 126 pounds) was loaded with talent: Johnny Dundee, Eugene Criqui (a Frenchman), Louis "Kid" Kaplan, Benny Bass, and Christopher "Battling" Battalino, who won the title in September 1928 and held it until March 1932. In the lightweight class (not over 135 pounds) Benny Leonard is ranked as one of the greatest fighters of all time. On 28 May 1917 at age twenty-one, Leonard won the world lightweight championship by knocking out Freddie Welsh at the Manhattan Athletic Club in the ninth round. Leonard held onto his title for the next seven years and retired undefeated. Among his most memorable bouts were those with left-hander Lew Tendler. They first fought on 27 July 1922 at Boyle's Thirty Acres in Jersey City. Tendler buckled Leonard's knees with a smashing left in the eighth round, nearly knocking him out. Leonard, struggling to maintain his feet, held on to his opponent and asked if that was as hard as he could hit. Tendler, evidently surprised by the remark, did not take advantage of his opportunity, and Leonard won by a decision. In their next bout in 1923 Leonard won easily. The welterweight division (not over 147 pounds) included several excellent fighters. Edward "Mickey" Walker won the title in a fifteen-round decision over Jack Britton in New York in 1922. Four years later, on 20 May 1926, Pete Latzo decisioned Walker for the welterweight crown in Scranton, Pennsylvania, only to lose on 3 June 1927 to Johnny Dundee in New York. In 1929 Jackie Fields took the title from Dundee in Detroit.

**The Middleweights and Heavier.** Among the middleweights (not over 160 pounds) were Tiger Flowers, Mickey Walker (who had moved up from the welterweight division), and Harry Greb. Flowers, the first black to hold the title, defeated Greb for the championship in February 1926, successfully defended against Greb in August in a fifteen-round decision, and then lost in Chicago to Walker on 3 December 1926 in a controversial ten-round decision. In addition to Gene Tunney — who relinquished his light-heavyweight crown on 23 February 1923 to enter, in 1925, the heavyweight division — the light-heavyweight division (175 pounds) featured memorable fighters. Mike McTigue defeated the Senegalese Battling Siki for the crown on 17 March 1923 (Saint Patrick's Day) in Dublin, Ireland. The light-heavyweight title passed from McTigue to Paul Berlenbach to Jack Delaney to Tommy Loughran, who won it in New York on 7 October 1927 and retained it for nearly two years until he moved up to the heavyweight division.

**The Heavyweights.** The heavyweights have always had more crowd appeal than boxers in other weight classes, and Dempsey and Tunney were the dominant

For the second Dempsey–Gene Tunney fight in 1927 the gate was more than $2 million, with Tunney receiving the record sum of $990,445 as his cut. Rickard's efforts increased the "take" of fighters in general as well as turning boxing into a sport that drew larger and larger crowds throughout the decade.

## RECEIPTS AND ATTENDANCE FOR DEMPSEY'S MAJOR CHAMPIONSHIP FIGHTS

DEMPSEY-WILLARD

4 July 1919, Bay View Park Arena, Toledo, Ohio

Scheduled for Twelve Rounds

RESULT: The bout ended when Willard could not answer the bell for the fourth round.

Official attendance — — 19,650

Official gross — — $452,224

Willlard's share — — $100,100 guarantee

Dempsey's share — — $27,500 guarantee

Promoters — — Tex Rickard and Frank Flournoy

DEMPSEY-CARPENTIER

2 July 1921, Boyle's Thirty Acres, Jersey City, New Jersey.

Scheduled for Twelve Rounds

RESULT: Dempsey knocked out Carpentier in the fourth round.

Official attendance — — — 80,183

Official gross — — — $1,789,238

Dempsey's share (guaranteed) — — — $300,000

Dempsey's share (from movies) — — — $4,000

Carpentier' share (guaranteed) — — — $200,000

Promoter — — — Tex Rickard

DEMPSEY-FIRPO

14 September 1923, Polo Grounds, New York

Scheduled for Fifteen Rounds

RESULT: Dempsey knocked out Firpo in second round.

Official attendance — — — 82,000

Official gross — — — $1,188,603

Dempsey's share (including movies) — — — $509,000

Firpo's share — — — $156,250

Promoter — — — Tex Rickard

DEMPSEY-TUNNEY

26 September 1926, Sesquicentennial Stadium, Philadelphia

Scheduled for Ten Rounds

RESULT: Tunney won a ten-round decision.

Official attendance — — — 120,757

Official gross — — — $1,195,733

Dempsey's share — — — $717,000

Tunney's share — — — $200,000

Promoter — — — Tex Rickard

DEMPSEY-TUNNEY

22 September 1927, Soldiers Field, Chicago

Scheduled for Ten Rounds

RESULT: Tunney won a ten-round decision.

Official attendance — — — 104,943

Official gross — — — $2,658,660

Dempsey's share — — — $425,000, plus $25,000 from film rights

Tunney's share — — — $990,445

Promoter — — — Tex Rickard

Source: Nat Fleischer, *Jack Dempsey* (New Rochelle, N.Y.: Arlington House, 1972).

figures of the decade. Dempsey was heavyweight champion from 4 July 1919 until 23 September 1926, a remarkable seven years. Tunney beat Dempsey twice and, defending his title only once, retained the heavyweight crown from 23 September 1926 until his retirement in August 1928. Jack Sharkey became the third heavyweight champion of the decade when, on 27 February 1929, he won a ten-round decision over William L. "Young" Stribling. The Golden Age of boxing was over.

Sources:

James P. Dawson, "Boxing," in *Sport's Golden Age*, edited by Allison Danzig and Peter Brandwein (New York: Harper, 1948), pp. 38–85;

*The Encyclopedia of Sports*, fourth edition, edited by Frank G. Menke (New York: Barnes, 1969).

1924 gag photo of the Notre Dame Four Horsemen: (left to right) Don Miller, Elmer Layden, Jim Crowley, and Harry Stuhldreher

## FOOTBALL: COLLEGE

**Post–World War I.** Football in the 1920s was the quintessential college game. Certain strategies had been developing since before World War I to encourage a more wide-open style of play and to create spectator excitement, although the most important strategies actually had been available before 1910. Yet many coaches and players of the 1910s dismissed the forward pass as unmanly and unsportsmanlike until Gus Dorias threw to Knute Rockne in a 1 November 1913 game with powerhouse Army and helped Notre Dame pull off a 35–13 upset. It took the 1920s to turn such strategies into electrifying plays that became a necessary feature of every game. This new approach to football appealed as much to the general public as it did to students and alumni. In 1927 thirty million spectators paid more than $50 million for tickets to watch the September-to-Thanksgiving season of games. Huge stadiums were built that held seventy thousand and eighty thousand spectators. Voices of discontent accompanied the rise in spectator zeal and investment, but these voices complained not so much about the physical punishment to players or about its effects on academic environments but instead about its possible commercialization of an allegedly pure amateur amusement. College football challenged professional baseball as the nation's true spectator sport. It became part and perhaps symbol of exciting, noisy campus life during the decade and spread its intoxicating charm well beyond red brick buildings and Gothic spires.

**Eastern Bias.** Probably because of the game's origins in an intercollegiate rivalry between Rutgers and Princeton, the Ivy League football teams were long held to be the nation's most important. In 1920 twenty-one of the thirty-three players selected for first-, second-, and third-team All-America honors were from eastern colleges, while seven came from the Midwest, three from the South, and two from the Pacific Coast. Newspapermen in the large eastern metropolitan centers focused their attention on the Ivys with only a passing nod to the rest of the country. In 1920 these writers unanimously voted Princeton, led by All-Americans Don Lourie at quarterback and Stan Keck at tackle, the best team of the year. Princeton's 1922 team, coached by Bill Roper, captained by guard Mel Dickenson, and quarterbacked by Johnny Gorman, was dubbed the "Team of Destiny." Army was undefeated in 1922, and Cadet Edgar Garbisch was selected as an All-America center. In 1923 every team in the Ivy League was building or had built a new, larger stadium, and during that same year Yale went undefeated because of the gridiron heroics of Century

## RED GRANGE'S COLLEGE GRIDIRON RECORD

| Opponent | Touchdowns | Minutes played | Yards Gained | Passes & Yards |
|---|---|---|---|---|
| **1923** | | | | |
| Nebraska | 3 | 39 | 208 | |
| Iowa | 1 | 60 | 175 | |
| Butler | 2 | 28 | 142 | |
| Northwestern | 3 | 19 | 251 | |
| Chicago | 1 | 59 | 160 | |
| Wisconsin | 1 | 30 | 140 | |
| Ohio State | 1 | 60 | 184 | |
| Total | 12 | 295 | 1,260 | |
| | | | | |
| **1924** | | | | |
| Nebraska | 0 | 60 | 116 | 6 for 116 |
| Butler | 2 | 16 | 104 | 2 for 30 |
| Michigan | 5 | 41 | 402 | 6 for 64 |
| Iowa | 2 | 45 | 186 | 3 for 98 |
| Chicago | 3 | 60 | 300 | 7 for 177 |
| Minnesota | 1 | 44 | 56 | 3 for 39 |
| Total | 13 | 266 | 1,164 | 27 for 524 |
| | | | | |
| **1925** | | | | |
| Nebraska | 0 | 51 | 49 | 1 for 18 |
| Butler | 2 | 41 | 185 | 2 for 22 |
| Iowa | 1 | 60 | 208 | 2 for 24 |
| Michigan | 0 | 60 | 122 | |
| Pennsylvania | 3 | 57 | 363 | 1 for 13 |
| Chicago | 0 | 60 | 51 | |
| Ohio State | 0 | 48 | 235 | 9 for 42 |
| Total | 6 | 377 | 1,313 | 15 for 119 |
| | | | | |
| Total 1923–1925 | 31 | 928 | 3,737 | 42 for 643 yards |

**Source:** Gene Schoor, with Henry Gilfond, *Red Grange: Football's Greatest Halfback* (New York: Messner, 1952).

Milstead, as did Gil Dobie's Cornell team because of the play of George Pfann. Yet the rise of football greats in the rest of the country foretold the gradual decline in preeminence of eastern teams.

**Midwest.** The midwestern universities — Notre Dame, Illinois, Iowa, Michigan, Chicago, and others — experienced an embarrassment of riches in legendary coaches and players during the decade: Notre Dame's Rockne directed George Gipp in 1920 and the Four Horsemen from 1922 to 1924; from 1923 to 1925 Bob Zuppke and Red Grange dazzled Illinois's opponents; Howard Jones coached Iowa's Duke Slater and Aubrey Devine in 1921 and 1922; Michigan's Fielding H. (Hurry Up) Yost made his quarterback Benny Friedman and his end Bennie Oosterbaan the first famous passing combination in college football, particularly during the 1925 season; Amos Alonzo Stagg, football coach at the University of Chicago from 1892 to 1933, directed his Maroons to the 1924 Big Ten championship; in 1927, 1928, and 1929 Dr. Clarence Spears's Minnesota offense centered around his great end, tackle, and fullback Bronislau "Bronco" Nagurski. These legendary coaches and players helped refocus the sports pages away from regional to national coverage.

**South and West.** While the midwestern schools dramatically proclaimed their prominence, the South and the West, too, had their share of coach and player glory. The South's elite became Tennessee, Alabama, Vanderbilt, and Georgia Tech. Tennessee coach Bob Neyland from 1926 through 1935 established a record of seventy-five wins, seven losses, and five ties. In 1925 and 1926 Wallace Wade brought Alabama national prominence. The first southern team to play in the Rose Bowl, Alabama showcased quarterback Pooley Hubert, halfback Johnny Mack Brown, and passer Grant Gillis, who led in the defeat of Washington 20–19 in 1926. The following year Alabama and Stanford played to a 7–7 tie in the same bowl. Vanderbilt was undefeated through the 1922 and 1923 seasons, and coach Dan McGugin's best player was end Lynn Bomar, who helped Vandy upset Minnesota 16–0 in 1924. Losing their previous coach, John Heisman, to the University of Pennsylvania, Georgia Tech in 1920 hired new coach Bill Alexander, who accumulated a record of twenty-three wins, four losses, and one tie in his first three seasons and stayed at Tech for twenty-five years. His star back was an outstanding runner, David "Red" Barron. In the West the University of California, Berkeley's "Wonder Team" of 1920 introduced a decade of such teams. Coach Andy Smith developed an extraordinary passing combination in quarterback Harold "Brick" Muller and running back Howard "Brodie" Stephens, who contributed to California's 28–0 victory over Ohio State in the 1921 Rose Bowl. In 1923, though undefeated, California declined to play at Pasadena, giving the University of Southern California's team of Elmer "Gloomy Gus" Henderson national prominence. University of Washington teams, starring George Wilson and Elmer Tesreau in the backfield, gave their coach, Enoch Bagshaw, an 11–1 1923 record; they tied Navy 14–14 in the 1 January 1924 Rose Bowl. The coaching legend Glenn Scobie "Pop" Warner, who began his career at Stanford in 1924, attained national eminence as did his fullback Ernie Nevers. The single most famous (or infamous) event in Western Conference and college football history came when California's Roy Riegels picked up a fumble and ran the wrong way in a play that set up Georgia Tech's 8–7 victory in the 1 January 1929 Rose Bowl.

**The Southwest.** Football in the southwestern region of the country did not gain national distinction until late in the decade, particularly when Southern Methodist University's "Flying Circus" nearly upset powerful Army on 6 October 1928; coached by Ray Morrison, SMU's Redman Hume passed to end Sammy Reed in a dazzle of plays that outmaneuvered the Cadets throughout the game, though SMU lost 13–14. The Southwest Conference's greatest player of the decade was Texas A&M's halfback Joel Hunt, who became an all-conference choice from 1925 to 1928; coached by the wonderfully named Dana Xenophon "D. X." Bible, the Aggies had up-and-down seasons throughout the 1920s. Edward "Doc" Stewart's 1923 University of Texas team was considered by many to be the uncrowned champion of the conference; undefeated but twice tied, Texas had a great running back, Oscar Eckhardt. However, the Southwest Conference would have to wait for Texas Christian's Sammy Baugh to arrive in the mid 1930s before they received the national recognition they deserved.

**The Great American Game.** In all parts of the country, college football gained momentum with each season. The broadcasting of games over radio and the showing of filmed highlights in local theaters helped advance the sport beyond the individual campuses and well beyond the confines of a mere game. In his 1928 *Harper's Weekly* article, "The Great God Football," John R. Tunis correctly described the elevation in the 1920s of football to the level of art, science, combat, and religion. Tunis writes: "For where is the game to thrill and move the observer as can our modern football, where is the game to bring your heart up suddenly as the back catches a punt in an open field, sidesteps a charging end, swings past another, straight-arms a third, and sets out at last a free man while the stands rise with a spontaneous roar and the goal posts loom directly ahead? Where is the game to bring forth the art of war with none of its destruction, to combine strength and skill, strategy and science? Football in its place, football as a game, has no rivals; with all its faults it is much too fine a sport and much too splendid an entertainment to lose. . . . In short, why not take football as what it is: The Great American Game?"

Sources:
Dr. L. H. Baker, *Football: Facts and Figures* (New York: Farrar & Rinehart, 1945);

Harold Claassen and Steve Boda, eds., *Encyclopedia of Football*, third edition, (New York: Ronald Press, 1963);

Braven Dyer, "Football in the Far West," in *Sport's Golden Age*, edited by Allison Danzig and Peter Brandwein (New York: Harper, 1948);

Weldon Hart, "Football in the Southwest," in *Sport's Golden Age*, edited by Danzig and Brandwein (New York: Harper, 1948);

Fred Russell, "Football in the South," in *Sport's Golden Age*, edited by Danzig and Brandwein (New York: Harper, 1948);

Preston W. Slosson, "The Business of Sport," in *The Great Crusade and After 1914–1928* (New York: Macmillan, 1930);

John R. Tunis, "The Great God Football," *Harper's Weekly* (November 1928): 742–752;

Arch Ward, "Football in the Middle West," in *Sport's Golden Age*, edited by Danzig and Brandwein (New York: Harper, 1948);

Stanley Woodward, "The Football Panorama and Football in the East," in *Sport's Golden Age*, edited by Danzig and Brandwein (New York: Harper, 1948).

## FOOTBALL: PROFESSIONAL

**From Rags to Riches.** At the beginning of the 1920s professional football was in disarray. The play-for-pay sport was twenty-five years old in 1920, but few people took notice. Tickets to games could hardly be given away. Players met in the lobby of a hotel on a Sunday morning, discussed some plays, and then put them into the game that afternoon. A teammate in one game might be an opponent in the next. What league organization existed was merely a loose confederation. Four men changed the game into a popular, rapidly growing spectator sport before the decade was over: Joe E. Carr, Tim Mara, Red Grange, and George Halas.

**The National Football League.** On 17 September 1920 the American Professional Football Association was founded in Ralph Hays's automobile agency in Canton, Ohio. The great former Olympian and football star Jim Thorpe was elected president; Stanley Cofall, the former Notre Dame star and coach of the Massillon Tigers, was elected vice president. George Halas was also among those present. Each of the eleven franchise teams paid $100 to be part of the organization. These eleven teams were the Canton Bulldogs; the Cleveland Indians; the Dayton Triangles; the Akron Professionals; the Massillon Tigers; the Chicago Cardinals; the Chicago Staleys; and yet unnamed clubs in Rochester, New York; Rock Island, Illinois; Muncie, Indiana; and Hammond, Indiana. The association, however, lacked direction until 1921 when Joe E. Carr, an experienced sports promoter, transformed it into the well-managed National Football League, as the association was renamed in 1922. Carr realigned teams, and Green Bay, Buffalo, Detroit, Columbus, and Cincinnati franchises replaced Massillon, Muncie, and Hammond teams. Although it was in the smallest market, the Green Bay team, founded in 1921 by Earl Louis "Curly" Lambeau for $500, provided one of the most consistent spectator markets in the league.

**True League Prosperity.** The turning point for professional football occurred in 1925 when Tim Mara paid $2,500 for the New York Giants franchise although he had not seen a football game in his life. His purchase of the franchise proved to be a brilliant business venture, for it coincided with Red Grange's entry into the pro game. The huge New York sports market provided 76,000 paying customers to watch Grange and the Chicago Bears play the New York Giants on 6 December 1925. Such a crowd helped insure financial stability for Mara, Grange, and George Halas's Chicago team.

**Halas and Grange.** Grange was signed to play professional football by George Halas, the former University of Illinois great. When Halas finished playing college football, his coach, Bob Zuppke (later Grange's coach), bemoaned his player's graduation, saying, "Just as a player begins to get good and learn something about this game, he graduates." Zuppke's words stuck with Halas, who decided to remedy the absence of postgraduation foot-

ball. Halas, hired as the athletic director and football coach of the Staley Starch Works of Decatur, Illinois, formed the Chicago Staleys. He approached his professional team with a college coach's sense of organization, demanding daily practice, for example. Halas at first served as coach, captain, and end for the team. Later he became the team owner and in 1922 renamed his team the Chicago Bears. With Grange on the team, the Bears became a powerful club and financial success. Grange, who had been the most publicized college player in the country, created national interest and drew front-page newspaper coverage — the boost the sport needed to ensure its financial future. From 1925 on, professional football succeeded and eventually grew into one of America's greatest spectator attractions.

Sources:
Arthur Daley, "Professional Football," in *Sport's Golden Age*, edited by Allison Danzig and Peter Brandwein (New York: Harper, 1948);

*The Encyclopedia of Football*, edited by Roger Treat (New York: Barnes, 1959).

## GOLF

**Golfing Popularity.** Like virtually every other sport in America during the 1920s, golf experienced an extraordinary increase in popularity. The number of weekend golfers doubled between 1916 and 1920 to a high of one-half million. The sheer volume of players meant that new golf courses, private and public, had to be constructed. In the past golf often had been viewed as an exclusive game for the upper classes, but during the 1920s the game increasingly appealed, as a participant and a spectator sport, to the middle class, who enjoyed more leisure time and relative prosperity than ever before. These were the same people who thrilled to the exploits of a trio of American golfing heroes.

**America's Golfing Dominance.** Bobby Jones, who was the dominant golfer from 1923 to 1930, is widely regarded as the sport's greatest practitioner. Jones's two major rivals during the 1920s were Walter Hagen and Gene Sarazen, and this trio of Americans became known as the Three Musketeers. Together they overshadowed everyone else in U.S. and international golf. Two of the Musketeers were largely responsible for an astonishing accomplishment between 1921 and 1930. In 1921 Jock Hutchison, a Scotsman who had moved to the United States, won the British Open at St. Andrews as an American. From that point on, American golfers claimed the tournament nine times out of ten. Hagen took the title in 1922, 1924, 1928, and 1929; Jones won it in 1926, 1927, and 1930; and English-born American resident Jim Barnes carried it home in 1925. Only one British golfer, Arthur Havers in 1923, broke the string of American wins.

**Walter Hagen.** Hagen was the most colorful member of the Jones-Hagen-Sarazen trio, and his 1922 victory in the British Open made him the first American-born player to attain the championship. Golf historian Mark H.

Bobby Jones tees off as Walter Hagen watches.

McCormack notes that "Hagen was indisputably a genius. He must have been to have hit so many bad shots while winning so much and so often. . . . He made golf look difficult, and because most golfers find the game difficult they were able to identify with Hagen." He was noted for his natty attire on the links but more notably for his boldness in the game and in life. He was a persistent voice for admitting professionals to all the major tournaments; he loathed the time-honored notion that gentlemen should play for the pure joy of sport rather than pay. Hagen won the British Open four times, the U.S. Open twice, and the PGA title five times, which included four consecutive titles between 1924 and 1927.

**Gene Sarazen.** Sarazen was the most durable of the Three Musketeers. He was still competing at age fifty-six when he finished four rounds in the 1958 British Open Championship at Saint Anne's. Sarazen was the best "little man" playing golf. An ex-caddy from a humble background, he had changed his name from Eugene Saraceni because he thought it made him sound like a violinist. Sarazen claimed the golfing world's attention when, at the age of twenty-two, he won the 1922 U.S.

Open; turning professional, he took the PGA title that same year and then brashly challenged and defeated Hagen in a one-on-one match for the unofficial championship of the world. In one year Sarazen had come from obscurity to international fame. He would become the first golfer to win all four major professional titles: the U.S. Open (1922), the British Open (1932), the American PGA (1922, 1923, and 1933), and the Masters (1935).

**Other Golfing Stars of the 1920s.** There were, of course, other notable golfers, both American and European, during the 1920s. Great Britain's Joyce Wethered took the British Women's Amateur title four times, in 1922, 1924, 1925, and 1929, and France's Simone de la Chaune in 1927 became the first European to win the British women's championship. (She married tennis star René Lacoste, and their daughter, Catherine Lacoste, would win both the U.S. and the British Open titles in the mid 1960s.) Glenna Collett (later Glenna Collett Vare), one of America's best-known female golfers, won the U.S. women's crown in 1922, 1925, 1928, and 1929 (and again in 1930 and 1935). Jim Barnes claimed the

**W**alter Hagen, known as "the Haig," attracted crowds with his flamboyance. He began caddying at the age of seven and one-half in his native Rochester, New York. At twelve, he was in school one afternoon when he felt the call of the links. He waited until the teacher's back was turned, then jumped out the window and hurried to the golf course. That, in effect, ended his formal education. He caddied for several years, then obtained a succession of jobs in pro shops, eventually becoming a professional golfer, which carried very low status in the 1920s. Pros were, in effect, servants. They gave lessons to golf-club members, made clubs, and did various other chores, but they did not mix with the gentry. Hagen changed all that.

Three British Opens made the difference. In one, Hagen was told he had to eat his meals in the pro shop with the other hired hands. The next day he rented a chauffeured limousine to drive him to the front of the pro shop. He sat in regal splendor in the back of the car while a liveried footman served him an elaborate luncheon with the appropriate wine for each course. On another occasion, when he was made to dress in the pro shop instead of the club locker room, he again hired a chauffeured limousine, which drove him to the front of the pro shop; he changed into his beautifully tailored golfing clothes in the back of the car. These antics attracted attention, but they would not have changed anything had it not been for the fact that the Prince of Wales, later King Edward VIII, invited him to have lunch in the clubhouse at an English course. When the club attendants whispered to the prince that Hagen, as a golf pro, was not allowed in the clubhouse, the prince replied loudly that if Hagen left he, too, would go. From that point forward, the social distinction between pros and amateurs ceased to exist.

Source: Ron Fimrite, "Sir Walter," *Sports Illustrated*, 70 (19 June 1989): 75–82.

U.S. title in 1921, and Cyril Walker, a 118-pound club professional from Englewood, New Jersey, won it in 1924. Edmund R. Held of Saint Louis took the first USGA-sponsored Amateur Public Links championship in 1922. Leo Diegel won back-to-back PGA championships in 1928 and 1929. The 1920s were clearly a decade blessed by golfing talent.

Sources:

O. B. Keeler, "Golf," in *Sport's Golden Age,* edited by Allison Danzig and Peter Brandwein (New York: Harper, 1948), pp. 183–207;

Mark H. McCormack, *The Wonderful World of Professional Golf* (New York: Atheneum, 1973);

Michael Williams, *History of Golf* (Secaucus, N.J.: Chartwell, 1985);

Herbert Warren Wind, *The Story of American Golf* (New York: Simon & Schuster, 1956).

## OLYMPICS: THE SEVENTH OLYMPIC GAMES

**Olympic Site and Timing.** Because the small country of Belgium had displayed extraordinary courage during World War I, Antwerp was selected as the site for the Seventh Olympic Games, held in August 1920. Though admirable in sentiment, the choice of Belgium was unwise since the country had neither the finances nor the time to construct proper facilities for the games; moreover, most of the competing nations were fielding underprepared and underfunded teams.

**America's Preparation.** To raise money quickly, the United States developed an extensive system of spectator-financed tryouts throughout the country. As a result, $163,113.45 in gate receipts and contributions were raised, an amount that exceeded the eventual team costs of $149,261.46. Transporting the team to Europe posed a major difficulty. Many of the large American ships were still in poor condition because of their war duties, but eventually the main group of 254 athletes set out on 20 July aboard a troopship, the *Princess Matioka,* that had last been used to bring home American war dead.

**Mutiny after the *Matioka*.** The ship had cramped dining and sleeping quarters and reeked of formaldehyde. American team members protested loudly during their voyage, and following their arrival in Antwerp, their expectations for improved living conditions were dashed when they were moved into schoolhouses and barracks, where they slept on small, hard cots. Athletes and officials held angry meetings — with the team threatening to boycott competition — after jumper Dan Ahearn was suspended from the team for having moved to another room. Following heated exchanges, Ahearn was reinstated, and the team agreed to participate in the games, though their relatively few medals reflected their low morale.

**American Track-and-Field Medals.** The U.S team won nine of the thirty track-and-field events, which also featured the first Olympic appearance of nineteen-year-old Paavo Nurmi, the Flying Finn, who would have his best performance in the 1924 games. Aileen Riggins, a thirteen-year-old, won the gold medal in the diving competition; she remains the youngest female gold medalist in the history of the Olympics. Charley Paddock, the first man to be called "The World's Fastest Human," took the 100-meter dash but came in second to teammate Allen Woodring in the 200-meter sprint. Both Frank Foss, who won the pole vault, and Frank Loomis, who triumphed in the 400-meter hurdles, broke world records. Pat McDonald won the fifty-six-pound weight throw, and Pat Ryan took the hammer throw. The U.S. won the

Harold Abrahams setting an Olympic record of 10.6 seconds in the 100-meter event against Charles Paddock and Jackson Scholz in 1924

3,000-meter team race, and Dick Landon collected the ninth United States gold medal by jumping 6 feet 4⅕ inches in the high jump, an Olympic record.

**More Records, More Gold.** Hawaii's Duke Kahanamoku set an Olympic swimming record of 1 minute 1.4 seconds in the 100-meter freestyle, and Norman Ross, a rebellion leader, won both the 400-meter and 1,500-meter freestyle. The U.S. boxing team took more titles than any other team but scored second in total points to Great Britain. Although featherweight Charles Ackerly was the only American to win an individual wrestling title, the high number of second and third places brought a first-place team finish to the U.S. wrestlers. John Kelly, a Philadelphia bricklayer, who "may have been the greatest individual oarsman in history," according to Richard Schaap, won the single sculls championship and, with his cousin, Paul Costello, the double sculls. Kelly was subsequently barred from competing at Great Britain's Henley Regatta on the grounds that he was not a gentleman. His son, John B. Kelly Jr., won Henley in 1947 and 1949, and his daughter became Princess Grace of Monaco.

**Olympic Firsts.** The Seventh Olympic Games marked the first time women competed as members of the U.S. team. These games also saw the first unfurling of the five-ring Olympic flag. Moreover, during the 14 August opening ceremonies at Antwerp, athletes for the first time took the Olympic oath of amateurism and fair play.

Sources:

James Coote, *A Picture History of the Olympics* (New York: Macmillan, 1972);

Richard Schaap, *An Illustrated History of the Olympics*, second edition (New York: Knopf, 1967);

Alexander M. Weyand, *The Olympic Pageant* (New York: Macmillan, 1952).

## OLYMPICS: THE EIGHTH OLYMPIC GAMES

**Birth of the American Olympic Association.** To honor retiring International Olympic Committee Chairman Baron de Coubertin, the man responsible for proposing the modern Olympic Games in the early 1890s, the Eighth Olympics were held in Paris in July 1924. To resolve a power struggle among organizations hoping to direct the U.S. team, the American Olympic Association — composed of representatives from the competing groups — was created on 25 November 1921 as a permanent controlling board for American Olympic teams.

**High Olympic Spirits.** With funding of $350,000, the 417-member American team departed from Hoboken, New Jersey, on 16 June on the luxurious S.S. *America.* The experience of the 1924 team was the antithesis of that of the 1920 team. Spirits and morale were high on the way to the games and were further buoyed by American successes.

**Outstanding American Performances.** The U.S. track-and-field team won twelve gold medals, more than any other team at the Paris Olympics, yet the 1924 Olympics belonged to two athletes, Finland's Paavo Nurmi, a distance runner who won four events, and America's Johnny Weissmuller, who claimed three gold medals in swimming. Weissmuller took the 100-meter in 59 seconds, an Olympic record, and in the process beat the two-time defending champion, Duke Kahanamoku. He also finished the 400-meter freestyle in 5 minutes 4.2 seconds, bettering the previous Olympic record by a full twenty seconds. He was, in addition, a member of the 4 x 200 (800-meter) relay team — with Ralph Breyer, Wallace O'Connor, and Harry Glancy — who won their event in 9 minutes 53.4 seconds. An All-American water polo player, Weissmuller also won a bronze medal as a member of the U.S. water polo team.

**More Records and Gold.** Although two American favorites, Jackson Scholz and Charles Paddock, were beaten in the 100-meter race by Great Britain's Harold Abrahams (his story became the basis of the 1981 movie *Chariots of Fire*), the American track-and-field team made a strong showing. Harold Osborn and Clarence "Bud" Houser emerged as stars for the United States. Osborn leaped 6 feet 5 15/16 inches in the high jump, an Olympic record that stood for twelve years. He became the only man to win a gold medal for the decathlon and for an individual event. Houser won gold medals in the discus throw and shot put. Lee Barnes, a seventeen-year-old California high-school student, won the pole vault event. Ben Spock, the seventh rower on the Yale crew that won the eight-oar event, later gained fame as Dr. Benjamin Spock, the author of child-care books.

**Other Key Winners.** Swimmer Gertrude Ederle won a gold meal as a member of the U.S. 400-meter relay team and two bronze medals for her third places in the 100-meter and 400-meter freestyle events. In 1926 Ederle became the first woman to swim the English Channel. The tennis stars Helen Wills and Vincent Richards were standouts on a U.S. team that swept all five tennis titles. The 1924 games were the last in which tennis appeared as an Olympic event until 1988. Fidel LaBarba, the most gifted American boxer, won the flyweight division and then turned professional and soon became the world's flyweight champion.

**First Separate Winter Olympic Games.** The first Winter Olympic Games were held from 25 January through 4 February at Chamonix, France, with sixteen nations entering a total of three hundred athletes, including eleven-year-old Norwegian skater Sonja Henie, who finished last in her competition. American skaters and skiers fared poorly, though the U.S. hockey team finished second to Canada.

Sources:

James Coote, *A Picture History of the Olympics* (New York: Macmillan, 1972);

Richard Schaap, *An Illustrated History of the Olympics*, second edition (New York: Knopf, 1967);

Alexander M. Weyand, *The Olympic Pageant* (New York: Macmillan, 1952).

## OLYMPICS: THE NINTH OLYMPIC GAMES

**American Preparations.** In 1928 the tryout system developed in 1920 received its most enthusiastic response with twelve thousand to fifteen thousand athletes competing for places on the 320-member Olympic team. The U.S. Olympic Committee raised $415,696 and spent $330,465. The U.S. Olympic Committee president, Maj. Gen. Douglas MacArthur, expressed absolute faith in the American team who would travel to Amsterdam for the July–August summer games and to Saint Moritz in Feb-ruary for the winter games: "Without exception our athletes have come through the long grind of training into superb condition. They are prepared both mentally and physically for the great test. Americans can rest serene and assured," MacArthur asserted. Buoyed by self-confidence, money, and talent, the Americans anticipated great success in the games. But although the United States won more gold medals than any other team — twenty-four — they did not live up to their own or others' expectations and came home disappointed.

**Poor Track-and-Field Showing.** The American men's track-and-field team won eight gold medals, its worst performance in Olympic history. The United States failed to place in seven major races — the 100-meter, 200-meter, 800-meter, 1,500-meter, 5,000-meter, 10,000-meter, and the marathon. American gold medal winners were Ray Barbuti, who took the 400-meter race in 47.8 seconds; he was also a member of the gold-medal U.S. 1,600-meter relay team with Emerson Spencer, George Baird, and Fred Alderman, who finished in a time of 3 minutes 14.2 seconds. Robert King won the high jump; Edward Hamm took the broad jump; Sabin Carr claimed the pole vault; John Kuck won the shot put; and the dentist Clarence Houser, who had taken both the discus and the shot put in 1924, repeated as discus champion. The Americans also took the 400-meter relay in 41 seconds.

**U.S. Female Athletes.** In 1928 female track-and-field athletes competed for the first time in modern Olympic history. Elizabeth Robinson won the 100-meter dash in 12.2 seconds and was the only American female gold medalist. American women swimmers and divers, on the other hand, had an excellent showing, winning five of seven events: Albina Osipowich won the 100-meter freestyle; Martha Norelius, the 400-meter freestyle; Helen Meany, low springboard diving; Elizabeth Becker Pinkston, high diving; and Adelaide Lambert, Eleanor Garatti, Norelius, and Osipowich, the 400-meter relay.

**U.S. Men's Swimming.** The American men won five of eight events in swimming. The 800-meter relay race was won by Austin Clapp, Walter Laufer, George Kojac, and Johnny Weissmuller. Peter Desjardins dominated both the low springboard diving and the high-diving competition; Kojac claimed the gold in the 100-meter backstroke; and Weissmuller won the 100-meter freestyle. After the 1928 Olympics Weissmuller retired from competition and during the 1930s became Hollywood's most famous Tarzan.

**Other Outstanding Performances.** In rowing the University of California's eight-oared shell defeated the Thames Rowing Club for the gold medal. Paul Costello, with partner Charles McIlwaine, won a gold medal in the double sculls for the third straight Olympics. Although Americans reached the finals in every wrestling weight class, only Allie Morrison, a featherweight, won a gold medal. The United States won no championships in boxing.

**Winter in Saint Moritz.** In the Saint Moritz, Switzerland, winter games, the United States showed surprising strength but finished a distant second to Norway in overall points, 109.5 to 51. John Heaton won the skeleton bobsled race, while his brother, Jennison Heaton, finished second. Seventeen-year-old Billie Fiske led the American five-man bobsled team to victory in 3 minutes 20.5 seconds.

**Mixed Results.** In his official if somewhat ineloquent summation of the 1928 Olympics, General MacArthur adopted a positive stance in regard to the American team's quite mixed results: "Nothing is more synonymous of our national success than is our national success in athletics. The team proved itself a worthy successor of its brilliant predecessors." The United States did outscore other nations in the competition, but its expectations were not met by its actual accomplishments.

Sources:

James Coote, *A Picture History of the Olympics* (New York: Macmillan, 1972);

Richard Schaap, *An Illustrated History of the Olympics,* second edition (New York: Knopf, 1967);

Alexander M. Weyand, *The Olympic Pageant* (New York: Macmillan, 1952).

## TENNIS

**Tilden and Wills.** During the 1920s Bill Tilden and Helen Wills largely dominated tennis in America and abroad. The pair provided models of athleticism and mastery that appealed to their fellow citizens who were flocking to private and public courts in unprecedented numbers. Alongside these two tennis giants of the decade were other talented players who won major championships and who provided Tilden and Wills with the competition they required to develop their own enormous talents. Moreover, these figures were intimately involved in the explosion of interest in team play that occurred in the 1920s, whether in the women's Wightman Cup competition or the men's Davis Cup matches.

**Wightman and Mallory.** Among the best of the U.S. women players were Hazel Hotchkiss Wightman and Molla Bjurdstedt Mallory. Wightman, a fierce competitor, had won four U.S. Championships between 1909 and 1919 and in the course of her long career took more than sixty titles (she also claimed in 1930 the women's squash rackets championship and won second place in a mixed-doubles badminton championship in 1936 when she was fifty). Past her prime as a player when Helen Wills emerged, she still provided able competition to the younger woman. Mallory, a Norwegian-born American, was a stronger rival, though she, too, had already seen her best tennis years when Wills arrived. Mallory had been the most powerful American woman player between 1915 and 1922. She had won seven U.S. Championships and

---

### WILLIAM TATEM TILDEN II'S RECORD

**U**.S. Singles — 1920, 1921, 1922, 1923, 1924, 1925, 1929.

U.S. Doubles — 1918, 1921, 1922, 1923, 1927.

U.S. Mixed Doubles — 1913, 1914, 1922, 1923.

U.S. Clay Court Singles — 1922, 1923, 1924, 1925, 1926, 1927.

U.S. Indoor Singles — 1920

U.S. Indoor Doubles — 1919, 1920, 1926, 1929.

Wimbledon Singles — 1920, 1921, 1930.

Wimbledon Doubles — 1927.

World Hard Court Singles (Paris) — 1921.

*Record in Davis Cup Singles (1920–1930)*

| Matches | | Sets | | Games | |
|---|---|---|---|---|---|
| Won | Lost | Won | Lost | Won | Lost |
| 17 | 5 | 54 | 31 | 459 | 392 |

---

would take another in 1926, a year in which Wills did not compete. Mallory had never won Wimbledon, though in 1922 she had met Suzanne Lenglen in the finals. She would have beaten Lenglen in the first round of the U.S. Championships in August 1921, but Lenglen — ill and unnerved by Mallory's aggressive play and the goading of Mallory's friend Bill Tilden — defaulted in the match after the first set. Both Mallory and Wightman were still active players and fine opponents for Wills.

**Wightman Cup.** Furthermore, the two women were very much part of the women's team competition that became popular during the decade. In 1923 Wightman had established the Wightman Cup, which was originally intended to promote friendly competition between American women's tennis teams and women's tennis teams from a variety of European countries. In fact, because most European countries still felt economically unable to support teams because of their war debts, only England and the United States competed. The first American team in 1923 was composed of Wightman, Mallory, Wills, and Eleanor Goss; their opponents on the British team were Kathleen "Kitty" McKane (who would defeat Wills in the 1924 Wimbledon final), Mrs. Alfred E. Beamish, Mrs. R. C. Clayton, and Mrs. B. C. Covell. The Wightman Cup format featured five singles matches and two doubles, and in the first year of competition the Americans won 7–0. The next year the British won 6–1, and in the eight years of Wightman Cup play during the 1920s, the two teams exactly split the contests, which always sparked considerable public interest.

**Johnston, Williams, and Richards.** Among the fine American male tennis players who were Tilden's contemporaries and competitors was "Little Bill" Johnston, who won Wimbledon in 1923, had taken the U.S. Championship in 1915 and 1919, and had lost to Tilden in five other U.S. finals. The wealthy, cultured Richard Norris "Dick" Williams, who had won the U.S. Championship in 1914 and 1916, was known for his apparently effortless execution and for his superb doubles play. Vincent Richards, a rising young star who would shock the tennis world by turning professional in 1926, had a strong all-around game and, like Williams, with whom he often paired, was an impressive doubles player. In 1925 Tilden, Johnston, Richards, and Williams were ranked 1, 2, 3, and 5 in the world.

**Davis Cup.** The Davis Cup competition, begun in 1900, was a source of interest for Americans during the 1920s, because their country was able to field a superb team in the international competition and because this team dominated Davis Cup play from 1920 through 1926, taking all of the events during the period by 5–0 or 4–1 scores. In 1927, however, the Americans met a French team composed of rising young stars called the Four Musketeers — René Lacoste, Henri Cochet, Jean Borotra, and Jacques Brugnon — and lost 3–2, including one loss by Tilden himself. During the final two years of the decade Americans again played against France in the Davis Cup finals, but both Williams and Johnston had retired from competition, Richards was on the professional circuit, and Tilden was aging. The matches were often exciting and still stirred considerable interest in the American public, but the great days of American tennis in the 1920s were over.

Sources:

Parke Cummings, *American Tennis: The Story of a Game and Its People* (Boston: Little, Brown, 1957);

Frank Deford, *Big Bill Tilden: The Triumphs and the Tragedy* (New York: Simon & Schuster, 1976);

Lance Tingay, *Tennis: A Pictorial History* (New York: Putnam, 1973).

## YACHTING AND POLO: GENTLEMEN'S SPORTS

**Sports and Wealth.** During the 1920s the upper classes saw their control of American sports culture slip away. In the nineteenth century the wealthy had dictated both the type and tone of respectable athletic events, embracing such sports as cricket, track and field, golf, and lawn tennis. The principles of amateurism dominated, and sports were viewed as a means of protecting social status and instilling desired values in the young. After World War I, however, as athletic events attracted increasingly large audiences and began, in some cases, to feature professional stars, the influence of amateurism

Tommy Hitchcock Jr. and his father in the 1920s

faded. Golf and lawn tennis — once played only by the affluent on their estates and at summer resorts — became middle-class pastimes and began to attract followings as professional sports.

**Polo.** Polo had first been played in the United States in the 1880s, but its popularity among the wealthy increased greatly during the 1920s. The British, who had originated the game in India in the 1860s, dominated international play until World War I. The Americans then introduced a more aggressive style of play, bred faster ponies, abolished pony height restrictions, and eliminated the offsides rule that had given defensive teams an advantage. These changes were soon adopted for international matches by the primary polo-playing nations, including Great Britain and Argentina. As a result, polo became more exciting and — because of the high cost of maintaining large strings of ponies and better polo fields — more expensive. American teams soon won most of the major international tournaments, including the Westchester Cup versus Britain in 1921 and 1924 and the inaugural Copa de las Americas versus Argentina in 1928.

**Popularity.** Because of the success of the American international teams, the sport's popularity soared. By 1927 there were fifteen first-class polo grounds on Long Island alone. Collegiate teams became popular, particu-

## MAN O' WAR'S RECORD

### 1919 (2-year-old)

| Date | Track | Event | Finish |
|------|-------|-------|--------|
| 6 June | Belmont | Purse Race | First |
| 9 June | Belmont | Keene Memorial Stakes | First |
| 21 June | Jamaica | Youthful Stakes | First |
| 23 June | Aqueduct | Hudson Stakes | First |
| 5 July | Aqueduct | Tremont Stakes | First |
| 2 Aug. | Saratoga | U.S. Hotel Stakes | First |
| 13 Aug. | Saratoga | Sanford Memorial States | Second* |
| 23 Aug. | Saratoga | Grand Union Hotel Stakes | First |
| 30 Aug. | Saratoga | Hopeful Stakes | First |
| 13 Sept. | Belmont | Futurity Stakes | First |

*Lost to Upset by 1/2 length

### 1920 (3-year-old)

| Date | Track | Event | Finish |
|------|-------|-------|--------|
| 18 May | Pimlico | Preakness Stakes | First |
| 29 May | Belmont | Withers Stakes | First |
| 12 June | Belmont | Belmont Stakes | First |
| 22 June | Jamaica | Stuyvesant Handicap | First |
| 10 July | Aqueduct | Dwyer Stakes | First |
| 7 Aug. | Saratoga | Miller Stakes | First |
| 21 Aug. | Saratoga | Travers Stakes | First |
| 4 Sept. | Belmont | Lawrence Realization Stakes | First |
| 11 Sept. | Belmont | Jockey Club Stakes | First |
| 18 Sept. | Havre de Grace | Potomac Handicap | First |
| 12 Oct. | Kenilworth Park | Kenilworth Park Gold Cup | First |

Source: George Gipe, *The Great American Sports Book* (Garden City, N.Y.: Doubleday, 1978).

---

larly in the East. In 1929 the first intercollegiate match in the Midwest was played between Ohio State and the University of Chicago. Polo was taken up as well by army officers and by students at prep schools. Ironically, though wealthy Americans had embraced the game as an alternative to the professionalization and mass appeal of other sports, by the middle of the decade polo had become a spectator sport as well. Metropolitan newspapers and sophisticated magazines such as *Vanity Fair* and *The New Yorker* gave the sport broad coverage. International matches were highly publicized and drew crowds as large as forty thousand spectators. This popularity would fade with the onset of the Depression, but by the end of the 1920s polo had become the established sport of wealthy young Americans.

**Hitchcock.** The greatest polo player during the 1920s was Tommy Hitchcock. His father had helped popularize the game in the United States in the 1880s and 1890s. Tommy Hitchcock learned polo on his family's estates in Aiken, South Carolina, and Old Westbury, Long Island. During World War I Hitchcock joined the Lafayette Escadrille, a group of Americans who volunteered for the French air service, and in March 1918 was shot down and imprisoned in Germany. He escaped, made his way to France, and returned home a decorated war hero. Hitchcock enrolled at Harvard, where he gained recognition as a member of the United States Polo Association's championship teams in 1919, 1920, and 1921 and established himself as a ten-goal player — the highest ranking in the sport. After graduation Hitchcock captained the 1924 American Olympic team, which lost to Argentina in the gold-medal match, and led American victories in international championships against Great Britain in 1927 and Argentina in 1928. Hitchcock remained an active polo player until 1941 when, following the Japanese attack on Pearl Harbor, he volunteered for the Army Air Corps. He died in an air crash in 1944 while testing a P-51 Mustang.

**Yachting.** Though yacht racing had been popular since the eighteenth century, the sport changed markedly during the 1920s, primarily because of new design rules and advancing boat technology. Designer Nat Herreshoff's *Reliance* — a technologically advanced yacht — had easily won the prestigious America's Cup race in 1903, inspiring increasingly complex and fragile boat designs. The 1920 Cup was marred by the British captain's refusal to sail his *Shamrock IV* on the fifth day of racing, claiming the stormy sea conditions threatened to destroy his boat. The American yacht *Resolute,* another Herreshoff-designed craft, won handily in the make-up race, but critics decried the trend in recent boat designs, claiming their fragility made a mockery of the sport and elevated technology over seamanship. These protests led to changes in racing rules that made the 1920s the grandest era in American yachting.

**New Regulations.** Racing in the United States traditionally had been regulated by individual yacht clubs and local racing associations. In 1925 the North American Yacht Racing Union (NAYRU) became the first permanent legislative body on a national level. In 1927 NAYRU officials met with the International Yacht Racing Union in London and adopted the new design standards called the International Rule. Under these guidelines length, sail area, and hull shape were regulated to ensure safer, more seaworthy boats. Also instituted was a new rating system that established standardized classes of yachts based on water-line length. These new regulations led to the construction of "J-class" boats with seventy-five- to eighty-seven-foot water lines — the largest and most elaborate racing yachts ever designed.

**Culmination.** When the America's Cup committee announced that the next match would allow boats up to J-class to compete, groups of wealthy Boston and New York businessmen — enriched by the burgeoning American stock market — entered an aggressive competition to build the boat selected for the upcoming Cup defense. The trend of increasingly large, ornate, and advanced yachts culminated in 1930, when four J-class boats competed in a series of trials to select the American entry. Starling Burgess's *Enterprise* won easily and in the Cup race handily defeated the technologically inferior *Shamrock V* from Britain. Yachting — particularly the grandeur of J-class boat racing — would continue as a popular sport for the wealthy even through the Depression, fading only with the onset of World War II.

**Sources:**

Nelson W. Aldrich, *Tommy Hitchcock: An American Hero* (Gaithersburg, Md.: Fleet Street, 1984);

" 'Better and More Expensive Polo,' Thanks to American Players," *Literary Digest,* 94 (17 September 1927): 56;

A. B. C. Whipple, *The Racing Yachts* (Alexandria, Va.: Time-Life, 1980);

"Yachting to the Fore," *Nation,* 115 (20 September 1922): 272.

# HEADLINE MAKERS

## TYRUS "TY" RAYMOND COBB

### 1886-1961

#### MASTER HITTER AND BASE RUNNER

**Champion and Psychotic.** Tyrus "Ty" Raymond Cobb, "the Georgia Peach," was arguably the greatest and certainly one of the most controversial baseball players in the history of the game. His biographer, Al Stump, asserts that Cobb was probably psychotic throughout his adult life; he clearly exhibited psychotic behavior, for he played with a hostile aggressiveness that provoked fistfights with opposing players, fans, umpires, managers, and his teammates. He was a brilliant hitter and base stealer.

**Records.** Cobb began his baseball career in the so-called "dead ball" era, a time when baseball was primarily a game of strategic hits, bunting, and base stealing. Cobb elevated these skills to a fine art, especially as a singles hitter. He gripped the bat with his hands wide apart in order to control placement of hits. During his twenty-four seasons he played in 3,033 games, in the course of which he had 11,429 at-bats and 4,191 base hits. His 3,052 singles and 5,863 total earned bases are records that still stand in the mid 1990s. Cobb amassed a career total of 118 home runs at a time when they were valued less than they later were to become. His runs batted in totaled 1,901, and his lifetime batting average of .367 remains the highest in baseball history. Only in his first season — when his average was .234 — did he bat less than .300, and he hit .400 or better three times; from 1907 through 1915 he won nine consecutive batting championships. Cobb was an extraordinary base runner and base stealer. He led the American League in stolen bases six times and had a career total of 892 stolen bases, including a record 35 stolen home bases in regular-season play.

**Early Career.** Cobb's long baseball career represented a triumph of talent and will over self-created difficulties. The career started in 1904 when he was seventeen and

playing for the Augusta, Georgia, Tourists, who cut him from the team before he was placed on the payroll. His first paying position was with the Anniston, Alabama, semiprofessional team; in 1905 he again played for the Augusta team but was so hated by manager Andy Roth that he was sold for $25 to the Charleston, South Carolina, Tourists, whose owners rescinded the deal the next day.

**Major Leagues.** Called up to the Major Leagues by the American League's Detroit Tigers in 1905, Cobb remained with the Tigers as an outfielder and, later, manager through 1927, spending his final 1928 season with the Philadelphia Athletics. Although he hated Cobb and had even campaigned to have him thrown out of the league, Athletics owner Connie Mack signed Cobb in 1928 for a salary of $70,000, 10 percent of the preseason gate receipts, and a $20,000 bonus if the Athletics won the pennant — which they did not — for a total of $85,000. According to Stump, "Since Babe Ruth did not enjoy a share in Yankee preseason income, that left Cobb still the highest-paid individual in the profession." He officially retired from baseball on 11 September 1928 in Yankee Stadium but made his final appearance in an exhibition game in Toronto on 14 September. In 1936 he was the first of the original five players elected to the Baseball Hall of Fame, along with Babe Ruth, Honus Wagner, Christy Mathewson, and Walter Johnson.

**Personal Difficulties.** Cobb's brilliant baseball accomplishments were marred by his personal difficulties on and off the field. From the very beginning his fierce competitive nature raised hostilities in his teammates, opposing players, team managers, team owners, fans, and himself. He was infamous for, in full view of opposing teams, sharpening his spikes so that they would shred the clothes and limbs of infielders who tried to prevent his base stealing. He received such rough treatment from teammates that on 17 July 1906 he was hospitalized for an emotional breakdown. From that point on he was forever at war with everyone else involved with baseball. In 1919 Cobb challenged American League umpire Billy Evans to slug it out after a game. When Evans asked how he wanted to fight, Cobb answered, "No rules — I fight to kill." Cobb particularly hated blacks whom he thought might have shown signs of disrespect toward him: he physically attacked a black waitress over a $1.50 bill; he slapped a black elevator operator at the Euclid Hotel in Cleveland, and then nearly murdered the black night watchman who came to the operator's defense. George Napoleon "Nap" Rucker, one of the few players who ever agreed to room with Cobb, once returned to their hotel room early to take a hot bath; discovering Rucker in the bathtub, Cobb screamed, choked his roommate, and tried to yank him from the tub: "I've got to be first at everything — all the time." This desire always to be first and its accompanying attack mentality contributed to much of Cobb's troubles with others.

**Early Life.** Cobb's psychotic character undoubtedly was influenced by the circumstances of his early life, particularly the manner of his father's death. Born in a three-room, pine-and-clay cabin in Royston, Georgia, Ty Cobb was the first child of W. H. Cobb, a locally prominent educator and later state politician, and Amanda Chitwood Cobb. When they married in 1883, W. H. Cobb was twenty-nine and Amanda Chitwood was twelve; she was fifteen when she gave birth to Ty Cobb. On 19 August 1905 eighteen-year-old Cobb was called up to the Detroit Tigers to replace an injured outfielder; the day before he left for Detroit, Cobb received news that his father had been shotgunned to death by his mother, who allegedly mistook his father for a burglar and blasted him at close range with both barrels. Cobb had revered his father; he was the one man — besides Jesus Christ — whom he loved, Cobb was later to say. Throughout his life Cobb wept when expressing his regret that his father never saw his Major League successes. The death of W. H. Cobb and the complicity of his mother in that death no doubt contributed to Cobb's pathological personality and his subsequent wars with teammates and others.

**Emergence of Babe Ruth.** The character of baseball changed with the arrival of Babe Ruth, who brought to the Major Leagues his extraordinary home-run hitting, dubbed the "long-ball" approach to the game. The fans who had appreciated the earlier, more strategy-driven approach to baseball now gave way to those who wanted the dramatic excitement of the homer. Cobb was extremely jealous of Ruth, claiming that anyone could hit home runs: "I knew Ruth couldn't hit with me — that is, *real* hitting — or even run bases with me — or [play] outfield with me." Cobb also used virulently racist language to goad Ruth into a fistfight, but several Tigers separated the two before any blows were struck. From that point on, Cobb incurred the Yankee star's contempt.

**Wealth.** Though hated by other players, managers, umpires, and baseball fans, Cobb nonetheless counted celebrities as friends, including President Warren G. Harding and his cronies, with whom he played poker in the White House; Jack Dempsey, the heavyweight champion; and a variety of national business and political leaders. Through these connections and through his hard-headed negotiations with team owners, Cobb was able to accumulate a fortune, estimated at $12 million when he died. After his first season with the Tigers, Cobb insisted on a raise, and in January 1906 he was offered and signed a contract for $1,500, $300 dollars more than he had asked for. In 1921 his salary was raised from $20,000 plus bonuses to $35,000 a year when he became the team's player-manager. During the 1920s most players earned $4,000 to $10,000 a season. Cobb regularly negotiated his own salary and with the help of a banker friend was also able to obtain long-term bonuses and acquire stock in the team. By 1924 his income from baseball was nearly $60,000, while his earnings from investments closely matched this sum. Early on he bought stock in Coca-Cola, Hupmobile, and General Motors, and the value of his Coca-Cola stock alone made him a wealthy man during the 1920s. Moreover, his political connections helped him evade scandals late in his career, especially one that suggested Cobb and Cleveland manager Tris Speaker had taken part in a gambling conspiracy by fixing a game between Detroit and Cleveland on 25 September 1919. In the wake of the Black Sox Scandal, important baseball figures and Cobb's political friends prevailed on Judge Kenesaw Mountain Landis, newly appointed baseball commissioner, to acquit the two players of any wrongdoing.

**Death.** Cobb died of cancer on 17 July 1961 at age seventy-four. On 5 June he had signed himself into Emory University Hospital in Atlanta, undressed, and placed on his bedside table a brown paper bag filled with $1 million worth of securities and topped with a Luger pistol. Only three representatives from baseball came to his funeral — catchers Mickey Cochrane and Ray Schalk and his minor-league roommate, Nap Rucker. Even at his death, baseball officially shunned one of the most gifted and most difficult players in the game.

Sources:

Robert W. Creamer, *Babe: The Legend Comes to Life* (New York: Simon & Schuster, 1974);

Al Stump, *Cobb: A Biography* (Chapel Hill, N.C.: Algonquin Books, 1994).

# WILLIAM "JACK" HARRISON DEMPSEY

## 1895-1983

### HEAVYWEIGHT CHAMPION

**Accomplishments.** In 1950 Jack Dempsey, a member of the Boxing Hall of Fame, was selected, in a nationwide Associated Press poll, as the Fighter of the Half Century. Dempsey had come to stand for the poor, small man's triumphant battle against giant opponents and gigantic adversities; as such he was an embodiment of the 1920s pursuit of and admiration for success. After winning the heavyweight championship in 1919, Dempsey in 1921 attracted the first $1-million boxing gate on 21 July 1921 and drew four more million-dollar-plus bouts in the course of the decade. He fought six championship bouts in seven years, losing only to Gene Tunney, who defeated him twice. His career as a fighter over, Dempsey became an icon of American boxing and, as a restaurant owner in New York City, remained a favorite with literary, movie, and political celebrities.

**Early Life.** Dempsey developed his fighting style from his early years of riding the rails and living in hobo jungles after leaving, at age sixteen, his Manassa, Colorado, home where he worked with his father in various western copper-mining camps. His early hobo years taught him that a young man alone needed to protect himself quickly and decisively; thus, he threw brutal punches that ended bouts in early rounds, frequently in one round, and that later inspired his nickname "the Manassa Mauler." Between 1911 and 1914 Dempsey fought in saloon bouts as "Kid Blackie," earning the standard fee of $2.50 a bout.

**Kearns and Rickard.** During this period of all-comers bouts, Dempsey formed an alliance with Jack "Doc" Kearns, a flamboyant fight manager who helped Dempsey advance rapidly from barroom brawls to major matches. When they traveled to New York for bouts, Dempsey and Kearns teamed with George L. "Tex" Rickard, who later promoted Dempsey's $5-million gates for major matches. Though fortunes were made in these bouts, Dempsey realized only a small portion of the earnings, since Kearns squandered both his and Dempsey's shares of the gate. After cutting his ties with Kearns in 1925, Dempsey received and kept a large portion of the money his bouts earned.

**Dempsey–Fulton.** Throughout his early career before Dempsey gained real prominence, big-time boxers and promoters were somewhat reluctant to schedule matches with the young slugger, thinking him inexperienced as a fighter and lacking in crowd appeal with his rough-hewn, scowling appearance. Rickard agreed to arrange a match with the world heavyweight champion Jess Willard only if Dempsey could beat veteran Fred Fulton. After Dempsey knocked Fulton out in 18.6 seconds of the first round of a 27 July 1918 bout, Rickard arranged for Dempsey to fight for the heavyweight crown.

**Dempsey–Willard.** Jess Willard was one of several boxers to be called the "White Hope"; he earned this nickname during the promotion for his 5 April 1915 bout with black champion Jack Johnson, whom he defeated with a controversial knockout in the twenty-sixth round of their Havana, Cuba, title fight. When he met Dempsey some four years later, Willard was thirty-seven, six feet six inches tall, and an out-of-shape 245 pounds. Before the bout Willard made the six-feet-tall, 190-pound Dempsey sign an agreement that if Dempsey were severely injured or killed, Willard would not be held responsible. Fighting in 103- to 110-degree heat on 4 July 1919 in Toledo, Ohio, Dempsey knocked Willard to the canvas seven times in the first round. Referee Ollie Record counted to ten after the seventh knockdown and signaled that Dempsey had won; however, the timekeeper indicated that the bell had rung before the count was complete, and the ring had to be cleared of the crowd and Dempsey retrieved from the locker room to continue the fight. Willard could not answer the bell after round three, and Dempsey became the new world heavyweight champion.

**Outside the Ring.** After winning the title Dempsey spent much of his time making movies in Hollywood, appearing on stage, fighting exhibition bouts, and in general making a great deal of money from these activities and enjoying the life of the celebrity. However, the first of his four wives, Maxine Cates, a former dance-hall prostitute, in a 23 January 1920 letter to the *San Francisco Chronicle* accused her ex-husband of draft evasion during World War I; though acquitted of these charges by the San Francisco U.S. District Court in June 1920, Dempsey found his popularity waning. Such organizations as the American Legion voiced animosity toward the now-wealthy champion who lived in luxury while war veterans struggled to make a living.

**Dempsey–Carpentier.** Public sentiment against Dempsey rose and fell until his bout against the French war hero Georges Carpentier on 21 July 1921. Promoted by Tex Rickard, this bout became the first "million-dollar gate" in boxing history and, perhaps equally important to Dempsey, helped gloss over his reputation as a wartime slacker. Bringing the French contender and the American champion together created a surge of nationalistic support for Dempsey, especially after he won in the fourth round by a knockout.

**Dempsey–Gibbons and Shelby, Montana.** Perhaps the prospects of another million-dollar gate caused the newly rich ranchers of tiny Shelby, Montana — population 500 — to bid for a championship bout between Dempsey and Tommy Gibbons, an accomplished light heavyweight. Oil had been recently discovered in Shelby, and in 1921 bankers and town boosters guaranteed Dempsey $300,000 for the match. The town expected to gain a fortune that never materialized, since only 7,000 rather than the expected 40,000 spectators paid to see the 4 July 1923 fight. Dempsey easily won a fifteen-round decision, collected $200,000 of his $300,000 prize money, and left town. The town fathers and businesses went into bankruptcy.

**Dempsey–Firpo.** On 14 September 1923 Dempsey successfully defended his title against Argentinean Luis Angel Firpo, the Wild Bull of the Pampas. The Dempsey–Firpo bout earned an even bigger gate receipt than had the Dempsey–Carpentier match, but it also stirred controversy. In the first round Firpo knocked Dempsey through the ropes and onto the typewriter of

New York Tribune reporter Jack Lawrence. Lawrence and a Western Union employee, Perry Grogan, pushed the fighter back into the ring. In the process they created a noisy postmatch argument that Dempsey had received aid and therefore should have been disqualified. Such arguments were defused by the fact that in the second round Dempsey knocked Firpo down seven times before finally knocking him out.

**Dempsey–Tunney I.** Although Dempsey was criticized for not fighting such black boxers as Harry Wills, Rickard believed that a racially mixed bout would not draw as successfully as a Dempsey–Gene Tunney bout. Tunney was light heavyweight champion, a decorated World War I Marine, and a handsome man. He was also in superb condition, whereas the older Dempsey was not. On 23 September 1926, as part of Philadelphia's sesquicentennial celebration, Dempsey the slugger fought the boxer-strategist. The match, which took place in a driving rainstorm, went the full ten rounds, which Tunney won by a unanimous decision.

**Dempsey–Tunney II.** After losing the crown Dempsey considered retirement, but Rickard quickly made plans for a 21 July 1927 bout with Jack Sharkey, which Dempsey won in the seventh round and which rekindled his interest in a second match with Tunney, clearly Rickard's strategy. After losing his title to Tunney, Dempsey found his popularity increasing. When he faced Tunney in "The Second Battle of the Century," he became the favorite. In the seventh round of their 22 September 1927 bout in Chicago's Soldier Field, Tunney came close to knocking out Dempsey; however, Dempsey rallied and floored Tunney. But rather than going immediately to a neutral corner as rules dictated, Dempsey stood over his opponent. This action added at least four extra seconds to the normal ten-second count, resulting in the now-famous "long count" that saved Tunney from defeat. Tunney won in a unanimous decision as the match went its scheduled ten rounds.

**Retirement.** After his second loss to Tunney, Dempsey retired from major boxing events. Though he participated in a variety of exhibition bouts from 1931 to 1940, his active boxing career was essentially over. Though he started life working for four dollars a day, Dempsey earned a fortune through boxing. He estimated that his total income from his fights, the movie rights to bouts, refereeing, lectures, and radio appearances amounted to more than $10 million. He had risen from grinding poverty to become one of the extravagantly colorful and successful figures that so epitomized the 1920s.

Sources:

Nat Fleischer, *Jack Dempsey* (New Rochelle, N.Y.: Arlington House, 1972);

Randy Roberts, *Jack Dempsey: The Manassa Mauler* (Baton Rouge: Louisiana State University Press, 1979).

# HEINRICH LUDWIG "LOU" GEHRIG

## 1903-1941

### BASEBALL'S IRON HORSE

**Disaster.** Lou Gehrig, the New York Yankees first baseman nicknamed "the Iron Horse," on 2 May 1939 took himself out of the Yankees lineup and thereby ended his record for playing in consecutive games at 2,130 (he had broken the old record of 1,307 consecutive games in August 1934). His record had begun on 1 June 1925 when he was sent in to pinch-hit for shortstop Pee Wee Wanninger. The next day Gehrig replaced Wally Pipp, the starting Yankee first baseman, who had complained of a headache. Pipp never returned to the Yankees' first base, for Gehrig did not relinquish the position until May 1939 when his batting average had dropped to .143 and he told manager Joe McCarthy that he was hurting the team. He could not easily perform such ordinary tasks as tying his shoes or sitting in a chair or stepping off a curb. Just over a month later he learned that he had amyotrophic lateral sclerosis, an incurable form of paralysis that attacks the central nervous system. He was thirty-six years old, had completed his thirteenth full season as a Major League Baseball player, and had two years to live. The news of his affliction stunned the sports world.

**Triumph.** On 4 July 1939 the Yankees held an official Lou Gehrig Day at which 61,808 fans listened to Gehrig deliver a farewell speech to baseball, particularly to his 1927 Yankee teammates, including Babe Ruth, who were specially invited guests. In what has been called the Gettysburg Address of baseball, Gehrig said: "They say I have had a bad break, but when the office force and the ground keepers and even the Giants from across the river, whom we'd give our right arm to beat in the World Series — when they remember you, that's something. . . . I may have been given a bad break, but I have an awful lot to live for. With all this, I consider myself the luckiest man on the face of this earth." His teammates gave him a silver trophy at the base of which was inscribed John Kieran's poem "To Lou Gehrig," written at the request of the players and followed by their signatures. Soon thereafter, sportswriters and baseball officials unanimously elected Gehrig to the Baseball Hall of Fame.

**Records.** Though Babe Ruth eclipsed him throughout their Yankee careers, Gehrig amassed his own distinctive records. His mark of 2,130 consecutive games played stood for fifty-six years until Cal Ripken Jr. of the Baltimore Orioles surpassed it on 6 September 1995. Batting clean-up after Ruth, Gehrig became a key member of the powerful lineup of batters that a New York cartoonist had earlier named "Murderer's Row." He led the American League in runs batted in five times, was named the

American League's Most Valuable Player four times, won the home-run crown three times, and in 1931 set the all-time Major League record of 184 RBIs. He played in a total of thirty-four World Series games, achieving a Series batting average of .361, with 8 doubles, 3 triples, 10 home runs, 30 runs scored, and 35 runs batted in.

**Early Life and Career.** Born Heinrich Ludwig Gehrig in New York City to German immigrant parents, Gehrig grew up in the Yorkville and Washington Heights areas of Manhattan. He was a member of the Commerce High School baseball team that won the 1920 national high-school championship. His play drew attention from college and professional baseball scouts, and he won an athletic scholarship to Columbia University, where he became a pitching ace and alternated at first base and in the outfield. After a brief stint with a New York Giants minor-league club, he was signed in 1923 by the Yankees to a $3,500 midseason contract. Because he struggled as a fielder, the Yankees soon sent him to their minor-league team in Hartford, Connecticut, where his confidence and skills improved significantly. Between summer 1923 and fall 1924 he divided his time between Hartford and New York, rejoining the Yankees permanently in September 1924. Breaking into the powerful Yankee lineup seemed to Gehrig an especially daunting task but one he achieved in June 1925 when, as a replacement of Pipp at first base, he hit two singles and a double in his first three at bats, scored one run, had eight put-outs and one assist, and helped the Yankees end a losing streak.

**The 1927 Yankees.** The 1926 team, with a lineup including Babe Ruth and Gehrig — who came to be known as the Home-Run Twins — started the legendary dynasty that reached its zenith with the 1927 Yankees, regarded as the best team in the history of baseball. Their record of 110 wins in 154 games stood for twenty-seven years. During this season, in which Ruth hit his sixty home runs, Gehrig came also into his full maturity as a player. He was the new Yankee star while Ruth was the seasoned veteran who asserted his dominance at the plate. Until 10 August, Gehrig was three home runs ahead of Ruth, with thirty-eight to Ruth's thirty-five, but after that day, Gehrig hit only nine home runs while Ruth had twenty-five. This intrateam home-run rivalry created a box-office draw for the Yankees. Ruth set the home-run record, and Gehrig received the Most Valuable Player award that season. Almost as an afterthought the Yankees defeated the Pittsburgh Pirates in a four-game sweep of the World Series.

**The 1928 World Series.** In 1928 Gehrig enjoyed another outstanding year, with 142 RBIs and a .374 average, though his home-run total dropped to 27, which was still good enough to place him second in the league to Ruth. The Yankees won the pennant and defeated the Saint Louis Cardinals in four straight games. In this Series Gehrig and Ruth exhibited amazing power hitting, Gehrig averaging .545 and Ruth .625, records that still stand for averages achieved in World Series play. The

two men were opposites in personality: Gehrig was businesslike, reserved, and modest, while Ruth was legendary for his late-night carousing and headline making. Yet they were friends, often hunting and fishing together, except for a brief period in the 1930s when they were not on speaking terms.

**The 1930s.** In the 1930s Gehrig's career burgeoned. In 1931 he won his fourth consecutive RBI title; on 3 June 1932 he became the first American League player to hit four home runs in a game; in July 1933 he was chosen to play in the first All-Star Game; in 1934 he won the American League's Triple Crown for the best batting average (.363), the most home runs (49), and the most runs batted in (165) and was named the American League's Most Valuable Player; and in 1936 he won his third home-run crown and was again named the American League's Most Valuable Player. In 1938 he signed a contract for $39,000, his highest salary in baseball.

**Decline.** In 1939 he took a $4,000 pay cut, for he was beginning to show evidence of a decline in power and skills. As early as 13 July 1934, while running to first base after hitting a single, he suddenly doubled over, nearly falling but reaching the bag safely. For some time he had difficulty straightening up; he thought he had caught a cold in his back. These were the first obvious symptoms of the disease that would kill him seven years later. That he achieved many of his greatest baseball successes while enduring the early stages of ALS is a testament to his physical strength and desire to play. Gehrig died on 2 June 1941, sixteen years after his first appearance as a Yankee first baseman.

Sources:

Frank Graham, *Lou Gehrig: A Quiet Hero* (New York: Putnam, 1942);

Norman L. Macht, *Lou Gehrig* (New York: Chelsea House, 1993).

# HAROLD "RED" GRANGE

## 1903-1991

### STAR RUNNING BACK

**College Football's Best.** Known as "Number 77" or "the Wheaton Iceman" or "Red" or, later, as sportswriter Grantland Rice called him, "The Galloping Ghost," Harold Grange was the decade's most famous college football player and, more than any other figure, the player who made professional football a popular spectator sport. Grange grew up in Wheaton, Illinois, where he became a star high-school halfback, averaging five touchdowns a game. One of the best coaches in the college ranks, Bob Zuppke, recruited him to play at the University of Illinois, where, from 1923 through 1925, he achieved his greatest gridiron successes. From 1925 through 1934 he played professional football but never attained the dominance he had had in college. When he retired from football, Grange had played the game for sixteen years, appearing in 237 games. He had carried the ball 4,013 times, averaging 8.1 yards per carry and two touchdowns a game, for 531 touchdowns total. He had been named All-American during each of the three years he played varsity football at Illinois and had been selected to the first All-Pro team in 1931. Later, in 1963, he would be elected to the Professional Football Hall of Fame.

**First Varsity Game.** After the first day of practice for the freshman team at Illinois, Grange was so overwhelmed by the more than two hundred players trying out that he wanted to quit. "When I was a freshman at Illinois I wasn't even going to go out for football. My fraternity brothers made me do it." He made the seventh team. The following year Grange started at halfback and in the opening game against Nebraska on 6 October 1923 took a punt on his thirty-four yard line and ran for a touchdown. The Fighting Illini defeated Nebraska 24–7. In this first game he played thirty-nine minutes, gained 208 yards, scored three touchdowns, and drew national attention. By the end of his sophomore year he had rushed for 1,260 yards and scored twelve touchdowns — at least one in each of the seven games he played.

**"The Wheaton Iceman."** During summer breaks Grange rejected lucrative job offers, choosing instead to return home and work at Luke Thompson's icehouse, a job he had held throughout his early years; he delivered blocks of ice house-to-house for $37.50 a week. After a photographer published a picture of him at work, he became known across the country as "the Wheaton Iceman."

**The Michigan Game.** During the 1924 season Grange was to have a record-setting game on 18 October against a powerful Michigan team that had not been beaten since 1921. He scored the first four times he touched the ball in the first twelve minutes of the game. He took the opening kickoff for a ninety-five-yard touchdown, then scored on runs of sixty-seven, fifty-six, and forty-four yards. Convinced that Grange could not sustain his brilliant performance, Zuppke removed him from the game. He returned in the fourth quarter for a fifth, fifteen-yard touchdown run and passed for a sixth, contributing to the Illini's rout of the Wolverines 39–14. The legendary University of Chicago coach Amos Alonzo Stagg later wrote, "This was the most spectacular single-handed performance ever made in a major game." Before the season ended, Illinois faced Stagg's team, one of the nation's strongest. In that game Grange played the entire sixty minutes, scored three come-from-behind touchdowns, rushed for three hundred yards, and passed for 177 yards. The teams played to a 21–21 tie.

**National Star.** In 1925, his senior year, Grange was elected team captain and moved to quarterback because of injuries to the regular starter. Against the unbeaten University of Pennsylvania, the team many regarded as the champions of the East, Grange played fifty-seven minutes, passed for thirteen yards, rushed for 363 yards, and scored three touchdowns and set up a fourth. This 24–2 Illinois victory, particularly, established him as a national rather than regional star among influential eastern sportswriters. Wishing to continue his football career, Grange signed a contract to play professional football once the collegiate season ended, and following the Ohio State game, he boarded a train to Chicago and George Halas's Chicago Bears.

**Professional Football.** Since professional football was held in contempt by those who believed in the purity of amateur athletics, Grange's decision to turn professional was considered by many as unwise, if not disastrous; yet the gifted football player managed to bring respectability and a real audience to the pro game. After only three days of practice, he made his debut for the Bears against the Chicago Cardinals on Thanksgiving Day 1925. The game ended in a 0–0 tie, but thirty-six thousand fans paid to see it. The team played every two or three days for the next two weeks, until in the season closer, when the Bears met the New York Giants at the Polo Grounds before a sellout crowd. Sixty thousand tickets had been purchased, but more than seventy thousand fans filled the stands. Still more spectators were turned away, and riot police had to be called out to control the potential mob.

**Off-Season.** Grange finished his first pro season badly bruised and had hoped to recuperate during the off-season, but his agent, C. C. Pyle, had other plans for him. Pyle had signed him to tour the South and West in the winter and early spring months of 1926, during which he would play exhibition games with teams of players, including the aging Jim Thorpe, recruited from professional and semiprofessional clubs. After the exhibition tour, Pyle committed Grange to appear in two movies, *One Minute to Play* and *The Racing Romeo*. These extra assignments added $125,000 to his roughly $100,000-a-year salary, but he started the 1926 season physically drained. Pyle also advised Grange to quit the Bears team and join a new team, the New York Yankees, in a new professional league, the American League, that Pyle was organizing. The team and league fared well until 1927 when Grange severely injured his right knee in a game between the Yankees and the Chicago Bears. The injury kept him out the entire 1928 season, and as a result the Yankees and the American League folded.

**Final Years as a Pro.** Grange returned to the Bears in 1929. Because his bad knee greatly hampered his running and cutting ability, he considered retirement. Halas, however, convinced him to continue playing, which he did until the end of the 1934 season. These five additional seasons of professional football took such a great physical toll on him that he was reduced finally to a utility player. During his professional career he scored 162 touchdowns and kicked eighty-six conversions. In 1935 Grange wrote a letter to Arch Ward, the *Chicago Tribune* sports editor, in which he stated: "I say that a football player, after three years in college, doesn't know any thing about football. Pro football is the difference between the New York Giants baseball team and amateur nine. . . . Pro football is smart. It is so smart you can rarely work the same play twice with the same results. Competition is keen. There are no set-ups in pro football. The big league player knows *football,* not just a theory or system."

**The Gift.** After football Grange started a successful insurance business and also became a respected radio and, later, television sports announcer. Throughout his life and career he remained genuinely modest, asserting that what he did as a runner was a gift for which he should not be accorded any special praise: "I could carry a football well, but I've met hundreds of people who could do their thing better than I. I mean, engineers, and writers, scientists, doctors — whatever. I can't take much credit for what I did running with a football, because I don't know what I did. You can teach a man how to block or tackle or kick or pass. The ability to run with a ball is something you have or you haven't. If you can't explain it, how can you take any credit for it?"

Sources:
W. C. Heinz, "Ghost of the Gridiron," in *The Fireside Book of Football,* edited by Jack Newcombe (New York: Simon & Schuster, 1964), pp. 129–136;

Gene Schoor with Henry Gilfond, *Red Grange: Football's Greatest Halfback* (New York: Julian Messner, 1952).

## ROBERT "BOBBY" TYRE JONES JR.

### 1902-1971

#### CELEBRATED AMATEUR GOLFER

**Amateurism.** In a decade when athletes were frequently lured away from amateur athletics by the small fortunes promised by professional sports, Bobby Jones spent his entire golfing career as an amateur. He felt that his potentially violent temper, fueled by his desire for the perfect shot and directed toward himself, worked against his succeeding as a professional. Consequently, although he was a consummate golfing artist and acclaimed worldwide, he did not earn money from his sport until after he retired from competition at age twenty-eight.

**Accomplishments.** In his entire fourteen-year career, Jones played in only fifty-two tournaments, twenty-three of which he won. He hated to practice and sometimes went as long as three months without playing golf at all. He averaged no more than eighty rounds a year, and when he did play it was most often with his father or friends, as if he were any other weekend golfer. Jones did not win a single national tournament in his first ten attempts, but in the summer of 1923 his career took off

when, at the age of twenty-one, he became the U.S. Open champion, playing against both professionals and amateurs. He then won the 1924 and 1925 U.S. Amateur titles and, in 1926, became the first player to win the British Open and the U.S Open in the same year, an accomplishment that earned him his first ticker-tape parade down Broadway. He again won the British Open in 1927, the U.S. Amateur in 1927 and 1928, and the U.S. Open in 1929. In all, he took thirteen major titles — four U.S. Opens, three British Opens, five U.S. Amateurs, and one British Amateur. His greatest golfing triumph occurred in 1930, when he won the British Amateur, the British Open, the U.S. Open, and the U.S. Amateur — the Grand Slam of Golf — a feat that no other player matched. In 1950 an Associated Press poll judged Jones's Grand Slam "the Supreme Athletic Achievement of the Century."

**Early Career.** Jones was introduced to the game while he was recovering from a series of childhood illnesses at East Lake, a resort near his hometown of Atlanta. His only golf lessons came from watching and copying the East Lake club professional, Stewart Maiden. Jones won his first children's tournament at East Lake at age six. At nine he took the Atlanta Athletic Club Junior Championship, beating a sixteen-year-old, and at thirteen he won, in Birmingham, Alabama, an invitational tournament in which his father also competed. At fourteen he reached the third round before losing to the defending champion in the U.S. Amateur.

**Later Career.** From 1923 to 1930 Jones won thirteen of the twenty-one national championships he entered in the United States and Great Britain. During this period he captured five of the eight U.S. Amateur titles for which he contended, all three of the British Opens he entered, and one of the two British Amateurs in which he played. No amateur golfer ever beat him twice in match play, and the two leading professionals of his time, Gene Sarazen and Walter Hagen, never won an Open in which Jones also completed, although Hagen beat him in their only matchup, a seventy-two-hole contest in 1926. During 1923 to 1930 Jones played in only seven tournaments that were not national championships: two amateur events and five tournaments now part of the professional tour; he won four of these events. In a qualifying round for the 1926 British Open, Jones played a "perfect" round of 66 — 33 out and 33 in, 33 shots from tee to green, 33 putts. In 1928 he played 12 straight subpar tournaments rounds, in only two of which he scored over 70. That same year he broke within a single week four course records in the Chicago area.

**Education.** After winning the Grand Slam in 1930, Jones felt that he had nothing else to accomplish in competitive golf and thus retired from the game at age twenty-eight. He had no difficulty occupying himself in retirement. While dominating golf Jones had also attended college, earning a degree in mechanical engineering from Georgia Tech, taking another degree in English literature from Harvard, and finally pursuing a law degree at Emory University. In the middle of his second year of law school, he sat for the Georgia State Bar exam to find out how difficult it was; passing easily, he left law school to join his father's law firm.

**Retirement.** Designing the first matched set of irons for Spalding in 1932, Jones also turned his interest to golf-course design. With Clifford Roberts, a Wall Street broker, and Alister Mackenzie, a British golf architect, Jones began construction on the Augusta National course in 1931 and completed it in 1933. The course became known as The Masters, though Jones thought the title pretentious. Its first Invitational Tournament was held in 1934. Additionally, Jones wrote extensively about golf, including *Down the Fairway* (1927, with O. B. Keeler) and *Golf Is My Game* (1960).

**Final Years.** In 1948 Jones began to suffer atrophy and pain on his right side. In July 1956 his ailments, unrelieved by two surgical procedures, were diagnosed as syringomyelia, a nervous-system disease similar to amyotrophic lateral sclerosis, which killed Lou Gehrig. A member of the World Golf Hall of Fame, Jones has often been called the greatest golfer of all time.

Source:
Ron Fimrite, "The Emperor Jones," *Sports Illustrated*, 80 (11 August 1994): 104–116.

# MAN O' WAR

## 1917-1947

### THOROUGHBRED CHAMPION

**Popular Legend.** Nicknamed "Big Red" for his deep chestnut color, Man o' War was America's legendary thoroughbred racehorse. Beautiful, powerful, and seemingly invincible, he so appealed to the general American public that he is credited with popularizing a sport that had often been regarded either as a diversion for the wealthy or as a sinister lure to those addicted to "immoral" gambling.

**Early History.** Man o' War was bred by August Belmont I, the great American turfman for whom Belmont Park was named. The colt, a son of Fair Play, was foaled in Kentucky and sold as a yearling to Samuel D. Riddle at a Saratoga, New York, race meeting for $5,000, a notable bargain since the horse earned $249,465 in purses and, later, even more in stud fees. During 1919 and 1920, when he was two and three years old, Big Red won twenty of his twenty-one races.

**Career.** Man o' War's only loss — to the appropriately named Upset — came in the August 1919 Sanford Memorial Stakes, his seventh race as a two-year-old, during which he was slowed by a bungled start, by an obvious foul, and by the 130 pounds he was carrying to Upset's 117 pounds. As a three-year-old he won all eleven of the races he started. He did not run in the Kentucky Derby because Riddle thought the distance too long for a three-year-old early in the racing season, but he did take the other two races in the Triple Crown, the Preakness and the Belmont. Man o' War set track records in at least two of his races as a three-year-old, despite carrying increasingly heavy weights, often more than 130 pounds. When his horse's weight requirement advanced to 138 pounds, Riddle decided to retire him. In the last contest of his career, the Kenilworth Gold Cup in Canada, Man o' War easily beat the Canadian champion and 1919 Triple Crown winner, Sir Barton, in a match race.

**Dwyer Stakes.** Sportswriter Grantland Rice regarded the match race between Man o' War and John P. Grier as one of the greatest thoroughbred races in history. The two horses confronted each other on 10 July 1920 in the Dwyer Stakes at Aqueduct. Clarence Kummer rode Man o' War, and Ed Ambrose was up on John P. Grier. Riddle instructed Kummer to "Lay alongside of Johnny Grier — use the whip only when you need it. Just once is enough — if you have to." Kummer followed these orders explicitly. The horses ran neck-and-neck, and their times were spectacular: 23.24 seconds at the first quarter; 57.24 seconds at the five-furlong pole; 1 minute 9.24 seconds at the six-furlong marker; and 1 minute 35.36 seconds at the mile pole. In the stretch Kummer touched Man o' War once with the whip, and the horse responded by taking a huge twenty-four-foot stride (the standard stride of the thoroughbred racehorse is eighteen to twenty feet) that thrust him into a one-length lead. Man o' War won the race by nearly two lengths and set a new world record of 1 minute 49.12 seconds for the mile-and-one-sixteenth course. This race particularly captured the public's imagination.

**Retirement.** Riddle retired Man o' War to Faraway Farms in Lexington, Kentucky, where he was named Leading Sire in 1926, a year in which his offspring won forty-nine races. Among his most famous colts were American Flag, who won the 1925 Belmont Stakes; Crusader, who took the Belmont in 1926; and War Admiral, who won the Triple Crown in 1937. Man o' War's birthday party each year was almost always attended by the governor of Kentucky. Before his death on 1 November 1947 at the age of thirty, more than one million visitors came to see the thoroughbred who had been labeled by Will Harbut, his groom, "the mostest hoss that ever was."

Sources:
Bryan Field, "Horse Racing," in *Sport's Golden Age,* edited by Allison Danzig and Peter Brandwein (New York: Harper, 1948), pp. 86–110;

George Gipe, *The Great American Sports Book* (Garden City, N.Y.: Doubleday, 1978), pp. 251–252;

Grantland Rice, "Big Red: 'The Mostest Horse,'" in *Esquire's Great Men and Moments in Sports* (New York: Harper, 1962), pp. 87–88;

Wells Twombly, *200 Years in Sports in America: A Pageant of a Nation at Play* (New York: McGraw-Hill, 1976), pp. 164–166.

## KNUTE ROCKNE

### 1888-1931

#### LEGENDARY FOOTBALL COACH

**Creator.** Notre Dame football coach Knute Rockne was a primary creator of modern football and of the modern college football hero. An astute promoter of the game, Rockne had an actor's gift for dramatic oratory and gesture, with which he inspired his players to near-religious fervor and captivated the popular press and throngs of spectators who felt themselves part — perhaps for the first time — of the drama played out weekly on the gridiron. Rockne changed the spectator's connection to the game, making the play literally more visible to large crowds. In the process he produced athlete-heroes for whom audiences could cheer and with whom they could identify: George Gipp, the Four Horsemen, and the Seven Mules.

**Smart Football.** Before the 1920s football formations characteristically featured tight knots of players smashing together in contests of strength that resembled rugby scrums. Rockne opened up the game by instituting his famous "box formation" and a system that emphasized speed and deception rather than brute force. His "smart football" plays were designed for long, game-breaking — and crowd-pleasing — touchdowns rather than the standard slow, grinding, three-yard power plays. He introduced "brush" or "influence" blocking that allowed smaller but faster linemen who complemented his small, fast backfield. These slighter, quicker athletes were necessary for the Notre Dame "shift," a carefully choreographed movement of players designed to spread the offense and defense. The shift worked so well that the rules committee of the Coaches Association twice tried to have it banned.

**Early Life.** Born in Voss, Norway, Rockne moved with his family to the north side of Chicago when he was five years old. The boy loved athletics, particularly football and track, and when he cut high-school classes to practice for a track meet, school officials suspended him and told him to transfer to another school. Instead, although he was an excellent math and history student and was close to graduation, Rockne dropped out of high school in 1905. He worked at various odd jobs and in 1907 decided to take the Civil Service Examination. His essay for the written section of the exam, "The Advisability of Our Having a Larger Navy Is Becoming Greater Since Japan Whipped Russia," revealed his interest in history and his colorful style. Later, proud of his writing skills, he would publish one nonfiction book, *Coaching* (1925), and a novel, *The Four Winners* (1925).

**Student Athlete.** Though a Lutheran, Rockne enrolled at Notre Dame, a Roman Catholic college, because the school had a history of providing employment for poor but bright students. He worked as a janitor in the chemistry laboratory and, at five feet eight inches and 165 pounds, started at left end on the 1911, 1912, and 1913 teams. The undefeated Notre Dame teams of 1911–1913 won twenty and tied twice, scored 879 points to their opponents' 77, defeating them by an average of forty to three a game. The team's greatest moment was Notre Dame's stunning 35–13 victory over powerhouse Army on 1 November 1913, the win that, according to Michael R. Steele, "changed forever the game of football." Rockne, a team leader and primary originator of the strategy, faked a limp, causing the Army defenders to neglect him as a receiver. At a key moment quarterback Gus Dorias threw a long pass to Rockne, who caught the ball in full stride. From then on, when Army defended against the pass, Notre Dame ran the ball; when Army defended against the run, Notre Dame passed. It was this balanced attack and use of deception (the pass used to set up the run) rather than a nearly exclusive use of the forward pass, as most accounts have it, that surprised Army and changed the strategy of college football. Rockne graduated from Notre Dame magna cum laude with a major in chemistry and pharmacology and applied to Saint Louis University's medical school. He was denied admission since school officials believed that coaching football — one of Rockne's stated intentions — and studying medicine were incompatible.

**Early Coaching Career.** After graduation Rockne was hired by Notre Dame as a chemistry instructor, head track coach, and assistant football coach. He served as an assistant for four years until 1917, when head football coach Jesse Harper resigned and Rockne assumed his position. Because young men were volunteering in large numbers for military service, the 1918 season was virtually canceled, but after the war American sports began its Golden Era, with the return to campuses of veterans and with the public's growing demand for athlete-heroes.

**George Gipp.** The decade of the 1920s was Rockne's greatest period, as he perfected his teams' running and passing games and their mastery of deceptive strategy. He also created football idols who captured the American imagination. George Gipp was one. By nature he was a rebel, willing to be indulged by rich, powerful alumni and disdainful of the somewhat sentimental, golden boy image of athletes espoused by his coach. He broke training rules, missed practice for three weeks, gambled openly, and was a superb halfback. In his first college game, Gipp was told to punt but instead drop-kicked a sixty-two-yard field goal from his thirty-eight yard line, giving Notre Dame its margin of victory over Western State Normal. This kick remains one of the longest field goals in college records. In his twenty-six varsity games,

Gipp ran for more than one hundred yards on ten different occasions and accumulated 4,833 total yards as a ballcarrier, passer, receiver, and returner, a total of 185 yards produced every time he played a game.

**Gipp's Death.** In his senior year, the Notre Dame–Northwestern game was designated "George Gipp Day." Gipp, who had a high fever, did not play for three quarters, but the crowd chanted for his appearance. Rockne put him in during the fourth quarter, and he threw two long touchdown passes. However, the hero's days were numbered; his illness turned into pneumonia, and he died on 14 December 1920. The legendary deathbed conversation between Rockne and Gipp has been met with skepticism, but eight years later Rockne did use the famous "Win one for the Gipper" to inspire Notre Dame to a 12–6 victory over a tough Army team during his worst season as a coach.

**The Four Horsemen.** In 1922 Rockne brought in Elmer Layden at fullback to join Jim Crowley at left halfback, Don Miller at right halfback, and Harry Stuhldreher at quarterback. Though small and light, averaging 158.5 pounds, this backfield was one of the greatest in college football history. Quick and resourceful, the four backs functioned as not individual stars but instead as a well-organized unit, thereby providing the perfect vehicle for executing Rockne's sophisticated plays. The Notre Dame backfield became known as the Four Horsemen, so-named in sportswriter Grantland Rice's famous description: "Outlined against a blue-gray October sky, the Four Horsemen rode again. In dramatic lore they were known as Famine, Pestilence, Destruction, and Death. These are only aliases. Their real names are Stuhldreher, Miller, Crowley, and Layden." To complement the Four Horsemen and perhaps to emphasize their crucial but less glamorous function, the Notre Dame linemen were nicknamed the Seven Mules. The 1924 team was undefeated in nine regular season games and scored 258 points to their opponents' 44, beating them by an average of 28–5. Notre Dame was invited to play Pop Warner's Stanford team led by Ernie Nevers in the 1925 Rose Bowl game. Though Stanford outgained Notre Dame 310 to 182 yards, the Irish won 27–10.

**Final Years.** Toward the end of his career, as Rockne became increasingly concerned with insuring the financial security of his family, he made himself a familiar voice on the lecture circuit and began to explore opportunities in Hollywood. On 31 March 1931 during a flight to California, his plane crashed, killing all aboard. At his memorial service Rockne was eulogized as one of America's greatest college football coaches and as a molder of young men. He clearly belonged to a decade in which heroes were created and adored as embodiments of the American dream of success and glory.

Sources:
Ken Chowder, "When Notre Dame needed inspiration, Rockne provided it," *Smithsonian,* 24 (November 1993): 164–177;

Michael R. Steele, *Knute Rockne: A Bio-Bibliography* (Westport, Conn.: Greenwood Press, 1983);

Wells Twombly, *Shake Down the Thunder* (Radnor, Pa.: Chilton, 1974).

# GEORGE HERMAN "BABE" RUTH

## 1894-1948

### HOME-RUN KING

**Greatest Hitter in Baseball History.** Babe Ruth single-handedly changed the character of baseball through his home run prowess, altering the game from an exercise in base-hitting, bunting, and base-stealing to a drama of long-ball hitting. For thirty-nine years he held the record for career home runs — 714 — which stood until 8 April 1974, when Henry Aaron hit his 715th home run in Atlanta for the Atlanta Braves. At Baseball's Hall of Fame in Cooperstown, New York, an entire room is devoted to Ruth's accomplishments and memorabilia. Ruth was also the first player to earn huge sums of money from baseball, an estimated $1 million in salaries and bonuses and at least another $1 million from endorsements and other enterprises.

**Early Life.** The legend surrounding Ruth's life and career has its origins in his troubled upbringing. When he was eight years old he was sent for a few weeks to Baltimore's Saint Mary's Industrial School for boys, a home for "incorrigibles." At the age of ten he was returned to the reformatory and from age ten to twenty, he spent at least seven years there. While at Saint Mary's, Ruth came under the influence of Brother Mathias, who in 1914 asked Jack Dunn, a scout for the Baltimore Orioles, then in the Federal League, to watch the nineteen-year-old left-hander pitch. Dunn signed Ruth on 14 February 1914 to a $600 contract with the Orioles.

**Early Career.** The Federal League collapsed, and Ruth was sold to the Boston Red Sox on 10 July 1914. Ruth won eighteen and lost six in his first season under Bill Carrigan, Ruth's favorite manager among the seven he played for in the course of his career. With the Red Sox he became an all-around player. During the 1917 season Ruth won twenty-four and lost thirteen, with a 2.02 earned run average; in 1918 he hit eleven home runs and set a World Series record by extending his scoreless inning streak to twenty-nine and two-thirds, a record that held until Whitey Ford broke it in 1961. He also began playing in the outfield on the days he did not pitch.

**A Crowed Pleaser.** Ruth's home run capabilities increasingly drew large crowds wherever he played. Partly because of his ability to attract paying customers and partly because of his continual run-ins with managers and owners about curfews, fines, and suspensions, the Red

Sox sold him to the Yankees, a deal that was finalized on 3 January 1920. The New York Yankees owners, "Col." Jacob Ruppert and Colonel Tillinghast Huston, paid Boston owner Harry Frazee, who was in desperate need of funds because of other business ventures, $125,000 cash and granted him a loan of $300,000. Ruth's salary, with bonuses and gate percentages, came to about $41,000 per season for 1920 and 1921.

**In Pinstripes.** Once in the Yankees organization, Ruth truly began building his legend. In 1920 he batted .376, hit fifty-four home runs, nine triples, and thirty-six doubles; scored 158 runs; batted in 137 runs; and stole fourteen bases. His "slugging average" was .847, still the major-league record. His biographer Robert W. Creamer maintains that 1921, his second season with the Yankees, was a better hitting year for him than 1927, when he hit his record sixty home runs. In 1921 he played in 152 games, hit 59 home runs, had 177 runs batted in, 204 singles, forty-four doubles, sixteen triples, and a batting average of .378. In 1927 he played in 151 games, hit sixty home runs, had 164 runs batted in, 192 singles, twenty-nine doubles, eight triples, and a batting average of .356. In 1923 he was the unanimous choice for Most Valuable Player in the American League, batted .393 (the highest average of his career, though it was second in the league to Harry Heilmann's .403), and led the league in home runs at forty-one. He negotiated his salary to $52,000 that year. When asked why he insisted on this figure, Ruth replied that he had always wanted to say he made $1,000 a week.

**The House that Ruth Built.** In 1923 Yankee Stadium, built at a cost of $2.5 million, opened. The new stadium stood on a plot of land bought from the Astor estate and located in the Bronx across the Harlem River from the Polo Grounds, the stadium that had been shared by the Yankees and the New York Giants. Yankee stadium had sixty-two thousand seats, and all were filled on opening day in 1923 when Ruth hit a home run, the first in his new locale, later to be dubbed "The House that Ruth Built."

**The Great Years.** In 1926 the Yankees won the American League pennant and met the Saint Louis Cardinals in the World Series. Ruth hit three home runs in one game, the first time that feat had been accomplished in Series play. However, the Yankees lost the series four games to three, when Ruth attempted to steal second in the seventh game with two outs in the bottom of the ninth and the Yankees behind in the score, three to two. His being called out ended a Yankees rally that might have changed the outcome of the game and the series. For this play Ruth came under a barrage of criticism.

**Winners.** During the next two years the Yankees gained dramatic revenge against the entire National League by sweeping the Pittsburgh Pirates in the 1927 World Series and the Saint Louis Cardinals in the 1928 World Series. From 1926 to 1931 Ruth led the American

League in home runs. The 1927 Yankees are considered by many to be the greatest team ever assembled. As a team they batted .307 and won 110 games and lost 44, a winning percentage of .714. Their famous "Murderer's Row" label predates Ruth, but once he and his teammate Lou Gehrig began their home-run rivalry in 1927, the name seemed especially applicable. In the four-game 1928 Series, Ruth had ten hits in sixteen at bats for a .625 batting average, still a World Series record. His salary was now raised to $70,000 a year for the next three years.

**The Glory Years.** The 1920s with the Yankees were Ruth's glory years. He led the American League in home runs from 1926 to 1931. A bearlike, fun-loving, and much-loved figure, Ruth was legendary for his public rowdiness and his eating, drinking, and womanizing. He missed the first two months of the 1925 season with a "stomach-ache heard round the world," the result of his eating dozens of hot dogs washed down with beer. He remained a boisterous child-man throughout the decade, and his prodigious appetites soon exaggerated his famous physique — a bulging belly atop spindly legs.

**More than the President was Paid.** In 1930 Ruth's salary was raised to $80,000, a salary even higher than President Herbert Hoover's ("I had a better year than the President," he said, and was no doubt correct as the Great Depression had begun). Ruth's abilities began to wane in 1932, though the most famous of his legends occurred that year when in the third game of the World Series against the Chicago Cubs, with the scored tied 4–4, Ruth allegedly pointed his bat toward center field and hit the next pitch — low and away — deep into the center-field bleachers. Whether he had "called" this home run or not is still much discussed, though he clearly had called home runs before, once in 1927 and again in 1931. Whether or not the 1932 "call" actually occurred, it quickly became part of baseball lore.

**The Declining Years.** Ruth had always expected to manage the Yankees when his playing days were over, but his history of carousing and rebellion against management defeated his ambition. Instead, he signed with the Boston Braves as a player–assistant manager for the 1935 season; on 25 May 1935 he hit three home runs for his new National League team, but the Braves were losing money, and Ruth quarreled with the team owner. In June 1935 Ruth was given his unconditional release. He coached for the Brooklyn Dodgers in 1938, but his brief nonplaying baseball career was drawing to a close.

**Death.** In 1946 Ruth developed a cancerous growth on the left side of his face; the following year he underwent radiation treatment, which caused him to lose nearly eighty pounds. On Sunday, 13 June 1948, in celebration of the twenty-fifth anniversary of Yankee Stadium, Ruth and other Yankee veterans of the 1923 season were invited to attend a special ceremony. Ruth, the last former player to walk out onto the field, was greeted with tumultuous applause. When he died on 16 August 1948, thousands of fans filed past his bier at Yankee Stadium.

Source:

Robert W. Creamer, *Babe: The Legend Comes to Life* (New York: Simon & Schuster, 1974).

## WILLIAM TATEM TILDEN II

### 1893-1953

#### TENNIS GIANT

**Accomplishments.** William "Big Bill" Tilden dominated men's tennis in the 1920s. Through his dramatic play he attracted public attention to a sport that had often been regarded as unmanly, snobbish, and boring. He won the U.S. Championship for six consecutive years from 1920 through 1925 and again, at the age of thirty-six, in 1929. On 3 July 1920 he became the first American to win the men's singles title at Wimbledon, a title that he successfully defended the following year and recaptured in 1930, when he was thirty-seven. He was a member of the U.S. Davis Cup team from 1920 to 1930, leading the team to seven championships until a strong French team emerged in 1927 and beat the Americans in the finals for four years straight. In Davis Cup play he lost only one doubles match and five of the twenty-two singles matches he played, all of his losses coming after 1925. In 1925 he ran off fifty-seven winning games that, as his biographer Frank Deford notes, was "one of those rare, unbelievable athletic feats — like Johnny Unitas throwing touchdown passes in forty-seven straight games or Joe DiMaggio hitting safely in fifty-six games in a row — that simply cannot be exceeded in a reasonable universe no matter how long and loud we intone that records are made to be broken."

**Early Career.** Born into a wealthy Philadelphia family, Tilden began playing tennis as a child but despite his obvious talent did not develop a strong game until he was twenty-seven. In 1915, when he was twenty-two, he was ranked seventieth in the world and was notorious for his first-round losses, usually the product of lackadaisical play. After he was rejected for military service in 1917 because of flat feet, he devoted himself to improving his game through sharpening his strategy and his technique — his individual strokes, his footwork, the spin of the ball. In so doing he was making himself into "the first real intellectual of the game, and the first to introduce elements of psychology, tactics, and even ballistics" into his game, as Gianni Clerici has written. As a result of his new discipline, Tilden reached the finals of the U.S. Championship in 1918 and 1919.

**"Big Bill" and "Little Bill."** His victorious opponent in the 1919 finals was William M. Johnston, whom Tilden would also face in five of his six U.S. Championship finals between 1920 and 1925. Fierce competitors and close friends, Tilden and Johnston played thrilling five-set championship matches in 1920, 1922, and 1925. The pair were known as "Big Bill" and "Little Bill," and together they were a study in contrasts: Tilden, at just over six feet and 155 pounds, was tall, thin, and an eastern aristocrat; Johnston stood five feet six inches tall, weighed 121 pounds, and was a California commoner. Together these two led the U.S. Davis Cup team during its 1920s glory years.

**Officialdom.** Throughout his career Tilden mocked and fought with tennis's governing bodies and officials, calling for rules changes that were often later effected and attacking what seemed to be absurd restrictions. Because Tilden had agreed to write a tennis column for *The New York Times*, the United States Lawn Tennis Association (USLTA) banned him as captain of the 1928 U.S. Davis Cup team just before the finals were to be played in Paris. When the French players learned that they would not be allowed to compete against him, they insisted that he be reinstated. The USLTA reluctantly returned Tilden to the team, but only after a U.S. ambassador intervened.

**Sportsmanship.** Contemptuous toward officialdom, Tilden was scrupulously fair and sportsmanlike to opponents. If a linesman made a bad call in his favor, Tilden would often purposely miss the next shot to rectify the mistake. During Davis Cup play he once gave away a complete set to Australian James Anderson to correct a line call that had awarded Tilden a set point in error. He regarded sportsmanship as crucial to the game and to his own patrician image.

**Style of Play.** Tilden's style of play was athletic, graceful, and dramatic. Essentially a baseliner, he was blessed with an enormous serve and with devastating forehand and backhand drives. In October 1922 Tilden's career was threatened by a cut on his right middle finger that became infected and that, in those prepenicillin days, ultimately required amputation just below the second joint. He retained enough of the finger that the power and placement of his shots were not noticeably affected.

**Professional Tennis.** With the stock-market crash of 1929, athletes in general were being pressured to turn professional. An outspoken advocate of amateur athletics throughout the 1920s, Tilden acquiesced to financial realities and turned pro in 1931. He won the men's professional singles championship in his first year on the tour and again in 1935. He retired from tennis in 1936 at the age of forty-three but returned in 1945 to win the pro doubles title with Vincent Richards. Tilden was then fifty-two.

**Other Pursuits.** Tilden was throughout his life passionate about the arts. He loved opera, painting, and the theater and counted among his friends movie stars Charlie Chaplin, Mary Pickford, and Douglas Fairbanks. He hoped to become an actor but proved to have little thespian talent, though he did once play the role of Dracula in a sixteen-week road show. He published a substantial amount of bad fiction, most of it populated by impossibly noble or evil characters, and wrote several excellent books on tennis, including *The Art of Lawn Tennis* (1923).

**Final Years.** Tilden's final years were difficult. He had, while he was still playing tennis, surrounded himself with attractive teenaged boys, and twice in the late 1940s he was arrested and served prison time for child molestation. Ironically, a few days before his release from his second jail term in December 1949, he was named by the Associated Press the greatest athlete in his sport for the first half of the twentieth century. Yet he could not recover his former glory or respect. Proud, financially pressed, and virtually friendless, he lived in a small apartment near Hollywood and Vine and tried to make ends meet by teaching tennis. He was invited to play in the U.S. professional tournament in Cleveland in June 1953, but the evening before the tournament began, he died of a heart attack. Only a few people attended his funeral, and no official or other form of tribute was sent by the USLTA.

Sources:

Gianni Clerici, *The Ultimate Tennis Book,* translated by Richard J. Wiezell (Chicago: Follett, 1975), pp. 154–163;

Frank Deford, *Big Bill Tilden: The Triumphs and the Tragedy* (New York: Simon & Schuster, 1976);

Lance Tingay, *Tennis: A Pictorial History* (New York: Putnam, 1973), pp. 52–57.

# HELEN NEWINGTON WILLS

## 1905-

### TENNIS CHAMPION

**Bright New Star.** On 19 August 1923 seventeen-year-old Helen Wills achieved national prominence when she won the women's singles final at the U.S. Championships, defeating the powerful Norwegian-born, seven-time U.S. champion, Molla Bjurdstedt Mallory. In the process Wills captivated the American public with her athleticism, her youth and striking beauty, and her poise both on and off the court. In fact, she exhibited so much public reserve that in 1922 *New York Evening Mail* columnist Ed Sullivan had dubbed her "Little Miss Poker Face." Wills soon became the dominant American woman tennis player of the 1920s.

**Democratic Tennis — a New Wave.** Wills launched a new trend in U.S. tennis. Unlike many of the players of her own and earlier generations, she was not from the privileged eastern upper classes with their private-school training. She was, instead, the daughter of a California doctor who had handed her a racquet when she was eight years old and practiced with her on public dirt courts. When her skills outstripped his own, he asked Pop Fuller, a veteran tennis coach, to be her instructor. She soon outplayed female opponents and turned to stronger, older males for competition. She was later to claim that she developed her fast, powerful ground strokes and charging volleys through these early years of play on public courts; she mastered the finer points of defensive play and pinpoint shot-making in actual match play with established women players. Her athletic approach to the game, as well as her hard-muscled, five-foot-seven-inch, 150-pound frame and her adoption of a rather unglamorous trademark — a white visor pulled down to her eyes — seemed to proclaim her origins in the ambitious, energetic American middle class. Whatever the accuracy of the image she projected, Wills proved enormously attractive to Americans in general, who began to flock not only to her matches but also to the public tennis courts that were being built in large numbers during the 1920s.

**To England and France.** In 1924 Wills attracted international attention when she played in the Wightman Cup competition and at Wimbledon in Great Britain and then moved on to the Olympics in Paris. Though the American team lost 1–6 to the British women in Wightman Cup play, Wills reached the singles finals at Wimbledon where she took a set from England's Kathleen "Kitty" McKane before losing to McKane 6-4, 4–6, 4–6. Wills and her partner, Hazel Wightman, defeated McKane and Mrs. B. C. Covell in the Wimbledon ladies' doubles, 6–4, 6–4. Later that same summer Wills, as a member of the U.S. Olympic tennis team, won the gold medal for women's singles by defeating France's Didi Vlasto, 6–2, 6–2, and, with Wightman, another gold for ladies' doubles.

**Tennis and Other Pursuits.** In the fall of 1923 Wills had enrolled at the University of California, Berkeley, where she had received a scholarship to study art. (She insisted throughout her life that painting was her true vocation and tennis a mere pastime.) While at Berkeley she published a book of poetry, *The Awakening* (1926), and earned both Phi Beta Kappa honors and a letter in tennis, becoming the first woman at the California university to letter in sports. She had repeated as U.S. champion in 1924 and 1925 but did not play at Wimbledon in either 1925 or 1926; illness and injuries troubled her during the 1926 season and prevented her from defending her U.S. Championship title that year.

**Lenglen.** By early 1926, however, the public was eagerly anticipating a match between the talented young American and the reigning queen of tennis, Suzanne Lenglen, the "French Goddess" who had taken two national titles in her native country and six Wimbledons. Lenglen — hardliving, temperamental, supremely gifted — seemed the antithesis of the hardworking, undemonstrative Wills, who traveled with her mother, kept regular hours, and avoided public attention whenever possible. On 16 February 1926, following massive ballyhoo that drew royalty, nobility, and the rich and famous from Europe and America to Cannes where the match was held, Wills and Lenglen met. Their play was excellent, but the results were disappointing for the American: her power game was finally dismantled by Lenglen's strategy and finesse, and Wills lost the match 3–6, 6–8. She did not play Lenglen again, since in the summer of 1926 the French star turned professional and was therefore prohibited from playing in the major tournaments. As a consequence of her loss to Lenglen, Wills returned to California from Cannes determined to improve her strategy, her footwork, and the diversity of her game.

**Dominance.** From 1927 into the mid 1930s when illness and injuries again began to plague her, Wills dominated women's tennis. She won singles titles in the French Championships four times (1928, 1929, 1930, and 1932), in the U.S. Championships seven times (1923, 1924, 1925, 1927, 1928, 1929, and 1931), and at Wimbledon eight times (1927, 1928, 1929, 1930, 1932, 1933, 1935, and 1938). Her record eight titles at Wimbledon stood for fifty-two years until 1990 when Martina Navratilova won her ninth singles title. In 1928 Wills had become the first player of either sex to win the singles titles of the United States, France, and Great Britain within one calendar year, and in 1929 she again claimed all three titles. Astonishingly, between 1927 and 1933 she did not lose a set in singles competition anywhere in the world, and she won 180 matches in succession.

**Retirement.** Wills briefly retired from tennis in 1936 but then returned to competition until she left the game permanently in 1939. Her 1929 marriage to stockbroker Frederick S. Moody ended in divorce in 1937, and in 1939 she wedded Aidan Roark, a polo player, from whom she was divorced in the early 1970s. A notably private person, Wills has spent most of her retirement years in California where she has written, painted, and played the occasional tennis match with friends.

Sources:
Gianni Clerici, *The Ultimate Tennis Book,* translated by Richard J. Wiezell (Chicago: Follett, 1975), pp. 189–196;

Parke Cummings, *American Tennis: The Story of a Game and Its People* (Boston: Little, Brown, 1957), pp. 140–144;

Larry Engleman, *The Goddess and the American Girl: The Story of Suzanne Lenglen and Helen Wills* (New York: Oxford University Press, 1988).

# PEOPLE IN THE NEWS

In 1929 University of Florida student **Walter "Red" Barber** delivered his first radio broadcast of a baseball game when he provided the play-by-play for his university's team. He later became known for his colorful down-home style while announcing first Cincinnati Reds' and then Brooklyn Dodgers' games.

On 16 September 1924 **Jim Bottomly** of the Saint Louis Cardinals set a single-game record of twelve runs batted in.

**Frank Boucher,** with seven goals and one assist in the nine-game playoffs, led the New York Rangers to their Stanley Cup victory in 1928. The Rangers were the first U.S. team to win professional hockey's most prestigious prize.

In 1928 **Avery Brundage** was named president of the Amateur Athletic Union (AAU), which divided control and direction of amateur athletics with the National Collegiate Athletic Association (NCAA).

**Frank Carauna** of Buffalo, New York, bowled consecutive perfect games on 4 March 1924.

On 18 February 1928 **C. C. Davis** won his third consecutive national horseshoe-pitching championship with thirty-one victories and three losses.

In 1922 **Clarence DeMar** won his first Boston Marathon in 2 hours, 18 minutes, 10 seconds, a time that would not be bettered until 1956. In all DeMar claimed the Boston title six times between 1922 and 1930.

**Leo Durocher,** who in the 1930s would become a member of the Saint Louis Cardinals' legendary "Gashouse Gang" and, later, a colorfully outspoken manager for the Dodgers, Giants, and Cubs, was called up from the Yankees' farm club in 1928. During the two years he played at shortstop and second base for the Yankees, he averaged just over 31 RBIs per season, for a .258 batting average.

Following her 6 August 1926 swim across the English Channel, nineteen-year-old **Gertrude Ederle** was greeted by a ticker-tape parade and public adulation. Later she toured as a professional swimmer but dropped out of sight in the early 1930s when back injuries virtually ended her swimming career.

Between 1920 and 1923 **Adeline Gehrig,** sister of baseball's Lou Gehrig, reigned as women's national foil champion in fencing.

**Dr. Graeme M. Hammond** retired in 1925 as president of the Amateur Fencers League of America, a position he had held since 1891. He had won the U.S. épée title in 1893 and the U.S. saber title in 1893 and 1894.

In 1927 **Willie Hoppe,** who would win fifty-one billiards titles in his forty-six years of competition, beat Young Jake Schaefer in a Chicago challenge match, 1500–1196; Edouard Horemans in a New York match, 1500–958; and Welker Cochran in a Boston match, 1500–1189.

Between 1920 and 1925 **Rogers Hornsby** of the Saint Louis Cardinals led the National League in batting. During three of these six seasons his average was over .400, including his unmatched .424 in 1924.

**Eric Krenz** of Palo Alto, California, became, on 9 March 1929, the first man to throw the discus farther than 160 feet; his throw reached 163 feet, 8 3/4 inches.

On 5 September 1923 flyweights **Gene LaRue** and **Kid Pancho** threw simultaneous punches and knocked each other out.

In January 1921 American professional wrestling champion **Ed "Strangler" Lewis,** whose real name was **Robert Friedrich,** defended his title three times: against Earl Caddock in New York; against Dick Daviscourt in Rochester, New York; and against Gustav Sulzo in Kansas City.

On 31 January 1920 **Joe Malone** of the Quebec Bulldogs scored seven goals, a record, in a game against the Toronto Pats. During the 1919–1920 season Malone was ice hockey's leading scorer with thirty-nine goals, six assists, and forty-five total points.

**Bo McMillin,** quarterback for tiny Centre College in Danville, Kentucky, ran thirty-two yards for the game's only touchdown and a stunning 6–0 upset of Harvard on 30 October 1921. The whole town of Danville and the governor of Kentucky joined the celebration for the returning heroes.

On 6 May 1929 sixty-year-old **A. L. Monteverde** left city hall in New York City and ran 3,412 miles in seventy-nine days, ten hours, and ten minutes; he arrived at his San Francisco destination on 24 July.

Race-car driver **Jimmy Murphy** became in 1921 the first American to win the Grand Prix of France in an American automobile, a Duesenberg, and in 1922 took the Indianapolis 500 in a Murphy Special. Murphy died on 15 September 1924 in a crash during a race at Syracuse, New York.

**Ernie Nevers,** fullback for the Chicago Cardinals, scored all the points in his team's 28 November 1929 40–0 victory against the Chicago Bears.

On 18 June 1921 **Charles Paddock,** who had won the 100-meter run in 10.8 seconds at the 1920 Antwerp Olympics, ran 110 yards (a longer distance) in 10.2 seconds; his record held for twenty-nine years.

On 1 May 1926 **Satchel Paige** pitched Chattanooga to a 5–4 victory over Birmingham in Negro League play. The game marked Paige's first professional appearance.

Forty-five-year-old goalie **Lester Patrick** saved the 7 April 1928 game for the New York Rangers when he was forced to play against the Montreal Maroons because of injuries to regular goalie Lorne Chabot.

On 26 May 1928 **Andrew Payne,** a nineteen-year-old from Oklahoma, won the first Bunion Derby. Devised by C. C. Pyle, the race started on 4 March in Los Angeles with 275 runners bound for Madison Square Garden in New York City, 3,422 miles away. Payne took eighty-four days to reach the finish line. He received the $25,000 first prize from Pyle, who believed he would make a fortune as spectators along the route purchased programs and tickets to see this strange contest. Unfortunately, few people took any notice of the runners, and Pyle lost about $100,000. He tried to recoup his losses by staging the event again the following year but lost even more money.

In October 1926 tennis star **Vincent Richards,** angered by a U.S. Lawn Tennis Association ruling that players could not be paid to report on tournaments in which they were competing, announced that he would turn professional. Richards, with a wife and family to support, had an $8,000-per-year contract to write about tennis for King Features Syndicate. In the fall of 1926 he and five colleagues made a profitable three-month tennis tour promoted by C. C. "Cash and Carry" Pyle, and in September 1927 he was one of the founders of the Professional Lawn Tennis Association of the United States.

**Earle H. Sande,** one of the great jockeys of the 1920s, rode two Kentucky Derby winners during the decade — Zev in 1923 and Flying Ebony in 1925. Known as "Big Feet" for his habit of "nudging" other jockeys during tough races, Sande briefly retired in 1928 but returned in 1930 to ride Gallant Fox to the Triple Crown. Damon Runyon toyed with his poem about Sande for the rest of his life:

Sloan, they tell me, could ride 'em;
Maher, too, was a bird.
Bullman a guy to guide 'em —
Never much worse than third.
Them was the old time jockeys;
Now when I want to win,
Gimme a handy
Guy like Sande
Ridin' them hosses in.

In January 1927 **Abe Saperstein** founded the Harlem Globetrotters, a team of black basketball players who combined amazing basketball feats with comic routines.

**Eleonora Sears** became the first U.S. women's squash racquets singles champion on 19 January 1928 at the Round Hill Club in Greenwich, Connecticut.

In 1922 **Charles Dillon "Casey" Stengel,** who would later become a legendary manager for the New York Yankees and the New York Mets, had a batting average of .368 — the highest of his career — while playing for the New York Giants. When he ended his playing career in 1931, he had a lifetime average of .284.

**Harold Stirling Vanderbilt** won the King's Cup with his schooner *Vagrant* in 1922. It was the first of his eleven major yachting victories between 1922 and 1938, including three successful defenses of the America's Cup during the 1930s. Vanderbilt is also credited with inventing contract bridge while on a yachting trip in 1926.

On 2 July 1923 welterweight champion **Mickey Walker** was defending against **Cowboy Padgett** when both fell out of the ring and landed on the press table. Padgett broke two ribs and was unable to continue the fight.

**Christy Walsh** began ghostwriting newspaper articles for Babe Ruth in 1923. Walsh, who may have been the first sports agent, arranged vaudeville and barnstorming tours for Ruth.

In Saint Louis, Missouri, **Lt. Al Williams** flew a Curtis racer 243.7 MPH to set a new air-speed record on 6 October 1923.

In 1920 **Garfield "Gar" A. Wood,** the foremost inboard motorboat driver of the decade, set a Gold Cup race record of 70 MPH, a record that stood until 1946. Wood won the Gold Cup, an American race, four times between 1917 and 1921 and, in a succession of boats called *Miss America,* claimed the international Harmsworth Trophy seven times between 1920 and 1933. He was largely responsible for popularizing motorboat racing as a spectator sport in America.

Kentucky Derby and Belmont Stakes winner **Zev** beat the English champion Papyrus in a match race at Belmont Park on 20 October 1923.

# AWARDS

1920

**Major League Baseball World Series** — Cleveland Indians (American), 5 vs. Brooklyn Dodgers (National), 2

**Rose Bowl** — Harvard, 7 vs. University of Oregon, 6

**Stanley Cup, Hockey** — Ottawa Senators

**Bantamweight Championship, Boxing** — Joe Lynch over Pete Herman

**Middleweight Championship, Boxing** — Johnny Wilson over Mike O'Dowd

**Light Heavyweight Championship, Boxing** — Georges Carpentier over Christopher "Battling" Levinsky

**Kentucky Derby, Horse Racing** — Paul Jones, Jockey: T. Rice

**Preakness Stakes, Horse Racing** — Man o' War, Jockey: C. Kummer

**Belmont Stakes, Horse Racing** — Man o' War, Jockey: C. Kummer

**National Open Champion, Polo** — Meadow Brook, 12 vs. Cooperstown, 3

**Indianapolis 500** — Gaston Chevrolet in a Monroe, Average Speed: 88.62 MPH

**U.S. Golf Open Champion** — Edward Ray

**United States Auto Club National Champion** — Thomas Milton

**Davis Cup, Tennis** — United States, 5 vs. Australia, 0

**Men's Tennis Champion** — William Tatem Tilden II

**Women's Tennis Champion** — Molla Bjurdstedt Mallory

**Wimbledon — Men's Champion** — William Tatem Tilden II

**Wimbledon — Women's Champion** — Suzanne Lenglen

**Boston Marathon Winner** — Peter Trivoulides

America's Cup — *Resolute*, United States, beat *Shamrock IV*, England, 3 races to 2

Boating Gold Cup — *Miss America*, Owner/Driver: Gar Wood, Average Speed: 70 MPH

AAU Champion, Handball — Max Gold

Squash National Champion — Charles C. Peabody

## 1921

Major League Baseball World Series — New York Giants (National), 5 vs. New York Yankees (American), 3

National Football League Champion — Chicago Staleys (Bears)

Rose Bowl — California, 28 vs. Ohio State, 0

Stanley Cup, Hockey — Ottawa Senators

Bantamweight Championship, Boxing — Pete Herman over Joe Lynch

Bantamweight Championship, Boxing — Johnny Buff over Pete Herman

Kentucky Derby, Horse Racing — Behave Yourself, Jockey: C. Thompson

Preakness Stakes, Horse Racing — Broomspun, Jockey: Coltiletti

Belmont Stakes, Horse Racing — Grey Lag, Jockey: E. Sande

National Open Champion, Polo — Great Neck, 8 vs. Rockaway, 6

Indianapolis 500 — Tommy Milton in a Frontenac, Average Speed: 89.62 MPH

United States Auto Club National Champion — Thomas Milton

U.S. Golf Open Champion — James M. Barnes

Davis Cup, Tennis — United States, 5 vs. Japan, 0

Men's Tennis Champion — William Tatem Tilden II

Women's Tennis Champion — Molla Bjurdstedt Mallory

Wimbledon — Men's Champion — William Tatem Tilden II

Wimbledon — Women's Champion — Suzanne Lenglen

Boston Marathon Winner — Frank Zuna

Boating Gold Cup — *Miss America*, Owner/Driver: Gar Wood, Average Speed: 56.5 MPH

AAU Championship, Handball — Carl Haedge

Squash National Champion — Stanley Pearson

## 1922

Major League Baseball World Series — New York Giants (National), 4 vs. New York Yankees (American), 0

Baseball Triple Crown — Rogers Hornsby — Saint Louis (National League)

National Football League Champion — Canton Bulldogs

Rose Bowl — California, 0 vs. Washington & Jefferson, 0

Stanley Cup, Hockey — Toronto St. Patricks

Bantamweight Championship, Boxing — Joe Lynch over Johnny Buff

Welterweight Championship, Boxing — Mickey Walker over Jack Britton

Light Heavyweight Championship, Boxing — Battling Siki over Georges Carpentier

Kentucky Derby, Horse Racing — Morvich, Jockey: A. Johnson

Preakness Stakes, Horse Racing — Pillory, Jockey: L. Morris

Belmont Stakes, Horse Racing — Pillory, Jockey: C. H. Miller

Indianapolis 500 — Tommy Murphy in a Murphy Special, Average Speed: 94.48 MPH

United States Auto Club National Champion — James Murphy

National Open Champion, Polo — Argentine, 14 vs. Meadow Brook, 7

U.S. Golf Open Champion — Gene Sarazen

Davis Cup, Tennis — United States, 4 vs. Australasia, 1

Men's Tennis Champion — William Tatem Tilden II

Women's Tennis Champion — Molla Bjurdstedt Mallory

Wimbledon — Women's Champion — Suzanne Lenglen

Wimbledon — Men's Champion — Gerald Patterson

Boston Marathon Winner — Clarence DeMar

Boating Gold Cup — *Packard-Chris-Craft*, Owner: J. G. Vincent, Average Speed: 40.6 MPH

AAU Championship, Handball — Art Shinners

Squash National Champion — Stanley Pearson

## 1923

Major League Baseball World Series — New York Yankees (American), 4 vs. New York Giants (National), 2

National Football League Champion — Canton Bulldogs

Rose Bowl — University of Southern California, 14 vs. Pennsylvania State, 3

Stanley Cup, Hockey — Ottawa Senators

**Flyweight Championship, Boxing** — Pancho Villa over Jimmy Wilde

**Featherweight Championship, Boxing** — Eugene Criqui over Johnny Kilbane

**Featherweight Championship, Boxing** — Johnny Dundee over Eugene Criqui

**Middleweight Championship, Boxing** — Harry Greb over Johnny Wilson

**Light Heavyweight Championship, Boxing** — Mike McTigue over Battling Siki

**Kentucky Derby, Horse Racing** — Zev, Jockey: E. Sande

**Preakness Stakes, Horse Racing** — Vigil, Jockey: B. Marinelli

**Belmont Stakes, Horse Racing** — Zev, Jockey: E. Sande

**National Open Champion, Polo** — Meadow Brook, 12 vs. British Army, 9

**Indianapolis 500** — Tommy Milton in an H.C.S. Special, Average Speed: 90.95 MPH

**United States Auto Club National Champion** — Eddie Hearne

**U.S. Golf Open Champion** — Robert T. Jones Jr.

**Davis Cup, Tennis** — United States, 4 vs. Australasia, 1

**Men's Tennis Champion** — William Tatem Tilden II

**Women's Tennis Champion** — Helen Wills

**Wimbledon — Men's Champion** — William Johnston

**Wimbledon — Women's Champion** — Suzanne Lenglen

**Boston Marathon Winner** — Clarence DeMar

**Boating Gold Cup** — *Packard-Chris-Craft*, Owner: J. G. Vincent, Average Speed: 44.4 MPH

**AAU Championship, Handball** — Joe Murray

**Squash National Champion** — Stanley Pearson

## 1924

**Major League Baseball World Series** — Washington Senators (American), 4 vs. New York Giants (National), 3

**National Football League Champion** — Cleveland Bulldogs

**Rose Bowl** — University of Washington, 14 vs. Navy, 14

**Stanley Cup, Hockey** — Montreal Canadiens

**Bantamweight Championship, Boxing** — Abe Goldstein over Joe Lynch

**Bantamweight Championship, Boxing** — Eddie Cannonball Martin over Abe Goldstein

**Kentucky Derby, Horse Racing** — Black Gold, Jockey: J. D. Mooney

**Preakness Stakes, Horse Racing** — Nellie Morse, Jockey: J. Merimee

**Belmont Stakes, Horse Racing** — Mad Play, Jockey: E. Sande

**National Open Champion, Polo** — Midwick, 6 vs. Wanderers, 5

**Indianapolis 500** — L. L. Corum and Joe Boyer in a Duesenberg Special, Average Speed: 98.23 MPH

**United States Auto Club National Champion** — James Murphy

**U.S. Golf Open Champion** — Cyril Walker

**Davis Cup, Tennis** — United States, 5 vs. Australia, 0

**Men's Tennis Champion** — William Tatem Tilden II

**Women's Tennis Champion** — Helen Wills

**Wimbledon — Men's Champion** — Jean Borotra

**Wimbledon — Women's Champion** — Kathleen McKane

**Boston Marathon Winner** — Clarence DeMar

**Boating Gold Cup** — *Baby Bootlegger*, Owner: Caleb Bragg, Average Speed: 46.4 MPH

**AAU Championship, Handball** — Maynard Laswell

**Squash National Champion** — Gerald Robarts

## 1925

**Major League Baseball World Series** — Pittsburgh Pirates (National), 4 vs. Washington Senators (American), 3

**Baseball Triple Crown** — Rogers Hornsby—Saint Louis (National League)

**National Football League Champion** — Chicago Cardinals

**Rose Bowl** — Notre Dame, 27 vs. Stanford, 10

**Flyweight Championship, Boxing** — Fidel LaBarba over Frankie Genaro

**Bantamweight Championship, Boxing** — Phil Rosenberg over Eddie Martin

**Featherweight Championship, Boxing** — Louis "Kid" Kaplan following Johnny Dundee's retirement from the division

**Lightweight Championship, Boxing** — Jimmy Goodrich following Benny Leonard's 1924 retirement

**Lightweight Championship, Boxing** — Rocky Kansas over Jimmy Goodrich

**Light Heavyweight Championship, Boxing** — Paul Berlenbach over Mike McTigue

**Kentucky Derby, Horse Racing** — Flying Ebony, Jockey: E. Sande

**Preakness Stakes, Horse Racing** — Coventry, Jockey: C. Kummer

**Belmont Stakes, Horse Racing** — American Flag, Jockey: A. Johnson

**National Open Champion, Polo** — Orange County, 11 vs. Meadow Brook, 9

**Indianapolis 500** — Peter DePaolo in a Duesenberg Special, Average Speed: 101.13 MPH

**United States Auto Club National Champion** — Peter DePaolo

**Stanley Cup, Hockey** — Victoria Cougars

**U.S. Golf Open Champion** — William McFarlane

**Davis Cup, Tennis** — United States, 5 vs. France, 0

**Men's Tennis Champion** — William Tatem Tilden II

**Women's Tennis Champion** — Helen Wills

**Wimbledon — Men's Champion** — René Lacoste

**Wimbledon — Women's Champion** — Suzanne Lenglen

**Boston Marathon Winner** — Charles Mellor

**Boating Gold Cup** — *Baby Bootlegger*, Owner: Caleb Bragg, Average Speed: 46.4 MPH

**AAU Championship, Handball** — Maynard Laswell

**Squash National Champion** — W. Palmer Dixon


1926

**Major League Baseball World Series** — Saint Louis Cardinals (National), 4 vs. New York Yankees (American), 3

**National Football League Champion** — Frankford Yellow Jackets

**Rose Bowl** — Alabama, 20 vs. University of Washington, 19

**Stanley Cup, Hockey** — Montreal Maroons

**National League Champion, Hockey** — New York Rangers

**Lightweight Championship, Boxing** — Sammy Mandell over Rocky Kansas

**Welterweight Championship, Boxing** — Pete Latzo over Mickey Walker

**Middleweight Championship, Boxing** — Tiger Flowers over Harry Greb

**Middleweight Championship, Boxing** — Mickey Walker over Tiger Flowers

**Light Heavyweight Championship, Boxing** — Jack Delaney over Paul Berlenbach

**Heavyweight Championship, Boxing** — Gene Tunney over Jack Dempsey

**Kentucky Derby, Horse Racing** — Bubbling Over, Jockey: A. Johnson

**Preakness Stakes, Horse Racing** — Display, Jockey: Maiben

**Belmont Stakes, Horse Racing** — Crusader, Jockey: A. Johnson

**National Open Champion, Polo** — Hurricanes, 7 vs. Argentine, 6

**Indianapolis 500** — Frank Lockhart in a Miller Special, Average Speed: 95.90 MPH

**United States Auto Club National Champion** — Harry Hartz

**Davis Cup, Tennis** — United States, 4 vs. France, 1

**U.S. Golf Open Champion** — Robert T. Jones Jr.

**Men's Tennis Champion** — René Lacoste

**Women's Tennis Champion** — Molla Bjurdstedt Mallory

**Wimbledon — Men's Champion** — Jean Borotra

**Wimbledon — Women's Champion** — Kathleen Godfree

**Boston Marathon Winner** — John Miles

**Boating Gold Cup** — *Greenwich Folly*, Owner: G. H. Townsend, Average Speed: 49.22 MPH

**AAU Championship, Handball** — Maynard Laswell

**Squash National Champion** — W. Palmer Dixon


1927

**Major League Baseball World Series** — New York Yankees (American), 4 vs. Pittsburgh Pirates (National), 0

**National Football League Champion** — New York Giants

**Rose Bowl** — Alabama, 7 vs. Stanford, 7

**Stanley Cup, Hockey** — Ottawa Senators

**National League Champion, Hockey** — Boston Bruins

**Bantamweight Championship, Boxing** — Bud Taylor named by National Boxing Association

**Featherweight Championship, Boxing** — Benny Bass over Red Chapman

**Welterweight Championship, Boxing** — Joe Dundee over Pete Latzo

**Light Heavyweight Championship, Boxing** — Tommy Loughran over Mike McTigue

**Kentucky Derby, Horse Racing** — Whiskery, Jockey: L. McAtee

**Preakness Stakes, Horse Racing** — Bostonian, Jockey: A. Abel

Belmont Stakes, Horse Racing — Chance Shot, Jockey: E. Sande

Indianapolis 500 — George Souders in a Duesenberg, Average Speed: 97.54 MPH

National Open Champion, Polo — Sands Point, 11 vs. Army-in-India, 7

U.S. Golf Open Champion — Tommy Armour

Davis Cup, Tennis — France, 3 vs. United States, 2

Men's Tennis Champion — René Lacoste

Women's Tennis Champion — Helen Wills

United States Auto Club National Champion — Peter DePaolo

Wimbledon — Men's Champion — Henri Cochet

Wimbledon — Women's Champion — Helen Wills

Boston Marathon Winner — Clarence DeMar

Boating Gold Cup — *Greenwich Folly,* Owner: G. H. Townsend, Average Speed: 48.65 MPH

AAU Championship, Handball — George Nelson

Squash National Champion — Myles Baker

## 1928

Major League Baseball World Series — New York Yankees (American), 4 vs. Saint Louis Cardinals (National), 0

National Football League Champion — Providence Steamrollers

Rose Bowl — Stanford, 7 vs. Pittsburgh, 6

Stanley Cup, Hockey — New York Rangers

National League Champion, Hockey — Boston Bruins

Featherweight Championship, Boxing — Tony Canzoneri over Benny Bass

Featherweight Championship, Boxing — André Routis over Tony Canzoneri

Kentucky Derby, Horse Racing — Reigh Count, Jockey: C. Lang

Preakness Stakes, Horse Racing — Victorian, Jockey: R. Workman

Belmont Stakes, Horse Racing — Vito, Jockey: C. Kummer

National Open Champion, Polo — Meadow Brook, 8 vs. United States Army, 5

Indianapolis 500 — Louis Meyer in a Miller Special, Average Speed: 99.48 MPH

United States Auto Club National Champion — Louis Meyer

U.S. Golf Open Champion — John Farrell

Davis Cup, Tennis — France, 4 vs. United States, 1

Men's Tennis Champion — Henri Cochet

Women's Tennis Champion — Helen Wills

Wimbledon — Men's Champion — René Lacoste

Wimbledon — Women's Champion — Helen Wills

AAU Championship, Handball — Joe Griffin

Boston Marathon Winner — Clarence DeMar

National Men's Duckpin Bowling Champion — Howard Campbell

National Women's Duckpin Bowling Champion — Irene Mischou

Squash National Champion — Herbert N. Rawlins Jr.

## 1929

Major League Baseball World Series — Philadelphia Athletics (American), 4 vs. Chicago Cubs (National), 1

Rose Bowl — Georgia Tech, 8 vs. University of California, 7

National Football League Champion — Green Bay Packers

Stanley Cup, Hockey — Boston Bruins

National League Champion, Hockey — Boston Bruins

Featherweight Championship, Boxing — Battling Battalino over André Routis

Welterweight Championship, Boxing — Jackie Fields

Kentucky Derby, Horse Racing — Clyde Van Dusen, Jockey: L. McAtee

Preakness Stakes, Horse Racing — Dr. Freeland, Jockey: L. Schaefer

Belmont Stakes, Horse Racing — Blue Larkspur, Jockey: M. Garner

National Open Champion, Polo — Hurricanes, 11 vs. Sands Point, 7

Indianapolis 500 — Ray Keech in a Simplex Special, Average Speed: 97.58 MPH

United States Auto Club National Champion — Louis Meyer

U.S. Golf Open Champion — Robert T. Jones Jr.

Davis Cup, Tennis — France, 3 vs. United States, 2

Men's Tennis Champion — William Tatem Tilden II

Women's Tennis Champion — Helen Wills

Wimbledon — Men's Champion — Henri Cochet

Wimbledon — Women's Champion — Helen Wills

Boston Marathon Winner — John Miles

Boating Gold Cup — *Imp,* Owner: R. F. Hoyt, Average Speed: 48.45 MPH

AAU Championship, Handball — Al Baneut

National Men's Duckpin Bowling Champion — Sam Benson

National Women's Duckpin Bowling Champion — Marjorie Smith

Squash National Champion — J. Lawrence Pool

# DEATHS

Adrian Constantine "Cap" (later "Pop") Anson, 71, baseball player for the Philadelphia Athletics and player-manager for the Chicago Cubs, who during his record twenty-seven seasons as an active player in the Major Leagues had a lifetime batting average of .399 and more than 3,500 hits, 14 April 1922.

George Archibald, 37, American steeplechase jockey who won more than one thousand races in Europe, including 180 in England, two of which were for King George V, 5 April 1927.

Louis P. Bayard Jr., 46, a Princetonian who was the first National Intercollegiate Individual Golfing Champion in 1897, 3 July 1922.

August Belmont Jr., 72, New York City subway developer, financier, thoroughbred breeder, and chairman of the American Jockey Club, 10 December 1924.

Lee Bible, 42, dirt-track racer killed while attempting to set a world's automobile speed record in a 1,500-horsepower Triplex at Daytona Beach, Florida, 13 March 1929.

Thomas E. Burke, 54, runner who as a Harvard undergraduate won Gold Medals in the 100-meter and 400-meter races at the 1896 Olympics, the first Olympic Games of modern times, 14 February 1929.

Walter Chauncey Camp, 65, football authority who in 1888 became Yale's athletic director and the following year selected the first of the annual All-American football teams. Camp was largely responsible for giving football its modern form and rules, including the gridiron field, the eleven-man team, the quarterback position, and the four-down structure. His books on football and other sports stressed strategy and clean play, 14 March 1925.

Robert L. Cannefax, 37, one-legged billiards player who in 1917, 1919, and 1924 was the world's professional three-cushion champion, 27 February 1928.

Major Winthrop Astor Chanler, 62, who served in the Spanish-American War and World War I and who

devoted much of his life to hunting in Canada, the Austrian Tyrol, and Sardinia, 24 August 1926.

Col. Ezekiel F. Clay, 79, owner of Runnymede Stock Farm in Bourbon, Kentucky, and president of the Kentucky Racing Association, 27 July 1920.

Alexander Smith Cochran, 55, carpet-fortune heir, philanthropist, and yachtsman, whose schooner *Westward* in 1910 defeated Kaiser Wilhelm's *Meteor* for the Jubilee Prize at Kiel and in 1911 won the Astor Cup, 19 June 1929.

Jimmy Delaney, 26, light-heavyweight boxer who fought sixty-seven bouts, twenty-nine of them no-decision exhibition matches; of his other thirty-eight fights, he won twenty-nine and lost nine. Delaney, who had served as a sparring partner to Tommy Gibbons and Gene Tunney before their title fights with Jack Dempsey, died of blood poisoning resulting from injuries suffered in a bout with Maxie Rosenbloom, 4 March 1927.

Budd Doble, 85, for more than thirty years beginning in 1865 owner and driver of great trotting horses, including Dexter, Goldsmith Maid, Axtell, and Nancy Hanks; in his poem "How the Old Horse Won the Race," Oliver Wendell Holmes included the couplet "Budd Doble, whose catarrhal name / So fills the nasal trump of fame," 29 March 1926.

William Earl Dodge, 43, wealthy New York socialite and avid speedboat racer, 4 May 1927.

William Edward "Wild Bill" Donovan, 47, pitcher for the Detroit Tigers from 1903 to 1912 and manager of the New York Yankees from 1915 to 1918; he died in a train wreck at Forsyth, New York, 9 December 1923.

Charles H. Ebbets, 66, president and part owner of the Brooklyn Dodgers who moved the Dodgers' playing field to Brooklyn and for whom it was later named, 18 April 1925.

**Frank J. Farrell,** 60, in 1903 cofounder with William S. Devery of the New York Highlanders, the American League team that later became the Yankees; after the partners sold the club to Col. Jacob Ruppert in 1915, Farrell became heavily involved in horse racing and gambling enterprises, 10 February 1926.

**Charles Addison Ferry,** 76, engineer who designed the Yale Bowl, 31 July 1924.

**Theodore "Tiger" Flowers,** 32, the only black boxer to win a major title during the 1920s; he defeated Harry Greb for the middleweight championship in February 1926, defended his title against Greb in August of that year, and lost in a highly controversial decision to Mickey Walker in December 1926. Of his 149 fights, Flowers won 115, lost 19, and had 15 no-decision contests, 16 November 1927.

**Margaret Crozer (Mrs. Caleb F.) Fox,** 67, the "Grand Old Lady of Golf," who had played in the first national championship for women golfers in 1895 and who, when she was sixty-two years old, beat the reigning women's champion, Glenna Collett, in a Florida tournament with a score of 77, 10 August 1928.

**Harry H. Frazee,** 48, theatrical producer (whose shows included *No, No, Nanette* in 1925) and former owner of the Boston Red Sox, whose team won the World Series in 1918; on 3 January 1920 Frazee sold Babe Ruth to the New York Yankees for $125,000 plus a substantial loan, 4 June 1929.

**Eugene J. Giannini,** 55?, champion rower who was on the New York Athletic Club's national-championship crews for eight-oared sculls in 1891 and 1892, who won more than thirty races in single and double sculls, and who served as a rowing coach both at Yale and at the New York Athletic Club, 3 March 1923.

**Charles Jaspar Glidden,** 70, telephone and telegraph executive, who in the first years of the twentieth century organized round-the-world and United States motoring tours; sponsored by the American Automobile Association, the U.S. tour, which between 1905 and 1913 included twenty-five to fifty entrants annually, covered one thousand miles, and had as its prize the Glidden Trophy, 11 September 1927.

**Harry (Henry Berg) Greb,** 32, boxer who, of his 291 bouts, won 114, lost 9, and fought 168 no-decision contests. In May 1922 Greb beat Gene Tunney for the light-heavyweight title, which Tunney reclaimed in February 1923. In August 1923 Greb took the middleweight title from Johnny Wilson, a title he successfully defended until February 1926, when he lost it to Tiger Flowers, 22 October 1926.

**Irving Grinnell,** 81, a grandnephew of Washington Irving, an inaugurator of rowing at Columbia University, and a yachting enthusiast who at one point served as commodore of the New York Yacht Club, 11 May 1921.

**Captain Harry P. Haff,** 61, skipper of world-class racing yachts for such owners as William E. Iselin, Henry I. Lippitt, Alexander Smith Cochran, and the Belmont family, 1 February 1922.

**Fred "Pop" Hanlon,** 65, for twenty-three years secretary and business manager of the Brooklyn Dodgers and an authority on baseball rules, 2 August 1927.

**John A. "Jack" Highlands,** 51, in the 1890s a notable Harvard pitcher who later had interests in a motion-picture company and in a cotton-production plant in Haiti, 15 April 1920.

**Samuel Clay Hildreth,** 63, trainer of thoroughbred racing horses for such breeders as Harry F. Sinclair, James Corrigan, William C. Whitney, and the Belmonts; among the horses Hildreth trained were Grey Lag, Purchase, Stromboli, and Zev, 24 September 1929.

**Samuel Shaw Howland,** 75, inheritor through birth and marriage of New York banking fortunes, who was a patron of both flat-track and steeplechase racing and a founder of the American Jockey Club and the National Steeplechase and Hunt Association, 27 April 1925.

**Miller J. Huggins,** 50, legendary manager of the New York Yankees from 1918 to 1929; between 1921 and 1928 Huggins led the Yankees — including Babe Ruth and, after June 1925, Lou Gehrig — to six American League pennants and three World Series championships, two of them sweeps in 1927 and 1928, 25 September 1929.

**Hugh Ambrose Jennings,** 56, baseball player who batted .300 or more for twelve seasons, most of them with the Baltimore Orioles, in the 1890s and early 1900s; an aggressive plate hugger, he was regularly hit by pitched balls. In 1907 Jennings began a distinguished career as a baseball manager, leading the Detroit Tigers to American League pennants in 1907, 1908, and 1909; he remained with Detroit until 1921, when John McGraw hired him as field manager for the New York Giants, who won National League pennants from 1921 through 1924. In 1925 he became the Giants' full-time manager but retired the following year because of ill health, 1 February 1928.

**George M. Kelly,** 80, champion jumper with American circuses; he was the first man to perform a triple-somersault leap over eight animals — horses, camels, and elephants — lined up in a circus ring, 4 April 1921.

**John Walker "Jack" Lapp,** 35, former catcher for the Philadelphia Athletics who had played a substantial role in the Athletics' World Series championships from 1910 through 1913, 6 February 1921.

**George H. "Kid" Lavigne,** 58, from 1893 to 1899 lightweight boxing champion, whose opponents included Joe Walcott, Dick Burge, and Young Griffo; though he had reportedly earned a small fortune in the ring,

Lavigne spent his final years as a night watchman at the Ford Motor Company plant in Detroit, 10 March 1928.

**Thomas Le Boutillier II,** 50, president of the Dubois Fence Company, pistol marksman, and member of the Old Westbury, Long Island, club polo team; he died of a heart attack while playing in the Autumn Plate Polo Tournament at Westbury, Long Island, 18 September 1929.

**Captain Martin J. Lyons,** 88, yacht skipper for James Gordon Bennett and winner of many races between 1866 and 1900, 21 July 1920.

**John E. Madden,** 73, financier, turfman, and, in his youth, amateur runner and boxer who was a sparring partner and "second" for John L. Sullivan. Most notably, Madden founded and operated a Kentucky racing stable, Hamburg Place, where he bred many famous horses, among them six Kentucky Derby winners: Plaudit (1898), Old Rosebud (1914), Sir Barton (the first Triple Crown winner, 1919), Paul Jones (1920), Zev (1923), and Flying Ebony (1925), 3 November 1929.

**Christopher "Christy" Mathewson,** 45, legendary New York Giants and Cincinnati Reds pitcher who was among the first five players named to the Baseball Hall of Fame. Mathewson played four seasons in which he won thirty games or more and eight others in which he won twenty games or more. During the 1903 season, while playing for the Giants, he pitched 267 strikeouts, a record that stood for more than fifty years. Mathewson was a master of the fadeaway pitch (later called the screwball); by the time of his retirement as a player in 1916, his win-loss record stood at 372–187, and he had struck out 2,499 batters. His early death was in part the result of gassing during World War I army service, 7 October 1925.

**Joseph Jerome "Iron Man" McGinnity,** 58, baseball player who, in the 1900 National League pennant race, pitched and won seven games in six days, helping his team, the Brooklyn Trolley Dodgers, beat out the Pittsburgh Pirates for the title; in 1904 he won thirty-five of the fifty-one games he pitched for the Baltimore Americans. McGinnity continued pitching for major- and minor-league teams until he was fifty-four years old, 14 November 1929.

**James Pilkington,** 77, New York subway contractor and all-around athlete who in 1879 won amateur heavyweight boxing and wrestling titles in a single evening, in 1889 won the national doubles sculling championship with Jack Nagle, and for twenty years served as president of the National Association of Amateur Oarsmen; a longtime member of the American Olympic Committee, Pilkington was known as the "father of amateur rowing," 25 April 1929.

**Myer Prinstein,** 46, broad jumper who won gold medals in the 1900, 1904, and 1906 Olympics (the latter a special event held in Athens to placate the Greeks who felt that Athens should be the permanent Olympic site). In 1900 Prinstein placed second in the running broad jump because his university, Syracuse, refused to allow him to compete in the Sunday finals; the following day he took the gold in the running hop, skip, and jump. In 1904 he won first place in both events and, in 1906, the gold in the broad jump, 10 March 1925.

**Paul J. Rainey,** 46, independently wealthy big-game hunter, whose tracking of African lions with American bear hounds became a favorite subject of early newsreels, 18 September 1923.

**George Lewis "Tex" Rickard,** 58, legendary fight promoter who turned boxing into a glamorous sport by making attendance at bouts popular among the rich and fashionable. Beginning as a gambling-house operator and speculator in the Klondike and Nevada, Rickard had his initial boxing success with the 1910 James J. Jeffries–Jack Johnson title fight, which he promoted as a contest between the first black heavyweight champion (Johnson) and a "white hope" (Jeffries) and which Johnson won. In 1919 Rickard arranged a championship fight for Jack Dempsey — the Dempsey–Jess Willard bout, which brought Dempsey the heavyweight crown. Other title fights that Rickard promoted included the 1921 Dempsey–Georges Carpentier contest (which produced the first "million-dollar gate"), the Dempsey–Luis Firpo bout in 1923, the 1926 Dempsey–Gene Tunney fight (with receipts of nearly $2 million), and the 1927 Dempsey–Tunney rematch, which grossed more than $2 million. Dempsey, who was with Rickard when he died of peritonitis, reported that among the promoter's final words were, "Jack, I've got this fight licked," 6 January 1929.

**Arnold Rothstein,** 46, gambler and racketeer indicted for fixing the 1919 World Series. Known as "The Brain" and "The Bankroll," he was never convicted of a crime. He was found shot to death on a stairwell in Manhattan's Park Central Hotel following a high-stakes card game. His murder was not solved, 6 November 1928.

**Sir Mortimer Singer,** 65, American-born British citizen and an heir to the sewing-machine fortune; he was a pioneer in cycling, motoring, and flying, and his racing stables produced several English racing champions, 24 June 1929.

**George Stallings,** 63, who managed the Boston Braves from 1913 to 1920; his 1914 team went from last place in the National League in late July to pennant winner on 25 September to a sweep of the World Series over the Philadelphia Athletics. Stallings' dying words were supposedly, "Bases on balls did this to me," 13 May 1929.

Walter J. Travis, 65, Australian-born American golfer who in 1904 became the first American to win the British amateur championship; he also took the American amateur championship in 1900, 1901, and 1903 and throughout his career served as a notable golf-course architect, 31 July 1927.

William Kissam Vanderbilt, 70, railroad heir, arts patron, and sportsman; in 1895 he sailed the yacht *Defender* that retained the America's Cup for the United States, 22 July 1920.

Pancho (Francisco Guilledo) Villa, 23, Filipino flyweight champion of the world since 18 June 1923; he died of an infected tooth ten days after a bout with Jimmy McLarnin, 14 July 1925.

Ellis Ward, 77, one of nine Ward brothers who were famous rowers, served for thirty-five years as the University of Pennsylvania crews coach, 25 August 1922.

Freddie Welsh, 41, lightweight boxing champion from 1914 to 1917, who died pennyless and alone; his wife, from whom he was separated but on good terms, said of other boxers, "This is a hard-boiled age. . . . Freddie knew them all when he was on top, but none of them knew him when he was down and out," 28 July 1927.

Edward Payson Weston, 90, long-distance walker; over the course of five decades he participated in walking tours and races, including a walk from New York City to San Francisco and back (3,895 miles in 103 days 7 hours), when he was in his early seventies, 12 May 1929.

Howard Frederic Whitney, 52, longtime member of the New York Stock Exchange and avid golfer, who as a member and officer of the United States Golf Association had been largely responsible for bringing about agreements between the U.S.G.A. and the Royal and Ancient Golf Club of Saint Andrews, Scotland. At the time of his death Whitney and Bobby Jones were the only Americans to hold honorary memberships in the Saint Andrews club, 30 June 1927.

Payne Whitney, 51, multimillionaire financier and sportsman who had been a champion rower at Yale and who with his wife, Helen Hay Whitney, and brother, Harry Payne Whitney, was active in thoroughbred horse racing, 25 May 1927.

Walter Winans, 68, independently wealthy world-champion marksman and huntsman who had won a gold medal in the running-deer double-shots competition of the 1908 London Olympics and had taken first prize for a sculpture in the new fine-arts division of the 1912 London Olympics; he was also a hackney- and trotting-horse fancier who died while driving a sulky in a London trotting race, 12 August 1920.

# PUBLICATIONS

Forrest Claire Allen, *My Basket-Ball Bible* (Kansas City, Mo.: Smith-Grieves, 1924);

Thornton Whitney Allen, *Intercollegiate Song Book: Alma Mater and Football Songs of the American Colleges* (New York: Intercollegiate Song Book, 1927);

Lou Eastwood Anderson, *Tennis for Women, with Reference to the Training of Teachers* (New York: Barnes, 1926);

Elmer Berry, *The Philosophy of Athletics, Coaching and Character, with the Psychology of Athletic Coaching* (New York: Barnes, 1927);

Sverre O. Braathen, *Ty Cobb: The Idol of Baseball Fandom* (New York: Avondale, 1928);

Mary Kendall Browne, *Top-Flite Tennis* (New York: American Sports Publishing, 1928);

William H. Carter, *The Horses of the World: The Development of Man's Companion in War Camp, on Farm, in the Marts of Trade, and in the Field of Sports* (Washington, D.C.: National Geographic Society, 1923);

Abel Chapman, *Savage Sudan: Its Wild Tribes, Big-Game and Bird-Life* (New York: Putnam, 1922);

Carrol Blaine Cook, *Goin' Fishin': Weather and Feed Facts, the Fresh-Water Game Fish, the Natural and Artificial Baits and Their Use* (Cincinnati: Stewart & Kidd, 1920);

John Duncan Dunn, *Intimate Golf Talks* (New York: Putnam, 1920);

Henry Grady Edney, *Theodore "Tiger" Flowers: A Biography* (Biltmore, N.C.: Country Club, 1928);

Sophie C. Eliott-Lynn, *Athletics for Women and Girls: How to Be an Athlete and Why* (London: R. Scott, 1925);

Bernard Cuthbert Ellison, *H.R.H. the Prince of Wales's Sport in India* (London: Heinemann, 1925);

Helen Frost, *Basket Ball and Indoor Baseball for Women* (New York: Scribners, 1920);

Frost, *Field Hockey and Soccer for Women* (New York: Scribners, 1923);

Alice Willetta Frymir, *Basketball for Women: How to Coach and Play the Game* (New York: Barnes, 1928);

*The Grip in Golf* (Chicago: Golfers Magazine, 1922);

Stanley Harris, *Baseball, How to Play It: Practical Instruction for Each Position Together with the Strategy and Tactics of the Game* (New York: Stokes, 1925);

A. H. W. Haywood, *Sport & Service in Africa: A Record of Big Game Shooting, Campaigning & Adventure in the Hinterland of Nigeria, the Cameroons, Togoland &c., with an Account of the Ways of Native Soldiers & Inhabitants & a Description of Their Villages & Customs as Well as of the Fauna & Flora* (Philadelphia: Lippincott, 1926);

*High School Athletics* (Columbia, S.C.: University of South Carolina, Extension Department, 192?);

Robert G. MacDonald, *Golf* (Chicago: Wallace, 1927);

Alexander Mackenzie, *Golf Architecture: Economy in Course Construction and Greenkeeping* (London: Simpkin, Marshall, Hamilton, Kent, 1920);

Evelyn George Martin, *Deep Water Cruising* (New York: Yachting, 1928);

John J. McGraw, *My Thirty Years in Baseball* (New York: Boni & Liveright, 1923);

Elmer Dayton Mitchell, *Intramural Athletics* (New York: Barnes, 1925);

Jay Bryan Nash, *The Organization and Administration of Playgrounds and Recreation* (New York: Barnes, 1927);

*Olympic Games Handbook: Containing Official Records of the Seventh Olympiad, Winners in Previous Olympiads, the 1924 Olympic Games, Official Olympic Athletic Rules and the Official World's Records and Noteworthy Performances* (New York: American Sports, 1921);

Jahial Parmly Paret, *Lawn Tennis Lessons for Beginners* (New York: American Lawn Tennis, 1926);

Paret, *Mechanics of the Game of Lawn Tennis* (New York: American Lawn Tennis, 1926);

Samuel L. Parrish, *Some Facts, Reflections, and Personal Reminiscences Connected with the Introduction of the Game of Golf into the United States* (New York, 1923);

Harford Willing Hare Powel, *Walter Camp, The Father of American Football: An Authorized Biography* (Boston: Little, Brown, 1926);

Henry Reynolds, *Spanish Waters* (London: Hurst & Blackett, 1924);

Louis Rhead, *Fisherman's Lures and Game-Fish Food, with Colored Pictures from Life of Various Creatures Fish Eat and New Improved Artificial Imitation Floating Nature Lures and Chart-Plans to Show the Haunts Where Fish Feed on Them in Lake and Stream* (New York: Scribners, 1920);

Grantland Rice, *The Duffer's Handbook of Golf* (New York: Macmillan, 1926);

Knute Rockne, *The Autobiography of Knute Rockne* (Indianapolis: Bobbs-Merrill, 1931);

Rockne, *Coaching* (New York: Devin-Adair, 1925);

Frantz Rosenberg, *Big Game Shooting in British Columbia and Norway* (London: Hopkinson, 1928);

Leslie Schon, *The Psychology of Golf* (London: Metheun, 1922);

Clifton Scollard, *The Epic of Golf* (Boston: Houghton Mifflin, 1923);

Amos Alonzo Stagg, *Touchdown! As Told by Coach Amos Alonzo Stagg to Wesley Winans Stout* (New York: Longmans, Green, 1927);

Seward Charles Staley, *Games, Contests and Relays* (New York: Barnes, 1924);

Frank J. Sullivan, *The Science of Swimming* (New York: American Sports Publishing, 1924);

Bill Tilden, *The Art of Lawn Tennis* (New York: Doran, 1921);

Tilden, *Better Tennis for the Club Player* (New York: American Sports, 1925);

Tilden, *The Common Sense of Tennis* (New York: Simon & Schuster, 1924);

Tilden, *Match Play and the Spin of the Ball* (New York: American Lawn Tennis, 1925);

Tilden, *Singles and Doubles* (New York: Doran, 1923);

John R. Tunis, *Sports, Heroics and Hysterics* (New York: John Day, 1928);

Nathaniel Louis Willet, *Game Preserves and Game of Beaufort, Colleton, and Jasper Counties, South Carolina: Hunters' Paradise, Manly Sports* (Beaufort, S.C.: Charleston & Western Carolina Railway, 1927?);

Paul Benjamin Williams, *United States Lawn Tennis Association and the World War* (New York: Robert Hamilton, 1921);

Helen Wills, *Tennis* (New York: Scribners, 1928);

Harry Leon Wilson, *So This Is Golf!* (New York: Cosmopolitan, 1923);

Milton Cooper Work, *Contract Bridge* (Chicago: Winston, 1927);

*Athletic Journal*, periodical;

*Baily's Monthly Magazine of Sports and Pastimes*, periodical;

*Golfdom*, periodical.

# GENERAL REFERENCES

---

## GENERAL

Frederick Lewis Allen, *Only Yesterday: An Informal History of the Nineteen-Twenties* (New York: Harper, 1931);

*The American Heritage History of the 20's and 30's* (New York: American Heritage, 1970);

Mary Kupiec Cayton, Elliott J. Gorn, and Peter T. Williams, eds., *Encyclopedia of American Social History*, 3 volumes (New York: Scribners, 1993);

*Chronicle of the Twentieth Century* (Mount Kisco, N.Y.: Chronicle, 1987);

John W. Dodds, *Everyday Life in Twentieth Century America* (New York: Putnam, 1965);

Paul Johnson, *Modern Times: From the Twenties to the Nineties*, revised edition (New York: HarperCollins, 1991);

Irving S. and Nell M. Kull, eds., *An Encyclopedia of American History*, revised and updated by Stanley H. Friedelbaum (New York: Popular Library, 1965);

Charles D. Lowery and John F. Marszalek, eds., *Encyclopedia of African-American Civil Rights: From Emancipation to the Present* (Westport, Conn.: Greenwood Press, 1992);

Iwan W. Morgan and Neil A. Wynn, *America's Century: Perspectives on U.S. History Since 1900* (New York: Holmes & Meier, 1993);

Barbara Sicherman and Carol Hurd Green, with Ilene Kantrov and Harriette Walker, eds., *Notable American Women: The Modern Period, A Biographical Dictionary* (Cambridge, Mass.: Harvard University Press, 1980);

*Statistical History of the United States from Colonial Times to the Present* (Stamford, Conn.: Fairfield, 1965);

*This Fabulous Century* (New York: Time-Life Books, 1988);

*Time Lines on File* (New York: Facts On File, 1988);

James Trager, *The People's Chronology*, revised edition (New York: Holt, Rinehart & Winston, 1994);

Claire Walter, *Winners: The Blue Ribbon Encyclopedia of Awards* (New York: Facts On File, 1982);

Leigh Carol Yuster and others, eds., *Ulrich's International Periodicals Directory: A Classified Guide to Current Periodicals, Foreign and Domestic, 1986–1987*, twenty-fifth edition, 2 volumes (New York & London: Bowker, 1986).

## ARTS

Daniel Aaron, *Writers on the Left* (New York: Harcourt, Brace & World, 1961);

Chris Albertson, *Bessie* (New York: Stein & Day, 1972);

Shelley Armitage, *John Held, Jr.: Illustrator of the Jazz Age* (Syracuse, N.Y.: Syracuse University Press, 1987);

Louis Armstrong, *Satchmo: My Life in New Orleans* (New York: Prentice-Hall, 1954);

H. H. Arnason, *History of Modern Art: Painting • Sculpture • Architecture* (Englewood Cliffs, N.J.: Prentice-Hall / New York: Abrams, 1968);

Carlos Baker, *Ernest Hemingway: A Life Story* (New York: Scribners, 1969);

John I. H. Baur, ed., *New Art in America: Fifty Painters of the 20th Century* (Greenwich, Conn.: New York Graphic Society, 1957);

Sylvia Beach, *Shakespeare & Company* (New York: Harcourt, Brace, 1959);

Laurence Bergreen, *As Thousands Cheer: The Life of Irving Berlin* (New York: Viking, 1990);

Walter Blair and Hamlin Hill, *America's Humor* (New York: Oxford University Press, 1978);

Daniel Blum, *A New Pictorial History of the Talkies*, revised and enlarged by John Kobal (New York: Putnam, 1982);

Paul S. Boyer, *Purity in Print* (New York: Scribners, 1968);

Milton W. Brown, *American Painting from the Armory Show to the Depression* (Princeton: Princeton University Press, 1955);

Matthew J. Bruccoli, *Some Sort of Epic Grandeur: The Life of F. Scott Fitzgerald*, revised edition (New York: Carroll & Graf, 1993);

Bruccoli, ed., *F. Scott Fitzgerald: A Life in Letters* (New York: Scribners, 1994);

Charlie Chaplin, *Charlie Chaplin's Own Story* (Bloomington: Indiana University Press, 1985);

Chaplin, *My Autobiography* (New York: Simon & Schuster, 1964);

*The Collected Catalogues of Dr. A. S. W. Rosenbach, 1904–1951* (New York: Arno/McGraw-Hill, 1967);

James L. Collier, *Louis Armstrong: An American Genius* (New York: Oxford University Press, 1988);

Collier, *The Making of Jazz: A Comprehensive History* (New York: Dell, 1979);

Louise Cowen, *The Fugitive Group: A Literary History* (Baton Rouge: Louisiana State University Press, 1959);

Malcolm Cowley, *A Second Flowering: Works and Days of the Lost Generation* (New York: Viking, 1973);

Donald Elder, *Ring Lardner: A Biography* (Garden City, N.Y.: Doubleday, 1956);

Hugh Ford, *Published in Paris: American and British Writers, Printers, and Publishers in Paris, 1920–1939* (New York: Macmillan, 1975);

Michael Freedland, *Jolson* (New York: Stein & Day, 1972);

Philip Furia, *The Poets of Tin Pan Alley: A History of America's Great Lyricists* (New York: Oxford University Press, 1990);

Herbert G. Goldman, *Jolson* (New York: Oxford University Press, 1988);

Ron Goulart, *The Hardboiled Dicks: An Anthology and Study of Pulp Detective Fiction* (Los Angeles: Sherbourne, 1965);

Horace Gregory and Marza Zaturensha, *A History of American Poetry, 1900–1940* (New York: Harcourt, Brace, 1946);

*The Harlem Renaissance: An Historical Dictionary of the Era* (Westport, Conn.: Greenwood Press, 1984);

Margaret Case Harriman, *The Vicious Circle: The Story of the Algonquin Round Table* (New York: Rinehart, 1951);

Trudier Harris, ed., *Afro-American Writers from the Harlem Renaissance to 1940; Dictionary of Literary Biography*, volume 51 (Detroit: Bruccoli Clark/Gale Research, 1986);

Frederic Hoffman, *The Twenties; American Writing in the Postwar Decade*, revised edition (New York: Collier, 1962);

Nathan Irving Huggins, *Harlem Renaissance* (New York: Oxford University Press, 1977);

Huggins, ed., *Voices from the Harlem Renaissance* (New York: Oxford University Press, 1995);

Langston Hughes, *I Wonder as I Wander: An Autobiographical Journey* (New York: Rinehart, 1956);

Edmund Jablonski, *The Gershwin Years* (Garden City, N.Y.: Doubleday, 1958);

Walter Kerr, *The Silent Clowns* (New York: Knopf, 1975);

Bobby Ellen Kimbel, ed., *American Short-Story Writers, 1910–1945*, series 1 and 2; *Dictionary of Literary Biography*, volumes 86 and 102 (Detroit: Bruccoli Clark Layman/Gale Research, 1989, 1991);

Richard Koszarski, *An Evening's Entertainment: The Age of the Silent Feature Picture 1915–1928* (New York: Scribners, 1990);

Felice F. Lewis, *Literature, Obscenity, and Law* (Carbondale: Southern Illinois University Press, 1976);

Richard Dyer MacCann, *The Silent Comedians* (Metuchen, N.J.: Scarecrow Press, 1993);

John MacNicholas, ed., *Twentieth-Century American Dramatists; Dictionary of Literary Biography*, volume 7 (Detroit: Bruccoli Clark/Gale, 1981);

Ethan Madden, *Better Foot Forward: The History of American Musical Theater* (New York: Grossman, 1976);

James J. Martine, *American Novelists, 1910–1945; Dictionary of Literary Biography*, volume 9 (Detroit: Bruccoli Clark/Gale Research, 1981);

Samuel Marx, *Mayer and Thalberg: The Make-Believe Saints* (New York: Random House, 1975);

Marc H. Miller, ed., *Louis Armstrong: A Cultural Legacy* (New York: Queens Museum of Art / Seattle: University of Washington Press, 1994);

Raymond Moley, *The Hays Office* (Indianapolis: Bobbs-Merrill, 1945);

*The Most of John Held Jr.*, Introduction by Carl J. Weinhardt (Brattleboro, Vt.: Stephen Green Press, 1972);

David Perkins, *A History of Modern Poetry from the 1890s to the High Modern Mode* (Cambridge, Mass.: Harvard University Press, 1976);

Peter Quartermain, ed. *American Poets, 1880–1945*, series 1–3; *Dictionary of Literary Biography*, volumes 45, 48, and 54 (Detroit: Bruccoli Clark/Gale, 1986–1987);

John Raeburn, *Fame Became of Him: Hemingway as Public Writer* (Bloomington: Indiana University Press, 1984);

Arnold Rampersad, *The Life of Langston Hughes* (New York: Oxford University Press, 1986);

Walter B. Rideout, *The Radical Novel in the United States 1900–1954* (Cambridge, Mass.: Harvard University Press, 1956);

David Robinson, *Chaplin: His Life and Art* (New York: McGraw-Hill, 1985);

Karen Lane Rood, ed., *American Writers in Paris, 1920–1939; Dictionary of Literary Biography,* volume 4 (Detroit: Bruccoli Clark/Gale Research, 1980);

Deena Rosenberg, *Fascinating Rhythm: The Collaboration of George and Ira Gershwin* (New York: Dutton, 1991);

Leland M. Roth, *A Concise History of American Architecture* (New York: Harper & Row, 1979);

Louis D. Rubin Jr., ed., *The History of Southern Literature* (Baton Rouge: Louisiana State University Press, 1985);

Gunther Schuller, *Early Jazz: Its Roots and Musical Development* (New York: Oxford University Press, 1968);

Mack Sennett, *King of Comedy* (Garden City, N.Y.: Doubleday, 1954);

Louis Sheaffer, *O'Neill: Son and Artist* (Boston: Little, Brown, 1973);

Sheaffer, *O'Neill: Son and Playwright* (Boston: Little, Brown, 1968);

Scottie Fitzgerald Smith and others, eds., *The Romantic Egoists: A Pictorial Autobiography from the Scrapbooks and Albums of Scott and Zelda Fitzgerald* (New York: Scribners, 1974);

John L. Stewart, *The Burden of Time: The Fugitives and Agrarians . . .* (Princeton: Princeton University Press, 1965);

Deems Taylor, *A Pictorial History of the Movies* (New York: Simon & Schuster, 1943);

Walter Terry, *The Dance in America* (New York: Harper, 1956);

Bob Thomas, *Thalberg* (Garden City, N.Y.: Doubleday, 1969);

Frederic Thrasher, ed., *Okay for Sound . . . How the Screen Found Its Voice* (New York: Duell, Sloan & Pearce, 1946);

Barry Ulanov, *A History of Jazz in America* (New York: Da Capo, 1972);

Herman Wasserman, ed., *George Gershwin's Song-book,* revised edition (New York: Simon & Schuster, 1941);

Ian Whitcomb, *Irving Berlin and Ragtime America* (New York: Limelight, 1988);

Edwin Wolfe II and John F. Fleming, *Rosenbach* (Cleveland & New York: World, 1960).

## BUSINESS AND THE ECONOMY

Bernard Baruch, *The Public Years* (New York: Holt, Rinehart & Winston, 1960);

Marilyn Bender and Seliq Altschul, *The Chosen Instrument: Pan Am, Juan Trippe, the Rise and Fall of an American Entrepreneur* (New York: Simon & Schuster, 1982);

John Brooks, *Once in Golconda* (New York: Norton, 1969);

Brooks, *Telephone: The First Hundred Years* (New York: Harper & Row, 1975);

Stuart Bruchey, *Enterprise: The Dynamic Economy of a Free People* (Cambridge, Mass.: Harvard University Press, 1990);

Karl Brunner, ed., *The Great Depression Revisited* (Boston: Martinus Nijhoff, 1981);

Keith L. Bryant Jr. and Henry C. Dethloff, *A History of American Business,* second edition (Englewood Cliffs, N.J.: Prentice Hall, 1990);

Bryant, ed., *Encyclopedia of American Business History and Biography: Railroads in the Age of Regulation, 1900–1980* (New York & Oxford: Manly/Facts On File, 1988);

Alfred D. Chandler Jr., *Giant Enterprise: Ford, General Motors and the Automobile Industry* (New York: Harcourt, Brace & World, 1964);

Chandler and Stephen Salsbury, *Pierre S. du Pont and the Making of the Modern Corporation* (New York: Harper & Row, 1971);

Walter P. Chrysler, *Life of an American Workman* (New York: Dodd, Mead, 1927);

Ed Cray, *Chrome Colossus: General Motors and Its Times* (New York: McGraw-Hill, 1980);

John M. Dobson, *A History of American Enterprise* (Englewood Cliffs, N.J.: Prentice Hall, 1988);

William S. Dutton, *Du Pont: One Hundred and Thirty Years* (New York: Scribners, 1942);

Ralph Epstein, *The Automobile Industry: Its Economic and Commercial Development* (Chicago: University of Chicago Press, 1928);

Irving Fisher, *The Stock Market Crash — and After* (New York: Macmillan, 1930);

John Kenneth Galbraith, *The Great Crash* (Boston: Houghton Mifflin, 1961);

Galbraith, *The New Industrial State* (Boston: Houghton Mifflin, 1971);

Carol W. Gelderman, *Henry Ford: The Wayward Capitalist* (New York: Dial, 1981);

George Gilder, *The Spirit of Enterprise* (New York: Simon & Schuster, 1984);

Charles E. Gilland Jr., ed., *Readings in Business Responsibility* (Braintree, Mass.: Mark, 1969);

Thomas Gordon and Morgan Witts, *The Day the Bubble Burst* (Garden City, N.Y.: Doubleday, 1979);

James R. Green, *The World of the Worker: Labor in Twentieth-Century America* (New York: Hill & Wang, 1980);

Gerald Gunderson, *A New Economic History: America* (New York: McGraw-Hill, 1976);

Lawrence Gustin, *Billy Durant* (Grand Rapids, Mich.: Eerdmans, 1973);

Leon A. Harris, *Merchant Princes: An Intimate History of Jewish Families Who Built Great Department Stores* (New York: Harper & Row, 1979);

S. H. Harris, *Twenty Years of Federal Reserve Policy* (Cambridge, Mass.: Harvard University Press, 1933);

Robert Heilbroner and Aaron Singer, *The Economic Transformation of America* (New York: Harcourt Brace Jovanovich, 1977);

Stewart Holbrook, *Age of the Moguls* (Garden City, N.Y.: Doubleday, 1954);

Jonathan Hughes, *The Governmental Habit* (New York: Basic Books, 1977);

F. Cyril James, *The Economics of Money, Credit and Banking,* third edition (New York: Ronald Press, 1940);

J. M. Keynes, *The General Theory of Employment, Interest and Money* (London: Macmillan, 1936);

Charles P. Kindleberger, *The World in Depression, 1929–1939* (Berkeley: University of California Press, 1975);

Joseph Stagg Lawrence, *Wall Street and Washington* (Princeton: Princeton University Press, 1929);

William Leach, *Land of Desire* (New York: Pantheon, 1993);

William M. Leary, ed., *Encyclopedia of American Business History and Biography: The Airline Industry* (New York & Oxford: Manly/Facts On File, 1992);

Edwin Lefevre, *Reminiscences of a Stock Operator* (Garden City, N.Y.: Doubleday, 1930);

William E. Leuchtenburg, *The Perils of Prosperity, 1914–1932* (Chicago: University of Chicago Press, 1958);

David L. Lewis, *The Public Image of Henry Ford* (Detroit: Wayne State University Press, 1976);

H. H. Liebhafsky, *American Government and Business* (New York: Wiley, 1971);

Eugene Lyons, *David Sarnoff: A Biography* (New York: Harper & Row, 1966);

George S. May, ed., *Encyclopedia of American Business History and Biography: The Automobile Industry, 1920–1980* (New York & Oxford: Manly/Facts On File, 1990);

Forrest McDonald, *Insull* (Chicago: University of Chicago Press, 1962);

John J. Nance, *Splash of Color: The Self-Destruction of Braniff International* (New York: Morrow, 1984);

Hugh S. Norton, *Economic Policy: Government and Business* (Columbus, Ohio: Merrill, 1966);

Ferdinand Pecora, *Wall Street Under Oath* (New York: Simon & Schuster, 1939);

Glenn Porter, ed., *Encyclopedia of American Economic History: Studies of the Principal Movements and Ideas,* 3 volumes (New York: Scribners, 1980);

Joseph C. Pusateri, *A History of American Business* (Arlington Heights, Ill.: Davidson, 1984);

John B. Rae, *The American Automobile: A Brief History* (Chicago & London: University of Chicago Press, 1965);

Doris Rich, *Amelia Earhart: A Biography* (Washington, D.C.: Smithsonian Institute Press, 1989);

Graham Robinson, *Pictorial History of the Automobile* (New York: Smith, 1987);

Larry Schweikart, ed., *Encyclopedia of American Business History and Biography: Banking and Finance, 1913–1989* (New York & Oxford: Manly/Facts On File, 1990);

Bruce E. Seely, ed., *Encyclopedia of American Business History and Biography: Iron and Steel in the Twentieth Century* (New York & Oxford: Manly/Facts On File, 1994);

David A. Shannon, *Twentieth Century America* (Chicago: Rand, McNally, 1963);

Alfred P. Sloan Jr., *Adventures of a White Collar Man* (New York: Doubleday, Doran, 1941);

Sloan, *My Years with General Motors* (Garden City, N.Y.: Doubleday, 1964);

Henry Ladd Smith, *Airways* (New York: Knopf, 1942);

George Soule, *Prosperity Decade: From War to Depression, 1917–1929* (New York: Rinehart, 1947);

Marvin Traub, *Like No Other Store: The Bloomingdales Legend* (New York: Times Books, 1993);

Thurman W. Van Metre, *Transportation in the United States* (Chicago: Foundation Press, 1939);

D. S. Watson, *Business and Government* (New York: McGraw-Hill, 1958);

Bernard M. Weisberger, *The Dream Maker* (Boston: Little, Brown, 1979);

Arch Whitehouse, *The Sky's the Limit: History of U.S. Airlines* (New York: Macmillan, 1971);

Irvin G. Wylie, *The Self-Made Man in America: The Myth of Rags to Riches* (New Brunswick, N.J.: Rutgers University Press, 1954).

## EDUCATION

James D. Anderson, *The Education of Blacks in the South, 1860–1935* (Chapel Hill: University of North Carolina Press, 1988);

Howard K. Beale, *A History of Freedom of Teaching in American Schools,* Report of the Commission on the Social Studies, American Historical Association, part 16 (New York & Chicago: Scribners, 1941);

Lynn G. Beck and Joseph Murphy, *Understanding the Principalship: Metaphorical Themes, 1920s–1990s* (New York: Teachers College Press, Columbia University, 1993);

John S. Brubacher and Willis Rudy, *Higher Education in Transition* (New York: Harper & Row, 1976);

Nicholas Butler, *Across the Busy Years: Recollections and Reflections,* 2 volumes (New York: Scribners, 1939, 1940);

H. Warren Button and Eugene F. Provenzo Jr., *History of Education and Culture in America* (Englewood Cliffs, N.J.: Prentice-Hall, 1983);

Robert L. Church and Michael W. Sedlak, *Education in the United States: An Interpretive History* (New York: Free Press, 1976);

Lawrence Cremin, *American Education, The Metropolitan Experience, 1876–1980* (New York: Harper & Row, 1988);

Cremin, *The Transformation of the School: Progressivism in American Education, 1876–1957* (New York: Knopf, 1961);

Cremin, *The Wonderful World of Ellwood Patterson Cubberley: An Essay on the Historiography of American Education* (New York: Columbia University Teachers College, Bureau of Publications, 1965);

Howard A. Dawson and M. C. S. Noble Jr., *Handbook on Rural Education: Factual Data on Rural Education, Its Social and Economic Backgrounds* (Washington, D.C.: National Education Association of the United States, Department of Rural Education, 1961);

William Clyde De Vane, *The American University in the Twentieth Century* (Baton Rouge: Louisiana State University Press, 1957);

Foster R. Dulles, *America Learns to Play* (Englewood Cliffs, N.J.: Prentice-Hall, 1940);

Martin Dworkin, *Dewey on Education* (New York: Columbia University Teachers College Press, 1959);

George Dykhuizen, *The Life and Mind of John Dewey* (Carbondale: Southern Illinois University Press, 1973);

William Edward Eaton, *The American Federation of Teachers, 1916–1961: A History of the Movement* (Carbondale: Southern Illinois University Press, 1975);

Richard Hofstadter and Wilson Smith, *American Higher Education: A Documentary History,* 2 volumes (Chicago: University of Chicago Press, 1961);

Thomas James, *Public versus Nonpublic Education in Historical Perspective* (Stanford, Cal.: Institute for Research on Educational Finance and Governance, School of Education, Stanford University, 1982);

Clarence J. Karier, *Roots of Crisis: American Education in the Twentieth Century* (Chicago: Rand, McNally, 1973);

Herbert M. Kliebard, *The Struggle for the American Curriculum, 1893–1958,* second edition (New York: Routledge, 1995);

Edward A. Krug, *The Shaping of the American High School,* volume 2: 1920–1941 (New York: Harper & Row, 1972);

Marvin Lazerson, ed., *American Education in the Twentieth Century: A Documentary History* (New York: Teachers College Press, Columbia University, 1987);

Abbott L. Lowell, *At War with Academic Tradition in America* (Cambridge, Mass.: Harvard University Press, 1934);

Lowell, *What a College President Has Learned* (New York: Macmillan, 1938);

Albert Marrin, *Nicholas Murray Butler* (Boston: G. K. Hall, 1976);

Harry Morgan, *Historical Perspectives on the Education of Black Children* (Westport, Conn.: Praeger, 1995);

Samuel Eliot Morison, *The Development of Harvard University Since the Inauguration of President Eliot, 1869–1929* (Cambridge, Mass.: Harvard University Press, 1930);

Majorie Murphy, *Blackboard Unions: The AFT and the NEA, 1900–1980* (Ithaca, N.Y.: Cornell University Press, 1990);

John D. Pulliam, *History of Education in America,* third edition (Columbus, Ohio: Merrill, 1986);

Samuel Tenenbaum, *William Heard Kilpatrick: Trail Blazer in Education* (New York: Harper, 1951);

Vivian Trow Thayer, *Formative Ideas in American Education, from the Colonial Period to the Present* (New York: Dodd, Mead, 1965);

Rena L. Vassar, *Social History of American Education* (Chicago: Rand, McNally, 1965);

Robert Westbrook, *John Dewey and American Democracy* (Ithaca, N.Y.: Cornell University Press, 1991);

Henry A. Yeomans, *Abbott Lawrence Lowell, 1856–1943* (Cambridge, Mass.: Harvard University Press, 1948).

## FASHION

C. Edson Armi, *The Art of American Car Design: The Profession and Personalities* (University Park: Pennsylvania State University Press, 1988);

Michael Batterberry and Ariane Batterberry, *Mirror, Mirror: A Social History of Fashion* (New York: Holt, Rinehart & Winston, 1977);

Herbert Bayer, Walter Gropius, and Ise Gropius, eds., *Bauhaus 1919–1928* (New York: Museum of Modern Art, 1938);

Patricia Bayer, *Art Deco Interiors: Decoration and Design Classics of the 1920s and 1930s* (Boston: Bullfinch Press/Little, Brown, 1990);

Kevin Brazendale and Enrica Enceti, eds., *Classic Cars: Fifty Years of the World's Finest Automobile Design* (New York: Exeter, 1981);

Helen L. Brockman, *The Theory of Fashion Design* (New York: Wiley, 1965);

John Burchard and Albert Bush-Brown, *The Architecture of America: A Social and Cultural History* (Boston: Atlantic Monthly/Little, Brown, 1961);

Stephen Calloway, *Twentieth-Century Decoration: The Domestic Interior from 1900 to the Present Day* (London: Weidenfeld & Nicolson, 1988);

Calloway and Elizabeth Cromley, eds., *The Elements of Style* (New York: Simon & Schuster, 1991);

Richard Burns Carson, *The Olympian Cars: The Great American Luxury Automobiles of the Twenties & Thirties* (New York: Knopf, 1976);

Ernestine Carter, *The Changing World of Fashion* (New York: Putnam, 1977);

*The Changing American Woman: Two Hundred Years of American Fashion* (New York: Fairchild, 1976);

Edna Woolman Chase and Ilka Chase, *Always in Vogue* (Garden City, N.Y.: Doubleday, 1954);

Clifford Edward Clark Jr., *The American Family Home, 1800–1960* (Chapel Hill: University of North Carolina Press, 1986);

Mila Contini, *Fashion: From Ancient Egypt to the Present Day* (New York: Odyssey, 1965);

Donald W. Curl, *Mizner's Florida: American Resort Architecture* (New York: Architectural History Foundation / Cambridge, Mass.: MIT Press, 1984);

Diana de Marly, *Fashion for Men: An Illustrated History* (New York: Holmes & Meier, 1985);

de Marly, *The History of Haute Couture, 1850–1950* (New York: Holmes & Meier, 1980);

Maryanne Dolan, *Vintage Clothing, 1880–1960: Identification and Value Guide* (Florence, Ala.: Books Americana, 1984);

Meredith Etherington-Smith, *Patou* (New York: St. Martin's Press/Marek, 1983);

Elizabeth Ewing, *History of Twentieth Century Fashion*, revised and updated edition (London: Batsford, 1992; Lanham, Md.: Barnes & Noble, 1992);

James J. Flink, *The Automobile Age* (Cambridge, Mass. & London: MIT Press, 1988);

Jane Gaines and Charlotte Herzog, eds., *Fabrications: Costume and the Female Body* (New York: Routledge, 1990);

Paul Gallico, *The Golden People* (Garden City, N.Y.: Doubleday, 1965);

Paul Goldberger, *The Skyscraper* (New York: Knopf, 1981);

Ben M. Hall, *The Best Remaining Seats: The Story of the Golden Age of the Movie Palace* (New York: Clarkson N. Potter, 1961);

Jacqueline Herald, *Fashions of a Decade: The 1920s* (New York: Facts On File, 1991);

Grant Hildebrand, *The Architecture of Albert Kahn* (Cambridge, Mass.: MIT Press, 1974);

Alan Jenkins, *The Twenties* (New York: Universe Books, 1974);

Alva Johnston, *The Legendary Mizners* (New York: Farrar, Straus & Young, 1953);

Edgar R. Jones, *Those Were the Good Old Days: A Happy Look at American Advertising, 1880–1930* (New York: Simon & Schuster, 1989);

Walter H. Kilham Jr., *Raymond Hood, Architect: Form Through Function in the American Skyscraper* (New York: Architectural Book Publishing, 1973);

Lena Lençek and Gideon Bosker, *Making Waves: Swimsuits and the Undressing of America* (San Francisco: Chronicle, 1989);

Sandra Ley, *Fashion for Everyone: The Story of Ready-to-Wear, 1870–1970* (New York: Scribners, 1975);

Chester H. Liebs, *Main Street to Miracle Mile: American Roadside Architecture* (Boston: Little, Brown, 1985);

Valerie Lloyd, *McDowell's Directory of Twentieth Century Fashion* (Englewood Cliffs, N.J.: Prentice-Hall, 1985);

Diane Maddex, ed., *Master Builders: A Guide to Famous American Architects* (Washington, D.C.: Preservation Press, 1985);

Elsa Maxwell, *R.S.V.P.: Elsa Maxwell's Own Story* (Boston: Little, Brown, 1954);

Virginia McAlester and Lee McAlester, *A Field Guide to American Houses* (New York: Knopf, 1992);

Caroline Rennolds Milbank, *New York Fashion: The Evolution of American Style* (New York: Abrams, 1989);

Alan Mirken, ed., *The 1927 Edition of the Sears, Roebuck Catalogue* (New York: Bounty, 1970);

Jane Mulvagh, *Vogue History of 20th Century Fashion* (Harmondsworth, U.K.: Viking, 1988);

Maggie Pexton Murray, *Changing Styles in Fashion: Who, What, Why* (New York: Fairchild, 1989);

David Naylor, *Great American Movie Theaters* (Washington, D.C.: Preservation Press, 1987);

Ave Pildas and Lucinda Smith, *Movie Palaces* (New York: Clarkson N. Potter, 1980);

Mary Jane Pool, ed., *20th-Century Decorating, Architecture & Gardens: 80 Years of Ideas & Pleasure from House & Garden* (New York: Holt, Rinehart & Winston, 1980);

Meyric R. Rogers, *American Interior Design: The Traditions and Development of Domestic Design from Colonial Times to the Present* (New York: Norton, 1947);

Leland M. Roth, *A Concise History of American Architecture* (New York: Icon Editions/Harper & Row, 1979);

Mary Shaw Ryan, *Clothing: A Study in Human Behavior* (New York: Holt, Rinehart & Winston, 1966);

O. E. Schoeffler and William Gale, *Esquire's Encyclopedia of 20th Century Men's Fashion* (New York: McGraw-Hill, 1973);

Franz Schulze, *Mies van der Rohe: A Critical Biography* (Chicago: University of Chicago Press, 1985);

Vincent Scully, *American Architecture and Urbanism* (New York: Praeger, 1969);

Ethel Davis Seal, *Furnishing the Little House* (New York: Century, 1924);

Stephen W. Sears, *The American Heritage History of the Automobile in America* (New York: American Heritage, 1977);

Marion Sichel, *History of Men's Costume* (London: Batsford Academic & Educational, 1984);

Louis William Steinwedel and J. Herbert Newport, *The Duesenberg: The Story of America's Premier Car* (Philadelphia: Chilton, 1970);

Robert A. M. Stern, with Thomas P. Catalano, *Raymond Hood* (New York: Institute for Architecture and Urban Studies/Rizzoli, 1982);

Donald Stowell and Erin Wertenberger, *A Century of Fashion 1865–1965* (Chicago: Encyclopaedia Britannica, 1987);

Jane Trahey, *The Mode in Costume* (New York: Scribners, 1958);

Trahey, ed., *Harper's Bazaar: One Hundred Years of the American Female* (New York: Random House, 1967);

Anne V. Tyrrell, *Changing Trends in Fashion: Patterns of the Twentieth Century, 1900–1970* (London: Batsford, 1986);

Marcus Whiffen and Frederick Koeper, *American Architecture 1607–1976* (Cambridge, Mass.: MIT Press, 1981);

Barry James Wood, *Show Windows: Seventy-five Years of the Art of Display* (New York: Congdon & Weed, 1982).

## GOVERNMENT AND POLITICS

Richard C. Bain and Judith H. Parris, *Convention Decisions and Voting Records,* second edition (Washington, D.C.: Brookings Institution, 1973);

William J. Barber, *From New Era to New Deal: Herbert Hoover, the Economists, and American Economic Policy, 1921–1933* (New York: Cambridge University Press, 1985);

Irving L. Bernstein, *The Lean Years: A History of the American Worker 1920–1933* (Boston: Houghton Mifflin, 1960);

William Henry Chafe, *The American Woman: Her Changing Social, Economic, and Political Roles, 1920–1970* (New York: Oxford University Press, 1972);

David M. Chalmers, *Hooded Americanism: The History of the Ku Klux Klan* (Durham, N.C.: Duke University Press, 1981);

*Congressional Quarterly's Guide to U.S. Elections,* second edition (Washington, D.C.: Congressional Quarterly, Inc., 1985);

Robert A. Divine, *American Immigration Policy, 1924–1952* (New Haven: Yale University Press, 1957);

Charles W. Eagles, *Democracy Delayed: Congressional Reapportionment and Urban-Rural Conflict in the 1920s* (Athens: University of Georgia Press, 1990);

Gilbert C. Fite, "The Farmer's Dilemma, 1919–1929," in *Change and Continuity in Twentieth-Century America: the 1920s,* edited by John Braeman (Columbus: Ohio State University Press, 1968);

William Keylor, *The Twentieth-Century World: An International History* (New York: Oxford University Press, 1984);

Stephen J. Kneeshaw, *In Pursuit of Peace: The American Reaction to the Kellogg-Briand Pact, 1928–1929* (New York: Garland, 1991);

Robert K. Murray, *Red Scare: A Study in National Hysteria, 1919–1920* (Minneapolis: University of Minnesota Press, 1955);

Burl Noggle, *Teapot Dome: Oil and Politics in the 1920s* (Baton Rouge: Louisiana State University Press, 1962);

Arthur M. Schlesinger Jr., ed., *History of American Presidential Elections 1789–1968,* 3 volumes (New York: Chelsea House/McGraw-Hill, 1971);

Schlesinger, ed., *History of U.S. Political Parties* (New York: Chelsea House, 1973);

Andrew Sinclair, *Era of Excess: A Social History of the Prohibition Movement* (New York: Harper & Row, 1962);

Ralph Stone, *The Irreconcilables: The Fight Against the League of Nations* (Lexington: University Press of Kentucky, 1970);

Bascom N. Timmons, *Portrait of an American: Charles G. Dawes* (New York: Holt, 1953);

U.S. Congress, House Committee on Rules, *Ku Klux Klan Hearings, October 11–17, 1921, 67th Congress, First Session* (Washington, D.C., 1921).

## LAW

Henry J. Abraham, *Justices and Presidents: A Political History of Appointments to the Supreme Court* (New York: Oxford University Press, 1985);

Paul Avrich, *Sacco and Vanzetti: The Anarchist Background* (Princeton: Princeton University Press, 1991);

Clare Cushman, ed., *The Supreme Court Justices: Illustrated Biographies, 1789–1993* (Washington, D.C.: Congressional Quarterly, 1993);

Martin L. Fausold, *The Presidency of Herbert Hoover* (Lawrence: University of Kansas Press, 1989);

Steven R. Fox, *Blood and Power: Organized Crime in the Twentieth Century* (New York: Morrow, 1989);

J. C. Furnas, *The Life and Times of the Late Demon Rum* (New York: Putnam, 1965);

Ray Ginger, *Six Days or Forever? Tennessee v. John Thomas Scopes* (Boston: Beacon, 1958);

Richard Kluger, *Simple Justice* (New York: Columbia University Press, 1967);

William M. Kunstler, *The Minister and the Choir Singer: The Hall-Mills Murder Case* (New York: Morrow, 1964);

Max Lerner, ed., *The Mind and Faith of Justice Holmes* (Boston: Little, Brown, 1943);

John Charles Livingston, *Clarence Darrow for the Defense* (New York: Garland, 1988);

Alpheus Thomas Mason, *The Supreme Court from Taft to Burger* (Baton Rouge: Louisiana State University Press, 1979);

Richard L. Pacelle Jr., *The Transformation of the Supreme Court's Agenda* (Boulder, Colo.: Westview Press, 1991);

Francis Russell, *Sacco & Vanzetti: Case Resolved* (New York: Harper & Row, 1986);

Russell, *Tragedy in Dedham* (New York: McGraw-Hill, 1964);

John T. Scopes and James Presley, *Center of the Storm: Memoirs of John T. Scopes* (New York: Holt, Rinehart & Winston, 1967);

Mary Lee Settle, *The Scopes Trial: The State of Tennessee v. John Thomas Scopes* (New York: Watts, 1972);

Page Smith, *Redeeming the Time, A People's History of the 1920s and the New Deal* (New York: Penguin Group, 1987);

Robert Stevens, *Legal Education in America from the 1850's to the 1980's* (Chapel Hill: University of North Carolina Press, 1983);

Irving Stone, *Clarence Darrow for the Defense* (Garden City, N.Y.: Doubleday, Doran, 1941);

Kevin Tierney, *Darrow: A Biography* (New York: Crowell, 1979);

Jerry R. Tompkins, ed., *D-days at Dayton: Reflections on the Scopes Trial* (Baton Rouge: Louisiana State University Press, 1965).

## LIFESTYLES AND SOCIAL TRENDS

Dorothy M. Brown, *Setting a Course: American Women in the Twenties* (Boston: Twayne, 1987);

William Chafe, *The American Woman: Her Changing Social, Economic, and Political Roles, 1920–1970* (New York: Oxford University Press, 1972);

Ellen Chesler, *Women of Valor: Margaret Sanger and the Birth Control Movement in America* (New York: Simon & Schuster, 1992);

Lela B. Costin, *Two Sisters for Social Justice: A Biography of Grace and Edith Abbott* (Urbana & Champaign: University of Illinois Press, 1983);

Nancy M. Cott, *The Grounding of Modern Feminism* (New Haven: Yale University Press, 1987);

Ruth Schwartz Cowan, *More Work for Mother* (New York: Basic Books, 1983);

Paula Fass, *The Damned and the Beautiful: American Youth in the 1920s* (New York: Oxford University Press, 1977);

Peter Feline, *Him/Her Self: Sex Roles in Modern America* (New York: Harcourt Brace Jovanovich, 1974);

Eleanor Flexner, *Century of Struggle: The Woman's Rights Movement in the United States* (Cambridge, Mass.: Harvard University Press, 1959);

James Flink, *The Automobile Age* (Cambridge, Mass.: MIT Press, 1990);

Flink, *Car Culture* (Cambridge, Mass.: MIT Press, 1975);

John Hope Franklin and Isidore Starr, *The Negro in Twentieth Century America* (New York: Random House, 1967);

Estelle B. Freedman and John D'Emilio, *Intimate Matters: A History of Sexuality in America* (New York: Harper & Row, 1988);

J. C. Furnas, *Great Times: An Informal Social History of the United States* (New York: Putnam, 1974);

James R. Grossman, *Land of Hope: Chicago, Black Southerners, and the Great Migration* (Chicago: University of Chicago Press, 1989);

Margo Horn, *Before It's Too Late: The Child Guidance Movement in the United States, 1922–1945* (Philadelphia: Temple University Press, 1989);

David M. Kennedy, *Birth Control in America: The Career of Margaret Sanger* (New Haven: Yale University Press, 1991);

Alice Kessler-Harris, *Out to Work: A History of Wage-Earning Women in the United States* (New York: Oxford University Press, 1982);

Mark Edward Lender and James Kirby Martin, *Drinking in America* (New York: Free Press, 1987);

Earl Lifshey, *The Housewares Story: A History of the American Housewares Industry* (Chicago: National Housewares Manufacturers Association, 1973);

Robert S. Lynd and Helen Merrell Lynd, *Middletown: A Study in American Culture* (New York: Harcourt, Brace, 1929);

John Madge, *The Origins of Scientific Sociology* (New York: Free Press of Glencoe, 1962);

Steven Mintz and Susan Kellogg, *Domestic Revolutions: A Social History of American Family Life* (New York: Free Press, 1988);

John Modell, *Into One's Own: From Youth to Adulthood in the United States, 1920–1975* (Berkeley: University of California Press, 1989);

Charles H. Page, *Fifty Years in the Sociological Enterprise: A Lucky Journey* (Amherst: University of Massachusetts Press, 1982);

Edwin Post, *Truly Emily Post* (New York: Funk & Wagnalls, 1961);

Rosalind Rosenberg, *Divided Lives: American Women in the Twentieth Century* (New York: Hill & Wang, 1992);

Paul Sann, *Fads, Follies and Delusions of the American People* (New York: Bonanza Books, 1968);

Barbara Miller Solomon, *In the Company of Educated Women* (New Haven: Yale University Press, 1985);

Judith Stein, *The World of Marcus Garvey: Race and Class in Modern Society* (Baton Rouge: Louisiana State University Press, 1986);

Susan Strasser, *Never Done* (New York: Pantheon, 1982);

Viviana Zelizer, *Pricing the Priceless* (New York: Basic Books, 1985).

## MEDIA

Gleason L. Archer, *History of Radio to 1926* (New York: Arno/New York Times, 1971);

John Bambridge, *Little Wonder, or, The Reader's Digest and How it Grew* (New York: Reynal & Hitchcock, 1946);

Erik Barnouw, *A Tower in Babel: A History of Broadcasting in the United States, Volume I, to 1933* (New York: Oxford University Press, 1966);

A. Scott Berg, *Maxwell Perkins: Editor of Genius* (New York: Dutton, 1978);

Edward L. Bernays, *Crystallizing Public Opinion* (New York: Boni & Liveright, 1923);

Bernays, *Propaganda* (New York: Liveright, 1928);

Simon Michael Bessie, *Jazz Journalism: The Story of Tabloid Newspapers* (New York: Dutton, 1938);

*The Book of the Month: Sixty Years of Books in American Life* (Boston: Little, Brown, 1986);

Noel Busch, *Briton Hadden: A Biography of the Co-founder of Time* (New York: Farrar, Straus, 1949);

Bennett Cerf, *At Random* (New York: Random House, 1977);

Jan Cohn, *Creating America: George Horace Lorimer and The Saturday Evening Post* (Pittsburgh: University of Pittsburgh Press, 1989);

Tom Dardis, *Firebrand: The Life of Horace Liveright* (New York: Random House, 1995);

Susan J. Douglas, *Inventing American Broadcasting, 1899–1922* (Baltimore: Johns Hopkins University Press, 1987);

Roy S. Durstine, *This Advertising Business* (New York: Scribners, 1928);

Peter Dzwonkoski, ed., *American Literary Publishing Houses, 1900–1980: Trade and Paperback; Dictionary of Literary Biography*, volume 46 (Detroit: Bruccoli Clark/Gale Research, 1986);

*Editor to Author: The Letters of Maxwell E. Perkins* (New York: Scribners, 1950);

Melvin Patrick Ely, *The Adventures of Amos 'n' Andy: A Social History of an American Phenomenon* (New York: Free Press, 1991);

Raymond Fielding, *The American Newsreel, 1911–1967* (Norman: University of Oklahoma Press, 1972);

Hugh Ford, *Published in Paris: American and British Writers, Printers, and Publishers in Paris, 1920–1939* (New York: Macmillan, 1975);

Neal Gabler, *Winchell: Gossip, Power, and the Culture of Celebrity* (New York: Knopf, 1994);

Roland Gelatt, *The Fabulous Phonograph: From Edison to Stereo* (New York: Appleton-Century, 1966);

Ron Goulart, *Cheap Thrills: An Informal History of the Pulp Magazines* (New Rochelle, N.Y.: Arlington House, 1972);

Emanuel Haldeman-Julius, *The First Hundred Million* (New York: Simon & Schuster, 1928);

John Heidenry, *Theirs Was the Kingdom: Lila and DeWitt Wallace and the Story of the Reader's Digest* (New York: Norton, 1993);

Frederick J. Hoffman, Charles Allen, and Carolyn F. Ulrich, *The Little Magazine: A History and a Bibliography* (Princeton: Princeton University Press, 1946);

William R. Hunt, *Body Love: The Amazing Career of Bernarr MacFadden* (Bowling Green, Ohio: Bowling Green University Popular Press, 1989);

John Kobler, *Luce: His Time, Life, and Fortune* (Garden City, N.Y.: Doubleday, 1968);

Sidney Kobre, *Development of American Journalism* (Dubuque, Iowa: Braun, 1969);

Dale Kramer, *Heywood Broun* (New York: Current Books, 1949);

Thomas Kunkel, *Genius in Disguise: Harold Ross of the New Yorker* (New York: Random House, 1995);

Charles Lee, *The Hidden Public: The Story of the Book-of-the-Month Club* (Garden City, N.Y.: Doubleday, 1958);

Ivy Lee, *Publicity: Some of the Things It Is and Is Not* (New York: Industries Publishing, 1925);

Eugene Lyon, *David Sarnoff* (New York: Harper & Row, 1966);

William Manchester, *Disturber of the Peace: The Life of H. L. Mencken* (New York: Harper, 1951);

H. L. Mencken, *My Life as Author and Editor* (New York: Knopf, 1992);

Frank Luther Mott, *American Journalism: A History, 1690–1960,* third edition (New York: Macmillan, 1962);

Richard O'Connor, *Heywood Broun* (New York: Putnam, 1975);

William S. Paley, *As It Happened: A Memoir* (Garden City, N.Y.: Doubleday, 1979);

Theodore Peterson, *Magazines in the Twentieth Century* (Urbana: University of Illinois Press, 1956);

Jerry Robinson, *The Comics: An Illustrated History of Comic Strip Art* (New York: Putnam, 1974);

Samuel L. Rothafel and Raymond F. Yates, *Broadcasting, Its New Day* (New York: Century, 1925);

Sally Bedel Smith, *In All His Glory: The Life of William S. Paley* (New York: Simon & Schuster, 1990);

Robert Sobel, *RCA* (New York: Stein & Day, 1986);

Christopher H. Sterling and John M. Kittross, *Stay Tuned: A Concise History of American Broadcasting,* second edition (Belmont, Cal.: Wadsworth, 1990);

W. A. Swanberg, *Luce and His Empire* (New York: Scribners, 1972);

John W. Tebbel, *American Dynasty: The Story of the McCormicks, Medills, and Pattersons* (Garden City, N.Y.: Doubleday, 1947);

Tebbel, *George Horace Lorimer and The Saturday Evening Post* (Garden City, N.Y.: Doubleday, 1948);

Tebbel, *A History of Book Publishing in the United States,* volume 3 (New York: Bowker, 1978);

Tebbel and Mary Ellen Zuckerman, *The Magazine in America, 1741–1990* (New York: Oxford University Press, 1991);

James Thurber, *The Years with Ross* (Boston: Little, Brown, 1959);

Alexander Walker, *The Shattered Silents: How the Talkies Came to Stay* (London: Elm Tree Books, 1978).

## MEDICINE AND HEALTH

Gerald Astor, *The Disease Detectives: Deadly Medical Mysteries and the People Who Solved Them* (New York: New American Library, 1984);

Herbert Bailey, *The Vitamin Pioneers* (Emmaus, Pa.: Rodale Books, 1968);

Barbara Bates, *Bargaining for Life: A Social History of Tuberculosis, 1876–1938* (Philadelphia: University of Pennsylvania Press, 1992);

Michael Bliss, *Banting: A Biography* (Toronto: McClelland & Stewart, 1984);

Bliss, *The Discovery of Insulin* (Toronto: McClelland & Stewart, 1982);

Ruth Bochner, *Clinical Application of the Rorschach Test* (New York: Grune & Stratton, 1942);

James Bordley and A. McGehee Harvey, *Two Centuries of American Medicine, 1776–1976* (Philadelphia: Saunders, 1976);

Allan M. Brandt, *No Magic Bullet: A Social History of Venereal Disease in the United States Since 1880* (New York: Oxford University Press, 1985);

Daniel E. Carmichael, *The Pap Smear: Life of George Papanicolaou* (Springfield, Ill.: Thomas, 1973);

James H. Cassedy, *Medicine in America: A Short History* (Baltimore: Johns Hopkins University Press, 1991);

John Duffy, *The Healers: The Rise of the Medical Establishment* (New York: McGraw-Hill, 1976); republished as *The Healers: A History of American Medicine* (Urbana: University of Illinois Press, 1979);

Mary Erlichman, *Electroencephalographic (EEG) Video Monitoring* (Rockville, Md.: United States Department of Health and Human Services, 1990);

Elizabeth Etheridge, *The Butterfly Caste: A Social History of Pellagra in the South* (Westport, Conn.: Greenwood Press, 1972);

Abraham Flexner, *Abraham Flexner: An Autobiography* (New York: Simon & Schuster, 1960);

John Farquhar Fulton, *Harvey Cushing: A Biography* (Springfield, Ill.: Thomas, 1946);

Kenneth F. Kiple, ed., *The Cambridge World History of Human Disease* (New York: Cambridge University Press, 1993);

Lois A. Magner, *A History of Medicine* (New York: Marcel Dekker, 1992);

Geoffrey Marks and William K. Beatty, *The Story of Medicine in America* (New York: Scribners, 1973);

Wayne Martin, *Medical Heroes and Heretics* (Old Greenwich, Conn.: Devon-Adair, 1977);

Elmer V. McCollum, *From Kansas Farm Boy to Scientist* (Lawrence: University of Kansas Press, 1964);

McCollum, *A History of Nutrition* (Boston: Houghton Mifflin, 1957);

Ralph W. Moss, *Free Radical: Albert Szent-Gyorgyi and the Battle over Vitamin C* (New York: Paragon House, 1988);

Claude Puetel, *History of Syphilis* (Baltimore: Johns Hopkins University Press, 1992);

L. J. Rather, *The Genesis of Cancer: A Study in the History of Ideas* (Baltimore: Johns Hopkins University Press, 1978);

Donald F. Scott, *Understanding EEG: An Introduction to Electroencephalography* (Philadelphia: Lippincott, 1976);

Peter Sebel and others, *Respiration: The Breath of Life* (New York: Torstar, 1985);

John C. Sheehan, *The Enchanted Ring: The Untold Story of Penicillin* (Cambridge, Mass.: MIT Press, 1982);

Wrynn Smith, *A Profile of Health and Disease in America: Cancer* (New York: Facts On File, 1987);

Charles W. Taber, *Taber's Cyclopedic Medical Dictionary*, sixteenth edition, edited by Clayton L. Thomas (Philadelphia: F. A. Davis, 1989);

Tyler Wasson, ed., *Nobel Prize Winners* (New York: Wilson, 1987);

Allen B. Weisse, *Medical Odysseys* (New Brunswick, N.J.: Rutgers University Press, 1991).

## RELIGION

Sydney E. Ahlstrom, *A Religious History of the American People*, 2 volumes (Garden City, N.Y.: Doubleday, 1975);

Catherine Albanese, *America, Religions and Religion* (Belmont, Cal.: Wadsworth, 1981);

Nancy T. Ammerman, *Bible Believers: Fundamentalists in the Modern World* (New Brunswick, N.J.: Rutgers University Press, 1987);

Randall Balmer and John R. Fitsmeier, *The Presbyterians* (Westport, Conn.: Greenwood Press, 1993);

Daniel W. Bjork, *The Victorian Flight: Russell H. Conwell and the Crisis of American Individualism* (Washington, D.C.: University Press of America, 1979);

Edith Blumhofer, *Aimee Semple McPherson: Everybody's Sister* (Grand Rapids, Mich.: Eerdmans, 1993);

Jerald C. Brauer, *Protestantism in America: A Narrative History* (Philadelphia: Westminster, 1953);

Samuel McCrea Cavert, *The American Churches in the Ecumenical Movement, 1900–1968* (New York: Association Press, 1968);

Robert D. Cross, *The Emerging of Liberal Catholicism in America* (Cambridge, Mass.: Harvard University Press, 1958);

Virginius Dabney, *Dry Messiah: The Life of Bishop Cannon* (New York: Knopf, 1949);

Jay P. Dolan, *The American Catholic Experience: A History from Colonial Times to the Present* (Garden City, N.Y.: Doubleday, 1985);

George W. Dollar, *A History of Fundamentalism in America* (Greenville, S.C.: Bob Jones University Press, 1973);

Lyle W. Dorset, *Billy Sunday and the Redemption of Urban America* (Grand Rapids, Mich.: Eerdmans, 1990);

Daniel M. Epstein, *Sister Aimee: The Life of Aimee Semple McPherson* (New York: Harcourt Brace Jovanovich, 1993);

James J. Hennesey, *American Catholics: A History of the Roman Catholic Community in the United States* (New York: Oxford University Press, 1981);

Arthur Hertzberg, *The Jews in America: Four Centuries of an Uneasy Encounter — A History* (New York: Simon & Schuster, 1989);

Darryl Hudson, *The Ecumenical Movement in World Affairs* (London: Weidenfeld & Nicolson, 1969);

Winthrop S. Hudson, *Religion in America: An Historical Account of the Development of American Religious Life* (New York: Scribners, 1981);

George Marsden, *Reforming Fundamentalism: Fuller Seminary and the New Evangelicalism* (Grand Rapids, Mich.: Eerdmans, 1987);

Martin E. Marty, *Pilgrims in Their Own Land: Five Hundred Years of Religion in America* (Boston: Little, Brown, 1984);

William G. McLoughlin, *Billy Sunday Was His Real Name* (Chicago: University of Chicago Press, 1955);

Robert Moats Miller, *Harry Emerson Fosdick: Preacher, Pastor, Prophet* (New York: Oxford University Press, 1985);

*Modern Revivalism: Charles Grandison Finney to Billy Graham* (New York: Ronald Press, 1959);

John K. Nelson, *Peace Prophets: American Pacifist Thought, 1919–1945* (Chapel Hill: University of North Carolina Press, 1967);

Frederick A. Norwood, *The Story of American Methodism: A History of the United Methodists and Their Relations* (Nashville, Tenn.: Abingdon, 1974);

Howard M. Sachar, *A History of the Jews in America* (New York: Knopf, 1992);

Ned B. Stonehouse, *J. Gresham Machen: A Biographical Memoir* (Grand Rapids, Mich.: Eerdmans, 1954).

## SCIENCE AND TECHNOLOGY

Hugh G. J. Aitken, *The Continuous Wave: Technology and the American Radio, 1900–1922* (Princeton: Princeton University Press, 1985);

Garland Allen, *Life Science in the Twentieth Century* (Cambridge: Cambridge University Press, 1978);

Enzo Angelucci, *Airplanes from the Dawn of Flight to the Present Day* (New York: McGraw-Hill, 1973);

Gleason Archer, *History of the Radio to 1926* (New York: American Historical Society, 1938);

Isaac Asimov, *Asimov's New Guide to Science* (New York: Basic Books, 1984);

Neil Baldwin, *Edison: Inventing the Century* (New York: Hyperion, 1995);

Roger Billstein, *Flight in America* (Baltimore: Johns Hopkins University Press, 1985);

Bryan Bunch and Alexander Hellemans, *The Timetables of Technology* (New York: Simon & Schuster, 1993);

Roger Burlingame, *Henry Ford: A Great Life in Brief* (New York: Knopf, 1954);

Carnegie Library of Pittsburgh, Science and Technology Department, *Science and Technology Desk Reference* (Detroit: Gale Research, 1993);

Dorothy Cochrane, Von Hardesty, and Russell Lee, *The Aviation Careers of Igor Sikorsky* (Los Angeles: Washington University Press for the National Air and Space Museum, 1989);

Joseph J. Corn, *The Winged Gospel: America's Romance with Aviation, 1900–1950* (New York: Oxford University Press, 1983);

Corn, ed., *Imagining Tomorrow* (Cambridge, Mass.: MIT Press, 1987);

Hamilton Cravens, *The Triumph of Evolution: American Scientists and the Heredity-Environment Controversy, 1900–1941* (Philadelphia: University of Pennsylvania Press, 1978);

Carl N. Degler, *In Search of Human Nature: The Decline and Revival of Darwinism in American Social Thought* (New York: Oxford University Press, 1991);

Harold Dick and Douglas Robinson, *The Golden Age of the Great Passenger Airships* (Washington, D.C.: Smithsonian Institution Press, 1985);

George H. Douglas, *All Aboard! The Railroad in American Life* (New York: Paragon House, 1992);

Eduard Farber, *Nobel Prize Winners in Chemistry, 1901–1961* (London & New York: Abelard-Schuman, 1963);

Derek Freeman, *Margaret Mead amd Samoa: The Making and Unmaking of an Anthropological Myth* (Cambridge, Mass.: Harvard University Press, 1983);

Charles Coulston Gillespie, ed., *Dictionary of Scientific Biography*, 18 volumes (New York: Scribners, 1970–1990);

Stephen B. Goddard, *Getting There: The Epic Struggle Between Road and Rail in the American Century* (New York: Basic Books, 1992);

James J. Halley, *The Role of the Fighter in Air Warfare* (London: Barrie & Jenkins, 1979);

Richard P. Hallion, *Legacy of Flight: The Guggenheim Contribution to American Aviation* (Seattle: University of Washington Press, 1977);

C. Dean Hanscom, ed., *Dates in American Telephone Technology* (New York: Bell Telephone Laboratories, 1961);

Guy Hartcup, *The Achievement of the Airship: A History of the Development of Rigid, Semi-Rigid and Non-Rigid Airships* (Newton Abbot, U.K. & North Pomfret, Vt.: David & Charles, 1974);

Niels H. de V. Heathcote, *Nobel Prize Winners in Physics, 1901–1950* (New York: Schuman, 1953);

Alexander Hellemans and Bryan Bunch, *The Timetables of Science*, updated edition (New York: Simon & Schuster, 1991);

David A. Hounshell and John Kenly Smith Jr., *Science and Corporate Strategy: Du Pont R&D, 1902–1980* (Cambridge & New York: Cambridge University Press, 1988);

Herbert T. Kalmus and Eleanore King Kalmus, *Mr. Technicolor* (Absecon, N.J.: MagicImage Filmbooks, 1990);

G. Kass-Simon and Patricia Farnes, eds., *Women of Science* (Bloomington: University of Indiana Press, 1990);

Daniel J. Kevles, *In the Name of Eugenics: Genetics and the Uses of Human Heredity* (New York: Knopf, 1985);

Kevles, *The Physicists: The History of a Scientific Community in Modern America* (New York: Knopf, 1978);

H. F. King, comp., *Kitty Hawk to Concorde: Jane's 100 Significant Aircraft* (London: Jane's Yearbooks, 1970);

Frank N. Magill, ed., *Great Events from History II, Science and Technology Series, Volume 2: 1910–1931* (Pasadena, Cal.: Salem Press, 1991);

Ernst Mayr, *The Growth of Biological Thought: Diversity, Evolution, and Inheritance* (Cambridge, Mass.: Harvard University Press, 1982);

Mayr and William B. Provine, *The Evolutionary Synthesis: Perspectives on the Unification of Biology* (Cambridge, Mass.: Harvard University Press, 1980);

*McGraw-Hill Encyclopedia of Science and Technology*, fourth edition, 14 volumes (New York: McGraw-Hill, 1977);

Ellis Mount and Barbara List, *Milestones in Science and Technology*, second edition (Phoenix: Oryx Press, 1993);

David Nye, *American Technological Sublime* (Cambridge, Mass.: MIT Press, 1994);

Claudia M. Oakes and Kathleen L. Brooks-Pazmany, comps., *Aircraft of the National Air and Space Museum*, fourth edition (Washington, D.C.: Smithsonian Institution Press, 1991);

George P. Oslin, *The Story of Telecommunications* (Macon, Ga.: Mercer University Press, 1992);

Carroll W. Pursell, ed., *Technology in America* (Washington, D.C.: USIA Forum Series, 1979);

Ronald Rainger, Keith Benson, and Jane Maienschen, eds., *The American Development of Biology* (Philadelphia: University of Pennsylvania Press, 1988);

Douglas H. Robinson and Charles L Keller, *"Up Ship!" A History of the U.S. Navy's Rigid Airships, 1919–1935* (Annapolis, Md.: Naval Institute Press, 1982);

Margaret W. Rossiter, *Women Scientists in America: Struggles and Strategies to 1940* (Baltimore: Johns Hopkins University Press, 1982);

Daniel L. Schodek, *Landmarks in American Civil Engineering* (Cambridge, Mass.: MIT Press, 1987);

Paul Schubert, *The Electric Word: The Rise of Radio* (New York: Macmillan, 1928);

Lowell Thomas and Lowell Thomas Jr., *Famous First Flights That Changed History* (Garden City, N.Y.: Doubleday, 1969);

Ethlie Ann Vare and Greg Ptacek, *Mothers of Invention, From the Bra to the Bomb: Forgotten Women & Their Unforgettable Ideas* (New York: Morrow, 1988).

## SPORTS

Nelson W. Aldrich, *Tommy Hitchcock: An American Hero* (Gaithersburg, Md.: Fleet Street, 1984);

Charles C. Alexander, *Our Game: An American Baseball History* (New York: Holt, 1991);

Sam Andre and Nat Fleisher, *A Pictorial History of Boxing*, revised edition (Secaucus, N.J.: Citadel Press, 1987);

Eliot Asinof, *Eight Men Out: The Black Sox and the 1919 Series* (New York: Holt, Rinehart & Winston, 1977);

Dr. L. H. Baker, *Football: Facts and Figures* (New York: Farrar & Rinehart, 1945);

John Rickards Betts, *America's Sporting Heritage: 1850–1950* (Reading, Mass.: Addison-Wesley, 1974);

Erich Camper, *Encyclopedia of the Olympic Games* (New York: McGraw-Hill, 1972);

Harold Claassen and Steve Boda Jr., eds., *Ronald Encyclopedia of Football*, third edition (New York: Ronald Press, 1963);

Dick Clark and Larry Lester, eds., *The Negro Leagues Book* (Cleveland: Society for American Baseball Research, 1994);

Gianni Clerici, *The Ultimate Tennis Book*, translated by Richard J. Wiezell (Chicago: Follett, 1975);

Tim Cohane, *Great College Football Coaches of the Twenties and Thirties* (New Rochelle, N.Y.: Arlington House, 1973);

James Coote, *A Picture History of the Olympics* (New York: Macmillan, 1972);

Robert W. Creamer, *Babe: The Legend Comes to Life* (New York: Simon & Schuster, 1974);

Parke Cummings, *American Tennis: The Story of a Game and Its People* (Boston: Little, Brown, 1957);

Allison Danzig and Joe Reichler, eds., *The History of Baseball* (Englewood Cliffs, N.J.: Prentice-Hall, 1959);

Frank Deford, *Big Bill Tilden: The Triumphs and the Tragedy* (New York: Simon & Schuster, 1976);

John Durant, ed., *Yesterday in Sports* (New York: Barnes, 1956);

Larry Engleman, *The Goddess and the American Girl: The Story of Suzanne Lenglen and Helen Wills* (New York: Oxford University Press, 1988);

Nat Fleischer, *Jack Dempsey* (New Rochelle, N.Y.: Arlington House, 1972);

J. C. Furnas, *Great Times: An Informal Social History of the United States* (New York: Putnam, 1974);

George Gipe, *The Great American Sports Book* (Garden City, N.Y.: Doubleday, 1978);

Frank Graham, *Lou Gehrig: A Quiet Hero* (New York: Putnam, 1942);

Will Grimsley, *Golf: Its History, People and Events* (Englewood Cliffs, N.J.: Prentice-Hall, 1966);

Grimsley, *Tennis: Its History, People and Events* (Englewood Cliffs, N.J.: Prentice-Hall, 1971);

John M. Gross and the editors of *Golf Magazine, The Encyclopedia of Golf,* revised edition (New York: Harper & Row, 1979);

Allen Guttman, *The Olympics: A History of the Modern Games* (Urbana: University of Illinois Press, 1992);

Guttman, *A Whole New Ball Game: An Interpretation of American Sports* (Chapel Hill: University of North Carolina Press, 1988);

Leo Katcher, *The Big Bankroll: The Life and Times of Arnold Rothstein* (New York: Harper, 1959);

Ivan N. Kaye, *Good Clean Violence: A History of College Football* (Philadelphia: Lippincott, 1973);

Norman L. Macht, *Lou Gehrig* (New York: Chelsea House, 1993);

Mark H. McCormack, *The Wonderful World of Professional Golf* (New York: Atheneum, 1973);

Will McDonough and others, *75 Seasons: The Complete Story of the National Football League, 1920–1995* (Atlanta: Turner, 1995);

Tom Meany, *Baseball's Greatest Players* (New York: Barnes, 1953);

Frank G. Menke, ed., *The Encyclopedia of Sports,* fourth edition (New York: Barnes, 1969);

Jack Newcombe, ed., *The Fireside Book of Football* (New York: Simon & Schuster, 1964);

Robert W. Peterson, *Only the Ball Was White* (Englewood Cliffs, N.J.: Prentice-Hall, 1970);

Benjamin G. Rader, *American Sports: From the Age of Folk Games to the Age of Spectators* (Englewood Cliffs, N.J.: Prentice-Hall, 1983);

Mark Ribowsky, *Don't Look Back: Satchel Paige in the Shadows of Baseball* (New York: Simon & Schuster, 1994);

Randy Roberts, *Jack Dempsey: The Manassa Mauler* (Baton Rouge: Louisiana State University Press, 1979);

Max Robinson and Jack Kramer, eds., *The Encyclopedia of Tennis: One Hundred Years of Great Players and Events* (New York: Viking, 1974);

Richard Schaap, *An Illustrated History of the Olympics,* second edition (New York: Knopf, 1967);

Richard Scheinin, *Field of Screams: The Dark Underside of America's National Pastime* (New York: Norton, 1994);

Gene Schoor with Henry Gilfond, *Red Grange: Football's Greatest Halfback* (New York: Messner, 1952);

Preston W. Slosson, *The Great Crusade and After, 1914–1928* (New York: Macmillan, 1930);

Murray Sperber, *Shake Down the Thunder: The Creation of Notre Dame Football* (New York: Holt, 1993);

Michael R. Steele, *Knute Rockne: A Bio-Bibliography* (Westport, Conn.: Greenwood Press, 1983);

Al Stump, *Cobb: A Biography* (Chapel Hill, N.C.: Algonquin Books, 1994);

Lance Tingay, *Tennis: A Pictorial History* (New York: Putnam, 1973);

Roger Treat, ed., *The Encyclopedia of Football* (New York: Barnes, 1959);

Hy Turkin and S. C. Thompson, eds., *The Official Encyclopedia of Baseball,* sixth edition (New York: Barnes, 1972);

Wells Twombly, *Shake Down the Thunder* (Radnor, Pa.: Chilton, 1974);

Twombly, *200 Years in Sports in America: A Pageant of a Nation at Play* (New York: McGraw-Hill, 1976);

David Wallenchinsky, *The Complete Book of the Olympics* (New York: Viking, 1984);

Alexander M. Weyand, *The Olympic Pageant* (New York: Macmillan, 1952);

A. B. C. Whipple, *The Racing Yachts* (Alexandria, Va.: Time-Life Books, 1980);

Michael Williams, *History of Golf* (Secaucus, N.J.: Chartwell, 1985);

Herbert Warren Wind, *The Story of American Golf* (New York: Simon & Schuster, 1956).

# CONTRIBUTORS

ARTS
    MATTHEW J. BRUCCOLI
    *University of South Carolina*
    ARLYN BRUCCOLI
    *Columbia, South Carolina*

BUSINESS AND THE ECONOMY
    HUGH NORTON
    *University of South Carolina*

EDUCATION
    VINCENT A. LACEY
    *Southern Illinois University*
    GEORGE S. REUTER JR.,
    *Arkansas Institute of Technical Research*
    JOHN E. KING
    *University of South Carolina*

FASHION
    JUDITH S. BAUGHMAN
    *University of South Carolina*

GOVERNMENT AND POLITICS
    JANET HUDSON
    *University of South Carolina*

LAW AND JUSTICE
    MILES RICHARDS
    *University of South Carolina*

LIFESTYLES AND SOCIAL TRENDS
    MARGO HORN
    *Los Altos, California*

MEDIA
    MATTHEW J. BRUCCOLI
    *University of South Carolina*
    ARLYN BRUCCOLI
    *Columbia, South Carolina*

MEDICINE AND HEALTH
    SUZANNE CAMERON LINDER
    *Columbia, South Carolina*
    EMILY LINDER JOHNSON
    *Columbia, South Carolina*

RELIGION
    JOHN SCOTT WILSON
    *University of South Carolina*

SCIENCE AND TECHNOLOGY
    ALLAN CHARLES
    *University of South Carolina — Union*

SPORTS
    RONALD BAUGHMAN
    *University of South Carolina*

# INDEX OF PHOTOGRAPHS

# GENERAL INDEX

American Society for the Control of Cancer 361

American Society of Composers, Authors and Publishers (ASCAP) 76

American Society of Landscape Architects 189

American Sociological Society 289

American Surgical Association 361

American Telephone and Telegraph (AT&T) 99, 101–102, 268, 292, 325, 399–400

American Tobacco Company 114–115, 298

*An American Tragedy* (Dreiser) 24, 34, 40, 309

*American Weekly* 297

*The Americanization of Edward Bok* (Bok) 73, 308

"The American's Creed" 213

America's Cup (yacht race) 116, 428, 461, 477, 484

Amherst College 139, 141, 384

Ammons, Elias Milton 226

Amos 'n' Andy 307

*Amos 'n' Andy* (radio show) 295, 312, 317–318

Amoskeag Textile Mill, Manchester, N.H. 77

Amplitude modulation (AM) 398, 415

Amyotrophic lateral sclerosis 465, 468

& (Cummings) 24, 56

Anderson, Carl 421

Anderson, James 473

Anderson, Mary 281

Anderson, Maxwell 24, 27, 32, 37

Anderson, Paul Y. 329

Anderson, Sherwood 20, 22, 31–32, 40, 55, 66, 309, 318

Andrews, James DeWitt 258

Andrews, John D. 284

Andrews, Roy Chapman 422

Andromeda galaxy 401, 418–419

Anesthesia 332, 360

Angelus Temple, Los Angeles 365–366, 387–388

*Animal Crackers* (Ruby and Kalamar) 28

*Anna Christie* (O'Neill) 21, 36, 59, 68, 74

Annenberg, Moses 327

Ansley, Clarke Fisher 327

Anson, Adrian Constantine "Cap" 481

Antheil, George 22–23, 26, 37

*Anthony Comstock* (Broun and Leech) 300

Anthropology 140, 284, 401, 420

Anti-Lynching Bill 193

Anti-Lynching Crusade 263, 280

Anti-Saloon League 195, 238, 258, 278, 368, 385

Antibiotics 335, 345, 347

*Antoine de Paris (Antek Cierplikowski)* 149, 185

Aphrodite 391

*Appalachian Spring* (Copland) 31

Apperson Automobile Company 171

*The Apple of the Eye* (Wescott) 23

Appleton, Daniel 329

Appleton, W. W. 329

"April Showers" (Jolson) 21, 67

Aragon Ballroom, Chicago 269, 273

*Arba'ah Turim* (Asher) 393

Arbuckle, Roscoe "Fatty" 41, 58, 62, 72, 292, 381

Arcadia Ballroom, Saint Louis 25

Archibald, George 481

*Architectural Forum* 320

Architectural League of New York 179

Architecture 35, 81, 88, 137, 146–150, 153, 161–164, 167–168, 170, 178–190, 289, 377, 433

*Archy and Mehitabel* (Marquis) 26, 57

Arden, Elizabeth 158

*Argosy* 310

Arlen, Michael 185

Arlin, Harold W. 327

Arlington National Cemetery 188, 292, 306

Arliss, George 75

Armistice Day Address (Harding) 292

Armory Show, New York City (1913) 31, 54

Armour, Philip D. 319

Armour, Tommy 480

Armour Institute of Technology 141

Armour meatpacking 319

Armstrong, Benjamin L. 188

Armstrong, Edwin Howard 327, 399, 415

Armstrong, Lil 60

Armstrong, Louis 23, 25, 29, 31, 49–50, 60–61, 70, 307

Armstrong, Will 60

Arno, Peter 57

"Arrow Collar Man" (Leyendecker) 159

*Arrowsmith* (Lewis) 24, 57, 72, 74

Art Deco 45, 81, 88, 149, 156, 164, 168–169, 180, 184, 186, 402

Art Moderne 168–169

*The Art of Lawn Tennis* (Tilden) 473

Arthur, Chester A. 258

Articles of Confederation 70

*Arts & Decoration* 168, 173

*As Thousands Cheer* (Berlin) 61

Asbury, Herbert 40, 327

Ashcan School 54

Asher, Rabbi Jacob ben 393

Ashland Auditorium, Chicago 247

Associated Press 328–329, 463, 468, 473

Associated Publishers, Inc. 138

Association for the Study of Negro Life and History 138

Association to Promote Scientific Research 140

Astaire, Adele 24, 27

Astaire, Fred 23–24, 26–27, 61, 64

Astor Cup (yachting) 482

Astronomy 402, 415, 418–419, 422–424

AT&T. *See* American Telephone and Telegraph 399

Atherton, Gertrude 309

Atlanta Athletic Club Junior Championship (golf) 468

Atlanta Braves 471

*Atlanta Constitution* 329

Atlanta University 139

Atlantic Coast Line Railroad Company 115

*Atlantic Monthly* 226, 269, 377

Atlas, Charles 288

Atomic bomb 417

Attell, Abe 443–444

*Atwater Kent Hour* 313

Atwater Kent Radios 311, 313

"The Auburn Affirmation" 365

Auburn Automobile Company 171, 174

*Auction Bridge Game* 313

Auditorium Theater, Chicago (Sullivan and Adler) 189

Audubon Ballroom, New York City 22, 263, 275

Augusta Tourists 462

Austin, Gene 24, 26–27

Auteur theory 32

Auto racing 114, 174, 475, 481

Auto-suggestion 263, 274

Cochrane, Elizabeth (Nellie Bly) 329

Cochrane, June 24

Cochrane, Mickey 440–442, 463

*The Coconuts* (Berlin) 25

Cocteau, Jean 176–177

Cofall, Stanley 453

Coffin, Henry Sloane 366

Cohn, Edwin J. 356

Cohn, Harry 31, 327

Cohn, Jack 327

Colby, Bainbridge 208

Cold War 197

Cole, Dr. Rufus 334, 357

Cole, Dr. W. H. 359

Cole Swimwear 160

Colgate, Col. Austen 188

Colgate College 386

Colgate company 188

*Collected Poems* (Robinson) 21, 74

*Collected Poems of H. D.* (Doolittle) 309

*College Humor* 65

College of Cardinals 370

College of Physicians and Surgeons 139

College of Wooster, Ohio 417

"Collegiate" (Pennsylvanians) 24

Collegiate style 65, 147, 150, 153, 158, 160, 282

Collett, Glenna 430, 433, 435–436, 454, 482

*Collier's* 155, 277

Collingwood, Charles 322

Collins, Eddie 439

Collins, Floyd 288

Collins, Herbert Seward 114

Collins, Morgan 255

Collip, James 332–333, 335, 342–343, 359

Collis P. Huntington Memorial Hospital 356

Colman, Ronald 25

*Color* (Cullen) 24, 47

Colorado State Supreme Court 285

Colored Waifs Home, New Orleans 50, 60

Colosimo, James "Big Jim" 232, 249

Colosimo's Café, Chicago 249

Colt, LeBaron Bradford 227

Coltiletti (racehorse) 478

Columbia Broadcasting System (CBS) 294, 312, 314, 318, 321–322, 325

*Columbia Encyclopedia* 327

*The Columbia Jester* 57

Columbia Pictures 31, 327

Columbia Records 296, 307

Columbia University 66, 127, 132–136, 140–141, 152, 284, 286, 317, 360, 420–421, 465, 482

— College of Physicians and Surgeons 360

— Law School 233, 256

— School of Architecture 189

— Teachers College 133–134, 136

Columbia University Press 327

*Columbus Enquirer Sun* (Ga.) 328

Columbus Platform 371

Combs, Earl 442

Comic books 292

Comic strips 65, 304, 317, 322–323

*Coming of Age in Samoa* (Mead) 401, 420

Comiskey, Charles A. 444

Commerce High School, New York City 465

Commercial Cable Company 294, 325

Commercial Law League of America 311

Committee of Forty-Eight 213

Committee on Federal Legislation for Birth Control 360

Committee on Negro Problems 264, 280

Commodity Exchange Act of 1922 77

Communism 58, 67, 199–201, 213, 222, 244, 247, 256, 263, 267, 323, 326, 367, 404

Communist Labor Party 200

Communist Party 120, 222, 293

Communist Third International of 1919 207

*Companionate Marriage* (Lindsey) 265, 285

*The Complete Bible: An American Translation* (Goodspeed and Smith) 393

*The Complete Poems of Keats and Shelley* 317

Compton, Arthur Holly 399, 417, 421, 423

Compton Effect 399, 417

Computer science 103, 401, 413

Concerto for Organ, Strings, and Harp (Hansen) 21

Concerto for Piano and Orchestra (Copland) 26

Concerto for Piano, Clarinet, and String Quartet (Harris) 26

Concerto in F for Piano and Orchestra (G. Gershwin) 25, 64

Conference for Progressive Political Action 213, 222

*Confidential Chats with Husbands* (Lay) 308

Confrey, Zez 21

*Confusion* (Cozzens) 23

Congregational Church 289

Congress Cigar Company 321

Congressional Medal of Honor 241

Conklin, Chester 58

Connecticut Agricultural Experiment Station 355

Connecticut Supreme Court 226

*A Connecticut Yankee* (Rodgers and Hart) 27, 54

Connelly, Marc 32, 36

Connie's Inn, New York City 60

"The Conning Tower" (Adams) 57, 305

Conowingo Bridge, Md. 306

Conrad, Dr. Frank 414

Conrad, Joseph 70, 321

Conservationism 218–219, 221

Conservatism 162, 213, 222, 378

Consolidated Exchange 115

Consumer Protection Laws 90

*Contact* 303

Contact Editions (publishing house) 37, 327

Continental Baking Company 78

Contract Plan 123, 127–128

Conwell, Russell H. 385–386

Conwell School of Theology 386

Cook, George Cram 76

Cook County Criminal Court, Ill. 242

Cookman Institute for Men 139

*Cook's Travelogue* 313

Coolbrith, Ina 76

Cooley, Charles Horton 289

Coolidge, Archibald Cary 140

Coolidge, Calvin 78–81, 83–84, 89–90, 112, 162, 193–195, 197, 199, 202, 204, 206–207, 209–211, 213–215, 218–222, 224–225, 228–229, 233–235, 241, 256–257, 268, 294, 308, 400, 405, 420

Coolidge, Grace (Mrs. Calvin) 173

Cooper, Gary 27

Cooper, Merian C. 24

Cooperative Analysis of Broadcasting 314

Cooperative capitalism 204, 221

Copa de las Americas (polo) 459

Copher, Dr. G. H. 359

Copland, Aaron 22–23, 26, 31, 45

Daugherty, Harry M. 197, 206, 218–219, 221, 225, 233, 256

*A Daughter of the Middle Border* (Garland) 74

Daughters of the American Revolution (DAR) 367

Daven Corporation, Newark, N.J. 295

David, John 80

Davidson, Donald 52

Davidson, Jo 20, 45, 57, 182

Davis 313

Davis, C. C. 475

Davis, Charles 21

Davis, David 108

Davis, Elmer 322

Davis, Harry P. 414

Davis, John W. 194, 202, 208, 212–214, 217, 222–224

Davis, Katherine Bement 263

Davis, Owen 22, 74

Davis, Stuart 21, 55

Davis Cup (tennis) 429–435, 458–459, 472–473, 477–481

*Davis Saxophone Octette* 313

Daviscourt, Dick 475

Davisson, Clinton J. 399

Dawes, Charles Gates 79, 112–113, 194, 199, 210–211, 213, 225

Dawes Plan of 1924 79, 194, 199, 211

Dawson, Howard A. 122

Day, Clarence 324

Day, William Rufus 227, 258

Dayton High School, Tenn. 250

Dayton Triangles 453

Dayton-Wright Airplane Company 406

Daytona Normal and Industrial Institute for Negro Girls 139

*Dear Judas* (Jeffers) 29, 309

*The Dearborn Independent* 371, 373–374

*Death Comes to the Archbishop* (Cather) 26

*Death in the Afternoon* (Hemingway) 66

*Death of the Machines* (Antheil) 22

DeBeck, Billy 304

De Broglie, Louis 399

Debs, Eugene Victor 114, 192, 207, 227, 232, 253–254, 267, 371

Declaration of Independence 70

*Decline and Fall of the Roman Empire* (Gibbons) 317

Deems, E. M. 394

Deering, Charles 114

*Defender* 484

Deford, Frank 472

De Forest, Lee 412

*The Degradation of the Democratic Dogma* (Adams) 76

Dehnert, Dutch 447

De Koven, Reginald 76

De Kruif, Paul 359, 400

Delacorte, George T. Jr. 292

Deland, Margaret 269

Delaney, Jack 448, 479

Delaney, Jimmy 482

Dell, Floyd 34, 58

Dell Publishing Company 292

Delmar, Viña 27, 34

DeMar, Clarence 475, 478–480

DeMille, Cecil B. 22, 26, 32, 54, 365, 382, 413

*Democracy and Education* (Dewey) 135

Democratic National Convention of 1920 192, 208, 223–224, 256

Democratic National Convention of 1924 194, 212, 224, 271

Democratic National Convention of 1928 195, 223

Democratic Party 192, 195, 197–199, 202–217, 219–221, 223–225, 228, 244, 249, 255–257, 265, 278, 285, 303, 366–367, 369, 377, 379, 385, 390–391

Dempsey, Jack 294, 312, 429, 431, 434–435, 437–438, 445, 447–448, 463–464, 479, 482, 484

*Dempsey and Firpo* (Bellows) 23

Demuth, Charles 21, 27–28, 31, 55

Denby, Edwin 197, 218–219, 225, 227

Denishawn School of Dance, Los Angeles 25, 42–43

Denison House, Boston 286

Dennett, Mary Ware 263, 327, 364

Dennett, May Ware 34

*The Denver Post* 304

DePaolo, Peter 479–480

Depew, Chauncey Mitchell 227

Derby hat 160

Derham (coach-making company) 177

*Des Moines Register And Tribune* 328

Des Moines University 390

*The Desert Song* 26

Designers' Gallery Show 150, 168

*Desire Under the Elms* (O'Neill) 24, 36, 68, 309

Desjardins, Peter 457

Deskey, Donald 168, 185

Deskey-Vollmer (interior design firm) 185

De Soto Motor Company 96

Destinn, Emmy 296

DeSylva, B. G. 27

*Detective Classics* 311

*Detective Fiction Weekly* 311

*Detective Tales* 311

Detroit Athletic Club Building (Kahn) 181

Detroit Cougars 433

Detroit Tigers 430, 439, 462–463, 482–483

Devery, William S. 482

Devine, Aubrey 451

Dewar Trophy for Automotive Excellence 95

Dewey, John 120, 126–127, 133–136

De Wolfe, Elsie 185

Dexter (racehorse) 482

Dey, Frederick Van Renssalaer 76

De Young, M. H. 329

Diabetes 332, 335, 341–343, 356, 359

Diaghilev, Sergei 45, 149, 176

*The Dial* 292

Dial Press 307

*Dialogues in Limbo* (Santayana) 308

"The Diamond as Big as the Ritz" (Fitzgerald) 63

Diamond Match Company 113

*Diaries of Boyhood and Youth* (T. Roosevelt) 308

Dick, Dr. George F. 332, 335–337, 352

Dick, Dr. Gladys H. 332, 335–337, 352

Dick Test 335, 337, 352

"Dick Tracy" 323

Dickenson, Mel 450

Dickinson, L. J. 205

*Dictionary of American Biography* 295

Diegel, Leo 436, 455

*Diet and Health with Key to the Calories* (Peters) 147, 154

Dietrich, Raymond H. 146, 149, 172, 177–178

Dietrich, Inc. 149, 173, 178

Dighigo, Martin 446

Dillon, Read and Company 79

DiMaggio, Joe 472

"Dinah" (Waters) 24

Diocese of All America and Canada 365

"Fascinating Rhythm" (G. and I. Gershwin) 23, 64
Fascism 66, 326
Fashion Academy, New York City 186
Fashion Publicity Company 189
Fate Marable Band 60
Faulkner, William 25, 29, 32, 51–52, 309, 317–319
Fauset, Jessie Redmon 38, 47–48
Faust, Frederick 311
Fawcett, Wilford H. 302
Fawcett Publications 292, 301–302
Fay, Frank 26
Feasley, Milton 327
Featherweight Championship (boxing) 478–481
Federal Bureau of Investigation (FBI) 193, 234, 237–238, 241, 256–257
Federal Council of Churches of Christ 367, 383
Federal League (baseball) 471
Federated Department Stores 100
Fedora hat 160
*Feelings and Emotions* (Frank) 284
Felsch, Oscar "Happy" 443
Felton, Rebecca 193
Feminism 56, 269, 279–280, 300, 335, 341, 366, 377
*Fence Rail* 389
Ferber, Edna 23, 25, 301
Ferguson, James E. 213
Ferguson, Miriam A. "Ma" 194, 213
Fermi, Enrico 400
Fermi-Dirac Statistics 400
Fernow, Bernhard Edward 139
Ferris, Woodbridge Nathan 227
Ferriss, E. N. 122
Ferriss, Hugh 146, 151, 164, 178–179
Ferry, Charles Addison 482
*A Few Figs from Thistles* (Millay) 20, 56
*Fiddler's Farewell* (Speyer) 74
"Fidgety Feet" (Beiderbecke) 23
Fields, Dorothy 28
Fields, Jackie 448, 481
"The Fifty-First Dragon" (Broun) 316
*Fifty Million Frenchmen* (Porter) 29
Filene's department stores 100
*Film Daily* 365
*Filterable Viruses* 357
*Fine Clothes to the Jew* (Hughes) 26, 38, 47, 67

Finger, Charles 73
*Fire!!* 38, 48, 303
*Fire Fighters* 311
*The Fireman* 62
Firestone, Harvey S. 112
Firestone Tire and Rubber Company 112
Firpo, Luis Angel 431, 464, 484
First Baptist Church of Fort Worth 378, 388–389
First Baptist Church of Minneapolis 378, 389
"First Fig" (Millay) 56
First National City Bank 116
First National Studio 62
First Presbyterian Church of New York City 364, 378–379, 386–387, 391
First Ward, Chicago 322
Fish, Stuyvesant 114
Fishbein, Morris 359
Fisher, Dorothy Canfield 300
Fisher, Irving 102, 112
Fisher, Judge 359
Fisher (coach-making company) 173, 181
Fiske, Billie 458
Fiske, Gertrude 187
Fitzgerald, Dr. 344
Fitzgerald, F. Scott 20–21, 24–25, 32–33, 39, 44, 63–64, 66, 68, 71, 153, 159, 308, 319, 323
Fitzgerald, Zelda Sayre 63
Fitzpatrick, D. R. 328
"Five Foot Two, Eyes of Blue — Has Anybody Seen My Girl?" (Autry) 24
*Five Little Peppers and How they Grew* (Sidney) 76
Five Points Gang 253
Five-Power Treaty of 1922 192
*Fix Bayonets!* (Thomason) 308
Flagler, Henry M. 100
Flaherty, Robert 21, 327
Flanagan, Father Edward Joseph 393
Flanner, Janet 45
Flappers 65, 155–157, 159, 168, 246, 263, 269, 278, 282
*Flappers and Philosophers* (Fitzgerald) 20, 308
Fleetwood (coach-making company) 173
Fleischman, Julius 114
Fleischmann, Raoul 324
*Fleischmann Hour* 60, 295, 312
Fleischmann's Yeast 312

Fleming, Alexander 332–333, 335, 344–345
*Flesh and the Devil* 26, 71
Fletcher Henderson Orchestra 60
Flexner, Abraham 334, 353–354
Flexner, Simon 353–354, 357
Flexner Report 334, 353
*Flight of Europa* (Manship) 24
*The Flight of a Moth* (Post) 287
*Floating Figure* (Lachaise) 51
*Floating Figure* (Zorach) 51
*The Floorwalker* 62
*The Florentine Dagger* (Hecht) 309
Florey, Howard Walker 345
Florida East Coast Railroad 100, 113
Florida House of Representatives 121
Floto, Otto 329
Flower, Lucy 289
Flowers, Theodore "Tiger" 434, 438, 445, 448, 479, 482
Flying Ebony (racehorse) 476, 479, 483
*Flynn's* 311
*Flynn's Weekly* 311
*Flynn's Weekly Detective Fiction* 311
Flyweight Championship (boxing) 478–479, 484
Foerster, Norman 53
*Fog Horns* (Dove) 29, 55
Fokine, Michel 23
Folger, Henry C. 69
Folger Shakespeare Library, Washington, D.C. (Cret) 69, 185
Fontanne, Lynn 72
*Foolish Wives* 21
Football 132, 250, 277, 293–294, 305–306, 311–312, 359, 437–438, 444, 450–453, 466–467, 469–470, 481
*For Whom the Bell Tolls* (Hemingway) 66
Forbes, Charles R. 197, 218, 225, 234
Forbes, Esther 301
Ford, Charles Henri 303
Ford, Edsel 147, 167, 172–173, 178, 181
Ford, Edsel B. 95, 110, 112
Ford, Ford Madox 66, 303
Ford, Henry 82, 88, 92–95, 99, 108–110, 112, 114, 146–147, 150, 153, 171–172, 181, 265, 268, 270, 371, 373–374, 402–403
Ford, Henry II 110
Ford, John 23, 32, 54

Grand Island College, Nebraska 282

*Grand Ole Opry* 293, 314

Grand Prix of France (auto racing) 475

Grange, Harold "Red" 150, 277, 432–433, 437, 451, 453, 466–467

Grant Memorial (Shrady) 57

Grant's Tomb (Duncan) 188

*Graphic* 293, 304

*Grass* 24

Grasty, Charles H. 329

Grauman, Sidney Patrick 150, 170

Grauman's Chinese Theater (Meyer and Holler) 150, 170

Grauman's Egyptian Theater (Meyer and Holler) 170

*Graustark* (McCutcheon) 77

Gray, Charles W. 114

Gray, Harold 304

Great Depression of the 1930s 48, 64–65, 70, 91, 95, 160, 164–165, 173–174, 178–179, 183, 197–198, 204, 217, 220–221, 223, 268, 272, 284, 286, 314, 316, 371, 375, 382, 391, 415, 460–461, 472

*The Great Dictator* 62

*The Great Gatsby* (Fitzgerald) 24, 44, 63, 308, 323

*The Great God Brown* (O'Neill) 26, 69

*The Great God Brown, The Fountain, The Moon of the Caribbees, and Other Plays* (O'Neill) 309

"The Great God Football" (Tunis) 452

*The Great Meadow* (Roberts) 52

Great Northern Railroad 82

Greb, Harry 431, 434, 448, 478–479, 482

*Greed* 23, 32

Greek Orthodox Archdiocese of North and South America 364

Green, Frederick Robin 360

Green, Paul 26, 52, 74

Green, Ruzzie 185

Green Bay Packers 453, 481

*The Green Bay Tree* (Bromfield) 23

*The Green Hat* (Arlen) 185

*Green Hills of Africa* (Hemingway) 66

Greenbaum, Wolff, and Ernst (law firm) 254

Greenberg: Publisher 307

*The Greene Murder Case* (Van Dine) 308

*Greenwich Folly* 480

Greenwich Village, New York City 44, 178

*Greenwich Village Follies* 22

Gregory, Montgomery 38

Grey, Zane 20

Grey Lag (racehorse) 478, 483

Greyhound Corporation 80

Greystone Ballroom, Detroit 273

Griffin, Hugh Reed 360

Griffith, Albert "Young Griffo" 483

Griffin, Joe 480

Griffith, D. W. 20–21, 32, 54, 62

*Grim Youth* (Held) 65

Grimes, Burleigh 440–442

Grinnell, Irving 482

Gris, Juan 45

Grofé, Ferde 23

Grogan, Perry 464

Groody, Louise 24

Gropius, Walter 35, 162–163, 186

Gross, Ben 327

Grosset & Dunlap (publishing house) 297

Grosvenor, Hugh Richard Arthur, Duke of Westminster 177

Groton School 322

Grove, Lefty 440–442

*The Growth of the American Nation* (Judson) 141

Gruman Aircraft 81

Guerin, Camille 332, 337

Guest, Edgar A. 51

Guggenheim, Daniel 407

Guggenheim, Harry F. 407

Guggenheim, Isaac 114

Guggenheim, Simon 139

Guggenheim Fellowships 25, 48

Guggenheim Foundation 139

Guggenheim Fund for the Promotion of Aeronautics 407, 423

Guinan, Texas 326, 388

Guiney, Louise Imogen 76

*The Gulf Between* 413

"Gulf Coast Blues" (B. Smith) 22, 70

Gulf Oil 90

"The Gumps" 323

Gunsaulus, Frank Wakeley 141

Gusenberg, Frank 249

Gusenberg, Pete 249

"Gut Bucket Blues" (Armstrong and the Hot Five) 25

Gutenberg Bible 70, 393

Guy's Hospital, London 350

Gye, Dr. W. E. 359

H

Haas, Robert K. 300

Hadden, Briton 91, 319–320, 329

Haedge, Carl 477

Haff, Capt. Harry P. 482

Hagen, Walter 158, 430, 432–437, 453–455, 468

Haggerty, Horse 447

The Hague, Netherlands 235, 283

Haines, Jesse 432

"Hair Cut" (Lardner) 68

*The Hairy Ape* (O'Neill) 22, 69

*The Hairy Ape, Anna Christie, The First Man* (O'Neill) 309

Halas, George 430, 453, 467

Haldeman-Julius, Emanuel 308

Haldeman-Julius Publishing Company 292, 307

Hale, George Ellery 418, 422

Haley, Margaret 125

Hall, Adelaide 28

Hall, Rev. Edward Wheeler 239

Hall, Frances Stevens 239–240

Hall, Granville Stanley 139, 289, 360, 424

Hall, Grover Cleveland 329

Hall, Radclyffe 34, 39

Hall, Wendell 22

Hall-Edwards, J. F. 360

Hall-Mills Murder Case 239, 304

Hall-Scott (engine manufacterers) 406

*Hallelujah* (Lubitsch) 28

Hallimond, John G. 394

Halsted, William Stewart 351, 360

Hambleton family 91

Hamburger and Sons 77

Hamilton, Alice 288

Hamilton County District Court, Neb. 252

Hamm, Edward 457

Hammerstein, Oscar II 25–28, 54

Hammett, Dashiell 29, 32, 56, 310–311

Hammond, Dr. Graeme M. 475

Hanan, John H. 188

Hanan Shoe Company of New York 188

*Handbook of Automobiles* 173

*Handbook on Rural Education* (Dawson and Noble) 122

Handy, W. C. 50, 327

Hanlon, Fred "Pop" 482

Hanover College 389

Hansen, Howard 21–22

Hanson, Earl Charles 398

Hanson, Vic 447

Happiness Boys (Billy Jones and Ernie Hare) 22, 293, 307, 312

Happiness Candy Company 312–313

Harbach, Otto 24–26, 54

Harbut, Will 469

Harcourt, Brace (publishing company) 307, 400

Hard-boiled detective fiction 48–49, 310–311

*The Hard-Boiled Virgin* (Newman) 34, 52, 77

Harding, Dr. George T. 359

Harding, Nelson 328–329

Harding, Warren G. 41, 76, 78, 83–84, 89–90, 112, 146, 162, 173, 192–193, 197, 205–211, 215, 218–221, 223, 227–228, 232–234, 237, 256–257, 292–293, 327, 359, 368, 381, 463

Hardy, Oliver 54, 58, 72

Hare, Ernie 293, 307, 312

Harkins, William D. 398

Harkness, Mrs. Edward 70

Harland, Marion (Mary Virginia Hawes Terhune) 77

Harlem Globetrotters 476

"Harlem on my Mind" (Berlin) 61

Harlem Renaissance 33, 38, 47–48, 51, 67, 139, 263, 271

*Harlem Shadows* (McKay) 48

Harlem Suitcase Theatre, New York City 67

Harmon, Judson 258

Harmon Medal 48

*Harmonium* (Stevens) 22, 56

Harmsworth, A. C. W. 322

Harmsworth Trophy (boating) 476

Harper, Jesse 470

Harper, William Rainey 134

*Harper's Bazaar* 155, 168, 175, 187

*Harper's Weekly* 452

Harriman, E. H. 114

Harris, Frank 34

Harris, Marion 23

Harris, Mary Belle 288

Harris, Roy 26, 29

Harrisburg Giants 446

Harrison, Benjamin 228

Hart, Harry 188

Hart, Joseph 278

Hart, Lorenz 25–27, 54, 61, 326

Hart, Louis 28

Hart, Schaffner & Marx 188

Hartford Theological Seminary 364

Hartley, Marsden 31, 54–55

Hartman, Emil Alvin 186

Hartman, Frank A. 333, 359

Hartnett, Gabby 440–442

Hartz, Harry 479

Harvard Classics 139, 309

Harvard Heresy Trial 258

Harvard House Plan 137

*The Harvard Lampoon* 57

Harvard University 53, 69, 100, 105, 131–132, 136–140, 248, 257, 310, 316, 323, 343, 351, 353, 356, 358–359, 370, 401, 424, 428, 460, 468, 475, 477, 481–482

— Architecture Department 186

— Board of Overseers 257

— Law School 137, 257, 265

— Library 140

— Medical School 288, 334–335, 343, 351, 356, 360

— Observatory 399

— School of Business 76

— Society of Fellows 137

Hastings, Thomas 149, 162, 187–188

*A Hasty Bunch* (McAlmon) 327

Hat Corporation of America 185

"Hatrack" (Asbury) 40, 327

Haugen, Gilbert 205

Havemeyer, Mrs. H. O. 72

Hawes, Charles 73

Hawley, Joyce 288

Hay-Adams Hotel, Washington, D.C. 80

Hayes, Helen 71

Hayford, John Fillmore 424

Haynes, Elizabeth Ross 288

Haynes, Elwood 114

Haynes-Apperson Company (later Haynes Automobile Company) 115

Hays, Arthur Garfield 244, 251, 257

Hays, Ralph 453

Hays, Will H. 41, 292, 381

Hays Office. *See* Motion Picture Producers and Distributors of America (MPPDA)

Haywood, William Dudley "Big Bill" 115, 253–254

Hazelton, George Cochrane 258

H'Doubler, Margaret 26

*He Who Gets Slapped* 23

*Head of a Young Girl* (Vermeer) 173

*Health Magazine* 360

Healy (coach-making company) 177

Hearne, Eddie 478

Hearst, William Randolph 106, 186, 239, 297, 303–304, 322–323, 326

Hearst, Mrs. William Randolph 175

Hearst Metrotone News 295, 297, 306

Hearst Press 293

Heart disease 338

"Heat Wave" (Berlin) 61

Heaton, Jennison 458

Heaton, John 458

Heavyweight Championship (boxing) 479, 463–464, 484

Hecht, Ben 28, 32, 34, 36, 303, 309

*Heebie Jeebies* 25, 38, 60

Heilman, Harry 471

Hein, Silvio 76

Heisman, John 452

Hekanakht Papers 422

Held, Edmund R. 455

Held, John Jr. 65, 155, 159

Helicopters 409–410, 423

*Hell-Bent fer Heaven* (Hughes) 23, 74

Hellinger, Mark 326

*Hello, Dolly!* 60

Helm, Rev. Adelbert J. 393

Helm, Marcus 115

Hemingway, Ernest 22–25, 29–30, 32, 40, 44–46, 55, 65–66, 295, 308–309, 318, 323, 326

Hemingway, Hadley Richardson 65

Hemophilia 357

Henderson, Elmer "Gloomy Gus" 452

Henderson, Fletcher 50, 60

Henderson, Lawrence J. 334

Henderson, Ray 27

Hendrick, Burton J. 74

Henie, Sonja 457

Henley Regatta, Great Britain 456

Herbert, Evelyn 27

Herbert, Victor 76

*Heretic* (Humphrey) 43

Herman, Pete 429–430, 448, 477

Hermès 184

Herndon, Charles 244

Herreshoff, Nat 461

Hess, Alfred 358

Hess, Victor 399, 421

Hewitt, William D. 188

*Hey Rub-a-Dub-Dub* (Dreiser) 309

Heyer, Adam 248

Heylander, John 444

Heyward, Dorothy 37

Heyward, DuBose 37, 52, 64

Hibbard, Thomas L. 146, 177
Hibbard & Darrin (coach-making company) 177
*The Higher Study of English* 140
Highlands, John A. "Jack" 482
Hildreth, Samuel Clay 482
Hill, George Washington 298
Hill, James J. 82
Hill, Percival S. 115
Hilldale Giants 446
Hillquit, Morris 371
"The Hills of Zion" (Mencken) 379
Hilton, Conrad 112
Hilton Hotels 112
*Him* (Cummings) 309
Hippocrates 344
Hires 313
*Hires Harvesters* 313
Hirsch, Emil G. 141
Hirschfeld, Albert 72
*The History of Education* (Cubberley) 120
*History of English Romanticism* 140
*History of Procedure in England from the Norman Conquest* (Bigelow) 140
*A History of the American Frontier* (Paxson) 74
*History of the Modern World* (Browning) 140
*The History of the Negro Church* (Woodson) 138
*The History of the United States* (Channing) 74
*Hit the Deck* (Youmans and Robin) 27
Hitchcock, Raymond 76
Hitchcock, Tommy 437, 460–461
Hitler, Adolf 326, 374
*Hod Carrier* (Baizerman) 29
Hoffenstein, Samuel 57
Hoffman, Malvina 57
Hofmann, Josef 296
Hofstadter, Richard 224
Hokinson, Helen E. 170
Holabird, William 188
*Holiday* (Barry) 28, 36
Holland, Clifford Milburn 115
Holland Tunnel 115
Holley, Marietta 76
*The Hollow Men* (Eliot) 24
Holloway, Emery 74
Holloway, Sterling 24
Hollywood Palladium 269, 273
Holman, Libby 29, 72
Holmes, Oliver Wendell 482

Holmes, Oliver Wendell Jr. 195, 200, 237, 241, 244, 248, 250, 257
Holst, Axel 348
Holt, Guy 39
Holt, Henry 329
Holt, Luther Emmett 139, 340, 360
Holy Name Catholic Cathedral, Chicago 249
*Home to Harlem* (McKay) 47
Homer 320
Homestead Grays 445–446
Homosexuality 40, 47, 242
"Honeysuckle Rose" (Waller) 29
Hood, Raymond M. 32, 147–148, 151, 163–165, 169, 179–181
Hookworm 346
Hooper, Charles 358
Hoover, Herbert 77, 80–83, 90–91, 96, 106–107, 112, 162, 168, 195–196, 197, 206, 210–211, 215, 217, 219, 221–222, 224–225, 236, 241, 258, 293–294, 340, 367, 370, 385, 398, 400, 405, 412, 472
Hoover, J. Edgar 193, 234, 237–238, 241, 256–257
Hoover Dam 221
Hoover Sentinels 311
*Hoover* v. *Intercity Radio Co., Inc.* 293
Hoover vacuum cleaners 311
Hope, John 139
Hopkins, Sir Frederick Gowland 332–333, 348, 356, 358
Hopkins, James 187
Hoppe, Willie 475
Hopper, Edward 24, 26, 29, 55
Hopwood, Avery 76
Horace Liveright (publishing house) 307
Horemans, Edouard 475
Hornsby, Rogers 432–433, 439, 442, 475, 477
Horse racing 327, 444–445, 468, 476–477, 483–484
*Horses and Men* (Anderson) 22
*The Hostess* (Calder) 58
*Hot Chocolates* 60
Hot Five 25, 60
Hotchkiss School 319
Houdini, Harry (Ehrich Weiss) 76, 289
Hough, Emerson 21, 76
Houghton, G. C. 394
*Hound and Horn* 303
House, Dr. R. E. 359
*House Beautiful* 168

*The House Beautiful Furnishing Annual 1926* 168
*House by the Railroad* (Hopper) 24, 55
House of Kuppenheimer 189
*House of Mystery* (Burchfield) 55
*A Houseboat on the Styx* (Bangs) 76
Houser, Clarence "Bud" 457
Houston, Charles Hamilton 257
Houston Eagles 446
Hovey, Alvah 394
Hovey, Richard 76
"How the Old Horse Won the Race" (Holmes) 482
"How to Help Your Child in School" (Lawrence and Mary Frank) 284
*How to Write Short Stories (with samples)* (Lardner) 23, 63, 308
Howard, Ralph 422
Howard, Sidney 24, 32, 36, 74
Howard Johnson restaurant 288
Howard University 47, 138–139, 355
— Law School 237, 257
Howe, George 151, 165
Howe, M. A. DeWolfe 74
Howell, William 398
Howells, John Mead 35–36, 147, 163–164, 180
Howells, William Dean 76
Howland, Samuel Shaw 483
Hoyt, R. F. 481
Hubbard, Gardiner G. 113
Hubbell, Carl 436
Hubbell, Jay B. 72
Hubble, Edwin 399, 401, 416, 418–419
Hubble's Law 418–419
Hubert, Pooley 452
Hudnut, Richard 188
Hudson Motor Car Company 78, 80, 94, 171, 262
*Hudson River Bracketed* (Wharton) 29
Hudson View Gardens, New York City 165
Hudson-Essex Company 171
Huggins, Miller J. 442, 483
*Hugh Selwyn Mauberley* (Pound) 20, 46
Hughes, Brian G. 115
Hughes, Charles Evans 199, 221, 225
Hughes, Dudley Mays 227
Hughes, Hatcher 23, 74
Hughes, Langston 25–26, 38–40, 61–62

Ipana toothpaste 311, 313
Ipana Troubadours 293, 311, 313
Ireland, Archbishop John 390
Iribe, Paul 177
*The Iron Horse* 23, 32
Iron lung 333, 343, 401
Iroquois Theatre 329
Irving, Washington 482
*Is 5* (Cummings) 56, 309
*Is Sex Necessary?* (Thurber and White) 57
"Is the Younger Generation in Peril?" 154
Iselin, William E. 482
Isolationism 197, 199, 213, 215, 222, 319
Isostasy 424
*It* 26
"It Ain't Gonna Rain No Mo' " (Hall) 22
"It Ain't Necessarily So" (George and Ira Gershwin) 64
"It All Depends on You" (Etting) 26
"It Don't Mean a Thing If It Aint' Got That Swing" (Ellington) 50
"It Had to Be You" (Harris) 23
"It Seems to Me" (Broun) 305, 316
"It's Right Here for You" (M. Smith) 307
Ives, Charles 21, 23

J

J & P Coats thread-manufacturing company 114
J. C. Penney Company 80, 99–100
J. I. Case & Company 102, 113
J. P. Morgan Building, New York City (Trowbridge & Livingston) 189
J. Walter Thompson (advertising agency) 298
Jackman, Ernest 120, 127
Jackson, "Shoeless Joe" 442, 444
Jackson, Travis 439
Jacobs, Helen 435–436
Jaffe, Louis Isaac 329
Jaffe, Solomon E. 394
James, Henry 30
James, Will 73, 308, 324
James, William 134
*Janet March* (Dell) 34
Janeway, Col. Jacob J. 189
Janeway & Carpenter Wall Paper Manufacturing Company 189
Jannings, Emil 26, 74
Jantzen Swimwear 146, 160

"Japanese Sandman" (Bayes) 20, 307
Jarvie, James N. 115
Jaundice 358
Jazz 31, 33, 49–50, 60–61, 63–65, 71, 149, 154, 264, 269, 271, 307, 380
Jazz Age 33, 50, 63, 65, 84, 89, 246, 303, 318
"Jazz Me Blues" (Wolverines) 23
Jazz Orchestra Pieces (Carpenter) 24
*The Jazz Singer* 26, 59, 67, 306, 400, 412
Jazz suit 160
Jeffers, Robinson 23–24, 27, 29, 56, 309
Jefferson, Thomas 72, 213
Jeffries, James J. 445, 484
Jenks, Jeremiah Whipple 424
Jenney, William Le Baron 188
Jennings, Hugh Ambrose 483
Jernegan, Marcus W. 138
Jesus Christ 79, 365, 372, 375, 377, 382–386, 462
"The Jewish Exploitation of Farmers' Organizations" (Ford) 374
Jewish Institute of Religion 365
Jewish Publication Society of America 394
Jewish Theological Seminary, New York City 393
Jim Crow laws 60, 237, 244, 246, 271, 438, 444–445
Joe Bren Producing Company 317
*John Brown's Body* (Benét) 27, 74
John Day (publishing house) 307
John McCormick Institute for Contagious Diseases 336, 352
John Newbery Medal for Children's Books 73
John P. Grier (racehorse) 428, 469
John Simon Guggenheim Foundation. *See* Guggenheim Foundation
Johns Hopkins University 134, 136, 139, 141, 351–354, 398
— Hospital 351, 354, 356–357
— McCollum-Pratt Institute 356
— Medical School 357–358
Johns-Manville Company 115
Johnson, A. 478–479
Johnson, Alva 328
Johnson, Alvin Saunders 139
Johnson, Ban 444
Johnson, Bunk 50

Johnson, Herbert Lansdowne 393
Johnson, Hiram 201, 206–207, 210
Johnson, Howard 288
Johnson, J. Rosamond 38
Johnson, Jack 445, 463, 484
Johnson, Jackson 115, 189
Johnson, James P. 23
Johnson, James Weldon 38, 47
Johnson, John Lester 445
Johnson, Lyndon Baines 255
Johnson, Wallace 429
Johnson, Walter 428, 440–442, 462
Johnson, William Julius "Judy" 446
Johnson and Johnson 239
Johnston, Bill 428, 430–433, 435, 459, 472, 478
Johnston, Dr. William J. 233
Jolas, Eugene 294, 303
*Jolly Wonder Bakers* 313
Jolson, Al 20–21, 23–27, 29, 50, 59, 67, 307, 412
*Jolson Sings Again* 67
*The Jolson Story* 67
Jones, Billy 22, 293, 307, 312
Jones, Bob 366, 379
Jones, Bobby 153, 158, 431–437, 453, 467–468, 484
Jones, George H. 115
Jones, Howard 451
Jones, Isham 21, 23, 307
Jones, James 324
Jones, John Price 26
Jones, Paul 477
Jones, Robert T. Jr. 478, 480–481
Jones, William L. 115
Jones and Hare 22, 313
Jones and Laughlin Steel Company 115
Jones College, Clearwater, Fla. 366
Jones-White Act of 1928 81
Jordan, Edward S. 298
Jordan, Robert 66
Jordan Playboy Automobiles 298
Josephson, Matthew 303
Josiah Macy Foundation 284
*Journal of Educational Psychology* 140
*Journal of Experimental Medicine* 354
*Journal of Forestry* 139
*Journal of Negro History* 138
*Journal of the American Medical Association (JAMA)* 346, 359–360
Joy, Henry B. 181
Joyce, James 21, 32, 34, 40, 44, 50, 70, 255, 263, 317
Jubilee Prize (yachting) 482

Mencken, H. L. 52, 68, 251, 276, 293, 310, 320–321, 327, 379–380, 383

Meningitis 354

Menninger, Karl 276

*Men's Conference* 313

*Men's Wear* 158

Mental illness 234, 240, 242, 275–276, 289, 346, 461–462

Mercedes-Benz 96

Mercer College (later University) 136, 391

Mercer Motor Car Company 173

Merchant Marine Act of 1920 76

Mercury Car Company 178

Meredith, Edwin Thomas 147, 208, 228, 302

Merimee, J. 478

*The Merry Widow* 24, 71

Merseles, Theodore Frelinghuysen 189

*Messer Marco Polo* (Byrne) 76

*Meteor* 482

Methodist Episcopal Church 365

Methodist Episcopal Church, South 225, 380, 385

Methodist Wesley Foundation 364

Metro-Goldwyn-Mayer (M-G-M) 23, 31, 54, 58, 64, 71, 75, 185, 268, 295, 306, 327, 329, 412–413

*The Metropolis of Tomorrow* (Ferriss) 151, 179

Metropolitan Museum of Art, New York City 72, 151, 169, 422

Metropolitan Opera House, New York City 72–73, 149, 186, 296

Meyer, Adolf 163

Meyer, John 343

Meyer, Louis 480–481

Meyer, Robert T. 252

Meyer and Holler (architectural firm) 150, 170

*Meyer* v. *Nebraska* 120, 125, 252

Miami Biltmore Hotel, Coral Gables, Fla. 78, 100

Michael, Joseph 404

Michelson, Albert A. 398, 420–421, 424

Michigan State Department of Health 347–348, 355

Mickey Mouse 28, 295

*The Microbe Hunters* (de Kruif) 359, 400

Middlebury College 140

*Middletown* (R. and H. Lynd) 150, 266, 270, 281, 285–286, 369, 381

*Middletown in Transition* (R. and H. Lynd) 285–286

Middleweight Championship (boxing) 477–479, 482

Midgley, Thomas Jr. 398, 403

The Midland Theater, Kansas City, Mo. (Lamb) 170

*Midnight* 311

*Midnight Mysteries* 311

Mies van der Rohe, Ludwig 147, 150, 162, 169

Mikhail Mordkin Ballet Company 22

Milam Building, San Antonio 150

Milburn Electric 262

Miles, John 480–481

Milestone, Lewis 74–75

Milhaud, Darius 45, 72

Milky Way galaxy 399, 402, 415–416, 418, 423

Millar, Moorhouse F. X. 390

Millard House, Pasadena (Wright) 187

Millay, Edna St. Vincent 20–22, 56, 74, 265

Miller, C. H. 478

Miller, Don 277, 305, 431, 470

Miller, Hannah Benedict 135

Miller, Harry L. 127

Miller, Henry 77

Miller, James 135

Miller, Marilyn 25, 28

Miller, William Burke 328

Millikan, Robert A. 399, 418, 421, 423

Milliken, Seth M. 115

Million Dollar Movie Palace, Hollywood (Woollett and Martin) 170

Mills, Eleanor 239

Mills, Florence 38, 77

Mills, James F. 239

Milton, Tommy 477–478

*The Mind in the Making* (Robinson) 140, 383

"The Mind of the South" (Cash) 383

Minnesota Mining and Manufacturing (3M) 401

Minot, George Richards 333, 350, 356–358

Minter, Mary Miles 41, 381

Minton, Balch (publishing house) 307

El Mirasol, Palm Beach, Fla. (Mizner) 146

Miró, Joan 45

Mischou, Irene 480

*Les Miserables* (Hugo) 317

*Miss America* 476–477

Miss America pageant 263

Miss Graham's Finishing School 287

*Miss Lulu Bett* (Gale) 20, 73

"Miss Thompson" (Maugham) 22

*Mrs. Wiggs of the Cabbage Patch* (Wiggin) 77

Mississippi flood of 1927 221

Mississippi General Assembly 246

*Mississippi Suite* (Grofé) 23

Mississippi Valley Power Boat Association 432

Missouri Pacific Railroad 114

*Mr. and Mrs. Haddock Abroad* (Stewart) 57

"Mr. Gallagher and Mr. Sheean" (Gallagher & Sheean) 21

"Mr. Jelly Lord" (Morton) 22

*Mr. Pope* (Tate) 27

*Mr. President* (Berlin) 61

*Mistress Nell* (Hazelton) 258

Mitchel Field, Long Island 429

Mitchell, Charles E. 112

Mitchell, Clarence 446

Mitchell, Lucy Sprague 284

Mitchell, Wesley C. 284

Mitchell, Brig. Gen. William 79, 405–408

Mizner, Addison 146, 148, 167, 182–183

Mizner, Wilson 182–183

Mizner Industries 183

"Moanin' Low" (Holman) 29, 72

Modern Language Association of America 140

Modern Library (publishing house) 307, 317–318

*The Modern Quarterly* 303

*Modern Times* 62

Modernism (architecture) 151, 162, 164"165, 167–168, 180, 185, 189

Modernism (art) 50–51

Modernism (interior design) 150–151, 153, 169, 185

Modernism (literature) 42, 47-48, 297

Modernism (religion) 364, 370, 372–373, 375, 378–381, 384, 386, 389–390, 393

Moline Plow Company 205

*Monsieur Beaucaire* 23

*Monsieur Verdoux* 63

*Montage of a Dream Deferred* (Hughes) 67

Montessori, Maria 127

University of Vienna 355
University of Virginia 141, 303
University of Washington 132, 432–433, 437, 452, 478–479
University of Western Ontario School of Medicine 342
University of Wisconsin 26, 127, 132, 139, 346, 356–357
— Experimental College 139
University Place Presbyterian Church 386
*The Unspeakable Gentleman* (Marquand) 308
*Upper Deck* (Sheeler) 29, 55
Upset (racehorse) 468
Urban, Joseph 168–169, 186
Urban League 38, 66
Urbanization 79, 87, 153, 161–162, 165–166, 178–180

V

Vactuphone 398
Vaculain, Samuel 113
*The Vagabond King* (Friml) 25
*Vagrant* 476
Vail, H. H. 141
Vail, Theodore M. 268
Valentina (Nicholaevna Sanina Schlee) 187
Valentino, Rudolph 20–21, 23, 25, 54, 77, 177, 185, 304
Vallee, Rudy 27, 29, 295, 312
Van Alen, William 81, 149, 164, 180
Van and Schenck 20–22
Vance, Dazzy 433
Vanderbilt, Cornelius 116
Vanderbilt, Cornelius Jr. 297
Vanderbilt, Harold S. 146, 476
Vanderbilt, William Kissam 101, 116, 484
Vanderbilt family 170, 183
Vanderbilt University 52, 452
Van Dine, S. S. 26, 29, 308, 324
Vanguard Press 307–308
Van Heusen, John Manning 146, 159
*Vanities* (Carroll) 54, 288
*Vanity Fair* 65, 159, 165, 167, 178, 184, 263, 460
Van Loon, Hendrik 73, 309, 383
Van Raalte, Zealie 189
Van Raalte (silk company) 189
Van Vechten, Carl 47, 70
Vanzetti, Bartolomeo 58, 232, 235, 247–248, 255, 257, 265, 316

Vardaman, James K. 246
*Variety* 105
The Varsity Drag 269
Vassar College 135
Vatican 364, 370, 390
Vatican Choir 306
*The Vaudeville News* 326
Vedder, Elihu 77
*The Vegetable* (Fitzgerald) 308
Velie, W. L. 116
Velie Motors 94
Venereal disease 345, 347, 354
Verdi, Giuseppe 73
Verdun (World War I battle) 30
Vermeer, Jan 173
Vernacular art 31
*Vers une architecture* (Le Corbusier) 149, 185
Verville Scout 405–406
Veterans' Bonus Bill 193, 223
Vicious Circle 57
Victor Animatograph 399
Victor Records 292, 307
Victor Talking Machine Company 295, 306, 325
Victoria Cougars 479
Victoria of Great Britain 189
Victorian (racehorse) 480
*The Victory at Sea* (Sims) 74
Victrola 306
*Video Age International* 321
Vidor, King 28
Vigil (racehorse) 478
*The Viking* 413
*The Vikings* 313
Villa, Pancho 431, 448, 478, 484
Villa de Sarmiento, Palm Beach, Fla. (Mizner) 146
Vincent, Boyd 394
Vincent, J. G. 478
Vincent, John Heyl 395
Viola Concerto (Piston) 29
Vionnet, Madeleine 152, 154–155
*The Virgin Man* 41
Virginia General Assembly 240
*The Virginia Quarterly Review* 303
Vitamins 332–333, 335, 348–350, 356–358, 398, 400–401, 422
Vitaphone 59, 412
Vito (racehorse) 480
Vlasto, Didi 474
*Vogue* 149, 155, 168, 175–176, 184–185, 187
Volstead Act of 1919 194, 203, 215, 232–233, 262, 368
Voltaire 317

Voluntary Parenthood League 263, 364
Von Braun, Werner 418
Von Stroheim, Erich 21, 23–24, 27, 32, 54
Vorhees, Gmelin, and Walker (architectural firm) 164
Vorticism 32
*The Voyages of Doctor Dolittle* (Lofting) 73

W

W. K. Kellogg Company 288
W. T. Grant stores 99
W. W. Norton (publishing house) 307
"Wabash Blues" (Jones) 21, 307
Wade, Horace A. 328
Wade, J. H. 116
Wade, Wallace 452
Wagnalls, A. W. 330
Wagner, Honus 439, 446, 462
Wainwright Building, St. Louis (Sullivan) 189
"Waiting for the Robert E. Lee" (Jolson) 67
Walcott, Charles Doolittle 424
Walcott, Joe 483
Waldorf Hotel, New York City 95
Walgreen's drug stores 99
Walker, Cyril 432, 455, 478
Walker, Edward "Mickey" 430, 448
Walker, Jimmy 40, 266
Walker, Mickey 433–434, 476–477, 479, 482
Walker, Ralph 180
Walker, Stanley 305
Walker Cup (golf) 430
Wall Street, New York City 76, 78, 81, 84, 90–91, 101–102, 104–107, 111–112, 196, 214, 222, 256, 319
*Wall Street Journal* 113, 222, 329
Wallace, DeWitt 292, 315
Wallace, Henry Cantwell 228
Wallace, John Findlay 424
Wallace, Lila 292, 315
Wallach, Samuel 116
Waller, Fats 29, 60
Walsh, Christy 476
Walsh, David 214
Walsh, Ernest 66, 303
Walsh, Thomas J. 219
Walt Disney Studios 28, 295, 412
Walter, Eugene 293

Walter Camp's Book of College Sports (Camp) 437
Walton, J. C. 193, 233
Wambsganss, William "Wamby" 428, 446
Wanamaker, John 116, 189, 395
Wanamaker, Lewis Rodman 189
Wanamaker department stores 116, 154, 179, 189, 325
Wanamaker family 183
Wanderer of the Wasteland 413
Wanninger, Pee Wee 433, 465
War Admiral (racehorse) 469
War and Peace (Tolstoy) 317, 323
The War in the Air (Wells) 318
The War of the Worlds (Wells) 418
The War with Mexico (Smith) 73
Warburg, Paul 102
Ward, Arch 467
Ward, Ellis 484
Waring, Fred 24
Waring, Orville Taylor 116
Warner, Albert 328
Warner, Glenn Scobie "Pop" 452, 470
Warner, Harry 328, 412
Warner, Herbert Baxter 382
Warner, Hulbert Harrington 116
Warner, Dr. Ira De Ver 190
Warner, Jack 328
Warner, Dr. Lucien C. 190
Warner, Sam 328, 330, 412
Warner, Sylvia Townsend 294, 300–301
Warner Bros. 31, 54, 67, 294–295, 328, 400, 412–413
Warner Brothers Corset Company 157, 190
Warner Chemical Company 190
Warner Theatre, New York City 59
Warren, Charles 74
Warren, Francis E. 228
Warren, Lloyd 165, 190
Warren, Robert Penn 32, 52–53, 317
Warren and Wetmore (architectural firm) 165
Wash Tubbs (Crane) 304
Washburn, Robert C. 341
Washington, George 72
Washington and Jefferson College (later University) 430, 477
Washington Conference on arms reduction 192
Washington Memorial Chapel, Valley Forge (Medary) 189
Washington Palace Five 447

Washington Redskins 447
Washington Senators 428, 432–433, 440–442, 478–479
Washington Times-Herald 322
Washington University 178, 417
The Washingtonians 24
Wassermann, August von 347, 354, 361
Wassermann Test 347–348, 354, 422
The Waste Land (Eliot) 21, 55, 309
Watch Your Step (Berlin) 61
Waterbury, John Isaac 116
Waters, Ethel 24, 29, 307
Watson, John B. 279
Watson, P. H. 436
Watson, Thomas Edward 193, 228
Watson, Thomas John 79, 113
Watterson, Henry 330
The Wave (Scott) 52, 58, 303
Way Down East 20, 32
"Way Down Yonder in New Orleans" (Creamer and Layton) 21
The Way of All Flesh 26, 74
The Ways of White Folks (Hughes) 67
WEAF Musical Comedy Hour 313
The Weary Blues (Hughes) 25, 38, 47, 66
Weaver, George "Buck" 442, 444
Webb, Clifton 25, 72
Webb, W. S. 116
Weber, Max 54
Webster, H. T. 305
The Wedding March 27
Weeks, John Wingate 228
Weidman, Charles 28
Weinshank, Albert 249
Weir, Robert Fulton 361
Weird Tales 311
Weiss, Hymie 258
Weissmuller, Johnny 158, 434, 436, 456–457
Welch, Elisabeth 22
Welch, William H. 354
The Well of Loneliness (Hall) 34, 39
Wellesley College 139, 141, 285
Wells Fargo Express 113
Wells, H. G. 265, 309, 318, 418
Welsh, Freddie 448, 484
Welterweight Championship (boxing) 477, 479–481
Welty, Eudora 317
Wescott, Glenway 23, 45
Wesley, Charles H. 138
Wesson, Joseph H. 116
Wesson, Walter H. 116
West, Mae 41

"West End Blues" (Armstrong) 60
West Side Tennis Club 437
West Virginia State College 138
Westchester Cup (polo) 459
Western Air Express 80
Western Electric 306, 412
Western Federation of Miners 254
Western State Normal University 470
Western Union 464
Westinghouse 102, 294–295, 325, 327–328, 414, 417
Westminster Confession of Faith 365, 372
Westminster Seminary 367, 378, 393
Weston, Edward Payson 484
Westover, Russ 304
West-Running Brook (Frost) 27
Westward 482
Wethered, Joyce 454
Wharton, Edith 20, 23, 26–27, 29, 32, 73, 308
What Can a Man Believe? (Barton) 384
"What Can I Say After I Say I'm Sorry?" (Lyman) 25
What Of It? (Lardner) 68, 308
What Price Glory? (Anderson and Stallings) 24–25, 37
"What'll I Do?" (Moore and Steel) 23
What's O'Clock (Lowell) 24, 74
Wheeler, Burton K. 194, 213
Wheeler, Frank P. 116
Whelpley, H. M. 361
"When My Baby Smiles at Me" (Lewis) 20, 307
"When the Moon Shines on the Moonshine" (Williams) 20
"When the Red, Red Robin Comes Bob, Bobbin' Along" (Tucker) 25
When Tutt Meets Tutt (Train) 308
Whipple, George Hoyt 332–333, 350, 356, 358, 399
Whiskery (racehorse) 480
"Whispering" (Whiteman) 20, 307
Whistler, James 30
White Buildings (Crane) 25, 51, 309
White Castle hamburgers 77
"White Christmas" (Berlin) 61
The White House (Bellows) 22
The White House, Washington, D.C. 293
White, E. B. 57, 324
White, Edward D. 259